THE CAMBRIDGE ANCIENT HISTORY

EDITORS

VOLUME X

THE
CAMBRIDGE
ANCIENT HISTORY

VOLUME X

THE AUGUSTAN EMPIRE

44 B.C.—A.D. 70

EDITED BY

S. A. COOK
LITT.D., F.B.A.

F. E. ADCOCK
M.A., F.B.A.

M. P. CHARLESWORTH
M.A.

CAMBRIDGE
AT THE UNIVERSITY PRESS
1966

PUBLISHED BY

THE SYNDICS OF THE CAMBRIDGE UNIVERSITY PRESS

Bentley House, 200 Euston Road, London N.W.1
American Branch: 32 East 57th Street, New York, N.Y. 10022
West African Office: P.M.B. 5181, Ibadan, Nigeria

First Edition   1934
Reprinted with corrections   1952
1963
1966

Printed in Great Britain at the University Printing House, Cambridge
(Brooke Crutchley, University Printer)

PREFACE

THE present volume describes the transition from the Roman Republic to the Principate. The institutions of the old Republic had already failed to control the great military chiefs so that, potent as were still the forms under which Rome had conquered the Mediterranean world, the Republic must have seemed to many, as to Caesar, '*imago sine re.*' On the other hand, despite the steady attraction of power to the *princeps*, the constitution of Rome had not ceased, when the volume closes, to employ the forms of the Republic. Yet within the century or rather more that followed the death of Caesar, there had been effected a profound change which gave to the ancient world a stable framework, a part of which both the Middle Ages and Modern Europe have inherited.

For this change one man may claim most of the credit—the first *princeps*, Augustus. Beginning his career in revolutionary times and in a revolutionary way, he ended it the first citizen of a Rome that had not to fear the fruits of military ambition or civil disorder. In the opening chapters of the volume he is seen on the way to power, the avenger of Caesar, the supplanter of Antony, the conqueror of Cleopatra. Then follows the story of his adaptation of the Roman State to the need for the unchallenged primacy of one man within the frame of the Republic, and of the first stages in the building up of an Imperial administration that could serve both Rome and the *princeps* where the older institutions failed. The army, that had threatened to be the deciding factor in politics, was reduced to being the instrument of defence alone. Behind this shield the frontiers were made secure whether by advance or by judicious renunciation of enterprises. While the provinces in general were divided, though not equally in point of power, between the immediate control of the *princeps* and the administration of the Senate subject to the overriding powers of the emperor, Egypt occupied a somewhat especial position as a Caesarian preserve. Here may be seen a new form of adaptation which took over the essentials of the government of the Ptolemies. Nor was this the only survival within the ambit of Roman power. Monarchy, if rejected in Rome, lived on in client-kingdoms under Rome's shadow, and the figure of Herod, the one of these client-princes of whom any clear record has been preserved, affords a kind of foil to the unobtrusive policy of his Roman overlord.

After the survey of the control and defence of the empire it is proper to consider other achievements of this age which were to be even more lasting in their effects. With the Mediterranean world secure, and with the dislocations due to Rome's past removed, there began an era of vigorous industrial advance and widespread commerce. Of even greater moment was the creation of a new Roman People, as Italy was made the home of a unified Roman nation capable of spreading and rooting Roman civilization in the West in a measure denied to the Greeks in the East after Alexander the Great. To make the heart of this Roman People sound was a prime care of the first emperor, and he pursued this end with a resolute tenacity. At this point may be considered the religious and philosophical trend of this period and of the age that immediately preceded it. The most striking feature of this was the development of the cult of the ruler, which set Rome and the Emperor in its due place, neither too exalted nor too visionary, in the consciousness of mankind. Herein was to be planted the conception of a religion of the State which transcended but did not challenge the deeper emotions of worship. Yet the two were destined to blend, until the victory of Christianity was sealed by the adoption of the State by the Church and of the Church by the State. Closely linked with the social and religious ideas of the Augustan age arose a literary movement which reflected the hopes and aspirations of the new Italy. Latin literature became at once national and imperial, and the same is true of Roman art, which assumes a character which may be called Virgilian. Rome became, at last, architecturally worthy of its place in the world, while at the same time in the provinces, especially of the West, there arose visible monuments of the greatness of the Empire.

Thus, in many ways, the principate of Augustus marks a turning point in the history of the world. How great was to be its effect cannot have been revealed at the time even to its author, and this part of the volume ends with an attempt to sum up what has been written in earlier chapters of the achievement of Augustus according to the ideas of his own day and within the limits of his personality so far as that can be divined.

When Augustus died he left some questions unstated or unsolved, though his career had indicated his own methods of solving them. The great prestige of his name and his long exercise of authority limited both the choice and the actions of his successor, and for half a century bound Rome to a family and a tradition. In the political sphere Tiberius made patent the elimination of the People in favour of the Senate, but in the administration both of

Italy and the provinces the control of the *princeps* prevailed more and more over that of the Senate. The personal link that joined the senatorial aristocracy to the emperor was broken by his long absence from Rome, while the fact that the world could be controlled from the island of Capri revealed that autocracy was possible. Gaius in a last year of extravagant self-expression betrayed the length to which the claims of an emperor might pass beyond the convention of the Principate. Claudius set his hand to the task of developing the Imperial administration in such a way that, while it depended less on senators and knights, it was also less affected by the personality of the emperor of the moment. Foreign policy and government were made positive and active, as they had not been under Tiberius. The danger to the central power that might arise from the concentration of legions on the Rhine was lessened by the diversion of military strength to the conquest of a part of Britain, which thus finds a fixed place in the history of the ancient world. Client-kingdoms were more and more absorbed into provinces, and provinces were more and more the sole care of the emperor. The revenge of the Roman aristocracy for the deflation of its power was a caricature of the personality of Claudius, no less a caricature that every feature in it was drawn from life.

With the advent of Nero there was an appeal from Claudius to the first *princeps*. The young Emperor posed before an artful drop-scene of the Augustan age painted by Seneca. But the reconciliation with the Senate was short-lived; and although the Imperial machine was too strong to be put out of gear by the vagaries of a *princeps* who deprived himself of worthy advisers, the goodwill bequeathed to the Julio-Claudian house was rapidly dissipated. The tact which had provided that generals should not have at once the power and the will to challenge the *princeps* failed, and the crowning ingratitude that rewarded with death the victories of Corbulo broke down the loyalty and aroused the dangerous fears of the army chiefs. The stirrings of nationalism on the Rhine and in Palestine were no longer repressed by the knowledge that the Roman State was united in a strong hand, so that the Julio-Claudian dynasty went down amid rebellion and civil war. Yet the work of Augustus and of Claudius survived the dynasty. The power of Rome quickly crushed rebellion even amid the distractions of civil war. The system of Imperial government remained unshaken, waiting for the right emperor. As by a kind of natural selection the Year of the Four Emperors ended in the promotion of the claimant who possessed most of the qualities of Augustus, and with the accession of Vespasian the Principate resumed its task of governing the Mediterranean world.

The political unity of the Mediterranean world under the control of Rome had become a fact accepted without question. In the war between Antony and Octavian the East was ranged against the West, and the day of Actium decided the issue. It may well seem doubtful whether a victorious Antony, even with the high genius of Cleopatra at his side, could have imposed a Hellenistic monarchy on Rome and lands beyond Rome. An Actium in which the East prevailed might have been the prelude to a Western and an Eastern Empire. Octavian's victory made certain that the ancient world should remain politically one. The manner in which the victory was used meant that during the principate of Augustus the face of Rome was turned towards the West. So far as there had been an Eastern reaction it was checked, and the Parthian Empire, though it remained a great power, was not active or strong enough to challenge the easy mastery of Rome. The world had one capital, *Roma aeterna*. But the *pax Romana* made possible the penetration of the West by the enterprising traders of Asia Minor, Syria and Egypt. Gradually there began once more the slow infiltration of Eastern ideas. However little Rome may have wished it, the provinces began to react upon the heart of the Empire. The days of their full effect were still in the future. But here and there an administrative device found entrance into the counsels of the Imperial government; here and there an Eastern cult began to strengthen its position despite the suspicions of the emperors. Gaius and Nero began to dream of something more like divine kingship than would have been acceptable to Augustus and Tiberius. The nationalist movement in Palestine was crushed, and with the destruction of the holy city of Jerusalem the history of the Jewish State, if not of Judaism, was ended. On the Rhine the fleeting idea of an 'Empire of the Gauls' vanished. The romanization of the West steadily advanced. Yet both West and East began to make their contribution to the intellectual and emotional life of the Empire, so that during the century that followed the death of Nero the Roman Empire did not cease to be Roman but at the same time became more universal in thought and tendency, especially in those spheres in which the native genius of the new Roman People was not most clearly dominant.

The period described in this volume witnessed the first beginning of movements which were soon to become significant. The Augustan age of literature died before Augustus. The sense of deliverance and of regeneration that inspired Virgil and a part of Horace grew faint, so that before the Julio-Claudian line was ended the time had come for a new movement in letters. The growth of the practice of declamation, the restriction of rhetoric to less worthy ends, and the absence of any great intellectual currents of thought conspired to clear the way for the silver age of Latin literature, which will be described in the next volume. There, too, will be found the account of Roman art in the phase that begins with the reign of Nero when the impulse of Augustan art had passed. In the period covered by the present volume there was not only an activity in legislation which has been recorded, but advances in the science of Roman jurisprudence. These advances, together with some developments in private law, will be estimated in the account of Roman law which will be given in connection with the great achievements of its classical maturity. In the sphere of religion the phenomenon of Christianity had been observed, but the story of its rise will be told at the moment when its importance was first felt definitely and continuously by the Empire as a whole. Finally, although enough is here said of the peoples outside the Empire, especially the Parthians, to make plain the springs of Roman foreign policy, an account of them and of their civilization is reserved for treatment in Volume Eleven, in which will also be found a survey of the several provinces during the two centuries that end with the Antonines.

In the present volume the first chapter is by Mr Charlesworth; chapters II to IV are shared by Dr Tarn and Mr Charlesworth, who have had the advantage of each other's help on all matters of common concern. To Dr Tarn we owe, in particular, the worthy portrayal of the brilliant figure of Cleopatra. Sir Henry Stuart Jones has described the constitutional position of the *princeps* and of the Senate and People of Rome in the age of Augustus. Mr Stevenson writes on the Imperial administration and the Army and Navy. The frontier policy of Rome in the East is described by Professor Anderson in chapters IX and XXII, that in the West by Mr Syme in chapters XII and XXIII. The Roman advance into Britain is the topic of a separate treatment by Mr Collingwood. In chapter X Dr Bell writes on Egypt under the early Principate, in chapter XI Professor Momigliano gives an account of Herod the Great, and in chapter XXV describes the Jewish rebellion and its defeat. Professor Oertel writes on the economic unification of the Mediterranean region in chapter XIII, Mr Last on the social policy of Augustus in chapter XIV. Professor Nock has discussed the religious and philosophical movements of this period and of that immediately preceding it, Mr Glover the literature of the Augustan age. Mrs Strong has continued her interpretation of Roman art in chapter XVII. Chapter XVIII, entitled the Achievement of Augustus, is by Professor Adcock. In the second part of the volume the reigns of Tiberius, Gaius and Claudius are the theme of two chapters by Mr Charlesworth; Professor Momigliano describes the principate and personality of Nero. To Mr Stevenson is due the account of the Year of the Four Emperors (chapter XXIV) and of the revolt on the Rhine which occupies a part of the concluding chapter of the volume. Mr Charlesworth has written the Appendix on Literary Authorities, and Professor Anderson, Professor Momigliano and Mr Last the Notes that deal with special problems within their contributions.

Readers are reminded that the maps in this volume cannot wholly remove the need of occasional reference to an Atlas. They are rather designed to assist to make clear the narrative at points where geographical factors are of especial importance. More space than has been usual is devoted to bibliographies. This is in part due to the fact that with the Empire begins a new body of scientific literature, in part to the assembling in this volume of bibliographical material, such as that on the historians and on Egypt, which will also serve the purposes of the next volume. In the text italics have generally been used to differentiate a technical from a non-technical use of a word. Thus '*princeps*' means the holder of certain powers whereas 'Princeps' is used of particular Emperors. It may be remarked that, in accordance with English literary usage, 'emperor' is freely used as a variant of '*princeps*' and the word is not to be interpreted in any other sense. We have used 'Empire' rather than 'empire' to denote, not the territories controlled by Rome, but the system which superseded the Republic. Complete consistency in these matters is not easily attainable, and where occasional inconsistencies may offend, the censure must fall not on contributors but wholly on the Editors. In this as in all preceding volumes the Editors owe much to the ready co-operation of the several writers, who have from time to time sacrificed their own practice in these and other formal matters to make possible such uniformity as has been attained. Of far greater importance has been the readiness to make their contributions serve the construction of the volume, without, it is hoped, lessening their individual value. In all this we have been exceptionally fortunate, and we trust that their efforts will make more difficult the generalization that a composite work must be *opus incompositum*.

Dr Tarn wishes to thank Mr S. R. K. Glanville and Mr H. W. Fairman for knowledge of the Cleopatra stele from Armant, and M. Cumont for information about then unpublished material at Susa. He and Mr Charlesworth owe a like debt to Professor P. Roussel for the communication of inscriptions from Rhosos. Dr Bell also would acknowledge the assistance of Mr Glanville, Mr Charlesworth the generous help and advice of Professor J. G. C. Anderson and Mr H. M. Last in the chapters dealing with the successors of Augustus. Professor Anderson thanks M. Jean Babelon, Sir G. F. Hill and Mr E. S. G. Robinson for assistance in numismatic matters. Mr Syme wishes to record his indebtedness to Mr M. Holroyd. Mr Last desires to express his thanks for ready help and friendly criticism to Professor W. W. Buckland and Professor F. de Zulueta. Professor Nock acknowledges a like debt to Professor W. S. Ferguson, Professor H. J. Rose and Mr Last. Mrs Strong, to whom the volume owes much for her assistance with the Sheets of Plans and the illustrations, is in turn greatly indebted to the late Senator Corrado Ricci and to Professor G. Q. Giglioli for unfailing generosity in the matter of plans and photographs, and wishes to thank Professor L. Curtius and Professor Boethius for help in the discussion of points of difficulty. Professor Adcock is grateful to Professor W. Weber for allowing him to see a part of his unpublished *Princeps, Studien zur Geschichte des Augustus*. Mr Collingwood would acknowledge the kindness of Dr R. E. M. Wheeler in allowing him to make use of the manuscript of his report on the excavation at Verulam.

The volume is indebted to contributors for the bibliographies to their chapters. Professor Momigliano has supplied the Genealogical Table of the House of Herod; for the other Tables the Editors accept responsibility, but they would gratefully acknowledge the assistance of Mr G. B. A. Fletcher. No Table of the Parthian Dynasty is given, for the problems concerned with that, so far as they do not affect Rome, are reserved for treatment in Volume Eleven. In the preparation of maps Mr Syme supplied material for Map 11 and Mr Stevenson for Map 15. Mr Syme and Mr Stevenson are responsible for Map 13, Dr Bell for Map 8, Mr Collingwood for Map 14: Map 4, which is repeated from Volume Nine, is due to Dr Tarn. In the construction of other maps the Editors have had the benefit of the opinion of other contributors on certain points. For the plans that accompany this volume we have to acknowledge the courtesy of the publishers of the *Enciclopedia Italiana Treccani* for Plan 1, of Professor Giglioli and the publishers of *Capitolium* for Plan 2 and of the Ufficio Antichità e Belle Arti of the Governatorato of Rome for Plan 4. We wish, together with Mrs Strong, to thank Signor Barocelli for permitting us to use his Plan of Aosta (Plan 3) and would acknowledge also the courtesy of the Società storica subalpina, from whose publications it is taken. We have to thank Mr Seltman for his assistance with the plans, for his co-operation in the illustrations of the volume, and for his most valuable advice on questions of numismatics. He has prepared the fourth Volume of Plates, which illustrates this and the preceding volume. Mr D. E. W. Wormell translated the chapter of Professor Oertel, Mr Charlesworth the contributions of Professor Momigliano. The General Index, the Index to Maps and the Index of Passages are the work of Mr Benham, who has spared no pains in a task of exceptional complexity. In this, as in former volumes, we have every reason to be grateful to the helpful skill and resource of the Staff of the University Press.

We have given to this volume the title of The Augustan Empire to indicate the fact that in the period covered by it the work of Augustus is the outstanding fact, and we have placed upon the cover the head of the Augustus of Prima Porta.

S.A.C.
F.E.A.
M.P.C.

September, 1934

TABLE OF CONTENTS

CHAPTER I

THE AVENGING OF CAESAR

By M. P. CHARLESWORTH, M.A.

Fellow of St John's College, Cambridge, and Laurence Reader in
Ancient History in the University of Cambridge

CHAPTER II

THE TRIUMVIRS

By W. W. TARN, Litt.D., Hon. LL.D. (Edin.), F.B.A., Trinity College, Cambridge,
and M. P. CHARLESWORTH[1]

[1] Sections I, II, IV and V are by Dr Tarn, Sections III, VI and VII by Mr Charlesworth.

CHAPTER III

THE WAR OF THE EAST AGAINST THE WEST

By W. W. TARN and M. P. CHARLESWORTH[1]

[1] Sections I–III, VI and VII are by Dr Tarn, Section IV by Mr Charlesworth, and Section V is by both in collaboration.

CHAPTER IV

THE TRIUMPH OF OCTAVIAN

By W. W. TARN and M. P. CHARLESWORTH[1]

CHAPTER V

THE *PRINCEPS*

By Sir HENRY STUART JONES, M.A., D.Litt. (Oxon.), Hon.D. Litt. (Wales),
Hon. Litt.D. (Leeds), F.B.A.

Honorary Fellow of Brasenose College, Oxford, and formerly Camden Professor of
Ancient History in the University of Oxford

[1] Section I is by Dr Tarn, Sections II and III by Mr Charlesworth

CONTENTS

CHAPTER VI

SENATUS POPULUSQUE ROMANUS

By Sir HENRY STUART JONES

CHAPTER VII

THE IMPERIAL ADMINISTRATION

By G. H. STEVENSON, M.A.

Fellow of University College, Oxford, and University Lecturer in Ancient History

CHAPTER VIII

THE ARMY AND NAVY

By G. H. STEVENSON

CHAPTER IX

THE EASTERN FRONTIER UNDER AUGUSTUS

By J. G. C. ANDERSON, M.A., Hon. LL.D. (Aberdeen)
Fellow of Brasenose College, Oxford, and Camden Professor of Ancient History
in the University of Oxford

CHAPTER **X**

EGYPT UNDER THE EARLY PRINCIPATE

By H. Idris Bell, M.A., Hon. D. Litt. (Wales and Michigan), F.B.A.
Keeper of Manuscripts in the British Museum

CHAPTER XI

HEROD OF JUDAEA

By A. Momigliano
Professor of Greek History in the Royal University of Rome

CHAPTER XII

THE NORTHERN FRONTIERS UNDER AUGUSTUS

By RONALD SYME, M.A.
Fellow of Trinity College, Oxford

CHAPTER XIII

THE ECONOMIC UNIFICATION OF THE MEDITERRANEAN REGION: INDUSTRY, TRADE AND COMMERCE

By F. OERTEL, Phil. Dr.

Professor of Ancient History in the University of Bonn

CHAPTER XIV

THE SOCIAL POLICY OF AUGUSTUS

By HUGH LAST, M.A.

Fellow of St John's College, Oxford, and University Lecturer in Roman History

CHAPTER XV

RELIGIOUS DEVELOPMENTS FROM THE CLOSE OF THE REPUBLIC TO THE DEATH OF NERO

By A. D. NOCK, M.A., Hon. LL.D. (Birmingham)
Frothingham Professor of the History of Religion in Harvard University

CHAPTER XVI

THE LITERATURE OF THE AUGUSTAN AGE

By T. R. GLOVER, M.A.

Fellow of St John's College, Cambridge, and Public Orator in the University of Cambridge

CHAPTER XVII

THE ART OF THE AUGUSTAN AGE

By EUGÉNIE STRONG, C.B.E., M.A., Litt.D. (Trin. Coll. Dublin),
Hon. LL.D. (St Andrews), Hon. Litt.D. (Manchester), F.S.A.

CONTENTS

CHAPTER XVIII

THE ACHIEVEMENT OF AUGUSTUS

By F. E. ADCOCK, M.A., Hon.D.Litt. (Durham)

Fellow of King's College, Cambridge, and Professor of Ancient History
in the University of Cambridge

CHAPTER XIX

TIBERIUS

By M. P. CHARLESWORTH

CHAPTER XX

GAIUS AND CLAUDIUS

By M. P. CHARLESWORTH

CHAPTER XXI

NERO

By A. MOMIGLIANO

CHAPTER XXII

THE EASTERN FRONTIER FROM TIBERIUS TO NERO

By J. G. C. ANDERSON

CHAPTER XXIII

THE NORTHERN FRONTIERS FROM TIBERIUS TO NERO

By R. SYME and R. G. COLLINGWOOD, M.A., F.S.A., F.B.A.

Fellow and Tutor of Pembroke College, Oxford, and University
Lecturer in Philosophy and Roman History[1]

[1] Sections I, II and V are by Mr Syme, sections III and IV by Mr Collingwood.

CHAPTER XXIV

THE YEAR OF THE FOUR EMPERORS

By G. H. STEVENSON

CHAPTER XXV

REBELLION WITHIN THE EMPIRE

By G. H. Stevenson and A. Momigliano[1]

[1] Sections I–III are by Mr Stevenson, sections IV–VII by Professor Momigliano.

BIBLIOGRAPHIES

NORTH ITALY

Scales

0 10 20 30 40 50 60

English Miles

0 10 20 30 40 50 60 70 80 90 100

Kilometres

CHAPTER I

THE AVENGING OF CAESAR

I. ANTONY IN POWER

THE Ides of March closed in a night of fear and trembling; none knew what might happen. The panic-stricken senators had fled from the scene of the murder; Antony, the surviving consul, fortified himself in his house in fear of an attempt on his life also, Lepidus, the *magister equitum*, withdrew across the Tiber; even the exultant assassins, who had rushed out proclaiming Liberty, were forced to retire on to the Capitol by the hostile attitude of the people. Yet they held the key to the situation; all Rome waited to see what they would do; vigorous and decisive action on their part could effect much. In this expectation Cicero visited them; it was on his name that Brutus had called, as he held

On the ancient authors who wrote on the period covered by this volume see the Appendix on Sources, pp. 866 *sqq.*

Note. The sources for the western half of the Empire in the period covered by these four chapters (44–27 B.C.) diminish both in quantity and quality the farther we get from 44. At the beginning there is first-rate contemporary material, Cicero's own *Letters* and *Philippics* and (embodied in the *ad familiares*) letters to and from the leading generals of the time, Lepidus, Pollio, Plancus, Cornificius, and Brutus and Cassius. When these cease in the summer of 43 there remain only secondary sources; the *Epitomes* of Livy show roughly the view that he took, but little more; Velleius Paterculus presents a short 'official' narrative making Antony the villain of the piece; both writers probably drew a good deal of their material from Augustus' own *Memoirs.* These are lost, but the *Res Gestae*, in its curt references to this period, represents Augustus' view and occasionally gives information otherwise lacking, as *e.g.* the *coniuratio Italiae.* The later parts of Plutarch's *Lives* of Cicero and Brutus are relevant but add little of real value; his Antony however is useful (and see p. 31, n. 1). Suetonius' *Augustus* offers important information, the more so as the authorities are often cited by name, but lacks precision especially in chronology.

In the main any connected narrative must depend on the later compilations of Appian and Dio Cassius. Appian's *Civil Wars*, II, 116–v, 145 (based mainly on Asinius Pollio, but also on other contemporaries such as Messalla and Augustus himself), are extremely valuable in their facts and figures, but unfortunately end at 35 B.C. Dio is not at his best: books XLV, 20–LIII, 3 provide a convenient framework but are full of rhetoric and motivation of his own and of the propaganda of both sides (see also p. 31).

The relevant coins and inscriptions are referred to in the text.

his dagger aloft, for that name stood for constitutional government. But though Brutus was determined there should be no more bloodshed, he was determined on nothing else; in the fond belief that the Republic would immediately be itself again, once Caesar was removed, neither he nor his fellow-conspirators had any plan of action or scheme for the future.

The first thing needful was to call the Senate and get the machinery of government in motion once more: during the day after the murder messengers passed between Antony and the assassins, and on 17 March the senators assembled at the summons of the consul in the temple of Tellus, which was conveniently near his house. An enthusiastic Republican like Tiberius Nero might propose rewards for the tyrant-slayers, others might clamour for the casting of Caesar's body into the Tiber, but more moderate counsels soon prevailed, for Antony's speech revealed clearly the unpleasant fact that the cancellation of Caesar's *acta* meant that many of those present would have to forfeit their position and hopes of a career. Cicero used all his influence in favour of a general amnesty, Munatius Plancus and others supported him, and the illogical compromise was finally reached that, while no inquiry should be held about the murder, Caesar's will and *acta* (not only those already published, but also those projects which could be found among his papers) should be confirmed, and a public funeral granted to the body. After the meeting the conspirators were invited by the Caesarians to dine with them and relations thus re-established.

But at a stroke the initiative had now passed to Antony, and he was quick to take advantage of it. Something of his previous career has already been seen (vol. IX, chaps. XVI–XVII): his early years had revolved around the exuberant pleasures of an aristocratic life in the capital, amid love-affairs and debt and rioting, followed by campaigns in the East wherein he had distinguished himself. But Caesar's insight had appraised his vigour and courage and found a use for him, and though for some time he fell into disfavour, after the battle of Munda he was received back and even chosen to ride next to Caesar himself on the journey through Italy. He was the most trusted of Caesar's lieutenants, colleague in the consulship with Caesar himself, and likely enough (as he had hoped and hinted) to be Caesar's heir and son[1]. Hence his zeal for the confirmation of the *acta* and will, and bitter must have been his disappointment when the will was opened in his house and he

---

[1] Cicero, *Phil.* II, 29, 71: 'testamento, ut dicebas, filius'; and cf. *Phil.* III, 5, 12.

learnt that Caesar's great-nephew had been preferred to him and that he was only mentioned among the *heredes secundi*. But his opportunity had come now and he meant to seize it; in the prime of life[1], of proved bravery and resourcefulness in action, a ready speaker, popular with the soldiery for his easy-going ways, splendidly impulsive and direct, he must have appeared the natural leader for the Caesarian party: what fate had yet to manifest was whether under this dashing exterior lay a unity of purpose or a controlling intelligence that might mark him out as a great statesman. For the moment the bankruptcy of counsel displayed by the conspirators gave him the very chance he needed; his first aim obviously was to conciliate the assassins and get them out of the way, to bind his fellow Caesarians to himself by tactful concessions, to satisfy the Senate by a semblance of constitutionality, and then to gain an important command for himself in some province near Italy. He had (with the consent of Calpurnia) already taken possession of all Caesar's papers and funds and during the next few weeks he worked with notable energy and success.

Each item on this programme was carried out smoothly. The news of Caesar's lavish benefactions to the Roman people had spread quickly[2], and when on 20 March the procession escorting the body of the dictator defiled into the Forum, amid all the pomp and moving ceremonial of a Roman funeral, the mob needed little rousing: as it listened to the recital of the honours heaped upon him and the oath that the whole Senate had taken to protect him, as it saw the toga in which he had been murdered, sympathy was soon excited and Antony had but to add a few words[3]; a transport of fury against the assassins seized it, and fire and rioting broke out. Urged on by various leaders the populace soon became so formidable that within a month Brutus and Cassius found it prudent to leave the city[4]. Antony demonstrated his friendliness by procuring a decree allowing Brutus to be absent from the city for more than ten days, which was the legal limit for the urban

---

[1] His birth falls either in 82 or 81 B.C. (Appian, *Bell. Civ.* v, 8, 33); his birthday was 14 January, as recorded by the Verulae calendar.

[2] The will was opened after the meeting of the Senate on the 17th; Caesar had bequeathed his Transtiberine gardens and 300 sesterces per man to the citizens of Rome: Suetonius, *Div. Iul.* 83, 2.

[3] Suetonius, *Div. Iul.* 84, 2; and see M. E. Deutsch, *Antony's Funeral Speech*, Univ. California Publ. in Class. Phil. IX, 1928, no. 5, p. 127.

[4] The date would seem to lie between 9 April and 13 April: Cicero, *ad Att.* XIV, 5, 2 and 7, 1.

praetor. To the Caesarians he was all favours: when Dolabella abruptly assumed the consulship (to which Caesar had intended him to succeed in his place) he made no objection, though a few months ago he had opposed it bitterly, and for Lepidus, who had already promised him his support on 16 March, he gained by an irregular election the coveted office of *Pontifex maximus*. Finally he won over the senators, who had been shocked at the consequences of the funeral, by a motion abolishing for ever the dictatorship, such as Sulla or Caesar had held, and by empowering Lepidus, who was on the point of setting out for his provinces of Old Gaul and Nearer Spain, to negotiate with young Sextus Pompeius, who was still at large with six legions in Spain[1]; to Cicero too he wrote in the most amicable and flattering terms. As Decimus Brutus had left for his province of Gallia Cisalpina in early April, Antony was now free of the embarrassing presence of the conspirators, and could feel he had conciliated all; the Senate showed its gratification by decreeing the province of Macedonia to himself and that of Syria to Dolabella. But unfortunately Antony could not rest here; the possession of Caesar's papers gave him opportunities, too tempting to lose, of winning supporters and raking in money: though he published much which was genuine (as, for instance, the drafts which were given the force of law by the Lex Antonia de actis confirmandis in June) or had been among Caesar's intentions, he invented more; Roman citizenship was bestowed on the Sicilians, Deiotarus given the kingdom of Armenia Minor, possible helpers smuggled into the Senate, privileges and exemptions sold, and a steady process of embezzlement of the treasure in the temple of Ops began. But in the long run he must rely upon Caesar's veterans: he and Dolabella had carried a law assigning land to them, and towards the end of April, with his beard grown long in symbol of mourning for the murdered dictator, he left for Campania to supervise personally the work of allotment and to assure himself of their fidelity. Some weeks before[2], Cleopatra, bereft of her protector, had left with her young son in flight for Egypt.

Within two months of the murder of Caesar his chief lieutenant had, by skilful manœuvring, gathered the State into his hands and rendered his opponents helpless. Cicero lamented that despotism

[1] See Vol. IX, p. 717: Sextus was apparently coining at Salduba on the Ebro, see L. Laffranchi in *Riv. Ital. Num.* XXV, 1912, p. 511.

[2] Before mid-April: Cicero, *ad Att.* XIV, 8, 1. What the rumour was about her that so pleased Cicero is unknown: *ad Att.* XIV, 20, 2; XV, 1, 5; 4, 4.

still lived though the despot was dead, but he could do nothing. For a time he was consoled by news of the repressive measures taken by Dolabella against the enthusiastic mob, who, urged on by an adventurer Herophilus, had erected on the site of Caesar's pyre a pillar at which they made offerings, but it was small recompense for lack of freedom. But as May was ending the announcement that a claimant to Caesar's fortune, who might disturb his plans, had appeared in Rome, impelled Antony to return to the city.

II. THE YOUNG OCTAVIUS

The new arrival, C. Octavius, was for nearly sixty years to play a leading part in the history of Rome and of the world. Ancient writers, struck by the contrast between the alleged villainies of the early Octavius and the acknowledged beneficence of the later Augustus, elaborated the picture of a young man for whom no wickedness was too base but who, through sheer satiety, turned to mildness and wisdom: many moderns, rejecting the rhetoric but retaining the contrast, postulate a change somewhere but leave it unexplained. Yet such a conception violates the laws of psychology and probability alike: anyone who would understand the character and achievement of Augustus must realize from the outset that most of the charges commonly brought against his youth or early manhood—immorality, cowardice, treachery—are based on no firmer foundation than the accusations and polemic of his personal enemies and are worthless[1]. This fact cannot be too strongly stressed, and once acknowledged, it is not difficult for the historian to discern, from careful and sympathetic study, how the boy Octavius could develop into the future Augustus.

His father, C. Octavius, belonged to an old and respectable, but not distinguished, family from Velitrae; his mother Atia, a niece of Julius Caesar, had borne to her husband two children, the elder a girl, Octavia, and Octavius himself, whose birth fell on 23 September

---

[1] The charges against his youth and morals come from Sextus Pompeius, Mark Antony and his brother Lucius (Suetonius, *Aug.* 68 and 69, 1, 2); they can be met by comparing Cicero, *Phil.* iii, 6, 15 and xiii, 9, 19, and Nicolaus of Damascus, βίος Καίσαρος, 3–13 (Jacoby). Charges of cowardice, as *e.g.* at Mutina, and repeated for Philippi, come from Mark Antony (Suetonius, *ib.* 10, 4), and are refuted by Cicero (*Phil.* xiv, 10, 28). The *canard* about the poisoning of Pansa hardly needs refutation, but see *ad Brutum*, 1, 6, 2. For the supposed butchery of the *arae Perusinae* see note 1 on p. 29, and for the Antony-Octavian propaganda p. 91 *sq.*

63 B.C., in the consulship of Cicero[1]. Four years later the father died and Atia, though she married L. Marcius Philippus, devoted her time, like a Cornelia, to the education of her children. For Octavius was not strong constitutionally; time and again he was attacked by serious illnesses, and his health always needed careful nursing[2]. From his mother he imbibed the veneration for the traditions and religion of Rome that is so marked a trait in his character, and learnt the glories of the clan to which she belonged. His teachers were some of the most celebrated of the day, M. Epidius, Apollodorus of Pergamum, and Arius of Alexandria; the affection he felt for them may be gauged by the fact that he gave his old *paedagogus* Sphaerus a public funeral and recognized later as just causes for freeing a slave devoted service as nurse or teacher. The promise he showed, his exceptional beauty and nobility of bearing[3], and a discretion and intelligence beyond his years, no less than the family connection brought him to the notice of his great-uncle. From a boy the name and fame of Julius Caesar can never have been far from his thoughts, and he made him the pattern of his ambition, for it was Julius who introduced him to political life, allowing him at the age of twelve the honour of pronouncing the *laudatio* over his grandmother Julia (including as it would the past history and glory of the *gens Iulia*), and promoting him to a place in the pontifical college. Like any Roman boy brought up on the tradition of *pietas* and *gloria* he longed to accompany his great-uncle, but his mother refused to let him go to Africa on the ground of his ill-health; still he received the *dona militaria* and rode in the triumph of 46 B.C. Next year illness again almost prevented him going to Spain, but he joined Caesar after the culminating victory at Munda and came back with him to Italy. Greatness calls to greatness: it is idle to speculate what he may have learnt from Caesar even in that short period of association, but the impact of so tremendous a personality upon the lad must have been overwhelming; on the other side, too, it is noteworthy that Caesar (unknown to him) in September 45 had decided to make him his heir. In the late autumn Caesar sent him over to Apollonia, accom-

[1] The coincidence was made significant later: for the omens and miracles that were found for his birth and childhood see Suetonius, *Aug.* 94.
[2] We hear of illnesses in 45 (Suetonius, *Aug.* 8), at Philippi in 42 (Dio XLVII, 37; Suetonius, *ib.* 13), in 41 (Appian, *Bell. Civ.* V, 12, 45), in 35 (Appian, *Ill.* 27), in 29 (Dio LI, 22, 9), in 26 during the Cantabrian War (Dio LIII, 25, 7) and in 23 (p. 136 *sq.*).
[3] Nicolaus 9 and 13 (Jacoby); Suetonius, *Aug.* 79, 'forma fuit eximia et per omnes aetatis gradus venustissima.' See Vol. of Plates iv, 146–50.

panied by friends such as M. Agrippa and Q. Salvidienus Rufus, to complete his studies, and to pick up army-life amid the officers and men of the legions in training there; the eighteen-year-old boy could look forward to having his taste of war at last in the coming Parthian campaigns.

Such had been his upbringing and career when on a late March evening came the terrific news that his great-uncle had been murdered, among the very senators who had sworn an oath to protect his life, by men whom he had spared, pardoned, and even promoted. All the ambitions and hopes of a delicate boy at the very moment when life seemed opening for him, all the love and admiration which had centred for so long in his great relative, were now suddenly fused by horror and pity into a white heat of fury against his murderers; everything bade him avenge his death, but so deep and strong was his passion that it called for delibera- tion, where a lesser passion would have rushed into action. He even rejected as untimely the suggestion of some officers that he should march on Rome at their head (for the men were ready), though he thanked them for their loyalty: instead, with a few friends, uncertain how he would be greeted, he determined to come to Italy, and landed obscurely near Brundisium.

Now came the second shock. Welcomed by the garrison at Brundisium, he learned for the first time that Caesar had left him heir to three-quarters of his estate and had adopted him as his son[1]. He was already resolved to avenge the murder; the news that Caesar had thought him worthy of his name and (who could tell?) of his position, gave the final edge to his resolution. To his mother, who tried to dissuade him from entering upon a perilous inheritance, he replied with Achilles' cry to Thetis when she too warned him of danger[2]; to all his elders' prudent cautionings he could only repeat that he dared not think himself unworthy of that name of which Caesar had thought him worthy[3]. Hence- forward he could not go back: the image of the murdered dictator was ever present to his mind; to avenge his death and then to complete his work became the sacred object of his life[4].

Yet in the pursuit of that object he was to meet many obstacles: his own ill-health he overcame by the sheer courage of a will

---

[1] Vol. IX, p. 724 *sq.*   [2] *Iliad*, XVIII, 98 *sq.*

[3] Appian, *Bell. Civ.* III, 13, 46–47; Vell. Pat. II, 60, 2.

[4] See the fragment, six words but decisive, of his November speech quoted by Cicero, *ad Att.* XVI, 15, 3: 'iurat *ita sibi parentis honores consequi liceat* et simul dextram intendit ad statuam.' The obvious protasis to the *ita* clause is some such phrase as *e.g.* 'ut eius mortem ulciscar.'

that refused to give in; against enemies or against those who (as he considered) would not further or misunderstood his father's plans he was to struggle for some fifteen years, sometimes openly and in strength, sometimes with the weapon of weakness, deceit, but always with one overmastering motive and with the clear consciousness of work reserved for him. And that consciousness came to him early, a consolation in perplexity (as to many another great man): in mid-July, when, against opposition and backed only by a few, he was celebrating the Ludi Victoriae Caesaris, a comet appeared in the heavens: the populace took it as a proof of Caesar's final reception among the gods, and he naturally encouraged this belief; but with an inner joy he recognized it as a sign for himself and knew his manifest destiny[1].

Meanwhile to work. He sent agents to secure the funds that Caesar had deposited in Asia for the Parthian war. Near Naples, in mid-April, he met Cicero, who despite his mistrust was impressed by his modest bearing and flattered by his attentions: 'he is completely devoted to me,' he wrote to Atticus, though he agreed (perhaps with some malicious anticipation) that there was bound to be 'a terrible *fracas* between him and Antony[2].' As Octavius entered Rome, towards the end of April, a halo round the sun seemed to promise divine favour[3], and his advent was welcomed by veterans and populace alike, and by a few true friends of Caesar such as Matius, who found in him 'a young man of the highest promise and well worthy Caesar[4].' He was allowed to address the people, and in doing so made no secret of his claim to Caesar's name and Caesar's money or of his views about the assassins; as soon as Antony returned he lost no time in visiting him; in the gardens of Pompey he placed his claim before him and asked for his help, but found himself treated with patronizing contempt and rebuffed.

---

[1] The account of this in Pliny, *N.H.* II, 93, quotes both Augustus' published words and his own private interpretation. A convenient conspectus of the literature about the *sidus Iulium* will be found in H. Wagenvoort, *Vergils Vierte Ekloge und das Sidus Julium*, but most writers are more concerned with the star than with Octavius.

[2] Cicero, *ad Att.* XIV, 10, 3 (the corrupt ριξόθεμιν in this letter does not disguise the general sense); 11, 2.

[3] Vell. Pat. II, 59, 6; Dio XLV, 4, 4; Seneca, *Nat. Quaest.* I, 2, 1, and Obsequens 67. See the careful investigation of this phenomenon by H. Kleinstück in *Festschrift zu Franz Polands fünfundsiebzigstem Geburtstag* (= *Phil. Woch.* LII, 1932, nos. 35/38), col. 244.

[4] Cicero, *ad fam.* XI, 28, 6.

For to Antony Octavius' arrival was likely to prove an embarrassing factor; up to now, while he had been the obvious leader for all who were devoted to Caesar, his reasonable and tactful bearing had averted any serious division in the State[1]. But if he upheld the boy's claim, apart from the annoyance of having to surrender the great riches he had so easily acquired he would almost certainly offend Senate and 'Liberators,' which was far from his intention: if he did not, the boy would win support from Caesar's friends and veterans, who might well ask why nothing had been done to avenge the murder. However intelligible his irritation it betrayed him into a blunder which was to have far-reaching consequences: he was after all the person to whom Octavius would naturally turn for support, the trusted colleague and friend of Julius Caesar, and from the day that Octavius found himself set aside and despised he could never trust Antony fully again. Antony had allowed his resentment to cloud his judgment, when tact and forbearance might have achieved much; and the appearance of a rival so disturbed him that he determined to grasp at once the power and the provinces he desired. On 3 June[2] a resolution of the people was passed giving him a provincial command for five years in Cisalpine and Transalpine Gaul, in exchange for Macedonia, though he was empowered to keep the Macedonian legions; at the same time his fellow-consul Dolabella received a similar command in Syria, and a commission which had been proposed in order to decide upon those unpublished intentions of Caesar which should become law was now revealed as consisting of the two consuls alone. In order to get rid on a specious pretext of Brutus and Cassius, the senators were induced on 5 June to give them charge of the corn-supply from Asia and Sicily, and to assign provinces to them to be named at a later date[3]. Finally a new agrarian law was carried distributing all the available land in Italy to veterans and poor citizens. By these measures Antony fortified his position for the present and secured a large command near Italy for the future, and already P. Ventidius Bassus, a man of ignoble birth but a capable soldier,

---

[1] It was not until October that Antony made any really hostile utterance against the 'Liberators.' It was then that he shocked Cicero by referring to them as men 'quibus se salvo locus in civitate esse non posset,' *ad Fam.* XII, 23, 3. Cf. also *ad Fam.* XII, 3.

[2] For the date see the discussion in M. A. Levi, *Ottaviano capoparte*, I, p. 77 and notes.

[3] In July Crete was assigned to Brutus, and Cyrene to Cassius. See W. Sternkopf in *Hermes*, XLVIII, 1912, pp. 381 *sqq.*

had begun raising recruits for him. He was irresistible, and Cicero in despair decided to leave Italy for the remainder of the year and return in 43 B.C. when Hirtius and Pansa would be consuls.

Octavius was not so easily disheartened, though he was meeting with nothing but opposition obviously inspired by Antony; first a tribunician veto held up the *lex curiata* which he needed to formalize his adoption, and then another prevented him displaying at the Ludi Cereales (which were held a month late) the golden chair and the diadem which had been granted to Caesar. Undaunted he paid such legacies as were due out of his own private funds, helped too, it is said, by his friends, and let slip no chance of demonstrating his *pietas* towards his father; he undertook personally the celebration (20–30 July) of the Ludi Victoriae Caesaris (for Thapsus) since the officials in charge of them dared not, and though Antony again would not permit him to exhibit the chair and diadem, the veterans and the people acclaimed him and were vexed at Antony. In return the consul denounced Octavius, but his soldiers remonstrated with him, and in the end patched up a reconciliation between the two on the Capitol. But though Octavius treated Antony with all the respect due to a consul and an older man, the reconciliation was hollow, and more than a year was to pass before Antony realized how essential concord was.

In the meantime Brutus and Cassius were busy collecting fleets before setting out, for there were rumours of pirates on the sea. Cicero had quitted Italy in disgust, but on the voyage contrary winds constrained him to put in at Leucopetra, and here the news of an attack made by L. Calpurnius Piso Caesoninus in the Senate of August 1 upon the conduct of Antony—and possibly the impression that dissension between Octavius and Antony might be encouraged—induced him to return. At Velia (17 August), on his way northwards he met Brutus, who announced he was leaving Italy to prevent any possibility of civil war, and a few days later Cassius with his fleet also set sail—not to the provinces allotted to them, but to Macedonia and Syria. But though Cicero reached Rome in time for the meeting of the Senate on 1 September, he did not dare attend for fear of coming into collision with Antony; the next day, in Antony's absence, he appeared and delivered the first of the series of speeches known as *Philippics*. Though it was temperate in tone, and subjected the consul's acts to a criticism that seems mild in comparison with later efforts, it may be doubted whether Cicero would have adopted so definite an attitude unless he was already meditating support from Octavius; by November they were exchanging letters almost daily, and must have been in communication before.

Antony's position was now far less strong: true, he had had the satisfaction of registering several shrewd hits on Cicero's target, when he replied to him on 19 September, but his relations to Octavius had not improved. He made some effort to attract Caesarian sentiment by erecting on the Rostra a statue of Caesar with the legend PARENTI OPTIME MERITO, but when there occurred a vacancy in the tribunate for which Octavius supported a friend, and the rumour grew that Octavius wanted to be tribune himself, Antony not only pointed out the illegality of such a candidature but threatened he would use all his consular authority to prevent it[1]. The reconciliation was breaking and early in October came a sensation; Antony put some of his bodyguard into custody at Suessa Aurunca and later had them executed on the ground that they had been tampered with; the suggestion that Octavius had tried to assassinate him was obvious; whether there was any substance to this charge it is impossible to determine; so rash a step seems unlike the caution of Octavius, who must early have realized how important Antony's existence was to him, and Antony may himself have fabricated the whole story[2]. But now, pretending his life was in danger, he determined on more decisive action; he would go to Brundisium to meet the legions he had recalled from Macedonia, extort what decrees he wanted from a subservient Senate, and occupy the provinces granted to him by the plebiscite of 3 June. But Octavius was equal to the occasion; he too left Rome on a visit to his father's veterans and dispatched agents to Brundisium to work on the Macedonian legions by speeches and (a characteristic touch) by propaganda leaflets. In consequence Antony had a stormy time, for the troops asked why Caesar's assassins had not been punished, and contrasted the small bounty they had been offered with the generous sums Octavius had distributed to the veterans of Calatia and Casilinum; he was compelled to execute the leaders and promise further payments for the future, and so persuaded the men to march to Ariminum, while he himself advanced on Rome with the legion *Alaudae*.

[1] Appian, *Bell. Civ.* III, 31, 120 *sqq.* It is interesting how early Octavius realized the usefulness of tribunician power.

[2] Cicero himself did not know the truth, *ad Fam.* XII, 23, 2, and our other authorities are completely at variance; see Appian, *Bell. Civ.* III, 39, 157 *sqq.*; Nicolaus 123; Plutarch, *Ant.* 16; Suetonius, *Aug.* 10; Vell. Pat. II, 60, 3.

It was high time, for Octavius had returned to Rome with three thousand loyal veterans[1] raised without authorization and was openly inveighing against Antony. He was in constant touch with Cicero, asking his advice and urging him to come to Rome, but still Cicero hesitated. He had spent the previous month fuming with resentment over Antony's attack and planning an elaborate and crushing reply, the famous *Second Philippic*; there is a certain irony in the reflection that while he was working feverishly on this tremendous piece of invective, he also found time to polish and complete his treatise 'On Friendship.' But between lingering distrust of Octavius and fear of possible violence from Antony he waited at Arpinum, and Octavius, hearing of Antony's approach, quitted Rome for Arretium, raising levies on his own account in Etruria as he progressed.

Events now began to move quickly. Shortly after mid-November, Antony arrived in Rome with the intention of declaring Octavius a public enemy, but alarming news suddenly reached him that the *legio Martia* and the Fourth legion had gone over to his rival. There was no time to be lost: he hastily summoned the Senate for November 28 to an evening meeting (which was illegal), redistributed provinces among his supporters, and set off for Cisalpine Gaul to dislodge Decimus Brutus, whom he formally ordered to leave. Decimus replied with defiance, declaring that he would uphold the authority of Senate and People, and after these admirable sentiments shut himself into Mutina to stand siege there. However weak he may have felt, to submit tamely, without striking one blow, to being besieged was scarcely the way to inspirit his troops, and Antony completed the investment of the city before the year was out.

But the departure of Antony from Rome and his discomfiture by Octavius at last emboldened Cicero to emerge from his retirement. News began to be more cheering: Brutus had occupied Macedonia and Cassius was rumoured to have reached Syria; Lepidus had brought over Sextus Pompeius[2]; from Gaul Munatius Plancus was replying to his letters in exemplary Latin, and best of all Octavius had made no objection to the assassin Casca—'the envious Casca'—holding the office of tribune. The young man was 'sound,' and Cicero arrived in Rome in time to attend a meeting of the Senate on 20 December, at which he delivered the *Third Philippic*. Both in this speech and in the following one to the populace he urged the instant prosecution of war with Antony and energetic support for Decimus in Mutina: for Octavius he

---

[1] Cicero, *ad Att.* XVI, 8, 2.   [2] Cicero, *ad Att.* XV, 29, 1.

had nothing but praise; the young man (whom he now addressed as 'Caesar' publicly for the first time) had, 'by his own initiative and exertions[1],' raised forces and freed Rome from the domination of Antony; all honour to him and his gallant legions.

So the eventful year 44 drew to its close. The prospects for the Republicans were sensibly brighter, for the consuls for 43, Hirtius and Pansa, were not bound by their service under Caesar to be partisans of Antony, and Cicero could write to Decimus Brutus in a tone of encouragement and hope. The apathy and timidity of the past few years fell away from him, to be replaced by much of his former energy and something of his old ambition; it may be surmised that he was once more toying with an idea, that had always proved attractive, of acting as political mentor to a successful general, guiding the State by his counsels while it was defended by the strong arm of a soldier; he had failed with the great Pompey, might he not succeed with a younger man, whose deference to and admiration for him were so apparent[2]? For the moment he was the centre, though not the chief, of the constitutional party, in close touch with Brutus and Cassius, writing to all (Lepidus and Plancus in Gaul, Pollio in Spain, or Cornificius in Africa) who would or could lend support. The issue was defined and clear— a contest between the claims of Antony and the State, but there was still one uncertain element, the mind of Octavius, who was playing his difficult hand with an adroitness that deceived all save a few shrewd observers.

III. MUTINA

On New Year's Day 43 B.C. the Senate gathered under the presidency of the new consuls to consider the situation. In spite of the insistence of Cicero, who saw clearly the importance of legalizing Octavius' position, members were not disposed to take the precipitate step of declaring Antony a public enemy, and after some days' debate a moderate motion by Fufius Calenus, that an embassy should be sent to Antony requiring him to withdraw and submit to the wishes of Senate and People, finally won approval.

---

[1] Cicero, *Phil.* III, 2, 5, '*privato consilio*' (and cf. 1, 3), a phrase which Octavius was glad to borrow for his own account in *Res Gestae*; so too the '*dominatio*' of Antony duly appears.

[2] Cf. such passages as Cicero, *Phil.* III, 8, 19; *ad Fam.* XII, 25, 4; *ad Brut.* I, 3, 1; 10, 3, and 15, 6, where he avows his responsibility in guiding Octavius. It is worth noting that Octavius was later ready to acknowledge this claim of Cicero's; see Plutarch, *Cicero*, 45, and *Compar. Dem. cum Cic.* 3.

But Cicero carried his point that honours should be conferred both on Lepidus (for winning over Sextus Pompeius) and on Octavius, in whom he now professed complete confidence; 'I know the inmost secrets of his heart,' he assured his hearers, and claimed that Providence itself had intervened to produce this divine young man who had delivered them from the tyranny of Antony[1]. The listening Senate decreed that Octavius should be given the rank of senator and should, together with the two consuls, join in command, as pro-praetor, of the force that was to be dispatched against Antony. February brought the return of the embassy with the news that their mission had been fruitless, for Antony far from showing submission had counter-claims to put forward, and the *senatus consultum ultimum* was formally passed. But Antony could still rely on his supporters at Rome to protract proceedings, and it was only after another proposal for an embassy had been mooted and quashed that Pansa marched out on 19 March, with four legions, to join his colleagues, of whom Hirtius was at Claterna and Octavius at Forum Cornelii. In addition Antony had written to the two consuls protesting against their attitude, jeering at Octavius as 'a boy who owed everything to Caesar's name[2],' and declaring that he himself was in understanding with both Lepidus and Plancus: evidence for this last assertion was soon seen in the arrival of letters to Cicero from these two advocating negotiations and peace, though publicly Plancus assured the Senate of his unwavering loyalty.

During the early spring Brutus had begun to feel the pinch of hunger in Mutina, and Hirtius and Octavius had moved nearer. Warned of Pansa's approach, Antony determined to attack him before he could join his colleagues, and marched up the Aemilian Way; but Hirtius had foreseen this move and had dispatched the *legio Martia* (which had already suffered from Antony at Brundisium) and two praetorian cohorts to aid his fellow-consul. On 14 April they came into conflict near the village of Forum Gallorum, where Antony had laid an ambush: Pansa was badly wounded, Antony's troops carried the day and were returning in victorious disorder when in their turn they encountered Hirtius coming up in support, who routed them. Octavius, who had been left to defend the Republican camp, for his bravery in repelling an attack won the praise of the veteran Hirtius; both of them were

[1] Cicero, *Phil.* v, 16, 43: 'quis tum nobis, quis populo Romano obtulit hunc divinum adulescentem deus?' This phrase too found later echoes.
[2] Cicero, *Phil.* XIII, 11, 24: 'et te, o puer, qui omnia nomini debes.'

acclaimed as *Imperatores* (15 April)[1]. Six days later Antony again offered battle, but Octavius and Hirtius forced their way into his camp, Brutus made a vigorous sally from Mutina itself, and his only course was to retreat. Decimus, with his famished troops, could not initiate a pursuit at once, and even when he did he was misled by false information. Meanwhile Antony, with one legion (V Alaudae) and the ill-armed remnants of several others, made for Gaul and Lepidus, and was joined by Ventidius Bassus and three legions raised in Italy[2]; a harassing march awaited him over the Alps, but his courage was superior to all hardships, and the real worth of the man showed itself here; by mid-May he had reached Forum Julii. But though the Republicans had triumphed, Hirtius had fallen in the moment of victory, Pansa was fatally stricken by his wound, and Octavius was left in possession of the field.

This unwelcome truth was not however immediately apparent to the senators: in their first reaction from fear they were prepared to be masterful. Antony was formally declared a public enemy, and all his opponents encouraged. At earlier meetings in March Cicero had succeeded in getting the position of Brutus in Macedonia legalized, though he had failed to secure a *maius imperium* for Cassius in Syria. But now the Senate was inspirited to grant more: Brutus and Cassius were confirmed in their provinces and given a *maius imperium* over all governors in the East; Sextus Pompeius was summoned from Massilia to be put in charge of the fleet and of the coast of Italy[3]; Decimus Brutus was actually given a triumph. To Octavius they were less generous: he was not allowed the *ovatio* that Cicero proposed, his own troops and those of the consuls were to be transferred to the sole command of Decimus, a commission of ten men to distribute bounties to the troops was appointed from which he was excluded, and the despatches were addressed not to him but direct to the legionaries. The majority would doubtless have agreed with what Marcus Brutus wrote to Atticus[4], that there was a risk that the boy might become difficult to hold in check, and that Cicero's enthusiasm for him was a blunder.

Octavius naturally made no effort to pursue Antony; rather through various channels he offered reconciliation. He would not

---

[1] Cicero, *Phil.* XIV, 10, 28; Dessau 108.

[2] Cicero, *ad Fam.* X, 34, 1.

[3] On coins henceforward Sextus calls himself *praefectus classis et orae maritimae*: Babelon, *Description Historique...*, pp. 352 *sqq.*

[4] Cicero, *ad Brut.* I, 17.

surrender Pansa's legions to Decimus; the rest refused outright to
serve under a leader whom they loathed for his treachery to
Caesar[1]. Thus the hopes of the Senate rested on Lepidus and his
seven legions; Plancus on hearing of the news of Mutina promised
to influence Lepidus in the right direction, but on reaching the Isère
in early May he was greeted by confident despatches from the
man he had come to save, for Lepidus affirmed he was quite
capable of dealing with Antony by himself. The next news was,
naturally enough, that the soldiers of Antony and Lepidus had
fraternized and that the two leaders had joined forces; Lepidus
now dispatched a letter of pious resignation to the Senate. Such
were the tidings that reached Decimus Brutus, toiling in pursuit,
early in June, and all he could do was to join Plancus, who had
retreated to Cularo. Lepidus was of course declared a public
enemy and Cicero lamented his 'criminal folly' in letters to
M. Brutus, through which a growing note of despondency sounds;
nowhere could he discern honest selfless Republican patriotism,
and Octavius would no longer listen to him[2].

It was true enough: in July a party of centurions entered the
Senate-house to demand the consulship for their general. Octavius
had eight legions to back him, he had played long enough with
Cicero to prevent the Senate taking united action against him[3], he
was in touch with the other Caesarian leaders, and the time was
ripe. Various reasons were advanced in ancient times for this change
of attitude, but all—whether irritation at being referred to as a
boy, or Pansa's death-bed exhortation, or a reputed witticism of
Cicero's—are trivial when weighed against the calculation that in
order to avenge his father's death and attain his honours Octavius
was bound eventually to combine with Antony, but must meet
him on equal terms; last year Antony had been consul, this year
it would be Octavius. The Senate temporized by offering a praetorship; he replied by marching on Rome and resistance collapsed.
Once assured that his mother and sister were safe and unharmed,
and after distributing from the treasury the promised bounties
to his troops, he could wait outside the city till the elections were
over; some difficulties were felt, for while one patrician magistrate
remained the *auspicia* could not return to the *patres*[4], but the praetor

[1] Cicero, *Phil.* x, 7, 15.   [2] Cicero, *ad Brutum*, I, 10.
[3] The story in Appian, *Bell. Civ.* III, 82, 337 *sqq.*, that Octavius
negotiated with Cicero about the consulship and played on his vanity is not
impossible, though full of Pollio's bias against Cicero: Brutus heard a rumour
that Cicero had actually been elected, *ad Brutum*, I, 4 A, 4.
[4] Cicero, *ad Brutum*, I, 5, 4; see vol. VII, p. 530.

nominated two proconsuls to hold the election, and on 19
August Octavius and his uncle Q. Pedius were duly announced
consuls. He had reached the highest honour Rome could offer at
an age younger even than Pompey, and it was reported that at his
first taking of the auspices twelve vultures were seen, as on the
first *auspicium* of Romulus[1]. The *lex curiata* necessary to confirm
his adoption was at last passed; henceforward he was Gaius Julius
Caesar Octavianus. The full significance of this—which Antony
well realized—is obscured for modern readers by the convention
of describing him as Octavian, a term only employed for him by
his enemies or by those who wished to be less than polite[2]. To the
Roman people and to the legions he was now Caesar, and the name
was magical[3]. A Lex Pedia, which pronounced sentence of outlawry upon all assassins after a form of trial had been gone through,
was passed as a signal for all Caesarians, and with his army
increased to eleven legions Octavian drew out of Rome for the
north[4]. Pedius easily persuaded the Senate to revoke the decrees
against Antony and Lepidus.

The collapse of Republicanism in Italy was followed by its
collapse in the West. The danger of a possible collision between
the Caesarians in Gaul and the recently united forces of Plancus and
Decimus Brutus was soon averted; Asinius Pollio, arriving from
Spain with two legions, preferred to join Antony, and succeeded
in bringing over Plancus as well. Decimus found himself
deserted; his legions joined the victors; in a vain effort to reach
Aquileia (? and Macedonia) he was captured by a Gaulish chief
and put to death. It is easy to brand the vacillation of a Lepidus
or Plancus or Pollio, but hard to descry what other course than

---

[1] Suetonius, *Aug.* 95. This report was to be of great importance afterwards, when he was hailed as the second founder of Rome. He was not yet
augur, though he certainly was by 41/40, as his coins show, with the legend
C. CAES. COS. PONT. AVG. and the augural *lituus*; see Volume of Plates
iv, 196, *a, c,* and on the whole question cf. J. Gagé, *Mélanges d'arch. et
d'hist.* XLVIII, 1931, pp. 79 *sqq.*

[2] See Mommsen's note upon *C.I.L.*[1] no. 683. An analogy, though not
an exact one, is to be found in Nero's indignation at being saluted as
'Domitius,' after he had been adopted into the Claudian family: Tac. *Ann.*
XII, 41. The title 'Octavius Caesar' on the Annecy *patera* is a freak; W
Deonna in *Rev. Arch.* XI, 1920, pp. 128 and 180.

[3] Fear of the effect of this name occasioned the large gifts Brutus and
Cassius made to the Caesarian veterans in their army: Appian, *Bell. Civ.* IV,
89, 374. A modern parallel would be the usefulness of the name Napoleon
to the rising Louis Napoleon.

[4] Three more joined him in Rome: Appian, *Bell. Civ.* III, 92, 381.

joining Antony was feasible for them. All three were men of distinction who had served under Julius Caesar and owed their rank and provinces to him, and Plancus was certainly carrying out the great dictator's plans when he founded the colonies of Raurica and Lugdunum (Copia Felix Munatia) in his province[1]: the sacred name of the Republic meant little to those who had seen one man's genius supersede it, and in a period when none was secure realism sought the protection of big battalions; in addition it was highly doubtful whether their men would fight against their fellows in Antony's army, for one of the most remarkable features of these years is the 'war-weariness' of the troops and their constant efforts to secure conciliation.

The only menace now left was in the East, where the Republicans had succeeded beyond expectation. As Syria at the beginning of 44 B.C. was held by a Pompeian general, Caecilius Bassus, Caesar had dispatched M. Crispus and Staius Murcus to deal with him and assigned the province of Asia to Trebonius, later one of his assassins. At the end of the year Dolabella set out to assume the government of Syria, and on his way through Asia killed Trebonius, who resisted him. But he was not to have peace, for Cassius, also bound for Syria, outstripped him travelling by sea, and won over not only the forces of the Pompeian Bassus but also those of the Caesarian Murcus, and at the same time pounced on four legions which Cleopatra had sent from Egypt to assist Dolabella. With a total of twelve legions he had no difficulty in blockading Dolabella in Laodicea and driving him to suicide. Urgent messages now reached him from M. Brutus (aware of the issue at Mutina) to meet him at Smyrna; he renounced a punitive expedition against Cleopatra, and after extorting 700 talents from the Jews, enslaving the inhabitants of four towns, and setting up various tyrants in the cities of Syria[2], he marched to join his colleague.

Brutus, too, had been fortunate. Landing at Athens he was warmly received and young men such as M. Cicero or M. Valerius Messalla Corvinus or Q. Horatius Flaccus enrolled themselves under him in a transport of Republican fervour; in Illyricum the legions of Vatinius went over to him, and he managed to bring C. Antonius (who had tried to occupy Macedonia, which the Senate

---

[1] The exact dating is doubtful: Raurica probably belongs to 44 B.C. and Lugdunum almost certainly to the autumn of 43 B.C. See Dessau 886; Th. Burckhardt-Biedermann, *Die Kolonie Augusta Raurica*, and C. Jullian, *Histoire de la Gaule*, vol. IV, pp. 42 *sqq.* The actual order for the foundation was apparently given by the Senate: Dio XLVI, 50.

[2] Josephus, *Ant.* XIV [11, 2], 272 and [12, 1], 297.

had assigned to him on November 28 and had ordered him on December 20 to give up) to surrender. He was in continuous correspondence with Cicero, and his letters display a calm lenity in curious contrast with Cicero's vehemence. He did not wish to drive Antony to extremes, and he repeatedly cautioned Cicero against the bestowal of excessive honours on young Octavian, in which he foresaw danger; 'we should be more keen on preventing the outbreak of a civil war than in glutting our anger on the defeated' was his message, and he spared the life of Antony's brother Gaius, though later he had to put him to death in reprisal for the proscriptions. The news of Mutina heartened him considerably, and during the campaigning season of 43 he not only collected recruits from Asia but also received the submission of several Thracian chieftains, and conducted a victorious expedition against the Bessi, for which he was greeted by his soldiers as *Imperator*. With the booty gained and the treasure contributed by the Thracian chiefs he issued a series of coins proclaiming symbolically his action as liberator of Rome[1], and in the autumn made his way into Asia in order to collect a fleet, money and recruits, and meet Cassius. By the end of the year the two Republican leaders were at Smyrna and by this date the Caesarians too had come to a meeting and agreement.

IV. TRIUMVIRATE AND PROSCRIPTION

By the autumn of 43 B.C., when Octavian, leaving Pedius in charge of Rome, marched out northwards, his object must have been clear: however great the disparity of character and purpose among the Caesarian leaders, however deep their mutual distrust, a year's experience had shown that concord and a common policy were essential. Antony and Lepidus had agreed to meet him; on the appointed day, early in November, the three arrived at their rendezvous near Bononia, accompanied by the officers of their staff, such as Pollio and Ventidius, and by their troops[2], and (after elaborate precautions against treachery) conferred together during two fateful days in full view of the soldiery on a small island in the river Lavinius[3]. The solution reached amounted to a triple dictatorship, like the informal compact of 60 B.C. (vol. IX, pp. 513 *sqq.*),

---

[1] See Vol. of Plates IV, 12, *j*.

[2] Antony and Lepidus brought 17 legions with them; 6 were left in Gaul under Cotyla (Plutarch, *Ant.* 18). Octavian when he left Rome had 11; and the 6 new-levied legions of Decimus Brutus joined him on the way (Appian, *Bell. Civ.* III, 97, 402).

[3] See the just remarks of Levi, *op. cit.* I, p. 218, n. 3.

but whereas that had been a secret and personal arrangement, this was to be public and statutory: the three were to be appointed *tresviri reipublicae constituendae* for a long term of years, superior to all magistrates, with power to make laws and to nominate magistrates and governors. Each Triumvir was also to have a province, Antony taking Cisalpine and Transalpine Gaul, Lepidus Old Gaul and all Spain, Octavian Africa, Sicily, and Sardinia; the division demonstrated Antony's predominance, for his possession of Cisalpine Gaul gave him the mastery of Italy and he left to his partners those lands which were most vulnerable by naval operations and in which Sextus Pompeius (deprived of his command by Octavian but still master of a considerable fleet[1]) might cause trouble. In the meantime, while Antony and Octavian dealt with the Republican forces in the East, Lepidus was to govern Italy. But to carry out this programme funds would be needed, not only for the expenses of war, but also to meet the demands of the veterans. These were satisfied by the allotment of land from eighteen of the richest Italian towns (Capua, Beneventum, Rhegium, Vibo, Cremona, and Venusia were among the number), while in order to replenish their war-chest and to rid themselves of their enemies the three determined on a proscription. There should be no clemency such as had ruined Caesar: with unflinching logic and on approved 'Sullan' methods they would uproot all opposition.

Such were the terms of this unholy alliance, and after they had been communicated to the exultant troops, they were embodied in a written compact formally sealed and signed by the partners. Octavian now resigned his consulship in favour of Antony's legate, Ventidius Bassus, and was to receive Antony's step-daughter, Claudia, to wife[2]; Asinius Pollio was left in Transpadane Gaul to supervise the assignment of land there to the veterans—a step momentous for literature (p. 540)—and the three leaders marched on Rome, where a tribunician law of 27 November (the Lex Titia) gave them the legal status they desired for a term of a little over five years, till 31 December 38 B.C. The next day a table of 130 proscribed was posted in the city, with a preamble intended to justify it; but a short preliminary list of the most important had already been issued, with no fine phrases, and the hunt was up. Nights and days of unendurable horror followed: the consul Pedius, who tried to allay the rising panic, died of sheer exhaustion; victims

[1] It was over 100 vessels; see Kromayer in *Philologus*, LVI, 1897, pp. 426 *sqq.*

[2] She was his wife in name only, and Octavian sent her back to Fulvia in the wrangles preceding the Perusine War (Suetonius, *Aug.* 62).

were cut down without mercy, for the rewards offered were large and payment prompt; terror ruled. Yet amid the wreck of civilized life there were still some whom rewards could not tempt or torture affright, slaves sons and wives who dared greatly and whose heroism triumphed over all obstacles[1].

A few, who were guilty of great possessions, attracted the triumvirs' cupidity (though the prudent kindness of the wealthy Atticus to Fulvia had ensured his safety and Varro was exempted by the intervention of Fufius Calenus), but the majority of the proscribed belonged to the old aristocratic order, who had supported Pompey and the Senate, and notable among these was Pompey's surviving son, Sextus, who during the winter was able to lay hold upon some towns in Sicily. Proscribed himself he made every effort, by the dispatch of ships and men, to rescue the unfortunate fugitives and bring them safely out of Italy. Many escaped to him, others lay hidden till better days dawned, but even so the number of those murdered—three hundred senators and two thousand knights—was appalling. Only those who believe that the triumph of a party deprives its opponents not only of the rights of citizens but also of human beings will find phrases to defend the proscription. Rome may have ultimately profited, but a crime it remains, and none of the three triumvirs can escape responsibility. Indeed it is false to history and to psychology alike to exempt Octavian; granted he was young, yet in pursuit of an object to which both his duty to his murdered father and his own ambition pointed, there could be small room for pity; he may have tried to avoid proscription at first, but he was the most ruthlessly logical in carrying it out, once it had been determined[2].

Among the first to fall was Cicero: worn out by his feverish exertions, his hopes and ideals crumbling around him, he had quitted Rome in August. A few fragments of letters to Octavian remain, the rest is silence. When the news of his proscription reached him he meditated flight, but the wintry weather and his own indecision drove him back. The soldiers overtook him; his slaves were ready to fight, but he forbade them; life had no more to offer, and gazing firmly on his executioner he met the supreme moment as a Roman should. There can be few whose character has been more bitterly impugned or more warmly

---

[1] Various exempla are preserved in Appian and Dio, or in such collections as Valerius Maximus. For the 'Turia' inscription see *C.I.L.* vi, 1527 and 31670 (Dessau 8393), and cf. R. S. Conway in *The Vergilian Age*, pp. 1 *sqq.*

[2] This is the view of Suetonius, *Aug.* 27.

defended, and fate ironically ordained that his own matchless power of expression (as exemplified in his *Letters*) should survive as the most relentless witness against him. His native horror of bloodshed and of 'Sullan' cruelty, his legal training, and his humanism as a scholar all gave him a traditionalist standpoint, making him an admirer of a stable constitution, where life could be lived in peace and reasonableness, and of this he saw a pattern in the times of Scipio Aemilianus before the Gracchi disturbed the State. It was his peculiar misfortune to be thrust into an age when all the arts of peace were powerless against brute ambition, which left no choice to a reasoning and sensitive nature save that between two evils. His vacillation was as much the consequence of his time as of his temperament, for in a real crisis he was no coward. In an age of apathy and corruption he could sympathize with the needs of the provincials and strive for better government: in his treatises his insight so gauged the trend of politics that, as Nepos remarks, 'he foretold even the things which are coming to pass now[1].' Yet it is not as consul or statesman that he vindicates his claim to fame, but by the influence that his speeches and writings exerted after him, so that (in the generous phrase of Julius Caesar) he 'advanced the boundaries of the Latin genius[2],' and fashioned Latin into an enduring and universal speech.

V. PHILIPPI

An impressive act marked the opening of the year 42, for on 1 January the Senate recognized Julius Caesar as a god, and the triumvirs not only themselves swore to uphold his *acta* but also administered the oath to magistrates and Senate: henceforward Octavian, the young Caesar, was *divi filius*. The final arrangements for the coming campaign were made: the three triumvirs had at their disposal an army amounting to forty-three legions; while sufficient forces were left to guard the provinces, Lepidus with three of his legions was to maintain order in Italy; to Antony Lepidus lent four, to Octavian three, and it appears that the two mustered between them twenty-eight legions with which to face Brutus and Cassius[3]. Eight legions were sent on in advance under Decidius Saxa and Norbanus Flaccus, and during the early summer the rest were transported across the Adriatic[4]. Difficulties,

---

[1] Nepos, *Atticus*, 17, 4 (written *c.* 30 B.C.).   [2] Pliny, *N.H.* VII, 117.
[3] For the calculations see Groebe-Drumann, *Geschichte Roms*, vol. I, pp. 468 *sqq.*, T. Rice Holmes, *The Architect of the Roman Empire*, vol. I, p. 217 *sq.*, and Levi, *op. cit.* p. 240, n. 3.
[4] Two, including the *legio Martia*, were being transported on the day of the first battle of Philippi: Appian, *Bell. Civ.* IV, 115, 479.

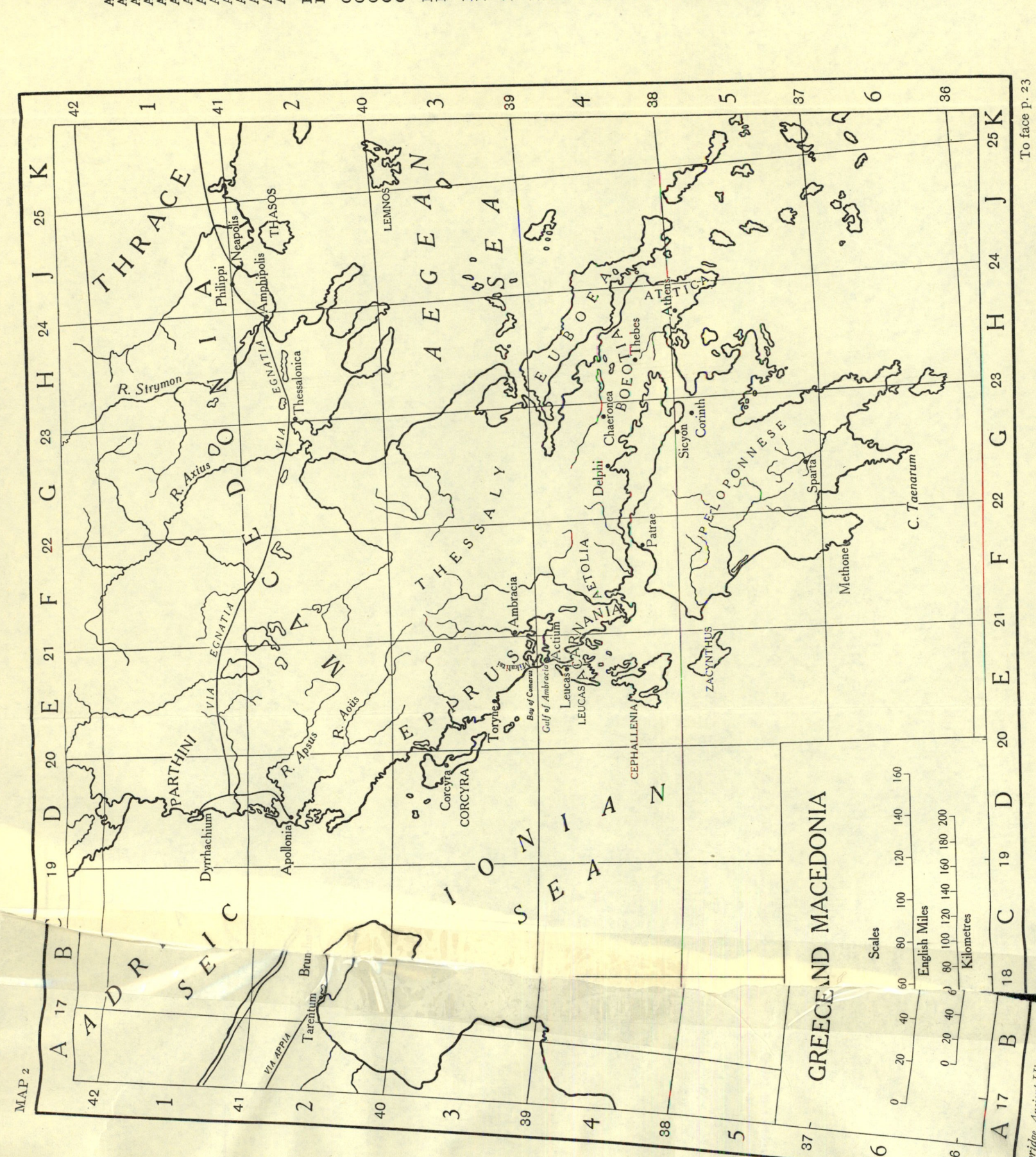

GREECE AND MACEDONIA

Scales

English Miles

Kilometres

MAP 2

however, were many: the proscriptions not only brought hatred upon the three, but had actually failed to provide sufficient funds for the campaign, and the imposition of property taxation met with strenuous resistance. During the winter Sextus Pompeius gained control of Sicily and began to give trouble, but though he repulsed a small squadron sent against him under Salvidienus Rufus, his own inertia prevented him from joining the two Republican admirals, Staius Murcus and Domitius Ahenobarbus, in harassing the transport of the triumviral forces. Octavian fell ill and had to be left behind at Dyrrhachium, but Antony moved rapidly eastwards to link up with Saxa and Norbanus, who after taking up an advanced position had been outflanked by Brutus and Cassius and so had fallen back upon Amphipolis.

Since meeting at Smyrna the Republican leaders had dealt determinedly with all open or suspected enemies. Brutus had summoned the cities of Lycia to contribute to his war-chest; Xanthus, proud of its century-old independence, refused and when the legions encompassed it, sooner than surrender, men and women destroyed themselves and their city; the other cities gave in and paid. Cassius was more extortionate still; Laodicea had to pay for its resistance, Tarsus was fined 1500 talents; the Rhodians saw their temples and citizens robbed of 8000; upon the cities of Asia he imposed the burden of ten years' tribute. It was the last expiring act of old Republican brutality, but it supplied the sinews of war, and the two reached the Hellespont together in September, in command of nineteen legions, whose fidelity was carefully reinforced by a share of the booty gained. They had sent Q. Labienus to ask for assistance from Orodes of Parthia—a mission that was to have far-reaching consequences—and now marched westwards, turning the flank of Saxa and Norbanus, towards Philippi. Prospects were good, for their fleets, under Murcus and Ahenobarbus, commanded the sea and had their base at Neapolis; winter was approaching and if an engagement could be postponed hunger might work havoc among the Caesarians. But it was not to be: though the Republicans had the better ground, though the two armies were approximately equal in numbers[1], the Caesarians possessed in Antony the most vigorous and resourceful general of the time, and now that Octavian, despite his illness, had joined the camp they had a living

---

[1] Antony left one legion, under Pinarius, at Amphipolis (Appian, *Bell. Civ.* IV, 107, 447); Appian says each side had 19 legions (*ib.* 108, 454), but two out of the Republican total were serving with the fleets of Murcus and Ahenobarbus (*ib.* 74, 315; 86, 367, and 99, 415), and six of the Caesarian were presumably guarding communications or on other duties.

reminder of the name and cause for which they fought. Against this personal element the Republicans could offer nothing.

Brutus and Cassius had pitched their camp, to the west of Philippi, on either side of the *via Egnatia* and in easy communication with their fleet at Neapolis. A large marsh lay to the south, a defence against outflanking of their camps and a barrier to any enemy who tried to cut their communications. Antony saw that the only way to foil the waiting tactics of the Republicans was to pierce this barrier, and started building a causeway across; when Cassius replied with counter-works Antony organized a simultaneous attack here and on the camp of Cassius. His dash and courage carried all before him, the troops of Cassius were routed and his camp plundered. In the dust and confusion Cassius, ignorant that Brutus' troops had rushed into battle unordered and actually stormed the camp of Octavian, chagrined at defeat and despairing of the future, committed suicide. It was a heavy loss to the Republican cause, for Cassius was a better disciplinarian and more experienced general than his colleague, who found it difficult to hold his troops in check, and now, fearing the effect of a public burial on his men, dispatched the body to Thasos. For the present he moved into Cassius' camp and carried on the uninspiring policy of inaction.

The only course for the Caesarians was to cut off Brutus' supplies; their own were running low, and winter was beginning. Propaganda leaflets were thrown into Brutus' camp, which induced some to desert, and taunts and abuse were hurled at the Republicans; men and officers alike chafed under inaction, and at last Brutus, against his better judgment, perhaps afraid that his lines would be cut, perhaps mistrustful of the continuing loyalty of his men (to whom it is said he had promised the plunder of Thessalonica), late on the afternoon of 23 October[1] led his legions out to accept the challenge. Octavian's troops played their part manfully and finally turned the Republicans to rout, Antony carried on the pursuit with brilliance, and night brought complete victory. But Octavian was still so weak in health that he handed over the guarding of the camp to Norbanus. Some of the leading Republicans committed suicide, some fled to join the fleet, a few obtained pardon; the troops, naturally enough, enlisted under the Caesarian generals.

Escorted and defended by a few faithful companions Brutus had escaped towards the hills, only to realize as the night wore on

[1] The date is now certain: see O. Marucchi, *Not. degli Scavi*, XVIII, 1926, pp. 277 *sqq.*

the hopelessness of further resistance; crying out, like some ancient Hildebrand, upon that righteousness which he had followed so unswervingly and which had at last left him destitute, he fell upon his sword. So passed away 'the noblest Roman of them all,' the last representative of the aristocratic tradition, and with him died the Republican spirit, for henceforward men fought for a leader. His is one of the most famous figures in antiquity, yet the fame seems factitious and the figure has suffered strange distortions. To the oppressed and to revolutionaries he has seemed the ideal combination of patriot and philosopher, his name one 'before which tyrants tremble'; modern critics, emphasizing his dourness of manner, his bluntness of speech, and that superior expression[1] which Cicero noted, heap scorn on *virtus* that could prey on provincials and kill a benefactor for the sake of principle. All this is beside the mark, for Brutus was a more ordinary man and no unfair specimen of the late Republican senator; what held admiration in antiquity was his steadfast adherence to a creed (however narrow) and his intense earnestness of purpose[2]. It is to his credit too that the murder of Caesar did not degenerate into a massacre of Caesarians; he would willingly have spared C. Antonius, and throughout he remained true to the principle he had enunciated to Atticus of unconditional warfare against extraordinary commands, tyranny, and all 'power which would place itself above the laws[3].' But firmness of character and loyalty to an ideal, however admirable in themselves, are no sufficient guides through changing political conditions, unless based upon an equipment of intellect, and intellectually Brutus was in no way superior to his fellow-nobles. When all is said, his was a creed of negative principles, lacking any trace of constructive policy to meet the needs of the time, ineffectual too against those who fought for a person and a memory.

VI. PERUSIA AND AFTER

Philippi finally shattered Republican hopes: Murcus and Ahenobarbus might gather in the irreconcilables and depart, the one to offer his services to Sextus, the other to maintain himself in the Adriatic with 70 ships and two legions, but there was no party

---

[1] Cicero, *ad Att.* XIV, 20, 5: 'Non te Bruti nostri *vulticulus* ab ista oratione deterret?'

[2] Caesar's comment, 'magni refert hic quid velit, sed quidquid volet valde volet' (Cicero, *ad Att.* XIV, 1, 2), is criticism, not enthusiasm. Cf. Plutarch, *Brutus*, 6, and see M. Rothstein in *Rh. Mus.* LXXXI, 1932, p. 324.

[3] Cicero, *ad Brutum*, I, 17, 6.

and no leader of the prestige of Brutus left. Caesar's murder was avenged; forty years later the inauguration of the temple of Mars Ultor fulfilled Octavian's vow before the battle[1]. But much remained to be done: the two immediately urgent problems were to bring the East into order again and to deal with the great mass of men who were or had been under arms. A start was made by planting a colony at Philippi[2] and by disbanding all but eleven legions, and of these eleven at least two were composed of Brutus' and Cassius' old troops; for the future the two partners agreed to a division of duties and provinces, witnessed by a signed compact of which each kept a copy. The division showed that Antony was still the predominant partner: while Octavian had been ill and carried about the camp in a litter Antony's courage and resource had won both battles; the prestige was his and he could impose his will. But Octavian held second place, for Lepidus was rumoured to be in negotiation with Sextus and, until he could clear himself, was to receive no provinces or troops. In the new allotment Antony took the two Gauls[3], together with the more important task of settling the East and of collecting the money which was required for the settlement of the disbanded troops; ultimately, he meant to carry out Caesar's plan of attacking Parthia. Octavian received Spain, Sardinia and Africa; this last on condition that he would pass it over to Lepidus, if he proved satisfactory; we may assume that Lepidus would also receive back the seven legions that he had lent to the other two (p. 30 n. 1)[4]. In addition Octavian was to supervise all the assignation of land and also deal with Sextus. Italy was to be common ground.

Of the eleven legions left Antony's share was six, but he borrowed two more from Octavian, thus taking eight legions with 10,000 horse, and leaving three legions and 4000 horse with his colleague. He left six of his eight legions under L. Marcius Censorinus in Macedonia, as the Illyrian Parthini were threatening, and took two with him to Asia. In the two Gauls he already

---

[1] *Res Gestae* 21; Suetonius, *Aug.* 29; Dio LV, 10.

[2] Strabo VII, 331 (frag. 41); Pliny, *N.H.* IV, 42.

[3] That is Old Gaul (later Narbonensis) and Gallia Comata, for, on the request of Octavian, Cisalpine Gaul was now left without a governor and became finally part of Italy; see vol. IX, p. 643 *sq.*

[4] Appian's account (*Bell. Civ.* V, 3, 12, and 12, 47) is here preferred; presumably, had Lepidus failed to satisfy, Antony and Octavian would have taken *Africa vetus* and *Africa nova* respectively. For a discussion of the problem see F. L. Ganter, *Die Provinzialverwaltung der Triumvirn*, Strassburg Diss. 1892, p. 3; Rice Holmes, *op. cit.* I, p. 218 *sq.*; S. Gsell, *Histoire Ancienne de l'Afrique du Nord*, 1928, p. 191 *sq.*

possessed large armies, eleven legions under Fufius Calenus, and thirteen divided between Ventidius Bassus, Pollio and Plancus, but he was going to lose touch with his generals there.

So the two triumvirs separated, Antony to the East, Octavian to the West; he was not fully recovered, and the fatigues of a winter journey brought on a recurrence of his illness which nearly proved fatal, but somehow he reached Brundisium. Arrived in Italy he showed Antony's representatives the written compact and gained their consent. To safeguard his provinces he sent Salvidienus Rufus with six legions to Spain to replace C. Carrinas, while in Sardinia he had two. Africa had been held for the triumvirs by T. Sextius, a soldier of extraordinary resource, who had succeeded in routing Cornificius and all other Republican commanders; he now handed over to the successor sent by Octavian, T. Fuficius Fango, but apparently still remained in the province[1]. Such were the resources with which Octavian faced his task.

It was no easy one: Sextus Pompeius was daily gaining strength from victims of the proscriptions or runaway slaves, and Murcus with his 80 ships brought a considerable accession to his fleet; the soldiers knew their power and were in dangerous mood; the veterans demanded immediate satisfaction; evicted townsfolk or landowners raised every possible obstacle; hundreds of poor wretches driven from farm and home were drifting about Italy or emigrating in despair; some few, such as Virgil, found protection, but the remainder mingled with the other malcontents and only needed a leader. But, despite all, Octavian's faith in his mission was unshaken; he was beginning to feel his feet, and could already afford to pardon some of the proscribed[2], and he had friends upon whose loyalty he could depend to the last. Such were M. Agrippa, who had been with him at Apollonia and was soon to manifest his ability as general and administrator, and C. Cilnius Maecenas, a rich and cultivated Etruscan noble, whose diplomatic gifts and talent for negotiation were increasingly at the disposition of his friend; these two were to be of inestimable service to him. Important too was the fact that they were contemporaries of his, unfettered by inconvenient memories of the Republic, unafraid to tread new paths.

---

[1] For the complicated course of the war in Africa, which was of small historical importance, the sources are Dio XLVIII, 21–3, and Appian, *Bell. Civ.* III, 85, 351; IV, 53, 226–56, 243; v, 12, 46; 26, 102–3; 75, 321. For modern accounts see F. L. Ganter in *Philologus*, LIII, 1894, p. 142, and Gsell, *op. cit.* pp. 184–94.   [2] Cf. Dessau 8393, ll. 21–8.

As the work of settlement went steadily on, friends of Antony began to realize that he had made a mistake in leaving the execution of it, and the resultant popularity with the veterans, entirely to Octavian. Lucius Antonius, the brother of the triumvir, who became consul in 41 and celebrated a triumph for victories over some Alpine tribes, first gave trouble; he claimed to be a Republican, and not only championed the cause of the evicted but attacked the triumvirate itself, and by so doing won considerable support. Fulvia, Antony's wife, was at length persuaded by a steward called Manius that her husband's interests were at stake, and the three joined in fierce opposition to Octavian; Lucius, pretending his life was endangered, collected a bodyguard from his brother's veterans, Asinius Pollio blocked Rufus' march westwards, and orders were sent to Bocchus, king of the Maurusii, to attack and detain the legions under Carrinas in Spain, and to T. Sextius to contest Africa with Fango[1]. The leaders of the legions, in alarm, tried to effect a reconciliation at Teanum Sidicinum, in the early autumn; the terms agreed on, as reported by Appian[2], are mysterious—including apparently the restoration of the consular power and an equal division between the two parties of the legions of Antony and the confiscated property—but they remained a dead letter from the start. The legionaries made a desperate last effort to bring the two parties together at Gabii; but Lucius, either through fear, or affecting to despise 'the hobnailed Senate of soldiers,' did not keep the appointment. There was nothing for it but to fight.

The only excuse to be urged for Lucius and Fulvia is that they honestly thought they were acting in Antony's interest; indeed Lucius assumed the name *Pietas* as a symbol of his loyalty[3]. But Octavian was in a most delicate situation, for how could he be sure that the whole business might not be due to Antony's prompting? Both parties wrote to Antony, but winter made communication slow, the news did not reach him till spring, and in any event he could not oppose his colleague without overthrowing the pact to which he had set his seal after Philippi. The actual course of the war demands no long narration; Octavian sent a legion to Brundisium to guard against possible reinforcements from the East, recalled Rufus and his legions, entrusted

[1] Dio XLVIII, 22, 3 and Appian, *Bell. Civ.* v, 26, 102–3.
[2] Appian, *Bell. Civ.* v, 20, 79–80.
[3] For coins of L. Antonius, giving the name and head of his brother, and with the legend PIETAS COS, see Vol. of Plates iv, 196, *b*, and cf. H. A. Grueber, *Coins of the Roman Republic in the Brit. Museum*, II, pp. 400 *sqq.*

another command to Agrippa, and placed Lepidus with two legions
n charge of Rome—a charge where he signally failed, since he
a lowed Lucius to break into the city. Fulvia was tireless; she and
Lucius had six legions of their own, she recruited two more which
she gave to Plancus, she wrote for assistance to Bassus and Pollio;
but the position of the three lieutenants of Antony was difficult, for
no one knew what Antony really wanted, and Plancus succeeded in
infecting the other two with much of his native caution. Lucius,
closely pursued by Rufus and Agrippa, flung himself into Perusia:
the old town with its Etruscan walls crowning a hill 1500 feet
high was impregnable by assault but all the more easy to blockade.
Octavian promptly drew great lines of circumvallation round it,
and detached some forces to watch the movements of the three
legates of Antony; in the end they retired and left the town to its
fate. That could not be long; the investment was close and
hunger—*Perusina fames* became a byword—soon drove the besieged to desperation; Lucius vainly attempted to break out on
New Year's Eve, some of his more notable supporters deserted,
and by the end of February, 40 B.C., he was forced to surrender. His
excuses were bound to be accepted, for Octavian could not afford to
offend Antony by harsh treatment of his brother; he was dismissed
unharmed, his soldiers were pardoned. Pollio retired northwards,
Bassus and Plancus towards Brundisium, and Agrippa succeeded
in bringing over two of Plancus' legions; but no serious obstacle
to escape was offered, and at Brundisium Plancus and Fulvia took
ship for Athens.

Far different was the fortune of Perusia; the city was given up
as plunder to the soldiery, stripped and burnt; the ordinary
citizens were allowed to go free, but to the senators and to the
remnant of Republicans taken there Octavian was pitiless, and the
last traces of opposition were stamped out[1]. An attempt at a slave
insurrection in Campania, led by the ardent Republican Tiberius
Claudius Nero, was soon crushed; with his wife Livia and son
Tiberius he fled to Sicily, and Octavian by a strange irony expelled
from Italy the woman who was to be his wife and the boy whom
he was to choose as his successor.

But the twenty-two-year-old leader had other difficulties to face:

[1] Inscriptions such as *Mars Ultor* and *Divus Iulius* found on sling-bullets
(*C.I.L.* I[1], 686 and 697, and cf. C. Zangemeister Eph. Ep. VI, 1885,
pp. 52–78) show that the siege was represented as part of the vengeance for
Caesar's murder. The alleged human sacrifice of the *arae Perusinae*, reported
with hesitation by Suetonius, *Aug.* 15, 2 and Dio XLVI, 14, 4, is hostile
invention; see J. S. Reid in *J.R.S.* II, 1912, pp. 41–4.

uncertainty whether Antony would return as friend or enemy made it imperative to deal quickly with Sextus and Lepidus, for either, if unsatisfied, might combine with Antony against him. Calenus had not yet given up two legions in exchange for those Antony had borrowed after Philippi (p. 26), and Octavian therefore bent his steps towards Gaul. Opportunely enough Calenus died, his son was too young to be left in charge of the army there, and Octavian took control for the moment of the eleven legions. So large a force could only be given to a man whom he trusted implicitly, and so Salvidienus Rufus was placed in supreme charge of Gaul, though L. Antonius was made governor of Spain; in addition Octavian could now present Lepidus with the two provinces of Africa and six legions from Antony's Gallic army wherewith to control them[1]. The acting governor of Africa, T. Sextius, who had succeeded in eliminating Fango, surrendered his four legions to the triumvir, and for the next few years Lepidus remained there inactive, though not without schemes of his own[2].

There remained Sextus Pompeius; here Maecenas used his skill in negotiations of which the upshot was that Octavian married Scribonia, the sister of L. Scribonius Libo, whose daughter was the wife of Sextus. To modern eyes the connection seems remote enough, but such alliances were an accepted part of Roman political life, and this one might be taken as affording Octavian some hold upon Sextus. What Octavian could not know was that Sextus, equally anxious for security, had himself opened communications with Antony and offered his services. Antony was returning to Italy; the prestige of the victor at Philippi still counted for much; all would depend upon his attitude and will.

[1] After Philippi Octavian still owed three and Antony four legions to Lepidus (p. 22): it is possible that Octavian claimed that in giving Lepidus six legions he was paying off not only his own debt (for he had already given Lepidus another two to defend Rome, p. 29), but also Antony's. Whether he had any authority (under the pact after Philippi) to act for Antony, and whether Antony acquiesced in Octavian's paying his debts for him or continued to claim these four legions of Calenus cannot be said; possibly at Brundisium the matter was left in abeyance and only settled at Tarentum (p. 54). (According to Appian, *Bell. Civ.* v, 75, 321 Antony sent an agent to Sextius in 38 for these very legions.) But the whole question of Lepidus' legions is obscure: what happened to the three which he retained in Italy in 42 and to the two that Octavian gave him in 41 is simply unknown.

[2] The only information about Lepidus' governorship, in Dio LII, 43, 1 and Tertullian, *de pallio*, 1, is too vague to warrant any precise statement, though it suggests some injury inflicted on the colonists of Carthage. He raised six legions more at least, for in 36 B.C. he started for Sicily with sixteen (Appian, *Bell. Civ.* v, 98, 406, and 104, 430), though Velleius (II, 80, 1) describes them as *semiplenae*.

MAP 3

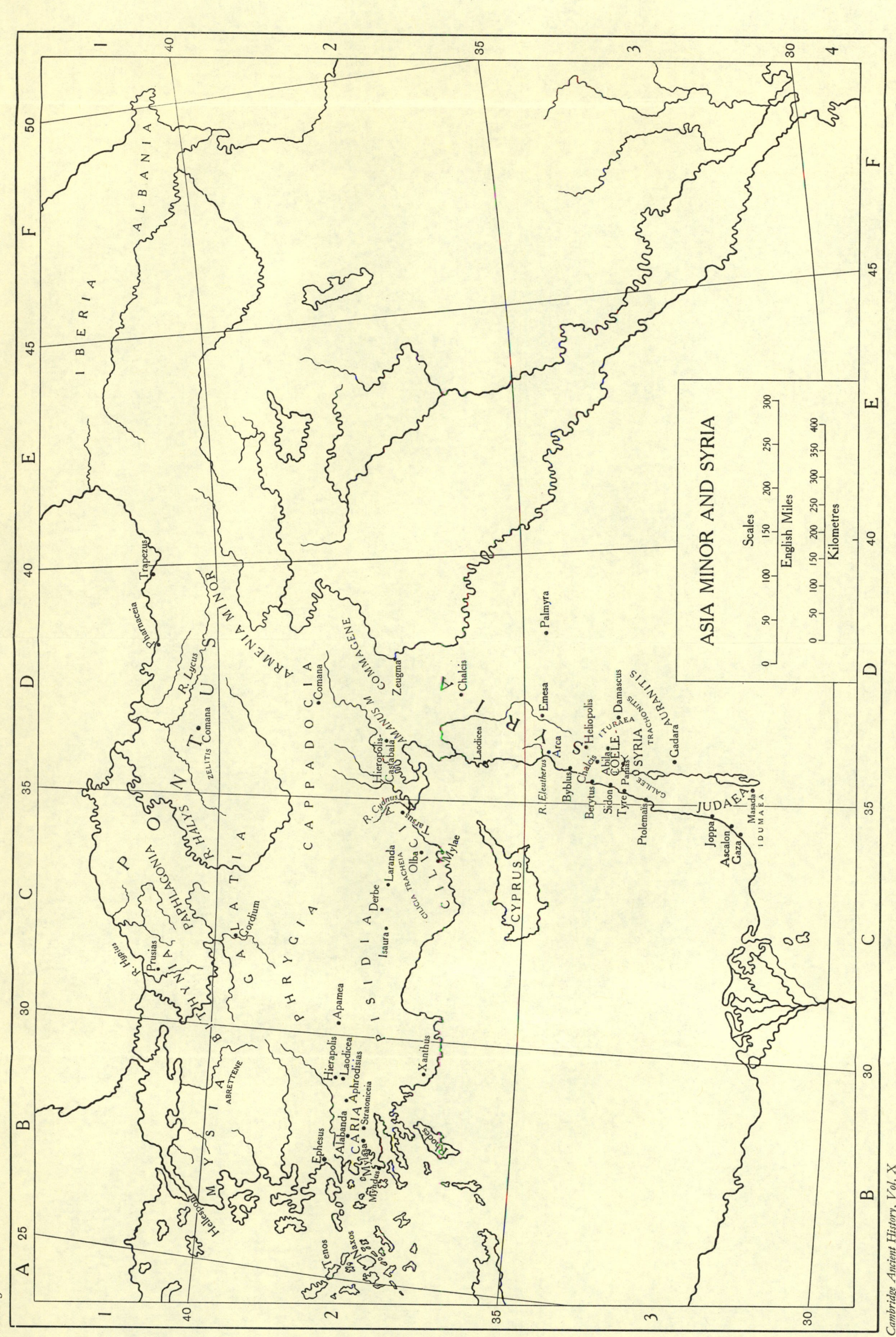

ASIA MINOR AND SYRIA

Scales

English Miles

Kilometres

MAP 4

INDEX TO NAMES

Adiabene, C 2
Albani, D 1
Anthemus, B 2
Antioch, B 2
Apamea?, D 3
Apamea?, D 3
Apavarktikene, FG 2
Araxes, R., CD 1, 2
Arbela, C 2
Aria, G 3
Arius, R., G 2, 3
Armenia, B-D 1, 2
Artaxata, C 1
Artemita, D 3
Assak, F 2
Ashur (Libba), C 2
Astauene, F 2
Atrek, R., EF 2

Babylon, C 3
Babylonia, CD 3
Bambyce, B 2
Belik, R., B 2
Bokhara, G 2
Borsippa, C 3

Carana, C 2
Carrhae, B 2
Caspian Gates, E 2
Caspian Sea, DE 1, 2
Characene, Kingdom of, D 3, 4
Charax, D 3
Charax, E 2
Choarene, E 2, 3
Comisene, E 2, 3
Commagene, B 2
Ctesiphon, C 3
Cyrrhestice, B 2
Cyrus, R., CD 1

Dahae, F 2
Dara, F 2
Doura, C 3

Ecbatana, D 3
Edessa, B 2
Elburz Mts., E 2
Elymais, Kingdom of, DE 3, 4
Euphrates, R., B-D 2, 3

Gabae, E 3
Gabiene, E 3
Gordyene, C 2

Hamun, L., G 3
Hatra, C 2
Hecatompylos, E 2
Helmund, R., G 3
Herat, G 3
Hyrcania, EF 2

Iberi, D 1
Ichnae, B 2
Indo-Parthian Kingdom, FG 3, 4

Kasaf-rud, R., FG 2

Libba, C 2

Mardi, E 2
Margiane, G 2
Massagetae, E-G 1
Media, D 2, 3
Media Atropatene, C-E 2
Merv, G 2
Mesopotamia, BC 2

Neapolis, C 3
Nicephorium, B 2
Nippur, D 3
Nisa, F 2
Nisibis, C 2

Ochus, R. (or Arius), G 2, 3
Orchoi, D 3
Ormuz, Strait of, F 4
Osrhoëne, B 2
Oxus, R., GH 1, 2

Palmyra, B 3
Parthian Empire, B-G 1-4
Parthyene, F 2
Persepolis, E 4
Persian Gulf, DE 3-5
Persis, Kingdom of, E-G 3, 4
Phraaspa, D 2
Portus Macedonum?, F 4

Rhagae-Arsacia, E 2
Rhagiane, E 2, 3

Sacaraucae, GH 1
Samosata, G 3
Seistan, G 3
Seleuceia, C 3
Seleuceia?, D 3
Seleuceia, E 3
Singara, C 2
Sinnaca?, B 2
Sippar, C 3
Skenite Arabs, C 2, 3
Sophene, BC 2
Susa, D 3
Syria, B 2, 3
Syrian Desert, B 3

Tabriz, D 2
Tapuri, E 2
Tapuria, F 2
Tejend, R., G 2, 3
Tigris, R., CD 2, 3
Traxiane?, G 2

Uruk (Orchoi), D 3
Urumia (Urmia), L., D 2

Van, L., C 2

Yueh-chi, GH 2

Zab, Lesser, R., CD 2
Zagros Mts, D 3
Zenodotium, B 2
Zeugma, B 2

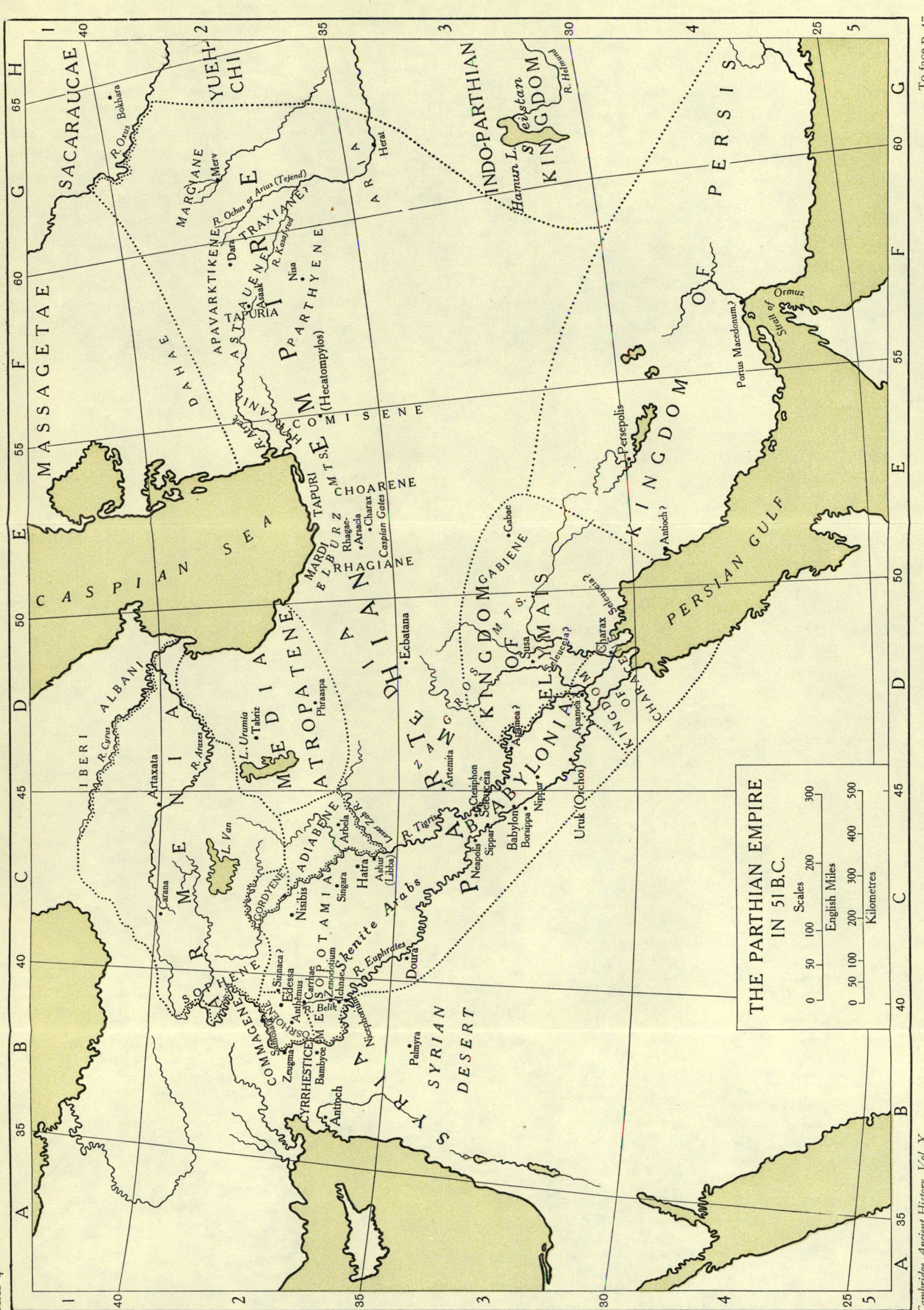

THE PARTHIAN EMPIRE
IN 51 B.C.

Scales
English Miles
Kilometres

To face p. 47

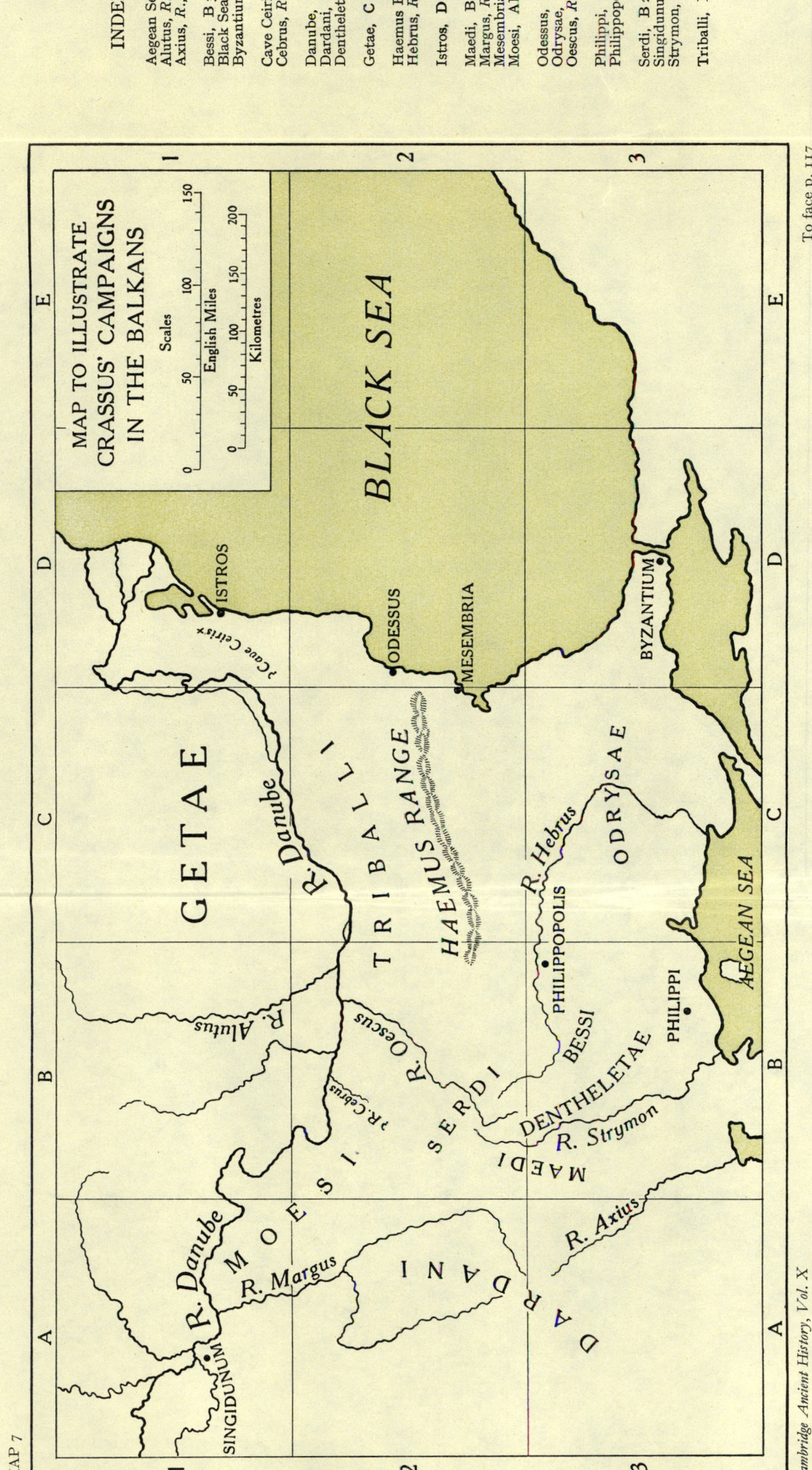

INDEX TO NAMES

Aegean Sea, BC 3
Alutus, *R.*, B 1, 2
Axius, *R.*, AB 3

Bessi, B 3
Black Sea, DE 1–3
Byzantium, D 3

Cave Ceiris?, D 1
Cebrus, *R.?,* B 2

Danube, *R.,* A–D 1, 2
Dardani, A 2, 3
Dentheletae, B 2, 3

Getae, C 1

Haemus Range, BC 2
Hebrus, *R.,* BC 2, 3

Istros, D 1

Maedi, B 2, 3
Margus, *R.,* A 1, 2
Mesembria, C 2
Moesi, AB 1, 2

Odessus, D 2
Odrysae, C 3
Oescus, *R.,* B 2

Philippi, B 3
Philippopolis, B 3

Serdi, B 2
Singidunum, A 1
Strymon, *R.,* B 2, 3

Triballi, BC 2

MAP 7

MAP TO ILLUSTRATE
CRASSUS' CAMPAIGNS
IN THE BALKANS

Scales

English Miles

Kilometres

Cambridge Ancient History, Vol. X

To face p. 117

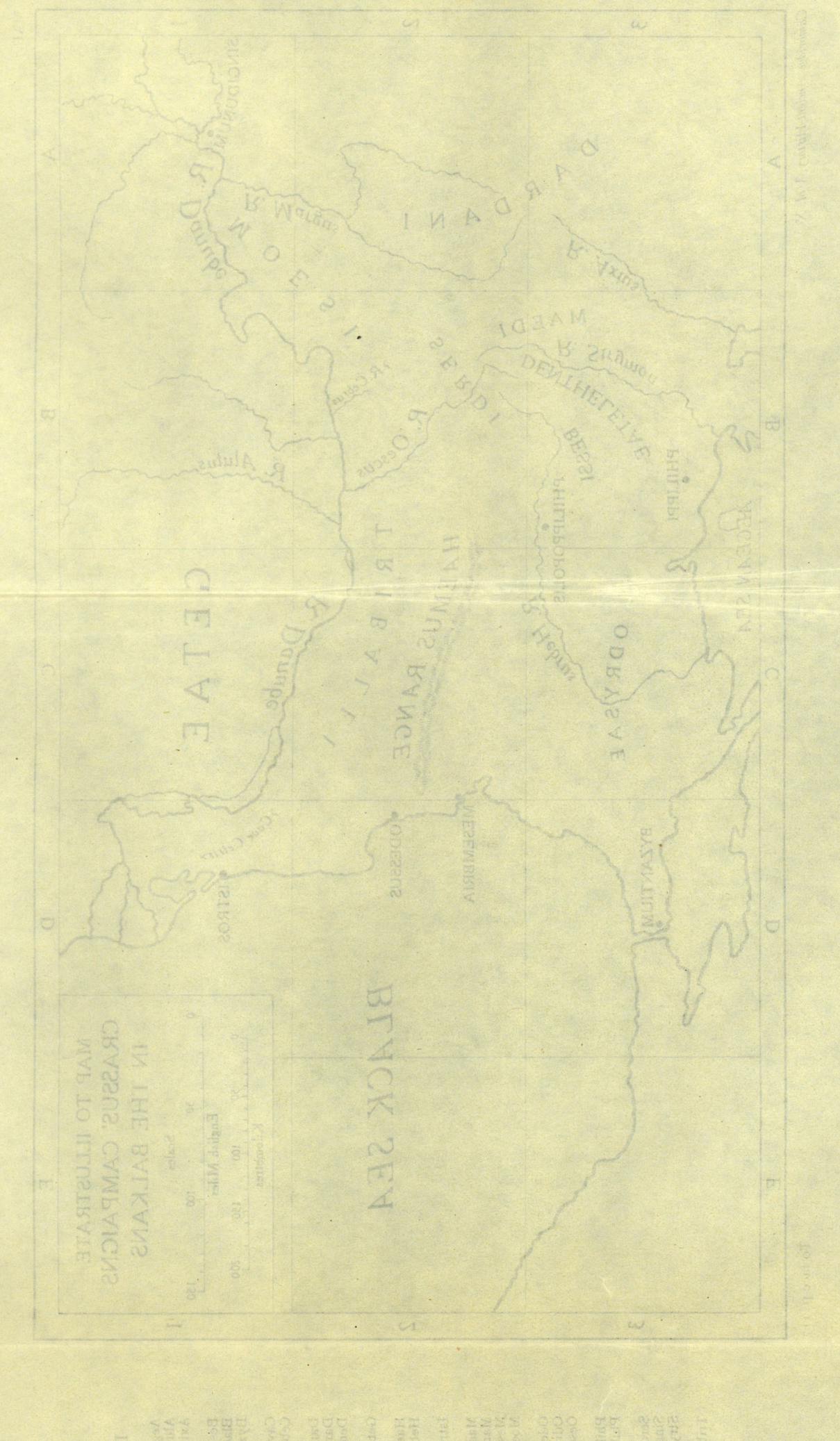

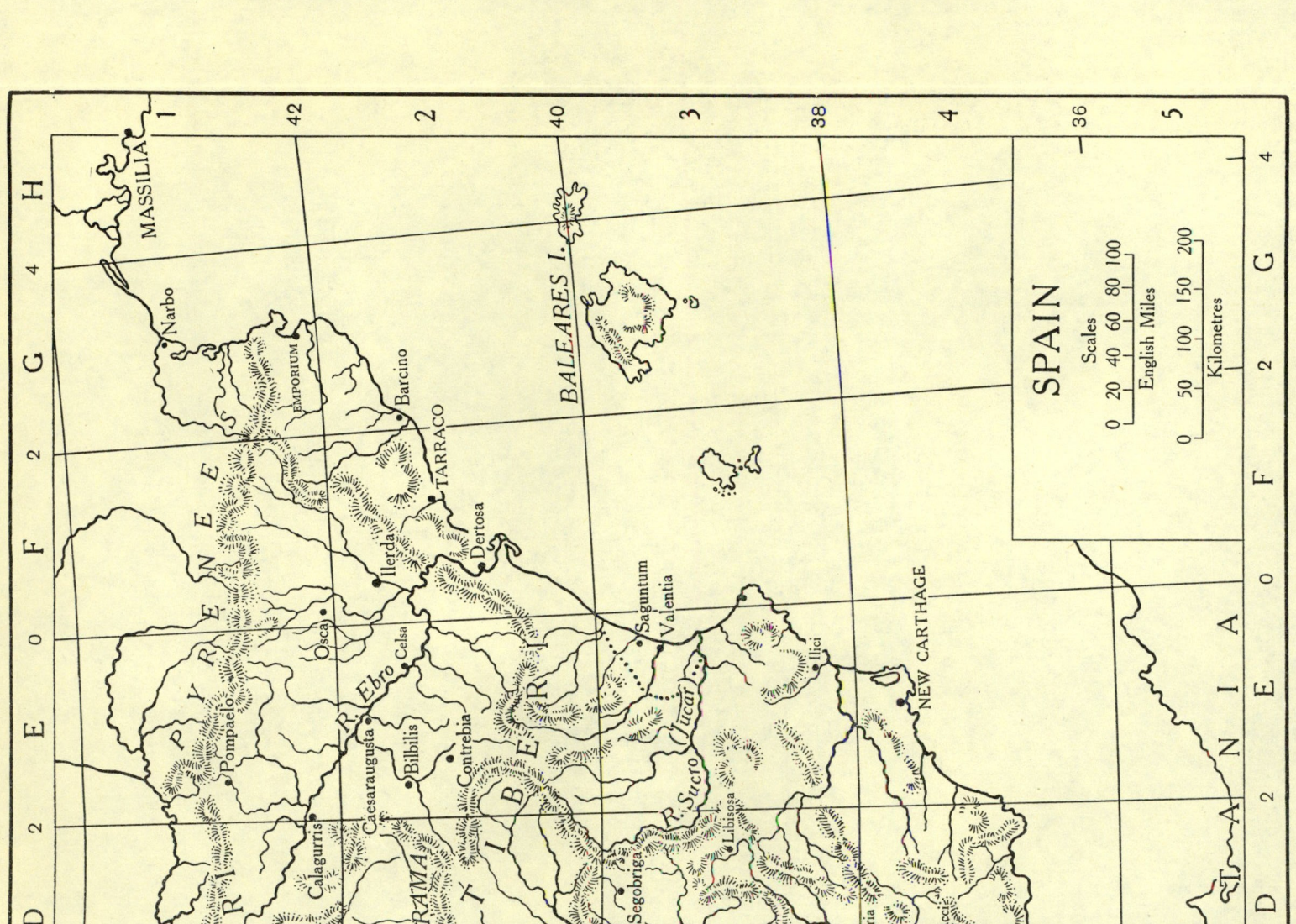

SPAIN

Scales

English Miles

0 20 40 60 80 100

Kilometres

0 50 100 150 200

MAP 10

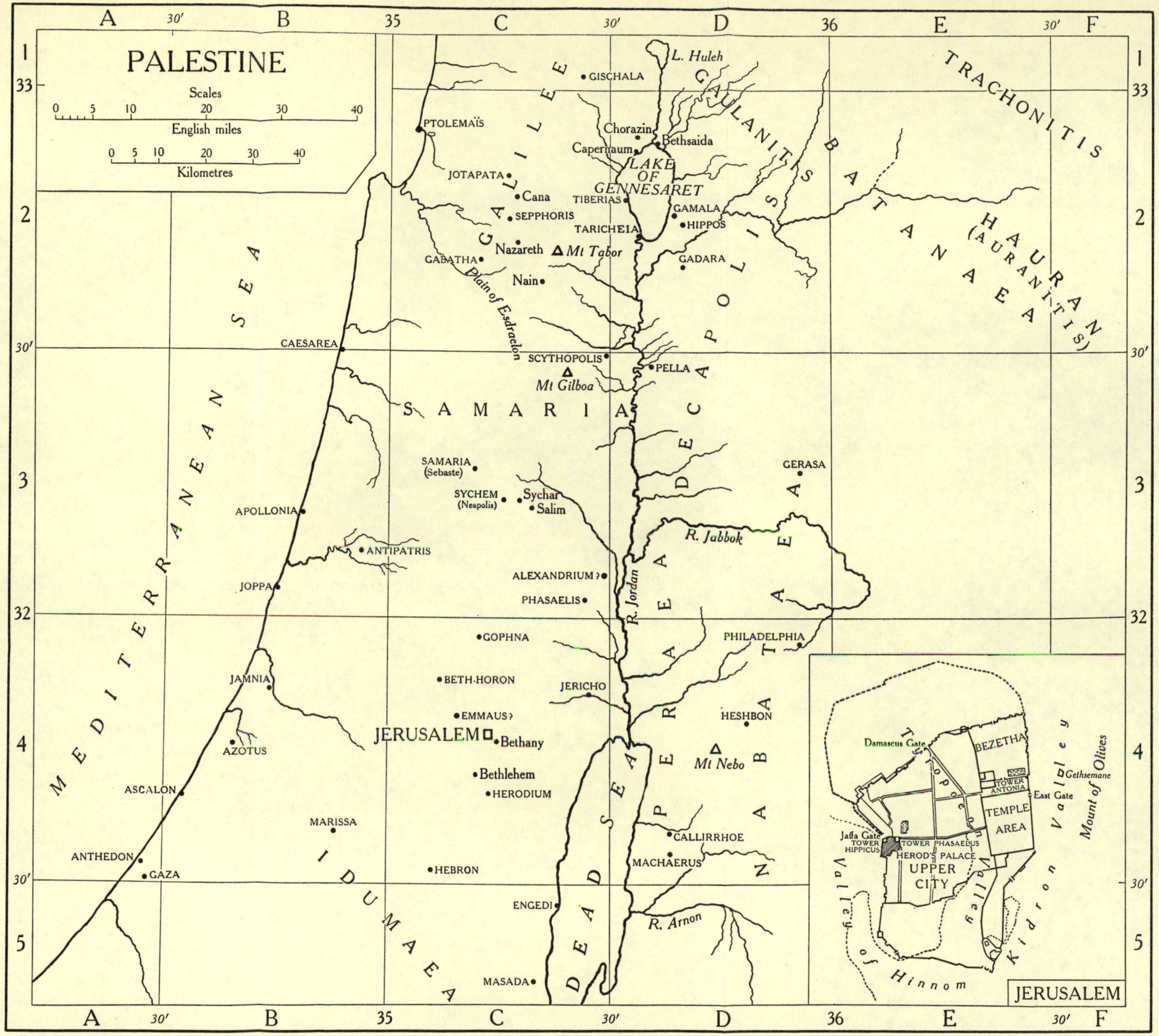

INDEX TO NAMES

Alexandrium?, C 3
Anthedon, A 4
Antipatris, B 3
Antonia, Tower, E 4 (inset)
Apollonia, B 3
Armon, R., D 5
Ascalon, B 4
Ashdod, *see* Azotus
Ashkelon, *see* Ascalon
Azotus, B 4

Batanaea, DE 2
Bethany, C 4
Beth-horon, C 4
Bethlehem, C 4
Bethsaida, D 2
Bezetha, E 4 (inset)

Caesarea (Stratonis Turris), B 2, 3
Callirrhoe, D 4
Cana, C 2
Capernaum, D 2
Chorazin, D 2

Damascus Gate (Jerusalem), E 4 (inset)
Dead Sea, CD 4, 5
Decapolis, D 2, 3

East Gate (Jerusalem), E 4 (inset)
Emmaus?, C 4
Engedi, C 5
Esdraelon, *Pl.*, C 2, 3

Gabatha, C 2
Gadara, D 2
Galilee, C 1, 2
Gamala, D 2
Gaulanitis, D 1, 2
Gaza, A 4
Gennesaret, *L.*, D 2
Gerasa, D 3
Gethsemane, F 4 (inset)
Gilboa, *Mt*, C 3
Gischala, C 1
Gophna, C 4

Hauran (Auranitis), EF 2
Hebron, C 4
Herod's Palace (Jerusalem), E 4 (inset)
Herodium, C 4
Heshbon, D 4
Hinnom, Valley of, E 4, 5 (inset)

Hippicus, Tower, E 4 (inset)
Hippos, D 2
Huleh, *L.*, D 1

Idumaea, BC 4, 5

Jabbok, *R.*, DE 3
Jaffa Gate (Jerusalem), E 4 (inset)
Jamnia, B 4
Jericho, C 4
Jerusalem, C 4, E 4, 5
Joppa, B 3
Jordan, *R.*, D 1–4
Jotapata, C 2

Kidron, Valley of, EF 4, 5 (inset)

Machaerus, D 4
Marissa, B 4
Masada, C 5
Mediterranean Sea, AB 1–5

Nabataea, D 3, 4
Nain, C 2
Nazareth, C 2
Nebo, *Mt*, D 4

Olives, *Mt*, F 4 (inset)

Pella, D 3
Peraea, D 3, 4
Phasaelis, C 3
Phasaelis Tower, E 4 (inset)
Philadelphia, D 4
Ptolemais, C 2

Salim, C 3
Samaria, CD 3
Samaria (Sebaste), C 3
Scythopolis, C 3
Sepphoris, C 2
Sychar, C 3
Sychem (Neapolis), C 3

Tabor, *Mt*, C 2
Taricheia, D 2
Temple Area (Jerusalem), **E 4**
Tiberias, D 2
Trachonitis, EF 1, 2
Tyropoeon, Valley of, E 4, 5 (inset)

Ulatha (district of L. Huleh, *q.v.*), D 1
Upper City (Jerusalem), E 4 (inset)

PALESTINE

Scales

English miles

Kilometres

JERUSALEM

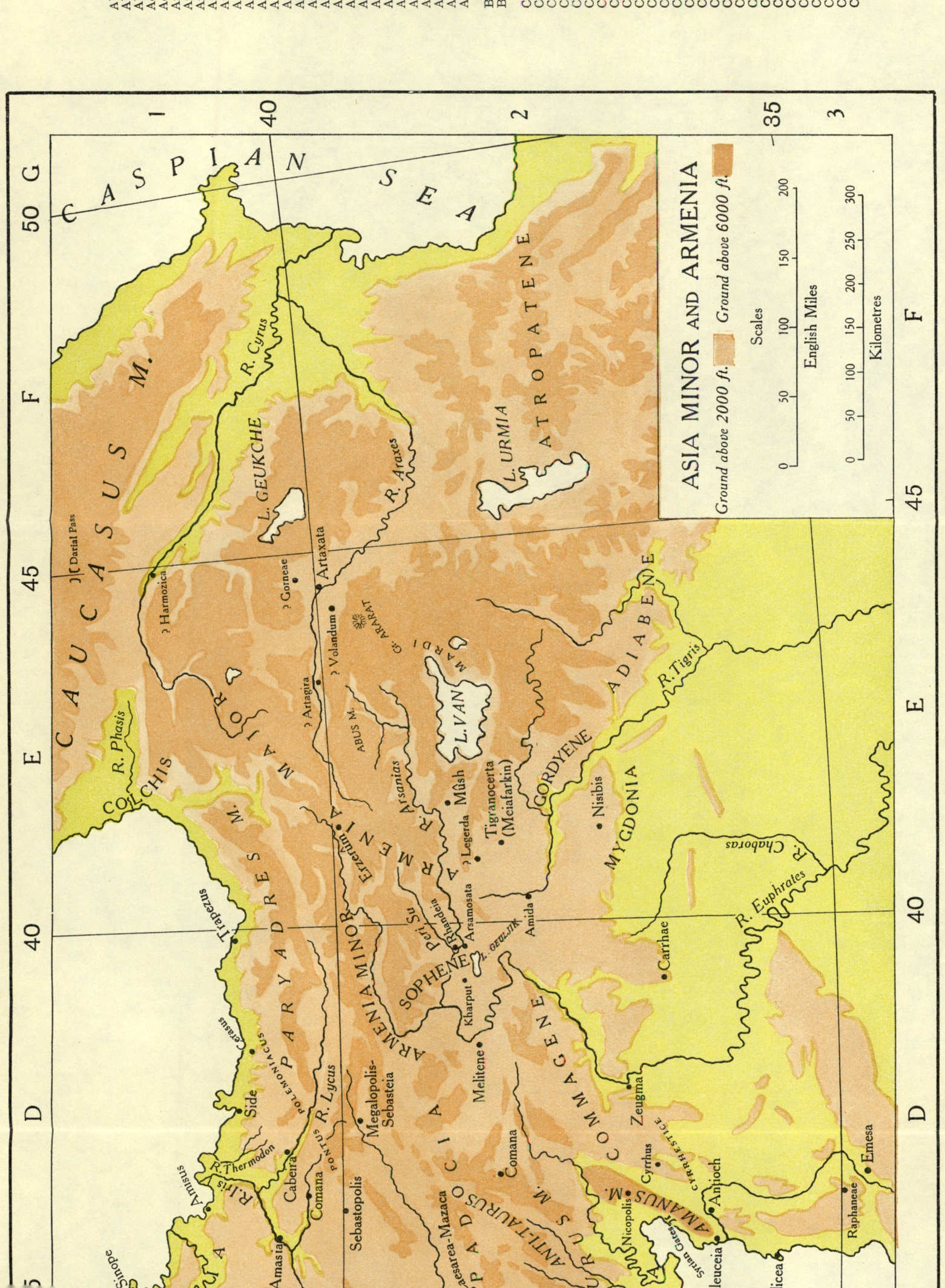

ASIA MINOR AND ARMENIA

Ground above 2000 ft. Ground above 6000 ft.

Scales

English Miles

Kilometres

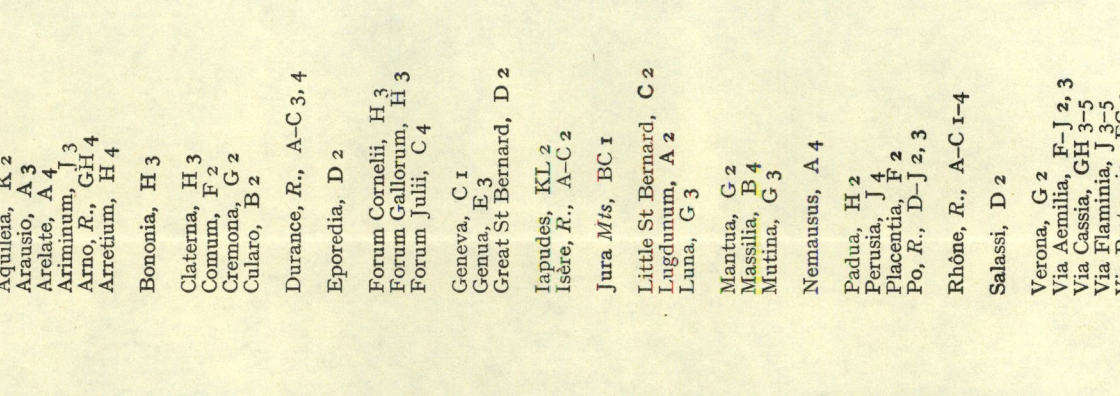

NORTH ITALY

Scales

English Miles
0 10 20 30 40 50 60

Kilometres
0 10 20 30 40 50 60 70 80 90 100

To face p. 1

CHAPTER II

THE TRIUMVIRS

I. ANTONY IN THE EAST

THE true story of Antony and Cleopatra is largely lost[1]. Something can be made of Antony down to 35, where Appian ceases; but of Cleopatra we know comparatively little until the last scenes in Alexandria, when Plutarch, heretofore hostile, begins to use the *Memoirs* of her physician Olympus. The surviving accounts of her in our late sources largely represent the victor's version; they freely pervert motives and reasons, and have incorporated much of the débris of an unscrupulous propaganda war; contemporary evidence from the East is very scarce, but what exists hints at something so different from the Cleopatra of Roman tradition that, in the present writer's opinion, there is small chance of the usual portrait of her being true. But there is little to put in its place; the material does not exist. The excellence of Appian on the Civil Wars might lead one to regret the loss of his *Aegyptiaca*, which portrayed Cleopatra; but though Appian of Alexandria, who still referred to the Ptolemies as 'my kings,'

[1] The contemporary material for Antony and Cleopatra (*i.e.* the Eastern side of things) during the years 42–30 consists of a few papyri and inscriptions, including the Fasti; coins, especially those of Antony and Octavian; some fragments; and several poems, the most important being Horace, *Epode* IX and *Odes*, I, 37, Virgil, *Eclogue* IV, and (in the writer's view) *Oracula Sibyllina* III, 350–61, 367–80. Of the secondary sources the best is Book V of Appian's *Bella Civilia*, which stops with 35; the excellent military details, and the comparative impartiality towards Antony, seem to the present writer to show that its main source can only be Pollio (see also above, p. 1). Plutarch's *Life* of Antony is notable among his *Lives* in being unsympathetic towards its subject—towards Antony throughout, towards Cleopatra down to chap. 77, where he begins to use Olympus; apart from his own family traditions his other sources are unknown, except that the invasion of Parthia is from Dellius and parts of Actium from an eyewitness on Octavian's fleet who had deserted from Antony. Dio Cassius XLVIII–LI, 19, partially represents Livy (also represented by his usual epitomizers), and thus in part goes back ultimately, with whatever modifications, to Augustus' *Memoirs*; but his value for Antony and Cleopatra is small. Josephus, *Antiquitates*, XIV [12], 301–XV [7], 218, *Bellum Judaicum*, I [12], 242–[20], 397, has preserved some valuable facts, but his chronology is most confused. For Parthia, beside the classical writers, the only materials are coins, the Susa poems, of uncertain interpretation, and a parchment from Doura (see Bibliography).

might have given a more sympathetic account, he would no longer have had Pollio behind him, and the *Aegyptiaca* might well therefore have been no better historically than the *Syriaca*.

Philippi showed that the Caesarian party was dominant in the State and Antony was the most powerful man in that party. In the written compact drawn up after the battle the prestige of the victory gave him first place and first choice. What that choice was has already been seen (p. 26); but though Italy was to be common ground and the settlement of the veterans a common task, Antony in taking the East made the mistake of allowing Rome to accustom itself to Octavian as ruler and the veterans to look to him as settler. Provided that he and Octavian did not come into conflict the East offered him certain advantages— science and administration, wealth and commerce (both somewhat impaired), potential sea-power; but in fact, though not on paper, he surrendered the most effective sources of man-power to Octavian. And whatever compacts might be made, there were already observers who saw that two men attempting to share the supreme power must ultimately fight for it.

But years were to pass before Antony should seek the supreme power for himself, and then not of his own initiative. He was born to be second, not first; as he had been with Caesar, so he was to be with Cleopatra and Octavian. Though he remained a blunt jovial soldier, the darling of his troops, whom he understood and cared for, he had some statesmanlike qualities; in politics at Rome since Caesar's murder he had shown rapidity of decision and resource, he could pick capable subordinates, and much of his ultimate organization of the East was to endure, though under another. But his nature was full of contradictions. Cruel enough when roused, he soon returned to his usual goodnature; sometimes great in adversity, in prosperity he preferred luxury and amusement; straightforward and often loyal himself, he trusted others and was easily flattered and deceived. His worst trouble was women; they existed, he believed, for his pleasure, and they had given him ample reason for his belief. He boasted his likeness to Hercules, but his strange disharmonic face[1], too long between eyes and mouth, reflected the discontinuity of his life; outbursts of energy alternated with periods of self-indulgence, and he could not follow an unswerving course or lay solid foundations for what he sought to build. For though he desired power, it was largely for the sake of pleasure; hence he himself might have

---

[1] Volume of Plates iv, 196, *c*.

been content with half the world, had he not been caught between two stronger natures.

He landed at Ephesus, where the people welcomed him as a new Dionysus; Roman governors had long been worshipped in Asia, and the Ephesians were only trying to please their new ruler and expressing the hope that he would be as beneficent as the god. The greeting did not affect Antony's own position or make him divine, but it chimed with his mood; he wished to be accepted in Asia as a philhellene and man of culture, and he rewarded Ephesus and some other cities which had suffered at Cassius' hands; Athens received Aegina and some small islands; Rhodes got Andros, Naxos, Tenos, and Myndus; Lycia was freed from taxation and invited to restore Xanthus; Laodicea and Tarsus were made free cities and Tarsus was presented with a gymnasium. He summoned delegates from the cities to Ephesus: they represented the Diet (*koinon*) of Asia, model for many other Diets, but whether Antony now founded it or whether it already existed is uncertain; certainly its function as a vehicle of the official religion dates from Augustus. But the delegates found him anything but beneficent; as he told them, he had to have money, and after praising the generosity of the Roman (*i.e.* Seleucid) system of taking a tenth of the harvest (which made the Government true partners with the peasantry, sharing losses) as against the Attalid system of a fixed payment (vol. VIII, p. 608), he ended with a brusque demand for the same sum as they had paid to Cassius, ten years' taxes down. The orator Hybreas of Mylasa had the courage to voice the general despair, and Antony reduced the demand to nine years' taxes, to be paid in two years; probably he never got so much, for Cassius had plundered well. After leaving Ephesus he made the usual governor's tour of Asia Minor, holding courts in the chief cities; his judgments were equitable enough, though cities and dynasts were alike called upon for money; he was however slack with his followers, who plundered freely, and what money he did get he sometimes, in his easy fashion, gave away. But he had realized the weakness of the triumvirs at sea, and he used part of the money to build 200 ships.

In Bithynia he met Herod. Hyrcanus, the High Priest governing Judaea, had sent to Ephesus to ask for the return of Cassius' Jewish prisoners, which was granted. Emboldened by this, Hyrcanus—or rather the Jews, for he was a cipher—sent again to Antony in Bithynia to accuse Herod, the son of Hyrcanus' dead Idumaean vizier Antipater, of aiming at sole power, and Herod came to defend himself. He made on Antony an impression of strength and usefulness which was never to fade, and the complaints against him were dismissed (see below, p. 318 *sq.*).

As regards the client-kings, Antony's policy was to make no change till he learnt better how things stood; in a peaceful age this would have been sensible, but after the recent troubles drastic reorganization was needed, and his policy gives an unfortunate impression of laziness. These subject-allies were important to Rome, for in return for the title of king and a free hand in internal matters they guarded the frontier or bridled the local hill-tribes, sparing Roman officials and Roman lives. Their armies were at Rome's disposal, they often paid tribute, and Rome could remove them at pleasure; but it was fixed Roman custom that, if one were removed, the crown was given to another member of the royal house[1]. When one died, his successor had to be approved by Rome. The two important client-states in Asia Minor at this time were Galatia and Cappadocia. Galatia, besides the country properly so called, included inner Paphlagonia and the eastern part of what had once been the kingdom of Pontus, the country about Pharnaceia and Trapezus; while the kings of Cappadocia also ruled Armenia Minor, which made them responsible for the safety of the frontier along the Upper Euphrates. The king of Galatia, the old Deiotarus, had sent his troops to Cassius under his secretary Amyntas; but Amyntas had gone over to Antony at Philippi in time, and Deiotarus kept his kingdom. But on his death in 40 Antony divided it; Deiotarus' grandson Castor succeeded to Galatia proper, while another grandson, Deiotarus Philadelphus, received Paphlagonia; Galatian Pontus Antony gave to Darius, a grandson of Mithridates Eupator. In Cappadocia Ariarathes X had succeeded in 42, but the line of priest-kings in Comana had long been pretenders to the crown. Comana was at present occupied by a young man, Archelaus (Sisines), grandson of the Archelaus who for a moment had been king of Egypt, together with his mother Glaphyra, whom Greek cities called queen[2]. Whether Antony had an intrigue with Glaphyra or not (the evidence is poor), it did not affect his policy, for he confirmed Ariarathes on the throne; Appian's story that he encouraged Archelaus without removing Ariarathes, *i.e.* staged a civil war in Cappadocia with Parthia threatening, is impossible.

But there was a client-queen of Rome[3] who stood on a different

---

[1] Josephus, *Ant.* XIV [14, 5], 386, τοῖς ἐκ τοῦ γένους ἔθος ἔχοντας αὐτὴν (the kingship) διδόναι.   [2] *O.G.I.S.* 361.

[3] Client-queen in fact; but whether in law Egypt was *in fide Populi Romani* may be doubtful, though Livy XLV, 13, 7 uses the phrase (168 B.C.).

footing from these petty rulers, Cleopatra VII of Egypt. Antony summoned her to Cilicia to answer the charge that she had aided Cassius; and in the late summer of 41 he was at Tarsus, awaiting her coming.

II. ANTONY AND CLEOPATRA

Cleopatra was now 29, the age, says Plutarch, at which the Graeco-Macedonian woman was at her best, both in mind and body. By descent half Macedonian and (apparently) half Greek[1], with a slight tinge of the Iranian, she was by instinct, training, and pride of race a Macedonian princess; Romans called her an Egyptian simply as a term of abuse, like Dago, for she had no Egyptian blood. She was not especially beautiful, but she had a wonderful voice and the seductiveness which attracts men, and she was intensely alive, tireless and quite fearless; even her wretched coin-portraits have occasionally preserved traces of the eager vitality of her face[2]. Apart from her attractions, she was highly educated, interested in literary studies[3], conversant with many languages, and a skilled organizer and woman of business. Brought up at a corrupt Court, she knew no conventions and few scruples; the moral code had little meaning to her; she was her own law. But she was to be a loyal wife to Antony, though certainly she did not love him; perhaps she never loved any man; her two love affairs were undertaken quite deliberately, with the same purpose as all her actions. For the key-note of her character was not sex at all[4], but ambition—an ambition surpassing that of any other princess of her ambitious Macedonian race; and the essence of her nature was the combination of the charm of a woman with the brain of a man, both remorselessly bent to the pursuit of that one object, power.

The belief that she was unpopular in Egypt is unfounded. She was unpopular with the faction in the capital which had supported her sister Arsinoe, and probably unpopular with some Alexandrian

[1] The facts of Lathyrus' life show that his mistress, Cleopatra's grandmother, must have been a Greek from Syria; one cannot therefore absolutely exclude the possibility that Cleopatra had a little Syrian blood, though it is unlikely.   [2] Volume of Plates iv, 196, *d, e.*

[3] Philostratus, *Vit. Soph.* 1, 5, for the fact (his comment is valueless); also Suidas, Θεόδωρος ποιητής.

[4] To bring sexual accusations against those you disliked (see p. 98 *sq.*) had been common form for three centuries. As there is no trustworthy instance of any princess of the blood royal in any Macedonian dynasty ever having a lover (doubtless from pride), it is obvious that there was some overmastering reason, other than sex, for Cleopatra's relations with Caesar and Antony.

Jews (not with all Jews), perhaps because they, as non-citizens, had once been excluded by her, as they were later by Germanicus (p. 309), from a distribution of corn to citizens of Alexandria during a famine[1]; but the evil spoken of her by the Jewish Josephus is largely taken from Nicolaus, who after her fall had gone over to her enemy Herod, and only represents what was current at Herod's court. But outside Alexandria she was certainly popular in Egypt[2], especially with the native Egyptians. From 216 to 86 native risings against the dynasty, centred in Upper Egypt, had been endemic; not only were there none in her reign, but at the end Egypt offered to rise *for* her[3], and, though she forbade it, Upper Egypt rose against the Romans as soon as she was dead. In her relations with the native Egyptians she seems to stand close to Alexander; and in some way she had won their confidence. One reason may have been that she could speak to them in their own language, a thing unique among monarchs of Macedonian blood; but much more important, probably, was her sympathetic attitude towards the native religion, which had laid its spell upon her (p. 68). Alexander had sacrificed to Apis, but she went further: she began her reign by going to Upper Egypt, to the very centre of the old disaffection, and in person, at the head of her fleet and of the burghers and priests of Thebes and Hermonthis, escorted a new Buchis bull to his home[4]; for Buchis, the sacred bull of Hermonthis, was the manifestation of the Sun-god Re, whose daughter she was (p. 110, n. 4). At Hermonthis she built a temple and her figure appears as the goddess Hathor in the temple at Dendera.

These facts amply disprove Dio's story that she acquired her wealth by plundering native temples. Indeed in the first century A.D. it was believed that she was skilled in alchemy and could make gold, having been taught the sacred mystery of the philosopher's stone by a 'philosopher' named Comarius; the illustrations to her recipe for making gold still survive[5]. The truth is that

[1] U. Wilcken, *Grundzüge*, 1, p. 364, *Hermes*, LXIII, p. 51. Not with all Jews: *O.G.I.S.* 742, and see pp. 70 *sq.*, 84.

[2] The caricature from Abydus (J. G. Milne, *J.E.A.* 1, p. 99), *if* it be Antony and Cleopatra, naturally does not affect this. Contrast the dedication by an Egyptian given by F. Preisigke, *Sammelbuch*, 1570.

[3] Pseudo-Acro on Horace, *Odes*, 1, 37, 23 (ed. Keller, 1, p. 133): 'dum omnis in auxilium eius Aegyptus conspiraret...contempsit amorem vel devotionem suorum.' Cf. *Aeneid*, VIII, 713, and Servius' commentary.

[4] The Armant stele (see Bibliography) 10, in her first year.

[5] Κλεοπάτρας χρυσοποία. On this and the 'Dialogue between Cleopatra and the philosophers' see F. S. Taylor, *J.H.S* L, 1930, p. 116.

she possessed a great treasure accumulated by her predecessors, the famous Treasure of the Ptolemies; her father may have diminished it somewhat, but he had met most of his difficulties by debasing the coinage, a process she continued[1]; she intended that her treasure should serve other ends than the restoration of a sound currency. Later times ascribed to her the authorship of a treatise, extracts from which survive, on weights, measures, and coinage in Egypt[2]. Modern statements that the two famines in her reign were caused by the canals silting up through her neglect cannot be supported, for famine in Egypt depended upon the Nile not rising above the 'cubits of death[3],' and there had been a great famine under Ptolemy III when presumably the canals were in good order. No doubt the agricultural system had deteriorated under the later Ptolemies, and Augustus found it advisable to clean out the canals; but one point of his measures was the deepening of them, which made a rise of 12 cubits at Memphis a full Nile as against the 14 of Ptolemaic times[4] (see p. 292). But though Cleopatra did not attempt to restore the agricultural position to what it had been under the earlier Ptolemies, there seems no reason to suppose that she was negligent in her working of the system which she actually inherited; for in 32 and 31 she not only fed Antony's great army and fleet (p. 100) but also presumably supplied the grain for his depôts in Greece, which shows that Egypt was still producing a considerable surplus of corn. She put on her coinage the double cornucopiae of Arsinoe II[5], 'Lady of Abundance,' and her one certain surviving rescript[6] attests a care for agriculture, and relieves from unauthorized local taxation some Alexandrians engaged in that business[7].

---

[1] J. Desvernois, *Bull. Soc. Arch. d'Alexandrie*, VI, fasc. 23, 1928, p. 338; Th. Reinach, *R.E.G.* XLI, 1928, p. 182; W. Giesecke, *Das Ptolemäergeld*, pp. 69 *sqq.*

[2] Fr. Hultsch, *Metrologicorum scriptorum reliquiae*, I, p. 253, no. 78: ἐκ τῶν Κλεοπάτρας περὶ στάθμων καὶ μέτρων. Obviously a different work from the κοσμητικά (p. 39, n. 6), of which, in the title of a second version, *ib.* p. 233, no. 60, it is made to form part.

[3] Seneca, *Quaest. Nat.* IV, 2, says explicitly that the famine of 42 B.C. was due to a low Nile, as does Pliny, *N.H.* v, 58, of the famine of 48 B.C.

[4] Strabo XVII, 788; W. L. Westermann, *C.P.* XII, 1917, p. 237.

[5] Volume of Plates IV, 196, *f.* On its significance see Athen. XI, 497 B.

[6] *B.G.U.* 1730 cannot be ascribed with certainty to Cleopatra.

[7] G. Lefebvre, *Mélanges Holleaux*, 1913, p. 103. The references in the treatise on weights and measures to a *Georgica* without any author's name may conceivably mean that a work on agriculture was ascribed to her.

Many things after her death show what Egypt, whether Greek or native, really felt for her. One man gave 2000 talents to ransom her statues from destruction. For a generation she remained 'the queen,' whom there was no need to name[1]; two generations later the Alexandrian grammarian Apion was championing her memory; her cult was still a living thing in the third century[2]. Alone of Alexander's successors she became a legend, like Alexander himself; and, besides her alchemy, there were attributed to her for centuries many of the great works of the past—the building of the palace and the lighthouse, the construction of Alexander's Heptastadion, the creation of the canal which brought water into Alexandria[3]. Even in the seventh century a Coptic bishop, John of Nikiu, said that none of the kings who preceded her wrought such deeds as she, and praised her as 'the most illustrious and wise among women,' 'great in herself and in her achievements in courage and strength'[4]. But it is not only in her legend, or in her policy towards the native Egyptians, that she recalls Alexander. Mystically daughter of Re as he had been mystically son of Ammon, near to the gods as he had been, with dreams of empire that matched his own, there burnt in her a spark of the fire from his own flaming spirit, perhaps the only one of all his heirs whom his fire had touched.

The Roman story that she drank to excess[5] may be noticed here, as it doubtless originated in a misunderstanding of her ring. She wore a ring with a figure of the goddess Drunkenness (Μέθη) engraved on an amethyst, the stone of sobriety; and a contemporary epigram explains the contradiction to mean that on her hand Drunkenness herself had to be sober (νήφειν)[6]. This gives the meaning of the figure; it was that Sober Drunkenness (μέθη νηφάλιος), 'mother of virtue,' which was to play such a part in Philo of Alexandria, and for long afterwards, as the expression of the Mystic Wisdom or divine Joy of

---

[1] *B.G.U.* 1182, 1198. Arsinoe II had become simply Βασιλίς at Arsinoe-Methana by the second century B.C. (F. Hiller von Gaertringen, Ἀρχ. Ἐφ. 1925–6, p. 72 l. 16, p. 74); but that was a cult-name and therefore hardly a parallel.

[2] E. Breccia, *Iscriz. greche e latine*, p. 32, no. 48ᵃ; U. Wilcken, *Chrestomathie*, no. 115 l. 10; perhaps *P. Oxy.* XII, 1449 l. 4. See A. D. Nock, *J.H.S.* XLVIII, 1928, p. 36.

[3] Ammianus XXII, 16, 9; Malalas IX, 218; *Excerpta Barbari*, p. 212, Schoene; John of Nikiu (next note).

[4] R. H. Charles, *The Chronicle of John, Bishop of Nikiu*, ch. 67.

[5] Plutarch, *Ant.* 29; Horace, *Odes*, I, 37, 14; Propertius III, 11, 56.

[6] *Anth. Pal.* IX, 752.

Life[1]. In origin it was connected, on the Greek side, with the 'drunkenness without wine' of the Bacchic women[2]; and what the ring, which is called a 'sacred possession', presumably did signify was that Cleopatra, like Arsinoe II[3], was an initiate of Dionysus.

It is said that Antony, when in Egypt as Gabinius' lieutenant (vol. IX, p. 604), had been attracted by her as a girl of fourteen; but since then she must have often seen him in Rome, and she thought she knew what manner of man he was. She intended now to make use of him; as to his personality she had no choice, for if she wanted power she could only get it through the Roman governor of the East, whoever he might be. Had Antony been a different character, we might have seen a different Cleopatra—perhaps the friend of philosophers[4], perhaps the business woman who ran a wool-mill with her slave girls[5]; as Antony loved pleasure, we see too much of the Cleopatra who, legend said, wrote a book on coiffures and cosmetics[6]. But how far she really understood Antony's contradictory nature may be doubtful; it was four years before she acquired any real influence over him, though of course events in Italy hampered her. She knew what she wanted, and thought she knew what Antony wanted; that she gave him, casting her bread upon the waters; she found it indeed after many days—when it was, for her, too late.

She had been in turn exile, client-queen, and potential mistress of the Roman world; she was now a client-queen again, but she did not mean to remain one. She came to Cilicia in response to Antony's summons, and sailed up the Cydnus to Tarsus, adorned as Aphrodite, in her golden barge; Shakespeare has drawn that wonderful picture once for all. She took the upper hand with Antony from the first; when he invited her to dinner she declined, and made him come to her—the judge to the accused. All the resources of Greek imagination were lavished on the description of her banquets; if true, she would have needed to bring half the transports in Egypt. With the actual charge she hardly troubled herself; she had not in fact helped Cassius, as

---

[1] On Philo see H. Lewy, *Sobria Ebrietas*, Giessen, 1929. He does not notice Cleopatra's ring.   [2] Plutarch, *Qu. Rom.* 112, *Mor.* 291 A.

[3] M. R. Vallois, *C. R. Ac. Inscr.* 1929, p. 38.

[4] Philostratus an Academician (Philostratus *loc. cit.*) and Nicolaus of Damascus the Peripatetic (*F. Gr. Hist.* II A, p. 324, fr. 2, *i.e.* from Sophronius) are known.   [5] Orosius VI, 19, 19.

[6] Κλεοπάτρας κοσμητικά, Hultsch, *op. cit.* p. 233; Κλεοπάτρας οὐλοποία, and κομμωτικὴ τέχνη, H. Usener, *Rh. Mus.* XXVIII, p. 412. Doubtless all refer to the same book, a later work attributed to her.

she proved without difficulty; but she wanted Antony at Alexandria, and took the shortest way by becoming his mistress. To be the lover of a queen flattered his vanity; he was ready to give her what she asked, provided it was no trouble to himself. She had never forgiven her sister Arsinoe (who *had* favoured Cassius) for her attempt on the crown of Egypt; she asked Antony to put Arsinoe to death for her, and that he did, tearing her from sanctuary. The Ptolemies had long practised dynastic murder, and Cleopatra had seen her father murder her elder sister, herself a murderess; in this matter she ran true to type, and the Antony of the proscriptions had no objections to offer. He also at her request executed her former governor in Cyprus, Serapion, for aiding Cassius, and a man who pretended to be her dead brother, Ptolemy XII. Before she left Tarsus she had his promise to visit her at Alexandria.

Antony spent little time in Syria. He confirmed on their thrones the two principal dynasts, Ptolemaeus of Chalcis, who ruled all central Syria with Damascus, and Iamblichus of Emesa; but he expelled some petty tyrants, who fled to Parthia. The Jews again tried to get Herod removed, but after consulting Hyrcanus he made Herod and his brother Phasael tetrarchs (p. 319). He imposed heavy contributions, against which one city, Aradus, revolted, and he tried to get some money by a cavalry raid upon Palmyra, but the Palmyrenes had removed themselves and their belongings into Parthian territory. He made Decidius Saxa governor of Syria, left with him his two legions, composed of Cassius' men, and hurried on to Alexandria, which he reached by winter. Caesar had entered Alexandria as a Roman magistrate, with the lictors before him; Antony entered without the lictors as a private man, Cleopatra's guest, and the queen had achieved the first step; she was no longer a client-queen, but by Antony's fiat an independent monarch.

They did spend the winter in extravagant festivities and amusements, and Antony did become leader of some gilded youths who called themselves 'The Inimitables,' but exaggeration has entered into the things they did, both at Alexandria and later at Samos; for example, Cleopatra did not drink a pearl dissolved in vinegar, for vinegar does not dissolve pearls, and an acid that would destroy one, had she known of such, would have destroyed her also. What she was seeking was to make herself indispensable to him, both to guarantee her existing rule and to pave the way to something larger; she was his good comrade in all he did, whether hunting or fishing, whether the lecture room or the streets at night, though she did remind him that these things were folly and that his true quarry was thrones and empires. She probably suggested marriage, as she was ready to marry him without parley in 37; doubtless she impressed upon him the advantage to himself of controlling the wealth, resources, and organization of Egypt. But beyond that she could not go. Antony was not thinking of marriage; he was enjoying himself, as a successful warrior might; she did not even succeed in making herself indispensable. The two things certain are that he did not fall in love with her and that he got no money from her Treasury; she was keeping it for a definite purpose, but of that she naturally gave him no hint, for as yet he was loyal to his compact with Octavian.

That loyalty explains his attitude towards events in Italy. He had known in the autumn that his wife Fulvia and his brother Lucius were making trouble, and during that winter the Perusine War was fought (see above, p. 28 *sq.*); but he did not intervene. The theory that he let Fulvia attack Octavian, meaning to reap the benefit if she won, supposes a duplicity quite foreign to his character; the theory that he dared not face the troops in Italy without the money he ought to have collected for them overlooks the fact that he did face them empty-handed a few months later. In fact he knew nothing of the war[1]; his last advices from Italy before navigation closed were sent off just after the arrangement of Teanum, when all seemed settled. He did not seek further information, because Octavian had accepted the task of settling Italy, and to deal with any troubles which arose was not only his duty but his right; and with that right Antony did not propose to interfere. What drew him from Alexandria was the news, received in February or early March, that the Parthians had invaded Syria. He hurried north at once, and nearly four years were to pass before Cleopatra saw him again. She kept herself informed of his doings through an Egyptian astrologer in his train, whose business was to impress upon him, in carefully veiled language, that to get free play for his own lofty personality he must break loose from Octavian. Probably she believed, from the political position, that he would have to return to her; but the world had no reason to think so, and only saw in her another of his discarded mistresses. After he left she gave birth to twins, a boy and a girl.

Antony sailed to Tyre, learnt of the defection of Saxa's troops (p. 47), and went on to Asia Minor, collecting his fleet. Cens-

---

[1] Appian, *Bell. Civ.* v, 51, 216 proves that he first heard of it in the spring of 40.

orinus in Macedonia was facing an invasion of the Parthini, and
there was nothing Antony could do till he got men from his
western provinces, where he had twenty-four legions—eleven in
Gaul under Fufius Calenus, seven in Cisalpine Gaul under
Asinius Pollio, and six divided between Ventidius Bassus and
L. Munatius Plancus, all seasoned troops except two legions of
Plancus' force which had been newly raised by Fulvia. But in Asia
Minor he heard of the Perusine War and Octavian's victory.
Asia had to take its chance; he must return to Italy. He did not
blame Octavian; he had been within his rights. He crossed to
Athens, where he met Fulvia and Plancus, who had fled from
Italy, and also envoys from Sextus Pompeius, seeking his alliance. He must, too, have heard that Pollio had reached the Po
delta, while Ventidius was near Brundisium; Plancus had lost
two legions to Agrippa and had fled, leaving his remaining troops
to join Ventidius. Fulvia told Antony that he must ally himself
with Sextus; but Antony merely overwhelmed her with bitter
reproaches. She had been a masterful woman, ambitious, and no
more moral than her world was; but she had been devoted to him
and his interests as she understood them, and what *she* saw was
that, while she had tried to make him master of the world, he had
first failed to support her and had then reproached her for trying
to serve him. Whatever her faults, Antony treated her brutally
enough; he left her ill in Greece without a farewell, and, with
nothing left to live for, she died. To Sextus' envoys he said that,
if Octavian kept his compact with him, he would try to reconcile
him with Sextus; but if he did not he would accept Sextus'
alliance.

By the time he reached Corcyra Antony must have heard that
Calenus was dead and that his inexperienced son had, on Octavian's demand, handed over to him Calenus' legions. It seemed
to Antony that Octavian had broken his compact with him; he
had taken from him Gaul and eleven legions, and that meant
alliance with Sextus and war. But Sextus was not the only sea-
king. Pollio on reaching the Adriatic coast had got into touch
with Domitius Ahenobarbus, and now told Antony that Domitius
would join him; and Antony, who wished to show the outlaw
that he was trusted, fearlessly set out with only five war-ships
and met Domitius' whole fleet bearing down upon him. There
was a moment of tense anxiety, and Plancus was terrified; then
Domitius' flag came down and he turned his galley broadside on
to Antony's ram. They went on to Brundisium together, to find
the gates of the town closed against them.

III. BRUNDISIUM AND MISENUM

In closing their gates against Antony and Domitius Ahenobarbus, which they did without Octavian's knowledge or order,
the townsmen of Brundisium had acted unfortunately, but their
action was natural enough: Domitius had been condemned by the
Lex Pedia as one of Caesar's murderers[1], he was technically an
outlaw, and only the previous year his fleet had attacked Brundisium and ravaged its territory[2]. Antony's reaction was equally
natural: convinced that this was Octavian's order, he immediately
set about blockading the town and sent forces up the coast to
seize strategic points such as Sipontum; at the same time he passed
the word to Sextus, and Sextus too began operations; he himself
attacked Thurii and Consentia in South Italy, while four of his
legions easily overpowered Octavian's smaller garrison in Sardinia.
Octavian marched hastily southwards and encamped opposite
Antony; Agrippa rescued Sipontum, and Sextus was repulsed
from Thurii; at Brundisium there was a deadlock. But though
Antony, by a brilliant cavalry exploit near Hyria, showed that the
name of the victor of Philippi could still inspire terror, Octavian
had already won a hold over the veterans he had settled: they
did not wish to fight, for they intended to reconcile Antony to
Octavian, but if Antony refused, fight they would.

Fortunately the deadlock did not continue long: the veterans on
each side began to fraternize; the news of Fulvia's death at Sicyon,
though it came as a shock to Antony, meant that one of the chief
causes of war was gone; it was not too late to think of peace and
L. Cocceius Nerva, a tactful and moderate man, went between the
two leaders, eliciting their grievances and trying to ease them. All
would be well could suspicion but be allayed; Antony suspected
Octavian of intending to keep Gaul and Calenus' legions and of
having deliberately shut him out of Italy; Octavian suspected that
Antony had been behind the Perusine War and was now making
common cause with outlaws such as Ahenobarbus and Sextus.
Characteristically, Antony made the first gesture, for he told
Sextus to return to Sicily and discreetly sent Domitius Ahenobarbus away to be governor of Bithynia. The soldiers chose two
more envoys, Pollio on behalf of Antony and Maecenas to represent

---

[1] The definite assertion of his complicity by Cicero, *Phil.* II, 11, 27 and 12,
30, outweighs later denials, as *e.g.* in Suetonius, *Nero*, 3. For an explanation
see J. D. Denniston's edition of the first two *Philippics*, p. 115.

[2] Appian, *Bell. Civ.* v, 26, 104.

Octavian; negotiations went well, the two triumvirs embraced, the past was to be wiped out, and as a token of restored friendship Octavian gave his own sister Octavia to Antony in marriage.

Naturally a fresh partition of territory between the masters of the Roman world followed; Antony agreed that Lepidus should be undisturbed in Africa, but the rest of the Empire the two divided between them, Antony taking the East and Octavian the West; though the dividing line passed through Scodra in Dalmatia both were to have equal recruiting right in Italy. Like Julius Caesar they nominated consuls for some years in advance (p. 46), and so secured honours and commands for their chief supporters. Antony soon gave an earnest of his reconciliation; not only did he put Manius to death for his share in the Perusine War but he informed Octavian of a piece of unexpected treachery. Salvidienus Rufus had been Octavian's most trusted general and rewarded with the governorship of all Gaul; the possession of a large army apparently turned his head[1]; he meditated revolt, but was imprudent enough to sound Antony, and Antony as in duty bound warned his partner. Salvidienus was hastily summoned to Rome on some plausible pretext, accused of treasonable designs before the Senate, and condemned to death—the first of a long line of army-commanders in the provinces to arouse suspicion and suffer the consequences. In his turn Octavian gave to Antony the remaining five legions of Calenus' army[2], and recognized the agreement with Ahenobarbus, from whom the ban of outlawry was now formally removed; he could also point to the fact that Antony's brother Lucius was governor in Spain.

The Pact of Brundisium, which can be dated securely to the first days of October[3], 40 B.C., was greeted with an outburst of jubilation by soldiers and civilians alike which reveals how deep had been the dread of civil war; the cloud had rolled away, peace was secured[4]. Of all that human excitement and hope, too soon

---

[1] No exact figures are given; Appian, *Bell. Civ.* v, 66, 278 simply says that he commanded the army of the Rhône. But the whole story presumes a very large force.

[2] Appian, *Bell. Civ.* v, 66, 279 implies that Octavian handed over the whole army, but this is impossible. It is more reasonable to assume that he gave Antony simply the five legions that he still owed him from Calenus' army, that is eleven legions *minus* the six given to Lepidus (p. 30).

[3] J. Carcopino, *Virgile et le mystère de la IVe Églogue*, ed. 3, Paris, 1930, pp. 111–23.

[4] Cf. *C.I.L.* x, 5159, on the re-erection of a *signum Concordiae* at Casinum, which Pais dates to a few days after the actual treaty; *Dalle guerre puniche a Cesare Augusto*, I, pp. 369–73.

to be dashed, one echo remains, for Virgil fashioned out of the joy of that moment the famous Fourth Eclogue. Some seven years before he had greeted the rising hope of the young Octavius, a fellow-pupil under Epidius; then had come civil war, a reign of brute force, and eviction; now in the union of the two great houses he foresaw the end of faction and warring and predicted the birth of a son who would bring back the age of gold; with this return he could link the name of his protector, Asinius Pollio, who had brought about the reconciliation and who in the last months of the year assumed the consulship[1].

'teque adeo decus hoc aevi, te consule, inibit,
    Pollio, et incipient magni procedere menses.'

But joy was short-lived, for the triumvirs had not sufficiently reckoned with Sextus, who feeling that Antony had played him false and untroubled by the marriage-connection into which Octavian had recently entered, determined to assert himself. The addition of Sardinia to Sicily gave him two bases for harrying the Italian coast: a raid was made on Etruria, corn-supplies were threatened. Such were the tidings that damped the festivities that had greeted the marriage of Antony and Octavia in Rome and the *ovatio* granted to the two leaders, and depression sharpened to exasperation as the cost of living rose and the triumvirs, in view of a war with Sextus, imposed fresh taxation, notably on slaves and on inheritances. The passing of the Lex Falcidia, which corrected some unfairnesses in the existing laws as to testamentary disposition by guaranteeing the heir at least a quarter of the estate, came opportunely enough for the new taxes[2]. But at the Ludi Plebeii in mid-November the populace broke into open riot and could only be repressed by the use of the soldiery. For the moment obviously Sextus must be satisfied, and at last he had achieved his aim; a first interview near Puteoli proved abortive, for he claimed more than the triumvirs would give, but in the spring of 39 B.C. a concordat was reached off Misenum[3]. In return for concessions made by Sextus, that he would keep the peace, give safe conduct to the corn-supply, and stop receiving runaways or planting garrisons in Italy, he was to be given a large

---

[1] See W. W. Tarn, in *J.R.S.* XXII, 1932, esp. pp. 151–7 and below, p. 472.

[2] Dio XLVIII, 33, 5; Appian, *Bell. Civ.* v, 67, 282; Rotondi, *Leges publicae pop. Rom.*, p. 438 and references cited there.

[3] For Puteoli as the place of meeting see *Rev. Arch.* XXII, 1913, p. 253 and cf. *ib.* XXIII, 1914, p. 340. For convenience the conventional title of Misenum is used in reference.

command for the duration of the triumvirate; Octavian was to yield him Corsica, Sardinia and Sicily (most of which he possessed already), and Antony the Peloponnese; he was to receive substantial monetary compensation for his confiscated property, to be an augur (like the other two leaders), and hold a future consulship[1]. In addition all exiles were to be free to return to Italy, and this provision restored to their homes and eventually to political life such notable men as Cn. Calpurnius Piso Frugi, Tib. Claudius Nero, L. Arruntius, M. Iunius Silanus, C. Sentius Saturninus and the younger Cicero. The terms were signed, and the treaty deposited with the Vestal Virgins; to celebrate the pact dinners were given to which the three came with friendly looks and concealed daggers.

Sextus sailed off proudly to his province; Antony and Octavian returned to Rome, hailed on their journey as saviours and protectors, and with all their popularity regained. To gratify Octavian Antony now consented to be designated priest of the deified Julius[2], and both triumvirs made arrangements for the defence and pacification of their respective regions. The north and the west of Gaul had been disturbed recently and to fill the place of Salvidienus there was only one man whom Octavian trusted sufficiently, Agrippa; he was given the governorship of Gaul, while Cn. Domitius Calvinus, a stern disciplinarian of the old school, was sent to Spain to deal with an insurrection of the Cerretani[3]. Beyond the Adriatic the Illyrian Parthini had been troublesome, and Antony dispatched Pollio against them. Far more grave was the menace of the Parthian invasion of Syria and

[1] The explanation given by G. Ferrero (*Grandezza e Decadenza di Roma*, III, p. 359, n. 5) of the discrepancy between Appian, *Bell. Civ.* v, 73, 313 and Dio XLVIII, 35, is here accepted. L. Cocceius Nerva, the peace-maker, was already consul, and among the arrangements for future years the most important were—Agrippa in 37, Sextus Pompeius in 35, Antony II (or his nominee) in 34, Octavian II in 33, and Domitius Ahenobarbus and C. Sosius (both Antony's men) in 32. Antony and Octavian were to be consuls for the third time in 31, and this may be the source for Appian's notion that the Triumvirate was to expire at the end of 32.

[2] Plutarch, *Ant.* 33. See L. R. Taylor, *The Divinity of the Roman Emperor*, p. 118.

[3] An inscription from Emporiae, *C.I.L.* II, 6186, proves that he went to Spain before the consular year of 40 was out. In fact both he and Pollio had resigned their consulships before the end of the year to make room for P. Canidius and Cn. Cornelius Balbus, probably by 1 December; cf. Carcopino, *op. cit.* p. 126 *sq.* The army of Gaul was far too important to leave for long without a commander, and Agrippa also may have left before his year of office as praetor was over.

Asia Minor; early in the year Ventidius Bassus was sent eastwards, and in the autumn Antony himself with Octavia crossed the Adriatic to winter at Athens. For about a year exhausted Italy enjoyed a respite from war or rumours of war.

IV THE PARTHIAN INVASION

The Parthian invasion of Syria in 40 B.C. was much more than a raid. Cassius had not disdained to seek Parthian help, and at the time of Philippi one of his officers, Q. Labienus, son of Caesar's general, was at Orodes' court. Philippi marooned Labienus in Parthia; but in the winter of 41, with Asia Minor denuded of troops, only two disaffected legions in Syria, and Antony in Alexandria, he persuaded Orodes' brilliant son Pacorus that a real conquest of these provinces was possible; probably the fugitive Palmyrenes, good trade customers, added their voices. Labienus and Pacorus entered Roman Syria very early in 40; Saxa was defeated, Cassius' old troops going over to Labienus, and Pacorus got his eagles; Saxa held out for a time in Apamea, but finally it surrendered, as did Antioch, and he fled to Cilicia and was killed. In Cilicia the allies separated, Labienus going west and Pacorus south. Antony's neglect to reorganize the client-kings now bore its fruit; hardly one stood by the triumvirs. Ariarathes of Cappadocia and Antiochus I of Commagene were pro-Parthian, while Castor of Galatia made no attempt to stop Labienus, who moved rapidly westward, enrolling men from the Taurus tribes. Cleon of Gordium, a brigand chief in Mysia, killed his emissaries; but no city closed its gates till he reached Laodicea-on-the-Lycus, which the orator Zeno and his son Polemo, soon to be famous, held against him. In Caria Hybreas tried to hold Mylasa, but it was taken and razed, though Hybreas escaped to rebuild it later; Alabanda was also taken; Stratoniceia and Aphrodisias alone resisted successfully. Zeus indeed saved Panamara by performing a miracle, but Hecate, less efficient, saw her sanctuary at Lagina violated. This half-hearted opposition did not mean that men remembered Cassius with favour; it was disgust with Roman misrule, by whomsoever exercised. The Parthians named Labienus 'the Parthian general,' and he put the shameful title, *Parthicus Imperator*, on his coins[1].

Pacorus swept southward through Syria. He could not take Tyre on its island; otherwise all Syria joined him, including Lysanias of Chalcis, who had just succeeded his father Ptolemaeus, and even Malchus of Nabataea was ready to be friendly.

[1] Volume of Plates iv, 8, *o*.

Pacorus perhaps was now joint-king with his father and struck coins[1], which may point to an intention to hold Syria permanently. The Hasmonaean Antigonus (Mattathias), Aristobulus' son, pretender to the throne of Judaea, now offered Pacorus 1000 talents and 500 women—the families of his political opponents—to make him king. The Jews, who hated the rule of the Idumaeans, welcomed Antigonus, and a Parthian force entered Jerusalem and seated him on the throne. He cut off Hyrcanus' ears so that he could never again be High Priest and gave him to Pacorus, who left Syria and took him to Parthia; there Orodes treated him kindly and gave him a residence in Babylonia. Antigonus struck bilingual coins with 'King Antigonus' in Greek and in Hebrew 'Mattathias the High Priest, the Commonwealth of the Jews'[2]; and for a century the Jews regarded the Parthians with affection as saviours, for they had delivered the people from Rome and her Idumaean friends. The tetrarchs, Herod and Phasael, held the castle till Phasael fell into the Parthians' hands and committed suicide; then with courage and skill Herod collected the threatened women, who included his mother and sister, Hyrcanus' widowed daughter Alexandra and her daughter Mariamme, his betrothed and got them away to his fortress of Masada in Idumaea. He left his brother Joseph to hold it, which he did successfully, and, after being refused help by Malchus, took the road to Egypt. To Cleopatra he was just a young man struggling to uphold Antony's interests; she gave him a ship, and he sailed to Rome to find Antony. He was fortunate in arriving after the peace of Brundisium; Antony agreed with him that only he could maintain Rome's cause against Parthia, and interested Octavian, who remembered his father Antipater's services to Caesar (vol. IX, pp. 404, 671); and an obedient Senate made Herod king of Judaea. This the first breach in the Roman custom that a new client-king must be chosen from the old line was thus made by Antony and Octavian in concert. From that day, whatever Herod did to his subjects, he never faltered in loyalty to Antony. He now returned to Palestine, raised mercenaries, and attacked Antigonus.

The legions at Antony's disposal[3] after the peace of Brundisium were six brought from Macedonia, seven under Pollio, four under

[1] Perhaps the bearded coin, Allotte de la Fuye, *Rev. Num.* 1904, p. 194. The youthful beardless heads usually assigned to him cannot be his: W. W. Tarn, *Mélanges Glotz*, 1932, p. 834 *sq.*

[2] Vol. IX, p. 405, Volume of Plates IV, 2, *i.*

[3] For Antony's troops throughout this chapter and the next see Tarn, *Antony's Legions*, C.Q. XXVI, 1932, p. 75, slightly modified on one point.

Ventidius, two from Domitius (who was sent with them to Bithynia as governor), and five once under Calenus (see p. 30, n. 1). Antony's army down to 36 consisted of these twenty-four legions only[1], no extravagant force with which to safeguard the Balkan frontier, manage the whole East, and conquer Parthia, and sufficient proof that he was not aiming at the sole power. He had retained 10,000 cavalry after Philippi, largely Gauls and Spaniards; how much more Ventidius and Pollio brought him cannot be said. Besides the Parthians, he now had to deal seriously with the Illyrian trouble. The Illyrian Parthini had invaded Macedonia in 40 and been expelled by Censorinus, who triumphed 1 Jan. 39; Antony now gave Pollio eleven legions and sent him to Macedonia to subdue them. Pollio successfully reduced the Parthini, retook Salonae, and celebrated his triumph on 25 Oct. 39 or 38[2]; Antony then divided Pollio's army, stationing four legions in Epirus and leaving seven to guard Macedonia and Illyria. The other eleven legions not with Pollio or Domitius he gave to Ventidius, with a strong force of cavalry and slingers, and sent him against the Parthians; he himself was urgently needed in Italy, and with more than one campaign to watch he naturally did not take the field himself. Either he or Ventidius had realized that the sling, with leaden bullets, would outrange the Parthian bows; but what neither knew was that there had been a change in Parthia's tactics and that it was not the archers whom Ventidius would meet. Carrhae had been won by the common man, trained and led by a genius; the nobility had felt slighted—hence perhaps Surenas' fall—and they were now going to show the Romans what they could do themselves. It was a great stroke of luck for Ventidius; no archers are mentioned in his campaigns, and his battles show clearly that Pacorus was relying on heavy cavalry, the cataphracts (see vol. IX, p. 601). Antony appointed Plancus to be governor of the province of Asia when cleared.

Our accounts of Ventidius' victories go back to a rhetorical panegyric written for his triumph by Sallust from material supplied by himself after Antony had cashiered him[3]; and Antony's

---

[1] A new factor was introduced when Lepidus took over four legions from Sextius in Africa, which Antony claimed as his (Appian, V, 75, 321, and see p. 30, n. 1); possibly therefore at Tarentum Antony claimed that Octavian, one way or another, did owe him four legions, and Octavian, though not admitting the claim, agreed to give four legions in exchange for ships (pp. 54, 59).

[2] The year before Ventidius; see p. 53, n. 4.

[3] O. Hirschfeld, *Mélanges Boissier*, p. 293.

opponents glorified him at Antony's expense. He landed in Asia early in 39 and surprised Labienus, who evacuated Caria and fled to Cilicia with Ventidius' cavalry in pursuit; he fortified a camp on the Taurus slopes and summoned the Parthians, while Ventidius camped on rising ground and waited for his legions, who arrived first. The Parthians evacuated Syria, but were too confident merely to join Labienus, and attacked Ventidius by themselves. Their cataphracts charged the Roman camp up the hill and met the legions hand to hand; they were thrown down the hill in rout, and Ventidius discovered that at short range his slingers could penetrate their armour. He then attacked Labienus' camp; Labienus lost his nerve and fled, and was subsequently killed. The retreating Parthians stood at the Amanic Gates, and must have dismounted men to hold the pass; it was easily forced, the defenders fled across the Euphrates, and Ventidius had cleared Roman Asia as quickly as it had been overrun. Antony took the title of *Imperator* for the second time[1] for the victories of Ventidius and Pollio, and Ventidius marched through Syria to dethrone Antigonus. But Antigonus bribed him[2], and he did nothing; he went into winter quarters with his army strung out from Judaea to Cappadocia, that country being a danger-point should Artavasdes of Armenia, Parthia's ally, enter the war.

The new Parthian tactics were obviously wrong; but Pacorus had not been with the army, which seemingly was not numerous, and did not recognize its defeat as decisive. Early in 38 he assembled a larger force; he may have brought every cataphract in Parthia. Ventidius, to gain time to collect his troops, skilfully let him hear that he was afraid he might cross the Euphrates, not at Zeugma, but to the south; Pacorus, perplexed and suspicious, apparently avoided both courses and made a détour to the north, crossing perhaps at Samosata; by the time he entered Cyrrhestice Ventidius was ready and had fortified a camp on rising ground near Mt Gindarus. Again the Parthian chivalry charged the camp, with the same result as before but with heavier loss, for Pacorus was killed and some of his men died fighting round his body; the main force escaped across the Euphrates. Ventidius became extraordinarily popular, for he was held to have avenged

---

[1] Following H. A. Grueber, *Coins of the Roman Republic in the British Museum*, II, p. 505, as against M. von Bahrfeldt, *J. I. d'A. N.* XII, pp. 89, 93, who makes this the *third*; in his view Philippi is the *second*, not the first, while *iterum*, which should appear on the coins after Philippi, is omitted.

[2] Josephus, *Ant.* XIV [14, 6], 390 is explicit as to the bribery; *cf.* Dio XLVIII, 41, 5.

Carrhae; but the story that Gindarus was fought on the anniversary of that battle is probably an invention. Pacorus' death was a loss to Parthia, for he is highly praised, not only for energy and valour, but for his moderation and equity, which everywhere attracted much support. But, except for that, the defeat of Gindarus was Parthia's salvation; it taught her not to rely upon cataphracts against a Roman army.

V. ANTONY AND OCTAVIA

At the beginning of November 40 the seal had been set to the treaty of Brundisium by the marriage of Antony and Octavian's sister Octavia, Marcellus' widow, the pledge that the two sides were henceforth one; Fulvia's death had left Antony free, and though Octavia had not completed the obligatory ten months mourning for her husband the Senate obediently gave her permission to re-marry. Through the murk of the civil wars Octavia shines like a star; in an age when every restraint was relaxed, and Roman virtues seemed likely to go down in a welter of license and cruelty, no evil about her was ever even hinted by anybody. Beautiful[1] and still young, highly cultured, the friend of the honoured philosophers Athenodorus (who dedicated a book to her) and Nestor, she preferred her home to politics; but she was a match for her brother in diplomacy, as she was to show at Tarentum by her quiet but conclusive handling of his accusations against Antony. Her gentleness and goodness, and her devoted obedience to her husband, sprang from strength, not from weakness; what she saw to be her duty, that, quite simply, she did. She made no complaint of Antony's treatment of her; she helped him as long as he would let her, and when the end came she took charge of his children by the rival who had ousted her and brought them up with her own, the crowning heroism of perhaps the loveliest nature which the ancient world can show.

Antony did not leave Italy till after the birth of Octavia's daughter, the elder Antonia, about August or September 39; then he and Octavia went to Athens, which for the next two years was his headquarters. The Senate had confirmed in advance his measures in the East[2], and the disaffection among the client-kings revealed by the Parthian invasion invited a complete reorganization. He made a partial one only. Labienus had got help from the Taurus peoples, and Antony took advantage of the breach

---

[1] Volume of Plates iv, 166, a.
[2] Appian, *Bell. Civ.* v, 75, 318.

made in Roman custom in Herod's case (p. 48) to pick out two
good men who did not belong to any dynasty but who had given
their proofs[1], Amyntas from Galatia, the former secretary of
Deiotarus (p. 34), and Polemo of Laodicea (p. 47), and put
them in authority over the tribes. Amyntas' kingdom was western
Pisidia and Phrygia-toward-Pisidia. Polemo had his seat at
Iconium and ruled Cilicia Tracheia, a wild country which had
once been part of the Roman province of Cilicia but which was
difficult to manage. Antony strengthened Tarcondimotus, a
dynast in the unruly Amanus, by making him king, with his
capital at Hieropolis-Castabala; on his coins he called himself
Philantonius. Cleon, the brigand chief who had defied Labienus,
was confirmed in his rule of the Mysian Olympus. Aphrodisias
received freedom and immunity from taxation; Antony's grant
is remarkable as containing (in simple form) a most-favoured-
nation clause, apparently its first appearance in history[2]. He also
raised his fleet to five squadrons of the line (300 ships), partly by
incorporating Domitius' fleet; if it came to trouble, he did not
mean to be weaker than Sextus. He made fleet-stations of
Cephallenia and Zacynthus, convenient for keeping watch over
Sicilian waters, and posted detachments there under Proculeius
and C. Sosius, who acted as lords of their respective islands and
struck coins; the coins of Antony's fleet-prefects of this period
are notable for their naval symbolism[3]. Either now or in 38
he brought to Asia the four legions from Epirus, leaving seven
in Macedonia.

He spent the winter at Athens with Octavia in the enjoyment of
a new sensation, the company of a virtuous woman. He became
respectable; he dressed simply, went with his wife to philosophers'
lectures and the public festivals, and served as gymnasiarch
(minister for education); perhaps it was now that he projected a
universal association of victors in the games. Athens gave Octavia
many honours, and the Panathenaia of 38 bore the added name
Antonieia. But, if more decorous, Antony was as self-indulgent
at Athens as he had been at Alexandria; he put aside all business
till the spring, though apparently he meant to conquer Armenia in
38 as the prelude to the invasion of Parthia. For his eastern subjects he now assumed divinity like a Hellenistic king and pro-

[1] Appian, *Bell. Civ.* v, 75, 319, ἴστη βασιλέας οὓς δοκιμάσειεν,—who
satisfied his δοκιμασία.
[2] *O.G.I.S.* 455, ll. 8, 9; the Senate's decree reproduces the wording of
Antony's grant.
[3] Volume of Plates iv, 196, *g, h.*

claimed himself a New Dionysus, the god who had conquered
Asia (p. 69). The story that he married Athene and exacted from
the Athenians a million drachmae as her dower first appears in a
rhetorical exercise[1] and reads like a refurbishing of the story of
the marriage of Antiochus IV with Atargatis; to 'woo Athene'
was almost a proverb for the insolence of power[2].

Antony's plans for 38 were altered by a message from Octavian,
who was having trouble with Sextus and asked Antony to be at
Brundisium on a given day for a conference. Antony came, but
Octavian did not; and Antony, naturally angry at what he considered an insult, went back again, after advising Octavian to
keep his treaties. Pacorus' second invasion (p. 50) prevented
further thought of the conquest of Armenia, and Gindarus was
followed by a fresh complication. Some fugitive Parthians had
taken refuge with Antiochus of Commagene, and Ventidius
marched on Samosata; but Antiochus, in imitation of Antigonus,
offered him 1000 talents to mark time, and the siege made no
progress. This second scandal created an impossible position, and
Antony was forced to supersede him and take command in person.
Samosata surrendered to him[3], and he presumably removed
Antiochus, who is not heard of again, and made his brother
Mithridates king; and he took the title of *Imperator* for the third
time, really for Gindarus. He sent Ventidius to Italy for the well-
earned triumph which the people had voted him and of which he
was too generous to deprive him in spite of his misdoings. Ventidius triumphed 27 Nov. 38 or 37[4], and is not heard of again;
naturally Antony could not employ him, and as Octavian never
did he probably died soon afterwards.

After Gindarus Ventidius had detached a force to help Herod;

---

[1] Seneca, *Suasoriae*, 1, 7.

[2] Rhianus l. 14 in Powell, *Collectanea Alexandrina*, p. 9; cf. Theopom-
pus, *Frag. Gr. Hist.* no. 115 fr. 31, and see O. Weinreich, *Hermes*, LXVII,
1932, p. 361. S. Eitrem, *Symbolae Osloenses*, XI, 1932, p. 14 takes Antony's
marriage seriously.

[3] Josephus' passing references (*Ant.* XIV [15, 9], 447; *Bell. Jud.* I [16, 7],
322) to the surrender as well-known cannot be wrong, and are confirmed
by Orosius (*i.e.* Livy) VI, 18, 23, vix uno castello expugnato (only one was in
question) and by the attitude of the Senate, Dio XLVIII, 41, 5. Were the
absurd story in Plutarch, *Ant.* 34 (repeated in many modern works) true,
Antony's prestige must have suffered enormously; of this there is no sign.

[4] The tables in *C.I.L.* I², pp. 54, 76, 180, give 38, which is probable.
But the *Acta triumphorum Capitolina*, p. 50, can equally well read DCCX[V or
DCCX[VI, and nothing else actually decides the question. The same uncer-
tainty affects Pollio's triumph (p. 49).

but Antigonus again bribed the Roman commander, and Herod, in despair of getting anything done, went himself to Antony, who was before Samosata. As soon as Samosata had surrendered, Antony put Sosius in command with strict orders to deal with Antigonus, and Sosius sent Herod on ahead with two legions, a rare instance of a foreigner commanding Roman troops. Herod defeated Antigonus' men at Jericho and formed the siege of Jerusalem, and when Sosius arrived the siege was energetically pressed by the entire Roman army. Jerusalem held out manfully, but was taken in July 37 B.C. (p. 321 n. 1); Herod prevented the desecration of the Temple and ransomed the town from pillage, saying that he wanted a kingdom, not a desert. Antigonus surrendered to Sosius, who subsequently took him to Antony; and Herod, who had married Mariamme, the last Hasmonaean princess, began his long reign as king of Judaea. Sosius commemorated his success by striking a coin with the figures of Antigonus and of Judaea as a captive woman[1]. But some Jews at once revolted against Herod, and that winter (37) Antony executed Antigonus lest he should become a centre of disaffection.

After taking Samosata Antony returned to Athens and again spent the winter (38) with Octavia. He was still not fated to reduce Armenia, for Octavian, after his disaster at Cape Scyllaeum[2], sent Maecenas to him with an urgent request for naval help. Antony's star was in the ascendant; three of his generals had recently celebrated or been granted triumphs, and that of Sosius was to come, while Octavian's campaign against Sextus in 38 had been a failure. Antony stood loyally by his colleague, and in the spring of 37 sailed to Tarentum[3] with Octavia and his whole fleet, only to find that Octavian, who had built a new fleet during the winter, now intimated that he no longer required his help. What followed is related elsewhere (p. 58); Octavia prevented war, and the result was the treaty of Tarentum, under which Antony handed over to Octavian two complete squadrons—120 ships of the line and their 10 scouts—against Octavian's promise of four legions, which Antony perhaps claimed that he owed already (pp. 30, 49); Antony agreed because he was short of money and wished to get rid of the upkeep of the ships. The treaty itself was only an uneasy truce; the legions were never given; and when in

---

[1] Volume of Plates iv, 2, *j*.   [2] See p. 57.

[3] Plutarch, in making Antony excluded from *Brundisium* (*Ant.* 35), seems to have transferred to this year a statement in his sources relating to 40 B.C., for παροξυνθείς fits Antony in 40 but not in 37, when he came συμμαχήσων (Appian, *Bell. Civ.* v, 93, 387).

the autumn (37) Antony quitted Italy for Greece he had already reconsidered his position. So far, he had been loyal to all his agreements with Octavian; but he felt that Octavian had not been loyal to him. As he saw it, he had been shut out of Brundisium in 40, though Italy was common ground; Octavian had called him to a conference and had never appeared, and had asked for and then rejected his help; for two years he had been prevented from beginning the conquest of Parthia; his treaty right of recruiting in Italy was a dead letter; and now Octavian had his ships and he had not his legions. He had become convinced that further co-operation with Octavian was impossible; and a personal motive was reinforcing that conviction. He was tired of Octavia. He could not live on her level; his was a nature which no woman could hold unless she had something of the devil in her. His mind, reacting from Octavia's virtues, had gone back to a very different woman; memory, which glosses all defects, presented Cleopatra as more desirable even than the reality; he fell in love with her during, and perhaps because of, his absence from her. From Corcyra he sent Octavia back to Italy, for which her approaching confinement and his coming Parthian campaign provided an excuse, and summoned Cleopatra to meet him at Antioch. She came, and he married her forthwith; he had burnt his boats.

VI. SICILY AND THE END OF SEXTUS POMPEIUS

Between the treaties of Brundisium and Tarentum a little less than three years had elapsed, yet actual peace in Italy lasted but an uneasy twelve months, and the troubler of it was, as before, Sextus Pompeius. Ancient historians were often unfair to unsuccessful candidates for power, and our sources combine to depict Sextus as the degenerate antithesis of his father, cruel and boorish, deficient alike in initiative and intellect, and wholly dependent on the brains of his Sicilian freedmen, Apollophanes, Demochares and Menas. In spite of the character of these sources—and much of Sextus' wickedness was perhaps that of the animal which, if attacked, defends itself—it is hard to find much in his favour. Neither before nor after Philippi had he the sense to co-operate with other anti-Caesarian leaders, and though the heritage of a great name attracted to him clients and nobles alike, he was unable to hold for long the loyalty of any Roman of note. His freedmen might win victories, but he himself had not enough energy or insight to follow them up. In all, his actions betray little beyond the limited purpose and outlook of a guerilla leader[1]. But at the time he had a genuine grievance: though Octavian acquiesced in yielding the islands to him, there was some difficulty over the transference of the Peloponnese, which was to come from Antony; Sextus declared that it had been granted him unconditionally and that Antony was deliberately lowering its value by extortion and taxation, to which Octavian replied that Antony had stipulated that Sextus should either pay over the tribute owing to him from Achaea or delay entry till it had been collected. Whatever the truth (and it looks as though there had been negligence on Antony's part[2]), Sextus immediately let loose his pirate squadrons; captured pirates confessed under torture that Sextus had instigated them, and Octavian determined on reprisals. To justify his action he published the terms of the treaty of Misenum; if war had to be made it would open with advantage for him, since Menas (Sextus' governor in Sardinia) deserted, bringing over the island and three legions; in addition he was sure of the loyalty of two of the most important South Italian towns, Vibo and Rhegium, for he had exempted them from the assignations of 43 B.C. (p. 20), and had guaranteed their territories. To mark the end of the hollow pact with Sextus he divorced Scribonia ('utterly disgusted,' as he wrote afterwards, 'with her contrary temper')[3] on the very day that she bore him a daughter, Julia, who was destined to cause him more trouble than all her mother's tempers.

He now entered into an alliance very different from the coldly political one he had just thrown off, though this new one perhaps indicated a desire to appease and come nearer to that old senatorial aristocracy, with whom Caesar had so signally failed. He had fallen in love passionately with Livia, the wife of Tiberius Nero, and the ardour of his passion no less than the complaisance with which Nero divorced his wife to give her to Octavian be-

[1] The ordinary 'official' view is seen in Livy, *Epit.* cxxvii–cxxxi, and in Vell. Pat. ii, 73. Of Romans who joined with him, Sextus Bithynicus and Staius Murcus were treacherously murdered, Tiberius Nero left him in disgust (Suetonius, *Tib.* 4, 3), and most returned after the treaty of Misenum; after that, the only known Roman commanders are L. Plinius Rufus, Tisienus Gallus and, possibly, Cn. Cornelius Lentulus Cruscellio (E. Groag in *Klio*, xiv, 1914, pp. 51–7).

[2] The Antonian coins found in a hoard at Olbia in Sardinia (Taramelli in *Not. degli Scavi*, 1904, p. 158) do not prove that Antony was supplying Sextus with money at this time.

[3] Suetonius, *Aug.* 62; Dio xlviii, 34, 3.

came a target for the wits of the day[1]. The marriage took place on 17 January, 38 B.C., three days after Livia had given birth to her second son Drusus; he and his three-year old brother Tiberius were to be reared in Octavian's house. Livia was nineteen, ambitious, beautiful, discreet; of aristocratic Republican stock, herself earlier a victim of the triumvirs' orders, she was a fit symbol of the reconciliation that was to come; throughout a devoted married life of fifty years she remained an influence for moderation and forgiveness.

Though Lepidus vouchsafed no reply to the appeals that Octavian sent out, Antony naturally promised help, and a meeting was arranged at Brundisium. Unfortunately, on the appointed day, Octavian did not turn up[2], and Antony, declaring that Parthian affairs allowed no delay, returned to Athens, leaving a curt message to Octavian not to violate the pact. Sextus immediately interpreted this as proof that Antony could not justify his colleague, and Octavian had to assure the populace that he and Antony were in full sympathy, and that Antony's reason for not surrendering Achaea was his annoyance at Sextus' piracies. But the events of the year went wholly in favour of the 'pirate.' The plan of campaign was to invade Sicily in force: as Agrippa was away in Gaul, Octavian appointed C. Calvisius Sabinus as his admiral (with Menas under him), gathered legions from Gaul and Illyricum, and ordered L. Cornificius to bring a fleet from Ravenna to Tarentum. An action off Cumae was indecisive, but Octavian, who had himself brought Cornificius' fleet from Tarentum to Rhegium in order to join with Calvisius, refused through excessive caution to attack the smaller squadron of Sextus; as he was sailing northwards through the Straits the ships of Sextus flashed out and drove him back towards land, the rocky promontories of Cape Scyllaeum; there followed a night of confusion, and next morning a strong south wind turned confusion into complete disaster. Octavian had lost half his fleet and had to abandon any attempt on Sicily; Sextus' exultation was correspondingly great; proclaiming himself 'son of Neptune'[3] he offered sacrifices to his

---

[1] A keen analysis of the traditional version, incorporating the new evidence from the Verulae calendar, is given by J. Carcopino in *Rev. hist.* CLXI, 1929, p. 225.

[2] This may possibly have been merely lateness on Octavian's part, due to some cause unknown; later he reproached Antony for not waiting longer: Appian, *Bell. Civ.* v, 80, 339.

[3] Hence Octavian's cry 'etiam invito Neptuno se victoriam adepturum,' Suetonius, *Aug.* 16, 2. For denarii of Sextus with legend NEPTUNI see Vol. of Plates iv, 196, *j*.

father, but strangely enough made no effort to follow up his victory.

Though the year closed thus in humiliation for Octavian the labours of his devoted friends gave promise of better things for 37. The mob at Rome murmured against war, but cities and well-wishers, to show their confidence, promised money towards the construction of ships, and Maecenas, who had journeyed to Greece in the previous autumn to discuss disputed points with Antony came back with the glad assurance that he was willing to help. Best of all, Agrippa returned from Gaul with a splendid record: he had been the second Roman general to lead troops across the Rhine, he had settled the Ubii on the site of Cologne and had won a brilliant victory over the insurgent Aquitani. He was to be consul for 37 and was offered a triumph, but with rare sympathy refused the coveted honour while his friend was in such distress. Octavian immediately entrusted him with the preparation and exercise of a fleet for next year, and shipbuilding was soon in full swing, but as Italy did not possess a harbour or manœuvring area sufficiently spacious Agrippa crowned his work by making the famous roadstead of Lakes Lucrinus and Avernus and connecting the two lakes with the sea; here there was ample room and for over a year freed slaves were practised at the oar, while experiments were carried out with a device of Agrippa, whereby grapnels were shot from a catapult to make it easier to hold and board an enemy ship. Even Lepidus finally consented to help.

As the spring of 37 B.C. was ending Antony duly appeared off Tarentum with 300 ships[1]; he badly needed recruits for his Parthian campaigns, he could not obtain them without Octavian's co-operation, and he hoped to exchange ships for men. But Octavian hesitated: he was mistrustful and angry, he had heard that Antony was in negotiation with Lepidus, and confident in Agrippa and the new-built fleet he probably felt ashamed of his appeals for help in the previous year. Days passed. Octavia, in anguish, obtained leave from her husband to mediate between him and her brother; to each and every plaint or suspicion of Octavian she had a sufficient reply, and thanks to her the two at last met near Tarentum. Twice she had saved Rome from civil war; a third time she was not to be so fortunate. But concord was restored: as the term fixed for the Triumvirate by the Lex Titia had expired with the last day of

---

[1] For the date see pp. 51–7 of Kromayer's *Die rechtliche Begründung des Principats*.

38 the two agreed upon an extension of their powers[1]; they also agreed to deprive Sextus Pompeius of what they had granted him, and to give each other mutual assistance. Antony offered 120 ships from his fleet to Octavian and was in return promised four legions[2]; through Octavia's good offices her brother received in addition ten *phaseli* and offered Antony the choice of one thousand picked men from his bodyguard. The two now parted: what happened to Antony and Octavia has already been told; in the West, though preparations went on vigorously, Menas—vexed at being kept in a subordinate position—returned to his old master, Sextus, and Octavian used this as a pretext for depriving Calvisius Sabinus of the command of the fleet and handing it to Agrippa.

By the end of spring in 36 the time had come to put the new fleet and new methods to a test, but operations did not begin immediately. Octavian with characteristic caution had prepared a complex scheme of attack, involving the co-operation of three distinct fleets, and orders had to be communicated and acknowledged; the campaign was to begin on 1 July, the month of Julius Caesar. The plan was that Agrippa with his fleet should smash the Sextian fleet and render possible the invasion of Sicily in overwhelming force; yet the crossing of the Straits against a resolute enemy has always been a difficult problem and one to tax the genius even of a Murat or a Garibaldi. Octavian was to start from Puteoli, Statilius Taurus with 102 ships from Tarentum (leaving some empty keels there), and Lepidus was to bring from Africa sixteen legions and 5000 horse. Against this formidable converging offensive Sextus had (at most) 300 warships and ten legions: he stationed himself at Messana with the best of his fleet and troops,

---

[1] The texts are notoriously contradictory. Dio XLVIII, 54, 6, says the Triumvirate had come to an end, Appian, *Bell. Civ.* v, 95, 398, that it was coming to an end, and no reconciliation is possible. The most reasonable hypothesis seems to the present writer to be that the term fixed by the Lex Titia expired on Dec. 31, 38 B.C., but that all the triumvirs carried on, as they might do on the ground that their powers could not lapse until they formally laid them down. At Tarentum Octavian got Antony to agree to some form of extension, and later on tried to validate that by getting a law passed granting a second five-year term (Appian, *Ill.* 28). Henceforward, Octavian was careful to call himself triumvir *iterum* and emphasize the constitutionality of his conduct, Antony simply continued to call himself triumvir without any suggestion of a second term, and what Lepidus did is unknown. See further, below, p. 94.

[2] Appian, *Bell. Civ.* v, 95, 396: Antony's coins of the period figure the heads of himself, Octavia and Octavian, galleys, and a *triskeles* (Sicily); see Volume of Plates, IV, 196, *i*.

and entrusted the defence of Lilybaeum and the west to L. Plinius Rufus[1]. But he could not hold out long once Octavian's legions landed in the island; his main hope must lie in the capture or killing of the directing will behind the armament, Octavian himself.

The new fleet was solemnly purified, and on 1 July the three great expeditions started, to meet with very different fortunes. Lepidus landed twelve legions safely, blockaded Plinius in Lilybaeum, and overran the western half of Sicily[2], but on 3 July a terrific storm burst over South Italy and Sicily and though Taurus crept back discreetly to his base Octavian met the full brunt of it. The damage would need a month at least to repair, the season was getting late, but Octavian did not relent. The crews of the shattered vessels were sent to fill the 28 empty keels at Tarentum, Octavian went the round of the colonies and the veterans, and Maecenas hurried to Rome to allay the superstitions of the populace, who felt that Sextus had indeed the gods on his side. But Sextus again made no effort to exploit Neptune's favour, and Menas in disgust registered his third desertion.

Mid-August saw the attack resumed[3]. This time Octavian made Vibo his head-quarters; it was close to Sicily and within less than thirty miles (by land) of Scolacium, where Taurus now lay. Agrippa and his fleet were to attack Sicily from the North and keep Sextus' attention engaged, while Octavian, helped by M. Valerius Messalla Corvinus (who had recently joined him) and by Statilius Taurus, was to transport his legions from Scolacium to Leucopetra, thence across to Tauromenium under cover of night, link up with Lepidus coming from the West, and fall on Messana; three legions under C. Carrinas at Columna Rhegia were to wait on events[4]. But Sextus had learnt, or guessed, this plan of attack and made a skilful counter. Off Mylae Agrippa attacked a squadron under Demochares, and his larger and heavier-built ships had the advantage; Sextus sent reinforcements and finally appeared himself with the main body of his fleet; the Straits were left temptingly clear. Octavian seized the chance to ferry three legions across from Leucopetra and camped them on the lava spit of Naxos. The trap

[1] Dessau 8891 records fortification work at Lilybaeum carried out by Plinius Rufus as legate of Sextus.

[2] Of four more legions following Lepidus two were cut off and destroyed by Demochares, Appian, *Bell. Civ.* v, 104, 430–2. (Drumann's identification of Demochares and Papias is here accepted.)

[3] See map 5 facing p. 55. For works of detail upon the campaign see the Bibliography, Part I, section II, H.

[4] Appian, *Bell. Civ.* v, 103, 428 is corrupt, but the general sense is clear; see G. Grasso in *Riv. Stor. Ant.* XII, 1908, p. 19.

could now close: Sextus had managed to withdraw his ships in good order, Agrippa was resting his men. Before Octavian could return for the rest of the legions Sextus with fleet and cavalry swooped down upon him. Handing over the command of the three legions to L. Cornificius Octavian decided to risk a sea-fight, but the superiority of Sextus' seamanship was crushingly demonstrated; Octavian's ships were burnt or wrecked, and though some survivors were rescued by Cornificius, Octavian himself only just managed to evade capture in the gathering darkness and reached the mainland with but one friend to be by him during the night. So near had Sextus come to success.

Octavian was utterly exhausted both in body and soul; for one moment even his will and belief broke and he begged his companion to kill him. His position was critical in the extreme: again Sextus had triumphed, Cornificius was isolated, he could not tell how Agrippa was faring, he could not be sure of Lepidus, for he was rumoured to have begun negotiations with Sextus; such was the outcome of five years' patient work. But dawn brought help and a renewal of hope; he was seen, recognized and escorted to Messalla. His first thought was for Cornificius and urgent messages were sent to Agrippa and all other commanders. Agrippa had by now attacked again, and had captured Tyndaris, one of the keys of the island; he threw out reconnoitring parties, and after a harassing march across the western slopes of Mt Aetna Cornificius and his three legions reached him unscathed.

The legions once securely in the island the surrender of Sextus could be merely a matter of time; he was cooped up into the northeastern corner, and while Lepidus and Octavian sat down to blockade Messana Taurus was dispatched to capture the towns that supplied him. Tradition records that the final battle took place after a challenge, as a result of which 300 ships from each side faced each other off Naulochus, while the troops watched from the shore. Though the incident of the challenge may be matched from the period it seems impossible that Sextus could muster 300 ships and the whole story smacks of rhetorical invention[1]. However that may be the final battle was fought on 3 September; the

---

[1] Orosius alone adds any figures of value to those provided by Appian. *Bell. Civ.* IV, 115, 480 compared with 117, 494 shows that in 42 B.C. Sextus cannot have had much more than 130 vessels. After Philippi add Murcus' 80 and allow for piratical and other craft, but he can scarcely have had more than 300. Orosius VI, 18, 21 says Menas deserted with 60 ships; at Mylae 30 were lost, Appian, *ib.* V, 108, 447. It may be reasonably doubted whether Sextus had more than 200 at Naulochus.

fight was long, but Agrippa's invention, the *harpax*, proved its value, and in the evening victory remained with the fleet of Octavian. Twenty-eight of Sextus' fleet were sunk, the rest were burnt or captured or ran aground, and only seventeen escaped to Messana[1]. Sextus sent a desperate summons to Plinius Rufus to join him there, but time was short and without waiting for the arrival of his lieutenant he changed into civilian dress and with the remnant of his fleet fled from Sicily to throw himself on Antony's mercy; yet the ruling passion was strong even in flight and on the way he stopped to pillage the rich temple of Hera at Cape Lacinium. The rest of his career demands no long telling: though he had sent envoys to Antony, the news of Roman failure in Media made him pause and he decided to offer his services to the king of Parthia as well; these messengers fell into Antony's hands, and though at first no active steps were taken against him, he soon made himself so troublesome in Asia Minor that Titius, Antony's legate, had him executed. It is possible that the fatal order was given by Plancus, but it was Titius who had to bear the blame, and the name of Pompey was still sufficiently revered in Rome for the whole populace later to drive him from the theatre by their execrations.

VII. THE END OF THE CIVIL WARS

Victory, complete and definite, had come at last, thanks to the skill and fidelity of Octavian's helpers, but due even more to the indomitable tenacity he himself had exhibited. Yet in the very hour of success a new menace faced him. Lepidus, who had for years acquiesced perforce in his subordination, now judged himself strong enough to strike for what he thought his rightful place; the large force with which he had left Africa suggests that he had carefully planned his *coup*, and now, while he and Agrippa combined to urge the blockade of Messana, luck suddenly placed the means and the moment in his hand. For Plinius, who had taken charge of the city, offered to surrender: Agrippa advised waiting for the arrival of Octavian, who was at Naulochus, but Lepidus overrode him, accepted the surrender, and then allowed his own fourteen legions to join with the eight Sextian in plundering Messana during one long night of licence. Next morning Octavian arrived to remonstrate, but Lepidus, strong in the backing of twenty-two legions, demanded the restoration of his rights and ordered Octavian to quit Sicily. But the issue could not long be

[1] Appian, *Bell. Civ.* v, 121, 503. Florus II, 18 [IV, 8], 9 for rhetorical effect makes the master of 350 ships flee with a mere six or seven.

doubtful: the soldiers were weary of civil war and still less inclined to enter one for Lepidus, whose sluggishness they despised, against Octavian, whose achievements were visible and splendid. Gradually they deserted, the Sextians first, then the men and officers of Lepidus' own legions, till at the last he was reduced to beg for mercy. Octavian spared his life but apparently forced him to resign his office of Triumvir, and dismissed him to drag out the remainder of his days as Pontifex Maximus in honourable captivity at Circeii. His brief greatness was ended, and in the momentous developments of the next decade he was to take no share.

There now remained, crowded together into the north-eastern corner of the island, a host of over forty legions; though their loyalties had been different, Sextian, Lepidan, or Caesarian, all were one in their longing for release from service and their numbers made them formidable indeed. Mutinous spirits fanned their discontent, and though Octavian reminded them of their oath and offered promises, they clamoured for something more substantial, for instant and profitable dismissal. But one of their ringleaders, a centurion, mysteriously disappeared, his fate deterred others, and finally Octavian disbanded twenty thousand, who had fought at Mutina and Philippi, and bestowed bounties on the rest with promise of early demobilization. Tribunes and centurions were given the rank of decurion in their native town[1], and Agrippa, for his magnificent services, was awarded a *corona rostrata*—a golden crown adorned with ships' prows—an honour never bestowed before. Finally Octavian arranged for the settlement of the territories that had fallen to him: of Sardinia little is known, though a colony was apparently founded at Turris Libisonis; in Sicily a colony was planted at Tauromenium[2], and though Catana, Centuripa and Syracuse were rewarded for good service during the war[3], the other Sicilian cities had to face a demand for sixteen hundred talents. The former Sextian commanders were pardoned, and runaway slaves restored to their masters. After a year spent in pacifying Sicily Statilius Taurus crossed over to organize the two provinces of Africa[4].

[1] For an edict of Octavian's, dating between 40 and 37 B.C., granting various privileges to veterans, see H. Malcovati, *Caesaris Augusti Imperatoris operum fragmenta*[2], xcvi, p. 36, and the literature cited in the Bibliography, Part I, section II, F.

[2] For a possible colony in the Lipari Islands see P. Orsi in *Not. degli Scavi*, v, 1929, pp. 98–100.

[3] Strabo vi, 272. A settlement at Rhegium, *ib.* 259: a later colony at Syracuse, *ib.* 270.

[4] Utica was given full citizenship; Dio xlix, 16, 1. Taurus himself triumphed in 34 'ex Africa.'

Having made the necessary arrangements Octavian could at last return to Rome, and his return was a triumphal progress, for nobles and commons alike flocked out in festal garlands and dress to escort him into the city. He did not however enter until 13 November, when he celebrated the *ovatio* which the Senate had decreed, but in the meantime other honours had been crowded upon him by a grateful people. The anniversary of Naulochus was to be a festival, a triumphal arch was to be erected, and a golden statue set up with an inscription celebrating the restoration of peace after long disturbances on sea and land. An official residence was voted to him, close to the ground which he himself reserved for a temple to his patron deity Apollo. Like his father he was given the right of wearing the laurel-wreath of the conqueror, and, most important of all, he was granted a sacrosanctity similar to that enjoyed by the tribunes—a privilege which two years later he had conferred upon his wife and sister[1]; thus already his own person was marked out as something hallowed and eminent, and this tribunician sacrosanctity foreshadowed the *potestas tribunicia* which was to be one of the great props of the coming principate.

The long horror of the civil wars was over, peace and prosperity should return once more—such was the burden of the speeches which Octavian made to the Senate and the People, in which he defended his acts as due to the necessity of the times. In conformity with these utterances he remitted a large number of public debts, cancelled some taxes, burnt the documents relating to the civil wars, and hinted that the Republican constitution would be restored when Antony returned from his Parthian campaigns. Too long had Roman fought against Roman; the time had come to turn against the barbarian. These speeches were not meant only for Rome; they had a message for all Italy, for Octavian published and circulated them throughout the peninsula: men could labour on their farms and homes in security, all could return to the normal business of life. The famine and misery produced by Sextus' raids and interception of the corn-supply had taught one lesson, the dependence of Italy upon foreign corn; it cannot be coincidence only that Varro's treatise upon agriculture appeared in 36 B.C. and that while an imperial freedman, Hyginus, was compiling practical handbooks for farmers in plain prose, Virgil at the prompting of Maecenas was beginning with loving care the great epic of the Italian countryside, the *Georgics*.

Caesar's murder had been avenged, his last enemies routed, but for the man who had accepted Caesar's heritage a loftier task

---

[1] Dio XLIX, 38, 1, and see further, p. 121.

remained. Whatever projects Caesar may have had for the East, his main achievement—whether as general or statesman—had been in the West, in Spain and Gaul and Italy. Octavian's reverence for Italian tradition and religion was deep implanted—as witness his refusal to take the office of Pontifex Maximus from Lepidus—and during nine long years of schooling he had grown to see what Italy and the empire needed and to believe that he was fated to give it. Time and again he had been near death, from illness or enemies, yet his life had always been spared, and the consciousness that destiny was guarding him for a great work must have been continually strengthened[1]. This consciousness and this singleness of purpose explain the devotion that he was able to inspire in his peers; the ordinary soldier might be fascinated by the magic of a splendid name, but it was something high and essential in the man himself that bound men of the calibre of Agrippa and Maecenas in such unquestioning and selfless loyalty or gained the respect and service of the Republican Messalla Corvinus, or of Statilius Taurus and others who were won over to his side. Because he stood for something more than mere ambition he could draw a nation to him in the coming struggle.

For struggle there must be. The Roman realm now lay in the hands of two men; the statutory Triumvirate had dwindled to an unauthorized duovirate. Octavian's treatment of Lepidus—little though his lethargic personality had counted in the coalition—and appropriation of the provinces of Sicily and Africa could not be defended on any constitutional grounds and could not be overlooked by Antony, even though his own conduct had not been impeccable. Herein lay dangerous chances of dissension between characters so disparate, and the influence Octavia might exert for peace was more than balanced by the imperial designs of Cleopatra. In that struggle few could foretell the result. The legions, weary of interminable fighting, would not always follow a leader's ambition against countrymen and comrades: the victor must possess not merely name or prestige, but above all a cause and a battle-cry that would rally waverers to his side and convince not only soldiers but citizens also that the unity of the Roman world was at stake.

---

[1] From the fragments of his Autobiography it looks as though Augustus himself laid special stress upon these escapes and the notion of a special providence preserving him. See Plutarch, *Apophth. reg. et imp., Aug.* 10 (*Mor.* 207 E); for literature upon 'the luck of Augustus' and the Augustuslegend see the Bibliography, Part I, section II, c.

CHAPTER III

THE WAR OF THE EAST AGAINST THE WEST

I. CLEOPATRA AND ANTONY

ANTONY'S marriage to Cleopatra in the autumn of 37 was the turning-point of his career, the beginning of his breach with the West. He did not propose to attack Octavian; he merely meant to go his own way without reference to his colleague. His pre-occupation at present was Parthia: its conquest would prove him Caesar's true heir and would outweigh any prestige Octavian could acquire. But his marriage had no connection with this scheme of conquest. Egypt was wealthy; but he drew nothing from Egypt for his invasion of Parthia, of which Cleopatra disapproved (p. 75); and the modern belief that he married her for her money is certainly untrue. Had it been money, he had only to raise his hand and she was dethroned and Egypt and the money his, amid Roman applause; he could not do it, because he had fallen in love with her. For this he married her, though he knew that it meant a general assent to her point of view. For the shock to Roman opinion he now cared nothing; and however strongly one condemns his treatment of Octavia, one must also sympathize with his scorn of an outlook which had no objection to the queen as his mistress but every objection to her as his wife. He married her in the form the Ptolemies used, presumably the Macedonian, and to every one east of the Adriatic she was his legitimate wife; but, as a Roman citizen, he could not in Roman law either have two wives at once or contract a valid marriage with a foreigner[1], and this enabled Octavian for the present, whatever he felt, to take no official notice of the marriage. Antony's is a strange story. Two women had been devoted to him. Had he followed Fulvia, he might perhaps have been master of the Roman world; had he followed Octavia, he could have ruled his half in peace, too popular to be attacked; instead, he had broken Fulvia's heart and made Octavia homeless. Now he had married a woman whose only devotion to him was as the instrument of her ambition; and her he would follow, and follow to his ruin, because he loved her. That is what redeems his memory, that at the end he did lose half the world for love.

[1] The controversy whether Antony had two wives at once or not is misconceived. In every law but Roman he had, in Roman law he had not.

Cleopatra had acted as though she expected his summons, and she started to build up a position which should end in her being what she had hoped to have been had Caesar lived. She took the upper hand at once, as at Tarsus, and requested a royal wedding gift, the foreign empire of her great predecessor Ptolemy II. Antony gave her all he could. He executed Lysanias for his treason in 40 and gave her Lysanias' kingdom of Chalcis, together with everything between Chalcis and Herod's realm (Hippos and Gadara are expressly mentioned); it was the old Coele-Syria in the narrower sense, and comprised all central Syria. He gave her the greater part of the coast of Palestine and Phoenicia from Egypt to the river Eleutherus, the original Ptolemaic boundary (vol. VII, p. 700); Tyre and Sidon alone remained free cities. He gave her Cyprus, which had once been Roman territory, but had already been alienated by Caesar. And he took from Polemo Cilicia Tracheia, which had likewise once been Roman territory, and gave it to her also (except the city of Seleuceia), so that she might get ship-timber from the Taurus, as Arsinoe II had done. The former Ptolemaic possessions on the Aegean being out of the question, there now remained only Judaea and Galilee, which were Herod's, and the one-time Ptolemaic part of Nabataea. She begged hard for Herod's kingdom, but here Antony was adamant, and all she got was Herod's deadly enmity. But he gave her the best morsel of Herod's realm, the balsam gardens of Jericho with the balsam monopoly, and (it seems) what of Nabataea Ptolemy II had had—the land east of the Dead Sea with the monopoly of the bitumen fishery, so important to Egypt. Nabataea, Egypt's secular enemy, was not really a client-state; but Malchus would hardly venture to oppose Antony. The son whom Cleopatra bore in the autumn of 36, when Antony was in Media, was named by her Ptolemy Philadelphus, to commemorate her re-establishment of Philadelphus' empire.

Antony was popular in Alexandria, where it was remembered that he had once prevented Ptolemy Auletes from killing his Alexandrian prisoners; and Cleopatra presently began to build a temple to him, which was unfinished at her death and was turned into one to Augustus. She and Antony put each other's heads on their coins (she was the only Ptolemaic queen who coined in her own right); and since Antony had already, for a very different reason, proclaimed himself Dionysus (pp. 53, 69), they were able to pose as a divine pair, as the Hellenistic East expected; to Greeks they were Dionysus and Aphrodite, to Egyptians Osiris and Isis. To Antony this was a deliberate political measure, but to

Cleopatra it was probably something more. Her attitude towards
the religion of Egypt has already been indicated, and just as her
death shows that she believed herself to be a daughter of Re, so
she perhaps took herself seriously as Isis; she wore her robes on
state occasions, and in disputes in other kingdoms she sided with
the woman—with Aba at Olba, Alexandra in Judaea—as became
one who was Isis, goddess and champion of women.

Cleopatra had brought her twins to Antioch, and when Antony
married her he acknowledged them as his and re-named them
Alexander Helios and Cleopatra Selene, the Sun and the Moon[1].
The names of all Cleopatra's children are significant, but especially
that of Alexander Helios. Helios and Selene in conjunction
possibly had a political meaning; the Parthian king was 'Brother
of the Sun and Moon,' and if the sun and moon really typified
the Iranian *fravashi* and *hvareno*, Antony, by annexing these
luminaries to his own family, was perhaps symbolically depriving
Phraates of the supernatural adjuncts of his royalty. As to the
name Helios, Antony's coin-type after Philippi had been the Sun
radiate[2], and his momentary revival of that type late in 37[3] shows
that he was passing on to the boy whatever the Sun meant to himself. Probably it meant to him the supreme deity of Asia, but it had
other connotations also; an Egyptian oracle had derived prosperity
from the Sun, in the prophecy of the Cumaean Sibyl the rule of the
Sun was to precede the Golden Age, and for Greeks Iambulus, in the
story of his Sun-state, had definitely connected the age of gold
with the Sun. As, in addition, it was Cleopatra's privilege, as a
New Isis, to bear the Sun, and as she herself was the Sun-god's
daughter (p. 110, n. 4), the boy could not really be called anything else; he was the Sun-child who should inaugurate the
Golden Age. The name Alexander referred primarily to Antony's
coming conquest of Parthia. Antony, like many Romans, had
dreamt of being a new Alexander—had he not at Philippi covered
Brutus' body with his purple cloak?[4]—but this too he now transferred to the boy, and became himself only the warrior king who
should precede the king of the Golden Age and pacify the earth
with his sword. But there was more than this. In the writer's

---

[1] See W. W. Tarn, *Alexander Helios and the Golden Age*, J.R.S. XXII,
1932, pp. 144 *sqq.* where the evidence for the whole of this section is given
and discussed at length. It is impossible to summarize it here.

[2] Volume of Plates iv, 196, *k*.   [3] *Ib.* iv, 196, *l*.

[4] As Alexander had covered the body of Darius, vol. VI, p. 386. Cf. the
similar action of Cleomenes III, vol. VII, p. 754.

view, Virgil's Fourth Eclogue was an epithalamium for the marriage of Antony and Octavia, and the child who should be a new Alexander and inaugurate the Golden Age was the son to be born to them. A coin of Antony's may reflect this union of the two houses[1]; but the child of the Eclogue had never been born, for Octavia's child had been a girl, and that is why after its birth Antony returned to the idea of Asiatic conquest, proclaimed himself Dionysus, conqueror of Asia, and did his best for Octavia by putting her head on his Dionysus-coinage[2]. But when he left Octavia for Cleopatra, the whole symbolism was transferred; though his assumption of divinity as Dionysus had been connected with Octavia, not with Cleopatra, it now fell most conveniently, for Dionysus could be Osiris and he and Cleopatra could be the divine pair Osiris-Isis; and Virgil's ideas could, through the boy's name, be transferred to Cleopatra's son, for whom they were never meant, but whom they fitted well, for he was the destined king of a golden age (though not of Virgil's) and a new Alexander, and he was *cara deum suboles*, the dear offspring of the gods Antony-Dionysus and Cleopatra-Isis, who would rule an Asia pacified by his father's valour. These are some of the ideas which seem to play round the name of the boy who was never to fulfil his destiny; how one Greek in the East was to envisage the coming age of gold will appear later (p. 82).

Antony spent the winter of 37–6 at Antioch with Cleopatra, not in amusement, but in strenuous preparation for the Parthian campaign. Before starting he had to secure his rear. Syria south of the Roman province was safe in the hands of Cleopatra and of Herod; but Antony now undertook the long-delayed reorganization of Asia Minor (was the impulse Cleopatra's?), and used to the full his new liberty of choosing the best men without regard to dynastic considerations. His system in Asia Minor was built up on three men, Amyntas, Archelaus, and Polemo. The strong Amyntas, who was already ruling western Pisidia and Phrygia-towards-Pisidia, was made king of Galatia, and also received Lycaonia and part of Pamphylia; this, with his existing Pisidian kingdom, placed the whole centre of Asia Minor in one hand. The Galatian cavalry, the best in the Roman East, was valuable to Antony, and at some period he rewarded two Galatian chieftains, Adiatorix with the rule of the Roman part of Heraclea and Ateporix with part of Zelitis. He executed Ariarathes of Cappadocia for his treason in 40 and gave Cappadocia to Archelaus of

[1] Volume of Plates iv, 198, *a*; type with two opposed cornuacopiae on a globe.   [2] *Ib.* iv, 198, *b*.

Comana, but without Armenia Minor. Archelaus was a student
and writer of the type of Juba II; and while previous kings of
Cappadocia had called themselves 'Friends of Rome,' he called
himself Philopatris, 'Friend of his country.' Polemo's kingdom
of Cilicia Tracheia had been given by Antony to Cleopatra, but
Eastern Pontus was apparently vacant, which may mean that Darius
was dead. Antony now sent Polemo to Pontus, but gave him
much more than Darius' realm; he reconstituted for him the old
kingdom of Pontus from Armenia to the Halys, which gave him
part of the Roman province of 'Bithynia and Pontus,' and he
added to it Armenia Minor[1], which carried the wardenship of
the Upper Euphrates. Of Antony's four important discoveries
who now ruled the principal client-kingdoms—Herod of Judaea,
Amyntas of Galatia, Archelaus of Cappadocia, and Polemo of
Pontus—all had successful reigns from the Roman point of view,
and all but Amyntas (who was killed in war in 25 B.C.) had very
long ones. At Olba in Cilicia Cleopatra restored Aba, a Teucrid
by marriage, to the priest-kingship; it had been usurped by her
father Zenophanes, a local tyrant who was not of the royal line.

In spring 36 Antony left Syria to join his army; Cleopatra, who
was expecting the birth of Ptolemy Philadelphus, accompanied
him to Zeugma and then returned to Egypt. On her way back
she visited Herod, to arrange about her monopolies; doubtless she
enjoyed the knowledge that her courteous host, a barbarian beneath his varnish, would have killed her but for the certainty of
Antony's vengeance. She understood business; she leased to
Herod his balsam gardens for 200 talents a year, and she leased
the bitumen monopoly to Malchus for a similar rent and made
Herod guarantee it and collect it for her; the arrangement would
cause bad blood between her two enemies. Herod paid punctually, for he dared not do otherwise, but after Antony's failure in
Media he got little from Malchus. He seemingly took a belated
revenge upon Cleopatra by stating in his *Memoirs* that she made
love to him, so that, should he trip, she might force Antony to
kill him; naturally Herod upon Cleopatra is not evidence, and the
story is certainly untrue.

Herod had begun his reign by making one Ananel High-Priest;
but Alexandra had asked Cleopatra to use her influence with
Antony for her son, the young Aristobulus, grandson of Aristo-

[1] Dio XLIX, 44 says that Polemo did not get Armenia Minor till 34. As
this frontier province could not have been left vacant for three years, this
would mean that Antony gave it to Archelaus in 37 and took it from him
in 34, which seems impossible.

bulus II and last male representative of the Hasmonaean line; and early in 36[1] Herod did make Aristobulus High-Priest, whether because Antony requested it or because he wished to conciliate the Hasmonaean interest. Whether Alexandra subsequently began to intrigue for the crown for her son is uncertain; but that autumn she thought that she and the boy were in danger, and sought Cleopatra's help. Cleopatra sent a ship to bring them to Egypt, but their attempt at flight was frustrated; the people however showed such favour to the boy that late that year, Antony being far away, Herod had him murdered. Alexandra he did not touch, it is said through fear of Cleopatra, and she again appealed to the queen, this time for vengeance; and when in January 35 Cleopatra met Antony in Syria on his return from the Parthian expedition (p. 75) she urged him to punish Herod. But though Antony sent for Herod, he had too much trouble on his hands to think of removing his loyal and capable supporter, and yielded to his argument that, as he had been made king, he must be allowed to act as such.

II. THE INVASION OF PARTHIA

In 38–7 a new king ascended the Parthian throne. Orodes, broken by the death of his beloved son Pacorus, had made another son, Phraates (IV), his heir; but the old man died slowly, and Phraates murdered him and seized the crown. He is called cruel, and he had trouble with his nobles; some he killed, others fled from Parthia. But the trouble was probably connected with the same difficulty which had brought down Surenas, the jealousy between noble and commoner, cataphract and horse-archer. The nobles had had their chance against Ventidius and had failed completely, and Phraates meant to rely on the horse-archers against Antony; fortunately for Parthia he was strong enough to have his way. He had the support, among others, of Monaeses, the powerful Warden of the Western Marches (vol. ix, p. 588), who owned great estates in Mesopotamia and was designated for the supreme command. Monaeses played the common trick of fleeing to Antony in simulated fear and offering him his services, with a view to discovering his plans. Antony welcomed him, gave him the one-time kingdom of Alchaudonius (vol. ix, p. 604), and

---

[1] The dating here adopted fits events better than the more usual 35, though that also is possible. For the arguments see W. Otto, *s.v. Herodes* in *P.W.* Suppl. ii, cols. 39 *sqq.*

promised him the throne of Parthia, but whether he was really
deceived does not appear; certainly Monaeses did not inform
him of Parthia's change of tactics. In spring 36 Monaeses
suddenly lost his fear of Phraates and returned to Parthia to take
command; throughout the war Phraates never took the field
himself[1].

Antony was a good tactician and cavalry leader, but he had
never tried to plan a great campaign. As he had Caesar's papers,
none could gainsay his claim to be carrying out Caesar's scheme;
but it is certain that he was not. Caesar no doubt had meant to
strike at the Parthian capital Ecbatana through Armenia, but he
would never have left an uncertain ally of some power between
himself and his base; even Crassus had been too wise to do that.
Caesar presumably meant first to reduce Armenia and create
there an advanced base; after that, it may be conjectured that he
intended to take Ecbatana and cut off Babylonia from Parthia
proper, and finally to annex Babylonia and establish his new frontier[2]. But Antony, who had been prevented for two years by events
in Italy from making a start, had become impatient and perhaps
tried to do too much the first year, though it is not known whether
it was early or late in 37 that Canidius Crassus was sent to carry
out the preliminary conquest of Armenia; if the latter, Antony
had in mind Alexander's winter campaigns. Canidius defeated
Artavasdes in a battle, and the king, who had been Parthia's
ally since 53, formally submitted and again became the ally of
Rome. Either Canidius or Antony was mad enough to think that
this sufficed; there were no guarantees—no towns were occupied,
no hostages taken, no garrisons left; in spring 36 Canidius passed
on and, like Pompey, reduced the Albani and Iberi of the Caucasus, and Antony struck a coin with the Armenian tiara[3] as though
Armenia were his. Armenia's regular policy was to maintain
independence by playing off Parthia against Rome, but as between
them her sympathies, like her civilization, were Parthian; Artavasdes had lightly deserted Rome in 53, and though he submitted to Antony he maintained an understanding with Phraates;
Antony had failed before he started. For his preparations had
thoroughly alarmed Asia; the other Artavasdes, king of Media
Atropatene (hereinafter called Media), had joined Parthia, as

---

[1] Plutarch, *Ant.* 44, οὐδεμιᾷ μάχῃ παρέτυχεν.
[2] Trajan's campaign may be a better guide to Caesar's intentions than
Plutarch, *Caesar* 58, which merely reflects the Alexander-legend.
[3] Volume of Plates iv, 198, *c.*

perhaps Elymaïs did also[1]; Asia was closing her ranks against the Roman, and Armenia could not well hold aloof.

Early in May 36 Antony left Zeugma and went northward through Melitene and along the Euphrates to Carana (Erzerûm), where Canidius joined him; our sources imply that he started too late, but it was no use reaching Carana before Canidius was ready. At Carana he reviewed his army, the best he ever commanded. He had left seven legions in Macedonia and one at Jerusalem, but none in Syria; in face of his attack, Parthia could hardly spare men for a diversion on the Euphrates. He had sixteen seasoned legions of about three-quarter strength, totalling 60,000 men; 10,000 Gallic and Spanish horse; and 30,000 auxiliaries, which included Artavasdes with some 16,000 Armenian cavalry and the forces of some client-kings; among his legates were Domitius and Canidius, and Plancus' nephew Titius was quaestor. He brought an enormous siege-train, including an 80-foot ram, for he was going to operate in a country devoid of good timber. The large force of legions shows both that he expected to meet the cataphracts and that he meant to garrison Ecbatana and other towns till Phraates submitted; there was no question of one summer sufficing. His first objective was the Median capital Phraaspa, on his road to Ecbatana; but whether he hoped to reach Ecbatana before winter, or meant to winter in Media, cannot be said.

Leaving Carana, he marched through the open country east of Lake Urumia, but his train of wagons, extending for many miles, made progress slow, and he divided his army; he left Artavasdes, Polemo, and Oppius Statianus with two legions to escort the wagons, and pushed on ahead with his main force. Alexander too had sometimes divided his army; but he had always left his best general and a majority of the troops with the wagons. Moreover Antony was marching blind; he had no idea where the Parthian army might be, while Monaeses had accurate information of his movements, proof of Artavasdes' understanding with Phraates. Monaeses in fact with 40,000 horse-archers, and the Median king with another 10,000, were quite close; the subsequent campaign shows that they must have had some system of a reserve of arrows (vol. IX, p. 607). With their perfect intelligence they eluded Antony and came down on the wagons. Artavasdes, whose troops formed the greater part of the escort, rode off home before the attack; the two legions were annihilated and their eagles added to

---

[1] This depends on the uncertain interpretation of the Susa poems (see Bibliography). On the relations of Parthia, Elymaïs, and Susa see Fr. Cumont, *C.R.Ac.Inscr.* 1932, pp. 247 *sqq.*

the Parthian collection; Polemo was captured by the Medes; the siege-train was burnt, the food burnt or carried off; the victory was as decisive as could be, and Antony found himself in mid-August helpless before Phraaspa, a strong fortress well garrisoned and provisioned.

But he was too proud to retreat. He threw up a mound against the wall, but his attacks were repulsed, and what machines he could improvise proved useless. The army soon ate up all the food in the neighbourhood and had to go far afield, while the Parthians shot down every weak foraging party. As a last resource Antony offered battle; Monaeses accepted, but could not shake the legions and just rode away again; Antony claimed a victory, but the Parthians only lost 80 killed, and meanwhile the garrison in a sortie had burnt his machines. It was now October, and the cold was beginning; even his stubbornness had to recognize that retreat was inevitable. The story that, at some time after the equinox, he sent envoys to Phraates, who received them seated on the golden throne of the Arsacids (which was in Ecbatana) and promised them peace if they retired, seems impossible, in view of the time needed to reach Ecbatana and return; for the retreat cannot have begun later than mid-October. A Mardian deserter[1], one of his race settled in Media, offered to guide the Romans back by a different way, avoiding the plains; Antony wisely accepted, and the man saved them, taking them through the hills by Tabriz.

The terrible retreat to the Armenian frontier lasted 27 days. The army marched in square; in spite of the hilly ground, Monaeses hung on its rear, cut off stragglers and foragers, and attacked at every opportunity; there were frequent desertions, and though the slingers made themselves respected in skirmishes there was one regular battle in which the Romans had 8000 casualties. They suffered from disease, thirst, and hunger, and ate 'unspeakable food'; but through it all the veterans remained too steady to be overwhelmed. The danger brought out all that was best in Antony; once more, and for the last time, he was the Antony of the retreat from Mutina, the worshipped leader who shared every privation and never lost heart. One night the army did get out of hand and he prepared for suicide, but in the morning he recovered control. At last, at a river six days from the frontier, the victorious Parthians turned back, after shouting a tribute to their enemies'

---

[1] The story in Vell. Pat. ii, 82, 2 that the guide was a soldier of Crassus may be due to a confusion of *Mardus* and *Marsus*, cf. Horace, *Odes*, iii, 5, 9, Marsus et Apulus (of Crassus' men).

courage; they had established a tradition of the invincibility of Parthia in defence which lasted till Trajan. It may or may not have been a consequence of his victory that Phraates appears later in Greek poems from Susa as 'god omnipotent,' a unique title quite outside the sphere of the Mazdean religion[1].

On entering Armenia Antony sent off a message to Cleopatra, which somehow reached her. He could not winter in that hostile country; he would have had to divide his army into detachments, and would have courted the fate of Antiochus Sidetes (vol. IX, p. 581). He spoke Artavasdes fair, for there was no alternative, and got food; and the worn-out men started afresh on their long march through the snow-bound land. He stayed with them till he was sure that Artavasdes would not attack them, and then, like Napoleon from Russia, pushed on ahead, leaving Canidius and Domitius to bring the army home. Syria might already be in Parthian hands and every city in revolt; that was why he had told Cleopatra to meet him, not at one of the great sea-ports, but at Leuke Kome, a village where she could force a landing. Even though he found Syria safe he was terribly anxious, for he did not know in what temper the army might arrive; it was only an army of the Civil Wars, whose allegiance sat lightly on it; it had already mutinied once, and in fact another 8000 men died in the Armenian snows. The story goes that day after day at Leuke Kome he would rush from dinner to scan the horizon for the Egyptian ships. But Cleopatra did not fail him; dangerous as winter navigation was, she arrived in time, bringing what he had asked for—masses of clothing and comforts for the troops; thanks to this help, the army was got quietly into winter quarters. But she brought little money; though Antony somehow supplemented it, it only sufficed to give the men some 28 shillings apiece; it was her method of explaining to him that her Treasury was not at his service for useless adventures. His expedition had indeed been worse than useless; he had lost some 37 per cent. of his army, including over 22,000 of his veteran legionaries. True, Xenophon had lost nearly as high a percentage on his much-praised retreat from Cunaxa to Trapezus, and he had not had to face Parthian arrows. But to Antony the loss was irreparable; he could get no more seasoned Roman troops, and probably the men who did return were never quite the same again. Meanwhile Octavian had conquered Sextus and removed Lepidus, and controlled forty-five legions.

[1] θεὸς παγκράτωρ. See Fr. Cumont, C. R. Ac. Inscr. 1931, p. 244: Ahura is never 'omnipotent.'

III. THE DREAM OF EMPIRE

Antony returned to Alexandria with Cleopatra and sat down to consider the position. Octavian might send the promised four legions, which would largely replace his losses; but any illusions on that subject were dispelled in the early spring, when Octavian sent him, not the legions, but what remained (70) of his 130 ships. Octavian's policy must have seemed to them clear: cut off from recruiting in Italy, Antony's power was to die like a ring-barked tree; Octavian only had to wait till the tree fell of itself. Cleopatra seized her opportunity; the sequel shows that it was now that she won Antony over to her own scheme. Parthia (she must have argued) mattered nothing; his enemy was Octavian. Sooner or later he would have to fight him, and he must mobilize all his resources for one great effort while success was still possible; that victory once won, Parthia or anything else he wanted would follow. Doubtless she knew that it was very late in the day and that the chances were against them; but it was the only chance she had had since Caesar's death of realizing her supreme ambition to rule the Roman world[1], and, whatever the odds, her courage was equal to taking that chance. She had of course no more right to conquer Rome, supposing she could, than Octavian had to conquer Egypt, but she had a right to resent Rome's treatment of her country and her line; it had broken the spirit of her predecessors, but it did not break hers. But she could only work through Antony; that was why she had married him. Her design of attacking Rome by means of Romans was one of such stupendous audacity that we must suppose that she saw no other way. There was indeed an alternative—to try and raise a semi-religious Graeco-Asiatic crusade; this was what Rome feared[2], but we cannot say whether she considered it, though Virgil, who made the whole of the Asia of the Alexander-tradition—Bactria, India, Sabaea—follow her to Actium[3], shows that some Romans thought she did. As for Antony, had he himself ever desired to oust

[1] Her son's name, Ptolemy-who-is-also-Caesar, and her oath, Dio L, 5, 4, witness to this ambition. It was believed by Romans (Horace, *Odes*, I, 37, 6 *sqq.*; Livy, *i.e.* Florus II, 21 [IV, 11], 2 and Eutropius VII, 7; Propertius III, 11, 27–46; Ovid, *Met.* XV, 828), by Jews (*Sibyll.* III, 75 *sqq.*), and, more important, by a Greek who supported her (see p. 82). But the best evidence is the actions of herself and Antony, pp. 80 *sqq.*

[2] Tarn, *J.R.S.* XXII, p. 141, and see p. 82, n. 2. There is not the least indication anywhere that Rome ever feared Antony; Rome can hardly therefore have feared Cleopatra's influence over him.

[3] *Aen.* VIII, 685–8, 705–6.

Octavian he would never have let Sextus and Lepidus fall as he had done, and his inactivity during 33, a wasted year, shows that his heart was not in the business; he was being driven on by two stronger natures, on the one side Cleopatra, on the other Octavian, and all Cleopatra's gifts both of mind and person must have been lavished on securing his assent. He had however first to punish Artavasdes for his treason; both knew that to be imperative.

Antony had written to Italy that the Parthians had been defeated, and Rome held festival accordingly; but Octavian knew the truth, as did his sister. Octavia held that Antony's purported marriage with a foreign woman did not make herself any the less his wife; it was enough that he needed help, and in March 35, as soon as navigation opened, she started to go to him, as Cleopatra had done, with large stores of clothing and necessaries for his army and 2000 picked men given her by her brother. Probably the troops really were meant as an invitation to Antony to leave Cleopatra and return to Octavia; Aeneas' treatment of Dido, who in some aspects recalls Cleopatra, may show what kind of conduct was expected of him. Octavia reached Athens, and there found a message from Antony ordering her to send on her troops and supplies and go back herself to Rome. It was brutal; a man between two women is likely to be brutal. She obeyed, and went back. Octavian, naturally furious, told her to leave Antony's house, but she refused; as his wife, her place was there till he himself told her to go. So she stayed, and looked after his political interests and his children; not only her own two daughters, but also Fulvia's two sons, whom she had taken charge of, though the elder soon afterwards went to Antony. The sight of her unselfish goodness did Antony much harm in Italy, though to harm him was the last thing she would have wished.

Probably Antony meant to rest his troops for some months and invade Armenia in summer 35; but he lost that year through Sextus Pompeius, whose activities in Asia compelled Antony to send against him the legions from Syria under Titius (p. 62). Titius ultimately hunted him down and killed him, whether with or without Antony's knowledge; it shows Antony's changed position that the surviving murderers of Caesar, Turullius and Cassius of Parma, who had been with Sextus, now joined him. Antony could not ask his troops to do any more that season; but he began to arm. He had now twenty-five legions, some very weak in numbers,—seven in Macedonia, thirteen in Syria (including one at Jerusalem), two in Syria or Bithynia, and three mixed legions of recruits taken from Sextus; he raised five more, giving him thirty in all. He could get some Italians from Caesar's colonies and the numerous Italian traders; but the inscriptions show that he also enlisted many Asiatics or Greeks, who took Latin names. Following Caesar's practice, he did not fill up the gaps in the legions of the Parthian campaign, using his recruits solely for the new legions; but he brought from Macedonia six of the veteran legions there, now the strongest he had, and replaced them by six legions of recruits. He also started shipbuilding on a great scale, and began to strike thirty series of coins, each giving the number of one of his thirty legions and on the reverse his flagship[1]. He further flouted Roman opinion by marrying his daughter Antonia (by his first wife) to a wealthy Greek, Pythodorus of Tralles; their daughter was the notable Pythodoris (see p. 112, n. 5).

The Parthians had not invaded Syria after Antony's retreat because, with the external danger removed, internal troubles had broken out again; Phraates' dated tetradrachms fail from 36 to April 34. Also they had quarrelled with the Medes over the booty, and the Median king, in anger and fear, released Polemo and sent him to Antony with an offer of his alliance against Parthia. Antony had no intention of attacking Parthia again, but he welcomed the alliance as proof that his expedition had not been fruitless. This was the position when early in 34 Antony, who on January 1 had taken and laid down the consulship, invaded Armenia, mastered the country, and captured Artavasdes and his younger sons Tigranes and Artavasdes; the eldest son, Artaxes, escaped and tried to raise the people, but was defeated and fled to Phraates; Antony gave a section of Armenia to the Median king and betrothed Alexander Helios to that monarch's little daughter Iotape. A story remains that he only captured Artavasdes by inviting him to a friendly conference and then seizing him— 'Antony's crime'; but as Octavian is also accused of having instigated Artavasdes' treachery towards Antony, the two stories are obviously charge and counter-charge in the propaganda war of 33 and are both untrue. For two years Armenia became a Roman province, and 'Roman' traders, i.e. subjects of Rome, flocked into it. Antony left his legions to winter there and returned to Alexandria before autumn, bringing with him Artavasdes and his sons and much booty, including the solid gold statue of Anaitis from her temple in Acilisene. The effect of his arming was now seen, for the reason was known or guessed at Rome, and while Rome

---

[1] Volume of Plates iv, 198, d, e.

had celebrated his earlier successes she ignored the conquest of Armenia; it was as though he were no longer her general.

The subsequent developments beyond the Euphrates may be anticipated here. Early in 33, in response to an urgent message, Antony again hurried to the Median frontier and saw the king, who feared a Parthian attack; he restored his share of the Roman eagles, and possibly Antony, who took Iotape back with him as hostage, gave him temporary help[1], for he did not withdraw his legions from Armenia till the autumn; but the Mede really secured himself for a time by an alliance with Tiridates. Tiridates, perhaps a general of Phraates in the war with Antony[2], revolted in 32 or early 31, and in summer 31 expelled Phraates; but Phraates came back in 30 with help from 'Scythians,' probably the Sacaraucae (vol. IX, pp. 582–7), and Tiridates, who was not an Arsacid, could not maintain himself; he and the Median king fled to Syria (p. 115), then in Octavian's hands, and Phraates took Media and also restored Artaxes to the Armenian throne[3]. Artaxes promptly massacred all the Roman traders in Armenia, and that country and Media were definitely lost to Rome.

To come back to the main story. In the autumn of 34, after Antony's return from the conquest of Armenia, Alexandria witnessed two extraordinary spectacles. He staged a triumph in the city, a thing hardly ever before celebrated by a Roman except in Rome[4]. High above the people Cleopatra sat in state on a golden throne, and Antony entered the city in a triumphal car, followed in procession by his Armenian captives, whom he presented to the queen. The presiding deity of a Roman triumph was Juppiter Optimus Maximus of the Capitol as the embodiment of Rome; and, whatever Antony may have meant[5], men naturally saw in his act the glorification of Cleopatra as an embodiment of the 'god-

---

[1] Dio's story, XLIX, 44, that Antony secured some Median cavalry by treachery, is clearly untrue, for he makes the Mede remain faithful to Antony's interests, LI, 5, 5.

[2] Conceivably he was Monaeses (Tarn, *Mélanges Glotz*, p. 836), but the matter is too uncertain to build on.

[3] An undated tetradrachm of Phraates IV (G. F. Hill, *Num. Chron.* 1927, p. 207), overstruck on a coin of Attambelos I, shows that at some time Phraates reconquered Characene, which may therefore have been Tiridates' ally; but this more probably belongs to Tiridates' second attempt (Tarn, *loc. cit.*) in 27–26.

[4] For an earlier instance see vol. IX, p. 152.

[5] Possibly he had in mind the triumphal procession of Ptolemy II. In any case, Hellenistic influences were affecting the Roman triumph: A. Bruhl, *Mélanges d'arch. et d'hist.* XLVI, 1929, p. 77.

dess Rome,' and attributed to him (almost certainly wrongly) the intention of shifting the capital from Rome to Alexandria[1]. In one other respect his triumph differed from the Roman form; he spared Artavasdes' life, even though he had been a traitor.

The triumph was followed by the ceremony generally known as the Donations of Alexandria. A great concourse of people gathered in the gymnasium[2]; above them Antony, and Cleopatra robed as Isis, sat on thrones side by side, and somewhat lower, on other thrones, sat their three children and Ptolemy Caesar (whom Alexandrians nicknamed Caesarion, little Caesar). Antony first harangued the people; he said that Cleopatra had been Caesar's wife (*i.e.* by a Macedonian marriage), that Ptolemy Caesar was Caesar's legitimate son, and that what he was going to do was a tribute to Caesar's memory. He then declared Cleopatra Queen of Kings and Ptolemy Caesar King of Kings, joint monarchs of Egypt and Cyprus and overlords of the kingdoms or overlordships of Cleopatra's other children. To Alexander, who wore the dress of the Achaemenid kings and received an Armenian bodyguard, he gave as his kingdom Armenia and the overlordship of Parthia and Media, that is, everything east of the Euphrates. To Ptolemy Philadelphus, who wore Macedonian dress and received a Macedonian bodyguard, he gave as his kingdom the Egyptian possessions in Syria and Cilicia and the overlordship of all client-kings and dynasts west of the Euphrates 'as far as the Hellespont'; the most westerly dynast known is Cleon in Mysia, but the phrase may pass. To Cleopatra Selene he gave as her kingdom the Cyrenaica and Libya. To commemorate the ceremony he struck a coin[3] bearing on one side his own head and the legend 'Armenia conquered' and on the other the head of Cleopatra with the legend 'Queen of kings and of her sons who are kings'; she was therefore overlord of the whole hierarchy, including Ptolemy Caesar (p. 81, n. 6). It was a glorious house of cards; whether it could be solidified might depend on the answer to one prosaic question— would the legions fight?

Antony's own position in the new hierarchy of powers was carefully not defined, for he was filling a double rôle. It was necessary, for his Roman supporters and his Roman troops, that

---

[1] The supposed coin (Eckhel, *Doctrina numorum veterum*, IV, p. 44; it is in Paris) which V. Gardthausen (*Augustus* II, p. 167, n. 12) cited in support of this idea is, Dr J. G. Milne tells the writer, a sixteenth-century fabrication.

[2] Had Alexandria had a Senate (see p. 294), it must (it would seem) have been mentioned as playing some part in this ceremony.

[3] Volume of Plates IV, 198, *f*.

he should remain Marcus Antonius, Roman magistrate. But to Greeks and Asiatics he was a divine Hellenistic monarch, Antony who is Dionysus-Osiris, consort of Cleopatra-Isis, queen of Egypt. What was this position of his which could not be defined because of Roman susceptibilities? It was something which could be inherited; for he had already (1 Jan. 34) struck the first of the coins[1] bearing his own head and the head of his elder son by Fulvia, Marcus Antonius the younger (nicknamed by Alexandrians Antyllus, little Antony), which shows that this boy was his destined heir. Again, it was something which dated an Era, like a king's reign. Documents of the joint rule of Cleopatra and Ptolemy Caesar in Egypt are always dated by a single date, the year of her reign; but in 34 there begins to appear in Egyptian papyri a double dating, the year of Cleopatra equated with another year, and this double dating, found also in Syria, continues till her last year, 22 which is also 7[2]. In the writer's opinion the meaning of this second Era is not now in doubt; it denotes Antony's regnal years[3], and though the first instance so far known of its use is in August 34[4], it was reckoned as from his marriage with Cleopatra in 37. Antony then at the time of the Donations was royal and had named his successor. But he was not king of Egypt; Ptolemy Caesar was that. And he was not King of Kings; he was greater than that, for he had given that title away to others, which shows that it was not his design to divide the Roman realm and become king of a Hellenistic kingdom in the eastern half. Only one possibility therefore remains: Antony, supreme ruler of the inhabited world, of the East and of Rome alike—that is, Roman Emperor[5], with the *oecumene* under his feet, like Caesar. And where he was, there Cleopatra would be beside him, she also supreme ruler of the inhabited world; that is, Roman Empress[6].

[1] Volume of Plates iv, 198, *g*.   [2] List in Bibliography, Part II, 1, c.
[3] *P. Oxy.* XII, 1453 and the notes. Of the two alternative views formerly put forward, that which referred this Era to the territorial gifts in Syria in 37 (a curious basis for an Era) became untenable once its use in Egypt was discovered, and that which referred it to Ptolemy Caesar was always impossible, as he was joint-king with Cleopatra long before 37.
[4] *P. Ryl.* II, no. 69: 9 Mesore of year 18 which is also 3, *i.e.* 3 August 34 B.C. Probably this antedates the Donations.
[5] Whether this meant that, if successful, he would have made the whole realm a kingdom on Hellenistic lines, or something more in accord with Roman ideas, cannot be said.
[6] The coin (Volume of Plates iv, 198, *f*) shows that she was overlord of the whole East, including Ptolemy Caesar king of Egypt; naturally Rome could not be mentioned, but her position must follow from Antony's. She was therefore two separate things, Queen of Egypt and Roman Empress.

The form of oath now attributed to Cleopatra, 'so surely as I shall one day give judgment in the Capitol,' only underlined what was already plain[1].

There was some weakness in Antony which led him to represent intentions as accomplished facts. He had celebrated the conquest of Armenia on a coin two years before it was really conquered; he had given away Parthia when Parthia had just defeated him; and now he represented himself, or let Cleopatra represent him, as world-ruler because he was going to defeat Octavian. Cleopatra must have known just what the Donations and Antony's Era were worth; but her object was victory, and anything was worth while which might drive Antony forward or influence opinion. She did influence opinion; prophecies of the overthrow and enslavement of Rome by Asia were recalled or renewed[2], and some Jews foretold that her victory would be the signal for the end of the current world-period, to be followed by the reign of the Messiah[3]. Octavian for his part cared little if Antony gave Roman territory to client-kings—he did it himself later—but Cleopatra as Roman Empress was another matter. It brought the day of battle very close. He had already a larger army and fleet than he could use, but he needed money, and public opinion behind him. He understood very well what Cleopatra and Antony meant, and gave himself forthwith to making Rome understand also.

Statements that Cleopatra drove Antony to ruin are not impressive, as he need not have been driven; it would be more important to know her own mind. Was it only ambition with her, or was there something greater behind? Did she share the vision of one of her followers, who saw in her the destined leader of a great uprising of Asia against Rome, of the oppressed against the oppressor, not for vengeance only, but for a better world to follow? What she herself thought we may never discover; we only know the great prophecy of that nameless Greek[4], who foretold that after she had cast Rome down from heaven to earth she would then

[1] It would be of the first importance if she really coined in Antioch, the capital of Roman Syria, as supposed by J. N. Svoronos, Tὰ νομίσματα τοῦ Κράτους τῶν Πτολεμαίων IV, p. 389; but this may be doubtful, see K. Regling, Z. f. Num. xxv, 1906, p. 397.

[2] On these prophecies, of which Augustus afterwards burnt a large number, see generally Fr. Cumont, Rev. de l'hist. des religions CIII, 1931, pp. 65–72 (primarily on the oracle of Hystaspes). The earliest known, that of the 'mad praetor' (Phlegon, Mirabilia 32), may be second century B.C.

[3] Sibyll. III, 46–54, 75–92; see Tarn, J.R.S. XXII, 1932, p. 142.

[4] Sibyll. III, 350–61, 367–80, on which see Tarn, loc. cit. p. 135.

raise her up again from earth to heaven and inaugurate a golden age in which Asia and Europe should alike share, when war and every other evil thing should quit the earth, and the long feud of East and West should end for ever in their reconciliation and in the reign of justice and love. It was surely no unworthy cause that could give birth to such a vision, or make men, even one man, see in Cleopatra the ruler who should carry out Alexander's dream of a human brotherhood. We know what Augustus was to do, and how Virgil in the *Aeneid* was to interpret it for all time; but if Antony was to be Roman Emperor, and Cleopatra was to be the instrument of Alexander's idea of the reconciliation[1] of East and West, can we say that the ultimate ideals of the two sides were so very far apart after all? What were far apart were the actual possibilities. Past history had shown that if such ideals were ever to be realized, however imperfectly, it could only be done from the West, by a Roman through Romans; no one, Roman or Macedonian, could have done it from or through the East, for he could never have carried Rome with him. In that sense, but perhaps in that sense alone, the common verdict is just, that it was well for the world that Octavian conquered.

IV. THE WINNING OF ITALY[2]

But in the West too something great had been coming to birth, the consciousness of an united Italy. The statesmanship of two generations before had produced out of civil war a people and made a nation from what had been a city: the labours of the scholars and poets of the Ciceronian age had given that nation a language and a culture; all it now needed was a leader, and that leader would be one who could promise and bring above all peace and relief from Civil War, but he must give as well the assurance that the hard-won heritage of the Italian people would not be wasted. At the end of 36 Octavian had declared to his rejoicing hearers that the Civil Wars were over; disbandment began immediately, and while some of the veterans were planted in overseas colonies (as the men of the Seventh Legion at Baeterrae in Narbonese Gaul), others were settled on land for which a proper purchase

[1] Arrian VII, 11, 9, read with Plutarch, *de fort. Alex.*, *Mor.* 329 C (from Eratosthenes), διαλλακτὴς τῶν ὅλων. See Tarn in *Proc. Brit. Acad.* 1933.
[2] The two main literary authorities for the Illyrian Wars are Appian, *Illyrica*, 13 and 15–28 (parts of which may be derived from Augustus' own memoirs), and Dio XLIX, 34, 2 and 35–38. For the modern literature see the Bibliography, Part I, section II, I.

price or compensation could now be offered[1]. But the winter of
36–5 was scarcely past before Octavian was on the move. The
suggestion of campaigns against Britain or Dacia can hardly
have been seriously intended, save as a proof that the young
Caesar had not forgotten any of his father's plans or conquests,
for what Italy most needed was security against attack. In the
north-west the Alpine Salassi were continually giving trouble,
from the north-east the Iapudes and kindred tribes had raided
Tergeste and Aquileia unscathed, the colony of Pola had been
destroyed about 40, Liburnian pirates infested the Adriatic,
and though Pollio had been granted a triumph for his successes
against the Parthini (p. 49), the Delmatae still held standards
captured from Gabinius (Vol. IX, p. 667). For the proper defence of Italy it was essential to gain the Alps as a boundary
and bring the mountain tribes into subjection, whether Salassi
in the north or Iapudes in the east, while control of the Ocra
pass and of the upper Save meant that Italy would be freed
from the inveterate fear of invasion from the east. True, the
Dacians were no longer formidable, for the empire of Burebista had split up into four warring kingdoms[2], but other
enemies might try that line of attack. Most important of all
was that Octavian must himself preserve his prestige as a
soldier and leader, must keep his numerous legions employed
and in fighting trim, and must rivet to himself the loyalty and
goodwill of the whole Italian people for deliverance from raids.
Herein lies the importance of these Illyrian campaigns. Great
expectations had been aroused, and Octavian elaborated his
favourite plan of a complex offensive; the fleet, possibly under
Menas, was brought round from South Italy, and while Octavian's
legates were to advance north-east from Aquileia towards Emona
(Ljubljana) and the head waters of the Save, he himself marched
south-east from Tergeste to Senia (Senj) in order to strike across
the range of the Kapela and descend by the valley of the Kupa
upon the Save.

The region in which the campaigns of the next three years were
to be waged corresponds roughly to the western half of the modern
kingdom of Yugo-Slavia, but its condition was then very different
from the pleasant valleys of Croatia or the stony uplands of the
Karst as they now appear to the traveller. There was little culti-

---

[1] *E.g.* Capua was recompensed by land in Crete and a new aqueduct:
Dio XLIX, 14, 5; Vell. Pat. II, 81, 2; Dessau 6317.
[2] Strabo VII, 304.

vation: thick and tangled forest prevailed, with sparse clearings where the native villagers grew the spelt and millet upon which they relied[1]. The population was a mixture of races with the Illyrians as a substratum: upon this mixture conquering bands of Celts (such as the Taurisci) had imposed themselves, but though their influence was strong—some tribes, for instance, had adopted Celtic weapons and armour—it was not everywhere dominant. Civilization was in an early stage: many of the tribes practised tattooing, some of the Delmatae used to redistribute their land every seven years, and though fortress-towns built of wood crowned hills here and there for shelter and defence in time of war, there were as yet no cities, no common councils and no possibility of united action[2]. In a remarkable passage the historian Dio suddenly breaks into personal reminiscence to record the rigours of the climate and the worthlessness of the land; the tribes are brave fighters and reckless of peril just because they can find nothing in their country which makes life worth living; 'I know,' he adds drily, 'for I have been a governor there myself[3].'

The programme for the year was carried out with complete success. The fleet, as it sailed northwards, dealt faithfully with the piratical Liburni and the islanders of Melite (Mljet) and Corcyra Nigra (Korčula), killing or enslaving, and received the submission of the tribes on the coast such as the Taulantii: in the North Octavian's *legati* brought over such tribes as the Carni and Taurisci (who became allies and supplied boats for use on the river) and reached Emona. Octavian had chosen the hardest part, the subjugation of the warlike Iapudes amid their rocky and close-timbered valleys; a few strongholds such as Monetium (Brinje) and Avendo (Crkvina) surrendered[4], but henceforward progress was slower, for the troops had to hack their way through the dense growth that encumbered the valley, while reconnoitring bodies advanced fanwise on the ridges above; an attempted ambush was repulsed and after the capture of Terpo (Gornji Modruš) the army moved on to the capital Metulum where greater

---

[1] Strabo VII, 315; Appian, *Ill.* 22: Dio XLIX, 36. For the effects of deforestation see C. Patsch, *Bosnien und Herzegowina in römischer Zeit*, p. 6 *sq.*

[2] Strabo, *loc. cit.* Cf. the 'Norica castella in tumulis' of Virgil, *Georg.* III, 474–5. On the Illyrians see Fluss, *s.v.* Illyrioi in *P.W.* Suppl.-Band v; on the archaeology V. G. Childe in *The Bronze Age* and the article *Die Illyrier* in *Reallexikon der Vorgeschichte.*   [3] Dio XLIX, 36.

[4] The identifications of G. Veith (*Die Feldzüge des C. Julius Caesar Octavianus in Illyrien*) are here accepted.

resistance was to be encountered[1]. Octavian erected a mound against the wall; the Iapudes, using Roman engines captured in previous campaigns, undermined it. Two more were raised from which four gangways were constructed for the final assault on the wall. But the desperate defenders succeeded in cutting away the supports and gangway after gangway collapsed till only one remained; the Romans wavered and stood still. The crisis in the assault had come; from the tower, whence he had been directing operations, he rushed down, seized a shield and (followed by Agrippa and a few of his bodyguard) advanced across; shamed into courage the soldiers crowded behind, but the weight was too great and the gangway gave way. Though badly injured by the fall, Octavian showed himself at once; his example was enough and the soldiers at the sight of their young general's bravery and danger found themselves again[2]. More gangways were run out, and to this indomitable resolution the doomed town surrendered; even so there was one last maddened sortie and the wooden walls and houses of Metulum went up in flame. The remainder of the Iapudes now submitted and M. Helvius was left to guard against outbreaks, while the main Roman force headed eastwards for Siscia (Sisak) lying near the confluence of the Save and Kupa. The headmen at first offered hostages and corn, but the sight of this tribute proved too much for the people; they made a furious rush to close the gates and prepared the town to stand a siege. But against such numbers resistance was unavailing, on land and on the rivers the Romans beat off attempts at relief and in thirty days Siscia fell[3]. In late autumn Octavian returned to Rome, leaving a garrison of over two legions in Siscia under the command of Fufius Geminus; the winter-quarters of the others are unknown, but were presumably in Northern Italy.

Rumours of an attack on Siscia forced Octavian to leave Rome before winter was finished; but the garrison had resisted successfully and he turned south into Dalmatia, where Agrippa and other *legati* had been assigned their tasks. He next appeared before Promona (Teplju), a hill-fortress which had been occupied

---

[1] The site of Metulum has been hotly disputed; the likeliest appears to be the modern hill of Viničica, not far from Munjava.

[2] The incident was famous and is important: cf. Pliny, *N.H.* VII, 148, 'Pannonicis bellis ruina e turri'; Suetonius, *Aug.* 20; Florus II, 23 [IV, 12], 6.

[3] At Siscia, in 35 or 34, Octavian probably received the Dacian embassy mentioned in Dio LI, 22, 7, 8: cf. Suetonius, *Aug.* 63, 2.

by the Dalmatian leader Versus[1]. Again sheer weight of numbers rather than any tactical skill prevailed and the stronghold, together with the positions on the surrounding ridges, was soon stormed. Marching southwards Octavian passed through the defile in which a few years previously Gabinius had been entrapped and so took all the necessary precautions against surprise. He captured Synodium[2] and began the blockade of Setovia (Sinj) on its impregnable rock, but the season was by now far advanced, a wound he had received in the knee was slow in healing and so, leaving Statilius Taurus in command, he journeyed to Rome to enter upon the consulship for 33 B.C. His own campaigns had taken him to the Cetina, but his *legati* had pressed even farther, for Appian's mention of the Derbani and of the Docleatae (whose capital appears to have been the modern Duklja, north of Podgorica), shows that at least the northern half of Montenegro was reached and that his forces came very near to the dividing-line between Antony and himself, the town of Scodra[3].

But in the past two years events had been occurring which brought a breach with Antony ominously near (pp. 79 *sqq.*), and it became important to husband his resources and bring the campaigns to a close quickly. Octavian accordingly laid down his consulship on the very first day, just as Antony had done a year previously, and began operations in Dalmatia in early spring. Setovia was forced by famine to surrender, and the Dalmatians at last made their submission, giving 700 hostages, promising to pay tribute and—best of all—yielding up the lost standards of Gabinius. In the west he put a stop to the indecisive campaigns which Antistius Vetus had been waging against the Salassi; Terentius Varro Murena was to settle the account six years later (p. 348). Apart from this minor check Octavian had every reason to be satisfied with his achievements; the garrisons at Emona and Siscia controlled and guarded a route of great antiquity and barred any invasion from the north-east; his conquests in Dalmatia had secured the eastern Adriatic coast and won him a splendid

[1] The beginning of this campaign *may* have involved the subjugation of the Glintidiones (? by the headwaters of the Una and Glina), but not of the Daesitiatae, who are not mentioned for certain by Appian, since in *Ill.* 17 Δαισιτιᾶται is Schweighäuser's emendation of the impossible Δαίσιοί τε. See J. Dobiáš, *Studie k Appianově knize Illyrské*, p. 208.

[2] On the site of Synodium see Veith, *op. cit.* and D. Gribaudi, *Synodium*, Riv. Fil. N.S. III, 1925, p. 413.

[3] Appian, *Ill.* 16, and see E. Swoboda, *Octavian und Illyricum*, p. 74 *sq.*

recruiting-ground for the Roman navies[1]. Illness had prevented him from carrying out the whole of his projects, but he had delivered Italy from a great fear, he had displayed courage and skill as a leader, and he could recite a lengthy list of tribes conquered—Iapudes, Docleatae, Carni, Taurisci, Naresii, Glintidiones, Interfrurini, Oxyaei, Bathiatae, Cambaei, Cinambri, Taulantii, Meromenni—many of them mere names to the Italians as to us, but which he could set in profitable contrast to what he called the inactivity of Antony[2]. And in the North the consolidation of the gains made was begun by the planting or refounding of colonies; to Tergeste (Trieste), which Caesar had made an Italian colony, he presented new fortifications[3], Pola rose again from its ruins as Colonia Pietas Julia, and Emona became in 34 B.C. Colonia Julia[4]; from their garrisons the soldiers faced eastwards towards the great river that was to be the boundary of their Empire, and the linking-up of communication between Danube and Rhine would tax the skill of Roman generals for many years to come.

It was not only in military prestige, not only in the heightened loyalty and improved discipline of his troops that Octavian had gained: by beautification of the city during these years he carried out yet another of his father's projects, and by a steady revival of pride in the past of Italy and her religion he filled the people with some of his own feeling and fostered a national consciousness (p. 456 *sq.*). The Romans saw their city adorned by the efforts of Octavian or his friends and lieutenants. From the booty won in the recent campaigns he himself rebuilt the Porticus Octavia in which he deposited the recaptured eagles of Gabinius[5]; at great expense he restored the theatre of Pompey, without adding his name, in 32 B.C.[6] L. Aemilius Lepidus Paullus, who had been on his staff during the Sicilian campaigns, completed the reconstruction, begun by his father, of that Basilica Aemilia which Pliny reckoned among the most beautiful buildings in the world[7], while

---

[1] See R. Vulpe, *Gli Illiri dell' Italia imperiale romana*, Ephemeris Dacoromana, III, 1925, pp. 136–44.

[2] Appian, *Ill.* 16, 'ἐν παραβολῇ τῆς ἀπραξίας Ἀντωνίου.'

[3] Dessau 77, 'Imp. Caes. cos. desig. tert., IIIvir r. p. c. iter., murum turresque fecit,' is to be dated to 33 B.C.

[4] Probably we should date to this period the sending of a colony to Iader and a grant of citizenship to Senia. See J. W. Kubitschek, *Imp. Rom. tributim discriptum*, p. 234 and p. 232, and the relevant articles in *P.W.*

[5] Appian, *Ill.* 28; Vell. Pat. II, 81, 3–4; *Res Gestae* 19; not to be confused with the Porticus Octaviae, for which see p. 574.

[6] *Res Gestae* 20.

[7] Pliny, *N.H.* XXXVI, 102

Statilius Taurus, after his triumph 'ex Africa' in 34, began work upon a great stone amphitheatre in the Campus Martius[1]. Maecenas, who had been in charge of the city during the Illyrian Wars and entrusted with Octavian's seal, cleared away a hideous stretch of burial ground on the Esquiline close by the Servian *agger*, and transformed it into a spacious park and walks for the populace[2]. Still greater was the energy of Agrippa who at his own expense assumed in 33 the unwanted office of aedile: by restoring the century-old Aqua Marcia and by raising a new aqueduct, the Aqua Julia, he increased and assured the water-supply of Rome, where hundreds of new basins and fountains, adorned with marble, facilitated distribution[3]: he repaired public buildings, reconditioned the drainage system, relaid streets, and spent money lavishly in providing amenities such as free baths and theatrical performances for the people.

Deeper and nobler was the sentiment that inspired Octavian in rekindling pride in the old Roman religion and institutions and in counteracting foreign practices. Greek cults were not banned for they had been long known to the people, Apollo was his protecting deity, and later, by his initiation, Octavian was to manifest his approval of the 'augusta mysteria' of Athens; but Asiatic, Syrian or Egyptian rites were not to be allowed. In every way men were encouraged to restore the sacred buildings and so reawaken belief: Octavian himself, on the prompting of the aged Atticus, undertook the repair of one of the most hallowed spots in Rome, the temple of Juppiter Feretrius wherein reposed the original *spolia opima* dedicated by Romulus[4], Cn. Domitius Calvinus from the spoils of his Spanish campaign rebuilt the Regia, adorning it with statues provided by Octavian[5], L. Marcius Philippus restored the temple Herculis Musarum and L. Cornificius took charge of the temple of Diana on the Aventine[6]. Already Horace, shedding his Republicanism, could write of Octavian as one whose care it was to protect 'Italy and the shrines of the gods,' and could advise a *parvenu* freedman to make good use of his pile by spending it on decaying temples[7]. Nor were

---

[1] F. W. Shipley, *Chronology of the Building Operations in Rome*, p. 24.
[2] Horace, *Sat.* 1, 8, 14, and the ancient commentators *ad. loc.*
[3] Pliny, *N.H.* xxxvi, 121; Platner-Ashby, *A Topographical Dictionary of Rome*, pp. 23 *sqq.*
[4] Nepos, *Atticus*, 20; *Res Gestae* 19.
[5] Dio xlviii, 42, 4–6; cf. Dessau 421.
[6] Suetonius, *Aug.* 29, and cf. Shipley, *op. cit.* pp. 29 *sqq.*
[7] Horace, *Sat.* 1, 6, 34–5 and ii, 2, 105 *sqq.*

the great priesthoods or the aristocratic families that supplied
them forgotten. Octavian was himself an augur and his reward
to the ex-Republican Messalla Corvinus for his services during
the Sicilian War was the grant of an *extra numerum* place in
the college of augurs; in 33 he was empowered by the Senate
to create new patrician families for the express purpose of
filling the priesthoods[1]; the children of these noble families had
been accustomed to take part in a ceremony (of supposedly
great antiquity) called the Lusus Troiae, and this was celebrated
by young men in 40 and again in 33 B.C.[2] By every possible
means, small and great, material and spiritual, Octavian was
slowly educating Italy to his own faith and giving it strength
for the coming struggle. Significant was the edict that in the
year 33 expelled from Rome astrologers and fortune-tellers and
magicians, those poor Greek or Asiatic charlatans whose antics
Horace used so to enjoy watching[3]: the time was not so far distant
when Octavian as fetial priest of an united Roman people would
demand reparation from a queen whose more formidable magic
menaced the existence of the Roman State.

V. THE BREAK

The agreement reached between Antony and Octavian at
Tarentum was not to last for long. By the winter of 34 B.C.
ominous signs had appeared, yet it is unlikely that the inner
history and exact truth of the important period lying between 37
and 30 will ever be discovered, because the facts have been obscured and distorted by the propaganda of both sides, propaganda
which has survived (and still defies complete analysis) in our
sources. Some discussion of these sources is imperative, therefore,
at this point, for though Octavian's ultimate victory did not
succeed in obliterating versions and traditions hostile to himself
or favourable to Antony, the conquering cause naturally pleased
the majority of Augustan historians[4]. In the earliest narrative
available, the brief history of Velleius Paterculus, the tone is
'official'; Antony has scarcely a redeeming feature and is wrong
almost from start to finish[5]. Still the fact that both Gaius and

[1] Dio XLIX, 43, 6.   [2] Dio XLVIII, 20, 2 and XLIX, 43, 2.
[3] Dio XLIX, 43, 5; Horace, *Sat.* 1, 6, 110 *sqq.*
[4] For writers favourable to Antony see the mention in Plutarch's *Moralia*
(*Quomodo adulator ab amico internoscatur*), 56 E–F; for a specimen of the anti-
Augustan tradition see Tacitus, *Ann.* 1, 10.
[5] See Vell. Pat. II, 56, 60, 61, 66, 67, etc. In II, 74 Antony is allowed
'virtutes quae interdum in illo erant,' and cf. II, 87, 1.

Nero could claim descent from Antony must have exercised a restraining influence upon writers, and the ordinary orthodox view is probably represented by Seneca's verdict that 'a great man and of notable ability was turned to foreign ways and un-Roman vices by his love for drink and his equal passion for Cleopatra[1].' But the fall of the Julio-Claudians made such circumspection unnecessary; Tacitus readily reproduces traditions hostile to Augustus and in Plutarch, Suetonius, Appian and Dio both sides are to some extent represented. Sometimes the name of an authority is given and the tendency is clear, but usually the strands are more closely interwoven, and it may be suspected that much which now passes for fact is merely an echo from this war of recrimination; on the other hand merely to reject on suspicion all favourable notices (or alternatively all unfavourable notices) as obvious propaganda leads to impossible reconstructions.

A few instances will show something of the problem: the existence of the society of the 'Inimitables' (p. 40) might be questioned as sheer Caesarian invention were it not confirmed by an inscription[2]; on the other hand the fishing exploit of Antony, which Plutarch sedulously chronicles among his 'Follies,' was obviously an attempt by Cleopatra to stir him to war and action (p. 41). But when Dio, speaking of the banquets that followed the pact of Brundisium, asserts that Octavian entertained 'in a soldierly and Roman fashion' but Antony 'in an Asiatic and Egyptian manner,' the cautious will scent a Caesarian writer, especially when in the next sentence Octavian is portrayed as rescuing Antony from the violence of soldiers who were demanding bounties promised after Philippi[3]. And though it is easy to see through such absurdities as the suggestion that Antony was never engaged in the first battle of Philippi and only took part in the pursuit[4], or the charges made against Octavian's early life[5]—mere stock-in-trade of Italian polemic—other passages do not disclose their origin so readily. What, for example, is to be made of the statement that the triumvirs in the winter of 43–2

[1] Seneca, *Epist. Mor.* 83, 25.

[2] Plutarch, *Ant.* 28 compared with *O.G.I.S.* 195.

[3] Dio XLVIII, 30; the counterpart is Appian, *Bell. Civ.* v, 85, where Antony saves Octavian from the mob.   [4] Plutarch, *Ant.* 22.

[5] Suetonius, *Aug.* 68 and 69. These charges, together with those of low birth thrown at him by Antony all recur in the Pseudo-Ciceronian *Epistula ad Octavianum*, 9, of uncertain date. See M. P. Charlesworth in *Class. Quart.* XXVII, 1933, p. 173; and cf. K. Scott in *Mem. Amer. Acad. in Rome*, XI, 1933, p. 7.

seized large sums of money deposited with the Vestal Virgins[1]?
Is it simply true? Or is it a convenient fiction utilized afterwards
to defend Octavian's extortion of Antony's will? (p. 97). Even
though it were possible to track down with absolute certainty the
narrative sources that underlie such works as the *Antony* of
Plutarch, the *Augustus* of Suetonius, the last three volumes of the
Bella Civilia of Appian, or books XLIV to L of the History of Dio
(for Velleius presents no serious problems) we should be little
nearer a solution, as both Asinius Pollio and Livy, to mention
the two most favoured candidates[2], were men of independent
judgment and not mere partisans. In such circumstances all that
the historian can hope to do is to set forth a probable story based
upon close examination of the sources and a sympathetic study
of the chief actors.

The pact of Tarentum had included among other clauses two
pledges of good faith for speedy fulfilment: Antony was to provide Octavian with a fleet for the Sicilian War, Octavian was to
give to Antony in return four legions (pp. 54, 59). Antony fulfilled
his part immediately, Octavian did not, and mutual suspicion
began again its fatal work. A year and a half elapsed before
Octavian gave thought to his pledge, but he went about it in
a manner that revealed his resentment over Antony's abandonment of his sister; in the spring of 35 some seventy of Antony's
ships were returned to him (which he had neither asked for nor
desired) and Octavia started eastwards with 2000 legionaries and
funds. Antony's reply was direct and brutal: he accepted the men
and money but bade Octavia come no farther; she must have returned to Rome in the winter of 35–4 and her brother tried to
persuade her to leave Antony's house. But he was met by a
determination and passion as great as his own; she remained
loyally in the house, attending to Antony's interests, receiving his
friends and lieutenants and looking after his children. But the
facts that Octavian continued his Illyrian campaigns and celebrated the death of Sextus Pompeius by the conferment of fresh
honours upon Antony, show that, however perturbed inwardly,
he was still prepared to preserve the outward semblance of concord.

But Antony must have felt differently: Octavian's pledges were
worthless, a breach was bound to come; let it come quickly before

[1] Plutarch, *Ant.* 21.
[2] Recently E. Kornemann in *Klio*, XVII, 1920, p. 33, has tried to make a
case for Cremutius Cordus.

his armies weakened yet further and before Octavian gained
greater strength and favour in Italy. In the winter of 34, therefore, he staged the famous Donations (p. 80), wherein he declared
that Cleopatra had been the wife of Julius Caesar and that
Ptolemy Caesar (Caesarion) was their acknowledged son[1]. This was
a definite step against his fellow triumvir, for it suggested that
Octavian was usurping the place and title of another and had no
real claim to the allegiance of the soldiers. Such news, reaching
Rome in the spring of 33, moved Octavian to angry remonstrance
in a letter; he reproached Antony with his ill-treatment of Octavia,
his *liaison* with a foreign queen, and his support of her son[2].
Antony, genuinely surprised, replied that Cleopatra was his wife;
if he was married to an 'Egyptian,' had not Octavian been ready
to offer his daughter Julia to a Dacian[3]? And what of Octavian's
own love-affairs? There followed more serious grievances: in accordance with the treaty of Brundisium Antony claimed half the
recruits levied in Italy and allotments for his veterans, and asked
where were the promised legions; finally he declared that Octavian
alone stood in the way of the restoration of the Republic[4]. To these
fair demands Octavian would not reply: rage at the insult offered
to his sister, mingled with his previous mistrust, had made him
determined that until Octavia was righted there should be nothing[5]. Instead he suggested sneeringly that Antony should find
land for his veterans from his conquests in Parthia and attacked
him for his enslavement to the Egyptian queen. This response
reached Antony in the autumn while he was still in Armenia
(p. 79), and although he made no immediate move in hostilities—for it was not until November that Canidius brought
his army to Ephesus—he realized that it was essential for
him to reach the Senate and win its approval in the struggle
that was bound to come; he addressed to it a despatch, asking
for the ratification of his *acta* (which would include the Donations), and intimating his willingness to lay down the powers of

---

[1] This follows from Dio XLIX, 41 and L, 1, 5; Plutarch, *Ant.* 54, and
Suetonius, *Div. Iul.* 52, 2. In his later despatch to the Senate Antony
declared that this acknowledgement had been hushed up; hence the pamphlet
of Oppius to disprove Cleopatra's claims for her son, Suetonius, *loc. cit.*
[2] Antony replied to this in his 'Quid te mutavit?' letter, and it can be
reconstructed accordingly; see Suetonius, *Aug.* 69.
[3] Suetonius, *Aug.* 28. The rest of the letter may be reconstructed in outline from Dio L, 1 and Plutarch, *Ant.* 55.   [4] Suetonius, *Aug.* 28.
[5] His devotion to Octavia was caricatured in the atrocious charge that he
was merely using her as a pawn in the game; Plutarch, *Ant.* 53.

the Triumvirate if Octavian would do likewise. From now on began a campaign of vituperation in which partisans of both sides joined, among them Cassius of Parma for Antony and Oppius and Messalla for Octavian[1]; amid such activities the year 33 closed and with the last day of December the legal term fixed for the second period of the Triumvirate expired[2].

It is especially at this point that we regret the meagreness and inexactitude of our sources. Precedents were few, if any, but it looks as though both surviving members of the Triumvirate (or rather the legal-minded among their supporters) could argue with some show of justice that the law merely fixed a day up to which they could hold their powers and that after that only a formal act of abdication on their part or a vote of termination by the original granting body, the Roman People, could end their tenure. Antony certainly kept the title and continued to act as triumvir[3]; Octavian dropped the title, though whether he made use of his powers or not is uncertain. But his tribunician right gave him sacrosanctity, he had the advantage of holding Italy, he knew he would be consul in 31, the position of *privatus* was not likely to terrify one who, twelve years ago, in equal certainty of the justice of his cause, had appealed to force and raised armies on his own authority, and he must have been aware that whatever illegalities or unconstitutionalities he might commit would be covered (if he emerged victorious) by retrospective legislation—as actually happened in 29 and 28 B.C. It seems likely therefore that while Antony continued to use both the powers and the title of Triumvir (for which he had at least an arguable case), Octavian dropped both and relied upon other means, and so could write in his *Res Gestae* that he was a member of the Triumvirate for 'ten consecutive years' and no more.

The consuls who entered office on 1 January 32 B.C., C. Sosius and Cn. Domitius Ahenobarbus, were both supporters of Antony, and as Octavian had prudently withdrawn from Rome before the new year came in[4], it looked as though Antony could at last gain the hearing of the Senate free and unfettered. But there was a difficulty; the consuls did not dare read to the Senate the full contents of the despatch they had received from their leader, for

---

[1] As Asinius Pollio remained neutral (Vell. Pat. II, 86, 3), the speech attributed to him by Charisius (p. 100, 20 B), *contra maledicta Antonii*, must have been a piece of self-defence and not propaganda.

[2] For the literature on this controversial question see the Bibliography, Part I, section II, J.

[3] This is proved both by his coins and by his offer to lay down his powers, if victorious, after six months; Dio L, 7.   [4] Dio L, 2, 3.

they guessed how damaging an effect the reiteration of the gifts and titles bestowed upon Cleopatra and her children would have upon public feeling in Rome. So they tried different methods: Sosius, the more fiery of the two, delivered a harangue in praise of Antony and would have made a motion against Octavian had not Nonius Balbus interposed the tribunician veto. Octavian did not delay his answer long, though he surrounded himself with a bodyguard of his friends and soldiers before he took his seat in the Senate-house; there he defended his own acts and attacked gravely both Antony and Sosius, offering to prove by written documents to be produced to the fathers on a fixed day the justice of his cause. None dared utter a word in reply and the meeting dissolved, but before the fixed day arrived both consuls and some four hundred senators had left Rome for the East.

Antony had made no overt move during 33, but with the return of his army from Armenia in November he had finally decided upon war. He and Cleopatra wintered at Ephesus (33–2) amid strenuous preparations; and on the arrival of the consuls he set up a counter-Senate. He removed many works of art from Asia Minor to Alexandria, and gave Cleopatra the library of Pergamum in compensation for the books burnt by Caesar[1], but it is doubtful if it was ever transferred. The great fleet was mobilized (p. 100); besides her squadron of warships, she supplied half of the 300 transports and probably a large force of rowers[2]. She had undertaken to pay and feed the army and navy, and she started the war-chest with 20,000 talents; this was what she had been working for, and she was ready now to throw in everything she possessed. Antony called up all the client-kings in his sphere except Polemo and Herod, and took an oath of allegiance from them. Polemo was left to guard the Armenian frontier; and though Herod came to Ephesus Cleopatra would not have him with the army, and at her request Antony told him to punish Malchus for withholding her rent. He did defeat Malchus after a hard struggle, but was nearly baulked of victory by Cleopatra's general in Coele-Syria, who knew that she only wanted the pair to damage each other. But before leaving Ephesus, Herod, who had grasped Antony's situation, tried to take his revenge by telling him that the path to success was to kill Cleopatra and annex Egypt[3].

[1] See above, vol. IX, p. 671.
[2] Some Egyptian Greeks from Antony's crews were settled later at Nemausus; see *C.I.L.* XII, p. 382.
[3] Josephus, *Ant.* XV [6, 6], 191 seems to put this after Actium; but that would be meaningless, and also Herod never saw Antony again after leaving Ephesus. Josephus misplaces several events of this period.

This abominable advice was sound, for at Ephesus the radical impossibility of Antony's dual position had become patent: he could lead Romans against Romans as a Roman, but not as a Hellenistic king, the husband of Cleopatra. There were fierce quarrels between some of his Roman supporters, who wanted the queen sent back to Egypt and kept out of sight and mind, and Cleopatra, who meant to fight in her own war. Antony's officers were of many minds. Some, like Canidius and Turullius, had to follow him whatever he did, as they could expect no mercy from Octavian. Some, like Domitius, were ready to fight for him, but only if they approved of his policy. Some, like the hardened deserters Titius and Dellius, merely meant to be on the winning side at the end. And there were plain honest men who had no wish for war at all; they preferred Antony to Octavian, but their real allegiance was to the Roman State. Cleopatra had the hardest struggle of her life. At one moment Antony ordered her back to Egypt, but she refused to go; the feeling aroused was shown when Canidius, who supported her, said that a woman who was paying and feeding the army and had a better head than most of them could not be sent away, and was at once told that she had bribed him. She strained her influence over Antony to carry her point, and she did carry it once for all, but the trouble was only glossed over, for the cause remained; Antony did his best by declaring that six months after victory he would lay down his powers. In April 32 headquarters were transferred to Samos, and she got him into good humour again with the usual banquets and amusements, while the transports were ferrying the army across to Greece; the whole body of Dionysiac artists were gathered in the island, and Antony rewarded them with Priene. In May they crossed to Athens, and the city gave Cleopatra the honours once given to Octavia. Antony's supporters in Italy sent him a message begging him to send away Cleopatra, but she was strong enough now to have the messenger turned out.

Meanwhile in Rome, though the consuls had left, Octavian had the advantage of holding the capital; he convened what was left of the Senate and read a detailed defence of his position and acts, attacking those of Antony (especially the Donations), and contrasting his own campaigns in Dalmatia and Pannonia with the failures of Antony. For the coming war he must be secure of two things, money and loyalty, the more so since Antony had the support of Egypt's wealth and boasted that gold could win him many friends in Italy. Fresh taxation was imposed, one-quarter of the annual income from all citizens and a capital levy of one-eighth on all freedmen, and a great effort was made to stir up national feeling. Some thirty years ago Pompey had persuaded Naples to pass a resolution urging the recall of Cicero from exile and bidding other municipalities follow suit[1], and now representatives began to move among the more important towns and municipalities in Italy, with rumours that Antony was drugged and dominated by a foreign sorceress, and suggesting that they should pass votes of confidence in Octavian, as leader of Italy. The movement slowly gathered impetus, and in May or June Antony took a step which alienated sympathy from him; he sent Octavia formal letters of divorce. For over two years, despite pressure from her brother, she had refused to leave Antony's house; now his messengers expelled her weeping, with the children she was mothering, and the sight and act roused in her brother such a fury of resentment that he did not hesitate to seize an opportunity suddenly placed in his grasp.

At Antony's headquarters the divorce of Octavia was taken to mean that Cleopatra was irresistible; and Plancus and Titius left and went over to Octavian, the first of many desertions. They had been trusted followers; they brought not only information about plans, but also news that Antony had recently drawn up a will (details of which they professed to know), which he had entrusted to the keeping of the Vestal Virgins. Octavian thus learnt that there was in Rome a document which would prove authoritatively to Italy all he wished to prove but had been unable to do owing to Sosius' withholding of Antony's official despatch to the Senate. The Vestals naturally refused to surrender the will to his request, and he seized it by force, risking the indignation which this act excited. A first glance convinced him that the will did indeed contain what would serve his purpose, and he read it publicly to the Senate. Among other clauses it is said to have included a declaration that Ptolemy Caesar was the true son of Cleopatra and Julius Caesar; but it certainly gave great legacies to Antony's children by Cleopatra, and it directed that he should be buried beside her in Alexandria[2].

This last provision roused Rome to fury, for it was taken to mean that Antony intended to transfer the capital to Alexandria: he was no longer a Roman, but the tool of the foreign woman. There was a fresh outburst against him, much of it pitiful enough: he had given Cleopatra a Roman bodyguard (they were in fact

---

[1] Cicero, *post red. in Sen.* 11, 29; *in Pisonem*, 11, 25; and *pro Milone*, 15, 39.
[2] Dio L, 3, 3–5; Suetonius, *Aug.* 17; Plutarch, *Ant.* 55.

Galatians)[1], he had acted as gymnasiarch in Alexandria (as he had done without comment in Athens), he walked by her litter or rode with her; the real charge was that he was a traitor to Rome, ready to lead strange foes against her, like a second Pyrrhus[2]. But against Cleopatra was launched one of the most terrible outbursts of hatred in history; no accusation was too vile to be hurled at her, and the charges then made have echoed through the world ever since, and have sometimes been naïvely taken for facts. This accursed Egyptian was a sorceress who had bewitched Antony with drugs, a wanton who had sold herself to his pleasures for power; this one and that one had been her paramours; Caesar's alleged son was the bastard of an unknown father. She was a worshipper of beast-gods, a queen of eunuchs as foul as herself, a drunkard and a harlot; later she was to be called a poisoner, a traitor and a coward.

Some indeed of these jackal-cries needed the assurance of victory before they were voiced at their loudest, but even so the effect of the publication of the will was decisive. A vast body of hitherto uncertain sympathies now swung round definitely to Octavian; by October the discontent, culminating in some regions in rioting and arson, that the new taxation had stirred up had practically subsided and money began to flow in. In the late autumn the whole of Italy, town after town, joined in a solemn *coniuratio*, swearing allegiance to Octavian as its general in a crusade against the menace of the East, a demonstration of the solidarity of that new citizen-body which had been created by the wise statesmanship of two generations before, and this oath was taken also by the municipalities in the provinces of the West, Sicily, Sardinia, Africa, and the Gauls and Spains[3]. Fortified by this public vote Octavian could take the final steps: Antony was deprived of his triumviral power and of his right to hold the consulship for 31[4], and Octavian himself, as fetial priest of the Roman people, before the temple of Bellona went through the impressive ritual that accompanied the formal proclamation of a *iustum bellum*. But he declared war on Cleopatra alone, not on Antony; partly because he had in 36 announced that the Civil

[1] Josephus, *Ant.* xv [7, 3], 217.

[2] For stories about Gonatas and Pyrrhus transferred to Octavian and Antony see Tarn in *J.R.S.* xxi, 1931, p. 181.

[3] *Res Gestae* 25; Suetonius, *Aug.* 17, 2 does not imply that the oath was taken under compulsion; for literature see the Bibliography, Part I, section II, J.

[4] Unfortunately Dio L, 4, 3, 'καὶ τὴν ἄλλην ἐξουσίαν πᾶσαν ἀφείλοντο,' gives no indication of the means employed.

Wars were at an end, but chiefly because opinion would be solid against a foreign enemy. And it corresponded to the facts; it was her war. Nor need we doubt that Octavian believed both in the mandate given him and in himself.

During the turn of the year Antony with his fleet and army was wintering in Greece, while the fleets of Octavian gathered at Brundisium and Tarentum. Though diplomatic interchanges had ceased publicity and propaganda continued unabated; the legal position of both protagonists was not strong, and no effort that might win support could safely be neglected. Charges and counter-charges now took their final and grossest shape: Antony was ridiculed for posing as Dionysus, Octavian for posing as Apollo; Octavian was a coward; Antony was a madman and a drunkard, a charge which stung him to a personal defence[1]; he abused Octavian's ancestors, and Octavian abused Cleopatra's ministers; political crimes were alleged on both sides, like the Artavasdes matter (p. 78); there were the sexual accusations which for centuries had been a commonplace of propaganda. Unsavoury in itself, this exchange of invective cannot be omitted from the history of the period and must even be stressed, because it had a definite effect upon historical writing of the next century and a half, and through these upon modern works, and it is not too much to say that both the conventional portraits—of Antony as a drunken sot occasionally quitting Cleopatra's embraces for disas-trous campaigns, of Octavian as a cowardly runaway, cruel and treacherous in his dealings—are due mainly to this propaganda and are wholly unreal. But they served their purpose.

The beginning of the year 31 greatly strengthened Octavian's constitutional position, for he entered upon his third consulship (which he was to have shared with Antony), having as his colleague M. Valerius Messalla Corvinus. Within a few months everything was in readiness: Maecenas was left in charge of Italy and the capital, all disturbances in the peninsula had been suppressed, the coasts of the Western provinces were protected by naval squad-rons[2], and Cornelius Gallus was dispatched to guard Africa against attack from the East[3]. As soon as the spring sea was fit for navi-gation, with fleet and transports and accompanied by a large number of senators Octavian crossed the Adriatic.

---

[1] The famous *de ebrietate sua*, published by Antony shortly before Actium (Pliny, *N.H.* xiv, 22). Cf. K. Scott, '*Octavian's Propaganda and Antony's de sua ebrietate*,' in *Class. Phil.* xxiv, 1929, p. 133.

[2] Dessau 2672 (*C.I.L.* xi, 623); a tribune of a legion, 'praef. orae marit. Hispan. citerioris bello Actiensi.'   [3] Dio li, 5, 6; cf. 9, 1.

VI. THE ACTIUM CAMPAIGN[1]

Antony's forces reached the coast of the Ionian Sea, his western boundary, about September 32. His fleet, which had picked up the detachments at Cephallenia and Zacynthus, totalled eight squadrons of the line of 60 ships each (one being Cleopatra's, led by her flagship *Antonia*) with their complements of light scouts, normally five to a squadron—over 500 warships; no such fleet had ever yet been seen. He had noted the advantage which Octavian had had over Sextus in the size and weight of his ships, and had outbuilt him; his ships ranged upward to vessels of nine men to the oar, the flagship having ten[2], while the larger vessels had belts of squared timbers bound with iron to prevent ramming; the crews might number some 125,000–150,000 men. His land army comprised nineteen legions, doubtless the seven of the old army of Macedonia and twelve, now very weak, which had been in Media—about 60,000 to 63,000 men, all Italians and well-seasoned troops; with the light-armed, partly Asiatics, he perhaps had some 70,000–75,000 foot, the latter an outside figure, and perhaps 12,000 horse, partly the remnant of his original cavalry and partly supplied by the client-kings[3]. That Cleopatra undertook to feed an army and navy of these dimensions shows that Egypt was still producing a large surplus of corn (p. 37); but he had formed food depôts in Greece and elsewhere. Of his remaining eleven legions, four under Scarpus were in the Cyrenaica to watch Octavian's army of Africa under Cornelius Gallus, and the rest were distributed between Alexandria, Syria (under Q. Didius), and the Macedonian frontier. There was some disaffection in his rear, but of little account; Sparta under Eurycles, whose father he had executed, joined Octavian, as did Lappa and Cydonia in Crete; and during the winter Berytus revolted from Cleopatra[4].

The army wintered on a line extending from Corcyra to Methone in Messenia, the largest force occupying the Actian peninsula, the southern of the two promontories flanking the narrow entrance to the Gulf of Ambracia, which was well fortified;

---

[1] See Map 2, facing p. 23. For the reconstruction of the battle of Actium here used, and the evidence, see Tarn, *J.R.S.* xxi, 1931, p. 173.

[2] His legionary coins (Volume of Plates iv, 198, *d, e*) give a picture of this vessel, of course much shortened.

[3] For the figures see Tarn, *Class. Quart.* xxvi, 1932, p. 75.

[4] Change from regal to city coinage: U. Kahrstedt, *Klio* x, 1910, p. 277.

Antony's headquarters were at Patrae, where Cleopatra struck coins. The life-nerve of the army was the Egyptian corn-ships, which rounded Cape Taenarum and came up the Peloponnesian coast; their route was guarded by stations at Leucas and elsewhere, the most southern being Methone, which was commanded by Bogud (vol. ix, p. 703), driven from Mauretania by his brother Bocchus in Octavian's interest. It was a bad position, for it surrendered the Via Egnatia and all good land communication with Macedonia and the East, and was very vulnerable from the sea; it gives the impression of being chosen by one whose aim was, not to crush his enemy, but to cover Egypt.

To challenge Octavian for the mastery of the world and then stand on the defensive was strange strategy, and Antony has naturally been blamed for not invading Italy in the early autumn of 32, while Octavian still had trouble there. But in fact he had no choice; he could not invade Italy, not because the season was late or the ports guarded, but because he could not go either with or without Cleopatra. To take her with him meant that the whole peninsula, including his friends, would stand solid against the foreign invader; and she would not let him go without her and perhaps, through Octavia's mediation, come to another accommodation with Octavian, at her expense. As he could not go to Octavian, he must make Octavian come to him; hence the surrender of the Via Egnatia, while in winter he withdrew from Corcyra, leaving free the passage to Dyrrhachium. Octavian, he thought, had not the money for a long war, and must seek a decision.

But if we understand why Antony surrendered the initiative, much of the ensuing campaign, as given in our secondary sources, is incomprehensible. Why did Antony not use his great fleet to attack Octavian when crossing? Why was that fleet never used at all till too late? And how came it, when he meant Octavian to cross, that Octavian surprised him—if he *did* surprise him? None of these questions can be answered. We might conjecture that his position and the quarrels in his camp had paralysed his will; that he only wanted to end it somehow, and believed that, given any sort of a land battle, his own generalship must prevail; but it would remain conjecture. Even the details are wrong; Turullius' coins[1] prove that Antony won some victory after which he was hailed *Imperator* for the fourth time, but it cannot be fitted into the

---

[1] Volume of Plates iv, 198, *h*. A coin of Scarpus (Grueber, ii, p. 583) showing a Victory may refer to the same thing.

extant secondary tradition. Till we come to Antony's final defeat
on land, no satisfactory account of the campaign is possible.

Octavian had mobilized 80,000 foot and 12,000 horse, and
something over 400 ships; the bulk of his fleet was formed by the
large heavy ships which had defeated Sextus, strengthened like
Antony's by belts of timber and equipped with catapults for firing
Agrippa's *harpax* (see p. 58); his fleet organization is unknown,
but he perhaps had more Liburnians (light scouts) than the usual
complement. As he possessed far more men and ships than he
mobilized, he must have decided that these numbers would
suffice, as they did. The land forces he meant to command himself, but the fleet he wisely entrusted to the tried skill of Agrippa.
Maecenas he left in Rome to manage Italy, but he brought most
of the Senate with him, except Pollio; Pollio had broken with
Antony on his marriage to Cleopatra and was living in Italy, but
he refused to fight against his former friend, and Octavian respected his scruples. Octavian crossed very early in 31, while
Antony's army was still in winter-quarters. Agrippa with half the
fleet attacked the Peloponnese, stormed Methone, Bogud being
killed, and thus secured a base for his cruisers on the flank of
Antony's corn-ships; and under cover of this diversion Octavian
with the army landed in Epirus, moved southward very fast, tried
but failed to surprise Antony's fleet from the land (perhaps
Antony's victory comes in here), and seized a position on the high
ground at Mikalitsi in the northern of the two promontories
which enclose the Gulf of Ambracia. Perhaps Antony was not
really surprised—witness Cleopatra's unconcern at the capture of
Toryne in Epirus; perhaps his fleet was a bait to draw Octavian
into a position where he thought he could trap him; but, if so,
things did not go according to plan. For by the time he had
collected his army in the Actian peninsula Octavian had fortified
his position and connected it by long walls with the roadstead of
Comarus, while Agrippa had stormed Leucas and destroyed the
squadron there; from Leucas and Comarus the fleet could now
blockade the Ambracian Gulf, so far as galleys could blockade,
and prevent the entrance of corn-ships. Agrippa subsequently
took Patrae and Corinth and cut Antony off from the Peloponnese.

An unsuccessful sortie of part of Antony's fleet, in which the
dynast Tarcondimotus was killed, may show that, as a dynast was
on board, Antony was refusing legionaries to the fleet and depending entirely upon his land operations. He crossed from
Actium and camped in face of Octavian; then he shipped troops up
the Ambracian Gulf, sent his cavalry round it, and attempted by a

combined attack to close Octavian in and cut off his water-supply, the weak point of his position. The attack was defeated by the failure of Antony's cavalry, who formed the northern (outer) wing of the encircling force, and two dynasts, Rhoemetalces of Thrace and Deiotarus of Paphlagonia, went over to Octavian; 'I like treason' said Octavian to Rhoemetalces when he abused Antony, 'but I don't like the traitors.' Antony made an effort to recruit more cavalry and led a second attempt in person; Amyntas, the man he had made, went over to Octavian with his 2000 Galatian horse[1], and the attempt was completely defeated. Amyntas and the other dynasts may have objected to the alteration of their position under the Donations; but their allegiance was due to Rome, not to a party, and they may merely have believed that Octavian would be victor. Antony recognized the defeat as decisive for the operations on land, and withdrew to Actium.

Instead of besieging Octavian, he was now virtually besieged. The troops and crews who had wintered on the low ground about the Gulf had suffered from disease; his press-gangs provided more rowers, but that did not help the troops. Rations were short; Agrippa had cut him off from Egypt and the Peloponnese, and food had to be brought on men's backs across the mountain paths of Aetolia (Plutarch's grandfather was pressed as a carrier, which helps to explain Plutarch's want of sympathy for Antony), and even this resource might fail, as Octavian had sent detachments eastward. Officers and dynasts alike were now deserting to Octavian, and Antony's attempt to stop the movement by severity —he executed Iamblichus of Emesa and a Roman senator—only increased it; even Domitius himself, desperately ill, left and went to Octavian to die. Dellius followed; and Antony called a council of war. Canidius wished to abandon the ships, retire into Macedonia, and fight in the open; Cleopatra insisted on using the fleet, and Antony agreed; Octavian learnt his decision from deserters. Cleopatra was right in theory; but it was much too late. At sea, with about 400 ships left—seven squadrons of the line, some under strength—they were on paper still at least as strong as Octavian; what came in question was the legions to man them. In those civil wars in which no principle is at stake, only personal ambition, men easily change sides wholesale; the wars of Alexander's Successors supply many instances, and Antony's troops had seen Lepidus' legions go over. Antony had been beaten on land, and the men, weakened by disease and short rations, disheartened by

[1] Horace, *Epode* IX, 17–18; Servius on *Aen.* VI, 612, 'per quos est victoriam consecutus.'

the desertions of officers, and suspicious that they were really fighting for Cleopatra, were thinking that it was time to end it. Antony knew that all was not well, but believed that the common man would always follow him in battle.

On that coast in summer the wind in the morning normally comes in from the sea, but about mid-day shifts to the north-west and blows with some force. Antony knew that when he came out he would find Octavian's fleet to seaward of him, and he meant to use the wind when it shifted to turn their left and drive them southward (down wind) away from their camp; were they broken or dispersed, he could starve the camp out. As rowers could not pursue far, he took his sails on board, an unusual course. But in case the battle miscarried he had a second plan, probably known only to Cleopatra and Canidius (certainly Octavian knew nothing of it): they would break through to Egypt with what ships they could, and Canidius would bring the rest of the army back overland. The war-chest was accordingly shipped in secret upon some of Cleopatra's transports, which shows that Antony contemplated the possibility of not returning to his camp; otherwise he would not have risked the money going to the bottom. Probably what actually decided the troops was his order to take the sails; this, to them, obviously meant flight, and they were not going to Egypt to fight for Cleopatra.

The number of Antony's ships shows that he shipped some 35,000–40,000 legionaries[1], more than half his strength; Octavian shipped about the same force, eight legions and five cohorts. Agrippa commanded Octavian's fleet, Octavian being on a Liburnian. After stormy weather it fell calm on September 2nd, and Antony's fleet came out and lay on its oars, waiting for the wind to veer; he had six squadrons in line, with Cleopatra's squadron, manned by her own mercenaries and trustworthy, in the rear, to stop any preliminary attempts at desertion. He commanded the three squadrons of the right, 170 ships, with himself on the extreme right to lead the turning movement; he had two squadrons on the left and one in the centre, but when the right stretched out to turn Agrippa Cleopatra was probably meant to come up into the gap, completing the centre. Well out at sea Agrippa also lay on his oars, waiting for the wind; he was on his own left, to counter Antony's move and if possible turn him instead and cut him off from his camp. When the wind shifted, Antony and Agrippa raced to turn each other and the ends of their two lines

1 The 20,000 of tradition, like the 170 ships, refers only to the right wing, his own command.

met; here there was fighting, and Antony ultimately lost some ten to fifteen ships, while his flagship was grappled; what Agrippa lost is not recorded. At this point the three squadrons of Antony's centre and left backed water and returned to harbour[1]; the two inner squadrons of his right, unable to follow because of Cleopatra, raised their oars and surrendered; and Antony was left with nothing but his personal squadron on the extreme right, which was engaged, and Cleopatra's, which was isolated. He signalled Cleopatra to carry out their second plan; she hoisted sail and stood southward, waiting for him once she was out of enemy reach; Agrippa's right, which may have followed Agrippa, was nowhere near her. Antony could not extricate his flagship; he transferred himself to the first ship of the line which was free, and with the rest of his squadron, some 40 ships, followed Cleopatra. He boarded her flagship and sat on the prow with his head in his hands, forgetting even her and staring at the sea, but what he saw was not the sea but his ships returning to harbour; he knew now that all was over, for there was scarcely anyone in the world whom he could trust to follow him. From that hour he was a broken man.

Octavian could hardly realize what had happened, and remained at sea all night; but in the evening he had sent a despatch to Maecenas in Rome with the bare facts, and from this Horace wrote his ninth *Epode*, which records the treachery of Antony's fleet. Next morning however he took over the five surrendered squadrons, the '300 ships' of his *Memoirs*[2]; he burnt the larger part, as was Roman practice, and used their bronze beaks to decorate the monument raised where his camp stood and the temple of Divus Julius in Rome; the rest he ultimately stationed at Forum Juliense (Fréjus) as one of the Imperial fleets. Canidius tried to get the army away, but though it did not surrender for seven days it was only negotiating terms; finally Canidius had to fly for his life, and went to Antony in Egypt.

Octavian was hailed *Imperator* for the sixth time, and Cicero's son had the satisfaction of reading to the Senate his letter announcing Antony's defeat. Some of Antony's prominent adherents were put to death, but some were spared, including Sosius; his corn was distributed to a hungry Greece, and his legions broken up; the veterans from both armies were sent back to Italy and the

---

[1] Horace, *Epode* IX, 19–20; see especially Bentley *ad loc.* This must be the kernel of any reconstruction. Cf. Appian, *Bell. Civ.* v, 17, 68–71 on mass desertion during this period, which implies some striking instance.

[2] *Res Gestae* 3 is conclusive that these 300 were warships, not transports, as M. A. Levi has supposed (*Ottaviano capoparte*, II, p. 258).

rest distributed in different places, lest they should mutiny. Octavian sent Agrippa to Italy to aid Maecenas, who during the campaign had had to deal with a plot by Lepidus' son, and himself went to Athens, where he was initiated, and thence to Samos; but the veterans sent to Italy saw themselves excluded from the plunder of Egypt and became so unruly that in January Agrippa urgently begged him to return. At great personal risk from storms he crossed to Brundisium; he distributed what money he had secured or could obtain, and took land for his own troops from communities which had favoured Antony, some of the dispossessed owners being settled at Dyrrhachium and Philippi, and from other communities which became military colonies; but he really tided over the trouble by promising to pay both troops and landowners in full from the treasure of the Ptolemies, and they agreed to wait. He then returned to Asia, with the knowledge that his career and perhaps his life depended on securing that treasure.

VII. ALEXANDRIA

Though Antony was broken by the catastrophe of Actium, Cleopatra was not. She sailed into the harbour of Alexandria with head erect and ships garlanded for victory; it gave her the few hours she needed, and she seized and executed all who might have raised a revolution against her. Antony went to Cyrene, but his legions there joined Gallus, and he went on to Alexandria. Cleopatra began to make plans; they might sail to Spain, seize the silver mines, and play Sertorius; they might found a new realm in the Indian seas, beyond reach of Rome. This was feasible enough, and she drew some ships over the isthmus to Heroônpolis; but Malchus joyfully attacked and burnt them. She executed Artavasdes to secure the Median alliance, in case they could defend Egypt. But every plan depended on Antony's co-operation, for she had no thought of abandoning him, and Antony was useless; as men had deserted him, he would desert men, and he was living alone in a house near the shore, playing Timon the misanthrope. The first necessity was to restore him to some sort of sanity, and she tried to do this by the only way she knew of, a fresh round of feasts and amusements, under the shadow of death. He did return to the palace; but as he never attempted to collect his remaining legions and hold the enormously strong line of the Nile, which had so often saved Egypt from invasion[1], he must have told her that

[1] Vol. vi, pp. 469, 499, cf. 146, 149. This, and the fact that Octavian was not hailed *Imperator* when he entered Alexandria, show that there was no 'Alexandrian war.'

defence was impossible; the troops would merely go over, as the legions at Cyrene had done and as Didius and the Syrian legions soon did. One body of men alone remained pathetically loyal to him; some gladiators training at Cyzicus to make sport for him after his expected victory started for Egypt to help him, but Didius prevented them passing through Syria and they were destroyed later by Octavian's general Messalla. Antony might have been expected to imitate Cato and Brutus and commit suicide; the sequel shows that he meant to live while Cleopatra lived, perhaps with some vague idea that he might yet be of use to her.

Cleopatra had to decide whether she would defend Egypt by herself; she faced the situation with her usual courage. After her two bids for supreme power she was again what she had been at the start, a client-queen of Rome. That she must lose her throne, if not her life, she knew. But if she fought, her children would fall with her, for the result was certain; if however she acted as client-kings did act in such circumstances—as Deiotarus had done and Herod was doing—and put her crown into Octavian's hands, there was a chance that he might follow Roman custom and give it to one of her sons. She made her decision accordingly, and when Egypt offered to rise for her she forbade it[1], giving as her reason that she would not inflict useless suffering on her people; it may well be true, though her primary reason was her children.

In the summer of 30 Octavian approached Egypt through Syria, while Gallus occupied Paraetonium; Antony went to Paraetonium, but merely lost his 40 ships. He sent envoys to Octavian[2], offering to kill himself and spare him trouble if that would save Cleopatra; Octavian did not answer. The stories of Cleopatra's attempted treachery to him (what was there to betray?) are all demonstrably untrue[3]. Following her decision, she sent Octavian her sceptre and diadem, asking him to crown one of her sons. Officially, he ordered her to disarm. But secretly he assured her that she had nothing to fear; for she still had one piece to play, the treasure of the Ptolemies. On the strength of it he had made many promises in Italy both to veterans and landowners; he still had to face the claims of his victorious army; if he failed to secure the last great accumulation of wealth in the world, army, veterans,

---

[1] See p. 36, n. 3.

[2] We can neither check nor criticize the story that he first asked for his life, but it sounds incredible enough; he was no coward.

[3] Analysed, Tarn, *J.R.S.* xxi, 1931, p. 196. Also they imply an 'Alexandrian war' (p. 106, n. 1). See also, on other lines, F. Blumenthal, *Wiener Studien* xxxvi, 1915, pp. 92–7.

and landowners would all turn on him in earnest. Cleopatra had built herself a mausoleum, not yet completed, near the temple of Isis; as Octavian approached, she shut herself up in the upper room with her two women, Iras and Charmion, while in the lower part was stored the treasure, gold and jewels, ivory and spices, heaped round with inflammable matter; should he refuse the crown to one of her sons, she could light a royal pyre and bring him to ruin.

On July 31 his advance cavalry reached the suburbs. Antony could not die without one fight; he fell on them and scattered them. But that night a sound was heard in the city not made by man, interpreted as the god Dionysus leaving Antony[1]; and when next day he drew out his forces, his cavalry and Cleopatra's ships (*i.e.* her mercenaries) went over to Octavian, and Antony, returning to the city, heard that Cleopatra was already dead. That was all he had waited for, and he stabbed himself, but did not die at once; then he heard that she lived, and begged to be taken to her. With much effort the three women drew him in at the upper window of the mausoleum, and Cleopatra mourned him as Briseis had mourned Patroclus, tearing her face and breasts with her hands[2]; and he died, as he would have wished to die, in her arms. That same day, the first of the month afterwards called in commemoration by his name, August, Octavian entered Alexandria. He was not hailed *Imperator* by his troops, as he entered without resistance; but it was publicly recorded in the Fasti that on that day he saved Rome from the most terrible danger, that is, from Cleopatra[3]. He at once sent his friend Proculeius with orders to take her alive. She spoke with Proculeius through a grating and named her terms, the crown for one of her sons; but he saw the window and returned next day with Gallus, and while Gallus held her in talk at the grating he and others climbed in at the window; she tried to stab herself, but was seized, disarmed, and carried off to the palace, and Octavian was safe at last; he had the treasure. When it was taken to Rome, the standard rate of

[1] H. J. Rose, *Annals of Archeol. and Anthrop.* XI, p. 25, treats this merely as Octavian's propaganda, to slay Antony's god-head. But gods usually left a city before it fell; so Troy (*Aeneid* II, 351), Athens (vol. VII, p. 708), and Jerusalem (Josephus, *Bell. Jud.* VI [v, 3], 299; Tacitus, *Hist.* V, 13).

[2] *Iliad* XIX, 284. It was sometimes done in Greece; Plutarch, *Solon* 12, 5 and 21, 4; Lucian, περὶ πένθους 16. Cf. *Aeneid* XII, 606.

[3] *C.I.L.* I², *Fasti Fratrum Arvalium* p. 214 and *Fasti Amiterni* p. 244, under August 1: q.e.d. (quod eo die) Imp. Caes. rem public. tristiss. periculo liberavit. He was only at war with Cleopatra.

interest at once dropped from 12 to 4 per cent., and Octavian was easily able to satisfy all claims of the army and the veterans and pay for all the land he took, though all prices doubled, and, after executing many public works, still distribute a large surplus in bonuses to the people.

He allowed Cleopatra to bury Antony, and he only put to death four men: Turullius and Cassius of Parma, Caesar's murderers; Ovinius a senator, manager of Cleopatra's wool-mill; and Canidius. But he killed the two boys, the young Antony as his father's designated successor, and Ptolemy Caesar (whom his mother had tried to send to the Indian sea for safety) because of his name and parentage[1]; the world must not hold two Caesars. It was the final brutality of a brutal age, and he meant it to be final; if the world was to have peace, he had to make an end of all who might yet trouble it. But there was still Cleopatra. Doubtless Rome expected her death, but he seemingly objected to killing a woman, or even to being thought accessory to her suicide; when on her removal to the palace she began starving herself he stopped her by threatening to kill her children. Yet she must die, both for what she had done and because she knew too much; Cleopatra on some Aegean rock writing her *Memoirs* might have been awkward for the future Augustus. His problem was to induce her to kill herself in such a way that he could not be blamed[2]. Had he really meant to preserve her for his triumph he would have given her a Roman gaoler, with trustworthy women never quitting her; instead, she was left in the palace with her own people in charge of his freedman Epaphroditus, who knew his wishes; if necessary, a freedman could always be disavowed and executed, as Antigonus I had executed the women he employed to murder another Cleopatra (vol. VI, p. 494).

Cleopatra, her first impulsive attempts at suicide having failed, desired now before dying to be sure that there was no chance of the crown for one of her sons—why had Octavian neither killed nor imprisoned her? Octavian knew her motive through Proculeius; he knew too, as did everyone, that she had declared that she would never be led in his triumph; she was not going to be shamed before the Roman mob, like her sister Arsinoe. On these facts he could work. Which of them sought the interview between them is immaterial; it was necessary to both. It was more than the meeting of two great antagonists; two civilizations, soon to be fused, stood face to face in their persons. What passed was never known but to

[1] That they had been declared of age was not the cause of their deaths.
[2] See E. Groag, *Klio* XIV, 1914, pp. 61 *sqq.*

their two selves; our accounts are merely rhetorical exercises[1]. But Octavian could only say what, if it became known, would not inculpate him, and the sequel shows something of what happened. He told her that he meant to annex Egypt, which removed her last reason for living; and he gave her some vague assurances which he knew that she would see through and would conclude that she *was* to be led in his triumph. Still she did not die, for she wished to die in one particular way; Octavian became impatient, and word reached her, as from a friend, that in three days time he would take her to Italy. Then she asked his leave to make a libation at Antony's tomb; and over the tomb she prayed—many must have heard—that, as they had not been divided in life, so they might not be divided in death. It was not acting; they could not have done and suffered together what they had done and suffered without her having *some* feeling for him; perhaps she did love him dead whom she had never loved living. One of her people used the occasion to arrange for the asp[2], and a peasant brought it to the palace in a basket of figs[3]. If the story we have be true—if no snake was seen after her death and yet Octavian at once sent the snake-charmers called Psylli to suck the poison from the wound—then he knew beforehand of the sending of the asp; but he would hardly have given himself away so glaringly, and doubtless the story of the Psylli is untrue. On receiving the snake, Cleopatra wrote him a letter, asking to be buried beside Antony; and Epaphroditus, with the palace slaves at command, quitted his post and took the letter himself, the final proof that Octavian intended her to have her opportunity.

Of the manner of her death no doubt should now exist, for it is known why she used an asp[4]; the creature deified whom it struck, for it was the divine minister of the Sun-god, which raised its

---

[1] The story that she made love to him was invented, on well-known lines, to glorify his continence; see Tarn, *op. cit.* p. 197.

[2] The tradition remembered this; *de viris illustribus*, 86.

[3] The story that she had snakes in the palace belongs to the shameful invention (see Spiegelberg, next note), originating in an anonymous Roman poem, *Carmen de bello Actiaco* (see Bibliography), that she tried them on slaves to ascertain what was an easy death, *i.e.* that she was a coward, the accusation which moved Horace to speak out (*Odes*, I, 37, 21–end). The basis of the story may be that criminals in Alexandria were sometimes executed by snake-bite: Galen XIV, 237, Kühn; G. Lumbroso, *Aegyptus* III, p. 46.

[4] W. Spiegelberg, *Sitzb. d. Bay. Akad.* 1925, II, nr. 1, pp. 3–6. His explanation is unaffected by E. Herrmann's criticism, *Phil. Woch.* 1931, col. 1100. Conceivably the broken papyrus *P.S.I.* VII, 760 referred to such 'divine deaths.'

head on the crown of Egypt to guard the line of Re from harm. Once she was alone she arrayed herself in her royal robes and put the asp to her breast; the Sun-god had saved his daughter from being shamed by her enemies and had taken her to himself. With her died her two women; of how many queens is it written that their handmaids disdained to survive them? So Octavian's men found them when they broke in: Cleopatra dead on her couch of gold, with Iras dead at her feet, and Charmion, half-dead and trembling, trying to adjust the diadem upon her head. One of the men burst out 'Is this well done, Charmion?' 'Aye,' said she, ''tis very well.'

The ancient world had little pity for the fallen; and it had little for Cleopatra. The hatred which Romans felt for her can be read at large in their literature; but through that literature there runs too another feeling, publicly recorded in the Fasti, and if Octavian's propaganda directed the hate, it did not create the fear. Grant all her crimes and her faults; grant that she sometimes fought her warfare with weapons other than those used by men; nevertheless it was the victors themselves who, against their will, raised the monument which still witnesses to the greatness in her. For Rome, who had never condescended to fear any nation or people, did in her time fear two human beings; one was Hannibal, and the other was a woman.

CHAPTER IV

THE TRIUMPH OF OCTAVIAN

I. OCTAVIAN IN THE EAST

CLEOPATRA died late in August[1] 30 B.C.; she was 39 years old, and had reigned 22 years. Octavian granted her last wish and buried her beside Antony; their tomb is covered by the modern city and will never be disturbed. Before it Octavian set up statues of her brave handmaids, whose names became a proverb for faithfulness unto death. Octavia took her three children and brought them up with her own; the little Sun and Moon walked in Octavian's triumph. The boys are not heard of again, though legend made one of them the ancestor of Zenobia, but the girl was married to Juba II of Mauretania; she made a little Alexandria on the Moroccan coast, but with the murder of her son Ptolemy by Gaius the known line of the Ptolemies ended. Antony's memory was formally obliterated; his name was expunged from the Fasti (though Augustus restored it later), his statues were overthrown, the decrees of honour passed for him by Greek cities were destroyed; the Senate passed a decree that the names Marcus and Antonius should not again be conjoined, though it soon became a dead letter. A village in Lydia continued to honour his memory[2], and a tribe bearing his name remained at Prusias on the Hypius[3], and perhaps at Ephesus[4]; otherwise the East retained little trace of him, except for Polemo, who afterwards married his granddaughter Pythodoris and named their elder son, the future priest-king of Olba, Marcus Antonius Polemo[5], and

---

[1] See U. Wilcken, *Griechische Ostraka*, I, 787 *sqq.*; B. P. Grenfell and A. Hunt on *P. Oxy.* XII, 1453; V. Gardthausen, *Berl. Phil. Woch.* 1920, col. 615. The day cannot be fixed.

[2] *I.G.R.R.* IV, 1375.

[3] G. Perrot and E. Guillaume, *Exploration archéologique de la Galatie*, etc., pp. 29 no. 20, 32 no. 22.

[4] *S.E.G.* IV, 535; it is Ἀντωνιανῆς on the stone, Ἀρχ. Δελτ. VII, 113.

[5] G. F. Hill, *Num. Chron.* 1899, p. 181; Sir W. Ramsay, *Hastings' Dict. of the Bible*, II, 1899, p. 86 (independently). This identification decides, as against H. Dessau, *Eph. Ep.* IX, 1913, p. 691, that Pythodoris *was* Antony's granddaughter, as Mommsen supposed.

their daughter, who married Cotys of Thrace, Antonia Tryphaena. But we may perhaps recall, as a problem in heredity, that from him and the gentle Octavia were descended the emperors Gaius and Nero.

Octavian set up many monuments of Actium. He ascribed his success to Apollo of Actium, whose temple he enlarged; the local Actian festival was made quinquennial and equal in honour to the Olympian, as the Alexandrian Ptolemaieia had been; and to Apollo he dedicated his unique 'ten-ship trophy,' a ship from each of the classes of Antony's fleet, headed by his flagship. Near where his own camp had stood he founded Nicopolis, a Greek city into which he synoecized most of the cities of Acarnania and Epirus, including Pyrrhus' capital Ambracia, thus degraded to a village by the defeat of the second Pyrrhus. His coins show that he consciously posed as the counterpart of the great Antigonids, who had vanquished the great Ptolemies, Cleopatra's ancestors, as he had vanquished her—Demetrius who had defeated Ptolemy I at Salamis, and especially Antigonus Gonatas, who had slain Rome's enemy Pyrrhus and had humbled Ptolemy II at Cos. His coin[1] showing Neptune with one foot on the globe recalls Demetrius' Poseidon, while Nicopolis was a copy of Demetrius' unique synoecism of all Magnesia into Demetrias; more important are the coins[2] which show on a ship's prow a copy of the Victory of Samothrace, the statue set up by Antigonus Gonatas to commemorate Cos[3], while his ten-ship trophy was the nearest he could get to Gonatas' dedication of his flagship *Isthmia* to Apollo, since at Actium he had had no flagship himself. This attitude soon obscured the truth about Actium, for if it were another Cos it must be a great battle, and a great battle it became; the overthrow of the queen who had restored the empire of Ptolemy II must be no less glorious than had been the defeat of her prototype[4].

From Egypt Octavian travelled back through Syria and Asia Minor, and restored to the cities of Asia most of the works of art carried off by Antony. Before returning to Italy he had to settle the matter of Antony's client-kings, and the settlement he now made may be treated as a whole, without distinguishing what was

[1] Volume of Plates iv, 198, *i*.   [2] Volume of Plates iv, 198, *j*.
[3] F. Studniczka, *J.D.A.I.* xxxviii–ix, 1923–4, p. 125; W. W. Tarn, Vol. vii, p. 714, and *Hellenistic Civilisation*, 2nd ed. p. 285; B. Ashmole, Vol. vii, pp. 675 *sqq.*, and Vol. of Plates iii, p. 126. H. Thiersch, in *Pro Samothrake*, Wien S. B. 212, Abh. 1, 1930, pp. 21 *sqq.*, took the same view, but has now altered it; *Gött. Nachr.* 1931, p. 337.
[4] See further on this paragraph, Tarn, *J.R.S.* xxi, 1931, pp. 179 *sqq.*

done before and what after the occupation of Alexandria; his arrangements in Egypt are described elsewhere (chap. x), and his colonies in general belong to a later period. The Donations were naturally cancelled[1], and Cyprus and Cyrene again became Roman provinces; otherwise he made little change in Antony's arrangements. Only two petty dynasts were executed, and that not for favouring Antony but for murder: Adiatorix of Heraclea for a massacre of Romans in his territory, and Alexander of Emesa for inciting Antony to kill his brother Iamblichus; the tyrant Strato, removed from Amisus, was not Antony's man.

In Asia Minor most of the dynasts had come over to Octavian in time. Deiotarus of Paphlagonia, like Rhoemetalces in Thrace, kept his kingdom; Cleon, the one-time brigand chief of Mysia, was made priest-king of Zeus Abrettenios in Aeolis, with Abrettene and Myrene as his domain. The priest-king of Comana Pontica, Lycomedes, although Caesar's man, was dethroned and his office given either to Adiatorix' son Duteutus or to one Medeus, who had revolted against Antony in Mysia. Tarcondimotus of the Amanus had fallen fighting for Antony, and had been succeeded by his son Philopator I; Octavian deposed him and administered the Amanus as part of Cilicia till 20, when he restored Tarcondimotus' line. Of Antony's three important kings, Amyntas had rendered much service to the victor; his kingdom was enlarged by the addition of Isaura and Cilicia Tracheia, which had once been Roman territory but had been given by Antony to Cleopatra; he also took Derbe and Laranda from a local tyrant, Antipater, and till his death was Augustus' right hand. Archelaus remained as he was, though his kingdom was enlarged later. How Polemo made his peace is unknown; but Octavian recognized his value and left him Pontus, and though for a special reason he deprived him of Armenia Minor (p. 115) he gave him as compensation an indefinite right of expansion north-eastward, of which he was to make full use.

In Greece, beyond giving freedom to Lappa and Cydonia in Crete, who had declared for him before Actium, and founding Nicopolis, Octavian did little, but that little was significant; he rewarded Sparta, his one ally in Greece itself, by enlarging her territory and giving her the conduct of the Actian games, but he also made Eurycles tyrant, thus imitating Antony, who had also set up one city-tyrant, Boëthus, in half-oriental Tarsus.

In Syria, the Phoenician cities regained their freedom, as did Ascalon; Berytus (p. 100), which had revolted from Cleopatra

---

[1] *Res Gestae* 31–3; coin with *Asia recepta* (Volume of Plates iv, 200, *p*)

before Actium, received (probably later) an enormous extension of territory. Emesa, vacant by the death of Iamblichus, was administered as part of Roman Syria till 20, when Augustus restored Iamblichus' son[1]. In Chalcis, lately Cleopatra's, Chalcis itself became a free city, but Zenodorus, the son of the former dynast Lysanias, was allowed to rule in Abila and to rent his father's possessions; subsequently he recovered much of the kingdom, but he governed badly and his dominions ultimately passed to Herod. In Judaea, Hyrcanus had foolishly returned from Parthia, and after Actium Herod killed him lest Octavian should make him king. Herod himself had made no submission after Actium, and Octavian sent for him. Like Cleopatra, he removed his diadem and laid it before Octavian, but he was too wise to make excuses; he said that he had been faithful throughout to his benefactor Antony, and if Octavian would try him he would be equally faithful to him. Octavian replaced his diadem with his own hand, restored to him his balsam gardens, and after Cleopatra's death gave him her Galatian bodyguard and all of Palestine except Ascalon which had been hers. The philosopher and historian Nicolaus of Damascus, who had been tutor to Cleopatra's children, now went to Herod and showed with his pen all the zeal of the new convert.

Beyond the Euphrates Octavian did not intend to interfere; he did not even avenge on Artaxes of Armenia his massacre of Roman subjects, beyond detaining his brothers as hostages. Parthia might keep her eagles; when the pretender Tiridates fled to him in 30 he gave him asylum in Syria but refused him support and gave a friendly reception to envoys from King Phraates. But he received Antony's friend the Median king with kindness, restored to him his daughter Iotape, and gave him Armenia Minor, which he took from Polemo; for the Mede was now Artaxes' irreconcilable enemy and the right man to guard the frontier.

Apart from the Donations, Antony's more important dispositions west of the Euphrates had thus stood the test, and Octavian's gift or confirmation of territory once Roman to Amyntas, Cleon, and Polemo followed his precedents. It has become a commonplace that Antony's arrangements were bad. Octavian did not think so.

[1] Octavian did not forget his friends: for recently discovered epigraphic evidence of correspondence of Octavian with Rhosus referring to the services of one Seleucus see P. Roussel in *Syria*, xv, 1934, pp. 33*sqq.*

II. WARS IN THE WEST AND THE BALKANS[1]

While men's eyes had been fixed upon the East and what was happening there, the western half of the Empire had been under the guidance of Maecenas; thanks to his tact and vigilance the administration went smoothly, and such an affair as the conspiracy of young Lepidus (p. 106) was easily suppressed. Some minor wars were necessary upon distant frontiers: in spite of Agrippa's campaigns in 39 Gaul was not yet completely settled in north and west, so Nonius Gallus had to punish an outbreak of the Treveri, while C. Carrinas put down the Morini and drove back the Suebi who had crossed the Rhine[2]: in 28 B.C. the Aquitanian tribes revolted and apparently invaded the old *Provincia*, and Messalla Corvinus won successes in this western region that earned him a triumph[3]. Britain was left unmolested, for Octavian had more serious problems to deal with, though rumours were abroad that in time he would renew and complete the enterprise of Caesar (p. 793). In Spain the beginning of the Provincial Era in 38 B.C. may have recorded the hope of peace, but within ten years there was a revolt of the north-western tribes, Cantabri, Vaccaei and Astures. These were crushed by the efficient Statilius Taurus, and from Spain too C. Calvisius Sabinus and Sextus Appuleius made good their claim to triumphs in 28 and 27. Thus Rome saw a succession of such spectacles, for in addition to Carrinas and Sabinus L. Autronius triumphed in 28 from Africa, and Messalla celebrated his triumph in the following year. The proceeds of the spoils were used on great public works, both on buildings and the repairing of roads (p. 133). Yet few of these campaigns can have roused more than passing interest in a Rome that was busied with greater issues; one, however, demands longer notice, not only on account of the importance of the operations for the defence of the North-Eastern frontier, but also because of its political consequences in Rome itself.

---

[1] The only continuous source of value for this period is Dio LI–LIII. Velleius Paterculus, Strabo, the *Res Gestae* and Suetonius' *Augustus* contribute occasional items.

[2] Possibly Gallus was acting as subordinate to the senior Carrinas; E. Ritterling, *Fasti des röm. Deutschland*, p. 4 (note by E. Groag).

[3] Appian, *Bell. Civ.* IV, 38, 162: Tibullus I, 7, 3–12, II, 1, 33: possibly the addition (mentioned by Strabo IV, 177) of fourteen tribes between the Loire and the Garonne to the territory of Aquitania took place at this time; see J. P. Postgate in *Class. Rev.* XVII, 1903, p. 112.

When Octavian in 30 B.C. entered upon his fourth consulship he had as his colleague M. Licinius Crassus, who tempered by prudence the ancient Republican tradition of his family: originally attached to Sextus Pompeius, he had joined Antony after Naulochus, and then deserted him to serve Octavian before Actium was fought[1]. He was undoubtedly a capable commander, and in the summer of 30 he was dispatched with an army of at least four legions to Macedonia, a province that badly needed a general. Its northern boundaries were always exposed to attack, and though the threat of a united Dacia had faded away (p. 84), there still remained the possibility of raids by the various petty Thracian and Getic chieftains; graver still was the threat from a migrating Germanic tribe, the Bastarnae, who some thirty years back had appeared in the region of the lower Danube and had inflicted near Istros a serious defeat (involving the loss of some Roman eagles) upon the unlucky C. Antonius[2]. The province offered obvious opportunities to an ambitious governor which Crassus was not slow to seize: so long as the Bastarnae crossed the Danube merely to harry Moesi, Triballi or Dardani, barbarian might kill barbarian, but when their masses broke over the Haemus range and attacked the Denthelete Thracians (in the valley of the Upper Struma), whose blind King Sitas was an ally of the Roman People, he had justification for interference. Early in 29 he drove them out of Sitas' territory towards the north-west and then—taking a leaf out of Caesar's diaries—when they sent him an embassy he made it drunk and so succeeded in entrapping the main body near the river Cebrus[3]. A fearful slaughter followed, in which Crassus had the distinction of killing the Bastarnian king, Deldo, with his own hand. Helped by a Getic chieftain, Roles, he next stormed a strong place occupied by some fugitive Bastarnae; the remainder of the year was spent in savage fighting against various tribes of the Moesi and in repelling attacks from Thracians who were supposed to be friendly. Enough had been done for the year, and he disposed his troops in winter-quarters: Octavian,

---

[1] Dio LI, 4, 3; 23–27; these last five chapters are the main source for the history of these campaigns. For modern work see A. von Premerstein, *Die Anfänge der Provinz Moesiens*, in *Jahreshefte*, I, 1898, Beiblatt, col. 158, and V. Pârvan, *Getica*, pp. 85–90.

[2] Dio XXXVIII, 10, 3; LI, 26, 5.

[3] Dio LI, 23, 5 and 24, 1 (reading Σελετικὴν and τῷ Κέβρῳ). The river Cebrus is probably to be identified with the Bulgarian Tzibritza, which flows into the Danube at Cibar, not far east of Lom Palanka; for another view see Pârvan, *op. cit.* p. 87, note 2.

perhaps in the late spring at Corinth, bestowed upon Roles the title of *socius et amicus*; the Senate awarded Crassus the honour of a triumph, and cities such as Athens offered him thanks and dedications[1]. In the next year he displayed as great activity: he drove back fresh bands of the Bastarnae who ventured to attack Sitas and his Dentheletae, routed the tribes of the Maedi and Serdi in the north-west, overran nearly all Thrace, helped Roles to counter the attack of a Getic chief, Dapyx, capturing finally the fort to which he had fled for refuge, and, advancing farther north into the realm of a chieftain Zyraxes, he fell on a strong place called Genucla; the fall of this brought with it the recovery of the standards that C. Antonius had lost[2]. Finally he turned westward and broke the power of the remnants of the Moesi.

The Triumphal Fasti record the celebration of a triumph by Crassus on July 4, 27 B.C. 'ex Thracia et Geteis.' He had shown great energy and rapidity and done much to restore the prestige of the Roman name. In two years he had repulsed the Bastarnae, broken the power of the Getae, and taught the wild tribes of the North-West that Rome would punish those who attacked her allies. Though the boundaries of Macedonia were not advanced and though a province of Moesia was not to be created for some years yet (p. 367 *sq.*), the frontiers were protected by various client-kingdoms, such as those of Sitas and Roles, and Crassus had increased the power of the kingdom of the Odrysian Thracians by giving it charge of the holy place of Dionysus, which had formerly belonged to the rival tribe of the Bessi: the Greek cities of the Black Sea, now that the dreaded Getic power was humbled, would look to the Romans or their allies as protectors. Crassus had every reason to be satisfied with his achievements and the triumph that he claimed and obtained was well deserved. But his request for another and a rarer honour met with a different fate; to understand why this was we must retrace our steps and see what had been happening in Rome since the year 30.

---

[1] Dessau 8810. Octavian probably received his seventh acclamation as *Imperator* now (*C.I.L.* VI, 783).

[2] Dio LI, 26, 5. The fact that Antonius had lost his standards near Istros, and that Crassus passed the cave Ceiris (in the region of the modern Gura Dobrogei) before reaching Genucla, shows it was a river fort in the Northern Dobrudja: Pârvan, *op. cit.* p. 89. The recovery of these standards is ignored in the *Res Gestae*.

III. THE FIRST CITIZEN

On January 1, 29 B.C., Octavian entered on his fifth consulship at his winter-quarters in Samos, where he was completing his re-organization of the East; that done, he set out for home. He passed through Corinth, and landed in early summer at Brundisium; ill-health compelled him to rest for some days in Campania, and at Atella Virgil recited the *Georgics* to him. Arrived in Rome he was at length able to celebrate—on August 13, 14 and 15—amid all the pomp and pageantry that the mind of Rome could devise, a triple triumph for Illyricum, Actium and Egypt.

> 'at Caesar, triplici invectus Romana triumpho
> moenia, dis Italis votum immortale sacrabat,
> maxima ter centum totam delubra per urbem.
> laetitia ludisque viae plausuque fremebant;
> omnibus in templis matrum chorus, omnibus arae;
> ante aras terram caesi stravere iuvenci.
> ipse sedens niveo candentis limine Phoebi
> dona recognoscit populorum aptatque superbis
> postibus; incedunt victae longo ordine gentes,
> quam variae linguis, habitu tam vestis et armis[1].'

A few days later came the solemn dedication of the temple of Divus Julius and the opening of the Curia Julia. The treasures of Egypt and the spoils of war were used, in accordance with tradition, upon great public works, which were carried out during the ensuing years in the capital and in Italy: the Via Flaminia was reconditioned as far as Ariminum, eighty-two temples were rebuilt[2], and on the Palatine the white marble temple of Apollo, Octavian's guardian deity, with its adjoining libraries for Greek and Latin books, could be hurried to completion and was dedicated on October 9, 28 B.C. Apart from the adornment of Rome Octavian was able to put his enormous riches to even more popular uses: towards his triumph the thirty-five tribes of the city had offered him a thousand pounds of gold each as *aurum coronarium* (a usage which had apparently begun with the triumph of L. Antonius in 41)[3]; Octavian not only refused to take it, but

[1] Virgil, *Aen.* VIII, 714–723.
[2] *Res Gestae* 20. Dio LIII, 2, 5 adds that he encouraged the descendants of the original builders to carry out restoration; doubtless Octavian helped them materially, just as he had helped Domitius Calvinus (p. 89).
[3] Dio XLVIII, 4, 6 records the offer to L. Antonius: it was an extension of the custom whereby, when a general triumphed, the communities of his province were expected to present him with gold crowns, and Octavian set his face against such an innovation.

distributed a handsome donative to the people, and during this and the following year lavished games and shows and made a fourfold distribution of corn. He paid in full all debts that he owed, and forgave all arrears of taxation; a year later all evidence for such arrears was publicly destroyed. Money was plentiful, interest dropped to one-third of the usual rate, impoverished Senators were helped by generous presents, and those who had formerly supported Antony were reassured by Octavian's declaration that all incriminating correspondence had been burnt: confidence began slowly to return to a world shaken by twenty years of civil war.

Among the many tasks facing the victor one had already been taken in hand, the reduction of the immense number of legions—some sixty—of which he had become master. In the years immediately following 30 B.C. over one hundred thousand veterans, with full bounties paid, were disbanded and either sent to older foundations or settled in new colonies, both in Italy and the provinces. The sites were selected with care: thus some veterans of Antony were settled at Bononia, a town of which he had been patron and which remained loyal to his memory[1]; Carthage, which had suffered at the hands of Lepidus, was repeopled; twenty-eight colonies in Italy owed their existence to Octavian, and in the provinces such towns as Acci Gemella in Spain, Parium in Mysia, Antioch by Pisidia and Berytus in Syria also received veterans as settlers. And these were only the first few of a carefully planned scheme, whereby not only were the claims of the soldiers met but mountainous and wilder regions, such as Western Spain or Pisidia, could be guarded and held in check[2]. Fair payment, as after Naulochus, for the land required was made to the municipalities concerned; the total cost of the settlement over a long period of years ran into hundreds of millions of sesterces[3]. Those soldiers who were retained in service—certainly not more than twenty-eight[4] legions—received gratuities after Octavian's triumph and were employed upon works of public utility, such as cleansing and deepening the canals in Egypt or making *levées* and embankments to curb the turbulent course of the Adige near Este[5].

[1] Suetonius, *Aug.* 17, 2; Pliny, *N.H.* XXXIII, 83.
[2] See the articles in *P.W.*, *s.v. Coloniae* (E. Kornemann) and *Legio* (E. Ritterling), for a full list of places settled and discussion of doubtful points.
[3] *Res Gestae* 16.   [4] See below, p. 221.
[5] *C.I.L.* V, 2603, as completed by *Not. degli Scavi*, XII, 1915, p. 137 and p. 141.

But disbandment was comparatively simple, granted the politic vision of Octavian: it was a question of time and money only, and he now had plenty of both. Far more complicated was the problem of his future position in the State; his victory, like that of Sulla or Caesar before him, had effectively placed the State within his control, and the honours and privileges that Senate and people crowded upon him at the slightest provocation had placed him on an eminence over-topping even theirs. We may agree with Dio that there is no need to dwell upon the decreeing of triumphal arches, images, games and holidays, but two honours of greater significance, belonging to the year 30, must be noticed here. The Senate enacted that in future priests and people should offer prayers for the saviour of the State and that libations should be poured to him at all banquets, an act that set him apart from other men[1], and the tribunician sacrosanctity granted him six years previously, and which he had had bestowed upon Livia and Octavia (p. 64), was now transformed into something more positive. Octavian was given a power and competence equal to the tribunes in *auxilii latio* (and presumably in *coercitio* and *intercessio*), and indeed more than equal, since his *auxilii latio* was extended to one mile beyond the city boundary and he received some form of appellate jurisdiction[2]. The full possibilities and significance of this *tribunicia potestas* were only to become apparent later (see further below, p. 139 *sq.*); here we need only admire the sure instinct that Octavian displayed in this new constitutional expedient. The tribunician board had been the only body to offer effective opposition to Caesar; as early as 44 Octavian may have sought to be elected tribune (p. 11), and as late as 32 it was the veto of Nonius Balbus that saved him from the attack of the Antonian consuls; now at one stroke he placed himself at the head, as it were, of the tribunes and beyond their reach[3], and also established the principle that the powers of an office could be separated from the title and conferred upon a person not holding that office, just as two years later censorial power was conferred on two men who were not censors.

On January 1, 29 B.C. the Senate confirmed all Octavian's *acta*,

---

[1] Dio LI, 19, 6 and 7: cf. *C.I.L.* IV, 5285.

[2] Dio, *loc. cit.* 'The Senate voted τὸν Καίσαρα τήν τε ἐξουσίαν τὴν τῶν δημάρχων διὰ βίου ἔχειν, καὶ τοῖς ἐπιβοωμένοις αὐτὸν καὶ ἐντὸς τοῦ πωμηρίου καὶ ἔξω μέχρις ὀγδόου ἡμισταδίου ἀμύνειν, ὃ μηδενὶ τῶν δημαρχούντων ἐξῆν, ἔκκλητόν τε δικάζειν κτλ.'

[3] In 29 he prevented a tribune elect, Q. Statilius, from proceeding to office, by what means we are not told, Dio LII, 42, 3.

and a few weeks later the news of the successful negotiations with Parthia produced a fresh crop of decrees: the temple of Janus was to be closed and the long-neglected ceremony of the Augurium Salutis revived. The meaning of these resolutions was unmistakable. Octavian had saved the Roman State, hence the dedication to him by Senate and People in this year of an arch RE PUBLICA CONSERVATA[1]: his final victory had put an end to all wars at home and abroad, an end which was symbolized by the closing of Janus; lastly, Octavian was himself an augur so that it was fitting that the college of augurs should ordain prayers for salvation for the State in the year in which its saviour returned to Italy[2]. There were not lacking other marks of his pre-eminence: the Senate voted that his name should be included in the litany of the Salii, the consul Valerius Potitus offered public sacrifices and vows on his behalf—a thing unprecedented—and at the triumph in August the magistrates and officials instead of guiding the *triumphator* into the city, as heretofore, followed behind his chariot. The praenomen of *Imperator* which Octavian (originally perhaps in answer to Sextus Pompeius' arrogation of the praenomen *Magnus* to himself) had been employing unofficially for some ten years he now assumed officially[3]; at the request of the Senate he was empowered not only to add as many members as he pleased to the priestly colleges, but also (under a Lex Saenia late in 30 B.C.) to create at his own choice new patrician families—for the ranks of these had been terribly thinned by years of civil war and proscriptions—and so aid in keeping alive the ceremonies and rites upon which the well-being of Rome depended.

Yet this accumulation of honours, which might have glutted the vanity of a Pompey, was a danger-signal to the more sober mind of Octavian, for he could not but remember that it was up this same dizzy path that Caesar had been led, to fall more fatally. However absolute his power—and it was no untruth when he

[1] Dessau 81.

[2] See especially J. Gagé in *Mél. d'arch. et d'hist.* XLVII, 1930, p. 138. On the Augurium Salutis see Dessau 9337, and G. Costa in *Bull. Arch. Com.* XXXVIII, 1910, p. 118; R. Cagnat in *C. R. Ac. Inscr.* 1911, p. 49, and F. Blumenthal in *Hermes*, XLIX, 1914, p. 246.

[3] Dio LII, 41, 3. The earliest evidence for use of this praenomen is provided by coins of Agrippa in Gaul, *c.* 39/38 (Volume of Plates iv, 198, *k, l*): the entry in the Capitoline Triumphal Fasti (*C.I.L.* I[1], i, p. 50), which gives the title to Octavian in 40, is subsequent to the foundation of the Principate and not so trustworthy; cf. L. Ganter, *Die Provinzialverwaltung...*, p. 61 *sq.* See also K. Mras in *Wiener Studien*, XXV, 1903, p. 288 and A. Rosenberg in *P.W.*, *s.v. Imperator*, cols. 1144 *sqq.*

claimed later that the State had been in his hand—it was essential to its continuance that he should not shock Republican tradition or sentiment; there must be nothing to point to a second Ides of March. On the contrary, all appearances indicated a gradual return to stability and the customary forms of government. In the year 28 he entered upon his sixth consulship, with the faithful Agrippa as his colleague; for the first time in twenty years two consuls held office together in the capital for the full twelve months, and Octavian shared the twenty-four lictors that accompanied him with his colleague so that each possessed the traditional twelve; at the end of his term of office he could take the customary oath that he had preserved the laws, a claim that was echoed by coins of the year with the legend LIBERTATIS P. R. VINDEX. With Agrippa he held a census of the whole people (a ceremony neglected since 70 B.C.), and carried out a revision of the list of the Senate, which had been swollen to an unwieldy number; it was now purged of its less worthy members, reduced from a body of 1000 to some 800, and Octavian himself was enrolled as Princeps Senatus.[1]

Yet while a return to constitutional correctness was foreshadowed by these proceedings there were signs of innovation. When Octavian and Agrippa carried out the census they had not been elected censors, nor did they act by virtue of any power originally inherent in the consulship; they received something new, a special grant of *censoria potestas*[2]—that is the conferment of the powers of the censorship upon persons not holding the office—and this development of the conception of *potestas* was soon to be put to important uses. And whereas formerly the *lectio Senatus* had always preceded the holding of a census, on this occasion it was performed while the census was already in progress. And though Octavian was nominally consul, coupled with a colleague of equal authority, the honours and privileges heaped upon him and the enormous prestige that he enjoyed proclaimed him something far higher than the ordinary Republican magistrate. The praenomen of *Imperator* was a perpetual reminder of the victories he had won, his tenure of the augurate and other

---

[1] In the previous year Octavian (perhaps through a *Senatus consultum*), in order to secure full attendances, forbade Senators to leave Italy without his permission; Dio LII, 42, 6.

[2] The statement of Dio LII, 42, that Octavian was censor with Agrippa is contradicted by an entry in the Fasti of Venusia (Dessau 6123), 'censoria potest(ate) lustrum fecer(unt),' upon which see Mommsen, *Res Gestae*[2], pp. 36–38.

priesthoods pointed to him as upholder and honourer of the old Roman religion, and the inclusion of his name in the Salian litany suggested something more than mortal. Like Romulus he had been favoured by the sight of twelve vultures when taking his first auspices, like Romulus he had chosen and created patrician families, the very stars that presided over his birth—so it began to be rumoured—were the same as those that had heralded Romulus' greatness[1]; he was the heaven-sent restorer and second founder of Rome. 'Quis populo Romano obtulit hunc divinum adulescentem deus?' Though he was nominally a consul and no more, in reality the State was his to remould as he wished.

The need for some remoulding was obvious from the tragical history of the past hundred years. For such a task Octavian had the advantage of a prestige greater than all his predecessors save only Caesar, and unlike Caesar he had now no active opposition to fear. Civil war and proscription had decimated the older Optimate families, the rest of Italy yearned for peace and stability, it mattered little under what name. But that was the negative side merely: no man can win and retain supreme power in a nation by the simple slaughtering of all opponents; he must be able to convince a majority of supporters that he has something definite and acceptable to offer them. This is what Octavian had done. Though his adoption by Caesar linked him to the noblest and oldest families in Rome, he had none of the narrowness that marred many a Roman aristocrat. By birth, upbringing and sentiment he was Italian, and had appealed to the deepest instincts and traditions of the population of Italy, which had stood steadfast for Caesar; that had brought him first the co-operation and fidelity of a band of able and devoted friends, and finally the overwhelming response of the *coniuratio totius Italiae*. But the very success of his appeal and the conscious sentiment it had aroused fettered him and circumscribed the area of political conceptions in which he could move; powerful though he might be he could not impose his will except in so far as his will interpreted the desires of the Italian people. In consequence it might be not unfairly urged against him that he was compelled to adopt a programme that was too definitely 'Western' in its outlook, and which placed Italy and things Italian too much in the centre of the stage.

[1] On the natal stars of Romulus and Octavian see Anton, *de sideribus Augusti nataliciis quae coniicienda videantur*, Halle Programm, 1861: A. Bouché-Leclercq, *L'Astrologie grecque*, p. 368: A. E. Housman, *Manilius, Augustus, Tiberius, Capricornus and Libra*, in *Class. Quart.* VII, 1913, p. 109.

For the time being, however, he had made no public decision as to the future form of the government, content with holding the consulship yearly and with the prestige and powers he possessed. How long this might have continued cannot be said, but an incident arising out of the victorious campaigns of Crassus almost certainly forced him to declare himself and accelerated a settlement. For his prowess in killing the Bastarnian king Deldo Crassus had claimed the right to deposit *spolia opima* in the temple of Juppiter Feretrius on the Capitol, the restoration of which had been begun by Octavian in 32 B.C. It was an honour that tradition granted to three Romans only, Romulus, A. Cornelius Cossus and M. Claudius Marcellus, the hero of Clastidium, for though an ordinary soldier might be awarded *spolia opima* for killing an enemy leader the privilege of dedicating the spoils in the temple of Feretrius had been by custom reserved for those generals who were fighting under their own auspices. But the awkwardness for Octavian of such a claim at such a moment needs no underlining; the new Romulus could ill afford to have a rival in military glory. To the objection, however, that the victory had been gained, not under Crassus' auspices but under Octavian's, Crassus was able to find an answer in the precedent of Cossus, who according to accepted tradition had been simply a *tribunus militum* and no independent commander when he was granted the privilege. It was therefore fortunate for Octavian that during the restoration of the temple of Feretrius, the actual spoils dedicated by Cossus were discovered, together with an inscription showing that at the time he was consul and not *tribunus militum*, and this new evidence was enough to bar Crassus' claim[1]. Though he was allowed to celebrate a well-merited triumph on July 4, 27 B.C., the title of *Imperator* was withheld[2]; in the ensuing years his services were no longer required.

But this occurrence and the negotiations in connection with it revealed clearly that some form of settlement was pressing, and that it was essential that in any such settlement the legions and

---

[1] The account given here is based on the article by H. Dessau, *Livius und Augustus*, in *Hermes*, XLI, 1906, p. 148, who first saw the connection between Livy IV, 19 and the claims of Crassus. But it would be rash to draw the inference that Octavian either forged or misinterpreted the evidence which came to light so luckily for him; on this point see above, Vol. VII, p. 507 *sq.*

[2] The fact that Crassus is called αὐτοκράτωρ (= *imperator*), in Dessau 8810, is merely proof of Athenian goodwill, and cannot be urged against Dio LI, 25, 2.

their commanders (or the greater part of them) should be under the acknowledged control of Octavian. In the next year, 27 B.C., he was to be consul for the seventh time, with Agrippa again as his colleague; there is some slight evidence that the work of reform had already been begun and that laws encouraging marriage and penalizing celibacy, fore-runners in fact of his later social legislation, were passed in this year, only to meet with such opposition that they had to be rescinded[1]. But their date and content, if indeed they happened, cannot be determined with any certainty, whereas Dio does record for us an important decree that met with universal favour: 'since Octavian had given many illegal and unjust orders during the strife of the civil wars, and especially during the triumvirate with Antony and Lepidus, he annulled all these in one edict, fixing his sixth consulship as the limit of their validity' (LIII, 2, 5). Details of this comprehensive measure are unfortunately lacking; it is possible that some grants already made had to be iterated in order to secure their validity[2], and we can safely infer that all disabilities attaching to the children of the proscribed and similar inequities were removed. But its general intent and effect cannot be doubtful; it was a fresh step towards that restoration of constitutional government that Octavian had promised after the victory at Naulochus. In sixteen years he had avenged his father's death and attained to more than his honours, he had surmounted all opposition and made himself master of the Mediterranean world. If he was to bring lasting peace, if he was to be called (as he longed to be called) 'the creator of the best constitution,' he must attack soon a problem that had baffled Sulla and Caesar. The wars were over; the period of constructive statesmanship could begin.

---

[1] P. Jörs, *Die Ehegesetze des Augustus*, pp. 3–28. The matter is, however, very doubtful. See below, p. 441, n. 3.

[2] *C.I.L.* x, 8038 (= Bruns *Fontes*[7], 80): Vespasian confirms to the Vanacini in Northern Corsica 'beneficia tributa vobis ab divo Augusto post septimum consulatum.' Recently discovered evidence reveals that a Lex Munatia Aemilia of 42 B.C. had authorized the Triumvirs to grant not only citizenship but exemption from taxation (see Roussel, *loc. cit.* pp. 34, 45), and these grants presumably held good.

CHAPTER V

THE *PRINCEPS*

I. THE RESTORATION OF THE REPUBLIC

THE stage was now set for the culminating act of the drama, to which the measures described in the closing pages of the previous chapter had been designed to lead. The coins of the year 28 had as their legend LIBERTATIS P. R. VINDEX, and gestures such as the cancellation of the illegal acts of the Triumvirate, which were declared to have validity only until the close of the year, seemed to illustrate the motto. The Senate, purged of its less worthy elements by the *lectio* carried out by Augustus and Agrippa, had been made once more fit to play its proper part in the constitution; and it has been shown (p. 125 *sq.*) that circumstances made it necessary for Octavian to clarify and define his position without further delay. This he did in January, 27 B.C.

Dio tells us that before taking the decisive step he prepared his more intimate associates for what was to come. He goes further, and represents him as seeking the advice of Agrippa and Maecenas, into whose mouths he puts speeches which form a strange contrast. The rhetorical artifice by which two alternative policies are clothed in the forms of oratory was a familiar one, not unknown to Dio[1]: but what is remarkable is that while Agrippa, taking the side of democracy, gives a rehash of the familiar commonplaces of Greek political writing, the speech attributed to Maecenas is a detailed study of the institutions of the Principate as they had developed by Dio's own time, and embodying some ideas which had not even then found concrete form. As such it is well worthy of close study; but it need not concern us here. Nor can we regard as historical the speech which Dio[2] puts into the mouth of Octavian himself

Note. The principal source of evidence for this and the two following chapters is the *Res Gestae* of Augustus himself. Velleius Paterculus, who wrote under Tiberius, contributes some details of importance, and the life of Augustus by Suetonius is useful in parts. The only continuous narrative is that of Dio, who doubtless used the work of Livy (which went down to 9 B.C.) and other good sources; but his statements on constitutional matters are often lacking in precision. The evidence of inscriptions is often of value, especially with regard to the Imperial Administration.

[1] See Schwartz in *P.W. s.v.* Cassius Dio, col. 1719.   [2] LIII, 3–10.

when he presented himself before the Senate at the opening of his
seventh consulship and declared his intention of laying down the
supreme power. That he should have claimed—not once but
twice—that while Caesar had refused the monarchy offered him,
he himself had laid aside that which had been conferred on him
and so 'transcended the deeds of man,' is foreign to all that we
know of his sober and dignified style. But we need not doubt
the mixed feelings with which those of the senators who were not
in the secret heard Octavian's announcement, whether they believed it sincere or not, and that even while his speech was being
read, cries of protest were heard begging him to retain his supreme
power, so that thus the way was prepared for a settlement which
had the appearance of being forced upon a reluctant ruler.

Octavian had placed at the free disposal of the Senate and
people all the provinces which were being administered by his
subordinates[1]; and he now consented to undertake the administration of a certain definite group—an arrangement for which, of
course, there were many precedents in the period following Sulla's
dictatorship. In 55 B.C. the greater part of the Roman dominions
had been parcelled out into three great military commands—the
Northern Command (the Gauls) under Caesar, the Western
Command (Spain) under Pompey, and the Eastern Command
(Syria) under Crassus[2]; and the effect of the act of January 27 B.C.
was to concentrate these (together with Egypt) in the hands of
Octavian and therewith to confer upon him the command of
almost the whole of the Roman army. This vast *provincia* he was
to hold for a period of ten years, and the Senate's allocation was
no doubt confirmed by a *lex*, such as those to which Caesar and
Pompey had owed their exceptional positions[3]. It is true that he
continued to hold the consulship in Rome, while governing the
several *provinciae* committed to him by means of his subordinate
legati: but this was not without precedent, for Pompey had been
in the same position in 52 B.C.[4]: and the personal inspections (and
military operations) which he carried out in East and West showed
that he regarded his special commission as one which entailed the
duty of direct supervision when such seemed to be called for. And
it was a Commission derived from the Senate and People of Rome.

In this sense he described the act of settlement in the following
terms in the summary of his *Res Gestae* (34) completed just before

[1] 'Redditaque est omnis populo provincia nostro' Ovid, *Fast.* 1, 589.
[2] Vol. IX, p. 617.
[3] Dio explicitly says (LIII, 12, 1) τὴν ἡγεμονίαν τούτῳ τῷ τρόπῳ καὶ παρὰ
τῆς γερουσίας τοῦ τε δήμου ἐβεβαιώσατο.   [4] Vol. IX, p. 626.

his death and preserved to us in the 'Monument of Ancyra[1].'
'In my sixth and seventh consulships, when I had put an end to
the civil wars, having acquired supreme power over the Empire
by universal consent, I transferred the Republic from my own
authority to the free disposal of the Senate and People of Rome.'
In the entry in the *Fasti Praenestini* (which, as is known, were
compiled by Verrius Flaccus, and are therefore specially authori-
tative) concerning the honours voted to Octavian by the Senate,
the ground is given in the words 'quod rem publicam populo
Romano restituit,' and the phrase is echoed in the *Laudatio Turiae*
in the words 'pacato orbe terrarum, restituta republica.' Writing
in the next reign, Velleius Paterculus waxes eloquent over the
restoration of constitutional forms and closes with the words
'prisca illa et antiqua rei publicae forma revocata[2].' We may take
it, therefore, that Octavian was determined that there should be
nothing in the constitution as remodelled by him—by a process
which we have still to trace—which should prevent a Roman of
the Romans, such as he himself was, from continuing to describe
it by the simple but pregnant designation hallowed by the tradition of centuries—*res publica*. In an Edict[3], which it is unfortunately impossible to date precisely, he wrote: 'Ita mihi
salvam ac sospitem rem publicam sistere in sua sede liceat atque
eius rei fructum percipere quem peto, ut optimi status auctor
dicar et moriens ut feram mecum spem, mansura in vestigio suo
fundamenta rei publicae quae iecero.' The words might have
been spoken by the most fervent upholder of the great Republican tradition; and it has been pointed out with justice that
they contain echoes of the language of Cicero himself[4].

Nor did Octavian accept any title inconsistent with his position
as the chief citizen of a free State. The evidence of the Calendars
seems to show that while the 'restoration of the Republic' and the
reassignment of the provinces took place on January 13, it was
not until three days later that the Senate decreed that as a recompense for his self-denying act various honours should be
granted to him. The door-posts of his house were decked with
laurel; a wreath of oak-leaves—the *corona civica* bestowed on a

---

[1] See Appendix on Sources (p. 870 *sq.*). Various theories have been put
forward regarding the dates at which its several portions were composed, but
these need not concern us. That the chapter from which the quotation in the
text is taken belongs to an early draft seems to the present writer a gratuitous
assumption.   [2] II, 89, 4.   [3] Suetonius, *Aug.* 28.
[4] See A. Oltramare, 'La réaction cicéronienne et les débuts du principat,' in
Rev. des ét. lat. 1932, p. 58.

soldier who saved his comrade's life in battle—was placed above
the door in token that he had preserved the lives of his fellow-
citizens (*ob cives servatos*, as the coins have it), and a golden shield
was set up in the Senate-house with an inscription commemorating
his 'valour, clemency, justice and piety[1]'; and above all, he was
given the name by which he was to be known in brief by succeeding generations—augustus[2]. Sulla had assumed the title of
'the Fortunate'; Pompey was to all Romans 'the Great'; it was
left for Octavian to discover an epithet which raised him in some
degree above ordinary human standards. Dio puts this in so many
words—'as being something more than human[3]'; and it has been
noted that in the early books of Livy, which were composed, as
it would seem, in the years following the settlement, the adjective
augustus is several times contrasted with *humanus*. But it had
other connotations. Suetonius tells us that a suggestion was considered and rejected, that he should take the name of Romulus in
token that he was the second founder of the city; but Romulus
had been a king, and that Octavian was determined never to be—
to the Romans. But the adjective *augustus* did in fact link him
with the founder; for Romulus (*optimus augur*, as Cicero calls him)
had established Rome *augusto augurio*, as Ennius put it in a line
which must have been in many mouths; Octavian, on first taking
the auspices in 43 B.C., had been vouchsafed the sign of the Twelve
Vultures which had accompanied the first auspices of Romulus;
he was himself an augur and learned in the *disciplina auguralis*,
and had in 29 B.C. celebrated the *Augurium Salutis*, a ceremony
which, like the closing of the temple of Janus, only took place in
time of profound peace; and the surname which he chose was thus
appropriate to one whose rule was consecrated by the expressed
will of the Gods of Rome[4]. The proposal was made in the Senate
by L. Munatius Plancus, one of the senior ex-consuls, whose
career earned for him the epithet 'morbo traditor'[5], but who was
now an unwavering adherent of the new régime. By a further

---

[1] *Res Gestae* 34; *C.I.L.* IX, 5811; see Volume of Plates IV, 198, *o*; see
E. Kornemann in *Klio*, XV, 1918, p. 214; A. v. Domaszewski in *Abh. zur
röm. Religion*, pp. 111 *sqq.*

[2] In the *Res Gestae* (34) Augustus explicitly says: 'Senatus consulto
Augustus appellatus sum': but Velleius writes (II, 91, 1) 'Planci sententia
consensus senatus populique Romani'; and Dio (LIII, 16, 6) has τὸ τοῦ
Αὐγούστου ὄνομα καὶ παρὰ τῆς βουλῆς καὶ παρὰ τοῦ δήμου ἐπέθετο.

[3] LIII, 16, 8, ὡς καὶ πλεῖόν τι ἢ κατὰ ἀνθρώπους ὤν.

[4] Ovid elaborates the theme in *Fast.* I, 607 *sqq.*

[5] Vell. Pat. II, 83, 1.

resolution the name of the month Sextilis was changed to Augustus, just as Quintilis had given place to Julius[1].

But 'Augustus' was a name, not a title, and its bearer was careful to assume no official style indicating that he held any exceptional office. In the *Res Gestae* (34), after recording the 'restoration of the Republic,' Augustus (as we must henceforth call him) writes as follows: 'post id tempus auctoritate[2] omnibus praestiti, potestatis autem nihilo amplius habui quam ceteri qui mihi quoque in magistratu conlegae fuerunt.' And in another passage (6) he lays stress on the fact that he refused to accept any office inconsistent with the *mores maiorum* (παρὰ τὰ πάτρια ἔθη). The significance of the term *auctoritas*[3] was plain to a Roman reader. It meant that Augustus' decisions in matters of policy carried greater weight than those of any other person or organ of State, although they might not take a legally binding form. Under the Republic a resolution of the Senate was termed *auctoritas*, until the legal step had been taken which made it a *consultum*; and if this step was barred by a tribunician veto, the resolution was entered on the minutes of the Senate and exerted such influence as the considered opinion of so eminent an assembly could command. This influence Augustus possessed in a supreme degree: and it mattered little that his magisterial power (*potestas*) was shared with others.

It is true that his statement hardly covers the facts. Who, it may be asked, were the 'colleagues' with whom, according to the fundamental principle of the Roman constitution, he was on equal terms? His fellow-consuls, no doubt, were formally his equals as the supreme magistrates of Rome; but, as we shall see, he soon relinquished that high office. He speaks in the *Res Gestae* (6) of 'colleagues' in the *tribunicia potestas*; but this can hardly be called a 'magistracy' in the historical sense of that term. As for the holders of the *imperium*, we shall see how he was in course of time granted powers which enabled him to override their decisions. We have here one of those disingenuous touches by which Augustus endeavoured to picture himself as no more than the first

---

[1] Livy, *Epit.* 134. The text is given by Macrobius (*Sat.* 1, 12, 35). Among the grounds are 'cum...Aegyptus hoc mense in potestatem Populi Romani redacta sit'. Augustus may have deferred formal recognition of the change until, as *pontifex maximus*, he regulated intercalation in 8 B.C. (Suetonius, *Aug.* 31; Dio LV, 6, 6; Censorinus, *de die nat.* 22). Cf. p. 483, n. 2.

[2] The Ancyra copy has ἀξιώματι, the Latin being missing. 'Auctoritate' is restored from the Antioch copy (see p. 870).

[3] Cf. R. Heinze in *Hermes*, LX, 1925, pp. 356 *sqq.*

citizen of a free community. And so he chose for himself no title expressive of an exceptional office, but preferred to describe himself by the term *princeps*, which we find three times in the *Res Gestae*[1]. The expression *principes civitatis*, 'leading men in the State,' was familiar to Roman ears;[2] and in the closing decades of the Republican era the singular form had been applied to eminent statesmen. In 49 B.C. Balbus wrote to Cicero that Caesar wished for nothing more than to live without fear 'principe Pompeio[3]'; three years later Cicero uses *princeps* as a matter of course with reference to Caesar: 'scito non modo me...sed ne ipsum quidem principem scire quid futurum sit[4].' It is therefore easy to see why Augustus chose this significant appellation; there is no need to suppose that he derived it from the political writings of Cicero (it is far from certain that it was used in the *De Republica*), and the notion that it was an abbreviation of the title *princeps senatus*—which of course Augustus was, as he tells us himself, for forty years—has nothing to commend it.

Was there then a restoration of the Republic? Some modern writers have taken Augustus' statements at their face value. Ferrero speaks of the 'Republic of Augustus.' Eduard Meyer believed that there was a genuine restoration of senatorial rule: Mommsen, who coined the term 'dyarchy' to describe the new constitution, devoted a section of his work to 'the *sovereign* Senate of the Principate.' Hirschfeld[5] believed that Augustus was only gradually driven, against his will and after the failure of his earlier experiments, to take the burden of government upon his shoulders. Mitteis[6] (with a closer approximation to fact) says that the principle of Augustus' rule was 'not so much to do away with the constitutional forms of the Republic as to supplement and support them by the addition thereto of an Imperial Administration.' But one thing is certain: he was resolved never to let slip the reins of power: as Dessau says, 'there never was a dyarchy and it was never intended that there should be[7].'

---

[1] *Res Gestae* 13; 30; 32; *princeps noster* is translated by ἡγεμὼν ἡμέτερος in the *senatus consultum* of the fifth Cyrene inscription, dated 4 B.C. (p. 167), and the derivatives *principalis* and *principatus* were soon established in literature (Vell. Pat. II, 124, 2, 3).

[2] Cf. *e.g.* Cicero, *II in Verr.* III, 90, 210.

[3] Cicero, *ad Att.* VIII, 9, 4.   [4] Cicero, *ad fam.* IX, 17, **3**.

[5] *Die kaiserlichen Verwaltungsbeamten*, p. 470.

[6] *Römisches Privatrecht*, p. 352.

[7] *Geschichte d. röm. Kaiserzeit*, I, 39, n. 1.

II. THE WORKING OF THE SYSTEM AND THE RE-SETTLEMENT

Augustus proceeded without delay to execute the commission entrusted to him by Senate and people, but before taking up his command in the provinces assigned to him he took a measure which showed his care for the well-being of Italy. The great trunk roads had fallen into disrepair during the civil wars, and Augustus took steps to recondition them. He himself assumed responsibility for the Via Flaminia, the Great North Road from Rome to Ariminum, and we possess in an incomplete form the inscription on the arch erected in his honour at the latter city[1]. It records the dedication of the monument to Augustus by the Senate and People of Rome on the ground that the Via Flaminia and the other most frequented roads of Italy had been put into condition 'by his initiative and at his charges.' Nor was Augustus alone active in the good work: the repair of the other roads was entrusted to those senators who had recently celebrated triumphs[2], and some milestones of the Via Latina[3] bear the name of C. Calvisius Sabinus, who triumphed in 28 B.C. 'ex Hispania' (p. 116). The expense was defrayed from the spoils of war.

In the latter part of the year Augustus set out for Gaul, accompanied (in all probability) by his stepson Tiberius and his nephew M. Claudius Marcellus, the son of Octavia by her first marriage with the consul of 50 B.C. Tiberius reached the age of fifteen in November, Marcellus was probably slightly older, and both boys had ridden beside Octavian in the triumph of 29 B.C. The conduct of affairs in Rome was left in the hands of Agrippa, who was succeeded as consul on 1 Jan., 26 B.C. by T. Statilius Taurus, one of Augustus' most loyal and efficient helpers[4], who had been rewarded for the construction of an amphitheatre in 30 B.C. by the conferment of the right to 'commend,' i.e. to designate for appointment, one member of the college of praetors.

We are not here concerned with the measures taken by Augustus in the frontier provinces of the West; it is not in fact certain which of the administrative arrangements made in Gaul belong to this date. We are told that Augustus contemplated an expedition to Britain, but this may be no more than an inference from the

---

[1] Dessau 81.   [2] Suetonius, *Aug.* 30; cf. Dio LIII, 22, 2.
[3] Dessau 889.
[4] Velleius Paterculus (II, 127, 1) places him second only to Agrippa.

courtly phrases of Horace (see p. 793). In any case he was
compelled by a serious rising in North-Western Spain to proceed
thither in person, reaching Tarraco in time to celebrate his entry
on his eighth consulship[1].

For the events of 26 B.C. our authorities are inadequate. To this
year belongs the fall of Cornelius Gallus, the first to occupy the
high post of the Prefect of Egypt. Both in his language and in
his acts he had failed to observe the respect due to Augustus: he
had set up statues of himself in all parts of Egypt and inscribed the
record of his exploits on the pyramids, and we possess a trilingual
inscription set up by him at Philae[2] in which he speaks grandi-
loquently of his achievements in suppressing a revolt of the
Thebaïd in fifteen days, conquering five cities and carrying his
arms to a point 'never reached by the Roman People or the Kings
of Egypt.' Augustus revoked his appointment and forbade him
to set foot in his house or in the provinces which he controlled;
and informations (the nature of which is not stated) were laid
against him by one Valerius Largus and others. What followed is
not made clear by Dio's statement that the Senate unanimously
voted 'that he should be condemned in the courts, deprived of
his estate and exiled[3].' Gallus was driven to suicide, and no trial
took place: nor can we accept the view that the Senate acted as
a High Court of Justice in virtue of the Settlement of 27 B.C. It
showed its subservience to the new ruler by voting that Gallus'
estate should pass to the Emperor and that sacrifices of thanksgiving should be offered. Augustus, we are told by Suetonius,
expressed his sorrow at the thought that 'he was the only man in
Rome to whom it was not permitted to set limits to his displeasure
with his friends[4].'

Finally, the chronicle of Jerome notes under the same year the
appointment of M. Valerius Messalla Corvinus to the post of
praefectus urbi, which he resigned, according to Tacitus[5], after a
few days 'quasi nescius exercendi': the chronicler tells us that he
held it for six days and laid it down as being an 'unconstitutional'
office. Messalla, one of the foremost representatives of the old
patriciate, who had fought for the Republic at Philippi, but had

---

[1] See below, p. 343.   [2] Dessau 8995. See below, p. 241.
[3] LIII, 23, 7.
[4] Dio (LIII, 24, 4) also assigns to this year the aedileship of Egnatius
Rufus, whose alleged conspiracy and execution took place in 19 B.C.; but
though Gardthausen, *Augustus*, II, p. 481, n. 11, accepts this dating, it
cannot be reconciled with the story as told by Velleius (see below, p. 136).
[5] *Ann.* VI, 11.

rallied to the Triumvirs, and had become one of Augustus' most loyal adherents, may well have felt that the creation of this office marked a departure from the ancient Republican tradition, and recalled the eight *praefecti* whom Caesar had appointed to discharge the duties of the Republican magistrates in 45 B.C. (vol. IX, p. 694). Not until he set out for his second expedition to the western provinces did Augustus repeat the experiment.

In 25 B.C., after the campaign in Northern Spain had been—as Augustus believed—brought to a successful conclusion, and a rebellion of the Salassi in the Western Alps had been crushed by A. Terentius Varro Murena, the temple of Janus was closed, and Augustus once more looked forward to an era of peace. He was, however, prevented from returning to Rome by illness. No doubt he contemplated the possibility that his life would not be prolonged, and it was now that he took the first step towards the establishment of a dynastic succession, though not a word was said to indicate that such thoughts were in his mind. He had no son, and the succession could therefore only be secured through the marriage of his daughter Julia, whose mother Scribonia he had divorced immediately after the child's birth (p. 56). She was now fourteen years of age, and was given in marriage to her cousin Marcellus, who had returned from Spain and assumed the *toga virilis*. Agrippa presided at the ceremony.

At the close of the year Augustus set out on his return to Rome; on January 1 the Senate confirmed his *acta* by oath; and a little later, on receiving the news that he proposed to distribute a largess of 400 sesterces per head to the Roman People, but would not publish the edict without the approval of the Senate, that body voted him, according to Dio[1], a general dispensation from the laws. It is impossible to believe that this is to be taken literally as placing the *princeps* above the law. The doctrine *princeps legibus solutus est*[2] belongs to a much later date; Augustus himself obtained a special dispensation from the marriage laws[3]; and it is implied in the *lex de imperio Vespasiani*[4] that he was only exempted from certain specific enactments.

Honours were now voted to Marcellus which indicated the future for which Augustus destined him. The Senate gave him a seat *inter praetorios* and reckoned him as a *quaestorius* for the purpose of proceeding to higher magistracies, so that he could be

---

[1] LIII, 28, 2.

[2] *Dig.* 1, 3, 31 (Ulpian; the reference is probably only to the Lex Julia and the Lex Papia Poppaea).

[3] Dio LVI, 32, 1.   [4] See below, p. 140.

elected aedile for 23 B.C.[1] It was also resolved that he might become a candidate for the consulship ten years before the normal age. At the same time Tiberius received permission to stand for office five years before the legal date, and he was in consequence elected quaestor for the following year.

The year 23 B.C. was a critical one in the history of the Principate, and the absence of any reliable narrative makes it difficult for us to trace the course of events with certainty. Dio[2] records under the following year a conspiracy against the life of Augustus, the ringleaders of which were A. Terentius Varro Murena and Fannius Caepio: we learn from Velleius[3] and Suetonius[4] that they were condemned by the *quaestio maiestatis*, Tiberius being the prosecutor. But, according to the Capitoline Fasti, Murena was consul with Augustus in 23 B.C. and died while holding this office, while other lists replace his name by that of his successor, Cn. Calpurnius Piso, a lifelong upholder of the Republican tradition, whom Augustus persuaded with difficulty to accept the consulship[5]. In view of this evidence we must reject Dio's chronology and place the conspiracy in 23 B.C.[6] Of Caepio we know scarcely anything: Murena (who has been mentioned above as the conqueror of the Salassi) was the brother-in-law of Maecenas, who incurred the displeasure of Augustus by communicating state secrets to his wife. The conspirators did not stand their trial and were condemned in absence: and it was enacted that in such cases the votes of the jurors should be cast openly.

Augustus was now stricken down by a serious illness and looked death in the face. He summoned the magistrates and senators[7] to his presence and, having addressed them on affairs of State, handed to his fellow-consul, Piso, a *rationarium imperii* giving details of the military and financial positions. At the same time he handed his signet-ring to Agrippa. It was generally thought that he would designate the young Marcellus as his heir and successor, but these expectations were disappointed, and the silence of the *Res Gestae*, in which (21) he is only called *gener* (as in

---

[1] These honours recall those conferred upon Octavian in 43 B.C., but he was given 'consularem locum...sententiae ferendae' according to his own version (*Res Gestae* 1).

[2] LIV, 3, 4.   [3] II, 91, 2.   [4] *Tib.* 8.

[5] Tacitus, *Ann.* II, 43.

[6] It follows that we must also assign to 23 B.C. the trial of M. Primus, governor of Macedonia, for *maiestas* on account of his having made war outside his province, though Dio (LIV, 3, 2) records it under 22 B.C.

[7] So Suetonius, *Aug.* 28: Dio (LIII, 30, 1) mentions 'the principal senators and knights.'

his epitaph in the Mausoleum[1]) makes it certain that he did not adopt his son-in-law.

But the end was not yet. The cold-water treatment of the Greek physician Antonius Musa brought Augustus back to life and health, and in the course of the summer measures were taken which profoundly modified the Settlement of 27 B.C. On July 1, at the celebration of the Latin games, Augustus resigned the consulship which he had held since 31 B.C., and his place was filled by L. Sestius Quirinalis. The choice was remarkable, for Sestius (the son of the Sestius defended by Cicero in 56 B.C.) was (like Piso) a staunch Republican, proscribed in 43 B.C. but amnestied, who never ceased to honour the memory of Brutus, under whom he had served in the civil wars: and the fact that Horace (who had fought by his side) dedicated an Ode (1, 4) to him and placed it immediately after those of which Maecenas, Augustus and Virgil formed the subjects, confirms the significance of his appointment. With both consuls adherents of the old régime the Republic seemed indeed to be restored.

But matters could not rest here. Augustus retained, it is true, the great *provincia* which had been voted to him in 27 B.C.; but he held his *imperium* no longer as consul but *pro consule*. Steps were therefore at once taken which compensated him for his abdication of the chief magistracy by restoring to him all that was necessary for his purposes of the power which belonged to that office. He was now no more than a proconsul, though his *provincia* embraced the whole group of frontier provinces, and therefore only the equal of other governors of the same rank; and like all holders of the *imperium* other than the city magistrates, he could not exercise his authority in Rome, but was obliged to lay it down on crossing the *pomerium*. Both these disabilities were now removed by special enactment. Dio[2] explicitly says that it was decreed that he should hold the *proconsulare imperium* (ἀρχὴ ἀνθύπατος) 'once and for all' (though this is incorrect), and should not lay it down on crossing the *pomerium* nor have it renewed on leaving the City, and that he should enjoy an authority superior to that of all provincial governors—i.e. a *maius imperium* such as had been proposed for Pompey in 57 B.C.[3], and had been conferred (for certain provinces) on Brutus and Cassius in 43 B.C.[4] There is no reason to dispute the truth of these last statements;

[1] *Ann. épig.* 1928, no. 88. The statements of Plutarch (*Ant.* 87) and Servius (on Virgil, *Aen.* VI, 861) are inaccurate.
[2] LIII, 32, 5.   [3] See vol. IX, p. 530.
[4] See above, p. 15.

it is evident from the edicts of Cyrene[1] (see p. 212) that Augustus did in fact intervene in the government of a senatorial province; nor can any argument be based on the fact that both he and his successor permitted the proconsul of Africa (so long as he had a legion under his command) to receive the *imperatoria salutatio* from his troops[2], for that simply meant that that commander fought under his own *auspicia* and not (like the *legati* of the Imperial provinces) under those of the Emperor.

Thus Augustus was invested with paramount authority throughout the Empire, and although Rome formed no part of his *provincia*, and was nominally under the rule of the consuls, he retained the *imperium* within its walls. But he had lost certain privileges enjoyed by the chief magistrate, particularly in relation to the Senate, and these were likewise restored to him by special enactment. In summoning the Senate and bringing business before that body the consuls enjoyed precedence over all other magistrates. Dio tells us that Augustus was empowered to 'bring forward one item of business at each meeting of the Senate[3]'; and after recording under 22 B.C. the trial of M. Primus (see above, p. 136 n. 6) he says that in recognition of his attitude in court he was given the right 'to convene the Senate whenever he pleased.' These enactments can have but one meaning, namely, that Augustus recovered the precedence which he had lost by his resignation of the consulship, and obtained the prior right of summoning the Senate which belonged to the consuls[4] and also what was later called the *ius primae relationis, i.e.* the right to introduce the first *relatio* at any meeting, by whomsoever summoned. Not until 19 B.C., if Dio is to be trusted[5], was Augustus granted the right to sit between the consuls of the year and to be attended by twelve lictors[6].

It is not surprising that Augustus should have restored the chief magistracy of the Republic, the natural goal of the ambition of every Roman senator, to the place which it had occupied before the foundation of the Principate. It was the symbol of constitutional government; it satisfied the aspirations of those who

---

[1] First published by G. Oliverio in *Notiziario Archeologico,* IV, 1927. See J. G. C. Anderson in *J.R.S.* XVII, 1927, pp. 33 sqq.

[2] In 19 B.C. L. Cornelius Balbus celebrated a triumph *ex Africa*—the last to be granted to one not a member of the Imperial house.

[3] LIII, 32, 5.   [4] Varro *ap.* Gell. *N.A.* XIV, 7.

[5] LIV, 10, 5.

[6] According to Dio (*loc. cit.*) he received *consularis potestas* for life: but this cannot be accepted.

were prepared to serve the new régime loyally; and it provided a succession of fit persons to occupy some of the leading positions in the new administration. But if the *princeps* ceased henceforth to hold the chief annual magistracy of the Republic, he adopted a new style which at once marked him out as the elect of the Roman People and at the same time gave to his rule the formal continuity associated with the reigns of legitimate kings.

We have seen that as early as 36 B.C. he had had conferred upon him the inviolability of a tribune, and that in 30 B.C. a *potestas tribunicia* wider than that of the members of the existing college, coupled apparently with an appellate jurisdiction based thereon, had been voted to him for life (see above, p. 121). As he puts it in the *Res Gestae* (10), 'sacrosanctus in perpetuum ut essem et quoad viverem tribunicia potestas mihi tribueretur statutum est.' To this act he assigns no date, but in chapter four he tells us that at the time of writing he was 'in the thirty-seventh year of his tribunician power,' that is to say, that it went back to 23 B.C.: and in fact all public documents are from that year onwards dated by the annual renewals of the *tribunicia potestas*, which normally appears after the titles of *pontifex maximus* (from 12 B.C.), *consul*, and *imperator*[1]. Dio[2] says that the Senate voted that he should be 'tribune for life,' but this is of course inaccurate; Augustus, as a patrician, could not be a tribune, but by one of those legal fictions which enabled the Romans to transform their constitution without doing violence to the principles on which it was nominally based, the prerogatives of the office were separated from its tenure and conferred on the *princeps*. Tacitus[3] speaks of the *tribunicia potestas* as 'summi fastigii vocabulum,' devised by Augustus because he would have none of such names as *rex* or *dictator*, yet desired a title which should be paramount over other *imperia*: and as such we shall find it conferred upon a colleague whom Augustus desired to designate as his prospective successor[4]. In the *Res Gestae*, as restored from the Antioch text, Augustus tells us that on five occasions he 'asked for and received a colleague in this power

---

[1] In the Cyrene edicts (p. 212) it follows the pontificate, and the other titles are (except *imperator* in one case) omitted.

[2] LIII, 32, 5.	[3] *Ann.* III, 56.

[4] Velleius tells us that Gaius Caesar, when invested with a *maius imperium* in the East, did homage to Tiberius, the holder of the *tribunicia potestas*, 'ut superiori' (II, 101, 1); and in II, 99, 1 he speaks of Tiberius as 'tribuniciae potestatis consortione aequatus Augusto'; but the former statement is inconsistent with those of other authorities (Suetonius, *Tib.* 12 and especially Dio LV, 10, 19 as restored from the epitomes), and the second may be exaggerated. Velleius is not free from bias when writing of Tiberius.

from the Senate[1],' but we read of its conferment by a legislative act of the popular assembly, described by the term *comitia tribuniciae potestatis*, in the records of the Arval brotherhood, which refer to it in relation to the accession of Otho and Vitellius[2].

It thus appears that in 23 B.C. the position of Augustus was defined by a law duly passed by the *comitia*, doubtless on the proposal of the consuls of the year: and Dio concludes his account of the prerogatives conferred upon Augustus with the words— 'As a result of this both he and the emperors after him by virtue of a certain law enjoyed the *tribunicia potestas* as well as their other powers; for the name itself of tribune was taken neither by Augustus or by any other emperor.' Now the classical lawyers, from Gaius onwards, trace the legislative powers of the emperor to the fact that he has received his *imperium* from the people by a *lex*[3]. And we possess a document which evidently forms the conclusion of a comprehensive enactment of this kind. This is the so-called *lex de imperio Vespasiani*[4], a bronze tablet discovered in the middle ages and set up by Cola di Rienzi in St John Lateran. We possess only the concluding clauses of the enactment and the *sanctio* which indemnifies all who act under it from prosecution for the contravention of other laws. In this *sanctio*, which was in the usual imperative form, the measure is called a *lex*, but the extant clauses are introduced by *uti* (depending on *censuerunt*) as in a *senatus consultum*, and no doubt reproduce the actual decree by which the Senate voted to Vespasian the various powers which went to make up the Principate, incidentally ratifying retrospectively all the acts done by him 'before this law was enacted.' We further note that in each clause the precedents of the grants made to Augustus, Tiberius and Claudius (Gaius and Nero being omitted[5]) are cited where applicable. It is natural to infer that such an act of legislation was passed for Augustus in 23 B.C. (as Dio seems to

<hr/>

[1] *Res Gestae* 6. Tacitus (*Ann.* III, 56) says that Tiberius sent a letter to the Senate asking for the *tribunicia potestas* for the younger Drusus. The word *collega* is preserved in the Antioch copy, and Velleius (II, 90, 1) speaks of Agrippa 'quem in...collegium tribuniciae potestatis principis evexerat.'　　　　　　　　　[2] Cf. Dessau 241.

[3] This is the *lex de imperio* of Ulpian (*Dig.* 1, 4, 1). The adjective 'regia' is added in the existing text, as also in the *Institutes* (1, 2, 6): but though Tribonian and Theophilus might so describe it, we cannot allow the expression to pass as Ulpian's (even by accepting Mommsen's suggestion [*Staatsrecht*, II³, p. 877 note] that he wrote 'rather as a Syrian than as a Roman').

[4] Dessau 244.

[5] The formal *damnatio memoriae* of Gaius was vetoed by Claudius (Dio LX, 3); Nero's memory was formally condemned by the Senate.

indicate) and that the powers conferred by it were enlarged or varied on the accession of subsequent *principes*.

It is unfortunate that the earlier portions of the law have not been preserved: the first of the extant clauses traces back to Augustus the right to make treaties with whomsoever he will and no doubt the preceding words gave him the power of making war and peace. In this connection we may note the striking passage with which Strabo concludes his *Geography*[1]. He observes that Augustus, when the nation had conferred upon him 'the primacy in rule' (προστασίαν τῆς ἡγεμονίας), *i.e.* the Principate, and he had been given for life authority to make war and peace, shared the provinces of the Empire with the People; and after explaining the distinction between the provinces he closes his work with the words 'and kings and dynasts and tetrarchies[2] belong and always have belonged to his share.' We should naturally infer that the right to make peace and war and the conduct of foreign relations in general date back to the restoration of the Republic in 27 B.C., but it would appear from the *lex de imperio* that provisions confirming this were embodied in the consolidating statute of 23 B.C. That statute further contains a clause—citing the precedent of Augustus—giving the *princeps* 'the right and power to do all such things as he may deem to serve the interest of the Republic and the dignity of all things divine and human, public and private.' The significance of this will appear later (p. 166).

We have seen that when threatened with the prospect of death, Augustus had given no clear indication of his view with regard to the situation which would arise if that prospect were realized. Having 'restored the Republic,' he would take no step implying the foundation of a dynasty; and on his recovery he proposed to read his last will and testament before the assembled Senate, in order to shew that he had designated no successor; but this the senators would not permit. Still, the marriage of Marcellus with Augustus' only daughter and the exceptional honours conferred upon him, the only less conspicuous privileges bestowed on his stepson Tiberius, and above all the fact that he had handed his signet-ring to Agrippa—the one outstanding figure in his entourage—could not fail to implant in men's minds the idea that when the *princeps* died, the principate would live. 'Men thought,' says Velleius[3], 'that should aught befall Augustus, Marcellus would succeed to his power, but that his security would be threatened by Agrippa;' and when Augustus dispatched the latter on a special mission to the East, it was assumed that he had taken

---

[1] XVII, 840.   [2] The text has δεκαρχίαι.   [3] II, 93, 1.

this step in order to ease the strained relations between his potential successors[1]. Our authorities can do no more than give us the rumours of the time: Suetonius tells us that Agrippa withdrew to Mytilene 'because Marcellus was preferred to him,' while he makes Tiberius (speaking of his own retirement to Rhodes) quote the precedent of Agrippa's withdrawal in order to avoid the appearance of standing in the way of Marcellus' career[2]. Later writers looked upon Agrippa's mission as exile—'pudenda Agrippae ablegatio', as Pliny the Elder calls it[3].

The case is not so simple. Dio's version is that Agrippa was sent as governor to Syria, but that 'with more than usual moderation' he remained in Lesbos and sent his lieutenants to the province. Josephus[4], however, says explicitly that Agrippa was sent out as 'deputy for Caesar (διάδοχος Καίσαρι) to the provinces beyond the Ionian Sea'—*i.e.* the *transmarinae provinciae*, as they were called, embracing the Eastern half of the Empire; and when recording his return to Rome from the East in 13 B.C.[5] he speaks of his 'ten years' administration of the Asiatic provinces.' As we shall find, the words just quoted cannot here be taken in their strict sense, for Agrippa returned to Rome in 21 B.C., and his work lay in the West until his resumption of the Eastern command in 17 B.C. But that his position in 23 B.C. is correctly described by Josephus there is no reason to doubt. He was invested with an *imperium* which made him the vice-gerent of the East under the *princeps*, and although direct proof is lacking that this was an *imperium maius* in relation to the governors of senatorial provinces (as was certainly the case after 17 B.C., when there is ample evidence that he intervened in the affairs of Asia and Achaia), it seems very probable that the institution of a 'secondary proconsular *imperium*' (as Mommsen called it)—the first of those experiments in co-regency which Augustus made in connection with the modification or renewal of his own powers—included the powers necessary to make the vice-gerent's power effective[6]. On the other hand, if we bear in mind the tentative methods of Augustus, we shall hesitate to adopt the view that the Senate now voted to Agrippa a general *proconsulare imperium* such as the *princeps* himself enjoyed and that 'from this time to the end of his

---

[1] Dio LIII, 32, 1.   [2] Suetonius, *Aug.* 66; *Tib.* 10.   [3] *N.H.* VII, 149.
[4] *Ant.* XV [10, 2], 350.   [5] *Ib.* XVI [3, 3], 86.
[6] In A.D. 17 a similar command was conferred on Germanicus covering the 'provinciae quae mari dividuntur,' and Tacitus (*Ann.* II, 43) expressly attributes to him a *maius imperium* as against both senatorial proconsuls and Imperial *legati*.

life Agrippa shared with Augustus the military and administrative control of the Imperial provinces of the Empire[1].'

III. FURTHER DEVELOPMENTS: THE NEW SAECULUM

Restored to health, and secured by the new settlement in the enjoyment of full control of the machinery of government, Augustus might well feel that he had guided the ship of State into smooth waters. But trouble was in store for him. In the autumn of 23 B.C. Marcellus fell sick of a disease which defied the treatment so successfully applied by Antonius Musa in Augustus' own case. His death was made immortal by Virgil in lines too familiar to quote[2] and his name was kept in memory by the theatre dedicated by Augustus, the remains of which still stand, and by the portico and library built by his mother Octavia.

The next blow was struck by the hand of Nature. In the winter of 23–22 B.C. the Tiber overflowed its banks, and the inundations were followed by an epidemic which caused lands to go untilled and brought scarcity in its train[3]. We are told that these calamities were connected in the popular imagination with Augustus' resignation of the chief magistracy, and that the mob besieged the Curia and threatened to burn it over the heads of the senators unless the *princeps* were appointed dictator. They then approached Augustus directly and begged him to assume the dictatorship and also the *cura annonae* in the form in which it had been conferred on Pompey in 57 B.C.[4] In the *Res Gestae* (5) he tells us that he refused the dictatorship when it was offered to him both in his absence and when he was present 'by the Senate and people,' but that he did not decline the control of the corn-supply in time of extreme scarcity and administered it with such effect that within a few days he relieved the whole people from panic and risk 'at his own expense[5].' Nevertheless the popular agitation continued. Augustus was offered, but declined, an 'annual and perpetual consulship,' and on being pressed to become censor for life, he caused Paullus Aemilius Lepidus (a nephew of the triumvir, who had, together with his father, been on the list of the proscribed in 43 B.C.) and L. Munatius Plancus (see p. 130) to be

---

[1] See M. Reinhold, *Marcus Agrippa, a biography*, p. 175.
[2] *Aen.* VI, 860–85.　　　　　　　[3] Dio LIV, 1, 1.
[4] Vol. IX, p. 529 *sq.*
[5] The nature and significance of the measures taken will be discussed elsewhere (p. 202).

appointed censors. They were the last to hold that magistracy under the Republican forms, but they did not celebrate the *lustrum*, and their disputes served to bring the office into discredit, while Augustus himself performed most of their functions.

In the autumn Augustus left Rome and went first to Sicily—possibly in order to take measures for the regulation of the corn-supply of Rome—and thence to Samos, where we find him in the following year. But Rome was not content with the new settlement, and the year 21 B.C. opened with only one consul in office—M. Lollius, one of Augustus' most faithful henchmen—the other seat having been left open in the hope that the *princeps* himself would consent to be elected. This, however, he refused to accept, and serious disturbances followed. The rival candidates for the vacant consulship, Q. Aemilius Lepidus, a son of the triumvir, and L. Junius Silanus, visited Augustus, who ordered that the elections should take place in their absence: in the end Lepidus secured a place in the Fasti. But Augustus felt that a strong hand was needed in Rome, and summoned Agrippa to return from the East and take control[1]. Nor was this all. Agrippa was married to Augustus' niece Marcella[2], whom he was now bidden to divorce in order to become the husband of the widowed Julia[3], with the prospect of securing the succession for the direct descendants of the *princeps*: a son, Gaius, was in fact born in the following year, and a second, Lucius, in 17 B.C. Augustus could now undertake the settlement of outstanding questions in the East, more especially the negotiations with the Parthian king for the recovery of the standards of Crassus, which (as is elsewhere related, p. 263) were handed over to Tiberius in 20 B.C.

---

[1] It has been held (*e.g.* by Gardthausen, *op. cit.*, I, 809) that Agrippa became *praefectus urbi*; but in that case the omission of his name in the list given by Tacitus (*Ann.* VI, 11) would be inexplicable. Nor can we accept Mommsen's view (*Staatsrecht*, II³, p. 1060, n. 2) that his authority in Rome and Italy was based on the *proconsulare imperium* conferred upon him in 23 B.C.; for this was (as we saw) limited to the *transmarinae provinciae*. He was the mouthpiece of the *princeps*, no more and no less (as he had been in 26 B.C.): and the word of the *princeps* was law.

[2] According to Suetonius (*Aug.* 63) there were children of this marriage. Marcella was married to Iullus Antonius, the son of Antony, after her divorce.

[3] Contemporary gossip may be illustrated by the story which Dio tells (LIV, 6, 6) that Maecenas advised the marriage and said to Augustus 'You have made him so great that he must either become your son-in-law or be put to death.' This is at any rate more credible than Plutarch's statement (*Ant.* 87) that Octavia suggested the divorce of her own daughter in order that Agrippa might marry Julia.

Agrippa's task did not, however, prove an easy one. In 21 M. Egnatius Rufus, whom Velleius describes as 'per omnia gladiatori quam senatori propior,' was aedile, and formed a fire-brigade from his own slaves, which gained him such popularity that he was elected praetor for the following year. On laying down his aedileship, he issued an edict in which he boasted that he had handed over the city 'unimpaired and intact' to his successor. Augustus thereupon transferred the duties of the fire-brigade to a corps of 600 public slaves, and imposed upon the praetors the charge of celebrating the games which had hitherto been held under the auspices of the aediles; he himself defrayed the expense incurred. Egnatius, however, was not lightly to be rebuffed; and in 19 B.C. he presented himself as a candidate for the consulship. As in 21, only one consul was in office, for again the second place had been left unfilled in the hope that Augustus would consent to be elected. The sole consul was C. Sentius Saturninus; and since Agrippa had been obliged to leave Rome towards the close of 20 B.C. in order to quell disturbances in Gaul and on the Rhine and had thence gone to Spain in 19, where the rebellion of the Cantabri called for his presence (see below, pp. 342 *sqq.*), Saturninus was left in a position of grave responsibility, to which he proved fully equal. His father had been among the proscribed, and he himself had followed the fortunes of Sextus Pompeius, and had been one of those whom the Pact of Misenum (p. 46) 'restored to the republic,' in the words of Velleius, who was his wholehearted admirer. He now refused to accept the candidature of Egnatius for the consulship, and went so far as to announce that even were he to secure a majority of the votes cast, he would decline to declare him elected. Again there were riots and bloodshed, and the Senate voted an armed guard for the protection of the consul, which he refused; and it was resolved to send envoys to Augustus, who was now on his return from the East; so he nominated one of these—Q. Lucretius Vespillo, who had been on the list of the proscribed,—to fill the vacant consulship. Meanwhile, as it would seem, a plot to kill Augustus was discovered, in which Egnatius played the principal part, and the ringleaders were executed in prison.

Preparations were now made to welcome Augustus on his return to Rome, and he was met in Campania by a deputation from the Senate, headed by the newly-appointed consul, and comprising representatives of the colleges of praetors and tribunes and other leading citizens (*principes viri*, as they are called in the *Res Gestae*), 'an honour which up to this time (he adds) had been decreed

to no one but myself[1].' But Augustus would have no triumphal
entry into the city. On the night of October 12 he slipped through
the Porta Capena, and the Romans awoke to find the *princeps* in
their midst. He would accept no honour save the erection of an
altar to Fortuna the Home-bringer (*Fortuna Redux*) without the
gate and the institution of an annual holiday, the Augustalia, on
the date of his return.

The year 18 B.C. marks a further stage in the development of
the Principate. The time was drawing near when the commission
granted to Augustus on the 'restoration of the Republic' would
expire; and its renewal (which of course was a foregone conclusion)
was made the occasion for certain significant measures. We have
already mentioned (p. 138) the restoration to the *princeps* of the
outward symbols of consular authority, which Dio inaccurately
calls 'the consular authority for life' and dates in 19 B.C. More
important for the future of the régime was the co-regency conferred
upon Agrippa for the same period—five years—for which
Augustus' tenure of the frontier provinces was extended. Dio
tells us that Augustus granted to Agrippa 'other privileges almost
equal to his own and therewith the *tribunicia potestas.*' It was the
first time that he had clearly indicated the means by which in the
event of his own death—and he feared assassination—the gap
might be bridged and the continuance of the principate assured.
The *tribunicia potestas* of Agrippa, like that of Augustus, was
annually numbered, so that we find him entitled *trib. pot.* III in
the inscriptions on the Maison Carrée at Nîmes[2] and the theatre
at Merida (Emerita) in Spain[3]. As for his *imperium*, we can only
say that on his return to the East in 17 B.C. he exercised control,
not only over the Imperial provinces, but also over those—such as
Asia—which had senatorial governors: for example, he restored
to Cyzicus in 15 B.C. the *libertas* of which Augustus had deprived
it in 20 B.C.[4] and in a letter to the Ephesians[5] he informs them that

[1] Mommsen (*Res Gestae*[2], p. 48) held that Augustus deliberately and
disingenuously confused and combined the two missions dispatched by the
Senate when he said that Lucretius Vespillo met him *as consul,* his object
being to conceal the disorders which led to the first deputation. This cannot
be admitted. It is, of course, true that Dio omits all mention of the complimentary delegation on which Augustus naturally laid stress. Vespillo, as we
learn from Suetonius, was consul when Virgil died on Sept. 21.
[2] As restored by E. Espérandieu, *Inscriptions Latines de la Gaule,*
no. 417.
[3] Dessau 130.
[4] Cf. *I.G.R.R.* IV, 146, 8.
[5] Josephus, *Ant.* XVI [6, 4], 167–8.

he has notified Silanus, the proconsul of Asia, that no Jew shall be constrained to furnish bail on the Sabbath day.

In the *Res Gestae* (6) Augustus tells us that both in 19 and 18 B.C. the Senate and People of Rome concurred in electing him to the *cura legum morumque* with supreme authority, but that he refused to assume this or any office inconsistent with the *mores maiorum*, and carried out the measures which the Senate desired to see put into effect by him in virtue of his *tribunicia potestas*. Dio goes farther and states (LIV, 10, 5) that in 19 B.C. Augustus received the *praefectura morum* and *potestas censoria* for five years[1]; but in the face of Augustus' explicit statement we cannot accept this account as historical[2]. He goes on to say that after voting these measures the people begged Augustus to 'set everything in order' and enact whatever laws he pleased, which laws should be called *leges Augustae* and be made binding by oath. There is here a clear reference to the *leges Juliae*, which belong to 18 B.C., and it is legitimate to interpret the words quoted above from the *Res Gestae* as meaning that these were proposed by Augustus to the popular assembly in virtue of his *tribunicia potestas*. In the eighth chapter of the *Res Gestae* he writes: 'legibus novis me auctore latis multa exempla maiorum exolescentia iam ex nostro saeculo reduxi,' thus stressing the moral reforms by which he hoped to earn the gratitude of posterity. It is to these that we must refer such expressions as those of Horace (*Ep.* II, 1, 1) 'cum...res Italas...moribus ornes, legibus emendes,' and Ovid's reference (*Trist.* II, 233) to 'legum...tutela tuarum et morum' means no more, and must not be taken to confirm Dio's version of the powers conferred upon Augustus.

The code of 18 B.C., so far as it relates to public morals, is fully discussed elsewhere (chap. XIV); we shall confine ourselves here to mentioning its most important provisions in other fields. It is not of course possible in every case to say whether a *lex Julia* was enacted by the dictator or by the *princeps*; but it can at least be said that considerable reforms were effected in the Criminal Law and in Legal Procedure. The Roman criminal code was made up of the laws establishing the *quaestiones perpetuae*, most of which were enacted by Sulla and hence called *leges Corneliae*. In the forty-eighth title of the Digest we have a series of chapters on these statutes; and most of them are now no longer *leges Corneliae*, but

---

[1] Suetonius (*Aug.* 60) says that he received 'morum legumque regimen... perpetuum'; but he connects it with the census (see below).

[2] Dio couples with this grant that of 'consular power for life' which, as we have seen, rests on a misconception.

leges Juliae, the presumption being that they were passed by Augustus[1]. Thus the statutes concerning *ambitus*, *maiestas*, *repetundae*, and *peculatus* were remodelled: and above all, two laws on *vis*—the Lex Julia de vi publica and de vi privata—were passed, which were of the first importance. This was especially true of the former: for Paulus tells us (*Sent.* XXVI, 1) that it rendered liable to the penalty of the law any person exercising authority who should execute, torture, scourge or condemn a Roman citizen 'antea ad populum, nunc imperatorem appellantem,' thus placing on a secure basis the appellate jurisdiction of the *princeps* in criminal matters.

Another important group of laws dealt with the reform of judicial procedure. These were the *leges Juliae* [*iudiciorum*] *publicorum* and *privatorum*. The number and nature of these enactments have been disputed: it has been held for example that there were two *leges Juliae privatorum*, one relating to procedure in Rome and the other to that in the *municipia*. It has also been suggested that these laws are not to be distinguished from the Lex Julia de vi publica and Lex Julia de vi privata mentioned above; but the passage cited from Ulpian in support of this view does not prove the point[2]; and the quotations from the twenty-sixth and twenty-seventh chapters respectively of the *lex publicorum* and *lex privatorum* in the Vatican fragments (sections 197, 198), taken in conjunction with other citations in the *Digest*[3], seem to make it clear that general forms of procedure were laid down.

In 18 B.C. Augustus also proceeded to hold a *lectio senatus*. It will be remembered that such a revision of the senatorial roll had been carried out (according to custom) in connection with the census of 29–28 B.C. In the *Res Gestae* (8) Augustus says quite baldly (perhaps because he did not wish to revive painful memories) 'senatum ter legi,' and then goes on to enumerate the three *census* at which the *lustrum* was celebrated, these being dated to 28 B.C., 8 B.C. and A.D. 14. It is clear that he did not regard the two

[1] The Lex Cornelia de sicariis and the Lex Cornelia de falsis were not superseded: nor, we may add, the Lex Pompeia de parricidis and the Lex Fabia de plagiariis.

[2] *Dig.* 48, 19, 32. It is quoted by Mommsen (*Strafrecht*, p. 655), who (p. 128) prefers to ascribe the laws to Caesar rather than to Augustus.

[3] Paulus (*Dig.* 48, 2, 3 *Pr.*) gives certain rules for proceedings taken under the Lex Julia de adulteriis, adding the words 'hoc enim lege Julia publicorum...generaliter praecipitur.' Rules of court 'ex lege quae de iudiciis privatis lata est' are referred to by Augustus in his edict concerning the aqueduct of Venafrum (Bruns, *Fontes*[7], 77, l. 68) and in the *s.c.* from Cyrene (p. 171) the νόμος Ἰούλιος δικαστικός is cited for the law of evidence.

functions—*lectio senatus* and celebration of the *lustrum*—as inseparable, and we are not in any way bound to suppose that (except in
28 B.C.) they coincided in time. Now Dio mentions four occasions
(excluding A.D. 14, where the text is mutilated) on which a
census and a revision of the senatorial roll or both took place—
in 29–28 B.C.[1], in 19–18 B.C.[2], in 13 B.C.[3], and in A.D. 4.[4]
Combining the statements of Dio and the *Res Gestae*, Hardy
attempted to construct a symmetrical scheme under which
census and *lustrum* were held at intervals of approximately twenty
years and *lectiones senatus* half-way through each period, *i.e.* in
18 B.C. and A.D. 4. But in any case the *census* of A.D. 4 must be
rejected, since the *Res Gestae* ignore it, nor can we count the *lectio*
of A.D. 4 among the three carried out by Augustus himself, since
(as we shall see) it was entrusted to Commissioners. Thus the
words 'senatum ter legi' must be taken as referring to 28, 18 and
13 B.C.[5] It remains true that both *census* and *lectio*, as also the
conferment or renewal of powers on the co-regents of the *princeps*,
coincided significantly with the successive renewals of Augustus'
own *imperium*[6].

In recording the *lectio* of 18 B.C., Dio describes an elaborate
scheme devised by Augustus in order to avoid the odium of
exercising compulsion on unworthy senators to resign their seats.
He first selected thirty senators, testifying on oath that they were
the fittest, and ordered each of them (also on oath) to write down a
list of five names. From each of these groups one was selected by
lot who was to draw up a further list of five. But this scheme
broke down in practice, and Augustus was finally compelled to
make his own selection, and to raise the number of senators to
six hundred instead of limiting it, as he would have wished, to
three hundred[7].

[1] LII, 42, 1.
[2] In 19 B.C., as we saw, Augustus (according to Dio, LIV, 10, 5) received
censoria potestas for five years: in 18 B.C. he revised the roll of the Senate
(LIV, 13, 1).
[3] The *lectio senatus* is recorded in LIV, 26, 3; no census is here mentioned,
but in LIV, 35, 1 it is said to have taken place in 11 B.C.   [4] LV, 13.
[5] In each of these cases Dio uses the words ἐξετάζω or ἐξέτασις.
Under A.D. 4, when Commissioners were appointed, the word used is
διαλέξαι.   [6] See the schedule drawn up by Pelham, *Essays*, pp. 64 *sqq.*
[7] It is worthy of note that one of the thirty, Antistius Labeo, the greatest
jurist of the time, and an incorruptible Republican, whose father had committed suicide after Philippi, set down the name of Lepidus the ex-triumvir,
and when Augustus threatened him with punishment for violating his oath
to select the fittest, replied, 'What have I done if I retain in the Senate one
whom even now you allow to remain Chief Pontiff?'

The time had now come to celebrate the coming of that golden age of peace and prosperity the dawn of which had been awaited with such fervent longing by a world weary of strife. More than once the cup had been dashed from Roman lips—in 49 B.C., when (according to the prevailing theory that the *saeculum* was precisely 100 years in duration[1]) the celebration of the Tenth Age should have taken place, in 44 when, after the murder of Caesar, the *sidus Julium* blazed in the heavens and (as Augustus related in his memoirs[2]) was interpreted by a *haruspex* named Vulcatius as signifying the beginning of the new *saeculum*—the seer paid the penalty for revealing the secret of the gods by instant death!— and again in 40 B.C., when the Fourth Eclogue of Virgil gave expression to the unvoiced thought of millions. Augustus, who had an eye for dramatic fitness, felt that the time was ripe for an imposing ceremony which should make as vivid an impression on Rome as the 'restoration of the Republic' ten years before, but should be religious rather than political. Virgil no doubt had been taken into his confidence, for before his death in 19 B.C. he had written the lines[3]

> Augustus Caesar divi genus aurea condet
> Saecula.

In the following year the promulgation of the new code betokened—as it might be supposed—a return to the purer morals of man's first estate; and due preparations were made for the staging of the celebrations. The Sibylline books were recopied by the hands of their guardians, the *xvuiri sacris faciundis*[4]; the interpretation of their oracles (and of the records of the Republic) in order that the Tenth Age might find its dawning in 17 B.C. was entrusted to Ateius Capito, the head of one of the great law schools, and a staunch supporter of the régime; and Horace, who, since the death of Virgil, was unquestionably the first poet of Rome, was commissioned to write the hymn to be sung by a choir of boys and maidens at the culmination of the ceremony; and in 17 B.C., on the third of June, prayers were duly offered for the 'seed of Anchises and Venus,' 'bellante prior, iacentem lenis in hostem.' It was not as fine a phrase as Virgil's 'parcere subiectis et debellare superbos,'

---

[1] Censorinus quotes, not only Valerius Antias, a *protégé* of the family connected by tradition with the first celebrations of *ludi saeculares*, but also Varro, for this doctrine (*de die natali*, 8).

[2] *Frag.* CLXVIII, Malcovati[2], p. 63.   [3] *Aen.* VI, 792.

[4] In the minutes of their proceedings (Dessau 5050) the name of the faithful Sentius Saturninus (see above, p. 145) appears next to that of Augustus.

but it served to mark the fact that the spirit of Rome (as Virgil had conceived it) was incarnate in the *princeps*[1].

IV. DYNASTIC POLICY AND THE CONSOLIDATION OF THE PRINCIPATE

In 17 B.C. Julia bore to Agrippa a second son, who was given the name Lucius, and, together with his elder brother Gaius, was almost at once adopted by Augustus, who thus gave a clear indication that it was reserved for his lineal descendants to carry on the family tradition and—presumably—to succeed in due time to the principate. In the meantime, however, there was work to be done for which he needed the help of his stepsons, Tiberius and Drusus, who had already received exceptional privileges. In 16 B.C. the elder brother was praetor, while the younger held the quaestorship; they were respectively in their twenty-sixth and twenty-third years of age. Agrippa had returned to the East for a second term[2], and Augustus had dedicated the restored temple of Quirinus[3] when he was once more needed in the West; M. Lollius, the *legatus* on the Rhine, had sustained a reverse at the hands of German tribes (see p. 360), and there was work to be done in Gaul. The *princeps* set out thither, accompanied by Tiberius, and was absent from Rome for the next three years. He appointed T. Statilius Taurus to the post of *praefectus urbi* which he filled with distinction (*egregie toleravit*, says Tacitus). We are not here concerned with the regulation of the Northern frontiers which is treated elsewhere; suffice it to say that Tiberius and Drusus gained undying fame by their campaigns, duly celebrated by Horace in the fourth book of the Odes. In 15 B.C. Drusus received the *ornamenta praetoria*, as Tiberius had done four years before, and in 13 B.C. became *legatus* of the Three Gauls.

In this year Agrippa returned from the East, having for the third time refused a triumph—in this instance voted to him for his settlement of the affairs of the Kingdom of Bosporus (p. 268). Tiberius was now consul, and presided in the Senate when the honours to be conferred upon Augustus on his return from the West were voted. The only one accepted by the *princeps* was the erection in the Campus Martius of an Ara Pacis Augustae. The 'Augustan peace' was indeed far from being established on a

---

[1] On the *ludi saeculares* see further below, p. 477 *sq.*
[2] Perhaps in 17 B.C.: the date cannot be determined.
[3] On 29 June, 16 B.C. (Ovid, *Fast.* VI, 795 relates to this dedication).

secure footing: but the monument represents the highest achievement of Imperial art (pp. 546 *sqq.*).

The second term of Augustus' *imperium* was now drawing to its close, and it was duly renewed, again for five years. At the same time Agrippa received an extension of his *tribunicia potestas* for the same period, and an *imperium maius* such as that which Augustus himself enjoyed, over all provincial governors[1]. Trouble was now brewing in the North-East, and Agrippa was dispatched to Pannonia (p. 357). Augustus also carried out a third *lectio senatus*, and the qualifications of the senatorial order were strictly examined: we shall deal with these later.

Dio[2] records that in the same year Lepidus the ex-triumvir died and that Augustus was elected to the vacant chief pontificate; but in the *Res Gestae* (10) we read: 'I refused to be created Pontifex Maximus in the place of my colleague during his lifetime, though the people offered me that priesthood[3], which my father had held. A few years later, when the man who, taking advantage of civil strife, had seized that priesthood was dead, I accepted it; and so great was the multitude that flocked to my election from all Italy that no such gathering at Rome had heretofore been recorded. This was in the consulship of P. Sulpicius [Quirinius] and C. Valgius [Rufus],' *i.e.* in 12 B.C. Augustus thus became at long last the head of the State religion, having with nicely calculated self-effacement refrained from doing violence to those institutions into which he laboured so tirelessly to breathe new life. The form of popular election to the chief pontificate was observed by succeeding Emperors, and we read, for example, of the *comitia pontificatus maximi* of Otho in the Acts of the Arval Brotherhood.

In the early spring Agrippa, having restored order in Pannonia, returned to Italy, and went to Campania, presumably for reasons of health. Soon, however, his condition grew worse, and in the third week of March tidings reached Augustus, who was exhibiting games in the name of his adopted sons, that he was critically ill. The *princeps* hastened to Campania, but found his colleague no longer alive. The body was brought to Rome, where Augustus delivered the funeral *laudatio* in the Forum and laid his friend to rest in his own Mausoleum. He had made the Emperor his principal heir, bequeathing to him his great estates—including the Thracian Chersonese—and the *familia* of slaves which he had formed to keep his buildings in Rome in condition: his baths and gardens he left to the Roman People.

---

[1] Dio LIV, 28, 1.   [2] LIV, 27, 1–2.
[3] In 36 B.C. (Appian, *Bell. Civ.* v, 131, 543).

Thus Augustus was deprived by an untimely death of his most loyal friend, the prop and stay of the Principate, just as he had given signal proofs of his confidence that in case of his own death the reins of power would remain in safe hands until the younger members of the Imperial house were able to take them up. For the time being the position on the Northern frontiers needed consolidation. This problem and the solution attempted is discussed elsewhere (see below, pp. 355 *sqq.*); here we must note that, although the work was of necessity entrusted to the stepsons of Augustus, he moved (as was his custom) cautiously in regard to the conferment of distinctions upon them as a reward for their military successes. The elder, Tiberius, was betrothed to Julia[1], now for the second time a widow, and shortly to become the mother of a child who was named Agrippa Postumus. We need not perhaps give credence to the story that she had endeavoured to engage Tiberius' affections during Agrippa's lifetime; there is less reason to doubt that her third marriage was at first happy, but that an estrangement took place after the death of the only child in infancy. But it was said that Tiberius never lost his deep affection for the wife whom he had been obliged to divorce for reasons of state—Vipsania, the daughter of Agrippa and granddaughter of Cicero's friend Atticus—and that on the only occasion when he was permitted to see her after his marriage with Julia it was noticed that his eyes filled with tears. In 12 B.C. he took command in Pannonia, and the Senate voted him a triumph for his successes, but Augustus would not permit him to celebrate it, nor did he recognize the *salutatio imperatoria* accorded to him by the troops. An important precedent, however, was created when the *triumphalia ornamenta*—the right to retain certain of the *insignia* of the *triumphator* for life[2]—were granted to Tiberius; and in the following year (11 B.C.), when Drusus (who was now praetor) gained conspicuous successes against the Germans, the triumph voted to him by the Senate was again refused, and the *ornamenta* conferred upon him instead. Tiberius earned them a second time in this year and both the brothers were now permitted to celebrate an *ovatio*, though neither was granted the use of the title *imperator*[3]. Their campaigns were not, however, at an end, and the culmination was reached when Drusus, as consul in 9 B.C., carried the Roman arms to the Elbe. Now at last, as it would seem, both the brothers were

---

[1] The marriage was celebrated in 11 B.C.

[2] For details see Mommsen, *Staatsrecht*, I³, p. 466.

[3] Dio tells us (LIV, 35, 5) that the Senate decreed that Drusus, at the close of his term of office as praetor, should rank *pro consule*.

allowed the coveted style of *imperator*. Such is the meaning of
Suetonius' words[1], and in an inscription[2] set up by Tiberius after
1 B.C., Drusus bears the title. He did not hold it for long, for on
September 14 he died as the result of an accident.

It was a shrewd blow to Augustus, who was thrown back on the
sole support of Tiberius until such time as his grandsons could
take up the position which he designed them to hold. He was
accordingly dispatched to Germany to complete the work begun
by Drusus, where he received a second *salutatio imperatoria* and
was at length permitted to enjoy a triumph; he was also elected to
the consulship for 7 B.C.[3]

The *imperium* of Augustus was renewed in 8 B.C., this time for
ten years, and a *census* was held, which, as he tells us, he carried out
solus consulari cum imperio; but it was not until 6 B.C. that he once
more sought a colleague in the *tribunicia potestas*, which was
conferred upon Tiberius for a period of five years. He was not,
however, minded to play the part which Agrippa had so loyally
sustained. It was evident that the Emperor's grandsons were
marked out for the succession to the Principate; and in fact the
first steps were now taken to give them an exceptional position.
Dio[4] tells us that in 6 B.C. it was proposed that Gaius should be
elected consul, but that Augustus expressed his disapproval and at
the same time his hope that no circumstances such as had arisen in
his own case[5] would compel the election of any one below the age
of twenty. Tacitus represents Augustus' refusal to accept the
proposal as insincere, and in fact there can be little doubt that the
demonstration was pre-arranged and was intended to lead to the
conferment of exceptional privileges upon the brothers. In 5 B.C.
Augustus assumed the consulship for the twelfth time, and introduced Gaius to public life by the time-honoured procedure of
deductio in forum on his assuming the *toga virilis*; he was then
designated as consul, to hold office after an interval of five years
(*i.e.* in A.D. 1); the Senate gave him the right to attend its meetings,
and the Roman knights saluted him as *princeps iuventutis*. These
precedents were precisely followed three years later, when
Augustus held his thirteenth and last consulship, Lucius receiving
the same privileges as his elder brother. The only distinction made
between the two princes was that while Gaius became *pontifex*,
Lucius received the augurate[6]. The title *princeps iuventutis* was

---

[1] *Tib.* 9; *Claud.* 1.   [2] Dessau 147.
[3] The organization of the *vicomagistri* and the administrative changes
connected therewith, which belong to this year, are treated elsewhere, p. 199.
[4] LV, 9, 2.   [5] See above, p. 17.   [6] Dessau 131, 132.

carefully chosen. It had Republican associations, for Cicero had used it, for example, in a letter writen in 50 B.C. to Appius Claudius Pulcher, in which, speaking of Pompey and Brutus, he describes the former as 'omnium saeculorum et gentium princeps' and the latter as 'iam pridem iuventutis, celeriter, ut spero, civitatis[1].' This phrase is paralleled by Ovid's apostrophe to Gaius Caesar, written in 2 B.C.

> nunc iuvenum princeps, deinde future senum[2].

If further evidence were needed that the *princeps iuventutis* was marked out as the future bearer of the title by which Augustus desired to be designated, it might be found in the words of what are known as the *cenotaphia Pisana*[3]. These are inscriptions set up by order of the municipal council of the colony of Pisa after the death of both the princes; and in the second, after Augustus has been termed 'maxsumus custos imperi Romani totiusque orbis terrarum praeses,' Gaius is referred to as 'iam designatus iustissimus ac simillumus parentis sui virtutibus princeps.'

To Tiberius the manifest intention of Augustus to base his dynastic policy on the line of direct descent was intolerable; he declined to carry out the mission which Augustus pressed upon him to settle the 'still vexed' question of the Armenian succession (p. 273), begged to be released from the burden of public life, and, in spite of the protests of Augustus and the entreaties of Livia, retired to Rhodes, where he remained for seven years, mainly engaged in literary pursuits and especially in the study of the fashionable pseudo-science of astrology. Of the true reasons for his retirement he said nothing at the time, and Roman gossip invented explanations which need not be repeated. Later, he defended his action by the precedent of Agrippa's withdrawal from Rome in 23 B.C., when the young Marcellus embarked on the career so soon to be cut short by death, and no doubt there was a certain resemblance between the circumstances, but it may well be believed that his unhappy marriage with Julia, who did not accompany him to Rhodes, influenced his decision.

In his absence the grandsons of Augustus filled the parts assigned to them in the dynastic system: in 4 B.C. Gaius took his seat at the Crown Council at which the future government of Judaea was debated (p. 337 *sq.*); and in 2 B.C. (when Lucius, as we saw, was introduced to public life) the office of *duoviri aedis*

---

[1] *Ad fam.* III, 11, 3. The expression is also used in Cicero's orations (*pro Sulla*, 12, 34, *II in Verr.* I, 53, 139).
[2] *Ars Am.* I, 194.   [3] Dessau 139, 140.

dedicandae was revived in order that the brothers might take part in the consecration of the temple of Mars Ultor, vowed by Octavian on the field of Philippi.

The year 2 B.C. was memorable for two events. The first was the conferment upon Augustus by Senate, Knights and People of the title of *pater patriae*—already in unofficial use, as the inscriptions show[1] and Dio expressly notes[2]. The titulature of the *princeps* was now complete. The other outstanding event of the year was the domestic catastrophe which befell Augustus when it came to his knowledge that his daughter had been guilty of flagrant offences against morality. It was impossible for the author of the Lex de adulteriis either to attempt the concealment of facts which were common knowledge or to fail to enforce his own law; Julia herself was banished to the island of Pandateria and her lovers were exiled—all except Iullus Antonius, the son of the Triumvir, who was driven to suicide[3].

In 1 B.C. the term of five years for which the *tribunicia potestas* had been conferred upon Tiberius expired, and so far from renewing the grant, Augustus refused permission to his stepson to return to Rome, so that he became a virtual exile, and only the entreaties of his mother induced the *princeps* to bestow upon him the honorary title of *legatus*. Gaius Caesar was now in his twentieth year, and Augustus caused him to be invested with a special proconsular *imperium* in the Eastern provinces. He was naturally provided with an efficient staff, at the head of which was M. Lollius, who has been mentioned above (p. 151). We have already spoken of the interview between Gaius and his stepfather (p. 139, n. 4); it was said (probably with truth) that Lollius did his best to sow seeds of discord between Tiberius and the young crown prince. He did not, however, long enjoy his position of confidence. Gaius soon discovered the real character of his adviser, and Lollius died in disgrace (p. 276). He was succeeded as Chief of the Staff by P. Sulpicius Quirinius (the Cyrenius of St Luke), a fine soldier and a man of proved integrity. Quirinius was a loyal friend of Tiberius, and an immediate result of his influence with Gaius was seen when Augustus—who was unwilling to recall Tiberius against the wishes of his grandson—now gave him permission to return to Rome, though for the time being he gave

[1] Cf. Dessau 96 and note; *parens patriae, ib.* 101.
[2] LV, 10, 10. The date was Feb. 5 (Ovid, *Fasti*, II, 127). On the precedent of Caesar see Vol. IX, p. 720.
[3] Tacitus (*Ann.* III, 24) implies that the offence was brought under the *lex maiestatis.*

him no part to play in public affairs[1]; when the powers of the *princeps* were renewed for ten years in A.D. 3, no co-regency was instituted.

Once more the Emperor's dearest hopes were disappointed. Lucius Caesar, to whom a commission in the West had been entrusted, died at Marseilles in A.D. 2 when on his way to Spain, and two years later, on Feb. 21, A.D. 4, his brother, as the result of a wound received in Armenia, met his end at Limyra in Lycia (p. 277). Augustus had now no choice but to designate Tiberius as his chosen successor, and four months after the death of Gaius he adopted him by the solemn ceremony of a *lex curiata* as his son. But this was not enough, for at the same time he adopted his only surviving grandson, the posthumous child of Agrippa and Julia, a boy deficient in every quality desirable in a possible heir[2], and insisted that Tiberius should adopt his nephew Germanicus, the son of Drusus by Antonia, in whose children's veins ran the blood of the *princeps*. Tiberius was, however, again invested with the *tribunicia potestas*, this time for ten years[3], and was dispatched (no doubt with a special *imperium*) to the Rhine frontier.

In the same year Augustus made a constitutional experiment which was not repeated. He felt that the time had come for a *lectio senatus*, but instead of carrying out the revision of the roll himself he set up a commission of *tresviri legendi senatus*, selected by lot from a list of ten proposed by himself[4]. It was doubtless at the same time that a second commission was called into being to revise the roll of the *equites*[5]. Although these commissioners were invested with the *censoria potestas*, there is no evidence that they celebrated the *lustrum*. This function was performed for the

---

[1] On the chronology of these events in the East see below, p. 275, n. 3.

[2] Agrippa Postumus, as he was usually called, was afterwards disinherited and exiled (by decree of the Senate, according to Tacitus, *Ann.* I, 6); the story ran that Augustus visited him on the Island of Planasia during the closing months of his life, but it is hard to believe this. On his execution in A.D. 14 see p. 609, n. 2.

[3] So Dio LV, 13, 2; Suetonius, *Tib.* 16 says five, but there is no trace of a renewal in A.D. 9, and in *Res Gestae* (6) Augustus speaks of *five* occasions on which a colleague was given him (*i.e.* 18, 13, 6 B.C., A.D. 4, 14).

[4] Suetonius, *Aug.* 37; Dio LV, 13, 3.

[5] This is mentioned by Suetonius (*Aug.* 37; a commission of ten senators appears *ib.* 39) and its existence is confirmed by Tacitus, who records the death of L. Volusius Saturninus ' censoria potestate legendis equitum decuriis functus' (*Ann.* III, 30)—one of his freedmen calls him *censor* in Dessau 1954— and also by an inscription (Dessau 9486) set up by a certain Favonius, whose offices show him to have belonged to the highest aristocracy, in which he describes himself as ' triumvir centuriis equitum recognoscendis.'

third and last time by Augustus at the close of his reign. His own words are (*Res Gestae* 8) 'tertium consulari cum imperio lustrum conlega Tib. Caesare filio meo feci,' the year being A.D. 14.

By this time Tiberius, whose services on the Northern frontiers (see below, pp. 368 *sqq.*) had gained him a triumph, had been placed in a position of co-regency with the *princeps* which went beyond previous precedent. In the year A.D. 13 Augustus received a fifth and final extension of his *imperium* for ten years 'against his will,' if Dio[1] is to be believed. Dio adds that the *tribunicia potestas* of Tiberius was renewed: but this was not all, for a law was passed in due form on the proposal of the consuls granting to him equal rights with his adoptive father in the administration of the provinces and command of the armies, and empowering him to conduct the *census* together with Augustus[2]. The duties of the censors closed with the celebration of the *lustrum* in May, A.D. 14, and Tiberius received a commission to proceed with the settlement of affairs in Illyricum. He parted from Augustus early in August at Beneventum, and went on his way northward; but he had no sooner reached his province than he was summoned to return to the deathbed of the *princeps*; Velleius and Suetonius[3] agree that he found him living, and for one whole day he remained in secret conclave with the dying Emperor.

At long last Augustus had made provision for the continuance of the system which he had perfected with infinite tact and patience. It was embodied in no written document, but had grown from precedent to precedent; and although the co-regency conferred on Tiberius had left no room for doubt where a *princeps* was to be found, it is going too far to say[4] that the Principate was conceived by Augustus as a dyarchy, not in the sense in which Mommsen used that word, *i.e.* a joint-rule of Senate and *princeps*, but as the 'dual sovereignty' of two rulers. What is of greater importance to consider is the part which the Senate and People of Rome were designed to play in the new system. This will be the subject of the following chapter.

[1] LVI, 28, 1.   [2] Suetonius, *Tib.* 21; Vell. Pat. II, 121, 1.
[3] II, 123, 2; *Aug.* 98; *Tib.* 21: the malicious gossip retailed by Tacitus (*Ann.* I, 15) and Dio (LVI, 31, 1) at Livia's expense is unworthy of mention.
[4] With E. Kornemann, *Doppelprinzipat und Reichseinteilung*, p. 6.

CHAPTER VI

SENATUS POPULUSQUE ROMANUS

I. FORMULA AND FACT

SENATUS censuit populusque iussit. The words of Rome's greatest constitutionalist[1] express with precision the theory of government which was the creed of all Romans. 'Commands' issue from the sovereign People; 'resolutions' are taken by the Senate[2]. The formal acts of the Roman State are registered in the name of both bodies: the order in which they are named varies, and in the earlier documents the People take precedence[3], but by the close of the Republican period the formula which stands at the head of this chapter had become stereotyped in public documents. It is the 'Senate and People of Rome' who in 29 B.C. set up in the Forum a monument (no doubt a triumphal arch) in honour of Octavian *re publica conservata*, and two years later the arch which marked the termination of the Via Flaminia at Rimini[4]; from 'Senate and People' Augustus received the powers of the Principate in 27 B.C. (p. 128); and at his request 'the Senate and People of Rome' conferred co-equal rights upon Tiberius at the close of the reign (p. 158). The traditional formula remained in use as long as the Western Empire lasted; and we naturally find it prominent on the coinage of the Civil Wars which followed the death of Nero, when Galba declared himself *Legatus senatus populique Romani* (p. 811).

Thus far the formula: what of the reality, especially as Augustus conceived it? To begin with, while the deliberative and legislative functions receive express recognition, the executive is not explicitly mentioned. Yet it was precisely the lack of adequate control over the holder of executive authority (*imperium*), derived as it was from the fount of popular election and subject to the guidance of an advisory council with ancient and glorious traditions, which had led to the breakdown of the Republican system. The story has been told at length, and there is nothing more to add save that Augustus deliberately set aside the solution of the problem which had been exemplified by the dictatorships of Sulla

---

[1] Cicero, *pro Plancio*, 17, 42.
[2] 'Senatus consulto populique iussu' on the monument of Bibulus (Dessau 862).   [3] Cf. Dessau 15.   [4] Dessau 81, 84.

and Caesar, and preferred to use the framework of the Republican constitution as the scaffolding of a structure adapted to the needs of the Mediterranean Empire of which the core was the city-state of Rome. We have seen that he was determined to be, beyond challenge, the wielder of supreme authority under the new conditions; but we have to ask what place he assigned in his system to the time-hallowed institutions which he desired to preserve. The genius of Rome had shown itself in the method by which, when change was called for, she set up new organs of State beside the old and left them to find their *modus vivendi*, often turning to new uses those which had outlived their original purpose. Would Augustus be able to carry this process a stage further, and harmonize the working of his new and elaborate administrative system, which compels our admiration, with the continued operation (with or without change of function) of the older organs?

That this was his intention is not to be doubted, and his successors were aware of the fact. Tiberius communicated to the Senate his political testament; and Dio[1], who gives a somewhat fuller version of his injunctions than other writers, makes him lay down the principle that public service should be rendered by all who were capable of understanding and managing affairs of State. Strabo tells us that Tiberius made Augustus 'the standard ($\kappa\alpha\nu\acute{o}\nu\alpha$) of his government[2],' and Tacitus reports him as saying that he regarded all his doings and sayings as law[3]; so that it might safely be assumed that such measures as were taken on his accession represent the considered judgments of his predecessor—even if we were not told that the oath of allegiance was taken in the form prescribed by Augustus[4], and that written instructions for the elections to magistracies had been drawn up by him before his death[5]. We are also entitled to regard the 'programme' speech composed by Seneca for Nero to deliver on his accession as embodying the principles which tradition regarded as those of Augustus: Suetonius, in fact, says that Nero asserted his intention of ruling *ex Augusti praescripto*[6]: and the keynotes of the speech, as recorded by Tacitus[7], are the right of the Senate to fulfil its 'ancient functions,' and the authority of the consuls over Italy and the public provinces. How far, we must ask, did theory correspond with fact?

Before, however, we examine this problem in detail a word

---

[1] LVI, 33.
[3] *Ann.* IV, 37, 4; for example, see I, 77
[4] Dio, LVII, 3, 2; see below, p. 611.
[6] *Nero*, 10.

[2] VI, 288.
[5] Vell. Pat. II, 124, 3.
[7] *Ann.* XIII, 4.

must be said with regard to the theory that the Principate was in essence a military despotism, based on the control of the army. It is evident that *in fact* the *princeps* could not maintain his authority unless the army was, for all practical purposes, at his command, and Augustus' use of the *praenomen Imperatoris*, although it was a personal appellation and not an official title, emphasized the relation between the troops and their *imperator*; but this does not alter the fact that the *legal* basis of the new constitution was the conferment upon the *princeps* of a special commission by the Senate and People of Rome. In the course of history it came about that the legions or praetorians, to whom an *imperator* was a necessity[1], imposed their will upon the Senate (which of course implied the formal consent of the People) when the succession was not clearly indicated: but such action was extra-constitutional, and was certainly not contemplated by Augustus as part of his system.

II. CONSTITUTION OF THE SENATE

We have seen how the Senate, once freely chosen by the censors, had become in the course of history a body of ex-magistrates, to which, since the reform of Sulla, entry was obtained by the holding of the quaestorship. In Republican theory candidates for public office required for their qualification a previous period of military service; but service with the eagles was not in practice obligatory in the last century of the Republic, and most of those who aspired to office seem to have secured posts on the staff of some provincial governor as *contubernales*; some, of course, served as *tribuni militum*. Augustus made service as an officer a necessary qualification for a public career; if not a *tribunus*, the aspirant to a senatorial career must serve as *praefectus alae* in a regiment of auxiliary cavalry. But this was not all. The senator's mark of distinction was the wearing of the broad purple stripe (*latus clavus*); and under Augustus, if not before, a senator's sons enjoyed the same privilege, which marked them off from the members of the *equester ordo*, who wore the narrow stripe (*angustus clavus*). To serve as a *tribunus* or *praefectus laticlavius* meant, in Augustus' system, to take the first step in the senatorial career; and Suetonius tells us[2] that he often placed two *laticlavii* in command of an *ala*, 'ne qui expers castrorum esset.' He could, moreover, bestow the *latus clavus* on young men not of senatorial birth and thus qualify them to serve as prospective

---

[1] Cf. the coins of Claudius with the legend *imper(atore) recept(o)* and the representation of the Castra Praetoria (Volume of Plates iv, 204, *a*).

[2] *Aug.* 38.

senators; and it was he who issued commissions and controlled promotions. Thus, from the outset of his career of public service, the young Roman under the Principate was imbued with the spirit of loyalty to the régime and to the ruler who exercised the chief command of the army.

Before, however, the aspirant entered upon the *cursus honorum* in the proper sense by holding the quaestorship, it was now necessary for him to be elected to one of the 'lesser magistracies,' a group of minor offices which had at one time been termed *vigintisexviri*, but which were reduced in number by Augustus to twenty[1]. These originally included the *tresviri capitales*, who performed police duties, the *tresviri monetales*, who had charge of the mint, the *quattuorviri viis in urbe purgandis* and *duoviri viis extra urbem purgandis*, whose names indicate their functions, the *decemviri stlitibus iudicandis*, who had jurisdiction in cases where the freedom of a citizen was in question, and, finally, the four *praefecti Capuam Cumas* (as they were called for short), a sinecure office, dating from the times when circuit judges administered law in Campania. In two or three inscriptions the holder of such an office describes himself as *XXVIvir*[2], but it is more usual for the office to be specified; patricians in particular appear as masters of the mint (*tresviri a(uro) a(rgento) a(ere) f(lando) f(eriundo)*)[3]. The way was now open for a qualified person to enter upon the *cursus honorum* by standing for the quaestorship[4]. Caesar had doubled the number of quaestors, which had been fixed by Sulla's law at twenty (vol. IX, pp. 287, 733); but Augustus reversed this; and he also fixed the age at which the office which gave admission to the Senate might be held at twenty-five[5].

---

[1] Dio, writing of the *lectio senatus* of 13 B.C. (LIV, 26, 5), says that before Augustus' return from Gaul it was resolved that the *XXviri* should be 'appointed from the knights,' and that no one was henceforth enrolled in the Senate without having held one of the qualifying offices. Such a step would not of course have been taken without Augustus' approval. Dio also explains that the fourth and sixth offices enumerated above had been abolished. Caesar had increased the number of the *tresviri capitales* and the masters of the mint to four; but this was only temporary.

[2] *E.g.* Dessau 908.

[3] It appears from Tacitus, *Ann.* III, 29, that even a member of the Imperial house (in this case Nero the son of Germanicus) required a special dispensation from serving one of this group of offices.

[4] If a *laticlavius* renounced the senatorial career, he resumed the 'narrow stripe'; 'clavi mensura coacta est,' says Ovid of himself (*Trist.* IV, 10, 35).

[5] The evidence is fully discussed by J. Stroux, *Sitzb. der Bay. Akad.* 1929, VIII, pp. 19 *sqq.*

The form of election by the Comitia was retained, both for the quaestorship and the other magistracies; but the influence of the Emperor, if and so far as he chose to exert it, was a decisive factor. In the first place, he examined the qualifications of candidates for office and put those who possessed them on the list to be submitted to the vote; this had always been the duty of the consul, as presiding officer, and it may still have been lawful for an aspirant to office to submit his name to the chief magistrate (*profiteri apud consulem*); but it seems that even after Augustus ceased to hold the consulship candidates approached him, with the request that he would 'nominate' them, *i.e.* formally approve their candidature. But he went further than this. Caesar had issued what may be called a *congé d'élire* to the tribes in favour of candidates whom he desired to see elected[1]; and Augustus took means to indicate those who enjoyed his support. Indeed, he followed the time-honoured Republican practice of canvassing the tribes in person in favour of 'his candidates' and cast his vote in the ballot 'ut unus e populo[2].' In his later years, however, he was unequal to the conduct of a personal canvass (a mere formality in any case) and from A.D. 8 onwards he resumed the practice of Caesar[3]. In the *lex de imperio Vespasiani* (see above, p. 140) it is enacted that any candidate for office whom the Emperor shall 'commend' to the Senate and people shall be considered *extra ordinem* at the *Comitia*; there is no reference to previous precedent in this clause, and it is permissible to infer that the right of *commendatio* had not previously been included in the Imperial prerogative without limitation. It is in fact doubtful whether, under the Julio-Claudian dynasty, the *congé d'élire* had been issued in connection with elections to the consulship[4], although it cannot be doubted that,

---

[1] The formula ran: 'Caesar dictator illi tribui commendo vobis illum et illum ut vestro suffragio suam dignitatem teneat.' Suetonius, *Div. Iul.* 41, 2.

[2] Suetonius, *Aug.* 56. That elections were not an empty form is implied by the fact that the penalties for bribery were made more severe by the Lex Julia de ambitu of 18 B.C., and by the requirement (instituted in 8 B.C.) that candidates should deposit a sum to be forfeited if corrupt practices were proved (Dio LV, 5, 3). Custom, however, had allowed a candidate to make presents to the members of his own tribe, and Augustus used to give a thousand sesterces to each elector from the two tribes with which he was connected (*Scaptia* as an Octavius, *Fabia* as a Julius).   [3] Dio, LV, 34, 2.

[4] An inscription (now partly lost) describes a person as 'per commendation(em) Ti. Caesaris Augusti ab senatu cos. dest(inatus)' (Dessau 944); but *commendatio* has no formal sense here. Tacitus makes it clear (*Ann.* I, 81) that Tiberius used indirect methods of indicating those whom he desired to see elected to the consulship.

at any rate after the troubles which followed Augustus' resignation of the office in 23 B.C. (p. 143 *sq.*), he made it clear whom he wished to see elected, especially since the highest commands in the army were filled by *consulares*. For the other offices 'Caesar's candidates' are proud to designate themselves as such on their monuments[1]. In the case of the quaestorship the *candidati Caesaris* furnished the two members of the college who were attached to the Emperor's personal staff as secretaries and read his messages to the Senate when he was absent from the sitting. *Candidati Caesaris* are also found in the higher grades, but rarely in those of aedile and tribune. During the Republican period these offices had not formed part of the regular *cursus honorum*, and it was common to pass from the quaestorship to the praetorship without holding either; but this was altered by Augustus, who made it necessary for all save patricians to hold one or other office[2]. The college of praetors numbered ten from 23 B.C. onwards[3] when Augustus placed two in charge of the Aerarium, feeling no doubt that its management called for the service of officials of more experience than the quaestors. We hear, however, that in A.D. 11, when there were sixteen candidates for the office, Augustus allowed all to serve, but that twelve was the *usual* number[4]; and it is consonant with this that Tiberius on his accession nominated twelve praetors, the number handed down from Augustus, of whom he selected four for *commendatio*, 'sine repulsa et ambitu designandos[5].' It so happens that Velleius informs us that among the four were himself and his brother—*candidati Caesaris*—whose names were on the list drawn up by Augustus before his death, so that they attained the distinction 'ut neque post nos quemquam divus Augustus, neque ante nos Caesar commendaret Tiberius[6].'

In examining the qualifications of candidates for office Augustus took property into account. As to this the statements of our

---

[1] We meet with the phrase 'per omnes honores candidatus Augustorum' or the like in inscriptions, *e.g.* Dessau 973.

[2] There are a few inscriptions (*e.g.* Dessau 906, 915) which record the tenure of both offices, but Cichorius has shown (*Römische Studien*, pp. 285 *sqq.*) that they are early in date and that the new rule probably came into force in 23 B.C. The object was partly to secure a sufficiency of candidates for these offices, which had ceased to be attractive; but this was not entirely attained, and in 13 B.C. and A.D. 5 compulsion had to be exercised (Dio LIV, 26, 7; LV, 24, 9, where he adds καὶ τοῦτο καὶ ἄλλοτε πολλάκις ἐγένετο).

[3] Vell. Pat. II, 89, 3; Dio LIII, 32, 2.

[4] Dio LVI, 25, 4. In his inaccurate review of Roman constitutional history Pomponius (*Dig.* I, 2, 2, 32) says that Augustus fixed the number of praetors at sixteen.   [5] Tacitus, *Ann.* I, 15.   [6] II, 124, 4.

authorities are conflicting: Suetonius informs us[1] that he 'raised the census of Senators from 800,000 sesterces to 1,200,000'; Dio on the other hand that he fixed it at 400,000 sesterces in 18 B.C. and raised it to 1,000,000 in 13 B.C.[2]. This last figure at any rate, may be accepted; for Tiberius, according to Tacitus, bestowed property of this value on an ex-praetor who begged for leave to resign his rank on the score of poverty; and the historian also tells us that Augustus had bestowed the same sum on the grandson of the orator Hortensius, 'ne clarissima familia extingueretur[3].'

III. LEGISLATION

Writing in the second century the jurist Gaius[4] enumerates the following sources of law—*leges, plebiscita, senatus consulta, constitutiones principum*, edicts issued by magistrates who possess the *ius edicendi*, and *responsa prudentum*. The third and fourth of these would not have found a place in a list drawn up in the Republican period; for although the Senate, through the advice which it gave to the magistrates, exercised great influence on legislation, it had no constitutional power of passing general enactments, and the *princeps* was yet to come. During the reign of Augustus the famous doctrine of Ulpian, *quod principi placuit legis habet vigorem*[5], would have seemed strange to a Roman jurist, although, by his use of the *ius edicendi*[6], his decisions on cases and petitions submitted to him, and his instructions to his subordinates, Augustus was in fact building up the body of law which Ulpian proceeds to analyse in the passage above quoted. Ulpian here expands the statement of Gaius (I, 5) that the Imperial *constitutiones*, which have the force of law, embrace edicts, *decreta* (judicial decisions)

---

[1] *Aug.* 41.　　　[2] LIV, 17, 3; LIV, 26, 3.　　　[3] *Ann.* I, 75; II, 37.
[4] I, 2.　　　[5] *Dig.* I, 4, 1.

[6] The edicts of the *praetor urbanus* and other magistrates continued, of course, to form sources of law under the Principate; but the *princeps* could also make law by edicts. Examples of these are to be found in the group of inscriptions discovered in the market-place of Cyrene (see p. 138, n. 1), and in the present context it is to be noted that in the first of these edicts, which deals with the constitution of the panel of *iudices* in the province of Crete-Cyrene, Augustus advises the governors to observe a certain procedure 'until the Senate shall deliberate on the question or I shall have devised a better plan'—in other words he recognizes 'dyarchy' in form. In his correspondence with Trajan, Pliny the Younger, writing as governor of Bithynia, refers to an edict of Augustus which modified the provincial constitution laid down by Pompey, and another which (if Hardy's conjecture 'Asiam,' in Pliny, *Ep.* x, 65, 3 is correct) related to the province of Asia. These would probably have been issued during Augustus' visit to the Eastern provinces (cf. Dio LIV, 7, 4, where Asia and Bithynia are mentioned).

and *epistulae* (replies to petitions): but we must add to these *mandata*, or instructions to officials, which are often cited in the Digest, and came to form a code of administrative law, to which additions were made from time to time. Ulpian (*Dig.* xxix, 1) quotes the clause inserted in this code by Trajan which finally legalized the 'military testament'; and the document known as the 'Gnomon of the Idios Logos,' in part based on Imperial *mandata*, illustrates the far-reaching effects of such instructions. The validity of the emperor's edicts and other dispositions was guaranteed by the clause of the *lex de imperio* that has already been referred to[1].

We saw in the previous chapter (p. 147) that in 19 B.C. Augustus was offered, but declined, the power to enact *leges Augustae* and embodied his reforms of the civil and criminal codes in a series of *leges Juliae*, which were no doubt submitted to the popular vote. Legislation proposed by magistrates also continued—it will suffice to mention such famous enactments as the Lex Fufia Caninia, the Lex Aelia Sentia, and the Lex Papia Poppaea, which are discussed elsewhere. But beside these we meet with enactments in the form of *senatus consulta*, which often bear the name of the consul who proposed them[2]; the earliest and one of the most famous of which we have knowledge is the s.c. Silanianum, which takes its name from C. Junius Silanus, consul in A.D. 10. This dealt with the torture and execution of the slaves of a murdered owner and is the subject of a chapter in Ulpian's commentary on the edict[3], and there was a further enactment by the Senate in the following year concerning this matter.

It is to be observed that under the Julio-Claudians the Senate does not, strictly speaking, make law by its decree, but tenders advice to the magistrate who administers justice; this is clearly set forth in a *senatus consultum*, of which the text is preserved in the Digest[4], forbidding women to become answerable for the

[1] See above, p. 141; cf. J. G. C. Anderson in *J.R.S.* xvii, 1927, p. 42 *sq.*
[2] The s.c. Macedonianum, passed under Vespasian, who made loans to a *filiusfamilias* irrecoverable, was named after a scoundrel mentioned in the preamble (the text is quoted by Ulpian, *Dig.* xiv, 6, 1).
[3] *Dig.* xxix, 5, 1; it was also treated in a monograph by Paulus (*ib.* 14).
[4] After the usual preamble the decree continues: 'arbitrari senatum recte atque ordine facturos ad quos de ea re in iure aditum erit, si dederint operam, ut in ea re senatus voluntas servetur' (*Dig.* xvi, 1, 2, 1). This decree was passed in the consulship of M. Junius Silanus and Vellaeus Tutor (the proposers of a Lex Junia Vellaea referred to in the law-books) which seems to be dated to A.D. 46, and is hence usually described as s.c. Vellaeanum (p. 693).

debts of others, and giving a further extension to a principle which, as Ulpian tells us, had been laid down in edicts issued by Augustus and afterwards by Claudius. In time, however, the Senate acquired the right to make law directly, and this accounts for the fact that Gaius, when he tells us that 'what the Senate commands and lays down has the force of law,' adds the words 'quamvis fuerit quae-situm'; half a century later Ulpian can write 'there is no doubt that the Senate can make law[1].' But it may well be asked whether the Senate's initiative in the matter of legislation was more than formal. In this connection it is instructive to examine the process by which a revised procedure *de repetundis* was set up in 4 B.C. In the fifth of the Edicts of Cyrene Augustus tells us that he has resolved to dispatch to the several provinces, and to append to his edict, copies of a *senatus consultum* which was passed in the consul-ship of Gaius Calvisius and Lucius Passienus, he himself being present and being one of the signatories[2], 'in order that it may be made clear to all who inhabit the provinces how great is the care taken by myself and the Senate that none of our subjects shall suffer injustice or extortion.' Then follows the decree, with the substance of which this is not the place to deal. The preamble, however, is most instructive, for it tells us that the consuls took the advice of the Senate 'Concerning the matters which Imperator Caesar Augustus, our *princeps*, in accordance with a resolution of the Advisory Board selected by lot from the Senate, desired to be brought before the Senate.' Here we have a reference to the privy council or cabinet the institution of which is mentioned by Dio[3] in his survey of the constitution which follows the account of the settlement of 27 B.C.; it consisted of the consuls, one member of each of the other colleges of magistrates, and fifteen other senators, selected by lot and serving for a period of six months. Suetonius[4] calls these bodies *consilia semenstria*, and tells us that their function was to prepare business for submission to the full Senate; and we may be very sure that no important measure was so submitted unless it had the Emperor's approval and had been drafted with the aid of his trained legal advisers.

Another example of the methods used by Augustus is to be found in the re-organization of the water-supply of Rome, of which a full account is fortunately preserved in the work of Frontinus

---

[1] *Dig.* I, 3, 9.
[2] συνεπιγραφόμενος in the Greek text indicates that Augustus was amongst those who *scribendo adfuerunt*, as the formula runs.
[3] LIII, 21, 4.   [4] *Aug.* 35.

de aquaeductibus[1]. As is mentioned elsewhere (p. 203), Augustus took this matter in hand after the death of Agrippa, who had bequeathed to him the company of slaves whom he had employed on the maintenance of the aqueducts built by him. Frontinus says that in a matter which up to this time 'quasi potestate acta certo iure eguisset, senatus consulta facta sunt ac lex promulgata,' and the texts of these are incorporated in his treatise[2]. First of all Augustus confirmed by edict the register (*commentarii*) compiled by Agrippa of those entitled to draw supplies of water. Then a series of *senatus consulta* were passed in due form, defining the duties, privileges, insignia and salaries of the *curatores* 'appointed by Caesar Augustus *ex consensu senatus*' (or *ex senatus auctoritate*); they are, amongst other things, to have powers of *iudicatio* and *cognitio* in cases where private persons have obstructed the course of the aqueducts with buildings. A further decree of the Senate provides that 'seeing that Augustus Caesar has undertaken to repair certain aqueducts at his own expense' he shall have rights of way over private property and a right to purchase materials at a fair valuation. All the above decrees were passed by the Senate in the year following that of Agrippa's death (11 B.C.), and two years later a law was proposed in due form by the consul T. Quinctius Crispinus and passed by the People voting 'in foro pro rostris[3]' imposing fines on persons obstructing or damaging the aqueducts and giving various powers to the commissioners. Thus Augustus is shown to have been careful to use the traditional constitutional machinery when legislation was required; but the initiative, we cannot doubt, rested with him who surpassed all others in *auctoritas*, and under his successors the *oratio principis*, pronounced by himself or read by his *quaestor* in the Senate, became the text of law[4].

[1] Frontinus (governor of Britain under Vespasian) was *curator aquarum* in Trajan's reign.   [2] *de aquaeductibus*, 99–130.

[3] This preamble furnishes direct evidence that *comitia populi tributa* continued to exist side by side with the *concilium plebis*. The first citizen to cast his vote, Sex. Virro, may perhaps be the person expelled from the Senate by Tiberius in A.D. 17 (Tacitus, *Ann.* 11, 48, where the MSS. have *Varronem*).

[4] Early instances of the *oratio principis* are to be found in the speeches of Claudius relating to certain reforms of procedure (*B.G.U.* 611, fully treated by Stroux, *Sitz. der Bay. Akad.* 1929, VIII). We possess the text of two *senatus consulta* which make it unlawful for speculators to demolish buildings in order to make a profit by selling the materials (Dessau 6043). The first—conveniently known as s.c. Hosidianum—may date from A.D. 45, and although it refers to the *providentia optimi principis*, it bears no sign of having been proposed on the initiative of the Emperor; the second, which belongs to A.D. 56, refers to it as passed 'auctore divo Claudio' (p. 695).

IV. THE ADMINISTRATION OF JUSTICE

It has been explained in a previous volume (IX, pp. 304 *sqq.*) how the *iudicium populi*, in which the Roman people assembled in *comitia* tried and decided cases arising from the appeal (*provocatio*) of a citizen against a sentence passed by a magistrate, gave place to the *iudicium publicum*, which took place in one of the Standing Courts (*quaestiones perpetuae*) set up by a series of statutes defining the several crimes of which the State took cognisance. These courts continued to function in the principate of Augustus; but, as we have seen, a general appellate jurisdiction was conferred upon the *princeps*, and from 23 B.C. onwards, when he ceased to hold the consulship annually, his proconsular *imperium* was retained even within the *pomerium* of the city, so that he could exercise in Rome itself the jurisdiction belonging to a provincial governor. Thus a new High Court came into being, and there is good evidence that Augustus took his duties as its president very seriously. Suetonius informs us[1] that he often sat in court until nightfall, and, in order to illustrate his leniency, tells the anecdote that he put to a prisoner clearly guilty of parricide the question 'Surely you did not kill your father, did you?' in order that he might avoid inflicting the well-known punishment of his crime, since only those who confessed were liable to it. Dio[2], on the other hand, speaks of his severity, and tells us how on one occasion Maecenas, seeing that he was about to pronounce a number of death-sentences, threw into his lap a tablet on which was written 'Rise at last, executioner!'

It is not so easy to determine when or how a second High Court of Justice, that of the consuls, acting with the Senate as their *consilium*, was called into being. The narrative of Tacitus makes it clear that under Tiberius trials in the Senate, especially on the charge of *maiestas*, were frequent. In A.D. 15 Granius Marcellus, governor of Bithynia, was brought before the Senate on this charge, and Tiberius (as Tacitus says) announced that he would pronounce his *sententia* openly and on oath; whereupon Cn. Piso asked him whether he would vote first or last, adding 'if first, I shall have a lead to follow, if last, I fear that I may unwittingly differ from your verdict'; and the Emperor agreed to a verdict of acquittal. In the following year Libo Drusus was charged with treasonable practices, and his accuser 'approached the consuls and asked that the Senate should take cognisance of the case.' In this case the accused committed suicide before the trial took place. In A.D. 19 Cn. Piso

---

[1] *Aug.* 33.　　　　　　　　　　　　[2] LV, 7, 2.

was tried on various charges, including the poisoning of Germanicus (see below, p. 623); we note that he expressed his willingness to stand his trial in the praetor's court *de veneficis*, but that his prosecutor, Fulcinius Trio, laid his information before the consuls and that the Senate requested the *princeps* to take up the case (*cognitionem exciperet*). Tiberius, however, declined to do so, and said that he would not place Germanicus above the laws, save in so far as his death should be investigated in the Senate and not before a jury-court; in this case also the accused committed suicide, and a vote of the Senate was taken, on the *relatio* of the Emperor, about the measures to be taken with regard to his honours and estate[1].

The impression which we gain from the accounts of these trials is that the new procedure was of recent growth, and not part of the system established on the 'restoration of the Republic' by Augustus. And indeed it would be hard to prove that the constitution of the Senate as a High Court of Justice dates back to so early a period. We have referred above (p. 134) to the case of Cornelius Gallus, where the fulminations of the Senate against the fallen favourite took the form of a demand that he should be condemned 'in the courts'; in 23 B.C. we find Tiberius prosecuting the conspirators Varro and Caepio for treason *apud iudices* and obtaining their conviction, and in the same year M. Primus was tried before the *praetor*, Augustus being summoned as a witness (p. 138), and several votes were cast for his acquittal[2]. The procedure in the case of Iullus Antonius and the other lovers of Julia is nowhere described in detail: Velleius would lead us to think that the Lex Julia de adulteriis was put into force, but Dio hints at a charge of *maiestas*[3]. Towards the close of the reign, however, cases are recorded by Tacitus in which the Senate appears to have acted in a judicial capacity[4]. A certain Cassius Severus, who had published *famosi libelli*, was brought to trial 'specie legis [maiestatis],' and was exiled to Crete 'iudicio iurati Senatus.' About the same time Volesus Messalla, the proconsul of Asia, who had been guilty of atrocious cruelty, was brought to trial and condemned, presumably under the *lex repetundarum*; and in A.D. 22, when a similar case came before the Senate, Tiberius ordered to be read the indictment drawn up by Augustus and the *senatus consultum* which was passed

---

[1] Tacitus, *Ann.* II, 28; II, 79; III, 10; III, 17.   [2] Dio, LIV, 3, 4.

[3] ὡς καὶ ἐπὶ τῇ μοναρχίᾳ τοῦτο πράξας (LV, 10); Tacitus hints (*Ann.* III, 24) that Augustus 'went beyond his own laws.' According to Suetonius (*Aug.* 65) he sent a report on the matter to the Senate.

[4] Tacitus, *Ann.* I, 72; IV, 21; III, 68.

inflicting penalties on Messalla. It has been supposed that a reference by the elder Seneca[1] to Furius Saturninus 'qui Volesum condemnavit' implies that Saturninus procured his condemnation in a jury-court, and that the decree of the Senate followed the verdict; but the inference is uncertain.

It seems therefore that the Senate's jurisdiction had become established before Augustus' death; and we may trace one of the steps by which this was brought about in the fifth edict from Cyrene, which (as has already been mentioned) covers a *senatus consultum* passed in 4 B.C. on the recommendation of the Emperor's *consilium*, laying down a new procedure to be adopted in cases of *repetundae* where the prosecutors claim only money damages and do not threaten the *caput* of the defendant governor. In the procedure the preliminary hearing of the case takes place in the Senate (which may be convened by any magistrate having the right to bring business before that body), and a commission consisting of four consulars, three praetorians and two other senators (which may be reduced to five if both parties exercise their right of challenging two) is set up, which is instructed to give a verdict within thirty days. In one sense this is no innovation, but a reversion to the procedure used before legislation *de repetundis* had taken place, for in effect it sets up a board of *recuperatores* to investigate the claim of the provincials, as had been done in 171 B.C. (vol. VIII, p. 310); but that this board should be made representative of the Senate shows the trend of constitutional development for which Augustus was responsible.

In what sense can it be said that there was precedent for this senatorial jurisdiction? Dio, it is true, in describing the working of the restored Republic (LIII, 21, 6) says that the Senate 'sat in judgment (ἔκρινε) as a body as it had done before'; but his statement finds no support in historical or legal tradition. Mommsen, who at first explained the facts by the hypothesis that the 'sovereign' Senate of the dynasty succeeded to the rights of the *comitia populi*, wrote later[2] of a 'dependence' (*Anlehnung*) of the new jurisdiction on the 'martial law' procedure set up in the last century of the Republic to deal with the threats to public security involved in the agitation of C. Gracchus and his followers and the conspiracy of Catiline, but admits that such emergency measures must not be confused with the proceedings of the 'consular-senatorial' court[2]. Augustus, in fact, was well aware that the man who never makes a precedent never makes anything; but here, as always, he was true

---

[1] *Contr.* VII, 6, 22.   [2] *Staatsrecht*, III, p. 1267 *sq.*; *Strafrecht*, p. 251.

to his motto *festina lente*. In effect he restored to the consuls—acting with the advice of the Senate—the plenitude of the *imperium*, such as he himself possessed. In the 'programme' speech of Nero (cf. p. 160) we read: 'consulum tribunalibus Italia et publicae provinciae adsisterent: illi patrum aditum praeberent'; and though these words of course cover much more than judicial functions, they indicate that the 'consular-senatorial' court was designed to try cases or hear appeals arising from its own sphere of administration. In fact, so long as the spirit of this programme was observed, we find that the Senate takes cognisance of offences committed by its own members, *equites* or provincials[1].

The Augustan system, in its completed form, thus provided for two High Courts of Justice, that of the *princeps*, and the Senate; and the result was to bring about far-reaching changes in procedure. The enquiries conducted by both courts are described by the term *cognitio*, as opposed to *iudicium*[2], and this made for elasticity, for the court was not bound by the formal restrictions of a suit promoted by a prosecuting party, nor (although it administered the laws by which the *quaestiones* were governed) was it precluded from dealing with several indictments in the same trial; and it could modify the penalty prescribed by statute[3]. Both courts, moreover, were courts of final appeal, and this was of special importance as regards the Emperor's court, for he delegated jurisdiction to his subordinates and representatives, from whom an appeal of course lay to himself. This applied to the provincial governors who held their commissions from him as *legati* and to the *praefecti* appointed by him to take charge of departments of State. Of these the most important was the *praefectus urbi*. We have already referred to Augustus' experiments in relation to this office, which was at first temporary. It is not quite clear when a permanent *praefectus* was appointed, but even if it was reserved for Tiberius to make their commander a permanent official, we cannot doubt that he was carrying out the expressed intentions of Augustus (see below, p. 201). The jurisdiction of the *praefectus urbi* arose from the fact that he was responsible for the maintenance of order in the City, but it was not long before he began to encroach on the functions of the civil courts, for as early as the reign of Nero we read of a case in which a prosecutor was exiled because he brought his case before the *praetor* in order to remove it from the jurisdiction of the prefect 'with a semblance of legality'; and eventually he took cognisance,

---

[1] A study of the trials recorded by Tacitus shows that the emperor could find means of influencing the Senate's decisions.   [2] Tacitus, *Ann.* I, 75.

[3] 'Senatui licet et mitigare leges et intendere' (Pliny, *Ep.* IV, 9, 17).

as Ulpian says, of all crimes committed 'up to the hundredth milestone' from Rome[1]. It is possible that Augustus, with his scrupulous adherence to constitutional forms, regularized the position of his delegates by legislation. This was certainly the case with the *praefectus Aegypti* (p. 288 *sq.*) of whom it is said by Ulpian[2] that he possesses an *imperium ad similitudinem proconsulis*, 'which was conferred upon him *by law* under Augustus'; and the jurisdiction exercised by the *praefectus annonae* (p. 202) was no doubt based on the Lex Julia de annona mentioned in the forty-eighth title of the Digest, which Dio seems to date to 18 B.C.[3]

A parallel development to that of the criminal courts may be seen in the field of civil jurisdiction. We have already mentioned the laws of 18 B.C. which regulated the procedure of the courts (p. 148) and finally abolished the antiquated procedure of the *legis actiones*[4]; but the formulary system itself which was characteristic of the praetor's court, and what it is convenient to call the *ordo iudiciorum*, gradually gave place to the more elastic *cognitio*, which took place *extra ordinem*[5], and was exercised by the holder of an *imperium* or a delegate appointed by him. The emperor naturally used this procedure in his own court, whether he tried a case in the first instance or on appeal from a lower court; for appeal in the proper sense of the word, which had not existed under the Republic, now became a regular institution. Suetonius (*Aug.* 33) says that it was the practice of Augustus to delegate the hearing of appeals arising in Rome (*urbanorum litigatorum*) to the *praetor urbanus*, and of those from the provinces to *consulares*. But the emperor and his delegates were not alone in using *cognitio*, for the consuls— using the Senate as their *consilium*—were also competent to exercise jurisdiction in this form and to hear appeals; and we read in Tacitus (*Ann.* xiv, 28) that Nero 'enhanced the prestige of the Fathers' by enacting that those who appealed from the findings of *iudices* in civil causes to the Senate should lodge the same caution-money as those who brought their cases before the emperor[6] (p. 705); up

---

[1] *Dig.* 1, 12, 1 (as emended).   [2] *Dig.* 1, 17.

[3] LIV, 17 (the word διενομοθέτει implies a legislative act); Mommsen (*Strafrecht*, p. 852, n. 1) refers this law to Caesar.

[4] 'per legem Aebutiam (cf. vol. IX, p. 862) et duas Julias sublatae sunt legis actiones' (Gaius IV, 30).

[5] *cognitio extraordinaria*, the term in common use, is not found in the jurists (except in the plural and in a non-technical sense in the rubric of *Dig.* L, 13). In Suetonius, *Claud.* 15 a distinction is drawn between *cognitio* and *ordinarium ius*.

[6] Suetonius, indeed, tells us (*Nero*, 17) that Nero enacted that *all* appeals from *iudices* should lie to the Senate; but he has evidently misunderstood the facts.

to that time, the historian tells us, no penalty was incurred by the unsuccessful appellant in the Senate's court. In jurisdiction, therefore, Emperor and Senate exercised concurrent functions; and it was natural that no appeal should lie from one court to the other[1].

V. FOREIGN RELATIONS

The Senate was no longer the 'assembly of kings' which had inspired awe in the peoples and potentates of East and West in the great days of the Republic. We have already seen that the power of making peace and war, and of concluding treaties with foreign States, was part of the imperial prerogative (p. 141); and that in the summary of the system of government with which his work ends, Strabo assigns the client-princes to the sphere of authority of the emperor; nor can it be doubted that this represents the facts of the case. In an interesting chapter of his life of Augustus (48) Suetonius tells us how the princeps pursued a policy of treating the protected rulers as 'members and constituents of the Empire' and encouraging friendships and matrimonial alliances between them, bringing up their children with his own and appointing advisers and guardians to such as needed such supervision. These statements can be abundantly illustrated from the history of the Eastern provinces[2], and the measures taken by Augustus are dealt with elsewhere. Here it will suffice to say that not only did he confirm in their principalities some of Antony's vassals, such as Herod the Great in Judaea, Archelaus in Cappadocia, Amyntas in Galatia and Polemo in Pontus, but gave a further extension to the system by bringing under his protection the kingdom of Bosporus and the Odrysian principality in Thrace[3]. At the same time it may be questioned whether he intended this system to be permanent. Galatia was annexed in 25 B.C. and Paphlagonia (hitherto ruled by the family of Deiotarus) was added thereto in 6 B.C.; and in A.D. 6 Archelaus, who had ruled Judaea on the death of Herod the Great, was deposed and his territory annexed (cf. p. 339). Nor can we doubt that in

---

[1] Ulpian writes: 'Sciendum est appellari a senatu non posse principem idque oratione divi Hadriani effectum' (*Dig.* XLIX, 2, 1); but we may be sure that this was the practice of Augustus and of the successors who ruled in his spirit.

[2] See pp. 113 *sqq.*, 276; the marriage of Antony's daughter Selene with Juba of Mauretania may also be noted, see p. 112.

[3] See pp. 265, 356. Intermarriage took place between these dynasties (p. 268).

annexing Cappadocia and Commagene (p. 620), Tiberius was carrying out a policy of absorption which he knew to be in accordance with the intentions of Augustus.

What part, if any, did the Senate play in the execution of this policy? There is no sign that it was in any way responsible for the decisions taken by Augustus, though he may have communicated them to it as a matter of courtesy. He speaks of the measures which he took to regulate the affairs of Armenia as his own acts, and it is evident that the Senate had no part in determining his policy[1]. Nevertheless, Augustus contrived to preserve in some measure the fiction that the Senate was an organ of government in the field of foreign affairs. In 29 B.C. Antiochus of Commagene was charged with the murder of an envoy sent to Rome by his brother, Mithridates II; Augustus summoned him to Rome, brought him before the Senate and secured his condemnation[2] and execution. This precedent was followed by Tiberius in two cases—those of Archelaus of Cappadocia in A.D. 17 and of Rhescuporis of Thrace in A.D. 19 (pp. 643, 645). It should be noted, however, that in his youth Tiberius had defended Archelaus against charges brought against him 'in the Emperor's court[3].' Again, it may be assumed that it was by a vote of the Senate that the title of 'friend of the Roman People' was, according to Republican custom, conferred upon Polemo, King of Pontus, in 26 B.C., for the King returned the compliment by granting to Roman Senators the right to occupy seats of honour in the theatres of his realm[4].

That embassies from the Senatorial provinces were admitted to audience by the Senate was natural enough. In the procedure for claims *de repetundis* laid down in the *senatus consultum* of Cyrene (p. 171) the first step is for the envoys to lay their complaint before one of the magistrates who have the right of convening the Senate, and he is instructed to bring them before that body as soon as may be and nominate a senator to present their

[1] *Res Gestae* 27. He here speaks of Tiberius and Gaius Caesar as his agents; and if special *imperia* were conferred upon them by decree of the Senate (as in the case of Germanicus under Tiberius) this was a constitutional formality.

[2] The circumstances of the case are not very clear; see Geyer in *P.W.* s.v. Mithridates (33).

[3] 'Augusto cognoscente' Suetonius, *Tib.* 8: he was accused by his subjects (Dio LVII, 17).

[4] The precedent was followed in the reign of Tiberius, when the Senate passed complimentary votes for Ptolemy of Mauretania (Tacitus, *Ann.* IV, 26).

case. But foreign relations are not involved here. Dio relates[1] that when a Parthian embassy came to him in 23 B.C. Augustus presented the envoys to the Senate, but that body referred the decision to him. Towards the close of his reign, when old age and infirmity restricted his powers of transacting business, it is said that Augustus 'entrusted to three ex-consuls the embassies sent to Rome by peoples and kings; these sat separately and gave audience to the envoys and replied to their requests except in cases where it was necessary for the final decision to be taken by the Emperor and the Senate[2].' When taking decisions on foreign policy Augustus might—and doubtless as a rule did—summon a *consilium* of advisers. We read, for instance[3], that, on the death of Herod the Great, Augustus took the opinions of his 'friends' (*i.e.* the *consilium amicorum*) on the question of the succession in Judaea: Gaius Caesar, then sixteen years old, was amongst those who attended this meeting. But no real responsibility rested on the shoulders of the Senate in such matters[4].

VI. THE OLD AND THE NEW

We have seen that in the record of his acts which he bequeathed as his political testament Augustus laid stress on his restoration of Republican forms and his refusal to accept any office inconsistent with those 'customs of the ancestors' to which every Roman— whether sincerely or not—paid unquestioning homage. The document, however, must be admitted to be somewhat disingenuous in its selection and presentation of historical facts. We should be led by it to think that the constitutional settlement of 27 B.C. was the organic measure by which the new régime took shape, whereas in fact the statute of 23 B.C., which profoundly modified the position of the *princeps*, had far greater importance for the future of the system: and the statement that Augustus 'added Egypt to the dominion of the Roman People' may have a formal truth, but obscures the fact that neither the People nor the Senate (whose members were expressly forbidden to set foot therein) had any part or lot in its government (p. 284 *sq.*). In order, therefore, to form a judgment on the new constitution it has been necessary to

---

[1] LIII, 33, 1.   [2] In the epitome of Dio LV, 33, 5.

[3] Josephus, *Ant.* XVII [9, 5], 229; in *Bell. Jud.* II [2, 4], 25, he speaks of a συνέδριον τῶν ἐν τέλει Ῥωμαίων.

[4] In the earlier years of his reign Tiberius, according to Suetonius (*Tib.* 31), made a practice of referring all matters of public policy to the Senate, including 'quid et qua forma regum litteris rescribi placeret.' He considered that in so doing he was carrying on the Augustan tradition; see below, p. 613 *sq.*

examine in detail the actual working of the system in respect of the principal functions of government.

The conclusion to which we are led is this: that Augustus, who preferred evolution to revolution, made such use as he could of existing institutions and practices, even when he foresaw the gradual decline in their importance or even their eventual disappearance, and at the same time built up beside them, gradually and often tentatively, a new fabric, subject to his own control, as the framework of the Imperial State. For the successful achievement of this task it was necessary to enlist the willing co-operation of the old governing order and also to tap the resources of administrative ability which the class hitherto excluded from the highest offices could supply; and in these respects his triumph was conspicuous. The hierarchy of orders and the *carrière ouverte aux talents* were his guiding principles, and they were well adapted to the needs of the time; but they could only be applied by one who, like Augustus, had a keen eye for the qualities which distinguish great administrators and was able to secure their loyal service. In an interesting passage Velleius Paterculus[1] illustrates the theme that 'great undertakings need great helpers' by reference to Agrippa and Statilius Taurus, who were not debarred by the *novitas* of their families from attaining the highest honours in the State—by the irony of fate the chapter concludes with a panegyric on his patron Sejanus! Seneca noted that Augustus 'enrolled the whole regiment of his intimates from the enemy's camp[2]'; we have already seen that when he laid down the consulship in 23 B.C., both holders of that office were men who had fought on the side of Brutus and Cassius and that in the following year Augustus had nominated one of the proscribed for the consulship and another for the censorship; and it is well to remember that in 2 B.C. the crowning honour of the salutation as 'Father of the Fatherland' was conferred on the *princeps* on the proposal of the famous orator M. Valerius Messalla Corvinus, who had commanded the Republican right wing at Philippi and had captured Octavian's camp[3]. In the following years the consulship was held by representatives of the Cornelii Lentuli and

---

[1] II, 127.

[2] *de clem.* I, 10, 1. He refers more especially to Sallustius Crispus, the nephew of the historian Sallust, M. Cocceius Nerva, the great-grandfather of the Emperor Nerva, and Dellius, probably the person addressed by Horace in *Odes,* II, 3.

[3] It will be remembered that he had pronounced the office of *praefectus urbi* to be unconstitutional (p. 134).

the Calpurnii Pisones; and if we add that only a few years before two brothers, Africanus Fabius Maximus and Paullus Fabius Maximus, whose *praenomina* attest their pride in tracing descent from the great Scipio and Aemilius Paullus, were among the proconsuls (in Africa and Asia respectively) who were permitted to issue coins bearing their own portrait[1], we have said enough to show that the reconciliation of the great families of the Republic with the new régime was an accomplished fact.

At the same time the promotion of 'new men' to Senatorial rank and their elevation to the consulship continued throughout the reign[2], and the increase in the number of holders of the chief magistracy brought about by the shortening of the term of office and the appointment of *suffecti*, which became regular from A.D. 2 onwards, enabled Augustus to recognize the claims not only of the old aristocracy but also of the families which had gained access to the circle of *nobiles* during the Civil War period by services rendered to the triumvirs, and of the men of marked ability whom he desired to employ in the most responsible administrative or military positions[3]. He needed *consulares* not merely to command his armies, but also to discharge other duties; we have seen that he allotted to them the hearing of appeals from the provinces (p. 173); in A.D. 6 he set up a Commission of three Senators of this rank, chosen by lot, to effect economies in public expenditure; and in the same year and in the next[4] two *consulares* were appointed to supervise the distribution of corn; and each of the Commissions or *Curae*, of which some account is given in a later chapter, had a consular for its president.

These Commissions may serve to illustrate Augustus' adaptation of old methods to new purposes. Under the Republic it had been found necessary to supplement the annual magistracies by the appointment of Commissioners (*curatores*) to carry out special administrative tasks, such as the repair of roads[5]; and Augustus

---

[1] Cf. Mommsen, *Staatsrecht* II[3], p. 261, Gardthausen, *Augustus*, I, p. 1109, II, p. 725.

[2] F. B. Marsh, *The Founding of the Roman Empire*, pp. 241, 247 *sqq.*, analyses the Fasti, so far as these can be restored, with a view to showing that the promotion of 'new men' was comparatively rare in the years following the 'restoration of the Republic.'

[3] Marsh, *op. cit.* pp. 246 *sqq.*, examines the facts regarding the employment of consulars in the service of the Emperor, and argues for a 'tightening of [his] control over the elections' (p. 251).

[4] Dio, LV, 25, 6; 26, 3; 31, 4.

[5] They possessed *potestas*, but not *imperium* (cf. Festus *s.v. curatores* and *cum potestate*): for instances see Dessau 45, 5799, 5800.

retained the title, but set up permanent Boards as Departments of State. Suetonius says[1] that 'in order to increase the number of those taking part in the administration of the Republic, he devised new offices,' amongst which he enumerates the *curae*; and there are several inscriptions which show that such boards were composed of Senators with a consular as chairman. It is probable that then, as now, administrative ability was confined to a limited number of those who took part in public life, for we find that the same names recur in different lists; for example, the two inscriptions[2] which give the names of the *curatores locorum publicorum* (with the consuls of A.D. 2 and A.D. 6 respectively as chairman) show that members of these boards also served on the Commission for regulating the Tiber[3]; and this latter department was in A.D. 15 entrusted to Ateius Capito and L. Arruntius[4], the former of whom (as we know from Frontinus) had been *curator aquarum* since A.D. 13. Capito, we may add, was one of the leading jurists of the time, and the fore-runner of the 'Sabinian' School; and we are justified in regarding him as the chief legal adviser of the *princeps*. It has been pointed out[5] that the new procedure set up for the trial of suits *de repetundis* in the edicts of Cyrene is clearly the work of a trained lawyer, and shows no trace of 'politically orientated innovation'; and this is what we should expect from one who, like Capito, was at once an enthusiastic supporter of the Imperial régime and at the same time notoriously conservative as a lawyer[6]. Augustus found in him and his like the type of public servant who can be trusted to reconcile order with progress.

Our finding, then, must be that Augustus was successful in adapting Republican institutions to the needs of the Imperial government and in creating a new governing class, into which the older aristocracy was absorbed. He must have recognized clearly that a Mediterranean empire could not be administered by the annual magistrates of an old-fashioned city-state; but the *cursus honorum* had a long and honourable tradition and had satisfied the ambition of the greatest of Romans in the past, and useful work could still be found for those who pursued it—under the control and supervision of the *princeps*. That the Senate had

---

[1] *Aug.* 37.   [2] Dessau 5939, 5940.
[3] Dessau 5893, 5925.   [4] Tacitus, *Ann.* I, 76.
[5] By J. Stroux in *Abh. der Bay. Akad.* XXXIV, 2, 1928, p. 112 *sq.*
[6] On the other hand his great rival, Antistius Labeo, was at the same time a staunch Republican and an original lawyer ('plurime innovare instituit,' says Pomponius, *Dig.* I, 2, 2, 47).

its part to play in his system is shown both by the assignment to it of new functions and by the attention which Augustus gave to matters of procedure and to the compulsion which he exerted upon the Senator to discharge his duties (p. 123, n. 1). In 17 B.C. he increased the existing fines for non-attendance[1], and though he reduced the quorum of four hundred necessary for the passing of a valid *senatus consultum* in 11 B.C.[2], in 9 B.C. he dealt with the whole question of procedure by a comprehensive measure, again increasing the fine for absence, but fixing a variable quorum in accordance with the nature of the business to be transacted[3]. But we should observe that Dio uses the word 'command' of the Emperor's regulations, and says in the passage last cited that 'he had the measures which he enacted (ἐνομοθέτησεν) inscribed on tablets and posted up in the Senate-house before bringing them forward, so that members of the Senate might, if they so desired, propose amendments.' It may be doubted whether any of them took advantage of the opportunity offered. And it must not be forgotten that from 29 B.C. onwards Augustus had reserved for himself the right of receiving requests from senators for leave of absence from Italy—which, if the object of their travel was a visit to Egypt, was refused on principle. He suspended the publication of the minutes of the Senate[4], which had been ordered by Caesar, and in the last year of his reign he modified the constitution of his Privy Council (see above, p. 167), which henceforth consisted of the consuls, twenty senators and such other persons (including members of the Imperial family) as he might summon, and secured for its resolutions the force of *senatus consulta*. These facts are significant.

As for the Roman People, it may be formally true to say that he 'restored the ancient rights of the assembly[5]' in 27 B.C., *i.e.* that the forms of election which had been suspended during the Triumvirate were once more brought into use. We have seen that legislation by the assemblies took place from time to time; and Suetonius[6] records a device by which the members of municipal senates could cast their votes in the elections of the city magistrates and forward them in sealed ballot-boxes to Rome (see below, p. 461 *sq.*). It is a characteristic example of Augustus' ingenuity— but it could have no practical significance when the *princeps*

---

[1] Dio, LIV, 18, 3. The principle 'senatori qui nec aderit aut causa aut culpa esto' had been laid down by Cicero (*de legibus*, III, 4, 11).
[2] Dio, LIV, 35, 1. [3] Dio, LV, 3 and 4, 1.
[4] Suetonius, *Aug.* 36. [5] Vell. Pat. II, 99, 3.
[6] *Aug.* 46.

'commended' to the electors the candidates whose election he desired.

Writing in the second century, Tacitus[1] summed up the trend of Augustus' government in the phrase 'he gradually absorbed into himself the functions of Senate, magistrates and laws': and this expresses the fact as seen from the standpoint of later times. Was Augustus himself conscious that this must inevitably ensue from the system which he adopted and especially from the establishment of a new administration which could not but overshadow the old? We shall never know: but Tiberius at least interpreted his injunctions in the sense that the Senate was to be consulted on all questions of policy, and followed them loyally in the earlier years of his reign (p. 613 *sq.*). Hirschfeld[2] believed that Augustus hoped that the welfare of the State might be secured by the harmonious co-operation of *princeps* and Senate, but his conclusion was that though we must give full recognition to his efforts 'we cannot acquit him of the grave reproach of having willed the impossible and set up the impermanent,' through an underestimate of the capacity of the twin pillars of his constitution. The history of his successors makes it hard to dissent from this judgment. Yet Tacitus, in the passage above quoted, recognizes that the provinces were ready to acquiesce in the new régime, since the 'rule of Senate and People' (*Senatus populique imperium*) had left them at the mercy of ambitious and avaricious rulers, and denied them the protection of the laws, 'perverted as they were by violence, intrigue and corruption.' And the judgment of Strabo[3], who had seen the old order giving place to the new, was that 'never had Rome and her allies enjoyed the blessings of peace and plenty in fuller measure than that which Augustus Caesar bestowed upon them from the time when he assumed absolute authority.'

---

[1] *Ann.* i, 2.   [2] *Die kaiserlichen Verwaltungsbeamten*, p. 468.
[3] vi, 288.

CHAPTER VII

THE IMPERIAL ADMINISTRATION

I. THE PROBLEM OF ADMINISTRATION

IN the speech of advice to Augustus which Dio Cassius[1] puts into the mouth of Maecenas, urging that a restoration of the Republic was neither desirable nor possible, it is pointed out that while Rome was a small State democratic institutions were efficient, but that with the growth of the Empire a strain was put upon them which they were unable to bear. 'The cause of our troubles is the multitude of our population and the magnitude of the business of our government; for the population embraces men of every kind, in respect both of race and endowment, and both their tempers and their desires are manifold; and the business of the state has become so vast that it can be administered only with the greatest difficulty.' 'Our city, like a great merchantman manned with a crew of every race and lacking a pilot, has now for many generations been rolling and plunging, a ship as it were without ballast.'

In this passage the historian puts his finger on the chief cause of the collapse of the Roman Republic. With their well-known conservatism the Romans had retained, though not without modifications, some institutions characteristic of the city-state, such as the annual magistracy and the popular assembly, which were ill suited to an imperial city forced to deal with problems calling for knowledge and experience. Republican Rome was not lacking in men possessing a high standard of efficiency and very well qualified to reform and administer the government of the Empire. But political conditions made it difficult for a Pompey or even a Sulla to do constructive work, and it is doubtful whether, even if he had lived longer, Caesar possessed the patience to undertake the task which occupied the long life of his adopted son. Cicero was undoubtedly right in protesting against the dictator's statement that his work was done, and in urging him to set his hand to the task of reconstruction[2]. It seems certain that Tacitus considered Augustus rather than Caesar to be the creator of the system of government under which he lived. In a short sketch of the history of the later Republic which he inserts into his Annals[3]

---

[1] LII, 15.   [2] *pro Marcello*, 7, 22–30.   [3] III, 28.

he passes from the third consulship of Pompey (52 B.C.) to the sixth consulship of Augustus (28 B.C.) with the dry comment: 'exim continua per viginti annos discordia non mos non ius,' without even mentioning the administrative measures of the dictator.

In an earlier chapter of this work (vol. IX, chap. X) an account was given of the methods employed by the Republic in the government of the Empire. It was shown that the provinces were inadequately garrisoned, were governed by men who were, at the best, well-meaning amateurs and, at the worst, unscrupulous scoundrels, and were taxed on a system which irritated the provincials without enriching the treasury. Nearer home the road system of Italy was neglected, and in Rome itself there was urgent need of supervision of the public buildings, of an improved water-supply, and above all of an organized police force. Thus the whole military, administrative, and financial machinery of the Republic required to be thoroughly overhauled, and a professional spirit introduced into the work of government. If this meant the sacrifice of such traces of democracy as still survived in Rome the price was a small one, for the popular assemblies had long ceased to represent adequately the citizen-body. Inefficiency had always been the curse of the city-state, and the time had come for Roman statesmen to look for guidance not to Athens or Sparta but to the Persian Empire and the Hellenistic monarchies which succeeded it. Even the cynical Tacitus[1] admits that the accession of Augustus to power was welcome to the provinces which had suffered so much under the old régime. If under the Principate there grew up an imperial patriotism and a genuine gratitude for the benefits conferred by Roman rule, the credit is mainly due to Augustus himself. He did much to secure that the representatives of Rome throughout the Empire should be competent and honest, and that the burden of taxation should not be excessive. Though the system which he founded was considerably developed and modified by his successors, the main features of the structure which he created remained unchanged for several centuries.

One of the greatest achievements of Augustus was that he attained to power without alienating, as Caesar had done, the sympathies of the senatorial class. The question of the place which he intended the Senate to occupy in the new constitution has been discussed elsewhere (chap. VI), and here we are only concerned with the part which he wished its members to play in the practical work of administration. Under the Republic the Senate owed its in-

[1] *Ann.* I, 2.

fluence and prestige mainly to the fact that it contained practically all of those who possessed administrative experience and a first-hand acquaintance with the problems of government. Even Caesar, though he showed himself high-handed and contemptuous towards the Senate as a corporation, had drawn from its ranks most of those who represented him in the provinces, for there is no reason to think that he introduced any fundamental change in the method of appointing governors. It is therefore not surprising that Augustus, who treated the Senate with the greatest respect and genuinely desired that it should take an important part in the work of government, reserved for senators most of the important posts to which he directly or indirectly controlled the appointment. Though the powers exercised by magistrates during their year of office were reduced and were often merely nominal, the tenure of the consulship or praetorship entitled a man to be reckoned among the *consulares* or *praetorii*, from whom the holders of the most responsible positions in administration and in the army were drawn. With few exceptions, which will be noted below, the Roman provinces were governed and Roman armies commanded by senators. It must, however, be noted that even under Augustus, and still more under his successors, senatorial rank ceased to be confined to a limited class of *optimates* (p. 177 *sq.*). From the beginning of the principate *novi homines* were far commoner than in the age of Marius and Cicero[1]. Two notable examples are P. Sulpicius Quirinius, consul in 12 B.C., who afterwards governed Asia and Syria, and C. Poppaeus Sabinus (consul in A.D. 9), whose career began under Augustus and who died in A.D. 35 after a very long tenure of the province of Moesia. Of the latter Tacitus tells us that his origin was humble, that he owed his consulship and triumphal honours to the friendship of Emperors, and that he governed important provinces for twenty-four years 'nullam ob eximiam artem sed quod par negotiis neque supra erat[2].' To men of this efficient and law-abiding type the change from republic to monarchy was an unmixed blessing, for it was now possible to hold responsible positions for a long period of years without being involved in political controversy and without being suspected of plotting the subversion of the state.

It was, however, as Augustus saw, undesirable and almost impossible to put the whole burden of administration upon the shoulders of the comparatively small senatorial class. In order to

[1] See F. B. Marsh, *The Founding of the Roman Empire*, chap. IX. Other notable examples are M. Lollius, M. Vinicius, P. Quinctilius Varus.

[2] Tacitus, *Ann.* VI, 39.

secure elasticity he decided to make use of sections of the population less hampered by Republican traditions and free from the requirements of a somewhat rigid *cursus honorum*. Although later on, when a regular bureaucracy had been developed, the career of a public servant of the non-senatorial classes was nearly as well-defined as that of a senator, this was not so at the time with which we are concerned. On the death of Augustus there existed only the rudiments of a Civil Service, but even in his reign posts had been created second to none in importance which were invariably held by non-senators, and a beginning had been made with the employment of equites and freedmen as subordinates to and colleagues of senators. Though later observers saw in Caesar's secretaries Oppius and Balbus predecessors of the civil servants of the Principate[1], the dictator did little to create a Civil Service and Augustus rather than he must be regarded as its founder.

It was noted above (vol. IX, p. 458) that a provincial governor of the age of Cicero had at his disposal no body of experienced assistants such as exists to-day under British rule in India and tropical Africa. The staff which he brought with him from Rome was no better informed than he was himself about the problems which confronted him. For local information he was dependent on the magistrates of the provincial towns and on the *publicani*, who were doubtless only too willing to offer their advice. But the latter were the servants not of the State but of profit-making companies, with whose services the government could not dispense, but whose interests often ran counter to those of the authorities and the provincials. These companies were very closely identified with the equestrian order, whose relations with the Senate had from the days of C. Gracchus rarely been cordial. It was only when life and property were seriously threatened, as at the time of the Catilinarian Conspiracy, that the senators and knights had closed their ranks. Cicero's ideal of a coalition government based on a *concordia ordinum* was thwarted by politicians who for the sake of personal advantage widened a breach which was largely artificial and need never have existed.

One of the most successful achievements of Augustus was to put an end to this disastrous conflict between the orders. He conceived the brilliant idea of so reorganizing the Ordo Equester that he would have at his disposal a body of men from whom he could draw officials to fill such of the new posts which he wished to create as for any reason it was undesirable to give to senators. The order which was traditionally associated with tax-collecting was

[1] Tacitus, *Ann.* XII, 60.

now to provide financial officials paid by the state who would either collect the taxes themselves or supervise their collection by others.

The history of the Equestrian Order under the Republic is a difficult subject which need not be fully discussed here[1]. Its nucleus consisted of the 18 Centuries of *equites equo publico* who were a survival of the time when the cavalry forces of the State were drawn from the younger members of the upper classes. These Centuries even in the later Republic consisted of men of military age, but the term *eques* was freely applied to many who were not and probably had never been enrolled in them. Membership of the order carried with it the right of wearing certain insignia, the gold ring and a narrow purple stripe on the tunic, and the privilege of serving in the equestrian *decuriae* in the jury-courts and of occupying the fourteen equestrian benches in the theatre. From 67 B.C., if not earlier, the property qualification for membership of the order was fixed at 400,000 sesterces. With the decline of the Censorship after the time of Sulla it is probable that the organization of the Order was neglected, and that the term *eques* was loosely used to include all who possessed the necessary property qualification. The privileges of the Order were usurped by men whom no censor would ever have admitted, like the freedman upstart attacked by Horace:

> Sedilibusque magnus in primis eques
> Othone contempto sedet.   (*Epod.* iv, 15–16.)

Though the cavalry of the Roman army was now drawn from other sources, the junior officers were taken from the *Ordo Equester*, which included sons of senators who had not yet held a magistracy. The *tribuni militum* and *praefecti* of Caesar's army were to a large extent men of this type. They had 'followed Caesar from the city for reasons of friendship and had little experience of warfare[2].'

When in virtue of the censorial powers which he *de facto* possessed Augustus undertook the re-organization of the *equites* he introduced no very fundamental change. As in his dealings with the Senate he merely attempted to secure that the members of the class from which he intended to draw his subordinates should be worthy of the honour. That he wished still to lay stress on the military character of the order is shown by his revival of a ceremony which had long fallen into disuse. Every year on July 15 was held the *travectio equitum*, at which the knights paraded

---

[1] See vol. IX, pp. 894–6.   [2] *B.G.* I, 39.

before the Emperor on horseback. About 5000 men are said to have taken part in the parade, divided into six *turmae* each of which was commanded by a *sevir equitum Romanorum*[1], who was generally a man of senatorial birth destined like many of those under his command to hold magistracies and enter the Senate after completing the requirements of the *militia equestris* (see p. 231). These *turmae* of the Principate must be regarded as the successors of the Republican *centuriae equitum*, which with the decay of the *comitia centuriata* were seldom if ever required to assemble for the purpose of voting, and they were under Augustus occasionally referred to as *centuriae*[2]. On reaching the age of thirty-five a man was entitled to resign his *equus publicus*, so that the *travectio equitum* definitely represented Roman youth of the upper classes. It was the young members of the order who elected Gaius and Lucius and later other members of the imperial house to be *principes iuventutis*. The annual *travectio* was associated with an inspection (*probatio*) which enabled Augustus and his board of three assistants to reprimand or expel any *eques* who seemed unworthy. At longer intervals there was held a *recognitio*, which probably concerned the order as a whole and not merely its junior members. The question has been raised whether all who called themselves Roman Knights had in their earlier days paraded in the Roman *turmae*. It is indeed almost certain that under the principate all equites were said to possess the *equus publicus*, but the large number of the equites who are known to have resided in the municipal towns of Italy and the provinces supports the suggestion that in these towns there was some organization of the younger members similar to that which existed in the capital[3]. There were 500 equites in Gades and more in Patavium[4], and an inscription from Narbonne[5] shows that in A.D. 11 equites could be numbered among the *plebs* of a city. It seems improbable that such men formed part of the comparatively small body which paraded before the Emperor, but they may have received in their native cities some physical and military training similar to that which was given to the members of the *turmae* in Rome.

As was said above, the senatorial class under the Principate was no narrow oligarchy but was constantly being recruited from below. The same is true of the Equestrian Order. Just as the gift of the *latus clavus* enabled a man possessing the necessary personal

---

[1] See L. R. Taylor in *J.R.S.* XIV, 1924, p. 158 *sq.*
[2] Dessau 1314, 9483.   [3] See L. R. Taylor, *op. cit.* p. 168.
[4] Strabo V, 213.   [5] Dessau 112.

and financial qualifications to stand for magistracies, so the gift of the *equus publicus* and the gold ring opened the equestrian career to those who did not belong to it by birth. Of the sources from which equites were recruited perhaps the most important was the legionary centuriate. It was a fundamental principle of army-organization that while the *legatus* of a legion was a senator and the *tribuni militum* equites, the soldiers must belong to neither order. If an eques wished to serve in the ranks he must resign his membership. But soldiers who became centurions, certainly all who reached the primipilate (p. 226), received on discharge the rank of *eques* and proceeded to hold posts in the *equestris militia*, such as tribunates in the city-troops, extraordinary prefectures in the provinces, and in the early days of the Principate the *praefectura cohortis* and the *tribunatus militum*. The prospect of such promotion must have been a powerful incentive to military service. Other sources from which members of the Equestrian Order were drawn were the wealthier inhabitants of country towns and the class of freedmen, of which more will be said below.

Even under Augustus considerable use was made of equites in civil administration as well as in the army. The greatest prizes were the prefectures of Egypt, the Annona, and the Vigiles, but much responsible work was done by equites who held the title of *Procurator*, a term which had under the Republic been applied to the agents of companies and wealthy individuals. In the early Principate it means little more than private servant of the emperor, and the sphere in which the duties were performed is less frequently mentioned in inscriptions than was afterwards customary. Many of these early procurators were destined to have distinguished descendants. The grandfather of the future Emperor Vitellius was an *eques Romanus et rerum Augusti procurator*. Agricola was the grandson of two natives of Gallia Narbonensis who held the same rank, and Q. Octavius Sagitta who was procurator under Augustus in three different provinces[1] was the ancestor of a senator of Nero's reign. To rise in the world was easier under the Principate than it had been under the Republic and many sons of successful equites aspired to senatorial rank, though this was not always the case, and we read that Augustus had sometimes to compel men to enter the Senate.

To complete the account of the classes from which Augustus drew his officials a word must be said about the freedmen, though it was not till the reign of Claudius that important posts in administration were opened to them. It has been shown else-

[1] Dessau 9007.

where (pp. 429 *sqq.*) that Augustus interested himself in the question of manumission and imposed restrictions on the right of masters to give freedom to their slaves. To individual freedmen however he showed himself generous, and often conferred on them equestrian rank, *e.g.* on the wealthy P. Vedius Pollio, on T. Vinius Philopoemen and on his own physician Antonius Musa. There was a reaction after his death, and in A.D. 23 the Senate passed a decree[1] (which did not however remain long in force) confining the gold ring to those who could show free birth for two generations. Even under the Republic freedmen had served the State as assistants to the magistrates and priests, and they continued to do so in the Principate. Augustus allowed them to serve in the fleets (which were usually commanded by freedmen) and in the cohorts of Vigiles, the fire-brigade and police of the city (see p. 200). A freedman could almost rank as a minor magistrate by becoming one of the *vicorum magistri* (pp. 459 *sqq.*) and in the municipal towns, though excluded from the magistracies, he was compensated by membership of the Augustales, who helped to celebrate the worship of the emperor. It was not till later that higher posts than these were conferred on freedmen. Early in his reign Augustus entrusted the financial administration of Gaul to the freedman Licinus with the title of procurator[2], but this man so grossly misused his position that the Emperor was probably discouraged from repeating the experiment. Yet even at this time much of the routine work of administration was in the hands of freedmen, and the importance of the class steadily increased in spite of the prejudice which existed against it in senatorial circles. In a speech delivered in the Senate in A.D. 56 it was stated that a large proportion of the senators and knights were ultimately of servile origin[3], and, though restrictions were imposed from time to time, it was fairly easy for descendants of freedmen, if not for freedmen themselves, to rise into the higher orders.

II. THE FINANCIAL REFORMS OF AUGUSTUS

Though there is no aspect of the work of Augustus about which so little accurate information is available as the details of his financial reforms, an attempt must be made to deal with the

[1] Pliny, *N.H.*, XXXIII, 32. For the question whether the gold ring conferred full equestrian status see A. M. Duff, *Freedmen in the Early Roman Empire*, p. 214 *sq.*

[2] Dio LIV, 21.

[3] Tacitus, *Ann.* XIII, 27.

subject, for there is no doubt that his achievements in this department were far-reaching and of lasting value.

Under the Republic the management of the finances of the State had been regarded as one of the most important functions of the Senate, which was thus enabled, as Polybius[1] points out, to exercise considerable control over the magistrates. When, for instance, a magistrate went to his province it was for the Senate to decide what sum was to be paid to him for the expenses of administration. Of the city magistrates those whose duties were primarily financial were the quaestors and the censors. The former were in charge of the old State Treasury, the *aerarium Saturni*, and supervised the public slaves attached to it, but they were young and inexperienced, and their duties cannot have involved much responsibility. The work of the censors was more important. By holding a census they determined the taxable resources of the citizen-body. They let out the contracts for the carrying out of the work for which the State was required to pay, and arranged the terms under which *publicani* would collect the provincial revenues. But it was difficult for them to exercise much influence on policy. Their period of office was by convention limited to eighteen months. A reforming censor was apt to be hampered by his colleague or by a tribune representing the interests threatened by the measures of economy which he wished to carry. Opposition to reform might come not merely from the *publicani* but from the Senate itself, as when the elder Cato tried to raise the assessments for property-tax. Any act of a censor might be cancelled by his successor, so that continuity of financial policy was difficult to secure, and during their short period of office the censors had duties other than financial to perform, *e.g.* revision of the list of the Senate and of the citizen-body. The Republican system of government thus provided small scope for a man of financial genius. Even the censorship fell into decay at the end of the Republic; Sulla's legislation struck it a blow, and though it was revived after his death, the spirit of the age was unfavourable to any vigorous measures of financial reform.

If the financial system of the Republic was unsatisfactory the explanation is not to be found in the cost of government. Much of the expenditure which must be incurred by a modern State was unknown to the Romans. There was no national debt and the 'social services' cost little. Even the army and navy were only expensive in time of war, and many wars paid for themselves out of booty. Little had to be spent on salaries, for the State was generally

[1] VI, 13.

represented by wealthy men, who were expected to spend their own money during their period of office. If they enriched themselves it was in irregular ways, and at the expense of the provincials rather than of the government.

The measures taken by Augustus to improve the government of the Roman world must have added a good deal to the cost of administration. By the end of his reign the army was a professional long-service force; the soldiers were well paid and received a liberal gratuity on discharge. The principle of payment for public service had been accepted, and probably all the representatives of the State except the actual magistrates received salaries. A beginning had been made with the creation of a Civil Service which, though an instrument of economy, increased the financial obligations of the treasury. Large sums were spent on providing the city of Rome with corn, water and police, and on erecting and repairing public buildings.

The extravagant system by which the provinces of the Republic were taxed has been explained in a previous volume (vol. IX, p. 467 *sq.*). The system aroused deep resentment among the provincials, and the treasury was not compensated by the amount of its gains, for too large a part of the yield of taxation went to the *publicani* and unscrupulous governors. It is probable, too, that the burden of taxation was unevenly distributed and fell too often on the wrong shoulders. What was wanted was that the *publicani* should be dispensed with or rigidly supervised, that the governors should be prevented from enriching themselves at the cost of the provincials, and that taxation should be imposed as equitably as possible. In all these respects excellent work was done in the reign of Augustus.

The great companies of *publicani*, which must have been almost ruined by the exactions made on them by Pompey during the Civil War, received a further blow when Caesar deprived them of the profitable privilege of collecting the *decumae* of Asia[1]. In what way he arranged for the collection of the forty million sesterces which he raised by taxation in Gaul is uncertain, but that he handed over the new province to the tender mercies of the *publicani* is unlikely. In any case on the accession of Augustus the equestrian order had lost much of its wealth and influence and was in a humble frame of mind. How he re-organized the Order and employed some of its members on administrative work has been shown elsewhere. But the time had not yet arrived when the State could dispense altogether with middlemen in the collection

[1] Caesar, *B.C.* III, 3; 31; 103; Appian, *Bell. Civ.* v, 4, 19.

of taxes. It is certain that while the direct taxes were, at any rate in the 'imperial' provinces, collected by the Emperor's procurator in collaboration with the governor, the indirect taxes were still let out to contractors. In the reign of Nero there were complaints of the 'immodestia' of the *publicani* who collected the *portoria*[1], and contractors were employed even in the collection of the new death-duties. The 'publicans' of the New Testament were humble examples of a type of man found all over the Empire: even in the time of Trajan *publicanus* was the normal Latin word for tax-collector[2]. But the *societates* of the Principate were on a comparatively small scale, were controlled by inspectors, and were no longer in a position to exercise political influence.

From the time of Augustus the provincials were much less likely than they had been to suffer from the depredations of an unscrupulous governor. The governors of provinces were carefully selected. They could be withdrawn from an 'imperial' province at any time if the Emperor so desired, and rarely governed a 'senatorial' province for more than a year. The machinery for bringing complaints to Rome was greatly improved, and a successful prosecution for *repetundae* would ruin a man's career.

In dealing with the *publicani* and the governors of provinces Augustus merely introduced an effective control which the Republic had been too weak to exercise. When by setting himself to acquire exact knowledge of the resources of the Empire he attempted to equalize the burden of taxation he undertook a much more difficult task. In collecting geographical information he received much assistance from Agrippa, who prepared a map of the known world which was after his death publicly displayed in Rome, while detailed information was embodied in *commentarii* which were freely used by the geographer Strabo and the elder Pliny. But for purposes of taxation it was necessary to have full information about the number and legal status of the inhabitants of each province and about the amount and sources of their wealth. This information could only be acquired by the holding of a *census* similar to but distinct from the census of Roman citizens which had been held periodically under the Republic, and was held by Augustus himself in 28 B.C. after an interval of forty-two years and on two subsequent occasions. In the older provinces where city life existed the census was a fairly simple affair, which could be carried through with the help of the municipal authorities. Even under the Republic a census had been regularly held in Sicily. By 7 B.C. in the province of Cyrene very exact information

[1] Tacitus, *Ann.* XIII, 50.   [2] Tacitus, *Germ.* 29: Pliny, *Paneg.* 37.

was available as to the number and wealth of the inhabitants. But the problem was much more difficult in regions where municipal life was as yet undeveloped, such as Gaul, Spain, and the new Danubian provinces. As the arrangements made by Caesar for the taxation of Gaul required revision, a census was held there as early as 27 B.C., another in 12 B.C. and a third immediately after the death of Augustus. Much of the time which the Emperor spent there in 16–13 B.C. must have been devoted to financial questions. Gaul was a region not of cities but of tribes, whose ruling classes cannot have welcomed the arrival of census officials, and things had not been improved by the behaviour of the notorious freedman Licinus who for some years early in his reign represented Augustus in Lugdunum. That the Emperor was not completely successful in reconciling the Gauls to the payment of tribute is shown by the complaints which were made under his successors[1]. Equal difficulties must have been faced in the more backward parts of the Spanish peninsula and in the Danubian provinces. The famous assessment of Judaea by Quirinius in A.D. 6 shows that the annexation of a new province was at once followed by a valuation of its taxable capacity. Little information is available as to the machinery employed by Augustus and the character of the returns required, which by the second century were very elaborate. In all probability the governor of a province was normally responsible for the census, and was assisted by subordinates of equestrian rank[2]. A good deal of information was available as early as 23 B.C. when Augustus during a serious illness handed to the consul Piso a book containing an account of the public revenues. On his death he left a *breviarium totius imperii* embodying the results of his investigations[3].

Augustus owed much of his popularity and influence to the generosity with which he devoted to public purposes money which he was entitled to regard as his own. He had inherited large sums from his father and from Julius Caesar, and in the course of his reign much was left to him by Agrippa and other friends. Moreover he treated as his own property the enormous 'spoils' which he raised in Egypt by confiscation after the deaths of Antony and Cleopatra. But when he died he was a comparatively poor man. In the *Res Gestae* he states that he gave 600 million denarii to the Aerarium, to the Roman plebs and to discharged soldiers, and to this must be added the huge sums which he spent on beautifying the city of Rome, on aqueducts, roads, and public games. In what

---

[1] Tacitus, *Ann.* III, 40. *Hist.* IV, 74.
[2] Dessau 2683 (but see p. 282 n. 1).   [3] For the census in Egypt see p. 304.

light he regarded the revenues of the provinces for whose government he was responsible is a question which has been much disputed. Under the Republic a provincial governor was expected to pay into the Aerarium any surplus which remained after the expenses of administration had been met, and it seems probable that this principle was accepted by Augustus. On his death he left a record of the sums deposited at the time not only in the Aerarium but in the *fisci* of the various provinces[1], mentioning the freedmen and slaves from whom an account could be demanded. It is, however, unlikely that much was left over when the Emperor had paid for the administration and defence of the provinces for which he was specially responsible. The cost of the army and of the wars which occupied so much of his reign fell primarily on the revenues of the frontier provinces. It was possible to tell the inhabitants of Gaul that the taxes which they so unwillingly paid were spent on providing them with security from the German peril[2]. But the wealthy senatorial provinces, such as Asia, Gallia Narbonensis, and Baetica must have contributed something to the cost of the frontier defence from which they derived so much benefit. Under Augustus Africa was not, as later, the only senatorial province in which troops were, at any rate occasionally, stationed. Before the annexation of Moesia the proconsul of Macedonia was often in command of an army, and Quirinius when governor of Cyrene seems to have undertaken operations against the desert tribes[3].

It was only equitable that the burden of imperial defence should be borne by the empire as a whole, and this end was secured by the preservation of the Aerarium as the central treasury which received any surplus revenues and assisted the poorer and more expensive provinces at the cost of the richer and more peaceful. Whatever may have been the case later, it is unlikely that Augustus applied the principle of dyarchy to finance, and created, as has often been assumed, an imperial *Fiscus* drawing its main revenues from the taxes of the imperial provinces. The money which he so generously expended on public objects was legally his own property and was not derived from provincial taxation. Any profits from the latter source would go not to him but to the Aerarium. That the revenue of the Aerarium was barely adequate is shown by the fact that on four occasions the Emperor made large payments to it from his private funds[4], and it might have been expected that he would insist on controlling it by an official

---

[1] Suetonius, *Aug.* 101, Dessau 1514; Dispensator ad fiscum Gallicum provinciae Lugdunensis.   [2] Tacitus, *Hist.* IV, 74.
[3] Florus II, 31 [IV, 12], 41.   [4] *Res Gestae* 17.

nominated by himself. But it was not till Nero's reign that two permanent *praefecti aerarii* were appointed. From 23 B.C. the supervision of the Aerarium was entrusted to two of the praetors chosen by lot, a system unfavourable to efficiency but tolerable if most of the public money was raised and expended in the provinces and the Aerarium was little more than a clearing-house in which surpluses were deposited and redistributed[1].

One of the most beneficent reforms of Augustus was his solution of the problem of the 'ex-service man' which had never been properly faced by the Republic (see below, p. 211). He realized that on discharge after sixteen or twenty years' service the legionaries had a moral right to a pension. During the early part of his reign the enormous cost of providing soldiers with land or gratuities was met out of his own resources, but in A.D. 6 a new system was introduced by the creation of a special treasury, the *aerarium militare*. Into this the Emperor paid 170 million sesterces and arranged that in future it should receive the yield of two new taxes, the death-duties (*vicesima hereditatum*) and a tax on sales (*centesima rerum venalium*). This new treasury was put under the charge of a body of three ex-praetors holding office for three years. Careful calculations must have been made of the probable yield of these taxes and of the sum which would be required for pensions, and these calculations would be upset by any change in the conditions of military service[2].

A feature of these taxes which made them unpopular was that they fell on Roman citizens resident in Italy; the death-duties indeed were paid by Roman citizens only, of whom the proportion resident in the provinces was still comparatively small. Augustus seems to have felt that the privileged position of Italy in the matter of taxation was unjustified. Since 167 B.C. no *tributum* had been paid by Italians, whose only contribution to the revenue was made indirectly through the *portoria* and an old tax on the value of manumitted slaves. Even under the Principate Italian land was exempt from taxation, and the greatest privilege which could be granted to a provincial community was what came to be called the *Ius Italicum*, which freed its soil from the land-tax. Before the end of the Republic a fair amount of provincial land was regarded as the property of the Roman State and was usually let out by the censors to regular tenants. But such land was put in a special

---

[1] Tacitus, *Ann.* XIII, 29. On the whole subject see U. Wilcken in *Sitz. der preuss. Akad.* XXVII, 1931, pp. 772 *sqq.* and Tenney Frank in *J.R.S.* XXIII, 1933, pp. 143 *sqq.*

[2] *Res Gestae* 17; Tacitus, *Ann.* I, 78.

category, and was sharply distinguished from the rest of the provincial soil. Though whole provinces (*e.g.* Asia, Bithynia, Cyrene) had been left to Rome by the will of their previous rulers, the idea that *all* provincial land was *ager publicus* was not definitely held in Republican times, nor probably till after the reign of Augustus[1]. When he founded colonies overseas he paid for provincial land exactly as he did in Italy. In his time full owner-ship of land *ex iure Quiritium* was possible in the provinces. It is not quite clear what theory underlay provincial taxation in the early Principate, but the view that the land-tax normally paid by provincial landholders was of the nature of rent and a charge on occupiers of land belonging to the State was only gradually developed until it was formulated by the lawyers of the Second Century. Even in Cicero's time the idea may well have occurred to those who remembered that the province of Asia, for example, had been the gift of king Attalus, and that the right of collecting its revenues was let out by the censors. In any case Italian land enjoyed a privileged position both under the Republic and in the Principate, and it was only right that Italians should in some other way make a contribution to the expenses of government. But it required all the authority possessed by Augustus to persuade the predominatingly Italian Senate to agree to the imposition of the death-duties, which were accepted as a less undesirable alternative to a tax on Italian land[2].

The distinction between direct and indirect taxes—*tributa* and *vectigalia*—was familiar to the Romans. As has been stated above, the former were from the time of Augustus normally collected by the governor of a province and his staff, while for the collection of the latter contractors were employed. In the senatorial provinces the direct tax was termed *stipendium* not *tributum*, but it is doubtful whether the distinction has any significance. It is possible that under Augustus the direct tax was collected by *publicani* in, at any rate, some of the senatorial provinces[3], but, if so, the method was soon abandoned. Though the main tax in every province was the *tributum soli*, paid by the occupiers of land, the owners of other forms of property were liable to a *tributum capitis*, and the value of their belongings was recorded by the census-officials. The *tributum capitis* was not in spite of its name a poll-tax: this was only raised in Egypt and perhaps in backward provinces, where an accurate valuation of property was difficult to secure[4]. In the collection of

---

[1] See Tenney Frank in *J.R.S.* XVII, 1927, pp. 141 *sqq.*
[2] Dio LVI, 28.
[3] Dessau 901; mancipes stipendiorum ex Africa.   [4] Dio LXII, 3.

tribute it was essential to receive assistance from the local authorities within a province, for the number of imperial officials was in the early Principate still small. The unwillingness of Rome at all periods to annex uncivilized districts may be explained by the difficulty of collecting taxes in a country devoid of the type of organization to which she was accustomed.

Of the indirect taxes the frontier-dues (*portoria*) were the most important. These were imposed simply for revenue purposes and were not intended to protect the products of certain areas against competition; no attempt was made to exclude provincial goods from Italian markets. A fixed but varying percentage was charged on the value of all goods crossing certain frontiers. For this purpose the Gallic, the Danubian, and perhaps the Spanish provinces were grouped together, but it is doubtful whether the details of the organization which is found in existence later can be attributed to Augustus. Of the other indirect taxes the *vicesima hereditatum* and the *centesima rerum venalium* have been already mentioned. The death-duties were not levied on property inherited from very near relations or on very small estates. The only other taxes calling for mention are the 5 per cent. tax on manumissions and the 4 per cent. tax on the sale of slaves, the latter of which was earmarked for the maintenance of the urban cohorts.

A word must be said in conclusion on the measures taken by Augustus to deal with the Roman coinage[1]. Nothing shows more clearly the all-pervasive power of the *princeps* in the new system than the fact that no coin above the value of a farthing (*quadrans*) was issued during his reign which does not bear his head or at any rate his name or some reference to his exploits. In the last days of the Republic the Senate lost control of the coinage, the right of issuing which was usurped by the great generals from Sulla onwards, and after Caesar's death the old chaos reappeared. Practically no bronze coins were minted between 80 B.C. and 23 B.C., when Augustus took the matter in hand.

During the earlier part of his reign gold and silver coins were struck in Asia and Spain and for a few years (19–12 B.C.) in Rome itself. The Spanish coins of 25–22 B.C. bear together with the name of the Emperor that of his *legatus* P. Carisius, but this experiment was never repeated. The years 15–14 B.C. are important in the history of Roman coinage, for about that time Augustus established at Lugdunum in Gaul an imperial mint, which was for the remainder of his reign practically the only source

[1] See H. Mattingly and E. A. Sydenham, *Roman Imperial Coinage*, I, pp. 1–92.

of the gold and silver coinage of the empire. The mint was under the charge of imperial freedmen and slaves and was protected by an urban cohort stationed in the city[1].

While the Emperor made himself responsible for the issue of gold and silver coins and except for a few years minted them in the provinces, the Senate was entrusted with the issue of the lower denominations. The coins of bronze (or *orichalcum*) issued in Rome between 23 and 4 B.C. bear the names of one or more of the *tresviri monetales*, a minor Republican magistracy now revived, the holders of which had under the Republic used the coinage as a means of glorifying the deeds of their ancestors, and such gold and silver coins as were issued in Rome also bear their names. But after the year 4 B.C. the names of the *tresviri* disappear even from the bronze coinage and do not reappear under the successors of Augustus. The provinces enjoyed a certain amount of freedom in minting copper, and occasionally silver, coins for local use, but the main issue of gold and silver was confined to the mint of Lugdunum. An interesting series of copper coins was issued in Gaul to commemorate the altar erected at Lugdunum to 'Roma et Augustus' in 12 B.C.[2], and at an earlier date coins had been minted by the Commune Asiae, which superintended the worship of the Emperor in that province.

It will be clear from this summary of the work of Augustus in the field of finance that he established a system which enabled the government of the empire to be carried on efficiently and economically. The resources of the empire were enormous, and it is unlikely (though exact figures are lacking) that the burden of taxation was excessively heavy. At any rate Augustus secured that it should be equitably distributed, and that the revenues of the State should be honestly collected and expended in such a way that the subjects of Rome might regard her rule as a blessing and not as a curse.

III. THE CITY OF ROME AND ITALY

The development of Rome into the capital of a great empire had not been entirely a source of advantage to the inhabitants of the City. Whereas in other Italian towns the municipal authorities were able to devote themselves entirely to local affairs, the Roman Senate and magistrates were so much occupied with questions concerning Italy and the provinces that they were apt to neglect the interests of the City itself. Republican Rome possessed no

[1] Dessau 2130; Coh. XVII Lugduniensis ad monetam.
[2] Volume of Plates iv, 210, *f.*

city-council and no municipal officials in the narrow sense. From time to time censors concerned themselves with the condition of public buildings and arranged for construction and repairs, but the duties which in a modern city are entrusted to highly trained experts were in the main allotted to aediles, who like other magistrates held office for one year only. The citizens of London would not welcome the transference of the duties of the London County Council to Parliament and the Cabinet. In the Rome of Augustus, not less than in the London of to-day, there was need of non-political bodies capable of dealing with the practical problems of local government. In no department of administration was the work of Augustus more successful than in this. He did not indeed create a city-council independent of the Senate, but by the end of his reign all the departments of local administration were in experienced hands, and Rome was a healthier and more peaceful city than she probably had been at any period of her history.

Some aspects of the work done by Augustus in Rome have been discussed in other chapters. There is, therefore, no need to describe here his activities as a builder and restorer of temples and public buildings, or to emphasize the skill with which he secured the loyalty of the poorer classes in the capital by his institution of the *vicomagistri*, who superintended the worship of the Lares Augusti at the crossroads and performed certain humbler tasks of administration[1]. By 7 B.C. the city had been divided into fourteen *regiones*, subdivided into 265 wards by which the *vicomagistri* were elected. Though almost invariably freedmen, they were entitled on certain days to wear the dress of a magistrate and to be preceded by two lictors. In all probability they were at first concerned in a subordinate capacity with such activities as the protection of their district against fire and the distributions of free corn. In this institution we can trace a desire on the part of the Emperor to inspire in the somewhat degenerate population of the capital a sense of responsibility and self-respect (p. 458).

Mommsen has remarked that when Tacitus states that Augustus gradually 'took over the functions of the Senate, magistrates and laws' what he had primarily in mind was the administration of the City[2]. In the early days of his principate Augustus was mainly concerned with provincial affairs, for in theory he was only one of the two consuls to whom an unusually large *provincia* had been allotted. After 23 B.C. when he resigned the consulship his position was less clearly defined and he was less hampered by

---

[1] See below, pp. 459 *sqq.* and p. 479 *sq.*   [2] *Staatsrecht*, II³, p. 1032.

Republican precedents. Though his building activities began earlier, it was not till 22 B.C., the year in which he refused the dictatorship and perpetual consulship, that he assumed any direct responsibility for the administration of the City. With characteristic caution he began by interfering intermittently and by modifying the existing system as little as possible. Not till nearly the end of his reign do we find the main departments of administration under the charge of *praefecti* or *curatores* nominated by him and holding office according to his pleasure.

The important task of protecting the City against fire had been grossly neglected under the Republic. It seems to have been included among the multifarious duties of the aediles and of the *triumviri capitales* or *nocturni*, who had at their disposal a body of public slaves. But their efforts required to be supplemented by private enterprise. We hear of privately organized fire-brigades, and as late as 21 B.C. the aedile Egnatius Rufus gained popularity by employing his own slaves in this capacity. In that year Augustus first intervened by putting at the disposal of the aediles a body of 600 slaves. This system continued till A.D. 6 when a succession of fires showed the need of a thorough reform. The important equestrian office of the *praefectura vigilum* was created, and to the prefect were allotted seven cohorts of Vigiles, each consisting of 1000 men drawn from the class of freedmen[1]. This institution was closely associated with the division of the City into fourteen *regiones*, for each cohort was made responsible for the safety of two of them. It is probable that the duties of the Vigiles, about which we have little information, were concerned with the prevention as well as with the extinguishing of fires, and that they performed the duties of police as well as of a fire-brigade. Though their officers were generally men who had served as centurions in the legions, they were not regarded as soldiers, for the possession of free birth was still regarded as an essential qualification for service in the army. There is reason to think that freedmen were not very eager to volunteer for membership of the Vigiles, for in A.D. 24 Roman citizenship was offered to Junian Latins who were willing to serve[2], and soon after free men are found among the members of the cohorts.

Every reader of the works of Cicero must have been struck by the almost complete absence in the Rome of his period of any machinery for the preservation of public order. Had an organized police-force existed the activities of some of his contemporaries,

---

[1] P. K. Baillie Reynolds, *The Vigiles of Imperial Rome*, pp. 22 *sqq.*
[2] Gaius I, 32 b. See below, pp. 431 *sq.*, 616.

such as Clodius, would have been seriously hampered, and the threats of Catiline and his associates would have caused less alarm. The public slaves allotted to the magistrates were ineffective, and in spite of the military attributes of the consulship there was seldom any organized body of troops attached to the consuls when resident in the city. It is probable that Augustus regarded himself as responsible for order in Rome, and by the end of his reign there had been created three *cohortes urbanae*, each probably consisting of 1000 men, and unlike the Vigiles, regarded as part of the army of the State. The early history of their commander, the *praefectus urbi*, is rather obscure. L. Calpurnius Piso, who died in A.D. 32, is said by Tacitus[1] to have held office for twenty years, but there is evidence that he received his office from Tiberius. Possibly Mommsen is right in holding that he was appointed about A.D. 13 when Tiberius was regarded as practically joint-ruler with Augustus. Under the Republic a *praefectus* had been appointed to take the place of the consuls when absent from Rome, and during his Spanish campaign Caesar had put *praefecti* in charge of the City. Maecenas had occupied a similar position when Octavian was at war with Antony, and it is probable that the appointments of Messalla Corvinus in 26 B.C. and of Statilius Taurus in 16 B.C. were connected with the absence of Augustus from Rome. Not till the very end of his reign did the *praefectura urbi* become permanent, though the urban cohorts certainly existed earlier. The *praefectus urbi* was regarded as a high military commander, and, unlike most *praefecti*, was always a senator of consular rank. Piso was not the only holder of the office to retain it for a long period of years. Tacitus says that it was the duty of the prefect of the city 'to overawe the slaves and that part of the population which, unless it fears a strong hand, is disorderly and reckless[2].' He can be described as the Chief Constable of Rome, and possessed a power of summary jurisdiction which was destined to come into collision with and eventually to supersede the older courts of criminal justice within the city[3].

To complete the picture of the garrison of Rome mention must at least be made of the Praetorian Guard (see pp. 232 *sqq.*), though it was not till the reign of Tiberius that all its cohorts were concentrated in the city. That the urban cohorts were regarded as a force supplementary to the Praetorians is shown by the fact that both forces were continuously numbered, and in case of need both would be available for the maintenance of order. If on the acces-

[1] *Ann.* VI, 10–11.   [2] *Ann* VI, 11, 3.
[3] Tacitus, *Ann.* XIV, 41.

sion of Augustus the police-force of Rome was almost non-existent, by the end of his reign it had attained dimensions which are probably unequalled in any modern city.

The task of feeding the population of the City was one of increasing difficulty, which even under the Republic had sometimes been beyond the capacities of the aediles, whose functions included the *cura annonae*. Extraordinary powers had been conferred on Scaurus in 104 and on Pompey in 57 B.C. in order to save Rome from starvation, and Caesar had created two new aediles Ceriales, who were specially concerned with the problem[1]. Since the days of Pompey the food-supply of Rome had again been threatened by pirates, for in 38–36 B.C. Sextus Pompeius had employed the weapon of blockade, and even in normal times the supply of corn from overseas was apt to be inadequate. The task of the aediles was complicated by the distributions of corn, whether beneath the market price or free, which had been introduced by C. Gracchus[2]. The problem was obviously one with which annual magistrates could no longer deal and a radical reform was wanted. In 23 B.C. when the City was threatened with famine Augustus at his own expense increased the corn-ration and in the following year accepted a *cura annonae* which, as he says, he administered with such effect that within a few days he relieved the whole people from the panic and risk to which it was exposed. It is however unlikely that as early as this the feeding of Rome was regarded as one of the functions of the *princeps*, and the responsibility for it probably remained with the *aediles Ceriales*. But when in A.D. 6 the situation again became acute a board of two consulars was created to supersede the aediles, and a few years later (the exact date is uncertain) the office of *praefectus annonae* was brought into existence and conferred on C. Turranius, a man of equestrian rank, who held it until the reign of Claudius. From this time onwards the emperor made himself responsible for the feeding of the City, and his equestrian prefect became the head of a large department with representatives in the ports and in the provinces. In 22 B.C. a board of two ex-praetors (raised in 18 B.C. to four) was appointed to supervise the free distributions of corn, and it seems probable that the administration of the 'dole' was not the affair of the *praefectus annonae* but of *praefecti frumenti dandi ex s.c.* who were not his subordinates though they must have stood in close relations with him. The Senate made itself responsible for the 'dole' and the expense of it fell directly on the

---

[1] See Vol. IX, pp. 165, 530, 699.

[2] *Ib.* pp. 57 *sqq.*, 95, 165, 301, 315, 328, 524.

Aerarium at any rate till the time of Nero. The number of recipients, which had been fixed by Caesar at 150,000, seems to have risen to 320,000 by 5 B.C. (if the 'plebs urbana' of *Res Gestae* 15 is to be identified with the 'plebs frumentaria'), but in 2 B.C. it was reduced to 200,000 and a system of registration introduced.

Under the Republic the care of the water-supply of the City had been entrusted to the censors. This department of administration seems to have been of special interest to Agrippa, who constructed two new aqueducts, the Aqua Julia and the Aqua Virgo, and trained a body of slaves who were qualified to deal with the matter. On his death in 12 B.C. they became the property of the Emperor, who might well have created an equestrian *praefectura*, as he did with the *annona* and the Vigiles. He preferred however to adopt another procedure which was applied to various spheres of administration (see above, p. 178 *sq.*). After consulting the Senate he appointed a board of three *curatores aquarum*, consisting of senators and presided over by a consular, Messalla Corvinus. These *curatores* received pay, wore the insignia of magistrates, and retained office for an indefinite period. Messalla remained in office till A.D. 13, and one of his successors did so from A.D. 74 till 97. The Senate was, at any rate till the reign of Claudius, responsible for the cost of maintaining the aqueducts, but the Emperor was prepared to assist in case of need, as he did in 5–4 B.C., when he repaired various aqueducts and doubled the supply available from the Aqua Marcia[1].

Another senatorial commission of the same type was created at an uncertain date (in any case after 11 B.C.) to supervise the condition of temples and public buildings. The expense of their erection and repair had been to a large extent borne by the Emperor, but the senatorial treasury was made responsible for the task of maintaining them in good condition. These *curatores aedium sacrarum et operum locorumque publicorum p.R.* were two in number, of praetorian or consular rank, and seem sometimes to have divided their functions, the one concerning himself with temples, the other with public buildings.

Another duty which fell upon Augustus was the protection of the City against inundations of the Tiber. Something was done to strengthen the banks in 8–6 B.C. (inscriptions show that the consuls of 8 B.C. were at work on the river bank)[2] and on at least one occasion the Emperor helped in the matter, but a permanent *cura* was probably not created till the first year of Tiberius (15 A.D.),

---

[1] *Res Gestae* 20; Dessau 98.
[2] Dessau 5923 *a–d*.

when a great flood led to the appointment of a board of five *curatores riparum et alvei Tiberis*, presided over by a *consularis*.

This brief summary of the work done by Augustus in the city of Rome well illustrates several features of his administration: viz. the substitution of experts for amateurs, his readiness to draw his subordinates from the senatorial or the equestrian orders as seemed best, and his unwillingness to make any change till the necessity for it was clear to all.

A word must now be said about the services rendered by Augustus to Italy. Though in the settlement of 27 B.C. Italy was not included in his special sphere of administration, it was inevitable that, as in the City, he should make his beneficent influence felt throughout the peninsula. In the period with which we are concerned Italy occupied a unique position among the lands subject to the rule of Rome. Caesar had extended the citizenship to the Alps, and in the period of the triumvirate Cisalpine Gaul had ceased to be regarded as a province. As is shown elsewhere (p. 195), residents in Italy were free from direct taxation. Everywhere there was active city life, into which Caesar had done something to introduce uniformity without interfering with the local autonomy of the communities (vol. IX, p. 699 *sq.*). Only to a slight extent had citizens of these municipal towns taken part in the political life of Rome, which was still merely the chief city of Italy. Interference of the kind which was accepted as a matter of course in the provinces would have been bitterly resented.

That the establishment of the Principate was as welcome to Italy as to any part of the empire is shown by the enthusiasm with which it was greeted by that good Italian Virgil (p. 512 *sq.*). The settlement of veterans in 'colonies' after the battle of Actium, unlike similar settlements made by Republican generals, was carried through in such a way as to cause the least possible offence. Augustus boasts that he was the first who had ever paid the townships for the land which he required for his soldiers[1]. Among the 28 colonies which he founded in Italy there must have been many cities which welcomed the new settlers. The presence of these old soldiers in Italian towns may perhaps be connected with the steps which we are told were taken to put down kidnapping and brigandage; they may have volunteered to serve in the garrisons stationed in regions where this evil was rampant[2].

Though the legions were now stationed on the frontiers it was as important for the Roman government as it had ever been that

---

[1] *Res Gestae* 16.   [2] Suetonius, *Aug.* 32.

the roads of Italy should be kept in good repair, and this was one of the first tasks to which Augustus set his hand. By 27 B.C. he had repaired the Via Flaminia at his own expense and had encouraged leading senators to take other roads in hand. But this was too costly a task to be left to private generosity, and accordingly in 20 B.C. the Emperor was entrusted with a regular *cura viarum*, which was administered, as was later the water-supply of the City, by a board of senatorial *curatores viarum* of praetorian rank, who, at any rate under his successors, divided the charge of the chief roads between them. The cost of the upkeep of the roads, as of the other curae, seems under Augustus to have fallen on the Aerarium (on a coin of 17–16 B.C. it is stated that the Emperor contributed a sum to the Aerarium for the purpose), but in 2 B.C. Augustus paid for the repair of the Via Aemilia from Ariminum to the river Trebia[1] and this was probably not the only occasion when he showed such generosity. By the Flavian period, however, the costs of the *longe series porrecta viarum*[2], like other expenses originally borne by the Aerarium, had been transferred to the imperial Fiscus.

IV. THE ADMINISTRATION OF THE PROVINCES

The claim that Tacitus makes Claudius advance in his speech advocating the admission of Gauls to the Senate[3] that throughout her history Rome, unlike Athens and Sparta, had shown generosity to her subjects is a little difficult to substantiate. It is true that in the earlier days of the Republic the Italian cities and tribes probably preferred to be allies rather than members of the Roman State, but the demand for incorporation with Rome arose long before it was granted. Its champions among Roman politicians, such as C. Gracchus and Livius Drusus, met with strong opposition, and Rome did not yield till the Italians had taken up arms. Even after the Social War the Transpadane region was denied the full privileges of citizenship, and did not receive them till the beginning of the Civil War (vol. IX, p. 643 *sq.*). In view of the fact that when the rule of Augustus began Italy had for barely twenty years been fully incorporated in Rome it is not surprising that he considered it his first duty to foster that Italian patriotism which is such a prominent feature of the poems of Virgil. He identified the interests of Italy fully with those of Rome, so that under his in-

---

[1] Dessau 9371.   [2] Statius, *Silvae*, III, 3, 102.
[3] Tacitus, *Ann.* XI, 24.

fluence the contempt which in the days of Cicero was felt in senatorial circles for natives of country towns, even if they possessed full Roman rights, gradually disappeared. Many such men were given important positions in the service of the state. Italy was, as we have seen, generously treated in the matter of taxation, and much was done to improve communications and to maintain law and order.

The extension by Caesar of citizen-rights to the Alps was only part of a larger policy. He had spent so many years of his life in the provinces that his sympathies extended far beyond the frontiers of Italy. The fact that during his dictatorship Cisalpine Gaul, though inhabited by Roman citizens, was still a province is significant, for it shows that to his mind there was no inconsistency between provincial status and the possession of the full franchise. On his death Antony claimed to have found among his papers a proposal that the whole of Sicily should be enfranchised[1]. How far he would have gone in this direction had he lived longer it is impossible to say. It is possible that he contemplated the full enfranchisement of Gallia Narbonensis in the near future, for those of its cities which did not become *coloniae civium Romanorum* by the settlement of his veterans seem to have received Latin rights[2], so that the status of the province was almost identical with that of Gallia Cisalpina between 89 and 49 B.C. In any case his policy of colonization finally put an end to the prejudice, so characteristic of the Republic, against the possession of citizen-rights by provincial towns. Gaul was not the only province in which he founded colonies. Many were established in Spain and in that province the city of Gades was made a Roman *municipium*. Farther east Carthage and Corinth were refounded as colonies and a few cities in Asia Minor, for example, Sinope, received the same status. All the great generals of the later Republic had been generous in the gift of the franchise to individuals. What is characteristic of Caesar is that he was not content to confer it on individuals whom he wished to honour, but established communities which he intended to serve as centres of Romanization[3].

Although in this matter Augustus was more conservative than Caesar circumstances made it inevitable that he should pursue in some respects a similar policy. In order to provide for the 300,000 soldiers whom he 'settled in colonies or sent back to their

---

[1] Cicero, *ad Att.* XIV, 12, 1. It is possible that Caesar's intention did not go beyond the conferment of Latinitas. See Vol. IX, p. 711.
[2] Vol. IX, p. 711.   [3] *Ib.* pp. 708 *sqq.*

towns' he had to have recourse to the provinces, in ten of which he planted colonies[1]. But these Augustan colonies differed from those of Caesar in the important respect that they were with a very few exceptions military, while Caesar had sent overseas not only soldiers but a large number of civilians including freedmen. Many of them were planted in backward provinces to act as a substitute for a legionary garrison, as in Pisidia which formed part of the new province of Galatia, in Mauretania which was not yet a regular province, and in Lusitania. The original settlers in these towns were as a rule men who had served in the same legions and were accustomed to co-operate with each other in putting down disorder.

The contrast between the methods of Caesar and Augustus is seen clearly in Sicily, which, as has been said, Caesar thought of raising to the level of Italy. At the end of the reign of Augustus the island probably contained 6 colonies, 6 *municipia*, and 3 Latin towns, so that out of 68 organized communities only 15 had received a privileged status. Even in the civilized province of Baetica the situation was much the same; about 46 out of 175 towns were included in one of the higher categories. It is characteristic of the Western sympathies of Augustus that he founded few colonies in the Eastern provinces, but even in the West he obviously wished to maintain the predominance of Italy. In every province the cities whose inhabitants possessed the full citizenship formed a small minority, and still smaller was the number of those which enjoyed the privileges of Italians in the matter of taxation.

The result of this policy was that the cities of a province were classified according to the privileges which they possessed. At the top of the scale stood the *coloniae civium Romanorum*, which in the time of Augustus were almost all towns to which military settlers had been sent, though later on the term merely denoted a certain status. Sometimes a colony was granted partial or complete immunity from taxation, but this was not usually the case. The other towns whose inhabitants possessed the franchise were called *municipia* or *oppida civium Romanorum*. Next came the interesting group of 'Latin' towns, where the franchise could be obtained by the holding of a magistracy, so that they possessed an aristocracy of Roman citizens. The other cities enjoyed no special privileges, but among them there were a few which still called themselves 'free' or 'federate' communities. This status was now an anachronism, although in the days of Cicero it had been a cherished

[1] *Res Gestae* 3, 28.

privilege. The provincials of the Principate, like the Italians of the Republic, regarded incorporation by Rome as something desirable, and realized that single cities could hardly be 'allies' of a State whose territories included most of the civilized world[1].

Though the Romans felt most at home in provinces whose inhabitants belonged to cities possessing institutions of a type with which they were familiar, they were too wise to impose the municipal system on regions accustomed to a different kind of organization. In Gaul, North West Spain, Africa and even in North Italy there were districts where no regular cities existed. The problem had to be faced on a very large scale in the newly conquered part of Gaul, where the unit of government was the tribe and not the city. Augustus wisely decided to recognize the old tribal institutions on condition that their authorities were willing to co-operate with the Roman representatives, especially in the matter of taxation. In Spain and Africa he adopted the same policy in dealing with districts which were not municipalized. In North Italy some of the Alpine tribes were 'attributed' to neighbouring cities; their inhabitants were subject to the authority of the local magistrates, but did not in the first instance receive the full citizenship[2]. In general it may be said that the policy of Augustus in the bestowal of the citizenship showed moderation and good sense. The fact that in the course of his reign the citizen population of the empire rose from about four to five million shows that he was not unduly conservative. While maintaining the primacy of Italy he won the support of the Western provinces by conferring the franchise on many communities, whose citizens were soon to obtain posts in the Civil Service or even seats in the Senate. In the East the franchise was given less freely to cities, for Augustus had won his victory over Antony as the champion of the West and wished his empire to have a Latin character. But citizenship was often given to individuals from all parts of the Roman world, though in every case their credentials were carefully examined. We are told that when his wife asked the Emperor to confer the citizenship on a certain Gaul he refused the request, but offered him immunity from taxation, saying that he preferred that the treasury should lose something than that the gift of the franchise should be made cheap[3].

As in dealing with the provinces it is impossible to avoid the use of the word 'Romanization,' the question must be raised how far it was the aim of Augustus and his successors to secure

[1] See Vol. IX, p. 465.   [2] Dessau 206.
[3] Suetonius, *Aug.* 40.

uniformity of law, government and civilization throughout the empire. The unification of so large a part of the world under the rule of Rome was bound in the long run to produce such uniformity, but in the period with which this volume is concerned this development was still far in the future. The distinction between Italy and the provinces was sharp, and there existed still sharper distinctions between the provinces. Unique problems were raised by the government of Egypt[1]. The other Eastern provinces were essentially Greek in language and civilization, and their inhabitants, though contented enough under Roman rule, probably regarded the civilization of Italy with something like contempt[2]. Among the Western provinces great differences existed. The southern parts of Gaul and Spain had come under Italian influence even in the Republican period, but much of Spain was not finally subdued till the reign of Augustus, and Gaul possessed a civilization of its own which it did not wish to lose. In North Africa Carthaginian influences were still strong and the Punic language was spoken by many. In these circumstances all that Rome could hope to do was to maintain internal peace and to win the gratitude of her subjects by protecting them against invasion. In the north the rivers Rhine and Danube formed a kind of *cordon sanitaire* round the Roman world, so that the inhabitants of the frontier provinces learned to regard their neighbours on the farther banks as barbarians who might not even set foot on Roman soil without special permission[3]. But, as has been said, no attempt was made to impose municipal institutions on unwilling subjects. The government did not interfere in religious matters unless, as in the case of Druidism, a religion contained features which were politically undesirable. At the same time it was inevitable that before long the political and economic advantages which the rule of Rome conferred on provincials should break down the barriers which originally separated one province from another and Italy from them all. In particular the improvements made by the Roman government in communications were bound to favour the development of a homogeneous culture. But in the time of Augustus the process of raising the provinces to the level of Italy had not gone far and was probably regarded with disfavour in some influential circles.

Though the status of the provinces varied they were effectively attached to Rome by the veneration which they felt for the person

---

[1] See below, chap. x.
[2] See C. S. Walton in *J.R.S.* xix, 1929, pp. 38 *sqq.*
[3] Tacitus, *Germ.* 41; *Hist.* iv, 64.

of the Emperor, whom they were prepared to treat as a god. It has been shown elsewhere[1] that the practice of offering divine honours to Augustus began in the East soon after Actium and in the course of his reign penetrated to all parts of the empire. What was originally an oriental practice was adopted with remarkable enthusiasm in the West, where the government was very conscious of its political value. The various centres of emperor-worship whether in provincial capitals or in smaller towns or in Gallic tribes provided a rallying-point for the friends of Rome, who were proud to hold the position of priest of a province or of flamen of Augustus in their own city. This tribute to the Emperor was nearly everywhere spontaneous. In Narbo, for example, the plebs erected an altar in the forum to the *numen Augusti*, at which on certain anniversaries offerings of incense and wine were made by a board of six men, none of whom were even members of the local Senate[2]. In newly conquered districts, however, the government took the initiative, as when the ara Ubiorum was erected on the Rhine, or when Drusus dedicated an altar to 'Roma et Augustus' near Lugdunum for the 'Three Gauls' in 12 B.C. By no means every province possessed a similar centre of worship before the death of Augustus, but there were probably few if any in which individual cities had not adopted this method of showing their gratitude. One of the defects of the provincial administration of the Republic had been that provinces as a whole had no recognized means of expressing their views to the government though particular cities might send embassies to Rome[3]. This defect was now remedied by the institution or recognition of *concilia* containing representatives of the various cities or tribes and meeting periodically to celebrate the worship of the Emperor. No doubt only 'loyalists' were elected, but they were allowed to exercise the right of criticism and to express opinions freely on the character of the administration. When a governor was prosecuted on his return to Rome the procedure was usually initiated by the *concilium* of his province. The institution of these *concilia* must have done much to inspire the leading inhabitants of provinces with loyalty to Rome.

As has been explained above[4], the arrangement made in 27 B.C. between Augustus and the Senate according to which for purposes of administration the provinces fell into two groups cannot be described as revolutionary. Under the Republic it had always been possible to suspend the ordinary system according to which each province had its own governor, and the sphere of authority

---

[1] See below, pp. 481 *sqq.*   [2] Dessau 112.
[3] See Vol. IX, p. 473.   [4] See above, p. 128.

entrusted to Augustus in 27 B.C., though larger than any hitherto known, was not so extensive as to imply a new principle. The provinces of Augustus, roughly speaking, comprised Gaul, Spain, Egypt, Syria, and the more backward parts of Asia Minor, while the Senate was responsible for the rest of the empire. In 22 B.C. Gallia Narbonensis was transferred to the Senate, and at an uncertain date Baetica was separated from the rest of Spain and surrendered by the emperor. On the other hand the wars waged by Tiberius against the Pannonians from 12 B.C. rendered it desirable that Illyricum should become an 'imperial' province, and it was therefore transferred to Augustus in 11 B.C.[1] The new provinces which were acquired in the course of his reign, Galatia, Raetia, Noricum, Pannonia, and Moesia, came, as was natural, directly under the control of the emperor.

It is commonly stated by historians, who can claim the support of the nearly contemporary Strabo[2], that the principle on which the division of provinces was based was that the Emperor undertook the rule of those among them which required military defence, while the senatorial provinces had no need of a garrison. But this statement requires some qualification. As is well known, legionary troops were stationed in Africa throughout the Principate and till the reign of Gaius were under the command of the proconsuls, who in the reigns of both Augustus and Tiberius undertook important military operations. What is less often noticed is that the same is true of the proconsuls of Macedonia and Illyricum, who during the earlier part of the reign of Augustus commanded armies consisting of several legions. The situation in these districts was altered by the annexation of Pannonia and Moesia. Macedonia became an 'unarmed province' before the death of Augustus, but till the Flavian period legions were stationed in Illyricum, which was now 'imperial.' In the three provinces which have been mentioned it is certain the armies were commanded by proconsuls and it is possible that this occurred elsewhere. There is some evidence for a war against a desert tribe conducted by Quirinius from the province of Cyrene[3]. These considerations make it probable that while the usual theory is true of later times it is not applicable to the greater part of the reign of Augustus, and that no rigid rule was laid down in 27 B.C. Under Augustus legions were employed where they were wanted, even

[1] Dio LIV, 34, 4. The date is a little uncertain.

[2] XVII, 840; cf. Dio LIII, 12.

[3] See above, p. 194. On the view of Groag that Quirinius waged his war against the Homanades as proconsul of Asia see Note 2, p. 877 sq.

in senatorial provinces, and not till later were they treated as a frontier garrison. Peaceful as Augustus was by temperament, more fighting occurred during his reign than under most of his successors[1].

The distinction between the two types of province was thus even in the reign of Augustus to a large extent illusory. As supreme commander of the army he could not remain indifferent to the administration of provinces requiring military defence even if they were not normally garrisoned by legions. Whatever may have been his legal position under the settlement of 27 B.C., there is no doubt that in 23 B.C. he received *maius imperium* over the whole empire. That his control of the senatorial provinces was a reality is shown by the important edicts dated between 7 and 4 B.C. which have been discovered in the province of Cyrene[2]. From these it is clear that Augustus considered himself entitled to introduce on his own authority reforms of judicial procedure in the interests of non-citizens. The wording of the edicts shows characteristic tact. The procedure which he favours is to be followed 'until the senate comes to a decision on the subject or I find a better plan.' His directions take the form of advice rather than of command. 'I think that the governors of Crete and Cyrene will do well in the future not to allow a Roman to be the prosecutor of a Greek.' The new method laid down for the settlement of charges of extortion is indeed enacted by a *senatus consultum*, but it is definitely stated that the consuls who proposed it did so on instructions from the Emperor and that it was signed by him. The embassies mentioned in the edicts as coming to Rome from the provincial cities probably went straight to the *princeps*. If, as has been suggested above, part at least of the revenues of senatorial provinces was expended by the Emperor it was impossible to apply to administration a rigid system of dyarchy. In the Cyrene edicts the Emperor and the Senate appear as two agents who act in friendly co-operation in the task of government[3].

Of all the problems which Augustus was called upon to solve perhaps the most urgent was that concerning the method by which provincial governors should be appointed. In the Republican period[4] the government of provinces had originally been a function of the annual magistrates, and, although the system had been modified, the connection between the magistracy and the adminis-

[1] See R. Syme in *J.R.S.* XXIII, 1933, pp. 21–5.
[2] On these edicts see especially above, p. 167.
[3] Especially no. 5, ὅσην φροντίδα ποιούμεθα ἐγώ τε καὶ ἡ σύγκλητος.
[4] See Vol. IX, pp. 452 *sqq.*

tration of provinces always remained close. Even Caesar had introduced no radical reform. The arrangements in force at his death show that he wished the provinces to be governed by men whose year of office as consul or praetor had just expired. In limiting by law the tenure of a consular province to two years and that of a praetorian province to one he took what was essentially a reactionary step[1], and the fear lest long provincial commands might lead others to follow the example which he had set showed a want of confidence in the stability of his system of government. The views of Pompey on this question seem to have been more radical than those of Caesar. His own extraordinary commands stood in little relation to the magistracy, and a law for which he was responsible interposed an interval of five years between the consulship or praetorship and a provincial command. What was wanted was the creation of a system whereby important commands could be held by the same man for a long period without danger to the state. In no other way was it possible to govern the provinces efficiently and to find scope for men who combined energy and capacity with loyalty and public spirit. Rome had always possessed such men, but full use could not be made of them so long as the Republic lasted.

The system of appointment which prevailed throughout the Principate is to a large extent the creation of Augustus. As has been already said (p. 183 *sq.*), he decided to retain the connection between the Senate and imperial administration, and to insist that the tenure of the consulship or praetorship must still be a qualification for the most important provincial commands. Though under the Principate the city magistracies became to an increasing extent sinecures, the fact that their tenure was a necessary preliminary to a governorship generally secured that enough candidates presented themselves. When a man had held the praetorship he was qualified to become proconsul or *legatus pro praetore* of one of the less important provinces, to command a legion, or to become a member of various administrative boards, while to have held the consulship opened to him the highest posts of all.

Of the senatorial provinces Asia and Africa were governed by consulars and the remainder by praetorians. To both types of province the principle laid down in Pompey's law of 52 B.C. was applied, so that an interval of time elapsed between the magistracy and the proconsulship, which in the case of praetorians was at least five years and in that of consulars at least ten[2]. The allocation

---

[1] Cicero, *Phil.* i, 8, 19; see above, Vol. ix, p. 698.
[2] Marquardt, *Röm. Staatsverwaltung*, i, p. 546.

of provinces among the qualified candidates was made by lot, and
the tenure was usually for a year, though exceptions were often
made, as when M. Silanus under Tiberius governed Africa for six
years. Under Augustus P. Paquius Scaeva was reappointed
proconsul of Cyprus after an interval *auctoritate Augusti Caesaris
et s.c.*[1], an interesting case of the interference of the Emperor in
the senatorial sphere. At this period it seems that the rules determining appointment were less rigid than they became later.
M. Lollius, for instance, probably governed Macedonia after his
consulship, though the province was normally praetorian. Under
the Republic the allocation of a province to a consul or praetor had
been determined by the circumstances of the case.

While the selection of the governors of the comparatively
civilized senatorial provinces could without any great risk normally
be left to the chances of the lot, it was otherwise with the provinces
for which the Emperor was directly responsible. In them it was
all-important that the right man should be appointed, and that, in
choosing the *legati pro praetore* whom, following the precedent set
by Pompey, he employed as his representatives, the Emperor should
not be hampered by rigid rules. As these *legati* were invariably
men of consular or praetorian standing it is not surprising to find
that by the end of his reign Augustus exercised much influence on
the election of magistrates, for it could not be a matter of indifference to him who obtained the necessary qualification[2]. When
once the requisite magistracy had been held, a man could at any
time obtain an appointment from the emperor and retain it for as
long a period as seemed desirable. Normally certain provinces
were governed by consulars and certain others by praetorians,
but under Augustus exceptions were sometimes made. There is at
least one example of the appointment of a praetorian to the command of Nearer Spain[3], and it is probable that what was later the
praetorian province of Galatia was governed by at least two consulars, L. Calpurnius Piso and P. Sulpicius Quirinius[4]. It is also
by no means certain that every province had at this period a
separate governor, though our ignorance may be due to the fact
that inscriptions frequently fail to record the names of provinces
governed by *legati* of Augustus. In any case, during the wars in
Germany the whole of Gallia Comata was probably under the
command of a single man, whether a member of the imperial

[1] Dessau 915.
[2] F. B. Marsh, *The Founding of the Roman Empire*, pp. 247 *sqq.*
[3] C. Furnius, 22 B.C., Dio LIV, 5, 1.
[4] See R. Syme, *op. cit.* p. 24, n. 74.

family such as Drusus, Tiberius or Germanicus, or a senator like Lollius or Quinctilius Varus, though later each of the 'Three Gauls' had its own governor. Similarly when Agrippa was in the East his authority may well have extended beyond the borders of Syria (see above, p. 142).

Though by far the greater part of the empire was governed by men of senatorial rank there were certain districts to which for one reason or another a different system was applied. Members of the equestrian order, the importance of which under Augustus has been discussed above (pp. 185 *sqq.*), were entrusted not merely with financial posts but with the government of several newly conquered provinces. The position of the *praefectus Aegypti* was unique, for though an *eques* he had a legionary force under his command (see below, p. 243). In other provinces governed by *equites* only *auxilia* or local militia would be found, and when legions were required application would have to be made to the nearest senatorial governor. The most important districts entrusted by Augustus to equestrian procurators were Raetia and Noricum and, in the East, Judaea after the dynasty of Herod came to an end in A.D. 6. Herod himself can almost be considered a procurator of Augustus though he bore a royal title. A parallel to his position can be found in the Cottian Alps, where a number of tribes were put under the rule of M. Julius Cottius, the son of King Donnus, with the title of *praefectus*. The adjoining region of the Maritime Alps was treated in a similar way, though the first *praefectus* of whom we know, C. Baebius Atticus, was not a local chief but a man who had served as *primus pilus* in a legion[1].

Augustus continued the policy of the Republic in leaving under the rule of 'client-kings' certain districts which, while in a sense included in the empire, were not ripe for annexation as provinces (see above, pp. 174 *sqq.*). This policy was applied to Armenia[2], to Judaea until A.D. 6, and to Thrace, Mauretania, and Cappadocia. In Thrace constant intervention was required to save the weak Odrysian dynasty (see below, p. 356), and it is rather surprising that Augustus did not anticipate Claudius in annexing the country. In Mauretania the scholarly King Juba, with his wife Cleopatra Selene apparently as co-regent, was entrusted with the difficult task of ruling a turbulent people, which would have been beyond his powers without the assistance of Roman troops. These client-kings were left free in their internal administration, and probably

[1] Dessau 94, 1349.
[2] *Res Gestae* 27. 'Armeniam maiorem...cum possem facere provinciam malui maiorum nostrorum exemplo regnum id Tigrani...tradere.'

paid no regular taxes[1]: at least we know that the annexation of Cappadocia by Tiberius increased the Roman revenues, but they might be required to provide troops and their foreign policy was determined by the Emperor. In case of need a Roman 'resident' might be stationed in their country[2].

The proconsul of a senatorial province was, as under the Republic, assisted in the work of administration by a quaestor and one or more *legati* of senatorial rank. In an imperial province the right-hand men of the governor were the *legati legionum*, who acted as his deputies in the districts where their legions were stationed (see p. 225). Each province too had its equestrian procurator who in the eyes of the provincials was almost as important as the governor himself[3]. These procurators were appointed by the Emperor quite independently of the *legatus* and the relations between the two were frequently none too friendly. A procurator of Augustus remained in Spain for ten years[4] and such cases were probably not uncommon. The supervision of taxation was almost entirely in their hands. The fact that imperial procurators are found also in senatorial provinces confirms the view taken above (p. 194) that a contribution was made by them to the funds administered by the Emperor.

The reforms introduced by Augustus into provincial administration were a source of great advantage both to the government and to the subjects of Rome. The method of administration was carefully adapted to the circumstances of each province. The burden of taxation was equitably distributed, and the revenue went to the treasury and not into the pockets of middlemen. The governors were selected with care, and competent men could attain to the highest posts even if their origin was obscure. The machinery for bringing complaints to Rome was reformed, and a charge of extortion was more likely to receive a fair hearing from a Senate which feared the Emperor's wrath than from the venal *quaestio repetundarum* of the age of Cicero.

Reference has already been made to the interest shown by Augustus in the roads of Italy and to his establishment of a regular *cura viarum*. But a very much larger problem was created by the re-organization of the empire and by the annexation of new and backward provinces. In order that the authorities in Rome might be kept informed of all that was happening the extension

---

[1] It may be argued that there were exceptions to this rule. See the view taken below (p. 330) in reference to Herod and his successors.

[2] Tacitus, *Ann.* II, 42; IV, 46, 67.   [3] Tacitus, *Agric.* 15.

[4] Dessau 9007.

throughout the empire of the network of roads starting from the 'golden milestone' in the City was a matter of prime necessity. Under Augustus are to be found the beginnings of the *cursus publicus* which enabled official despatches to be forwarded rapidly by means of posting-stations erected along the trunk-roads. Evidence from many provinces testifies to active road-construction at this period. The newly conquered north-west of Spain was opened up, and in the south of the peninsula a new road shortened the line of communication between Baetica and the north[1]. The road-system of Gaul was greatly improved by Agrippa, who made Lugdunum the centre from which four roads radiated, leading respectively to Aquitania, to the Rhine, to the northern Ocean, and down the Rhône to Massilia[2]. The conquest of Raetia was followed by the planning of a road from north Italy to the Danube[3]. As has been shown elsewhere (p. 352 *sq.*) the clue to the military operations on the northern frontiers of the empire is the desire of the Romans to control the road which ran down the Save to the Danube and thence to Byzantium, thus providing a land-route from Italy to the East. It is indeed true that the primary reason for the development of Roman roads was military: it might at any time be necessary to move legions rapidly from one part of the frontier to another. But of course their existence had far-reaching effects of another character. Not only was the exchange of commodities greatly facilitated, but the improvement of communications led to an interchange of ideas which gradually created a more or less homogeneous civilization throughout the vast area which recognized the overlordship of Rome[4].

[1] Dessau 102.　　　　　　　　　[2] Strabo iv, 208.
[3] Dessau 208. See W. Cartellieri, in *Philologus, Supplementband*, XVIII, 1926, i, pp. 45 *sqq.*
[4] See M. P. Charlesworth, *Trade Routes and Commerce in the Roman Empire*, and the present writer in *The Legacy of Rome*, pp. 141 *sqq.* See also below, p. 424.

CHAPTER VIII

THE ARMY AND NAVY

I. THE PROBLEM: THE MAIN FEATURES OF
THE AUGUSTAN SETTLEMENT

IN an earlier chapter of this work[1] it was shown that long before the end of the Republic the Roman State was called upon to face problems of government and administration which could not be satisfactorily solved without a complete re-organization of her army and navy, and that under the prevailing political conditions such a re-organization was almost impossible to realize. The military system which had been adequate to the needs of a small State whose wars were confined to Italy and which refused to bring under her direct control a great part even of the peninsula until practically compelled to do so by the Italians themselves, was ill adapted to the conquest and government of extra-Italian provinces. Rome was in no hurry to annex, but circumstances made annexation inevitable, so that by the end of the Republic she was mistress of the greater part of the lands facing the Mediterranean, and had by Caesar's victories extended her authority to the English Channel and the Atlantic. Many of the provinces of the Republic were exposed to attack from dangerous neighbours. Mithridates and the Parthians resented the presence of Rome in Asia Minor. Macedonia was constantly raided by Balkan tribes, and the invasion of the Teutoni and Cimbri showed the need of protecting the Mediterranean world from the barbarians of central and northern Europe. The problems thus raised were dealt with by the Republic in a very inadequate way. The size of the army was determined by the needs of the moment. In times of peace a province might be practically denuded of troops, and when trouble arose armies had to be improvised in order to meet it. Many disasters might have been avoided had the provinces been at all times garrisoned by a force capable of policing the country and of protecting it against invasion.

Such a situation called for the creation of a professional army consisting of long-service troops and commanded by generals who were primarily not politicians but soldiers. The professional soldier had existed *de facto* before the days of Marius, and after his reforms

[1] Vol. IX, p. 443 *sq.*

there can have been few soldiers who did not serve for a long period and did not look to the State or their general for provision on their discharge. But the size of the army varied according to the military situation, and a soldier on enlistment must have been very uncertain about his future. It is not even clear that he 'signed on' for a definite number of years, and there is no doubt that before the time of Augustus the problem of the 'ex-service man' was never properly faced.

As regards the officers things were even worse. Provincial commands were regarded as perquisites of the magistracy, with the result that the conduct of wars was often entrusted to men devoid of the necessary knowledge and experience. When the situation became very bad, the ordinary rules were suspended, and an extraordinary command conferred on a Marius, a Sulla, a Pompey, or a Caesar, but such commands were regarded in senatorial circles as abnormal and unconstitutional, and the holder of them tended to be viewed with suspicion. These generals were to a large extent the creators of the armies which they commanded, so that the loyalty of the troops was directed primarily to them. It has been said with truth that 'so far from there being a State army in the last century of the Republic, there was rather a succession of armies owing loyalty to their respective generals[1].'

Another defect of the Republican system of army administration was that the burden of military service and imperial defence was borne to an undue extent by Italians. Roman provincial rule was so unpopular that the government did not dare to arm the provincials, even to defend their own homes against invasion. It is true that specialist troops—archers, slingers, and especially cavalry—were provided by certain provinces, but not till the civil war between Pompey and Caesar are provincials to be found in any number in the legions and then only when Italians were not available[2]. Thus when a crisis arose it was necessary to raise an army in Italy and to transport it to the seat of war. This process took time, and in the meanwhile disasters occurred which might well have been avoided had the provincials been equipped with means of defence or an adequate garrison stationed in their midst. So long, however, as Rome's provincial subjects were treated in such a way that it was hard for them to identify their interests with those of the governing people there could be no question of calling on them to take any large part in the defence of Roman rule against attack. The words used by Cerialis in addressing the

---

[1] H. M. D. Parker, *The Roman Legions*, p. 26.
[2] See above, vol. IX, p. 710 *sq.*

revolted Gauls in A.D. 70 could not have been uttered under the Republic. 'You often command our legions, you govern these and other provinces: there is no narrowness, no exclusiveness in our rule. You benefit as much as we from good rulers though you live far off. Bad emperors attack only those who are near them[1].' As early as the time of Cicero[2] we find traces of the idea that Rome's subjects should be grateful for the blessings of the *pax Romana*, but it is unlikely that this claim found a responsive echo in the minds of men ruled by Verres or Gabinius. It is clear that the well-known tendency of the Romans to avoid revolutionary changes and to retain institutions which a less conservative people would have abolished had had an unfortunate effect on the army, and that the whole system required to be overhauled and to be adapted to the new conditions. In no other department was the work of Augustus of such permanent value. The system which existed at his death was modified only in detail by his successors during the first two centuries of our era, and traces of it remained till the last days of the Western Empire.

In this department, as in others, Augustus owed something at least to the example of Caesar. In no army of the Republic had professionalism and efficiency reached such a height as in the force which conquered Gaul and defeated Pompey and his lieutenants. Among Caesar's officers were men who had little connection with politics and could fairly be regarded as professional soldiers. His legions developed an *esprit de corps*, rare among the shortlived legions of the Republic, but a familiar feature of the armies of the Principate. Again, by his recognition of the military value of provincials Caesar foreshadowed the practice of the Principate. The chief recruiting-ground of his legions was the Italian province of Cisalpine Gaul, on which the full citizenship was not conferred till 49 B.C., and one whole legion (the Alaudae), recruited in Transalpine Gaul, did not receive the franchise till the period of the Civil War. Even greater use was made of provincials in those sections of his army which were not organized as legions. A large proportion of his cavalry consisted of Gauls and Germans, and when in 49 B.C. he encountered Pompey's lieutenants in Spain he made use of Gallic contingents led by their own chiefs. His example was followed by his opponents, who indeed, for the campaign of Munda, raised not only auxiliaries but legions among the natives of Spain. At this crisis the old prejudice against the arming of provincials was breaking down, and the way was being prepared for the creation of a regular auxiliary force as a permanent

---

[1] Tacitus, *Hist.* IV, 74.   [2] E.g. *ad. Q. Fr.* I, I, 11, 34.

element in the Roman army. Finally, the manner in which Caesar provided for his time-expired soldiers afforded an important precedent. Large bodies of them were settled in the provinces, especially in the south of Gaul. Most of these military colonists must have been men of Italian stock, and the importance of this step in removing the distinction between Italy and the provinces cannot be exaggerated. The Republic had objected on principle to transmarine colonization: C. Gracchus had made himself unpopular by championing an idea which was destined to have a great future.

The steps taken by Augustus to deal with the unwieldy body of troops (consisting of at least sixty legions) which was at his disposal after Actium have been described elsewhere (p. 120). Soldiers were settled in twenty-eight cities of Italy and in Africa, Sicily, Macedonia, Spain, Greece, Asia, Syria, Gallia Narbonensis, and Pisidia. This process was complete by 13 B.C. and from that date, if not earlier, the total number of legions did not exceed twenty-eight.

Although, as has been said, the professional soldier and even the professional general was not unknown under the Republic, not till the Principate was the army definitely organized on professional lines. The troops raised by Caesar and Pompey and by the Triumvirs had not enlisted for a definite period. They can only have hoped that when their services were no longer required a victorious general would see that they did not starve. But such a system was inconsistent with the ideas of Augustus, to whom the army was not primarily a field force raised for the purpose of a definite campaign, but a permanent garrison intended to protect the frontiers from invasion and to keep order in the provinces. Accordingly in 13 B.C. he decided that legionaries must serve for sixteen years and soldiers of the Praetorian Guard for twelve before they could claim discharge and a definite gratuity[1]. In A.D. 5 the period of service was raised to sixteen years for the praetorians and to twenty for the legionaries, and their allowances fixed at 20,000 and 12,000 sesterces respectively[2]. In the following year the financial burden of this provision for old soldiers, which had hitherto fallen on the emperor's private revenues, was transferred to a new treasury, the *aerarium militare*, into which were paid the sums raised by taxes on inheritances and sales. In this way the Roman army became what it was destined to remain, a body of long-service troops.

The government of the Principate claimed and occasionally

---

[1] Dio LIV, 25, 6.   [2] Dio LV, 23, 1.

exercised the right to compel its subjects to serve in the army, but this method of recruiting was unsuitable when military service lasted twenty years or more. Accordingly, compulsion was seldom enforced except at crises, such as the Pannonian Revolt of A.D. 6. Most soldiers were volunteers, of whom an adequate supply was generally available, especially when as a result of the new system families possessing military traditions had sprung up all over the Empire. Enlistment in the army offered good prospects and a secure future. The danger of death in battle was not great at a time when serious wars were rare.

As early as the time of Tiberius it was possible to say that the main strength of the army lay in the non-Italian element[1]. 'Nihil validum in exercitibus nisi quod externum.' This was indeed an exaggeration, but Augustus, profiting from the experience of the civil wars, had frankly accepted the principle that the defence of the Empire was a task in which provincials might be expected to take an important part. From the beginning the *auxilia*, whose place in the army was definitely recognized, were recruited entirely in the provinces, and even the legions, especially in the eastern provinces, contained many non-Italians. Nothing did more to create a feeling of imperial patriotism than this confidence shown by the government in the loyalty of provincials. In the Ciceronian age the subjects of Rome were frequently referred to as allies, but the word was not used in anything but a technical sense until the Principate. Provincials learned to feel that they participated in a civilization which it was a privilege to defend against barbarian attacks. The tribes of north-eastern Gaul, for instance, came in time to consider that their spiritual ties were with Italy rather than with their so-called kinsfolk across the Rhine.

Enough has been said to show that Augustus had a clear appreciation of the nature of the problem, and that his solution of it bears every mark of constructive statesmanship.

II. THE LEGIONS

The first task which confronted Augustus after his victory over Antony was to reduce the legionary forces to a manageable size. In the *Res Gestae* (3) he states that in the course of his reign he settled in colonies or sent back to their own towns over 300,000 soldiers, a number which probably does not include many of the troops of Antony and Lepidus, whose services he did not require. The most important years in this respect were

[1] Tacitus, *Ann.* III, 40.

30 and 14 B.C. In the latter year many of the soldiers whom he had retained after Actium had completed their period of service, and it was probably about this time that the principles which were to guide him were definitely accepted.

In deciding how many legions were to be retained in the army Augustus was guided by considerations both of policy and of finance. He must have been well aware that the contemplated extension of the Empire to the Elbe and the Danube could not be accomplished without much fighting. On the other hand he had decided in 20 B.C., when he recovered the standards captured at Carrhae, to abandon the aggressive policy of Caesar and Antony in the East, and to aim at establishing friendly relations with the Parthians. About the same time, as he says himself, he could have made Armenia a province, but preferred to entrust it to a king who recognized the suzerainty of Rome. Thus only in the North was it likely that actual fighting would occur. The long wars in Spain had come to an end in 19 B.C., and the campaigns in Africa and Arabia were not likely to be repeated. A decision was also very desirable from a financial point of view. Augustus had devoted years to the task of re-organizing the taxation of the Empire, and it was essential for him to know what he would have in the future to spend on the army, by far the most important item of expenditure in the Roman budget. Accordingly in 13 B.C. he reached a final decision about the number of the legions and the conditions of legionary service.

The discovery of a papyrus showing that a legion numbered XXII existed in 8 B.C. has definitely disproved the view of Mommsen that Augustus after Actium reduced the army to eighteen legions and raised many more in the troubled years A.D. 6–9. It is now generally agreed that from 14 or 13 B.C., if not earlier, the army contained twenty-eight legions, three of which were lost with Varus in A.D. 9, and not immediately replaced. Thus under Tiberius there were twenty-five legions. Two were added by Claudius (XV and XXII Primigenia) and by the time of the accession of Vespasian there were three more (I and II Adiutrix and I Italica). The foresight of Augustus is established by the fact that Trajan, the best soldier among his successors, was content with an army of thirty legions.

Although the principle that frontier defence was to be the main function of the legions goes back to Augustus, so many wars occurred during his reign that they were moved from province to province to a greater extent than was customary under his successors. The historian, Velleius Paterculus, who was attached as military tribune to a legion (probably V Macedonica) whose headquarters were in Macedonia, saw service in the eastern provinces. During the Pannonian revolt legionary reinforcements were brought from Macedonia and Syria. It is thus difficult to state with any accuracy the normal distribution of the legions at this period[1]. But from the accession of Tiberius the task is easier. In A.D. 23 there were three legions in Spain, eight on the Rhine, seven in the Danubian provinces, four in Syria, two in Egypt, and one in Africa[2]. This remained the normal distribution during the Julio-Claudian period, though the conquest of Britain under Claudius and Corbulo's operations in the East involved certain modifications. After the Flavian period only one legion is found in Spain, and none at all in Dalmatia. The majority of the provinces were unarmed, and the military forces were concentrated on the frontiers.

The wisdom of this military system cannot be discussed apart from the general problem of the frontier policy of the Principate. Here it must be enough to say that the absence of any reserve units which could have been sent as reinforcements to threatened points on the frontier might well have had grave consequences. In order to strengthen any one part of the long frontier it was necessary to weaken another, so that if the Empire had been attacked simultaneously on two or more fronts it might well have collapsed. Fortunately this situation was unlikely to arise. The tribes beyond the Rhine and the Danube were too disunited to be a serious danger, and by indirect means Rome fostered their natural tendency to disunion. In the East an unaggressive policy was pursued. No serious attempt was made to annex Armenia before Trajan, and few kings of Parthia were strong enough to contemplate any extension of their kingdom at the expense of Rome.

A more serious objection to the system is one which becomes obvious in the year of chaos which followed the death of Nero, during which the armies of the Rhine, the Danube, and the Euphrates supported different candidates for the throne. Nothing did more to secure the support of the eastern legions for Vespasian than the rumour that his rival had proposed to move them to the Rhine. The ties which bound groups of legions to each other and to the provinces in which they were stationed were inconveniently close: the soldiers, whatever their origin, tended to regard these provinces as their home[3]. But this development of *esprit de corps* in the separate armies was likely to cause trouble only

[1] See on this problem R. Syme in *J.R.S.* XXIII, 1933, pp. 14 *sqq.*
[2] Tacitus, *Ann.* IV, 5.   [3] Tacitus, *Hist.* II, 80; *Ann.* XIV, 27.

when the throne was vacant for all armies were usually loyal to the
emperor for the time being. At the same time it cannot be said
that in this period the army was a unit that was normally conscious
of its power or disposed to use it, or that the emperor was master
of the State by virtue of being the representative of the soldiers
and their interests.

The connection between the magistracy and military commands
long outlasted the Republic, and the higher officers of the legions
of the early Principate can hardly be described as professional
soldiers. Though no magistrate performed military duties during
his year of office, the commanders both of provincial armies and
of individual legions were (except in Egypt) men who had reached
a fairly definite stage in the senatorial *cursus honorum*. Each legion
was commanded by a *legatus*, who was at first an ex-quaestor and
later almost invariably an ex-praetor. This office was a creation of
Augustus, though he had to some extent been anticipated by Caesar,
who put sections of his army under carefully selected *legati*. The
post must have given its holder valuable experience, but no man
held it long enough to establish close ties between himself and
his soldiers[1]. After a year or two he returned to Rome to hold
another magistracy or was transferred to one of the numerous
provincial governorships held by men of praetorian rank. The only
opportunity of gaining military experience open to a man who
hoped to command a legion was in the office of *tribunus militum*,
which in the Principate, as in the later Republic, was held by
young men who had not yet entered the Senate and were considered to be members of the equestrian order. The duties of these
tribuni cannot have involved much responsibility, and they must
have been regarded primarily as learners. Rome possessed no
military colleges, so that the future governor of Britain or Pannonia
was expected to acquire military knowledge by practical experience
alone. Agricola's military experience before his governorship of
Britain consisted of about a year as military tribune followed after a
long interval by perhaps three years as *legatus* of a legion: yet his
son-in-law describes him at this stage of his career as a *vir militaris*[2].
If the foreign policy of Rome had not been so unaggressive, the
system just described might have had serious results. Usually
the governor even of an important frontier province was not an
experienced soldier[3]. At a critical moment a special appointment
had to be made: the position of Corbulo in the East during
Nero's reign recalls the extraordinary commands of the Republic.

[1] See, however, Tacitus, *Hist.* iv, 39.   [2] Tacitus, *Agric.* 9.
[3] Tacitus, *Hist.* ii, 86.

There is at least some truth in the suggestion of Tacitus that the emperors were unwilling that senators should have opportunities of gaining military distinction[1].

The absence of professional experience among the higher officers was to some extent remedied by the institution of the centurionate. Each legion had sixty centurions, six attached to each of its ten cohorts. The senior centurion was called *primus pilus*, and it was customary for the commander to consult a group of centurions known as the *primi ordines*, which consisted probably of all the centurions of the first cohort and the senior centurion of each of the others[2]. Many, perhaps most, of the centurions had risen from the ranks, but quite early in the Principate it was possible for men belonging to a higher social class than most of the private soldiers, and even for equites, to begin their military career as centurions. Such men were promoted rapidly and were transferred from legion to legion and from province to province, while their colleagues who had started in the ranks sometimes spent the whole of their military life in the same legion. All centurions however had an experience which must have been of great value to their nominal chiefs. On retirement a *primus pilus* had good prospects of interesting work. He might as an *eques* become tribune of a praetorian or urban cohort in the city of Rome, or receive a command in Egypt or in the auxiliary forces, or even in the early Principate become tribune of a legion. Many financial posts were open to him. Finally, he might settle in a town and hold municipal office. He normally received equestrian rank, and might well have sons who entered on the senatorial career.

On the whole then the legionary officers had much less professional experience than the rank and file. The *tribuni* and *legati* were almost amateur soldiers, and even among the centurions there were many who regarded their military service mainly as a preparation for a civilian career.

If in the early Principate the great majority of the soldiers, at least in the western legions, were men of Italian birth, the reason was that comparatively few of the provincials possessed the Roman franchise. With the extension of the franchise by colonization and other means the provinces came to provide a very considerable proportion of the legionaries, and from the Flavian period onwards the number of Italians in the legion steadily declines. From the beginning the eastern legions were mainly recruited in the eastern provinces, especially in Galatia, and the soldiers must often have been given citizenship on enlistment. Of 61 soldiers serving in the

[1] Tacitus, *Agric.* 39.   [2] Parker, *op. cit.* pp. 201, 281 *sq.*

Egyptian legions in the first century 53 are known to have been natives of Asia Minor, Syria, and Egypt. The division of the Empire into the Greek-speaking East and the Latin-speaking West is reflected in the army. The western legions were recruited in Italy and in such romanized provinces as Baetica and Gallia Narbonensis[1]. The Danubian army drew on both eastern and western provinces[2], while, as has been said, the eastern legions were almost entirely eastern in their composition.

It is probable that the conditions of service established by Augustus in A.D. 5–6 (p. 221) were not in the first instance strictly observed. One of the main grievances of the mutinous legionaries at the beginning of the reign of Tiberius was that they were retained with the colours sometimes for thirty or forty years, and that even after formal discharge military duties were imposed on them[3]. The Emperor was forced to make concessions which had almost immediately to be cancelled for financial reasons. Twenty years remained under the Julio-Claudian emperors the normal period of legionary service. Even in A.D. 23 the situation was not satisfactory. In that year Tiberius thought of visiting the provinces in order to raise new troops in place of the veterans who were clamouring for discharge. The cause of the trouble was probably financial. It took time before the *aerarium militare* established in A.D. 6 would contain sufficient funds to provide adequately for old soldiers, and in the interim it was simplest to retain them in the legions. The policy of settling veterans in colonies was not abandoned when in A.D. 5 the scale of gratuities was fixed. Colchester and Cologne are only two examples of the military colonies of the Julio-Claudian age. Sometimes old soldiers were expected to settle in Italian towns, but it seems that this policy was unpopular. Men settled by Nero in Tarentum and Antium drifted back to the provinces where they had served. It has already been noted that soldiers formed close ties with the inhabitants of the districts in which their legions were stationed. When the Germans in A.D. 70 urged the people of Cologne to kill all the Romans in their city the answer was: 'Soldiers who have been settled here and are united to us by marriage and the offspring of these unions regard this town as their home: you cannot be so unreasonable as to wish us to kill our fathers, our brothers, and our children[4].' Legal marriage between a soldier and a provincial woman was not permitted during active service.

---

[1] Galba raised a whole legion in Spain (Suetonius, *Galba*, 10; Tacitus, *Hist.* III, 25) and Clodius Macer in Africa (Tacitus, *Hist.* II, 97).

[2] Tacitus, *Ann.* XVI, 13.　　[3] Tacitus, *Ann.* I, 17.

[4] Tacitus, *Hist.* IV, 65.

The laws enforcing matrimony did not apply to soldiers. There were no married quarters in legionary camps. But the immobility of the legions led to the formation of alliances which were often legalized when the soldier got his discharge.

The life of a Roman legionary must often have been an unexciting one. He was usually attached for twenty years to the same legion, cohort, and century, and might well spend all his military life in the same camp. Important campaigns were so rare that a man might get his discharge without ever having fought in a battle. When Corbulo went to the East in A.D. 58 he found that discipline had become very slack. 'The soldiers, demoralized by a long peace, endured impatiently the duties of a camp. The army contained veterans who had never acted as sentry or guard, to whom the rampart and ditch were new and strange sights, men without helmets and breastplates, sleek money-making fellows who had served all their time in towns[1].' Sometimes generals employed their idle troops on useful work. Under Claudius the Rhine army, much against its will, was forced to dig for silver in the Taunus district, and a little later an enterprising commander proposed to construct with military labour a canal from the Moselle to the Saône which would have enabled ships to sail from the North Sea to the Mediterranean[2]. A certain proportion of the private soldiers might hope to reach the rank of centurion, and for others there were specialist jobs in the orderly-room or in the camp-hospital: some were despatch-riders and others horn-blowers. It was a great honour to bear the *signum* of a cohort or the *aquila* of the legion. Sometimes a soldier would have an opportunity of visiting another province through being seconded to a detachment sent to assist a governor whose army required temporary reinforcement.

III. THE *AUXILIA*

If the army of the Principate had consisted of legions alone it would have been too small to perform its functions. At full strength the twenty-five legions which existed at the death of Augustus contained only some 150,000 men. Accordingly, a second force of about the same size was raised from among the provincials, and organized on a different system. As was stated above (p. 219 *sq.*), the armies of the Civil War and the Triumvirate consisted not only of legions but of smaller units of both infantry and cavalry, recruited in the provinces and frequently commanded by their own chiefs. For instance, when Antony crossed the

---

[1] Tacitus, *Ann.* XIII, 35.   [2] Tacitus, *Ann.* XI, 20; XIII, 53.

Euphrates in 36 B.C. he was accompanied by some 10,000 Gallic and Spanish cavalry, some of whom took part in his final campaign against Octavian.

Thus after the battle of Actium Augustus was called upon to decide, not merely how many legions should be retained, but whether any, and, if so, how many of these irregular units should be given a permanent place in the army. What was his exact decision it is difficult to say, but it is certain that during his reign a very considerable number of auxiliary units existed. No less than 70 *cohortes* of infantry and 14 *alae* of cavalry helped to crush the Pannonian revolt: these constituted a force of about 50,000 men, and it is possible that the total number of auxiliaries under arms at this time did not fall far short of 150,000, and was roughly equivalent to the number of the legionaries. Whether many of these units had existed before Actium is doubtful, but the names borne by certain cavalry squadrons suggest that they had originally been raised in Gaul by Caesar's officers.

Without the creation of such a force full use could not have been made of the resources of the provinces in military material, for it was impossible to break suddenly with the tradition that Roman citizenship was a necessary qualification for service in the legions. Under the Republic few provincials possessed the citizenship, and even under Augustus there were many parts of the Empire where it was rare, but whose inhabitants were well fitted to be soldiers. It was in these regions that the great majority of the auxiliaries were recruited. With a very few exceptions only the imperial provinces were drawn upon, while the Romanized inhabitants of the senatorial provinces served in the legions.

The districts in which auxiliary units were originally recruited can usually be told from their titles *e.g. Ala I Tungrorum, Cohors II Raetorum, Cohors I Thracum*, but it is a mistake to suppose that the bodies of troops which bore such titles always retained their local character. In some districts the territorial system of recruiting was soon abandoned and at least as early as the reign of Tiberius recruits were accepted from among the inhabitants of the provinces in which the units happened to be stationed. It has been said that 'the nominal rolls of many cohorts formed under Augustus must a century later have represented a map of the regions in which they had at one time or another served[1].' Undoubtedly Pannonians are found in 'Spanish' *cohortes* and Germans in 'African' *alae* quite early in the Principate. In this way something was done to discourage purely local patriotism, to

[1] Dessau, *Geschichte der röm. Kaiserzeit*, I, p. 282.

foster a common allegiance to Rome, and to spread the use of the Latin language, which must have been necessary as a means of communication between the heterogeneous elements included in the *auxilia*.

But this point must not be exaggerated. There is no doubt that till the end of the Julio-Claudian period a very large proportion of these units retained their national character and were stationed not far from their homes. This is particularly true of the Rhine frontier, where troops of Gallic nationality were employed at any rate till the rising of A.D. 69–70. It is clear from Tacitus' account of this rising that the titles borne by these units can safely be used to determine their composition. The Batavian cohorts, for example, which are so frequently mentioned, were evidently homogeneous, and this is true of most of the other bodies of *auxilia* which bear Gallic or German names. That there was at this time strong feeling against service far from home is shown by what happened in Thrace under Tiberius. Thracians who were quite prepared to serve under their own leaders against neighbouring tribes, were infuriated when it was reported that they might be 'separated from each other, attached to other peoples and dragged away to distant lands[1].' A little later we find the same situation in Britain. British troops were willing to serve loyally under Agricola against the Caledonian tribes, but regarded it as a grievance to be called upon to serve elsewhere than in Britain. Accordingly it is not surprising that three-quarters of the Rhenish *auxilia* in 69 were drawn from Gaul proper or the Teutonic tribes of the Belgic province. It was probably in the Danubian provinces that the practice of the local recruiting of *auxilia* was first adopted. After the Pannonian Revolt, which demonstrated the danger of training what might be a national army in a province, many of the local auxiliary units seem to have been sent elsewhere and their place taken by troops from other provinces of the West, especially from Spain. But when new recruits were wanted for these Spanish units they were not always brought from home, and suitable applicants were accepted from the districts in which they were stationed.

The auxiliary forces of the Roman army were organized in cohorts of infantry and *alae* of cavalry. In the first century both cohorts and *alae* were normally composed of about 500 men, though units of 1000 occur, and later become common. The infantry commander was called *praefectus cohortis*, and the cavalry commander *praefectus equitum*, and later *praefectus alae*. During

----

[1] Tacitus, *Ann.* IV, 46.

the greater part of the Principate these posts together with that of *tribunus militum* in the legions constituted the so-called *militia equestris*, and were held by young men who aspired to a career in the equestrian *cursus honorum* (pp. 186 *sqq.*). Though an *eques* could never command legions (except in Egypt), the military experience gained in his youth as commander of a *cohors* and *ala* would stand him in good stead if he later became procurator of such a province as Mauretania or Thrace, which contained a considerable force of auxiliaries.

But at the beginning of the Principate the time had not come to entrust these commands to young men without military experience. Accordingly the earliest *praefecti* were taken mainly from two other sources, legionary *primi pili*, whose previous training must have qualified them admirably to keep order in a force raised in the less civilized parts of the Empire, and tribal chiefs. So long as the *cohortes* and *alae* consisted almost entirely of men belonging to one tribe or drawn from one district it was often thought best to put at their head a man of their own race who had been granted the Roman citizenship, but who did not intend to enter on the normal *cursus honorum*. The leaders of the revolt on the Rhine in A.D. 69 were *praefecti* of this type, and the experience gained by the African chief Tacfarinas as an officer of *auxilia* rendered him a dangerous opponent of Rome in the reign of Tiberius. From the Flavian period *auxilia* are not commanded by tribal chiefs, and the development of local recruiting rapidly deprived the units of their territorial character. Even in the Julio-Claudian period isolated examples occur of young *praefecti* of the later type, and the *militia equestris* seems to have been organized by Claudius. But before the reign of Vespasian the majority of the *praefecti* were probably derived from other sources.

The subordinate officers of the *auxilia*, the *decuriones* of cavalry *turmae* and the centurions of the cohorts were Roman citizens who were frequently promoted to the legionary centurionate. The private soldier seems to have had little prospect of promotion.

Most of our information about the *auxilia* is derived from the certificates of discharge, the so-called *diplomata militaria*, which were granted to a soldier on the completion of twenty-five years of service, and which record the gift of citizenship and the legalization of any marriage which he had contracted or might hereafter contract. It has been questioned[1] whether this privilege goes back to Augustus, who granted the citizenship sparingly, but it is certain that by the middle of the first century A.D. every ex-soldier

---

[1] Dessau, *op. cit.* p. 276.

of the *auxilia* was a Roman citizen. By this time the rates of pay and of retiring-allowances were no doubt fixed, but we have no detailed knowledge of the subject. This generous policy must have done much to promote the provincialization of the legions, for one cannot doubt that many sons of these enfranchised auxiliaries enlisted in them. In two or three generations the descendant of an inhabitant of a backward province might reach the highest posts in the senatorial career.

As the regularly constituted *cohortes* and *alae* could not absorb all the provincials who were qualified for military service, many others were at critical periods enrolled by Roman generals under officers who were usually termed *praefecti levis armaturae*. In his invasion of Germany Germanicus made use of these *tumultuariae catervae*, and so did Corbulo in his eastern wars. They are frequently mentioned in the *Histories* of Tacitus[1] and are found in Raetia, Noricum, the Maritime Alps and in Mauretania. In Switzerland the garrisoning of at least one fort was entrusted to troops of this kind[2]. They were distinguished from the regular *auxilia* by being liable to service only in their own districts. It is probable that they were disbanded at the end of a war.

Finally, it must be mentioned that Rome made demands for military assistance on such client-kings as were allowed to survive. Before the organization of the province of Moesia the defence of the lower Danube was probably entrusted to the kings of Thrace, one of whom gave valuable assistance in crushing the Pannonian revolt. This kingdom became a province under Claudius, but farther east several kingdoms survived whose rulers were called upon for assistance by Corbulo and offered their services to Vespasian when he decided to aim at the throne.

IV. THE GARRISON OF ROME

In other chapters mention is made of the important part played by the Praetorian Guard and its commanders in the history of this period, especially at times when the throne was vacant. This famous body of troops, which consisted of nine cohorts[3], each containing 1000 men, was in theory the body-guard of the *princeps*. It performed in Italy the duty of preserving law and

[1] 1, 68; II, 12, 58; III, 5.   [2] Tacitus, *Hist.* 1, 67.
[3] Inscriptions (*e.g.* Dessau 2031, 2701) show that the number was raised to twelve under Claudius and Nero, and Vitellius enrolled as many as sixteen, but a *diploma* of the year 76 (Dessau 1993) shows that Vespasian had reverted to the original number.

order which in the provinces belonged to the legionary and auxiliary forces. Holders of *imperium* under the Republic had been attended by a body of picked soldiers, drawn perhaps mainly from young men of the upper classes, who in this way satisfied the legal requirements of military service, but the resemblance of the Praetorian Guard of the Principate to such units was merely one of name. Under Augustus only three of the cohorts were stationed in Rome itself, the remaining six being quartered in various towns of Italy—three were for a time as far from the capital as Aquileia —but Tiberius concentrated all nine in a camp outside the northeast gate of the city. As the personal body-guard of the emperor the praetorians were not liable to active service except when he or some member of his family took the field, and as this rarely happened under the Julio-Claudian dynasty, it is not surprising that they were regarded with envy and perhaps a little contempt by the legionaries, whose conditions were less comfortable, whose period of service was longer, and who received less than a third of their pay[1].

The rank and file of the praetorians was in the early Principate recruited mainly from Central Italy, while the Italians who served in the legions were drawn to a large extent from Cisalpine Gaul. But some exceptions occur. We happen to know that members of certain Alpine tribes of the Trentino, whose very claim to the citizenship was doubtful, had reached the rank of centurion in the Guard under Claudius, and more than one praetorian of this period was a native of Macedonia or even of Asia Minor[2]. Though, as will be seen, the commanders of the praetorian cohorts had usually served with the legions, private legionaries could seldom hope to be transferred to Rome. The example set by Vitellius of enrolling legionaries in the Guard[3] was not followed till the end of the Second Century. The majority of the praetorians were infantry, but to each cohort a squadron of cavalry was attached.

The praefects of the Guard were normally two in number, but the office was held without a colleague by Sejanus during the greater part of the reign of Tiberius, and by Burrus from 51 to 62. The praefect was with rare exceptions a man of equestrian rank, and was often of very humble origin. Nymphidius Sabinus who aimed at the throne on the death of Nero was the son of a freedwoman, and the parentage of Tigellinus was obscure. Plotius Firmus, praefect under Otho, had served as a private soldier. It is probable that Burrus was not an Italian but a native of

---

[1] Tacitus, *Ann.* I, 17.   [2] Dessau 206, 2032.
[3] Tacitus, *Hist.* II, 93–4.

Narbonese Gaul. The important position gained by these men illustrates the fact that under the Principate the possession of high birth was by no means essential for success in public life.

The separate cohorts were under the command of *tribuni*, who had usually held the primipilate of a legion and had thereafter acquired equestrian rank. A tribunate in the praetorians or the other city-troops was a regular stage in the equestrian *cursus honorum* and often led to important procuratorships and praefectures.

The life of a praetorian of the Julio-Claudian period can hardly have been a very strenuous one, and the routine nature of his duties must have made it hard for him to distinguish himself. The inscription which records the career of a man who accompanied Claudius to Britain as a private of the Guard, and subsequently gained equestrian rank and the procuratorship of Lusitania is almost unique[1]. As a rule such a man could not aspire to more than a centurionate in his cohort or to admission to the body of 300 *speculatores* who formed within the Guard a *corps d'élite*. But the conditions of service were good. He served for only sixteen years, was paid two denarii (32 asses) a day, and on discharge was given a gratuity of 5000 denarii. The legionary served twenty years or more, was paid ten asses a day, and his gratuity amounted to no more than 3000 denarii.

It is a mistake to regard the praetorians as the city-police of Rome. This duty belonged to a separate group of *cohortes urbanae*, three and later four in number, under the command of the *praefectus urbi* (p. 201), a senator of consular rank whose duty it was to keep order in the city. Individual cohorts were commanded by *tribuni*, men of the same type as the *tribuni* of the praetorians. The urban cohorts were not exempt from regular military service —they were employed by Otho in his war against the Vitellians— but on the whole they were confined to the city to an even greater extent than the praetorians. The cohorts which garrisoned the important provincial cities of Lugdunum and Carthage were reckoned as belonging to the urban cohorts. The pay was lower than that of the praetorians, and the period of service lasted twenty years. Whatever may have been the case under the Republic, the force employed by the Principate to maintain law and order in the city cannot be described as inadequate.

In addition to the praetorian and urban cohorts there were created in A.D. 6 seven *cohortes vigilum* under a *praefectus vigilum*, whose primary duty was to act as a fire-brigade (p. 200). In 21 B.C.

---

[1] Dessau 2678.

this task had been assigned to an aedile with the assistance of 600 public slaves, but it was later decided that the work could be better performed by an equestrian nominee of the Emperor at the head of 7000 men. Each cohort was responsible for the safety of two of the fourteen regions into which Rome was divided. A peculiar feature of these units was that membership was open to freedmen, who were rigidly excluded from most departments of the army: a law of A.D. 24 conferred after six years of service the full citizenship on any of the vigiles who had not acquired it at the time of their manumission. The praefect of the vigiles was second only to the praefect of the praetorians among the equestrian officials of Rome, and frequently succeeded to his office. The *tribuni vigilum* later on usually held a similar post in the urban and praetorian cohorts.

Finally, mention must be made of the so-called German bodyguard which from the time of Augustus to that of Galba was closely attached to the persons of the emperor and of members of his family. It was recruited from tribes on the very fringe of the Roman Empire such as the Frisii, the Ubii and especially the Batavi. Its members were not citizens, but adopted such Greco-Roman names as Felix, Phoebus, Nereus, and Linus. In the reign of Nero a special burial-ground was allotted to them from which some stones survive. About the same time they were organized in a *collegium* under a *curator Germanorum*.

V. THE FLEET

The statement that 'every true Roman was afraid of the sea' contains this amount of truth that except at great crises the government of the Republic failed to realize the importance of sea-power. The successful termination of wars was postponed by the need of creating fleets[1], and little appreciation was shown of the fact that in the absence of a permanent navy seafarers in the Mediterranean were certain to be exposed to danger from pirates. If the Roman government of this period had, as has sometimes been assumed, been influenced by a desire to encourage commerce, it could hardly have failed to do more than it did to produce the conditions which make commerce possible. Naval service ranked lower than service in the legions, and the hastily improvised fleets consisted mainly of ships contributed by maritime cities in the provinces. No class of naval officers was created, so that when it was decided to take vigorous measures against the pirates, it

[1] See vol. IX, p. 495 *sq.*

was to a great soldier that the task was entrusted. Even Caesar does not seem to have realized fully the need of possessing a navy comparable in efficiency to his legionary forces.

But Augustus had learned valuable lessons in his wars against Sextus Pompeius and Antony, and the influence of Agrippa, the victor of Naulochus, must have been exercised in favour of the policy of retaining part at least of the fleets which had fought at Actium. It is very much to the credit of Augustus that, in spite of the decisive character of his victory, he did not follow the example of Republican generals in disbanding the fleet which had helped to secure it.

Early in his reign he organized the two Italian naval bases which were destined to remain for centuries the headquarters of the principal Roman fleets, Misenum on the Bay of Naples, and Ravenna, near the mouth of the Po, with which it was connected by a canal. A squadron consisting of ships captured at Actium was for some time stationed at Forum Julii in Gallia Narbonensis, and probably all provincial governors had some warships at their disposal; we happen to hear of *liburnicae* in Corsica in A.D. 69. Regular fleets are found early in the Principate at Alexandria, at Seleuceia the port of Antioch, in the Black Sea, and on the Rhine and Danube. The Rhine fleet played a prominent part in the operations in Germany conducted by Drusus and later by his son Germanicus, who in A.D. 16 had a thousand ships of one kind or another under his command. Communications between Britain and the mainland were maintained by a fleet which is mentioned in A.D. 70 and was used by Agricola in his campaign against the Caledonians.

The reign of Claudius probably marks an important stage in the organization of the fleet. Previously it seems to have been regarded as belonging less to the armed forces of the State than to the household of the princeps. In the war against Sextus Pompeius slaves had been freely employed as oarsmen by both sides, and the practice was continued by Augustus. Early inscriptions prove that even the trierarchs who commanded ships were slaves or freedmen of the emperor, and it cannot be doubted that the majority of the oarsmen at this period were slaves. But by the time of Claudius we find free provincials among the sailors, and at the end of the reign of Nero the servile element must have disappeared. For in A.D. 68–70 two whole legions I and II Adiutrix— were created out of men serving in the Italian fleets. Inscriptions show that the soldiers of these legions were mainly natives of Dalmatia, Pannonia, and Thrace. Tacitus emphasizes the fact that the support given to Vespasian by the fleet at Ravenna was due to the adherence of the Danubian provinces to his cause[1]. It is hardly likely that even during the civil wars slaves or freedmen would have been enrolled as legionaries. From the time of Claudius the fleet was evidently regarded as a part of the regular *auxilia*. Sailors received citizenship on discharge after twenty-six years of service, and their children would be able to serve in the legions.

Even under the Principate little seems to have been done to create a class of professional naval officers. In the Julio-Claudian period the *praefecti* who commanded fleets were either freedmen of the emperor like Anicetus who was in charge of the ships at Misenum when Agrippina was murdered, or ex-legionary *primi pili* of equestrian rank. Moschus, the commander of Otho's fleet, was probably the last freedman to hold this post, but the fact that in 79 the fleet at Misenum was commanded by a scholar like the elder Pliny suggests that the standard of seamanship was not a high one. Lucilius Bassus, to whom both the Italian fleets were entrusted by Vitellius, had commanded a squadron of cavalry, and hoped to be praefect of the praetorians.

Regular sea battles rarely occurred under the Principate, and the so-called 'soldiers' of the fleets must be regarded primarily as oarsmen: if actual fighting was expected it is probable that legionaries were taken on board. The fleets were normally employed on such duties as conducting governors to their provinces, bringing prisoners to Rome, and escorting transports and corn-vessels. Under Claudius sailors were employed in organizing a 'sea-fight' on the Fucine Lake, and later on so many of them were brought to Rome on various duties that special barracks were erected for them. As the work required of the navy called primarily for speed it is not surprising that it consisted mainly of light *liburnicae* with only two banks of oars, the value of which even in battle had been demonstrated at Actium. In a world dominated by the *pax Romana* there was no need for the huge warships of the Hellenistic age.

No aspect of the work of Augustus and his successors is more worthy of careful study than their organization of the defence of the Empire. The army and navy were potent instruments of Romanization. Though the troops often complained of the conditions of service and the provincials of the taxation rendered necessary by the need of defending the frontiers, such

---

[1] Tacitus, *Hist.* III, 12.

complaints became rarer with the lapse of time. The attempt of Gaul to throw off the Roman yoke in A.D. 69–70 was a half-hearted affair. As has been shown, the task of defending the Empire was entrusted to an increasing extent to the provincials themselves, who found in army service a means of acquiring the citizenship and often of rising to high positions in the service of the government. If Rome seems to have taken unnecessary risks in attempting to defend her long frontier with an army of some 300,000 men, it must not be forgotten that the size of an army is determined by policy, that Rome seldom aimed at territorial aggrandisement, and that her diplomacy was usually successful in preventing the consolidation outside the Empire of a power strong enough to threaten its security.

CHAPTER IX

THE EASTERN FRONTIER UNDER AUGUSTUS

I. THE DEFENCE OF EGYPT AND THE MILITARY OCCUPATION OF THE NILE VALLEY

WITH the fall of Alexandria on August 1, 30 B.C., the whole East lay at the feet of Octavian, and one of the immediate tasks confronting him was to provide for its security. Nowhere was the task so easy as in Egypt, which nature had surrounded with ramparts so formidable as to make it the most defensible of all Mediterranean lands. The physical geography of the country dictated the principles of the military policy to be adopted for its defence against external foes and for the maintenance of internal peace and order.

Egypt is a plane of limestone formation which slopes gradually down from the jagged crest of the mountain range that borders the Red Sea to the line marked by the chain of oases which stretches from the latitude of Assuân (Syene) north-westwards to Sîwa, the site of the oracle of Ammon. Linked at its north-east corner by the barren peninsula of Sinai to the deserts of Arabia and Syria, this plane is a waste expanse, almost devoid of vegetation save where the Nile, collecting its waters from the highlands of Abyssinia and equatorial Africa, has cut through the middle of it a deep trench, which it has overlaid with fertile alluvium, re-fertilized by annual inundation. From the first cataract above Assuân, the southern boundary of Egypt proper, the alluvial belt is narrow while the stream passes through a long tract of sandstone and limestone rocks which hem it in; but within about a dozen miles of Thebes (Luxor) it opens out into a broad valley, varying in width from twelve to thirty miles, which runs all the way to Cairo. Below Cairo, at the edge of what was once the coastline, the parting of the waters has expanded the alluvial ribbon into the fan-shaped Deltaic tract that spreads out between Alexandria and Pelusium. The whole sea base of the Delta is occupied by a string of marshy lakes, whose waters filter through sand dunes to the sea, except on the west, where Lake Mareotis is penned by a spur of sandy limestone which provides Alexandria with a dry site and a harbour on an otherwise practically havenless coast. Access to the old harbour, which can now be used only by fishing boats, was difficult in ancient times owing to the narrowness of the entrance and the existence of rocks under the surface of the water; while communication between the city and the interior was provided only by a strip of dry land between the lagoons, a strip much narrower in antiquity than it is to-day and easy to defend. It was not without justice that the ancients spoke of Alexandria as lying 'close to' Egypt rather than in it. Difficult of approach as it was from the Mediterranean, the valley of the Nile was protected on its western flank by the infinite waste of the Libyan Desert and on its eastern by the Arabian Desert—a sterile, calcareous, wadi-furrowed plateau, almost destitute of surface water and clothed with but little vegetation or none at all, which stretches away to the coastal range, whose eastern slopes fall steeply down to the desolate rocky shore of the Red Sea.

Egypt was truly an isolated land, 'walled about on every side,' in the phrase of Josephus[1]. Only on the south was there no better defined natural boundary than the first cataract of the Nile, and beyond it lay the kingdom of Ethiopia, a loose organization of desert tribes, which, though not powerful, was a potential source of trouble. Excavation has led to the belief that at the time of the Roman conquest Ethiopia was divided, as it had been in the third century B.C., into two kingdoms, a northern round Napata and a southern round Meroë; but it is more likely that there was then only a single kingdom with its capital at Meroë[2]. The establishment of settled relations with this neighbouring State was one of the duties which fell to the first governor, C. Cornelius Gallus, the friend of Virgil.

Before dealing with this matter, Gallus was called upon to crush two local insurrections in Egypt itself[3]. For the natives the Roman conquest merely meant one more change of masters, and they had offered no opposition to it; but the new yoke was to prove heavier than the old, and revolts broke out at Heroônpolis near the eastern edge of the Delta and in the district of Thebes of the Hundred Gates, where the rich and powerful priesthood of Ammon had proved a thorn in the side of earlier rulers. Probably in both cases, certainly in the latter, the outbreak was due to the pressure of taxation, the result either of stricter collection or of the imposition of a fresh burden, possibly the general poll-tax which was levied in the Roman period. The revolts were

---

[1] *Bell. Jud.* IV [10, 5], 610.   [2] See below, p. 243 n. 1.
[3] Strabo XVII, 819; and the inscription of Gallus, Dessau 8995 (*O.G.I.S.* 654; *I.G.R.R.* I, 1293).

easily suppressed by Gallus, who vaunted his exploits in a vain-glorious trilingual inscription which he erected on the island of Philae, close to Syene, on April 15, 29 B.C. In this document, which shows that his head was turned by vice-regal power, he boasts that he crushed the revolt of the Thebaïd within fifteen days, after winning two pitched battles and capturing by storm or siege five towns, three of which were, in fact, parts of the one city of Thebes.

Gallus then proceeded southwards to regulate the frontier. His instructions, no doubt, were to impose 'the friendship of the Roman people' on the Ethiopians, or in plain words to establish a protectorate, a favourite but precarious Roman method of covering a frontier. After a military demonstration beyond the first cataract—'a region which,' he avers, 'neither the Roman nor the Egyptian arms had ever reached'—he received at Philae envoys of the Ethiopian king and made a convention whereby the king was admitted to Roman protection and a subordinate *tyrannus* was appointed to rule the Triakontaschoinos, a district once under Ptolemaic rule[1], which perhaps extended from the first to the second cataract at Wadi Halfa. The purpose apparently was to create a buffer state under a chief whose dependence on Rome would be a guarantee of his loyalty. This settlement made, Gallus proceeded to indulge his vanity by setting up statues of himself throughout Egypt and inscribing a record of his achievements on the pyramids; he was recalled and disgraced by Augustus, and a deluge of accusations, followed by a decree of the Senate that he should be convicted in the courts and condemned to banishment and loss of property, drove him to suicide (26 B.C.)[2].

The inadequacy of this first frontier policy was proved some four years after its adoption, when a large number of the Roman troops left in Egypt had been withdrawn for an expedition to Arabia under the command of Aelius Gallus (p. 250). It was a favourable opportunity for a raid, which the Ethiopians were not slow to seize[3]. In 25 B.C.[4] they poured across the frontier, over-powered the garrison of three auxiliary cohorts planted there to defend it, and ravaged Philae, Syene and Elephantine, carrying off statues of Augustus as trophies and enslaving the inhabitants. The governor[5] of Egypt, C. Petronius, soon appeared with a

---

[1] *O.G.I.S.* 111.   [2] Dio LIII, 23; Suetonius, *Aug.* 66.

[3] Strabo XVII, 820; Dio LIV, 5; Pliny, *N.H.* VI, 181 *sq.*; *Res Gestae* 26.

[4] For the date cf. A. Maiuri, *La Successione 'Elio Gallo—C. Petronio' nella lista dei prefetti dell' Egitto.* Saggi di Storia Antica e di Archeologia (presented to Beloch), Roma, 1910, p. 326.   [5] See below, p. 247, n. 2.

force of not quite 10,000 infantry and 800 cavalry, drove out the invaders, and pursued them into their own land. The Ethiopians retreated up the river to Pselcis (Dakke), where Petronius forced a battle and easily routed the ill-organized horde, which had no better equipment than shields of ox-hide, axes and pikes; only a few had swords. After taking the town, Petronius advanced southwards and stormed Primis, a stronghold on the steep hill on the east bank of the Nile which is now crowned by the fort of Kasr Ibrîm. Thence he pushed on to Napata, the northern capital of the kingdom, where was the queen's son; the queen herself, a one-eyed lady of masculine character, had retired to a neighbouring fort, whence she sent envoys to negotiate; but Petronius stormed and destroyed the town, from which the prince effected his escape[1]. Deterred by the difficulty of the country ahead, he advanced no farther. Contenting himself with the recovery of the prisoners and the statues of Augustus, he retraced his steps to Primis, which he re-fortified and garrisoned with a force of 400 men, whom he supplied with provisions to last two years. Then he returned to Alexandria and dispatched a thousand of his prisoners to Augustus, who had recently returned from Spain to Rome, which he reached in the early months of 24. Two years later, in 22[2], towards the end of the period for which Primis had been provisioned, the Ethiopian queen returned in force to attack the fort, but Petronius succeeded in relieving it and strengthened its fortifications, with the result that the queen gave up the struggle and opened negotiations. Ethiopian envoys were sent to Augustus, whom they found at Samos during the winter of 21–20, and they obtained terms of peace, of which nothing is recorded beyond the fact that they secured what they wanted, including a remission of the tribute that had been imposed on them.

[1] The queen is called Candace, but Greeks and Romans mistook for a personal name what was really an Ethiopian title, *Katake*, which appears in Meroitic inscriptions attached to the personal name and may be translated 'queen.' (F. Ll. Griffith, *Meroitic Inscriptions*, Pt. I, 1911, pp. 55, 79 *sq.*) She was almost certainly queen-regent for her son, like other queens of the Ethiopian royal house. Another queen Candace is mentioned in *Acts of the Apostles*, viii, 27, and a third in Nero's time (Pliny, *N.H.* vi, 186). The mistake gave rise to the belief that the name was transmitted from queen to queen (Pliny, *loc. cit.*) and produced the impression that Ethiopia had been governed by a long line of queens, a view decisively disproved by the Harvard excavations near Napata and at Meroë. G. A. Reisner, *The Pyramids of Meroë and the Candaces of Ethiopia*, Sudan Notes and Records, v, 1922, pp. 173 *sqq.*
[2] Dio LIV, 5, 4.

The sequel of the Ethiopian war was the military occupation of the district called the Dodekaschoinos, which extended south-wards from Syene as far as Hiera Sykaminos (opposite Mahar-raka). This district had been granted by the Ptolemies to the temple of Isis at Philae as 'sacred land,' and it remained the property of the goddess, forming a zone intermediate between Egypt and Ethiopia, not included in the former, but attached for administrative purposes to its most southerly nome and guarded by a string of military posts, which prevented any violation of the southern frontier until the middle of the third century[1].

The establishment of a southern frontier zone made Egypt immune from invasion on every side. The nomadic inhabitants of the surrounding deserts might, indeed, raid a Nile village or a mining district or a caravan, but they were powerless to do more than produce a local disturbance of the peace. Egypt had thus no frontier region which required to be defended by a *limes*. The primary tasks of the Egyptian army were to guard the Nile valley against Arab raids and to maintain internal order. Once the country had settled down under the new régime, only a garrison of moderate size would be needed for such duties. Until then Augustus deemed it advisable, in view of the paramount economic importance of the country, to take no risks, and he placed under the command of the Prefect a force more than half the size of that which he probably left to face the Parthians, three legions with their complement of auxiliary troops, amounting to nine cohorts and three cavalry regiments, about 23,000 men in all. In addition to its garrison Egypt was provided with a naval squadron, *classis Augusta Alexandrina*, which shared with the Syrian fleet the duty of policing the southern coast of the Mediterranean and con-voyed the Alexandrian merchant ships which transported Egyptian grain to Italy. Augustus also took over the Ptolemaic institution of a river-patrol, which policed the Nile from Syene to the sea, and placed it perhaps under the orders of the prefect of the fleet, who certainly was in command of it at a later period.

The distribution of the troops at the outset is partially indicated

---

[1] Reisner, who holds that Candace ruled a Napatan kingdom, explains its subsequent disappearance by supposing that its power was broken by the Roman invasion and that the ruler of Meroë, at that time also a queen, seized the opportunity to re-unite the two kingdoms (*op. cit.* p. 190; *J.E.A.* IX, 1923, p. 73 *sq.*). But his archaeological inferences are not all sure, and his view disaccords with the inscription, *J.E.A.* IV, 1917, p. 159, which implies that Meroë was the centre of power at the time of the invasion.

by two brief notices of Strabo[1]. One legion, he tells us, was stationed at the capital Alexandria, and another near the apex of the Delta at Babylon (Old Cairo) on the east bank of the Nile, opposite the great pyramids; of the nine auxiliary cohorts three were stationed at Alexandria, three at Syene, and the other three 'in the rest of the country,' by which he perhaps meant Middle Egypt; as regards the three *alae*, no precise inference can be drawn from his superlatively vague statement that they were 'similarly posted at suitable points.' The Alexandrian legion was XXII Deiotariana[2], a Galatian regiment which had been armed and trained in the Roman style by King Deiotarus[3] and was taken over when Galatia was annexed in 25 B.C.; its fortress lay three miles from the east gate of the capital in the new suburb of Nicopolis, which Augustus founded in commemoration of his victory at the point where Egyptian resistance had been crushed in 30 B.C. The legion which was stationed at Babylon cannot be identified[4]. The quarters of the third legion are not mentioned by Strabo, but there is small room for doubt that they lay in Upper Egypt, at Thebes or Coptos, and that the legion in question was III Cyrenaica. The oldest monuments of this legion connect it with the Thebaïd, and although the evidence they furnish is not sufficient to prove the presence of the whole legion there, it is clear that a garrison was needed in this region. Coptos was the nodal point of the most important military and commercial roads in Egypt, and Thebes, with its powerful priesthood and celebrated cult, was a focus of native nationalism and had been a centre of disaffection in the early days of the Roman occupation.

Meagre as this evidence is, it enables us to discern the broad features of the military arrangements made by Augustus. The occupation of Lower Egypt was based on the triangle formed by Alexandria, Babylon, and Pelusium, communication between these three points being secured by river ways along the arms of the Nile, by canals, and by a network of roads not now traceable. Alexandria was the military, as it was the naval, base, and as time went on its importance steadily increased. The strategic value of Babylon lay in the fact that it commanded communications between the Delta and the upper valley of the Nile. Pelusium, 'the

[1] XVII, 797, 807.
[2] *B.G.U.*, 1104, 1108 (8, 5 B.C.); *C.I.L.* III, 399, 12,059 (Dessau 2274).
[3] *Bell. Alex.* 68, 2.
[4] Ritterling in *P.W.* s.v. *Legio*, col. 1706, suggests that it was perhaps leg. XII Fulminata, afterwards transferred to Syria; but it is more likely that this legion was in Africa (Dessau 8966; *J.R.S.* XXIII, 1933, p. 25).

key-position by land,' as Alexandria was by sea[1], always had a
garrison, and along the coastal road leading from it through the
sandy desert to Syria forts were always maintained as a defence
against Arab raids. Doubtless military posts, held by small
detachments of legionary or auxiliary troops, were soon established
along the eastern edge of the Delta on the route connecting
Pelusium with Babylon and Memphis by way of the Nile canal
and Heroônpolis, and on the road leading from Pelusium by
Serapeum to Clysma (Colzum) near the head of the Gulf of Suez;
and probably the roads from Alexandria to Memphis and towards
Cyrenaica were at all times held by detached posts. But on such
matters of detail no information has survived for the period of the
early Empire. After a time, and in all probability about A.D. 7—
although the fact is not definitely attested till A.D. 23—conditions
in Egypt proved to be tranquil enough to permit a reduction of the
garrison[2], and the legion at Babylon was withdrawn, its place
being taken by an auxiliary regiment (p. 743). The withdrawal of
the legion was not accompanied by any appreciable reduction of
the auxiliary establishment[3], so that the Egyptian garrison now
numbered about 17,000 men all told.

About the military dispositions adopted by Augustus in the
rest of Egypt there is little evidence. The conditions admitted of
so little variation of policy that we may presume that, as in later
times, garrisons were placed at suitable points in the Nile valley,
such as Hermoupolis Magna (Ashmunên), where there was a
customs station for goods brought down the river from Upper
Egypt[4]. A specially important point was Coptos, the collecting
and forwarding centre not only for goods landed at the Red Sea
ports of Myos Hormos (probably at Abu Shar) and Berenice
(Bender el-Kebir) but also for the products of the numerous
mines and quarries in the mountains of the Arabian Desert between the Nile and the Red Sea. This whole region was placed by
Augustus under the care of a military officer who bore the title of
praefectus Berenices (or *Berenicidis* or *montis Berenicidis*[5]). The first
recorded *praefectus* is described in A.D. 10–11 as director of all

---

[1] *Claustra terrae ac maris*, Tacitus, *Ann.* II, 59; *claustra Aegypti*, *Hist.* II,
82.
[2] Tacitus, *Ann.* IV, 5; Ritterling, *op. cit.* col. 1235; *J.R.S.* XXIII, 1933,
p. 31.
[3] *Dipl.* XV in *C.I.L.* III, *Suppl.* (to the units enumerated has to be added
cohors scutata c.R.) compared with Strabo's evidence.   [4] Strabo XVII, 813.
[5] *C.I.L.* III, 13580, Dessau 2698, 2700; a fuller description *praef.*
praesidiorum et montis Ber(e)nices is given in Dessau 2699.

the mines of Egypt[1]. He administered the district, supervising the working of the mines and quarries, with the assistance of a procurator, and commanding the military posts established to provide for the security of the mining centres and of the desert roads leading to them and to the Red Sea ports. To the improvement of the facilities of travel on the trade routes Augustus paid special attention. In the early years of his reign wells were dug and cisterns built; their existence was known to Strabo[2], whose information about Egypt was gained during his visit to his friend, the prefect Aelius Gallus, and further evidence is furnished by an inscription of Coptos, belonging probably to the later years of Augustus[3], which records the construction by legionary and auxiliary detachments of cisterns (*lacci*) at Myos Hormos and Berenice and at two points on the road connecting the latter with Coptos[4]. These reservoirs were no doubt constructed, as in later times, within a fortified enceinte, guarded by soldiers. It was always necessary to protect these roads against the robber Bedouin, and it may well be that the system of convoys and convoy-dues, which is attested in the reign of Domitian[5], owed its institution to Augustus.

To the south of Thebes, where the Nile valley becomes steadily narrower, communications with the frontier were secured in later time by the establishment at various points of forts placed opposite each other on either bank of the river, but whether this system was as old as Augustus, cannot be said. About the military occupation of Lower Nubia, which made it unnecessary to increase the strength of the garrison at Syene, no details are known. The establishment of a fort at the extreme southern point, Hiera Sykaminos, may be taken for granted; and it may be presumed that the northern and southern ends of the granite gorge through which the river flows between Tafis (Tafa) and Talmis (Kalâbsheh)—'the Gate,' *el-Bâb*, as the Arabs call it—were held by military posts, as well as Pselcis, the scene of Petronius' victory, where the presence of a legionary cohort is attested in A.D. 27–8[6].

In Egypt frontier defence was a simple task. The duties of the

---

[1] *Ann. épig.* 1910, no. 207.   [2] XVII, 815.
[3] Cuntz would assign it to the decade preceding 1 B.C. (*Jahreshefte*, XXV, 1929, p. 80), but the upper limit is too early; the evidence about the domicile of several of the soldiers points to a date subsequent to the annexation of Paphlagonia (6–5 B.C.) and of Sebastopolis (3–2 B.C.).
[4] Dessau 2483. The road Coptos–Berenice is described by Pliny, *N.H.* VI, 102–3.
[5] *O.G.I.S.* 674; *I.G.R.R.* I, 1183.   [6] *I.G.R.R.* I, 1366.

troops were primarily of a police character. A large number of the soldiers were at all times dispersed over the country, manning the military posts which studded the land from the Mediterranean to Lower Nubia. Those that were stationed at Nicopolis had many police duties to discharge in Alexandria, mounting guard over the corn magazines or the papyrus factories or the mint. From time to time, as in other provinces, detachments of the various units were set to execute works of public utility, such as clearing and deepening the irrigation canals and maintaining and improving the roads. Once the southern frontier had been regulated, there was no actual fighting in Egypt itself for two and a half centuries, and field service was seen only by the detachments which were drafted off now and again to strengthen Roman armies campaigning in other parts of the East. The conditions of service and of recruitment (pp. 226, 286) were not calculated to maintain a high standard of military efficiency in the army of Egypt.

II. THE ROMANS AND ARABIA[1]

The Ethiopian invasion of Egypt was prompted, as has been seen, by the withdrawal of about a third of the Egyptian garrison for an expedition which Augustus decided to launch against Arabia Felix under the command of Aelius Gallus, who had been the successor of Cornelius Gallus in the prefecture of Egypt[2]. The decision of Augustus to embark on this aggressive campaign against a country that lay beyond the proper limits of the Roman Empire was a striking exception to his general policy of abstaining from the annexation of territory in the East which was not essential for the security of the frontiers.

Arabia in Roman times was very like what it is to-day, except that some of the more favoured regions have long since fallen far below the standard of prosperity and civilization which they then enjoyed. The character of the land has not changed. From the Red Sea a strip of coral beach, the Tihâma, fringed with reefs and

---

[1] The sources are Strabo XVI, 780–2; XVII, 819; Dio LIII, 29; Pliny, *N.H.* VI, 160 *sqq.*; *Res Gestae* 26. For the date, Mommsen, *Res Gestae*[2], pp. 106 *sqq.*

[2] Whether Gallus was the second prefect and whether he was prefect when he conducted the campaign have been much disputed questions. There is little doubt that the first question should be answered (with Mommsen) in the affirmative, and the second (against him) in the negative: in 25 Petronius was already prefect. See P. M. Meyer (*B.P.W.* 1907, col. 462; *Klio*, VII, 1907, p. 122) and esp. A. Maiuri, *loc. cit.* and W. Otto, *Herodes*, in *P.W.* Suppl. II, col. 67 note.

volcanic islands, slopes up to the mountain range of varying altitude which enfolds the inland plateaux—the two sandy, water-less deserts of Nefud and Roba el-Khali, separated by the tableland of Nejd, which is nowhere utterly waste or wholly waterless and has numerous oases. The coastal regions towards the north get some rain in winter, but under the burning summer sun surface water disappears, except in the higher valleys, where there are some oases. The inhabitants have always been nomadic and pre-datory, save where there is water enough to allow of agriculture and settled life. Farther south, in Yemen and the adjoining region of Hadramût, conditions are more favourable. The coastal range, rising to 9000 or 10,000 feet, is high enough to catch the moisture of the two monsoons and to send copious streams down its slopes, to be finally lost in the torrid strand of the Tihâma on the seaward side and to be stored for the irrigation of the fields on the plateau or to lose themselves in the steppe.

Here in the south-west corner of the peninsula was Arabia Felix *par excellence*, the El Dorado of the ancients, a happy land by contrast with the surrounding wastes and by reason of its precious products. From the third century B.C. the kingdom of Saba, the Sheba of the Bible, which occupied the southern half of Yemen and reached the sea on the west and south, had been famous in the Mediterranean world as the richest and most powerful state in Arabia[1]. Its political organization was of a feudal type, and its prosperity was based on the cultivation of the soil and, above all, on the production and export of those aromatic substances—frankincense, myrrh, cinnamon and cassia—so highly prized by the ancient world for religious ceremonial and for the preparation of fragrant unguents, perfumes, spices and medicinal ointments. These articles and the Ethiopian (Somaliland) varieties of them, as well as gold, precious stones, pearls and other wares, were transported by the Sabaeans by land and sea to Egypt, Palestine and Syria. The overland route northwards traversed the desert to Leuke Kome, an entrepôt in the territory of the Nabataean Arabs, situated most probably at the mouth of the Wadi el-Hamd (south of El-Widj), whence it led through Aelana, at the head of the gulf of Akaba, to Petra; there it forked north-westwards to Gaza and Rhinocolura on the Egyptian border and northwards to Syria. As

[1] For the Sabaeans and their trade, Strabo XVI, 768–9, 778, 780–1. At the time of the Roman expedition the Sabaeans formed part of a Sabaean-Himyarite (Homerite) state under the rule of the 'king of Saba and Dû-Raïdân' (the latter being the old royal fortress at the Himyarite capital Saphar, near Yerim).

this route was exposed throughout its entire length to the attacks of Arab tribes, the trade could only be carried on by the native chiefs, who organized the caravans and provided them with military escort. But the land route was not the only artery of communication with the West. The Sabaeans had also a large carrying trade by sea. Not only were their exports partly conveyed by ship to Leuke Kome and to the Egyptian Red Sea ports, but they were the commercial intermediaries between India and the Mediterranean. At the time of the expedition of Gallus the port of Aden, then called Eudaemon Arabia, was a great mart both for the export of Arabian goods to Egypt, Syria, and India and for the import of Indian wares, which were brought by Arabian and Indian merchants and re-shipped partly to Leuke Kome for transport to Syria, partly to Berenice and Myos Hormos, whence they were conveyed by camel to Coptos and thence down the Nile to Alexandria. Egyptian ships had some share in the Red Sea traffic, but it was mostly in Arab hands.

Greek writers have left glowing descriptions[1] of the wealth and luxury of the Sabaeans (that is to say, the Sabaean aristocracy), which, if exaggerated, are not fictitious; they are supported by the existing remains of city walls and towers, temples, palaces, colonnades, sculptures and engineering works, of which the most striking is the great barrage drawn across the valley of the Wadi Dena, the river of Marib, to form a vast reservoir, from which the water was drawn off through sluices into strongly built channels to irrigate the land. Such pride in building and such constructive skill imply a developed civilization and a well-organized form of government with large financial resources; and this is confirmed by the coinage of the Sabaean and Sabaean-Himyarite kings, which from the third century B.C. was modelled on Athenian money, brought across the desert from Gaza, but adopted the Babylonian standard of weight[2].

Such was the state against which Augustus resolved to launch an expedition. His motives are indicated by Strabo, who owed his information to his intimate friend, Gallus. Encouraged by the promise of the co-operation of the friendly Nabataean Arabs, he proposed to make Arabia Felix a protectorate or a subject State and thereby bring its trade under Roman control, and inciden-

---

[1] They all go back to the account of Agatharchides in the fifth book of his work περὶ τῆς Ἐρυθρᾶς θαλάσσης, written c. 132 B.C. (Müller, Geogr. Gr. Min. I, pp. 186 sqq.), which was copied by Diodorus III, 46–7 and by Artemidorus (in Strabo).

[2] Hill, B. M. Cat. Arabia, pp. xliv sqq.; Volume of Plates iv, 198, m, n.

tally to get possession of the proverbial wealth of its inhabitants, who plied a one-sided trade selling their wares at high prices and buying nothing in return[1]. If the country became an annexe of Egypt, both the imperial exchequer and Roman subjects would profit materially by the substitution of maritime transport for the laborious and expensive transport by caravan, by the cheapening of Arabian products, and by the development of direct trade with India, which would be promoted by the control of the Arabian coast and Arabian waters. The potential financial gain may be gauged from the data supplied by Pliny for his own time[2].

The campaign opened in 25. The force at the disposal of Gallus amounted in all to about 10,000 men, composed of legionary and auxiliary troops, a contingent of 500 men sent by Herod, and one of 1000 furnished by the Nabataean king Obodas under the command of his vizier Syllaeus, who undertook to act as guide and to be responsible for the commissariat. Instead of concentrating his troops at the most southerly harbour of Egypt, Berenice, and transporting them under escort of a small fleet to the south Arabian coast, using his warships to secure his communications with Egypt, Gallus decided to assemble his men at Cleopatris (Arsinoë), close to Suez, and to transport them to Leuke Kome, the southernmost port within Nabataean territory, where he would have 900 miles of desert between him and his objective, the Sabaean capital Mariaba. He began by building 80 fighting ships before he realized that the enemy had no war fleet; then he proceeded to construct 130 transports. On these he embarked his troops, but the shoals and the coral reefs which the coast of the Gulf of Suez and the islands and shores of the Red Sea proved too much for his pilots, and before he reached Leuke Kome after a fourteen days' voyage, he lost many ships with their crews. No sooner had he arrived than his troops began to be attacked by scurvy and palsy of the legs, diseases endemic in the country owing to the scarcity of good water and vegetable food, and he was forced to spend the rest of the hot summer and the following winter at the port.

In the spring of 24 he started on his march. After many days' journey through wastes, where water had to be carried on camel back, he reached the land of Aretas, a kinsman[3] of Obodas, who

---

[1] See also Pliny, *N.H.* VI, 162.   [2] *N.H.* VI, 101; XII, 63–5.

[3] A. Kammerer, *Pétra et la Nabatène*, Paris, 1929–30, p. 199, suggests that συγγενής is really the court title used in Hellenistic and half-Hellenistic States, Aretas being viceroy of Obodas; but his name favours a literal interpretation of the term.

gave him a friendly reception but whose barren country could provide no supplies except coarse grain, dates and butter. A whole month was needed to traverse it, and ahead lay the roadless desert of Ararêne, where long detours had to be made to find food and water. A weary march of 50 days across it brought the army at last to the town of Negrana, which lay in the valley of Wadi Nejrân, within the borders of Arabia Felix. The king fled, and his city was taken and destroyed. Six days' further march led to a river, probably the Wadi Khârid, where the Arabs were waiting to offer battle. Their untrained host, equipped with double-edged axes or with bows, spears, swords and slings, was easily dispersed; Strabo gravely reports their losses as 10,000 men against two Roman casualties. This victory was followed by the capture of two other towns, Nasca[1], the Nashk of Arabian geographers and inscriptions, now el-Baidā, and Athrula or Athlula, probably the Iathul or Iathlul of inscriptions, represented by the ruins of Barâkish. In the latter town Gallus placed a garrison, and advanced to a city which Augustus and Pliny call Mariba, while Strabo calls it 'Marsyaba(e), belonging to the tribe of the Rhammanitae, who were subject to Ilasaros.' After six days' fruitless assault and siege he was forced by lack of water to retire. This city has usually been identified with the Sabaean capital Mariaba, now Marib, some days' march to the east of San'a, the modern capital of Yemen, but the identification can hardly be correct. Lack of water neither was nor is a feature of Marib, famous in antiquity for its great reservoir and still supplied with excellent water by the Wadi Dena; nor is it credible that, if Gallus had really reached the Sabaean metropolis, the reports of his expedition would all have failed to mention the fact, or that Strabo, who in two previous passages speaks of it under its correct name, would have described it here as a town of an obscure tribe elsewhere unmentioned in Greek literature[2].

On his retreat from Mariba Gallus took a more direct route northwards through Negrana and across the desert to Egra, an unidentified village on the sea within Nabataean territory, covering the whole distance in sixty days, while his outward march had taken six months. From Egra he shipped the remnant of his army to Myos Hormos, whence he marched to Coptos and descended the Nile to Alexandria.

[1] Aska in Strabo (*n* dropped by haplography), Nascus or Nesca in Pliny (VI, 154, 160).

[2] In Pliny's text, too, the Sabaean capital appears, not as Mariba, but as Marelibata, a corruption of Mareiaba. For a possible identification of Mariba, see Note 1 on p. 877.

So ended this abortive expedition, planned in total ignorance of the physical and climatic conditions of the country and of the difficulties it presented to an invader. Its failure was attributed to the treachery of Syllaeus, but the proofs of treachery given by Strabo, who naïvely reproduces the official version, are mostly proofs of the credulity of himself and his public. While it is impossible to believe that the Nabataeans can have welcomed Roman interference in Arabia or can have genuinely wished for the success of the campaign, which would have seriously affected their profits from the caravan trade, it is plain that without the services of Syllaeus the Roman army could never have traversed the peninsula from north to south[1]. Twenty years later he was tried and executed at Rome, but a belated charge of treachery in Arabia was not, as Strabo implies, one of the counts against him.

Doubtless the campaign of Gallus had a moral effect on people who had never known invasion, and it appears to have led to the establishment of friendly relations between the Sabaean-Himyarite kingdom and Rome[2]. It was not, however, a cause of the rapid development of the maritime traffic of Egypt with India. That development had begun even before Gallus entered Arabia, as Strabo's evidence shows. While on tour in Egypt during the prefecture of his friend, he learned that, whereas in the later Ptolemaic age not even twenty ships a year ventured to pass the straits of Bâb el-Mandeb, now as many as 120 Alexandrian merchant vessels sailed from Myos Hormos to the Somali coast and India, bringing back valuable cargoes to be re-exported from Alexandria and to enrich the exchequer by double duties, for import and for export. In describing the enforced stay of Gallus at Leuke Kome, he observes that, although merchandise from Arabia and India was still conveyed by way of that port to Petra and Rhinocolura, most of it was then landed at Myos Hormos; and speaking of Berenice, he says that 'all Indian and Arabian goods as well as those from Ethiopia that are brought down by the

---

[1] It was not unnatural to regard the contrast between the length of the outward and the return journey as a proof of treachery, but (as Glaser suggests) Syllaeus may have avoided the more direct route because he feared serious trouble from the Bedouin tribes through which it passed. Probably, too, the country south of their own territory was *terra incognita* to the Nabataeans themselves.

[2] Strabo's statement (XVI, 779) that the Sabaeans as well as the Nabataeans 'are now subject to the Romans' implies at least a nominal relation of clientship; and such a relation is attested at a later date by the *Periplus maris Erythraei* 23.

Arabian Gulf are now conveyed to Coptos'[1]. It is plain that before the Arabian campaign transport by sea was gaining ground at the expense of the caravan trade. This was a natural result of the establishment in Egypt of a strong government which brought the country into close contact with Rome, the greatest market for Oriental products. The Egyptian share in this maritime traffic steadily increased, especially after the discovery of the periodicity of the monsoons and the use to which they could be put enabled mariners to sail direct from the Red Sea straits to northern India. Egyptian competition naturally crippled the trade of the southern Arabs, but it did not paralyse it. The *Periplus of the Erythraean Sea*, written in all probability towards the middle of the first century[2], shows that the Arabs still maintained an active traffic not only in the Red Sea but also in Persian and Indian waters, while they still exported Arabian products by way of Leuke Kome to the Mediterranean. But direct intercourse between Egypt and India was bound to cause the steady decline of Aden as an entrepôt and the diversion of trade to Egypt was promoted by the measures which Augustus took to improve communications between the Red Sea ports and Coptos. Whether he took any further steps to foster maritime commerce and to protect it against the piracy which infested southern waters, we have no knowledge. There is no certain trace of a Roman fleet in the Red Sea before the reign of Trajan.

The experiences of 25–24 B.C. might have been expected to put an end to the idea of conquering Arabia, the more so as, within a few years of the retreat of Gallus, Augustus publicly adopted, and consistently adhered to, the policy of refraining from fresh conquests in the East. Yet in 1 B.C., when Gaius Caesar was sent on a mission to the East, there figured in his programme an Arabian expedition, which Pliny clearly understood to imply a revival of the old scheme of conquest[3]. He narrates that an Oriental Greek, Dionysius of Charax (the geographer Isidorus was probably meant[4]) was sent to the East by Augustus to put together all necessary information for the use of the crown prince, and that Juba, the learned king of Mauretania, dedicated to him volumes of literary material about Arabia, 'the fame of which had set his heart ablaze.' It is so difficult to believe that Augustus contem-

---

[1] II, 118; XVI, 781; XVII, 798, 815; cf. XV, 686.

[2] See Note 6, p. 881 *sq.*

[3] *N.H.* II, 168; VI, 141, 160; XII, 55–6; XXXII, 10. Mommsen believed that the intention was to deliver an attack by way of the sea from the mouth of the Euphrates.   [4] See E. Herzfeld, *Sakastan*, pp. 4 *sqq.*

plated such a departure from the policy he had pursued for
twenty years that there is something to be said for the view that the
real goal of the expedition was to be, not Arabia Felix, but Arabia
Petraea[1]. The Nabataeans took their obligations as clients of
Rome very lightly. On the death of King Obodas about 9 B.C.,
Aretas had assumed the kingship without asking the permission of
Augustus and nearly lost his throne in consequence. Moreover,
strained relations between the Nabataean vizier Syllaeus and King
Herod had led the former to abet a revolt against the latter in
Trachonitis and to shelter the rebels, who made plundering raids
into Judaea and Syria[2]. Herod appealed to the governor and the
procurator of Syria, who gave judgment in his favour, but instead
of complying with their verdict, Syllaeus set out for Rome. Herod
then made reprisals by invading Arabia with the consent of the
Roman officials. Syllaeus made capital out of this attack, and for a
time he won the ear of Augustus, but in the end he was condemned
to death for his misdeeds (among others the murder of an imperial
finance officer Fabatus) and was executed shortly before Herod's
death (4 B.C.). The death of Herod did not improve the stability
of the situation in this part of the East, and Augustus may have
thought it advisable to send Gaius thither to secure the subservience of the Arabs and the maintenance of peace and order in
the borderlands of Syria.

III. THE PARTHIAN AND ARMENIAN PROBLEMS: THE PERMANENT FACTORS IN THE SITUATION

In 30 B.C., after settling Egyptian affairs, Augustus proceeded
to Syria. The Roman world expected that the conclusion of civil
war would be followed by the chastisement, and even the conquest,
of Parthia and by the restoration of Roman supremacy in Armenia.
Its expectations were disappointed. Augustus left Syria for Asia,
where he spent the winter setting in order the affairs of the
peninsula, and he then returned to Rome, shelving for the moment
the settlement of Eastern questions.

Had Caesar been the victor of Actium, he would certainly not
have quitted the East without settling accounts with Parthia and
re-establishing Roman authority in Armenia. Augustus was of a
different mould. He was well aware that matters could not be left
as they were; not merely Roman sentiment but the interests of the
Empire demanded the restoration of Roman prestige and the

---

[1] Dessau, *Gesch. d. röm. Kaiserzeit*, I, pp. 379 *sqq.*
[2] Josephus, *Ant.* XVI [9], 271 *sqq.* See below, p. 334.

establishment of such relations with Parthia as would ensure the
security of the frontier lands. The circumstances of the moment
were favourable for vigorous action. Phraates had recovered his
throne, but he was not firmly seated on it. Augustus had a large
force on the spot. True, many of his soldiers were looking forward
to receiving their discharge and the rewards of service, and
probably they would not have been in a mood to face the hardships of campaigning beyond the Euphrates. But these were
hardly the considerations that weighed with Augustus. He had
made up his mind to refrain from war in the East, if it could be
avoided, and he believed that every vital interest could be secured
without it. He judged that there was no immediate danger to be
feared from Parthia or from Parthian influence in Armenia, now
that the Roman empire was united under a single control. Should
Phraates attempt any hostile action he had an instrument in his
hands wherewith to threaten his security, in the person of Tiridates, the defeated pretender to the Arsacid throne, whom he
permitted to live in Syria. He also held as hostages the brothers
of the Armenian king Artaxes, and he created a menace to his
western flank by establishing on the throne of Armenia Minor his
implacable foe Artavasdes, the fugitive king of Media Atropatene.
If danger from Parthia or Armenia might be regarded as negligible, the re-organization of the Roman empire was an urgent
task which could not wait. That accomplished, he would take
steps to secure the satisfaction of Roman honour and the establishment of stable relations with the Eastern monarchy, and he was
sagacious enough to foresee that the instability of political conditions in the Arsacid kingdom was likely to offer an opportunity of
attaining these objects by diplomatic methods, backed by a display of force. His line of policy was already foreshadowed when
during the winter of 30 to 29 B.C. he gave a friendly reception to
the envoys of Phraates and indicated that he would lend no
support to his defeated rival Tiridates[1]. Ten years were to elapse
before a settlement was reached. Meanwhile he left in Syria a
garrison of perhaps as many as four or five legions, supplemented
no doubt by auxiliary troops (p. 280). This was the only military
force assigned to the Eastern front. Where the legions were
quartered, is wholly unknown; but, judging from later arrangements, we may safely presume that none of them was stationed
on the Euphrates, which was the natural line of a Parthian
invasion.

Public opinion at Rome urged the subjugation of the East as

[1] Dio LI, 18, 3.

far as India or even, as the poets would have it, as far as China[1], just as it had hailed with joy Caesar's projected campaign to avenge the disaster of Carrhae, which it hoped would result in the subjection of Parthia[2]. Some have thought that Caesar's aim was to recover for the Mediterranean world and for Western civilization the eastern half of Alexander's empire, where Hellenic culture was being submerged by its Oriental environment. If such a grandiose scheme, wholly divorced from practical possibilities, was really cherished by Caesar, it was certainly never present to the mind of his successor. Augustus took a sane view of Rome's Eastern question, and if he could have freed himself from the shackles of political tradition, he might have brought about an understanding that would have saved the empire endless trouble and bloodshed without sacrificing any real Roman interest. He clearly realized that what the empire needed was, not expansion beyond the Euphrates, but consolidation and peace. He felt—instinctively perhaps, but none the less truly—that it was an empire based on the Mediterranean, and that that basis was the source of its strength and the condition of its cohesion.

The lands that surround the Mediterranean and the islands that stud it are uniform in climate and character, and they are knit together by the sea, which they dominate from Gibraltar to the Bosporus, as Napoleon saw[3]. The Roman Empire was thus a natural formation, but its proper boundaries were the limits of the Mediterranean belt. Once the Romans had established themselves in the province of Asia, they were bound sooner or later to advance eastwards to the Euphrates; physical geography left no alternative, and the intervening lands were all within the Mediterranean area, permeable by Greek civilization, and consequently capable of absorption into the empire. Farther south, too, the river marked a natural dividing line up to the point where it enters the great desert which stretches from central Mesopotamia through Arabia to Egypt. To overpass that limit was to leave the Mediterranean world behind and to enter the alien domain of Oriental nationality and civilization. It is true that the Euphrates did not mark a sharply defined cultural boundary. From the dawn of history the plains of Mesopotamia had been in close contact with Syria, and far beyond the river Hellenic civilization, disseminated by the conquests of Alexander, still enjoyed living strength and influence; while the border peoples of Asia Minor had been strongly

---

[1] E.g. Virgil, *Aen.* VII, 606; Horace, *Odes*, I, 12, 53 *sqq*
[2] Dio XLIII, 51, 1.
[3] A. Vandal, *Napoléon et Alexandre Ier*, I, p. 249.

affected by Iranian blood and influences and were hardly touched by Hellenism. Nevertheless the Euphrates was the natural limit of Roman expansion, and conquest beyond it was a false policy, which, if seriously pursued, would have resulted in an overgrown and unstable empire, impossible to weld together and, even if maintainable for a time by exhausting efforts, doomed to fall to pieces under its own unbalanced weight.

The feud between Parthia and Rome owed its origin to the acts and arrangements of Pompey in the East, and it was aggravated by the aggression of Crassus. But there was only one abiding cause of hostile relations, the establishment of Roman suzerainty over Armenia. Save for this apple of discord, there was no reason why the two empires should not have lived side by side in peace and amity. The recognition of the Euphrates as the frontier between them, to which Lucullus had agreed and Pompey also had at first assented, would have ensured peaceful relations. Parthia was anything but an aggressive power. Her organization (which has already been described[1]) was of such a character as to confine her almost entirely to a defensive rôle. The Arsacid kings never succeeded in welding their empire into a strong and united state. The vassal kingdoms which fringed their provinces (satrapies) were never brought under their effective sovereignty; the 'King of Kings' was no more than overlord of his feudatory princes, and overlordship, whatever it precisely implied, did not mean real control. All the Parthian institutions—political, social, and military—were of a feudal type. A landed aristocracy ruled over a population of half-free serfs and of slaves, and the most powerful of these magnates, owners of vast estates, governed the king's provinces and led his armies. While constant in their allegiance to the principle that only an Arsacid should rule, the Parthian nobles were fickle in their loyalty to the individual king and as ready to welcome a change of sovereigns as to regret the change[2]. Revolution and civil war were frequent, while the king, seated precariously on his throne, sought to safeguard his position by putting potential rivals and enemies out of the way, and his most dreaded foes were those of his own house.

Such internal disunion weakened the power of Parthia and rendered her incapable of a sustained offensive. Another cause of weakness was her military system. Parthia maintained no standing army; a field force consisted almost wholly of levies raised by nobles and landowners from their retainers, who were carefully trained to horsemanship and archery. Such a mobile force could

[1] Vol. IX, pp. 588 *sqq.*   [2] Tacitus, *Ann.* II, 2; VI, 36; XI, 10.

win decisive victories, but it could not be kept together for any great length of time. One reason was the neglect of any system of commissariat, a defect emphasized by Dio as a cause of the inability of the Parthians to wage a continuous offensive war[1]. Another was their invincible repugnance to prolonged campaigning even within their own dominions[2]; nothing except an unsuccessful war was more apt to cause a revolution[3].

The weakness of Parthia's offensive power and the absence of an aggressive tendency are facts of cardinal importance in judging the wisdom of the traditional Roman policy in regard to Armenia. Having conquered that country, Pompey had added it to the ring of vassal states on which Rome relied for the defence of her provinces in Asia Minor, hoping thereby to make it a counterpoise to Parthia and a barrier between her and Roman spheres of interest. This system of frontier defence was a convenient one for Rome, reluctant as she was to increase her responsibilities by expansion eastwards, and in itself it was sound enough as a provisional measure. In recording the assignment to king Archelaus of Cilicia Tracheia, a region which readily lent itself to brigandage and piracy, Strabo explains that the Romans deemed it better to place it under client-kings than under Roman governors, who would not always be on the spot nor have armed force at their disposal[4]. The principle here stated had a wider application. Not only where districts were unruly but where the native peoples were too backward in civilization to be conveniently incorporated in the empire, the Romans realized that the task of governing and civilizing them was better entrusted to princes born and bred in the country. Their function was to promote the political and economic development of their realms by stimulating the growth of city life and the improvement of agriculture. When that development was sufficiently well advanced, their fiefs could be incorporated as provinces or parts of provinces, and they could be annexed at any moment that seemed good to the imperial government. Vassal status was by its nature transitional, and, as a rule, it was destined to lead ultimately to absorption.

Pompey's action in applying this system to Armenia was not unnatural. For geographically Armenia is a continuation of the lofty plateau of Asia Minor. Towards the east of the tableland

[1] XL, 15, 6.   [2] Tacitus, Ann. XI, 10; cf. Herodian VI, 7, 1.

[3] The exaggerated estimate of Parthian power which prevailed among Romans at the close of the Republic, was due to the disaster of Carrhae and the Parthian successes of the Triumviral period.

[4] XIV, 671.

the mountain ranges which traverse it—apart from the Black Sea
chain and the long range of Taurus on the south—converge, as
they rise in height, towards the orographical roof of Armenia,
the broad mass of Bingeul Dagh (Abus mons), which fills the
space between the two arms of the northern Euphrates and, together with its prolongations towards Erzerûm on the north and
Great Ararat on the east, forms the watershed between the
Euphrates and its affluents and the rivers that flow towards the
Caspian Sea. Up to this central point the mountain ranges follow
an easterly direction, enclosing between them the valleys which
give access to the centre of Armenia. Then they trend south-
eastwards in a direction parallel to the Caucasus mountains,
affording easy communication with lesser Media (Atropatene, now
the Persian province of Azerbaijan). While, therefore, Armenia is
closely attached to Asia Minor, it is no less closely connected
through Media with the Iranian plateau; and it is easily reached
from the lowlands of northern Mesopotamia, where the Taurus
barrier becomes narrow and sinks so low as to offer no serious
obstacle to an army marching towards the Armenian plains.

Thus interposed between two great empires, Armenia was
bound to be under the effective influence of one or the other, if
it did not actually form an integral part of either. But beyond a
doubt its natural connection was with Parthia, not with Rome. Its
civilization was unaffected by Hellenism; its people had become
completely Iranized, although the basis of their language is held
to be Thracian. In manners, customs, and mode of life, in
political and military organization, in religion, in dress, and
through marriage ties, their affinities were with the Parthians[1].
Here was an insuperable obstacle to the success of the policy of a
Roman protectorate. There were other difficulties in the way. The
claim to suzerainty was naturally regarded by the Arsacids as an
encroachment on their domain and as a standing threat to the
security of their realm. It was wholly incompatible with lasting
peace between the two empires. Moreover, the lack of cohesion
and of the spirit of aggressive militarism in the Parthian empire
made the assertion of the claim superfluous; and it was in any
case a claim which Rome could not enforce when her actual
frontiers were far distant and she had no troops anywhere near to
overawe the vassal king, who might easily be induced by the
pressure of circumstances to transfer his allegiance. Even after
Actium, Rome had under her direct rule only the outer shell of the
peninsula of Asia Minor, and not quite all of that.

[1] Cf. Tacitus, *Ann.* XIII, 34, 5.

IV. THE POLICY OF AUGUSTUS AND THE SETTLEMENT OF 20 B.C.

Such were the difficulties involved in the traditional policy in regard to Armenia. How was Augustus to deal with the problem? If he were dissatisfied with the traditional policy, there were two courses theoretically open to him. He might have boldly cut the knot and abandoned Armenia to Parthia, taking any measures that seemed to him necessary for the defence of the border lands. No vital interest would have been sacrificed. Had there been a strong and militant power established in Iran, the cession of Armenia would indeed have furnished it with an avenue of attack on Asia Minor; but such a power Parthia was not, and could never become without a radical transformation. In itself Armenia was a poor country, which had little attraction for Romans. Though it contained numerous valleys and plains of great fertility, one of the most favoured of which lies round the ancient capital Artaxata, it is predominantly an Alpine land, with a rigorous winter climate and a short summer season, which is hot and dry; it offered no rich field for Roman capital to exploit. While, however, the abandonment of Armenia would have been the best solution of the problem, it was hardly a practicable policy even for a ruler with the prestige of Augustus. A national claim which has become historic is not easily renounced. Roman sentiment and pride would have been offended by the repudiation of a legacy associated with the memories of Republican victories and triumphs[1], and the *de facto* Armenian king had to be punished for his massacre of every Roman subject left behind in his realm[2].

The alternative policy would have been to annex the country, and at a later date Augustus proclaimed to the world that he might have done so[3]. This policy would have involved as a preliminary step the incorporation of all the dependent kingdoms of Asia Minor, most of which were not ripe for annexation. But the declaration of Augustus was merely intended to impress on the Romans the mastery of the situation which he had achieved by bloodless means. That he did not contemplate annexation is shown by the mere fact that he reduced his army at once to a size which was inadequate for the defence of the empire as it stood. The objections to conquests beyond the Euphrates have been already set forth. Geographical conditions would have compelled

---

[1] Cf. Tacitus, *Ann.* XIII, 34, 4.   [2] Dio LI, 16, 2. Above, p. 79.
[3] *Res Gestae* 27.

an advance beyond Armenia to the Caucasus and the Caspian, as
Pompey found; and strategic considerations would have required
the annexation of northern Mesopotamia as far as the river
Chaboras (Khabûr) and the range of Jebel Sinjar, which bounds on
the north the desert of central Mesopotamia. Such a frontier, even
with a well-affected population behind it, could only have been
held at the point of the sword; the military and financial burdens
of defence could not have been borne; the only result would have
been perpetual conflict with Parthia; and the unity of the empire
would have been broken by the eastward shifting of the centre of
gravity. The policy of annexation could not commend itself to a
sober statesman, and having rejected it, Augustus saw no alternative but to follow precedent.

His purpose, as has been said, was to settle the whole Eastern
question, if he could, without actual war. Immediately after
Actium he had held out a friendly hand to Phraates by declining
to abet the refugee pretender Tiridates. From his domicile in
Syria the latter made a second attempt to overthrow the Parthian
king, and, failing, fled a second time to Augustus in 26–25 B.C.,
bringing with him the king's youngest son, Phraates, whom he is
said to have kidnapped[1]. Augustus was then in Spain, from which
he returned to Rome in the early months of 24. In the previous
year he had advanced the Roman frontier in Asia Minor a considerable distance eastwards by annexing the kingdom of Galatia
on the death of Amyntas, who lost his life in the course of a
vigorously conducted campaign against the robber tribes of the
northern front of the Taurus range, which made life and property
insecure in the plains of southern Phrygia towards Pisidia and
Isauria (p. 270). The new province at first included the whole
kingdom of Amyntas, but its size was reduced in 20, when
eastern Lycaonia together with Cilicia Tracheia, to which it was
the key, was transferred to the rule of Archelaus, king of Cappadocia[2]; thereafter it comprised Galatia proper, Pisidia, Isauria and
western Lycaonia. By the annexation of this large tract of country
the whole interior of the peninsula as far as the borders of Pontus
and Cappadocia was brought under direct Roman administration.

No steps, however, were taken to bring the Taurus tribes under
effective control, and (so far as is known) no legionary troops were
stationed in the new province. As the Parthian question also

[1] Justin XLII, 5, 6; cf. Dio LI, 18, 3.
[2] Strabo XII, 535, 537; XIV, 671; Dio LIV, 9, 2. The city of Seleucia on
the Calycadnus, however, retained its autonomy.

remained in abeyance, Eastern affairs needed careful watching, and in 23 Augustus sent out Agrippa with secondary proconsular authority and a staff of legates to act as vice-regent in the East, a mission believed by the Roman public to be merely a pretext—not unwelcomed, according to one report, by Agrippa himself—for his temporary removal from Rome[1]. Some months later, if we may take the order of events in Dio's narrative as chronological, envoys from the Parthian king arrived in Rome with a demand for the surrender of Tiridates and the restoration of the young Phraates. Augustus declined to hand over the former, who might be useful to him as an instrument, but he gave an assurance that he would not lend him support against Parthia, and he sent back the king's son on condition that the Roman standards and prisoners of war should be restored[2].

A year passed, but Phraates gave no sign of complying with the condition, and Roman opinion, reflected by the poets, kept clamouring for vengeance on Parthia. Augustus decided that the time had come to apply pressure, and late in the year 22 he set out on a tour of inspection through Sicily, Greece, and the eastern provinces. From Samos, where he passed the winter of 21–20, he sent instructions to Tiberius, now twenty-one years of age, to bring a large legionary force, drawn no doubt from the armies of Macedonia and Illyricum, overland through Macedonia to Armenia[3]. In that country chronic disunion reigned among the nobles, a weaker section leaning on Rome and a stronger favouring Parthia. The former had sent an embassy to Augustus to prefer charges against king Artaxes and to request his deposition in favour of his younger brother Tigranes, who had lived for ten years in Rome; and the mission of Tiberius was to place him on the throne. In the spring Augustus crossed to the mainland and, after instituting reforms in Asia and Bithynia, proceeded to Syria. His arrival and the news of the approach of Tiberius' army, travelling with the rapidity with which news has always travelled in the East, had the desired

[1] Vell. Pat. II, 93; Dio LIII, 32, 1; Suetonius, *Aug.* 66, *Tib.* 10; Tacitus, *Ann.* XIV, 53 and 55; Pliny, *N.H.* VII, 149; Josephus, *Ant.* XV [10, 2], 350.
[2] Dio LIII, 33; Justin, *loc. cit.*, says *filium sine pretio remisit.* In *Class. Phil.* III, 1908, pp. 145 *sqq.*, D. Magie makes the ingenious but hardly convincing conjecture that the dispatch of the Parthian embassy was due to the diplomatic efforts of Agrippa, the object of whose mission to the East was to suggest secretly to Phraates that by offering acceptable terms he could secure his son, and who chose Mitylene as his place of residence in order to conceal the purpose of his mission.
[3] Strabo XVII, 821; Dio LIV, 9, 4–5; Vell. Pat. II, 94; Suetonius, *Tib.* 9, 1.

effect on the Parthian king. Faced by the threat of attack from two sides, and knowing that a Roman invasion was likely to cost him his throne, he resolved to yield and, risking the displeasure of his own people, he restored the standards and such of the prisoners as still survived and did not seek to elude discovery. On May 12, in all probability, they were handed over by his representatives, and Augustus was acclaimed *Imperator* for the ninth time[1].

It was a notable diplomatic success, which Augustus ranked higher than a victory in the field. 'I compelled the Parthians,' he proudly wrote[2], 'to restore the spoils and standards of three Roman armies and as suppliants to implore the friendship of the Roman People.' The submission of Parthia was sung by the poets with tedious iteration and immortalized by artists and by the Roman mints. On the cuirass of the fine statue of Augustus found in the villa of Livia at Prima Porta a relief depicting the surrender occupies the central place[3]. In 18 B.C. coins were issued with the legend *Caesar Augustus sign(is) rece(ptis)* inscribed round the figure of a Parthian on bended knee, proffering a standard with his right hand and holding out his left in an attitude of supplication[4]. In honour of Augustus the Senate decreed a triumph, which he declined, and a triumphal arch, which was erected in the Forum next to the temple of the deified Julius[5], and is figured on coins of 18–17 B.C. bearing the legend *Civib(us) et sign(is) milit(aribus) a Part(his) recup(eratis)*[6]. The standards were taken to Rome to be dedicated to Mars Ultor. They were placed temporarily in a small round temple which Augustus ordered to be built on the Capitol on the model of that of Juppiter Feretrius, and they were subsequently transferred to the splendid new temple of the god in the Forum of Augustus which was dedicated on August 1, 2 B.C. The memory of the event was kept alive till the fourth century by the annual celebration of a thanksgiving and of Circensian games on May 12[7].

The settlement with Parthia made the task of Tiberius easy. The threat of invasion gave the pro-Roman party the upper hand, and before he reached Armenia, Artaxes had been murdered by

---

[1] Dio LIV, 8, 1; Vell. Pat. II, 91; Livy, *Epit.* 141; Suetonius, *Aug.* 21, *Tib.* 9. The order of events is assured by the accounts of Dio and Velleius.

[2] *Res Gestae* 29.   [3] Volume of Plates iv, 148, *a*.

[4] *Ib.* 200, *a*; Horace, *Ep.* I, 12, 27: *ius imperiumque Phraates Caesaris accepit genibus minor.*

[5] Platner-Ashby, *Topographical Dictionary of Rome*, p. 34.

[6] Volume of Plates iv, 200, *b*.

[7] Ovid, *Fasti* v, 597; *C.I.L.* I², pp. 229, 318.

his own kinsmen. Tiberius entered the country without opposition and in the presence of his legions solemnly placed the diadem on the head of Tigranes. Augustus announced to the world that he had conquered Armenia but that he refrained from annexing it, preferring to follow established precedent and hand it over to a client-king. The claim to conquest was stressed by contemporary writers and by the Roman mints, which issued coins bearing the legend *Armenia capta* (or *recepta*) and displaying the figure of an Armenian on bended knee, extending his hands in an attitude of surrender, or other symbolic representations of conquest[1]. The restoration of Roman authority in Armenia was followed by a request from the people of Media Atropatene, now freed from the rule of Artaxes, that Augustus should choose them a king, and he appointed Ariobarzanes, son of their former king Artavasdes, who had died in Armenia Minor.

Such was Augustus' solution of the Eastern question. Peace was to be maintained with Parthia on condition of her recognition of Roman suzerainty over Armenia. Despite the applause which greeted his successes, the renunciation of all idea of conquest in the East was not what Romans had expected, and Augustus thought it well to justify his policy. This he did in a communication to the Senate, in which he declared that he regarded any further extension of the empire as undesirable[2].

The submission of Phraates was no doubt resented by his subjects and was not calculated to improve the security of his position. It has been supposed, on slender evidence, that he was once more driven from his throne[3]. Anyhow, about 10 or 9 B.C., he took the extraordinary step of handing over to M. Titius, the governor of Syria, his four legitimate sons—Vonones, Seraspadanes, Rhodaspes and Phraates—with their families to be permanently domiciled in Rome, where they were provided for in royal style at the public expense[4]. His motives were variously interpreted. The Roman official explanation was that they were sent as pledges of his friendship[5]. A sounder explanation is given

---

[1] Volume of Plates iv, 200, *c*   [2] Dio LIV, 9, 1.

[3] There is a gap in the series of his coins between 23 and 10 B.C., and Herod was falsely accused of having made a pact of friendship against Rome with 'Mithridates, King of Parthia,' some years before 7 B.C. (Josephus, *Ant.* XVI [8, 4], 253); but the gap is doubtless accidental, and Herod's accuser may well have been ignorant of the king's name (cf. W. Otto in *P.W.* Suppl. II, col. 134)

[4] Seraspadanes and Rhodaspes ultimately died in Rome (Dessau 842).

[5] *Res Gestae* 32; Vell. Pat. II, 94; Suetonius, *Aug.* 21, 43; Tacitus, *Ann.* II, 1, who, however, combines with this the motive given by Strabo.

by Strabo: Phraates was afraid of revolution, and as he knew that
no rebel could prevail unless he were allied with an Arsacid, he
removed his sons to deprive evil-doers of that hope[1]. A contributory motive is stated by Josephus. Phraates had an illegitimate son
Phraataces, by an Italian slave girl sent him by Augustus, whom
he afterwards made his legitimate queen under the name of
Thea Urania Musa, and she persuaded him to remove his legitimate offspring in order to secure the succession for her son, who
did in fact succeed[2]. The sons were evidently content to go to
Rome, as they made no attempt to resist or to escape, and their
willingness indicates that they were as afraid of their father as he
was of them. Fortune could have placed no more valuable gift in
the hands of Augustus than this supply of Arsacid princes, who
might be used to undermine the security of a hostile Parthian king,
and were so to be used by his successors. Augustus was gratified
by this crowning success of his Parthian policy, and did not fail
to take an opportunity of impressing it on the people of Rome by
showing off his hostages at a gladiatorial show[3].

V. THE BOSPORAN KINGDOM

Three years after his return from the East in 19 Augustus
decided to send Agrippa thither again with plenipotentiary
powers to superintend the government of the provinces and the
vassal states and to deal with all matters that required settlement[4].
One of the tasks that fell to him was the regulation of affairs in the
Bosporan kingdom. The effective control of this outpost of
civilization was a matter of importance for Rome. Alike for
political and economic reasons it was imperative that its government should be in capable and loyal hands. Flanked on the west
by the Scythians of the Crimea, and on the north and east by
Sarmatian tribes strung out over the South Russian steppes and
extending westwards as far as the Dniester[5], it was the only
barrier against the establishment of an Iranian domination of the
northern shores of the Euxine. It was even possible that such a
development might be promoted from within the Bosporan kingdom by the emergence of a ruler inspired by Mithridatic ambi-

---

[1] Strabo XVI, 748.   [2] Josephus, *Ant.* XVIII [2, 4], 41; see Volume
of Plates IV, 200, *d*.   [3] Suetonius, *Aug.* 43.
[4] Dio LIV, 19, 6; Josephus, *Ant.* XVI [2, 1], 12.
[5] Between the Dniester and the Dnieper Strabo enumerates the Iazyges,
Royal Sarmatians and Urgi; between Dnieper and Don the Roxolani; and
east and south of the Don the Aorsi and Siraci (Σιραχοί, *C.I.G.* II, 2132*e*)
towards the Caucasus (VII, 306; XI, 492; 506).

tions. The government of the State was purely monarchical, the Greek population had no voice in it; its rulers were of Iranian or semi-Iranian lineage, and its Greek subjects were no longer of pure Greek blood, while the nearer Sarmatian tribes had become partially hellenized through intensive commercial intercourse with their neighbours. Such conditions might throw up an ambitious prince bent on casting off the yoke of Rome and uniting the adjoining tribes into a formidable Graeco-Iranian state on the northern shores of the Black Sea.

There were other reasons for keeping a vigilant eye on the Bosporan kingdom. Its economic importance was great. It was still the main source of food supplies for the cities of northern Asia Minor and of the Aegean; and when Roman troops were required in the northern section of the eastern frontier, as they had been required in 20 B.C., their provisionment depended chiefly on the produce of South Russia. Moreover, the Black Sea had to be policed not only in the interests of indispensable trade but also for the protection of the coastlands within and beyond the limits of actual Roman territory; and for this work the co-operation of an efficient Bosporan government was essential. The sea was infested by pirates. The Tauri of the south coast of the Crimea were notorious wreckers and freebooters, but they were not so formidable as the wild tribes inhabiting the steep wooded slopes of the Caucasus, which made their living by piracy and slave raids[1]. The Caucasian pirates, says Strabo, were masters of the sea; and he adds that, while native rulers took punitive measures against them when their subjects suffered, Roman territory was attacked with greater impunity through the negligence of the governors. Until the imperial government made up its mind to take over the task of policing the waters of the Euxine, it had no alternative but to impose the duty on the client-kings of Bosporus and Pontus. There was plainly no lack of reasons why Rome should see to it that the government of the Bosporan kingdom was vested in strong and trustworthy hands.

Since Caesar's death the throne had been held by Asander, probably one of the half-Greek citizens of Panticapaeum (Kertch), who had overthrown Pharnaces[2] and secured the support of the people through his marriage with the late king's daughter Dynamis (which may, however, have taken place before her father's death). After crushing Caesar's nominee, Mithridates of Pergamum, and ruling three years as archon, he had succeeded, perhaps

---

[1] Strabo XI, 496; Ovid, *Ex Ponto*, IV, 10, 25 *sqq*.
[2] Strabo XIII, 625; Dio XLII, 48; Appian, *Mithr.* 120.

by a bribe, in obtaining the recognition of Antony and the title of King, which appears on his coins from 41 B.C. Either then or at a later date he was also recognized by Octavian and enrolled among the *amici populi Romani*[1]. He evidently proved a capable ruler, maintaining his territory against Scythian and Sarmatian invasion[2] and keeping piracy in hand. At the time of Augustus' sojourn in the East he was still on the throne, but shortly after a revolt was raised against him by an adventurer named Scribonius, who claimed to be a grandson of the great Mithridates; and it is said that, when he saw his troops beginning to go over to the usurper, he starved himself to death[3]. He died in or just before 17 B.C. at the great age of 93. Scribonius alleged that he had been chosen by Augustus as Asander's successor[4], and won the hand of the unscrupulous queen, who may be suspected of complicity in the plot; but she kept the sovereign power in her own hands, for she struck gold coins (of which only one, dated 17–16, survives) with her own head and name alone[5]. Who Scribonius was, is unknown; he may well have been a provincial of good social standing—possibly even, like Mithridates of Pergamum, of royal descent—who took a Roman name[6]; a low-class adventurer would not have been accepted by Dynamis as a husband.

When the news of these events reached Agrippa in Syria, he naturally declined to recognize the impostor and commissioned Polemo, king of Pontus, to attack him, promising him the throne and arranging, with the sanction of Augustus, that he should marry Dynamis; thereby his position would be legitimized, the acquiescence of the Bosporans would (it was hoped) be secured, and the re-union of the two parts of the old Mithridatic empire under the rule of an energetic and reliable vassal would obviate possible dangers and ensure stable conditions on the north-eastern fringe of the Empire. Before Polemo reached the Bosporus, Scribonius had been put to death by the Bosporans themselves, in the hope that his removal would save them from the rule of Polemo. Disappointed in their expectation, they offered resistance

---

[1] He bears the title φιλορώμαιος in an inscription erected by one of his admirals in commemoration of a naval victory, doubtless over the pirates (*Ios. P. E.* II, 25, *I.G.R.R.* I, 874). For the signification of the title, cf. R. Münsterberg, *Jahresh.* XVIII, 1915, pp. 315 *sqq.*

[2] Strabo XI, 495; VII, 311.   [3] Pseudo-Lucian, *Makrobioi*, 17.

[4] Dio's brief record (LIV, 24) gives the impression that Scribonius went to the Bosporus after Asander's death, but this may be due to his conciseness: he says nothing of the circumstances of the king's death, and the statement in *Makrobioi*, 17, can hardly be pure fiction.

[5] See Volume of Plates iv, 208, *j*.   [6] Cf. Dessau, *Eph. Epigr.* IX, p. 394.

to the invader and, in spite of defeats, persevered in the struggle until in 14 B.C. Agrippa sailed with a fleet to Sinope and threatened to take the field against them[1]. The threat sufficed. The Bosporans submitted, and Agrippa proceeded to order the affairs of the kingdom, imposing on it the obligation to supply contingents to the regular auxiliary forces of the imperial army[2], and arranging that the isolated city of Chersonesus, near Sebastopol, while retaining the autonomy which Augustus had apparently restored to it in 25, should place itself under the aegis of the Bosporan kingdom by the conclusion of an alliance which should secure it against the attacks of its Scythian neighbours[3]. The kingdom was then handed over to Polemo, who duly wedded Dynamis. The importance which Augustus attached to the settlement of Bosporan affairs is shown by the honours decreed to Agrippa, among them a triumph, which in accordance with his fixed practice he declined[4].

The marriage of Polemo and Dynamis proved unhappy. Both were masterful personalities, and each was determined to rule; they separated after little more than a year, and Polemo then took to wife Pythodoris, daughter of a rich citizen of Tralles in the Maeander valley, by whom he had three children[5]. Dynamis, as would seem most probable[6], fled across the straits and took refuge with a Sarmatian (or possibly Maeotian) tribe ruled by one Aspurgus, son of King Asandrochus[7], whose active support she secured by giving him her hand and with it the prospect of the Bosporan throne. With his help she organized a revolt against Polemo, which dragged on for several years. Despite various successes, among which is perhaps to be included the capture and destruction of the Greek colony of Tanais at the mouth of the Don[8],

[1] For the date, Dio LIV, 24, Euseb.-Hieronymus, p. 143, ed. Schöne (era of Abraham 2003, *i.e.* Oct. 14–13, while the Armenian version gives 2002, *i.e.* Oct. 15–14).

[2] A *cohors Bosporanorum* is mentioned soon after Agrippa's settlement, Dessau 9503; *ala I Bosporanorum*, which served in Syria in the first century, is first mentioned in A.D. 54 (*Ann. épig.* 1922, no. 109).

[3] Strabo VII, 309; *Ios. P. E.* I², 354, 419, 704; M. Rostovtzeff in *J.R.S.* VII, 1917, pp. 41 *sqq.*　　[4] Dio LIV, 24.　　[5] Strabo XII, 556.

[6] The reconstruction of Rostovtzeff (*J.H.S.* XXXIX, 1919, pp. 88 *sqq.*) is here followed; the paucity of evidence precludes certainty about several details.

[7] *Ios. P. E.* II, 36 (*I.G.R.R.* I, 879). By 'king' is meant tribal ruler, not king of the Bosporus: Asandrochus is not to be identified with Asandrus (cf. Kiessling in *P.W.* s.v. *Gorgippia*, col. 1628).

[8] Strabo XI, 493. If the destruction of the city was an episode of the struggle against Dynamis and Aspurgus, it presumably took their side; but the event may belong to Polemo's first war against the Bosporans.

Polemo failed to crush the revolt and in 8 B.C. he had recourse to the stratagem of attacking the rebels under the guise of friendship, but the ruse was discovered, and he was captured and put to death[1]. The tribesmen who formed the following of Aspurgus and styled themselves 'Aspurgians' were rewarded by being settled on the rich lands of the Taman peninsula between Phanagoreia and Gorgippia; the possession of these lands, which henceforth bore their name, ensured their support for the new régime[2].

Dynamis had won, but her position was critical; she had over-thrown the nominee of Augustus, and the last word was with him. At this time he had many preoccupations: his hands were full in the West; in southern Asia Minor the subjugation of the predatory mountaineers of the Pisidian Taurus was perhaps in progress (p. 271); and trouble may have already broken out in Armenia (p. 273). No doubt he also realized the attachment of the Bos-porans to the Mithridatic dynasty and their aversion from the Polemonian house, and he accepted the situation, recognizing the rule of the queen on condition that she should accept the full obligations of a Roman vassal. The condition was loyally observed. Dynamis received the title of 'friend of the Roman People,' which regularly appears on her monuments. Her head, name, and title now disappeared from her coins and were replaced by the heads of Augustus and Agrippa, with nothing more than a humble monogram to indicate that she was still ruler; and for the rest of the Julio-Claudian period the Bosporan kings, with one significant exception, placed on their gold coins only monograms and dates, never their full name and title. She died in A.D. 7/8 about the age of seventy.

During her lifetime her husband Aspurgus was not officially associated with her in the government of the kingdom, nor did he immediately succeed her. For two years the throne was held by a ruler whose name is unknown[3]. Then Aspurgus acceded to power (A.D. 10/11), but he did not bear the royal title till A.D. 14/15, when it was conferred on him by Tiberius together with that of *amicus Caesaris populique Romani*[4]. At the same time he received Roman

---

[1] Strabo XI, 495. The date is fixed by the commencement of the series of staters bearing the monogram of Dynamis. Volume of Plates iv, 208, *k*.

[2] Strabo, *loc. cit.* and XII, 556. The district assigned to the Aspurgians, with whose name Rostovtzeff aptly compares the 'sons of boyars' in Russia, was still called after them in the third century (*Ios. P. E.* II, 29, *I.G.R.R.* I, 871, etc.).   [3] See the list at the end of the volume.

[4] The grant of the royal title is marked by the addition of B($\alpha\sigma\iota\lambda\epsilon\upsilon\varsigma$) to his monogram; this numismatic inference is confirmed by the use of the title in an inscription of A.D. 16/17 (*Ios. P. E.* II, 364, *I.G.R.R.* I, 906).

citizenship and adopted the names of his benefactor, Tiberius Iulius, which were borne by his son Cotys and all his successors for centuries[1]. Aspurgus appears to have been a strong ruler as well as a loyal vassal; he maintained Bosporan territory intact as far as Tanais and is extolled by one of his officials as having 'subdued' the Scythians and the Tauri[2]. He died soon after Tiberius in A.D. 37/8, leaving two sons, Mithridates and Cotys, the former borne to him perhaps by Dynamis, the latter by his second wife, a Thracian princess Gepaepyris.

VI. THE HOMANADENSIAN WAR

Not many years after Agrippa had completed his mission in the East military operations on a considerable scale were required to establish peaceful conditions in the southern borderlands of the province of Galatia[3]. Between the province and the Levant stretched a broad belt of very wild country forming part of the great Taurus range, which walls off the central tableland from the sea. Lofty mountain ridges running athwart the general trend of the range from west to east and enclosing rough, rocky, rolling plateaux, seamed with precipitous ravines and deep cañons which have been cut by the rivers that drain to the Pamphylian and Cilician seas, make the whole belt exceedingly difficult to traverse and furnished a terrain ideally suited to be a nursery of brigands and pirates. The tribes that occupied the northern front of this mountainous tract—Pisidians on the west and, adjacent to them, two tribes racially akin to their southern neighbours in Cilicia Tracheia, the Homanades[4] in and round the valley of lake Trogitis and the Isaurians in the Lycaonian hills—were the scourge of the fertile countryside which Strabo calls 'Phrygia adjoining Pisidia[5].' Amyntas, the last king of Galatia, had made a gallant effort to reduce those lawless mountaineers and had achieved considerable success. After capturing Pisidian strongholds, among them Cremna, he proceeded to attack the Homanades and succeeded in storming most of their fastnesses, reputed to be almost impregnable, and in slaying their chief; but he fell into an ambuscade laid by the dead man's wife and lost his life.

[1] Ios. P. E. IV, 204 (I.G.R.R. I, 880).
[2] Ios. P. E. II, 36 (I.G.R.R. I, 879).
[3] Strabo XII, 569; Tacitus, Ann. III, 48; Pliny, N.H. v, 94.
[4] The evidence of Pliny and Byzantine documents suggests that this spelling more nearly represents the native name than the Graecizing form Homonadeis (Strabo) or Homonadenses (Tacitus).
[5] Strabo, loc. cit. and XIV, 671.

Although he left sons behind, Augustus decided to annex the kingdom (25 B.C.), whether because he thought that the interests of the empire demanded its incorporation or because for one reason or another he deemed none of the sons suitable for the throne[1]. For many years, however, he took no step to carry through the work of pacification which Amyntas had begun; he confined himself to the defensive measure of founding at Antioch, perhaps in 19, under the name of Colonia Caesarea, a garrison colony of soldiers discharged from two legions, V Gallica and VII (Macedonica), which was designed to aid in checking the raids of the mountain tribes[2]. To ensure the effective protection of territory which it has annexed is the first duty of any government, and the delay in taking decisive action is hardly to be explained by the consideration that much more urgent tasks were awaiting accomplishment or that the coercion of the Homanades, which Amyntas had nearly achieved, was so serious an undertaking that it had to be postponed until the reorganization of the empire was complete. It is more likely that the establishment of Roman administration had produced a lull in the marauding activities of the tribe; otherwise the inaction of Agrippa between 16 and 13 would not be intelligible.

If quiescent for a time, the Homanades must have caused serious trouble at some date between 12 B.C. and A.D. 1, and Augustus resolved to deal with them. He entrusted the task to P. Sulpicius Quirinius, a man of humble birth who had forced his way up by his military talents. Among his services was the successful conduct of a campaign which he had been commissioned, no doubt as proconsul of Crete and Cyrene, to wage against two tribes of the Libyan desert, the Marmaridae and the Garamantes, which had menaced the security of the Cyrenaic cities (cf. above, p. 211). As a reward he was given one of the two eponymous consulships for 12, an honour which about that time was reserved for members of the highest nobility, and some time thereafter he was chosen to carry out the subjugation of the Taurus region. The main attack on the offending tribe could be made only from the north, and in all probability Quirinius was

[1] Dio LIII, 26, 3. That Amyntas bequeathed his kingdom to Augustus is not a sure inference from Strabo XII, 577; in any case no testament was needed to entitle Augustus to terminate the status of clientship.

[2] Coin of Antioch (Z. f. N. XXXVIII, 1928, p. 56); Dessau 2237–8; C.I.L. III, 6826–8; J.R.S. VI, 1916, p. 90. On these legions cf. J.R.S. XXIII, 1933, p. 30. The colonia was in existence before 11 B.C. (C.I.L. III, 6843); the name Caesarea may have been given to Antioch by Amyntas.

appointed governor of Galatia and Pamphylia[1], which appear to have formed a single governorship in the time of Augustus. The inclusion of Pamphylia in his command gave him control of both sides of the mountain belt, the only way (as the Romans were well aware) of ensuring the subjugation of mountain tribes. About the forces employed there is no evidence, but it is probable that they included two or three legions, drawn from Syria and perhaps Egypt[2]. Nor is anything recorded about the course of the operations beyond the fact that Quirinius resorted to the method of blockading the mountain strongholds (*castella*) of the tribe, forty-four in number (which implies that he had a large force under his command), and starved them into submission, capturing 4000 men. He doubtless began by occupying the fertile but marshy valley of lake Trogitis, in which lay the chief tribal centre, Homana, and driving the tribesmen back on their hill forts, which he stormed when famine had exhausted their power of resistance. His prisoners, who represented the total number of the surviving adult tribesmen, were removed from the mountains to the plain and settled in the neighbouring cities. In recognition of his successful accomplishment of a difficult task Quirinius was awarded the triumphal insignia, and the colony of Antioch expressed its gratitude to him by electing him duumvir, an office in which he was represented by a deputy who was a distinguished citizen of the town[3].

A war of subjugation was usually followed by a reorganization of the country concerned, and this may have been the date of the establishment of five colonies of veteran soldiers which Augustus planted[4] in the region south of Antioch to assist in the maintenance of law and order, three of them in Pisidia (Olbasa, Comama and Cremna) and two in Lycaonia (Parlaïs and Lystra), all called Iulia Augusta (or Iulia) with added epithets. They were connected with the older *colonia* and administrative centre Antioch by a system of roads, officially designated by the hybrid name of *viae Sebastae*, which were in process of construction in 6 B.C. during the governorship of Cornutus Aquila[5]. The subju-

---

[1] See Note 2, p. 877 *sq*.
[2] Cf. R. Syme in *J.R.S.* XXIII, 1933, p. 24 and *Klio* XXVII, 1934, p. 144 *sq*.   [3] Dessau 9502–3.
[4] *Res Gestae* 28: *colonias in...Pisidia militum deduxi.* The name Pisidia was loosely used by Romans.
[5] *C.I.L.* III, 6974 (12217), 14185, 14401 *a–c.* Cf. *J.H.S.* XL, 1920, pp. 102 *sqq.* The possibility that the colonies had been founded and the roads made before the campaign (with the same defensive purpose as the earlier

gation of the Homanades was complete and final, but the severity of their treatment did not suffice to cow all the tribes of the mountain area. In A.D. 6 a fresh outbreak of brigandage on the part of the neighbouring Isaurians developed into a regular war, of which no details have survived[1]. Thereafter peace seems to have reigned in the Galatian borderlands, and its hill tribes settled down to assimilate Graeco-Roman culture; but their neighbours in Cilicia Tracheia, removed from civilizing influences, remained untamed barbarians, ready to descend from their mountains on plundering raids[2] and destined in later centuries, under the name of Isaurians, to emerge as a militant force and even to give an emperor to Constantinople.

VII. THE REVOLT OF ARMENIA AND THE MISSION OF GAIUS CAESAR

With the results of his policy in Armenia Augustus had small reason to be satisfied[3]. His nominee Tigranes II died, after a brief term of rule, at an uncertain date not later than 6 B.C., and then, in the words of Augustus, Armenia 'revolted and rebelled.' The anti-Roman faction placed on the throne his son Tigranes III and his daughter (perhaps by a different wife) Erato, who were joined in wedlock in eastern fashion. Augustus commissioned Tiberius to proceed to Armenia, and when he declined the commission and retired to Rhodes, he ordered the installation of Artavasdes, probably a younger brother of the late king, with whom he had been taken to Rome. He was supported by Roman troops, but his reign was short. Some time before 1 B.C. he was driven out by Parthian aid, together with the Roman troops sent to support him, and Tigranes regained the throne. It was a serious blow to Roman prestige, and the vexation of Augustus is reflected in his silence about this unfortunate nominee. Being deprived of the co-operation of Tiberius and being himself too old to undertake another journey to the East, he was forced to send the youthful Gaius Caesar to deal with the situation, causing to be con-

colony at Antioch), and that the campaign itself was subsequent to 6 B.C. is suggested by the silence of Dio about the war, which may be due to the fragmentary state of his narrative between 6 B.C. and A.D. 4.

[1] Dio LV, 28, 3.

[2] Cf. Tacitus, *Ann.* XII, 55 (A.D. 52), and Ammianus Marcellinus, XIV, 2 (fourth century).

[3] The main sources are *Res Gestae* 27; Tacitus, *Ann.* II, 3–4; Dio LV, 9, 4; 10, 18–21; 10a, 4 *sqq.* For Parthian affairs: Josephus, *Ant.* XVIII [2, 4], 39 *sqq.*

ferred on him the secondary proconsular power, with authority overriding that of provincial governors, which had formerly been wielded by his father Agrippa, and providing him with an advisory staff, headed by M. Lollius, who had acquired some knowledge of the East as organizer of the province of Galatia. This frontier province had in recent years crept a little farther eastwards; in 6 B.C. all inland Paphlagonia had been added to it on the death of king Deiotarus Philadelphus, and in 3–2 B.C. the adjoining principalities of Amasia and Sebastopolis in inland Pontus, with the city of Megalopolis-Sebasteia (Sivas)—an important nodal point in the system of roads, which hitherto had belonged to the Polemonian kingdom of Pontus—were incorporated in the province under the distinguishing title of Pontus Galaticus[1]. These districts carried the main road from the Bosporus towards Armenia, which was afterwards to become a great trunk-road connecting the Armenian frontier with Moesia. Roman territory was thus advanced a considerable way towards the Euphrates, though between the two there still intervened three vassal states, Polemonian Pontus now under the rule of Polemo's widow, the able queen Pythodoris, Armenia Minor, and the realm of Archelaus, king of Cappadocia.

All preparations completed, Gaius travelled by way of Athens across the Aegean. At Samos (or Chios) he met his stepfather Tiberius, who had come from Rhodes to pay his respects but was accorded a cold reception, thanks to the hostile influence of Lollius[2]. From Samos he went out of his way to Egypt, perhaps merely to gain personal knowledge of the most important economic dependency of Rome, just as he had previously been sent round European provinces[3]. There is no clear trace of any activity on his part in the country, and little probability in the view that the object of his visit was to set on foot preparations in the Red Sea ports for the Arabian expedition which was believed to be the intended climax of his triumphal progress[4]. From Egypt he

---

[1] *I.e.* the part of Pontus added to Galatia. The dates of annexation are derived from the Eras of the cities, which were reckoned from the date of their admission into the empire (see *Studia Pontica*, III, pp. 73, 109; *Anatolian Studies presented to Sir W. Ramsay*, p. 7 *sq.*).

[2] Suetonius, *Tib.* 12; Dio LV, 10, 19.

[3] Vell. Pat. II, 101; Suetonius, *Aug.* 64; Dio LV, 10, 17 (Danubian provinces).

[4] See above, p. 253. The fragmentary passage of Zonaras (Dio LV, 10a, 1, Boissevain), which seems to refer to operations against a marauding desert tribe under the command of a tribune of the praetorian guard, baffles interpretation (V. Gardthausen, *Augustus*, p. 1136, with note 7).

sailed direct to Syria[1], where he entered on his consulship for
A.D. I.

Two years earlier (2 B.C.) there had been a dynastic revolution
in Parthia, where the old king Phraates had been murdered and
succeeded by his son Phraataces[2]. The servile descent of the new
king made him unacceptable to the Parthian nobility, and his
policy of actively abetting the revolution in Armenia was probably
adopted in the hope of strengthening his position. On hearing of
the mission of Gaius, he had sought to negotiate with Augustus,
proffering an explanation of what had occurred and requesting,
as a condition of peace, the return of his four half-brothers
domiciled in Rome, who were a potential menace to his security.
Augustus naturally declined to part with those convenient
weapons of offence, and brusquely branding him as a usurper,
ordered him to withdraw from Armenia. Phraataces sent a
haughty reply, and for the time Armenia remained under Parthian
control; but its *de facto* king Tigranes, after the death of his
expelled rival Artavasdes, dispatched envoys to Rome with gifts
and a humble petition for the Armenian throne. Satisfied,
apparently, with this acknowledgment of Roman suzerainty,
Augustus accepted the gifts and bade Tigranes go with good
hope to Gaius in Syria.

Some time after the arrival of the crown prince in the province,
Phraataces, believing that resolute action was portended and
apprehensive of the disaffection of his own subjects, changed his
mind and determined to come to terms with Rome. He receded
from his demand for the return of his brothers and declared his
readiness to refrain from interference in Armenia. On these
terms a concordat was concluded, and in the following spring (as
would appear[3]) a personal interview between the Roman prince
and the Great King took place on the neutral soil of an island in
the river Euphrates, which was thereby definitely recognized as
the boundary between the two states. Velleius Paterculus, then a
young legionary tribune, describes the scene which he witnessed.
The Roman and Parthian armies were drawn up on either bank
and the representatives of East and West landed on the island

---

[1] Orosius VII, 3, 5–6.

[2] Josephus, *Ant.* XVIII [2, 4], 39; Dio LV, 10*a*, 4.

[3] The date is indicated by the fact that Tiberius was back in Rome
shortly before the death of L. Caesar on Aug. 20, A.D. 2 (Dio LV, 10*a*, 10);
he would not delay his return after receiving the permission of Augustus, and
the consent of Gaius was not accorded until after the fall of Lollius, which
was a sequel of the meeting (Suetonius, *Tib.* 13).

with an escort of equal size. An exchange of banquets followed, the Parthian yielding precedence to the Roman and dining first on the western bank, while Gaius crossed to the Parthian side to return the compliment. The meeting, which can hardly have taken place without the approval of Augustus, was significant as a public acknowledgement by the imperial government that it recognized the Parthian empire as an independent state subsisting side by side with the Roman, not indeed on a footing of equality, but with equal rights of sovereignty, however grudgingly they might be accorded[1]. Before taking his leave, Phraataces revealed to Gaius that Lollius had been abusing his high trust by accepting huge bribes from Eastern potentates; the charge proved to be true, and Gaius renounced his friendship. Within a few days thereafter Lollius died, probably by his own hand, and was replaced by P. Sulpicius Quirinius, whose military ability and experience well fitted him to act as adviser to the young prince[2].

Meanwhile Tigranes had fallen in 'a war with barbarians,' stirred up perhaps by the philo-Parthian nobles in resentment at his submission to Rome, and his death was followed by the abdication of his sister and wife Erato. The Armenian royal family was now extinct, and Gaius in the name of Augustus gave the crown to Ariobarzanes, king of Media since 20 B.C., who, says Tacitus, was readily accepted on account of his singularly handsome person and his noble character[3]. It was not merely for those qualities that he was chosen, but because the Median royal stock was connected with the Armenian by marriage ties, and both countries had been recently ruled by Artaxes[4]. The Parthian faction, however, refused to accept him and raised a revolt (A.D. 2), which Gaius proceeded to suppress. While

[1] The fact is expressed in the remark of Strabo (XI, 515) that the size of the Parthian empire has made it, in a way, a counterpoise to that of Rome, and in that of Pompeius Trogus: *Parthi penes quos velut divisione orbis cum Romanis facta nunc Orientis imperium est* (Justin. XLI, 1, 1).

[2] Vell. Pat. II, 102; Pliny, *N.H.* IX, 118; Tacitus, *Ann.* III, 48.

[3] His appointment appears to have followed the meeting with the Parthian king. The Pisan decree, Dessau 140, ll. 10–11, speaks of Gaius waging war in Armenia (*ultra finis extremas p. R.*) in A.D. 1; but Augustus evidently knew nothing of military operations nor even of the Parthian settlement on Sept. 23 of that year, when he wrote Gaius the letter preserved by Gell. *N.A.* XV, 7, while Dio explicitly dates the outbreak of war in Armenia to A.D. 2, and Velleius states that Gaius entered Armenia after the conference with Phraataces. The campaigning season in Armenia ended about October.

[4] Strabo XI, 523. Augustus favoured intermarriages among client-princes (Suetonius, *Aug.* 48).

attacking the fortress of Artagira (in the province of Ararat, perhaps near Kagyzman in the Araxes valley, some 80 miles west of Artaxata), he allowed himself to be lured on the 9th of September[1] to a conversation with the commandant of the fort, a man named Addon, who pretended to have secret information to give him concerning the treasures of the Parthian king and treacherously wounded him. Thereupon the fort was besieged and captured after a long resistance, and the revolt was crushed, but Gaius did not recover from his wound. His health, never robust, and his spirits were broken. He begged Augustus to let him retire into the seclusion of a Syrian city and was with difficulty persuaded at least to return to Italy. Thither he set sail on an ordinary merchant ship, and died at the Lycian port of Limyra on February 21, A.D. 4[2].

VIII. THE ECLIPSE OF ROMAN INFLUENCE
IN ARMENIA

Such was the tragic end of an expedition which had started with great pomp and high hopes. The net result was the establishment of a *modus vivendi* with Parthia and the restoration of Roman supremacy in Armenia. The understanding with Parthia lasted, despite dynastic changes, beyond the lifetime of Augustus, but ill fortune continued to attend his dispositions in Armenia. Soon after peace had been restored to that distracted country king Ariobarzanes died, to be succeeded by his son Artavasdes, who, like his father, was at the same time ruler of Media. Within a short time he was murdered[3], and Augustus then set on the throne Tigranes IV, whom he describes as a scion of the royal stock of Armenia. He was, beyond reasonable doubt, a grandson of Herod the Great, son of Alexander and Glaphyra, daughter of the Cappadocian king Archelaus, whose first wife was in all probability a princess of the Armenian royal house. With his appointment the record of Augustus ends, and as there appears to be no allusion in the *Res Gestae* to provincial and foreign affairs after A.D. 6, that year was perhaps the approximate date of his accession. He was evidently soon deposed by the Parthian faction[4]. His reign was so brief that Tacitus omits it altogether, naming as the successor of Artavasdes a queen called Erato, who was quickly expelled; she was clearly the wife of Tigranes III, brought back

[1] *C.I.L.* IX, 5290.　　　　　　　[2] Dessau 140, l. 26.
[3] *Res Gestae* 27; cf. Tacitus, *Ann.* II, 4.
[4] He subsequently lived in Rome; he is the Tigranes, *Armenia quondam potitus*, who in A.D. 36 was put to death there (Tacitus, *Ann.* VI, 40).

for a moment to power. Her fall was followed by an interregnum, which lasted till the death of Augustus.

Meantime dynastic revolutions had taken place in Parthia. Soon after the death of Gaius, Phraataces was driven from the throne and replaced by Orodes (Hyrodes), a prince of Arsacid descent, whose excessive cruelty and irascible temper quickly led to his assassination. A Parthian embassy was then sent to Rome to ask for the return of Vonones, the eldest of the sons of Phraates IV, who had lived with his brothers in the capital since 9 B.C., to fill the vacant throne[1]. The embassy was probably that which was sent on to Tiberius while he was engaged in completing the conquest of Germany (A.D. 4–6)[2], and the evidence of Parthian coins indicates that the reign of Vonones began between the autumn of A.D. 6 and A.D. 8–9. His popularity was short-lived: his foreign habits and his indifference to riding and hunting and the other interests of a Parthian gentleman excited the contempt of the nobility; it was intolerable to them that the Arsacid throne should be held by a slave who had brooked bondage for so many years and that it should be bestowed by the Roman emperor, as though Parthia were a Roman province. So they called to the throne Artabanus, an Arsacid on his mother's side, brought up among the Dahae of the steppe country north of Hyrcania, the original homeland of the Arsacids. According to Josephus, he had become king of Media (Atropatene), presumably after the death of the last representative of the native royal house[3]. After an initial defeat he succeeded in establishing himself in A.D. 11–12[4], and Vonones fled to Armenia, then without a ruler, in the hope of securing the crown.

Such was the position at the end of Augustus' reign. Armenia was kingless and had passed from Roman control. The whole involved story of failure after failure to keep the country under

---

[1] Res Gestae 33; Tacitus, Ann. II, 1; Josephus, Ant. XVIII [2, 4], 46 sqq.
[2] Suetonius, Tib. 16.
[3] W. Schur (Orientpolitik des Kaisers Nero, pp. 70 sqq.), developing Kiessling's view (P.W. s.v. Hyrkania, col. 507 sq.), holds that Josephus is wrong, and that the seat of Artabanus' power was the Hyrcanian country, which he had conquered in the dark period of Iranian history A.D. 5–15, while he had secured Media for his brother Vonones (king of Parthia in A.D. 51). This conjecture accords with most of the facts narrated by Tacitus concerning the connection of Artabanus and his son with Hyrcania and the steppe land of the north, but Ann. VI, 36 ascribes the connection to adfinitas. E. Herzfeld believes that Artabanus was an Atropatenian on his father's side, and that his sister married the king of Hyrcania (Sakastan, pp. 61, 74, 86).
[4] In that year the coinage of Vonones ends and that of Artabanus begins.

Roman influence, when all allowance has been made for ill fortune, shows the hopelessness of the task to which Rome had committed herself. The policy of setting a Romanized prince on an eastern throne, whether Armenian or Parthian, was doomed to failure, for a prince sophisticated by long residence in Rome could never win the favour of an Oriental aristocracy; and when, with the exhaustion of the supply of native princes, Augustus varied his policy by choosing nominees from an Eastern royal house friendly to Rome, such nominees, even if suitable in themselves, had to contend against the natural predominance of Parthian sympathies among the majority of the nobles. It was only by the rarest combination of personal qualities and tastes that a ruler appointed by Rome might succeed in maintaining his position; in general, there could be no guarantee of the stability of Roman arrangements unless a military force were stationed in the country or within striking distance of it.

IX. THE DEFENCE OF THE EUPHRATES FRONTIER

Augustus made the province of Syria the pivot of frontier defence in the East. In 27 B.C. he placed it under a *legatus pro praetore* of consular rank, combining with it Cilicia campestris, as geographical and political conditions suggested[1]. The Cilician plain is cut off from Asia Minor by the broad, high wall of Taurus, over which winds for nearly seventy miles the pass of the Cilician Gates, ascending to about 4300 feet at the summit. On the other hand, it is closely attached to Syria, and communication between the two is easy. Cilicia included the eastern slopes of the northern part of the Amanus range and it was joined to Cyrrhestice by the pass over the broad *col* (3140 feet) of Arslanli Bel which led to Nicopolis (Islahiyeh), while on the south it was easily reached from Syria by the 'Syrian Gates,' the Beilan pass, which barely reaches an altitude of 2000 feet. Politically it was separated from Roman territory on the west and north-west by a wedge of hill country which was not under direct Roman rule. The attachment of Cilicia to Syria was therefore natural.

The earliest evidence about the garrison of Syria, which relates to the time when Quinctilius Varus was governor (6–4 B.C.), puts its total strength at three legions. They are to be identified as III Gallica, VI Ferrata, and X Fretensis. In the later years of Augustus (in all probability[2]) a fourth legion, XII Fulminata, was

---

[1] The present writer in *C.R.* XLV, 1931, p. 190.

[2] The presence of a fourth legion is not actually attested till A.D. 23 (Tacitus, *Ann.* IV, 5).

added. From these facts it has usually been inferred that, after the battle of Actium, Augustus assigned to Syria only three legions, and that the garrison remained at that strength during the greater part of his reign. If the inference were valid, it would prove conclusively that Augustus never anticipated any serious danger of aggression on the part of Parthia. It is, however, in itself improbable that, at a time when the course of events in the East could not be foreseen and when no solution of outstanding questions was in sight, the military establishment could have been fixed on such a low scale; and certain facts, notably the transference of two legions from the oversea provinces to Illyricum[1] in A.D. 7 (one at least of which must have belonged to the garrison of Syria), indicate that the normal strength of the garrison was not less, and possibly more, than four legions, and that it had been temporarily reduced when Varus was governor by the absence of one or two legions on service in Galatia[2]. During the Julio-Claudian period the military establishment remained fixed at four legions with their complement of auxiliary troops. The relative smallness of the garrison is striking when it is remembered that the governor had to keep his eye not only on his own province and frontier but also on the various vassal states to north and south, and that there was no other force anywhere else in the East to undertake military operations in Asia Minor[3] or Armenia. The responsibility attaching to the Syrian command is reflected in the fact that it was the highest in rank of all imperial governorships and was held in the later stages, or at the end, of a senator's career.

The legions were quartered not in isolated fortresses, as in the West, but in or close to towns[4]. This was a result of the physical configuration of the country, which precluded the sharp division into civil and military areas that was so marked a feature of provinces like Gaul or Britain; for the fully and partially civilized parts of Syria, the coastal fringe and the inland valleys, were flanked by mountain ranges, which were occupied by robber tribes, and protection was needed against their depredations. The conditions of service made the soldier's life more agreeable than in the West, but they were not equally favourable to the main-

---

[1] Vell. Pat. II, 112, 4; cf. *Jahreshefte* XXI–XXII, Beiblatt, 468 *sqq.* It was probably at this time that XII Fulminata went to Syria.

[2] See p. 272 above. Considerations pointing to this view are set forth by R. Syme in *J.R.S.* XXIII, 1933, pp. 24, 29 *sqq.*

[3] Cf. Tacitus, *Ann.* VI, 41; XII, 55.

[4] *Militia per oppida expleta* (*Ann.* XIII, 35, 3).

tenance of a high standard of discipline and efficiency. Immediate contact with luxurious city life, easy and profitable service in a pleasant climate with no active foe on the frontier[1], the frequent breaking up of the units into detachments for police duties and for the execution of works of military and public utility, and the recruitment of the legions from eastern provinces—all these factors combined to relax military discipline and soon reduced the efficiency of the Syrian formations to a level far below that of the Western legions.

Concerning the distribution of the Syrian forces under Augustus our sources are silent, but the broad features of the system he adopted are indicated by the incidental mention of the standing quarters of two legions four years after his death. The military occupation was limited to the northern part of the province, which alone was under direct Roman administration. The defence of the rest against the raids of the Bedouins of the desert, as well as the maintenance of internal order, was entrusted to the vassal states of Emesa and Ituraea, which continued to rule all the southern portion of the province from Arethusa in the upper valley of the Orontes to the borders of Herod's kingdom. The Ituraean prince, the 'tetrarch' and high-priest Zenodorus, retained for a time almost the whole of his hereditary principality, the valley of Chalcis and Heliopolis with its two flanking ranges of Lebanon and Antilebanon, which were the home of robber tribes, and the adjacent region beyond the Jordan as far as the Haurân, where brigandage and the robbery of caravans were the chief occupation of the natives[2]. But his misgovernment and positive encouragement of robbery for his own profit led in 24 B.C. to military intervention and to the transference of the Transjordan districts of Trachonitis, Batanaea and Auranitis to Herod; and when he died in 20, the intervening district between Galilee and Trachonitis was added to Herod's territory. Six years later the principality was further broken up by the assignation of a large tract in the centre of it to the colonies of veteran soldiers which Agrippa established at Berytus (Beirût)[3] and Heliopolis (Baalbek) to act as

<hr/>

[1] Tacitus, *Hist.* II, 80; Suetonius, *Vesp.* 6, 4.

[2] Strabo XVI, 755–6; Josephus, *Ant.* XV [10, 1–3], 342 *sqq.*; *Bell. Jud.* I [20, 4], 398 *sqq.*

[3] Strabo XVI, 756 and coins (Eckhel, *Doctr. Num.* III, p. 356). 14–13 B.C. is the date given by Eusebius-Hieronymus, but the Armenian version gives 16–15. The colony at Heliopolis, which bore the same title *Col. Iulia Augusta Felix* and was formed from veterans of the same legions, V Macedon, and VIII Aug. (Eckhel, p. 335), was probably founded at the same time.

garrisons and assist in holding the Lebanon tribes in check. Nevertheless these hardy mountaineers continued to give trouble; about A.D. 6/7, during the governorship of Quirinius, a punitive expedition had to be sent against them[1]; but, if difficult to reduce to order, they furnished excellent material for auxiliary regiments. What remained of the Ituraean principality was subsequently divided into the three 'tetrarchies' of Chalcis, Abila in Antilebanon, and Arca at the northern end of Lebanon, which survived under separate or combined rule till the end of the first century[2].

The administrative and military headquarters of the province were at Antioch, which can hardly have been left without a legionary garrison[3], any more than its rival Alexandria, in view of the character of its inhabitants, light-hearted, frivolous, intransigent people, inclined to turbulence. The other legions were stationed on or near the main roads leading north and south from the capital, in positions from which they could doubtless be easily concentrated at need for operations in any direction, but which were plainly chosen with an eye to the maintenance of peace within the province rather than to its defence against external foes. On the north the city of Cyrrhus (Khoros) was selected as the military centre of the quadrilateral forming the northern corner of the province, which extended from Mt. Amanus and the Cilician border to the Euphrates and abutted on the southern boundary of the client-kingdom of Commagene, left by Augustus under the rule of its old dynasty. Cyrrhus, a Seleucid foundation, occupied a strong position commanding the roads to Commagene and to Zeugma (Seleuceia ad Euphratem), situated at Balkis Kaleh, five miles above Birejik[4], which derived its name from a famous pontoon bridge constructed by Seleucus Nicator across the Euphrates, but no longer existing in the Roman period.[5] It was a suitable station for a legion which had to serve the double purpose of covering the capital and of maintaining law and order in a

[1] If Dessau 2683 be genuine. The inscription, long considered a forgery, was ultimately accepted as genuine by Mommsen (*Eph. Ep.* IV, pp. 537 *sqq.*); but its remarkable style and formulae and the character of the lettering cast grave doubt on its authenticity.

[2] Beer in *P.W.* s.v. *Ituraea*; A. H. M. Jones in *J.R.S.* XXI, 1931, pp. 265 *sqq.*   [3] Cf. Josephus, *Bell. Jud.* II [18, 9], 500.

[4] Fr. Cumont, *Études Syriennes*, pp. 119 *sqq.* In the time of Augustus Zeugma belonged to Syria (Pliny, *N.H.* V, 82, based on the commentaries of Agrippa).

[5] No permanent bridge appears to have been maintained in Roman times, but materials for the construction of one were always available (Tacitus, *Ann.* VI, 37, 4; XII, 12, 3; XV, 9, 1).

region where brigandage had long been endemic[1]. The legion placed there was no doubt X Fretensis, which occupied the position in A.D. 18[2]. On the south of Antioch one legion, VI Ferrata, was quartered at or close to Laodiceia (Latakia) on the coast[3]; and we may presume that the remaining legionary site was, as in later times, at Raphaneae (Rafnîyeh) near the borders of the southern principalities, 15 miles north-west of Emesa, on the high ground which slopes down from the coastal range to the Orontes valley.

No legion lay on the Euphrates either in the reign of Augustus or for a long time after his death. It cannot indeed be supposed that there were no troops at all on the river. A position of the strategic importance of Zeugma, which was also a customs station for goods entering Syria from the East, cannot have been left undefended; we may suppose that it was guarded by an auxiliary force, but the distribution of the auxiliary troops is a blank in our knowledge. Scanty as the evidence is, it is sufficient to show that the disposition of the legionary forces was inspired primarily by considerations of internal security. Once a settlement with Parthia was reached and relations between the two empires were adjusted, the main function of the Syrian army was to maintain peace and order in the province and in the adjoining vassal states, not to stand on guard against a menacing foe ready to seize any opportunity of violating the frontier. The effect on the morale of the troops was soon to be revealed: when a serious campaign was contemplated, they always proved unfit to take the field and had to be reinforced by legions brought from the West.

---

[1] Cf. Strabo XVI, 751.   [2] Tacitus, *Ann.* II, 57, 2.
[3] Tacitus, *Ann.* II, 79, 3 (A.D. 19).

CHAPTER X

EGYPT UNDER THE EARLY PRINCIPATE

I. THE STATUS OF EGYPT IN THE EMPIRE

IT is unfortunately difficult, in the present state of the evidence, to determine in any detail the changes which Augustus introduced into the administration and economic machinery of Egypt[1]. Even the initial question of the relation between Egypt and the empire is not free from difficulties[2]. Augustus himself in his *Res Gestae* declares that he 'added Egypt to the dominions of the Roman People,' and more than one ancient author speaks of the country as a province; but a province of the same kind as the other provinces it can hardly be called, and some writers have even represented it as the property of the Emperor and its connection with the empire as personal only. This is to go too far. Egypt was held by a Roman army and in its turn supplied recruits alike to the legions and to the *auxilia*; it was administered not by a procurator of Caesar but by a Prefect, trained in the regular Imperial service; and its revenues went to the central treasury, where they were used, in common with the other moneys there accumulated, for the needs of the empire.

Nevertheless it differed markedly from other provinces in several respects. Its wealth and the importance to the Roman food-supply of the corn which it exported made it a possible source of danger in the hands of a rival; and Augustus, though he nominally handed it over to the Roman People, took special precautions to keep it under his own control. Alone among the provinces administered by him it was governed by an equestrian prefect instead of a man of senatorial rank; and the anomaly was the more obvious because this prefect was in command of a legionary army. Moreover (and in this Egypt stood quite alone in the empire)

---

[1] For abbreviations in the references to papyri see the Bibliography.

[2] For recent discussions of the question see M. A. Levi, *L' esclusione dei senatori romani dall' Egitto Augusteo*, in *Aegyptus*, v, 1924, pp. 231–5; B. A. van Groningen, *L'Égypte et l'Empire, ib.* VII, 1926, pp. 189–202; S. Solazzi, *Di una pretesa legge di Augusto relativa all'Egitto, ib.* IX, 1928, pp. 296–302. Groningen probably underestimates the differences between Egypt and the other Imperial provinces.

senators and *equites illustres* were expressly forbidden to enter the country without the Emperor's permission.

Within the country itself Augustus was frankly the successor of the Ptolemaic kings. In the Egyptian temples he and his successors replaced the divine Ptolemy, were represented on the monuments in the same manner as the Pharaohs of old, received the same divine honours, and were accorded the same titles, though the new position of the country as part of a wider empire was recognized by the addition of the title 'king of kings' to the old 'lord of the two lands.' On the other hand the Greek cult of the living ruler ceased to be a State cult and was continued merely as a communal institution. The Imperial titles usual elsewhere were in Egypt employed only in official Latin documents, and the consular dating was replaced, except in such documents, by the regnal years of the reigning Emperor, an apparent attempt to establish an Era by the *kratesis Kaisaros* or 'dominion of Caesar' having failed to establish itself[1]. The Emperor in fact, though under the early principate he did not, in Greek, bear the royal title, was to his Egyptian subjects no less a king than any of the Ptolemies. The prefect, his representative, who held office at his pleasure and not for a fixed term, was therefore a viceroy, and is indeed so described by both Strabo and Tacitus. On his official visits to the temples he was accorded royal honours; and he sent the traditional offerings to the Nile at Philae and was subject to the ancient taboo which forbade the king to navigate the river during the inundation. He was invested with proconsular powers, his enactments had the force of law, and he could manumit slaves and appoint guardians.

II. DEFENCE: CENTRAL ADMINISTRATION: THE LAND

Through the many centuries of Egyptian history the rulers of the country have always been faced by three main tasks, upon the performance of which the success of their rule has depended; and

---

[1] Wilcken would connect this with a decree of the Senate mentioned by Dio (LI, 19, 6), but see Gardthausen, *Berl. Phil. Woch.* XL, 1920, cols. 619–624. There are considerable difficulties in Wilcken's view. Dio's statement is somewhat obscurely worded, but there seems no reason for referring it to Egypt at all. Would a decree of the Senate have validity there? The reckoning by the *kratesis* occurs, in papyri, only in private documents, mostly from an out-of-the-way village and from the later years of Augustus; and the coins which have been taken to refer to this era do not contain the word *kratesis*. A recently published papyrus, however, *P.S.I.* 1150, is dated in the fourth year of the *kratesis*, and its evidence must now be reckoned with.

just as the surest sign of decay has been the neglect of these, so has a resolute handling of them been the first care of a conquering power. These three tasks are the maintenance of the irrigation system, the preservation of the country's internal unity, and its defence against attack from without. The last subject and that of the military organization generally are treated elsewhere (pp. 243 *sqq.*), but for the sake of completeness some reference must be made to them here.

The establishment, as a result of Petronius' war with the Ethiopians, of the frontier district known as the Dodekaschoinos, which was administered, under the ultimate authority of the *epistrategos* of the Thebaïd, by the *strategos* of the nome of Ombos and Elephantine, and garrisoned by detachments of legionary and auxiliary troops, prevented further trouble for many years to come; and the force left in Egypt by Augustus, three legions, nine cohorts, and three *alae*, was larger than any external danger demanded. Its size was probably dictated in part by a fear of the turbulence and insubordination for which the Egyptians were proverbial, but even so it was larger than was needed; and before A.D. 23 one of the legions had been withdrawn, though without an equivalent reduction of the auxiliary forces, which thenceforward stood in a rather high ratio to the legionary troops. The single legions were commanded not by senatorial *legati* but by *praefecti legionis* chosen from among those who had twice held the first centuriate (*primi pili iterum*) and had attained the highest rank in the equestrian military service. The commander in chief was, of course, the prefect of Egypt. The Egyptian like the Oriental legions generally were recruited largely in the East and as time went on were drawn more and more from Egypt itself. Their recruits were taken primarily from among the Romans and from the privileged Greeks, who were given the Roman citizenship as a preliminary to enlistment. The auxiliary forces were recruited, in principle, from the *peregrini*, in Egypt mainly the hellenized Graeco-Egyptians, who received the citizenship on their discharge; but in the course of time the distinction of status between legions and *auxilia* tended to disappear[1]. The veterans frequently settled as landowners in the villages or nome-capitals, where they played a considerable part, forming, socially if not economically, a sort of rural upper class.

Though Alexandria was the military base of the army, legionary detachments, as well as auxiliary units, were detailed for service

---

[1] If the readings can be trusted, we find in P. Oslo 30, as early as 20 B.C., a centurion (εκατονδρακει!) with the thoroughly Egyptian name of Anchoriphis.

in posts extending the whole length of Egypt to the southern
frontier of the Dodekaschoinos. The duties of the troops were not
merely military. They were employed in the construction and
repair of canals, of cisterns on the desert routes, and of other
public works; they acted as guards, perhaps also in an administrative capacity, in the mines and quarries; and it is probable that
even as early as the reign of Gaius or the later years of Tiberius
they were detached on occasion to assist in the collection of taxes,
thus inaugurating a practice which in the Byzantine age was to
occasion grave abuses. They were further used to augment the
local police. The coasts of Egypt and probably Libya as well were
protected by a fleet known as the *classis Augusta Alexandrina*,
which was also responsible for convoying the grain fleet to Italy.
It was commanded by a prefect, who was further responsible, at a
later date if not from the first, for the river police on the Nile.

In Egypt, which, apart from the Delta, consists in effect of the
long and narrow Nile valley, there has always been a pronounced
tendency, whenever the central authority has grown weak, for the
districts farthest from the seat of government to break away. Our
information as to internal conditions during the last half-century
of Ptolemaic rule is scanty in the extreme, but it may be doubted
whether during much of that time the royal authority was very
effective in Upper Egypt. Certain it is that on the arrival of the
Roman tax-collectors in 30–29 B.C. the Thebaïd, long accustomed
to defy the rulers at Alexandria, rose in revolt. But the rebels
soon found that the Roman army was of another calibre than the
Ptolemaic levies. In a campaign of fifteen days, which included
two pitched battles and the capture of five towns, the first prefect,
Cornelius Gallus, who had already[1] suppressed a revolt at Heroônpolis, crushed the rebellion so effectually that for a century and a
half we hear of no further trouble.

Augustus did not content himself with military measures, but,
like the Ptolemies before him and the Arabs later, reformed the
administrative system in the direction of greater centralization.
Under the later kings of the Ptolemaic dynasty the Thebaïd had
been governed by an official known as the *epistrategos*, who possessed both civil and military powers and towards the end of the
period enjoyed an almost royal authority. Augustus retained this
official and seems even to have left the existing Greek *epistrategos*
in office; but he deprived him of all military power, vesting in the
prefect the ultimate command over the army of Egypt. This

---

[1] That is, if we can assume that this affair, which Strabo XVII, 819
mentions before the revolt of the Thebaïd, actually preceded the latter.

reduction in the importance of the post was emphasized by the appointment, perhaps at the same time, of two similar officials. Egypt was in fact divided into three administrative districts, the Thebaïd, the Delta, and the intervening country, known officially as 'the Seven Nomes and the Arsinoite Nome,' with an *epistrategos* at the head of each. The functions of these officials, who were always (with the sole exception of the Greek just mentioned) Roman knights, were purely civil and administrative. They included the selection of persons nominated for certain liturgical offices, a supervision of the gymnasia, the admission of *ephebi* in the Greek cities, and some judicial powers of a secondary kind; but the *epistrategos*, though often delegated by the prefect to hear cases, had no independent jurisdiction.

In nothing indeed was the centralizing tendency of the new government more marked than in the administration of justice. The Ptolemaic itinerant courts were swept away, at least in their original form, and judicial power was concentrated in the hands of the prefect. He held an annual assize for each of the three areas (not identical with the districts of the *epistrategoi*) into which, for judicial purposes, Egypt was now divided. The venue of the assizes was announced each year; but normally the sessions were held at Alexandria for the nomes of the western Delta, at Pelusium for those of the eastern Delta, and at Memphis for the rest of Egypt. The business was by no means confined to judicial matters. It included a general survey of the local administration, and the various officials concerned were required to submit their accounts and records to audit.

The choice of the assize towns was presumably intended to prevent a time-wasting journey by the prefect into Upper Egypt; but it must have entailed great inconvenience to litigants from the remoter nomes, who had now to make the long journey to Memphis or even farther; for cases from the upper country seem at times to have been heard at Pelusium. This inconvenience was but slightly lessened by occasional changes in the venue of the court. As early as possible in his tenure of office each prefect made a tour of inspection in the Thebaïd, and no doubt sometimes took the opportunity to hold the assizes in that district; but since most prefects probably paid no more than one visit to Upper Egypt, it was but rarely that litigants from the southern nomes were able to have their suits heard locally. Of greater utility was the frequent practice of delegation. The prefect was assisted at the assizes by other officials, acting as his deputies; some suits were referred to local magistrates; and when very contentious cases arose they might be adjourned to the following year, with an injunction for the preliminary enquiries to be made locally.

The prefect was the sole magistrate in Roman Egypt possessing unrestricted independent jurisdiction; but there were others who had limited powers, though probably the prefect alone was competent in criminal cases. Of the officials with judicial power the chief was the Juridicus, who, like the prefect, was a Roman knight and received his commission direct from the Emperor, with authority extending over the whole of Egypt[1]. The Archidicastes also had an authority embracing the whole country, though he was intimately connected with Alexandria, from the leading families of which, usually those possessing the Roman citizenship, most holders of the office were drawn. He was not, as the title suggests, a Chief Justice nor, probably, a judge of appeal, and appears most often in connection with the process of execution and distraint for unpaid debts. He had authority over the *katalogeion* or Public Record Office, was concerned in the registration of *ephebi*, and was the responsible authority in the procedure for giving public validity to private contracts or chirographs. If he had any independent jurisdiction apart from the process of execution for debt, it was probably in cases arising out of contractual obligations.

Jurisdiction, in matters affecting their own departments, was possessed also by the two great financial officers, the *Dioiketes* and the *Idios Logos*. The former, who does not appear under this title in extant papyri until the second century A.D., is probably not to be connected directly with the high Ptolemaic official so called; but the office was clearly one of importance, and the holders of it seem always to have been Romans. Much more is known of the *Idios Logos* or *Idiologos*, an office certainly of Ptolemaic origin but continued by the Romans, apparently with little essential change of function, though with greatly increased importance. The holder of this office was always a knight. The title did not denote anything like our 'Privy Purse,' and is to be translated, not 'private' but 'special account'; the *Idios Logos* was in fact not so much a separate department as a term of book-keeping, and the sums collected went to the central treasury. Broadly speaking, the *Idiologos*, as the procurator at the head of the department was called, was responsible for all irregular or sporadic sources of revenue, notably those derived from ownerless and confiscated property and all species

---

[1] For the Juridicus, besides Mitteis, *Grundzüge*, p. 26 *sq.*, and Pauly-Wissowa, *s.v.*, see especially P. Jörs, *Z. d. Sav.-Stift*. Rom. Abt. xxxix, 1918, p. 102, n. 2; add *B.G.U.* 1019; H. Frisk, *Aegyptus*, ix, 1928, p. 285 *sq.*; *P.S.I.* iii, 222.

of fines. Land taken over, if fertile, was transferred to the category of royal land, but if unproductive was retained under his own control unless and until it could be sold. He claimed all dead trees or dry branches of living trees, even when in private ownership[1]. Fines, confiscations and licences for the unauthorized cultivation of land, for changes of name, for breaches of the laws of status, all fell within his competence; and he appears so often in matters affecting temples, as in the sale of priestly offices, the exaction of dues for the circumcision of priests' sons, and the collection of fines for infringement of regulations, that he was long supposed to be *ex officio* High Priest as well as *procurator idiu logu*; but this is probably an error, so far at least as the first and second centuries are concerned. Not only the local officials and his own special staff but a whole army of informers, some of whom appear to have occupied a semi-official position, aided him in his task; and though it was an exaggeration when the prefect Ti. Julius Alexander declared in an edict that Alexandria was almost depopulated through the activities of these gentry, there can be no doubt that in times of financial stringency the department of the *Idios Logos* was an instrument of fiscal oppression as efficient as it was all-pervading.

The other central officials, procurators, Imperial freedmen and the like, may be disregarded here; but something must be said as to Augustus's ecclesiastical policy, for not only does it further illustrate his centralizing tendency, but the control of the Egyptian church was as essential to the preservation of internal unity as centralization itself. Under the later Ptolemies the influence of the priests had grown steadily, and additional privileges, grants of lands, and extensions of the right of asylum to even minor temples had been wrung from the enfeebled government. Augustus, recognizing the danger of this State within the State, returned to the stricter control of the earlier Ptolemies, which he even strengthened. Considerable confiscations of the temple lands were made, probably in the main from the estates granted by the later kings and managed by the priests themselves. The ordinary sacred land was, as formerly, under the control of the State officials, the relations of its lessees being with them, not with the temples. Apart from particular exceptions, the priests continued to receive a stipend from the government, and the taxes paid for sacred purposes formed a special department of the revenue; but the

---

[1] See now P. Tebt. III, 1, p. 98, where the editors justly remark that all trees (alive or dead) *on public embankments* would naturally be under the supervision of the *Idiologos*.

very fact that the priesthood was dependent on State support was a guarantee against insubordination. It was probably to the same end that the management of the temples was transferred, in many cases at least, from the single overseer of Ptolemaic times to a college or committee of the priests; for a division of power seemed less dangerous than its concentration in the hands of one man. But the most effective measure was the subjection, either by Augustus himself or by a later emperor, of the whole ecclesiastical organization to a central authority, that of the 'High Priest of Alexandria and all Egypt.' This functionary, who, despite his title, was no priest but a Roman civil official, exercised a strict control over all the details of cult and temple organization. Each temple was required to send to the *strategos* of the nome an annual list of its priests and property, together with its accounts. The priests must even resign themselves to losing some of their special privileges. The exemption from poll-tax which they had enjoyed under the Ptolemies was continued, but in a restricted form, a fixed number of priests being assigned to each temple and all in excess of that figure being rendered liable to the tax. Priests were not even, in principle, exempt from liability to liturgical offices and the *corvée*, though particular cases of exemption are recorded. Yet effective as these measures were in curtailing the power of the priesthood, and though the interest of the Roman government in the religious organization of Egypt seems to have been primarily fiscal, it is by no means certain that the true drift of the new policy was perceived at the time. Not for nearly two centuries after the conquest do we hear of any disorders in which the priests were concerned. Augustus continued, like the Ptolemies, to protect the ancient religion of the country and to build or enlarge temples; and the strict control over the priests and their property, if it implied a limitation of their powers, at least guaranteed their subsistence. They were Danaan gifts that Caesar gave to the Egyptian church, but it may well be that only the more far-seeing priests knew them for such[1].

The third of the three great tasks which have always confronted the rulers of Egypt is the most vital of all; for upon the maintenance of the dykes and canals depends the very possibility of organized life in the rainless Nile valley. Times of political disorganization and economic decay have always been marked by a shrinkage of the cultivable area, necessitating, as soon as a more capable government was established, an attempt to reclaim the land

[1] Some useful material on the priests of Tebtunis will be found in the recently published vol. x of *P.S.I.*

which had fallen waste. It is clear that the state of agriculture had deteriorated in the later Ptolemaic period, and Octavian found it advisable, like the early Ptolemies before and the Arab conquerors after him, to undertake a reform of the irrigation system. He employed his troops in the task of cleaning and deepening the neglected canals, and so effective were his measures that, according to Strabo[1], whereas before the Roman conquest a time of abundance occurred only with a rise of fourteen cubits in the level of the Nile, and a rise of eight meant famine, in the prefecture of Petronius a rise of only twelve produced a record harvest and there was no scarcity when the rise was but eight cubits. For the further maintenance of the dykes and canals the immemorial *corvée*, by which the peasantry were compelled to give their labour, was maintained by the Romans, but with some changes, notably in the method of reckoning the quota of labour.

It was not sufficient to improve the irrigation; the lands which had fallen waste under the later Ptolemies must be brought into cultivation again. In the measures taken to this end Augustus followed essentially the methods employed by his predecessors, bringing to their logical conclusion tendencies already marked before the conquest. The Ptolemaic king, like the Pharaoh before him, was in theory sole owner of all the land in Egypt, and the fertile arable land was in fact for the most part retained under his control and cultivated on leases of indefinite duration by the 'royal tenants'; but considerable areas, chiefly of the less productive land, were 'released' from the direct control of the king. The released land included various categories, but all alike belonged ultimately to the king; nor, despite a tendency towards an increasing security of tenure, does it appear from our evidence that a true ownership ever developed under the Ptolemies.

On the conquest the whole land of Egypt fell to Octavian, who transferred it to the Roman People. The main categories continued, but considerable changes were made. The tenure of the katoikic land or military allotments of the Greek settlers naturally ceased to be military, and much of it was confiscated. The remainder was treated frankly as private property, subject to a tax in kind, and of the confiscated allotments portions were sold to private purchasers. This land continued, however, to form a separate category and was entered in a special register.

Just as the Roman government transformed the military tenures into full property (to the extent, that is, to which Roman law recognized private property in the provinces), so did it abandon the theory of the royal ownership of the so-called 'private' land.

---

[1] XVII, 788.

Indeed the formation of private property was actively forwarded, whether by selling barren or derelict land at a fixed price, with exemption from taxes for a given period and thereafter payment of the one-artaba tax, or by offering confiscated land for sale by auction to the highest bidder. Conditions no doubt varied greatly, but it is clear that the agrarian history of the Roman period was characterized by a great extension of private property in land and by the growth of a class of peasant proprietors. The policy was dictated less by any regard for the interests of the populace than by the desire to see the financial responsibilities of the cultivators backed by guarantees; for land was the most concrete and most accessible form of property.

The domain land still played an important rôle, comprising as it did the majority of the more fertile soil. As of old, it was leased to the 'royal' (now 'public') tenants on an indefinite lease; at irregular intervals fresh distributions were made, but a lease could be terminated at any time if an offer of higher rent was received. The rents varied according to the quality of the soil; and in times of depression, in order to attract tenants, special rates were offered. If voluntary tenants were lacking, compulsion, already employed exceptionally in a crisis by the Ptolemies, was resorted to; but this practice, which took various forms, and was eventually to become a burdensome abuse, hardly falls within the period covered by this chapter, though there are occasional indications of it in the first century.

Though a good deal of sacred land was confiscated, this category was not abolished. The Ptolemaic 'gift land' finds a Roman analogy in the domains (ousiai) which were created in great numbers during the early Principate, probably in part out of confiscated estates, and were granted to or purchased by members of the Imperial family, Imperial freedmen, and prominent private persons, Roman or Alexandrine[1]. These domains, which probably included a good proportion of fertile land, were leased partly to tenants of the same class as the royal tenants, partly to large-scale lessees. From the time of Claudius, and particularly in that of Nero, they fell in rapid succession into the possession of the emperor; and by the reign of Titus most, if not all, belonged to the Imperial *patrimonium*. Probably at that period a change was made in their administration, and it may have been then that the

---

[1] A list of these οὐσίαι (with new material later than in the English edition) is given by M. Rostovtzeff, *Gesellschaft und Wirtschaft im röm. Kaiserreich*, II, pp. 294–6. See also Italian edit. pp. 338 *sqq.* To this list add now: Claudius, P. Mich. Tebt. 121 Recto, I, xii (Tebtunis); Germanicus, P. Mich. Tebt. 123 Recto, xvii, 30 (Tebtunis).

office of *procurator usiacus*, to manage this class of land, was created. But the later history of the domains lies outside the scope of this chapter. Not so with regard to another class of public land, the so-called 'revenue land,' which can be traced back at least to the middle of the first century. Its nature is still in dispute, but it seems likely that it was land which had in some way passed, permanently or for a time, out of private into Imperial possession.

III. THE GREEK CITIES AND THE NATIONALITIES

After the fall of Alexandria Octavian, in a Greek speech, promised the citizens an amnesty, and he further pleased them by paying a ceremonial visit to the tomb of Alexander; but he declined to inspect the mummies of the Ptolemaic kings, and seems indeed to have made no extraordinary effort to conciliate Alexandrian loyalty. He confirmed all the privileges of the city, which he left, as he had found it, the capital of Egypt.

It is a striking example of the fragmentary and haphazard character of our evidence for the history of Graeco-Roman Egypt that we know so little of the constitution and administrative system of this city, the greatest in the eastern Mediterranean, and in the Empire second only to Rome. Even the question whether Octavian found a senate there is still in dispute. It is a reasonable supposition that Alexander established one, but we have no clear evidence of its existence during the Ptolemaic period, and it is certain that there was none under the Empire until the reign of Septimius Severus. It is often asserted that Octavian abolished it; but the weight of evidence favours the view that if Alexandria ever had a senate it had ceased to exist before the Roman period. If the Caesar mentioned in a recently discovered papyrus fragment is to be identified with Octavian, it would appear that the Alexandrines, either immediately after the conquest or, more probably, at a later period in his reign, made an unsuccessful attempt to obtain a senate, as we know that they did after the accession of Claudius[1].

We hear nothing of any popular assembly, but some machinery there must have been for expressing the corporate will of the city and electing the magistrates. Of the four magistrates whom Strabo mentions, the only one whom we can regard as certainly municipal was the *exegetes*, who seems to have been originally the chief

[1] Recent discussions of this subject are summarized and the above conclusions defended in detail by H. I. Bell in *Aegyptus*, XII, 1932, pp. 173–84. See further, P. Viereck, *Noch einmal die* ΒΟΥΛΗ *von Alexandreia, ib* pp.210–16; U. Wilcken, *Arch. Pap.* X, 1932, p. 255 *sq.*

of the Alexandrian magistrates, and who was particularly concerned with the enrolment of the *ephebi*. The gymnasiarch, who at an earlier time may well have been a private or semi-private functionary, is more prominent than the *exegetes* in the texts of the Roman period, and it is possible that Augustus reorganized municipal administration, giving the gymnasiarch the principal place. Associated with the gymnasiarch in his supervision of the gymnasium and the games connected with it was the *kosmetes*. Among others of whom we hear were the eutheniarch, responsible for the food-supply, the *agoranomos*, in charge of the market and notarial business, and the *hierothytai*. Whether all of these magistrates existed throughout the Roman period, what was their method of election, what the qualifications required, and whether their authority extended over the whole population or only over the full citizens—these are questions which may be answered with greater or less degrees of probability, but no certainty can be attained at present.

Under the Ptolemies Alexandria had its own law-courts, and two of these continued after the conquest, lasting at least till the 26th year of Augustus, after which they are not heard of again and probably disappeared; but even before that date the extant papyri of the reign of Augustus do not show them exercising any functions which can be regarded as strictly judicial, their activities being confined to a peculiar kind of legal contract known as *synchoresis*. Their place was taken later by the Archidicastes and his bureau, the *katalogeion*, which was also concerned in the enrolment of *ephebi* and during the Roman period developed from a municipal institution into a Record Office for Egypt at large.

It has already been implied that the actual citizens were not the only element in the population of Alexandria, and indeed they were certainly a minority there. Even among them there were grades. The full citizens were those enrolled in tribes and demes. The important and constant element was the deme rather than the tribe, and during the Ptolemaic and earlier Roman period it was customary, since the deme-names of Alexandria and Ptolemaïs differed, to describe a citizen of either city by his deme only. The tribe-names were more fluid; thus we know that Claudius sanctioned a proposal to name a tribe in his honour. Sweeping changes were made in the nomenclature from the reign of Nero onwards; at the same time the relations of demes and tribes were altered, and it became the practice to describe citizens by both tribe and deme.

Besides these deme-members there were citizens of inferior right, belonging to no deme. The letter of Claudius to the

Alexandrines shows, indeed, that the prerequisite for citizenship (special grants excepted) was not membership of a deme but admission to the ephebate, a privilege granted only to the sons of former ephebes, whose qualifications were examined before admission, and who were then enrolled in symmories.

In the absence of a senate and possibly of an assembly citizenship carried only limited political rights, but it offered substantial advantages. It was the essential preliminary, for natives of Egypt, to the Roman citizenship; it gave the right to enter the legions, as well as immunity from poll-tax and from the obligation to liturgies and similar burdens throughout the rest of Egypt; and it naturally carried much social prestige.

Alexandria had from the first contained a considerable Egyptian population, whose number probably grew with time. There were also many Greeks who were not citizens. The Macedonians formed a special class, outside the citizen body; and we hear of Phrygians and of Persians of the *epigone*; but it is doubtful whether any of these national groupings survived the reign of Augustus, with the one exception of the Jews. Settled in the city from an early period of its existence, at first in the 'Delta' quarter but spreading later to a second quarter also, the Jewish community enjoyed marked privileges. Not indeed citizens, they were to this extent actually superior to the Alexandrines, that they had a council of elders (*gerousia*). At the head of the community, perhaps the president of the *gerousia*, was an official called ethnarch or genarch, who enjoyed powers of jurisdiction. The Jews possessed a special archive and their own courts; but we have no documentary evidence as to the law and procedure which obtained there.[1]

Diodorus states on the authority of the registration officials that in his day the free inhabitants of Alexandria numbered over 300,000[2]. If we add to these the slaves and the floating population always present in a great commercial capital and seaport, we shall arrive at a figure of about half a million. Fierce, fickle, turbulent, pleasure-loving, flippant in speech and ready of wit, always apt to be stirred by some popular song or ribald jest into incalculable action, divided by racial feuds, and subject to sudden accesses of political violence or religious fanaticism, the people of Alexandria were a perpetual anxiety to their Roman rulers. But if they were

---

[1] E. R. Goodenough's attempt, in *The Jurisprudence of the Jewish Courts in Egypt*, to reconstruct from Philo's writings an outline of the law actually administered in the Jewish community seems to the present writer only partially successful.   [2] XVII, 52, 6 (of the time of Augustus).

unruly and licentious they were certainly industrious. Alexandria was now at the zenith of its fortunes; trade and industry prospered, the population increased, and the city, with its broad, well-lighted thoroughfares lined by colonnades and adorned with splendid public buildings, must have presented an impressive spectacle. Its intellectual life was centred in the Museum, now as under the Ptolemies a State institution, supported by a regular subvention and under the direction of an official of equestrian rank appointed by the emperor. Though it was probably an institute for research rather than for teaching, its professors were free to give instruction and no doubt often did so. It cannot be said at this period to have been responsible for any work of paramount importance, but it still boasted scholars of some standing; and its activity was paralleled in the Jewish community by a group of writers whose leading representative was Philo. It was in truth by no mere accident that Alexandria became later the seat of that Christian catechetical school to which the names of Clement and Origen have given an unfading lustre.

Besides Alexandria there were, before the founding of Antinoopolis, only two Greek cities in Egypt, Naucratis and Ptolemaïs. We know even less of them than of Alexandria, but concerning Ptolemaïs we may draw some inferences from what is known of it under the Ptolemies. It is certain that it then possessed both a senate and an assembly; and though we have no documentary mention of either between the Roman conquest and A.D. 202, there is no sufficient reason to suppose that Augustus abolished them. As at Alexandria the citizens were enrolled in tribes and demes; but there was no reorganization of these under Nero. It is likely that they enjoyed in general the same privileges as Alexandrines, but this cannot be proved in detail.

The position of the Greek cities was quite exceptional. The nome-capitals (*metropoleis*), though called *poleis*, were not to Greek conceptions cities in the proper sense, but merely glorified villages. They possessed none of the marks of a *polis*, neither senate nor assembly, no organization by tribes and demes, and originally no civic magistrates; and they were as much under the authority of the nome officials as any part of the nome. There was however, alike in them and in the villages, a non-Egyptian element, the military settlements established by the Ptolemies. The settlers, Macedonians, Phrygians, etc., were organized in racial unions or *politeumata*, both Greek and oriental; but all alike were more or less hellenized, were regarded by the natives as Greeks, and in course of time came to be in some sort a unified group of 'Hellenes' as opposed to the native 'Egyptians.' The prevailing view, that the effect of the Roman conquest was to reinforce the Greek element in Egypt and correspondingly to depress the status of the Egyptians, has recently been called in question[1]. Bickermann holds that from the reign of Augustus all inhabitants of Egypt except the citizens of the Greek cities were to the Romans 'Egyptians'; and though he has to admit some difficulties, for which no solution has yet been discovered, his theory seems in the main to be well-founded.

The Romans recognized and indeed emphasized a difference between Hellenic and Egyptian culture, but the actual distinction which they made for administrative purposes was one between the inhabitants of the *metropoleis* and those of the villages. Accustomed to self-governing municipalities in the provinces, they did introduce in Egypt certain elements which bore some resemblance to municipal institutions, though nothing that can properly be called municipal government. They initiated in fact a process of development which was to lead, with the grant of the senates in the reign of Septimius Severus, to at least a semi-municipalization, and later on to the transformation of Egypt from a country divided into nomes, each with a *metropolis*, into one of *poleis* or *civitates*, each with its *territorium*. On the assumption, doubtless justified to a considerable extent, that the inhabitants of the nome-capitals were likely to be more deeply imbued with Hellenic culture than mere villagers, the metropolites, though they paid poll-tax like other 'Egyptians,' were assessed, if of metropolitan descent on both sides, at a lower rate, which varied from *metropolis* to *metropolis*, but was always substantially lower than the standard rate paid by villagers. Simultaneously the *politeumata* seem to have been abolished, and a momentous change was made in the administration of the *metropoleis*. The typical expression of Hellenic culture and the centre of Hellenic life was the gymnasium, and its existence, wherever Greeks settled in any considerable number, was as much a matter of course as the club and cricket-field wherever the modern Englishman is found. In Ptolemaic Egypt gymnasia are widely recorded, not only in the nome-capitals but in country villages. In the more important centres they acquired a status which gave them a semi-official air;

---

[1] By E. Bickermann, in *Arch. Pap.* VIII, 1927, p. 239; IX, 1928, pp. 40–43. His theory is attacked by E. Schönbauer in *Z. d. Sav.-Stift.* Rom. Abt. XLIX, 1929, pp. 345–403 and V. Arangio-Ruiz, *Persone e famiglia*, pp. 23–43. Their arguments are very damaging to Bickermann's view so far as the Ptolemaic period is concerned but do not seem to invalidate his main conclusions as to Roman policy.

but nowhere in the *chora*, and perhaps not even in Alexandria, were they official institutions. It may have been Augustus who made the Alexandrian gymnasiarch a regular municipal magistrate; it was certainly he who gave official recognition to the gymnasiarchs of the nome-capitals, and with them, in imitation of Alexandrian institutions, to a group of magistrates who bore titles familiar in the Greek city-states, the *exegetes*, the *kosmetes*, the chief priest, the *agoranomos*, the eutheniarch, and the *hypomnematographos*. It is not certain that these magistrates formed a corporation from the first, but they certainly did later; and in them on the one side and the privileged metropolites on the other we may recognize the nuclei of a senate and an assembly or *demos*.

Not all metropolites were eligible for the magistracies. True to her principle of favouring everywhere an aristocratic form of government, Rome established a superior class within the metropolite body, that known as 'the gymnasium class.' Only members of this were entitled to that education in the gymnasium which was as much the hall-mark of social superiority as a public school education has been in England, and only they were eligible for election to the magistracies. They formed a closed hereditary caste within the community, probably corresponding with the class of ephebes at Alexandria; and like the Alexandrines they were eligible for the ephebate, to which they were admitted after an examination of their credentials. Yet this privileged aristocracy was not exempt from the reduced poll-tax and was not necessarily of pure Greek blood. As if to mark more decisively the difference between the 'Egyptian' villages and the hellenized *metropoleis*, the village gymnasia disappeared with the introduction of the new order in the latter[1].

All the available evidence converges to show that these changes were made about A.D. 4–5 and were part of a carefully thought-out policy. But we cannot speak dogmatically of a clean-cut distinction between Romans and citizens of the Greek cities on the one side and 'Egyptians' on the other nor, among the latter, between metropolites and inhabitants of the villages. As has been already mentioned, there are some unsolved problems. Among these is the question of the *katoikoi*, or military settlers. Though the katoikic land continued to be classed as a separate category, the *katoikoi* seem to occur as a special class only in the Arsinoite nome, where they were perhaps identical with a caste known as

---

[1] For the village gymnasia see F. Zucker, Γυμνασίαρχος κώμης, in *Aegyptus*, XI, 1930, pp. 485–96. The latest date yet recorded for such a gymnasium is A.D. 2 (*B.G.U.* 1201).

'the 6475 Greek men in the Arsinoite nome.' Practically nothing is known as to this body or as to the Greeks of the Delta and the Thebaïd, who are mentioned in an inscription; nor is it quite beyond doubt that the *katoikoi* were, as generally stated, exempt from poll-tax[1].

Naturally, in a population so nicely graded, some machinery for determining status was indispensable. The means adopted was the so-called *epicrisis*, in regard to which there were two somewhat different modes of procedure. The *epicrisis* of Roman citizens, whether veterans or youths, and of Alexandrines (possibly too the citizens of the other Greek cities, though this is doubtful), was conducted by the prefect, either personally or by deputy; that of the Graeco-Egyptians of various classes by local officials, varying in different nomes. The object was always the same, to determine status, though the ultimate motive was no doubt fiscal. It should be added that slaves were subject to *epicrisis* equally with their masters, whose condition, in this respect, they followed[2].

IV. LOCAL ADMINISTRATION: TAXATION

In the sphere of local government the Roman conquest brought little immediate change. At the head of the nome administration was still the *strategos*, now quite divested of military power but otherwise uniting in his own person all the functions of government. The *strategoi*, drawn most often from the wealthier Graeco-Egyptian class, though Roman or Alexandrian citizens are also found among them, were appointed by the prefect, normally for three years. The next to them in rank was not the nomarch, now a mainly financial official, but the royal scribe, who even in the Imperial period retained this immemorial title. His functions too were mainly financial, but he had some share in the general administration and usually acted as *strategos* during a vacancy in that office.

The nome was normally divided into toparchies, each with a toparch and a scribe; and below them in the administrative scale came the village scribe, who was charged with every kind of business affecting the financial administration. His counterpart in the *metropolis* was the scribe (or rather scribes, for there were

---

[1] See below, p. 302 *sq*. The *katoikoi* may have replaced in the Arsinoite nome the gymnasium class, which is not attested for Arsinoe. If so, they should, by analogy, have paid the reduced poll-tax. They are contrasted with λαογραφούμενοι; but that word probably means 'paying the *full* poll-tax.'

[2] For the *epicrisis* see, among many others, J. Lesquier, *L'armée romaine d'Égypte*, pp. 155–201; E. Bickermann, *Arch. Pap.* IX, 1928, pp. 30–5.

generally two) of the city; and in each of the quarters or *amphoda*
into which most *metropoleis* were divided was an amphodarch, to
whom, in the third century, was added a scribe of the *amphodon*.

All these were State officials, but there were others who may
be described as organs and representatives of the community.
Such were, in the nome-capitals, the semi-municipal magistrates
mentioned in the preceding section; in the village, the elders and
the guards of all kinds. There were of course many other officials
of various grades, charged with such special functions as the
inspection of crops, the labour on the dykes, the collection of
tolls and taxes, and so forth; but exigencies of space exclude the
mention of any but the *bibliophylakes*, who were in charge of the
Public Record Office of the nome, situated in the *metropolis*. This
was an innovation of the Roman period, probably introduced about
the middle of the first century. There was at first only one such
institution in each nome, but eventually (in the Arsinoite nome
not long after A.D. 72, somewhat later in other nomes) it was
divided, and henceforth there was one office for official documents,
such as census and taxation rolls, land registers, and the like, and
another for private contracts, particularly those concerning real
property, each under the supervision of two *bibliophylakes*.

Apart from these institutions and the incipient municipalization
of the nome-capitals referred to in the previous section, there was
to all appearance little that was new in the Roman administrative
system. The real and far-reaching change which Roman rule
brought, and that very gradually and hardly at all in the period
covered by this chapter, lay in the basis rather than in the details
of the system. The Ptolemaic bureaucracy was in the main a
professional one. In times of depression or political anarchy applicants for the administrative posts might be wanting, and then the
sovereign State did not scruple to resort to compulsion; but such
cases were quite exceptional. This salaried bureaucracy was at
first continued by the Romans, perhaps for nearly a century after
the conquest, but gradually recourse was had, at first sporadically
and then more and more generally, to the liturgical system, by
which all persons possessing the necessary property qualification
and not otherwise exempt were compelled to undertake certain
offices. The principle was of course no Roman invention; but its
substitution for the Ptolemaic bureaucracy was a change of fateful
importance. Beginning probably with the minor local offices, it
spread farther and farther up the administrative hierarchy; and
though there was always in theory a distinction between the
liturgy and the once coveted municipal offices, between *munera*

and *honores*, yet by the middle of the second century the principle of compulsion was already well established for the latter as well. In fact the only difference between liturgy and magistracy came at length to lie in the qualifications and social status of the persons conscribed. Along with the liturgical system went the principle of collective responsibility: the community, as in the case of the village officials, or the class, as with the municipal magistrates, was responsible alike for the proposal of the liturgists and for their proper performance of their duties. The system was disastrous in its effects; and just as the heavy burden of taxation crushed the poorest members of the community, so was the middle class, higher and lower alike, impoverished by the liturgies and liturgical magistracies. These developments fall, it is true, outside the scope of this chapter; but the edict of the prefect Tiberius Julius Alexander (A.D. 68) suggests that the principle was even then creeping into practice, though perhaps not yet officially recognized[1].

It is possible that the first introduction of the liturgical system was connected with a change in the method of tax-collection. Under the Ptolemies the taxes had been farmed, in accordance with the usual Greek practice; but at least as early as the reign of Tiberius we find some of them collected by *praktores*, acting directly under the State; and since these men were responsible with their property for the raising of the statutory amount, and at the beginning of the second century were certainly liturgists appointed by and in the community which formed the sphere of their work, it is at least a plausible suggestion that the reason for the change of machinery was precisely to secure that corporate responsibility which was the essence of the liturgical system as developed in Roman Egypt. The old method was retained for some taxes, and doubtless the employment of *praktores* was only gradually extended; roughly we may say that the indirect taxes in general were farmed, the direct ones collected by State officials.

The total quota of taxes was fixed by the emperor himself, and the prefect had no power to vary the amount. The actual taxes were for the most part the same as in the Ptolemaic period; and they were both numerous and, to the modern investigator, confusing. The chief novelty was the poll-tax (*laographia*); for though it is now known that a similar tax existed even under the kings, it had a different name, and its incidence was probably not the same as in the Roman period. As already said, the 'metropolites' were

---

[1] Philo's words of Lampon (*in Flaccum*, 130), ἠναγκάσθη γὰρ γυμνασιαρχεῖν, show that even at Alexandria, and as early as the reign of Tiberius, municipal office was not always entirely voluntary.

assessed at a lower rate. Romans and the citizens of the Greek cities, a certain number of priests and possibly the *katoikoi* and other 'Greeks' were wholly exempt. The rest of the male population between the ages of fourteen and sixty[1] paid the full poll-tax at rates which for some unexplained reason varied widely not only from nome to nome but even in different localities within a single nome.

The money taxes fell into various classes. Some, like the *laographia*, were assessed on a capitation basis, others were in the nature of licences; and there were also taxes on sales, on sacrifices, on domestic animals, and a 'crown tax,' in theory a gift to a new ruler, which became later a regular impost and was as burdensome an abuse as the 'benevolences' of Tudor and Stuart times in England. There was a developed system of tolls and customs, not only at Coptos, which formed the Egyptian end of the Red Sea route, or Schedia, where the traffic up and down the Nile paid toll, but at points like the chief exits from the Fayûm or Arsinoite nome.

Various kinds of land-tax are found, corresponding to the various classes of land and payable partly in money, partly in kind. The chief corn-tax varied in amount between one and two artabas per aroura[2]. On vineyards, orchards and garden-land generally were levied money-taxes, differing among themselves in amount and incidence. The corn-taxes were delivered to the *sitologoi* at the local granaries, whence the corn was conveyed by donkeys or camels to the places of embarkation for transport to Alexandria, the transport being managed by the 'public livestock-breeders,' who were organized as a guild and in later times discharged their functions as a compulsory liturgy, though they were paid fees for the carriage[3].

To the great quantities of corn collected for the corn-tax must be added the grain paid as rent in kind on the royal, sacred, public, and domain land, some at least of which was probably added to the tax-corn to make up the quota sent annually to Rome,

[1] But see P. Princ. Univ. 8, VII, 1, where a man of 62 is found paying *syntaximon*, which was probably a form of the *laographia* (see against the view taken in P. Princ. Univ., pp. xxi–xxiii, Clinton W. Keyes, *Am. Journ. Phil.* LII, 1931, pp. 263–9, 288–9; W. L. Westermann, *Class. Weekly*, XXV, 14 Dec. 1931, pp. 69–70; P. Col. II, p. 39). There may however have been some special reason for this.

[2] The aroura is rather more than half an acre. The artaba varies. A common measure under the Empire was about 30 litres.

[3] In addition to earlier treatments of the subject of transport (*e.g.* M. San Nicolò, *Äg. Vereinswesen*, I, pp. 111–24; F. Oertel, *Liturgie*, pp. 115–31), see H. Frisk, *Bankakten aus dem Faijûm*, pp. 10–36; P. Col. II, pp. 103–14.

where, we are told, a third of the year's supply came from Egypt. The conveyance from Alexandria to Rome was the task of the *classis Alexandrina*. The granaries at Alexandria, in which the corn was stored after receipt, were situated in the quarter known as Neapolis, and were placed under the charge of the *procurator Neaspoleos et Mausolei*[1].

These regular imposts were not the only burdens which the tax-payer had to bear. There were also requisitions of provisions and other necessaries for the periodic tours of inspection of the prefect, *epistrategoi* or other officials, or for the rarer visits of the Emperor himself or some member of the Imperial family. The needs of the army, not only in provisions but in clothing and other supplies, were met by similar requisitions, whether by way of tax or, as in the case of the *frumentum emptum*, by forced sales, the amount required being determined by the prefect and the distribution among villages and the single contributors carried out by the officials of the nome and of the village respectively. Not till the end of the second century do we find the *annona militaris* established as a regular tax.

This complicated system of taxation necessitated an equally elaborate system of registers and taxing-lists to determine the amounts due from each tax-payer. The personal registers rested ultimately on the fourteen-year census, which in the Roman period replaced the annual returns of Ptolemaic times. The earliest recorded instance of the census can be dated with practical certainty in the year A.D. 20, but it has been inferred (since the Ptolemaic institution of annual returns is known to have been in force as late as 18 B.C.) that the new system was introduced in 10–9 B.C.[2]

A return was required from every householder (usually from the owner), in which he specified all the occupants of the house; and hence the census was called 'the house-to-house registration.' The returns were addressed, generally in duplicate, to the ordinary local officials and to a special commission of *laographoi* or to some of them; and since personal attendance was required, the prefect issued an edict requiring all persons absent from home, unless

---

[1] On the Alexandrian granaries and corn supply see U. Wilcken, *Hermes*, LXIII, 1928, pp. 48–65.

[2] A. Calderini, *La più antica scheda di censimento romano proveniente dall' Arsinoite*, in *Rend. R. Ist. Lomb.* LXIV, 1931, pp. 551–8, holds that the census of A.D. 19–20 was the first of the fourteen-year series. His view rests in the main on a comparison of statements of age; but it is certain that these were often by no means exact, and it is hazardous to place so much reliance on them as Calderini does in this case.

specially exempted, to return for the enrolment. On the basis of the single returns were prepared elaborate registers showing, quarter by quarter, or street by street, and house by house, the whole population, with age and status and careful note of all exemptions[1].

The period of fourteen years was no doubt adopted because it was at fourteen that boys became liable to poll-tax; but between one census and another the registers were kept up to date by returns of births, probably compulsory, and of death, which, since their effect was exemption from the liability to poll-tax, were left to the initiative of the tax-payers. Voluntary too were the applications for the *epicrisis* of those claiming to belong to one of the privileged classes; and these returns also were united in composite rolls and used in the preparation of special registers.

Parallel with this personal registration was the procedure in respect of property. Annual returns of livestock were required; indeed, in the case of sheep and goats we hear of two returns in the year[2]. The census itself, since it was based on the returns of householders, furnished a register of house property; and among the duties of the property Record Office mentioned above was that of keeping a register of real property[3], which recorded not only ownership but all such liens as arose from hypothecation, dower rights, and government claims against State debtors. The official notarial offices periodically sent to the archives copies and abstracts of the contracts drawn up by them, and it was forbidden to alienate or encumber property thus registered without the authorization of the *bibliophylakes*. At intervals, whenever the registers of the office were found to be in disorder, which happened not infrequently, the prefect ordered general returns of property, on the basis of which new registers were prepared.

Even more meticulous and elaborate was the procedure in registering land of all categories, as was natural in a country where year by year the inundation not only obliterated landmarks but altered the relative fertility and even, by erosion or the deposition of silt, the conformation of holdings. Defect or excess of water or an accumulation of sand might justify partial or even total remission of taxes or rents due, and all such variations from the normal were reported to the responsible authorities, the statements being of course checked by an official inspection; and as in the Ptolemaic

---

[1] A useful list of extant returns and census lists is given by A. Calderini, *Le schede di censimento dell' Egitto romano* (Comitato italiano per lo studio dei problemi della popolazione, 1932), pp. 4–8.

[2] See P. Ross.-Georg. II, p. 54 *sq.*

[3] Slaves were also entered in the registers of the βιβλιοθήκη.

period, detailed registers were kept of all land, arranged both geographically, by areas, and personally, by holders.

V. INDUSTRY AND COMMERCE: CURRENCY

The Roman period was marked, as by a great extension of private property in land, so also by increased freedom of trade. The protective policy of the Ptolemies seems to have been abandoned; for though duties were certainly levied at the points of entry into the country, they were probably imposed for the purpose of revenue rather than as a protective tariff. The system of State monopolies, so characteristic of Ptolemaic Egypt, was maintained under the Emperors but in modified and restricted forms. Indeed, since licences were regularly granted for the exercise of monopolized industries, we should perhaps speak less of monopolies in the strict sense than of State-controlled undertakings, many carried on by private enterprise under official supervision[1].

In the country districts industry was usually on a small scale and served local needs only, but at Alexandria and perhaps in the Delta capitalistic enterprise was doubtless common enough, though the paucity of evidence forbids any insight into its methods. Alexandria was a manufacturing as well as a commercial centre, and a large proportion of the export-goods of Egypt (p. 398 *sq.*) must have been produced there. The mines and quarries were placed at first under the charge of an official known as the *archimetallarches*, who administered them through a procurator; but the title is not found in later times, when the same authority was exercised by the *praefectus montis Berenicidis*. The quarries were exploited in part directly by the State, in part through contractors or lessees; how far there was any private property in them or in the mines is doubtful. The actual work was performed by convicts, prisoners of war, and slaves, but also by free labourers. Egypt produced, besides emeralds, several kinds of stone, particularly porphyry and granite, which were valued abroad and which must therefore be reckoned among the exports.

The exports of Egypt were indeed greater than the imports, according to Strabo, who remarks that ocular demonstration of the fact might be got from a comparison between the lading of the ships entering and those leaving the port of Alexandria. Octavian's conquest, though it might hurt the pride of the Alex-

---

[1] See F. Heichelheim in Pauly-Wissowa, *s.v. Monopole.*

andrines, certainly benefited their pockets, and the commerce of the city had never been so great as in the early Roman period. There was also an extensive transit trade, particularly in goods from Somaliland and Arabia and from the Indies.

The Arabian expedition of Gallus was in part due to commercial motives, in which respect it was not unsuccessful; and though the later plan for an expedition under Augustus's grandson Gaius was dropped it is possible that the Romans succeeded about this time in occupying Aden, which would secure for the empire a valuable station and port of call for the Indian trade (see Note 6, p. 882 *sq.*). During the reign of Augustus repeated embassies from India came to Rome, and under Claudius we hear of one from Ceylon. The discovery of the monsoons, perhaps about A.D. 40, gave a further impetus to the eastern trade, and great fleets sailed annually for India, to return laden with the merchandise of the East. This was brought to the ports of the Red Sea, Myos Hormos or Berenice, whence they were carried by the desert roads[1] to Coptos, and so, after paying toll there, down the Nile to Alexandria. Merchants from all parts of Egypt shared in this trade and made the voyage to India; while in the multitudes which thronged the quays and streets of Alexandria Indians were no uncommon sight. In exchange for the imports, such commodities as slaves, wine, flax, corn, glass, and coral were sent to the East[2]; but the balance of trade would seem to have been against the empire (see p. 417 *sq.*), and there was much export of coin, a fact which attracted indignant comment from more than one writer, particularly as the Eastern imports were mainly articles of luxury.

The banking monopoly which had existed under the Ptolemies was relaxed, if not abolished, by the Romans. The royal (now called public) banks continued to function; but besides them we meet with numerous private banks. The machinery of banking was highly developed, and payments of all kinds were frequently made not in cash but by simple transfer of a credit from one banking account to another; we even meet with a form of order

---

[1] For these routes see J. Lesquier, *L'armée romaine*, pp. 417–58; G. W. Murray, *The Roman Roads and Stations in the Eastern Desert of Egypt*, in *Journ. Eg. Arch.* XI, 1925, pp. 138–50.

[2] Documentary evidence for the trade is furnished by the interesting group of ostraca, J. G. Tait, *Greek Ostraca*, 1930, Ostr. Petr. 220–304; see M. Rostovtzeff, *Gnomon*, VII, 1931, pp. 23–6, and H. Kortenbeutel, *Der äg. Süd- und Osthandel*, 1931, p. 63. On the eastern trade see also P. Jouguet, *Bull. Inst. fr. d'arch. or.* XXXI, 1930, pp. 12–26.

which may in some degree be compared with the modern cheque. The public granaries stored not only the grain paid as land-tax or rent on the State lands but the stocks of private owners as well; and in a country where natural economy had never been wholly ousted by the use of money, it is not surprising that a banking procedure, with book-payments and 'cheques,' established itself in them also.

The issue of the silver tetradrachm by the Alexandrian mint was stopped by Augustus, though a copper coinage continued to be minted; but in A.D. 19–20 Tiberius introduced a tetradrachm of debased silver, equated with the Roman denarius, which was thenceforth the main currency of Egypt throughout the Roman period, though its value gradually declined. The old Ptolemaic silver coinage continued, however, to circulate, and was indeed in great estimation; Roman coins, except the *aureus*, seem to have played but a small part in the monetary system. The Alexandrian mint was regularly used, with considerable skill, for purposes of propaganda, and a study of coin-types throws much light on the aims and currents of Roman policy in Egypt[1].

VI. HISTORICAL EVENTS

If it be true that that country is happy which has no history, Egypt must be counted fortunate during the reigns of the earlier emperors; for it is hardly a mere accident of tradition that it figures so little in the works of historians between the settlement of the southern frontier by Petronius and the reign of Nero. Only in Alexandria, the storm-centre of the eastern Mediterranean, did events occur such as would attract the attention of contemporary historians. The citizens could not forget that their city had once been the capital of the richest and most powerful of the Hellenistic monarchies; and their failure to obtain a Senate was the more galling because Augustus confirmed the rights of the Jews, with their council of elders. For the Jews, who had twice betrayed the national cause and helped the Roman invader, were already hateful to the Alexandrines; and the latter saw with growing exasperation the favour and protection accorded by Rome to their rivals. Thus it came about that the militant nationalism of Alexandria found expression in hostility to the Jews, and the literature which it evoked, though primarily inspired by opposition to Rome, has in fact a strongly anti-Semitic tone. This literature (often called 'Pagan Acts of the Martyrs') has been casually preserved in very

[1] See on this, J. Vogt, *Alexandrinische Münzen*.

fragmentary papyri, mostly of the age of Caracalla; but it is clear that the texts contained in these derive from contemporary accounts, and that the literary *genre* was of much earlier origin than the manuscripts themselves. Nevertheless we have no evidence, literary or documentary, of any collision between Greek and Jew during the reigns of Augustus and Tiberius.

In A.D. 19 Germanicus, disregarding the rule which forbade men of senatorial rank to enter Egypt without the Emperor's permission, paid a visit to the country. His action was reprimanded by Tiberius, and it was not made less exceptionable by his behaviour at Alexandria, where he appeared in Greek costume and took considerable pains to render himself agreeable to the citizens. The ostensible reason for his visit was a serious famine, which he relieved by opening the granaries and distributing corn to the populace. It is not surprising, particularly since he excluded the Jews from a share in the distribution, that he received from the Alexandrines such exaggerated homage as made it necessary for him to deprecate their excessive attentions and remind them that divine honours were appropriate to the Emperor alone[1]. It does not appear however that any special friction between Jews and Greeks followed his visit, nor did Sejanus's hostility to the Jews have any effect at Alexandria. Not till the reign of Gaius did serious disturbances occur.

The prefect at this time was A. Avillius Flaccus, a trusted servant of Tiberius and a friend of Gaius' co-regent Gemellus, and of Macro, the praetorian prefect. The leaders of the Alexandrian opposition were Dionysius, Isidorus, and Lampon, members of the civic aristocracy but turbulent and unscrupulous intriguers, and the last two personal enemies of Flaccus. When first Gemellus and then Macro fell victims to the Emperor's jealousy, Flaccus began to fear for his own position. He had the more reason to do so if the conjectural restoration of an unfortunately fragmentary papyrus, recently edited[2], can be relied on; for it would appear from this that Isidorus had (or claimed to have) a hand in the fall of Macro. The position was the more serious since Gaius felt a special affection for Alexandria, which he designed to visit, and Flaccus seems to have decided that a rapprochement with the nationalist party was necessary. In the existing state of feeling this meant hostility to the Jews; and not long afterwards events

---

[1] On this visit see, *e.g.*, C. Cichorius, *Römische Studien*, pp. 375–88, and, against him, U. Wilcken, *Hermes*, LXIII, 1928, pp. 48–65.

[2] H. I. Bell, 'A New Fragment of the Acta Isidori,' *Arch. Pap.* x, 1932, pp. 5 *sqq.*

occurred which precipitated a clash between the two factions. Julius Agrippa, the friend and boon companion of the Emperor, had been made by him king of the former tetrarchies of Philip and Lysanias; and tearing himself away from the dissipations of Rome in the early summer of A.D. 38, he set out for his kingdom by way of Alexandria, where his last appearance had been in the rôle of a bankrupt fleeing from his creditors. When the Jews, despite an attempt on his part to make an unobtrusive entry, gave him a royal reception, the irritated Alexandrines staged an elaborate parody of him and his suite, parading through the streets an idiot in royal robes. It was a gross insult to an intimate friend of Gaius, and alike to the demonstrators and to Flaccus, who had taken no action against them, and who had moreover suppressed a decree in honour of the Emperor which the Jews had asked him to forward, reflection brought considerable misgiving. When therefore the Alexandrines hit upon the idea of demanding that statues of Gaius should be placed in the Jewish synagogues conformably to Imperial order, Flaccus welcomed the move, and on the inevitable refusal by the Jews branded them in an edict as 'aliens and intruders.' Taking the hint, the city mob fell upon the Jews with the cry to restrict them to the 'Delta' quarter. Statues of the Emperor and a quadriga, dragged from the gymnasium, were introduced into the synagogues, several of which were burned, the Jewish houses were pillaged, and many of the Jews themselves were butchered with every circumstance of horror. Flaccus, who chose to throw the blame for these events on the Jews, had many members of their council publicly scourged, and forbade the exercise of their religion, closing the synagogues.

The Jews, however, were not without a defender. Agrippa procured a copy of their suppressed decree and sent it to Gaius, doubtless with a formal complaint against the prefect, whose complaisance to the Alexandrines had signally failed in its object, since Isidorus and Lampon now appeared at Rome as his accusers. Gaius needed no incentive to proceed against an official already suspect; a centurion from Rome arrested Flaccus as he was dining at the house of one of Tiberius's freedmen, and he was taken to Rome, condemned, banished to Andros, and later put to death there.

The Jews, impoverished by the pillage of their homes, denied the right of worship, and apprehensive of further outrages, sent an embassy to Rome, of which Philo, one of the envoys, has given a vivid account. They failed to obtain satisfaction but suffered no evil consequences beyond a rather terrifying display of Gaius' grim humour[1]. The Emperor was indeed occupied with a scheme, the erection of a statue of himself in the temple at Jerusalem, which for the Jews overshadowed even the events at Alexandria and, if persisted in, would certainly have provoked a revolt of Judaea; but the daggers of Chaerea and his associates ended the career of the tyrant before his intention could be carried out.

Meantime the Alexandrian Jews had been preparing for revenge; and the accession of Claudius, also a close friend of Agrippa, who was instrumental in procuring his recognition as Emperor, was the signal for an attack on their Greek neighbours. A desperate struggle followed, so obstinate and prolonged that Claudius had to send the prefect instructions for its suppression. Both parties sent embassies to Rome, ostensibly to congratulate the new Emperor on his accession but largely to exculpate themselves for their share in the disturbances. The Jews, dissatisfied with their privileged position, were agitating for the Alexandrian citizenship, and there can be little doubt that their envoys were instructed also to ask for this. Claudius had already, on his accession, issued two edicts, the one confirming all the privileges of the Alexandrian Jews, the other making similar provisions for the Jews throughout the empire. He now received the rival embassies and listened to their arguments; and a copy of the reply which he sent to the Alexandrines has fortunately been preserved on the back of a papyrus roll[2]. He accepted some but declined others of the honours voted to him, confirmed the Alexandrian citizenship to all who had become *ephebi* down to his principate except such as had been wrongly entered on the lists, accepted a proposal to make the municipal magistracies triennial, and diplomatically shelved the request which the Alexandrines had advanced for a senate by referring it to the prefect. In the last section of his letter, turning to the recent disturbances, he warned both parties that the aggressor in any subsequent outbreak would receive condign punishment, informed the Alexandrines that he had confirmed all the rights and customs of the Jews, and finally, in language of unexpected sharpness, bade the latter be content with what they had and not introduce into the city Jews from Syria or Egypt, lest he should be compelled to punish them for 'fomenting a general plague for the whole world.'

The settlement thus effected was not permanent if a law-suit brought by the Alexandrines against Agrippa, of which a record

---

[1] Some Giessen fragments, of which, by the kindness of Prof. Kalbfleisch, the present writer has been allowed to see a transcript, may refer to proceedings connected with this embassy.　　[2] P. Lond. 1912.

has been preserved in several papyrus fragments, is rightly referred to Agrippa II and to the year 53[1]. The exact grounds of the quarrel cannot be determined, but the real reason was no doubt the old racial animosity. The two Alexandrian leaders, Isidorus and Lampon, after a display (probably exaggerated in the propagandist tract) of astonishing insolence to Claudius, were both executed, and their memory was long cherished as that of martyrs to the cause of Alexandrian nationalism.

Egypt again comes into the light of history in the following reign. The army of occupation was required in A.D. 63 to furnish detachments for the Parthian war, and about the same time Nero is credited with contemplating a war against Ethiopia. There is some evidence for a concentration of troops at Alexandria, and an expedition was certainly sent up the Nile to Meroë to explore the sources of the Nile and possibly to report on the political situation there[2]. Any such schemes were, however, stopped by the revolt of Judaea. That event had its repercussions in Alexandria, where a meeting of the citizens, called to discuss an embassy to Nero, ended in a battle royal between them and the Jews. The prefect, Tiberius Alexander, a renegade Jew, after vainly attempting to make his countrymen see the folly of their intransigence, was compelled to employ against them not only the regular garrison but a newly arrived detachment from Cyrene; and Josephus declares that 50,000 of the Jews perished before order was restored. This severity was effective, and there was no further trouble till after the fall of Jerusalem, when some of the fanatical *sicarii*, fleeing to Alexandria, attempted without success to stir up a revolt there (see below, p. 863). Among the schemes which flashed through the disordered brain of Nero in the days during which he saw the empire falling away from him was one for a flight to Alexandria, where he thought to establish a new empire in the East; but he lacked resolution for that as for other projects and perished ingloriously near his revolted capital.

[1] The suit was heard by Claudius on 30 April and 1 May, but the year is lost. It is fairly clear that it must be either 41 or 53. For 41 see C. Hopkins, *Yale Class. Studies*, I, 1928, pp. 171–7, and W. Graf Uxkull-Gyllenband, *Sitzungsber. Preuss. Akad.*, Phil.-Hist. Kl., XXVIII, 1930, pp. 664–79; for 53, in addition to earlier discussions, A. von Premerstein, *Hermes*, LXVII, 1932, pp. 174–96.

[2] On the alleged plans of Nero, see further, below, Note 6, pp. 880 *sqq*

VII. THE SPIRIT OF ROMAN RULE IN EGYPT

It remains to ask what was the effect of the Roman conquest on Egypt. Scanty as our evidence is for the early period, there can be no doubt that it brought at first an increase in prosperity. An efficient defence of the frontier prevented raids from without, order and settled government were established internally, the repair and deepening of canals much increased the yield of agriculture, the new agrarian policy caused a great extension of private property, and trade and industry flourished. The resumption of a silver coinage by Tiberius is an indication of growing prosperity, and the activity of the Alexandrian mint was so marked in the early years of Claudius that it has been held to reflect the discovery of the monsoons, since it was probably due to a sudden expansion of the Indian trade. The municipalization of the nome-capitals no doubt stimulated communal activities and intensified Hellenic culture there, while the unprivileged Egyptians of the villages at least profited by the increased agricultural production. So far as we can judge from the combined evidence of excavation and papyrus records there was in the average household a reasonably high standard of comfort, though no doubt conditions differed widely, and archaeological material comes mainly from the Fayûm. The houses, constructed of mud-brick, were well built, the interior walls plastered and generally painted with ornamental patterns; many contained ornamental niches, steps and door-posts of stone are occasionally found, and the wood-work was usually good. Little furniture has been found, but it has perhaps perished or it was removed when the houses were deserted; but pottery, some of it of good design and workmanship, glass, wooden chests and coffers, bronzes, basket-work, terracotta lamps and figurines, jewellery, and hoards of coins, to say nothing of the sometimes high quality of the portraits so characteristic of the period, all attest some degree of refinement[1]. The use, even among peasants who paid the highest rate of poll-tax, of pure Greek names, not merely those familiar among the military settlers but such literary names as Hector, Pylades, Laertes or Meleager, shows a certain cultural assimilation of Egyptian to Hellenic elements; and in the larger

---

[1] A. E. R. Boak and E. E. Peterson's *Karanis* (1931), the preliminary report on the excavations at Kôm Aushîm, gives a good idea of conditions in a Graeco-Egyptian village or town of the period, now supplemented by *Karanis: Reports*, 1924–31 (1933); and see, too, *B.G.U.* vii, introduction, and P. Viereck, *Philadelpheia*, chap. i, and (for Tebtunis) *Aegyptus*, x, 1929, p. 295.

villages there were many people who could write, and some at
least who were familiar with Greek literature.

Yet this well-being was very insecurely based. The substitution
of a strong and efficient government for a weak and incompetent
one is bound, particularly in a country dependent like Egypt on a
proper control of the irrigation system, to produce at first greater
prosperity. How long this will endure depends on the spirit of
the government; and it was precisely in the spirit which inspired
it that Roman rule in Egypt was at fault. To the Ptolemies the
country was the personal estate of the ruler, its people were his
servants, their individual interest was subordinated throughout to
that of the State. This conception, when inherited to the full by the
Romans, was bound to be more harmful; for whereas the corn and
money wrung from his subjects by a Ptolemy remained for the
most part in the country itself, under the Romans much of both
went to Rome as tribute, and no corresponding advantage accrued
to the inhabitants. Egypt was, indeed, no more than a demesne
added to the empire by Augustus and administered for the
good of the Roman People. There is no reason to suppose that
the relative amount of taxes was substantially increased[1]; but the
very efficiency of the Romans made them more burdensome. The
exemption or partial exemption from poll-tax of the privileged,
who were in general the wealthier, classes threw the weight of this
impost on to the peasantry; and with the introduction, very likely
in our period and certainly soon afterwards, of the liturgical
system the middle classes also began to be burdened beyond their
strength. The principle of collective responsibility, in both spheres,
made the evil doubly disastrous. On the other hand, if the Roman
government was efficient—how efficient may be seen by studying
the evidence for the operations of the department of the *Idiologos*—
in collecting the last penny of its dues, it was much less successful
in controlling its own servants, the tax-collectors and other officials. There is plenty of evidence, documentary and literary, to
show that the gravest irregularities existed before the middle of
the first century. The better governors strove to get rid of these;
but a system which placed the fiscal interest before all else invited
abuse. And signs are not wanting that economic difficulties
were already making themselves felt. An edict of the prefect
Flaccus prohibiting the carrying of arms may indicate disturbances

---

[1] M. Rostovtzeff (*Journ. of Econ. and Business Hist.* I, 1929, p. 346 *sq.*)
argues that it was, but the revolt of the Thebaïd, on which he chiefly relies,
falls short of proving this.

or the threat of them; and when we read in a petition dating from about A.D. 55–60 of villages partially depopulated by the flight or death of tax-payers[1] we cannot doubt that there was something gravely wrong with the whole system. For though local causes may have been operative here, this piece of evidence, though specially striking, does not stand alone. The population was burdened to its utmost capacity, and any failure of the harvest or slump in prices, though some remission of taxes might be conceded, was bound to cause a crisis. From every such crisis recovery became progressively more difficult under a government whose one remedy for a failure in the policy of compulsion was to tighten up the system, and which met a default on the part of the tax-payer or liturgist by shifting his burden on to other shoulders. Thus the early Principate, efficient as was its administration and just as were its intentions, may fairly be held to have sown the seed whose harvest was to be the economic collapse of the third century and, in process of the years, the Byzantine servile State.

[1] S.B. 7462 (=P. Graux 2).

CHAPTER XI

HEROD OF JUDAEA

I. JUDAEA AFTER THE DEATH OF CAESAR

THE victory of Octavian over Antony and Cleopatra placed the client-kingdoms in Asia Minor and Syria, no less than Egypt, within his grasp. But it was no part of his policy to make far-reaching changes in these regions, and as has been seen (pp. 113 *sqq.*) he even maintained many of Antony's arrangements. Among the kings who were confirmed in their power there was one who by his personality stood out among the rest, and of whom the ancient sources permit a connected account[1]. This was Herod, whose kingdom of Judaea was to have more significance for history than its political importance warranted. In this chapter the history of the Jews will be resumed from the death of Caesar[2] and carried on beyond the reign of Herod to the moment at which Judaea was transformed into a Roman province.

Only a few weeks before his murder Caesar had reaffirmed his trust in the High Priest Hyrcanus II and his Idumaean minister Antipater by allowing them to rebuild the walls of Jerusalem and by granting, presumably in connection with the heavy expenses the rebuilding would entail, a remission in the amount of tribute due[3]. In spite of this, scarcely had Cassius won possession of Syria (p. 18), before the Jewish government afforded him help, and to the general reasons for their attitude one in particular should perhaps be added—the influence of Antipater's son, Herod. Young though he was[4], he early had political experience;

[1] Practically the sole source for this chapter is the two parallel accounts of Josephus (*Bell. Jud.* I [10, 10], 211–II [8, 14], 166 and *Ant.* XIV [11, 2], 271–XVIII). On the relation between these two narratives see Note 7, p. 885 *sq.* For other sources see the Bibliography. A genealogical table of the House of Herod will be found at the end of the volume. See also Map 3, facing p. 31.

[2] See above, vol. IX, pp. 404 *sqq.*

[3] Josephus, *Ant.* XIV [10, 6], 203–206 shows that Caesar did not free Judaea from the obligation to pay tribute, but made new regulations; in that passage the tribute in kind is ordered to be paid at Sidon, obviously either for dispatch to Italy or for disposal by the Roman governor. In XIV [10, 2], 195 and [10, 6], 204 the only immunity granted is from requisitions by armies passing through.

[4] He was born *c.* 73 B.C. See W. Otto in *P.W., s.v.* Herodes, col. 16.

he had to relinquish his governorship of Galilee (vol. IX, p. 404 *sq.*), but Sextus Caesar, then legate of Syria, had compensated him with an important administrative post in Coele-Syria[1]. But he could not regain influence in Palestine, and so naturally seized on the chances that the changed position after Caesar's murder offered him; once he had persuaded his father—and of course Hyrcanus —to support the Republicans, he got Cassius to give him the task of collecting that portion of the 700 talents extraordinary tribute imposed on Palestine which was due from Galilee, and so set foot again in the land from which he had been driven three years before. Here his energy in collecting the tribute was so much appreciated by Cassius that he not only retained his post in Coele-Syria, but was also apparently entrusted with the general collection of funds for the war in the whole province; more still, as a mark of his restored position he was given the 'Wardenship of the Armouries' in Judaea, that is, probably, the general supervision of all fortresses and stores of arms, the safety of which was essential to the Republicans[2].

The newly-won importance of Herod not only overshadowed his elder brother Phasael, the governor of Jerusalem, but disturbed the balance till now existing between Hyrcanus II and Antipater, which rested upon the willing co-operation of the two which Caesar had intended[3]; henceforward Herod could use his authority as a Roman official and, better still, the firm belief of the Romans that he was indispensable for their rule in Palestine, to advance his family. Among the discontented parties that troubled Judaea there now arose yet another: those who favoured Hyrcanus and did not wish to see his power decrease to the advantage of the Idumaean house. There ensued a constant crossing and sometimes actual fusion between three different revolutionary currents: one of these movements, a straight refusal to pay the extraordinary tribute levied by Cassius, was only checked by the wholesale enslavement of Gophna, Emmaus and lesser cities[4]; a second combined anti-Roman feeling with support for Antigonus, the son

[1] *Bell. Jud.* I [10, 8], 213 says definitely στρατηγὸς Κοίλης Συρίας καὶ Σαμαρίας; *Ant.* xv [9, 5], 180 only στρατηγὸς Κοίλης Συρίας. But later events show that Samaria fell within the competence of Herod, cf. *Bell. Jud.* I [11, 6], 229; *Ant.* xiv [11, 4], 284. The duties of the post are obscure.
[2] Josephus is not clear on the point: *Bell. Jud.* I [11, 4], 225 calls Herod Συρίας ἁπάσης ἐπιμελητής; cf. *Ant.* xiv [11, 4], 280. For the φυλακὴ τῶν ὅπλων in Judaea cf. *Ant.* xiv [11, 3], 278.
[3] B. Motzo, *Studi Cagliaritani di Storia e Filologia*, I, 1927, p. 1.
[4] R. Laqueur, *Der jüdische Historiker Flavius Josephus*, p. 216.

of the dispossessed Aristobulus (see vol. IX, pp. 403, 405); the third, headed by one Malchus, a friend and probably high official of Hyrcanus, was aimed exclusively against Antipater and his house. Malchus succeeded in getting Antipater assassinated, and Hyrcanus' complete failure to proceed against him gave some grounds for the suspicion that he had favoured the plot. But Herod, who must have been supported by his own armed bands, played a more active part: with Cassius' approval he succeeded in his turn in getting rid of Malchus and destroying his party.

Hyrcanus' only course, short of surrender to Herod, was to join with him, for Herod's forces were his only protection against the steadily increasing partisans of Antigonus, who now, in 42, backed by the Syrian dynasts, Ptolemaeus of Chalcis and Marion of Tyre, were left free in the confusion that prevailed in Syria before Philippi to do what they would; indeed, Marion had already seized some parts of Galilee. Party struggles, which broke up any firm feeling of loyalty to Hyrcanus, merely served to help Herod, and the results were soon visible. He routed Antigonus, and though he could not recover from Marion the lost Galilean lands, Hyrcanus—willingly or not—had to reward Herod with a crown and promise him the hand of one of his grand-daughters: this was Mariamme, the child of his daughter Alexandra and of Alexander, the son of Hyrcanus' brother Aristobulus; Herod dismissed, though he did not divorce, his first wife Doris, an Idumaean, who had borne him a son named Antipater. The political value of this alliance, which bound Herod to a descendant of two rival branches of the Hasmonaeans, is obvious; since Hyrcanus had no sons it practically gave Herod a title to the succession, though it ran counter to the aspirations of the great majority of the Jews, who hated him as a foreigner and philo-Roman.

The death of Cassius at Philippi did not entail the overthrow of his protégé, though the Jews hoped for it and twice sent embassies to Antony to accuse Herod, and implicitly or explicitly Hyrcanus as well (p. 33 *sq.*). But Hyrcanus and his advisers cleverly parried the charge of supporting the Republicans by representing themselves as their victim, and by begging Antony to free the Jews whom Cassius had enslaved and restore the territory Marion of Tyre had occupied—two petitions that could not fail of success. Moreover, these displays of Jewish discontent merely strengthened in Antony a belief which was strong in Roman circles, that Judaea could not be kept quiet under the rule of pure-blooded Jews, so that he was ready enough to uphold the authority of the house of Antipater and smooth its path in succeeding to Hyrcanus. The

coming marriage of Herod with Mariamme proved the feasibility
of the solution that was to prevail later—the setting-up of a
government that though nominally Jewish was in reality alien and
only able to survive by loyalty to Rome. So Antony gave Herod
fresh promotion by nominating him tetrarch, but—whether as a
punishment for having helped Cassius, or with the idea of creating
a permanently balanced power in Palestine—he deprived him of
the absolute pre-eminence that marriage with Mariamme offered by
bestowing the title of tetrarch on Phasael also. Many of the details
of this change are obscure, since we do not know what were the
relations of the tetrarchs to the ethnarch and between themselves[1].
It is clear, however, that the appointment of Herod and Phasael
as tetrarchs set the seal on the rise of the Antipatrid dynasty.

But the Parthian invasion swept away both the decisions and
the projects of Antony in Palestine. Scarcely had the Jews had
time to evince their disgust at the new order by a riotous demonstration, which was put down with bloodshed, before the Parthians
were called in by Antigonus in 40 B.C. (pp. 46 *sqq*.). Possibly, thanks
to memories of the Persian Empire and the existing relations with
the Babylonian Jews, the Parthians already enjoyed the sympathy
of all who looked for support in freeing themselves from Rome;
certainly their invasion, which not only gave Antigonus supreme
power and the High Priesthood, but prevented Hyrcanus ever recovering it and drove Phasael to suicide[2], seemed so providential
that, among the various Messianic legends that sprang up after
A.D. 70 one prophesied that it was the Parthians who would make
straight the way for the Messiah by conquering Palestine a second
time[3].

But Herod had no thought of joining Parthia, and Phasael's
death restored him the primacy he had recently lost. The Idumaean fortress of Masada still remained to him: he reorganized
its defences, and left there not only his relatives (and also his
betrothed Mariamme and her mother Alexandra), but a nucleus

---

[1] *Bell. Jud.* 1 [12, 4], 244 (cf. *Ant.* XIV [13, 1], 326) simply says,
τετράρχας ἀποδείκνυσιν τοὺς ἀδελφοὺς πᾶσαν διοικεῖν τὴν Ἰουδαίαν
ἐπιτρέπων.

[2] So Josephus, *Bell. Jud.* 1 [13, 10], 271; *Ant.* XIV [13, 10], 367;
according to Julius Africanus *ap.* Syncell. 1, 581 (Dindorf) Phasael was killed
in battle; this possibly derives from Justus of Tiberias, though no certain
valuation of its worth can be made.

[3] Cf. especially *Talmud bab.*, tract. *Sanhedrin*, fol. 98 *a–b* and J. Darmesteter, *Journ. Asiat. Soc.* IX, vol. IV, 1894, p. 43; J. Klausner, *Die
messianischen Vorstellungen des jüdischen Volkes im Zeitalter der Tannaiten*,
pp. 39–40; G. F. Moore, *Judaism*, II, pp. 354–5.

of devoted followers and the treasures of his family. Having thus
secured a base for the recovery of his power he at last succeeded in
reaching Rome. Here his cause was too closely bound up with
the restoration of Roman power in Syria for him not to be recognized at once as king—king and not ethnarch, either as a proof of
goodwill or more probably because, since as an Idumaean he could
never become High Priest, he must be given a title equal in
prestige to the priestly one[1]. At his coronation Herod, by
sacrificing to Juppiter Capitolinus, revealed for the first time how
lightly his Jewish religious convictions lay upon him. Samaria,
which he had already governed as an official of the legate of Syria,
was also added to his kingdom[2].

He was named king, but his subjects refused to acknowledge
the rule of one whom Rome had recognized as their sovereign and
Herod had to set about the conquest of Judaea with mercenary
bands. In 39, after a few early successes—the occupation of Joppa,
and the relief of Masada (which restored him control over most of
Idumaea)—Antigonus' resistance prevented further advance, and
Ventidius the legate of Syria, too busy elsewhere or bribed by
Antigonus (p. 50, n. 2), failed, despite Antony's orders, to support
Herod in strength. Nor did the situation show any substantial
change next year until at last Herod gained an interview with
Antony before Samosata and persuaded him to detach two legions
under Sosius to help him; as in Pompey's day Judaea needed a
regular Roman army to conquer it. With these two legions Herod
was able, in the autumn of 38, to set about the systematic re-
occupation of his kingdom.

An army sent by Antigonus into Samaria to divert Herod from
Judaea was routed, and by February 37 he was able to lay siege to
Jerusalem. Resistance was desperate since the governing classes,
usually favourable to Rome, faced with the danger of a non-Jewish
king, devoted all their skill and determination to prolonging the
defence; the protests of two famous Pharisees, Shemaya and

[1] It is to be remembered that Antigonus had assumed the title of High
Priest for the Jews and of king for the Gentiles (p. 48).

[2] Appian, *Bell. Civ.* v, 75, 319, mentioning Antony's reorganization of
the client-kingdoms (p. 52), refers to this assignation, ἴστη δέ πῃ καὶ
βασιλέας οὓς δοκιμάσειεν ἐπὶ φόροις ἄρα τεταγμένοις...Ἰδουμαίων δὲ καὶ
Σαμαρέων Ἡρῴδην. The mention of Samaria makes no difficulties;
granted that the old territory of Judaea was already tribute-paying (p. 316 n. 3),
it is understandable that Samaria, again included in the kingdom, should pay
tribute too. But the allusion to Idumaea, already part of the old territory and
so tribute-paying, is puzzling; either Appian has blundered or the territory
of Idumaea was rounded off with some addition for Herod's benefit.

Abtalyon, who saw that resistance was vain, went unheeded. But the siege was also prolonged by Herod himself, for he suddenly decided to marry Mariamme at Samaria; naturally it is hard to decide whether the celebration of the marriage in such circumstances was due to reasons of sentiment or of politics. So it took five months of siege before Jerusalem surrendered to Herod and the Roman legions, in July 37[1]. Though Antigonus' partisans were massacred, and Antigonus himself was put to death by Antony, Herod managed to save the city from general sack and to get the legions back to Syria without any further disorders. He was now, in fact as well as name, king of the Jews.

II. HEROD ON THE THRONE

To the hard task of being the king of the Jews Herod brought notable personal gifts. Undaunted, subtle, energetic, time-serving and politic without servility, he was both a soldier and a diplomatist, shrewd in his judgment of the weight of Roman power as of the probable limits in Rome's use of it. Yet, at his best, he fell short of greatness and, at his worst, he was little more than a creature of cruelty. Indeed, through all the acts of his reign it is hard to distinguish, as we have seen in the marriage with Mariamme, the part played by passion, often savage passion, and the part played by calculation. Passionate and calculating, he could sometimes make calculation serve his passions, at other times could ruin his calculations by passion. At bottom his desires were simple enough—power, glory, pomp and pleasure; they became complex because in satisfying them he had to reckon with two different worlds, Gentile and Jewish; he had to be a match for both and yet in neither of them did he ever feel at ease. He was no true Jew, he was not bound in firm and intimate loyalty to the Law; indeed he longed incessantly to break through its encumbrances and associate freely with that other world, to be sought out and admired for assimilating the culture, above all the opulence and elegance, of the Gentile. Yet though we cannot deny him a certain intellectual curiosity, this longing obviously arose from no deep understanding of the spiritual values of Graeco-Roman civilization; it was simply ambition, the restless ambition that strives to attain greatness by entering into a different tradition. With it all he retained not only the suspicion and cruelty of an

---

[1] For the date see Note 7, p. 886. The reckoning of Herod's regnal years began with Nisan (c. April) 37; see G. F. Unger, *Bay. S.B.* 1896, p. 391; E. Schürer, *Gesch. d. jüd. Volkes*, 1, p. 415. For a different hypothesis (autumn 37) see E. Schwartz, *Gött. Nach.* 1907, p. 266.

Oriental prince, but also a desire to uphold his own prestige among
the Jews (whether of Palestine or of the Diaspora) by being looked
on as their protector. So while he laboured to raise Judaea to the
rank of one of the greatest client-kingdoms of Rome, by secu-
larizing it as far as possible and giving it a definitely Hellenistic
structure, on another side his policy bore a strong Jewish imprint.
It was Herod's fate to be a great man *déraciné*, who lavished his
boundless energies on the contradictory tasks of hellenizing the
Jewish State and of enhancing the political prestige of Judaism.
His true forerunners were the sons of Tobiah, who like him were
Judaized rather than Jewish[1]. Though he apparently succeeded
better than they, because he had what they lacked in their struggles
with Syria and Egypt, the solid support of Rome, his political
failure was not far different. He could not transform the Jews,
still less turn his kingdom into a stable element in the Roman
system of client-states. The Tobiads made the first, Herod the
last, attempt to bring Judaea within the circle of Hellenistic (and
ultimately Roman) civilization; soon after began the tragedy
which led to the total overthrow of the Jewish State.

Herod's first care, once on the throne, was to crush the aristocracy. They had opposed him during and after his trial in 47[2], and
confirmed their enmity during the siege. His revenge was to kill
forty-five of the most influential members of the Sanhedrin, so that
its quota of 71 could now be filled up with more docile elements[3];
this massacre, accompanied by confiscation of property, dealt the
aristocratic opposition a blow from which it never recovered
during his reign, and further murders and confiscations were to
follow. The question of the High Priesthood was more difficult,
because it involved his relations with the surviving Hasmonaeans,
and so with Antony and Cleopatra. Though he liked to be regarded as of priestly family Herod could not be High Priest and
never tried to be[4]. Simply for this reason he set about destroying

---

[1] See vol. VIII, pp. 500 *sqq.*   [2] *Ib.* p. 404.
[3] For a different opinion on the rank of the forty-five victims see S. Funk
in *Monat. f. Gesch. und Wiss. d. Judentums*, LV, 1911, pp. 37–9.
[4] Strabo's assertion, XVI, 765, Ἡρῴδης, ἀνὴρ ἐπιχώριος, παραδὺς εἰς
τὴν ἱερωσύνην τοσοῦτον διήνεγκε τῶν πρὸ αὐτοῦ κ.τ.λ., is false. Nothing in
Herod's conduct authorizes the belief that he aspired to the High Priesthood
or had himself officially recognized as of priestly family. But he may well
have allowed the rumour to circulate that he was of priestly family, a rumour
which Strabo picked up, and this is confirmed by Justin, *Dial. c. Tryph.* 52,
Ἡρῴδην...ὅμως ἐν τῷ γένει ὑμῶν ὄντα λέγετε ἀρχιερέα. Parallel with
this is the story which he caused to be circulated among the Jews of the
Diaspora by his Gentile courtier Nicolaus of Damascus that his family
belonged to those Jews who had returned from the Babylonian exile.

that theocratic form of government which by now seemed to Jewish eyes the only lawful one. He needed a High Priest insignificant and yet belonging to the Zadokite family, reputed to be descendants of Aaron, who had held the office before the Hasmonaeans; this would give an appearance of legitimacy to the change. Herod found his man in Ananel (Hananeel), a priest of the Babylonian Diaspora[1]. But from his Hasmonaean relatives opposition at once broke out. His mother-in-law, Alexandra, wanted the nomination for her sixteen-year-old son, Aristobulus, but apart from the unprecedented youthfulness of the candidate it involved grave dangers. For the Hasmonaeans, who had had at first to bow to his will, were now trying to recover their lost position; Herod, who had sought their alliance, did not feel himself strong enough to break with them, and had in fact recently obtained the return of Hyrcanus from his Parthian prison just because his presence would imply acceptance of the new order. And there was another serious reason. Alexandra had contrived to interest Cleopatra in Aristobulus. But Cleopatra did not disguise her wish to extend the boundaries of Egypt to what they had been in Philadelphus' time (p. 67), and almost at the very moment of the discussions over the Priesthood, in 36, she had persuaded Antony to take the territory of Jericho from Herod for her[2], and wanted more. Herod had been compelled to rent the territory that had once been his and also to guarantee the rent of the lands that Cleopatra had taken from Malchus of Nabataea (p. 70).

In these circumstances to oppose a scheme supported by Cleopatra would have been dangerous indeed, and so Aristobulus was given Ananel's place (c. 35 B.C.). But after a year the position became intolerable for Herod: during that year Alexandra showed she would not forgo her intrigues with Cleopatra—who saw an opportunity for fresh gains in Judaea—and with her help concocted a scheme for the 'flight' of Aristobulus; this, with a short stay in exile, was obviously intended to smooth the way for his return as a candidate for the throne in Israel. But it failed and Herod, ruthless, had the young Aristobulus drowned. Summoned by Antony to Laodicea to clear himself he emerged unharmed, for he had arranged the murder skilfully and had chosen a moment when Antony badly needed an undisturbed Judaea be-

---

[1] Josephus, *Ant.* xv [3, 1], 40.

[2] It is unlikely that Gaza too was taken from Herod by Antony (Otto, *op. cit.* col. 45), for it could not have been Herod's till after 30. The phrase ἄρχων τῆς Ἰδουμαίας καὶ Γάζης in *Ant.* xv [7, 9], 254 though referring to 37 B.C. reflects the position after 30.

hind him. Thus the problem of the High Priesthood was solved; it was to be neither hereditary nor for life, and Herod could henceforward freely bestow or take away the highest priestly dignity; usually he reserved it for the members of those aristocratic families who supported him, the most favoured being the house of Boëthus[1], with which Herod later entered into a marriage alliance. To mark his mastery he now took into his keeping the garments which the High Priest wore at solemn functions and which were reputed to have magical powers[2], and only lent them out on these occasions, a practice which was to give rise to serious disturbances when the Romans took Herod's place (p. 850).

With the murder of Aristobulus the alliance with the Hasmonaeans was broken; the struggle between the two parties was to rage, sometimes openly sometimes underground, during his whole reign, involving in it all the opposition of the old Jewish tradition to the usurper, an opposition which in the end wrecked any hope of a lasting dynasty of Herod's family. At the beginning of 30 the aged Hyrcanus fell a victim, suspect, according to the official version[3], of conspiring with the king of Nabataea. In 29[4] Herod killed Mariamme, who had borne him five sons; it was the issue of a mysterious tragedy, in which the king's violent jealousy was turned to profit by his mother and his sister Salome against the hated Hasmonaean. In 28, Alexandra, who had tried to persuade Herod's officers, during an illness of his, to surrender to her the fortress of Jerusalem, was killed with a band of her followers. And this was only the beginning of the struggle.

Yet though it ultimately destroyed Herod's kingdom, at first this struggle did not openly weaken it, because the populace remained for long apathetic. The only attempt at a popular rising occurred when, during Herod's interview at Laodicea, the rumour spread that Antony had condemned him to death, and this attempt was quickly put down. His defensive precautions doubtless helped to give him a firm hold on the people; his mercenaries and his fortresses were posted all over the country, and two works certainly go back to the first years of his reign, the rebuilding of

[1] The house of Boëthus possibly gave its name to a not very clearly defined tendency in Sadduceeism, the so-called Boëthosaeans; these may originally have been the supporters of the Idumaean dynasty (but cf. vol. IX, p. 415, n. 2).

[2] J. Jeremias, *Jerusalem zur Zeit Jesu*, II B, 1, p. 3 *sq.*

[3] In Herod's own memoirs, Josephus, *Ant.* xv [6, 3], 174.

[4] For an incorrect version of Mariamme's execution, placing it too early (*Bell. Jud.* I [22, 4], 441 *sqq.*), see Otto, *op. cit.* col. 8.

the fortress Hyrcania[1] and the reconstruction of the citadel of the Temple (the so-called *Baris*), to which he gave the name Antonia. Yet perhaps the profound need for peace in Judaea, rent as it had been for nearly ten years by civil war—the same need that was being felt throughout the whole Roman Empire—contributed even more effectually to the rapid restoration of order in the country. Thanks to this Herod could face with calm the complexities of the final phase of the Civil Wars, and Cleopatra's interference in his relations with Antony actually profited him, for otherwise he must have helped Antony against Octavian and been involved in common ruin. Indeed in 32 he was on the point of joining Antony, when at Cleopatra's instance he was dispatched against Malchus, who was proving slack in his payment of rent (p. 95). The struggle was kept up during part of 31 without decisive result, for Athenion, the Egyptian commander in Coele-Syria, set himself to hinder any victory which might disturb the balance between the two combatants. In the end Herod had the better of it and seized the occasion, while Egypt's attention was elsewhere, to impose a kind of protectorate on the Arabs[2]. So the battle of Actium found him far from Antony's side, and it was easy for him to change with fortune and assist the legate of Syria in intercepting the gladiators, whom Antony had engaged to celebrate his expected victory, on their way from Cyzicus to Egypt (p. 107). This done, he could meet Octavian in the spring of 30 (p. 115), and Octavian, like Antony before him, had no reason for not confirming him. Indeed, either in reaction to Cleopatra's policy or because he thought it useful, for the defence of the boundaries of the Empire, to strengthen the realm of Herod above all with non-Jewish elements, after the death of Cleopatra he restored him Jericho and presented him with practically all the territory that had been taken from Judaea by Pompey and had not yet been given back[3].

---

[1] Otto, *op. cit.* col. 41.

[2] *Bell. Jud.* ɪ [19, 6], 385, and *Ant.* xv [5, 5], 159, state that Herod was nominated by the Arabs προστάτης τοῦ ἔθνους, but the precise meaning is obscure.

[3] The list, in Josephus, *Bell. Jud.* ɪ [20, 3], 396 and *Ant.* xv [7, 3], 217, of the cities given back (Gadara, Hippos, Samaria, Gaza, Anthedon, Joppa, Stratonis Turris) is partly incorrect and partly incomplete. Joppa had already been restored by Caesar (*Ant.* xɪv [10, 6], 202), Samaria by Antony (p. 320), while Azotus (Ashdod) and Jamnia, which were probably restored at this time (Schürer, *op. cit.* ɪɪ, pp. 103, 126), are not even mentioned.

III. THE ATTEMPTED TRANSFORMATION

As the years went on Augustus' favour for Herod showed no
diminution. In 23 B.C. he transferred the districts of Trachonitis,
Batanaea and Auranitis from the tetrarchy of Zenodorus to
Judaea, and on Zenodorus' death, in 20 B.C., he added the rest of
the tetrarchy, comprising the districts of Ulatha and Panias to
the north-east of Galilee (see above, pp. 115 and 281). The
appointment of Herod's brother, Pheroras, as tetrarch of Peraea
in this year implied no lessening of Herod's prestige, for Pheroras
was throughout subordinate, both *de jure* and *de facto*; as we shall
see, it must be viewed in connection with the domestic circumstances of Herod, and in any event was by his express nomination.
The reasons for Augustus' favour need not be sought so much in
any political contingencies, which might suggest alterations in
the client-kingdoms, as in the sympathy with which he followed
Herod's effort to bring Judaea out of its isolation and turn it into
a client-kingdom on which Rome could count as much or even
more than the others. Herod's aim was to reduce the Jewish State
to the normal type, to hellenize it and by so doing strengthen it
for the defence of the frontiers of the Empire. The progress of
this hellenization can be seen in every aspect of the State's life, and
all traces of the theocracy were systematically swept away.

Herod's coinage no longer bore legends in Hebrew; it is entirely Greek. His court assumed a Hellenistic character through
all its grades, from the Chancellor or Finance Minister Ptolemaeus[1] down to the numerous minor officials, and the customary
Hellenistic court-titles, *kinsmen*, *comrades*, *friends*, were all introduced[2]. On the model of the Hellenistic kingdoms, too, was the
new private Council of the king, the *Synedrion*, which took over all
the political and judicial functions of the old Sanhedrin, over which
the High Priest had presided, and whose competence was now
strictly limited to jurisdiction on religious questions[3]. The royal
favourites received grants of lands as fiefs according to the usual
Hellenistic practice[4]. Many of the highest posts were held by non-
Jews of Greek training. Literary men were specially favoured,

---

[1] The terminology employed in *Ant.* XVI [7, 2], 191 is ambiguous.

[2] Otto, *op. cit.* col. 82 *sqq.*; cf. vol. VII, p. 165.

[3] G. Corradi, *Il συνέδριον dei sovrani ellenistici*, in *Studi Ellenistici*,
pp. 231–55. For the commonly accepted view (*e.g.* Otto, *op. cit.* col. 114)
that Hyrcanus was only condemned to death after Herod had consulted the
old Sanhedrin, Josephus, *Ant.* XV [6, 2], 173 offers no support. The old
Sanhedrin cannot have been merely consulted; it was itself a judicial tribunal.

[4] Otto, *op. cit.* col. 59; see above, vol. VII, p. 172.

for they would introduce foreign modes of thought; the most famous was Nicolaus of Damascus, the adviser and historian of the king, but we hear of a rhetorician, Irenaeus, and Andromachus and Gemellus, to whom was entrusted the education of the king's sons, must have been rhetoricians too. So the king's sons received a Greek training, and furthermore, two of them, Alexander and Aristobulus, sons of the Hasmonaean Mariamme, were sent to Rome in 23 B.C. to complete their education, though they apparently roused great scandal by living in the house of a Gentile, Asinius Pollio[1]. Fifteen years later three sons, of different wives, Archelaus, Antipas and Philip, were also sent to Rome, but scandal was avoided this time since they probably lived in a Jewish household[2]. Herod himself displayed a fondness for Greek culture: he would discuss rhetorical or philosophic points with Nicolaus[3], declaring that he felt himself nearer to Greeks than to Jews[4], and he chose Greek as the language for his *Memoirs*. At Jerusalem, and in other cities, there arose theatres, amphitheatres and hippodromes, designed for spectacles unknown to and loathed by the Jews, and Greeks were always sure of a welcome at the Court, where some, like the Spartan notable Eurycles (p. 114), were for long guests of honour.

So too the structure of Herod's army was Hellenistic and composed of mercenaries; the Palestinian Jews were totally shut out, as disloyal, though there were plenty of Jews from the Diaspora, especially the Babylonian, and this must be connected with the popularity that Herod enjoyed in the Diaspora (p. 321 *sq.*). But the majority of the soldiers were Idumaeans, Celts, Thracians, Germans and citizens of various Greek cities, grouped in special units, and it is typical that Augustus should have given Cleopatra's Celtic bodyguard to Herod (p. 115). Possibly, too, there were Roman instructors, but we cannot trace their influence[5]. What with civil and military posts a swarm of foreigners must have invaded Judaea, as is shown by the agitation that broke out on Herod's death against 'the Greeks[6].'

For the defence of the frontiers there were military colonies: we hear of one at Esbon (Heshbon) in Peraea, another at Gaba in

---

[1] *Ant.* XV [10, 1], 343.

[2] *Ant.* XVII [1, 3], 20, with Niese's conjecture Ἰουδαίῳ.

[3] Nicol. Damasc. frag. 135 (Jacoby). The shallowness of Herod's interests betrays itself in this very passage.   [4] *Ant.* XIX [7, 3], 329.

[5] Otto, *op. cit.* col. 57. But cf. H. Willrich, *Das Haus des Herodes zwischen Jerusalem und Rom*, p. 181.

[6] Nicol. Damasc. frag. 136, 8 (Jacoby).

Galilee and two others, unnamed but important, in Batanaea and
Trachonitis. The system of colonies was completed by a chain of
fortresses, some in the interior of the country (p. 324), some on the
borders. Masada was rebuilt[1], as were Machaerus and Alexan-
dreum (this last near Jericho); Herodium was founded near
Jerusalem and another stronghold of the same name on the Nabataean frontier. Jericho received a new citadel-wall, called (after
Herod's mother) Cyprus, Jerusalem a whole series of fortifications in addition to the Tower of Antonia, while many of the
palaces that Herod built all over Palestine had the character of
fortresses. The transformation of the country was completed by
the foundation of Hellenistic cities. Samaria was rebuilt in 27
with the name Sebaste; Stratonis Turris was renamed Caesarea
and changed, by works that occupied twelve years from their inception in 22, into a great seaport, which could deal far better than
the small port of Joppa with the trade of Palestine. The rapid
growth of this city, with its harbour larger than the Piraeus—in
A.D. 6 it became the seat of the imperial procurators—shows how
well Herod chose the site. Anthedon was rebuilt with the name
Agrippeum or Agrippias, and two other cities were founded in
Judaea proper, Antipatris and Phasaelis. The inhabitants of these
new foundations were drawn, for the most part, from non-Jews.
This is certain for Caesarea[2] and for Sebaste; they were to some
extent military colonies, and furnished to the royal army a corps of
troops called after the cities from which they came[3]. Yet however
favourable Herod might be to Hellenistic cities, he must have
limited their autonomy considerably, for Gaza was placed under
the governor of Idumaea and other cities were probably treated in
a like way[4].

[1] A. Schulten, *Masada*, in *Zeits. Deutsch. Paläst.-Vereins*, LVI, 1933.
[2] The writer agrees with Willrich, *op. cit.* p. 176, in holding that the Jews
never had the right of citizenship at Caesarea; such, at any rate, was the view of
Nero's government (p. 854).
[3] A comparison of *Bell. Jud.* II [3, 4], 52 with III [4, 2], 66 and *Ant.* XIX
[9, 2], 364–5 leaves no doubt that Καισαρεῖς and Σεβαστηνοί made up
one corps only; under the Roman procurators, who retained these troops,
they were garrisoned together at Caesarea and called officially *Sebasteni*
(the epigraphic documentation in Schürer, *op. cit.* I, p. 460).
[4] There are other indications that Herod made considerable reforms in
the administrative divisions of Judaea. Thus the Elder Pliny, who almost
certainly reflects here the state of affairs under Augustus (*N.H.* v, 70),
numbers Herodium (cf. Josephus, *Bell. Jud.* III [3, 5], 54–5) among the ten
toparchies of Judaea in the strict sense; this implies that Herod must have
reorganized the system of toparchies in Judaea, which certainly existed before
(Schürer, *op. cit.* II, p. 234).

At the same time Herod spent huge sums outside his kingdom, to gain fame in the great centres of Greece and the Greek East and probably also to prove in a striking way that the Jews had broken with their traditional isolation and meant to take part in the life of the outer world: Sparta, Athens[1], Rhodes (where Herod rebuilt a temple of Apollo Pythius), Chios, Pergamum, Laodicea, Tripolis, Byblus, Berytus[2], Tyre, Sidon, Ptolemaïs, Ascalon, Damascus and Antioch (where the king repaved the main street and provided it with a colonnade), all experienced his royal munificence. He consented to be *agonothetes* at Olympia, where he established a fund for the upkeep of the games, and he made personal appeals to Agrippa on behalf of Chios and Ilium.

In all this activity his fidelity to Rome was implicit: it became open and expressed where his works were in the nature of homage to the imperial house, as at Caesarea and Sebaste, in the *portus Augusti* at Caesarea, or in the contribution he made towards the building of Nicopolis, which Augustus had founded in commemoration of Actium (p. 113). But there were more important aspects still of his loyalty, and they found a Hellenistic manifestation. About 17 B.C. Herod had made his subjects take an oath of allegiance to himself: some ten years later the name of the Emperor was given the first place in this oath[3]. Next, the imperial cult was established in all the non-Jewish lands of the kingdom, visible at its most splendid in the magnificent temple of Augustus at Sebaste[4], while for Jewish use Herod revived the practice—customary during the Persian and Seleucid overlordship—of daily sacrifice in the Temple for the sovereign; in this case it was for the Roman emperor[5]. In Jerusalem, too, quadriennial games in honour of Augustus were instituted. More than this, Herod entitled himself officially 'Friend of the Emperor' and 'Friend of the Romans[6],' and was always ready to go where he could

---

[1] See *I.G.* III, 550 (= *O.G.I.S.* 414) and 551. Otto, *op. cit.* col. 74, has shown that the second refers to this Herod.

[2] See *C.R. Ac. Inscr.* 1927, p. 243.

[3] The present writer agrees with Schürer, *op. cit.* I, p. 399, that the oath mentioned in *Ant.* XV [10, 4], 368 is not a doublet of that in *Ant.* XVII [2, 4], 42; for a different view see Otto, *op. cit.* coll. 61–2.

[4] *Harvard Excavations at Samaria*, I, pp. 170 *sqq.*

[5] The sacrifice took place twice a day. Philo's assertion (*Legatio*, 157) that it was on the order of Augustus reflects his interest in proving that Augustus recognized the Jewish worship, and is probably due simply to the fact that Augustus paid for it. Had Augustus ordered it, obviously he would not have felt bound to pay for it.

[6] φιλοκαῖσαρ, *I.G.* III, 551; φιλορώμαιος, *I.G.* III, 550 (= *O.G.I.S.* I, 414).

be useful: thus in 25 B.C. he sent 500 of his soldiers to take part in the Arabian expedition of Aelius Gallus (p. 250), and in 14 the little fleet, which he had had built, sailed into the Black Sea to help Agrippa who was threatening war on the Bosporan kingdom (p. 268). On his side Augustus displayed his sympathy for the new Jewish policy by taking on himself the expenses of the sacrifices in his honour in the Temple and by making other gifts to it, while his pleasure at the foundation of Caesarea took the form of a donation of over 500 talents from himself and from his family, at the inauguration in 10 B.C. His feelings were shared by his great helper Agrippa, who in 15 B.C. gave, in the name of the Roman government, an impressive demonstration of friendship by visiting Jerusalem, where he offered a hecatomb in the Temple and made a donation to the populace. In his turn Herod paid a state visit to Augustus in Rome about 18–17 B.C.

Such a policy must have been extremely expensive to finance, the more so that we have no good grounds for believing that Herod's kingdom had not to pay tribute to Rome. The obligation is proved for the territories added to Judaea in the time of Antony (p. 320 n. 2); it is hard to believe that, had conditions changed during the remainder of Herod's rule, the sources would not have mentioned it. Yet, apart from those families who suffered confiscation, we cannot say definitely that the expenses of the kingdom pressed very hardly on his subjects. We may pass over the fact that Herod twice (in 20 and 14 B.C.) remitted part of the taxes and that in 25, during a severe famine, he undertook the provisioning of the country, for these statements are capable of contrary interpretations. But the total of the yearly taxes paid to Herod, about 1000 Jewish talents[1], seems to have been two hundred talents lower than that which Agrippa I imposed on his smaller and poorer kingdom. On the other hand the public works undertaken all over the kingdom must have given employment to many, and this by itself, apart from the watchful police-system of Herod, explains why we hear nothing, as we do before and after his reign, of bands of brigands in conflict with the land-owners; this benefit would alone have been enough to justify an increase in taxation. Indeed the only economic unrest in this period was in a Greek city, Gadara (c. 20 B.C.), and its complaints were brusquely rejected by Augustus. Nor is it fair to suppose that Herod helped himself by manipulating the currency; on the contrary he improved it by reducing the amount of lead, which had risen to

[1] Otto, op. cit. coll. 91 sqq. For the talent on which Josephus bases his calculations see F. Hultsch, Klio, II, 1902, p. 70.

27 per cent. during the brief reign of Antigonus, to 12·8 per cent.[1]

The truth is that Herod had other sources of income than the taxes of his subjects; first and foremost large hereditary estates, increased by confiscations, and secondly revenues from his commercial and industrial ventures. About these we have only stray notices, but they must have been on a large scale, as for instance his contract for half the revenues of the copper-mines in Cyprus, for which he paid Augustus 300 talents in 12 B.C.[2] In his speculations Herod was simply developing his father's estate, for Antipater was above all a financier and contractor. The reports on Herod's will, in which he left huge legacies (among them 1500 talents to Augustus and the imperial family), show how great his economic resources were.

Generally, apart from a small group of nobles ruined politically and financially, the Jews had no reason for discontent from the economic standpoint. And in one way no ruler contributed so much as Herod to the prestige of the Jewish religion, for the reason given above that his ambition was too strong to forgo popularity with the Jews. Thus, as he remained a Jew in religion, though claiming to be more Greek than Jew, the prestige of the Jews' religion was always an element in his own. In spite of gathering so many foreigners to his court, he could yet demand that the Nabataean vizier, Syllaeus, who had asked for the hand of his sister Salome, should be converted to Judaism, thus rendering the marriage impossible; and though he built foreign temples, in 20 B.C. he began the rebuilding of the Great Temple at Jerusalem. A proof of the magnificence of this rebuilding—which was proverbial—is its long duration; some ten years passed before it could even be inaugurated, and it was not properly finished till A.D. 64, on the very eve of the war with Rome. But Herod also intervened on behalf of the Jews of the Diaspora whenever their religious liberties or political rights were in danger: in 14 B.C. he caused Nicolaus to plead, with success, for the rights of the Jews in Asia Minor before Agrippa at Ephesus, and at the same time— though not with the same success—for those of the Jews of Cyrene[3]; the echoes that Agrippa's visit to Jerusalem aroused among all the Jews can easily be imagined. Indeed, in the Diaspora, where men

[1] Willrich, op. cit. p. 84.

[2] Ant. XVI [4, 5], 128. We hear also of a loan to Obodas, the king who succeeded Malchus in Nabataea (ib. [9, 4], 279; [10, 8], 343).

[3] What the exact questions of right at issue before Agrippa were is uncertain. For an hypothesis see Willrich, op. cit. p. 93.

could better appreciate the advantages of Herod's prestige in the
Gentile world and where they cared less about scrupulous observance of the law, Herod enjoyed great popularity which lasted
long after his death[1], and it is worth noting that one of the Jewish
communities in Rome was called after him[2].

But in Palestine things fell out differently. Herod's work of
superficial hellenization, designed simply to impose a different
political structure, lacked the co-operation of the Jews and
naturally did not alter their convictions in the least. That Herod
was often eager to proclaim himself a Jew only rendered his
offences graver when he broke the Law. Two instances only of
such violations need be cited. As a penalty for theft Herod laid
down a new law permitting the sale of the guilty party as a slave
to a Gentile; the Mosaic Law did not permit a Jew to be enslaved
for more than six years and only in his own country[3]. He allowed
his statue to be set up in a Gentile temple in Batanaea[4]. In short,
hellenization, presented openly as diametrically opposed to
Judaism, would have met with unsurmountable obstacles. As it
was, owing to the incomplete detachment of Herod from Judaism,
alternating with efforts at conciliation, such as the rebuilding of
the Temple, which only helped to inflame national religious feeling
more warmly, hellenization seemed a series of outrages against
the Law by a disloyal convert and provoked the national conscience
to a reaction so violent as to overwhelm the effect of all the political
reforms.

IV. THE LAST YEARS OF THE REIGN: DOMESTIC AND RELIGIOUS QUARRELS

Religious hostility lay dormant so long as family strife did, and
this, after the murders of 30–28 B.C., could not flare up again
until a new generation of the Hasmonaean house, represented by
Mariamme's sons Alexander and Aristobulus, reached manhood.
By sending these two sons to the imperial court at Rome in 23

[1] Persius, *Sat.* VI, 179–83 mentions a feast called after him; perhaps the
monthly commemoration of his birthday or of his accession to the throne.

[2] See the inscription in Vogelstein-Rieger, *Geschichte der Juden in Rom*,
No. 124. The name was probably given to this community (συναγωγή) in
7 B.C. at the time of the reform of all *sodalicia* in consequence of the Lex
Julia de collegiis. See J. B. Frey, *Recherches de science relig.* XXX, 1930, p. 269
and XXXI, 1931, p. 129; A. Momigliano, *Rassegna mensile d'Israel*, VI, 1931,
p. 283.   [3] *Ant.* XVI [1, 1], 1 *sqq.*

[4] *O.G.I.S.* 415. Naturally this is only one example, accidentally preserved, of what must have happened in many temples. Herod's marriage to
the Samaritan Malthace was equally an offence to Jewish feeling (p. 333).

Herod had shown that he thought of them as successors, provided, of course, that Augustus, in whose right the choice lay, agreed. But from now onwards the domestic situation became complicated, and was to become even more so, owing to Herod's numerous marriages—ten in all—and the resultant rivalries between the several sets of sons. It will be enough to mention here that by a second Mariamme, daughter or sister of the High Priest Simon (Boëthus' son), the king had a son Herod; by a Samaritan, Malthace, besides a daughter, two sons Archelaus and Antipas; by a Jewess of Jerusalem, Cleopatra, a son Philip. That by 20 B.C. he was already aware of the difficulties intrinsic in the situation is shown by the nomination of his brother Pheroras to the tetrarchy of Peraea, a measure that must be interpreted in the sense that while he felt it necessary to secure the loyal support of his brother, he also believed a division of the kingdom between the members of his family unavoidable; though possibly this division was to be limited, according to an utopian idea to which he clung obstinately, by the elevation of one, as the true king, above all the rest.

About 17 B.C. the two heirs designate returned from Rome: Alexander was married to Glaphyra, the daughter of the Cappadocian king Archelaus, Aristobulus to Berenice, the daughter of Herod's sister Salome. These two obviously political alliances revealed Herod's intentions clearly, as also his desire that the sons of the Hasmonaean should be bound more closely to his father's family. But his attempt at peace-making failed: the old feud was now rekindled by both Salome and Pheroras, to whom the imperious temperament of the two young men possibly lent a handle. Herod certainly gave ear to their attacks, for he recalled to the court his wife Doris and her son Antipater (p. 318), who represented the pure Idumaean tradition among his children. His designs for Antipater are by no means clear, but as he soon sent him to Rome in the suite of Agrippa (13 B.C.), he presumably meant him to have a share—perhaps the chief share—in the succession. The hatred between Antipater and the two sons of Mariamme naturally knew no bounds; even from Rome Antipater tried to achieve the overthrow of his brothers. Eventually he and his messengers convinced Herod that the two were plotting against Herod's life. The king's violent and suspicious temper suddenly broke loose again, as fifteen years before, and all the worse because he loved so well the sons by whom he believed himself betrayed. Indeed the most pitiable side of Herod's cruelty is just this, that it blazed out so furiously against real or suspected treachery in those to whom he was most attached. He decided to charge both his sons before Augustus, and they were tried at Aquileia in 12 B.C. The Emperor, with his usual good sense, tried to reconcile Herod and his sons, and for the time being succeeded. It was agreed that all three claimants should be kings after Herod's death and all wear the insignia of royalty, but that Antipater should exercise a primacy (though not, to modern eyes, a very clearly defined primacy) over the other two. But the solution was only temporary, and intrigues soon began again, complicated by all the customary jealousies and gossip of the *harem*. For instance it is said that a coolness developed between Herod and Pheroras because the king wished to marry one of his daughters to him, while Pheroras refused to part from one of his mistresses. It is certain, however, that Pheroras and Alexander drew towards each other and were accused of conspiring together, and that it was only the timely intervention of Archelaus of Cappadocia, Alexander's father-in-law, that saved them.

But meanwhile all these quarrels had sickened Augustus. And just about this time a fresh incident occurred to sharpen his annoyance and prove that he was beginning to view Herod with a different eye. Syllaeus, the vizier of the Nabataean king Obodas and determinedly hostile to Herod, not only helped some rebels in the Trachonitis but also tried to relieve his country from paying a debt contracted with Herod, or rather to withdraw it from the economic and political influence that Herod had been exerting over it since Cleopatra's time (p. 323). Herod demanded the handing-over of the rebels from Trachonitis, whom he was sheltering, and the payment of the debt (12 B.C.). The dispute dragged on till Herod lost patience and in 9 B.C. got leave from the legate of Syria to invade Nabataea. The expedition was purely punitive, with no territorial gain in view, but it sufficed to waken the suspicions of Augustus, who was misled by Syllaeus; he intimated to Herod that their friendship was at an end; henceforth he would treat him no longer as an ally but as a subject. It needed all the eloquence of Nicolaus and the support of Aretas IV—who had just succeeded Obodas and bore no kindly thoughts towards the minister of his predecessor—to turn Augustus to gentler counsels: perhaps too it needed the establishment of the oath of fealty to the Emperor, the introduction of which about this time, c. 8/7 B.C., should probably be regarded as one of the means devised by Herod to recapture the Emperor's goodwill (p. 329). But though relations improved the old sympathy did not return; indeed it could not, for now the family feuds sheered downwards to such tragedy as to draw from Augustus the bitter jest that he would sooner be Herod's pig than Herod's son[1].

Fresh charges were brought against Alexander and Aristobulus about 7 B.C., the agent apparently being the Spartan Eurycles. Probably, in contrast to the previous occasion, the accusation was well founded, for Augustus gave leave for it to proceed, merely ordaining that the trial should take place outside Herod's territory at Berytus, before a court of which Roman officials must form part; the court sat, and condemned the two brothers to death. Disaffection at once appeared in the army, an indication that extensive propaganda for a *coup d'État* had been used on the soldiers, and though it was ruthlessly repressed it is likely that the fear provoked by the movement drove Herod to carry out the sentence on his two sons without delay.

This disaffection was one of the first signs of a new unrest creeping over the country. Apart from the unimportant rebellion in Trachonitis, the last outbreak that could have disturbed Herod was that of the governor of Idumaea, Costobarus, about 27 B.C. and even that was of small consequence. But now the various members of his family, looking for supporters for their designs, offered a chance of expression to hidden discontent and even created it where it had not been before. The army was restive: more serious was a revolt among the Pharisees. They had already refused to take the oath to the king in 17 B.C. and though that was definite political opposition—for unlike the Essenes they had no objection on principle to oaths—owing to their large numbers Herod had had to leave them unpunished.

Now, on the introduction of the new oath, which included the Emperor's name, the Pharisees to the number of 6000 again refused to swear. Herod could not again leave them unpunished and he imposed a fine. But Pheroras' wife sided with them and paid the fine for them. Though Herod recognized the gravity of the issue and killed several of the chief men he dared not proceed against his brother's wife. Old age and approaching death seemed to emphasize his aversion from the strict letter of the Law, and he lost the comparative self-control that he had so far shown. He transgressed the Mosaic prohibition of images by putting the figure of an eagle over the gate of the Temple[2]. Whatever was

---

[1] Macrobius, *Sat.* II, 4, 11. The jest, which gains if uttered in Greek ($\hat{v}s$–$vi\acute{o}s$), had its sting, for Herod, as a Jew, would never touch pig's flesh.

[2] Josephus, *Ant.* XVII [6, 2], 151, regards this as a breaking of the Law but says no more. In Syria the eagle with outstretched wings appears to represent the sky-god and to reflect the Syrian Ba'alim just as Juppiter Capitolinus

the precise religious motive that underlay his action—if indeed it was anything more than a last provocative gesture against the orthodox whom he loathed—we must probably add a deep difference in matters religious to the already numerous reasons for these domestic quarrels; while Pharisaism was gaining some members of his family, Herod was drawing farther and farther away from it.

Pharisaism certainly reappeared in the next stage of the conflict. Though we have only a confused account of the enmity that arose between Herod and Antipater, once the latter had got rid of his rivals, two points emerge clearly: the first that Pheroras, in growing aversion from his brother, was working with Antipater to oust Herod, the second, that through his wife he was coming under the influence of Pharisaic circles. More we do not know, but the upshot was startling. Antipater, who had been sent for the second time to Rome in 5 B.C. to win the approval of Augustus for his nomination as sole heir to the throne, lost his influence in a moment and was summoned back to stand his trial, while only Pheroras' death a few months before saved him from a like fate. Even here, it is worth noting, the extraordinary court set up, of which the legate of Syria was a member, accepted the proofs of the accusation adduced by Nicolaus and sentenced Antipater to death; nor did Augustus, in spite of the growing disgust in his heart and his loss of confidence in the kingdom of Judaea, think of refusing permission to carry out the sentence.

Antipater was executed only a few days before his father, seventy years of age and for long ailing, himself went down to the grave (end of March–early April, 4 B.C.). It may be that, thanks to Herod's perverse cruelty, the son's condemnation hastened the father's death. Certainly he never showed himself a more determined hater than in those last days when he turned his frenzied energies against all whom he suspected of anticipating the joy of hearing of his death. A group of Pharisees, who had been instigated by two scribes to pull down the sacrilegious eagle on the Temple, were punished with inhuman ferocity; many were condemned to death, some actually burnt alive. On the very eve of

(Fr. Cumont in *Syria*, VIII, 1927, pp. 163 *sqq.*). Or it might be taken to symbolize apotheosis (cf. Fr. Cumont, *Études Syriennes*, pp. 35 *sqq.*) and indicate that in his old age Herod was attracted by soteriological cults, as Otto thinks, *op. cit.* col. 102. It cannot be brought into connection with a Herodian coin of uncertain date which figures an eagle with closed wings; this is simply an imitation of a Ptolemaic type, just as Herod's anchor and cornucopiae imitate Seleucid models.

his death he had the notables of his kingdom shut up in the hippo-
drome at Jericho, presumably holding them as hostages to secure
an undisturbed succession to the throne for his sons; this seems
more probable, at any rate, than Josephus' assertion that he meant
to kill them and so smother the outbursts of joy his death would
otherwise have caused[1]. Such a measure might perhaps have
hindered a rebellion; but it was cancelled by Salome, who deemed
it more politic to set the hostages free as soon as Herod was dead.
So these men were allowed to spread through the country, exasperated by the outrage done to them and helping, quite as much
as the memory of the recent massacre of the Pharisees, to foment
fresh discontents.

V. JUDAEA BECOMES A ROMAN PROVINCE

Once again dynastic quarrels came to the rescue of the Jewish
nation. Herod had nominated Archelaus as his successor, though
he had assigned to Antipas the tetrarchy of Galilee and Peraea, and
to Philip that of Gaulanitis, Trachonitis, Batanaea and Panias,
while to his sister Salome he had bequeathed Jamnia, Azotus and
Phasaelis. But in a will drawn up a little before he had left the
throne to Antipas. The reasons for the change are unknown.
Naturally Antipas began working at Rome to gain Augustus'
recognition of the will that favoured him, and so Archelaus in his
turn got Nicolaus to champion his rights, and meanwhile organized
a campaign to win Jewish favour by offering an amnesty and
lower taxes. But the people felt its strength, grew bolder and
demanded more, above all the dismissal of 'the Greeks' from their
posts; the crowds that assembled at Jerusalem for the Passover of
4 B.C. were riotous and repressed with difficulty. A little later a
Jewish embassy arrived at Rome, asking for the abolition of the
monarchy and the reinstatement of the theocracy under a Roman
protectorate[2]. But its desires were no more welcome than the

---

[1] *Bell. Jud.* I [33, 6], 660; *Ant.* XVII [6, 5], 175 *sqq.* The substance of
the story is confirmed by rabbinical tradition (the scholium of the *Megillath
Ta'anith*, 11), cf. J. Dérenbourg, *Essai sur l'histoire et la géographie de la
Palestine*, I, pp. 164–5 or H. L. Strack and P. Billerbeck, *Kommentar zum
Neuen Testament aus Talmud und Midrasch*, I, p. 89; this tradition, however,
wrongly ascribes the act to Alexander Jannaeus.

[2] It is very likely that chapter 103 of the Ethiopic *Book of Enoch* refers to
this embassy and mirrors Jewish delusions. See B. Motzo, *Saggi di Storia e
Letteratura giudeo-ellenistica*, pp. 3 *sqq.* On the situation at this time see also
the *Assumptio Mosis*, composed a little after A.D. 6, especially chapter 6; cf.
R. H. Charles, *Apocrypha and Pseudepigrapha*, II, p. 41.

appeals of Archelaus, for Augustus' one anxiety now was to break up the kingdom of Herod—which he regarded as useless—and yet give the appearance of upholding his will. For this reason he granted the rank of autonomous States to the tetrarchies created by Herod for Antipas and Philip, and reduced the kingdom of Archelaus (Judaea, Idumaea and Samaria) to an ethnarchy; also, by taking away the cities of Gaza, Gadara and Hippos and annexing them to the province of Syria, he satisfied to some extent the wish of the Greek cities not to be under a Jewish State. But the territories which had been bequeathed to Salome were incorporated in the ethnarchy of Archelaus, because they were regarded (perhaps in accord with Herod's intentions) as her private property and not as her dominion.

Meanwhile the failure of the Jewish embassy at Rome provoked new and serious outbreaks in Judaea, and the procurator Sabinus, who had been placed there by Augustus to safeguard the interests of Rome and of the sons of Herod, merely aggravated them by his shuffling policy. Armed bands sprang up on every side and petty captains took the title of king. Varus, the legate of Syria, was forced to dispatch two legions to harry Palestine with fire and sword. At last the three sons of Herod were able to return to their territories[1]: the need to defend themselves against their subjects did something to lessen their rivalries, but a sign of the conflicting claims of Archelaus and Antipas is perhaps to be seen in their simultaneous adoption of the name Herod; by raising it to a dynastic name each presumably meant to show that he regarded himself as the true heir and successor of Herod[2]. The tetrarchies of Philip and Antipas remained intact (save for a brief interval between A.D. 34 and 37 in the former tetrarchy) until Agrippa I absorbed them in A.D. 41 in the larger Jewish kingdom that Claudius gave him, and then took on a new life in altered form under Agrippa II (p. 854); but the principality of Archelaus, comprising the majority of the Jewish population, had no chance of survival. The enmity of the people was rendered more bitter by the

[1] Samaria was rewarded for not joining in the rebellion by a reduction of one-quarter in her taxes; the phrasing in Josephus (*Ant.* XVII [11, 4], 319; *Bell. Jud.* II [6, 3], 96) which might be taken to refer to all Archelaus' ethnarchy, and not merely to Samaria, is certainly incorrect.

[2] Josephus, in setting out the genealogy of the House of Herod, gives him the title of ὁ μέγας (*Ant.* XVIII [5, 4], 130, 133, 136). This title is never found on inscriptions, coins, or even in Josephus elsewhere, and its position here lends colour to the hypothesis of H. Ewald, *Geschichte des Volkes Israel*, IV³, p. 546, that ὁ μέγας simply signifies 'the elder' (*maior*) in comparison with these sons of the same name.

hardships that followed the stoppage of the great public works begun by Herod, and for long the presence of a Roman legion was needed in Jerusalem. Archelaus married his cousin Glaphyra, who had been the wife of his brother Alexander and had then passed by a second marriage to Juba of Mauretania; but since Glaphyra had already had children by Alexander, the marriage was illegal according to Jewish law and only increased his unpopularity. Nor does the other evidence suggest any striking sagacity, for his only recorded achievements were the foundation of a village (*kome*) called after him[1] and some fresh palm-plantations at Jericho. Least satisfactory of all must have been his relations with Rome. Augustus had long ago lost any illusions as to the possibility of making Judaea a really strong client-kingdom. Consequently he readily gave a hearing in A.D. 6 to two embassies; one was Jewish, the other Samaritan, but they came with an unanimity that must have been unique to demand again the abolition of the monarchy. Archelaus was banished to Vienna in Gallia Narbonensis, and Judaea was transformed into a province under an imperial procurator, commanding a body of troops and with judicial powers (*ius gladii*).

The Jews had been unable to find any other way to escape the hated dynasty than by demanding direct administration by Rome: some years later, when this direct rule began to seem to them even less bearable than kingship, there were many ready to group together in a party, which aimed at the restoration of the monarchy of the Herods; they were the *Herodiani* of the Gospel texts[2].

[1] On the topography of *Archelaïs*, cf. H. Guthe, *Mitt. des Paläst.-Vereins*, 1911, p. 65; P. Thomsen, *ib.* 1912, p. 71; F.-M. Abel, *Rev. Bibl.* x, 1913, p. 236 *sq.*

[2] *Matt.* xxii, 16; *Mark* iii, 6; xii, 13. For the interpretation see Otto in *P.W.* Suppl. II, *s.v.* Herodianoi.

CHAPTER XII

THE NORTHERN FRONTIERS UNDER AUGUSTUS

I. THE PRINCEPS AND THE EMPIRE

ALTHOUGH Augustus had neither the instincts of a soldier nor the ambition of a conqueror, his Principate is a long record of military operations on almost every frontier, from the Northern Ocean to the shore of Pontus, from the mountains of Cantabria to the Ethiopian desert: and on the proud memorial of his achievements the Princeps claimed that he had moved forward the boundaries of every frontier province of the Empire.

While Heaven might promise to the Roman people dominion without limit of space or time, the dangerous extent to which the empire had already grown excited apprehension. Duration and security were surely preferable to breadth of empire. Yet if peace once established were to endure, if the empire were to stand firm for the future, it would have to be enlarged still further—only then would it be possible to reduce foreign policy to the protection of the frontiers, and to banish at the same time the occasion for warfare on a large scale and its unfailing concomitant or sequel, the menace of intestine strife. To the attainment of this end the wars of Augustus were devoted: and the consolidation of the far-flung and haphazard conquests of the Republic demanded a con-

Note. The only continuous histories extant, those of Dio and of Velleius Paterculus, are peculiarly inadequate, as is at once apparent whenever they describe the same events. Dio provides a chronological order, but neither his dates nor his opinions can always be accepted. Velleius is usually incoherent and soon degenerates into an enthusiastic biographer of Tiberius; even where he writes as an eye-witness, about the Pannonian Revolt, he must be checked and supplemented with the help of Dio, if a rational narrative is to be secured. Tacitus recounts at some length the campaigns of Germanicus. The *Res Gestae* of Augustus is unique; so is Strabo in another way—there is no part of the subject which his disinterested testimony does not illuminate. But where these fail us, scraps of information must be gleaned from the most various, often from the most miserable, of sources. Pliny the Elder, Suetonius, and the *Periochae* of Livy are naturally of value: but even Florus and Orosius cannot be neglected. (For other sources, see the Bibliography.)

Epigraphic evidence other than the *Res Gestae* now begins to be very important (*e.g.* Dessau 8965).

siderable annexation of new territories. The East might remain
more or less as Pompey and Antony had left it, but in Europe between the Rhine and the Black Sea there were only two dependent
kingdoms, Noricum and Thrace, and they might not always be
equal to the task of checking a barbarian invasion or controlling
their own subjects: for the rest, the ragged fringes of Roman
dominion could nowhere be dignified with the name of a frontier.
It was here that the Empire was to receive an extension that gave it
internal stability as well as defensible frontiers. While the principal
conquests of the Romans were achieved under the Republic,
Augustus not only designed and nearly carried out a plan of
annexation surpassing in magnitude anything attempted by Rome
before or since, but also, despite the abandonment of Germany,
was able to add to the Empire, in Western and Central Europe, an
area as great as that of the Gaul which Caesar conquered. Hitherto, though Rome had extended her sway from Tagus to Euphrates,
there had been more chance than design in the process. But when
at last the Empire had begotten an Emperor, when one mind and
one will directed the armies of the Roman People, it might be
expected that a vigorous policy would take the place of inertia
and acquiescence. The secret of the real intentions of the great
Dictator perished with him, yet it is hard to believe that he would
not have wished to do in Illyricum and the Balkans what he had
done in Gaul, and win the Danube as well as the Rhine. Be that as
it may, this necessary task was reserved for his successor: and it
was not until some fifteen years after Actium that the plan of
Augustus began to unfold—it had been long matured and well
prepared and was not to be launched until he had completed the
pacification of Spain, of Africa, and of the Alpine lands and the
organization of provinces east and west.

By the terms of his first settlement with the Senate the Princeps
took as his portion Spain, Gaul and Syria (with Cilicia and Cyprus),
almost the same provinces as those held by Pompey, Caesar and
Crassus, but with a significant difference—Cisalpine Gaul was not
among them. The most powerful of the provinces and by far the
greater number of the legions were his: but of the provinces in
which armies were stationed the Senate retained for its proconsuls
Africa, Illyricum and Macedonia, and with them about six legions[1].
Augustus could claim with some justification that he had restored
a free constitution—he was not the only proconsul with an army,

[1] Dio (LIII, 12) is anachronistic and misleading (see above, p. 211). For
the problem presented by the military protection of Northern Italy, see
below, p. 348 *sq.*

and, as he did not hold Cisalpine Gaul, he was not exerting undue pressure on Rome and Italy. No danger or inconvenience to his own position or to the needs of the Empire was to be apprehended: and though Illyricum or Macedonia might require the attention of the Princeps as much as Gaul or Spain, the arrangement was provisional in form and could be modified at need. It would be well for Augustus to depart to his provinces without delay, to remove from Rome a prestige and a power that might soon become burdensome, and to allow the revived rule of Senate and People to stand alone, without help and without hindrance. Moreover, though the Empire could have no other capital than Rome, its government could be directed, in so far as direction was advisable, by a Princeps residing for long periods in Tarraco, Lugdunum or Samos.

It was to the West that Augustus first turned. Towards the middle of the year 27 he set out for Gaul. There was some expectation that he would emulate the great Julius and invade Britain: but before the end of the year he was in Spain, no doubt his goal from the first.

II. SPAIN AND AFRICA

Of the provinces acquired by the Romans under the Republic, Spain was one of the earliest to be entered, one of the latest to be pacified. It is easy to invoke that inevitable explanation, the short-comings of Republican policy: it is more profitable to consider the character of the land and its inhabitants.

The definite bounds of the peninsula, the sea and the Pyrenees, lend to it a deceptive appearance of unity and compactness. It is a land of bare plateaus and tangled trackless mountains; roads are few, for the rivers and their valleys are seldom channels of communication, but only so many obstacles to surmount. Spain is indeed more similar to Asia Minor or North Africa than to Gaul. The population is split up into many small divisions, and though the natives cannot oppose a united resistance to an invader, they are, for that reason, all the more difficult to subdue—in which matter the contrast with Gaul is again evident. Warfare in Spain presents an unchanging face—it degenerates into brigandage on both sides. A small army will gradually waste away and finally be overwhelmed, a large force will starve. Nowhere is the country more difficult than in the north and north-west, ever the last home of Spanish independence. The Cantabrian mountains stand in serried masses severing the upland plain from the northern coast, and beyond to the west extend the tangled mountains of Galicia and

Northern Portugal, pierced, but not opened up, by the rivers Minho
and Douro. On the western coast the Callaeci, it is true, had been
more or less accessible to the influence of commerce and the arms
of Rome; but the interior and the northern coast were untouched
—the shepherds and huntsmen of the hills, the untamed Asturians
and Cantabrians, had not merely held their own but had turned to
their profit Rome's enforced neglect and had extended their sway
southwards over the agricultural population of the plateau of León
and Old Castile.

The final conquest was arduous to achieve and would be tedious
to record, even if the sources were satisfactory. The Princeps
directed in person only the Bellum Cantabricum, the first of the
two campaigns of 26 and 25 B.C. He recounted it in his autobiography, and a brief and obscure narrative has preserved a
few details[1]. The campaigns of his legates, however, are barely
mentioned, and, on the other side, except for a brigand called
Corocotta, the heroes of the last fight for Spanish freedom are
nameless and unknown. None the less, geography and the unchanging character of Spanish warfare can provide the outline
and the colours, even if most of the details are lacking. The
routes of armies and the paths of conquest present little variation.
There were two Roman armies, probably of three legions each,
those of Nearer and of Further Spain[2]; in 26 B.C. Augustus put
himself at the head of the former, and undertook the conquest
of Cantabria. A beginning had probably been made before this,
and it might be conjectured that some at least of the successes for
which six Spanish triumphs had been celebrated in the last ten
years had been earned in Navarre and had served to open up communications with Aquitania over the western Pyrenees; and the
western flank of his army may likewise have been made secure[3].

[1] Orosius VI, 21, 1–11, and Florus II, 33 [IV, 12], drawing upon a lost
epitome of Livy. Only a very radical treatment of these sources can yield an
intelligible narrative, and much must remain conjectural and controversial.
See D. Magie, 'Augustus' War in Spain' in *C.P.* XV, 1920, and the present
writer, 'The Spanish War of Augustus (26–25 B.C.),' in *A.J.Ph.* LV, 1934.

[2] It is evident that there were still, and for some time, two Spanish armies,
even if Further Spain had been divided as early as 27 B.C., with Baetica going
to the Senate, as Dio (LIII, 12, 4) holds. It can, however, be maintained that
in 27 B.C. Augustus took over the whole of Spain.

[3] Carisius the governor of Further Spain came up and prevented an
Asturian attack on the winter camps of the legions of Nearer Spain, and then
captured Lancia, a few miles south-east of León. This exploit is narrated by
Orosius and Florus after the close of the campaign of 25 B.C., but surely
belongs to the early spring of 26 or of 25 B.C.

However that may be, Augustus set out from his base at Segisama (west of Burgos), and the army marched northwards in three columns[1]. The Cantabrians were defeated in battle at Vellica, and the Romans forced their way through the pass which leads by Juliobriga (near Reinosa) down to the coast near Santander. A fleet now co-operated, bringing supplies and landing troops from Aquitania to take the enemy in the rear. Some of the Cantabrians took refuge on the Mons Vindius (perhaps the Peñas de Europa), where they were hemmed in and reduced. But there must have been many another band to be hunted down by the Romans as they contended with hunger, heat and flies, with all the discomforts as well as all the perils of mountain warfare against an elusive and resourceful enemy. Augustus, worn-out and dangerously ill, retired to Tarraco and left to his lieutenants Antistius and Carisius the conduct of the next year's campaign, the penetration and subjugation of Asturia and Callaecia. This would appear to have been the work of the two armies, advancing from their separate and distant bases. Antistius with the army of Nearer Spain marched westwards, past León and Astorga over the Montañas de León into the hill-girt basin of El Vierzo and the upper waters of the river Sil. In the meantime Carisius approached from the south-west. The armies met and beleaguered the Asturians on the Mons Medullius[2]: the fall of this position brought the campaign to a suitable and dramatic conclusion.

The war was now regarded as over, veterans were dismissed and the closing of Janus was decreed. Augustus returned to Rome, which he reached in the course of the next year, 24 B.C. It might appear at first sight that he had completed in two years the process of two centuries and had equalled if not surpassed, on their own ground, the achievements of a Scipio or a Pompey. But he had hardly departed when war flamed up once again and raged almost without intermission: it was not until Agrippa was called to Spain in 19 B.C. that the end came. Most intractable were the Cantabrians—captives sold into slavery slew their masters, escaped to the hills and raised the tribes. Insubordinate soldiers—many of them were elderly and weary of war—as well as a desperate and embittered enemy tried the patience and the resource of Agrippa. At last and at the cost of wholesale massacre the stubborn spirit of the Cantabrians was broken and a war of eight years was brought to an end.

[1] The route and the operations of only one of these columns appear to have been recorded.
[2] The site cannot be ascertained.

Such was often the fate of a freedom-loving people. Among those wild mountains and barbarous tribes peace could never be permanent unless conquest had been thorough and unrelenting. It will be convenient to mention in brief space the methods which were called for in the Alps, the Balkans and the Taurus as well, and carry forward by a few years the pacification of Spain to the time when Augustus again visited it during his second sojourn in the West in the years 16–13 B.C.

With calm majesty Augustus observes that he preferred not to wipe out utterly such tribes as could safely be spared[1]. Comprehensive enslavement and massacre were often the only remedy, but the desired end could sometimes be attained if the natives were enlisted in large numbers and transported abroad to spend their dangerous valour in the service of Rome. In this way many regiments of Spaniards came to the Rhine and to Illyricum. The survivors were encouraged or compelled to come down from their mountain strongholds and settle in new towns. This was an old device and it was employed elsewhere—in Gaul the Aedui now abandoned the hill of Bibracte and built Augustodunum in the plain. New urban centres appear in the north-west, Bracaraugusta (Braga), Lucus Asturum (Lugo), Asturica Augusta (Astorga). They were connected by a network of military roads, for the land did not yet appear quite secure, and a large garrison still remained, at first of four or five legions; even when troops were urgently needed on the Rhine after the disaster of Varus, Spain was allowed to retain three legions. These were not the only cities to be built in Spain—the veterans of the wars were provided for, either by new colonial foundations such as Emerita (Merida) and Caesaraugusta (Saragossa), or by the reinforcement of older colonies or towns. Urban civilization and the use of the Latin tongue could now spread over a great part of the peninsula; Roman and native could exploit in peace the wealth of its soil and the produce of its mines. It may have been now (in 16–13 B.C.) that Further Spain was divided, its southern and more civilized part, Baetica, being given to the Senate: the other part, Lusitania, was retained by the Princeps, and to Lusitania the western portion of the newly conquered territory, Asturia and Callaecia, was at first attached; it was subsequently assigned to Nearer Spain (Tarraconensis) when the two Spanish armies were fused into one[2].

Spain and Northern Africa are intimately connected in geo-

---

[1] *Res Gestae* 3 (not with reference to Spain).
[2] The dates of these changes are uncertain and controversial.

graphy and in history; and the provinces of the Senate no less than those of the Princeps have their place in the Augustan scheme of consolidation. The year of the final pacification of Spain, 19 B.C., witnessed the celebration of an African triumph that was long to be remembered. Cornelius Balbus made an expedition to the land of the Garamantes in Fezzan far to the south of the region of the Syrtes and reached Garama, their capital. It might be inferred that this distant expedition was not undertaken until some measure of order and security had been established nearer home. Triumphs had also been earned by Balbus' predecessor and by three earlier proconsuls between 34 and 28 B.C. A spectacular performance may eclipse but it cannot disprove more solid achievements. Hardly any details have been preserved in history—a fact which illustrates how capricious and fragmentary, in Africa as in other regions, is the record of the wars of the age of Augustus. Enough survives, however, to refute the opinion that only peaceful provinces had been left to the Senate in 27 B.C. The memory of Carthage and the food-supply of the capital magnified the importance of Africa: that Augustus should have resigned Africa to a proconsul is evidence both of the strength of his own position and of the art with which he disguised it.

Caesar converted the kingdom of Numidia into a province called Africa Nova (vol. IX, p. 688); and after the death of Bocchus in 33 B.C. all Mauretania lapsed to Rome. Though Augustus had founded a dozen military colonies in Mauretania, he can hardly have desired to retain this region as a province, if he could help it, and govern directly the whole of North Africa from the shore of the Atlantic to the Syrtes with a frontier nearly a thousand miles in length. A client-prince was required. The last king of Numidia had left a son. In the enforced leisure of exile the young Juba turned his mind to the pursuits of science and letters: at the bidding of a stern taskmaster he now assumed the cares of war and government. In 25 B.C. Augustus made him king of Mauretania, to which was attached a considerable part of the dominions of his father. In this same year another instrument of imperial policy, Amyntas the king of Galatia, met his end in the execution of his duty and was slain by the wild tribes of the Taurus. Juba was to enjoy a long reign—but not without risk of his life. His large Mauretanian kingdom covered and defended the Roman province of Africa on the west and south-west, and it was his task to exercise what control he could over the tribes of the plateau and the desert, the Gaetulians—for such was the name generally applied to all the nomad peoples on and beyond the ill-defined southern borders of Mauretania and Numidia. In Africa, as elsewhere, the settled agricultural peoples presented few problems —if they did not welcome Roman protection they could easily be harried and conquered: the tribes of the mountain, the steppe and the desert were elusive and intractable.

Cornelius Balbus had made the name of Rome known and respected among the proverbially distant Garamantes; and the Marmaridae who dwelt south of the province of Cyrene were dealt with by P. Sulpicius Quirinius at an uncertain date. Yet disturbances could not fail to occur. In A.D. 5–6 Cossus Cornelius Lentulus terminated with success a formidable Gaetulian War and bequeathed a cognomen to his son. The natives had revolted from the control of King Juba and had inflicted severe losses on Roman troops that had been dispatched against them. Next to nothing is known of these operations, but the analogy of warfare in North Africa before or since provides some idea of the difficulties that must have confronted the Romans, and permits the conjecture that they had lasted for some time[1]. In the reign of Tiberius the insurgent leader Tacfarinas pursued his depredations and evaded capture for seven years (see p. 643 *sq.*).

After A.D. 6 only one legion was stationed in Africa (III Augusta, probably at Ammaedara, near Theveste). During the revolt of Tacfarinas, however, another legion had to be summoned. It might therefore be doubted whether the African garrison had been quite as small as one legion in an earlier period of unrest[2].

III. THE ALPS

The first decade of the principate of Augustus was devoted to preparation and consolidation, the second to new and extensive conquest. These two periods are bridged by the subjugation of the Alpine regions which is at the same time the last stage of the one and the first of the other. In 16 B.C. begins Augustus' second sojourn in the provinces of the West. That a German raid across the Rhine in the previous year and a defeat which Lollius the governor of Gallia Comata suffered, but very soon retrieved, was the cause or even the occasion of his journey is highly doubtful. Eleven years before, Augustus had halted at Narbo on the way to

---

[1] Dio (LV, 28, 3–4) records the end of the War under the year A.D. 6. A few years earlier L. Passienus Rufus had been awarded *ornamenta triumphalia* and had assumed the title of *imperator* (Vell. Pat. II, 116, 2; Dessau 120).

[2] See *J.R.S.* XXIII, 1933, p. 25.

Spain, but his stay had been brief, and Gallia Comata must sooner or later claim his undivided attention. He now came to Lugdunum and during the next three years completed the organization of the Gallic provinces. He was also able to visit Spain once more. In these years his frontier policy begins to assume nobler proportions and a clearer outline.

While the legions made war and conquests far away, Northern Italy was still exposed to the raids of petty Alpine tribes; and although Gaul had been in Roman hands for a generation, the passes which provide the shortest and most convenient routes to Central Gaul and the Upper Rhine, the Little and the Great St Bernard, were not yet available for troops or traders. North of the Great St Bernard the tribes of the Vallis Poenina (the Valais) forbade access, to the south the Salassi of the Val d'Aosta. Caesar had tried, but in vain, to gain control of this all-important pass and quite recently the Salassi had defied armies sent against them (p. 87). Their impunity was short-lived: in 25 B.C. Terentius Varro applied the ruthless measures that were here and elsewhere necessary, and all but blotted out the very name of the Salassi. Forty-four thousand of them, almost all who survived the massacre, were sold into slavery in the market of Eporedia. In this way the approach from the south was secured: the northern side of the pass cannot have been neglected, and it is an attractive conjecture that a success won by Marcus Vinicius in this same year set the seal upon the pacification of the Valais[1]. After this nothing is recorded until 17 or 16 B.C. when P. Silius Nerva, proconsul of Illyricum, reduced the tribes of the valleys from Como eastwards to Lake Garda, and probably also the Venostes of the Upper Adige (Val Venosta, Vintschgau). Taking advantage of his absence, Pannonians and raiders from Noricum came down and harried Istria. This was the cause, or at least the pretext, of the incorporation of the kingdom of Noricum which followed either at once or after no long interval[2].

A more spectacular campaign could now be launched. The southward-facing valleys of the Alps had been occupied or blocked: to complete the work it was thought necessary to pass beyond the principal chain of the Alps, cut off and isolate the

[1] Dio LIII, 26, 4–5; cf. G. Zippel, *Die Römische Herrschaft in Illyrien*, pp. 252–3.

[2] Dio records the operations of P. Silius Nerva under the year 16 B.C. (LIV, 20, 1–2). It is not a serious difference that Strabo (IV, 206) should make the incorporation of Noricum a part of the campaign of Drusus and Tiberius in 15 B.C.

northern valleys and, by subduing the Raetians of the Tirol and eastern Switzerland and the Vindelicians of Bavaria, win possession of all the land that slopes down to the Danube. In 15 B.C. Tiberius was to march eastwards with legions from Gaul, his brother Drusus northwards, no doubt with a part of the army of Illyricum. Drusus appears to have used the route which the Via Claudia Augusta was to follow, up the broad Val Venosta and over the Pass of Resia (the Reschenscheideck) to the valley of the Inn[1]; and one of his columns may have crossed the Brenner, despite the gorges of the Isarco (Eisack) and the ferocity of the Breuni and Genauni. From the valley of the Inn his troops could march across the mountains by easy passes into Bavaria. In the meantime Tiberius, after winning a battle beside Lake Constance, was also ready to invade Bavaria. The brothers met, overran the land and carried their conquests as far as the Danube.

It was a signal triumph for the arms of Rome and the household of the Princeps, and Horace was persuaded to recall to service his ageing lyric Muse and celebrate the exploits of the stepsons of Augustus. It was the rapid termination of a long process, and while it crowned the exertions, it may have obscured the merits of others less fortunate. None the less this rapidity and ease of conquest admits of another explanation. In many parts the long, broad Alpine valleys provided attractive lines of march and lines of communication: and the Alps could be crossed by passes which were quite easy of access. For the natives who dwelt in the valleys there was no escape save to a death of hunger and cold on the high peaks. It was not so in the broken ravines and wooded hills of Northwestern Spain and the Balkans, or in the marshlands and forests of Germany.

High on the mountain side above Monaco was erected the Trophy of Augustus to commemorate the pacification of the Alps from end to end, from the upper to the lower sea, and to bear record of the names of the tribes that had been subdued[2]. Augustus claimed to have made war on none of them without just cause or provocation—a protestation which might perhaps have been spared. Italy at length had peace from their inroads and was no longer to require military protection. Cisalpine Gaul could now become in the fullest sense a part of Italy—its union with Italy in 42 B.C. (p. 26, n. 3) does not seem to have been maintained without

---

[1] *C.I.L.* v, 8003 (cf. *ib.* 8002 = Dessau 208), a milestone found west of Merano.

[2] *C.I.L.* v, 7817; Pliny, *N.H.* III, 136–7. Cf. *Res Gestae* 26.

interruption[1]. This region had always been fertile and populous; it was now to enjoy a period of exceptional prosperity, and develop its resources by trade with the lands beyond the Alps. Its thriving cities were the admiration of the traveller[2], and this breeding ground of legionary soldiers and civil servants was the very core of the strength of the Roman Empire.

The new territories were not organized in a uniform manner. In the valleys that slope southwards towards the Po the practice of placing the native population under the charge and control of the cities was continued and extended. For example in the Val d'Aosta a new colony, Augusta Praetoria, was built on the site of Varro's camp, and a few Salassi who had been spared were 'attributed' to it[3]. Brixia likewise received the tribes of Val Camonica and Val Trompia[4], Tridentum the Anauni[5]. In the West, the Maritime Alps had been reduced in 14 B.C. and were placed under an equestrian governor. In the Cottian Alps M. Julius Cottius, the son of a native prince, ruled with the name and rank of a Roman prefect. As the reward of a wise and timely submission, his dominions were preserved and even augmented: and, guided by gratitude or policy, he improved the road across the pass of the Mont Genèvre[6]. The peaceful and civilized kingdom of Noricum had long been in a position of amicable dependence; but its purpose had been served, and very soon after 15 B.C., if not just before that date, the Romans took charge of its destiny. The Raetians, Vindelicians and the four tribes of the Vallis Poenina were subsequently governed by an equestrian prefect or procurator. At first, however, there appears to have been a garrison of two legions in the land (until A.D. 9), at Augusta Vindelicorum (Augsburg)[7], in order to hold it in subjection, to protect it from invasion—the Marcomanni were still

---

[1] Cisalpine Gaul, or at least the Transpadana, may for a time have belonged to the *provincia* of a proconsul. Suetonius (*De Rhet.* 6) attests the presence of a proconsul at Milan; compare the operations of P. Silius Nerva (above, p. 348), who was proconsul of Illyricum (Dessau 899).

[2] Strabo V, 210 and 218.　　　　[3] Strabo IV, 206; Dessau 6753.

[4] Pliny, *N.H.* III, 134.

[5] Dessau 206. Cf. further, Comum, Dessau 206, and Tergeste, Dessau 6680.

[6] Dessau 94; Pliny, *N.H.* III, 138; Ammianus Marcellinus XV, 10, 2. On the Alpine roads see further Strabo IV, 204 and 209.

[7] Archaeological remains found at Oberhausen, a suburb of Augsburg, have been taken to imply a military occupation; and without the hypothesis of a garrison of two legions in Raetia, the distribution of the legions in A.D. 6 is baffling. Compare Ritterling in *P.W. s.v. Legio*, col. 1226, and his reading of Dessau 847, viz. ... [s]ub C. Vibio Pansa legato pro [pr. in] Vindol.

near at hand in the valley of the Main and had not yet migrated to Bohemia—and to co-operate, when the time should come, in the conquest of Germany.

With the annexation of Noricum Roman control now extended down the Danube as far as Vienna. Italy no longer needed the protection of the army of Illyricum, which was free to operate against the Pannonians and Dalmatians. It is time to discuss the reasons that may have moved Augustus and his military advisers to conceive the ambitious plan of conquest which now begins to unfold in Illyricum—and in Germany as well.

IV. THE NORTHERN FRONTIER OF THE EMPIRE

Northern Italy could never feel safe until the raids of Alpine tribes had been brought to an end; the coast lands of Dalmatia were exposed to like visitations, and the warlike peoples on the borders of Macedonia had seldom cheated a governor of his triumph. The security of these civilized regions, however, is only a partial explanation of the end which the policy of Augustus sought to attain. The watershed of the Alps might have provided Italy with a natural frontier on the north. But conquest passed beyond the Alps, and the extension of Illyricum to the Danube is also part of a larger plan. Nor is it to be believed that the security of the Gallic provinces demanded the conquest of Germany and Bohemia. Both before and after the wars of Augustus the Rhine provided an adequate frontier. If the Elbe were to replace it, the Elbe would have to be defended no less than the Rhine, and legions would still be required to hold down the Gauls. Such an advance would be no solution of the Gallic and German problems —if anything, an added danger. Yet it was contemplated by the sober intelligence of Augustus and prosecuted for twenty years. Other reasons must therefore be sought: they will perhaps be discovered if the European frontiers of the Empire are examined, not separately, but together, with Illyricum as central in position and foremost in importance.

Among the dangers revealed by the Civil Wars were two most ominous—that an army could make an emperor and that there might even be two Empires, an Eastern and a Western. The problems that confronted Augustus might perhaps be solved in the same way, in so far as they admitted a final solution: it was his design to make the Empire stable and secure by giving it a broad territorial basis and frontiers easily defended. The army had now become in fact, if not in name, a standing army. And, apart from the cost of its upkeep and the scarcity of recruits of a suitable stamp, the grave political menace which the army presented by its very existence was another good reason for keeping it as small as was safe. For the moment no enemy threatened the Empire: but what of the future? The Cimbri might come again, another Mithridates might rise, another Burebista, perhaps both at once. It would therefore be well to enlarge the Empire and create a continuous line of defence from sea to sea. What was required was a shortening not so much of frontiers as of communications, for it is not the mere length of a frontier that matters—it is the danger of its being attacked and the ease with which it can be reinforced. By their lines of communication both armies and empires stand or fall: the quicker the routes available between points of danger the fewer troops are required.

Hitherto the communications of Italy with Gaul and Macedonia had been deplorably circuitous and difficult. Before Augustus took in hand the conquest of the Alps, Roman armies had not been able to use the passes of the Little and the Great St Bernard leading to Central Gaul and the Upper Rhine. To Macedonia there was no land route at all in Roman hands, for the Dalmatian coast does not lend itself to the passage of an army even in times of peace[1]. Short of the valley of the Save there is no route—between the Save and the coast lies Bosnia, one of the most pathless and isolated regions in Europe. Of the old road from Italy to the valley of the Save, across the low eastern gateway of Italy, the Julian Alps, the Romans had long been aware. Here Italy was most vulnerable, here Philip V of Macedon had planned to send over a horde of Bastarnae[2]. It was a long time before the Romans ventured to advance beyond the Julian Alps and when they did it was for the better protection of Italy or in order to get into touch with the Dalmatian coast. It is indeed surprising that it was left to Augustus to win for Rome the overland route to the Balkans, the route which was to be the very backbone of the Empire. It ran from Aquileia to Emona, from Emona down the Save to Siscia, Sirmium, Singidunum and beyond to Naissus, and thence south-eastwards by Serdica to Byzantium. This is the only route by which in our day the kingdom of Yugoslavia can be traversed from end to end with

[1] The march of Raymond of Toulouse in A.D. 1096, from Istria to Albania, is a military curiosity.
[2] Livy XXXIX, 35 and XL, 57. Compare the fears of Augustus in A.D. 6, Vell. Pat. II, 110, 6.

some measure of rapidity and comfort. Control of this road—and of the other way to Sirmium, that from Poetovio down the Drave to Mursa—was a necessity which could no longer be postponed. The control of these routes brought with it the natural extension of Roman Illyricum as far as the Danube, from Vienna to Belgrade. By the conquest of Raetia and the annexation of Noricum the Romans had just won the south bank of the great river as far down as Vienna, and this further conquest might be expected to follow, and did follow, without delay. An enlarged Illyricum would thus bind Macedonia to Italy and, through easy passes in the Eastern Alps, bring it much nearer to Gaul and the Upper Rhine. A direct route between Bâle and Belgrade represents a considerable saving in time and therefore in troops.

The value of Illyricum is manifest, its conquest is the logical and necessary sequel of all that had gone before it. Not so Germany—it is almost an afterthought, a further development on a large scale, an experiment which if unsuccessful need not be ruinous. It had been found necessary to extend Illyricum as far as the Danube; it might also be profitable to advance in Germany at the same time, if thereby frontiers and communications could be shortened still farther. To the east the broad estuary of the Elbe gave promise of a river that might replace the Rhine as a frontier; and its sources southwards could not be far from the middle course of the Danube. Beyond the forests of Central Germany and the Böhmer Wald there might be open country, and it was no doubt known that there were fertile lands in Saxony about the middle course of the Elbe and in the heart of Bohemia. Imperfect geographical knowledge may well have encouraged undue hopes both of the ease with which such a conquest could be made and of the advantages which would accrue from it: but it was worth the attempt, and only invasion and exploration could give a final answer. Gaul had proved an acquisition of inestimable value. After a rapid conquest the natives appeared to acquiesce in their subjugation. Germans west of the Rhine were seen to be amenable to civilization and loyal to Rome—might not their wilder kinsmen to the east be subdued and incorporated? The annexation of Germany and Bohemia would provide a shorter frontier and a shorter line of communication, substituting for the line Cologne—Bâle—Vienna the line Hamburg—Leipzig—Prague—Vienna. It would also leave no room in Central Europe for a power to grow up dangerous to Rome, and it would broaden yet further and consolidate still more firmly the western half of the Empire and thereby ensure its preponderance, in peace as in war, over the East. But this grandiose design was subsidiary to the Roman advance in Illyricum. Even were it to be postponed or abandoned, the work of Augustus would not be incomplete. It was Illyricum that held the Empire together and bound East to West, whether the frontier was to follow Elbe or Rhine.

Reasons such as these must be invoked to explain the frontier policy of Augustus and the plan of conquest which began to unfold during his second sojourn in the provinces of the West. The time was now ripe, the army was ready. The pacification of Spain had set free several legions for service on the northern frontiers, and the conquest of the Alps enabled the legions of Illyricum to turn their arms eastwards. In 27 B.C. the armies of the Gallic provinces, of Illyricum and of Macedonia, probably did not number more than ten or eleven legions. Now, however, in 13 B.C., if we may assume that the armies had reached the strength which they probably had in A.D. 6, as there is some reason to believe, there were no fewer than fourteen or fifteen legions available[1]. Moreover it was in this year that the conditions of military service were for the first time made fixed and definite, so that the army was at last recognized as a standing army. The veterans of the old army had been used up in the Spanish wars or settled in colonies. For the future the legionary was to receive a bounty in money at the end of his period of service. A large number of soldiers were thus remunerated in the years 7–2 B.C., and it is tempting to infer that they represent the troops of the new army, recruited since Actium, well-chosen and well-trained, with all the qualities and none of the failings of veterans[2]. They had shown their mettle in the campaign of 15 B.C.; and Augustus intended to get good value from them in the great wars of conquest of 12–9 B.C., when they were at their best and just before they were due for dismissal.

It is therefore evident that the date 13 B.C. has a significance of its own. Augustus returned to Rome, and the Senate decreed that an altar of Pax Augusta should be set up. Drusus remained in Gaul, to open his campaigns in the following year. In Illyricum, Agrippa and Vinicius had already begun what the Romans called the Bellum Pannonicum.

---

[1] In A.D. 6 there appear to have been fifteen legions, namely five on the Rhine, two in Raetia, five in Illyricum and three in Moesia (if we may combine Tacitus, *Ann.* II, 46, Vell. Pat. II, 113, 1, and Suetonius *Tib.* 16).

[2] *Res Gestae* 16; see R. Syme in *J.R.S.* XXIII, 1933, p. 20 *sq.*

V. ILLYRICUM AND THE BALKANS

Of the wars against Pannonians and Dalmatians in 13–9 B.C., as a result of which the bounds of the province of Illyricum were extended as far as the Danube, the written record amounts to a few sentences, vague as well as brief[1]. It can, however, be interpreted and supplemented with the help of the fuller narrative of the second conquest of these same regions twenty years later, the suppression of the great revolt of the Pannonians and Dalmatians in A.D. 6–9 (see pp. 369 *sqq.*), for the same conditions of geography and therefore of warfare prevailed in conquest and reconquest alike. It was mainly for the sake of the land route to the Balkans that the conquest was required, and the first and necessary stage of the conquest was to win control of the valley of the Save. From the coast the interior cannot be conquered and has never been conquered—the huge mass of the Dinaric Alps severs Dalmatia from Bosnia, a Mediterranean from a Central European land. Roads are few and difficult, the rivers form gorges or waterfalls. It is only from the north that Bosnia can be invaded, and then not easily, from the valley of the Save along, or rather parallel to, its tributaries, the Una, Vrbas and Bosna. Before the Dalmatians, the Illyrian population in the heart of Bosnia, can be dealt with, the Pannonians, the Celtic agricultural population of Croatia and Slavonia, must first be mastered. An invader can occupy the valley of the Save either from the direction of Italy or from the Balkans, his base can be either Siscia or Sirmium; but, in order to win and control it, it may be expedient or even imperative that there should be an army at each of these positions.

To form some conception of the nature and extent of the conquest achieved it is necessary to estimate how much of the vast area which Roman Illyricum (the later provinces of Pannonia and Dalmatia) was soon to embrace, from the Adriatic to the Danube, was already in Roman hands, and how far the pacification of the Balkan lands had been carried forward. The campaigns of Octavian in 35–33 B.C. had been modest in scope and design, modest also, though solid and satisfactory, in achievement; and so, when war with Antony broke out, Northern Italy was secure and there was no fighting in Dalmatia. In the north, in Croatia, Octavian had seized the strong place of Siscia, which can serve as a base not only for a further advance, but also for the better protection of Italy. Farther than this his armies do not seem to have gone: in the

---

[1] Dio LIV, 31, 2–4 etc.; cf., however, *Res Gestae* 30; Vell. Pat. II, 96, 2–3; Suetonius, *Tib.* 9; Florus II, 24 [IV, II].

south, in Dalmatia, they did not pass beyond the Dinaric Alps (p. 87). Nor did Octavian come into conflict with the most populous and powerful of the Pannonians, the Breuci, below Siscia, about the middle course of the Save. He cannot therefore have conquered any of the great Bosnian tribes of the interior. These still remained to be dealt with by Tiberius, for it was Tiberius who subdued the 'nations of the Pannonians which no Roman army had ever approached[1]'. By 'Pannonians' are to be understood in the first place the tribes of the valleys of Save and Drave, especially the Breuci; but also some of the tribes of Bosnia such as the Ditiones, Maezaei and Daesitiates, which were usually called Dalmatian and which later belonged to the Roman province of Dalmatia, but which a well-informed contemporary reckons as Pannonian[2]. That a Roman army had approached any of these tribes before the campaigns of Tiberius is neither recorded nor credible. It appears therefore that after the campaigns of Octavian, Roman Illyricum comprised only Dalmatia, the Hercegovina, Carniola and most of Croatia: the greater part of Slavonia, Bosnia, and Serbia still maintained its independence.

In the south-east also much remained to be done. Crassus had broken the power of the Bastarnae and hurled them back over the river (p. 117 *sq.*). The eastern part of the region later known as Moesia had been the scene of his exploits, but it does not seem to have been brought directly under Roman administration, and farther west there were tribes still independent—the frontiers of Macedonia had been secured rather than extended. After Crassus there is obscurity, fitfully lit up by raids and risings here and there. Trouble might be expected from two sources. North of the Danube were the Dacians and other tribes, ever ready to profit by any disturbance, while to the south the Romans had to rely upon the kingdom of the Odrysian Thracians to maintain peace and hold down the wild tribes of Haemus and Rhodope. It was no easy task, and the intervention of Rome was often needed, especially against the Bessi, turbulent and resentful because the charge of the national sanctuary of Dionysus had been taken from them. Thus Lollius the proconsul of Macedonia had to help Rhoemetalces, uncle and guardian of the sons of Cotys, about 19–18 B.C. A year or two later came a Sarmatian raid across the Danube; and the Dentheletae of the upper valley of the Strymon and the Scordisci from Serbia harried Macedonia. When the Scordisci are next heard of they are friendly to Rome, acting in concert with Tiberius against the Pannonians in 12 B.C. It is therefore difficult

---

[1] *Res Gestae* 30.   [2] Strabo VII, 314.

to resist the conclusion that there had been some Roman advance
from the south-east, to secure firmly the Serbian bank of the
Danube and to occupy Sirmium as a base for an army to take the
Pannonians in the rear. In one of the years 13, 12 or 11 B.C. the
whole of Thrace rose in arms[1]. To the valour of barbarians the
natives united a religious fervour which made them scorn danger
or death. This inflammable material was kindled by a priest of the
Bessi. Rhescuporis the prince was slain, his uncle Rhoemetalces,
deserted by his troops, was pursued into the Chersonese. This
formidable rising was only quelled after three years of hard
fighting by L. Calpurnius Piso (*cos.* 15 B.C.), who was brought
from Pamphylia to Thrace. To account for the spread of the
revolt and the summoning of Piso it would be tempting, but perhaps unnecessary, to assume that the proconsul of Macedonia and
his army were occupied farther to the north-west, towards or near
Sirmium.

It is clear enough that the task which confronted the generals of
Augustus from the Alps to the Balkans was arduous and considerable. In 13 B.C. operations were begun against the Pannonians by Marcus Vinicius, and Agrippa was soon called to the
scene; after his death in the next year Tiberius took charge. With
the Scordisci as his allies he reduced the Pannonians. The road
from Siscia to Sirmium was now firmly in Roman hands, the tribes
of the interior cut off from the north, and Bosnia could be penetrated
and subdued. In the following year, 11 B.C., the Pannonians rose
again in his absence, but he reduced both them and the Dalmatians.
Only local rebellions are recorded in the next two years, and there
was not much left to be done in 8 B.C. by Tiberius' successor, Sex.
Appuleius. Roman armies may have traversed Bosnia, but there was
little fighting—the strategical superiority and rapid movements of
the conquerors compelled the natives to make a hurried submission
and seemed to render unnecessary a thorough subjugation, and a
thorough occupation. Fifteen years later the price of this optimism
had to be paid in full.

Northern Pannonia had fallen without a blow. The exact limits
of the kingdom of Noricum on its eastern side cannot be ascertained, but they may have extended as far as the great highway to
the North, the old Amber Route from Poetovio by Savaria and
Scarbantia to the Danube at Carnuntum. The rest of the land between Drave and Danube was either empty or occupied by small

---

[1] Dio (LIV, 34, 5–6) places the outbreak in 11 B.C., but the war lasted
three years (Vell. Pat. II, 98), and 11 B.C. may well be the last of these years,
not the first, cf. Livy, *Epit.* 140.

tribes and remnants of tribes, lacking the power or the desire to
resist. The dominion of Rome was preferable to the pitiless incursions of the Dacians.

In this way the frontier was advanced to the Danube and a vast
area was incorporated in the province of Illyricum. To the south-
east Piso had established peace and order in Thrace; it may have
been now, but it was perhaps not until more than a decade had
elapsed, that the army in these parts was transferred from the proconsul of Macedonia to an imperial legate of Moesia (p. 367 *sq.*).

In the meantime Drusus had been pursuing his triumphant
career in Germany.

VI. GERMANY[1]

Gaul had soon succumbed before the rapid and crushing blows
of Caesar. The calm of exhaustion passed into acquiescence in
the burdens and benefits of Roman rule, and the peace which
prevailed was such as to belie the old renown of the Gauls and
move Roman and German alike to surprise and even to scorn.
There were disturbances, it is true—Caesar, whose aim it had been
to strike at the most powerful tribes and seize the most important
lines of communication, had neglected the western extremities of
the land, and the pacification of Aquitania was not completed till
27 B.C. (p. 116): moreover, it was some time before the Roman
control was firm enough to prevent feuds and discords such as
those which more than anything else had delivered Gaul into their
hands. The exaction of tribute and the introduction of the census
provoked sporadic risings, even in 12 B.C. None the less Drusus
was able to invade Germany leaving behind him a Gaul that was
loyal and peaceful[2]—and so it was to remain, even when a Roman
army had been destroyed. Beyond the Rhine was freedom, but
how far that freedom excited envy or desire among the Gauls is
doubtful. The Roman dominion was irksome but inevitable: it
was supported and justified by the best of arguments, force of
arms and an experience of German invasions which was still recent
and which the Gauls had no wish to see renewed. The existence of
the Germans, then, was one of the surest bonds of Gallic loyalty.

[1] The sources are meagre and scattered. Dio (LIV, 32–3; LV, 1) provides
the outline of the campaign of Drusus and a few details. For what concerns
Tiberius here and later Velleius is a full but a prejudiced source. The confused
and rhetorical account of Florus (II, 30 [IV, 12]) is not very helpful. As far as
they go, the brief Livian *Periochae* are useful, and Strabo must not be neglected.
[2] Dessau 212 (*Oratio Claudi Caesaris*). Cf., however, Dio LIV, 32, 1 and
Livy, *Epit.* 139.

It has been maintained that the conquest of Germany was necessary if Gaul were to be both secure from invasion and loyal to Rome; on the contrary, it was the tranquillity of Gaul which made a conquest of Germany possible as well as desirable.

Caesar had made the Rhine the frontier of the Empire, the limit between civilization and barbarism. Though a river may be a convenient line of demarcation, it seldom deserves to be called a natural frontier. The Rhine was a German river: to the west of it dwelt many tribes of real or fancied German origin; they were firm in their allegiance to Rome, and their claim to German blood, for what it was worth, so far from being the expression of a community of sentiment or interest with the free Germans, was little more than an assertion of superiority over their Gallic neighbours[1]. The friendly Ubii had been transplanted by Agrippa at their own request; the Vangiones, Nemetes and Triboci, remnants of the hosts of Ariovistus, had been given lands in the Palatinate and Alsace and in return were expected to guard the bank of the Rhine. There was, indeed, little danger of another invasion. Caesar had broken the power of Ariovistus; his massacre of the Usipetes and his crossing of the Rhine had struck terror into the Germans and had arrested or diverted their westward advance for many generations. It was not in order to hold the line of the Rhine that legions were required in the Gallic provinces. In spite of apparent peace in Gaul the conservative Roman took no risks with any enemy known and feared for several centuries. When the ravages of war had been repaired and its memory forgotten the Gauls might take thought of their ancient glory and their present resources. The land was rich, its population abundant and vigorous. The Gauls had ever been devotedly loyal to their chieftains and brave with that headlong valour which was the wonder and the terror of the more civilized nations of antiquity. The great roads of Agrippa, radiating from Lugdunum, opened up the country, and, for some ten years or so after 27 B.C. there were two armies in the interior of Gaul, comprising five or six legions, the armies of Comata and of Aquitania (to which Narbonensis was attached between 27 and 22 B.C.[2]). Detachments of auxiliary troops were stationed at points of strategic importance. The Rhine however was lightly held—in the main by the militia of the native tribes. Though a serious invasion was unlikely, there might still come raiding parties of restless and

---

[1] Tacitus, *Germ.* 28.
[2] E. Ritterling, 'Zur Gesch. des römischen Heeres in Gallien unter Augustus' in *Bonn. Jahrb.* 114/5, 1906.

predatory Germans, as even later when the bank of the Rhine was guarded by a chain of Roman legions and *auxilia*.

A raid of this kind by the Sugambri and their allies the Tencteri and Usipetes had taken Lollius off his guard in 17 B.C.[1] They soon repented of what they had done and gave hostages for good behaviour in the future. Order was restored—and, if that were not enough, there might have followed a few punitive expeditions which would employ Gallic troops in Roman service against the common enemy and weld Gaul more firmly to Rome. But the Roman expeditions launched in 12 B.C. are of a different kind and on a greater scale—they are a part of a large and comprehensive design to secure a shorter frontier for the Empire and shorter lines of communication between Gaul or Germany and the Roman armies in the Danubian lands. How far the advance might proceed, no man could tell—exploration and invasion must go hand in hand. When Augustus departed from Gaul in 13 B.C. he had completed the organization of the Gallic provinces, and its crown and symbol, the Altar of Lugdunum, was to be dedicated by Drusus in the next year (p. 210). The legions had been brought up from their camps in the interior to bases on the Rhine, and with them and the levies of Gaul, Drusus was to invade Germany.

To a man from the Mediterranean Germany presented a forbidding aspect. He looked in vain for those fruits whose names meant civilization itself, the olive and the grape, and saw instead a waste of marsh and woodland, a realm of damp and cold. From the Rhine as far east as the land of the Dacians and beyond, it was averred, stretched one great forest, nine days' march in breadth from north to south. Error and exaggeration were prevalent both about the land and its inhabitants. Yet it was not all forest—in the Wetterau, the valley of the Neckar and parts of Saxony were fertile regions. Even within the Hercynian forest there were patches of open country, as in Bohemia[2]. The natives themselves, though moralists and rhetoricians for their own ends delighted to endow them with the ideal qualities of primitive virtue or primitive ferocity, were far from being nomads, unspoiled by the practice of agriculture and the habit of settled life. It might seem that they, like their kinsmen west of the Rhine, German or Celt (for there

---

[1] This date (Julius Obsequens *c.* 71) is to be preferred to 16 B.C., that of Dio, who includes in one chapter the events of several years (LIV, 20). The 'disaster' does not appear to have been as grave as Velleius (II, 97, 1) would have his readers believe. The fact that Tiberius and Lollius were bitter enemies explains his version. See *J.R.S.* XXIII, 1933, pp. 17 *sqq.*

[2] Strabo VII, 292.

appeared to be little difference)[1] might not prove impervious to civilization. Yet in this easy appreciation of them the Romans made a
profound miscalculation. The truth was that the Germans were
centuries behind the Gauls in material culture and that a better
comparison was with the Thracians and Dalmatae in their un-
readiness to accept either the culture or the domination of Rome.
Nor was it an easy task to penetrate and control the country, to
crush the resistance and curb the spirit of the warrior tribes. The
obstacles were so considerable and movement was so slow that
distances were easily multiplied[2]. The chief problem that confronts
a general, how to transport and feed an army, assumed formidable
proportions in Germany. Caesar in Gaul had been able to move
rapidly because he found roads, bridges and food wherever he
went; he had been able to bring the enemy to battle because they
had towns and property to defend. In Germany the invader had
to make his own roads and bring with him his own supplies: the
Germans were elusive and might be inaccessible. The army which
Drusus could transport from the Rhine to the Elbe was thus restricted to a size too small perhaps for a thorough conquest, while
the larger forces employed by Germanicus were slow and unwieldy,
despite his use of the approach by water up the great rivers—only
the urgent needs of transport would have induced the Romans to
brave the perils of the Northern Ocean.

The ultimate goal of the Romans appears to have been the Elbe
near or not very far above Magdeburg, and the routes which their
expeditions followed can be recognized in outline but cannot be
reproduced in detail. The winter camps of the legions were
established on the Rhine by Drusus, not in positions of defence
but as bases for invasion, and the principal, though surely not the
only, camps of Augustan date were Vetera (near Xanten) facing
the valley of the Lippe, and Moguntiacum (Mainz) opposite the
confluence of the Main and the Rhine; both Lippe and Main
could provide water-transport for some distance. From Vetera
the Weser near Minden could be reached in two ways, by going
north-east to the Ems and then keeping to the north of the
Wesergebirge and Teutoburger Wald, or by moving up the
valley of the Lippe and then through those wooded hills. Neither
of these routes was without difficulty, and the former was probably
avoided until a causeway had been built across the morasses between Rhine and Ems. But from Vetera by way of the Lippe it

[1] Strabo VII, 290.
[2] Strabo VII, 292. Both Strabo and Velleius overestimate the distance
between Rhine and Elbe.

was also possible to reach the Weser higher up, near Cassel where it takes its origin from the union of the Fulda and the Werra. Towards this region, however, the most easy and attractive route came from the south—from Mainz over the Rhine, across the fertile Wetterau and northwards through the Hessian Gap between Taunus and Vogelsberg. From these two most important strategic positions, Minden and Cassel, half-way between Rhine and Elbe, armies could proceed eastwards to the Elbe, from Minden passing north of the Harz to Magdeburg, or from Cassel south of it to the Saale near Halle and then to the Elbe.

After the preliminary exploration of his first campaign in 12 B.C., Drusus seems to have made the region near Cassel his goal, approaching it from Vetera (in 11 B.C.), then from Moguntiacum (10 and 9 B.C.). This, though in reverse order, was the method followed by Charlemagne—in his first campaign against the Saxons he marched north from Frankfort, in his second eastwards up the Ruhr. Germanicus, however, sought to reach the Elbe by way of Minden, partly because the unwieldy numbers he employed made necessary the use of the Ems (and perhaps the Weser) for transport. Drusus, it is true, built a canal to connect the Rhine with the Ocean through the lakes of Holland, but did not again use it after his first experiment[1]. It may be appropriate at this point to mention that among other measures taken by him was the erection of auxiliary forts along the Rhine and elsewhere, and the establishment of a base or bases for the fleet[2]. Moreover at the close of his second campaign he built a fort 'where the Elison joins the Lippe,' and another 'in the lands of the Chatti near the Rhine[3].' The site of the latter may be Höchst, where the Nidda runs into the Main just below Frankfort, or the low hill of Friedberg in the Wetterau[4]. The former presents a tangle of problems: the Latin historians mention Aliso as the site of a fort, and excavation has revealed at Haltern about thirty miles up the Lippe the remains of two forts, one by the water's edge, the other on the Annaberg close by, and of two legionary camps, the one above the other; and further, at Oberaden some twenty miles farther east, a camp for

---

[1] Unless a 'naval battle' on the Ems against the Bructeri (Strabo VII, 290) belongs to the operations at the beginning of his second campaign.

[2] Florus II, 30 [IV, 12], 26.

[3] Dio LIV, 33, 4.

[4] Both Höchst and Friedberg have yielded remains of Augustan date and both are important strategic positions on the line of an advance into Germany; the latter consideration excludes Wiesbaden from a claim to be the 'fort of Drusus.'

two legions. In the present state of knowledge it might be claimed that the remains at Haltern are numerous and varied enough to provide a localization both for the fort of Drusus and for the Aliso of Roman writers.

The tale of Drusus' campaigns is soon told. In 12 B.C. the Sugambri and their allies sought to forestall his attack but he fell upon them as they were crossing the Rhine, routed them and ravaged Westphalia. Later in the year he made a naval expedition in the North Sea and won over the Frisians—the Batavi were probably in alliance already: but the retreating tide left his ships stranded, and without the help of the Frisii he would have been in sore straits. In the next year he subdued the Usipetes north of the Lippe, bridged that river and marched eastwards through the territory of the Sugambri; he found the way open and was able to advance as far as the Weser because the Sugambri had turned their arms against the Chatti. They were waiting for him when he returned. He was trapped in a narrow defile at a place called Arbalo, but the overhaste of the barbarians robbed them of their prey. Drusus now made Moguntiacum his chief base instead of Vetera. He invaded the land of the Chatti in 10 B.C., and again in the next year, in his last and greatest campaign. Then he struck at the Marcomanni, turned northwards and marched as far as the Cherusci and from there eastwards to the Elbe. He did not cross it; and as he returned he succumbed to an accident and died in the summer camp, somewhere between the Saale and the Rhine[1].

Tiberius now took charge in Germany. The troublesome Sugambri were made to feel the resentment of Rome. Such as survived were transported across the Rhine to its western bank. No open resistance now raised its head and Tiberius could depart in 7 B.C. to enjoy his triumph and the prospect of a command in the East. Though the admiring Velleius claims that Tiberius had almost reduced Germany to the state of a tributary province, the conquest was far from complete. Many regions remained un- trodden and unsubdued, and there was no lasting occupation through the winter. By the swift marches of a small and highly trained army Drusus had traversed Germany and defeated or intimidated many of the tribes between Rhine and Elbe, but his expeditions were little more than raids; the slow and piecemeal process of permanent subjugation had not begun.

[1] Strabo VII, 291.

VII. MAROBODUUS

The second decade of the Principate now came to an end, and
the period of the great wars of conquest was to be succeeded by a
breathing-space. The policy of Augustus still moves forward in
ordered majesty—its slowness is that of strength, not of weakness
or indecision. In the years 7–2 B.C. many veterans who had served
in the campaigns of Drusus and Tiberius were dismissed. When
another ten or twelve years had elapsed many more would no
doubt be ripe for discharge—but they would not receive it until
they in their turn had been employed in warfare. And so this third
decade is a time of consolidation, of exploration and preparation for
a further great advance, the conquest of Bohemia, and, following
thereon, the annexation of South Germany.

Tiberius' departure to Rhodes in 6 B.C. deprived the Empire of
a general and the Princeps of a colleague. Though he was not
indispensable, though there were other Romans of birth and
ability on whose support Augustus could rely, the resentment of
Augustus is pardonable. It must have been a time of acute dis-
comfort. He was weary, ageing and disappointed. Agrippa his
trusted partner, Drusus the well-beloved were dead, Tiberius was
a morose and contumacious exile, the two grandsons were young
and untried. To Augustus the most critical, to the historian this
period is the most obscure portion of his Principate. The narrative
of Dio is fragmentary and defective; and it was hardly to be
expected that Velleius Paterculus would care to record the exploits of the men who usurped with the armies of Rome and in
the councils of the Princeps the position that had belonged to
Tiberius. L. Domitius Ahenobarbus, the husband of a niece of
Augustus, held in succession the commands in Illyricum and
Germany: to him and to Lentulus, likewise of noble birth, to the
new men Vinicius, Quirinius and others the safety of the Empire
in these years was committed. The date, sequence and significance
of events on the northern frontiers during this decade (6 B.C.–A.D. 4)
are for the most part obscure, but some attempt must be made to
elucidate or supplement the inadequacy of the written record. One
of the chief preoccupations of Roman policy in this period was
Bohemia; and though the empire of Maroboduus may not immediately have attained the extent and power that made it seem to
the Romans more dangerous indeed than the King's intentions
justified, it will be convenient to adopt it as the central theme.

In his last campaign (9 B.C.) Drusus had attacked the Marcomanni who dwelt in the valley of the Main, and it was perhaps then and with Roman aid or encouragement that a young noble called Maroboduus rose to power among them. He soon persuaded them to migrate to Bohemia to avoid that encirclement and annexation of South Germany which he saw to be the logical end of Roman policy. Here, in a fertile land of old civilization, once the home of the Boii, girt about, like Transylvania, with a ring of forest and mountain, was the seat which nature seemed to have designed for a great empire. The Marcomanni were ever conspicuous among the Suebian tribes, and in Maroboduus they had a leader of remarkable ability. He had been at Rome, he had probably served with Roman armies, like Arminius—and he knew how to use all that he had seen and learnt. He was not content to enjoy merely the respect due to birth or the temporary prestige of a successful adventurer—he set himself to build up a well-organized kingdom based on a large and disciplined army. Secure in his mountain bastion he inspired terror in all his neighbours, and before long extended his dominion northwards over Saxony, Brandenburg and Silesia; at one time or another the powerful nation of the Lugii, the fierce Langobardi and even the proud Semnones acknowledged his sway[1]. A power was rising in Central Europe that might threaten the Empire and Italy itself, a power that could be compared to that of Pyrrhus or Antiochus[2]. It appears to have been the aim of Roman policy not merely to prevent the extension of the empire of Maroboduus and then subvert it by force or diplomacy, but to annex that part of it, Bohemia, which they needed if they were to dominate Central Europe themselves and control the route from the Danube to the Elbe.

It is with reference to Bohemia and as preliminary to an attack on Maroboduus that the principal Roman operations of this obscure decade are best interpreted; no fewer than three great expeditions beyond the Danube appear to belong to this period. At some time between 7 and 2 B.C. L. Domitius Ahenobarbus (*cos.* 16 B.C.) crossed the Danube, came upon the Hermunduri who were wandering about in search of lands to settle in, established them 'in a part of the land of the Marcomanni,' crossed the Elbe and set up an altar there in honour of Augustus[3]. The Marcomanni had just vacated the region of the Main, and it is in Franconia and Thuringia that the Hermunduri are later to be

---

[1] Strabo VII, 290; Tacitus, *Ann.* II, 45.
[2] As it was by Tiberius (Tacitus, *Ann.* II, 63).
[3] Dio LV, 10 *a*, 2–3; Tacitus, *Ann.* IV, 44.

found[1]; the purpose and direction of the march of Ahenobarbus can therefore be explained. To the Elbe from the Danube the easiest and shortest route runs north-west from Carnuntum across Bohemia: had Ahenobarbus followed it, however, he would surely have encountered the Marcomanni and not the Hermunduri before he reached the Elbe. It would therefore appear that he crossed the Danube higher up, from the side of Raetia, perhaps at Donau-wörth or Regensburg, and so marched northwards to the sources of the Saale and down the Saale to the Elbe (if so far, for he may have mistaken the Saale for the Elbe)[2]: and though he was, or rather perhaps had just been, legate of Illyricum, he may have used the legions which were in Raetia. The purpose of his expedition was to find a way through for an army from the Danube as far as the western entrance of Bohemia and beyond, to the Middle Elbe; one of its results was to isolate Bohemia on the west and facilitate an invasion at some time in the future by interposing between Bohemia and the Chatti and Cherusci the friendly and grateful tribe of the Hermunduri.

A fragmentary inscription records the deeds of an unknown legate of Illyricum, who may, or may not, have been M. Vinicius (*cos.* 19 B.C.)[3]. After passing over the Danube he routed a host of Bastarnae and entered into relations of peace or war with the Cotini, the Anartii and other tribes whose names are not preserved. The Cotini, a Celtic tribe of miners, probably dwelt in the valley of the Gran, the Anartii in north-eastern Hungary, on the northern bounds of Dacia. The occurrence of Bastarnae is surprising but not in-explicable. Pushed away from the Lower Danube they may, like the Sarmatae Iazyges a generation later, have come round over the Carpathians to the Middle Danube. The purpose of this expedi-tion was to secure the Middle Danube, and, more than that, to isolate Maroboduus on the eastern side and cut him off from the Dacians by extending Roman influence and even control over the tribes south of the Tatra and the Carpathians. This was a necessary

---

[1] Tacitus, *Germ.* 41; Procopius, *B.G.* I, 12, 10, μετὰ δ' αὐτοὺς ἐς τὰ πρὸς ἀνίσχοντα ἥλιον Θόριγγοι βάρβαροι δοντὸς Αὐγούστου πρώτου βασιλέως ἱδρύσαντο.

[2] Some Roman writers appear to have regarded the Saale as the main stream, not as the tributary, of the Elbe, cf. Tacitus, *Germ.* 41, 'in Hermunduris Albis oritur.' Cf. also Vell. Pat. II, 106, 2.

[3] Dessau 8965. A. von Premerstein (*Ein Elogium des M. Vinicius*, Jahres-hefte VII, 1904) suggested Vinicius and argued for 14 B.C. as the date of his operations. For the date and the interpretation indicated in the text see *Class. Quart.* XXVII, 1933, pp. 142 *sqq.*

precaution—Bohemia and Transylvania in alliance was a danger that must be averted at all costs, as Domitian was to find. An expedition, or even diplomatic intervention, beyond the Middle Danube would have been pointless, if not impossible, before Tiberius' campaigns and the extension of Illyricum as far as the Danube, and so it probably belongs to this same period, 6 B.C.–A.D. 4. If the general were Vinicius, it could be more closely dated. Vinicius followed Ahenobarbus in Germany in A.D. 1, therefore he might also have been his successor in Illyricum a few years earlier.

After the murder of Burebista and the collapse of his empire the Dacians were broken and divided. Though no longer a menace they were still a nuisance, ever ready to indulge in raids, like the Sarmatians, their neighbours to the south-east. Moreover, they still possessed a part of the Hungarian plain and on this side they had crossed the frozen Danube in the winter of 11–10 B.C. and had carried off much booty. It would thus be necessary before long to humble both Dacians and Sarmatians. Augustus records that his army crossed the Danube and compelled the tribes of the Dacians to submit to the commands of the Roman people: and the Bastarnae, the Scythians, and the kings of the Sarmatae who live on both sides of the river Tanais sought his friendship[1]. This was in the main the work of Cn. Cornelius Lentulus (*cos.* 18 B.C.), at some date which cannot be accurately determined, but probably falls in this period[2]. From the west he attacked the Dacians, probably using the river Marisus for transport[3]: to the south and south-east he drove away the Sarmatians from the neighbourhood of the Danube. And it was perhaps about the same time (*c.* A.D. 1–3?) and in connection with these operations that Aelius Catus transported fifty thousand Getae across to the Thracian bank of the river, 'where they now dwell under the name of Moesians[4].' The area directly under Roman control in these regions would thus be increased, and the army of Illyricum, which hitherto had been available to help, would soon be moved farther north, for the invasion and conquest of Bohemia; so it was perhaps in these

---

[1] *Res Gestae* 30 *sq.* Strabo (VII, 305) regards the Dacians as almost subject.

[2] The only ancient evidence mentioning Lentulus by name (Florus II, [IV, 12], 27–8 and Tacitus, *Ann.* IV, 44) provides no indication of date. Modern suggestions have ranged between 14 B.C. and A.D. 11. It is here conjectured that he was legate of Illyricum *c.* A.D. 1–4.

[3] Strabo VII, 304.

[4] Strabo VII, 303. The operations of Catus (*cos.* A.D. 4) are, however, usually dated *c.* A.D. 9–10.

years (A.D. 3–4?) that the legions of Macedonia were taken from the proconsul and transferred to an imperial legate of Moesia.

But in Germany in the meantime all had not been tranquil. Ahenobarbus had trouble with the Cherusci (about 1 B.C.), and it was no doubt to render access to their land more easy from the west that he built his famous causeway over the marshy lands between Rhine and Ems, the *pontes longi*. Vinicius, who came after him, was confronted with a serious rising, and his efforts were not entirely successful. The firm hand of Tiberius was needed and it was once again at the service of Rome. At his coming the joy and confidence of the soldiers knew no bounds. In A.D. 4 he advanced as far as the Weser and as the result of a campaign that lasted into the winter he received the submission of the tribes of north-western Germany from the Bructeri and the Cherusci as far as the shore of the Ocean. The army passed the winter in quarters far up the valley of the Lippe[1]. The next year witnessed a great combined expedition by sea and land. Tiberius defeated the Langobardi and reached the Elbe, where he was met by the fleet which had explored the northern seas as far as the promontory of Jutland. A remnant of the Cimbri made atonement to Rome for the misdeeds of their ancestors, the Charydes and even the Semnones sought the friendship of Augustus[2]. All was now ready for the conquest of the Kingdom of Maroboduus. On the north he had been weakened by the detachment of the Semnones; on the east he had been cut off from the Dacians; on the west the Hermunduri would give passage to a Roman army.

Twelve Roman legions marched against Maroboduus in A.D. 6, as he was afterwards to boast—perhaps with some exaggeration: it was the total of the armies of the Rhine, Raetia and Illyricum. Sentius Saturninus was to march eastwards from Moguntiacum with some of the legions of the Rhine[3], the troops from Raetia were probably to come northwards in the direction of Nuremberg or Eger to meet him[4], while Tiberius was to invade Bohemia from the south-east with the army of Illyricum, crossing the Danube at Carnuntum. The campaign was a masterpiece of organization and deserves a proud place in the annals of the military art. The armies and the generals of Augustus have nothing to lose by a comparison with

[1] 'ad caput Juliae (*Lupiae*, Lipsius) fluminis,' Vell. Pat. II, 105, 3.
[2] *Res Gestae* 26; Vell. Pat. II, 106; Strabo VII, 293; Pliny, *N.H.* II, 167.
[3] 'per Cattos, excisis continentibus Hercyniae silvis' (Vell. Pat. II, 109, 3); but it would not be forest all the way, and he would soon come to the land of the Hermunduri.
[4] Cf. Ritterling, *P.W. s.v. Legio*, col. 1232.

those of any age in the history of Rome. The advance by separate routes to a common goal was a method which had already been practised on a grand scale and in the face of great natural difficulties, in Spain and in the Alps: but the invasion of Bohemia was to be the crowning achievement of Augustan strategy. In this hour the might of Rome had reached its climax; by their rapid marches and disciplined valour the legions had subdued Illyricum and overrun Germany; at the terror of their approach the nations beyond Elbe and Danube had done homage to the majesty of the Roman People. Only Maroboduus remained: but the short hour of triumph was already passing. When the armies of Saturninus and Tiberius were only a few days removed from their goal in the heart of Bohemia, the news came that Illyricum had risen. The situation was critical, but sound judgment was not lacking in Tiberius—or in Maroboduus. They came to terms, by which Maroboduus was recognized as a king and friend of the Roman People. Tiberius could turn southwards—not a moment too soon.

VIII. THE GREAT REBELLION

When some of the native levies were mustering for the campaign against Maroboduus they saw their own strength and the chance to exert it[1]. The insurrection which began far to the south-east among the Daesitiates, under their chieftain Bato, was at first neglected—the campaign in the north claimed precedence—and soon spread to the Pannonian Breuci who were led by Pinnes and another Bato. Roman merchants were massacred, legionary detachments overwhelmed, and before long the whole of the region conquered by Tiberius some fifteen years before had risen in rebellion. One of the prime movers of the revolt asserted that its cause was to be found in the injustices of Roman taxation and recruiting[2]. This interested and partial testimony cannot pass unchallenged—it must be supplemented by the observation that the original conquest had not been thorough and severe enough to ensure that when a new generation grew up it would not seize with alacrity the earliest opportunity that presented itself. The Dalmatians were a fierce intractable Illyrian people, never so happy as when defying law and order, the Pannonians had their share of the Celtic dash and delight in warfare, to which they now added some

---

[1] The following narrative is based on Velleius (II, 110–16) and Dio (LV, 28, 9–33, 4; 34, 4–7; LVI, 11, 1–17, 3). There is hardly any other evidence.   [2] Dio LVI, 16, 3.

familiarity with the language and discipline of Rome[1]. It was the first time that these tribes stood united in resistance; to subdue them engaged the generalship of Tiberius and the military resources of the Empire for three long years.

With sound strategic instinct Bato the Pannonian swooped down on Sirmium and its Roman garrison. Caecina Severus the legate of Moesia came up in time to rescue it, defeating the enemy, though not without heavy losses to the Romans. Had the Dalmatian been intelligent enough to join his Pannonian namesake, their combined hosts might have overwhelmed the army of Moesia and raised all the Balkans in revolt. Had he turned northwards, Siscia and the road over the Julian Alps into Italy were his: he preferred to waste precious time by attacking Salonae and by sending his raiding bands down the coast as far as Apollonia. When at last he marched northwards, it was too late—Tiberius was hastening back from Bohemia, with Valerius Messallinus, governor of Illyricum, and the Twentieth Legion in the van; after a reverse Messallinus was victorious in a battle fought against great odds, and the whole army reached Siscia. Five legions now stood between the insurgents and the approach to Italy. The Romans held the keys of Illyricum, Siscia and Sirmium, but all that lay between and to the south as far as the Adriatic was in the hands of the enemy, and for some time very little progress could be made against them. Tiberius stood firm in Siscia, taking no risks and waiting for reinforcements. But in the south-east the fate of Sirmium still hung in the balance; the rebels had occupied the Mons Almus (the Fruškagora) to the north of that city, and though defeated in a skirmish by Rhoemetalces the Thracian king, whom Caecina had despatched against them, were able to maintain their position when Caecina himself attacked them. Raids of the Dacians and Sarmatians compelled Caecina to return and protect his own province; he left Rhoemetalces behind to hold up the insurgents and prevent if he could an invasion of Macedonia. Such was the situation through the winter of A.D. 6–7, and indeed for a great part of the next year. The thorough devastation spread both by the insurgents and the Romans made the land a desert. Tiberius hoped to reduce the enemy by the slow process of famine rather than risk battle and the lives of Roman soldiers. He gradually extended his control from Siscia eastwards and southwards and held a large body of the enemy pent up in the hills between Save and Drave (the Mons Claudius).

In Rome, however, the voice of detraction whispered that

[1] Vell. Pat. ii, 110, 5; compare Dio's opinion of the Pannonians and Dalmatians (xlix, 36, 3–4).

Tiberius was prolonging the war for purposes of his own. Accustomed to the easy and spectacular successes that till now had crowned the conquests of Augustus, the ignorant or the malevolent despised this cautious strategy. Tiberius stands all the higher because his name is associated with no great battle; and Augustus cannot have wavered in his confidence in a general whose principles of warfare were his own[1]. It was the crisis of the Empire. A sudden turn of fortune shattered the proud hopes that prevailed on the eve of the march against Maroboduus, and revealed how narrow and insecure were the foundations on which that ambitious policy had been erected. It was only with difficulty that the rising in Illyricum could be prevented from spreading. One province arrested and wrecked the frontier policy of the Empire; but what would happen if Germany and Thrace rose at the same time, if Maroboduus threw off his allegiance, if the Dacians appeared in force? In those evil days Augustus is reported to have thought of putting an end to his life[2]. There was discontent at home, famine and pestilence raged in Italy as well as in Illyricum. The soldiers were weary and dejected. Most manifest and alarming was the military weakness of the Empire. There were no reserves of strength, recruits for the legions were hard to find, and so no new legions could be raised. Veterans were recalled to the standards, liberated slaves were enrolled in companies (*cohortes voluntariorum*). Some of these levies were brought to Siscia before the end of the year A.D. 6 by Velleius Paterculus, others in the course of the following year by Germanicus. But where could legions be found? Now as later the Empire worked with military resources which were cut down even below the margin of security. The provincial armies were expected to be more or less self-supporting. The price of this economy had now to be paid. It was not thought safe to move whole legions from the western provinces, and none came from these regions to Tiberius at Siscia: from the East, however, two legions might be temporarily withdrawn to reinforce the south-eastern theatre of the war. The army of Moesia by itself was not strong enough, and it was needed to hold down Thrace and ward off the Dacians and Sarmatians from the southern bank of the Danube: yet it was only with the co-operation of a strong army based on Sirmium that Tiberius could gain control of the valley of the Save, the first and necessary stage of the reconquest of Illyricum. The legions from the East,

---

[1] Compare his letter to Tiberius, Suetonius, *Tib.* 21.

[2] Pliny, *N.H.* VII, 149, 'iuncta deinde tot mala: inopia stipendi, rebellio Illyrici, servitiorum dilectus, iuventutis penuria, pestilentia urbis, fames Italiae, destinatio expirandi et quadridui inedia maior pars mortis in corpus recepta.'

however, did not arrive until late in the second year of the Revolt —Tiberius may at first have underestimated the resistance of the insurgents, or for some other reason these troops may not earlier have been available[1].

At last this army was ready to advance; its kernel was composed of five legions and it was led by Caecina Severus, legate of Moesia, and by Plautius Silvanus who came from some post in the East. But the enemy had concentrated in force under both the Batos and was waiting to dispute their passage westwards of Sirmium, in the direction of Cibalae (Vinkovci), where the road runs across the narrow neck of firm ground north of the marshes of the Lower Save. If they still held their commanding position on the Mons Almus to the north of Sirmium (and there is no evidence that they did not) they were able to choose the time and place of their attack. This would explain the surprise which they inflicted, but would not excuse the negligence of the Roman leaders. While the army was making ready to encamp the enemy suddenly fell upon it and almost overwhelmed it. Before their impetuous charge the Thracian cavalry broke and fled, and the auxiliaries, both horse and foot, were scattered. Even the legions wavered, and many officers fell; but at length the discipline and tenacity of the common soldier prevailed, and victory was snatched from defeat. Such was the Battle of the Volcaean Marshes—almost one of the greatest disasters in the annals of Rome. Caecina and Silvanus could at last bring their troops to Siscia. And there was now assembled a host such as had never been seen since the Civil Wars—ten legions and over eighty auxiliary regiments, to say nothing of ten thousand veterans, many *cohortes voluntariorum* and the cavalry of Rhoemetalces. But it was not for such a concentration that the reinforcements were required. After a few days Tiberius escorted them back again whence they had come, to Sirmium. Caecina with a part of the army was no doubt needed in Moesia, but Silvanus was to remain at Sirmium. At last Tiberius had in his hand the means of controlling the valley of the Save, and when he returned to Siscia and put the legions into separate quarters for the winter, it was with the rational confidence that in the next year the Pannonians would be reduced.

In the next year (A.D. 8) all the Pannonians capitulated at the river Bathinus[2]. Famine and the patient strategy of Tiberius had worn them down, treachery did the rest. Bato made the best of a

---

[1] For the Isaurian War in A.D. 6 (Dio LV, 28, 3), cf. *Klio* XXVII, 1934, pp. 139–42.

[2] Perhaps the Bosna, cf. B. Saria, *Klio*, XXIII, 1930, pp. 92–7.

hopeless cause, betrayed Pinnes to the Romans and as a reward became chieftain of the Breuci himself. He was not to enjoy the honour for long—the other Bato, the Dalmatian, captured and slew him and persuaded many of the Pannonians to take up arms again. They were crushed by Silvanus; Bato, giving up these parts for lost, retreated southwards and blocked the defiles leading into Bosnia. The penetration and subjugation of this difficult region, the Bellum Dalmaticum as it was called, was to be the work of the next year. Tiberius, leaving Aemilius Lepidus in charge at Siscia (while Silvanus remained at Sirmium), departed to Rome for the winter.

At the opening of the next campaigning season Lepidus led the army (or part of it) southwards to Tiberius in Dalmatia. The line of his march (Siscia to Burnum?) brought him into country as yet untouched by the war, but he fought his way through it successfully. The final conquest was to be effected by three separate armies; Lepidus was to operate from the north-west, Silvanus from the north-east, Tiberius from the side of Dalmatia[1]. With Tiberius was his young nephew Germanicus, to whose credit was already to be set the capture of three fortresses, Splonum, Raetinium and Seretium[2]; while the other two armies entered Bosnia from the north, Tiberius in the south hunted down the indomitable Bato. He threw himself into the rocky fastness of Andetrium hard by Salonae, but succeeded in slipping away before it was captured. When one after another the hill forts fell to the Romans, Bato resolved to make his submission. Tiberius spared his life and interned him at Ravenna.

The last embers of the revolt had been stamped out among the Daesitiates in the neighbourhood of Sarajevo and the Pirustae of Montenegro, and the long war was over at last. Scarcely was it known at Rome when there came like a thunderclap the news of disaster in Germany—Varus had perished and with him three of the best legions of the Roman army.

IX. ARMINIUS

After the last campaigns of Tiberius (A.D. 4 and 5) a deceptive tranquillity brooded over Germany. Even the crisis of A.D. 6 had called forth no echo, and some of the most formidable of the tribes, such as the Cherusci, seemed willing to accommodate themselves to foreign rule—for as yet there was nothing in the

---

[1] Dio (LVI, 12, 2) mentions a triple division and puts it down to fear of a mutiny.   [2] None of these sites have been identified with certainty.

Roman occupation that could be called thorough, permanent or oppressive. In the summer the legions might move forward as far as the Weser, but they returned to spend the winter in safety on or not far from the Rhine. Save in the valley of the Lippe no attempt seems to have been made to gain a firm hold on any part of the country by means of a network of roads and fortified positions. The land was not yet ready to be turned into a Roman province. Though an altar had been set up in the town of the Ubii on the western bank of the Rhine to serve as a religious centre for German nobles, very little else seems to have been done—it is difficult to believe that the methods of Roman taxation had been introduced.

From ancient times onward the circumstances surrounding the end of Roman rule in Germany have been an occasion for prejudice and rhetoric[1]. Varus was made the scapegoat for the miscalculations of Roman policy; the contrast between the inertia or benevolence of Varus and the energy or perfidy of Arminius, between the Roman governor and the native prince, was drawn in vivid colours, and artfully employed to personify the opposition between civilization and freedom. In the last emergency Varus does not seem to have displayed the qualities of a general—or even of a soldier; and he may have been better fitted to govern the rich and peaceful province of Syria than a Germany which was still unsubdued. But the shortcomings of Varus mask a more eminent culprit. The choice of Varus as commander of the Rhine army was that of Augustus (Varus had married his great-niece), and the policy of conciliation which appeared to have been responsible for his ruin must have been suggested and imposed by Augustus, anxious at all costs to avert a rebellion like that which was still raging in Illyricum.

On the other side stands Arminius, a figure welcome to the fervid patriot or to the romantic historian. The valour and resource of the young prince of the Cherusci admit of no dispute, his treachery needs no excuse. But in the estimate of his historical importance a certain caution is not out of place. Though it was due

---

[1] The only contemporary description of the disaster of Varus, that of Velleius (ii, 117–120), though unduly prejudiced against Varus, is of primary importance: but it does not claim to be a complete narrative. Dio is fairly sober and credible, but lacking in details of time, place and direction. Florus (ii, 30 [iv, 12]) is worthless. Tacitus (also a source for the Varian disaster, see p. 374) has lavished all the resources of his art on the person and on the exploits of Germanicus. His good faith and even his accuracy have been called into question by modern critics: at the very least he cannot be absolved from the charge of magnifying and distorting both the character and the results of his hero's campaigns.

in a large measure to his efforts, now and later, that the Romans did not conquer Germany, he was only the leader of a faction even among his own tribesmen, not a champion of the German nation, for no such thing existed. The very name was of recent date, an alien appellation; there was among the Germans little conscious-ness of a common origin, of a common interest none at all. Arminius himself was a Roman citizen and a Roman knight, and his own people did not preserve the memory of their liberator.

About the disaster, and about its site, there is not much that needs to be said. By the report of a rising some distance away the conspirators persuaded Varus to march out of his summer camp. When the Roman column, encumbered by a heavy baggage-train, was involved in wooded country, the Germans fell upon it. The Romans struggled forward as best they could, but everything was against them. The resolution of Varus failed him and he took his own life. The cavalry fled, but did not escape. One of the *praefecti castrorum* fell fighting, the other made a capitulation which ended in a massacre. Like the disaster to which Caesar's legates, Sabinus and Cotta, succumbed (vol. IX, p. 563), it was the result of an attack on the army while it was marching through difficult country. That is a danger which can befall a good general, and from which he may be lucky to escape, as were Drusus at Arbalo and Caecina Severus on the *pontes longi* (pp. 363, 377); but the plight of the Varian legions, like those of Sabinus and Cotta, was aggravated by treachery and incompetence. The summer camp of Varus might be sought near Minden on the Weser, the site of the disaster in a wide region between Osnabrück and Detmold, in or between the Teutoburger Wald to the south and the Wiehengebirge to the north—the only indication of locality is the vague statement of a writer who had no occasion to be precise[1]. The Germans swept on to capture the Roman posts east of the Rhine; they fell with-out a blow, except Aliso. After a tenacious defence the garrison slipped out and made its way safely to the Rhine. Asprenas, the legate of Varus, had already hastened down with his two legions from Mainz, but the enemy made no attempt to cross.

It had not been a general uprising of the nations of Germany and so no invasion of Gaul was to be feared. Arminius sent the head of Varus to Maroboduus, inciting him to war. Maroboduus wisely declined to serve the ambition of another. At Rome, how-ever, there was consternation. Augustus lamented the loss of his

[1] Tacitus, *Ann.* 1, 60, 'ductum inde agmen ad ultimos Bructerorum, quantumque Amisiam et Lupiam amnes inter vastatum, haud procul Teuto-burgiensi saltu in quo reliquiae Vari legionumque insepultae dicebantur.'

legions—and well he might, for they could not be replaced. Again came the call for recruits—but where were they to be found? Of raising new legions there was as little prospect as there had been three years before[1]. Forced levies and inferior material were used, and once again freed slaves were enrolled in separate formations. Tiberius had to postpone his Pannonian triumph and betake himself to the Rhine. Five legions had sufficed for the campaigns of Drusus; the garrison was now, however, raised to the total of eight legions, which were henceforth divided into two armies, each under the command of a consular legate. To supply this total the garrison of two legions was withdrawn from Raetia, and four legions were taken from Spain and Illyricum.

The Roman occupation beyond the Rhine had been so incomplete and superficial that after the loss of the army of Varus nothing was left save some control of the coastal regions, perhaps as far as the mouth of the Elbe—the Frisii remained loyal, perhaps also the Chauci. Augustus' own statement about his German policy is studiously vague[2]; it may fit the facts—but it may also mask them. If he still laid claim to Germany, the presence of eight legions on the Rhine seemed to show that the claim was to be asserted. It has often been assumed that the disaster of Varus marks the turning point in Rome's career of conquest, but, even though Tiberius may already have felt what he was before long to express, the renunciation of the conquest of Germany and all that that plan implied was not yet made manifest. After the calamities of the years A.D. 6–9 Rome needed a respite; the great age and the infirmities of Augustus were a warning that the political crisis which his death would provoke could not be far off. So in A.D. 10 and 11 Tiberius and Germanicus did not venture far beyond the Rhine, but contented themselves with raiding and ravaging.

Germanicus was fired by a youthful ambition to emulate the exploits of his father Drusus and make himself worthy of the name which he had inherited; but he had neither the good fortune of his father nor the ability of his uncle. The death of Augustus and the mutiny of the Rhine legions (p. 618) gave him the chance for which he had prayed. The repentant soldiers clamoured to be allowed to expiate their fault in blood, and so Germanicus led them over the Rhine against the unsuspecting Marsi. The Romans fell upon them, butchered many, and succeeded in returning without much danger. Germanicus was not content with this easy victory.

[1] Unless *legio I* (cf. Tacitus, *Ann.* 1, 42) be regarded as an entirely new formation.

[2] *Res Gestae* 26. Cf. U. Wilcken in *Sitz. d. preuss. Akad.* 1932, XI, pp. 232 *sqq.*

In the course of the following winter he appears to have gained the permission, though perhaps not the enthusiastic approval, of Tiberius for a series of operations on a larger scale: but in their estimate of the purpose which these campaigns were to serve, Tiberius and Germanicus may have differed quite as much as they did two years later about the value of the results achieved. In the spring of A.D. 15 he crossed the Rhine at Mainz. While Caecina Severus from Lower Germany engaged the attention of the Cherusci and defeated the Marsi, Germanicus was to deal with the Chatti. He marched north-eastwards up the Wetterau, rebuilt his father's fort, crossed the river Adrana (the Eder) and burned Mattium, the capital of the Chatti[1]. He now turned back and was moving towards the Rhine, but on the news that Segestes, the father-in-law and bitter enemy of Arminius, was being beleaguered, he rescued him, and secured a precious hostage, Thusnelda the wife of Arminius. There was still time for another campaign, this time in Lower Germany. Caecina with four legions marched through the lands of the Bructeri, Pedo with the cavalry farther to the north-west, through the Frisii, while Germanicus transported four legions by sea; the three forces met at an agreed point on the river Ems (probably near Rheine). The Bructeri were defeated, and the army marched east or south-east till it came within reach of the Saltus Teutoburgiensis. After visiting the melancholy scene and erecting a tumulus over the unburied bones, Germanicus pursued Arminius eastwards into difficult country. After an indecisive battle he returned to the Ems, where the army broke up again. The cavalry returned in safety; but two of the legions of Germanicus marching along the shore of the Ocean were almost overwhelmed by a high tide, and the army of Caecina was assailed by Arminius as it was crossing the *pontes longi*. In a vision of the night Caecina saw the ghost of Varus rise from the marshes and beckon him to destruction. It was no idle apprehension—a general with less experience, with less control over himself and over his troops, would have given his name to a second disaster. So after many labours, many risks, and with little to show for it all, the troops returned to their winter quarters.

Germanicus, impressed by the difficulties of transport and provisioning, resolved to make a greater use of the approach by sea. The order went out to build a thousand ships. Before the great expedition was to start, however, he sent a force against the Chatti, and himself, after relieving the fort of Aliso on the Lippe, repaired the road and causeway leading thither. At last all was

---

[1] Perhaps the Altenburg near Niedenstein, south-west of Cassel.

ready. With a prayer to his father Drusus, Germanicus sailed
down the canal, through the lakes of Holland, and round to the
mouth of the Ems. Here he landed the troops, apparently on
the western bank, so that time was wasted in crossing the river[1].
Then suddenly the Roman army appears at the Weser a hundred
miles away; beyond are seen the hosts of Arminius. The Romans
forced the passage of the river and established themselves on the
eastern bank. On the following day was fought a great battle at a
place called Idistaviso, probably not far east of Minden. Arminius,
holding the hills to the south on the right flank of the Romans,
sought to prevent them from marching eastwards towards the
Elbe. Though it was claimed that the battle was a defeat for the
Germans, Arminius was not dismayed. He now took up a position
to the north, on the left flank of the Romans, at the boundary
wall of the Angrivarii; the battle which followed does not appear
to have been a decisive victory for Germanicus.

The victories of civilized powers over native tribes are commonly
due to a superior organization which enables troops to be concentrated rapidly and surely, and at once secures a strategic advantage.
Yet Arminius could bring together and could keep together a
considerable force of Germans. To have entrapped Varus and his
three legions was indeed no mean achievement—but to withstand
a Roman army of eight legions and numerous *auxilia*, to compel it
to fight on ground which he had chosen, to arrest its advance, this
was military genius[2].

In comparison Germanicus cuts a poor figure. He set up a
trophy with an inscription which asserted that he had conquered
the nations between Rhine and Elbe, and then gave the signal for
retreat. On the return voyage a great storm arose and scattered
the ships. Most of the crews were eventually rescued—but in the
eyes of Tiberius that would be no excuse for the risks that had
been run. Germanicus—or at least his panegyrist—might affect
to believe that the resistance of the Germans had been broken and
that another year would complete their subjugation. Tiberius was
not to be deceived: he wrote suggesting that Germanicus should
now return to celebrate the triumph which he had earned. The
arguments of Tiberius were those of good sense itself—honour
had been satisfied, risks enough had been taken, diplomacy was
a more effective weapon than arms in dealing with the Germans[3].
Germanicus had no choice but to obey.

[1] Tacitus, *Ann.* II, 8. A textual corruption is not the only difficulty here.
[2] Cf. the final verdict of Tacitus, *Ann.* II, 88, 'proeliis ambiguus, bello
non victus.'   [3] Tacitus, *Ann.* II, 26.

The enterprises of Germanicus had served only to reinforce the caution of Tiberius; it could no longer be doubted that the conquest of Germany must be postponed for a generation if not abandoned for ever.

Until A.D. 6 the Augustan plan of conquest had been carried out with an ease and rapidity that seemed to justify the boldness of its design. The Pannonian Revolt was a grim warning; and might alone have brought about a gradual and peaceful retirement from Germany. After the disaster of Varus and the illusory victories of Germanicus there was no choice. The task was seen to be more difficult in every way than had been imagined; it would take many years yet to penetrate the land and subdue its inhabitants. The Germans had at first been intimidated by the rapid movements of the Romans and circumvented by their strategy. But now came a change—it was much more than a Roman army that perished with Varus. The spell of Roman prestige was shattered. The Germans under a leader of great military talent had been emboldened to face the legions in open battle. A succession of Roman blows such as those struck by Germanicus, so far from breaking down their resistance, might only weld them more firmly together. A German nation, a German national resistance did not exist—the impact of the foreigner might create it. To keep the Germans disunited and harmless an occasional intervention of Roman diplomacy would be more than sufficient.

Moreover, however strong might have been the arguments in favour of conquest, the risks and the cost were enough to deter the prudent parsimony of Tiberius. The earlier campaigns in the north had been swift and bloodless: but in the Pannonian Revolt many legionaries had fallen in battle, and the Empire could not afford another disaster like that of Varus. To achieve the conquest of Germany and to make it permanent, more legions would be required. But they could not be found—the crisis of the years A.D. 6–9 revealed a deplorable weakness; and an intelligent contemporary had drawn a melancholy comparison with the reserves of men that Rome had been able to command in an earlier age[1]. The three legions of Varus were not replaced; even the normal demands of legionary recruiting in the reign of Tiberius were far from easy to satisfy, as reputable evidence attests[2]. But if the person and the privileges of the Roman citizen had to be spared,

---

[1] Cf. Livy VII, 25.
[2] Tacitus, *Ann.* IV, 4; Vell. Pat. II, 130, 2; Suetonius, *Tib.* 48.

were there not native levies in abundance whose employment would serve a double purpose? It is true that without the help of this excellent fighting material the wars and conquests of Augustus could not have been planned and achieved, the frontiers could not have been protected later. But there was a limit to their use, as the Pannonian Revolt had shown.

Therefore, despite the disproportion in population and resources between the Roman Empire and the free Germans, the conquest was postponed, if not renounced. Had it been as desirable or necessary to Rome as the possession of Germany between Rhine and Elbe was to Charlemagne, it would no doubt have been achieved, and by the use of similar methods, whatever the cost. But it was not necessary. Possessing Illyricum, the Empire could dispense with Germany; however desirable may have been the control of the route from the Elbe to the Danube, there were certain disadvantages, especially in the annexation of so much rough and forested country close behind the intended frontier. An Empire which embraced the fairest regions of the globe could cheerfully forgo an extension without purpose or profit; and Rome had acquired so much territory in Europe that a pause was imperative. Moreover should the time ever come for a renewal of aggression, it might not take the form of a resumption of the adventures of Germanicus in Northern Germany. Here the broad stream of the Rhine could be a barrier as well as a boundary: but in South Germany the need for a more rapid route between Mainz and the Danube lands might suggest an advance like that made by the Flavian emperors, or even further, to a natural frontier in the Thüringer Wald. Nor was the Danube to be neglected. In the decade before A.D. 6 the Romans had not only secured the line of the Danube, but had extended their influence, if not their control, far beyond it: Dacia had been humbled, Bohemia was to be annexed. The plan failed: and it is to be regretted that Trajan's conquest of Dacia was never completed by that of Bohemia, so as to carry forward the frontier to the Carpathians and enclose the whole of the Danube basin. Such an advance at some time in the future may once have been contemplated by the advisers of Augustus—but his political testament forbade all expansion; and it was not likely that his successor would neglect it.

Though failure and disaster had arrested the progress of Roman conquest, what had been achieved was none the less great. Province had been bound to province, army to army[1]. In this

---

[1] *Ann.* 1, 9, 'mari Oceano aut amnibus longinquis saeptum imperium; legiones, provincias, classes, cuncta inter se conexa.'

system Illyricum was the indispensable link; and when civil war
comes again, the decision is not fought out in Thessaly, Epirus
or Macedonia, but farther to the north, on the great highway
between West and East; the mastery of the sea loses its importance, no legions pass along the Egnatian Way; the sieges of
Byzantium and Aquileia stand large in the pages of history,
Cibalae and Mursa give their names to momentous battles.

The value of Illyricum is not at first manifest, for very little
happens on the Danube for some time. The Rhine after Varus,
like the Parthian Question after Crassus, is accorded in annals
ancient and modern a prominence that exceeds its deserts. By the
end of the first century, however, the Danube provinces begin to
come into their own. In Hadrian's time they have ten legions, the
Rhine has only four. It is to Pannonia that Hadrian sends his
adopted son Aelius Caesar, and it is Pannonia that raises Septimius
Severus to the purple. In the third century Illyricum, its soldiers
and its emperors, are the salvation of the Empire.

It had once been the belief of Augustus and his advisers that
fifteen legions would be enough to achieve great conquests, and
hold in subjection not only Gaul and the Danube provinces but
Germany and Bohemia as well. It was now evident that the same
number of legions would be needed to protect the frontiers of
Rhine and Danube—or rather to hold down wide regions within
those frontiers, Gaul, Bosnia and the Balkans. Beyond the great
rivers, the barbarians had been isolated and intimidated. They
might be left to their own quarrels—here the open secret of
Roman policy was to divide but not to conquer.

It was not long before the policy of Tiberius was triumphantly
vindicated. German turned against German, and within a few
years Arminius was dead, Maroboduus an inglorious exile.

CHAPTER XIII

THE ECONOMIC UNIFICATION OF THE MEDITERRANEAN REGION: INDUSTRY, TRADE, AND COMMERCE

I. THE GENERAL EFFECT OF THE CHANGE FROM THE REPUBLIC: A WORLD AT PEACE

IN industry, trade, commerce, and the economic unification of the Mediterranean region, as in other fields, the Principate meant the coming of a new age. The Republic had, it is true, especially towards its close, done much to prepare the way. A capitalistic spirit of enterprise was not wanting, and from the beginning of the third century B.C. grew steadily stronger. Italian merchants worked in the Levant, and became increasingly numerous in Delos; they pressed also into Gaul and Germany, and sought to extend their activities to Britain[1]. Indeed the conditions prerequisite to an extensive trade, and consequently to an industry working for export, were satisfied. There was a steady rise in demand: the rich Romans, whose wealth was derived from their landed property, from war-contracts and the profits of booty, from the exploitation of the provinces through administration, taxation, the practice of usury among the provincials and so on, wanted the merchandise which the world had to offer. And, through the creation of the *Imperium*, this world had become a very comprehensive one, more closely bound together than Alexander's empire. Roman proconsuls made improvements in the road system everywhere; Servilius Isauricus and Pompey gave security to commerce, at least for a time, through their wars with the pirates; the economic life of the Roman East, of Italy, and already, to some extent, of the West also, reached a respectable height.

Yet everywhere there remained barriers and obstacles. They were inherent in the very structure of society. The Romans were in origin a warlike peasantry that needed land and gained it by conquest; subsequently, in the course of their great military successes, and through the imperialism which these fostered,

---
[1] Strabo IV, 194.

they became more accustomed to political domination and political exploitation of other nationalities and peoples. The capitalism which ensued developed, accordingly, along agrarian lines, or else went hand in hand with political oppression. Cato furnishes an instance of the first process, the *nobiles* and knights, who exploited the provincials, of the second. These openings, however, were in themselves very great, and apart from them the Roman capitalist, generally speaking, confined himself to the extraordinarily lucrative field of activity which his connection with politics more or less offered him, namely to speculation (*negotiatio*). In consequence, industrial and commercial enterprise was generally left to that part of the population which was not Roman, but preponderatingly Greek, in origin. This element contained both Italian Greeks, who had later become Roman citizens, and also those who had come as aliens from the Greek Orient, or even as slaves, subsequently to gain their freedom and to constitute an ever-growing section of society. Under these circumstances a truly energetic economic policy is found only in the spheres of agriculture and politics. Thus the interests of the great land-owners, who formed the ruling aristocracy, were protected by the ban imposed from time to time on the production of wine and oil in the provinces[1]; and the interests of the knights as tax-farmers and speculators played an important part in the expansion of the Empire. Nothing is heard, however, of a corresponding policy which might have directly favoured industry and trade. The trader was welcome because he advanced Roman prestige and pacification, and hence exerted a political influence. Use, moreover, was made of these middlemen, who brought merchandise, food-supplies and luxuries, from distant sources, and it was observed with pleasure that in Italy itself business activity and production were increasing. But that was all: the aristocracy, in which the power was vested, in reality took very little notice of the business men, whom it disdained; they were merely treated with tolerance, in Italy as in the provinces. The suggestion that from the second century onwards a 'Roman commercial spirit' can be observed is mistaken[2]; the equation of imports with booty came almost as naturally to a Mummius and his successors as to the overlords of Homeric times. A policy of protective tariffs, such as the Ptolemies practised, was wholly lacking. There is no

[1] For example, in South Gaul, at the end of the second century B.C. Cicero, *de Re pub.* III, 9, 16.
[2] J. Kaerst, 'Scipio Aemilianus, die Stoa und der Prinzipat,' in *Neue Jahrb.* 1929, pp. 653 *sqq.*

trace of an attempt to secure a favourable balance of trade for Italy, and such an attempt is not to be expected, since the voice of the interested parties went unheard.

But the worst obstacle to a full development of trade and industry was the general political situation. In the closing years of the Republic, though the economic area was, indeed, large, it was in a state of unrest. A world-wide economic system, however, cannot develop when it is constantly disturbed through political discontent and interference by the State in production and in the give-and-take of trade. It was precisely such difficulties that had dislocated the economic life of the Greeks in the classical age, and equally in Hellenistic times, when they were constantly preparing armaments against each other and against Rome. With Rome's violent entry on the scene, such convulsions had certainly not become rarer; the reverse was true, since during the time of the Civil Wars the scale of events had actually increased. Italy had suffered much through the lasting social upheavals—in consequence of which Capua alone, during the years when Pompey and Caesar were in power, had received some twenty thousand new colonists[1]—and was bleeding from many wounds. Far deeper were the wounds inflicted on those provinces which had been dragged into Mithridates' war of liberation, and which, thereafter, debased to fields for exploitation by Roman generals striving for power, had often come to the very brink of the abyss. Campaigns, fresh piratical raids, devastations, debt and impoverishment, disturbances and revolutions—all played their part, with especial effect in the East: in Greece, the Islands, and Asia Minor, and to some extent also in Syria and Egypt. To a greater or lesser degree, varying with the locality, they choked the economic life which was spontaneously beginning to develop. An atmosphere of instability and uncertainty clung to the whole period until the close of the Civil Wars.

A fundamental change took place after Augustus had given to the world the *pax Romana* and the *quies Italiae*, and had thus created an economic area characterized by an extent and peacefulness such as mankind had not previously seen. His aim was to create a corporate unity from the whole of the civilized part of the globe. The road system had been steadily developed, and was kept in excellent order. It permitted the rapid passage to and fro of armies, and of troops for police purposes, and the dissemination of news with the aid of the State postal-service.

---

[1] Vell. Pat. II, 44, 4; Suetonius, *Div. Iul.* 20; Appian, *Bell. Civ.* II, 10, 35.

Hence it constituted a guarantee of peace and order. On the Mediterranean the plague of piracy had vanished; Roman flotillas where necessary guarded the inland water-ways, and garrisons protected all frontier districts where danger could possibly threaten. These outward manifestations were matched by inward peace and security. It resulted from a policy which understood how to leave unaltered all that could possibly be pre-served, and to steer clear of a radicalism which would inevitably evoke distrust. The feeling of happiness, which sounds in so many voices of the times, both from Italy and the provinces, is an additional proof of Augustus' sureness of touch, and of his clever-ness in appreciating the importance of incalculable factors. This applies not only to his purely political measures, but also to those for the regulation of social and economic life. Once the Empire was consolidated there was, with few exceptions, no interference in the ownership of property. The time of the *leges agrariae* was past. The distinctions marked out by the old social order were retained. No alteration was made in Italy's predominant position in relation to the provinces, and, if the provincials had an equal share with Italy in the blessings of the new age, this was due not to any marked change in their legal standing, but largely to the removal of oppression.

There was also the least possible interference in the internal affairs of the provinces. Much though the imperial government desired and encouraged the advance of civilization and the transition of savage hill-tribes to agriculture and stable economic activity (if only because this must conduce to pacification and prosperity, and, in part, to better administration and increased revenue), yet, over the Empire as a whole, it did not contemplate any artificial romanization and urbanization. In general, in this sphere also, Augustus was at pains to make no sweeping change, to provide the framework, merely, and the milieu through which things might develop of their own accord. Naturally this did not prohibit the occasional planting of colonies in the East as in the West—in Asia Minor, Syria, Spain, and elsewhere—with a view to greater security, or as a means of settling veterans on the land. In the Mauretanian settlements it is, indeed, possible that the idea of spreading civilization may have been a primary motive, but this was not the normal policy. If we disregard the effect of political pacification and subjection, the means by which the romanization of the West was accomplished were that the pro-vinces of themselves admitted the superior Roman culture, and that Roman civilians and veterans of their own free will migrated into new and rising districts, there to seek their fortunes and to settle.

Still more important in this connection is the fact that the existing organization of labour and of economic life was not subjected to disturbance. Caesar might summarily transplant Roman freedmen to Corinth, to create a new trading colony; he might refound Carthage, with, perhaps, the same end in view; he could interfere with the rights of the employer by his decree that one third of the labourers on a farm must be free; he could, in fact, manifest in various ways a disposition towards control which might easily have strengthened into a system of State socialism. But there is no trace of similar tendencies under Augustus and his immediate successors. The old economic principle of *laissez faire, laissez aller* was left unchanged; indeed certain limitations of the principle, which the aristocratic régime had introduced, were removed, in so far as the one-sided policy which favoured the interests of the large-scale agricultural producers was abolished. Free competition was to prevail throughout the Empire, and free trade. It is not inconsistent with this that the imperial government, long before Nerva's alimentary legislation, took suitable measures for the protection of agriculture[1]; and if it later attempted to influence the kinds of agricultural produce grown (cultivation of corn or production of oil and wine), this must be regarded as an emergency measure, connected with the general problem of an adequate food-supply, a matter to which an alert government had always to give heed.

Beside the principle of *laissez faire* there was the belief in the old doctrine of private enterprise. The victory of Augustus and of the West meant, then, a repulse of the tendencies towards State capitalism and State socialism which might have come to fruition earlier, had Antony and Cleopatra been victorious, than was thus the case. Apart from the exceptional conditions in the imperial domains, and in the mines, which counted as part of them, and apart from the special circumstances prevailing in the corn-trade which resulted from the conception of food-supply, the principle of private enterprise remained supreme. The armament industry itself was privately owned during the Augustan age and even later, and it is symptomatic that even in Egypt, although it was administered on the model of one of the great imperial estates, considerable areas of landed property were liberated from State ownership, and that the highly developed Hellenistic system of monopolies was weakened through the

---

[1] As in A.D. 33, Tacitus, *Ann.* VI, 17, and see p. 642.

substitution by the government of the licence-system, thereby making room for Western ideas. It was all the easier for Augustus to refrain from developments along oriental lines, and to abide by the fundamental principles of the West, because he himself in the course of the Civil Wars had accumulated, by more or less honest means, an immense private fortune, and had become a leading individual capitalist, and because it accorded far better with the subtle cleverness of his policy to pose as a private benefactor to the State, and not as its exploiter.

II. THE QUICKENING OF ECONOMIC LIFE

All these circumstances, the size of the Empire, the removal of disturbances and upheavals, to which must be added the maintenance of a sound and stable currency, could not but act as an exceptional stimulus in the whole field of economic life. The roads not only served for military, police, and postal purposes, but enabled traders, on their two- or four-wheeled carts, to penetrate with their wares deep into the interior: from Aquileia through the Alps to Linz, or by Siscia and Poetovio to Carnuntum; from Milan by Bregenz to Augsburg, or from Turin to Lyons and beyond to the shores of the English Channel, or to Mainz and Cologne; from Ephesus via Tralles and Laodicea to Apamea on the Maeander, and so on. Indeed certain roads, such as those in the Spanish mining districts, may perhaps have done more to satisfy economic than military needs. The security in the Mediterranean and on the rivers must have stimulated commerce in the same way: it was possible to reckon on being in Rome some eighteen days after leaving Alexandria, or, under favourable conditions, to be in Puteoli a mere nine days later; from Gades to Ostia took seven days; from Egypt to Crete three days and nights[1].

Such were the circumstances which indirectly encouraged revival; to these must be added what may rather be called direct influences. This applies, above all, to the general advancement of the bourgeoisie, a policy which is to be connected with Augustus' desire to create a new social stratum on which his new State was to be based. Since he was obliged to reduce the power of the old *nobiles*, and since for him the proletariate did not come into the question, there remained only the middle class. This social

---

[1] Cf. *e.g.* Pliny, *N.H.* xix, 3 *sqq.*; Strabo x, 475.

stratum was mainly composed of the soldiery and their descendants, or derived from other branches of the citizen-farmer class
—Roman, Greek, or sometimes non-Greek in origin—; a considerable percentage consisted of freedmen, mostly of Greek
nationality, who had a flair for business and had become wealthy,
a type brilliantly ridiculed by Petronius; and the knights also, being
recruited largely from the municipal aristocracy, which in its turn
drew on the bourgeoisie, are to be counted in this class. It was,
then, the active business section of the community, deeply interested in industry and trade, which now grew in importance, or,
at least, was not as formerly pushed into the background. It
was, indeed, to the Emperor's advantage to encourage this pre-
occupation with professional and business matters, since it induced political apathy (as the tyrants of former ages had well
understood), or alternatively a limitation of interest to parochial
politics, which amounted to the same thing. Even the imperial
officials were really salaried civil servants, and the imperial
soldiery earned its living through its professional services. The
gap which had formerly separated the *homo politicus* and the *homo
oeconomicus* became steadily smaller, and the centre of gravity was
shifted increasingly towards a sound business activity. The big
capitalist interests, the Knights, turned more and more from the
speculative contracts for tax-farming, which had declined, to
industrial and mercantile enterprises; the *negotiator* changed from
a speculator to a business man. Professions formerly frowned
upon now became open to gentlemen, a change in standards for
which modern history can furnish many parallels. This rise in
the repute of trade and industry, which coincided with the
closing of some of the more questionable opportunities for
money-making, could not but be a great stimulus to industrializa-
tion and commercialization.

There was yet a further factor. The State had the greatest
interest in trade, not only because of its policy of promoting
the welfare of the people in general, and of encouraging the
bourgeoisie in particular, but also on account of the revenue
involved. Exploitation had always been a force in Roman policy
in the past, and it was partly, at least, with this in view that she
extended her power over provinces with fertile soil, or rich
deposits of precious metals. But trade also was a field for exploitation, and of this the Romans were as fully aware as the early
Corinthians, or the Ptolemies, or the rulers of Petra, Axum, or
Saba. Customs duties, chiefly, but also harbour dues, enabled
the State to appropriate its share of the revenues accruing from

trade, and at the same time it could afford to finance the making and upkeep of harbours which, from the State's standpoint also, were necessary. This explains the direct promotion and encouragement of trade by the Caesars, the building not only of roads but also of harbour-works, with moles, quays, and lighthouses, the construction of canals, the consideration of the project of piercing the isthmus of Corinth, and the relaxation of passport regulations. It explains also the establishment of international relations, such as those with Maroboduus, or, during Claudius' time, with the king of Ceylon[1], and the possible creation of a kind of consulate, such as that in Palmyra[2], for the protection of merchants. The emperors showed the keenest interest in the exploration of new trading areas, whether it was a question of the silk route through Bactria to Zeugma, of Aethiopia, or of the northern amber-producing region[3]. Maps and the description of trade routes were needed; and the imperial government constantly held a protecting hand over ventures which aimed at supplying this need. Augustus' famous attempts, for example, to advance towards Arabia had that motive. Though not too fortunate, the expedition of Aelius Gallus[4] succeeded at least in so far as it won strategically vital trading posts for Rome, and established a Roman protectorate over the passage of the Red Sea, thereby safeguarding the interests of those engaged in trade to the South-east, among whom the Alexandrines were predominant. Indeed we hear that from that time onwards the trade with India had increased to an exceptional degree[5]. The emperors were active in seeking to gain a control of trade, while weakening such control where it lay in foreign hands, Parthia being a case in point; and they even took steps to erect their own customs stations, wherever possible, under the protection of Roman soldiery, as at Leuke Kome in the Red Sea[6]. Pliny's biting epigram[7] that campaigns had been undertaken in order that Roman ladies and gentlemen might have a better choice of perfumes is, of course, a deliberate exaggeration, but an element of historical truth is latent in it all the same.

These conditions, which promoted the general development

---

[1] Pliny, *N.H.* VI, 84 *sqq.*

[2] *I.G.R.R.* III, 1056 IVa 42. 57. Cf. M. P. Charlesworth, *Trade-routes and Commerce of the Roman Empire*, p. 48 *sq.*

[3] Isidore of Charax, Müller, *Geogr. Graec. Min.* I, pp. 244–56; Pliny, *N.H.* VI, 181; XXXVII, 45.

[4] See p. 252 *sq.*   [5] Strabo II, 118.

[6] *Peripl. mar. Erythr.* 19.   [7] *N.H.* XIII, 23.

of economic life, must also have added momentum to particular tendencies which are innate in all systems of capitalism, tendencies towards expanding the enterprises, and increasing the efficiency of the working organization, in order to achieve a more intensive output with mass export, where possible, as the goal of production. A highly capitalistic striving after profits, and a readiness to speculate had long existed; even in ancient times men knew that the occidental understands better than the oriental how to make use of the resources at his disposal[1]; and improvements in technique, as in glass-blowing or dyeing, proved them right. New markets for exports had been opened, and were constantly being added. The standard of living was rising not only in Italy and in Alexandria; the demand for luxuries had sometimes reached fantastic heights, and extended in part to the middle and lower classes. 'Every peasant's wife of the country beyond the Po wears amber trinkets,' we are told, and 'every servant girl has a silver mirror'[2]. There were also changes in fashion: now metal, now glass drinking cups were in use; the favoured shades of purple might be first violet, then red; in Claudius' time it was essential to have marble panels and mosaics in the bedroom in order to be up-to-date[3], and so on. There was an immense rise in consumption, quite apart from the vast demands of the standing army.

The comparative ease with which raw supplies could be imported loosened even more than before the ties which had been apt to bind industry to the locality where its materials were to be found. This, of course, does not apply to the clay for making bricks and pottery, or to vitreous sand, but it is very often applicable in the case of drugs and spices. As the element of risk in commerce lessened the transport rates naturally became lower, and, as the customs dues within the Empire were commonly reasonable (there existed, it is true, duties payable on the provincial frontiers and for transit, but no protective taxes), the freight charges, especially on goods sent by sea, were not so high as to stifle production. Producers and exporters alike were thus able to base their calculations on a margin of profit, and could contemplate the mass production of certain articles. We find large-scale capitalistic concerns in the most varied branches: in the production alike of raw supplies and of finished goods—in the pottery, metal, glass,

---

[1] Pliny, *N.H.* VI, 89: 'ipsorum opes maiores esse dicebant (*sc.*, the envoys from Ceylon) sed apud nos opulentiae maiorem usum'; even though the author may be rather thinking in the first instance of a more sophisticated enjoyment.   [2] Pliny, *N.H.* XXXVII, 44.   [3] Pliny, *N.H.* XXXIV, 160.

and paper industries, and perhaps also to some extent in textiles (though here we must think also of a domestic system with manufacturers[1]), and in the provision trade; we find them engaged in the supplying of articles for mass export, but also in mass production to satisfy the local demand. A man of sufficient initiative living in a large town might find even the position of miller and baker, tanner or brick-maker a useful start towards the building-up of an intensive wholesale business. The dimensions attained, on occasion, are very notable: we are told of works with many hundreds of employees; and the great farms producing oil, wine, and fruit, are, in the last instance, nothing but agricultural manufactories[2].

The workers in the large-scale concerns, whether agricultural or industrial, are mostly slaves; the managers, too, are drawn, in general, from the slave class. Only in regions where the lower class of the free population was almost as dependent, and received almost as low wages as slave labour elsewhere—in Egypt, that is, or in districts inhabited by Celts (even, to some extent, in Celtic north Italy)—was this semi-free population used for mass production. Otherwise, the free workers constitute merely a supplementary labour force, for occasional (seasonal) employment; they were drawn on when it was not worth while spending business capital on a slave, who would then have to be permanently supported, when, in fact, the temporarily higher expense of hiring a free workman proved, in the long run, more profitable.

The concentration of many workers under one management naturally brought with it a certain degree of specialization of labour; in the pottery industry, for instance, the processes of modelling, throwing, firing, and painting, were assigned to different craftsmen, and a similar differentiation of sifting the grain, grinding, kneading, rolling, and baking, occurred in the great bakeries. The manufacture of part of an article is also known.

[1] 'Manufacturer' is here used in the sense of the German *Verleger* (*i.e.* a capitalist who finances and controls the production of outworkers and disposes of their products). In what follows 'factory' represents the German *Fabrik, i.e.* a workshop for a system of production with a strongly marked division and re-assembling of work; 'manufactory' (with the adjective 'manufacturing') is used to denote the German *Manufaktur, i.e.* a workshop in which division and re-assembling of work is much less advanced, where skilled craftsmanship is much more markedly preserved and often only grouped together.

[2] Rightly emphasized by T. Frank, *An Economic History of Rome*[2], pp. 265 *sqq.*

The metal mountings for the furniture made in Pompeii came from Capua, particularly beautiful feet for *triclinia* from Delos. Candelabra were constructed from two parts, the lower of which had been made in Tarentum, the upper in Aegina[1].

Although the incitement to achieve an output still more in excess of immediate needs, and to develop local varieties into specialities produced on a large scale, must have existed almost everywhere, yet there were admittedly great variations in the speed, degree, and individual characteristics of the process; it could hardly have been otherwise, seeing that these factors were dependent on considerations of economic geography and of history. In some places all that was needed was to continue a process already far advanced; in others it was possible to reweave the fabric with the old threads, torn though it were; elsewhere a first beginning must be made.

III. THE OUTPUT OF ITALY

The country which was the most advanced in this respect was undoubtedly Italy. To rich natural resources, and a central position, she could add all the advantages resulting from victory. The wounds which the two decades before Actium must have inflicted have left no visible scars in the archaeological remains of Pompeii. Italy could without difficulty have become self-supporting, had this been the goal in view, as is time and again stressed by the moralists, whose cherished dream it was. The potential corn-growing area was sufficient to satisfy the demand, and corn was, in point of fact, grown, not only by peasant proprietors, but also on the big estates, more especially in the North. There was an abundance of fish and meat, fruit and cheese, wood and stone, some iron at least, and these commodities were interchanged within Italy, either on shipboard along the coast, or else making use of the rivers, the Po, Ombrone, Tiber, Arno, and so on.

More important, however, are those products which were not intended for the home market. The reason why the demand for corn was no longer covered by the supply is that agricultural production was still, to a large extent, organized on highly capitalistic lines, the export of wine and oil on a large scale being the end in view, so that full use was made of the advance achieved in the last century B.C. The *villae rusticae* in the neighbourhood of Pompeii, with their wine and oil presses, their storehouses

[1] Pliny, *N.H.* xxxiv, 11.

and forwarding departments, their slaves' dormitories, and their buildings for the masters or directors, make this clear; for Falernian wine was not only retailed in local taverns, or sent by sea to Rome and other places in Italy; inscriptions on the amphorae show that the lands of the Danube, Roman Germany, and Britain, and, to some extent, Gaul, Spain, and Africa, were also supplied with Campanian wines and oils. To this must be added the large-scale consumption of the army. Such production was not limited, however, to central Italy; the South also had a share in it, and the North exported westwards and northwards its own as well as Campanian brands; Venetian wine and oil crossed to Illyria. Far to the East, in distant Alexandria, and even beyond, in Axum and northern India[1] there was a demand for Italian wine. We are told that in the southern Po valley the wine was matured in immense vats—bigger than houses[2]; and Pliny proudly announces that two-thirds of the world output in choice wines derives from Italy[3]. The Italian wine trade must, then, have been highly remunerative, and the estimated profit of twenty per cent. is, perhaps, not far wrong[4].

Export industry did not lag behind agriculture here. Nothing sheds a clearer light on the enterprise of the Italian, who still modelled his activities on Greek economic conceptions, than to stroll through the streets of the business section at Pompeii, with their industrial establishments, artisans' quarters, and combined workshops and stores, and, at the same time, to observe with the insight of a Rostovtzeff the frescoes and pictured amoretti in the houses of the rich business men[5]. Here again we are less interested in what the cobblers, tailors, potters, bakers, and other tradesmen produced to satisfy the local demand, than in what might be exported (even though it is the result of individual craftsmanship) as some sort of speciality. We cannot say whether the products of the goldsmiths' workshops of Campania, Rome and Aquileia, were exported in bulk; but the amber industry in Aquileia, which made necklaces, small bottles, boxes, and similar articles from German amber, besides distributing this

---

[1] *Peripl. mar. Erythr.* 6, 49.   [2] Strabo v, 218.

[3] Pliny, *N.H.* xiv, 87.

[4] Frank, *op. cit.* p. 425 *sq.* (following Columella iii, 3, 9). Cf. Pliny, *N.H.* xiv, 48 *sqq.*, where a vineyard near Nomentum, which was bought for 600,000 sesterces, is sold to Seneca, ten years from the time when it was planted—and, it should be added, after a series of improvements—at four times the original price, with a yearly revenue of 400,000 sesterces.

[5] *Social and Economic History of the Roman Empire,* p. 96.

popular luxury locally and reaching the markets of Rome and Pompeii, exported it also to the Dalmatian coast, to Africa, to Belgium and even as far as Egypt. Cloth-weaving and other branches of the textile industry flourished in Campania, Tarentum, Brundisium, and also in the vicinity of the Po, where sheep-breeding sometimes furnished the raw material. The Cloth Hall at Pompeii shows that the drapery trade had reached a high degree of development, and Pompeii's architectural history testifies to an increasing expansion, although, admittedly, we have here no certain evidence of export to very distant markets. Nevertheless there was a lively commerce within Italy, not only in fine wares, such as Paduan carpets and the Paduan garments which were transported to Rome, but also in the Ligurian and Insubrian coarse wool, 'from which most of the clothing for the Italian slaves is made[1].' Pompeian furniture, too, which apparently got as far as Rome, will have supplied the needs of a somewhat small trading area.

The situation is very different in the Italian precious metals, pottery, and glass industries, which certainly manufactured for large-scale export to distant markets. Wholesale firms in Capua and Tarentum produced silverware, specimens of which have been recovered in Denmark. Vessels of copper and of bronze were made in Capua, Puteoli, Aquileia, and north-west Italy. The Capuan art-foundries, the names of whose owners are still known to us, were huge concerns, working on a methodical system with specialized labour, which distributed their wares throughout Italy, and beyond to Germany, Denmark, Scandinavia, Finland, and southern and north-eastern Russia. The large-scale manufacture of pottery likewise had its home in Campania, Capua, Puteoli, and Cumae, and farther afield still in Italy, for example in Adria (where a particularly durable ware was made), in Rhegium, and in the valley of the Po. Above all Arretium's pottery, with its red glaze, enjoyed a world-wide reputation. Throughout the Empire save the South-east this famous table-ware was in every-day use in many houses; it constituted, in fact, a genuine article of mass consumption, and in the remains we possess there constantly recur the trade marks of the Perennii, of Ateius, Cornelius, Calidius Strigo or some other owner of the workshops at Arretium. These are the manufactories mentioned above (p. 391) in which there were mixing vats with a capacity of ten thousand gallons[2].

---

[1] Strabo v, 218; cf. v, 213. Unfortunately it is not certain whether it was the raw material or the finished article that was exported.

[2] *Not. degli Scavi*, 1896, p. 455 (quoted by Frank, *op. cit.* p. 222, n. 5).

Similar conditions prevailed in the glass industry. Strabo's mention[1] of epoch-making inventions, made, according to him, at Rome—perhaps by a Greek from Sidon or Alexandria—and of a consequent simplification in the production of glass, is probably to be taken in conjunction with Pliny[2], and to be understood as a reference to the substitution of the technique of glass-blowing for the use of moulds. A result of this was the reduction of prices to a *chalcus* (about a halfpenny) per cup and saucer, so that developments in technique in this way exercised a decisive influence on the formation of a world-market. In Campania also, where the river Volturnus provided suitable beds of sand, glass of a brilliant colour and with patterned reliefs was made. Conditions equally favourable for production existed in Aquileia, so that here too an industry manufacturing glass on the largest scale for export could develop. Campanian glass was distributed widely throughout the Empire, and also, like copper and the bronze wares, is encountered in south Russia, in north Germany, and in the Scandinavian countries.

About the iron industry (weapons, knives, agricultural implements, and so on, and articles of sheet iron) opinions differ. The question is whether the exports under consideration were organized on a small scale, and consist in specialities, produced by individual craftsmen[3], or were meant for a world-wide export, and are products of large-scale manufacturing concerns[4]. The description in Diodorus[5] looks more like occasional labour, dependent on the arrival of an excess of raw materials, more like a capitalistic system with home work and 'manufacturer' than a stable and permanent organization of 'manufactory'; indeed, it would almost seem as if the same traders (*emporoi*) who brought the crude iron from Elba later carried the finished articles through the world. It is, then, in the writer's opinion, more prudent not to draw too striking a picture of huge iron works, with specialized labour, roaring with activity. However, that there was an iron industry, which exported its products, cannot be denied: its centres were in Campania, and again, above all, at Aquileia, where crude iron from Noricum was worked into articles of iron and steel, and may even have been re-exported to Dalmatia and the lands of the Danube[6].

[1] XVI, 758.   [2] *N.H.* XXXVI, 193.   [3] So Frank, *op. cit.* pp. 232 *sqq.*
[4] So Charlesworth, *op. cit.* p. 6 *sq.*; Rostovtzeff, *op. cit.* p. 71 *sq.*   [5] V, 13.
[6] Rostovtzeff, *op. cit.* p. 533, n. 25. It is doubtful if the *fibulae* stamped with the name 'Aucissa' and found over a wide area are really an Italian product: they are more probably Gallic (p. 405).

Another problem which as yet defies solution is concerned with the manufacture of terracotta lamps. In this connection a special importance attaches to the workshops of Fortis at Mutina, who lived in the time of Augustus. His lamps are found in quantities in all parts of the Empire, notably in Gaul, Roman Germany, the Danubian provinces[1] and Britain. If these all derive from Mutina, then we have before us a firm with truly world-wide connections—and this view is widely adopted. A different theory is that casts were made in the provinces copying the Fortis type of lamp and his trade-mark[2]. If in any way, certainty here can only be achieved through chemical analysis of the materials employed; but even if we are dealing with imitations, it remains probable that the specimens which served as models came from the original firm into the regions concerned.

This catalogue, to which perhaps might have been added the Pompeian manufacture of attar of roses (so finely illustrated by a fresco in the house of the Vettii), and of fish-sauce (*garum*), may suffice to show how generally not only agricultural, but also industrial centres of production on a large scale were to be found in Italy. Campania, Etruria, and the north of Italy were pioneers in this, and conclusive evidence can be drawn from the plan of Pompeii for the advance of industrial development. The proof lies in the buildings for industrial purposes and no less in those connected with trade. It was trade which made it possible to obtain raw materials, so far as they were not to be found in the immediate vicinity, either from Italy itself, or from abroad. It is, however, not only imports of raw materials which throw light on production, but equally what we learn about activity in exports. Reference has already been made to the wine-trade of Campania. The style of decoration in the houses of the Pompeian aristocracy in this age, which points to the influence of Alexandria, indicates that the wholesale merchants of Pompeii themselves visited the East, and, incidentally, formed their tastes there. And yet Pompeii (the port for Nola, Nuceria, and Acerrae) was a place of secondary importance, and lagged far behind the centres of the export trade, Puteoli, or Aquileia, 'the Puteoli of the North,' as it has been called[3]. Finally, the wealth of the producing and exporting classes is itself a proof of their business success. Its reality is attested by the splendid remains found at

---

[1] *Germania*, XVI, 1932, p. 310, records a new specimen from Ingolstadt.
[2] See E. Loeschke in *Mitt. d. Altertumskomm. f. Westf.* V, p. 211.
[3] Rostovtzeff, *op. cit.* p. 72. For Augustus' interest in Aquileia cf. A. Calderini, *L'Aquileia Romana*, pp. 32 *sqq.*

Aquileia and Pompeii, and is reflected by the growing sump-
tuousness in architecture, which, for the middle of the first century A.D., finds expression in the Fourth Style at Pompeii.

The long list given by the authorities of luxuries imported into
Italy tells the same tale. Many of these, it is true, went to the
world's capital, Rome, which, although producing articles extensively for local use, was still, in the last instance, a city consuming
more than it could itself supply; but enough remained over, and
this surplus found its way to exporting cities of the type of
Aquileia, Padua, Capua or Pompeii. Moreover, the increase in
the population of the large cities reacted on the organization of
business whose concern was with local production. Large-scale
mills and bakeries, such as are mentioned above, of a type which
existed in Rome as early as the first century B.C.[1], can be recognized in Pompeii also (their owners being Popidius Priscus and
Paquius Proculus), and the same is true of large-scale tanneries
and brick-yards. Italy may have had an unfavourable balance
of trade, as might be expected in view of the vast consumption
of the dominant nation, which derived a greater revenue from
taxation than did the provincials; and Strabo[2] gives explicit
testimony of the disparity between Italy and Egypt in this connection, when he says that Alexandrine ships are heavily laden
when they sail to Puteoli, whereas they carry little on the return
voyage. But, firstly, Egypt possessed an unusually flourishing
active trade, and, secondly, the main stream of Italian export flowed
not to the East, but to the West and North, so that the greater
part of Italian imports could, in reality, be paid for in goods and
not solely in cash, that is not solely with the aid of wealth drawn
from mines which were won by conquest, or from the purse of
the provincials.

IV. THE OUTPUT OF EASTERN LANDS

From Italy we turn to a brief survey of the economic value of
the various provinces of Rome under the early Principate. It is
more convenient to begin with the regions that had known
civilization for centuries, and here pride of place is claimed by
Egypt. Strabo declares that Egypt, which had suffered an
economic decline under the later Ptolemies[3]—and the debase-
ment of the coinage reinforces the verdict of a man who had

---

[1] See vol. IX, p. 822 and Volume of Plates iv, 72.
[2] Strabo XVII, 793.   [3] Strabo XVII, 797 sq.

himself seen the country in the retinue of the governor Aelius Gallus—was again placed on its feet through systematic reclamation of the land. Trade, and with it the industries exporting their products, was revived by the re-establishment of openings for export (above, p. 389). The surplus of corn was vast, far greater even than that which a past-master of economic policy, Ptolemy Philadelphus, had squeezed from the land. Twenty million modii went each year to Rome[1], and this sufficed to supply the needs of the city for a space of four months[2]. Wine and oil served, in general, only to satisfy local demands; but grape juice, which was prepared in Diospolis (Thebes), was exported, together with some corn, to the South-east. There was a demand for Egyptian stone: Syenite, basalt and granite, marble, porphyry, and serpentine, were transported from Syene, Memphis, and the Mons Claudianus (on the shore of the Red Sea) to Italy[3], and beyond, to the West and North-west even as far as Belgium. Even sand was exported to remote distances, that from Coptos being used in sawing marble, while Nile-sand was used for the wrestling-schools in Rome. The jewel-mines of upper Egypt produced emeralds, topazes, amethysts, onyxes, and similar gems. Herbs and drugs for ointments, for medicinal purposes, or as dyes, of which an exhaustive account is given by Pliny, also came from Egypt. Egyptian alum ranked as the best; while soda was especially plentiful in the soda-lakes near Momemphis in the Delta.

A far greater rôle, however, was played in the world-market by the products of the Egyptian and especially the Alexandrine workshops. Industrial activity, once so intense under the Ptolemaic system of State capitalism, surmounted the temporary depression, and revived with twice its former energy. In principle, it is true, the Caesars avoided the policy, which a narrow mercantilism might have prompted, of crushing the competition of other producers within the Empire; the numerous monopolies had, as we saw (above, p. 306), been given a less oppressive form, thus stimulating the initiative of those engaged in business ventures whether on a large or small scale. This did not, however, prevent the emperor, who was himself here acting, to some extent, as head of a large-scale industrial undertaking, from taking an energetic share in the competition for markets.

In the large-scale export of commodities, whose inner organiza-

---

[1] Aur. Vict. *epit.* 1. [2] Josephus, *Bell. Jud.* II [16, 4], 386.
[3] But the attempt, made during Claudius' reign, to popularize porphyry statues did not succeed; Pliny, *N.H.* XXXVI, 57.

tion is unfortunately not clearly known to us, the papyrus industry holds a commanding position, for Egypt here possessed a world-monopoly so complete that the greatest embarrassment resulted, when, as in the reign of Tiberius[1], the Egyptian papyrus-harvest failed. But the inhabitants of the Delta, where the papyrus-plant grew, were aware of the advantages of their position, and kept the price high; hence they did not hesitate to cut down a proportion of the plants[2] (though this may well have happened only when there was a notably abundant harvest), actuated by the same motives as recently caused the Brazilians to dump their coffee in the sea. Like the manufacture of papyrus, the glass industry was very ancient, thanks to the beds of vitreous sand in the country, of whose existence Strabo learnt from the Alexandrine glass-workers themselves[3]. Expensive many-hued glasses were put on the market, but cheap articles as well, small bottles, glass paste, sham pearls, and glass imitations of *murrena* vases[4]. Axum and the coast of Somaliland, India and even China bought these products, and the Empire preferred Alexandrine glass, or at least glass of the Egyptian type, and the discovery of the glass-blowing technique must have helped, here as in Italy, to increase the output. The textile trade, also, although apparently organized on a basis of individual craftsmanship, worked for mass export. Barbarian clothing was made specially for Axum, the Sabaeans, and the natives of the Somaliland coast, while a particular type of ready-made sleeved garment was worked up at Arsinoe (near Suez). To these we must add the original Egyptian fine linens, which found purchasers in the Empire and India alike, and fabrics, woven out of Indian cotton and Chinese silk, which were highly prized in the West. Alexandrine metal-ware and metal utensils (especially of silver, which had to be imported for the purpose) competed with the Campanian, and were widely distributed throughout the world. They, too, reached as far as India; and specimens have been found in south Russia. Products of the jeweller's art, and ivory articles, round off the list, and, last but not least, the famous scented essences, perfumes, and ointments, subtly blended from native and foreign ingredients and embodying much medical lore, but also much quackery, which were made into a remunerative item of Mediterranean trade. Thus Alexandria was not only in the first rank as a focus for the transit trade—of this aspect more will be said later—but also a maritime centre of industry and export on a very large scale,

[1] Pliny, *N.H.* XIII, 89.   [2] Strabo XVII, 800.   [3] Strabo XVI, 758.
[4] *Peripl. mar. Erythr.* 6 (manufactured in Diospolis).

whose produce circulated in the civilized world of those days over a wide area and with great effect.

From early times Syria was a vigorous rival of Egypt, not only because of her transit trade, which, incidentally, brought raw materials, such as crude silk and drugs, into the land in bulk, but mainly because of her highly developed industry, which regained its former eminence through the establishment of settled conditions. Her soil was naturally fertile and had been rendered still more productive through the development of artificial irrigation, so that it too played its part in supplying the needs of foreign customers. The wine drunk in Alexandria came mostly from Syrian Laodicea, and the lords of Axum and the Indians knew its quality. Even in Rome it sometimes appeared, for variety, on the table, together with olives from Damascus. Syrian fruit preserves, dried plums and figs, dates from Jericho, truffles from Jerusalem, and onions from Askalon, were a special delicacy. The output in precious stones was less than the Egyptian; on the other hand, there was an abundance of spices and drugs, among which we may make especial mention of the balsam from Jericho, which was unique, and of the asphalt from the Dead Sea, which was used in Egypt for embalming the dead.

All this, however, came second to the textile industry of Tyre and Sidon, of Berytus, Laodicea and Byblus, stimulated as it was by the purple-dyeing trade. Trimalchio's treasurer wears Tyrian woollens as a matter of course. The linen woven from local raw materials was distributed throughout the whole world and competed with the Egyptian product. Syrian silks satisfied much of the demands of fashionable society, which existed everywhere. The purple murex, dredged up off the Phoenician coast, constituted the raw material from which the loveliest purple in the world was derived, and then was either exported direct, or used to dye Syrian fabrics. Dyeing was carried on in countless works, especially at Tyre 'as a result of which the city, while becoming a most unpleasant place to live in, at the same time grew rich[1].' The importance of Syrian glass is shown by the legend that glass was originally invented by Sidonians[2]. Glass bearing a Syrian stamp is found in the distant West, penetrating as far as the Rhine, and also in the graves of south Russia, together with the Campanian product. Finally, Syria had also a high reputation in the perfume industry; the best cyperus-oil, for instance, was prepared in Sidon[3]. The number of important and wealthy com-

[1] Strabo XVI, 757.   [2] Pliny, *N.H.* XXXVI, 191.
[3] Pliny, *N.H.* XIII, 12.

mercial cities was even greater here than in Egypt, since in Syria the centralization was less thorough; and, although from the earliest times pride of place had been taken by wholesale trading operations, thanks to the old Phoenician heritage, yet the manufacture of exports, a branch of more recent growth, could claim an honourable position in contemporary world production.

Asia Minor (including the adjacent islands) resembles Syria in this respect. Here too the coastal inhabitants had long been merchants, an activity to which the unique economic geography of the country—its position making it a bridge, thrust far forward between East and West—was still a significant contributory factor. As in Syria, trade gave rise to the utilization of the country's rich resources for export purposes, the chief difference being that the tendency towards subdivision into a conglomeration of moderate-sized productive centres, in which old Greek cities frequently survived, was still stronger in Asia Minor. Inscriptions and remains, and the texts of Strabo and Dio of Prusa enable us to discern the gradual regeneration, which was even more marked in the industrial than in the agricultural sphere. Corn was not exported by Asia Minor, as the country could barely satisfy its own needs, but vast quantities of excellent wine and oil were sent abroad, which sufficed to cover the demand of the East and North-east; some wine went also to Italy, in return for which Italian wine would be exported to Asia Minor[1]. Further articles of export are raisin-wine, dried figs—transported in boxes[2]—pure honey, first-class truffles, dried funguses, used for medicinal purposes, cheese (from the Salon plain in Bithynia), tunnyfish—which were caught at Pharnaceia, Sinope, and Byzantium, and then salted down—, oysters from Ephesus, and shellfish from the Troad. There was also wood, which grew plentifully throughout Asia Minor, both ship-timber and that of finer grain, such as boxwood; copper, especially from Cyprus, which supplied even the Indian market, silver, lead, and iron; the widest variety of precious and semi-precious stones, ranging from diamonds and emeralds to onyxes, all in great demand among the Roman jewellers; all kinds of transparent rock crystal, such as the Cappadocian mica, which was split into sheets before being exported to serve as window panes; a bright-hued marble which was quarried in bulk at Synnada, and brought as far as Rome; drugs,

---

[1] Dio of Prusa, *Or.* XLVI, is cited by Rostovtzeff (*op. cit.* p. 511, n. 10) as showing the transition from arable land to vineyards in the time of Dio's father.　　　　　　　　　　　　[2] Pliny, *N.H.* xv, 82.

including dyes such as 'Sinopian earth' (red chalk)[1], various medicinal wares, and Lycian funguses.

All this, however, was overshadowed by the magnificent textile industry, Asia Minor's special pride and craft from time immemorial. Here she was fully able to hold her own against Syrian and Egyptian competition. Now, however, Laodicea instead of Miletus took the lead. Once again the connection with the dyeing industry made itself felt. The method was to employ vegetable dyes, as at Hierapolis, or else purple-dye, supplied by the purple fisheries of the Anatolian coast, as at Thyatira. Immense quantities of coloured fabrics and clothing crossed the sea, mostly of a high quality, for Milesian wool had always been an esteemed article, commanding as ready a sale as the pedigree Milesian sheep themselves. Anatolian cloths were stocked by the fashion-houses of Pompeii, Anatolian carpets and woolly blankets were known everywhere. The Coan silks, though coarser in texture than the genuine Chinese product, nevertheless were very popular. Two kinds were brought out: delicate fabrics for women's wear, the raw material for which was derived from the Assyrian silk-worm farms, and a coarser fabric for men's attire, which was made from the cocoons of the local Coan silkworm. Linen from Colchis also was exported far afield, and in Italy rough coats of Cilician goats' hair were prized.

The regions adjacent to the West, which lay in the same longitude as the Greek homeland, showed a greatly reduced economic activity in comparison with the countries we have named, and with their own earlier history. Cyrene, it is true, yet retained some of her importance in the African trade[2], and her agriculture was still flourishing, but she had forfeited her position as a centre of production and export since the famous and valuable aromatic herb called *Silphium* had become extinct[3]. Only one or two other drugs come under consideration in this connection, among them a good white dye, the *paraetonium*, which, like the Cretan product, was used in Rome. Greece, always a poor country, had sunk still lower during the Hellenistic age and under the Roman Republic, and the opening years of the imperial régime could bring little change. Together with the

[1] Strabo XII, 540; exported at this time not from Sinope but from Ephesus.
[2] As is shown also by no. 3 of the new Cyrene edicts, H. Malcovati, *Caesaris Aug. Imp. Operum Fragmenta*[2], p. 42; J. Stroux and L. Wenger, *Die Augustus-Inschrift auf dem Marktplatz von Kyrene*, Abh. Bay. Akad. XXXIV, 2, pp. 10 *sqq.*
[3] Well before the time of Pliny (*N.H.* XIX, 39).

Greek islands she exported as in the past wine and oil with which the East was supplied, and honey from Hymettus and the islands; rare marbles, sometimes quarried far below the earth's surface and often sent to Italy to adorn rich men's palaces; emeralds from Taygetus; mussel-pearls from Acarnania; various drugs, including Melian alum and a series of dyes, such as Attic and Achaean ochre, and Laconian purple. Among industrial products art-bronzes, made in Corinth, Aegina, and Delos, brought a high price at Rome; very fine linen for women's wear was made in the vicinity of Elis and at Patrae, by women weavers; perfumes in Boeotia. But the general impression left by such writers as Strabo and Dio of Prusa, by Plutarch also and later by Apuleius, is not very different from the picture painted by a Polybius. Better conditions prevailed in Macedonia alone. For whereas in Greece proper the silver-mines at Laurium, which had once been so productive, were exhausted, the mines on Pangaeum remained 'gold-mines' indeed. Diamonds also were found there, and a valuable by-product of the mines was the Macedonian *chrysocolla*, a pigment of a rich green hue. Finally the timber of the Macedonian pine retained its former reputation.

V. THE OUTPUT OF WESTERN LANDS

The blessings of the imperial régime made themselves still more clearly felt in the West than in the East. There it was often a question simply of removing débris so that life could spring into being again; in the West there was almost a new creation, and in districts on the outskirts of the Empire culture and more advanced forms of economic life arose as distant responses to stimuli emanating from the older centres of Gallia Narbonensis, Baetica, Africa, and the northern border of Italy.

The three islands of Sicily, Sardinia, and Corsica call for notice first. Sicily sustained her old reputation as 'Rome's storehouse,' for with the exception of a few products, which are consumed in the land itself, everything is brought to Rome. This includes not only agricultural produce, but also cattle, hides, wool, and similar commodities[1]. Among agricultural produce, the first place was taken by corn in Sicily as in Sardinia; the cattle may have been drawn for the most part from the great ranches of which Horace speaks[2]. The volcanic soil near Etna furnished the fiery wine it does to-day. From Sicily came also honey, and

---

[1] Strabo VI, 273.　　　　[2] *Odes*, II, 16, 33; *Ep.* I, 12.

from Corsica wax, while Agrigentum supplied cheese made from
goats' milk. Some further specialities are blocks of stone, and
jewels (emeralds); vitriol from Lipari, and Sicilian sulphur,
which was produced in bulk, and was used everywhere by vine-
growers; among drugs, the excellent Sicilian saffron, which went
to Rome, alum, Sardinian chalk for use as fuller's earth, and
so on.

We now turn to consider, in Gaul, the first of those regions
radiating cultural influences, in which the growing diffusion of
civilization (p. 405) is realized. Strabo expressly tells us how
in Gallia Narbonensis the inhabitants had abandoned their warlike practices for agriculture and urban life[1]. The land was
fertile, and invited a more intensive cultivation. In the southern
belt, which extended northwards about as far as Lugdunum
(Lyons), the growth of vine and olive was now successfully
resumed, and not only supplied the rest of Gaul, but also Ireland
and even Italy, as amphorae-fragments at Rome prove. Vines,
olives, and figs, did not thrive in the North, but this was all the
more reason for growing corn, of a good quality and in such
quantity that part of the Roman *annona* could be provided from
it. Equally flourishing was stock-farming, both in Gallia Narbonensis, and in the Three Gauls; from the surplus products,
hides, pickled meats, hams, sausages, and cheese, were supplied
to the wholesale trade, which then brought them to Italy. The
carrots which Tiberius ordered each year from the vicinity of
Düsseldorf, and the geese which in Pliny's time were driven in
flocks all the weary way from Belgium to Italy for their goose-
liver, are doubtless instances of expensive delicacies, though
Pliny remarks that the carrot had become a fashionable vegetable
since Tiberius[2]. On the south coast of France fishing had
brought in its train establishments utilizing the catch at Forum
Julii and Antipolis where the simpler sorts of *garum* were prepared. The corals of the Stoechades, the pinewood from the Jura
and Vosges mountains, and drugs such as Gallic nard, vegetable
purple-dye, and Rhenish cassia, were probably the concern of
local trade only, and similarly it is difficult to determine to what
extent the mineral treasures were exported. In Strabo's time, it
is true, there was an abundance of gold, especially in the South;
he says of the Tarbellian mines (in Aquitania) that they are the
best in the whole world[3]. There was also silver, copper, lead,
and tin, and an abundance of iron, especially on the lower Loire

---

[1] IV, 189.
[2] Pliny, *N.H.* XIX, 90; for the geese see X, 53.   [3] IV, 190.

and in the valley of the Sambre, as is proved by the many traces of iron-workings discovered there. In all probability, however, the metal-bearing regions of Spain, Britain, and Noricum constituted too strong a competition for the crude metal to be exported on a large scale. But in the land itself the working-up of metal was carried on extensively. Caesar notices this iron-working in Gaul[1]; the art of the local gold- and silver-smiths was known beyond the Gallic frontiers; and if the Aucissa-fibulae (which date from the first half of the first century A.D., and are spread over an area comprising Gaul, Britain, Italy, the Tyrol, and Asia Minor, and even extending to the Don and the Caucasus), were Gallic products[2], we should be dealing with a leading article of wholesale export.

In any case, Gallic industry shows other instances of the tendency to expand and to dominate the market (below, p. 406). The textile industry, at whose disposal local agriculture placed an embarrassing quantity of raw materials—good crude wool, and flax—proceeded to build up its production of the woolly coats, which were a feature of the country, with a view to supplying distant markets, a policy which met with response in Italy and Rome[3]. Bolsters and quilts stuffed with flax counted as Gallic inventions; and the weaving of linen was so widespread—*Galliae universae vela texant*—that this was a direct source of Gaul's importance[4]. Most interesting, however, are the conclusions to be derived from the evidence of pottery. Through finds in the Roman forts of west Germany, we can trace accurately from decade to decade the progressive emancipation during the first half of the first century A.D. from domination by imported Italian terra-sigillata. Originating perhaps in branch settlements of Arretine firms, there gradually developed at the end of the Augustan age great manufactories (as for instance that of a certain Mommo) in the La Graufesenque district of southern Gaul. Then, after the middle of the century, follow those in central Gaul, situated at Lezoux. Production was still intended, in the first instance, for the local Gallic and German market; but ultimately the wares were distributed farther afield, to Britain and the Danubian provinces, and even to Italy, as is shown by a

---

[1] *B.G.* VII, 22, 2; cf. III, 21, 3.

[2] As Keune suggests: *P.W.* Suppl. III, col. 183.

[3] But the Romans apparently introduced a breed of sheep with a finer fleece and thinner wool, Strabo IV, 196.

[4] Pliny, *N.H.* XIX, 8; 'itane et Galliae censentur hoc reditu': *loc. cit.* 7 (however 'censentur' be translated).

consignment which reached Pompeii from Gaul via Rome, but remained unopened as a result of the catastrophe in 79[1]. In the glass industry analogous conditions prevailed. The first Gallic glass-blowing works arose apparently at Lugdunum in the middle of the first century of our era. At a later stage, however, this branch too of Gallic industry, especially after its centre had been transferred to Cologne, competed successfully with Syrian, Alexandrine, and Italian glass.

Though this development and the climax of Gallic civilization generally lie outside the period we are considering, the impulse everywhere dates from the opening years of the imperial régime. Centres of production and export sprang into being, which took over the conduct of trade not only with the South, via the ports of Gallia Narbonensis (chiefly Narbo and Massilia), but also with the North, for which Lugdunum constituted the focal point. A prosperity ensued which became proverbial. In A.D. 64 Lugdunum sent four million sesterces to Rome as a contribution towards repairing the ravages of fire in the capital. To make his countrymen see the madness of a revolution, Agrippa II in A.D. 66 asks them whether they fancy themselves richer than the Gauls, a people who, according to his description, have all the means of production in their own land, and flood almost the whole world with their merchandise[2]. The imported luxuries, the numerous foreigners who brought them, the sumptuous architecture and art[3], the highly developed local handicrafts and the local trade, of which we learn from the inscriptions in the twelfth volume of the Corpus of Inscriptions—all this shows that Agrippa did not exaggerate too greatly.

Britain, though wealthy, stands in marked contrast to Gaul. It is the opening period of British culture; hence besides animals and foodstuffs only raw materials, and not products made up from them, served as objects of trade. In exchange, articles characteristic of a higher plane of living, such as wine, oil, bronze utensils, pottery, glassware, and so on, were brought by foreign traders. Strabo (IV, 199) gives a kind of statement of trading returns: 'exports comprised corn, cattle, gold, silver, and iron... and also hides, slaves, and very good hounds.' If to this list we add tin and lead, the two chief articles of export, it gives the essentials. The omission is due solely to the fact that Strabo,

---

[1] D. Atkinson in *J.R.S.* IV, 1914, pp. 27 *sqq.*

[2] Josephus, *Bell. Jud.* II [16, 4], 364 and 372.

[3] Pliny, *N.H.* XXXIV, 45, mentions a colossal statue of Mercury, which was cast in bronze to the order of the tribe of the Arverni, during Nero's reign, which cost forty million sesterces in wages alone.

following a recurrent misconception of the ancient world, groups together those regions of the West which export tin, and applies to them the mythical collective term of 'Tin islands[1],' which he conceives to be situated off the coast of Spain. Diodorus, however, who elsewhere adopts a similar localization to that of Strabo (the common source of both writers being Posidonius), knows, perhaps from Timaeus, that there were rich tin deposits in Cornwall[2]. Finally, Pliny[3] and many inscriptions testify to the exceptionally plentiful and easily accessible veins of lead[4].

The second great radiating centre was ancient Spain, comprising southern Spain, and the eastern coastal region, which had long since attracted the attention of the Massiliotes and Phoenicians. This remote peninsula, favoured by the climate, with a fertile soil, and abounding in precious metals, was associated in men's minds with age-old legends of infinite wealth. This was especially true of Baetica; the Fields of the Blessed were perhaps thought to be here, and the story ran that even horses fed from silver mangers[5]. Yet here too the full and rational utilization of the natural riches of the country as a whole first came about through the policy of pacification and unhampered development pursued during the early years of the Empire, and we must bear the effects of this policy in mind in order to understand Pliny's remark[6] that after Italy and India Spain is the most productive region in the world. Some part in this more intensive utilization was, it is true, played by Italians. There were colonists and veterans, who had been transplanted to Spain, partly by Caesar (and before him), but chiefly later by Augustus, as a means of pacification and settlement. Further, there were Italians who migrated into the province of their own initiative, as early as the first century B.C. and whose example was now followed by many others—all of which contributed to the romanization and urbanization of this area (see above, p. 385 sq.) Yet the natives were the core, and among its members the Phoenicians, especially those of Gades, were outstanding as enterprising business men; from their ranks also most of those engaged in the export trade were drawn. In density of population and in prosperity an exceptionally advanced stage had here been reached; Strabo calls

[1] Haverfield in *P.W.* x, col. 2332, *s.v.* κασσιτερίδες.

[2] Diodorus v, 22 and 38. Cf. Pliny, *N.H.* iv, 104 (from Timaeus) and Haverfield in *P.W.* ix, col. 857 sq. On Cornwall as the leading tin-producing area of the earlier Mediterranean world see R. Hennig, in *Rh. Mus.* LXXXIII, 1934, pp. 162 *sqq.*　　　　　　　[3] *N.H.* XXXIV, 164.

[4] Strabo (III, 175) treats British lead in conjunction with the 'Cassiterides.'　　　　[5] Strabo III, 150 *sq.*　　　　[6] *N.H.* XXXVII, 203.

Gades the second city of the Empire, the number of its capitalists (knights) being equalled in Patavium only.

According to a list given by the same author, the chief articles of export from Baetica were wax and honey, pitch, dyes (kermes and minium), and especially quantities of corn, wine, and excellent oil, products which were already exported in the closing years of the Republic. Whether the ban imposed upon Gallic oil- and wine-production (p. 383) had been later extended to all the western provinces, and whether it was the lifting of this ban that made possible the renewal of intensive cultivation of vine and olive is a question that cannot be answered either for Africa or Spain[1]. At any rate Spanish wine and oil were welcome in Italy and Rome, as the numerous sherds of vessels and jars from the 'Monte Testaccio' at Rome show[2]. Spanish wine came also from other centres, from Tarraco, for instance, and the Balearic Islands. Baetican artichokes were a special luxury for epicures. But greater importance in the economic system as a whole attaches to the immense quantity of jars and pots full of pickled fish and *garum*-sauce which were daily shipped overseas by the great fishing concerns. For here we are dealing with genuine large-scale enterprises[3], in which whole companies (*socii*[4]) were involved, and which yielded a substantial profit.

A still more lucrative economic system than that of the coastal regions prevailed in the mountainous area comprising the Sierra Morena and Gallaecia, where the numerous mines were located. These were mostly State-owned, but individual capitalists, often from Italy, dealt with the contracting and exploiting. Mining plant with a high standard of technical development, or a system of washings for alluvial gold, was used to recover the metal. Thus gold, silver, copper, lead, tin, and iron were put on the world market in huge quantities. The yearly yield of gold in Asturia (the site of the richest gold-field), Gallaecia, and Lusitania, amounted, according to Pliny, to twenty thousand pounds[5]. The figures for the silver-mines near New Carthage, which in Polybius' time had a circuit of forty-six miles and in which forty thousand workers were employed, came at that time to no less than twenty-five thousand drachmae daily[6], implying a yearly output of more

[1] Frank, *op. cit.* p. 116, n. 19; Rostovtzeff, *op. cit.* p. 22, 492, n. 17.
[2] Though the chief finds on the Monte Testaccio belong to a later period, the earliest certainly fall in the middle of the first century of our era.
[3] Strabo III, 156, calls them ταριχεῖαι μεγάλαι.
[4] Pliny, *N.H.* XXXI, 94.   [5] Pliny, *N.H.* XXXIII, 78.
[6] Strabo III, 147 *sq.*; cf. Diodorus V, 36.

than eight and a half thousand kilograms ($=8\frac{1}{3}$ tons); and there are no grounds for assuming that production had declined. Single lead-mines were let at a yearly rent of two million denarii[1]. Lead and tin penetrated as far as India[2]. The iron, of which there was an abundant outcrop in Cantabria, was converted into steel, in places where the water supply favoured this process, as in the Ebro valley, and, moreover, worked up into finished articles, it seems, at Dianium; it was exported principally to Italy, a country notoriously deficient in iron. But this does not exhaust the list of Spain's exports: there were dyes (other than those from Baetica mentioned above): cinnabar, scarlet, azure, black, and copper-green; esparto-grass from the region to the north of Carthago Nova, 'which was used for cordwaining and was exported to all parts, especially to Italy[3]'; linen yarns in quantity from Zoela (Gallaecia), fine linen fabrics from Emporiae, Tarraco, and Saetabis, places which set the standard of quality for the European manufacture of these materials[4]; and beautiful woollens from Salacia[5]. There was thus an abundance of wares to be sent out into the world by the Spanish export-firms of the interior, and more especially of the countless maritime cities of the South, though they also occur at New Carthage and elsewhere. Producers and exporters grew ever wealthier through this trade, and from decade to decade the number of citizens in the hundreds of Spanish cities went on increasing.

The special position of Africa was based to a far greater extent than was the case with Spain on her grain, and on the corn-trade deriving from it, which was under State control. The fertility of the soil is often praised. It would seem that crops sometimes flourished there under a kind of terraced cultivation: palms, fruit trees bearing olives, figs, and pomegranates, vines, and corn—all prospered at different levels on the same terrain—and in the lowest region, when the corn was over, leguminous plants and cabbages could be cultivated in the same year. The wheat, it was maintained, gave between one and a half and four times as heavy a yield as the best Sicilian, Baetican or Egyptian product[6]. After

---

[1] Pliny, *N.H.* xxxiv, 165.

[2] Pliny, *N.H.* xxxiv, 163; *Peripl. mar. Erythr.* 7.

[3] Strabo III, 160; cf. Pliny, *N.H.* xix, 30.

[4] Pliny, *N.H.* xix, 9.

[5] Strabo III, 144; Pliny, *N.H.* viii, 191. In Strabo's day, at any rate, the Baetic export of the raw wool was more important than that of the finished product.

[6] Pliny, *N.H.* xviii, 95; cf. however, Varro, *de re rust.* i, 44, 2.

Thapsus, Caesar announced that Rome would in future receive
each year two hundred thousand Attic medimni of corn, and three
million *litrae* of oil from Africa[1]; oil, therefore, ranked second as
an article of taxation, and hence of wholesale export. In view
of the imperial government's constructive policy, which was
everywhere in operation, it is *a priori* probable that the pioneer
work of Gaius Gracchus and of Caesar was extended and that
production was stimulated. But it is also directly deducible from
the account of the African export trade to Puteoli and Ostia in
the Augustan age, which would seem to have been even more
vigorous than that from southern Spain[2]. Its volume, moreover,
can be at least approximately determined[3]. The remains from
Ostia and the 'Monte Testaccio' afford confirmatory evidence
for the close of our period; foreign immigration and the balancing
list of imports (raw materials and finished articles) make the
circle complete. In addition to corn and oil, articles of export
on a somewhat larger scale such as *garum* from Leptis, and the
African dyes, especially purple[4], may be noticed. The rest must
be regarded as specialities of secondary importance only: African
figs, which feature in Trimalchio's housekeeping, cucumbers,
truffles, and Numidian fowls; marble from Numidia; wax, cumin,
and medicinal wares and so on. On the other hand, there was
next to no export of wine[5], with the exception of a little grape
juice, which came into fashion through Tiberius.

From Mauretania, a land which, with the aid of colonies,
began to make headway from the time of Augustus, and which,
in the West, was naturally influenced by Spain, came oil from
Tubusuctu[6], wild beasts for the games, the famous citron-wood

[1] Plutarch, *Caesar*, 55.   [2] Strabo III, 145.

[3] Josephus (*Bell. Jud.* II [16, 4], 386) states that Egypt's contribution
to the corn-supply suffices for four months, whereas that of the African
nationalities (reaching, it may be remarked, from the Atlantic Ocean and
the pillars of Hercules to the Red Sea and Aethiopia) suffices for eight.
As the Egyptian *annona* came to 20,000,000 modii (see p. 303 *sq.*), or about
2,900,000 Attic medimni, it is clear that in Agrippa's lifetime the African
annona must have been far in excess of the 200,000 medimni of Caesar's time,
although the deduction that it amounted to 5,800,000 medimni (Frank,
op. cit. p. 430, Charlesworth, *op. cit.* p. 144) may overshoot the mark.

[4] Horace, *Odes*, II, 16, 36: Grosphus' robes were twice dipped in African
purple.

[5] This must be the source of Pliny's curious statement (*N.H.* XV, 8)
that nature had denied oil (*sic*) and wine to the province of Africa, in order
to reserve it wholly for corn.

[6] According to the testimony of amphorae-inscriptions from the Monte
Testaccio.

for fine tables and also citron-tables themselves, precious stones, pearls, and ivory, doubtless also Gaetulian purple—the manufacture of which together with purple dyeing had been developed by Juba II—asphalt, and copper. Juba's new foundation of Iol Caesarea grew into a splendid royal residence, and at the same time into a busy port and lively centre of local industry and of export, so that here, as in the other colonies, the traditions of Phoenician Carthage were actively maintained.

To complete our survey of the productive countries of the world-empire there remains only the newest sector in the circle of civilization, namely the Danubian lands, to which we append the barely cultivable country of Illyria. Admittedly the primary motive that underlay the pushing forward of the frontier to the North, was the desire to obtain an advance area of strategic importance (pp. 351 *sqq.*); yet the mineral wealth of the Alpine lands, and the iron- and gold-fields of Noricum had long been known, so that here again, as so often, occupation and exploitation joined hands[1]. Iron came to Italy in the crude state, and also, to some extent, after manufacture. Horace praises Norican swords, and Trimalchio gives his cook a Norican knife, much to his guests' admiration and astonishment. At Noreia (Steiermark) in addition to the iron-works[2] there was gold, both alluvial and mined. Further, gold- and silver-mines are mentioned in remote Dalmatia, while semi-precious stones were found at Virunum. All this went, mostly as raw materials, to Aquileia, to balance the mass export of agricultural and manufactured products from that town (pp. 393 *sqq.*). Here, too, there were specialities: a certain amount of Raetian and Illyrian wine, Illyrian oil, excellent cheese from the Alps and Dalmatia, pickled fish from the Illyrian inland lakes (east of Epidamnus), fish-liver furnished by the *mustelae* of Lake Constance, and by Pliny's time Dalmatian *muria* was making a name[3].

But there is no need of an exhaustive list: it is sufficient for our purpose to have demonstrated that in every region there existed, in more or less advanced forms, production in excess of immediate local needs for export. Sometimes the production was primary, as in Africa, Spain or Britain, sometimes the result of

[1] Strabo IV, 208. The discovery of gold among the Norican Taurisci in Polybius' lifetime caused a gold-rush in which Italians took part as well as the native inhabitants; by Strabo's time all the gold-mines were in Roman hands.

[2] σιδηρουργεῖα: Strabo V, 214.

[3] Pliny, *N.H.* XXXI, 94.

several processes, as in Italy, Egypt, Syria and Asia Minor or Gaul. But all had their place in the world market.

VI. THE RANGE AND METHODS OF COMMERCE

All these varied products of the Empire, apart from those which, as taxes in kind, stood directly at the disposal of the State, went to swell the stream of trade: an increase in production necessarily involved an increase in trade, and probably also in the forms of commercial organization. Trading cities received a new stimulus, not only the great ports, such as Alexandria, the centre of the world's trade, Puteoli, Aquileia, and (after Claudius' time) Ostia, Narbo, Massilia, Gades, Tyre, and Ephesus, but also river ports and inland cities such as Rome, Antioch, Corduba, Lugdunum, and Damascus. To these centres of the first importance we must add a vast number ranking lower: Pompeii, Brundisium, and the cities of the Po valley, in Italy; Coptos, Myos Hormos, Aradus, Berytus, and Seleuceia, in the East; the two Carthages, Arausio, Nemausus, in the West; and countless more. Businesses dealing with the export, import, and transit trades here came to their full development: for the import trade the chief business centres were Rome and Ostia, for the transit trade the great commercial cities of the East, and also Aquileia. The harbours could cope with the highest demands made upon them[1].

Naturally the peddler still hawked his wares, as before, and many tradesmen made their rounds in the old-fashioned way, buying their wares from the producers themselves, or at markets and fairs, loading them on ships, on mule-back, or on waggons, and transporting them to some other district, where they set them out and sold them. Such was in all probability the way in which C. Gracchus, the outlaw's son, who, in Tiberius' time, travelled to and fro between Africa and Sicily, eked out a humble existence[2]. Trimalchio is another case in point: he suddenly determines to embark on a trading venture, builds ships, buys wine and other commodities at a low rate, and makes at random a journey to Rome, to dispose of them at a high price[3]. He too is not far removed from an itinerant tradesman, for if he fails to

[1] Strabo v, 245, observes that the largest merchantmen can moor safely in Puteoli.

[2] Tacitus, *Ann.* IV, 13: 'per Africam et Siciliam mutando sordidas merces sustentabatur.'

[3] Petronius, *Sat.* 75 *sq.*

get rid of his wares at Rome, he, or else his representatives, must travel farther afield with them.

Yet alongside this primitive economic form there were higher developments: export and import firms, with great warehouses, which did not solely depend on chance sale or chance supply, but maintained steady business connections; and trading concerns, or producing and trading companies, which had their agencies, at various centres, such as Puteoli, Rome, Ostia, and Alexandria, and at countless other points within and without the Empire. The discoveries at Ostia give us a vivid picture of this development, though the bureaux there in the vicinity of the theatre belonged not only to traders, but also, in part, to ship-owners and shipping companies. For traders and shipowners, whose vessels plied the seas and rivers, were not always the same people. The more specialized differentiation that existed between trading and shipping operations is illustrated with exemplary clearness in the *navicularii*, who saw to the transport of the *annona* on behalf of the State. In conjunction with this transport, a system operating with a certain regularity along more or less fixed trade-routes came into being, which made possible at least a secondary carrying trade, and a passenger service, and permitted merchants with a reasonably small quantity of wares to use the travel facilities. The tonnage of the vessels, in spite of variations in individual instances, was quite large, in some cases—we must remember that sailing ships only are in question—really remarkable and suggestive of the advance the carrying trade may have made. The ship on which the Apostle Paul was brought to Rome, had 276, that of Josephus about 600 persons on board[1]. The general aim was to build as big ships as possible. 'Scitis, magna navis magnam fortitudinem habet,' says Trimalchio[2]. 'The biggest (and most numerous) trading vessels' were owned in Strabo's time by the inhabitants of Gades[3]; travellers to India and Arabia also sailed in 'large ships[4].' The vessel in which Gaius caused an Egyptian obelisk to be transported to Rome, which was ballasted with a hundred and twenty thousand *modii* (more than a hundred thousand litres) of lentils, could take a cargo of 1335 tons[5], and her length was almost as great as that of the left side of the newer harbour at Ostia[6]. Her capacity must, then, have exceeded a

---

[1] *Acts* xxvii, 37. (On the reading cf. H. v. Soden, *Die Schriften des Neuen Testaments in ihrer ältesten erreichbaren Textgestalt*, I, p. 1656 *sq.*); Josephus, *Vita* [3], 15.   [2] Petronius, *Sat.* 76.
[3] Strabo III, 168.   [4] *Peripl. mar. Erythr.* 10, 56.
[5] A. Köster, *Das antike Seewesen*, p. 163.   [6] Pliny, *N.H.* XVI, 201.

thousand tons register. We may well regard Trimalchio's ships as having been equally large[1].

Thus throughout the length and breadth of the Empire, there developed an extraordinary life and activity, and a commercial intercourse with foreign countries, which may well have sometimes been comparable with the Leipzig Fair a century ago. Foreign tradesmen were encountered in all parts. Numerous inscriptions still testify to this—in Rome, Ostia, and Puteoli, just as in Delos, Narbo, Brigetio (Pressburg), where the slave of a tax-farmer set up an inscription to the *genius commercii et negotiantium*[2], or otherwhere. Italians travelled in the West and East, and they also stayed as settlers: two Calpurnii in Puteoli are the subjects of an honorary inscription from *mercatores, qui Alexandriai Asiai Syriai negotiantur*[3], which implies connections with the East; in Tiberius' time Roman *negotiatores* strolled about the streets of Gythium[4]; a *conventus civium Romanorum qui in Asia negotiantur* existed in A.D. 43/4 at Ephesus[5]; there must have been many merchants from Pompeii in Alexandria during the first century A.D.; and many Romans were to be found in Petra and in Palmyra[6].

Still more numerous than the occidentals in the East, were the orientals of Greek and semi-Greek origin in the West. Anatolians, Syrians, Alexandrines, and even Palmyrenes, travelled in large numbers with their carpets, silks, fruits, glass, cosmetics, spices, and other merchandise, not only in the cities of the East, but also of Italy, and beyond in Gaul, on the Rhine, in the Alpine lands, in Britain, and in Spain; and glib-tongued as they were they disposed of their wares at such a profit that the Italians were more and more thrust into the background even in their native land by the Levantines. Only the Carthaginians, and the southern Spaniards of Phoenician stock, held their own with the peoples to which they were linked by age-old ties of kinship. Thus at the focal points of economic life traders of every nationality and clime mingled in kaleidoscopic confusion. Naturally the leading

---

[1] The cargo of wine for five ships represents a value of 30,000,000 sesterces. If we follow Pliny, *N.H.* XIV, 56, in reckoning 100 sesterces to an amphora, we get an average per ship of 60,000 amphorae, or 150,000 litres, which, in itself, if the wine was poured into the ship's hold, would require a capacity of 555 tons register.

[2] Dessau 1861.   [3] Dessau 7273.

[4] S. B. Kougeas, Ἑλληνικά, I, 1928, p. 9.

[5] J. Keil, *Forschungen in Ephesos*, III, p. 110.

[6] Alexandria: above, p. 397. Petra: Strabo XVI, 779. Palmyra: above, p. 389.

merchants themselves did least travelling, though even they from time to time must have accompanied their wares and looked after their agencies. 'Most of the population of Gades is constantly at sea,' says Strabo[1], so some portion of her five hundred knights must have been abroad; and the leader of a trade expedition to the Baltic coast of Germany to fetch amber, was a Roman knight[2]. But these merchant princes were exceptions, not the rule. In general the independent tradesmen, who travelled with their wares, will have belonged to the middle class, and the same is true of the agents and supercargoes, who maintained the connection of the larger trading firms with the outside world. The travelling buyers, who visited the manufacturing firms, the commercial travellers and agents of these firms, and the branch officials employed as local managers (typified in the *negotians vestiarius civis Gallus* in Pola[3]), if they showed any distinguishing marks of class, are more likely to have borne the brand of slavery than the *angustus clavus*. With all this coming and going commercial intercourse became progressively livelier. The hotels in the large cities must have flourished: even in sequestered places (such as Berenike Trogodytike) accommodation was to be found, and there were hostelries at the caravan stations.

An exchange of information about market openings and values had been customary in earlier times. In Rome and elsewhere the traders met regularly, and it was in answer to such a demand that special exchange buildings were erected, as those behind the theatre at Ostia, or near Trajan's Forum at Rome. Only the banking system remained comparatively undeveloped. Exchange counters on a small scale were, indeed, to be found everywhere, extensive money-lending businesses were carried on, and there had been signs of a tendency towards more complicated monetary transactions[4]. The reason, however, for the retarded development of banking is to be found in the fact that apart from those instances in which the State was helpful—in the contract for the imperial domains, for example, or for tax-farming, or for the transport of corn—Roman financiers never achieved the organization of a syndicate, which might have broken down the simple system of guilds, companies or personal partnership. Consequently, despite the money-lending operations of a Seneca, said

---

[1] Strabo III, 168.   [2] Pliny, *N.H.* XXXVII, 45.
[3] Dessau 7576.
[4] Thus Cicero got Atticus to open 'a credit account' for the young Cicero with his agent Xeno in Athens: Cicero, *ad Att.* XV, 15, 4 and XVI, 1, 5.

to involve millions[1], the foundation of large banking institutions, whose capital should not be personally owned, never came to be attempted.

Yet even without systematized banking the existence of commercial intercourse on a large scale was fully established; it may be conveniently divided into three categories: inter-district, inter-territorial, and inter-national, and the second category, inter-territorial trade, was of paramount importance for the unification of the Empire. Inter-district trade was, of course, in existence everywhere. How true this was of Italy has already been shown[2], and Pliny never tires of repeating his demonstration that Italy is essentially self-supporting[3]. Papyri show there was a similar linking of the Egyptian land divisions with one another and with the great centre of Alexandria, the centre of wholesale buying and selling, and Strabo tells the same tale about both Gaul and Noricum[4].

Even connection with foreign countries was but the continuation of old traditions: the great innovations were a further extension of the trading radius, and an increasingly direct contact with the demands and products of even remote lands. In this way the chain of middlemen could in part be eliminated, or at least diminished, customs barriers circumvented, prices lowered, and marketing possibilities increased. In all this the emperors played a great part (p. 388 *sq.*): Claudius and Nero seem to have followed the model of Augustus. Strabo tells of the chain of middlemen controlling the overland trade from southern Arabia through Syria to Mesopotamia[5], and from Pliny we learn how high an expenditure it involved: a camel-load of incense over the stage from Thomna (in southern Arabia) to Gaza incurred charges amounting to 688 denarii for transport, customs, and bakshish, not counting the customs dues of the Roman Empire[6]. It is a safe assumption that the route by water from Kane or Muza to Berenice Trogodytike or Myos Hormos, and thence to Coptos and down the Nile to Alexandria, was much cheaper. Hippalus' discovery in the first century B.C. of the regularity of the monsoons in the Arabian Gulf came gradually to be fully utilized, and in three stages a progressively shorter passage to India was found, until finally, at the time of Nero, trade took the direct overseas

---

[1] Tacitus, *Ann.* XIII, 42; see below, p. 714.
[2] See above, pp. 392 *sqq.*, and cf. Strabo IV, 202 (Liguria and the rest of Italy).
[3] Pliny, *N.H.* XXXVII, 202.
[4] Strabo IV, 189 and 207.
[5] Strabo XVI, 778.
[6] Pliny, *N.H.* XII, 65.

route to Muziris—a journey of forty days from Ocelis. Plainly
the leaders in these enterprises to the South and South-east were
the Alexandrian traders, and they drew upon three regions:
eastern Africa (including Aethiopia, Axum and the coast of
Somaliland), Arabia and India, and China. But whereas they
were in direct touch with Arabia and India, the vagueness of the
Graeco-Roman ideas about China shows that connections were
only indirect, and that their merchandise took complicated routes.
It might come through eastern Turkestan and Bactria, and
by Taxila down to the mouth of the Indus, and so by the Red
Sea, or—by ways along which Arabian and Indian wares, too,
were transported—crossing Arabia from Gerrha to Petra, or up
the Euphrates to Ctesiphon and across the desert to Palmyra
and Damascus. But the Romans had no desire to enrich Parthia
by trade, and there are indications that in order to avoid the
transcontinental highway through Parthia, they encouraged the
use of a more northerly route, from Maracanda (Samarkand) by
the Oxus and the Caspian and across the Caucasus to the Black
Sea.

Such were the main routes between Rome and the South-east,
along which western products could be sent, mainly metals, a
certain amount of wine, and cheap Egyptian manufactures such
as textiles, glass, ornaments and perfumes. The cargo from the
South-east was varied and luxurious: gold and silver, steel,
precious and semi-precious stones, fine woods, ivory, ostrich-
feathers, tortoise-shell, pearls, and spices and, above all, drugs of
every kind, and textiles, whether Chinese silks or Indian cotton
and calico, whether raw materials or manufactured fabrics. Even
this brief list shows that trade must have been carried on with
great intensity. India's yearly quota of exports into the Empire,
after the establishment of direct communication along the short
route, was estimated to amount to a minimum export value of
1,500,000 sesterces (with a retail value of 150,000,000 sesterces[1]).
From the Roman standpoint India took second place among producing regions, outstripping Spain, and surpassed by Italy alone[2].
On the other hand India, China, and Arabia, together, are stated,
'after careful computation,' to take the sum of 100,000,000
sesterces annually from the Empire[3]. This admittedly sounds as
if the account was liquidated wholly in money payments, and
Pliny's references to India and Arabia do, in fact, point in this

[1] Pliny, *N.H.* VI, 101.
[2] Pliny, *N.H.* XXXVII, 203.
[3] Pliny, *N.H.* XII, 84: *nostro imperio adimunt.*

direction[1]. But his moralizing lamentations[2], which are not always consistent, seem exaggerated, and it is hard to believe that the 'great fleets' which Strabo records as sailing to India went eastwards with empty holds[3]. It is nevertheless true that the Romans did not hesitate, when a luxury import was in question—and it is with such, on the whole, that we are dealing—to make inroads on the Empire's stock of precious metals, and to barter Indian diamonds, for example, for Roman denarii. The numerous Roman coins found in India, mostly minted in Tiberius' reign, and the fact that the king of Ceylon could get possession of various issues, prove that this was so[4]. The truth, then, probably lies midway between the two extremes. For the rest, in the numerous trading centres and ports of the South-east, some of which had made the most up-to-date provision for commerce (including a pilot service), we encounter not only Arabs and Indians, but also Greeks and other occidental merchants, corresponding to the Arabian trading agencies at Coptos, and the Arabs and Indians, who could doubtless be seen before the time of Dio of Prusa in the streets of Alexandria.

While doubt may exist whether there was a favourable or unfavourable balance of trade with the South-east, direct interchange of wares with the North is much more certain, thanks to archaeological finds. In return for wine, oil, and manufactured articles, south Russia still provided corn, salted fish, furs, hides, and slaves, while from north-east Germany, Scandinavia and the Baltic, in return for Italian manufactures (especially from Capua), came slaves, furs, and especially amber. The routes to south Russia ran via Panticapaeum and Tanais (on the Don), or farther to the East via Dioscurias and Phasis; while the Baltic region could be reached by the all-sea passage from northern Gaul, or from the Black Sea up the Dnieper, or again from Aquileia through Carnuntum and Bohemia. For though in the Augustan age Roman merchants had not penetrated beyond the Elbe[5], by Nero's time they had

---

[1] Pliny, *N.H.* VI, 101: *HS |D| imperii nostri exhauriente India et merces remittente*; VI, 162: *vendentibus* (sc. *Arabibus*)...*nihil invicem redimentibus.* Cf. also *Peripl. mar. Erythr.* 6 (Axum), 8 (Malao), 49 (Barygaza).

[2] Cf. also Tacitus, *Ann.* III, 53 *sq.*

[3] Strabo XVII, 798. It has been proposed to reach a lower valuation of this trade by dividing the μεγάλοι στόλοι into journeys to India, and journeys to Somaliland, because the latter are also referred to here. But from II, 118 it is clear that Strabo is thinking principally of the journeys to India.

[4] Pliny, *N.H.* VI, 85.   [5] Strabo VII, 294.

become bolder, as the Roman knight sent to get amber proved by his expedition (p. 415).

Thus the trading connections of the Empire extended far beyond its own frontiers to the regions on the margin of the *oikoumene*, often but dimly known. But although all parts of the world helped to supply Trimalchio's table, and although Italian apothecaries needed ingredients mostly of non-European origin[1] to blend their ointments, vital necessities were not, on the whole, imported from abroad. The rich could manage with fewer emeralds on their fingers or pearls in their ear-rings. In the inter-territorial exchange of trade within the Empire, however, we are not, in general, dealing with such *deliciae*, and hence this was ultimately more important than international trade. The system of commercial communication, by land and sea, within the Empire, which was operating with growing efficiency created a milieu most favourable to such an exchange of trade. It linked up in the eastern frontier districts with the ends of the old high-ways of world trade—it developed the transverse route, connecting Asia Minor and Egypt, with great success, and in the western frontier districts, in the Alpine and Danubian lands, in Gaul, on the Rhine, and in Spain, it sometimes opened up wholly new arteries of commerce.

Thus in the stream of trade those wares which were produced for known markets in nearer or remoter areas, or were handed over for unknown markets to itinerant vendors, brought in return from near and far not only foreign wares but also imports from within the Empire, including products of primary production—food-supplies and raw materials—and also of finishing processes. We may be certain that the primary production of the Empire was sufficient for its needs. Although Strabo is explicit on this point only for Europe[2], the inclusion in our consideration of those parts of Africa and Asia which belonged to the Empire only makes this sufficiency more pronounced. The production of corn and crops in each country was generally adequate to solve the problem of its food supply. Greece and Italy were exceptional: Greece, because here even after the drop in the numbers of the population in Hellenistic times the old difficulties in providing a sufficient supply still prevailed; Italy, because the inhabitants were un-willing to cultivate corn, although there was no lack of oppor-tunities. The deficiency was supplied by the lands of the Empire with a surplus of corn. Greece need not have drawn on a foreign country, the Crimea, for Egypt was exporting corn to lands

---

[1] Pliny, *N.H.* xxiv, 4 *sq.*   [2] Strabo ii, 127.

outside the Empire (see above, p. 398). As for other food-supplies, we have seen that the most varied products of the most varied countries were imported to the great consuming centres such as Italy.

The imports of raw materials present a more complicated problem. Here, if we concentrate on what was typical, three main classes of territory can be discerned. First came stretches of land which were more or less self-sufficing in raw materials, and which also generally worked up these materials themselves into articles for home consumption or export. The most representative example of this type was Gaul, especially in later times; her leading position was directly due to the fact that she had at her disposal large natural means of production (above, p. 404 *sq.*). The occasional import of Corinthian carbuncle[1] or Egyptian syenite is not an exception, for there had always been a brisk interchange of such specialized raw materials. The second class comprises countries with a deficiency, which, while themselves possessing quantities of raw materials, needed still more, partly because a densely concentrated population with high demands meant a large consumption, and also because their technical skill was so high that it was possible to satisfy the needs not only of the land itself, but of others also, and to manufacture articles from foreign as well as native raw materials. Such was the situation in the leading industrial countries of Italy, Egypt, Syria, and Asia Minor, and this explains their heavy import of metals, stone, wood, hides, raw materials for textiles and cordwaining, ingredients for ointments, and so on. The eastern industrial areas, however, occupied an exceptional position, in as much as they—more than the western—received a good part of their raw materials not from within the Empire but from foreign countries. As a complement to the highly industrial regions we have the third division, comprising the lands specifically limited to the production of raw materials, which did not themselves absorb in manufacture the greater part of their surplus output. The reason for this might be that the raw materials were present in such abundance that the available supplies of civilized labour were fully occupied in the process merely of tapping these riches, or, alternatively, in disposing of them. Such was the state of affairs in many parts of Spain, and doubtless also in Sicily; it is significant that in the Spanish branch of the textile trade the processing of wool was at times dropped in favour of exporting the raw material[2]. Another important reason for supplying raw materials (including

---

[1] Pliny, *N.H.* XXXVII, 97.   [2] Strabo III, 144.

human beings) lay in a lack of technical experience. This applies not only to a great number of Orientals, whose limitations in this respect are explicitly stressed by our authorities[1], but also to a whole series of members of the Empire: the Dalmatians, the inhabitants of the Alpine and Danubian lands, the Britons, and the natives of Central Spain and Central Asia Minor. Here Italians, Greeks, or Graeco-Orientals, were often the first to discover the existence of new raw materials, to recognize their value, or to bring supplies of them into circulation. We call to mind the Roman gold-miners in Noricum, and the 'mercatores, qui ulteriora Aethiopiae scrutantur[2].'

Lands producing raw materials were the complement of industrial countries in so far as the former drew on the latter's output of manufactured wares, and especially on articles of mass consumption, comprising the products of industry and of industrialized agriculture, such as pottery, lamps, glass and metal ware, wine and oil. Admittedly, the import of such mass-produced articles was not limited to industrially backward regions. Egyptian paper and oriental glass are found in Italy, occidental lamps in Corinth, Italian ware in Gaul, and, later, Gallic ware in Italy. There is an interchange of wines from Italy, Greece, and southern Spain and also of oils from Italy with those of Gaul, Spain and Africa. The reason for this is partly that certain large-scale industries enjoyed a more or less complete monopoly (as did the Egyptian papyrus industry), and partly that the idea of exchanging individual specialities was already exerting an influence. How attractive to try Coan wine for once as a change from the good Falernian usually drunk, or to sample Spanish, Gallic, even Dalmatian *garum* as a sauce in place of that familiar Pompeian! In the same way there was a trade in other manufactured specialities (particularly luxuries): in choice foods, textiles, dyes, perfumes, articles of bronze and silver, or similar goods.

There was, then, a specialization of labour over a wide area, and strong ties bound the various parts of the Empire together, and linked the Empire with the outside world. The whole *orbis terrarum* seemed united into one trading area by the bonds of commerce and import, and 'even the most obscure product was brought into the sphere of world consumption[3].' The constantly recurring emphasis on the ideal of self-sufficiency shows that its practical realization was unknown, that everywhere, but above all at those centres which were the focal points of civilization in its

[1] *E.g.* Strabo xv, 706.   [2] Pliny, *N.H.* vi, 173.
[3] Pliny, *N.H.* xiv, 2.

highest form—at Rome[1], Pompeii, Ostia, Aquileia, Alexandria, Antioch, and elsewhere—what actually prevailed was the most colourful range and variety of imports imaginable. The geographical disposition of raw materials in one place, and skilled workmanship in another (a contrast which was sharply marked in some instances), in itself determined the creation of this interlocking system, whereby the one found its counterpart in the other.

Admittedly this simultaneity set a limit to the possibilities of development. The incorporation of backward peoples in the Empire must inevitably have exposed them to civilizing influences and led them to the conception of utilizing their raw materials themselves for production. We hear of travelling industrial experts[2], and of the establishment of branches and industrial settlements. Industries could be transplanted as well as plants and domestic animals; the glass industry moved from Syria and Alexandria to the West, the ceramic industry from Arretium to Gaul. This acted as a decentralizing factor, and so reduced the radius of activity of the old large-scale industries. Other influences were also at work which hastened this development instead of retarding it. One of these was the system of commercial intercommunication. Relatively speaking this was highly developed, but judged by absolute standards it was still primitive. A journey by land, and, above all, a voyage by sea, was still exposed to numerous dangers[3]. Overseas trade was on the whole a risky business, and freight charges still remained high, or at least fluctuating[4]. Secondly there was no possibility of obtaining compensation for the effects of decentralization, through a reduction of running costs. Machines, in our sense of the word, were unknown. The slave market actually began to run dry in consequence of the *pax Romana*. Finally, economic activity, in spite of all the advances under the imperial régime, had never wholly lost its characteristic insecurity. This was due to two facts: first, credit facilities for productive enterprises, which might have tided them over times of crisis, were either non-existent, or else but weakly developed; secondly, personal capital only, not joint-stock capital, was sunk in business. Tendencies towards State

---

[1] Pliny, *N.H.* xi, 240: *Romae, ubi omnium gentium bona comminus iudicantur*; cf. iii, 54.

[2] Dessau 7648. Cf. Gummerus in *P.W.*, *s.v.* Industrie, col. 1478.

[3] Pliny, *N.H.* xii, 88: *negotiatores multos interire*; Tacitus, *Ann.* iii, 54: *incerta maris et tempestatum*; cf. the shipwreck of St. Paul, *Acts* xxvii, of Josephus, *Vita* [3], 15, or of Trimalchio, Petronius, *Sat.* 76.

[4] Pliny, *N.H.* xxxiii, 164: constant fluctuation of prices, in particular *prout navigatione constiterint*.

socialism on oriental lines, that were gaining ground by the
middle of the century, and for which the outflow of the reserves
of precious metal from the Empire may have been one of the
causes, brought no improvement in the situation.

In fine, the basic structure of economic life—as in classical
Greek antiquity—tended ultimately to rest on the old foundations of agriculture, skilled craftsmanship—perhaps on a large
scale (involving many trained hands)—or speculation. The safest
capital investment is still always real estate (it is only necessary
to remember Trimalchio's profits from speculation); then, as
before, the inclination to income from rent is marked. Hence
large-scale industry, for all its positive achievements, some of
which are amazing enough, did not develop into a truly typical
form of economic activity, but, if we disregard the Alexandrine
paper industry, remained limited to particular branches (the
ceramic, metallurgic, glass, and perhaps the *garum* industries),
branches which were based on the possession of a certain
technique, on the exercise of a certain artistic skill, and, apart
from these, at best on the special enterprise of individual indus-
trialists, instead of on the impulse, inherent in a definite working
method, towards the attainment of a progressively greater
efficiency—a development which is only found with the coming
of 'factories.'

Within the boundaries, however, which the ancient world set
itself, and which it did not transgress, the early Principate marks
a rise to the highest point that was ever to be reached. An
economic system flowers in which the sap of life flows strong.
In the conflict of forces, competing rivals measure each other's
strength, and do not shrink from imitation and forgery of each
other's products. In the North-west, Italian and Gallic, in the
North-east, Alexandrine and Campanian industries strive with
each other for the prize. Some branches of local production are,
it is true, crushed out of existence by the presence of the mono-
polist large-scale industries. Common table ware cannot be made
in Pompeii because the mass import from Etruria, or even from
Puteoli, chokes the local output. But other institutions working
to satisfy local needs, and organized on a broader basis than the
normal artisans' or small tradesmen's businesses, struggle into
being, as is shown by the example of the Roman and Pompeian
large-scale bakeries. Municipal centres, implying a concentrated
demand, grew up on all sides. The wealth of the cities, and luxury
in private and public life, steadily increased, in Italy as, above all,
in the provinces (Greece being again an exception), though their

golden age, in the West at any rate, still lay in the future. Through
this multiplication of the individual centres, the life of the community as a whole blossomed into a greater activity. There was
a constant passing to and fro of merchandise and travellers.
'Miscentur sapores...miscentur vero et terrae caelique tractus[1].'
Throughout the world there was an interpenetration, and a
smoothing-out of differences, to an extent undreamed of before.
The nationalistic Roman moralists lamented 'vincendo victi sumus;
paremus externis[2].' They advocated a rejection of capitalism and
luxury, and a return to self-sufficiency and agriculture. Yet if we
contemplate the facts from the standpoint of the Empire, our
verdict must be that, in spite of all the dangers that an exaggerated capitalism has latent in it, industry, trade and commerce
accomplished the task, which Augustus set them, the task of
welding the Empire into a unity, thereby rendering possible its
survival for centuries to come.

[1] Pliny, *N.H.* xv, 105.   [2] Pliny, *N.H.* xxiv, 5.

CHAPTER XIV

THE SOCIAL POLICY OF AUGUSTUS[1]

I. THE SOCIAL PROBLEM

SIXTY years before Actium a large part of the Italian population was engaged in an attempt to throw off the leadership of Rome. Justice demanded that an empire won by the joint efforts of Rome and the Italians should be regarded as the empire not of Rome but of Italy: yet for over a century Rome had been always more openly treating it as her own. For the Roman Republic the Social War marked the crisis of its history and the culmination of its achievement. By its outbreak Italian unity was threatened: its end was secured by a daring innovation which was the most valuable contribution made by Rome before the Principate to the political ideas of Western Europe. The citizenship of a single city was turned into the citizenship of the whole peninsula. The Allies were retained because they became Romans; and, if the empire remained Roman in name, that was only because the extension of the Roman franchise made Rome and Italy politically identical.

The reception of the Italians into the body politic of Rome was a momentous step. When the *civitas Romana* was made the common citizenship of Italy, the nature of the citizenship itself was changed. It grew into an imperial citizenship, recognized as compatible with active membership of smaller communities within the whole. Indeed, the local citizenships lost little of their importance; for it was still through them that men controlled their own affairs and retained that sense of responsibility for their surroundings which is the most valuable product of political freedom. The public rights of a Roman citizen could only be enjoyed at Rome; and, though 'civis Romanus sum' were words which a man might utter when he was in danger from the law, to the inhabitants of Italy at large their Roman citizenship in practice implied few of the activities for which citizenship had stood during the earlier ages of Graeco-Roman civilization. Its extension to the whole of Italy went far towards emptying the Roman *civitas* of meaning:

---

[1] In this chapter, when a statement rests on the evidence of two or more jurists of whom Gaius is one, a reference to the relevant passage of Gaius alone is given.

and though the enfranchisement of the Allies was a long step towards their final unification, the unity of which their Roman citizenship might become a symbol would not be complete until the people of Italy came to think of themselves, no longer primarily as members of this small community or that, but as parts of a single whole—the body politic of Rome. Only when a strong and universal consciousness of Italian solidarity had been called into being would Italy be ready to assume with confidence the 'patrocinium orbis terrae[1].' And, as has been seen again in the years since 1860, to create a political unity in Italy is one task, to create Italians a second.

From its earliest days the power of Rome had been built round the solid core of Roman patriotism: in war the Romans had never asked their friends to do more than they would do themselves. And now that the Italians had won their way to partnership in empire, Italy at large must be stirred by the spirit for which Rome had been famous in the best days of the Republic. To awaken Italy to a consciousness of itself was a task imposed on the statesmanship of the early Empire, not by any doctrines of nationalism like those which have spread wide since the days of the reaction against Napoleon, but by the sound instincts of a people with a gift for the tasks of government. When the Gallic rebellion of 52 B.C. was afoot, Julius Caesar had sent home for re-inforcements, 'magni interesse etiam in reliquum tempus ad opinionem Galliae existimans tantas videri Italiae facultates ut, si quid esset in bello detrimenti acceptum, non modo id brevi tempore sarciri, sed etiam maioribus adaugeri copiis posset[2].' If Italy was to be equal to its burdens, it must be convinced of its imperial mission; and to create that conviction something more was needed than a mere statement of Rome's destiny—even if the statement came from Virgil himself.

The history of Hellenism since Alexander had shown that an ecumenical State could only be constructed round the solid core of a people strong in numbers, with a culture of its own and a tenacity of the traditions of its native land which would save that culture from submergence when it came to be carried into the empire at large, and preserve it to be the common property of stocks which were ethnically distinct. The non-Greek populations of the Hellenistic kingdoms in the East were never hellenized: they did not look to Greece as the home of their civilization. But

[1] Cicero, *de off.* II, 8, 27.

[2] Caesar, *B.G.* VI, 1, 3. A comment of some interest is made on this passage by General Gouraud in *Pro Alesia*, 47–48, 1927, p. 100.

the problem which had baffled the Greeks in Asia was solved in
Europe by Rome. The non-Roman populations of Western Europe
were romanized: the time was to come when Gauls and Illyrians
would show themselves more zealous Romans than the inhabitants
of Italy itself. And this romanization of Western Europe was of
all Rome's achievements by far the richest in its effects on later
history. The task of Rome was, indeed, easier than that which
Asia had presented to the Greeks: the Celts were nearer akin to
the Romans than were the Asiatic peoples to the Greeks, and
Rome was challenging no culture so ancient or so high as that
which was to be found in the dominions of the Persian king. But,
more than that, the Greek effort was made by a disunited homeland whose culture was already past its prime, the Roman was
based on an Italy which stood solid, believing in its mission and
with a civilization, despite disquieting symptoms, still in essence
sound. For the choice of Rome's method the man responsible
was Augustus, and it is in his social programme that the manner of
his choosing is revealed.

When Augustus became supreme, much still remained to be
done before Rome could be ready to guide an empire into a new
phase of its development. The age of war was ended; the world
for the first time was to be organized for peace; the period of
romanization was to begin; and in the Romans themselves
patriotism of the mere martial order would no longer be enough.
The imperial people must be taught its mission, and the duties
which the Roman *civitas* implied must not need the stimulus of
war to bring them into conscious recognition. The first step of all
was to unify the Roman People. Italy had been the foundation
of Octavian's resistance to Antony, and men did not doubt that
the conflict which reached its end at Actium was a struggle between West and East. To that extent Italy and the provinces
which had looked to the young Caesar for a lead could claim a
certain character in common; but the most superficial glance
would reveal that even then Italy could make no adequate reply
to the taunt that it was still a geographical expression. Politically
its free inhabitants were all citizens of Rome: yet Virgil's stress
on the promise which Juppiter is made to give[1] is only one of
many reminders that in Augustan days the promise had yet to be
redeemed. In Southern Italy large parts of the population still
spoke Greek. Farther North, it was only after the Social War that
Latin had begun to make rapid headway in the regions where

----

[1] *Aen.* XII, 837: '. . . faciamque omnis uno ore Latinos.'

Oscan or Umbrian was the native speech[1], and the evidence from Pompeii is enough to show that at the beginning of our era Oscan was by no means dead[2]. In a land where such variety prevailed, where more than half the population belonged to stocks which had been brought into the Roman State less than sixty years before, and where these men had still to learn that their Roman citizenship was something more than a mere protection against the whims of Roman magistrates, much had to be changed before it could be said with truth that the peoples had been welded into one.

This was the end which Augustus sought. His method for its attainment was to instil into the peoples of Italy the great traditions of the Roman past, to make them the conscious heirs of a proud inheritance, and so to implant a sense of responsibility to their successors which might supply an adequate ideal for their future conduct. His work, however, was made more difficult by the peculiar conditions which prevailed at the end of the Civil Wars. Besides other influences more local in their effects, there was one potent factor affecting the whole peninsula alike. Slavery, which had played its part in creating the unemployment of the second century (Vol. IX, p. 7), and had also threatened to make the countryside unsafe (ib. p. 11), was now producing a still graver result. Julius Caesar had twice taken steps to encourage parenthood, and some hint of his reason may be found in the rule that at least one third of the herdsmen employed on the ranches of Italy must be drawn from the free population[3]. Abounding supplies of slaves seem to have restricted the demand for free labour, and this restriction was reflected in the birth-rate among the humbler sections of the citizen-community. However remote, the threat which had already proved disastrous to Greece was now hanging dangerously over Italy[4].

It is not to be supposed that there was any dearth of men legally entitled to be called 'cives Romani.' Apart from the vast additions which had been made to the citizen body after the Social War, its numbers were being constantly recruited by the enfranchisement of slaves, and it appears that manumissions on which the *vicesima libertatis* was paid amounted during the period between 80 and 50 B.C. to a total in the neighbourhood of half a

[1] See R. S. Conway, *The Italic Dialects*, I, pp. 234, 258, 289, 396.
[2] *Ib.* p. 55 and pp. 70 *sqq.* (nn. 61 *sqq.*).
[3] Suetonius, *Div. Iul.* 42, 1.
[4] On this question see J. Beloch, *Die Bevölkerung der griechisch-römischen Welt*, p. 504 *sq.*

million[1]. Nor was this all. If, as is highly probable, this tax was not levied on informal manumissions[2], there was a further mass of people whose slavery had in practice been terminated by this process and who, although in the eyes of the law they were still not free, had progressed so far along the road to liberty as to secure praetorian protection against any arbitrary recall to effective servitude[3]. The steady flow of slaves into Italy and their prolific unions[4] meant that the country was in no danger of desolation; and the frequency of manumission was a guarantee that the total number of the free inhabitants would not decline. The menace to a programme like that of Augustus was different: if the population of Italy was only maintained by immigration, it must soon become a nondescript farrago, with the Roman element too weak to leaven the whole lump. The traditions which were to be the foundation of Italian nationality were the traditions of the Latin stock, and they would not readily be communicated to the rest of Italy if the free population of the country were penetrated by heirs of the Hellenistic culture who affected to regard Italy as barbarian[5]. The first business of Augustus was to define the limits of his task: so far as circumstances allowed, he must mark off the material which he was to mould into an imperial people. For this reason he was involved in measures which, by arresting the extension of the Roman *civitas* and above all by setting limits to the numbers of those Greeks and Orientals who, coming to Italy as slaves, were merged on manumission into the general body of Roman citizens, would preserve that material from uncontrolled contamination. The second part of his work was to raise the *morale* of Rome itself and, having done so, to pass on its ideals to the rest of the Italian people.

II. INFORMAL MANUMISSION[6]: THE LEX JUNIA

The steady importation of slaves and the readiness with which these slaves were freed—often without regard to their moral fitness

---

[1] See T. Frank, 'The Sacred Treasure and the Rate of Manumission' in *A.J.Ph.* LIII, 1932, p. 360.

[2] See below, p. 430.   [3] Gaius III, 56; *Frag. Dos.* 5.

[4] On the frequency of marriage among slaves and on the size of their families see T. Frank, 'Race Mixture in the Roman Empire,' *Am. Hist. Rev.* XXI, 1915–16, especially pp. 696 *sqq.*

[5] See *e.g.* Dion. Hal. I, 4, 2 *sqq.*

[6] For criticism of the familiar phrase 'informal manumission' see M. Wlassak, 'Die prätorischen Freilassungen' (*Z. d. Sav.-Stift.*, Rom. Abt. XXVI, 1905, pp. 367 *sqq.*).

for a place in any ordered State[1]—had confronted Italy at the end
of the Civil Wars with two distinct problems. One concerned the
Italian civilization, which was threatened by this invasion of men
whose culture had its roots elsewhere and to whom Italy was at
best a step-mother. The other was a question of law, but not of
law alone; for the structure of Roman society would remain to
some extent disordered until this question received a satisfactory
answer. The process of formal manumission was neither easy nor
cheap. Since its result was legally to confer the Roman citizenship
on a slave, it was an act which demanded the cognizance of the
State: for this reason it had in theory to be performed in the
presence of a magistrate, and, though *manumissio vindicta*—the
normal variety of this procedure—was often made before praetors
out of court, a praetor even in his leisure hours was not always
readily to be found. Again, five per cent. of the value of a slave
thus formally set free seems to have been claimed by the
aerarium sanctius[2]. Both the trouble and, in all probability, the
expense might be avoided by 'informal' manumission, of which
the essence was an announcement by the *dominus*, made in a way
which would allow the slave to prove it by evidence if the *dominus*
thereafter attempted to deny his word, that the slave might for the
future regard himself as free. This process in theory did no more
than establish a private arrangement between master and slave;
and, since it made no claim either to admit him to Roman
citizenship or even to terminate his slavery before the law, there
was no reason for the State to take notice of the ceremony
and no good cause why it should levy the tax set upon formal
grants of liberty[3]. Nevertheless the results of this institution
forced themselves on the notice of the administration. It produced
a large body of persons legally bond but in practice free; and at
some uncertain period of the Republic the praetors had implied
a recognition of the system by giving a measure of protection to
the class which it created[4]. Yet much remained to be done,
especially for the sake of the children of such persons. So long
as the parents, despite informal manumission, remained legally

[1] Dion. Hal. IV, 24, 4–5. The contemporary account of manumissions in
the time of Augustus which Dionysius gives in this chapter is of the greatest
value for an understanding of the resultant legislation.

[2] Livy VII, 16, 7; XXVII, 10, 11 *sq.*

[3] The evidence on this point is not explicit; but, since informal manumission did not confer liberty, it is perhaps reasonable to assume that slaves
subjected to this process did not incur liability to the *vicesima libertatis*.

[4] See above p. 429, n. 3.

slaves, they were incapable of any union which the law would
recognize as marriage, and they could not of right pass on their
quasi-liberty to the next generation.

The many anomalies caused by informal manumissions were
at length removed by a Lex Junia—a measure of which both date
and authorship are uncertain. But if, as well may be, the author
was Augustus himself, this law must take a leading place in the
story of his social legislation[1]. It did not, indeed, bear directly
on his central task of creating an Italian nation, but, by raising
to liberty a body of men and women who hitherto had floated
uncertainly between slavery and freedom, it simplified and
strengthened the structure of society; and the new status which
it created played a large part in the social history of the Roman
world until, having served its purpose, it was abolished by Justinian
in A.D. 531[2]. The essential provision of the Lex Junia was to confer
statutory freedom on persons informally manumitted, and to
define the legal position which they should hold. Their rights,
known as 'Latinitas Juniana,' from their resemblance to those of
the contemporary Latin colonies, brought them definitely within
the category of *personae liberae* and gave them a limited capacity
to acquire, hold and alienate property in accordance with the Civil
Law. But the restrictions on this capacity were serious. Though
Latini Juniani enjoyed what was tantamount to usufruct of their
property during life, they could not receive inheritances or legacies
(except in a roundabout and evasive way as beneficiaries of *fideicommissa*); nor could they make any kind of independent will, and
their property at death reverted to the patrons under rules which,
until A.D. 42, were indistinguishable from those governing the
peculium of a slave[3]. Justinian is not unfair when he describes
them as men 'qui licet ut liberi vitam suam peragebant, attamen
ipso ultimo spiritu simul animam atque libertatem amittebant[4].'
Hence, since the patron's interests were protected by the usual
rules against fraudulent alienation of property by freedmen, the
patronage of Junian Latins acquired a very special value. Against
this, however, must be set the provisions about children. If in
the matter of property the Junian Latin was assimilated to the
slave, his offspring were unmistakably those of a freedman.
Though, if we should follow Gaius[5] rather than 'Ulpian[6]' the Lex

[1] A brief statement of the considerations which lead the present writer to
think that 17 B.C. is not improbably the year in which this measure was
passed will be found in Note 9, pp. 888 *sqq.*
[2] *Cod. Just.* VII, 6.   [3] Gaius III, 63 *sqq.*; *P. Gnomon*, 22.
[4] *Inst.* III, 7, 4.   [5] I, 29.   [6] *Ulpiani Epit.* III, 3.

Junia itself did nothing to allow the Latins it created an avenue to any higher position, children who took their status from a parent holding Junian Latinity counted as free-born Latins and were far on the road to Roman citizenship.

Such in outline were the provisions of a measure chiefly notable for its contribution to the ordered arrangement of society. It cannot be said to have made an addition to the free population of the Roman State, because the freedom of the people it affected was already protected in principle by the praetors. Indeed, if it had any influence on the number of manumissions at all, that influence perhaps rather tended to their diminution. Evidence is lacking: but if the *vicesima libertatis* is properly so described—if, that is, the tax was a charge for freedom and not for admission to the Roman *civitas*—it may reasonably be conjectured that, when the Lex Junia granted liberty with the full authority of the Roman People to slaves informally set free, opportunity was taken to make all manumissions liable to this charge and thereby to discourage reckless gifts of freedom. But this, like the date and authorship of the law, is not a matter on which the material justifies more than a tentative conclusion.

III. SLAVES AND THE ROMAN CITIZENSHIP: THE LEX FUFIA CANINIA AND THE LEX AELIA SENTIA

Distinct from the problem presented by domestic manumission, with which the Lex Junia had to deal, was the threat made to the character of the Roman People by the numbers in which slaves were set free by the full procedure which converted them forthwith into Roman citizens. Unlike the Lex Junia, the measures whereby Augustus sought to reduce this unwelcome recruitment of the citizen-body are well attested. In 2 B.C.[1], by a Lex Fufia Caninia, Augustus fixed limits to the reckless generosity with which masters freed their slaves by will. Testamentary manumission, which carried with it both liberty and the Roman citizenship, was an attractive form of charity. It postponed the gift till the donor could not feel the cost, and, by releasing his pent-up benefactions on his death, ensured the concentration at his funeral of the gratitude due to the liberality of a lifetime. So potent were motives such as these that men had been known to leave wills which ordered the manumission of all their slaves without exception[2]. This abuse the Lex Fufia Caninia countered with an arrangement whereby the number of slaves a master might liberate

---

[1] For the date see Dessau 9250.   [2] Dion. Hal. IV, 24, 6.

by will was limited to a stated fraction of the number which he owned, and this fraction diminished as the size of the *familia* increased. At one end of the scale, which did not apply to those with fewer slaves than three, the man who had ten slaves or less might free half, at the other the wealthy proprietor of slaves between one hundred and five hundred might liberate one fifth, provided always that each beneficiary was explicitly named by the testator[1]; and in no case was it possible for more than a hundred to gain liberty by any single will[2]. Thus one of the broadest channels by which foreign blood flowed into the community of Roman citizens was so far dammed as to leave its stream of manageable dimensions, with consequences of which the value may be gathered from the care which was taken to prevent their frustration[3].

Five years after he had regulated manumissions at death Augustus completed his programme for curbing the enfranchisement of slaves with a measure which cut down the rights of masters to grant liberty during life. This capacity, which had been left untouched by the Lex Fufia Caninia[4], was drastically curtailed by an elaborate statute known after S. Aelius Catus and C. Sentius Saturninus, consuls in A.D. 4. One of its provisions, framed on a somewhat different principle from the rest, completely shut off a certain class of slave from access to the Roman citizenship. Those who had been condemned to certain specified forms of punishment either by their masters or by the State were consigned on manumission to the status of surrendered enemies (*peregrini dediticii*)[5]. They were compelled to live at least a hundred miles from Rome under pain of return to slavery for life[6], they could neither take under the will of someone else nor (according to the best opinion) make one of their own[7], and at death their property passed according to various rules of intestate succession[8]. On the other hand, towards candidates for enfranchisement against whom no moral objection could be urged the law adopted a milder attitude, and its effect, drastic though it might be, was merely to withhold the citizenship in cases where manumission might be reckless. Always provided that the slave was not disqualified by character, if the *dominus* was over twenty years of age and the slave over thirty, full enfranchisement was possible in the normal way by the

---

[1] Gaius II, 239.   [2] Gaius I, 42–45.
[3] Gaius I, 46.   [4] Gaius I, 44.
[5] Gaius I, 13 and 15. These are the ὀνείδη μεγάλα καὶ ῥύποι δυσεκκάθαρτοι whose former admission to the Roman citizenship Dionysius stresses with especial regret in *Ant. Rom.* IV, 24, 7.
[6] Gaius I, 27.   [7] Gaius I, 25.   [8] Gaius III, 74–6.

ceremony with the *vindicta* in the presence of a praetor or some other appropriate magistrate. But when either of these two requirements of age was not fulfilled enfranchisement only followed if, before the ceremony, special reasons for the proposed manumission had been adduced and these reasons had been approved by a body of investigators, composed in Rome of five senators and five *equites* who sat for this purpose on stated days and in the provinces of twenty Roman citizens who were available to hear such cases at the end of each assize[1]. In the absence of a successful *causae probatio*, if the *dominus* was under twenty no result of any kind could follow[2]: indeed, such was the insistence that the *dominus* must be of age that a man of less than twenty could not even set a slave free by will[3]. If on the other hand, he was over twenty but the slave was less than thirty, the manumission must be treated as 'informal' and the slave became a Latinus Junianus[4].

The effect of these enactments, which were by no means all that the Lex Aelia Sentia laid down[5], was to complete the work begun by the Lex Fufia Caninia. These two measures had a common aim—to check the number of manumissions which involved the enrolment of slaves in the ranks of Roman citizens. The earlier measure had brought testamentary manumission under control: the Lex Aelia Sentia curbed manumission during the lifetime of the owner: and together these laws cannot have failed to secure a drastic reduction in the number of persons alien both by culture and by blood, whom the body politic of Rome was called upon to absorb.

IV. THE STATE OF ROMAN SOCIETY

Thus far the way of Augustus was easy: there was no difficulty in passing laws which would cut down, or even stop, the contamination of the Populus Romanus from outside. But what remained was a harder task—to restore the *morale* of an enervated people and to rid them of their own inherent ailments. The causes of the social distemper were two. First the influx of wealth, from small beginnings in the third century B.C., had grown to the dimensions of a torrent and had swept away the whole superstructure of the old agrarian community, leaving the place free for a mercantile plutocracy new to the use of money. And then

---

[1] Gaius I, 18–20 and 38.   [2] Gaius I, 38.   [3] Gaius I, 40.
[4] Gaius I, 31 (and 29). Cf. *Ulpiani Epit.* I, 12, where 'Caesaris' is certainly corrupt.
[5] See further below, p. 450.

had come half a century of domestic war, with all the familiar consequences of a sudden transference of wealth, a dislocation of the economic system and a general loss of responsibility among men reduced to a precarious tenure of their property, and even of their lives. In Italy at large the damage is easy to exaggerate. Since the rising of the Allies in 91 B.C. the country had, indeed, seen frequent wars, but it had not been subjected to widespread or continued devastation. Nevertheless, warfare had wrought a change. The volunteers of the Marian army, who enlisted because the army offered more attractions than any they could find in civil life, were men whom unemployment had driven to the towns; and, if they were not all drawn from the proletariate of Rome itself, at least they had made closer acquaintance with an urban society than was possible for farmers living scattered over the territory of some agrarian community. For such men, when they had spent their active lives as soldiers, pensions had to be provided on discharge, and the grants of land which served this purpose scattered these carriers of a Roman outlook far and wide.

As a contribution to the unification of Italy such settlements of ex-service men cannot be deplored; but their numbers were so large that their claims were only met at the cost of considerable hardship to the civil population. Sulla had found homes for over 100,000 of his men by ruthless seizure of land[1], and, though Caesar, both as consul and dictator[2], had shown great consideration for vested interests, in the period of the Second Triumvirate drastic confiscations were renewed: it was not till 30 B.C. that gentler methods were resumed (p. 120). That the sufferings of the time were severe is beyond dispute; but their severity can be exaggerated, though not excused. The dispossessed were not all condemned to destitution: the farmer Ofellus, a sturdy tenant of the land he once had owned[3], is not to be regarded as unique. Indeed, the most alarming changes on the land were due to other causes than the return of soldiers from the wars. It was not to them that Virgil sang the praise of Italy and extolled the dignity of the soil. The audience to which the *Georgics* were addressed was one strange to landed estates—an audience composed of men who had made fortunes in the wars and had rushed to invest their capital in real property, the one gilt-edged security of the ancient world. Interest was all they sought, and it was not likely that their incomes would be sacrificed to the social duties of a landlord. But in Italy, where the physical structure of the country is peculiar, such men might

---

[1] Appian, *Bell. Civ.* I, 104, 489; see vol. IX, p. 302 *sq.*
[2] Vol. IX, pp. 515 *sq.* and 706.   [3] Horace, *Sat.* II, 2, 112 *sqq.*

do much harm. Bitter experience had proved that in large parts of the peninsula ranching would yield higher profits than arable cultivation, and experience had shown as well that these profits were won at the expense of the community. For under grass the country needed fewer hands to work it than when it was under plough; and, if town-bred landlords in their zeal for gain recklessly increased the grazing, the land of Saturn would cease to be a great mother of men because it would no longer be a great mother of crops[1].

Though there were anxious symptoms, it was not the countryside or the smaller towns of Italy which presented Augustus with his hardest task. Despite the advent of new owners, whether large proprietors or private soldiers with their humble plots, the character of the rural population was not greatly changed. The newcomers were largely parasitic: they might impoverish the people on whom they battened, but the sturdy virtues of the Italian peasant survived. The crucial problem lay elsewhere. From the earliest beginnings of its history Rome had owed its greatness to an oligarchy. If Italy was to be the heart of an empire, it was no less true that the heart of Italy was, and would remain, the aristocracy of Rome; and at the end of the Civil Wars that aristocracy showed ominous signs of collapse. Until the middle of the second century B.C. its vicissitudes had offered no reason for alarm: as old families sank into insignificance and new ones rose to fame, the heritage of political experience which each generation held in trust was passed on intact to its successor. But now for at least a hundred years signs had not been wanting that more dangerous forces were at work. The eastward advance after the Second Punic War brought wealth to certain sections of the Roman population in a sudden profusion which, even in a society where capital might find employment more easily than it ever could in a world which had not been industrialized, would have given its owners no time to learn its proper use. When conquest yielded wealth and wealth opened prospects of life on a scale unknown before, men trained to the narrow outlook of a rustic folk took time to find their bearings; and, while they sought, much mischief was done. In his penetrating sketch of the Republic in decay, Pliny is not mistaken: 'posteris laxitas mundi et rerum amplitudo damno fuit[2].'

The moral consequences of this economic change have been

---

[1] For a more detailed statement of the reasons why pasturage spread in certain parts of Italy, see vol. IX, pp. 3 *sqq.*

[2] *N.H.* XIV, 5.

described at length elsewhere (Vol. IX, pp. 792 *sqq*.). To the modest aristocracy of the agrarian Republic there succeeded a body of men whose wealth was essential to their position and whose leisure was largely spent on a competition in extravagance. The cost of public life became enormous. Crassus, indeed, is recorded to have said that for a man of high political ambition no amount of wealth could be enough[1]; and it is the prevalence of such an attitude which gives significance to the peremptory demand for a return to financial sanity which is implied in the senatorial census fixed by Augustus (see p. 164 *sq*.). Private life, too, was affected no less: wealth would not lie idle, and men who could find no salutary employment for their capital spent it in ways less easy to defend. Luxury took hold of the upper class; and rivalry in ostentation, even more effectively than the mere prudential motives of other times, provoked that money-madness which, to Horace at least, seemed the most vicious feature of his age.

The effects of this demoralization were many, and among them was one which calls for special mention here. A generation which has seen the spread of motor-cars among the many needs no more reminder that, when opportunities for expenditure increase and fashion allows pleasure to justify its cost, the price of luxuries is found by economies practised in the home. When the standards of living rise faster than incomes, the birth-rate falls; and, though in Rome there were individuals whose fortunes were prodigious, the financial drain of public life was so severe that, until a man had made himself, like Julius or Augustus, master of the Roman world, he could never afford to despise opportunities of saving in the comfortable assurance that his money was enough. Cornelia, the mother of the Gracchi, had borne a family of twelve[2], but in the Ciceronian age the great ones were rare whose children numbered more than two or three. By the end of the Republic the old conception of marriage and its obligations to the State had long vanished from the places where it was most to be desired: when Propertius exclaims

> nullus de nostro sanguine miles erit[3],

he is distinguished from many of his nobler contemporaries by nothing save the cynical frankness of his defiance.

The financial inducements to parsimony at home were re-inforced by two other powerful considerations. The first was the result of a feature in Roman life which can claim a greater significance than is generally allowed. Provided that his will was made

---

[1] Cicero, *de off.* I, 8, 25.　　　[2] Pliny, *N.H.* VII, 57.　　　[3] II, 7, 14.

in proper form, a citizen was under no obligation to choose an heir from his own family; and, more important still, he might diminish the inheritance by legacies which in size and number at first were unrestricted. This latitude of the law was a necessary condition of the custom whereby the wealthier citizens left generous tokens of affection to their friends—a custom which had grown, until to be omitted from the will of an acquaintance could be taken as a calculated insult. It was reckoned a sign of high principle in Pompey that he protected the body of Sulla from dishonour though the Dictator had left out his name from the list of his legatees[1]. The abuses which this practice provoked are a commonplace of the early Empire. When testators were so prodigal with their bequests, the temptation to seek mention in a will grew strong enough to break through the restraints of decency and even honour. If men like Crassus and Hortensius, though they were not its authors, stooped to profit by a testament which was known to have been forged[2], smaller people might be pardoned the use of flattery in an attempt to win some tangible mark of gratitude from the object of their attentions. Cicero already had condemned the 'malitiosae blanditiae' by which inheritances were won[3], and Horace in the most satirical of his *Satires*[4] holds up the hunt for dead men's shoes as the shortest and most certain road to wealth.

When a livelihood could be made from bequests and their acquisition had gained a recognized place among the professions of the age[5], the practitioners of the art naturally bent their energies with especial zeal to those of the rich whose generosity was not trammelled by the claims of children. Catullus knows the way in which the arrival of a male descendant, even if only a grandson,

suscitat a cano uolturium capiti[6];

but it was not long before the ingratiating servilities of the *captator* found victims to whom they were so welcome that celibacy seemed to offer attractions greater than any to be found in marriage. In his shrewd remarks on the lack of intellectual interests at Rome the elder Pliny notices that one of the results produced by the worship of money was to put *orbitas* 'in auctoritate summa et potentia[7].' Celibacy was made seductive; the satisfaction which

---

[1] Plutarch, *Pomp.* 15, 3.   [2] Cicero, *de off.* III, 18, 73.
[3] Cicero, *de off.* III, 18, 74.   [4] II, 5.
[5] See Seneca, *de benef.* VI, 38, 4—'...qui captandorum testamentorum artem professi sunt.'
[6] LXVIII, 124 (LXVIII A, 84).   [7] *N.H.* XIV, 5.

vanity might derive from the obsequiousness of aspiring legatees was added to the expense of self-indulgence as a motive for declining the ties of parenthood; and the evidence for the effect of *captatio* on the birth-rate among the wealthy is clear enough to show that, besides a certain humour, there was a large measure of justice in the enactment of Augustus to the general effect that, whatever the condition of the testator, people of any substance, other than near relatives, who were to benefit under a will must at least be married themselves (see below p. 450 *sq.*).

There remains one other potent force among the factors which combined to discourage marriage. The high conception of the relation between husband and wife attained in early Rome is scarcely more remarkable than the lack of legal regulations to protect it. All unions, except the negligible minority contracted by the elaborate process of *confarreatio*, might be dissolved without the intervention of the State, and in marriage even the formalities which brought the wife under the *manus* of her husband had ceased to be necessary before the time of the Twelve Tables[1]. Not only did the woman remain in the *potestas* of the *paterfamilias*, but in course of time arrangements were devised whereby her dowry ceased to pass irrevocably to the husband. Cases, of which the most famous is that in which Licinia, the widow of Gaius Gracchus, recovered her portion from his heirs[2], show that by the second century B.C. the rights of the husband had been curtailed, and even a legislator so conservative in his outlook as Augustus was ready not only to accept, but to extend, the principle that the *dos*—and consequently the bride who brought it—at the beginning of the union was to be regarded as no more than a loan to the husband[3]. With the passage of time he might, indeed, extend his ownership to a larger fraction of the property. If children were born and the wife subsequently became the guilty party in a divorce, he was entitled to retain one-sixth of the dowry for every surviving child up to a maximum of three[4]; but beyond this point nothing short of the wife's death could increase his claim, and the wife herself remained absolutely free to end the union at her discretion.

The change in the status of the dowry marks a change in the position of women themselves. Though they had enjoyed an honourable prominence in daily life from the earliest times of which records are preserved, there are elements in the Roman law

---

[1] Gaius I, 111; Bruns, *Fontes*,[7] p. 25.   [2] *Dig.* XXIV, 3, 66, *pr.*
[3] For the Augustan rule about *fundi dotales*, see Gaius II, 63.
[4] *Ulpiani Epit.* VI, 10.

which clearly assume a high degree of subjection to the husband: most famous of all is the denial of remedy for adultery by the husband, though adultery on the other side was an act for which the husband might even put his wife to death[1]. But by the last century of the Republic, females had in practice obtained their independence, and nothing but social convention and a sense of responsibility barred the way to a dangerous exploitation of their privilege. Under the demoralizing temptations of great and sudden wealth the barrier at length broke down, and fashion took a form which could not be safely tolerated. The performances of Clodia and her like, political unions which were marriages in nothing more than name, and the whole development first revealed by Catullus and seen at its climax in the world of Ovid, all have their place in a story which boded ill. Nor were the effects of the new manners confined to those who lived loose themselves. The exaggerated freedom of the womenfolk, which enabled the greatest of them to take their part even in high political concerns, had its repercussions in circles which might even have been called old-fashioned. Neither Quintus Cicero nor Atticus was a moral revolutionary: yet the experience of Quintus with his wife Pomponia, Atticus' sister, was of a kind to warn prudent bachelors against experiments with a mate whom the law would leave immune from a husband's control. When free women were apt to be froward partners, in wide sections of society men were tempted to seek a substitute for marriage in life with an enfranchised slave over whom they might still retain the authority of a *patronus*.

Thus in an age when the distinction between wedlock and mere cohabitation was fine, and when it could be seriously argued that bigamy was impossible because a second marriage was by itself a valid dissolution of the first[2], the stability of the family was endangered by the threat that marriage would be made to serve the pleasure of the parties rather than the needs of the community as a whole. It is not, indeed, to be supposed that the moral outlook of Italy at large had changed: the evidence, though scanty, is enough to show that outside Rome the old ideals had not lost their power. And even in the City itself the new frivolity was confined to a single class. But that class, the governing nobility, was the one which it was essential to preserve; and by the end of the Republic signs were plain that, if it was to survive, the aristocracy must be recalled to some kind of moral sanity. Marriage

[1] Cato, in Gellius, *N.A.* x, 23, 5.
[2] Cicero, *de or.* I, 40, 183; 56, 238.

must be raised again to the dignity of a duty to the State, the hampering activities of the *captatores* must be curbed, and the licence which had deposed children from their place as the final cause of wedlock must be restrained. Only so would the nobility preserve the solid strength which was essential in the keystone of the whole imperial structure.

V. THE CHRONOLOGY OF THE LAWS ON THE MARRIAGE OF ROMAN CITIZENS

The sequence of the measures by which Augustus sought this moral reformation cannot be recovered in all its details. Two passages in the poems of Propertius, neither of which can well be dated to a year later than 23 B.C., have been adduced as evidence that legislation on marriage was mooted in the earliest period of the Principate[1], and Propertius is perhaps confirmed in this by Livy[2]; but the proposal, whatever it may have been, was postponed, if not withdrawn[3], and the first positive enactment was reserved for the eve of the new era. The Lex Julia de maritandis ordinibus was in force by 23 May 17 B.C.[4], and not long afterwards Horace, who had already revealed in the *Secular Hymn*[5] that morality was a matter of active interest in the highest quarters, provides the first clear evidence for the effects of the Lex Julia de adulteriis[6]. A closer dating of these two fundamental statutes cannot be proved; but the appearance of evidence for their existence in 17 B.C. and soon afterwards lends support to the suggestion of Dio that they belong to the period immediately following the return of Augustus from the East in the autumn of 19 B.C.[7] According to the account of Augustus himself, it was towards the end of this year that he was first offered the *cura legum et morum* by the Senate and Roman People[8]; but, since the offer had to be repeated within twelve months, it may be inferred that the mea-

---

[1] I, 8, 21, if 'taedae' be the right reading, which however is doubtful; II, 7, 1–10.

[2] *Praef.* 9. On this see H. Dessau, 'Die Vorrede des Livius' in *Festschrift zu Otto Hirschfelds sechzigstem Geburtstage*, p. 461.

[3] Propertius II, 7, 1. In the opinion of the present writer, Mommsen (*Strafrecht*, p. 691, n. 1) is rightly sceptical of the attempt made by P. Jörs (*Die Ehegesetze des Augustus*, pp. 4–28), who is followed by V. Gardthausen (*Augustus und seine Zeit*, I, p. 902), to show that a law on marriage was actually passed in 28 B.C.

[4] *C.I.L.* VI, 32323, l. 57.

[5] Ll. 45 *sqq.*

[6] *Odes*, IV, 5, 21 *sqq.*; cf. *Ep.* II, 1, 1 *sq.*

[7] LIV, 16, 1–2.

[8] *Res Gestae* 6.

sures which justified his claim to have carried out the wishes of
the Senate without accepting any extraordinary office and on the
authority of the *tribunicia potestas* alone cannot have been complete,
at earliest, before the year 18 B.C. was well advanced. Legislation
may well have started soon after the consuls of 18 B.C. took office;
the Lex Julia de maritandis ordinibus at least had been enacted
by the early summer of 17 B.C.; and the passage of the whole
programme may thus plausibly be placed in the months when the
world was approaching the New Age to be inaugurated by the
Festival begun on 26 May 17 B.C.

The next measure to be dated with precision is the law which
brings the tale of the social legislation to its end—the Lex Papia
Poppaea of A.D. 9; but it is clear that this was only the culmination
of legislative activity spread over several years, if not over the
whole period since 17 B.C. Suetonius seems to imply that the Lex
de maritandis ordinibus was amended after its passage[1], and Dio
represents the Lex Papia Poppaea as a concession to protests
against a harsher enactment which had been suspended, first for
three years after its passage, and then for two more[2]. If it might
be assumed that the period of suspension was about to expire at
the time when the Lex Papia Poppaea was framed, the severities
which it mitigated would belong to a law passed five years before,
in A.D. 4; and this may conceivably be true[3], though it is perhaps
more likely that the five years were a period immediately following
17 B.C. during which some provisions of the recent legislation
were kept in temporary abeyance[4]. But the common assumption
that it is the whole truth has less to commend it: Augustus himself[5] seems to record that in 11 B.C. there was a repetition of the
demand that he should accept extraordinary powers for the purpose of social reform and that, as in 18 and 17 B.C., he so far met
the wishes of the Senate as to introduce the desired measures in
virtue of his *tribunicia potestas*. Certainty cannot be attained; but
it would be rash to deny the possibility that between 17 B.C. and
A.D. 9 the scheme of social legislation was modified and extended
more than once. The loss of the evidence for the experiments made
during these years is to be regretted. Had it survived, it would

---

[1] *Div. Aug.* 34, 1.   [2] Dio LVI, 1, 2; 7, 3; 10, 1–3.

[3] For a discussion of the evidence in detail see P. Jörs, *Die Ehegesetze des
Augustus*, pp. 49 *sqq.*: it must be remembered that part of Dio's remarks on the
year A.D. 4 stood in the section, now lost, which followed LV, 11, 2.

[4] It is to be noticed that *C.I.L.* VI, 32323, l. 57 shows the Lex Julia de
maritandis ordinibus to have been applied, in part at least, forthwith.

[5] *Res Gestae* 6.

have yielded a clue to the stages by which Augustus reached his final conclusions on the proper attitude of the State towards the private lives of its citizens; but, since his enduring contribution to the Civil Law of marriage was made in the measures of 18 B.C. and A.D. 9, it is with these alone that the jurists are concerned, and history is therefore condemned to be content with a knowledge of the finished result, divorced from any adequate information about the experiments from which it was evolved.

VI. THE REHABILITATION OF MARRIAGE: THE LEX JULIA DE ADULTERIIS COERCENDIS

The social laws affecting Roman citizens were all designed to secure the permanence of the Italian stock, and for this reason it may be agreed that the stimulation of the birth-rate was their common end. Nevertheless a distinction must be made. The *caelebs* and the *orbus*[1] were not the same: it was one thing to encourage marriage, and another to make it productive. But, if marriage could be restored to its pristine honour, some degree of fertility would doubtless follow of itself, and the positive inducements which Augustus offered to parents may reasonably be regarded as a re-inforcement of the measures designed to revive the prestige of the family. The success of Augustus must be judged by his attempts to restore the respect for marriage, and it is because artificial aids to the birth-rate were a mere supplementary undertaking that humour at the expense of the *ius liberorum* cannot pass for proof that he failed in his main endeavour.

In the story of the social legislation the measure which laid the foundation of reform and can claim the first importance was the Lex Julia de adulteriis. The significance of this famous statute lies in its extension of the field of law by bringing under the protection of the courts an institution which had hitherto been defended by merely private sanctions. Precedents for such intervention were not wholly lacking. At Rome, as in Greece[2], moral laxity had never been condoned, and the censors had freely penalized persons of notoriously evil life. Traditions were even found to support the more drastic efforts of Augustus to enforce the obligation of marriage. Marriage was said to have been compulsory in ancient times[3], and in assigning duties to the censors of his ideal Rome so

---

[1] I.e. the childless: see Quintilian, *Inst. or.* v, 10, 26—'parens liberorum an orbus.'

[2] [Demosthenes], LIX, 87: νόμος μοιχείας.   [3] Dion. Hal. IX, 22, 2.

sound a Whig as Cicero was prepared to include among their instructions 'caelibes esse prohibento[1].'

The ill-attested custom of the Republic seems to have offered the husband an embarrassing choice of remedies against a peccant wife. If she had been taken in adultery he might kill her, either on his own responsibility[2] or after the death-penalty had been approved by a domestic council[3]: but, if death seemed too drastic, his only alternative was divorce, and her consequent release from a man to whom she had been unfaithful involved no punishment for the wife beyond the forfeiture of her dowry, wholly or in part[4]. The objection to this rough-and-ready system was grave: in an age when puritanism was ill seen it left free opportunity for adultery to be condoned. Public opinion would rarely tolerate a penalty so severe as death, and the only alternative offered nothing but the findings of a family tribunal to protect the husband against the taunts that his own pecuniary profit had increased with the punishment of his wife. The whole institution must be cleared away before the control of social morals could effectively pass to the State, and this Augustus achieved without formally destroying a jurisdiction which could claim the authority of age. The powers of the husband, and of the father, were so hedged about with restrictions that their effective use became difficult, if not dangerous. A husband might not kill his wife even if taken in the act[5], and he was discouraged from violent vengeance on the paramour by the threat of arraignment for murder unless various conditions had been fulfilled[6]. Moreover, the largest fraction of the dowry which he might retain for damages on divorce was fixed at only a sixth of the whole[7]. The father of a married woman still in his *potestas*[8] had somewhat greater rights. Unlike the husband, he might in certain circumstances kill the woman as well as the

---

[1] *De legibus*, III, 3, 7.

[2] Cato, in Gellius, *N.A.* X, 23, 4.

[3] Dion. Hal. II, 25, 6: cf. Suetonius, *Tib.* 35, 1; Tacitus, *Ann.* XIII, 32, 4.

[4] It seems clear from Val. Max. VIII, 2, 3 and, more particularly, Pliny, *N.H.* XIV, 90 that in Republican times a husband might be awarded any part of the dowry up to the whole by a *iudicium de moribus mulieris*.

[5] Paul, *Sent.* II, 26, 4; Papinian in *Collatio*, IV, 10.

[6] The most restrictive of these required that the adulterer, unless he was a slave or freedman of the family, should be *infamis* or one 'qui corpore quaestum facit': Paul, *Sent.* II, 26, 4 = *Collatio*, IV, 12, 3.

[7] *Ulpiani Epit.* VI, 12: this was additional to any *retentio propter liberos* or for other causes.

[8] Or, according to Paul (in *Collatio*, IV, 2, 3) and Papinian (*ib.* IV, 7), if she had passed into the *manus* of her husband.

adulterer; but the privilege was turned into a deterrent[1] by the rule that the death of the paramour at his hands would expose him to the penalties for murder unless he killed his own daughter at the same time[2].

With such limitations the jurisdiction of relatives became finally inadequate to maintain the morals of society, and in the New Age its place was to be taken by a public court[3], armed with authority to pass sentences up to banishment (in the form of *relegatio*) both on the principals and on those who aided or abetted the offence[4]. The gravest danger was discerned in the fickleness of women, and against this, though Augustus chiefly cared for the manners of the nobility, the court was to protect the dignity of marriage in every section of society: indeed, so comprehensive was the law that, besides covering marriages which were recognized as such in the fullest sense, it extended its sanctions to all those unions which for one reason or another fell into the category of *matrimonium iniustum*[5]. The general form of procedure was for the husband to divorce his wife and start a prosecution for adultery; and this by itself involved an innovation of importance. The most common form of marriage, which did not transfer the bride to the *manus* of her husband but left her in her father's *potestas*, was one which could be dissolved with little ceremony or none[6]; and this absence of formality, besides encouraging contempt for the marriage tie, caused obvious difficulties in proving that divorce had actually occurred. Augustus accordingly ordered a set form to be ob-

---

[1] *Dig.* XLVIII, 5, 23 (22), 4 (Papinian).
[2] *Dig.* XLVIII, 5, 24 (23), 4 (Ulpian).
[3] See Dio LIV, 30, 4.　　　　　　[4] *Dig.* XLVIII, 5, 9 (8)–11 (10).
[5] Africanus quoted by Ulpian in *Dig.* XLVIII, 5, 14 (13), 1. It is doubtful, however, whether the law went even further and sought to preserve relationships in which *maritalis affectio* was absent. The view, based mainly on *Dig.* XXV, 7, 1, 4 (Ulpian) and XXV, 7, 3, 1 (Marcian), that in the Augustan legislation *concubinatus* was for the first time recognized as a union, inferior indeed to marriage, but still in some sense legal has found wide acceptance; and, in a modified form, it is adopted by P. Meyer in *Der römische Konkubinat nach den Rechtsquellen und den Inschriften*. The weakness of the evidence for any such theory is emphasised by J. Plassard, in *Le concubinat romain sous le Haut Empire*, especially pp. 53–84; and to the considerations there adduced may now be added the clue to the attitude of Augustus himself offered by the diptych from Karanis (*Ann. épig.* 1929, 13, ll. 9 *sqq.*) in which it is revealed that the Leges Aelia Sentia and Papia Poppaea forbade the registration of *spurii* in the *album professionum liberorum natorum*. It is at least probable, though the conclusion is still controversial, that among *spurii* are included the offspring of *concubinatus*: with *Frag. Vat.* 194 contrast *ib.* 168.　　　　　[6] See above p. 440, n. 2.

served; and this procedure, presumably among other demands, is alleged to have included a requirement that the party taking action should give notice of divorce in the presence of at least seven Roman citizens[1]. Thereby no room was left for doubt that the marriage was at an end, and at the same time it may be surmised that light-hearted divorces were discouraged by the reflection that the necessary witnesses would expose the whole transaction to the judgment of public opinion.

Divorce was an essential preliminary to any charge of adultery. In the rare cases where the husband had caught his wife *in flagranti* and had killed her paramour it must be made at once and the affair put into the hands of a magistrate within three days[2]; but in more normal circumstances, when the evidence had to be weighed with care, the right to prosecute was reserved to the husband (and his father-in-law) for sixty *dies utiles*, at the end of which any accuser more than twenty-five years old might act[3]. If, however, the husband had not divorced his wife, she was immune from prosecution for adultery until the husband had been convicted of condonation[4]—a charge which could only be substantiated if the husband was shown to have taken his wife in the act or to have made profit by her adventure[5]. When such proofs were lacking and the husband shut his eyes to the failings of his wife, prosecution was barred[6]. The reason for this mildness is to seek; but it may perhaps be found in a remark of Ulpian's that a wife approved by her husband and a peaceful marriage ought not lightly to be disturbed[7]. Augustus was no puritan himself; he was legislating on subjects where intervention by the State might be resented; and he knew better than to risk his main purpose by letting accusers loose among the peccadillos of the aristocracy.

The penalties on conviction were heavy. Both parties were relegated to different islands for life, the paramour losing half his

---

[1] *Dig.* xxiv, 2, 9 (Paul): see Suetonius, *Div. Aug.* 34, 2, where, however, 'modum' more probably means 'measure' or 'limit' than 'method' or 'procedure', and *Dig.* xxxviii, 11, 1, 1 (Ulpian). Both these passages from the *Digest* are suspect: see E. Levy, *Der Hergang der römischen Ehescheidung*, pp. 21 *sqq.*, who brings heavy criticism to bear on the suggestion that Augustus established a procedure for divorce in marriages without *manus*. Less radical interpretations of the texts will be found in S. Solazzi, 'Studi sul divorzio' (*Bullettino dell' Istituto di diritto romano*, xxxiv, 1925, p. 295), at pp. 312 *sqq.* and in P. E. Corbett, *The Roman Law of Marriage*, pp. 231–9.   [2] Paul, *Sent.* ii, 26, 6.

[3] *Dig.* xlviii, 5, 15 (14), 2 (Scaevola); 16 (15), 6 (Ulpian).

[4] *Dig.* xlviii, 5, 27 (26) (Ulpian).   [5] *Dig.* xlviii, 5, 2, 2 (Ulpian).

[6] *Dig.* xlviii, 5, 2, 3 (Ulpian).   [7] *Dig.* xlviii, 5, 27 (26).

property and the woman a third, as well as half her dowry[1]; and the woman at least was forbidden subsequent marriage with a free-born citizen[2]. But though a wife's adultery was a major crime, a married man was in no necessary danger merely because he had intercourse with some female acquaintance. Even if he brought himself under the law of adultery, his wife could not accuse him, though husbands were so far expected to set a good example that a man of loose life might find himself in jeopardy if his wife were arraigned on this charge[3]. Nevertheless the responsibilities of men in general were increased. Apart from the penalties of adultery which they incurred by affairs with other people's wives, by casual intercourse with any free woman not registered with the aedile as a prostitute[4], or engaged in one of those occupations where moral laxity was assumed, they exposed themselves to equally severe punishment for *stuprum*[5]—an offence defined and extended by Augustus so as to include a large number of sexual acts subversive of the family which men might commit and to which the provisions against *adulterium* did not apply. Thus the prohibition which it was the object of the statute to impose—the prohibition 'ne quis posthac stuprum adulterium facito sciens dolo malo[6]'—had the widest reference, and *adulterium* and *stuprum* together were charges which fitted every act by which the permanence of the family might be endangered. This Lex Julia de adulteriis coercendis was an outstanding piece of legislation, and one which endured as the basis of Roman law on the subjects with which it was concerned. By bringing the family as an institution under public protection it marked a notable advance in the conception of the proper functions of the State, and, by penalizing the practices of an age when men and women had begun to seek their own pleasure alone, it opened the way for a return to the ancient view of marriage as a union 'liberorum quaerundorum caussa[7].'

---

[1] Paul, *Sent.* II, 26, 14.
[2] *Ulpiani Epit.* XIII, 2; *Dig.* XLVIII, 5, 12 (11), 13 (Papinian).
[3] *Dig.* IV, 4, 37, 1 (Tryphoninus); XLVIII, 5, 14 (13), 5 (Ulpian).
[4] See Mommsen, *Staatsrecht*, II³, p. 511, n. 2.
[5] See Mommsen, *Strafrecht*, p. 694.
[6] *Dig.* XLVIII, 5, 13 (12) (Ulpian).
[7] See *e.g.* Plautus, *Captivi*, 889; Livy, *Epit.* 59.

VII. THE STIMULATION OF THE BIRTH-RATE: THE LEX JULIA DE MARITANDIS ORDINIBUS

Whatever its effects on the size of families, the attempt of Augustus to restore the dignity of marriage was his boldest project in the social sphere. But by itself it was not enough: positive inducements were thought necessary to check celibacy and encourage procreation, and these were enacted in the Lex Julia de maritandis ordinibus of 18 B.C. and the Lex Papia Poppaea of A.D. 9. The second of these statutes amended and completed the first, and together they supplied the abiding basis of the law. But so closely were they connected with one another that the jurists rarely distinguished them[1], and their habit of treating what they name the 'Lex Julia et Papia Poppaea' as a single set of rules makes it impossible to disentangle the provisions of the two measures in detail[2]. Nevertheless, there is no room for doubt that the three essential principles of the programme—the removal of unnecessary restrictions on marriage, the use of the law of inheritance to favour parenthood, and the special stimulation of child-bearing in the upper classes by the offer of privileges in public life to the fathers of large families—were all to be found adopted in the law of 18 B.C.

The most valuable of these proposals, and the one most closely allied in aim to the Lex Julia de adulteriis, was the first; but the magnitude of the change it involved is difficult to estimate, because the evidence for the law before this time is defective at the most vital point. Authorities are unanimous that henceforward marriages between free-born and freed were to be valid, with the significant reservation that unions of this kind, and also with play-actors and their families, were denied to senators, their children and their descendants down to the third generation in the male line[3]. The State was to take advantage of the readiness with which men found a mate in their own households, but this concession to

[1] The distinction is made in *Ulpiani Epit.* xiv, and by the author of *Frag. Vat.* 216 and 218, but its only value is to show that the Lex Julia, though amended by the Lex Papia Poppaea, was not entirely superseded.

[2] For an elaborate attempt see P. Jörs, *Ueber das Verhältnis der Lex Julia de maritandis ordinibus zur Lex Papia Poppaea.*

[3] The words of the law are quoted by Paul—*Dig.* XXIII, 2, 44, *pr.*; cf. Dio LIV, 16, 2 and LVI, 7, 2. It appears from *e.g. Dig.* XXIII, 2, 16, *pr.* (Paul) and *Ulpiani Epit.* XVI, 2 that marriages by members of senatorial houses in contravention of these regulations were not at first treated as null but were *nuptiae iniustae*, penalized by certain disabilities.

custom stopped short of the point at which it would contaminate the governing class with blood necessarily derived from regions outside Italy. The degree of novelty which this implied has been variously assessed. If Mommsen[1] were justified in his belief that it was Augustus who first raised unions between slave-born and *ingenui* to the status of legal marriage, the reform would have been great: but strong objections can be brought against this theory. When Cicero records that a certain Gellius Publicola, step-son of one consul and probably brother of a second, 'libertinam duxit uxorem[2],' he does so in language which certainly suggests that such a match cannot have been due to any honourable cause; but his words imply scarcely less clearly that the union was a legal marriage. A clue to the position both before the time of Augustus and after is perhaps rather to be found in a remark of Ulpian—that, if a patron takes one of his freedwomen as a partner, it is more decent[3] for her to be a concubine than a *materfamilias*. Though it was not forbidden by the law, formal marriage in these circumstances was not well seen in the stricter circles of society, and this prejudice, for his own good reasons, Augustus so far encouraged as to deny the privileges of marriage to members of the nobility who indulged so coarse a taste. Nevertheless, he made no effort to check the practice elsewhere; and he even confirmed its legality, if this had ever been in doubt, by enacting that a freedwoman married to her patron should not have the right to divorce[4]. The bar laid upon the nobility is no sign of failing in the enthusiasm of Augustus for matrimony. Marriages of freedwomen into senatorial houses cannot have been many: their prohibition would not make for celibacy to any serious degree, and it cannot have failed to serve a useful purpose by emphasizing the need for the aristocracy to keep itself free from dangerous admixtures of foreign blood. But, if they were out of place in high society, wives of servile birth were not to be discouraged elsewhere.

The general regulations of the Lex Julia which forbade fathers of whatever station to put vexatious obstacles in the way of their children's marriage[5] and invalidated conditions in general restraint

---

[1] *Staatsrecht*, iii, pp. 429 *sqq.*   [2] *Pro Sestio*, 52, 110.
[3] 'Honestius': *Dig.* xxv, 7, 1, *pr.*   [4] *Dig.* xxiv, 2, 11, *pr.*
[5] *Dig.* xxiii, 2, 19 (Marcian). The value of this excerpt in its present form is doubtful: see P. E. Corbett, *The Roman Law of Marriage*, pp. 64 *sqq.* and 153 *sq.*, with the literature there cited. It certainly does not justify the statement that Augustus was the author of the legal obligation to provide dowries for their daughters under which fathers were ultimately laid, though Gaius i, 178 shows that he was not indifferent to the need for arrangements to secure that dowries should be forthcoming.

of matrimony attached to bequests[1] were followed in A.D. 4 by clauses in the Lex Aelia Sentia directly benefiting manumitted slaves. For their sake it was enacted that similar restrictions should be set aside when a *dominus* sought to include them in the terms of his grant of freedom[2], and that a freedman who was a Junian Latin because he had been manumitted before the age of thirty might obtain the Roman citizenship for himself and his child, if his wife were a Roman citizen—and for his wife as well if she were a Latin—so soon as there was a child of the marriage a year old[3].

Barriers to matrimony were thus broken down; the way lay open; and all that remained was to guide the flock into the path prepared. This Augustus essayed by using the law of succession with a courage to be measured by the strength of the almost superstitious respect in which Romans were accustomed to hold the dispositions of the dead[4]. For the purpose of the State it was assumed that marriage was a duty for men between the ages of twenty-five and sixty and for women between twenty and fifty[5]. Matches between persons of whom one was still within these limits and the other had left them behind were discouraged by confiscation of the dowry on the husband's death[6], and anyone who had passed these periods of life was penalized for a failure to shoulder the burdens of parenthood by partial disability to take under the terms of wills. Like the *vicesima hereditatum* (see p. 197), which was designed in the same spirit as the more strictly social measures, these pains did not affect inheritance and legacy within the immediate family: blood relatives of the testator up to the sixth, or even the seventh, degree were exempt[7]. But outside these limits the law was severe, and its reply to the parasites who built their highest hopes on the wills of the childless was to debar all but those worth less than 100,000 sesterces from the right to benefit if they had remained incorrigible bachelors themselves[8]. The rules

---

[1] See *e.g. Dig.* XXXV, 1, 64 (Terentius Clemens); *ib.* 79, 4 (Papinian).

[2] *Dig.* XL, 9, 31–2 (Terentius Clemens).

[3] Gaius I, 29–30; *cf. ib.* 72 and 80, and below, p. 889.

[4] In legal circles Augustus' radical attitude to the principles of the existing law seems to have met with criticism: see Gellius, *N.A.* XIII, 12, 2.

[5] *Ulpiani Epit.* XVI, 1.   [6] *P. Gnomon*, 24 and 25.

[7] *Frag. Vat.* 216.

[8] Gaius II, 111. The details of this regulation may perhaps illustrate the interest of Augustus in the richer classes. It seems that men worth less than 100,000 sesterces were not disqualified by celibacy from taking under a will until they reached the age of 60 (*P. Gnomon*, 32). After that age celibacy was a bar to all alike (*P. Gnomon*, 27).

for women were similar but more rigorous. Spinsters and wives
without children lost all capacity to take under wills when they
reached the age of fifty[1], though in earlier life they were only
deprived if they had property amounting to 50,000 sesterces[2];
but, unlike men, they were also subject to a direct financial tax. By
a rule which may well be Augustan, though its authorship is not
recorded, women with property exceeding 20,000 sesterces paid
to the State a yearly levy of one per cent. on their capital until such
time as they might find a husband[3].

Relief from these restrictions began with marriage, increased
with the birth of the first child and became complete with the
arrival of the third or fourth. The details of this arrangement
cannot be assigned with certainty to the Lex Julia of 18 B.C. It is
beyond dispute that the promotion of child-bearing among women
was a principal object of the subsequent Lex Papia Poppaea, and
many of the recorded rules framed with this purpose may consequently not be earlier than A.D. 9; but the grant of the *ius trium
liberorum* to Livia in 9 B.C.[4] is evidence enough that similar regulations had been enacted before, and it is a plausible suggestion
that they were to be found in the Lex Julia itself. Whether in
18 B.C. or later, it was established that, when a child was born,
both parents recovered the right to benefit by wills without regard
to their wealth[5], though in the woman—who naturally gained
immediate exemption from the spinster's tax by marriage—this
right only became indefeasible if by the age of fifty she had a
family of three (or four, if she were a manumitted slave[6]); and it
may well have been in 18 B.C. that some beginning also was made
in the use of release from the troublesome duties of *tutor* and
curator[7] or, for freedmen, of dispensation from the performance of
operae[8] as a reward for contributions to the population. But, whatever the provisions of the Lex Julia on these subjects, it is certain
that they proved so far inadequate as to receive drastic re-inforcement in the Lex Papia Poppaea.

[1] *P. Gnomon*, 28. On the interpretation of this clause see E. Seckel and
P. M. Meyer, 'Zum sogenannten Gnomon des Idioslogos' in *Berl. S.B.*
1928, pp. 438 *sqq.* and, especially, p. 442 *sq.*

[2] *P. Gnomon*, 30.   [3] *P. Gnomon*, 29.

[4] Dio LV, 2, 5.   [5] *P. Gnomon*, 30 and 32.

[6] *P. Gnomon*, 28: see above, n. 1. It appears from Dessau 6089, § 56 *sq.*
that children who died before they had been named did not count in these
calculations, that those who died before puberty were reckoned as each a
half, and that those who had passed that age but had died thereafter were not
distinguished from those still living.

[7] *Dig.* XXVII, 1, 2, 2 (Modestinus).   [8] *Dig.* XXXVIII, 1, 37, *pr.* (Paul).

The last feature of the programme was the set of provisions designed to encourage families among the most important class of all—the class which took active part in public life. The details are ill recorded, but it is apparent that in general the regulations gave precedence to fathers, when they came to stand for office, in a measure determined by the number of their children[1]. If votes were equal, the candidate with the larger family was elected[2], and by this criterion the seniority of the consuls was fixed[3]. But the most cogent use of office as a reward for domestic patriotism lay in an elaboration of the *leges annales* to make them play on men's sense of rivalry with their contemporaries. In the senatorial *cursus* candidates were allowed to stand for the various magistracies as many years before the minimum age otherwise required as was the number of their children[4], and parents were also given some preference in the appointment of governors to the public provinces[5]. These were not negligible inducements, but they scarcely deserve the prominence they have received in accounts of the Augustan legislation. Their field of application was narrow, and their cogency was small: in days when office no longer brought unlimited opportunities for gain, men knew how to wait their turns. As later history was to show, the social legislation of 18 B.C. was far from being treated as failure; but its success in the encouragement of families was due less to the hopes it held out of a quick career than to the steady pressure of the law of succession.

VIII. THE BIRTH-RATE AGAIN:
THE LEX PAPIA POPPAEA

The development of the social programme in the years after 17 B.C. is almost wholly unrecorded. Though Augustus claims that the measures of 18 B.C. were passed at the Senate's request, and though there is no reason to doubt that a certain body of opinion was urgent in its demand for an attack on the moral anarchism of the more advanced, the reforms were not carried without resistance. To his own persuasions Augustus thought well to add the arguments of Metellus Macedonicus, whose speech *de prole augenda* (Vol. IX, p. 38) he recited to the Senate at length[6], the drafts of the laws were amended, and the most offensive proposals were toned down[7]; but, even so, the opposition remained

---

[1] See Dio LIII, 13, 2.
[2] Dessau 6089, § 56 *sq.*
[3] Gellius, *N.A.* II, 15, 4.
[4] *Dig.* IV, 4, 2 (Ulpian).
[5] Dio *loc. cit.*
[6] Suetonius, *Div. Aug.* 89, 2.
[7] Suetonius, *Div. Aug.* 34, 1.

strong, and it is probably to the period immediately after 18 B.C. that there should be assigned the successive suspensions by which the application of the rules about inheritances and legacies was postponed, first for three years and then again for two[1]. There may also have been some minor additions to repair flaws in the original enactments. Attempts were made to secure the benefit of marriage without the burden by men who engaged themselves to children, and the rules by which betrothal was forbidden to girls below the age of ten and marriage was required to follow within two years may only have been established when the defects of the Lex Julia had been revealed in practice[2]. But, with the exception of the measures on manumission passed in 2 B.C. and A.D. 4 (see above, pp. 432 *sqq.*), after 17 B.C. no new statute is recorded before the Lex Papia Poppaea of A.D. 9.

By that year prolonged agitation, in which the *equites* played a foremost part[3], had reached a pitch which must have revealed to a less sensitive observer than the Princeps that, if all concession was refused, public opinion would range itself so solidly against the existing rules that the whole scheme would scarcely survive its author. The first object of the Lex Papia Poppaea was to mitigate the Lex Julia de maritandis ordinibus to a degree which would win it acquiescence: the second was to offer still stronger inducements to marry[4]. From the nature of the new regulations it is clearly to be inferred that the Lex Julia had been less successful with women than with men, and the opportunity provided by the need for fresh legislation seems to have been taken to bring even heavier pressure than before to bear upon potential wives.

Among the changes made to lighten the incidence of the Lex Julia by far the most generous was a widening of the field in which celibacy and spinsterhood did not debar from succession. Not only various blood-relatives, as before (see above, p. 450), but certain connections by marriage were now exempt[5]. The demand thus met was not without an element of reason; and there was a

---

[1] Dio LVI, 7, 3: see p. 442, nn. 2 and 4.

[2] Suetonius (*Div. Aug.* 34, 1) represents some such clause to have been a later addition, and this account is confirmed by Dio LIV, 16, 7 and LVI, 7, 2.

[3] Dio LVI, 1, 2.

[4] According to Tacitus (*Ann.* III, 25, 1), a third purpose was to increase the public revenue. But, though the State gained income—as well as unpopularity—by forfeiture of monies from which the heirs and legatees were debarred by celibacy, it is not to be supposed that financial considerations played any considerable part in the framing of the Lex Papia Poppaea.

[5] *Frag. Vat.* 218.

second like it. In his own experience as a husband Augustus might find reminder enough that sterility was not always a pretence: yet the laws in force before A.D. 9 treated the childless as if they were unmarried[1]. By the Lex Papia Poppaea the hardship of this method was admitted, and *orbi* were allowed for the future to take under the terms of wills half the amounts they would have received if their marriages had not been barren[2]. Moreover, the periods of six months and a year, within which the Lex Julia had required women to find a new husband after divorce and widowhood, were extended to eighteen months and two years respectively[3]; and there may have been yet another change found necessary in the rules of succession. Roman lawyers held a doctrine expressed by Paul in the formula 'quod initio vitiosum est non potest tractu temporis convalescere[4]', and it is possible that ingenious opposition might have invoked this principle to deprive legacies of their value to the social programme. Had it been applied, a legacy only accessible to a husband would have been no inducement to him to marry if he was a bachelor when the will was witnessed. The gravity of this danger is doubtful; but it is clear that, if any such difficulties threatened, they were swept away[5]. Legacies became yet one more encouragement to wedlock, and legatees debarred by celibacy were allowed an interval after the testator's death in which to remove their disability by marriage[6].

The spinsters remained. To break down their hesitation the inducements to wedlock offered by the Lex Julia were vigorously re-inforced. According to Dio[7], whose word there is no reason to doubt[8], some women—and these may be presumed to have been the mothers of three children—were either partly or completely exempted from the operation of the Lex Voconia—the law of 169 B.C. which had set strict limits to the extent to which

---

[1] This uncharitable view of *orbi* (the married but childless) was probably adopted already in 18 B.C. For an attempt to show that it was first taken in some measure subsequent to that date but earlier than A.D. 9 see P. Jörs, *Die Ehegesetze des Augustus*, p. 55 *sq.*   [2] Gaius II, 286 *a.*
[3] *Ulpiani Epit.* XIV.   [4] *Dig.* L, 17, 29.
[5] Perhaps cf. *Dig.* XXXIV, 7, 1, *pr.* (Celsus) and XXXIV, 7, 5 (Ulpian).
[6] In the third century the period was the normal 100 days allowed to the *heres* for deliberation (*Ulpiani Epit.* XVII, 1), and it may well have been so from the start. The year's grace vaguely mentioned by Dio (LVI, 10, 1) possibly refers only to a suspension of the measures there described for twelve months after their passage into law.   [7] LVI, 10, 2.
[8] The belief that the Lex Voconia was repealed by the Lex Papia Poppaea rests on no ancient authority.

females might benefit by wills. Again, the claims of women, whether *patronae* themselves[1] or daughters of *patroni*[2], to the estates of manumitted slaves were greatly increased for the benefit of mothers, and the rights of a *patrona* with three children were assimilated to those of a *patronus*[3], whom praetorian intervention had long given an interest, unknown to the Twelve Tables, in his freedmen's property. Nor did the freedmen themselves escape attention. Three children were now required by the richest and most vulnerable members of that class to destroy the patron's hold over some part of their estates[4], and freedwomen had to reduce the patron's portion by bearing children. Four gave the mother exemption from *tutela*, so that she could make an independent will, but the portion of her estate due to the patron was only reduced as the size of her family increased[5].

Thus, twenty-six years after its inception, the work begun in 18 B.C. was at an end. Augustus had made an attempt of unprecedented daring to change the outlook of society—to raise marriage again to its old esteem and to restore children to their place as its end and object. His purpose was to preserve the strength of the imperial people, and in particular of that vital stock which was to spread the traditions of Rome through Italy, so that Italy might hand them on to the empire at large; and his success or failure is to be judged rather by the part which Italy came to play in the history of succeeding centuries than by the tales of criticism in Rome or the resentment which fell on *delatores* who made profit out of offences against these laws. Dio has been followed by many in his remark that of the two consuls who gave their names to the Lex Papia Poppaea both were bachelors[6], but it is certainly no less relevant to observe that one of the sponsors whom Augustus chose for this last addition to his plans for maintaining the Roman race was a namesake, and almost certainly a relative, of that Papius Mutilus who a century before had been leading the Samnites in the Social War. Nor was the work a failure. The laws of 18 B.C. and A.D. 9 endured, and the care with which they were elaborated from time to time proves more than that they fell short of perfection. Tiberius (p. 615 *sq.*), Claudius (p. 694), Nero (p. 704), Vespasian, Hadrian, the Antonines and the Severi all revealed their conviction that the social legislation,

---

[1] Gaius III, 50 and 52.

[2] Gaius III, 46 and 47: a corresponding and even more generous concession was made to the sons of a *patrona*.

[3] *Ulpiani Epit.* XXIX, 7.   [4] Gaius III, 42.

[5] Gaius III, 44.   [6] LVI, 10, 3.

even down to the rewards for families, must be developed and enforced; and of an achievement which was found good by men responsible for the government of the world for two centuries and more it is impossible to say that it failed. Not until Christianity climbed the imperial throne and impressed its exalted view of celibacy on Constantine were any of the principles adopted by Augustus called into question, and even then the destruction of his work was slow.

IX. *URBS ROMA*

In the social programme of Augustus the laws on marriage and enfranchisement justly hold the foremost place; and even they did not exhaust his faith in statutes. By sumptuary measures, some of which may well have been passed in 18 B.C.[1], the size of houses was limited[2] and the cost of meals prescribed[3] in a way doubtless designed to encourage a return to the modest ideals of a bygone age when Rome was still merely Roman[4]. But to secure this end no amount of prohibitions would be enough, and the fame of the legislative enactments must not obscure the other means which were pressed into service of the cause. Elements are not lacking in the constitutional and religious reforms which belong to the story of the revival of the Roman ideal. By the *lectio senatus* of 29–8 B.C. (p. 123) the Senate regained some measure of that select distinction which had been the basis of its prestige in the days before it was vulgarized by Julius Caesar; and the creation of fresh patricians in 29 B.C. under the terms of the Lex Saenia (p. 122) was another mark of deference to the Roman past. So too in religion Augustus aimed above all at a revival of the national cults, and even when he was compelled to compromise with ideas (like some about the relation of his own position in the scale of being to that of ordinary humanity) which had their origin in the Hellenistic East, the alien conceptions were so deftly transmuted that they could be taken up unnoticed into a whole which was unmistakably Italian. The loyalty of Augustus to the traditions of Italy did more than give its character to the Augustan Age. It endowed the Roman Empire with its significance in the history of Western Europe; and all its expressions consequently

---

[1] Dio LIV, 16, 3 *sqq.*   [2] Suetonius, *Div. Aug.* 89, 2.

[3] Gellius, *N.A.* II, 24, 14–15.

[4] It is generally agreed that the length at which Livy (XXXIV, 1, 1–8, 3) sets out the arguments alleged to have been used in 195 B.C., when the Lex Oppia sumptuaria of 215 B.C. was repealed, is due to the interest in this type of legislation provoked by the social programme of Augustus, and particularly by those measures which affected women.

deserve the closest scrutiny. The Italian bias of the constitutional
reforms and the Italian inspiration of the religious revival are
noticed elsewhere (pp. 124, 476 *sq.*); but, though it is in his religious and constitutional policies that the mind of Augustus
stands most clearly revealed, the legislation on freedmen and
marriage was not the only undertaking in the social sphere which
had the creation of an Italian patriotism as its end.

It was Augustus who first gave the city of Rome that character
which is still conceded by phrases like 'the Eternal City[1].' During
the Hellenistic Age the visible centres of men's loyalty had been
many. The claims of Alexandria could only be acknowledged
where Ptolemaic influence was supreme, and in regions under
Seleucid control the allegiance of the inhabitants was divided between Antioch, Sardes and Seleuceia-on-the-Tigris. But when the
Romans came to end the period of political pluralism, Rome itself
inevitably became unique. To the peoples of the eastern provinces
it was now the one city of the world hallowed by the presence of
a ruler whom it was natural for them, in accordance with the
established custom of the Hellenistic world, to regard as in some
sense God Manifest; and to the whole empire alike Rome was
the one and only source of governmental authority. But to Italy
the City clearly stood in a more intimate relation, and that relation
called for definition with special insistence since the political
structure of the Italian peninsula had been changed beyond recognition by the results of the Social War.

> Alme Sol, curru nitido diem qui
> promis et celas aliusque et idem
> nasceris, possis nihil urbe Roma
> visere maius.[2]

The hope of Horace was the intention of Augustus. Rome was to
become the focus and the stimulus of Italian patriotism, and it
was to make the City worthy of the people whose inspiration it
should be that Augustus and his friends undertook the works
which are described at length elsewhere (chap. xvii). Cassius Dio,
indeed, emphatically asserts that, in claiming to have left of stone
the Rome he found of clay, Augustus referred to the solidity of
the empire rather than to the physical aspect of the capital[3]; but

---

[1] See R. Heinze, *Die Augusteische Kultur*[2], pp. 66 *sqq.*

[2] Horace, *Carm. Saec.* 9 *sqq.*

[3] Dio LVI, 30, 3–4; cf. Suetonius, *Div. Aug.* 28, 3, where the juxtaposi-
tion of this remark with that contained in section 2 suggests that, whatever
Augustus may have meant by the words he used about the City, it was not
left for Cassius Dio to invent the interpretation which he accepts.

in their literal meaning the words were not untrue as Rome slowly became 'urbs pro maiestate imperii ornata[1].'

The exaltation of the City conferred a new dignity on its inhabitants: the people whose home was the capital of the world must neither merit nor receive the treatment which had justly been the lot of the 'faex Romuli' in the declining years of the Republic. If the new city was to inspire them with a new self-respect, the government must abandon that attitude to the *plebs* which the meanness of the masses had richly merited in the days of Cicero. The problem of the surplus proletariate was not less pressing than it had been for the last century and more, but when its members were to be flattered with the suggestion that they formed a valuable part of the imperial race the cavalier methods by which Julius had treated the urban mob must be abandoned. Instead of providing colonies abroad wherein these people might earn their livings and then coercing the desired number to emigrate by curtailing the lists of those to whom free corn was given, Augustus had to keep them in Italy, if not in the City itself. Colonies in the provinces were now designed for veterans alone[2], and the unemployed remained to await provision at home. The task of protecting them from the destitution which makes men dangerous was still difficult enough, even if it was soon rendered less formidable than it had been in the past by the success of Augustus in his central undertaking. Among the many effects of the Augustan Peace was a severe restriction of the supply of slaves from abroad: by the beginning of our era slaves seem to have grown so scarce, and consequently so dear, that the profits gained by *suppressio* (kidnapping) of innocent travellers made the practice common enough to call for drastic action by the government[3]. With servile competition thus reduced the demand for free labour grew, and the problem of the *plebs urbana* remained within reasonable dimensions. Nevertheless the numbers of those who lived on public charity tended to rise, and when Augustus at length called a halt, as he seems to have done between 5 and 2 B.C., he was compelled to fix a maximum higher by about a third than that which had been enough in the time of Julius[4].

To these humble inhabitants of the City Augustus made himself

---

[1] Suetonius, *Div. Aug.* 28, 3.

[2] *Res Gestae* 28, with Mommsen's remarks *ad loc.* (*Res gestae divi Augusti*,[2] p. 119).   [3] Suetonius, *Div. Aug.* 32, 1; *Tib.* 8.

[4] A little over 200,000 (*Res Gestae* 15; cf. Dio LV, 10, 1) instead of the 150,000 to which the total had been reduced by Julius (Suetonius, *Div. Iul.* 41, 3).

both friend and mentor. To the regular dole of corn were added special gifts of food at his own expense, and besides these, to mark occasions of note, there were lavish distributions of cash, on which between 29 and 2 B.C. he seems to have spent a sum of more than three hundred million sesterces. But these imperial dependents were no pampered pensioners: in return for favours received they were expected, if not to perform any positive service to the State, at least to abandon their mischievous activities of the past. The Assemblies were not, indeed, abolished; but the dwindling functions they retained were to be exercised under the threat of increased penalties for corruption[1]. At public spectacles praetors were charged with the preservation of order[2]; special seats were reserved for senators and *equites*[3]; and the descendants of senators were forbidden to demean themselves by performing for the delectation of the mob[4], which itself was now compelled on occasion to appear wrapped in the dignity of the *toga*[5]. In the days of this new respectability it was wholly appropriate that the weapons of Clodius should be destroyed: by an enactment of the first importance the most dangerous of the old clubs were abolished[6], and for the future toleration was promised to none but those which had gained a licence under the provisions of the Lex Julia de collegiis[7].

There remained one grave problem. In the time of Augustus Rome was in the strange position of being the only city of the Empire whose inhabitants enjoyed no effective citizenship of their own. After the Social War their franchise had become the common franchise of the whole peninsula: its wide extension made it no longer capable of any but the most formal use, and yet in its place they had nothing to put which would correspond to the rights enjoyed by people living in the country-towns under the municipal constitutions of the various communities. For this defect Augustus seems to have sought a remedy: the evidence for his intention, indeed, is to seek, but the end at which he aimed may be divined by conjecture not wholly rash. On 1 August 7 B.C.[8] there was inaugurated the system whereby Rome was

---

[1] Suetonius, *Div. Aug.* 34, 1; 40, 2: Dio LIV, 16, 1; LV, 5, 3: Paul, *Sent.* V, 30 A.

[2] Dio LIV, 2, 3; cf. Suetonius, *Div. Aug.* 44, 1.

[3] Dio LV, 22, 4.

[4] Dio LIV, 2, 5.   [5] Suetonius, *Div. Aug.* 40, 5.

[6] Suetonius, *Div. Aug.* 32, 1; Dio LIV, 2, 3.

[7] See Dessau 4966; it is possible that the relevant law was the Lex Julia de ui.

[8] For the date see G. Gatti, 'Ara marmorea del "vicus Statae matris"' in *Bullettino della commissione archeologica communale di Roma*, XXXIV, 1906, pp. 198 *sqq.* and Dessau 9250. See above, p. 199, and below, p. 479 *sq.*

divided into fourteen *regiones*, each of which was divided again into a number of smaller districts known, by a name familiar, at least unofficially, under the Republic[1], as 'vici[2].' The *regiones* were put under the charge of (apparently) fourteen magistrates drawn by lot from the praetors, aediles and tribunes of the year[3], and below them each *vicus* had annual *magistri*, normally four in number, chosen by some method now unknown from the inhabitants of the *vicus* itself[4]. Thus there was erected an organization capable of being used as machinery, however rudimentary, for the purposes of local administration, and there was a possibility that the inhabitants of Rome might find in domestic politics a vent for the political energies which could no longer be dissipated on the affairs of the Populus Romanus.

The measure of responsibility which Augustus intended to lay upon the wards and their officers is impossible to estimate with confidence; but there is no room for doubt that he was alive to the necessity that men, to be contented, must have some interest in institutions which belong to the structure of the State, and it is a plausible conjecture that the organization of the *vici* was intended to provide a focus for that parochial patriotism which adds a salutary interest to lives otherwise in danger of being wholly self-regarding. The functions of the *vici* were modest. Until the creation of the Vigiles in A.D. 6, the *magistri vicorum* were in charge of the arrangements for dealing with fires—a fact which explains their early concern with Volcanus[5] and with Stata Mater, the goddess who stayed the conflagration[6]; and in A.D. 4/5 and 12/13 they are found supervising the weights used in handling gold and silver[7]. But this promise of a system which might in time have allowed the masses some slight independence in their local government was soon belied. The disastrous fire of A.D. 6[8] seems to have convinced Augustus that a fire-brigade to be effective must be under central control, and the responsibilities of the *vicomagistri* in this respect were thereupon transferred to the Praefectus Vigilum. Indeed, the organization of the *vici* had not passed beyond the stage of experiment when it lost even such small administrative significance as it had boasted at the start, and the

---

[1] Livy xxxiv, 7, 2.   [2] Pliny, *N.H.* III, 66.
[3] Suetonius, *Div. Aug.* 30, 1; Dio LV, 8, 7.
[4] Suetonius, *ib.*
[5] Dessau 3306 (3/2 B.C.); cf. 3305.
[6] Dessau 3307 (7 B.C.); *C.I.L.* VI, 764 (6/5 B.C.); Dessau 3306 (3/2 B.C.); 3308 and *C.I.L.* VI, 765 (A.D. 12). Cf. Festus, p. 416 L.
[7] Dessau 5615.   [8] Dio LV, 26, 4.

vicomagistri, so far as we can say, soon found themselves left with none but religious duties. From a date before the death of Augustus himself until the whole system disappeared in the third century, their only business seems to have been with the various shrines and chapels in their respective districts. The divinities to which this allegiance is recorded are many, but only one of the cults under their care could claim any serious importance. It was the *vicomagistri* who controlled the worship of the Lares Compitales. This was the cult which, when to these deities Augustus added his own Genius, took on so definitely political an air that its objects came to be known as the 'Lares Augusti[1],' and which thus came to serve an invaluable purpose by offering the masses a regular occasion for simple ceremonial, which was at the same time a reminder of their obligation to the man who embodied the ideals of the new Italy wherein they were asked to make themselves worthy of a place. (See further, p. 479 *sq.*)

X. ITALY

In this new Italy at large the strongest single bond was the common citizenship of its people, but here too Augustus was the author of some minor measures by which the growth of their nascent solidarity can scarcely have failed to be encouraged. Like Rome itself, the focus of their patriotism, the country as a whole was divided into *regiones*, of which in the case of Italy there were eleven[2]. What part they played in the administrative system cannot now be ascertained: it is a plausible conjecture that they served as a foundation for the machinery by which the census was taken and by which the indirect taxes were collected[3], but their service to the social programme of the day is to be seen, if anywhere, in the reminder which they supplied that the whole area included in the system—the peninsula from the Straits of Messina to the Alps—was one. The same tendency is to be found again in a remarkable scheme in which Augustus is said to have sought means whereby the opinion of the country towns in Italy might find expression at the elections of the magistrates of the Populus Romanus. According to Suetonius[4], the *decuriones* of his new colonies in Italy were to be given the opportunity of recording their votes for the election of magistrates at Rome without leaving their native cities, and these votes were then to be sent under seal

---

[1] Dessau 3611 *sqq.*   [2] Pliny, *N.H.* III, 46.
[3] See J. Marquardt, *Röm. Staatsverwaltung*, I², p. 220.
[4] *Div. Aug.* 46.

to the capital. It must be admitted that no trace of this arrangement in practice is to be found either during the principate of
Augustus himself or in the times of his successors, but the suggestion that he at least toyed with the idea of its introduction is
entirely in accord with what is otherwise known of his political
ideals. Whatever may have been the difficulties in the way of its
execution, a plan which could connect the aristocracy[1] in communities scattered up and down the peninsula by a common
interest in the affairs of Rome was typical of Augustus' hopes for
Italy in general, as well as of the part for which he cast the capital
itself.

There remains the Juventus—a memorable institution which
served at once to unite the youth of Italy and to remind it of the
burdens to be borne by an imperial people. Though in course of
time they were doubtless influenced by the Greek ἐφηβεία, the
origin of the *collegia iuvenum* is almost certainly to be sought far
back in Italian history[2]; and their revival at the beginning of the
imperial age could with justice be regarded as the revival of something not alien but native. It appears that the custom was for boys
of the upper classes, even before they assumed the *toga virilis*, to
join clubs or societies which provided them with some kind of
physical exercise and training in horsemanship, the results of
which it was their habit to display in the so-called 'Lusus Troiae[3].'
At this stage they remained perhaps until they were seventeen,
when they passed into the Juventus proper and their activities
took a more definitely martial turn, giving some preliminary acquaintance with the use of arms to youths of whom many would
soon be serving as officers in the army. The religious aspect of
these clubs and the few extant facts about their organization and
their officials add little to our knowledge of the social function
which it was their business to discharge[4], but the authorship of
the revival which brought them into the prominence they enjoyed
during the early Empire is a matter of more moment. That they
were under the high patronage of Augustus himself is proved by

[1] The emendation of Suetonius (*loc. cit.*) proposed by V. Gardthausen
(*Augustus und seine Zeit*, II, p. 315) in order to make this right of voting for
Roman elections available, not only to the *decuriones*, but also to the whole
citizen-body of the colonies in question, if palaeographically unobjectionable,
is repugnant to everything recorded about Augustus' views on the value of
democracy in the central government

[2] See *e.g.* Livy IX, 25, 4; R. S. Conway, *Italic Dialects*, I, no. 42.

[3] Cf. Virgil, *Aen.* V, 545 *sqq.*

[4] The origin and the nature of the institution is discussed at length by M.
Della Corte, *Iuventus*, chaps. I, II.

ample evidence, above all by his choice of 'Princeps Iuventutis' as a title of honour for his grandsons Gaius and Lucius[1]; but it is less certain that he was the first to encourage the spread of this ancient institution. The Lusus Troiae, which seems to have been closely connected with the Juventus, had already made an isolated appearance under Sulla[2]; but it is not until the dictatorship of Julius that signs of an interest in its revival become marked. According to Dio[3] the game had been performed at the triumph of 46 B.C., and something of the same sort is implied again in Suetonius' account[4] of the displays by *iuvenes* and *pueri* which the Dictator had made part of the ceremonies at the inauguration of his improvements to the Circus Maximus. After his death it is recorded in the shows given by Agrippa both as praetor in 40 B.C.[5] and as aedile in 33 B.C.[6] (p. 90), and the prominence it receives at Virgil's hands suggests that its position was assured at a time earlier than any to which the enactment, if not the first formulation, of other social measures in the Augustan programme can be assigned. Thus indications are not lacking that the Juventus had found favour before the establishment of the Principate; and, if the evidence allows a conjecture that Julius Caesar had not been without some share in the responsibility for its new importance, the conjecture may gain support both from the inclusion of the Trojan game in the contests arranged by Octavian to celebrate the dedication of the Aedes Divi Iuli on 18 August 29 B.C.[7] and from the propriety with which a man whose convictions about the burden of empire were such as those of Julius are known to have been[8] might concern himself with an institution designed to prepare the high-born youth of Italy for the military duties proper to an imperial race. But, if a doubt remains whether it was the Dictator or his adopted son who took the first steps to revive its popularity, there can be no dispute at all that the Juventus found a champion in Augustus, and scarcely more that he saw in it a means of fostering throughout Italy the consciousness of common interests and common obligations. 'Legibus novis me auctore latis multa exempla maiorum exolescentia iam ex nostro saeculo reduxi, et ipse multarum rerum exempla imitanda posteris a me [?] tradidi[9].' Thus Augustus sums up a large part of his social pro-

---

[1] See also Suetonius, *Div. Aug.* 43, 2.
[2] Plutarch, *Cato min.* 3, 1.   [3] Dio XLIII, 23, 6.
[4] *Div. Iul.* 39, 2.   [5] Dio XLVIII, 20, 2.
[6] Dio XLIX, 43, 3.
[7] Dio LI, 22, 4; cf. *C.I.L.* 1,[2] p. 248 (*Fasti Ant.*).
[8] See above, p. 426.   [9] *Res Gestae* 8.

gramme; and of these 'exempla' not the least valuable was the Juventus.

Augustan Italy and Augustan Rome were personified on the slabs which formerly flanked the eastern entrance to the enclosure of the Ara Pacis[1]. Italy was to be one, in spirit as in name, and it was to be strong through the fertility of its mothers. By the limitations of his art the sculptor was debarred from an explicit reference to the laws on slavery—the Lex Junia, the Lex Fufia Caninia and the Lex Aelia Sentia—whereby the infiltration of foreign blood was brought under control, but the Roman dress and Roman details of the procession carved on the side-walls of the precinct serve as reminders of the ideal set before the population as a whole. All alike were recalled to a sense of moral responsibility by the Lex Julia de adulteriis coercendis, and in the Lex Julia de maritandis ordinibus and the Lex Papia Poppaea the demand for a return to the ancient ways was addressed with special emphasis to the nobility. They were the trustees of the traditions which were to become the traditions of all Italy, and in them was vested the experience of government by the methods which were to be followed throughout the Roman world. They were the custodians of the Latin culture which, under the fostering care of Augustus and his successors, was to grow into the Latin civilization of the West—the civilization of which the new Italy, 'rectrix parensque mundi altera[2],' was the seat, and the new Rome,

cui par est nihil et nihil secundum[3],

the symbol.

[1] For this interpretation of the southern relief, which is not universally accepted, see J. L. Ussing, 'Ara Pacis Augustae' in *Kgl. Danske Videnska-bernes Selskabs Forhandlinger* 1903, No. 1, and A. W. Van Buren, 'The Ara Pacis Augustae' in *J.R.S.* III, 1913, pp. 134 *sqq.* See also Volume of Plates iv, 120, *a*.

[2] Pliny, *N.H.* XXXVII, 201.   [3] Martial XII, 8, 2

CHAPTER XV

RELIGIOUS DEVELOPMENTS FROM THE CLOSE OF THE REPUBLIC TO THE REIGN OF NERO

I. *FIN DE SIÈCLE*

ROMAN religion is in its essence a matter of cult acts[1]. These acts, whether of the household, or of the *gens*, or of the State, are thought of in a juristic way as obligations incumbent on an heir or on the people, or as contractual dealings in which the human party, if he fulfils his obligations, may look to the divine party to do its share, in which, moreover, the human party takes legal precautions to prevent the invalidation of what he does. The State or its official representatives can decide without reserve what is necessary or adequate. It stands between the individual and the supernatural, just as the head of a household stands between the gods and those set under him. The State's official representatives have full powers. It was so in the Greek city, but in Rome the conception is carried out with peculiar consistency.

What results has little to do with the emotion or imagination or speculation of the individual. From time to time there arose in the masses a fear that traditional observances were in some way deficient. The ruling class regarded this as an epidemic to be met by the introduction of some new rite or cult (vol. VIII, pp. 451 *sqq.*). Two religious emotions and two only were valued, the *religio* of just scruples against breaking an oath and its positive complement, *pietas*, a strict and loyal readiness to perform all the obligations of a Roman and a son. Speculation and imagination were not conspicuous. The official system was part of the political framework of life, and the use of its auspices and omens to block an agitator's actions was not regarded as blasphemous. Yet we must not conclude that the whole thing was a mere convention. When we hear of a man obeying the omens to his personal disadvantage, that may be just conformity to etiquette; but it is clear that down to the fourth century A.D. it was widely held that the prosperity and even the safety of Rome depended on the accurate performance of traditional ceremonies. Men cannot be keeping up appearances

---

[1] The development of Roman religion during the Early and Middle Republic has been described in vol. VIII, chap. xiv, but it is convenient here to take note of elements of importance for the period of this chapter.

all the time, and we have probably to reckon with a psychology of association. On the face of it Rome had practised these worships and had succeeded, and when a disaster happened some ritual omission could often be discovered to account for it.

From the end of the third century B.C. this religion was quickened by Greek anthropomorphism and interpreted by Greek speculation, Polybius in particular helping the ruling class to realize the pragmatic value of their view of religion as an official institution. Apart from this inward transmutation, there were other consequences of Rome's advance to supremacy in the Mediterranean world. In the first place, Romans and, even more, Italians moved freely in the Hellenistic East as soldiers and merchants, and as merchants often settled there, as for instance at Delos (vol. VIII, pp. 644 *sqq.*). When so established they clung together, preserving their national individuality and reverencing the old household gods, above all the Lar and the Genius. At the same time, many of them as individuals worshipped local gods, and might on their return bring back their cults[1]. Secondly, Romans who went to the East in positions of authority found themselves treated with the honours accorded to Hellenistic kings. Flamininus received a cult and a priest at Chalcis, M'. Aquilius a priest at Pergamum[2]. Not merely the man but his personified attributes might be worshipped: Cicero wrote to his brother Quintus 'You see your virtues consecrated and set in the number of the gods[3].' So the idea of deification was early introduced to the Roman ruling class. Finally, Rome itself attracted numerous immigrants, bringing their own cults and their own points of view. We can see manifestations of this in the statues set up in 86 B.C. to a popular praetor M. Marius in the quarters of the city and the offering to him of incense and wine, as well as in the cultus of alien gods satirized in the *Eumenides* of Varro.

Thus there came to Rome both the higher and the lower elements of the Greek East. The Hellenistic religious world contained a curious mixture of different elements, civic conservatism, individual mysticism, and scepticism. New deities, and above all Isis and Sarapis, became absorbed (as we see in their annual priesthoods of the Greek type) and obtained full civic recognition, even where there was no such motive as a desire to win Ptolemaic favour. From the cults of Cybele and Isis the Greeks formed initiations of their own type. These acquired importance,

---

[1] Cf. J. Hatzfeld, *Les trafiquants italiens dans l'orient hellénique*, pp. 265 *sq.*, 341 *sqq.*   [2] H. Seyrig, *Rev. Arch.* 2 Sér. XXIX, 1929, p. 95, n. 4.   [3] *ad Q.F.* I, I, 31.

but it must not be forgotten that the cult of Isis was not primarily a religion of initiations: they were an 'extra' for the devotee who could afford them. Many cult societies were formed, giving to the individual a substitute for family and local associations from which he was separated, many foundations also to secure the upkeep of his grave, which could not depend on relations and descendants. The tone of thoughtful men was marked by a certain weariness, as we see it in the end of Catullus LXIV: when our ancestors were pious, things went well; now the gods are far away and there is nothing in particular that we can do about it; 'I a stranger and afraid, in a world I never made.'

We are primarily concerned with the effect of these contacts on the ruling class, which in antiquity set the tone of society in a way in which it does not now. Paradoxical as it may sound, the jejune nature of Roman religion made for its preservation. It was in no sort of rivalry with new ideas but lived on as it were in a separate compartment. In Greece philosophy was not incompatible with conformity with civic tradition, and here that tradition was yet more closely connected with the community's well-being. When Scaevola distinguished civil, mythological and natural theology he did not for a moment suggest that civil theology was to be abandoned. If you had asked him whether the ceremonies of public cult were in any *rapport* with the supernatural—which he doubtless conceived in the Stoic way as the fiery life-breath of the universe—he would probably have replied that he was not in a position to deny it. Man makes reservations in his scepticism as well as in his belief, and rationalism did not then rest on the solid mass of sure and digested information which can be invoked in its support to-day. Again, the Roman temperament inclined towards an attitude which may be characterized by Schweitzer's phrase 'Yes, but—.' So it is that in Cicero's *De natura deorum* and *De divinatione*, after the inconsistencies and illogicalities not merely of mythology but of the whole system of auspices have been fully revealed, the conclusion is always that tradition must be maintained. Here as in Varro we see a non-rational element of conservative feeling, coloured by the national pride conspicuous in literature and life from the Sullan epoch onwards and also by the turn which Stoicism was then taking in the hands of Posidonius, a turn at once conservative and Platonizing.

Posidonius held the Stoic conception of the immanent life-force with the warmth of religious conviction. He was a traveller and an ethnologist and found, as he thought, in the most diverse peoples traces of a simple primitive belief overlaid by later super-

stition. Yet he did not, like Panaetius, reject the idea of divination:
it held together only too well with his doctrine of the sympathy of
all the parts of nature. The fact that his Platonizing tendency
made the idea of the essential divinity of the human soul very
congenial to him is important, for Posidonius had a great influence
on his contemporaries: Cicero gives one the impression of wanting
to believe him to be right. This conservative turn was not limited
to Stoicism. Antiochus of Ascalon introduced Stoic views in the
Academy, and a fragment, which may be his and which certainly
reproduces Academic views, says that the building of temples in
the most conspicuous places is a primary duty of statesmanship,
an instructive contrast with the banning of temples and images
from the ideal state of Panaetius[1]. Again, Philodemus is concerned both to show that Epicurus performed his religious duties
as a citizen and to distinguish the true piety of the enlightened
Epicurean from the beliefs of the crowd and the complexities of
the Stoic.

It has been usual to represent the last decades of the Roman
Republic as a period of religious decay. The state of feeling of the
masses can hardly be estimated. The impression which we form
from Cicero and Varro is that their works set forth an ideal for
others, and that those around them were prone either to *superstitio*,
emotional personal religion, or to a shallow and subversive scepticism. The path of *pietas* resembles that of a tight-rope walker. If
we turn to the conduct of the ruling class we see disorder in this
as in every department of public life. Auspices were shamelessly
misused for political ends and the augural discipline was not
carefully maintained, except by an enthusiast like Appius[2]. Pro-
digies, says Livy[3], were commonly neither announced nor recorded
because of that same negligence through which men commonly
now believed that the gods did not give signs of the future; the
calendar was allowed by the *pontifices* to sink into hopeless disorder; temples were not repaired when they fell into decay (and
ancient buildings needed very frequent restoration, to judge from
the inscriptions on aqueducts[4]); the Capitoline temple, burnt in
83 B.C., was not fully restored for twenty-one years; the meaning
of many ceremonies was forgotten; the office of *flamen Dialis*,
which involved its holder in tedious taboos, was not filled from
Sulla's dictatorship till 11 B.C.; provincial temples were robbed to
satisfy the greed of governors or the needs of war; the disposal of

---

[1] Stobaeus II, p. 152, ed. Wachsmuth; H. Strache, *Der Eklektizismus des
Antiochus von Askalon*, p. 65.
[2] Cicero, *de div.* I, 16, 29.   [3] XLIII, 13, 1.   [4] *E.g.* Dessau 218.

pauper dead on the Esquiline was as shocking as it was in-
sanitary.

All this is just disorder, like the disorder in civil life. Roman
religion was made up of traditional practice, and animated by
patriotic spirit; it was not a matter of belief. Scepticism might
lead to carelessness, if men suspected that neither the performance nor the neglect of ritual had any effect on the course
of events. Yet the strongest spirits favoured conservatism in
observances, and acted in a way which suggests that religious
things retained a certain prestige. When Caesar set the calendar
in order, he showed scrupulous respect for the traditional sanctity
of certain days, and in the *lex coloniae Iuliae Genetivae* minute
provision was made for the organization of public worship
(vol. IX, p. 709). We have, perhaps, some indication of the ideas
current in his circle in the account of Romulus given by Dionysius
of Halicarnassus, which may be based on a Caesarian pamphlet[1]
and certainly reflects the mood of the time. In this Romulus is
represented as the founder of Roman religion, careful not to give
State countenance to the extravagance of exotic cults. It cannot
be said that Caesar, in the days of his autocracy, pursued a
deliberate religious policy (*ib.* p. 722), but his insistence on the
divine origin of his family, his watchword of Venus Victrix at
Pharsalus, his new temple to Venus Genetrix as his patron-
goddess, and the planning of a temple to Mars show that an aura
of religion was not unacceptable to him (*ib.* pp. 616, 701, 713).
Sulla had claimed to be the favourite of the same goddess and had
cared for the restoration of the temple of Juppiter; Pompey had
dedicated to Venus Victrix a temple attached to his theatre—a fact
which perhaps gave additional point to Caesar's battle-cry—and
the poem of Lucretius attests the emotional response which the
forms of religion might evoke. The prestige of the State cults is
illustrated by the coins struck by Roman magistrates with representations of the temples built by their ancestors.

Something like the Augustan restoration would probably have
been undertaken by any responsible Roman if he had had absolute
power; it would have seemed to him an integral part of any
bringing back of public order. Cicero, in the second book of
his work *On laws*, lays down that there are to be no private
unrecognized worships: sanction is given only to civic rites in
temples or groves and to family rites. Worship is to be directed
to the Lares, to the old gods, to those who are recognized as

---

[1] *Ant. Rom.* II, 7–29. See M. Pohlenz, *Hermes*, LIX, 1924, pp. 157 *sqq.*

having reached heaven for their merits, and to personified virtues. Emphasis is laid on the maintenance of the priestly colleges and the Vestals, on the augural system (including the observance of the *augurium salutis*), on the control of prophecies (the number must be limited), on the official nature of worship, and on the use of fetials—just as by Augustus (see below, p. 475). Sacrifices by night are prohibited, with one time-honoured exception (that of Bona Dea): so also initiations except those of Ceres, and religious begging except in honour of the Idaean Mother. In the commentary which he then gives he speaks of the nature of purity and of the acceptability of a simple rite, he urges that old temples to evil deities such as Febris should be abolished, and he defends divination by the common custom of humanity.

The most illuminating commentary on the time is provided by the fragments of Varro's *Antiquitates divinae*. This work was a sequel to his *Antiquitates humanae* and was deliberately so placed from the conviction that religious institutions are man-made or rather State-made, Varro remarking that he wrote so because he wrote for Rome and not from an absolute point of view. In the same spirit discussion of the *personnel* and paraphernalia of religion precedes that of the gods. Varro adopts Scaevola's classification of the three kinds of theology. His own belief is that there is one god, the soul of the universe, who may be identified with Juppiter Capitolinus or with the god of the Jews; the other gods are his parts or virtues. If Varro were founding a new State he would have consecrated the gods and their names in accordance with the scheme of nature: but as it was, the State being long established, he wrote with the purpose that the masses might be willing to worship the gods rather than despise them. He regrets image-worship. For over one hundred and seventy years Rome did without it, and if those conditions had continued the gods would be worshipped with greater purity. Sacrifice is not wanted by the real gods. Yet there are many things which the masses should not know, many delusions which are useful: that is why the Greeks walled off the mysteries in silence. Again, though the eternal gods are to be distinguished from deified men, for States it is useful, even if it is false, that brave men should think themselves to be descended from gods. He endorses the Polybian axiom that Roman power is due to Roman piety: religious observance and fasts can save us from peril. He is indignant at the worship of the Alexandrine gods in Rome. Religion means respect of the gods as of parents, superstition fear of them as of enemies.

Throughout he writes with patriotic emotion, avowing that he is afraid lest the gods should perish, not from the attack of

enemies, but through the neglect of citizens: from this destruction
he is freeing them and storing them in the minds of the loyal
with a care more praiseworthy than that of Metellus for the *sacra*
of Vesta, or of Aeneas for the Penates. He emphasizes the duty
of maintaining family rites as well as civic rites. Like Virgil he
has a genuine sentimental attachment to the old Italian deities,
as we see in the invocation opening his *De re rustica*, and in the
setting of the first book in the temple of Tellus on the occasion
of the Feriae Sementivae.

We are told of Varro that he wished to be buried in the Pythagorean way. Here we touch another element in the religious
life of the time. Pythagoreanism had not been much in evidence
after the end of the fourth century, but it had no doubt continued
in a subterranean way, and about the beginning of the first
century B.C. it enjoyed a revival, represented in Rome by Nigidius
Figulus. Nigidius, a friend of Cicero, was a man of wide learning
and astrological and religious inclinations. Cicero's speech against
Vatinius indicates that the movement was regarded as of the
nature of a sect, with magical interests. In Varro there converge
the interests which are of most importance for the Augustan age,
the wish for revival and restoration in religion, the value set on
Italian tradition and legend—which bulks large in him—and the
importance attached to a doctrine of the soul[1]. Virgil owed more
to him than we can now realize.

II. THE TIME OF THE TRIUMVIRATE

The death of Julius evoked much popular emotion. The comet
which appeared during the games given by Octavian in his honour
was thought to be his soul now received in heaven, and in 42 B.C.
Senate and People voted that he should be included among the
gods of the State. This came, says Suetonius (*Div. Iul.* 88), not
only from the lips of those who passed the measure but also
from the conviction of the masses. Though his temple was not
dedicated till 29 B.C., the celebration of his festival began at
once, and the fact that he was to be reckoned as a god and not a
man was signalized by the prohibition against the carrying of his
imago in funerals of his *gens*. He was *divus*, a word earlier used
as a synonym of *deus* and appropriate because of its adjectival
nature. This step was made easier by the dissemination of Eu-
hemeristic ideas and above all by the notion that the old god
Quirinus was in fact the deified Romulus. Another significant
event, dated in 43, was the decision of the triumvirs to build

[1] A. D. Nock, *Cl. Rev.* XLI, 1927, pp. 169 *sqq.*; XLIII, 1929, pp. 60 *sq.*

a civic temple to Isis, a reversal of senatorial policy, no doubt intended to win the favour of the lower orders, and probably never put into effect.

The time between 43 and 31 was one of disquiet and disorder. This evoked panic and portents and prophecies[1]. Some of the moods of the time are preserved by Virgil's Fourth Eclogue and Horace's Sixteenth Epode. The first is written under the emotions aroused by the Peace of Brundisium. An end had been made to the Perusine war, and the marriage of Antony and Octavia set the seal on the new hope of enduring concord. The poem heralds the birth of a child of human parents and yet of divine origin, whose coming marks the beginning of a new period of the world's life: as he grows up, the evil habits of humanity will gradually disappear. As in Isaiah vii, his growth is contemporary with deliverance, but he is not a Messiah who by his action brings that deliverance. The common assumption among Virgil's contemporary readers was probably that this child was the son to be expected from Antony and Octavia[2]: but if this assumption was correct the point was not expressly stated, and the application was in any case a particular use of an earlier prophecy associated with the name of a Sibyl. What is foretold rests upon one of the many schemes of the Ages of the World; but it differs from current philosophic theory in that between one cycle and the next there is no cosmic disaster, and in that the Ages return upon themselves. From the degradation of the present we pass to an improved Heroic Age, and from that to the Golden Age[3]. Coins show that the ideas involved were in the air at the time[4]. How serious the Eclogue is we do not know. Virgil is at this time an Epicurean: he cannot consistently look for divine interference in human affairs. Yet in his own life Octavian's intervention has been miraculous. When all seemed lost, his farm was restored to him, and he can in the

---

[1] For prophecies of Rome's downfall, cf. Fr. Cumont, *Rev. hist. rel.* CIII, 1931, pp. 64 *sqq.*

[2] See on this W. W. Tarn, *J.R.S.* XXII, 1932, pp. 135 *sqq.*, and above, p. 45: for the literature see Bibliography to chaps. I–IV, II, C. Ancient tradition referred the poem to Pollio's son Saloninus: but if Pollio was the father it is hard to see why Virgil says *te duce* and never alludes to the paternity. On the other hand, it is likely that when the hopes of a son of Antony and Octavia and of a peaceful joint rule by Antony and Octavian failed, any appropriation of the prophecy for Saloninus would be welcomed.

[3] The most interesting analogy is in Plato, *Politicus*, 269 c *sqq.* For the possibility of a Neopythagorean source, cf. J. Carcopino, *Virgile et le mystère de la quatrième églogue.*

[4] A. Alföldi, *Hermes*, LXV, 1930, pp. 369 *sqq.*; Volume of Plates IV, 200, *e, f, g.*

transparent allegory of the First Eclogue say of his deliverer
namque erit ille mihi semper deus. Perhaps this is really the beginning of a new era; perhaps something like this supposedly old
prophecy will really come to pass. Here is the dream—from the
gate of ivory or the gate of horn.

The Sixteenth Epode is closely related to the Fourth Eclogue.
The question of priority is disputed, but it seems reasonable to
suppose that the Epode was written before, not after, the Peace
of Brundisium. Horace speaks the language of despair. No foe
from outside could shake Rome's power, but we by our civil
strife leave the city an easy prey to the barbarian. The only help
is for us to depart and seek the Islands of the Blest. When the
Golden Age gave place to the Bronze, Juppiter set aside those
shores for the righteous. The poem reduced to this summary
sounds like a mythological commonplace, but it is anything but
that. The geographical knowledge of antiquity always left the
chance of some happy haven just beyond the edge of the map.

In 40 Virgil might look to Octavian as the saviour of Italy, but
the view cannot have been common. His success against Sextus
Pompeius in 36 did, however, make him something of a national
hero. Appian says 'the cities set him up with their gods,' an
ambiguous phrase which should mean that images or statues of
him (as earlier of Julius) were set in the chief temples of Italian
municipalities, but might mean only, 'gave divine honours to
Octavian,' or 'included his name in prayer formulas[1].' Further,
we see Octavian in this period foreshadowing the religious policy
of his principate by his refusal to depose Lepidus from the office
of *pontifex maximus,* his encouragement of temple restoration,
and his celebration of the Troia (p. 89 *sq.*). Early in the Second
Triumvirate Livineius Regulus struck coins with a head of Octavian
and Aeneas bearing Anchises; of the same period is a coin struck
by P. Clodius with the head of Octavian and Venus Genetrix,
doves, and Cupid[2]. In the year 36 Octavian's house on the
Palatine was struck by lightning: he at once dedicated the site to
Apollo, a god perhaps chosen because of the old Roman tradition
of turning to the Sibylline books of his prophetess or to his shrine
at Delphi in times of need. Apollo was a god of purifications and
of healing: such was Octavian's mission. The temple was dedicated 9 October 28, when the fact of Actium having been fought,
as it were under the eyes of Apollo, had given to him a new

---

[1] Appian, *Bell. Civ.* v, 132, 546: αὐτὸν αἱ πόλεις τοῖς σφετέροις θεοῖς
συνίδρυον; G. Wissowa, in *Hermes,* LII, 1917, p. 101.

[2] Volume of Plates iv, 200, *h, i.*

prestige. Further, in 33 Octavian's lieutenant Agrippa expelled from the city magicians and astrologers.

The campaign of Actium was preceded by a brisk exchange of calumny between Antony and Octavian (see above, pp. 97 *sqq.*). Octavian taunted Antony, justly indeed, with posing as a new Dionysus. Antony retaliated with the allegation that Octavian had dined with eleven others, taking himself the part of Apollo and leaving to the rest the characters of the other gods, a parody of a *lectisternium*. That this is invented is clear. Octavian would hardly have suffered another to play Juppiter to his Apollo. But it is significant that such stories were regarded as discrediting their object. In actual conduct Octavian took every care to pass as the champion of Roman ways and Roman gods: he declared war on Cleopatra with the old fetial ceremony, and the court poets represented the struggle as one between the gods of Rome and those of Egypt. Was the *sistrum* of Isis to sound upon the Capitol?

Once more Virgil helps us to realize something of the mood of the hour. His Georgics occupied him from 37 till 29 B.C. The prayer at the end of the first Book—whenever it was written—registers a state of mind belonging to the time before or soon after Actium. Virgil has spoken of the ravages of civil war and turns to passionate supplication: 'O ancestral native gods, and Romulus, and mother Vesta that guardest the Tuscan Tiber and Roman Palatia, at least do not prevent this warrior with life before him[1] (he has not been named) from coming to the help of our shattered generation. We have long paid to the full in our blood for the perjuries of Laomedon's Troy. The palace of heaven has long grudged thee to us, O Caesar.' With these words he picks up the other prayer with which the book opens—a prayer to twelve gods[2] and 'thou too Caesar—whichsoever part thou choosest, sea, sky or underworld.' Laomedon's Troy! It sounds like the most frigid mythological commonplace. But it is not: it is to be taken quite seriously in the light of ancient ideas about the guilt which a city, as a living organism, retains through the succession of human generations. Horace had voiced the sentiment earlier in *Epodes* VII, 16, 'Harsh fates drive on the Romans, and the guilt of brother's murder, ever since the blood of innocent Remus flowed on the ground bringing a curse on those yet unborn.' Later comes the reconciliation: *cana Fides et Vesta, Remo cum fratre Quirinus* (*Aen.* 1, 292).

---

[1] *iuvenem* is hardly translatable. It is not 'young man': but it implies that Octavian should, if preserved, have life enough to do what Rome needs.

[2] Subtly varied from Varro's invocation, mentioned above, p. 471; cf. Wissowa, *op. cit.* pp. 92 *sqq.*

III. THE AUGUSTAN RESTORATION

After Actium Octavian had the task of rebuilding national faith and faith in the nation. In 30 he was given the privilege of creating new patricians, which was not only a way of honouring his supporters but also a necessity for the filling of certain priestly positions. In 29 he, like Julius, was empowered to create—theoretically, no doubt, to recommend—priests beyond the number traditional for the priestly colleges[1]. The dignity of their office was enhanced. The priesthoods of greater eminence were open only to senators, the position of Lupercus and other minor places to knights[2], and in general priestly honours, though separated from magistracies in the *cursus honorum*, were among the greatest distinctions and were used to mark out possible successors to the principate. The *princeps* was himself a member of the four great colleges. Two old organizations, that of the *sodales Titii*, of whom we know little, and that of the *fratres Arvales*, concerned with ceremonial performed in spring to promote the crops, were revived by him, the latter between 36 and 21. They were now a very dignified corporation of which the Emperor was a member but not necessarily *magister*. Their ceremonies included vows in January to Juppiter, Juno Regina, Minerva, Salus publica p(opuli) R(omani), Dea Dia (later omitted), and (after his death) to Divus Augustus on behalf of the *princeps* and the payment of the vows made in the previous January. The exhaustive records of their proceedings inscribed on stone show a careful archaism of language and ritual.

In this institution we see a characteristic combination of conservatism with innovation, calculated to confer on the new régime the prestige of old religious sentiment. The same spirit appears in the taking of the *augurium salutis* in 29 B.C.[3], in the closing of the temple of Janus in 29 and 25 and on a later occasion, and in a reform of the Lupercalia. In 28 the Senate entrusted to Octavian the restoration of all temples in the city which needed it, and he claims to have rebuilt eighty-two[4].

So the past was once more set upon its throne. At the same

[1] In 36 Octavian had made Messalla an augur *supra numerum*: in 17 there were at least 21 members of the *quindecimviri*.

[2] Mommsen, *Staatsrecht*, III, pp. 566 *sqq.*

[3] For a list of the major and minor occasions of this see Dessau 9337; cf. F. Blumenthal in *Hermes*, XLIX, 1914, pp. 246 *sqq.*

[4] For his personal interest in their rebuilding, cf. Livy IV, 20, 7; *Res Gestae* 19.

time, the new order received religious expression in new foundations which outshone the old. We have spoken of the temple of
Divus Julius and of that of Palatine Apollo. To these should be
added the temple of Juppiter Tonans on the Capitol commemorating the deliverance of Augustus from peril in Spain, the Pantheon,
consecrated to Mars and Venus, the divinities of the Julian house,
the temple of Mars Ultor dedicated on Imperial property in the
new Forum Augustum in 2 B.C. (a small round temple on the
Capitol had been erected for him in 20 B.C.), and the new temple
of Vesta on the Palatine (dedicated 28 April, 12 B.C.). The temple
of Mars Ultor was given special prominence: triumphal insignia
and captured standards were here deposited, discussions on war
and triumphs by the Senate were conducted here, magistrates
going to their provinces made this their starting-point, censors
drove into its wall the commemorative nail at the end of a *lustrum*.
The temple thus received what had been privileges of the Capitol
and, while members of the Imperial house and the young of the
senatorial and equestrian classes when enrolled as *iuvenes* still put
on the garb of manhood at the older shrine, they proceeded thence
to the new[1]. Again, the Sibylline oracles, hitherto kept in the
Capitol, were transferred to the temple of Apollo on the Palatine
after their revision and recopying by the *quindecimviri* in 18 B.C.;
and in 4 B.C. Augustus received Jewish envoys in that temple.

Julius Caesar had acted without greatly troubling himself about
popular feeling. For the success of the Augustan purpose it was
of the first importance that sympathy should be enlisted and the
appropriate spirit created. The buildings contributed to this, and
the men of letters did perhaps even more. The Princeps himself
and his loyal friends Agrippa and Maecenas managed with great
skill to convey to the writers of the time the not unwelcome conviction that their support was of real value. So one and all they
glorify Actium as a victory of Roman culture, of the Roman
spirit; one and all they extol plain living and patriotic thinking,
the Trojan origins of Rome and the Julian *gens*, Apollo and Mars,
the gods of the new order. In Propertius and Ovid we may
suspect this of being a cliché—not that clichés are without
influence—but in Virgil and Horace and Livy it is serious. The
'Roman odes' of Horace's Third Book, included in the collection
published by him in 23 B.C., insist on the ideals of simplicity and
the military virtues, on the rejection of Eastern ideas, on purity
of home life, on the need of rebuilding temples. The *Aeneid* is an

---

[1] See Wissowa, *Religion und Kultus der Römer*, p. 78, who has pointed out
the significance of the policy as a whole.

apotheosis of the Augustan system which is not the less effective
for being indirect. Its theme is Roman history viewed as a process
culminating in the world-power of the Eternal City, a process
willed by heaven and secured by *pietas*; its story is one of the
sacrifice of personal inclination to duty, of the defeating of arrogant self-assertiveness, of reconciliation after conflict. Apollo and
Actium, the Augustan peace, the mission of Rome are with us in
this ancient setting. Varro's enthusiasm for Italy and Italian tradition and the mysticism of Posidonius here find an expression
which could stir the common man: inscriptions show how well the
masses knew their Virgil. The same lessons were conveyed by the
statues in the Forum Augustum, by the sculptures in the temple
of Mars Ultor, and by the other art of the period (pp. 571 *sqq.*).

The most effective outward and visible sign of the new régime
was the Secular Games of 17 B.C., which marked the close of an
epoch (p.150). The *saeculum* was Etruscan but not only Etruscan[1],
and though in 249 B.C. *ludi saeculares* were an innovation prescribed by the Sibylline Books in time of stress, they were a
Greek shoot grafted on a native stock.

We are fortunately able to reconstruct the order of ceremonies,
culminating with the words—'When the sacrifice was completed
those thereunto appointed, twenty-seven boys and twenty-seven
girls who had lost neither father nor mother, sang a hymn, and so
likewise on the Capitol. The hymn was written by Q. Horatius
Flaccus.'[2] The ideas behind the Augustan celebration are clear
and important. The nocturnal ceremonies, performed at full moon
to be more impressive, correspond to the old festival and maintain
a cathartic character, though even here the offering to Terra Mater
looks to the birth of a new and better age, and the victims and
deities are different: they are deities who excite reverence and not
dread. The rites done by day are directed to the old Capitoline
protectors of the State and to the new Imperial deities. Mars is
absent, for he is not appropriate to this context; we are not now
thinking of war or of vengeance for Julius. That is over and done:
and, as the children sang, 'Now the Median fears the Alban axes
supreme on land and sea: now the proud Scyths, yes, and in these
last days the Indians, beg for an answer (to their embassies).'
Divus Julius likewise can have no express mention. In this con-

---

[1] For calculations of the *saeculum* see M. P. Nilsson in *P.W. s.v. Saeculares
Ludi, etc.* cols. 1696 *sqq.*

[2] The first half of the copy on stone which we possess (*C.I.L.* VI, 32323;
Mommsen, *Ges. Schr.* VIII, pp. 567 *sqq.*: part in Dessau 5050) has suffered
serious mutilation, but Zosimus II, 5, fills in some gaps.

text the nocturnal ceremonial takes a new sense. It is the burial of the bad past. And though Augustus is no king, though he is the first citizen, and not yet *pontifex maximus*, though the *quindecimviri* administer all the proceedings just as the college from which they grew did in 249, none the less he stands as spokesman between his people and their gods.

Horace's ode was written to be sung, both on the Palatine and on the Capitol, and is a liturgical text but like some ancient and many modern prayers it is addressed to the public as much as to the gods. It gives pregnant expression to the contemporary ideal fully stated in the Aeneid. Sol, Ilithyia, the Parcae, Apollo and Luna are asked to hear the prayers now uttered:

'If Rome is your handiwork and Ilian squadrons reached the Etruscan shore, being those of the folk who were bidden to change their homes and city on a blessed voyage, those for whom pure Aeneas, surviving his country's fall, made a clear path through Troy that blazed from no treachery: (he was to give them more than they had left behind)—grant, oh ye gods, to the young a spirit to learn and righteous conduct, grant to the old peace and calm, grant to the race of Romulus wealth and offspring and all glory. And may there be full answer to the prayers offered with white oxen by the splendid scion of Anchises and Venus triumphant over foes who war, kindly to the prostrate.'

Parcere subiectis et debellare superbos. There is peace, continues the poet, and the old lost qualities are returning. May Phoebus prolong the Roman State and Latium in blessedness to another cycle and ever improving ages; may Diana hear the *quindecimviri* and the children: I carry home a sure hope that Juppiter and all the gods have this purpose. The vision of the future is a vision of what may be accomplished by co-operation with Augustan social and religious policy. It is a conscientious if laboured attempt to produce the right atmosphere, like Horace's earlier poem (*Odes*, IV, 6) addressed to the choir which was to sing the ode.

Both the legends and the types of the coinage of 17 B.C. and the following year emphasize the ceremonial. We see the young laureate head with a star (the rejuvenated Divus Julius and the *sidus Julium*); Augustus distributing to the people the means of purification; Apollo on a platform ornamented with prows and anchors, the description of the *princeps* as *quindecimvir*, the dedication to Juppiter Optimus Maximus by the Senate and People of Rome for the safety of Augustus because he had given tranquillity to the State[1].

In this way Augustus gave visible expression to his ideals and

---

[1] See Volume of Plates iv, 200, *j–n*.

surrounded his rule with a religious nimbus. It is in a peculiarly
Roman way an alliance of the throne and the altar, and such an
alliance means that the altar is not at the time in question a political
creation devoid of significance. The idea was given further expression by the Senate's dedication *c.* 9 B.C. of the Ara Pacis Augustae
in the Campus Martius to celebrate Augustus' return from Spain
and Gaul four years earlier. The reliefs on it are perhaps the best
surviving artistic expression of the spirit of the moment, linking
once more the piety of the present to the tradition of the past[1].

After the death of Lepidus, Augustus succeeded him as *pontifex
maximus* on 6 March, 12 B.C. The way in which he magnified
this office is shown by two things: it became a regular part of
Imperial titulature, and the day of his assumption of it was one
of the *feriae publicae*[2]. Augustus now ceded part of his house to
become public property. He did not live in the old house of the
pontifex maximus: he had made the Palatine his own, and the
new temple of Vesta on it was ready by 28 April, 12 B.C. Then
follow further reforms. Senators were ordered to offer incense at
the beginning of each meeting. Again, the office of *flamen Dialis*
had been vacant since the dictatorship of Sulla. This was partly
due to the burdensome taboos which weighed upon its holder.
Augustus made some modifications in these—once more we see in
use the Roman State's absolute authority to make such changes—
and in 11 B.C. secured a new holder. Again, he increased the
dignity and privileges of the Vestals, making over to them the old
house of the *pontifex maximus*. Later, when there was a shortage
of candidates for the position, he strongly urged the people to
offer their daughters, saying that if any of his granddaughters
were of the right age he would have offered them. He was, however, compelled in A.D. 5 to admit the daughters of freedmen to
their ranks. Throughout the Principate their prestige was maintained, and in A.D. 24 it was voted that whenever Livia went to
the theatre she should sit among the Vestals[3].

In 7 B.C. the redivision of the city into districts was complete.
With these districts had been associated the only Roman cult

---

[1] Cf. p. 548 *sq.*, and Volume of Plates iv, 112–120, *a*, 122.

[2] Further, though each successor became *pontifex maximus* the dignity of
the office in the first century at least was maintained by the fact that this was
done by a special election, and did not go with the principate automatically.
Cf. Volume of Plates iv, 200, *o*.

[3] Tacitus, *Ann.* iv, 16. The institution of two *curatores* in charge of
temples and of other public buildings probably belongs to this period
(Kornemann, *P. W. s.v. Curatores*, cols. 1787 *sqq.*).

which belonged to the poor, the worship of the *Lares compitales* at the cross-roads under the supervision of *magistri vicorum*. Augustus with consummate skill turned this into a support for his rule by enlisting in his service the instinct of self-importance in humble folk. The cult was now made official: the *magistri vicorum* were elected by the *vici*, four by each annually, and the cult was directed to the *Lares compitales* and the Genius of Augustus. Augustus showed his support of the system by dedicating to the *Lares publici* images of other deities from the money ceremonially given to him in January[1]. The organization was not complete till 7 B.C. Horace indicates that the general idea was in the air well before that time; the *magistri* of one *vicus* describe themselves in A.D. 109 as *magistri anni* CXXI—but CXXI may be an error for CXVI, which would agree with our other evidence[2]. The *magistri* entered on office on August 1, and the institution may well be a sequel to the official re-naming of the month Sextilis. The significance of this for ruler-cult and its effect on the domestic Lar cult will be discussed later (p. 484 *sq.*): for the moment the point to emphasize is this giving of a suitable religious interest to a new social class. The worship of the *Lares Augusti* spread through Italy and the Empire. The popularity of the Lares in Rome is indicated by several reliefs, one of which shows the apotheosis of Julius, the portent of the Alban sow, and sacrifice to a Lar, another (the altar of Manlius) figures of Lares and a sacrifice, perhaps to the Genius Augusti and to Concordia Augusta[3].

Augustus thus won the poor to his ideas. Further, by creating or (as is more likely) revitalizing the associations of *iuvenes*, free born young men, in Rome and Italy he attracted a higher class. We find these associations closely related to municipal cults[4]. The interest now taken in traditional Roman religion is shown by the multiplication of copies of the *fasti* showing the festivals in Rome and in Italian municipalities: this we find from the middle of the principate of Augustus down to A.D. 51[5].

With other religious interests of this class Augustus was less

---

[1] G. Gatti, *Bull. d. commiss. archeol. comm. di Roma*, XVI, 1888, pp. 229 *sqq.*

[2] *Odes*, IV, 5, 34; Mommsen, *Ges. Schr.* VII, p. 181; Gatti, *op. cit.* XXXIV, 1906, pp. 186 *sqq.* The main object of the re-organization was administrative, but this, like any other local unit, needed a religious aspect.

[3] Volume of Plates iv, 128, 130, 132.

[4] M. Rostovtzeff, *Römische Bleitesserae* (*Klio*, Beiheft III), esp. pp. 80, 87; M. Della Corte, *Iuventus*.

[5] *C.I.L.* I², pp. 205 *sqq.* The Julian calendar demanded new *fasti*, but the number and chronological distribution are significant.

in sympathy. We have seen the banishing of astrologers and magicians in 33 B.C. The Egyptian rites, which interested above all the lower orders and the demi-monde, had time after time been repressed by the Optimate rule of the later Republic. These rites were further discredited as a result of the campaign against Cleopatra, in which Augustus had rallied in his support national sentiment and the old feeling against 'the beastly devices of the heathen,' dog-headed gods, and the like. So in 28 he 'did not receive the Egyptian rites within the pomerium' and in 21 Agrippa 'curtailed the Egyptian rites which were again invading the city, forbidding their performance even in the suburbs within a mile of the city.' It is clear both that these prohibitions were not thoroughly and continuously enforced, and that they were what Varro or Cicero would have done[1]. To the official attitude on such questions we shall return later (p. 491).

IV. THE INSTITUTION OF RULER-WORSHIP

How it came to be that Hellenistic kings received the honours appropriate to divinity has been set forth in a previous volume (vol. VII, pp. 13 sqq.). Such honours were an expression of gratitude which did not involve any theological implications. This may sound a paradox. To the Greeks there was often a shading off of the distinction between man and god, and in addition to this general tendency of thought we have to reckon with two widespread ideas, the one that the gods of popular worship were men deified by grateful humanity, the other that the soul of a man or at least the soul of an outstanding man was in a sense divine. All the same a difference remains, for the old cults were there as an established part of life and no inferences or additions unsanctified by oracular or other revelation could hope to obtain the same standing. Countless as are dedications and acts of devotion to deified rulers, it is yet clear that they are all of the nature of homage and not of worship in the full sense, for worship implies the expectation of blessing to be mediated in a supernatural way. The touchstone of piety in antiquity is the votive offering, made in recognition of supposed deliverance in some invisible manner from sickness or other peril. This we do not find directed to rulers dead or living. Since ruler-cult was the expression of gratitude or the acknowledgment of power, the initiative normally lay with

---

[1] Cf. an ideal picture of early Rome in Propertius IV, 1, 17: *nulli cura fuit externos quaerere divos.*

the subjects and not with the ruler. There are exceptions—as for instance the demand made by Alexander to the Greek cities—but there the question is one of status and not of worship. In general, a ruler had no interest in the cult of himself except as a factor in the cohesion and organization of the State or as an element in his own standing in relation to a dependent city, or in competition with other dynasties. Between him and his subjects the issue was one of loyalty: he desired to be assured of it, to receive what soon became the standard form of homage, and they to express it. Hence on their side also the amount of emotion involved was slight except towards individuals who excited a deep-felt gratitude, the memory of which sometimes lasted for centuries. This was directed above all to those who, like the earlier founders of colonies, had established or re-established a city. The attitude in this instance was akin to that traditional towards the heroes.

Such a development was originally foreign to Rome. Rome had no native hero-cult and the Roman view of deities was far less sharply anthropomorphic than the Greek, so that such a shading off between the human and the divine was not likely to arise. Nevertheless, by the time of Augustus Rome had come very much nearer to this world of thought. The idea of heroization or deification for merit had come in with Ennius: many Romans had received divine honours in the East, which perhaps meant more to them by reason of their novelty than to the Hellenistic rulers whom they had superseded[1]: and the mixed population of the city now included many to whom such forms of compliment appeared natural and almost automatic.

Whatever had been done and thought about Julius in his life, after his death he was Divus Julius, and from 40 at latest Octavian was 'Divi filius,' a title in itself unique for a Roman and liable to lead to more. In 36 B.C. the gratitude of Italian municipalities had given to him a place in their temples. After Actium his standing called for some recognition in this as in other ways. So in 30 began the celebration of his birthday as a public holiday, which gained in solemnity, and the pouring of libations in his honour at public and private banquets, and in 29 it was voted that in hymns his name should be coupled with those of the gods and that the day on which he entered the city should be honoured with sacrifices and kept holy for ever[2]. In 28 quinquennial vows were established

---

[1] Thus note the feelings expressed by Cicero over the description of Verres as *soter* (II *in Verr.* II, 63, 154), commonplace as that was.

[2] For Hellenistic precedents see E. Peterson, *Zeit. f. system. Theol.* VII, 1929/30, pp. 682 *sqq.*

for his welfare. In 27 he was given the title of Augustus. It had been earlier used of mysteries and of things belonging to the gods and it had an auspicious sound, for it was thought to be connected with *augere* and *augurium*[1], the latter in its turn suggesting to a Roman the characteristic attribute of *auctoritas*. Between man and god it represents just such a compromise as does *princeps* between citizen and king. How appropriate it was felt to be we see from its application to the month Sextilis[2] and from its use by all successors (see further above, p. 130 *sq.*).

This compromise represents official policy. One apparent exception demands our attention. Augustan policy turned very much on the finding of a special function for each class of society[3]. One body within the State stood in a peculiar relation to the *princeps*; it was the army. If to civilians Augustus was *princeps*, to soldiers he was *imperator*, and he had on their loyalty a claim which was different and charged with a distinctive emotion, expressed in the direct and personal oath of loyalty taken to him as to his Republican predecessors in the field. The army occupied a peculiar position in the framework of Roman religion; essentially it was the Roman People acting in a military capacity and not an organization within the State. Its commander had the right and the duty to consult the gods by taking auspices before action; this was an inseparable concomitant of *imperium*. But the Roman army was not, like a Catholic or Mohammedan army, concerned with the carrying on of a regular scheme of religious observance; it did not observe the celebrations of the civil calendar[4]. They were the concern of the appropriate authorities at Rome. But any Roman army or military unit, at least from the early second century B.C. onwards, was highly conscious of itself as a permanent entity. Given the ancient interpenetration of what we regard as the secular and the religious spheres of life, and the ancient tendency for any group within the community to find a religious centre, it is natural that military

[1] The augural *lituus* is common in contemporary art as an attribute of Augustus.

[2] Seeck-Fitzler, in *P.W. s.v.* Julius (Augustus), cols. 361 *sqq.* and K. Scott, *Yale Classical Studies*, II, 1931, pp. 224 *sqq.* argue that this application was made in 27 but allow that its recognition by the *princeps* hangs together with his regulation of intercalation in 8 B.C.

[3] Cf. A. D. Nock, *Mélanges Bidez*, vol. II, p. 636.

[4] Pliny, *N.H.* XIII, 23, speaks of the anointing of the standards *festis diebus*; this probably refers to the *natalis aquilae* and to Imperial celebrations.

units also developed a focal point of this type[1]. For them it could not but be the standards, and the place in which they were kept came to be a *sacellum*[2]. To these was now added a representation of the reigning *princeps*, and his image was carried with standards both of the legion and of other units, and seems to have been used as the standard of cohorts of the legion. It thus received the homage of the troops and was presented for the veneration of submissive barbarian rulers. A military unit worshipped also a group of gods of war, though it must be said that the precise form which this took is not clear.

We must not over-emphasize the importance of all this. The Praetorian guards and the marine detachments were the only soldiers normally stationed in Italy, and there was no feeling against the participation of citizens in Emperor-worship outside Italy. Further, the association of these *imagines* with the eagles put them on a special footing; the civilian worshipped neither the one nor the other. The soldier gave to both adoration, but he did not expect supernatural aid from either, and many military dedications, both of individuals and of units, are addressed directly to the Emperor in his human capacity, as marks of honour, and do not use the form *Genio* or *Numini*[3].

We must now study the further ramifications of the official policy that has been described above. In Rome it did not go far. It was perhaps in 12 B.C. that the Genius of Augustus was in official oaths included between Juppiter Optimus Maximus and the Di Penates, and after the re-organization of the cult of the Lares publici this same Genius was worshipped together with them in their public shrines[4]. It was not deification, for the Genius of a private person, being the life-spirit of his family, received sacrifice on his birthday. The cult was therefore not new in principle and did not emphasize the individual. In 7 B.C. Tiberius vowed a temple to Concordia Augusta, a deified attribute of the new order: this was dedicated in A.D. 10 or 13, and in the latter year, probably, Tiberius dedicated an altar, also in Rome, *Numini Augusti*, at

[1] The *cohors XX Palmyrenorum* at Doura had a ἱερεὺς λεγιωνάριος (Fr. Cumont, *Fouilles de Doura-Europos*, pp. 375 *sqq.* no. 14; cf. p. 113).
[2] Cf. A. Schulten, *Zeit. d. deutsch. Pal.-Verein*, LVI, 1933, pp. 117 *sqq.*, for the *sacellum* found in the fort of Masada, of the time of Vespasian, with places probably for the standard of the unit and for those of two maniples.
[3] Cf. A. von Domaszewski, *Westdeutsch. Zeit.* XIV, 1895, pp. 1 *sqq.*; R. Cagnat, *L'armée romaine d'Afrique*[2], pp. 342 *sqq.*
[4] L. R. Taylor, *The Divinity of the Roman Emperor*, p. 191, n. 20.

which the four great priestly colleges were to do annual sacrifice.
This looks very like deification and yet it is not, for after death
Augustus still had to be voted *caelestes honores*. *Numen* had been
predicated both of the Senate and of the People by Cicero[1]: it is
the more than normal will perceived in Augustus. In Italy outside Rome there is one institution which must be mentioned here
as probably owing its origin to official inspiration: the various
positions concerned with the worship of Augustus which were
open to freedmen. There are several titles, *magistri Augustales*,
seviri, *seviri Augustales*, and *Augustales*. The first emerges in 13–
12 B.C. when the *princeps* was associated with the cult of the
Lares, and it too gave a function to citizens outside the governing class. It is therefore likely that its beginnings are to be sought
in some action of the central authority, although the diversity of its
forms indicates a free and uncontrolled development in detail[2].

In Rome and Italy care had to be taken neither to institute nor
encourage anything savouring of monarchy. In the provinces, on
the other hand, some sort of cult and organization were needed for
reasons of state. The Eastern provinces had vigorous city life, and
sometimes *Koina* or associations of cities sending delegates to
common assemblies, and they had been accustomed to worship
their rulers. There was nothing to gain by breaking with these
traditions. In 29 B.C. permission was given to the Romans in
Asia and Bithynia to dedicate temples at Ephesus and Nicaea to
Roma and Divus Julius jointly and to the Greeks to do as much
at Pergamum and Nicomedia for Roma and Augustus. Roma had
been worshipped by non-Romans since 195, sometimes in conjunction with local deities. This combination of the *princeps* with
her could wound no susceptibilities. The other Eastern provinces
followed suit. Roma was not always included: certainly not in
Cyprus and Pontus[3]. The provincial cult thus set up was generally administered by the *Koinon* and the presiding high priest held
what was for natives the chief post of dignity in local society[4]. In
this as in so much else Egypt formed an exception (cf. p. 285).
There was a cult in Alexandria and in various local temples, and

[1] *Phil.* III, 13, 32; *Or. post. red. ad Quirites*, 8, 18.
[2] See Nock, *op. cit.* pp. 628 *sqq.*
[3] A. von Domaszewski, *Abhandlungen zur römischen Religion*, pp. 234 *sqq.*;
Fr. Cumont, *Studia Pontica*, III, pp. 75 *sqq.*, no. 66 (= *O.G.I.S.* 532).
[4] The term Asiarch appears to have been applied to those high priests to
whose lot it fell to celebrate the quinquennial games (A. Schulten, *Jahreshefte*,
IX, 1906, p. 66; J. Keil, *Forschungen in Ephesos*, III, p. 146 *sq.*); but the
matter is open to dispute (cf. L. R. Taylor in Foakes Jackson and Kirsopp
Lake, *The Beginnings of Christianity*, V, pp. 256 *sqq.*).

certain honours were paid to the Emperor throughout the land but there was no provincial cult for the reason that Egypt was not allowed to have any self-consciousness as a unit and there was moreover no enthusiasm to regulate. Asia had been delivered from bondage but Egypt had merely passed into the hands of absentee landlords who kept strict bailiffs.

The function of Rome in the matter of ruler-cult in the East was to permit and to regulate. In the West, Rome created the institution *de novo* as an instrument for the spreading of her culture. In 12 B.C. Drusus dedicated at Lugdunum the altar of Roma and Augustus built by sixty tribes from the three Gauls[1]. Its cult was administered by the *concilium Galliarum* composed of delegates sent annually by the tribes to elect the *sacerdos*. It should be noted that there is here no distinction of citizens and non-citizens. A similar altar was built at Oppidum Ubiorum between 9 B.C. and A.D. 4 for the intended province of Germany. In Gaul and in the Germany of Rome's dreams the central authority took action. Elsewhere in the West development was gradual and spontaneous. Thus in Tarraconensis cult by local *conventus* or associations of cities preceded provincial cult. The main development followed on Tiberius' permission to that province in A.D. 23 to erect a temple to Divus Augustus. Between that date and 64 provincial cult was organized in Lusitania and probably Baetica, Alpes Cottiae, Alpes Maritimae, Mauretania Caesariensis and Tingitana, and perhaps Sardinia: in the Flavian period probably by Gallia Narbonensis. Africa, Dacia and the Danube provinces followed later[2].

What should be done in Rome or by the provinces acting as units called for official sanction. On the other hand such sanction was not called for in the matter of worships established by municipalities unless a ruler had strong personal feelings and even these were not always obeyed. Such civic cults began in the East, as at Mitylene about 27 B.C.[3], and spread through the Empire. They were directed sometimes to Augustus alone, sometimes to Augustus and Roma. The combination with Roma is not found for the names of later Emperors and only a few of them have

[1] Hirschfeld, *C.I.L.* XIII, pp. 227 *sqq.* Some evidence points to the year 10 B.C.: perhaps Drusus summoned the meeting of the chiefs of the tribes in 12 and the dedication took place in 10 (L. R. Taylor, *The Divinity of the Roman Emperor*, p. 209).

[2] E. Kornemann, *Klio*, I, 1901, pp. 117 *sqq.* Narbonensis may fall under Tiberius; cf. A. L. Abaecherli, *Trans. Am. Phil. Assoc.* LXIII, 1932, pp. 256 *sqq.*   [3] *O.G.I.S.* 456.

flamines reserved to themselves by name. *Flamen Aug.* refers in general to the worship of the ruler of the time whoever he was. It is a remarkable fact that the development of such cults in Italy occurs mainly from 2 B.C. onwards. It is not the product of a wave of popular emotion after Actium. Its origin at this time may be explained from the dedication of the temple of Mars Ultor and of the Forum Augustum and perhaps above all from the fact that the growing up of Gaius and Lucius appeared to secure the dynasty. Municipal cult was addressed also to Livia and to other members of the Imperial house in spite of the fact that Augustus did not give any special honours to those of his kinsfolk who died. There were, again, other ways in which a town could express its devotion. It sometimes took the name Caesarea or Sebaste or altered the names of its months to honour Augustus. On the other hand the assumption that in Asia Minor the Emperor was commonly associated in worship or identified with local deities is unjustified: there are only exceptional instances of this[1].

If a municipality was free to show its loyalty in forms not always sanctioned for larger political units, so was of course an individual. Any one could erect on his estate what shrines he would, as Cicero did for his dead daughter. We know temples at Pompeii and at Beneventum and another for the *gens Augusta* at Carthage[2]. Again, at Alexandria there was a cult society called the Augustan synod of the god Imperator Caesar, with a priest and other officials[3].

There were wide possibilities in worship. There were even wider possibilities for the language of literature and art. In these the comparison or identification of persons honoured with particular deities was old and natural, for the deities supplied the traditional types of beauty and power and benevolence. It was sometimes held that the ruler was a god come down on earth; so Horace suggests that Augustus may be Mercury. The other poets of the time are full of phrases which seem to us exaggerated and artificial. Yet we must remember that there was a deep and genuine sentiment in many hearts, an enthusiasm of gratitude which had to use the warmest ways of expression which it could find. It is revealed to us in the halo of legend which grew up around Augustus in and shortly after his life[4] and again in the

---

[1] Nock, *Harv. Stud.* XLI, 1930, pp. 37 *sqq.*
[2] Volume of Plates iv, 134.
[3] Fr. Blumenthal, *Arch. f. Pap.* V, 1911, p. 331 *sq.*
[4] A. Deonna, *Rev. Hist. Rel.* LXXXIII, 1921, pp. 32 *sqq.*, 163 *sqq.*; LXXXIV, 922, pp. 77 *sqq.*

impulsive act of veneration made towards him by some sailors at Puteoli in A.D. 14.

Demonstrations of loyalty were not confined to those who were citizens or subjects of Rome. The client-princes also showed their loyalty in religious forms: Herod named Samaria Sebaste and set on its highest point a temple of Augustus, built Caesarea and erected in it a temple for Roma and Augustus with quinquennial games; Juba dedicated to Augustus a grove with an altar and temple in his new Caesarea[1]. We hear also that the client-kings consulted together about completing the Olympieum at Athens and dedicating it to Augustus.

When Augustus died, his funeral, carried out in accordance with his directions, was just like that which he had ordered for Agrippa. The one novelty is the eagle released from the pyre and thought to be carrying his soul to heaven: this symbol of apotheosis was probably borrowed from Syria and perhaps Babylonian in origin, but not unfamiliar in the Graeco-Roman world[2]. Further, Numerius Atticus swore that he had seen Augustus ascending to heaven just as Proculus had seen Romulus. Even as *sidus Julium* showed that the real self of Julius was with the gods, so this was the tangible proof for Augustus. It corresponds to the miracles which justify a saint's canonization. But whereas the saint's earthly remains are venerated in his shrine, like the relics of a Greek hero, the Emperor's ashes remained in his mausoleum and were not taken to his temple[3].

On 17 September A.D. 14 the Senate decreed that Augustus should as Divus Augustus be accepted among the gods of the State. A golden image of him was set on a couch in the temple of Mars and received the honours later to be paid to his cult image. The house at Nola in which he had died was consecrated to him: the celebration of his birthday passed to the consuls; the college of Sodales Augustales was founded: and Livia became first priestess, Germanicus a *flamen*[4]. A precedent was thus set for the inclusion of other good Emperors after their death among the gods of the State. This inclusion was the culmination of a series of honours given in return for services rendered. It was not an automatic culmination. It was warranted by miracle and approved by the authority which was necessary for any addition to the official

---

[1] Vol. of Plates iv, 202, *a*, *b*.

[2] Fr. Cumont, *Études Syriennes*, pp. 35 *sqq.*

[3] E. Bickermann, *Arch. f. Rel.* XXVII, 1929, pp. 1 *sqq.* Contrast the veneration of the body of Alexander at Alexandria.

[4] Cf. the new coin-types in Volume of Plates iv, 202, *c, d.*

circle of worships. Further, it depended on the quality shown by the man and not on the fact of his having held the supreme position. Divinity hedged a *princeps* around but was not inherent in him, however much it might and did so appear to provincials and even to individual citizens. From the constitutional point of view he stood between the mass of citizens and the gods, on the godward side but without any loss of his humanity or of his ultimate responsibility before the bar of public opinion. The celebrations during his life of his birthday and of his accession were among the most prominent features of public life[1] and at every possible turn secular and religious foundations were made in his honour or for his welfare, but it remains certain that these things did not cause to the ancients that confusion of thought which they have often caused to modern students, and that Augustus would have smiled in a puzzled way if he had been informed that he had introduced Pharaonic divine monarchy at Rome[2].

V. OFFICIAL RELIGIOUS POLICY

We have discussed earlier (pp. 475 *sqq.*) the measures taken by Augustus to restore order in public worship and to give to the new order the consecration of religion, and we have noted the steps taken against the intrusion of alien cults within the old area of the city. We have now seen how the instinct making for ruler-worship was used and regulated. Our next task is to consider a matter of permanent importance in the religious history of the Empire, the obligations and freedom of Roman citizens in their relations to the gods of the State and to other gods. So far as we can see, no obligation whatever rested on the private individual. In 42 all citizens were compelled to celebrate the birthday of the deified Julius, wearing laurel and showing joy[3]; but that was a political demonstration. Later, acts of disrespect to Imperial statues could fall under the charge of *maiestas* and this category of indictable acts was capable of extension by prosecutors who had a desire to obtain a share of their victim's goods: a wise Emperor

---

[1] Cf. the Aboda Zara as edited by W. A. L. Elmslie, in J. Armitage Robinson's *Texts and Studies*, VIII, ii, pp. 5 *sqq.* The Jews had their own ways of commemorating these occasions (J. Juster, *Les juifs*, I, p. 345).

[2] It is to be noted that Plutarch makes outspoken criticisms of the self-deification of Hellenistic kings without any feeling that what he says might be taken as reflecting on Roman practice.

[3] Dio XLVII, 18, 5. In many civic festivals all citizens were bidden to come, but we do not usually hear of penalties.

like Tiberius restrained this tendency. On the other hand, an
official position imposed certain obligations. A Roman magistrate
had religious duties to perform. We have no indication of what
would have happened had he refused, and the case no doubt did
not arise: we hear of a prosecution of Aemilius Scaurus in 104 B.C.
'because by his neglect many *sacra* of the Roman people had
suffered,' but the prosecution took the form of an indictment by
a tribune before the people and it is clear that there was no regular
procedure provided for the contingency. Any dignitary who
belonged to the Emperor's entourage would be obliged to
attend religious functions. Again, a *decurio* in a municipality had
religious duties, such as filling the office of *flamen*: hence Jews
were exempt from the obligation of holding the office[1]. But in
private life the occasions for any sort of issue of irreligion being
raised were very few; a husband might be moved to take steps if
his wife became a Jewish proselyte (p. 495), or the former owner
of a slave if his freedman refused to take his part in family rites.
Again, an inheritance often carried with it the obligation of
maintaining certain *sacra* traditional in a *gens*, and they were in
effect a charge upon the estate. Neglect of them was a breach of
fas. It involved social disapprobation and the risk of degradation
by the censors, but could not apparently lead to a prosecution, at
least not in the period which we know. Even perjury was regarded
as a matter which it lay with the gods to avenge, except in cases
where the oath was taken by the Emperor's genius and could be
construed as *maiestas*[2].

Criminal law had no wide category of *laesa religio* or *sacrilegium*. Apart from proceedings against Christians as described
by their own writers, *sacrilegium* is applied only to overt acts of
sacrilege in the modern sense[3], *laesa religio* and its synonyms to
similar acts or again to the profanation of the ceremony of the
Bona Dea by Clodius (and there a special *quaestio* had to be constituted on the motion of a tribune); Augustus regarded adultery
by members of his own family as falling under the rubric of

[1] Tertullian, *de corona militis*, 11 in enumerating the unchristian acts
that a soldier may be obliged to do, does not mention pagan worship. That
was hard for a centurion, but not for a private soldier, to escape. But Jews
had no regular exemption from military service (Juster, *op. cit.* II, pp. 265 *sqq.*).

[2] A refusal to take an oath was no doubt punishable.

[3] An imperial rescript, or edict, said to come from Nazareth and called
Διάταγμα Καίσαρος, prescribes punishment for tomb-violation as being as
heinous as sacrilege (Fr. Cumont, *Rev. hist.* CLXIII, 1930, pp. 241 *sqq.*:
F. de Zulueta in *J. R. S.* XXII, 1932, pp. 184 *sqq.*).

laesae religiones[1]. If Horace had carried to its logical conclusion his policy of being *parcus deorum cultor et infrequens* no action could have been taken against him, and Tertullian's statement, *sed apud vos quodvis colere ius est praeter deum verum*, represents a general rule to which there are only certain specific exceptions.

These exceptions rest either on enactments of the Senate or People or on the exercise by magistrates of their general police jurisdiction or *coercitio*: they are not initiated by the Pontifex Maximus. A magistrate had in virtue of his *imperium* an extensive power of giving orders to citizens and an even more extensive power of giving orders to non-citizens. Disobedience was commonly punishable even though the action which had been commanded was in no sense a normal obligation[2]. Again, measures might be taken against any who appeared by their action to be exciting the popular mind or in danger of disturbing public order. The classic example is the suppression of the Bacchanalia in 186 B.C. Livy represents the consul as referring on this occasion to the frequency with which the magistrates had been charged to prohibit foreign rites, to ban sacrificers and soothsayers from the forum, to gather together and to burn books of prophecy, to abolish every mode of sacrificing other than the Roman[3]. Again, in 139 B.C. the Jews in Rome were banished for 'attempting to corrupt Roman morals by the cult of Juppiter Sabazius[4].' It is the proselytizers not the proselytes who are the object of attack. In general, religious professionals, like magicians and astrologers, and occasionally philosophers, were liable to be attacked in this way. It must be remembered that the lay character of most official priesthoods left a wide range of emotional needs to be satisfied by unofficial professionals. The great majority of these professionals would be non-citizens, and the legal rights of aliens who were not men of substance were somewhat tenuous in practice. There was of course nothing to prevent a man from having an image of Isis in his *lararium*, or frequenting a temple outside the mile limit, and we know that the temples were frequented[5]. It

[1] Tacitus, *Ann.* III, 24. R. Heinze, *Ber. sächs. Ges. Wiss.* LXII, 1910, p. 334 n. 2.

[2] Compare Pliny's remark, *Ep.* X, 96, 3: *pertinaciam certe et inflexibilem obstinationem debere puniri.*

[3] XXXIX, 16, 8; cf. IV, 30; XXV, 1.

[4] Val. Max. I, 3, 3.

[5] Dessau 3090 is notable: a dedication for Emperor, all ruled by him, Senate, and People, and the world outside by a freedman Zethus *Mercurio aeterno deo Iovi Iunoni regin., Minervae, Soli, Lunae, Apollini, Dianae, Fortunae...nae, Opi, Isi, Pietati, Fatis d[ivinis(?)]...iussu Iovis aram augustam*

is as in Spain under the old régime, when synagogues and Protestant churches might not be built in the main streets. The Romans indeed gave privileges to synagogues, but that was a measure necessitated in the main by the anti-Semitism of Alexandria and of other Greek cities and by the desirability of avoiding the disorders which might arise if it was not officially restrained, partly also by the State's insistence on its control over the formation of associations, partly by the need of protecting Jews against capricious interference by governors of provinces.

With the beliefs of subject races Augustus interfered very little. If he forbade Roman citizens to take part in Druidical worship, his purpose was political: to withdraw Gauls who had received the citizenship from a strongly nationalist influence. True, among foreign worships he had his preferences; he was initiated at Eleusis, refused to visit the Apis calf which appeared in Egypt during his presence there, and praised Gaius Caesar for not going to the Temple at Jerusalem. But he left, for example, Jewish privileges untouched. Their places of worship were protected from robbery, their sacred books or moneys from theft, and they were given free right to send offerings to Jerusalem[1]. Where Rome interfered, it was in matters of mundane consequence[2]. The right of temples in Egypt to afford sanctuary to criminals and runaway slaves was controlled but not abolished. Finance came very largely into the hands of the civil administration, for what may be called a national church had political significance, and the financial official in charge of the treasury department called the *Idios Logos* acquired perhaps as early as Augustus a considerable measure of control. This authority showed itself in the supervision of the personnel, even in such details as the fining of a priest who wore woollen clothing or allowed his hair to grow. The *princeps* was to the clergy Pharaoh[3]

---

posuit. Salus Semonia, Populi Victoria. Mercurio is a later addition, perhaps to correct an accidental omission: the last four words are also added. In them as in *Opi* and *aram augustam*, 'an altar deserving reverence,' we see the influence of Augustan archaism. *Isi* introduces an oriental element.

[1] Josephus, *Ant.* XVI [vi, 1], 162 *sqq.*; cf. J. Juster, *Les juifs*, 1, pp. 213 *sqq.*

[2] Or in answer to special appeals, as when the priest of the Cabiri at Miletus appealed to the proconsul Caecina Paetus (before A.D. 42) to secure for him the allowances previously made for the cult, and the proconsul wrote to the city saying that the claim seemed reasonable (A. Rehm, *Milet*, 1, ix, p. 177 *sq.*, no. 360).

[3] He has his cartouches. For an exceptional instance of old ideas in a votive Demotic stele, cf. H. Gauthier, *Livre des rois*, v, p. 59: 'le dieu grand, qui donne la vie à Parthénios' (of Claudius). Ordinarily Demotic texts give translations of Greek forms.

and is represented as completing or restoring temples[1], whether
he really did or is so shown in obedience to convention, but
in Egypt he was the stepfather of his people. The Pharaonic
equivalent of 'Caesaropapism' may have meant little enough
to the Ptolemies but it was a theory for their kingdom; to the
Roman rulers any such shows were no more than survivals.

But, in this as in other matters, Egypt remained a country
apart, and in general religion was left to itself. At the same time
the Empire was bound to make a difference. To the religious life
of the East Rome brought nothing new but the substitution of
the cult of the Emperor for that of earlier kings and the introduction of the Capitoline *cultus* of the Roman military colonies.
The claims of the older culture were not challenged. But the
West took the culture which the Empire brought as a superior
thing and hastened to assimilate its gods to those of Rome. Though
such names as Epona persisted, native gods in countless instances
appeared as Mars or Mercury. This was a spontaneous development, promoted above all by the imposing temples and monuments
built by the conquerors and by the influence of Latin literature[2].
Thus in later times Latin was the only language of Christian
liturgy in the West, while the East came to use its several ver-
naculars[3].

Augustan policy was followed or even exaggerated by Tiberius.
This we see above all in the matter of ruler-worship, which was
naturally the matter most in question under the early Principate.
Suetonius says of Tiberius (*Tib.* 26):

'He forbade the decreeing to himself of temples, *flamines* and priests, and
even of statues and representations without his permission, and he permitted
them only on the condition that they should be set, not among the images of
the gods, but among the decorations of the temple. He forbade men from
swearing allegiance to his *acta* and from naming the month September
Tiberius and October Livius.'

This represents the Emperor's personal preferences. In A.D. 23
he allowed the province of Asia to build a temple, erected in due
course at Smyrna, to himself, Livia and the Senate. There the
tradition was old, and it was hardly worth while to oppose it. But
in 25 when the Spanish province of Baetica proposed to build a
temple to Livia and himself he refused. We find municipal priests
of Tiberius in many places[4] and Dio[5] says of the time at which

[1] W. Otto, *Priester und Tempel im hellenistischen Ägypten*, I, pp. 386 *sqq.*
[2] Wissowa, *Arch. f. Rel.* XIX, 1918, pp. 1 *sqq.*; A. D. Nock, *Gnomon*,
VI, 1930, pp. 34 *sqq.*; cf. the Mainz column, Volume of Plates IV, 194.
[3] Cf. Fr. Cumont, *Mélanges Fredericq*, pp. 63 *sqq.*
[4] Cf. Rietra, note on Suetonius, *loc. cit.* (pp. 13 *sqq.*).   [5] LVIII, 4, 4.

Sejanus was powerful that men sacrificed to his images just as to those of Tiberius. What Suetonius records represents the wishes of the *princeps*, as expressed when a community asked his permission to establish a particular form of cult, the intention being no doubt the advertisement of their loyalty. How he answered on such occasions we know from an inscription of A.D. 15 or 16, parts of which are found on two stones at Gythium in Laconia[1]. The first stone prescribes that the ephors are to provide *eikones*—probably representations on painted panels for the wall of the stage or the orchestra—of Augustus, Tiberius, and Livia which the *agoranomoi* are to place in the theatre. Incense is to be offered in the theatre and a bull sacrificed in the Caesareum for the welfare of the rulers and there are to be six days of theatrical celebrations, one for each of the Imperial personages named, a fourth for the Victory of Germanicus, a fifth for the Aphrodite of Drusus, a sixth for Titus Quinctius Flamininus. The second stone begins by naming penalties for any one who proposes the violation of a cult, presumably Imperial, and then gives a letter of Tiberius.

'The envoy Decimus Turranius Nicanor, who was sent by you to me and my mother, gave me your letter, to which were appended the provisions made by you for the worship of my father and for our honour. I applaud your intentions and think that all men in general and your city in particular ought to reserve special honours suited to the greatness of my father's services to the whole universe; for myself I am contented with more modest and human honours. However my mother will give you an answer when she knows your decision about the honours to be paid to her.'

Since the texts appear thus on two stones, it is impossible to prove that the town of Gythium did not first pass a *lex sacra* which instituted direct worship of Tiberius and Livia and ended with the sanctions, and then, on receipt of the Emperor's letter, pass a second law, the one which is preserved. But if the town was making the validity of the law depend on Tiberius' approval we should expect it to end with provisions for the sending of the ambassador. It seems safe, therefore, to suppose that one law only was passed and a copy of it sent to Rome as a demonstration of loyalty. In that case it is the very modest provisions of the extant *lex sacra* which the *princeps* courteously deprecates. The attitude of Livia to the proposals, if not also that of Tiberius to Livia, remains enigmatic.

---

[1] First published by S. B. Kougeas in ΕΛΛΗΝΙΚΑ, I, 1928, pp. 7 *sqq.* and 152 *sqq.*

A letter to Cos in A.D. 15 in answer to an embassy, begins with thanks and then breaks off: it may well have been an answer to a proposal like that of Gythium; *I.G.R.R.* IV, 1042.

A striking illustration of the spontaneity of this attitude and of the official reaction to it is afforded by an edict issued by Germanicus to the Alexandrians during his stay early in A.D. 19[1]. He thanks them for their goodwill but says:

'I altogether deprecate those acclamations of yours which are invidious to me and put me on a level with deity, for they are appropriate only to him who is really the saviour and benefactor of the whole human race—my father, and to his mother, who is my grandmother. All that is mine is but a reflection of their divinity. Wherefore, if you do not obey me, you will compel me not to appear before you often.'

The natural inference from the phrasing is that the acclamations were simply 'saviour' and 'benefactor,' which, little as Germanicus may have known it, were readily given even to less exalted personages[2].

In other respects the policy of Tiberius conformed to that of Augustus. The rights of some Hellenic temples to grant asylum were examined and curtailed by senatorial decrees. In Egypt he, like Augustus and like his successors, is represented in temple relief (as for instance at Dendera and Philae) as making offerings to local deities: this again may either correspond to fact or purely to a convention[3]. Oriental cults at Rome were sometimes visited with his displeasure. In A.D. 19 an *eques* Decius Mundus gained his way with one Paulina, a devotee of Isis, priests of the goddess being bribed to inform her that Anubis wished for her company. The woman's credulity, not wholly shared by her friends, was later undeceived, and the *princeps*, being informed, crucified the priests, destroyed the temple, and had the image of Isis thrown into the river. In the same year a Roman matron Fulvia was persuaded to send a purple robe and gold to the temple of Jerusalem. The four Jews who persuaded her, appropriated the offerings, and, on the information of her husband, the Emperor expelled the race of Jews from Rome. Four thousand of them were enlisted for military service in Sardinia and recalcitrants were executed[4].

---

[1] Wilamowitz and Zucker, *S.B. Berlin*, 1911, pp. 794 *sqq.*; C. Cichorius, *Römische Studien*, pp. 375 *sqq.*; U. Wilcken, *Hermes*, LXIII, 1928, pp. 48 *sqq.*

[2] It should be noted that the dedication formula of the temple of Augustus at Philae uses σωτῆρι καὶ εὐεργέτῃ without θεῷ (*O.G.I.S.* 657).

[3] Cf. Gauthier, *op. cit.* v, p. 30 (offering to Pakysis).

[4] Josephus, *Ant.* XVIII [3, 4], 65 *sqq.* with Rietra's note on Sueton. *Tiber.* 36. The story of the Isis incident comes from hostile sources, but something must have happened to provoke intervention. Seneca, *Ep.* 108, 22 indicates a general suspicion of alien beliefs at this time. The expulsion may have been confined to Jews who were *peregrini* and at any time liable to such treatment (cf. E. T. Merrill, *Cl. Phil.* XIV, 1919, pp. 365 *sqq.*).

Early in his reign there were decrees for the expulsion of 'Chaldaeans,' astrologers, diviners and the like, an act of State by an Emperor who was himself a devoted student of the art, since the days when he was convinced of the powers of its notable professor Thrasyllus (p. 608), so much so that he is believed to have been logical enough to be careless about the gods and religious exercises.

In contrast to Tiberius, Gaius abandoned the Augustan wariness towards Oriental cults. It was in his reign that the Isiac festival was established in Rome[1] and, if we may trust Josephus, the *princeps* himself donned female garb and took part in mysteries which he instituted[2].

This conduct belongs to the period in which Gaius had broken with tradition. He started conventionally by proposing that Tiberius should be deified. The resentment of the senatorial class caused this to fall through[3], but Gaius as master of the Arval Brothers sacrificed in his memory on 25 May 38. Earlier in 37 he had dedicated the shrine of Augustus built by Tiberius. As for personal worship he started by forbidding images of himself and requesting the annulment of a decree ordering sacrifices to his Fortune. But honours were heaped on him because of his popularity: the day of his accession, March 18, was called the Parilia and treated as a refounding of Rome. When his sister Drusilla died in 38 she was consecrated by the Senate and given a priesthood and two images, one in the temple of Venus Genetrix, equal in size to that of Venus, another in the Curia; her birthday was made a public holiday on a par with the Megalesia and she was made the deity for women's oaths. Here, also, apotheosis was justified by the statement of a senator that he had seen her ascending to heaven. Drusilla was given the name Panthea and was declared a worthy recipient of divine honours in all cities[4].

Presently Gaius began to seek the most manifest worship. It was perhaps in June 40 that being provoked by the fact that the Jews of Jamnia had destroyed an altar erected to him by the Gentile inhabitants of the city, he ordered a statue of Zeus with his own features to be placed in the Temple at Jerusalem. An embassy of Jews from Alexandria coming by reason of the troubles

---

[1] Mommsen, *C.I.L.* I[2], p. 333 *sq.*   [2] *Ant.* xix [1, 5], 30.

[3] It perhaps follows from Seneca, *Apocol.* 2, that there was a witness of the ascension of Tiberius.

[4] At Athens we have a dedication probably to Gaius and a deified sister whose name has been effaced, either Drusilla or Livilla. (P. Graindor, *B.C.H.* xxxviii, 1914, pp. 401 *sqq.*) Drusilla was honoured by games in Cyzicus (Ditt.[3] 798) and by a priestess at Epidaurus. (*I.G.* iv, 1400.)

which started with the pogrom in 38 obtained a hearing, and were greeted with the words, 'You are the wretches who do not believe that I am a god, although I am recognized as such among all the rest of mankind.'[1] This formidable allocution was, however, followed by indulgence to such invincible ignorance. The order about Jerusalem was withdrawn and then again issued. Nor was it only Jewish susceptibilities that were shocked. Gaius is said to have appeared in the dress and with the insignia now of the Dioscuri, now of Dionysus, or again of Mercury, Apollo, Mars, Neptune, and even Juno, Diana, and Venus. Paeans were sung to him in his various divine characters. He gave orders—not put into effect—that the statue of Zeus at Olympia should be brought to Rome and have his head substituted for the original. He prolonged his palace to the Forum, turning the temple of Castor and Pollux into his vestibule: he appeared between the images of the twin gods to receive adoration; he uttered oracles from a lofty platform in the dress of Juppiter; he was hailed as Juppiter Latiaris. He instituted for his own godhead a special temple—Dio says two, one at the public expense, one on the Palatine at his own—and a priesthood and carefully thought out sacrifices. He invited the moon to his embraces[2]; he spoke to Capitoline Juppiter as one god to another, and threw a bridge over from the palace to the Capitol and commenced the building of a new house on the Capitol; he sought to appropriate Apollo's temple at Didyma (the truth being that he extended its asylum privileges by two miles[3] and that a temple was built in his honour at Miletus by an association of Lovers of Augustus (φιλοσέβαστοι) from the province as a whole)[4]; he set his daughter Drusilla on the knees of Capitoline Juppiter and gave her to Minerva to suckle.

Such is the tradition, which shows clear signs of exaggeration and sensationalism; but there is no doubt that Gaius received direct worship in Rome and it is possible that irritation with the Jews inspired him with the idea of this policy. Of the honours paid to Drusilla we have spoken. Livilla was honoured at Pergamum as a new Nikephoros, enthroned with Athena Polias and sharing a priest with her and Athena Nikephoros, but this is

---

[1] Philo, *Legatio*, 353. Cf. pp. 311 and 662.

[2] As she is said later to have come to those of Alexander of Abonuteichos.

[3] *O.G.I.S.* 473. It may be suggested that the privilege of ability to receive bequests possessed by this god (*Ulpiani Epit.* XXII, 6) was conferred on him at this time.

[4] Inscription published by Th. Wiegand, *Abh. preuss. Akad.* 1911, *Anh.* 1, pp. 65 *sqq.*

spontaneous and normal[1]. Even in this sphere the princeps showed his impulsive individuality. In 39, when he deported his surviving sisters to the Pontian islands, he forbade the awarding of honours to any of his relations.

The Jewish question and the question of ruler-worship were both raised before Claudius at the beginning of his reign. In 41 embassies from Alexandria evoked a letter addressed to that city (see below, p. 683). In his rescript he permits the keeping of his birthday as an Augustan day (ἡμέρα Σεβαστή), and the setting, in the places specified, of statues (ἀνδριάντες) of himself and of his family. He accepts a gold statue to Pax Augusta on condition that it shall be dedicated in Rome[2], but accepts the other statue offered, unfortunately without mentioning what it is (perhaps a statue of Messallina, perhaps one of himself), and certain other honours. A high priest and temple for himself he will not have, 'For I do not wish to seem vulgar to my contemporaries and I hold that temples and the like have by all ages been attributed to the gods alone.' After handling certain Alexandrian questions, he comes to the question of responsibility for the trouble between the Jews and Greeks of that city and speaks in the tone of a magistrate who binds over both parties to keep the peace. It is plain that Claudius was not an anti-Semitist; the Imperial interest lay solely in the maintenance of order.

His reserve in the matter of ruler-worship is a reversion to tradition. It is no breach of it that he consecrated Livia in 41, a fact to which the dedication of an altar to Pietas Augusta perhaps alludes, or that a temple was erected to him at Camulodunum: it was a necessary means of romanization in a new province. Naturally the usual language of courtly flattery continued. The very governor who published the letter to the Alexandrians says in his preamble 'that you may marvel at the greatness of our god Caesar[3].' Scribonius Largus refers to him three times as *deus noster Caesar*, Seneca speaks of his *divinae manus* (similar phraseology had been applied to Tiberius and had excited his irony), Phaedrus of *divina domus*, and Seneca in his *Consolatio ad Polybium* refers to him as a saviour.

In other matters of religion Claudius returned to tradition and we see in what he did the work not only of the follower of Augustus

---

[1] *Harv. Stud.* XLI, 1930, p. 24.

[2] ἐπὶ Ῥώμης ἀνατεθήσεται, as Wilcken reads for ἐπεὶ Ῥώμης.

[3] Cf. Gauthier, *op. cit.* V, pp. 50, 52, 54, for 'god', or 'god, son of god', in Demotic texts of the years 42 to 48: there are no Greek parallels from Egypt in the Emperor's life.

but also of the student of Roman and Etruscan history. His censorship of 47 was marked by special activity. In it he celebrated secular games in a year resting on calculations other than those of Augustus; he raised certain families to the patriciate in order to fill priestly offices; he also took steps to revive the Etruscan haruspices, always consulted in Republican times[1], denouncing in his speech thereon the encroachment of foreign rites. In 49 he celebrated the *augurium Salutis* and extended the pomerium. In his triumph over Britain in 44 he ascended the steps of the Capitol on his knees. He ordered an expiatory rite for the supposed incest of Silanus, he caused the praetor to announce public holidays on the occasion of earthquakes, and as *pontifex maximus* conducted an *obsecratio* when a bird of ill-omen was seen on the Capitol. He made treaties with the old fetial ceremony and always took an oath before co-opting priests. Motives of public convenience caused him in 43 to abolish many sacrifices and holidays, but that is fully in accordance with the Roman theory of the State's powers, just as much as his addition to the Saturnalia in 45 of the fifth day designated by Gaius and then dropped. He put down Druidism because of its political danger, and urged that the ruined temple of Venus at Eryx be restored at the cost of the Aerarium[2].

It is not inconsistent with this policy that he thought of transferring the Eleusinian mysteries to Rome, for, as we have seen, Augustus like many other conservative Romans had been initiated at Eleusis, and the identification of Demeter with Ceres might make the action appear to be no more than the addition of a foreign ceremony to this old cult. Nor is there any inconsistency in his introduction of the festival of Attis, a naturalized and romanized Attis, to be sure, for the position of *archigallus* now became a dignified priesthood held by a citizen and not a eunuch, not only in Rome but perhaps also in Pessinus[3]. The motives are not hard to find. In the Augustan age the emphasis laid on the Trojan origins of Rome in general and the Julian family in particular led to an emphasis on Cybele, and among the temples which Augustus restored was that of the Magna Mater on the Palatine[4]: Claudius had perhaps a personal interest in the cult because of the legend of the part played by Claudia Quinta in the arrival of the goddess at

[1] E. Bormann, *Jahreshefte*, II, 1899, p. 134 has shown that the *ordo* LX *haruspicum* existed in the time of Augustus.

[2] It is not irrelevant that Aeneas was said to have founded this shrine; *Aen.* v, 759.

[3] J. Carcopino, *Mél. d'arch. et d'hist.* XL, 1923, pp. 135 *sqq.*, 237 *sqq.*

[4] *Res Gestae* 19 speaks of it as *built* by him.

Rome. It is in no sense a surrender to the East. It is notable that, in the *Apocolocyntosis* of Seneca, Claudius is introduced to Olympus not by Attis, who could have been made the subject of much wit (the servant of Agrippina introduced by the servant of Cybele), but by the archaic Diespiter[1].

In his speech on the revival of *haruspices* Claudius had deplored the strength of foreign superstition, and in 52 a decree of the Senate was passed to expel astrologers from Italy: it arose out of the prosecution of Furius Scribonianus for having enquired into the time at which the Emperor would die. In 53, when Statilius Taurus was put on his trial before the Senate, the charges of extortion were aggravated by an allegation of magic superstitions. This statement would normally relate to something of the sort (just as in 66, when Soranus was accused of treason, his daughter was put on trial for having spent money on magicians: she had sought by their aid to find how her house would fare and whether Nero would be appeased). It has however been connected with the discovery of an underground place of worship near the Porta Maggiore in Rome on ground which has been thought to fall within the gardens of the Statilii. The symbolism of the remarkable stuccoes with which it is decorated appears to point to the idea of the liberation of the soul from the body and it is likely that the sect which used this chapel was Neopythagorean[2]. Those who were devoted to its teachings were particularly liable to be suspected of magic.

Claudius on his accession at once restored the Jewish immunities withdrawn by Gaius but in the same year, in view of their increase in numbers in Rome, he forbade them to hold meetings[3], disbanding also the active associations which Caligula had allowed to form anew. In 49 he banished from Rome the Jews who 'at the instigation of Chrestus continually raised tumults[4].' It is possible that the tumults in question arose from the presence among the Roman Jews of some who maintained not only that a Messiah had appeared and would shortly return to inaugurate the New Age but probably—what was far worse—that Gentiles

---

[1] This observation is due to Dr Scramuzza.

[2] J. Carcopino, *La basilique pythagoricienne de la Porte Majeure*. The scene in the apse (Vol. of Plates iv, 182) represents Sappho's leap into the Leucadian waters. Carcopino, p. 382, draws attention to Pliny, *N.H.* XXII, 20 as proving Pythagorean interest in this story; *ob hoc et Phaonem Lesbium dilectum a Sappho, multa circa hoc non magorum solum uanitate sed etiam Pythagoricorum:* but the second *hoc*, like the first, must refer to a particular charm for becoming lovable.

[3] Dio LX, 6, 6.   [4] Suetonius, *Claud.* 25.

might be admitted to table-fellowship without submitting to circumcision[1].

The death of Claudius was promptly followed by his deification. A clever skit by Seneca parodies the procedure (the witness of the ascent to heaven and the senatorial decision on the merits of the case), but is no more to be taken as an attack on the institution than are mediaeval parodies like the *Evangelium secundum marcas* on the New Testament. We hear now of *Sodales Augustales Claudiales*, of a *flamen* and *flaminica*. The honours to Claudius were later neglected by Nero and revived by Vespasian: a temple was commenced by Agrippina on the Caelian but 'almost completely destroyed by Nero,' probably in connection with the construction of the distributing section of the Aqua Claudia which Nero extended to the Caelian[2]. The new régime was in general normal and the new Emperor concerned to honour the memory of Augustus[3]. In 54 the Senate, in order to compliment the young Emperor on the measures taken to meet the Eastern situation, voted that a representation of him should be set in the temple of Mars Ultor and should be as large as the cult image of the god. There is no statement that worship should be paid to it, and as late as 65, when Nero's megalomania had fully developed, he refused the proposal that a temple should be built at public expense to Divus Nero; the omen was unpropitious. He called April Neroneus, but for this he had precedents, as also for the consecration of his dead child by Poppaea and of Poppaea herself. On the other hand, it cannot be denied that, as the reign proceeded, a tendency towards the deification of the Emperor as ruler of the world became more and more marked (see below, p. 732), even when allowance is made for the traditional element in the writings of poets and the decrees of the Greek communities. Nero ended by going beyond precedent in the erection of a colossus of the Sun with his own features in front of the Golden House, in his representation with a radiate crown on coins[4], and in the depicting of himself driving a chariot among the stars on the hangings over the theatre in 66.

Suetonius says of Nero that he disregarded all religious sanc-

---

[1] St Paul's epistle to the Roman church makes it quite clear that it at least contained a Gentile element (i, 13) and probable that questions of food ritually pure and impure had arisen in it (xiv: cf. G. Kittel, *Zeit. neutest. Wiss.* xxx, 1931, p. 155 *sq.*).

[2] Platner-Ashby, *Topographical Dictionary of Ancient Rome*, p. 120.

[3] Suetonius, *Nero*, 12; 25.

[4] Not apparently till A.D. 64; cf. Volume of Plates iv, 202, *e*.

tities save that of the Dea Syria and even her he subsequently despised, cleaving only to his devotion to the image of a girl given him by a plebeian as a talisman against conspiracies[1]: just after receiving it he discovered one and sacrificed to the image three times a day. There is, however, an interesting record of the impression made on him and on society in general by the visit of Tiridates in 66. He was strictly religious and had brought Magi with him, and he even initiated Nero in their ritual forms[2]. This should mean that Tiridates allowed Nero to be present at a Persian communion—such as we know not only in Persia but also in South Russia. Pliny further suggests that Nero made experiments in necromancy. It appears that he was possessed by the religious inquisitiveness common in the age. Like Tiberius he had an astrological confidant, Ti. Claudius Balbillus, perhaps the man whom we know as prefect of Egypt.

Under Claudius the phenomenon of Christianity was hardly known as a thing apart from Judaism. About the beginning of Nero's reign a Roman citizen named Paul, who had become involved in a riot at Jerusalem, insisted on his right of being heard by the Emperor. The charge against him was probably sedition, lying in the cause of a riot by the introduction of Gentiles into the Temple and perhaps aggravated by an insult to the high priest in the Sanhedrin: in the interests of peace the Romans were willing to sacrifice individuals to Jewish susceptibilities[3]. The case was not heard for two years. The result may have been an acquittal or a collapse of proceedings owing to the failure of the accusers to appear. The value of the tradition that Paul lived to visit Spain and was executed in the troubles arising out of the fire of Rome in 64 cannot be determined with certainty[4]. The persecution that followed the great fire shows Christianity as a known mass movement in Rome. After the fire supplications of the traditional type were held to the gods. Whatever be the precise interpretation of the narrative of Tacitus[5], it must imply that the existence of Christians in Rome was well known, as was

---

[1] *Nero*, 56, *icuncula puellaris*, very likely an image specially made in accordance with recipes such as we find in the magic papyri.

[2] Magos secum adduxerat, magicis etiam cenis eum initiaverat. Pliny, *N.H.* xxx, 17. Cf. Fr. Cumont, in *Riv. Fil.* LXI, 1933, pp. 145 *sqq.*

[3] So the killing of a sacred animal in Egypt was made a capital offence.

[4] Ed. Schwartz, *Nachr. Götting. Gesellsch.* 1907, pp. 288 *sqq.*, and others argue that the original trial ended in Paul's execution. From the Roman point of view there was a substantial case against him.

[5] *Ann.* xv, 44; on this, see below, p. 725 *sq.* and Note 8, p. 887 *sq.*

indeed natural, for inasmuch as the ancients read less than we do, they talked even more, and oral information spread rapidly, and we know from the Epistle to the Philippians (iv, 22) that adherents of the new movement were to be found in the service of the Emperor in Rome. However little credence we may attach to the suggestion of Nero's responsibility for the fire, it is clear that public opinion would demand scapegoats. Here as on previous occasions we see that special charges were needed to inspire action against the members of a particular sect. There is an apparent exception in 57 when Pomponia Graecina was accused of *externa superstitio* and left to her husband's judgment, who acquitted her. The gravamen of the charge may really have been adultery (we could have imagined such a charge against Paulina). It is hard to see why she was accused (Paulina or Fulvia had not been), unless perhaps the *senatus consultum* passed under Tiberius could still be invoked[1]. It is notable that Paul when in *libera custodia* at Rome was not prevented from teaching those who came to him. Certainty is not attainable, but it is likely that under Nero the name of Christian became punishable though the matter remained legally indefinite: so much may be deduced from Pliny's correspondence with Trajan (Book x, *Epp.* 96–7), and from Tertullian's statements.

VI. PERSONAL RELIGION

In considering personal religion we must begin with Rome, for Rome was now not merely the capital of the world of the time but also the centre in which intellectual religious and artistic movements converged. We know its atmosphere well from Augustan art and literature. We have seen their glorification of the new order: we may now remark on their strong emotional attachment to the rustic worships of Italian country life. Behind this last there lies an Alexandrian tradition partly due to the new life in great cities. But the worships were in fact alive, as we see in later dedications by soldiers, and they were the worships of the milieu from which the poets themselves came. It is something more than a convention which prompts Virgil's passionate outburst, 'Blessed is he who has won to the heart of the universe: he is beyond good

---

[1] She may have been accused of consulting astrologers about the Emperor, or of refusing to take part in some official celebration: but if either supposition were true we should expect Tacitus to make pathetic use of the facts. The immunity granted by Claudius as recorded in Josephus (*Ant.* xix [5, 3], 287–91) mentions only Jews, *i.e.* Jews by birth.

and evil. But that is too much for ordinary humanity to attain: it is a very good second best to know the gods of the country, to live the life of the country[1].' The same spirit appears in Horace's praise of the simple piety of Phidyle, in the prayers of Tibullus to the gods of his home, in Propertius' picture of the old rite at Lanuvium, in passages of the *Fasti*.

The poets know the new Oriental cults, above all that of Isis, as the favourite devotion of their mistresses from the demi-monde. Ovid betrays a certain fascination for the exotic; he prays to Isis, not to Lucina, to help Corinna in her travail, and he attaches to Isis and tells as a miracle of hers the story of Telethusa[2]. But these things, like the more influential phenomenon of astrology and like magic, are foreign to the educated as a class. In the Campana reliefs, belonging to this period, and in the stuccos of the Casa Farnesina there are numerous representations of scenes relating to the old-established Dionysiac and Eleusinian rites, but only very rare representations of Egyptian priestly figures, and they need not mean more than the commoner scenes of Nile life, which had then something of the interest which China possessed for Europeans of the eighteenth century. Again, Egyptian subjects are not common on the popular Arretine pottery[3].

Religious tendencies lay in the sphere of feeling, not of thought. The Augustan age in Rome is not one of creative religious thought, not one of creative thought in any sphere, but one of action and of feeling. The ideas with which men operate are inherited—Stoic, Epicurean, Neopythagorean. Both Horace and Virgil start from Epicureanism. Virgil's old self breaks out in Dido's cry, *scilicet is superis labor est, ea cura quietos sollicitat*; but it is mastered by the emotional values of Stoic-Platonic mysticism and by a conviction in Providential over-ruling, a conviction caused by the Augustan bringing of order out of chaos, which seemed to supply a reason which Cicero lacked for belief in a supernatural system—for it is that and not the mythology, always lightly held or allegorically interpreted, which is at stake. Some such change of mood is indicated by the ode of Horace (I, 34) which describes his conversion by a thunderclap out of a clear sky. We have seen earlier (p. 478) how he gave expression to the religious and moral ideas of the Augustan order in his Odes but even in them he sounds like a man who is repeating a lesson which he is trying to make himself believe, and his self-revelation in the Epistles shows him as one

---

[1] *Georgics*, II, 490 *sqq.*   [2] *Met.* IX, 667 *sqq.*
[3] M. Rostovtzeff, *Mystic Italy*, p. 124; G. H. Chase, *Catalogue of Arretine Pottery in the Museum of Fine Arts at Boston*, p. 70.

who thinks that in face of the uncharted there is nothing to do except to concentrate on the preservation of a calm and dignified attitude. This point of view looks purely intellectual, but it also contains a strong element of emotion—on the one hand, the feeling that certain practices and attitudes are Roman and worthy, certain others are un-Roman and contemptible, on the other hand, the distinction of *religio* and *superstitio*. This was philosophic in origin (in fact Academic), but had come to be a matter of class feeling, found outside speculative circles; in the beautiful eulogy on Turia we read that she was religious without superstition[1].

The feeling for rustic piety and for the past, as we see it in the sceptical Livy, was not confined to court circles. If we look at the mural paintings which in Pompeii correspond to our wall papers we find as the commonest scene of all a rustic shrine with a sacred tree in an enclosure. Cult was around you at every point; the possibility of its abandonment did not occur to you. Every city had its temples, every house its *lararium*. Horace's concept of eternity is

dum Capitolium
scandit cum tacita virgine pontifex.

And around cult there was now for many this emotional atmosphere which prepared the way for the piety of the Antonine age just as Gothic romanticism prepared the way for the Catholic revival of De Maistre and Montalembert. In any case rationalism was something superimposed, something a little on its defence. Religion, or we should rather say cult—which is what it was—was a fact of life, philosophy was an interpretation.

In society outside the ruling classes—the society from which the ruling classes of the Flavian and later ages came—there were fewer intellectual and aristocratic inhibitions on belief. The Egyptian cults made a more direct appeal to human emotion and won many adherents, though it would be a mistake to suppose that they bulked as large as older worships even in these circles[2]. Again, astrology revolutionized the world in which lived men with no tincture of philosophy by bringing them for the first time in touch with universals. The declamations of philosophers and satirists against *superstitio* bring home to us the fact that they and their class felt themselves to be, as indeed they were, a very

---

[1] Dessau 8393, 30, [*religionis*] *sine superstitione*: there can be no doubt of the correctness of the restoration.

[2] It is, however, interesting to see the festivals of Isis and Sarapis in rustic calendars which are not later than the Flavian period (G. Wissowa in *Apophoreton*, pp. 29 *sqq.*).

small minority surrounded by multitudes believing in strange miracles, in unreasonable vows and penances, in a supernatural with which you could strike amoral bargains. In his self-examination Horace asks, 'Do you laugh at dreams, at terrors inspired by magic, at wonders, at witches, at bogies by night, at Thessalian portents[1]?' and the question is put on a par with questions on fundamental human values.

The same division into an intellectual aristocracy and the masses we find in the Greek world of the time. On the one hand, there are philosophers carrying on the traditions of their schools, adapting them in a measure to the needs of the time by an emphasis on ethics rather than on metaphysics. Polemic has waned with the waning of the hope of new truth. Between Posidonius and Neoplatonism there is no fresh impulse and little if any experimental investigation[2], but in their place a consciousness of

> Dipping buckets into empty wells
> And growing old with drawing nothing up.

The result is commonly a detached theism with an interest in *faits divers*—such as we find in Strabo. The only strong desire in philosophy at this time is the desire to supply men with a reasoned way of life. Stoicism gave this with its concept of life in accordance with nature, with its idealization of the acceptance of Fate, with its doctrine of duties. Epicureanism gave it with its ideal of a liberation from the fear of death and of a capricious supernatural— the joy of a great simplification of life. The Cynics who preached to all and sundry offered the ideal of freedom, of the breaking of those undue attachments to rank or possessions which make men weak and afraid. The Neopythagoreans held up the possibility of life in a brotherhood with an other-worldly theology, and the hope that by discipline and prayer and sacrifice the soul might here in part and hereafter wholly be freed from the trammels of the body. All of them made their adherents, but all of them preached to a tired world.

The masses went on in the old way, using Greek or Oriental cults which promised security, going to civic temples, and also joining private associations which saved them from their dread of loneliness. There was here the possibility of new development, when the speculative and ethical interests of philosophy fused with popular religion. Of the incoming of ethical interests, perhaps

---

[1] *Ep.* ii, 2, 208 *sqq.*; cf. *Sat.* i, 5, 97 *sqq.*; ii, 3, 288 *sqq.*
[2] Cf. W. Kroll, *Studien zum Verständnis der römischen Literatur*, pp. 280 *sqq.*

coloured by Neopythagoreanism, we have a striking example in the ordinances of a private shrine of the Phrygian goddess Agdistis (with altars of other deities) at Philadelphia in Lydia, probably founded not later than the beginning of the first century before our era[1].

'Let men and women, slave and free, when coming into this shrine swear by all the gods that they will not deliberately plan any evil guile or baneful poison against any man or woman: that they will neither know nor use harmful spells: that they will neither turn to nor recommend to others nor have a hand in love-charms, abortives, contraceptives, or doing robbery or murder....Let not woman or man who does the aforementioned acts come into this shrine: for in it are enthroned mighty deities, and they take notice of such offences, and will not tolerate those who transgress their commands... These commands were set beside Agdistis, the most holy guardian and mistress of this shrine. May she put good intentions in men and women, free and slave alike, that they may abide by what is here inscribed; and may all men and women who are confident of their uprightness touch this writing, which gives the commandments of the god, at the monthly and at the annual(?) sacrifices in order that it may be clear who abides by them and who does not. O Saviour Zeus, hear our words, and give us a good requital, health, deliverance, peace, safety on land and sea.'

For the fusion of philosophy with religion we may point further to the Neopythagorean movement in general. It seems to have absorbed what survived of Orphism and to have made Orphic literature its own and to have produced more of it. A doctrine of hidden affinities led easily to an interest in magic, and the opponents of the school charged it with necromancy. When we look at the collections of magical processes which survive in papyri of the third and fourth centuries A.D., we find in them large elements which bear the marks of ultimate provenance from circles culturally far higher than the classes then mainly served by the practitioners who owned these manuals. There are hymns very much like the Orphic hymns in style and thought, directions for bloodless sacrifice, and rites originally intended to secure direct communion with the Sun god. The first extant ancient author who is familiar with these processes, as distinct from the older Greek magic, is Lucan. It is likely that Neopythagoreans are, in fact, responsible for some at least of the adaptation of Egyptian practice (e.g. threats to the gods) and Jewish exorcism[2].

---

[1] Ditt.[3] 985. See further, O. Weinreich, *S.B. Heidelberg*, 1919, XVI; A. D. Nock in *Cl. Rev.* XXXVIII, 1924, pp. 58 *sq.*; and "Early Gentile Christianity," pp. 72 *sqq.* in A. E. J. Rawlinson's *The Trinity and the Incarnation*.

[2] A. D. Nock, *J.E.A.* xv, 1929, pp. 219 *sqq.* and note 14 in Foakes Jackson and Kirsopp Lake, *Beginnings of Christianity*, v, pp. 164 *sqq.*

Certainly we know that the famous Neopythagorean Nigidius had some acquaintance with Persian eschatological speculation[1]. The full development of this process of fusion falls later in the first century and in the second century A.D., but we cannot deny the possibility of development within our period.

The new growth is due to certain psychological needs. The men of the Graeco-Roman world of this time were not oppressed by a sense of sin or a fear of demons. These are in general the product of the 'theologies' which offer an antidote. The majority of men were probably in an unreflective way content with traditional practice and unquestioning. Those whose needs were responsible for new creations were harassed, not by these troubles, but by a feeling of resentful helplessness in face of the order of Fate, written in or established by the stars, by an uncertainty as to the hereafter, and by a general inquisitiveness as to the supernatural. Hence arose a desire for security here and hereafter and a desire for some sort of revelation. These desires were met by a rise in the importance of initiatory sacraments, which gave a revelation and a new status to the initiate by some rebirth or reconstitution, also by the growth of small private mysteries, such as those of Hecate associated with the so-called Chaldaic oracles, and by the production of revelation literature claiming to come from Orpheus or Zoroaster or Thrice Greatest Hermes, the Egyptian god Thoth. Here we see the root-idea of *gnosis*, special revelation, special knowledge of the nature of man's soul and of the hereafter. The psychological factors which produced it led many to Judaism, which had a clear-cut theistic scheme of the universe and which in its synagogue worship had—what was then in religion unique—the sermon. Not a few Gentiles, some men and more women (who had not to face circumcision), became proselytes, that is to say naturalized Jews, others became *Sebomenoi*, that is to say that they worshipped in the synagogue and observed the commands which were held by Judaism to be binding on all humanity alike, others again became *Hypsistarioi*, that is to say that they practised, perhaps by themselves, a sort of Judaizing monotheism which was not wholly exclusive of Gentile elements.

Those who followed any of these paths had a definite belief as to the hereafter. Others, in general, vacillated between a conviction that the grave was the end and vague ideas derived from that Orphic picture of heaven and hell which had become common property. The most confident hope of bliss existed among Dionysiac initiates, and the symbolism of the hereafter on funerary

[1] Frag. 67, Swoboda, preserved by Servius on *Ecl.* IV, 10.

monuments is largely Dionysiac in character, as earlier in Etruscan tomb paintings. For the educated in general the prospect was *pulvis et umbra sumus*, with a mental reservation that Plato's myths might be true[1].

For the moods of the latter part of the period, again, we have excellent literary evidence. Petronius depicts for us the freedman life of an Italian coast town, its bourgeois feeling for the good old days of piety—the Augustan attitude has had time to work down through the social scale—its belief and superstition and disillusion; he parodies also the private mysteries of the time in his allusion to certain rites of Priapus: (ch. xvii) 'the secrets of so many years, which barely a thousand men know.' Seneca is a man whose youthful acquaintance with the philosopher Sotion and the Sextii had the emotional character of a religious experience. In the years of his exile and of his subsequent power he was a literary man with an ideal standard which was not the less real if it was at times inevitably compromised. On his retirement from public life he again turned to *vie intérieure*: he read busily, he heard the lectures of Metronax, and he sought to communicate to his friend Lucilius those teachings thanks to which he felt himself to be passing through a transformation. Philosophy is, he says, the great rite of initiation, giving admission to the great temple of the universe. With an evangelical fervour like Epicurus, whom he had at this time read closely, and to whom letters i–xxix are greatly indebted in form as well as in substance[2], he holds that the liberal arts, grammar and geography and the interpretation of poetry and even the abstrusities of metaphysics are a snare. Man's business is with the art of living: *non in dialectica Deo complacuit salvum facere populum suum*, he could say as well as St Ambrose. The good life means an avoidance of luxury and vice and superstition, and a whole-hearted acceptance of that which the world order has provided for us to do and to suffer; *ducunt volentem fata, nolentem trahunt*. To the attainment of this good life one must devote all one's energies, abandoning if it must be public duties, however important, that the soul may receive individual attention[3]. This attitude rests on an ethical theism with a deep feeling of the opposition of the body to the soul; there is the possibility of a happy

---

[1] It is noteworthy that in the *Aeneid* there is apart from book vi no reference to life after death except for Anchises, Aeneas and their descendants.

[2] H. Mutschmann, *Hermes*, L, 1915, pp. 321 *sqq.*

[3] *Dial.* x.

immortality for the virtuous, but it is only an accidental possibility, and popular religion is rejected as unworthy[1].

The contemporary antithesis of Seneca is M. Annaeus Cornutus, a Stoic active in Rome under Claudius and Nero. Cornutus wrote on the categories, on rhetoric, on spelling, on the exegesis of Virgil; he was devoted to those very liberal arts which Seneca condemned. We learn from a fragment that he taught the annihilation of the soul at death. We know him best from a treatise which professes to be an abridgement of the treatment of Greek theology by older philosophers, and handles the various deities, explaining their names in the way of ancient etymology which regarded a name rightly interpreted as containing the essential nature of a person or thing: myths and attributes also are allegorically explained as referring to physical phenomena. This jejune proceeding is animated by an excursus with a comparative point of view, maintaining that there lies behind all mythology a primitive wisdom which has been covered over by fiction, a view carefully to be distinguished from the theory that the whole is veiled wisdom. We see at the end how serious this is to Cornutus. He writes, he says, in order that the young may be taught to worship aright in piety and not in superstition. The divergence of his point of view from Seneca's is clear, and we are told that his pupil Persius was long before he made the acquaintance of Seneca and was not captivated by his intellect.

Yet Persius shows us how moving even the teaching of so seemingly arid a philosopher could be. The satires of Persius, while preserving the form of Lucilius and Horace, are heavily weighted with morality: several of them are Stoic sermons—the second, for instance, against superstition, a topic common in satire but particularly congenial to the pupil of Cornutus. The fifth depicts in the most moving terms what the writer's discipleship had meant to him. At the critical time of the first liberty of manhood, says Persius, I put myself under your direction and you straightened out my knotted soul. The resultant product is, after all, what Seneca would have desired.

One more figure of the period may be named in conclusion— Lucan. He died young, and in the poem which he has left we find a monotonous if powerful Stoicism which sounds like a cliché but does at times fascinate him as it were against his will. He has a host of references to religious ideas and practices regarded as

---

[1] *Epist. Mor.* 95, 47 *sqq.* and the fragments of the *De superstitione*, in which *civilis theologia* and Roman official practice are criticized as severely as Oriental worships.

faits divers, and incidentally a remarkable knowledge of magic: his attitude like that of Tacitus later is one of interested pessimism. The quality common to all these men—except Petronius, who is a good detached onlooker—is a certain emphasis on the significance of the individual's conduct[1]. Whether this conduct is viewed from the standpoint of the *beau geste* or of the Stoic idea of duty makes little difference. In either case there is the same feeling of tension, the same theatricality. The Stoic suicides in Tacitus, like the death of Vulteius in Lucan (iv, 402 *sqq.*), are vigorous demonstrations on the stage of the universe. They are pieces of acting which serve no purpose except the vindication of a principle or an attitude, the giving of examples to others who will be in like case, and the escaping of that oblivion which to the men of this time seemed so terrible. Their thinkers seek to justify two non-rational convictions, that 'let us eat, drink and be merry for to-morrow we die' is an inadequate formula, and that man matters in the universe and even to the universe; they seek to do this without at the same time surrendering to popular religion. The conviction remains and the refusal to surrender remains for a time and in certain circles, till social changes and the pressure of external phenomena reduce and ultimately destroy the division between the intellectuals and the masses. Whether Time is or is not, as Sophocles says, a kindly god, he is not wholly unjust; the intellectualism which was thus superseded was in a measure arid, in a measure a thing of class feeling, 'a small soul carrying a dead body.'

[1] Cf. C. H. Moore, *Harv. Theol. Rev.* ii, 1909, pp. 221 *sqq.*

CHAPTER XVI

THE LITERATURE OF THE AUGUSTAN AGE

I. THE AGE OF AUGUSTUS

THE Augustan age has become a type and a proverb for a period when letters flourish and men of letters prosper, when, in Aristotle's phrase, life is complete or perfect—the national life happy in great achievement and in great hope. A galaxy of talent or even of genius is thought of, and, commonly, a monarchical society. The periods have been few in human story when great poets have abounded; yet at times national character and circumstance have brought to full ripeness the creative power of a people; 'all at once and all in tune' a nation hears its poets speaking. There is no clear explanation why one generation should concentrate in itself the gifts that make a nation great in the creative arts. It seems that behind or underneath literature there must be some national consciousness; the men of letters may not speak of it; they may even revolt against national ideals; but there must be the atmosphere, the nidus, the 'leaf-mould,' that only a nation, race and a history can give. Yet national achievement by itself seems not enough. Sometimes, as in the decade of Napoleon, we find a common *floruit* for the literature of a number of nations together, a profound stirring of all that goes to make literature— sorrow, triumph, doubt, pain, obstinate questionings, endeavour, experience, hope, personality. Béranger, Wordsworth and Goethe are sufficiently unlike, but they all in their several ways interpret Europe. Our common talk labels these great creative ages not so much by the name of poet or thinker as by that of some other figure, it may be Pericles or Elizabeth. Yet in so saying we give more than date; we stumble into a half-explanation of what interests us. Augustus has more to do with the Augustan age than we should deduce from his historians. It is Virgil who gives the true picture, the true significance of Augustus, who 'created' him and made him a figure and a legend; and Augustus in turn did more for Virgil than perhaps Emperor or even poet recognized. In spite of such critics as Martial, the financial is the least causal of all links between Augustus and *Aeneid*; let it be struck out at once. It is the age of Augustus, it is unthinkable without him.

Elsewhere in this volume will be read the Emperor's history;

here we are not so greatly concerned with fact as with imagination. It is not so much what the Emperor did or even was, but what men divined in him, or through him. Here the haunting picture of Pliny the naturalist serves us best—the collector of facts, curious of phrase, illuminative in his spasms of insight and epigram. 'The unthinkable majesty of Roman peace' (*immensa Romanae pacis maiestas*)—word by word it has its value, its suggestion; the four words sum up the burden of the *Aeneid*, the real meaning of the work of Augustus.

To be able to judge aright of literature, Longinus tells us, is the last fruit of long experience. Harder still is it to trace influences, thoughts hardly to be packed into the narrow compass of word or even poem, the impulses of deeper birth which make poets; with long acquaintance the task grows not easier but harder. The great poets do not unlock their hearts in sonnets; the original impulse may be transformed more than once before it yields the poem that is to be immortal. When criticism is in its autocratic youth, with principles few and fixed, many things are possible, which to the old lover of Virgil seem rough and improbable. To assess the influence of his age upon the poet, of all people, is difficult; the touch of time is perhaps always unimaginable; the poet consciously or unconsciously reacts to it and against it. Sometimes it chiefly wakes the desire to escape to some other world of old romance, to some deeper world where he can handle the eternal, as readers of Virgil know. The poets tell us explicitly that they look before and after, that Memory is the mother of the Muses, that poetry is 'emotion re-collected in tranquillity'; no wonder then, a feeling for the past—the past of the man, the land, the human kind —tells in the shaping of a poet. But if he has no faith in the future, no reasonable hope, he will lose heart, and do nothing. Perhaps some ease of mind in the present must contribute to the needed tranquillity.

All these requirements are met in the age of Augustus. The collapse of the Republic witnessed, if it did not stimulate, a great antiquarian movement. Augustus gave the world new hopes. It was, men said, in the interests of all that the whole world should be ruled, and ruled by one man; it was the only remedy for a land divided against itself. The hope was in the main justified; for two centuries mankind had peace. With all his sensitiveness to pain, his indelible memories, Virgil shows the effect of this new hope. Yet in the marshalling of events, and their disentangling, we may be so absorbed by movement, or by personality, as to forget the slow influence of years too full of the dramatic and catastrophic, the ceaseless play of thought upon problems unsolved, the sheer pain that the disorder means for the sensitive nature.

There was immense literary activity, the poets especially being innumerable; they always are. Velleius Paterculus, a minor historian, but possessor of a pleasant style, the sole surviving admirer of Sejanus, runs rapidly over a series of great names. He links Virgil 'prince of poets' (*princeps carminum*) with Rabirius; with them he groups Livy, Tibullus and Naso; all of them 'superlatively perfect' is his almost illogical verdict (*perfectissimi*). He omits Horace. Ovid, in passing, pronounces Rabirius to have been 'mighty-mouthed' (*magni oris*). These compliments serve merely to remind us of men long forgotten, interesting only to those who find history in lists. But, above these, there are in penumbra round the great poets their friends whose genius they, more sympathetic than posterity, recognized as equal to their own. Yet, as Plato suggests, the greatest poets are not always the best critics. The minor poets of an age have what Matthew Arnold called a historical value; they reveal the common impulses and endeavours, the atmosphere of their day, sometimes more clearly than the greater men; for they are more obviously under its influence. They may even be more popular for the time. But the significant thing in History is constantly less obtrusive; it is creative, the seed of something to come, the force that is slowly making a new age, and contemporaries often miss it. Not always;

nescio quid maius nascitur Iliade;

though one wonders how often Propertius and his friends acclaimed epoch-making works.

The outstanding men of letters of the age of Augustus were born in Republican times. Virgil was nearly forty when Actium was fought. How the troubles of his country affected him, we read in the first *Georgic*; twice over Emathia's plains are drenched with Roman blood, shed in civil strife; right and wrong are confounded; the fields are left untilled, the ploughman is a soldier; Euphrates and Germany threaten war; neighbour cities draw the sword, each on the other; life and work have lost their appeal. In prose, it is Catiline, the disorders of Pompeian Rome, the Civil War, the strange promise of Caesar's rule, the Murder, Antony, Brutus, the whole chaos of factions and incapables; and then Actium. Posterity knows that Actium meant final peace; contemporaries did not. There were still conspirators; the Emperor's health was uncertain; the succession to the throne was a problem. Augustus maintained that his rule was a temporary expedient;

a policy that may have kept men conscious that he was needed, but left the strain of uncertainty not wholly relieved.

Thus for decades change had been menaced, such change as left men unable to forecast national or personal life. Custom was the very basis of life and of national character, and it was to be swept away. If freedom and self-government were to be lost, what were the alternatives? The Roman looked out on degenerate Macedonian despotisms, on old Greek cities garrisoned by conquerors, on citizen life reduced to nullity and all the chances of battle, murder and sudden death. It takes thought to realize the full effect of this upon sentient natures. A highly developed society, it has suffered much, and it is uneasy and restless.

The Roman world was repeating the experience of the Hellenistic age, when many elements of modern feeling, largely absent in the great classical art of Athens, begin to appear—a new delight in family life, a new interest in man as man, a new way of looking at love, a new sensitiveness to the beauty of external nature (as Virgil's old Corycian pirate among his flowers and fruits will remind us), a new interest in science; and, we may add, a new self-consciousness in the use of language and a highly developed antiquarianism. The human mind must have compensations, and the new interests replace in some measure the lost political life, and bring out new values in human experience. It is an endeavour to find as much to believe in, and to enjoy, as a changed world will allow. Something to believe in is sought by the greater minds; something to rub along on, by Horace and his school, something to forget with, by Ovid and his kind. The idealist looks back and looks within; but there is also the forward look. The *Aeneid* shows a happier and braver prospect than the *Georgics*; the promise of the new age is sustained through the opening years of imperial rule and the outlook brightens.

II. THE MOVEMENT AWAY FROM ALEXANDRINISM

Every kind of literature is attempted; the old Greek masterpieces, and the less masterly models of the Hellenistic period, where design is lost in workmanship, are studied and copied. The Emperor himself wrote a tragedy, or part of a tragedy, starting on it with great enthusiasm; but when his friends asked him what had become of Ajax, 'he has fallen upon his—sponge,' he said. Augustus had the gift denied to some great men, as Tacitus says[1];

[1] *Dial. de claris orat.* 21.

he might write poetry but he did not publish it. The age saw the gradual decline of 'the singers of Euphorion' as Cicero called them, the addicts of Alexandrinism.

Propertius indeed glorifies the land of his nativity on account of his own likeness to the chief of the Alexandrines—

> Umbria Romani patria Callimachi,

though Assisi prefers to remember a very different son. He, like others, loved to reproduce the tricks of the Hellenistic poetry, to shine as 'learned.' The whole of Greek mythology was absorbed; and an extreme allusiveness imbedded in Latin verse (without too much other distinction) Greek names, often long names and patronymics, as if large part of the charm of verse lay in the riddles that only a very full dictionary could explain. Of course its emotional value was slight, it could only live where useless learning was the ideal.

> Iam Pandioniae cessit genus Orithyiae,
>   a dolor ibat Hylas ibat Hamadryasin.
> Hic erat Arganthi Pege sub vertice montis
>   grata domus Nymphis umida Thyniasin.   (1, 20, 31–4)

The appalling difficulty found by the medieval copyists in reproducing these long words proves the point; it was not the language actually employed by men. The writer was not perhaps thinking of readers, vain as he was; he loved perhaps the long words so full of vowels, so free from consonants, the peregrinate movement of his lines, their freedom from elision, their unexpected structure. Catullus had done the same thing in monotonous hexameters, following closely the ingenuities and perversions of Callimachus; but much is forgiven to bright experimentalists of his sort. They may explore blind alleys, but they know enough to come out of them.

Something was gained by this variety of experiment. Ennius and Lucretius wrote ruggedly enough. Whatever their gifts of mind, and poetic feeling, few will feel that they had mastered their medium. Latin was not Greek; no language but has its own movements and music, and naturalization is a slow business. Homer's hexameter was Greek; and to do the same thing in Latin was to do something different; the poet must know his own language and prefer it. Spenser's letter to Gabriel Harvey about the hexameters is relevant here. Spenser was quite clear that English is not Latin, and he listened till he caught the native island accents, and wrote his *Faerie Queene* with that music in his heart. It is the same record that we read in Latin. Homer is

splendid, but not Latin; the Alexandrines were ingenious and
'writ no language.' The men who will write Latin hexameters
could learn from both, but they had to write by ear (*digito
callemus et aure*). Two men above all others trained the Latin ear.
Cicero, whose poems Tacitus and Juvenal ridiculed, and whose
verse Virgil studied, was one; and the other was Virgil himself.

But the other poets show the same movement. Horace is the
least Alexandrine of them all. With a scorn for the affectations,
the vocabulary and the tricks of the school, and a strong preference for older models, he always knew what he was doing; he
wrote his odes with a miraculous instinct for what was possible
and triumphed in sheer sound. His hexameters were deliberately
moulded on an old Roman pattern, but, with time and self-
criticism, he gradually responded there also to his own sense for
pause and movement. Ovid shows the same response. The years
reveal little change in his technique; the only difference is made
by the solitary and frost-bitten spirit. If elegiacs are to be written
in Latin at all, they must be written as Ovid wrote them. He too
has learnt from the modes of his predecessors. He can match
learning and polysyllables with Propertius; but he wears his
wealth of learning much lightlier, it never gets between his feet;
he does not go to Alexandria to learn how to turn a Latin sentence;
let the singers of Euphorion invert, contort and obscure any
meaning they labour with, Ovid writes to be understood at once.
He is quick where others lumber, gets three sentences into his
couplet, where they may take three couplets to a sentence—and
Heaven may know what it means then; Ovid's meaning leaps at
the most indolent reader. His verse is lighter in movement and
texture than could before him have been believed possible. He
plays with his learning and his mythology; no nymph among his
hundreds has the self-conscious solemnity of Pandionian Orithyia.
His hexameters, too, are of the newer period, but they show a
falling away from the great standards of Virgil; they are monotonous; perhaps because in his heart he preferred writing elegiacs.
At times his hexameters sound much more like elegiacs[1].

When it comes to hexameters, it was Virgil alone who wrote
Virgilian hexameters; there is a subtler art about them, beyond
imitation. There have been many studies of Virgilian verse, as to
sense-pause, caesura strong or weak, the interweaving of dactyl and
spondee, the strong control of elision (the most difficult of details);
and the conclusion of the whole matter is a new consciousness of
the master-hand, and a despairing realization that the rules of

[1] Cf. *Met.* IV, 306–9, 581, 610; V, 166, 345.

genius are very few or infinite. Virgil has assimilated Homer and Apollonius—'it was easier,' he said, 'to wrench his club from Hercules than to steal a line from Homer'; yes! it would still be Homer's, conspicuously stolen property. He has assimilated Lucretius, Cicero, Catullus; and, unlike the Greek poet, who did the right thing without knowing why, Virgil does know why and writes with the infinite variety and the supreme fitness of Nature herself. Charles Lamb did not wish to see the corrected manuscript of Milton; Virgil's premature death left passages unrevised in the *Aeneid*, or we should have said his verse was as 'inevitable' as the printed lines of Milton.

The story of Virgil shows his early interest in Alexandrinism. The *Eclogues* are obviously inspired by Theocritus; and the long passage in the fourth *Georgic*, telling the tale of Aristaeus and his bees, shows the influence of other Alexandrine models. The use of lovely proper names, which could indeed be omitted, the movements of the verse, the insertion of the beautiful story of Orpheus, and the handling of its central emotion, reveal the story of his mind. It is pleasant to think of the young Virgil enjoying the art of Catullus and imitating it, turning his lines with the happy and self-conscious cleverness of youth—a young poet among young poets, mannered with the studied graces of his day. But it means more to realize that, even in his cleverest and most youthful work, there were 'certain vital signs' of something far greater yet to develop.

> Drymoque Xanthoque Ligeaque Phyllodoceque...
> Cydippeque et flava Lycorias, altera virgo...
> Clioque et Beroe soror, Oceanitides ambae...
> Atque Ephyre atque Opis et Asia Deiopea....
>
> (*Georg.* IV, 336–44)

The names, the metrical structure of the second line, the open vowel and pentasyllabic ending of the last, are unmistakable. Spondaic endings Virgil never used with the lavish freedom of Catullus. It is remarked that Lucretius has none of them in his last book; his spondaic endings had been more apt to suggest Ennius than Alexandria, and there is perhaps something in the guess that he renounced them consciously, a contemptuous revolt from the fashion that captured Catullus. Virgil at all events uses both types of spondaic ending, the Ennian type in his later work; the lines of the mature man neither smell of the museum nor have a self-conscious air. The *Epithalamium* of Catullus is frankly imitative throughout, but Virgil never surrenders so completely. When Ovid uses a spondaic ending, it has a look of being dragged in;

like an irrelevant quotation, it is foreign to the movement of his thought and his lines.

But, in another way, the passage shows the Alexandrine influence, and comparison with others reveals how Virgil outgrew it; and both stages are in measure illustrative of the age. The Hades which Orpheus visits is picturesque, and amenable to song, not quite so deliberately charming as Horace's genial infernos— the pleasant limbo of poets and myths, to which the branch of the guilty tree so nearly sent him, and the other, where the daughters of Danaus rest to hear music, and Ixion and Tityos smile reluctantly—but it is a literary hell, not too unlike that one of fair women, at which Propertius hints, in a beautiful line, with a good double spondee to restrain excessive sorrow:

> Sunt apud infernos tot milia formosarum.   (ii, 28, 49)

It has all the right things in it; Orpheus sings, and the shades gather about him to listen, and we grow conscious, as the poet speaks, of deeper thoughts, which we are to think again:

> At cantu commotae Erebi de sedibus imis
> Umbrae ibant tenues simulacraque luce carentum,
> Quam multa in foliis avium se milia condunt,
> Vesper ubi aut hibernus agit de montibus imber,
> Matres atque viri defunctaque corpora vita
> Magnanimum heroum, pueri innuptaeque puellae,
> Impositique rogis iuvenes ante ora parentum.   (*Georg.* iv, 471–7)

When Virgil drew Hades in real earnest, the Hades that Aeneas visited[1], he used this passage again but with two changes. It is no casual storm or cold evening that drives the birds from the hills; it is the great migration of the birds to another shore altogether. The difference is profound. No Orpheus fetches up the idle companies of the dead to listen genially to his chance music; there is a new earnestness; the throngs are urging forward on an inevitable journey and in dire need. The lines, but for the change noted, and some slight re-arrangement, are the same; but they have become a new thing, and give the reader for ever one of the most moving pictures that the ancient world has to offer. It is a miracle of change, and it too speaks of movements of thought, intensified, and to become more and more urgent in the centuries of Roman life that follow.

A last point on the passage. Orpheus leads away his half-regained Eurydice, but he looks back, and loses her; and her last cry is in five lovely lines, too exquisite to be a transcript of the deepest emotion; too structured and intricate for translation with-

---

[1] *Aen.* vi, 305–12.

out changes, the art is conscious with the double *quis* and the rare and beautiful movement of the middle line:

> Illa 'quis et me' inquit 'miseram et te perdidit, Orpheu,
> Quis tantus furor? en iterum crudelia retro
> Fata vocant, conditque natantia lumina somnus.
> Iamque vale: feror ingenti circumdata nocte
> Invalidasque tibi tendens—heu, non tua—palmas.' (*Georg.* IV, 494–8)

Emotion uses other tones, as Virgil came to see, directer language.

> Do you see this? Look on her, look, her lips,
> Look there, look there!

So Lear; and it is with new directness, not unlike it, that Virgil in later years tells of death and loss. Simpler structures serve for the end of Palinurus, Mimas, Mezentius; and human sorrow under the passionless stars has its quietest telling toward the end of the *Aeneid*, and there significantly it is to Ennius and not Euphorion that Virgil turns:

> Tum litore toto
> Ardentes spectant socios semiustaque servant
> Busta, neque avelli possunt nox umida donec
> Invertit caelum stellis ardentibus aptum.   (*Aen.* XI, 199–202)

III. DIDACTIC POETRY

It was a persistent idea among ancient critics, professed experts or ordinary persons usurping the rôle in the light of nature, that the poet is essentially a teacher. To draw the inference that the object of poetry is information might be too abrupt; but some of the poets evidently thought so. It was the Muses, who can speak feigned things like to the true but can speak truth on occasion, who first gave this idea to Hesiod. Aristophanes chooses to suppose for the moment that Homer's glory lies in the value of the *Iliad* as a military handbook; Aeschines that Homer meant to warn Greeks against bad demagogues; but orators are often more naive than humourists. But even Plato calls for valuable poets, who can put into suitable verse the doctrines which the state would have instilled into childhood; he saw, with some regret it would seem, that poetry, in general, was a divine madness, carrying on an ancient quarrel with philosophy, and that, very oddly, the madman wrote verse which men sang with more abandon, and read with more love and reverence, than the lines which the sober-minded achieved; it was very strange.

But the sober poets took their function very seriously, and put all sorts of useful information into conscientious verse, taking care to slip in gay snatches of what they meant for real poetry, in the hope of coaxing the reader along. They had never read, nor imagined on their own account, that instructions may be conveyed too directly, too like a lecture, but that they should rather 'slide into the mind of the reader while he is imagining no such matter[1]'. When Nicander of Colophon indites his *Theriaca*, all about serpents and antidotes, the reader is left in no doubt as to what is intended, and if he cares for snakes or is nervous about them, he is the man who must hear Nicander; but the snake might be preferable. The modern reader may feel some surprise that a second copy of Nicander was ever made. Aratus wrote of astronomy, and found two men to translate him into Latin verse; Cicero was one of them, and it seems that Virgil read the translation as Milton read Sylvester's version of Du Bartas. The patience of great poets almost seems a phase of their divine madness.

The Roman character took instinctively to the idea of putting information into verse; Ennius perhaps started the mode with his *Annals*. Lucretius lifted the tradition of didactic poetry to a new level altogether, and as poet and thinker gave it a new life and a new warrant. Among his imitators, men of less genius, Manilius, Stoic, poet, exponent of astronomy, perhaps has the first place.

It is remarkable how at this time astrology captured the minds of men, coming re-inforced from the nearer East, and taught by 'Chaldaeans.' Horace warned Leuconoe to avoid 'Babylonian numbers' and take the days as they came, his own philosophy of life. But the Roman world was not to be put off by such genial sceptics. The sudden and widespread acceptance of the planet week in this period is significant; and the Northern names of the days prove how the new week overleapt the Imperial frontiers while paganism still prevailed. It is a very curious phenomenon. Posidonius, the fashionable philosopher, came to Rome in 51 B.C.; and to-day every kind of intellectual activity is traced to his inspiration, where it is not direct translation of his own books. He was, so St Augustine tells us (*de Civ. Dei*, v, 2), 'a champion of the fateful stars' (*fatalium siderum assertor*). Horace himself plays with these stars as he does with Hades and other things; his horoscope coincides with that of Maecenas. But astrologers in Rome were condemned by an edict of Tiberius in A.D. 16, and Manilius saved his poem from suspicion by leaving out the promised planets; a horoscope without planets is unthinkable.

Manilius then wrote of the stars, a poem less interesting to modern astronomers, who find it incoherent, obscure and below

---

[1] Charles Lamb to Wordsworth, February, 1801.

Greek standards, than to classical scholars. To-day he is perhaps more read for his editors than for himself. A poet who will grapple with 'dodecatemories' takes his life in his hands, even with the precedent of Lucretius and *homoeomereia*. Yet he has learnt in the same school as Ovid; which is to say that he can write good Latin gracefully, and will not spurn a quip. Bentley would have it that Manilius and Ovid alone among the ancients had wit.

> Ornari res ipsa negat contenta doceri.   (III, 39)

> Victorque Medusae
> Victus in Andromeda est. Iam cautibus invidet ipsis
> Felicesque vocat teneant quae membra catenas.   (V, 572)

That the Stoic can affect the stylist, every reader of Seneca knows. Manilius can turn off a Stoic dogma as neatly:

> Fata regunt orbem, certa stant omnia lege.   (IV, 14)

> Quis caelum poterit nisi caeli munere nosse
> Et reperire deum nisi qui pars ipse deorum est?   (II, 115)

But good lines and sound doctrine do not make a great poet, and mankind turns away from the unequal yoking of dubious science and respectable verse. Oddly enough Manilius has supplied Benjamin Franklin with an epitaph, or the best part of it. Reason, wrote Manilius,

> solvitque animis miracula rerum
> Eripuitque Iovi fulmen viresque Tonanti.   (I, 103)

Turgot took the last line, eliminated Jove, slipped in George III and the British, and there was the epitaph, Latin, concise, epigrammatic, and rhetorical:

> Eripuit caelo fulmen sceptrumque tyrannis.

But it is a dubious interpretation of literature, which includes in it everything written.

Another piece of the kind is the didactic poem *Aetna* which, as its name implies, deals with volcanoes, and explains that the cause is physical not divine, the gods have better things to do (32); the earth is hollow, full of chasms and wind-channels; wind and spirit jostle within Etna, they are blocked and explode. This also is a poem, whose author's only care is for the fact—*omnis in vero mihi cura* (92)—with digressions, though it may be relevant to urge that possessions can be an encumbrance when you are running away from an eruption (617–9). One line describing how two bold sons risked death to save their parents,

> Erubuere pios iuvenes attingere flammae   (633)

absurd as it is, may be the inspiration of the most famous line of

Crashaw[1]. The main interest, however, of the poem is that in ancient times it was attributed with some doubt (*de qua ambigitur*) to Virgil. It is not to-day, but Virgil's fame is not injured by the transfer.

Virgil wrote his own didactic poem, as all the world rejoices to remember— a song of Ascra for the towns of Rome. The epithet *Ascraeum* proclaims allegiance to Hesiod; but the poem is not in the least in Hesiod's vein; and it is read not so much for instruction as delight. No Roman had ever written anything like it, not Virgil himself in his *Eclogues*. In the *Aeneid* he does not mention Homer, nor the Meles, nor Chios' rocky isle, and he transcends the *Georgics* as in them he eclipsed his *Bucolics*. Horace also wrote a didactic poem, *de Arte Poetica*, derived it is said (by the commentator Porphyrion) from a Greek, Neoptolemus[2]. But, for all its sense and wit, it never made a reader a poet yet.

The didactic poem which has had most influence, the only one that has really taught men and women what it set out to teach them, is a very different work from any yet noticed; not one of the true didactic poets (for Virgil and Horace are not really of the order) could have tolerated the idea of such an outrageous parody, but none of them was ever so effective, so witty, or so readable as the infamous Ovid with his *Ars Amatoria*. The whole thing was a defiance, an outrage—and a revelation of life in Rome. It is not great poetry; but assume there is no such thing as morality, and nothing could be better done than the three books of the poem; though it would in reality lose a great deal by such an assumption, and Ovid knows it. He is too clever to use the ugly language of Juvenal or Martial; it is a graceful corruption; there never was such cleverness nor such wit so used. Ovid has to be at his worst to be at his best. The book deserves its bad name; yet, strange paradox, there is something likeable about the man himself. But that is the way with human beings.

IV. ANTIQUITIES AND ANTIQUARIANS

With the new interest in antiquity, that rose in the Republic's last years, came something akin to a national reaction. From the earliest days of civilization in Italy commodities and fashions had come from the South and the Sea; the North and the mountains had nothing to send but men—the last being the great naked magnificent Gauls, tallest and most beautiful of races, Polybius says,

[1] Boswell, *Johnson*, III, p. 304, n. 3. (Birkbeck Hill.)
[2] C. Jensen, *Philodemos über die Gedichte fünftes Buch*, pp. 93 *sqq.*

but not civilized. The Greek alphabet, the Greek arts, the Greek mason, Greek literature, Greek slaves, Greek wines, Greek fashions had followed one another. From the time of Cato there is a reverse movement—a growing interest in what is Italian, Latin, Roman, in ancient usage, custom, ceremony, in native legends and old Latin literature. *Origines* is the title of Cato's book, a significant name; and the form and texture of the book were significant, even ominous. The antiquary and the historian approach the past in different ways, because in fact they come to it in a different spirit. It is not *what* happened that is interesting, Polybius urges; it is *why* it happened. The antiquary is not greatly interested in 'causes of things,' in evolution; he loves the picture of the past because it is past, the old tools, the old furniture, the old usage; and his interests exclude order and encourage digression. The mode is set of a rambling sort of book with no more thread than the drifting mind of the antiquary; a gossip on old grammar may come before or after a discussion of the honours of old age, or ancient courtesy, or old farming ways. Those curious in such things will recall all sorts of books comfortably packed together on this scheme or absence of scheme—the works of Gellius, Aelian, Plutarch, and Clement— encyclopaedias with the loose-hung habits of a penny newspaper, but generally with an antiquarian flavour. The fashion spread widely and deserves notice; for the antiquary started it, and the all too easy structure fitted well with declining energy of mind.

Horace bears witness to the zeal for obsolete words, used by Catos and Cethegi in days of old, but long lost in the dust of antiquity, to the passion for old authors—no other merits beyond age were needed to make them literature. Horace himself is no archaizer, no collector of verbal curiosities. That rôle he left to such people as Verrius Flaccus whose assemblage of words, grammar and antiquities known as *de Verborum Significatu* sur- vives only 'in ruins,' of interest now, as in his own day, only to the learned. The practical Augustus despised what he called 'the odour of far-fetched words'; he pursued a middle path of lucidity with equal contempt for innovators and archaizers (*caco- zelos et antiquarios*), parodying the 'scented permanent wave' of Maecenas' style, and laughing at his stepson's quest for the obsolete; why should you want, he asked, to use the words that Sallust borrowed from Cato's *Origines*? Gellius, a century later, takes substantially the Emperor's position, when he bids culti- vate the character of the past and use the language of the present. *Vive ergo moribus praeteritis, loquere verbis praesentibus* (*N. A.* 1, 10, 4).

But the mode interested Virgil, who loved old words, old lines, old poets, and used the archaisms, but in his own way, *pudenter et raro*.

A great mass of writing, not all of it literature, grew up about old Roman usage. Varro is in the centre of it, a curious figure, dreaded a little by Cicero, denounced by Virgil's great commentator, Servius, as 'everywhere the enemy of religion,' yet claiming himself to be a sort of second Aeneas rescuing the gods and their rituals from sheer oblivion, as the first Aeneas saved them from burning Troy[1]. His work was a godsend to St Augustine and the Christians long after, and in the age of Augustus to poets and historians. When the poetic value of Cynthia was exhausted—it was never so high or of such universal significance as her poet supposed—Propertius announced a new departure. He would sing of sacred rites and sacred days, of the ancient names of famous places; and he wrote one or two elegies on these lines. But we need only contrast the grave and splendid scene of Evander and Aeneas in the Forum with the kind of cleverness that antiquity inspired in Propertius, to see that he was wise to give it up.

> Fictilibus crevere deis haec aurea templa.   (v, 1, 5)

He is more conscious of the clay than of the god; but it is the god that impresses Evander, and through him the reader of Virgil—*quis deus incertum est, habitat deus*, and the great conclusion follows *et te quoque dignum finge deo*, a note beyond Propertius, whose gift for bad taste, where no irreverence can give it a flavour, is still with him:

> Optima nutricum nostris lupa Martia rebus
> Qualia creverunt moenia lacte tuo.   (v, 1, 55)

Ovid took up the task, and wrote twelve books of *Fasti*, of which he destroyed six. The literary critic scarcely deplores the loss, but the archaeologist well may, and the humanist. That Ovid of all people should play the antiquary, is all the evidence we need for the popularity of the hobby. It takes him from his proper field; no one can entirely trust his data or his interpretations; and no doubt he was bored with it all at times. But the kindliness of the man, his humour, his humanity, are not excluded by his subject; and he can tell a story as charmingly as anybody. Yet the spiritual value of the past, for Virgil its very essence, was not to be expected to touch Ovid. He belonged to his own age:

> Prisca iuvent alios; ego me nunc denique natum
> Gratulor; haec aetas moribus apta meis.   (*Ars Am.* III, 121)

---

[1] See above, p. 470 *sq.*

Nothing could be truer; his day and his character were admirably matched; antiquity—well, Virgil was made for antiquity.

Horace wrote no *Antiquities*. No poet, once the crude days of Epode and Satire were over, ever made fewer mistakes. *Metiri se quemque suo modulo ac pede verum est*—he certainly observed his own rule and took his own measure. Antiquarian poetry, even if such a thing is actually possible, is inevitably a branch of didactic poetry; and, while Horace is as apt to preach as Coleridge, he knew better than to meddle with this form of double desiccation. Virgil, like Milton playing with the notion of King Arthur, had his dream of writing of Alban kings and their battles, but Apollo (as also in the case of Horace) happily intervened with an oracular reference to sheep. His biographer more bluntly says that he was displeased with his material and turned to the *Bucolics*. Later on his studies of old Rome and ancient Italy served a more glorious end in the *Aeneid*. Point by point Virgil absorbs, reflects and transcends his age.

Romulus and Remus are part of a normal English education, and have been for centuries; and so they are likely to be as long as Macaulay's *Lays of Ancient Rome* are available for children's recitation. But few realize how much was written by classical authors about the most ancient days of Rome. Dionysius of Halicarnassus is little read, seriously as he took his antiquarian work, and admirably as Edward Spelman translated (and printed) him. He is oftener cited as a critic—not one of the great epoch-making critics, but as an Augustan of great scholarship, highly trained, and possessed of a real sympathy for literature. On Homer, Herodotus, Thucydides, he writes what is still interesting. Of his history he tells us that he came into Italy, at the end of the Civil War; and spent twenty-two years at Rome, preparing materials for his work; scholars helped him and he drew upon such authors as Cato, Fabius Maximus, Valerius Antias, Licinius Macer, the Aelii, the Gellii and Calpurnii. Greeks are in general unacquainted with Roman history, though Greeks were Rome's first founders; so, 'as the most grateful return' for all Rome has done for him, he writes of 'that most beautiful part of the Roman history,' a story of brave men, who fulfilled their destiny and deserve immortal glory; of foreign wars and seditions; he will give an account of all the forms of government that Rome has used, and show the whole manner of living of the ancient Romans. 'I look upon that country as the best,' he says, 'which is the most self-sufficient and generally stands least in need of foreign commodities. Now I am persuaded that Italy enjoys this universal fertility beyond any other country.' So he too writes his *Salve magna parens*. A succession of beautifully designed speeches may accomplish his intent 'to afford satisfaction to those persons who desire to qualify themselves for political debates,' but no more than Livy's similar productions does it convince the modern historian. Yet he is a pleasant writer, not infallible, but possessed of abundance of matter—legend and usage, myth and religion, and boundless learning—eminently useful to the careful student of Livy and Plutarch, and for himself good to read, with the grave qualification applied to others by Quintilian (x, 1, 90)—*si vacet*.

A shorter space must suffice for Diodorus of Agyrrhium, better known as Diodorus Siculus, who compiled a universal history from the best available writers and preserved much that might otherwise have been lost, though E. A. Freeman, a severe judge, found his work often inaccurate and himself invincibly stupid.

The past and its achievements were bound to have a part in other literature than the antiquary's. Vitruvius must know the great traditions of the Greek architects before he could write the famous book on Architecture that has meant so much in the history of that art and is still full of human interest even for others than architects. Strabo, chief of geographers, abounds in ancient learning; his book is full of legend and literature. Geography is not for him all latitude and equator. Incidentally perhaps the great map of the Empire, set up in a colonnade by Vipsanius Agrippa, may be mentioned here, the first parent of many. That the great lawyers Antistius Labeo and Ateius Capito (to be treated of in the next volume) should draw upon antiquity, was inevitable; precedents imply the past.

But, of course, for the antiquities of Rome no author takes precedence of Livy and Virgil. In this interest also, they represent their contemporaries. 'A mere antiquarian,' said Dr Johnson, 'is a rugged being,' and so some of them were, Cato and Varro particularly; while Ovid shows that even a frivolous world could find the austere study, if handled aright, quite bright and amusing. In Livy and Virgil Roman antiquarianism falls into the hands of genius, and is transformed, and becomes the interest of the world for ever.

We hear from time to time—Cicero's letters and Horace's odes reveal it—of historians and poets who conceive that the history of their own times is full enough of vivid episode to yield theme for great writing, who would handle the Civil War, its causes, sins, alliances, and so forth, a task full of hazard, indeed to tread the lava with the volcanic fire below. It was no new idea; Thucydides had written of his own time; but it needs peculiar gifts; the struggle for life is perhaps as hard among historians as among poets, and the Romans who wrote contemporary history and survived are few. It is better for the historian to write of the past 'unmoved, and without reason to be moved, by anger or by party spirit.' The past is always apt to be better known than the present and more intelligible. As for the poets who would make epics of contemporary events, Plato's canon that madness is essential to poetry obviously excludes history. Virgil and Horace gave to posterity, each of them, a great deal of his age, and a great interpretation of it; and one has only to read Lucan to realize how much more wisely they conceived of poetry.

V. PERSONAL POETRY: ELEGY; PROPERTIUS

Homer, as Aristotle remarked, 'said as little as possible on his own account'; he kept himself out of his poetry. The next age of Greek poetry sees poets, men and women, who tell their own tales; rage, says Horace, armed Archilochus with the iambus that he made his own; Sappho has her complaints and writes her *Ille mi par*; Alcaeus resounds the stern sorrows of strife, of flight, of war. To these and to other poets Romans turned in this age of many interests, forgetful of what Horace notes, in the ode we are citing, that the mass of men prefer as themes of song battle and the tyrant driven forth; and Aristotle says the mass of mankind is apt to be right. *Securus iudicat orbis terrarum.*

All that Gallus wrote for Cytheris is gone with Cinna's *Smyrna* and other immortal works. Propertius survives in virtue of great promise in youth. He had an instinct for Latin and its rhythms and cadences, a love of phrase and of beautiful words, an ear for movement and variety—gifts that enabled him to reveal a new province for Roman poetry. His concentration on his own passion was not so new, and there are those who feel he was at heart less interested in Cynthia than in Propertius. But Cynthia filled his first volume of verse, and he tells us:

> Non haec Calliope non haec mihi cantat Apollo:
> Ingenium nobis ipsa puella facit.   (II, 1, 3–4)

A few lines lower, as so often, the case is given away by a line fatally susceptive of an unintended meaning:

> Maxima de nihilo nascitur historia.   (*ib.* 16)

Questions are asked about the transmission of his poems—is their order all wrong, are their pages shuffled, or is he beyond other poets inconsequent? It is conceded by his admirers that he lacks self-criticism, that he over-estimates the appeal of allusive learning, that Cynthia was after all only Cynthia, a monotonous type, abruptly as her moods vary. Those moods her poet records; and patient commentators try to make a story of them; she blazes out at Propertius and bids him be gone for a year; so a vacant year is marked in the annals. He tried other themes—the antiquities of Rome, as we saw. He writes an elegy for a friend lost at sea, strikes out a great line:

> Nunc tibi pro tumulo Carpathium omne mare est   (III, 7, 12)

and matches it with a clever conceit, which shows how little feeling there was in it all:

> Et nova longinquis piscibus esca natat.   (*ib.* 8)

Not so the greater poets:

> Nudus in ignota, Palinure, iacebis arena.   (*Aen.* v, 871)

Tibullus followed with elegies to Delia, a slighter force in the history of verse and perhaps of poetry, but a pleasanter and more congenial nature, with affinities to Virgil, and the friend of Horace, a poet graceful, delicate, refined, who loved the country. After them comes Ovid, the greatest of elegiac poets. His Corinna had the advantage of being perhaps an abstraction; so, safe from passion, Ovid can be safe from absurdity, the type that Horace drew (with no thought of him):

> urbani parcentis viribus atque
> Extenuantis eas.

He lived longer than the other elegiac writers; he had more range, more variety and more wit—humour, too, which the others lack.

VI. LIVY

So many interests, so many lines of original experience and deliberate imitation, meet in Augustan literature, and throughout it all is a strong consciousness of Rome. Rome *maxima rerum*, Rome *pulcerrima rerum*, Rome *populum late regem*—the beauty and the wonder and the power of this city on the seven hills, of this marvellous citizenship, of this world-wide empire—they never lose the sense of it, the passion for it. Rome is in all their thoughts, consciously or unconsciously. As the Englishman of the Victorian period moved about the continent, not saying that he was English, perhaps not thinking it, but being it, distilling it, announcing it, the Roman of this period, as we see him in his writing, is a citizen of no mean city, a fellow-citizen of Augustus. The doors of Janus were at last shut, and mankind had entered upon the unthinkable majesty of Roman peace. The world was one, united as it had hardly been under Alexander; Rome had achieved this, she was giving order and law, life and hope, to the world and she was its centre; and every man who thought knew it, and the greater men felt it.

'Whether I am likely to accomplish anything worth the labour, if I record the achievements of the Roman People from the foundation of the city, I do not exactly know, nor if I knew would I venture to affirm it; perceiving as I do that it is an old practice and hackneyed; all new historians believe either that they can produce higher certitude as to matter, or that by grace of style they will eclipse a rude antiquity.' So Livy begins the preface to his History—a work of infinite labour covering seven hundred years. His readers will wish to reach the account of their own day, when the might of a great people is its undoing; for himself, there are things he is glad to forget. To the earliest legends he will attribute neither truth nor falsehood; for the rest, he would have the reader consider as he goes, what life and character were age by age, by what men, by what policy or arts, in peace and in war, Rome's power was developed—and then the reader must reflect upon the decay of discipline and character; though Livy believes that there never was a State where poverty and thrift were so long honoured, and where luxury and avarice arrived so late with their fatal consequences.

The historian came from Patavium (Padua); twice over Quintilian tells us how Asinius Pollio (the friend of Virgil and the critic of Cicero) detected a certain 'Patavinity' in the historian's Latin. He was born in Caesar's first consulship (59 B.C.) and survived Augustus by three years; and full forty years of this long life he gave to his history, an accepted figure at the court of Augustus, for it was with his encouragement that the young prince Claudius embarked on History. It is something to have made an Emperor an historian. He lived to be famous, and his fame survived him. But in process of time his hundred and forty-two books seemed long, and fell into the hands of men who abridged them and finally were content with epitome; and then for centuries little is heard of him, till fame begins to return to him with John of Salisbury. Three-quarters of his work remains lost. Still an author who survives in thirty-five books has an immortality beyond most of his profession.

A higher certitude or a superior grace was Livy's antithesis. As we have not (with one signal exception) the work of the men from whom he drew, and do not in all cases know who they were, it is perhaps idle to dispute about the higher certitude. The one exception is Polybius, an author (Livy concedes) 'not to be despised[1]'— 'a reliable authority in all Roman history and especially where Greece is concerned[2].' Pleasant words and patronizing, but from them few would guess the amount of Livy's debt to Polybius or how closely he follows him. The students of history must be few who would not surrender a good many books of Livy for as many of Polybius; for no man who has spent his years with Herodotus, Thucydides, Xenophon and Polybius, can think of Livy as an historian in the same sense of the word. The speeches in Livy, particularly in the early period, 'the neat and eloquent harangues —pure inventions—lend an air of unreality to the whole narrative. But fashion rules and history had to be written thus[3].' So judges a great English historian of Rome, and most honest readers will have felt the same.

Matthew Arnold once spoke of a history of English literature being written to the tune of *Rule Britannia*. No one can follow Hannibal through Polybius and Livy and fail to make a similar judgment on the Roman. Polybius judges more dispassionately, and as a man who has actually taken a hand in politics, who has seen war in many lands, who has travelled and explored the world and lived in intimacy with statesmen and generals. Livy, like Timaeus (in Polybius' caustic criticism), had lived and worked in a study. His battle-pieces, written with gusto, are pronounced magnificent but not war. He is criticized for a similarly defective knowledge of Roman law, and for confusion in his account of constitutional struggles. The Emperor Gaius came near having the busts and writings of Livy removed from all public libraries, complaining that he was 'verbose and careless.' To be sure, Gaius was for doing the same by Virgil as 'a man of no genius and very little learning,' and asked why he might not, like Plato, turn Homer too out of his Republic. But critics of more admitted sanity make the same complaint of Livy's neglect of documents and monuments. He will not quote the hymn to Juno written by Livius Andronicus in the Second Punic War—'praiseworthy enough for the rude talent of those times, but to-day if quoted it would seem lacking in taste and finish[4].' He used Valerius Antias freely in his

---

[1] xxx, 45, 5.   [2] xxxiii, 10, 8.

[3] W. E. Heitland, *The Roman Republic*, i, p. 81.   [4] xxvii, 38.

first decade, to decide later on that he was not very reliable. He is believed not to have troubled to use the great antiquarian accumulations of Varro. In judging evidence, or statements that must pass for evidence, his canons of criticism are various; he will go by the majority, or the earliest, or he will harmonize, or he will choose the story that looks probable or tells best or fits best with Roman glory or statesmanship. 'In matters so ancient, if a story looks like truth, let it be taken as true.'

Traditur—there is something to be said for tradition, for folk-memory, as it is now called; and Livy would not have made much of a Record Office, if he had had it; nor did his public want a Latin Polybius—we have to remember that. For Livy knew the taste and temper of his day, and he gave his fellow-citizens quite evidently what they wanted. He too is a sign of the times; History is an art akin to Rhetoric, and more and more it will be written on Livy's lines, from Quintus Curtius and his *Alexander* on into the Middle Ages. Curtius may have belonged to this very age of Augustus—it is not certain; but he writes well in the Livian way, and posterity kept his book and did right to do so. Even the solider and sounder historians show the heritage of rhetoric—Eusebius and Ammianus Marcellinus are invaluable, but their style is incredible to those who only read in the great periods of literature. But who would care for a Thucydidean precision; does the stuff go well, does it carry you along, does the story march?

The answer is that Livy's story does carry you along. 'It is hardly too much,' wrote Macaulay's nephew, 'to assert that the demand for Macaulay varies with the demand for coal. The astonishing success of this celebrated book must be regarded as something of far higher consequence than a mere literary or commercial triumph. It is no insignificant feat to have awakened in hundreds of thousands of minds the taste for letters and the yearning for knowledge.' Something of the same kind may be claimed for Livy. Livy and Macaulay did what they intended; they carried History into the business and bosom of their nations. They taught men to find the past interesting, to believe in their people; they helped to mould their languages. It is something to consort with a man of genius, who so writes as to be always clear, always interesting, always illuminative. *Il parle d'or*, said Paul-Louis Courier of Livy.

Hannibal may be drawn amiss in Livy's pages; Romulus may lack a little of being historical; Valerius Antias may—but enough of this. Rome is the hero of Livy's book. Rome may not have been so uniformly wise and right—though few but Polybius and the author of *Revelation* said so with much emphasis. But Livy chose well, and he did his work. He made the history of Rome. Sainte-Beuve comments on some ancient work in the telling phrase that 'it made no heart beat.' Livy's work did make the heart beat; it helped to give men the sense of their country; it forced them to realize the grandeur of that old type which 'did not despair of the Republic.' Whatever our view of his limitations, it was of Livy's Rome and Virgil's that men thought, it was she that they loved, to her that they rallied, through the great centuries of the Empire and in the dark times that followed. Is this picture of Rome true? That after all is the final question. There is no doubt about the art with which it is drawn; it has fascinated mankind as well as the Romans; it lives; but is it true? Is it relevant to ask, does his picture agree with Virgil's?

VII. OVID

'In elegy,' wrote Quintilian, 'we can challenge the Greeks. In this Tibullus seems to me a writer in the highest degree terse and graceful, though there are those who prefer Propertius. *Ovidius utroque lascivior*.' Time developes some meanings in words and atrophies others; and the criticism may sound ambiguous, till the sentence is finished: '*sicut durior Gallus*.' Quintilian feels a certain stiffness in Gallus; no one has made this complaint of Ovid, either as regards style or matter; he is the gayest and most playful of Latin writers. Perhaps he has not more humour than Apuleius, but he did not feel it necessary to invent a new language; he was content to write Latin. No one wrote it with more grace; no one can be read with more ease; not Cicero himself is more definitely master of the art of saying precisely what he means and being entirely as lucid as he intends. The complaint is the other way; the writing is too easy, the meaning too quickly exhausted. 'A line of Wordsworth,' wrote Charles Lamb (and it is as true of Virgil) 'is a lever to raise the immortal spirit.' There are no undertones, no harmonics, about Ovid's work; it is all on the surface. Probably no writer, who refused depth, has ever had so wide a range of influence; and if complete mastery of his art entitles him to it, Ovid deserves it.

    Sulmo mihi patria est gelidis uberrimus undis. (*Trist.* iv, 10, 3)

Ovid (43 B.C.–A.D. 18) was born at Sulmo, ninety miles from Rome, in the Paelignian country, of a family whose equestrian rank was inherited, he says in this short account of himself, from ancestors of old (*usque a proavis vetus ordinis heres*), it was not the chance gift of Fortune in modern times. His elder brother's bent was oratory; he preferred the Muses, in spite of his father's frequent reminder that Homer left no estate. He dutifully tried to write prose, but in vain; verse came of its own accord,

> Et quod temptabam scribere versus erat.

He took the first steps in a legal career, but he gave up the hope of attaining the Senate; neither body nor mind inclined to energy; he lacked ambition—at least of that sort. So he lived a life of ease—without scandal, he points out; he wrote verse, associated with poets, heard Propertius recite, listened to *numerosus Horatius*; but *Vergilium vidi tantum*. He visited the East and Sicily. He was early famous, and everybody wondered who Corinna might be; it was a feigned name, he tells us. *Amores, The Letters of the Heroines*, the *Art of Love*, the *Remedy of Love*, the *Metamorphoses* in fifteen books, the *Fasti* originally in twelve, suggest that his life was not all idle, in spite of the evidence that his works offer so abundantly of the frivolity and worthlessness of the company he kept or pretended to keep. Suddenly in A.D. 8 Augustus ordered him to remove to Tomi on the Black Sea—Costanza to-day, where his statue stands. The cause for this removal was twofold—a book and a blunder. The book was the *Art of Love*; but that had been already published for ten years; then what was the blunder? All sorts of guesses have been made, with little agreement. Augustus never forgave him; and Tiberius, whose domestic happiness had been wrecked by compulsory marriage with Julia, was not likely to take a genial view of the poet of her school. So he had ten years of Tomi, writing letters and *Tristia*, with a heavy heart, to no purpose at all. His descriptions of barbarian life away on the Euxine are interesting; but the repeated picture of a broken spirit does not add to his fame.

To some of his books reference has already been made, his *Art* and his *Fasti*. His *Heroines* are graceful enough, and (he says) a novelty; no one would look for history or character in them—it would be as wise to grumble at the *Iliad* for failing of the brevity of an epigram; but a certain tenderness is sometimes felt in them not revealed in his other work. The *Heroines* show a wide reading in Greek literature, as does everything he wrote. The *Metamorphoses* make a book which one might call portentous, but that mankind owes so much happiness to it. Others had collected stories, and love tales in particular, like the solid Parthenius, who is supposed to have taught Virgil, and the dateless Apollodorus, both Greeks. Ovid has a sort of string for his series of tales, but the reader soon forgets it. At one point a group of sisters tell stories to one another, to while away the time, with a faint sug-

gestion of Boccaccio[1], but the grand merit of the book is that it is
a huge assemblage of stories, in Latin that will perplex nobody,
told with such vigour and brightness—and such utter absence of
any kind of reverence—that the reader is never taxed wherever
he picks it up. The only difficulty is to read it as a whole. It has
many famous lines:

> Fas est et ab hoste doceri   (IV, 428)
> Video meliora proboque, deteriora sequor   (VII, 20–1)
> Os homini sublime dedit caelumque videre: (I, 85)

and thousands more ranging from bathos to wit as unexpected—

> Et quia nuda fui, sum visa paratior illi: (V, 603)
> Hoc certe furtum coniunx mea nesciet, inquit,
> Aut si rescierit,—sunt o sunt iurgia tanti.   (II, 423–4)

This couplet is Juppiter's, who is here the Jove of the Pompeian
wall-pictures, which might have been designed to illustrate the
book. There are rhetorical passages of course, and proper names
in gratuitous heaps. Thirty-two of Actaeon's dogs are named before we reach the brute that bit him; in the Phaethon story twenty-
three mountains are listed and twenty-seven rivers. The poet plays
at his work, and a great deal of it is trifling. But when all this is
said, the main thing remains to be said.

The Middle Ages adopted the *Metamorphoses*; men had through
that great period 'a passion for monotony,' we are told; and the
book was read and re-read, probably by others, certainly by poets
who drew matter and inspiration from it. Few books can have
given so much pleasure to mankind directly or indirectly. We
read of Ovid as the favourite poet of Chaucer and Boccaccio—

> As saith Ovid and Titus Livius—

but Chaucer knew little of Livy beyond the tales of Lucretia and
Virginia. Throughout a long poetical activity Chaucer is constantly borrowing from Ovid, and on all sorts of subjects, especially
from the *Metamorphoses*. The Wife of Bath tells of her husband
Jankin and his comprehensive volume:

> He hadde a book that gladly, night and day,
> For his desport he wolde rede alway. . . .
> In whiche book eek ther was Tertulan,
> Crisippus, Trotula and Helowys,
> That was abbesse nat fer fro Parys;
> And eek the Parables of Salomon,
> Ovydes Art, and bokes many on,
> And alle thise wer bounden in o volume.

'Ovydes Art' is one of the strongest influences in Provençal poetry
and his other books contribute significantly to medieval romance.

---

[1] *Met.* IV, 55–385.

The *Heroines* are a sort of 'Saints' Legend of Cupid.' Stranger still, we read of Ovid being 'moralized' by Chrétien Légouais, a Franciscan, at the beginning of the fourteenth century, who allegorized the *Metamorphoses* in 70,000 lines; this or another effort of the kind was twice printed by Badius in the early days of printing. The *Art* itself was allegorized and lies behind the *Roman de la Rose*. As for 'wandering scholars' and the Goliardic tribe, Ovid was their obvious canon, and we are told of one Doctor of Divinity in Paris, who held that God hath spoken in Ovid even as in Augustine. But here we seem leaving literature for theology, and Phoebus may twitch our ears.

VIII. HORACE

It seems established, though it remains strange, that Chaucer had no knowledge of Horace, much as they have in common. In general it appears that Horace did not appeal to the Middle Ages as did Ovid, Statius, Lucan, and above all Virgil—a fact not altogether idle. Some great writers will stand translation, and even in very bad renderings will capture and influence readers: the *Odyssey* and *Don Quixote* are outstanding books of this kind. But others insist upon having readers of their own class and antecedents, and on being read in the original. Horace almost requires an Augustan age. Ben Jonson translated some of him into English. Burton found him congenial and constantly quotes him in *The Anatomy of Melancholy*. Herrick read him and copied him. Indeed it is well said that Horace is the patron saint, the ancestor and exemplar of all light verse in English from Prior to Praed. Perhaps we might count the essayists too from Addison to Thackeray among his descendants. The eighteenth century is his true *floruit*. It gave him a constituency with the same sort of culture, the same preference for taste, finish and sanity, and a strong sympathy for his *nil admirari*. Horace took clear precedence of Virgil throughout the century in England, and lived in ceaseless quotation. Steele and Fielding show his spirit; Lord Chesterfield and Horace Walpole have him at their fingers' ends; Burke, Pitt, Fox and Sheridan quote him, with consummate address. Indeed it might be said that Horace only lost his seat in Parliament when Gladstone retired from politics and solaced himself by translating the *Odes*. It was not a supreme version, but to be translated by a Prime Minister—

> Principibus placuisse viris non ultima laus est,

is Horace's own comment.

In his interesting essay on Béranger, Walter Bagehot compares him with Horace, but finds marked differences, which go far to explain Horace's eighteenth-century popularity. Sceptical and indifferent as both poets are, Béranger differs from Horace in having a real faith in liberty and belief in it. Horace was the friend of Maecenas, and was offered very high, if untitled, office by Augustus. Bagehot finds it hard to imagine why precisely Horace, the student at Athens, should have thought it worth while to serve with Brutus. Perhaps he was not yet the Horace we know. An American scholar has recently brought out the length of his service, the range of territory covered, and the rank attained with the inference, supported by the proposal of Augustus, that Horace was a far more capable and forceful person than some suppose[1]. But it is Horace's care to obscure all this. It is characteristic of him that he can write with humour of his wars against Augustus, of his military tribune days and his rout at Philippi. And there, says Bagehot, he touches Béranger closely; the most essential character of each is geniality. Pope endeavours to copy Horace, but there is always a bitter ingredient in the copy which the original lacks; for it is not commonly given to the children of men to be philosophers without envy, while Horace either never had it, or outgrew it. He has a genius for friendship— though not necessarily with pushing people like Propertius, he seems to say, who must in any case have been thoroughly distasteful to him, an extravagant, unbalanced person. Horace is the poet of the quiet mind, who gives the world in exquisite form its own view of itself, 'its self-satisfaction, its conviction that you must bear what comes, not hope for much, think *some* evil, never be excited, admire little, and then you will be at peace.' Ἔτι δὲ ἐν βίῳ τελείῳ—with a Sabine farm, a friend in Maecenas, and an Augustan age. So baldly stated, it does not sound quite attractive or very genial. But Horace, aloof from crusades and passions, is genially aloof, and very human and lovable in his Epicureanism.

His story is familiar; he tells it himself. The freedman father, the sound education, Athens, the war, Philippi, the 'clipped wings,' and then friendship with Virgil and Varius, with Maecenas and Augustus. It is curious how often he speaks of the sea. To Maecenas his tone is, to a surprising degree, that of a friend on equal terms, in a genuine friendship. For Virgil he has an obvious reverence; Virgil is among the 'white souls,' none whiter. But, after all, perhaps the man who stands highest with him is the freedman father, so described. There is an ode in the Fourth Book

[1] Tenney Frank, *Catullus and Horace*, chap. vii.

that has perplexed critics; it must be to another, an unknown, Virgil, *iuvenum nobilium cliens*? Could anyone so name *the* Virgil? Could anyone chaff Virgil about bartering nard for wine of Cales? Could the famous *dulce est desipere in loco* be addressed to the author of the *Aeneid*? Charles Lamb at any rate so addressed the author of the *Excursion*. 'Now, I think, in buffoonery I have a wider range than you.' It may well be an early ode, written when the words *iuvenum nobilium cliens* would not be shocking. But they never did shock Horace, nor did the freedman stigma of his father. Proud as he is of exalted patronage, he can write his *cuncta resigno* and *libertino patre natum*. That is the man; for genius is a strange compound, and Horace well illustrates what strange traits it can have, and how much it can lack.

The survival of his earlier works, *Epodes* and *Satires*, makes his greatness still stranger. If nothing else survived, few would wish to read him. Even among the *Odes* there are verses which could be spared; they are too like the *Epodes*; they may be old work, but there they are. Literary mode may, of course, be the explanation; even the admirable Pliny the Younger felt it fitting to endeavour on one occasion to write obscene verse, and no doubt wrote it conscientiously as he wrote everything. The *Epodes* are unpleasant, with a harshness, a coarseness of fibre, that surprises; but the more surprising thing is that Horace outgrew it all. His sense of humour suffers change into something rich and strange. The coarseness is gone; there is instead geniality, good taste, a delightful playfulness, a charm that is not artifice or mode, but comes from within, as Longinus says all greatness does, an echo of the nature. The development is in its way as wonderful as the result.

The *Satires* were imitations of Lucilius, in matter and metre, and the model was ill chosen; for in his *Epistles* it is his own genius that is seen, and it is incomparably pleasanter and wiser. The changes in metre we have noted. The matter is dictated by friendship instead of satire; and we have a mellowing poet's judgments upon books, and Homer, the schools of the philosophers, the ways of men; tale and fable and country scene vary the impression; and all is lit up by Horace's own philosophy of life. The book, indeed his whole work, gives a remarkably living picture of the times; he might be called the Boswell of his age, but that he has no Johnson, not even Maecenas, and that such parallels can only be partial and the wrong part would be emphasized. Still more the appeal lies in his having the late Elia's fondness for the first person; he reveals himself and we like him.

As for the *Odes* they form, it has been said, 'a secular Psalter for daily and yearly and age-long use.' The art of them for ever taxes the critics; the workmanship suggests the Matine bee, mosaic, painting in monochrome, jewel-work and so forth. His own 'golden mediocrity,' the shrewd word 'economy' and the like help us perhaps a little. No one quotes Plato about him; he is of all great poets least like an 'inspired idiot.' It has been sometimes said that Horace is the favourite poet of men who do not care for poetry; what women think of him is not so clear—probably, like Boswell, he is a man's author. But it takes a lifetime of acquaintance with Horace himself and the classical poets to realize how great an achievement is his handling of verse. The old technical term 'inevitable' recurs to the mind. His ear is quick, and he has trained it, and in lyrics he is as infallible as Virgil in hexameters. Perhaps the achievement would not be possible in any language but Latin. The modern tongues have to make shift with characterless monosyllables, where Horace had to his hand case-endings, a conjugated verb and the mysteries of the subjunctive. But even in Latin he has no real imitator; Prudentius has real lyric gifts, and writes Sapphics, but he has other aims, another feeling for life. No one really gets very far beyond the two famous criticisms of Petronius and Quintilian—*Horatii curiosa felicitas* and *plenus iucunditatis et gratiae et varius figuris et verbis felicissime audax*. There we may leave it; there is consolation in St Augustine's phrase, if we may detach it, *alii disputent, ego mirabor*.

IX. VIRGIL

In our survey of the main factors and interests in Augustan literature, we have found at every point that Virgil is master of all that lives, that he touches every phase of national life and movement. Elegy excepted, it may be said; but the ancients judged otherwise, for where love is concerned they set Dido before Corinna; the one represents merely an amused animalism, the other is tragedy, and her story raises every question that pain and happiness can bring home to the human heart. St Augustine was assuredly not alone in shedding tears for *Didonem extinctam ferroque extrema secutam*[1]. If the modern reader makes the confession *mens immota manebat*, it merely means the triumph of scholarship over humanism and helps to explain the decline of classical studies. For in judging Virgil the reader judges himself;

---

[1] *Confessions* I, 13, 21.

his comments merely tell a sentient world what he himself is fit for; what follows is written in that consciousness.

Virgil was born on 15 October 70 B.C.—*Octobres Maro consecravit Idus*. He was born by the roadside, we are told; he grew up on a farm at or near Andes, a village not very far from Mantua. His father was a man of energy, among other things a lumberman, and his son vividly pictures the felling of the forest and the flight of the birds.

> Antiquasque domos avium cum stirpibus imis
> Eruit; illae altum nidis petiere relictis.   (*Georg.* II, 209)

Deforestation had its usual effects, and to-day men miss the birds that Virgil knew in his country. Virgil's intimate knowledge of woodcraft is remarked, not by the ancients who loved to augment his omniscience, but by the modern expert; and he is always very near the farm and the farm-people; the wars of Antony and Turnus wreck the settled low content and all that it means of work and happiness. To the end, we are told by Melissus, a professional humourist, Virgil looked like a rustic and would be taken for one. He remained shy and uneasy; and, when he was suddenly recognized and applauded in the theatre, he left Rome for the neighbourhood of Naples. There his character won him the nickname *Parthenias*, which suggests that the Neapolitans may have pronounced his name, as it afterwards became current, and as it passed into the languages and literature of Europe.

Nos patriae fines et dulcia linquimus arva stands in the forefront of his work, an experience indelible for such a nature; for, quickly as Pollio, Maecenas, and Octavian in turn come to the poet's aid, he has shared the common lot. So in his way had Horace; but Horace, unlike the greater poets, had ways of protecting himself, *et mea virtute me involvo*, and lived free from the past and careful to avoid fresh trouble. The greater poet discards no experience; and a tenderness for human suffering, little familiar in Roman literature, is always to be felt in his work by those who have known suffering. Some imagination is needed for the interpretation of a poet, and it may not be mere fancy to believe that this painful contact with the common problem reacted upon Virgil's attitude to letters and to thought. A poet does not read as ordinary men do, witness Keats reading Chapman's *Homer*; Virgil was never done with his poets, their text was written over again within him. But life gave fresh clues. He had his clever period, like an undergraduate, and clearly loved the sheer cleverness of the Alexandrines. And he meant to be an Epicurean, to gather the learned lore of Siro and free his life from all care in the havens of the blest. Martial implies in his senseless way that Virgil found those havens; Tennyson thought not—'the doubtful doom of human kind' is never absent from him. Neither Hellenistic poetry nor philosophy was deep enough to explain his experience, and he went back to the greater poets and thinkers of an earlier day—to Euripides and Pythagoras, and, of course, to Hesiod and Homer. Plato, in one of his greatest sentences, speaks of 'the ancient quarrel between poetry and philosophy[1].' It is a useful thought for the student of poets; for the greatest poets all know that quarrel between intuition and reason, as well as Plato knew it; it is fought out within them; and if it be not, there is no great poetry. 'Prolong that battle while his life shall last,' or you will hardly have a Virgil, a Dante, a Shakespeare. There are other views of poetry, but probably to the extremest champion of pure poetry, of sheer music (if he can feel Latin), Virgil will speak as securely.

Without stopping to analyse poems so familiar as the acknowledged writings of Virgil, or to guess (fond amusement) about the disputed works, let us sum up in outline what Virgil has meant to his friends, ancient and modern, remembering that no great poet can be explained by any such process. An index never gives the living spirit of a book, nor will it here; but it may tell a reader what to look for. To begin, then, Horace affixes to Virgil two epithets, which mean little to the casual reader unless it be a question.

> Molle atque facetum
> Vergilio adnuerunt gaudentes rure Camenae.   (*Sat.* 1, 10, 44)

The Muses of the country-side, all would admit at once; the adjectives need closer care. Exquisite tenderness and playfulness is what they seem to connote; the one is soon obvious, the other is still subtler. *It nigrum campis agmen*—Ennius would have stared; it is ants that march in file in Virgil, but the line was Ennius' own, and he wrote it of elephants; how came Virgil to borrow it? The reader must answer that, not forgetting the *dulce est desipere in loco* discussed above. No lover of Virgil but recalls the antithesis:

> Felix qui potuit rerum cognoscere causas. . . .
> Fortunatus et ille deos qui novit agrestes.

The lines are poetry; they chronicle opinion—fact, too, perhaps— but far more an attitude to life, a spirit in which life is handled, for which fresh discoveries mean much, but a tireless expectancy much more. Virgil is never done with life, with human experience

---

[1] *Republic*, x, 607 B.

and history; they are as fertile as Nature of surprises and revela-
tions; and he pursues life both ways. To these add the untranslated

Sunt lacrimae rerum et mentem mortalia tangunt.

Here many comments recur to the mind—the higher truth and
the higher seriousness of poetry, which Aristotle and Arnold emphasize; the conception of poetry as the echo of a great soul, which
Longinus gave; the common man's realization that a man cannot
be human who has 'no capacity for tragedy.' But Virgil only
speaks to those who know him in his fulness and are long intimate
with him.

Our index would seem to require some listing of what Virgil
did for his Roman readers and has ever done. He gave, then, beyond all other poets, a new revelation of the beauty of Latin; and
here Longinus' 'old experience' is needed. There is so much in his
Latin—all the values of sound—consonant, vowel and syllable,
none astray—word with word, line with line, the paragraph and the
page. Other men are best quoted in lines; Virgil's page, better still
the book or the whole epic, are needed to give his music. It is like
Don Quixote, so little quotable, everything in the spirit and the
fabric. 'The rich Virgilian rustic measure of *Lari maxime*'; all the
suggestions of word and sound, the harmonics that echo from the
great phrase—all these have to be reckoned. For some unaccountable reason, says his friend, R. L. Stevenson's favourite line of
Virgil from boyhood was

Iam medio apparet fluctu nemorosa Zacynthos.

Was it unaccountable? Look at the last words; think of the sea
and sea-faring; and there is Homer behind and Samoa to come;
from Sertorius to Sancho it is in the Isle that men look for happiness. The great poets are frank enough in linking their music to
those who went before them, and Ennius is best known in Virgil;
his verse serves to patch the sense out for those who do not know;
but for those who do know there is a depth of feeling unspeakable
—music, reminder, old story, reconciliation—

nox umida donec
Invertit caelum stellis ardentibus aptum.

But once again it is the passage that gives the interpretation.
'Virgil,' writes J. W. Mackail, 'stands out as having achieved the
utmost beauty, melody and significance, of which human words
seem to be capable[1].'

---

[1] *The Aeneid of Virgil*, p. lxxxvi.

Virgil goes farther. Romance in his day pointed to Greece, to Troy, to the Orient; Italy was a land of prose. Virgil revealed its beauty for ever, and taught other men beside the Italians to see their own lands. *Sed neque Medorum silvae*—no, there is no land to match Italy:

> praeruptis oppida saxis,
> Fluminaque antiquos subterlabentia muros...
>   te, Lari maxime, teque,
> Fluctibus et fremitu assurgens Benace marino.
>   (*Georg.* II, 156–7, 159–60)

Whatever Homer's catalogues meant to the Greek, they were Virgil's warrant for showing Italy to his people. The Italians, too,

> quibus Itala iam tum
> Floruerit terra alma viris—   (*Aen.* VII, 643–4)

Marsian, Sabellian, Ligurian, the heroes, Decii, Marii and all, the settler from overseas, the old Corycian, and the great figure of Evander:

> Me pulsum patria pelagique extrema petentem
> Fortuna omnipotens et ineluctabile Fatum
> His posuere locis—   (*Aen.* VIII, 333–5)

he thinks of them all and interprets them, and all that they have done in the beauty of the land, the growth of civilization, the development of character, the turning to account of work and pain and happiness. It is long since Matthew Arnold pronounced literature to be an interpretation of life—the noble and profound application of ideas to life; and other things are said. But Virgil's work at least warrants Arnold's view, and will never be quite understood without it.

The *Aeneid* some have reckoned a mistake, and cited the dying poet's sense of incompleteness to support a shallow judgment. Here again the criticism chiefly reveals the critic—has he known an empire, a national history? Does he look only to youth, or are middle age and old age also part of life? *Aeneas* is no young Achilles; he has his *barbarus has segetes* written on his heart—*et campos ubi Troia fuit*—and Augustine's line

> Infelix simulacrum atque ipsius umbra Creusae;

he lives for no purpose of his own, *Italiam non sponte sequor, ego poscor Olympo*; and he is tenderer than the old type of hero, witness the killing of Lausus, and *pacem me exanimis*. He becomes an interpretation of all Roman history. Into the story are woven— and they belong there, are an integral part of it—the great names of Rome, heroes and statesmen, the house of Julius with its great service of mankind, the Roman Empire ('the best thing that Fortune ever did for the world,' says Polybius), and the 'unspeakable majesty of Roman peace.' If Virgil's interpretation of these things is true, the poem must have meaning for others than Romans; it must interpret the world, life, the human heart; it must be more philosophic, more in earnest, than any history. All this men through the centuries have found in the *Aeneid*, and it is still to be found there; but not by casual readers, nor in fragments. Poetry and Nature are not so read to any purpose; they ask for devotion and they repay it.

CHAPTER XVII

THE ART OF THE AUGUSTAN AGE

I. CHARACTERISTICS OF IMPERIAL ART

WITH Augustus Roman art definitely acquires an Imperial and universal value. In the Augustan programme the art of Rome, predestined capital of a new unified dominion, must primarily be Italic and Roman in character: the Italic tradition was now so deeply rooted in the national consciousness that the Emperor could fearlessly exalt it and complete its romanization. This is not to say that Hellenism was repudiated, far from it; but it was to be admitted only as an element deliberately accepted and absorbed. The question was no longer one of conflicting principles, but of complementary factors. What to Cato and his followers had appeared a peril to be avoided at all costs[1] had now become a necessary and intrinsic part of the complex Roman fabric. The formation of Roman civilization and art was 'not the result of the simple combination of foreign elements, but of the combination of these with an element preponderant among them all, the Latin element itself[2].'

Roman Imperial art was thus no sudden phenomenon. Its Italic origins are revealed in its themes which remain man and his doings; hence it excelled in portraiture and in the rendering of *res gestae* whether public or private. Its sphere was still the life of the city, of the camp and of the soil. For the Romans ideas had little value except in so far as they could be translated into actions; to them art was neither the expression of ideas nor the attainment of beauty, but a method of making actions known and of committing them to posterity. It was commemorative rather than historical, a record of contemporary events which only turned to the past or to legend when this seemed necessary to the enrichment of the present. A great representational art now came into existence, whose function was to enforce the lessons of Empire, and to glorify the doings of its rulers and its people.

[1] Vol. IX, p. 805.
[2] C. Q. Giglioli, *Roma e la Civilità del Mondo* in *Nuova Antologia*, Sept. 1, 1927, p. 6.

II. THE *ARA PACIS AUGUSTAE* AND KINDRED
MONUMENTS

These characteristics come out forcibly in the famous reliefs from the enclosing wall of the *Ara Pacis Augustae* which was put up between 13 and 9 B.C. as symbol of the *pax Romana* now established throughout the world by will of the Emperor. The occasion was a State thanksgiving for the safe return of Augustus from Gaul and Spain, in which the Emperor himself and his family, the priestly colleges, the Senate and the People appeared as participants. The altar was in the Campus Martius close to the Via Flaminia[1] by which Augustus entered the city on his return and, like the earlier altar of Fortuna Redux at the Porta Capena[2], was served according to a ritual fixed by the Emperor himself[3]. The inner and outer faces of the wall were divided horizontally into two zones. The lower zone of the outer face is covered by acanthus spirals; a ceremonial procession fills the longer sides of the upper frieze and allegories of Empire adorn the shorter panels on each side of the two entrances[4]. The sculptured reliefs, though found at different times and scattered in various museums of Italy and Europe, have survived almost complete.

As a visible memorial of the home policy of Augustus the processional friezes have a value second only to the Emperor's own account of his Principate—those *Res Gestae Divi Augusti* which were inscribed on tablets of bronze at the entrance to his Mausoleum. The first act of the pageant[5] opens as the Emperor, surrounded by his bodyguard, halts to offer libation; immediately follow the religious orders, the Vestal virgins, the priestly colleges and the Pontifex Maximus himself[6]. The religious organization of Augustus is here vividly portrayed in its two main manifestations —the liturgy, of which he showed himself a zealous observant[7],

---

[1] Actually under the modern Palazzo Ottoboni-Fiano, where the altar itself, its steps and one or two reliefs are still interred.

[2] Erected six years earlier (19 B.C.) at the gate by which Augustus entered the city from the Via Appia on his return from Syria with the standards recaptured from the Parthians. Unfortunately nothing is known of the decorative work, either on this altar or on the Arch put up to Augustus in the Forum on the same occasion.

[3] *Res Gestae* 11 (Fortuna Redux), 12 (Ara Pacis).

[4] See Plan 1, facing p. 582.   [5] Volume of Plates iv, 112, *a*.

[6] *Ib.* 114, *a*.

[7] Cf. his three nights' vigil on the occasion of the Ludi Saeculares of 17 B.C.

and the priesthoods, in which he himself held high office[1]. A small boy[2] who hangs on to the cloak of the Pontifex and looks back to the second part of the advancing procession, effects the needed shifting of the key from the religious solemnities to the animated couples who, accompanied by their children, represent the Imperial family and symbolize the dynastic continuity which Augustus believed to be interwoven with the life of the Empire[3]. The entrances divide these august presences from the second part of the procession shown on the parallel wall. A long file of senators, draped in their ample togas, fills some two-thirds of the space[4]. This prominence emphasizes the re-organization of the Senate, thrice purged by Augustus of alien or unworthy elements (see p. 149). If the ranks are a trifle monotonous they are at least impressive. As on the first frieze the mode changes gradually from grave to gay, and the pageant closes in a group of citizens with their wives and children[5]. They stand for the Roman *Populus* whose racial purity Augustus strove to safeguard from foreign contaminations, and whom he raised to a new sense of national dignity and importance as chief mainstay and support of the State. The technique of these friezes is not exempt from asperities, the movements often lack suppleness and ease, but the whole is harmoniously welded together by the unity of the pervading thought.

The representation of childhood on the balustrades of the Ara illustrates a purely Italic strain which has never died out of Western art. The children of the Imperial group, the little girl of the north frieze, who, holding a stiff nosegay, walks with childish self-importance[6], the baby who totters along, all but lifted off his fat legs by the firm hand of his father[7]—

> dextrae se parvus Iulus
> inplicuit sequiturque patrem non passibus aequis—

are familiar types that may be studied any day in the streets of modern Italy. The child, so often admitted on sufferance into Greek art as complement of a story, as attribute or even mere ornament, acquires independence in Roman art, and takes its place as an integral part of the life of the family. This strong feeling for childhood was doubtless fostered by the dynastic

---

[1] *Res Gestae* 8.
[2] Probably a *camillus* (text to Volume of Plates iv, 114, *a*).
[3] Volume of Plates iv, 114–16.
[4] E. Strong, *La Scultura Romana*, I, figs. 18, 19.
[5] Volume of Plates iv, 114, *b*.   [6] Strong, *op. cit.* I, fig. 21.
[7] Volume of Plates iv, 114 *b*, 118 *c*.

hopes of Augustus, by his love for those children and grand-
children who he proudly believed would succeed him, as also
by his insistence on the fertility of the family as a first condition of
national prosperity (pp. 443 *sqq.*).

It is not so much with the majesty of Empire that the Ara Pacis
strikes one as with that human and personal conception of the
Principate which Augustus wished to stress. There is nothing
monarchic about these friezes in the Oriental sense which places
the monarch above his subjects, though the dynastic idea is
manifest in the presence of the many descendants. Augustus, the
central figure of the ceremony, remains closely connected with the
action, thus maintaining his character of *primus inter pares*—the
visible counterpart of his title *princeps*. He is placed in three-
quarter view to the right[1], as participant in the action, and there
is no question as yet of giving him the frontal position which
would bring him out of the picture and relate him to the spectator,
while separating him from the other actors in the scene.

In the four panels on the entrance sides the subjects pass from
the realities of contemporary ceremonial to allegory and mythology. The best preserved is the well-known relief in Florence of
Terra Mater with her nurselings (a figure sometimes interpreted
as *Italia*) flanked by the spirits of Air and Water[2]. The goddess
sits on a rock above a stream, which flows from a reed-fringed
pool on the left, reminiscent of Virgil's Mincio,—

> Hic virides tenera praetexit arundine ripas
> Mincius—

while the cattle rest in the shade of the rock, and tall poppy-heads
and more reeds give a background to the charming composition.
Save in the accessories, the central group varies little from its
compeer in the Louvre[3]; both seem to derive from the same
statuary composition set up possibly in some chapel or sanctuary
of Tellus. Of the companion slab to the *Terra Mater* all we have
is a few fragments apparently of Roma seated on a pile of armour,
enough, however, to show that the power and glory of Rome as
fountain-head of the new prosperity faces the fertility of the
Orbis Terrarum under the Imperial rule.

The panel on the opposite side, representing the Arrival of
Aeneas in Latium[4], affords a good instance of the Roman power
of knitting the past with the present; this is effected in the person
of Aeneas, who appears here both as founder of the race and as

---

[1] Volume of Plates iv, 112, *a*.
[2] *Ib.* 120, *a* (with discussion of alternative interpretation).
[3] *Ib.* 120, *b*.   [4] *Ib.* 122, *a*.

double of Augustus, in token of which, though only just landed in
Latium, he performs his sacrifice in sight of a shrine of the Penates,
whose cult Augustus had restored[1]. The relief has something of the
sylvan beauty of the Tellus slab: from a cave an attendant drives
the sow to a rustic and garlanded altar, beside which stands a
camillus carrying a jug and a cup piled with fruit; on the right, the
commanding figure of Aeneas, bearded as befits an ancestor,
accompanied by Achates and perhaps by Iulus, looks benevolently
on, as he pours his libation at the altar. The corresponding relief,
on the right of the entrance, of which only the merest fragments
remain, apparently represented the Nurture of the Twins within
the Lupercal, a subject dear to Augustus, who had also restored
this ancient shrine[2]. The mythico-historical happenings of the
west side, localized in Rome, combine with the more generalized
allegories of the east side, to form a setting of cosmic significance
for the Imperial processions.

The technique of these friezes retains much of the old Republican harshness: the figures appear carved rather than
modelled and the folds of the drapery are rendered by means of
sharp ridges which produce contrasts of black and white, with little
attention to the rendering of texture or to surface transitions. The
processional arrangement likewise has Italic traits, the serried
ranks breaking up into groups of closely related figures who
move, so to speak, in space as well as along the surface. The
tridimensional principle had already made itself felt in Etruscan
art[3], but it was only with greater technical dexterity that it attained
full expression. A century of effort was needed before sculptors
produced the spatial illusion of the panels of the Arch of Titus.

The lower wall is richly decorated with an intricate pattern,
composed of four systems of interlacing acanthus scrolls, each
springing from a central stem. To cover the whole surface of a
wall with carved reliefs as with a carpet or tapestry-hanging was a
new and original device. A new sense of plasticity, lacking to the
processional friezes, makes itself felt here: the swelling stalks,
the petalled flowers, the opening buds, the rich foliage, the
Apolline swans poised with spreading wings on slender stems, all
these are modelled with minute attention to light and shade, and
to plastic form. So delicate is the carving that the pattern enriches
the wall-surface without detracting from its solidity. But there
is no monotony in the huge design, if only because the acanthus
stems appear grafted, as it were, with plants of another kind;
clusters of ivy, pansies and poppies flower happily on an alien

----

[1] *Res Gestae* 19.   [2] *Ib.* 19.   [3] Vol. IX, p. 117.

stem as if to illustrate the second *Georgic*[1]. The scrolls themselves became a typical Roman decoration; they were not only used as an architectural ornament, but often adorned furniture and small objects. A network of spirals similar to those of the Ara Pacis encircles a cup from Boscoreale in the Louvre and another in Berlin from the Treasure of Hildesheim. They could be infinitely varied; they were translated with equal effect into paint or mosaic and attained to a last splendid efflorescence in the art of Christianity.

Fine decorative effects are likewise provided by the swags of flowers, fruit and leafage which hang between *bucrania*, or ox-skulls, along the inner wall of the enclosure[2]. We have already seen similar festoons painted between the columns of the White Room of the so-called House of Livia (vol. IX, p. 828); they had also appeared at an earlier date carved on the tomb of Bibulus[3], later on that of Caecilia Metella; repeatedly and at all times along the friezes of tombs and temples—Roman art is almost unthinkable without them.

Fruit treated with the same rich naturalism as the swags of the Ara Pacis overflows from the numerous cornuacopiae symbolic of the fertility of the Empire, such as those held by the Genius Augusti in the Vatican[4], or carved on the altar of Carthage (p. 552) and on a relief in the Terme[5], while on the Ara Pacis itself the fruit in the cup held by the *camillus* in the Aeneas panel, and the delicate poppy-heads in the background of the Terra Mater panel show the same acute observation of natural forms. All these fruits and flowers were naturalistically coloured in the manner revived in the Renaissance by the Della Robbias and Crivelli (see further, below, p. 567). In time this naturalism became conventionalized and was replaced by the harder rendering of flower and plant forms already to be seen on the sarcophagus Caffarelli in Berlin which is datable to the Tiberian epoch[6].

In the dearth of monumental sculpture of the Augustan period besides the Ara Pacis, great importance attaches to the small altars set up in connection with the cult of the *lares* restored by Augustus. One of the most significant of these altars, datable to between 12 and 6 B.C., is in the Vatican[7]. It is primarily

---

[1] Volume of Plates iv, 122, *b*.   [2] *Ib*. iv, 124, *a*.
[3] Datable to about 60 B.C. (?); T. Frank, *Roman Buildings of the Republic*, p. 144; cf. Platner-Ashby, *Top. Dict. of Ancient Rome*, p. 477.
[4] Helbig-Amelung, *Führer durch die Sammlungen Klass. Alt. in Rom*, 1, no. 304.   [5] Volume of Plates iv, 124, *b*.
[6] *Ib*. 124, *c*.   [7] *Ib*. 130.

a record of the past and present claims to glory of Augustus. On the front face the Victory, who in Augustan policy appears as the pledge of perpetual victory to himself and his successors, hovers by the *clipeus*, which can be none other than the *clipeus aureus* granted to him in 27 B.C. by the Senate and hung on a pillar like a trophy[1]. The group is framed by two laurel bushes, identified as those that flanked the entrance to the house of the Princeps. The doctrine of Victory inculcated on the front face is balanced on the back panel by that of Apotheosis[2]; here Caesar, like Elijah, rises heavenward in a flaming chariot, within a cosmic setting defined by Sol, Caelus and the divine eagle in their midst, while members of the Imperial family look up from below. The shorter sides introduce us to scenes of more human and immediate interest; on the right, within a garlanded precinct, the ceremony of the reconsecration of the *lares* takes place; on the opposite side the Mother of the *lares*, reading out of the prophetic scroll, presides over the prodigy of the Laurentian sow, while Trojan Aeneas looks on. This mythological episode connects in the Augustan manner the present with the legendary past. Apart from this significance, the altar is remarkable for its finish, for the purity of its linear style, and for a severity of composition characteristic of an early date; the figures grouped round the altar in the scene of sacrifice are intent on the business in hand, and no attempt is made to correlate them either by action or by glance with the spectator.

An altar in the Uffizi, dedicated by the *vicomagistri* of the *Vicus Sandalarius* (Cobblers' Lane) in 2 B.C., has on the front face Augustus, marked out by his staff as *augur*, an office which he held in the greatest honour, with Livia on his left and an Imperial prince on his right, all three apparently imitations of statues in the round, a common device of Augustan and Julio-Claudian art[3]. At the back is the crown of oak, *ob cives servatos*, and a sacrificial *patera* to indicate the sanctity of the spot. Here the Augustan Victory appears on the right narrow side, balancing herself on a trophy, while on the left side are two *lares*. A third altar, in the Palazzo dei Conservatori, was dedicated in A.D. 1 by the *magistri* of the *Vicus Aesculetus* (Oak-tree Lane), who are shown on the front face offering sacrifice, two on each side of an altar[4]. At the back are traces of an oak-wreath, and at the sides the Augustan *lares*. The personages show little variety of attitude as contrasted with the animated groups on the altar of Manlius, with which we may

---

[1] See J. Gagé in *Mél. d'arch. et d'hist.* XLIX, 1932, pp. 61 *sqq.*
[2] Volume of Plates iv, 130, *a.*   [3] *Ib.* 136, *a.*   [4] *Ib.* 132.

close the series of *Lar* altars[1]. On the front face is carved a sacrificial scene within a garlanded precinct, and at the back, in place
of the more usual Victory or wreath, a ceremony in honour of
Fortuna, who sits on a high-backed throne raised on a rock. The
lares are repeated, one on each of the shorter sides of the altar. The
complicated composition both of the sacrificial scenes and of the
ceremony, in which Fortuna appears almost frontally, shows a
marked advance in tridimensional composition; it heralds the art
of the Flavian age and the reliefs of the Arch of Titus. Like the
relief of the Etruscan cities (p. 554), the altar of Manlius was
found at Caere; it therefore probably belongs to the efflorescence
of that city in the reign of Claudius, a date which would well
accord with its style.

In the provinces the same influences were at work. Art with the
Romans became an acknowledged system of religious and political propaganda; it was the beginning of that pictorial teaching
afterwards so fecund in the early ages of Christianity. The Imperial creed was made clear to Italy and the provinces by the same
means that inculcated it in Rome: the provincial monuments being
often, though not invariably, copied, imitated or borrowed from
monuments in the capital. The influence of the slabs of the Ara
Pacis, for instance, may be detected in the fine altar of the Gens
Augusta discovered not long ago at Carthage[2]. It is a shortened
catechism of the new doctrines: on the front face Roma, seated,
holds the familiar pillar supporting the Augustan Victory, as she
contemplates an altar on which are piled the Orb of the World,
symbol of universal power, and the cornucopiae, symbol of plenty,
the dominating ideas of the Tellus and Roma panels of the
Ara Pacis being here condensed into one picture. At the back
sits Apollo, the special protector of Augustus, holding out a
laurel branch towards a tripod: on one short side is shown the
flight of Aeneas from Troy: on the opposite side Augustus
sacrifices to the *Lares*. These three panels further illustrate the
desire of Augustus to associate the Roman cults with those gods
and heroes who, like Apollo and Aeneas, stand for the Trojan
ancestry of Rome. Further examples from Carthage itself are the
relief representing the divinities of the temple of Mars Ultor—
Mars, Venus and an Imperial prince[3], and the relief now in the
Louvre which reproduces the Terra Mater motive of the Ara
Pacis[4]; two reliefs which belong, according to a theory which it is
hard either to prove or to disprove, to one altar. Another altar,

---

[1] Volume of Plates iv, 128, *c*.   [2] *Ib.* 134.
[3] *Ib.* 136, *b*.   [4] *Ib.* 120, *b*, and text.

put up in honour of Augustus at Lugdunum in 12 B.C., bears witness in its remaining long swag of oakleaves and acorns to the same inspiration as the Ara Pacis[1].

A number of Augustan and Julio-Claudian undated reliefs can be linked up with historical events. With Actium is connected a fragment representing a fully manned bireme, found at Praeneste[2], still Italic-Etruscan in composition and carved with the Republican harshness and stiffness. The visit of Germanicus to Actium in A.D. 18[3] seems recorded on a fragment found at Nola which shows the young prince before the Actian Apollo[4]. Its fluid style and the attempt to stress space by placing the Apollo, for instance, in a three-quarter view, marks a great advance upon the stiffer composition of the Praenestine frieze. To the Pannonian triumph of A.D. 12[5], or else to that over the Sugambri in 7 B.C., should probably be referred the two Rothschild silver cups[6] representing, the one Tiberius as *triumphator*, the other Augustus receiving the homage of the conquered people. No doubt the composition is inspired by some monumental frieze or picture, but the elaborate foreshortenings, the clear sense of tridimensional space, the complicated groupings, the swinging rhythm of the sacrificial scene, make it probable that the cups represent a later version of an Augustan theme, datable to the Claudian period, when enthusiasm for the Augustan past was fostered to the utmost.

To the earlier decades of the first century A.D. may be dated, on the grounds of style alone, the five della Valle-Medici reliefs, from a frieze of the same character and size as those of the Ara Pacis[7]. Here again the subject is a procession; the officiating prince strongly resembles Claudius, but Claudius so young that the ceremony can only be referred to about A.D. 8 when he was invested with the office of Augur and could make his appearance as protagonist in a religious pageant. The date accords with the style: the compression of the groups, the introduction of onlookers amid the participants in the ceremony, the more nearly frontal pose of the sacrificing prince, the beauty of the sacrificial scene, no whit inferior to that on the Rothschild cup, show a grasp of artistic means far beyond anything attempted on the Augustan

---

[1] Volume of Plates iv, 210, *f*.

[2] Corner block of frieze; W. Amelung, *Skulptur d. Vat. Mus.* II, p. 65.

[3] *Cum recordatione maiorum* (Tacitus *Ann.* II, 53), in other words to do honour to the memory of the victor of Actium (suggestion verbally communicated by L. Curtius).   [4] Strong, *op. cit.* fig. 7.

[5] For the date see below, p. 609.   [6] Volume of Plates iv, 128, *a, b*.

[7] *Ib.* 126 and text.

altar. The actual period of Tiberius should be credited, it is
thought, with the frieze of the *Suovetaurilia* in the Louvre from
some altar enclosure or triumphal arch[1]. As in the Ara Pacis the
figures tend to fall into groups and to look towards one another
without for all that interrupting the flow of the composition, which
is unified and dominated by the tall, draped figure at the garlanded
altars; his face is much mutilated but seems to resemble portraits of
Tiberius, of whom the towering stature would be typical.

We are on safer ground with two works of art which are in-
dubitably Tiberian. The first is the sword in the British Museum
which is decorated with a scene—probably borrowed from a
larger triumphal composition—recently interpreted as Germanicus
giving homage to Tiberius after his victories of A.D. 15 and 16.
The Emperor, identified by the inscription on the shield at his side
(*Felicitas Tiberii*), sits enthroned, while behind him hovers Victory,
holding the dynastic shield with the inscription *V(ictoria) Aug(usti)*[2].
The second monument is the base in Naples erected in honour of
Tiberius in A.D. 30 by the Augustales of Puteoli and almost
certainly intended to carry the statue of the Emperor[3]. It is
adorned with allegorical figures in relief inscribed with the name
of certain cities of Asia Minor restored by the generosity of
Tiberius after the earthquake of A.D. 17. The types were evidently
borrowed from the statues which once surrounded the colossal
effigy of Tiberius, erected in Rome near the temple of Venus
Genetrix, as record of the Emperor's liberality. The individual
figures are possibly inspired by Graeco-Asiatic originals to be
seen in the restored cities, but their compressed arrangement in
depth and frontal poses are essentially Roman. We have here
again an interesting repetition made for a provincial city of a monument set up in Rome to commemorate an Imperial happening.

A fine example of Claudian sculpture in relief is afforded by the
fragment of the Etruscan cities in the Lateran[4]. Like the Puteoli
base it is a record of gratitude towards an Imperial benefactor—in
this instance Claudius who had restored the glories of the ancient
Etruscan League. Since two of the cities stand on bases it is
obvious that they were copied from statues in the round but instead
of being stiffly aligned like the Augustan statues on the *Lares* altar
in Florence, one of them at least is placed obliquely to the background to accentuate the spatial content. The effect is further
enhanced by the swaying movement from front to back of the
putto who holds up the garland—a motive already introduced into

[1] Volume of Plates iv, 138, *a*.   [2] *Ib.* 140, *a*.
[3] *Ib.* 138, *b*.   [4] Strong, *op. cit.* fig. 66.

the decoration of the monument of the Julii at St Rémy[1]. The fragment, found, like the altar of Manlius, at Etruscan Caere, may well have decorated the pedestal of a statue of Claudius, and would suit, for instance, the fine seated statue of this Emperor found at Caere itself[2].

III. THE SYMBOLIC VALUE OF AUGUSTAN ORNAMENT

The various patterns carved on altars and other monuments were rapidly elaborated and enriched; in the Augustan period festoons were simply suspended from ox-skulls or *bucrania*: under Tiberius and Gaius the ox-skulls were supplanted by an infinite variety of motives, including heads of Ammon as angle-supports for the wreaths, masks of Medusa as central apotropaic ornaments, heads and even groups of Eros and Psyche, and numerous animal designs, all used with evident protective intention. The heads of Ammon form an almost continuous series, and reappear carved against a rich foliated background in the centre of the imposing *paterae* which were added to the decoration of the Forum of Augustus during the Principate of Hadrian[3]. With the increasing wealth of the State and of private individuals, ornament became more and more lavish, but an underlying religiosity, the old Roman sense of the sacredness attaching to inanimate things, a relic possibly of the cult of the indwelling *numen*, acted as a check to profane or vulgar excess. An example of this sobriety in luxury is offered by the bronzes belonging to the ships of Nemi, whose recovery has given us back a treasury of works of art[4]. The ships, which date, it is believed, from the reign of Gaius and were designed as processional barges to parade the lake on the feast of the goddess, were adorned at vulnerable points by apotropaic heads of snake-haired Medusas, of lions with flaming manes, of spotted leopards and snarling wolves. No evil powers would dare to approach such guarding forces—they recall the series of the fictile figures that protected the ancient Italic temples[5]. As examples may be taken two heads of wolves from the latest finds[6]. The first with head as long as that of a greyhound, deep-set eyes that watch without terrorizing, tongue protruding to hide the lower teeth, recalls a good watch-dog rather than the more ferocious wolf. The wolf, with all that makes him still the terror of the Latin region, is represented by the other head with its fiercely

[1] Volume of Plates iv, 60, *b*.
[2] Helbig-Amelung, *op. cit.* no. 1169.   [3] *Capitolium*, 1930, pp. 173–7
[4] G. Cultrera in *Not. degli Scavi*, 1932, pp. 206 *sqq.*
[5] Vol. ix, pp. 807, 832.   [6] Volume of Plates iv 140, *b, c*.

open eyes, its snarling nose and its savage jaw showing the ravenous teeth. The workmanship of both is excellent: the skin round the jaws of the first wolf is rendered with mastery; so is the shaggy hair left standing in both beasts to frame the head while the smoother hair is indicated by short chisel-strokes on the bronze surface. This is animal sculpture of the first order such as the Romans always delighted in producing.

To the same class of apotropaic ornament belong the silver medallions from a military breastplate in Berlin, known as the Lauersfort *phalerae* from the place where they were found. The style is somewhat earlier than that of the Nemi bronzes and the technique more delicate, as appears if we compare the Medusa from Nemi with one of the two from Lauersfort[1]. Yet the full facial forms have much in common and both are modelled with a force that recalls the Italo-Etruscan Gorgons from Veii (see vol. IX, p. 807). Greek motives also are borrowed, but become romanized by the religious use to which they are put, and by the unusual compression into a closed decorative space: such the charming Psyche resting her chin on her hand as she looks back to the pursuing Eros of another medallion[2]. Likewise a bronze gladiatorial helmet at Naples, made for parade or as a votive offering, is richly embossed with groups taken with religious intent from the "Fall of Troy" (Cassandra, the Death of Priam and the like) to recall Rome's function as avenger of Troy[3]. The spirit is Augustan; the isolated groups seem borrowed from a larger composition; the actual date is uncertain.

This short survey may fittingly close with an example of Claudian decoration, interesting for its symbolism, and also as showing how, with a growing sense of tridimensional space, figures or objects were crowded up without fear of confusion. This is the relief at Mantua, dedicated, it would seem, to Juppiter, whose thunderbolt is flung across his heavily draped throne, while one end of the sceptre is seen on the ground on the right, and a large eagle issues forth from under the drapery on the left[4]. It is difficult to imagine a more impressive condensation of the attributes of a divinity; the god is not present, and yet he is suggested in all his awful majesty.

[1] Volume of Plates iv, 142, *a, b*.   [2] *Ib.* 142, *c*.
[3] *Ib.* 144, *a*.   [4] *Ib.* 144, *b*.

IV. PORTRAITURE

The factors that were to contribute to the greatness of Roman portrait art had been fixed by the last century of the Republic, but the influences were still lacking which should check defects, such as the Italic angularity and harshness, induced perhaps by a too ardent pursuit of detail. The corrective was now provided by the portraiture of the Princeps. Precisely as altars and other monuments reminiscent of those of Rome were erected in Italy and the provinces to impress on them the Imperial creed, so also was the Imperial effigy set up for the same purpose and multiplied indefinitely. The portraiture of the man who ruled over the *Orbis terrarum* accordingly demanded new qualities that should contribute to its universal significance. To attain to this conception, it was necessary to clarify and purify the Imperial effigy itself till it should reach its maximum of expressiveness, less by the Greek method of 'idealization' than by heightening the reality—a process likewise responsible for the excellence of much of the portraiture of private individuals.

In the portraiture of Augustus the old Italic element made itself strongly felt, modified by Hellenistic currents. The portrait at Chiusi has already been mentioned for its distinctly Italic derivation[1]. The bronze head in the Vatican[2] again seems the direct descendant, allowing for differences of period, age and personality, of the 'Brutus' of the Conservatori[3]. There is the same strong line of the cranium, modified in the Augustus by the more abundant hair. The serious concentration of gaze is combined, as in the Brutus, with an expression of strong will power, though the flexibility of the lips is free from Italic harshness. The Vatican head, which probably belonged to a statue, represents the Princeps at about the age of thirty. Of approximately the same date is the magnificent head in the Capitoline Museum with high cheek-bones, loose locks of hair, nervously closed mouth and severe scowling expression[4]. These contrasting presentments of the Emperor show that different aspects of his personality were beginning to impose themselves upon art and to triumph over set traditions native or foreign.

In the celebrated statue of Prima Porta[5], one of the most imposing creations of European portrait art, Augustus is shown in the prime of manhood and of power. The features of the Emperor are delicate and refined: the clear ossature of the face shows be-

[1] Volume of Plates iv, 44, *b* and vol. ix, p. 810.
[2] Volume of Plates iv, 146, *b*.   [3] *Ib.* 46, and vol. ix, p. 812.
[4] L. Curtius in *Antike*, 1931, p. 250, figs. 14, 15; O. Brendel, *Ikonographie des Kaisers Augustus*, p. 67, no. 15.   [5] Volume of Plates iv, 148, *a*.

neath the firmly modelled flesh; the luminous eyes look steadily
out into space; the mouth has the beauty of line familiar in
portraits of the Julio-Claudians; the comparatively small chin is
without weakness, the line of cranium and neck of incomparable
harmony. On the richly embossed cuirass the protecting powers
of the Empire appear in a grandiose composition which centres in
the group representing a Parthian handing over the standards to
the Roman Mars, who is accompanied by his dog[1]. The surrender
episode of 20 B.C. being certain, the statue, or its original, is
commonly dated to about this time. On the other hand, the advanced
technique, subtlety of modelling, careful gradations of light and
shade, and the elaborate composition of the cuirass, in which
certain figures appear fore-shortened, seem out of the question at
a date ten years earlier than the Ara Pacis. It is therefore reasonable to look upon the Prima Porta Augustus as executed much
later with the help of contemporary portraits. A style so much in
advance of the purely Augustan and a view of the events of the
Principate so comprehensive, would tally exactly with the more
accomplished art of the Claudian age, and with that insistent
glorification of Augustan policy that was encouraged by Claudius
himself. By the side of this military statue of undoubted Roman
origin it is interesting to set the famous bronze head of Augustus
from Meroë which must likewise have belonged to a statue in
armour[2]. It is judged as a rule to be Hellenistic, which is not
improbable considering its provenance. Certainly a Greek touch
pervades it, working up individual features into an idealized
presentment illumined by the flashing eyeballs of onyx which shine
with all the majesty of greatness.

In contrast with these Imperial and military effigies of the
Princeps, the statue from the Via Labicana, in the Terme, shows
him at a more advanced age, togate and offering sacrifice[3]. Head
and body though of different marble are in perfect harmony; the
slightly bent shoulders and solemn gait suit the pensive and poetic
quality of the head. Once again another side of the Emperor's
personality has imposed itself upon the artist. The draperies
superbly hold together the composition and show to what a degree
of grave dignity the Roman toga had by now attained. With the
head of the Via Labicana statue ranks one at Ancona, which—as
the drapery drawn over the back of the head shows—also belonged
to a statue of Augustus sacrificing[4]. It is an untouched original,

---

[1] Volume of Plates iv, 150 and text.
[2] H. B. Walters, *Select Bronzes in the British Museum*, pl. 61.
[3] Volume of Plates iv, 148, *b*.   [4] *Ib.* 146, *c, d.*

only recently published, in which the features of the Emperor are rendered with evident precision: the nose is long and aquiline; the delicate nostrils and the full lips have a vivid line not weakened by convention or copying; the serious expression is heightened by the furrows round the mouth and by the clear-cut eyebrows beneath the richly modelled forehead.

The bulk of the portraits of Augustus belongs roughly—it would seem—to a period between Actium and the Ara Pacis. From the large number that have survived we can form some estimate of their multitude in antiquity. They still exist as single statues, both of marble and of bronze, as busts, in groups, carved in precious stones, like the charming turquoise head in Florence[1], engraved as intaglios or carved as cameos. The image of the Founder of the Empire was venerated throughout the *Orbis Terrarum* and the demand for reproductions of every kind was unending long after his death. Few of these, it is clear, could have been studied from the Emperor himself, though one or two direct likenesses certainly existed, upon which were based replicas, copies and innumerable adaptations. Among the most remarkable is the young Augustus shown at the age of about sixteen[2], though from its accomplished Augustan technique it can hardly be contemporary; it must have been executed at a later period, no doubt posthumously, when the growing cult of the Divus called for portraits of him at all periods of his life.

The influence of the portraiture of the Princeps naturally affected that of the Imperial family, of the court, of the Emperor's closer friends and to a less extent that of private individuals. In fact it dominated its epoch. The portraiture of even so strong a personality as Agrippa, minister, son-in-law, fellow-student and life-long friend of Augustus, was brought into the Augustan orbit. The likeness between the portraits of the two friends is difficult to define, but it is there: it has been well remarked that one or two 'Agrippas' only save their identity by the evidence of the inscriptions, and might otherwise pass for indifferent effigies of Augustus[3]. Very different is the head found in the theatre of Butrinto[4] (Buthrotum), which from the provenance we must believe to have been executed immediately after Actium—a portrait therefore of Agrippa in his prime and at the height of success. The broad forehead with eyebrows already meeting in a determined frown, the

[1] R. Delbrueck, *J.D.A.I.* 1925, pp. 13 *sqq.*, figs. 6, 7; p. iv.
[2] Volume of Plates iv, 146, *a*.
[3] A. W. Lawrence, *Classical Sculpture*, p. 333.
[4] Volume of Plates iv, 154, *a*.

keen glance of the deep-set eyes, the finely shaped nose and lips and the powerful line of the jaw reveal the steadiness of purpose and moral strength of the man who was co-founder of the Empire. The same traits, accentuated by experience, recur in the best portraits of him in later life (Louvre, Florence and Capitol). In nearly all Agrippa's portraits a certain sensuousness about the mouth befits one who was not only a great statesman and soldier, but also a lover of literature and of the arts, to whose liberality and good taste Rome owed much of her Imperial magnificence. From the double likeness to Agrippa and to Augustus it is easy to recognize in a bust of the Capitoline Museum, still misnamed Caligula, their son and grandson Gaius Caesar. The line of brow and jaw are those of Agrippa, while the profile is strongly Julian[1].

Tiberius, another strong personality, like Agrippa with no blood-relationship to Augustus, and with whom, moreover, he had little in common, shows in his portraits so marked a resemblance to his stepfather that it is difficult at times to decide which of the two Emperors is intended[2]. This assimilation of the effigy of one ruler to that of another is a common phenomenon of court portraiture; in reality the facial differences between the two Emperors were deep enough. The squarer face of Tiberius, the broader jaw, the mouth thin-lipped and pinched, the hair cut straight above the massive forehead, and tending to become a fringe, are essential points that distinguish him from Augustus. They are already patent in the lovely head of the young Tiberius in Boston[3], save that the mouth has a soft freshness retained in the earlier portraiture of his prime—for example, in the head from Veii in the Vatican, and in the beautiful head from Caere in the Lateran[4], which has fortunately never been separated from its body—but lost in the later portraits, such as the seated statue from Privernum in the Vatican[5], where the confidence of youth has vanished and his Imperial mien, largely borrowed from Augustus, is clouded by a bitter misanthropy. That Gaius, like Gaius Caesar, should resemble both Augustus and Agrippa might seem sufficiently accounted for by family relationship, and the likeness comes out clearly in the head at Ny Carlsberg[6], probably the finest of his portraits, with features as yet untouched by religious or any other mania.

Many portraits of the Julian and Claudian eras easily come within the Augustus-Tiberius-Gaius group. They include what

---

[1] Volume of Plates iv, 154, *b*.   [2] Text to *ib.* 158, *a* (cameo in Vienna).
[3] *Ib.* 152, *a*.   [4] *Ib.* 152, *c*.
[5] *Ib* 152, *b*.   [6] *Ib.* 154, *c*.

seems a well accredited portrait of Nero Drusus in armour at the Lateran—and a head wearing the *corona civica* in the Capitoline Museum, formerly known as Augustus, but from its resemblance to the head of the Lateran statue almost certainly Drusus[1]. Both heads have the same energetic profile and both show a natural inbred melancholy, in contrast to the bitterness of the middle-life portraits of Tiberius, though the two brothers apparently inherited much of the renowned beauty of their mother Livia, as we see her for instance in the lovely portrait at Pompeii[2].

Assimilation and repetition might have reduced Imperial portraiture to mere academism (as happened in too many instances) but for the appearance on the scenes of so original a personality as Claudius. What little assimilation there is here is subordinate to the Emperor's strong individuality, though in both his standing and seated statues he carries his dignities as his hereditary right. It is perhaps the consciousness of the line of Emperors behind him that lends him an *auctoritas dignitasque formae* which even Suetonius grants him so long as he is still[3]. Certainly in the seated portrait in the Lateran, wisdom and penetration are shown in the face, and majesty in the whole figure[4]. The same thoughtful brow overhanging the deep-set eyes, the fine aquiline nose and sensitive mouth are seen in profile on the cameo at Windsor[5], and on the famous cameo of the Four Cornuacopiae in Vienna[6]. Nor is this dignity absent from what is presumably the earliest of his possible portraits, that of the sacrificing prince on the Della Valle reliefs[7]. Only in the posthumous statue of Claudius as Juppiter, in the Vatican Rotonda, is the dignity endangered by the absurdity—a common one in effigies of deified Imperial personages—of combining an aged head with the eternal youth of a godlike body. As we look through the portraiture of this learned and amiable Emperor, it becomes evident that Claudius, unlike Tiberius, had not allowed the maltreatment and neglect from which he suffered up to his accession to embitter his outlook on life. Whatever Claudius had endured, he forgot it in his veneration for the Julian family and especially for Augustus. Of this devotion we have an example in the Claudian frieze at Ravenna[8] showing Augustus deified, in the attitude of the bronze Augustus as Juppiter at Naples[9], accom-

---

[1] For the statue Bernoulli, *Röm. Ikonographie*, II, 1, pl. XIII; for the Capitoline head see Delbrueck, *Antike Porträts*, pl. 33, where it is still named Augustus.   [2] Volume of Plates, iv, 168.
[3] *Claud.* 30.   [4] Volume of Plates, iv, 154, *d*.   [5] *Ib.* 158, *d*.
[6] *Ib.* 158, *b*.   [7] *Ib.* 126, *b*.   [8] *Ib.* 160, *a*.
[9] R. West, *Römische Porträt Plastik*, no. 162; pl. 38.

panied by Livia and two princes who are very variously interpreted, though the one in armour might well be Tiberius. The
style is magnificently Claudian, as appears from the almost
Flavian character of the sacrificial group at the left, and from the
oblique pose of the female seated figure—perhaps a goddess—
which recalls the seated Fortuna of the Manlius altar (p. 552).
Above the whole group towers the godlike personality of Augustus
—an Augustus who has grown in stature as in prestige since the
simpler presentation of him on the Ara Pacis.

Imperial portraiture acquires by a process of purgation something of the quality of great religious art. If it be a just reproach
that the Roman genius was unequal to creating the image of a god,
the answer must be that it created the image of the Imperator,
though an elaboration of several centuries was needed before its
full significance was made manifest in the Constantine of the
Basilica Nova or the so-called Valentinian[1] of Barletta.

A more human and intimate quality which necessarily drops out
of Imperial portraiture distinguishes that of private individuals.
Three examples may be singled out, each characteristic of its
period. The first is the admirable bronze in the Metropolitan
Museum[2] of a man in early middle age portrayed with that sure
and tranquil mastery which brings out essential traits without
over-accentuation or under-statement. The expression is calm but
lit up by the eyes with inset eye-balls. A good portrait of the
Tiberian epoch, though only recently recognized as non-Repub-
lican, is afforded by the bronze bust of the actor Norbanus Sorex
from Pompeii[3] (not to be confused with the actor Sorix of the time
of Sulla). The face has none of the angularity of the Republican
period to which it was once confidently attributed; the cut of the
hair is surely Tiberian; the droll and ugly face with the pushed-up
chin, the wide mouth with protruding underlip and long upper-
lip, the wide-awake eyes and arrogant profile belong to the man
of the people rather than to the patrician. On the other hand the
third example[4], from the Claudian period, has a distant resemblance to the Claudian family itself. In a recent penetrating
analysis the head has been likened to Dostoievsky's 'Idiot.' It is
a face in which inherited traits are shown in full decadence: the expression is obstinate; the mouth discontented and weak; the eyes no
longer keen but merely staring; the over-developed forehead fails

[1] Now called Marcian. See Delbrueck, *Spätantike Kaiserporträts*,
p. 219 *sq.*
[2] Volume of Plates iv, 162, *a.*
[3] *Ib.* 162, *b.*   [4] *Ib.* 162, *c, d,* and text.

to dominate the face but only overpowers it; the furrows at the base of the nose divide the face in two instead of contributing to its unity, while in the profile view, nose, mouth and receding chin seem to hang only loosely together. It is the degeneracy of a whole race. But there is no degeneracy of technique, which already has some of the subtlety of Flavian art.

Equestrian statues, always popular with the Romans, had long been granted as a sign of special honour to distinguished men. Under the Empire these statues became legion, but no examples survive, if we except the somewhat mediocre statues of the two Balbi father and son, at Naples, datable to the last quarter of the first century B.C.[1], and the numerous equestrian effigies of Imperial and other personages on coins. Of even greater importance were the quadrigae of the gods or of the triumphing Emperors (cf. the Tiberius cup from Boscoreale) drawn by a team of four horses, a type of monument to which many of the portraits we have been considering probably belonged. The magnificent horses of St Mark's in Venice[2]—a purely Augustan work—afford an idea of the splendour to which this statuary had attained under the early Empire. Their original function is uncertain: they may have belonged to an Imperial chariot or to the chariot of the Sun, have adorned a temple-pediment, or stood on a base as votive offerings, much like the quadriga erected in honour of Augustus in his forum in 2 B.C.

The women of the Ara Pacis only give a very inadequate idea of the female portraiture of the Augustan period, so slightly are they individualized. Yet long before the Ara Pacis we find portraits full of vitality and promise dating from the late Republic or early Empire. Occasionally we come upon one of such originality that it is difficult to place it exactly: the bust of a girl in the Museo Torlonia, only a little earlier in date than the Octavia portraiture, is a case in point[3]. This might be described in the words of a modern writer as possessing 'the daintiness and intoxicating line of adolescence' and some have felt inclined to attribute it to the Renaissance or to a modern chisel: the lovely sweep of shoulder and neck, best seen in the back view, and the dainty movement of the upper lip have a fragile beauty without exact parallel in ancient art, but the bust as a whole is essentially non-modern, while definite Italic traits come out in the strong architectural line of the head, accentuated by the severe Republican coiffure, with its heavy flattened chignon and bandeaux, left unchiselled as if to be

[1] R. Paribeni, *Il Ritratto nell' arte antica*, pls. 162, 163.
[2] Volume of Plates iv, 160, *b*.   [3] *Ib.* 164.

covered by a plait. Probably the head had its compeers, if only we knew where to look for them. At Parma, for instance, is another delightful presentment of girlhood[1]; the lips are softly closed; the eyes were once made vivid by inset pupils; in front the hair was arranged over a raised pad; at the back it is severely combed and drawn into a pigtail such as is worn in more elaborate fashion by the ladies of the late Republic and of the early Empire.

The female portraiture of the time of the Second Triumvirate is characterized by the wavy bandeaux, the cushion of hair over the forehead, and the little chignon worn low on the nape of the early portraits of Octavia, the finest of which is in the Louvre[2]. This austere coiffure was soon exchanged for the flattened wavelets of hair which gradually grew into deep hot-iron waves with tiny curls peering from under the bandeaux, such as came into fashion in the Principate of Augustus. The Imperial ladies brought in complicated and interesting styles, used with excellent effect by their portraitists to emphasize character or mood. The ageing beauty of the Livia at Ny Carlsberg[3] is framed in a setting of waves and curls which add to her Imperial mien. In the head of the elder Agrippina recently discovered in Cyrene[4], the harsh regularity of the hair waves bring out the severity of the features. In the portrait at Ny Carlsberg, said to be of the sorrowing Agrippina, the parted hair pulled over the forehead enhances the grief of the tear-stained face[5].

The coiffure in superimposed ringlets distinctive of the Claudian period is seen in the portraits of the younger Agrippina best represented in a tragic head recently found in Rome[6]. It is likewise familiar from the so-called portraits of Messallina, the third wife of Claudius, though in the famous Paris cameo where she appears with her two children[7] her coiffure assumes a simpler style. Varieties of mode were innumerable: hair curled up at the sides into bunches of ringlets as in the charming portrait of Minatia Polla at the Terme[8] or twisted into corkscrew curls that entirely cover the head[9]. We are far yet from the tower-like erections of Flavian and Trajanic hairdressing; yet these Julio-Claudian court ladies already might justify the saying of Apuleius, that 'there is such a dignity in the hair, that whatsoever she be, though she be never so bravely attired with gold, silks, precious

---

[1] Volume of Plates iv, 166, *d*.   [2] *Ib.* 166, *a*.   [3] *Ib.* 166, *b*.
[4] *Ib.* 166, *c*.   [5] Hekler, *Greek and Roman portraits*, pl. 213.
[6] In the *Antiquario comunale* (unpublished).
[7] Volume of Plates iv, 158, *c*.
[8] Strong, *Rom. Sculpture*, fig. 221.   [9] Strong, *Art in anc. Rome*, I, fig. 242.

stones, and other rich and gorgeous ornaments, yet if her hair be not curiously set forth, she cannot seem fair[1].'

As already appears from the Ara Pacis the portraiture of children strongly attracted Augustan artists. A new understanding of infancy inspires the rendering of the tiny Cupid who so gallantly rides the ancestral dolphin by the side of the Augustus of Prima Porta[2]. That this is a real infant, neither little man nor conventional *putto*, appears from the soft still formless nose and chin, the bulging forehead, the uncertain line of the skull which has not yet hardened. This picture of healthy babyhood may be contrasted with the admirable head in the Munich Glyptothek—also of the Augustan period—of a sick infant[3]. Boyhood too, was represented in its many moods; for example the jolly little head of a laughing child in the Museum of Toulouse[4]—from the perfection of its technique probably an Imperial princeling, or again the portrait with alert determined expression in the Museo Barracco, doubtless another princeling since it was found in the Imperial Villa of Prima Porta[5]. No less attractive than these representations of infancy or early childhood are those of adolescence, of that touching age of transition from boy to man, of which we have an admirable rendering in the bronze statue in New York of a young Julio-Claudian prince, portrayed in serious meditative mood[6].

The tombstones which show several members or several generations of one family stiffly aligned within an architectural frame deserve a passing mention, if only because they afford incomparable matter for the study of popular Roman portraiture. They had made a first appearance in the closing decades of the Republic (Vol. IX, p. 814 *sq.*) and continued to be the favourite form of tombstone down to the period of Trajan. Their numbers are legion. For the period of the Second Triumvirate a good example is provided by the stele of the Furii in the Lateran[7]; for the period of Augustus by that of Ampudius in the British Museum[8]. These severe, mostly frontal, figures that face the spectator as if to demand homage *in perpetuum*, have a further sig-

---

[1] Apuleius, *Met.* II, 18. Trans. Adlington. Cf. Ovid, *Ars Amat.* III, 133–52.
[2] Vol. of Plates, IV, 118, *d.*   [3] Hekler, *op. cit.* pl. 216, *a*, *b.*
[4] E. Espérandieu, *Bas-reliefs de la Gaule romaine III*, No. 2537; to be shortly published by L. Curtius, in *Röm. Mitt.*, with a new interpretation.
[5] Volume of Plates IV, 170, *b.*
[6] *Ib.* 170, *a.*   [7] *Ib.* 170, *c.*
[8] A. H. Smith in *J.R.S.* VIII, 1918, pp. 179 *sqq.*; Paribeni, *op. cit.* p. 18, fig. 19.

nificance as symbols of the Roman belief in the solidarity of the family and in the sacredness of family ties. The informing conception is that which governs the Imperial groups on the Ara Pacis Augustae.

V. PAINTING

Little remains of Augustan painting in Rome. No trace survives of the mural decorations that covered the walls of porticoes or of temples; we can little more than guess their style or how far Pompeii can be accepted as the measure of what was produced in the capital. The second or 'architectural' style known from the so-called House of Livia (Vol. IX, p. 828) presumably continued in fashion, being gradually transformed into the fantastic 'architectures' of the fourth style which in Rome made their appearance in Nero's Golden House. Between the second and the fourth styles, or perhaps parallel to them, intervened a system of wall decoration known as the third style. It represented an effort to assert the value of the wall as flat surface[1], by substituting for the vistas and prospects disclosed through openings in the wall, framed picture panels, or *aediculae*, affixed to the surface in imitation of real pictures. The history of Roman mural painting is one of conflict between the decorative element which strives for the illusion of space beyond the wall, and resistance offered by the mechanical forces of the wall itself. The story is repeated in the mural paintings of the Italian Seicento.

All this would be difficult to illustrate fully in Rome. For the gap of nearly one hundred years between the pictorial triumphs of the House of Livia and those of the Golden House of Nero, examples in Rome are comparatively few. To about 38 B.C. and to the second Pompeian style belongs a masterpiece of Roman illusionism—the garden enclosure painted on the walls of a room in the Villa of the Empress Livia at Prima Porta[2]. The conquest of the 'space beyond' is here an accomplished fact—the sense of the confining wall is annulled; it is as if the closed door, beyond which in certain Pompeian paintings we see trees waving and birds flitting, had suddenly burst open and we had entered the enchanted garden. It is an *hortus inclusus* of purest delight, where the flowers bloom, the birds sing and the butterflies flutter, without intrusion of any human element. In the Prima Porta fresco it is no longer the wall that encloses the room, but the garden itself that defines the space by means of a well-trimmed path running between

[1] Cf. L. Curtius, *Die Wandmalerei Pompejis*, p. 191.
[2] Volume of Plates IV, 172, *a*, with text.

two railings, the innermost of which breaks now and again into
exedrae adorned by tall conifers. So also in the 'Casa dell' Efebo'
at Pompeii, the lovely fragment of a pomegranate garden has an
exedra with fountains surmounted by a majestic bronze peacock[1].
The same type of decoration carried out in mosaic appears in the
charming fountain niche of the Fitzwilliam Museum at Cambridge[2]. This 'garden painting' hangs together with the flower
and fruit pieces already noted as characteristic of Augustan reliefs
(p. 550); of the brilliancy of the original colouring we may form a
notion from the basket of flowers in mosaic found in the second-
century 'Villa dei Quintilii,' obviously from its extreme naturalism
the copy of an Augustan model[3].

Columbarium painting, though overlooked and neglected because of its humble character, can throw much light on mural
decoration. Of special interest are the friezes running between the
rows of *loculi* in a columbarium of the ancient Via Aurelia which is
dated to the first years of the Empire. The mythological episodes,
copied from larger compositions for their symbolic value, are, it is
true, ineffective as art, but the painter's light and rapid touch is
admirably suited to the rendering of the numerous landscape
scenes. These include farmyards, poultry yards, duckponds, the
'wayfarer' theme, and a series of sacred and sepulchral enclosures
marked by trees and statues raised on high pillars, within which
women tend the tombs and deck the altars; all this belongs to
the same school of miniature landscape as the gold-brown frieze
in the House of Livia, the style of which has been traced back to the
topiaria opera of the landscape painter Studius who 'introduced a
delightful style of decorating walls with representations of villas,
porticoes, landscape-gardens, sacred groves, woods, hills, fishponds,
straits, streams and shores: any scene, in short, that took the
fancy[4].' Next in order of time comes the decoration in stucco and
colour of the Columbarium of Pomponius Hylas, near the Porta
Latina, datable to the time of Tiberius[5]. The central niche is
decorated with a number of mystical subjects; the conch of the
apse and the vaulted ceilings are covered by a delicate network of
flowering vine tendrils, enlivened by symbolic figures and birds:
a grim chamber of death sunk several feet below the ground is
thus transformed into a gay and flowering arbour. Fragments of

[1] Phot. Alinari 39386.
[2] Volume of Plates iv, 172, *b*.   [3] *Ib.* 178, *a*.
[4] Pliny, *N.H.* xxxv, 116. Above 'porticoes'=*porticus* (Mayhoff); others
prefer to read *portus* = 'harbours' with Detlefsen.
[5] Volume of Plates iv, 180, *b*.

wall-paintings from a house of Claudian date on the Quirinal show kindred motives of Erotes clambering among cherry branches where fruit and leaves are represented with botanical precision[1].

Stucco decoration, so closely connected with painting that the two are all but interchangeable, was likewise extensively used for the patterning of walls and ceilings. To the period of Caesar belong the stuccoes from a vaulted ceiling in the Villa Farnesina; scarcely later are the remains of a stuccoed vault in the garden room of the Prima Porta Villa; the magnificent series in the recently destroyed Tomb of the Arruntii is datable to about 10 B.C.[2] Finally to the Claudian period may be assigned the stuccoes that entirely cover the walls and vaults of the *hypogeum* of the basilica of Porta Maggiore. The transformation here is of an underground chamber into an Elysian hall, against the white translucency of which are silhouetted scenes and figures of the Soul's adventures in her quest after Immortality[3].

Painting, no less than sculpture, must have been called upon to commemorate the *res gestae* of the Augustan period, and to give expression to its dynastic aspirations. The pictures are lost, but from cameos and metal-work one may catch at least some echo of their style. The famous *Gemma Augustea* in Vienna, for instance, held to represent an incident in a triumph of Tiberius[4], is essentially pictorial in its well-knit composition—in the flow of the lines which unite the chariot group on the left and the allegorical figures on the right with the central group of Roma and Augustus —pictorial also is the frieze of the captive prisoners, though sharply divided off from the principal scene. In the 'Grand Camée de France'[5] the whole composition is still harmoniously blended: the seated group of Tiberius and Livia forms the focal point of interest; on either side are grouped the living princes of their house; soaring figures of dead and deified Julian heroes unite the personages of the central zone with the Divus Augustus who, supported by a figure who may be the ancestral Iulus, looks protectingly from heaven on his descendants; the frieze of captive barbarians of the lower zone, less completely isolated than in the Vienna Cameo, seems worked into the body of the picture—all Pompeii has scarcely left us a more compact and purely pictorial design. The original models for both cameos may well have been mural paintings or else large panels made to be carried, banner-

[1] P. Marconi, *La Pittura dei Romani*, fig. 133, p. 101.
[2] For date and description see *Mem. Amer. Acad.* IV, 1924, p. 35. It was put up for his family and freedmen by L. Arruntius, the friend of Augustus.
[3] Volume of Plates IV, 180, *a*, 182.   [4] *Ib.* 156, *a*.   [5] *Ib.* 156, *b*.

like, in procession on solemn occasions and exhibited in public places to stimulate enthusiasm for the Imperial dynasty. They are the counterpart of the triumphal pictures of the Republican period (Vol. IX, p. 825) and presuppose the same principles of design as on the 'Grand Camée,' a central figure, or a group, surrounded by attendant personages and above a protecting divinity. The formula reappears in the 'allegory of conquest' of the cuirass of the Prima Porta Augustus[1], and in the 'allegory of the fecundity of the Empire' on the silver patera from Aquileia[2], both compositions being of triumphal character and originally displayed, we may imagine, on a larger canvas. The Four Cornuacopiae Cameo in Vienna[3]; the Paris Cornucopiae Cameo of Messallina and her children[4]; the lovely fragment in the British Museum of Livia enthroned amid the fruits of a cornucopiae[5], seem likewise to derive from pictorial compositions which exalted the Imperial family as source of all prosperity to the State.

That painting was made a means of propagating the new creeds is evident even at Pompeii, a provincial town outside the sphere of great political or religious happenings. The many episodes from the 'Taking of Troy' must, like the second book of the *Aeneid*, have been inspired by a reawakened interest in the Trojan ancestry of the Romans; the pictures of the loves of Mars and Venus recall the honour in which these patron gods of the Julian race were held in Rome; two paintings recently discovered show the one the group of Aeneas with Anchises and Iulus, the other Romulus shouldering the spoils of Acron, both evident copies of the statues in the Forum of Augustus described by Ovid (p. 578)[6]; ornamental details, the tripods and other Apolline emblems, the dolphins and the ships so profusely introduced among the 'fantasies' of the Pompeian Fourth Style, obviously refer to the Augustan cult of Apollo and the naval victories of Actium[7]. Still another Pompeian picture—a landscape of the 'Third Style'— offers a glorified version of the Romulean legend of the Palatine exalted by Augustus[8]. The Palatine Lupercal which is seen in the foreground is also represented, with its inmates and protectors, on the interesting marble intarsia (*opus sectile*) in the Palazzo Colonna found in the neighbourhood of Rome[9].

---

[1] Volume of Plates iv, 150.   [2] *Ib.* 184, *a.*
[3] *Ib.* 158, *b.*   [4] *Ib.* 158, *c.*
[5] *Brit. Mus. Cat. of Gems*, No. 1977 (1571).
[6] Volume of Plates iv, 176, *a, b*; Ovid, *Fasti*, v, 563–8.
[7] L. Curtius, *op. cit.* p. 159 and *passim*.
[8] Volume of Plates iv, 176, *c.*   [9] *Ib.* 178, *b.*

In the Augustan and in other periods examples of portrait painting are surprisingly few in comparison with the overwhelming number of portraits in stone or bronze still extant. This is partly due to the perishable nature of the material and also to negligence on the part of a bygone generation of excavators. In Pompeii alone many more portraits were found than is generally known, but precious examples were allowed to perish at a time when only pictures with mythological subjects were valued. Of what little remains one of the best is the portrait-group of a young couple[1] in the Naples Museum, which from the coiffure of the lady may be assigned to the Claudian period; these are simple and straight-forward transcripts of the face, lifted however above commonplace likeness by the luminous glance of the large eyes—a trait noted in early Italic heads (Vol. IX, p. 809) and familiar at a later date from the long series of Fayûm portraits. We are again in the Italic tradition with the portrait of Virgil seated between Two Muses on the celebrated mosaic in the Bardo[2]. The theme of seated poet or philosopher is of the commonest and doubtless Hellenistic in origin, but in the Virgil it is transposed to a Roman key; the differences between the Hellenistic and Roman handling of the motive is evident if we compare the strong taut silhouette, the stiff angular draperies and the intense glance of the Virgil with the soft and sinuous lines and dreamy expression of the portrait of Me-nander, recently discovered at Pompeii[3].

Of Imperial portrait groups something has already been said in connection with the triumphal pictures of which the effigies of the *Imperator* and his family formed an integral part. Of the more intimate family group—at all times a favourite subject of portrait painting—we can gain some idea from the pictorial composition of certain cameos and glass pastes—for example, the well-known blue paste in Vienna of Germanicus or a Julio-Claudian prince with three young sons[4], a charming type of composition which persists with slight modifications and variations down to the period of Constantine.

VI. THE ROME OF AUGUSTUS AND OF HIS IMMEDIATE SUCCESSORS

Rome after the murder of Caesar was long pictured as a city of dreadful night where, in the general turmoil of the Civil Wars, monuments were allowed to fall into decay till such time as the

---

[1] Volume of Plates, iv, 174, *c.*   [2] *Ib.* 174, *a.*
[3] *Ib.* 174, *b.*   [4] *Ib.* 184, *b.*

Pax Augusta made possible the emergence of a city of marble out of the ruinous material. This dramatic contrast, inspired by the laudatory poetry of the Augustan age, is no longer true to fact. Excavations and a more careful reading of the texts show, for instance, that during the closing years of the Republic victorious generals continued, like their predecessors, to erect or restore temples on the occasion of their triumphs[1] and, as will appear, much else was done besides. What is true, however, is that after the death of Caesar, any systematic legislation for the improvement of the City had been swept aside and that before the town-planning policy introduced by Augustus when still Octavian, edifices were erected at haphazard without concerted plan. When Augustus took matters in hand he came forward as upholder of the old Italic and Republican traditions. The very year of his three-fold triumph he decreed the restoration of the fallen temples—in his *Res Gestae* he himself gives the number as eighty-two—an act of piety towards the gods of the State, on a par with the rest of his religious policy (p. 475). He combined his own schemes within the limits of the possible with those of Caesar but here he proceeded cautiously. Loth to impose too heavy a burden on the newly re-organized finances of the State, he took upon himself a large proportion of the colossal building expenditure, paying for it out of his own fortune[2]. Opposition to his schemes on the ground of cost was thus disposed of, while the monuments erected appeared as Imperial benefactions which redounded to the glory of himself and the Julian dynasty.

The aims of Augustus in the re-planning of Rome are clearly brought out in the Campus Martius. Without going the length of Caesar who had projected to deflect the course of the Tiber, so as to extend the Campus up to the Monte Mario, Augustus applied himself to its neglected northern region which he transformed from an unkempt swamp into a splendid monumental zone—largely aided in this by the liberality of his co-adjutor Agrippa, like himself possessed of great wealth. At its upper end, between Tiber and Via Lata, Augustus began to erect as early as 28 B.C.—the year of his consulship with Agrippa—the Mausoleum which was to be the memorial of himself and the dynasty. It was characteristic of him that he chose for his family tomb the circular drum

[1] See F. W. Shipley, 'Chronology of building operations in Rome from the death of Caesar to that of Augustus' in *Mem. Amer. Acad. in Rome*, IX, 1931, for a careful dating of these monuments.

[2] On the expenditure cf. U. Wilcken, *Sitz. d. preuss. Akad.* 1931, pp. 773 *sqq.*; Tenney Frank, *J.R.S.* XXIII, 1933, p. 146 *sq.*

with conical tumulus of Italic-Etruscan origin rather than borrow from the splendours of foreign architecture. The huge mound which was crowned by the statue of Augustus, contained on the ground level a comparatively small sepulchral chamber divided into niches for the ash urns of the Imperial family[1]—the earliest to be placed here being that of Marcellus, nephew and son-in-law of Augustus, the first flower of the dynasty to be cut off[2]. The Mausoleum was representative rather than unique. It had its Republican prototypes and was itself only a more splendid example among other circular tombs of the period such as those of Munatius Plancus at Gaeta, of Caecilia Metella and of Lucilius Paetus just outside Rome, to which we may add the cenotaph of Nero Drusus at Mainz and the *Tropaeum Augusti* in Provence, the latter a record of victory the shape of which recalls the Mausoleum[3]. The small park surrounding the Mausoleum contained the crematory chapel of the Imperial family; near by stood the *Ara Pacis Augustae* as witness to the blessings of peace brought about by the Imperial rule; and near by again rose the obelisk from Heliopolis, erected by Augustus in 9 B.C. as needle of a great sundial inlaid with bronze.

Agrippa opened out, east of the Via Lata, a park known as the *Campus Agrippae* which was at once promenade and field for military manœuvres; it was crossed by the Aqua Virgo, also a work of Agrippa's and the first Imperial aqueduct of Rome, while a portico, completed after his death by Agrippa's sister Polla, contained the famous map of the *Orbis Terrarum* based on the notes and plans of Agrippa himself. Farther down, on the west side of the Via, Agrippa built in 25 B.C. a large portico in thanksgiving for 'the naval victories[4],' *i.e.* Actium and his own in Sicilian waters, appropriately decorating it with a picture of the 'Expedition of the Argonauts,' after which the portico was named. Farther down again, on the same side, he completed, in homage it is said to Augustus, the huge *Saepta Julia* planned by Caesar to be carried out wholly in marble[5]. Somewhat to the west, close to the tomb of the Dictator (Vol. IX, p. 841), Agrippa, again desiring to honour the Julian house of which he had become a member by his marriage with Marcella, put up in 27 B.C., according to the still

---

[1] See Plan 2, facing p. 582.

[2] For the inscriptions for Marcellus and Octavia, see *Ann. épig.* 1928, no. 88.

[3] Volume of Plates iv, 188, *a*.   [4] ἐπὶ ταῖς ναυκρατίαις, Dio LIII, 27, 1.

[5] According to Cicero, *ad Att.* IV, 16, 14. The remains of the *Saepta* foundations, under the modern Palazzo Doria, are of travertine, but it is possible that the Agrippan superstructure was of marble.

extant inscription, the first Pantheon. It contained statues of Venus and Mars, divine ancestors of the Julian House, and one of Caesar—the Triad later venerated with even greater splendour in the Augustan temple of Mars Ultor, while statues of Augustus and of Agrippa himself were placed at each side of the entrance to guard the shrine which stood, it has been well said, as 'true symbol of the house of Augustus and its future[1].' This Agrippan Pantheon which was later obliterated under Hadrian's rotunda, is generally held to have been of rectangular shape, occupying a little less than the space of the actual Hadrianic vestibule. It is a moot question however, whether like its successor it too may not have been of circular shape, conceived as pendant to the Mausoleum, on the model of the earlier round temple with rectangular porch of the Largo Argentina (Vol. ix, p. 833). Of the architectural splendours of the Augustan Pantheon nothing survives, nor can the Baths of Agrippa, erected south of it in 9 B.C., be perfectly made out; what remains is of paramount importance, these being the earliest of those huge public baths which are reckoned among the typical achievements of Roman Imperial architecture. To the west of the Baths stretched another park with portico, and a canal known as the Euripus. An Agrippan complex which centred in the Pantheon thus balanced the Augustan Mausoleum and its surroundings[2].

The new Augustan-Agrippan zone formed the northern extension of the area laid out in the southern part of the *Campus* by the great Republican town-planners (Vol. ix, p. 836). With vast spaces still unoccupied and numerous monuments needing repair or enlargement, it had continued to afford a field for the building energies of victorious generals and others between the death of Caesar and the Principate. Thus in 34 B.C. Statilius Taurus had built in this region a stone amphitheatre; Cn. Domitius Ahenobarbus, at a date which is still uncertain, built or rebuilt the Temple of Neptune *in circo Flaminio*[3], and about 32 B.C., after his Jewish triumph, C. Sosius rebuilt, apparently from its foundations, the ancient temple of Apollo which though frequently restored dated back to 433 B.C.[4] Even before the Principate Octavian took a leading part in the improvement of the Campus. In 32 B.C. he had seen to the total restoration of the Theatre of Pompey. The ancient precincts and porticoes south of the theatre were re-

---

[1] L. R. Taylor, *Divinity of the Roman Emperor*, p. 167.
[2] Cf. Shipley, *Agrippa's building activities in Rome*.
[3] Volume of Plates iv, 210, *b*.
[4] Recent excavations on this site have brought to light columns of Augusto-Hellenistic type.

fashioned or improved by his care and that of his friends. He rebuilt the old *porticus Octavia*, allowing the name of the first owner of the site to be retained[1]. His step-cousin[2] L. Marcius Philippus added a portico round the temple of *Hercules Musarum*. The old *porticus Metelli* was likewise rebuilt and renamed after restoration *porticus Octaviae* in honour of his sister, who had enriched it with a library in memory of Marcellus, her son and the son-in-law of Augustus. Close by, a large theatre, rival of that of Pompey, originally decreed by Caesar, was constructed by Augustus and dedicated by him in 13 B.C. to the memory of the same Marcellus, thus completing a dynastic group of buildings, evidently planned by Augustus on the southern end of the Campus to correspond with the Mausoleum and the new buildings on the north.

The recent clearance of the Theatre of Marcellus has revealed the full beauty of the arcaded façade of the *cavea* in which the combination of Roman arch and Hellenistic column, since the Tabularium (Vol. IX, p. 838) a canonical form of wall decoration, breaks the inert mass of the wall, multiplies its latent vertical forces, and gives life to the huge pile[3]. The site chosen for the Theatre of Marcellus was no doubt largely determined by the neighbouring temple of Apollo[4], long a centre of the liberal arts, including theatrical performances and recitations. With the accession to power of the Julian house, the cult of Apollo, protector of the ancestral Trojans in their struggle against the Greeks, and Lord of the Sibylline books, continued in the ascendant, and the god himself was soon chosen as religious centre of the Augustan programme. As early as 36 B.C. Octavian had vowed to Apollo— till then kept as a foreign divinity outside the Pomerium—a temple on the Palatine, which was dedicated in 29, the year of the threefold triumph, in thanksgiving for the victory of Actium won by the grace of the god. Above the pediment Apollo as *Sol* rode in his chariot illuminating the *Orbis Romanus* with his rays. Within the temple the divine Triad—Apollo between Latona and Diana, with the Sibyl at their feet[5]—stood for the new spiritual forces of the Empire, the logical counterpart of that older Triad that held

[1] *Res Gestae* 19.
[2] On the relationship see Shipley, *Chronology...*, pp. 29 *sqq.*
[3] Volume of Plates IV, 188, *b*. A third theatre, situated somewhere between that of Pompey and that of Marcellus, had been erected by L. Cornelius Balbus on the occasion of his African triumph in 19 B.C. and dedicated by him the same year as the theatre of Marcellus; for the site see Platner-Ashby, *op. cit.* p. 213.   [4] This seems to be implied in *Res Gestae* 21.
[5] The group, which was by Greek artists, appears on the Sorrento base; see E. Rizzo, *La Base di Augusto*, p. 19, pl. III.

sway on the Capitoline hill opposite. But of the Palatine temple, one of the most significant of the religious foundations of Augustus, nothing remains, beyond the description of its splendours by the poets; even its location is uncertain. The balance of evidence is in favour of placing both the temple and the house of Augustus on the western summit of the Palatine[1] overlooking the Velabrum, Augustus as 'new Romulus' undoubtedly coveting for his Palatine edifices a site traditionally associated with the founder of the city, whose cult it was part of his policy to erect into a State dogma.

The holy places of the Palatine Augustus made his special care. In 3 B.C. he restored after a fire the Temple of the Magna Mater which was situated on the Cermalus side of the hill[2], and he adorned as a nymphaeum the ancient Lupercal at the foot of the Scalae Caci. Within the actual grotto might be seen, as in some pagan *praesepe*, the wolf with her divine nurslings, Faustulus keeping watch and the shepherds looking on in amazement, while a statue of Nero Drusus[3] linked the dynasty with the most sacred traditions of the City's foundation.

The Augustan programme proved itself not one of destruction but of fulfilment. If Apollo ruled over the Augustan Palatine, Juppiter Capitolinus, still supreme god of the Roman State, was not forgotten. Besides restoring the god's chief temple, Augustus rebuilt *c.* 31 B.C. the ancient Capitoline shrine of *Juppiter Feretrius* and erected one to him as *Tonans* in 22[4]. In 20 B.C. he erected close to these Capitoline sanctuaries a round temple to *Mars Ultor* for the temporary custody of the standards recovered from the Parthians[5], adopting for the war god, who was also a primitive agrarian divinity, the circular form of temple reserved as a rule for cults of great antiquity (Vol. ix, p. 833).

The Roman Forum, already carefully replanned by Caesar, received under Augustus the configuration which it retained throughout the Empire with but few changes. The great centre of civic life had grown irregularly without definite plan, and by the time of Caesar had become a mere agglomeration of temples needing repair, of shops and small basilicas. Already under the Second Triumvirate much had been done to remedy this state of affairs,

---

[1] For the identification of the temple with the ruins of the temple on Augustan podium, formerly thought to be that of Juppiter Victor, see Platner-Ashby, *op. cit.* p. 18 *sq.*; against this view see Rizzo, *op. cit.* and Bartoli, *Il Valore Storico delle recenti scoperte al Palatino e al Foro*; and cf. Vol. ix, p. 828, n. 1.

[2] For its Augustan façade see Volume of Plates iv, 190, *a.*

[3] *C.I.L.* vi, 31200.   [4] Volume of Plates iv, 210, *a.*   [5] *Ib.* 210, *d.*

but it was the Principate that set its mark on the whole. The temple to the deified Caesar decreed by the Senate in 42 and dedicated by Augustus in 29 B.C., the year of the threefold triumph, formed the dominant element of a new plan. It was placed as nearly as possible on the long axis of the Forum, facing the Tabularium, and being raised on a double podium produced a commanding effect, well seized by Ovid as he prays that the god Julius may continue to protect Forum and Capitol from his lofty shrine:

> Fac iubar, ut semper Capitolia nostra forumque
> Divus ab excelsa prospectet Iulius aede![1]

The low platform, prolonged to form an orator's tribune, contained the altar. The upper structure—a shallow Ionic cella with six-columned vestibules, the decorative detail of which is not free from the stiffness and angularity of Republican work—was of marble from the newly discovered quarries of Carrara[2].

Monuments built or restored between the death of Caesar and that of Augustus enclosed the temple of the *Divus* as within a sacred precinct. At the back was the ancient *Regia*, or public office of the *Pontifex Maximus*, as rebuilt in marble by Domitius Calvinus in 36 B.C. The three-passage arch over the Via Sacra, on the left of the temple of Caesar, which is probably identical with that erected by Augustus in 19 B.C. in honour of the surrender of the Parthian standards, balanced the old Arch of Fabius, north of the temple. The same architectural scheme of temple between two arches was thus obtained which we get in the Forum of Pompeii and in the later Forum of Augustus. Beyond the arch rose on its high podium the ancient temple of the Castores, restored in marble with soaring columns and with a vestibule modelled on that of Mars Ultor—a magnificence due to Tiberius, who rebuilt the temple in A.D. 6, inscribing it with his own name and that of his dead brother Nero Drusus. Farther north, on the same side, stood the Basilica Julia begun by Caesar and dedicated by him before completion, but rebuilt in marble by Augustus after a fire and renamed by him after his grandsons[3]. Beyond the *Vicus Jugarius* rose, again on a high podium, the ancient temple of Saturn which had been restored as early as 43 B.C. by L. Munatius Plancus. Immediately below the Tabularium might be seen the historic temple of Concord, restored on a magnificent scale in A.D. 10 by Tiberius, who dedicated it to the *Concordia Augusta* in the name,

---

[1] Ovid, *Met.* xv, 341 *sq.*   [2] Volume of Plates iv, 210, *c.*
[3] *Res Gestae* 20.

once more, of himself and of his dead brother. Coins show the temple pediment crowned in Italic fashion by three upstanding figures with arms interlocked as symbol of concord[1], and splendid fragments survive of the architectural decoration.

The line of monuments was continued on the east side by the Senate house planned by Caesar and completed by Augustus. Though repeatedly restored—what we now see is mainly as late as Diocletian—the main lines of the Augustan structure seem to have been respected, including the actual *Curia* with the stepped tiers that supported the wooden Senatorial benches. Next came the ancient *Basilica Aemilia* restored in 14 B.C. to correspond to the *Basilica Julia*; it was fronted by a long portico ending on the south in a *sacrarium* or chapel dedicated in honour of the two young princes, Gaius and Lucius, that the dynasty might once more be emphasized. This brings us back to the Arch of Fabius and completes the zone encircling the Temple of Caesar. Finally, at the north-west end of the Forum area rose the Rostra, transferred here from the old Comitium by Caesar and dedicated by Octavian in 42 B.C., the year of Philippi, though the incurving steps were added later. The essential features of the Forum were now fixed; new monuments were repeatedly introduced, but the main lines were never substantially altered.

Augustus was no more able than Caesar before him to remedy the congestion of the old Forum, save by building auxiliary fora[2]. He completed that of Caesar[3] and opened a second and more spacious Forum as forecourt to the temple vowed at Philippi to Mars, Avenger of Caesar. The site, which was scooped out of a densely populated spur of the Quirinal, cost the Imperial purse vast sums, though, even so, the new forum does not appear to have been of the large proportions originally intended by the Emperor. But the site was pre-ordained: obviously the temple, vowed at Philippi to the Avenger, must be in close proximity to the temple vowed to the Genetrix at Pharsalus, and the Forum of Augustus must be made to appear the complement of that of Caesar.

In the Forum Augusti the Italic conception of forum as temple

---

[1] Volume of Plates iv, 210, *i*.   [2] See Plan 4, facing p. 582.
[3] Volume of Plates iv, 186, *b*. To what has been said in Vol. IX, p. 841 must be added a reference to the inscription found at Ostia which records that the Temple of Venus Genetrix was 'built' by Trajan (G. Calza in *Not. degli Scavi*, 1932, pp. 188 *sqq.*), which probably means rebuilt on the old lines. The structure as revealed by the excavations of 1933 only allows a comparatively narrow passage between its back wall and that of the Forum itself, sufficient however to justify Appian in saying, somewhat quaintly, that Caesar 'placed a precinct round the temple' (περιέθηκε), *Bell. Civ.* II, 102, 424.

enclosure is carried out in perfection: here the temple apse abuts against the back wall of the huge court, whence it dominates the whole emplacement, while on each long side the enclosing wall itself curved out into deep semicircular exedrae as if to give lungs to the space about the temple and to afford extra protection from a crowded neighbourhood. The straight regular lines of the older porticoes are here abandoned, apse and exedrae forming in plan an harmonious trefoil pattern, a remarkable advance on anything hitherto attempted. The scheme is already that of the colonnade of St Peter's.

The temple, which was Corinthian octostyle, followed the Italic norm; high podium and steps only in front[1], no columns at the back; the broad cella had a deep vestibule, later imitated in the Temple of Castor in the Forum. The apse of the spacious nave contained a long base which supported the statue of the Avenger brandishing his sword, between Venus Genetrix, divine ancestress of the Julian race, on his right and on his left Caesar, marked out by the Julian star[2]. This dynastic triad, which raised to a higher key an already familiar motive (p. 548), appeared as fresh assertion of the perpetual renewing of the spiritual forces of the Empire. It was under the shadow of these divine presences that the cult of the deified Augustus found shelter till the *templum Divi Augusti*, begun by Tiberius and Livia and consecrated by Gaius in A.D. 37, was ready to receive it.

The surrounding Forum matched the Temple in magnificence: the pavements were resplendent in coloured marbles; its exedrae were curtained by columns of precious marble, and adorned with niches containing statues of the Roman *triumphatores*, from Aeneas founder of the *gens* and Romulus founder of the City down to Caesar founder of the Empire. The two first statues, one showing Aeneas with Anchises and Iulus, the other Romulus bearing away the spoils of Acron, are known from the coin representing the *templum Divi Augusti*[3] and from two Pompeian paintings[4]. Between the *exedrae* and the central area ran long colonnaded porticoes which were later linked to the temple of Mars by the two small arches put up by Tiberius in A.D. 19 in honour of the younger Drusus and Germanicus whose statues they bore. These arches completed the architectural scheme at the temple end of the Forum on the model already known from the Forum of Pompeii and possibly from that of Caesar[5].

---

[1] Volume of Plates iv, 190, *b*.   [2] *Ib.* 196, *a*.
[3] *Ib.* 204, *d*.   [4] *Ib.* 176, *a*, *b*.
[5] See above, p. 576 and Volume of Plates iv, 186 *a*.

The arch as monumental entrance to a defined area is common in Italy and the provinces, where numerous arches of Augustan date functioned as ornamental screens to city gates, or else were worked into the town wall as city gates themselves. Fine examples are to be seen at Fano, Rimini, Pola, Aosta, Susa and Orange[1]. They were of the so-called 'triumphal' type and carried statues or chariot groups, their façades being often, though by no means invariably, adorned with reliefs or statue niches[2]. Honorary arches of Augustan date have disappeared in Rome, save for one or two ground plans, but there still stands a charming aqueduct arch of the period, which spanned the old Via Tiburtina. Under Augustus the arch continued to develop in the service of engineering, showing its great adaptability to the most exacting problems of bridge construction, whether in the soaring arches of Narni or in the low arcaded bridges of Rimini and of Merida. Again, the superposed tiers of the Pont du Gard in Provence—generally referred to the Augustan period and to Agrippa, though the date is still uncertain—are not only a great piece of engineering, but a notable architectural achievement which owes its beauty of effect to the variations in the size of the arches and of their piers.

After the death of Agrippa in 12 B.C., Augustus had received loyal support from Tiberius in all his building projects; whatever their other discords, both princes worked harmoniously together for the improvement of Rome and of the cities of the Empire. Among other collaborators were Asinius Pollio who remodelled the old Atrium Libertatis and fitted it with Greek and Latin libraries, and Maecenas who converted the Esquiline, a malarial district covered with disused cemeteries, decaying houses and refuse heaps, into a fine park and gardens as counterpart to the work of sanitation and improvement carried out by Augustus and Agrippa in the Campus Martius. Besides the public baths, the theatres and the libraries, numerous works of public utility were erected in the Rome of Augustus, which bore the same witness to the new economic prosperity of the Empire, that the temples did to its renewed spiritual life. Market places were built for the disposal of wares from all parts of the world; granaries to receive the produce of a revived agriculture; docks to meet the increase in shipping; immense *horrea* or warehouses for the products of the new industrialism. But to discuss these is impossible within the brief space at our disposal. What was accomplished in the Campus

---

[1] Volume of Plates iv, 192.
[2] For these honorary arches see M. Nilsson in *Corolla Archaeologica*, pp. 132 *sqq.*; and I. A. Richmond in *J.R.S.* xxiii, 1933, pp. 149 *sqq.*

Martius and in the heart of the City sufficiently illustrates the principles upon which Augustus remodelled Rome, and justifies his boast that he had found it of brick and left it of marble. The glittering white material from the rich quarries of Carrara contributed to the new aspect of the city; the crude brilliance was happily tempered by the retention for the older buildings of rose-brown travertine and of tufa faced with softly glowing stucco—while the whiteness of the newer edifices was itself relieved by the introduction of coloured marbles for floors and revetments. The scale of buildings was enlarged and tall columns rose from the high Italic podium in obedience to the Roman love of verticalism. The heavy entablatures and pediments of Italic architecture were reduced to lighter proportions at the greater height. The open Italic pediment of the old tufa and terra cotta temples disappeared, and pediments in the Greek manner became the rule. Greek also, as often as not, were the architectural trimmings and refinements, though coins show that pedimental cornices continued to be crowned in Italic fashion with tall upstanding figures which caught up the vertical movement of the columns and carried it upwards into infinite space[1]. The Italic-Roman type of temple was adopted throughout the Empire—witness among many others Nîmes, Vienne, Pola and Ancyra, all still standing on their Italic podia.

In one respect Augustus' neat epigram as to his city of marble needs correction. It applied doubtless to the civic edifices, the temples and temple areas but it glided over the question of the big blocks of tenement houses built of sun-dried bricks and wood—the many-storeyed *insulae* set in a network of crooked narrow streets. Regular planning was limited, as under the Republic, to certain monumental areas, but there was no thought as yet of cutting Imperial roadways through densely populated quarters, or of running streets from one monument to another to obtain a vista. The omission of any street-planning effort or housing reform in the building policy of Augustus is all the stranger in that he showed himself most zealous in planning the new Imperial cities of Italy such as Aosta[2], and of the provinces on the regular system derived from the *castrum*[3]. In Rome the hills certainly formed an obstacle then as now, yet the level Campus Martius offered an opportunity for wider streets which was neglected and so did the parts south of the Forum, afterwards laid out by Nero in long porticoed avenues leading to the Golden House. The Via Lata, a piece of the Flaminian road accidentally drawn within the city, was there to show the

---

[1] Volume of Plates iv, 210, *i*.   [2] Plan 3, facing p. 582.
[3] Vol. ix, p. 836, n. 1.

fine effect of a roadway bordered by monuments, but the hint was only taken later.

The building policy of Augustus was taken up by his Julio-Claudian successors. To the Principate of Tiberius belong, besides a number of minor works, two buildings of outstanding importance—the temple of the god Augustus at the foot of the Palatine which was begun under his auspices, though not dedicated till after his death, and the *Castra Praetoria*, the great military fortress erected in A.D. 21–22, for the concentration of the Praetorian troops into one vast city camp; often though the Castra were restored traces may still be made out of the original brick and concrete walls with their battlements, gates and chain of turrets[1]. While following as a rule in the steps of Augustus, Tiberius in one noteworthy instance abandoned his predecessor's example; by erecting on the Palatine the first of those sumptuous Imperial residences for which the hill afterwards became famous—a contrast to the 'modest house' of Augustus 'without marble decoration or handsome marble pavements,' praised by Suetonius, and it was Tiberius likewise who enlarged Augustus' pleasant villa at Capri into a splendid country-seat whose elegant porticoes and sunny terraces are now being scientifically explored[2].

Few traces remain of the buildings put up by Gaius. The private circus which he erected on the right bank of the Tiber, in the gardens inherited from his mother Agrippina, were destined to be the scene of the earliest Christian martyrdoms and to be eventually absorbed in the great basilica of Saint Peter. On the Palatine he enlarged the imperial residence, projecting, it is said, to connect it with the Capitol by means of a bridge, but the addition, if ever it existed, has disappeared. His name however remains honourably connected with the dedication in A.D. 37 of the *Templum Divi Augusti*, as recorded on a fine contemporary bronze[3]. The coin shows the young Emperor in front of a six-columned Ionic temple, garlanded for the occasion. Within the pediment Romulus, prototype of the now deified New Romulus, stands between Venus Genetrix and Mars Ultor, an assemblage of Julian divinities which is completed by the acroterial figures of the cornice. Here the flaming chariot of the apotheosis, symbol of the new god, appears in the centre, flanked by two crown-bearing Victories, between Romulus on the left bearing away the spoils of Acron and the

---

[1] I. A. Richmond in *Pap. Brit. School at Rome*, 1927, p. 12.

[2] A. Maiuri, 'Il palazzo di Tiberio detto "Villa Jovis" a Capri' in *Atti d. 3° Congresso di Studi Romani*, 1934.

[3] Volume of Plates iv, 204, *d*.

group of Aeneas with Anchises and Iulus on the right—evident imitations these of the Romulus and Aeneas of the Forum of Augustus[1].

Claudius was the first emperor to devote his building energies almost exclusively to works of engineering and public utility: the reclaiming and drainage of land, the creation of harbours, and the extension of the aqueduct system which he brought up to the same level of efficiency as that of the roads. Under Claudius the simpler aqueduct arch was elaborated: magnificent twin arches of rusticate masonry carried two aqueduct channels across the fork of the Via Praenestina and Via Labicana (modern Porta Maggiore), while the triumphal arch erected across the Via Lata in A.D. 46 to commemorate Claudius' conquest of Britain was in reality but the monumental transformation of an arch of the Aqua Virgo which spanned the road at this point. That fresh architectural forces were stirring under Claudius is evident from the new and striking use of vaulted and arched construction that makes its appearance in the now famous hypogeum near the Porta Maggiore[2]. This hall, dedicated to a mystery religion—unless it be merely the meeting place of some funerary college—is composed of barrel-vaulted nave and aisles separated by two rows of pilasters connected not by a straight trabeation but by arcading; the nave is preceded by a pronaos with coved ceiling and arched doorway, and ends in an apse with the indication of the officiant's seat. We thus have at this comparatively early date, and in the service of a pagan cult, a building on the same principle—ante-chapel or narthex, nave, aisles and tribune with throne—as the later Christian basilica.

In essentials the Rome of the Julio-Claudians is one with the Rome of Augustus. New temples, arches, civic halls and palaces might be built, but no substantial change had occurred in the general outlay of the city itself. Its housing system, save for the palaces and homes of the wealthy, remained mean and ugly, its streets narrow and congested. The time was at hand when some improvement must be seriously contemplated. The great fire and the undoubted town-planning abilities of Nero were soon to make possible the desired changes, but the *forma aedificiorum urbis nova* for which Tacitus[3] praises Nero belongs to another chapter of this history.

[1] Volume of Plates iv, 176, *a*, *b*.
[2] Volume of Plates iv, 180, *a*, and above, p. 568.
[3] *Ann.* xv, 43; see A. Boethius in *Corolla Archaeologica*, pp. 84 *sqq.* ('The Neronian *Nova urbs*'); Strong, *Art in Ancient Rome*, i, p. 175.

CHAPTER XVIII
THE ACHIEVEMENT OF AUGUSTUS
I. THE NEW ORDER

IT is beyond doubt that during the principate of Augustus there was a widespread belief that a new page had been turned in the history of mankind. The belief was not everywhere the same nor due to the same causes. In the client-kingdoms men regarded Rome as the power that upheld the ruling houses and may have judged Rome according to the good or bad government of the kings. Yet it must have been observed that in the main the influence of the *princeps* was on the side of good government, that the expensive ambitions of kings in foreign policy were prevented, that contingents from client-kingdoms were less and less called upon as the system of *auxilia* was developed, and that deference to Rome forbade over-ostentatious extravagance. In the provinces of the Hellenistic East the Principate brought good government and relief from wars. Vague aspirations after a new era for which the leader should be found in the East[1] were reduced to unreality by Actium and the fall of Egypt, and there can have been few who did not recognize that the new order, for all its insistence on the primacy of Italy and the supremacy of *cives Romani* over all other inhabitants of the world, permitted the Hellenistic East to live its own life with security and self-respect. The freedom to be judged by their own laws which the Greeks prized almost above political independence was not infringed by Rome. Greek culture was admired, though Roman culture claimed its independence. In religion Rome stood by the older gods of Italy and Greece, but permitted freedom of cult and worship in all the provinces.

The seas and roads were secure, and everywhere men could pass freely on their lawful occasions. Beyond the Danube and the Euphrates there might be enemies, but Rome stood on guard on every frontier. For generations before, the provinces and client-kingdoms had seen the power of Rome and had sought to find in it protection even at the price of dependence. The worship of Rome

---

Note. This chapter is intended to stress certain points already made by other writers in earlier contributions to the volume, and to add general reflections that arise from their interaction.

[1] See p. 82.

had evinced the desire to find a lasting protector, as the honours paid to Roman generals and governors had evinced the desire to find protection for the moment. But Rome had pursued no steady policy, and the great generals and governors had passed or had fallen. Now stability had entered into Roman affairs, and the provinces and kingdoms that readily realized power in terms of persons saw that the keystone of this stable Rome was the *princeps*, Augustus. Thus it was not illogical for them to combine the cult of Rome with that of Augustus, the combination of the two ensuring their security and in so far deserving their gratitude. This was not a personal religion in the sense that it had any meaning for the spiritual life of the worshippers, or that it was tinged with any emotion other than gratitude and an interested solicitude for the preservation of the new order. Nor was it directed to a person in the sense that it attributed to Augustus any qualities or powers other than those of a man. Apart from Egypt, where the native Egyptians had for centuries imagined their Pharaohs to be nearer the gods than men[1], the Hellenistic East in general had seen in rulers the source of benefits or injuries and in the cult of them the placation or laudation of a power that was wholly of this world. To them, as to Virgil, '*deus nobis haec otia fecit*,' and so long as he did so, '*erit ille mihi semper deus*.' The all-embracing power of Rome was a necessary part of the beneficence of Rome and both of these could readily be personified in the *princeps*. It is this simple conception that lies behind such dedications as that of the people of the petty town of Myra in Lycia[2] to Augustus as 'ruler of land and sea; benefactor and saviour of the whole *kosmos*.'

In the western provinces, especially in Spain and Gaul, Rome had another meaning. To the Gauls outside the old Provincia and to the tribes of northern and western Spain, Rome was a new master. A ruthless war against these tribes had made safe the more civilized parts of Spain[3] and they were becoming romanized. The sentiment of the more urbanized Spain was becoming more akin to that of Italy, whence had come many settlers; elsewhere no violence was done to national or tribal feeling[4]. The Roman *auxilia* offered a career to Spaniards who could not endure the *pax Romana*, the rest of Spain welcomed security and order. In Gaul the tribes and their chiefs were won by gentle handling and by protection against the Germans beyond the Rhine. The advance of material civilization and comfort was hastened by the facilitation of trade between

[1] See p. 285.   [2] *I.G.R.R.* III, 719.   [3] See p. 344 *sq.*
[4] See C. H. V. Sutherland in *J.R.S.* xxiv, 1934, pp. 37 *sqq.*

the ends of the Empire. The Gauls might well feel that they had sacrificed little more of liberty than the name, and that they had received a high price. Indeed, Rome offered to them a sense of national unity within the Empire; and when Drusus dedicated to Rome and Augustus the altar of Lugdunum built by sixty tribes from the three Gauls he made the new Rome the foster mother of Gallic unity[1]. Rome had divided in order to conquer; now she united in order to rule.

In Rome, Italy, and among the Roman citizens who lived outside Italy, the Principate meant something far more, and the new order aroused deeper emotions. Civil wars, the proscriptions and requisitions, the dread some men had of an autocrat, the dismay some felt when the removal of the autocrat brought no more than the name of freedom as a losing battle-cry, the fear that Rome itself was to yield pride of place to a queen from the East with a Roman as her led-captain—all these had induced a sense of guilt and insecurity. The Romans had felt the stirring of a new emotion, doubt of themselves and despair of the Republic. In such moments a people will turn with unquestioning and almost savage loyalty to a man who sets himself to exorcize these emotions. Whatever Octavian may have been, however ruthless and self-seeking, he stood for Rome, and all else was forgotten. Caesar had embodied faith in his own star and his own genius; Octavian stood for faith in Rome. At Ilerda, Pharsalus, Thapsus, Munda, it was Caesar who had conquered; at Actium it was Rome and Italy. Caesar had pardoned his enemies; Octavian had watched them perish, and now could honestly declare that he had no enemies among Romans who held by Rome. Policy alone would have dictated to him the championship of Rome and Italy;

> 'The same arts that did gain
> A power, must it maintain'—

but Octavian was no mere adventurer exploiting emotions which he did not share. The faith which was placed in him was not misplaced. The new order meant the revival of Roman primacy, the assertion of Roman culture, the restoration of Roman self-confidence, the exaltation of Roman religion as the reflection of the State. Yet this nationalism was not ungrateful. What Greek thought and letters and art had meant to Rome was not denied. It was retained and honoured, but only as having become a part of Roman culture. Apollo on the Palatine might match, even outshine, Juppiter on the Capitol, but he must do so as a god of Rome.

[1] See p. 486.

New elements from without, such as Oriental cults or old elements of the same kind which had not been taken into the Roman State religion, were kept in their place. Whoever would, might find comfort in the service of Isis and the like, but as Romans and Italians men must recognize the gods of Rome and Italy.

Least of all was Augustus prepared to permit the worship of the State gods to be replaced or rivalled by worship of himself. Rather he prided himself on being the first and the most devout of all their servants and worshippers in the name of Rome. The cult of Divus Julius was another matter: Caesar now belonged to the past of Rome, as would Augustus himself when he was gathered to his fathers. A like sanctity rested on the Senate and the magistracies which had been the channels of Roman power and tradition[1]. These were to remain, and the citizens were to be their own masters within the forms which had been consecrated by time. To Romans faith in their past was the larger part of their faith in their future. There were to be no innovations which would shake this faith. To them the new age meant that they were to wake from a nightmare to find that they were themselves after all. Yet the nightmare had been so long drawn and horrible that much had to be done to drive out its memory and to restore tone to the shaken nerves. Herein the personality of Augustus played a great part. His serenity and his very matter-of-factness combined to assist the cure.

We thus find in the first years of the Augustan age a consciousness of the greatness of the Republic. In the early books of Livy, in the *Odes* of Horace, and in the *Georgics* and *Aeneid* there is heard again and again the note of pride in the past, of belief in the people of Italy and in the sound old qualities of the Republican worthies[2]. Imperial art is full of the same theme, as of the dignity and composure of Roman ceremonial[3]. By the side of the martial spirit in which Rome so readily saw the spring of virtue there is also a new domestic gentleness, an enjoyment of simplicity. The arrogant luxury and self-seeking ambition of the nobles of the failing Republic were rebuked by the modest state kept by the *princeps* and by his untiring devotion to the plain path of duty. The appeal to virtue on the ground that vice was un-Roman linked the national spirit with the desire for a reform in morals. It was natural to connect the agonies of the last decades with a loosening of morality and neglect of religion[4]; it was equally natural to believe that in the revival of religion and morals lay security against such disasters. That one man should control the State had come

[1] See F. B. Marsh, *Founding of the Roman Empire*[2], p. 217.
[2] See above, p. 476.   [3] See pp. 546 *sqq.*   [4] See p. 474.

to be a political necessity; the necessity was made more easily a free choice when the man who was to control the State carried forward into the Principate what was believed to be the most precious heritage of the Republic.

As policy alone would have taught Augustus to champion, at the risk of narrowness, the primacy of Rome and Italy, so it would have inspired him to retain the forms of the Republic. Yet that retention was something more than a screen for effective autocracy. Caesar's dictatorship had been the crowning *reductio ad absurdum* of Roman constitutional forms: Augustus meant the old Republic to be a reality so far as it could. He had ever been willing to use and to acknowledge the talents of others and he realized that Rome needed, as he needed, the service of the aristocracy. He cannot well have planned to allow the State to escape from his control, or to stand aside and content himself with protecting a Republican government from dislocation from within or without. The position of a *moderator rei publicae* fell below his capacity and fell short of the needs of his generation. But he did intend to rule as one among many servants of the State, the greatest, the most powerful, the most permanent of them, but not alone. The last decades of the Republic had shown that the Senate was not equal to all the tasks that fell to Rome. The Senate at the beginning of the Principate was even less capable, for it had been weakened by the Civil Wars and the proscriptions. But for part of the old tasks it was still strong enough, and these it was left to carry on. The remainder the *princeps* took upon his own shoulders formally at the request of the Senate. It was his commission to provide for it, and he had the power to appoint his own helpers. But, so far as his commission went, he was responsible to the State for his own actions and those of the helpers. The State was no other than the Senate and People of Rome; the *princeps* was not a third estate by the side of these two. In any activity in which Augustus was a magistrate, he had no more powers than anyone associated with him as colleague[1]. To call the constitution of the Principate a dyarchy is to miscall it: there was no division of power; what there was, was a division of labour. There was no moment and there was no sphere of activity in which Augustus was not acting in the name of the Senate and People, except that, like other magistrates, he was his own master in his own *provincia* until his commission to deal with it expired.

[1] The theory that Augustus evoked for himself ancient wider powers from the consulship has been more than once refuted. See P. de Francisci, 'La costituzione Augustea' in *Studi Bonfante*, I, p. 25.

It is without doubt true that, in general, the armies of the Re-public were under Augustus' control, but it is inexact to describe his constitutional position as that of a military monarch. His effective control of almost all the army did indeed prevent the rise of a rival. But his power did not formally rest on the army, and the fact that he had assumed the *praenomen* of Imperator had no constitutional significance[1]. It is true that he had in his hands almost, if not all, the military patronage of the State. But this, in theory, only endured so long as he was entrusted with a commission to govern the provinces in which most of the legions were posted. With the end of that commission his legal control of the army would have ceased. Nor can any constitutional importance be attached to the word *princeps*[2]. As *princeps senatus* Augustus enjoyed primacy in the Senate, but outside the *Curia*, *princeps senatus* meant nothing, and within the *Curia* it was no more than primacy. *Princeps*, apart from *princeps senatus*, was, as it had always been, a complimentary title and no more. It reflected the fact that Augustus counted for most among the citizens of Rome: it was a convenient though un-official compendium for the authority which Augustus enjoyed. It was the noun which described what in the *Res Gestae* Augustus claimed, that he ranked before all others in *auctoritas*. Such was the setting in which the Principate began.

Yet from the year 23 B.C. onwards it must have been realized that Augustus did enjoy a constitutional position such as Pompey, for instance, had neither enjoyed nor even, perhaps, desired. He was not the colleague of the tribunes and he had a *tribunicia potestas* which overrode their office: he was not the colleague of proconsuls but he possessed a proconsular *imperium maius* which meant that his will went over the will of all proconsuls. Their *imperium* was derived from the same source as his, but on him was conferred an *imperium* which was greater than theirs, if their *imperium* and his came into conflict or comparison. Yet both the *imperium proconsulare maius* and the *tribunicia potestas* were powers which Augustus could share without forgoing their practical effectiveness. In the *Res Gestae* Augustus declared that he five times received from the Senate at his own request a colleague in the possession of the *tribunicia potestas*, and it is clear that those persons on whom the *imperium proconsulare* was specially conferred might possess it in the form of the *imperium maius*, though the sphere within which it was operative was limited by the sphere for which the *imperium* itself was granted. It is assumed by Mommsen that this *imperium* was subordinated to that of Augustus, but it may be argued that this distinction, which is nowhere formally attested, did not exist in strict law, but that it was deduced in practice from the superior *auctoritas* of the *princeps* and the fact that the appointment of officers within the imperial provinces seems to have remained in the hands of the *princeps*. How great was the effective validity of the *auctoritas* of the *princeps* is, indeed, shown by Augustus' very willingness to allow others to hold these powers on which his own position formally rested. Even when at the last Tiberius was vested with powers which were hard to distinguish from those of the *princeps* himself there can have been no doubt whose will counted for most in the State.

If men asked themselves the question whether Rome under the Augustan Principate was or was not a Republic the answer depended on what was contrasted with a Republic. It was not a monarchy in any sense in which the world had hitherto known the word. It was not an autocracy in the sense that the sole initiative in the State sprang from the will of the emperor. It was not a military tyranny in the sense that the emperor's power formally rested on the will of the army or on the command of the army, or that the emperor either represented or pursued the interests of the army as a power in the State. As against these alternatives the Augustan Principate was Republican. But, once this negative definition is abandoned, it becomes clear that Rome suffered a change from the régime of *Senatus populusque Romanus*. It has been argued above[1] that in the settlement of 23 B.C. a group of powers was conferred on the *princeps* by a legislative act which went beyond the powers inherent in the *imperium proconsulare maius* and the *tribunicia potestas*. If this be so, and if such powers as are ascribed to Augustus in the *lex de imperio* of the time of Vespasian are not rather the statement of what in fact he had come to do without question in the course of his reign, then from the year 23 B.C. onwards it must have been clear that the Senate and People of Rome had in certain matters abdicated in favour of the *princeps*. In any event, despite the renewals of the *proconsulare imperium*, which formally implies that the commission expired if it was not renewed, it is not easy, in the face of his *tribunicia potestas*, to see how any alternative commission to anyone else was possible. Even if it was, the administration of the Imperial provinces was so organized as a radiation of power from the *princeps*, that the only practicable alternative to one *princeps* was another. In fact, the

---

[1] See p. 140 *sq.*

government of this large part of the Empire was not Republican, if by that is meant that the governors were immediately responsible to the Senate and People of Rome. Nor is that all. If in senatorial provinces the will of the *princeps* could prevail over that of the governors by virtue of his *imperium proconsulare maius*, then these governors, too, were potentially subordinate to a power that was, in action, other than that of the Senate and People. Further, even within Italy itself there grew up a side of the administration which must be called imperial in character, and, as this grew, the centre of gravity in the State moved steadily away from the Senate and People (which in practice meant the Senate) and towards the *princeps*. During the fourteen years after the settlement of 27 B.C. Augustus acquired a firm grasp on the government of most of the provinces in the mere execution of his commission, and during the remaining twenty-seven years of his life his presence at Rome attracted to himself an increasing share of the administration of affairs at home, while he did not cease to extend his authority even within the senatorial provinces. Those who wished to believe that there had been no breach with the Republican constitution as it had existed for centuries might find some real and more formal grounds to encourage their belief, but in point of fact, the weight of evidence was against their conception of the State and refutes those modern scholars who would share it.

II. THE PERSONALITY OF AUGUSTUS

The record of Augustus' *res gestae* that was placed before his Mausoleum in Rome and has thrice been found inscribed in towns of Asia Minor attests his services to the State, above all to the Romans and the people of Italy. But the personality of the man that stood behind that great career is not easy to grasp. Between the passionate outcry from Homer[1] with which he faced his first great adventure and the actors' epilogue with which he claimed applause on his deathbed[2] many changes had altered his mind as well as his fortunes. The strong desire for security and high position working for and through revenge for Caesar, the politic instinct for

---

[1]   αὐτίκα τεθναίην, ἐπεὶ οὐκ ἄρ' ἔμελλον ἑταίρῳ
          κτεινομένῳ ἐπαμῦναι.   *Il.* XVIII, 98 *sq.*
See above, p. 7.

[2]   εἰ δέ τι
          ἔχοι καλῶς τὸ παίγνιον, κρότον δότε
          καὶ πάντες ἡμᾶς μετὰ χαρᾶς προπέμψατε.
                                          Suetonius, *Aug.* 99.

the way to conquer authority and to rally behind him the forces that made for permanence, the tact that revealed what men hoped for in the Principate and shunned what men might fear or resent, the conquest of bodily weakness and the long-drawn single-minded industry of the first servant of the State mark stages in the development of his character. We may suspect that the features of the Octavian of Mutina and of Philippi did not bear the serenity of the Augustus of Prima Porta. The courage to dare was transmuted into the courage to endure.

Security and success lulled to sleep and almost destroyed the cruelty and self-seeking that at times mastered him in the first decade of his career. How far in the struggle with Antony the championship of Italian and Roman ideals was an end rather than a means, we cannot say. But when the struggle was over the inspiration of the championship remained with him. More and more he displayed the hard-headed tenacity, the caution, the faith in the past together with the cool appreciation of the present that marked out the most solid parts of the Roman and Italian character.

It may be argued that apart from native shrewdness and painstaking thoroughness his guiding motives were negative; reaction from the dangerous sides of Caesar and of Antony, the ineffective side of Cicero, the unpractical side of Cato, the blind side of Pompey. But this interpretation does Augustus less than justice. His statecraft is not to be explained as dictated by a tradition, or the mere avoidance of refuted policies and expedients. It was the natural expression of his character, so far as we can discover what his own character was and became.

The few extracts from his private letters and the few authentic sayings that have been preserved[2] reveal a man of warm feelings, careful of appearances yet impatient of affectation, with a frank almost naïve liking for simple social pleasures, a humour not without a tincture of wit. This is one side of Augustus, something not unlike the figure of a middle-class Roman from the country. He stoutly believed in respectability and decorum and was prepared to face unpopularity to exact from the governing class at least a minimum of both. This is not to say that his own life was always above reproach: we can hardly doubt that there was some truth in Antony's imputations on his morals; but he was capable of strong devotion, if not entire fidelity, to Livia through their long married life, and he died with her name on his lips.

---

[1] See Volume of Plates iv, 148, *a*.

[2] H. Malcovati, *Caes. Aug. imp. operum frag*². pp. 5–22; Macrobius, *Sat.* ii, 4; Plutarch, *Apoph. reg. et. imp., Aug.* (*Mor.* 206 F–208).

One quality Augustus possessed by which his other qualities may in part be judged. He was able to hold the loyalty of friends eminent enough to have to make a sacrifice of ambition to serve him. In the last decades of the Republic friendship had been a weapon rather than a bond[1]. The *amicitiae* of Roman nobles had been jealous and exacting: only rarely, where the tastes of friends made way for each other as was true of those of Atticus and Cicero, was friendship lasting and loyal. Most men in history who have risen as Augustus rose have been very ready to be rid of their helpers, but there was in him a quality which evoked loyalty and was great enough to recognize and cherish it. In his earlier days there stood by his side two men of a different stamp, Agrippa and Maecenas. Of Agrippa it is not too much to say that, had there been no Augustus, he had capacities which might have made him the first man in Rome. A general and administrator of high distinction, his features display a man of resolute character not without subtlety[2]. More intriguing still is the shrewd and useful patron of letters Maecenas, cloaking with indolence and a certain preciosity a penetrating political dexterity. They were both far more than a Berthier or a Fouché or perhaps even a Talleyrand, more than a Bentinck or even a Sully. It may be said that Agrippa lacked the *cachet* of birth and that Maecenas was soft metal. But it cannot be denied that in arms or diplomacy they earned the right to be counted great men; and they spent themselves in the advancement of Augustus with an abnegation of self that even Caesar was not able to evoke in his friends. There remains one other helper and colleague, Tiberius. Between him and the Princeps, despite affectionate phrases[3], there was imperfect sympathy. Apart from the sacrifice of Tiberius' happiness to his stepfather's dynastic hopes, there was a disharmony between the Claudian by birth and the Julian by adoption[4]. The withdrawal of Tiberius[5] may have outraged the Emperor's sense of duty, though Tiberius did not fail in the end to show that, grimly and reluctantly, he would serve the State in his own way. Hard though it is to discover the truth through the cloud that suspicion raised around these two figures, it may be suggested that the relation of the two made shipwreck between the affection of Augustus for Livia and of Livia for Tiberius. But at the last, whatever the ingrained discord of their temperaments, their common service

---

[1] W. Kroll, *Die Kultur der Ciceronischen Zeit*, i, pp. 56 *sqq.*

[2] Volume of Plates iv, 154, *a*.   [3] See Malcovati, *op. cit.* pp. 8–12.

[4] For this contrast see also E. Kornemann in *Staaten, Männer, Völker*, p. 78.   [5] See p. 155.

refuted the easy epigram of *insociabile regnum*. One thing may be said, that if the greatness of Augustus is more attested by his achievement than by what the ancient evidence of his character permits us to deduce, there must have been in him a natural dominance of mind if he could be acknowledged as the leader of these men with a leadership which neither they nor others dreamt of challenging.

In the *Res Gestae* there is the chronicle of Augustus' services, achievements and benefactions with an interpretation of his career which is not all the truth, for truth is not all its purpose. Written to be made public in Rome when the author was beyond the reach of his enemies, it set out the credit side of the account and left others to make what detraction they could. The man who advised Tiberius not to be too greatly outraged at the thought that there could be anyone who spoke ill of him—'satis est enim si hoc habemus ne quis nobis male facere possit[1]'—had come to care little for detraction, but the *Res Gestae* reveals the intention to make it plain that no Roman who condemned him at his death could do so without incurring the reproach of ingratitude. How far the aged Emperor deceived himself about the acts of his early days, we shall never know. Nor can we complain that he presents his constitutional position with more attention to its formal correctness than its actual predominance[2]. So far as the *Res Gestae* is not a claim in the aristocratic manner to the one kind of immortality for which most Romans cared, it is a State Paper setting out the capital of good will and good services with which the new order was endowed, and Augustus was too good a man of business to understate the assets.

The *Res Gestae* is, then, concerned with positive and concrete achievements: what is not described is the general order and system which Augustus had brought into being. It is here to be supplemented by the pronouncement[3], already quoted, which will bear repetition: 'ita mihi salvam ac sospitem rem publicam sistere in sua sede liceat atque eius rei fructum percipere quem peto, ut optimi status auctor dicar et moriens ut feram mecum spem, mansura in vestigio suo fundamenta rei publicae quae iecero.' Here is a claim to an achievement and to a reward. Besides the motive thus indicated, there is evidence enough that Augustus

---

[1] Suetonius, *Aug.* 51.

[2] Indeed, the *Res Gestae* contains no reference to his *proconsulare imperium*.

[3] Suetonius, *Aug.* 28. See above, p. 129. With this may be compared Augustus' dictum on Cato (Macrobius, *Sat.* II, 4, 18)—*quisquis praesentem statum civitatis commutari non volet et civis et vir bonus est.*

was moved by a very strong sense of duty, that he regarded himself as a soldier at a post which it would be criminal to desert. Something of this idea is found in Hellenistic kings and much in Roman Stoicism[1] inspired in part by Augustus' own example. But there is no need to look beyond the Roman military tradition and the character of the *princeps* himself. It may fairly be said that in this constant unwavering laborious service of the State Augustus stood first even among Romans. The system of imperial secretaries had not developed so far as to relieve the *princeps* from personal care about a vast multiplicity of matters in which policy or justice were concerned. What remains of the records of his intervention in the affairs of provincial communities attests the directness of Augustus' own contact. In his letter to Cnidus[2] and in the decrees at Cyrene[3] can be heard the echoes of his positive practical fair-minded judgment. A generation of unostentatious unremitting activity justified the dictum, whether of Tacitus or of Tiberius—'solam divi Augusti mentem tantae molis capacem[4].'

Such an activity might be no more than the routine diligence of an imperial bureaucrat, but until the last few years of his principate, Augustus' acts show an elasticity of mind and a constructive statesmanship. Augustus himself, like most Romans, was ready to see in his achievements the hand of fortune, and his *felicitas* was proverbial in the days of his successors. But his determination to sacrifice others as well as himself to the needs of the State was visited with a series of mischances. It seemed as if he was never to be released from his duty and it has been well pointed out how the realization of approaching death induced in him a mood almost of gaiety[5].

In his misfortunes and in the way in which he met them can be detected the facets of his character. For reasons of State he forced Tiberius to divorce the wife he loved and to marry Julia and he advanced his grandsons, Gaius and Lucius Caesar, until Tiberius withdrew suddenly from public life. This desertion Augustus seems for long not to have forgiven. Yet when the death of his grandsons made it clear that Tiberius was the one man who could become *princeps* with the prestige of the Imperial House, he did not shrink from adopting him and finally making him the equal

---

[1] E. Köstermann, '*Statio principis*,' in *Phil.* LXXXVII, 1932, pp. 358 *sqq.*, 430 *sqq.*

[2] Ditt.[3] 780.

[3] See pp. 138, n. 1, 167, 212.   [4] Tacitus, *Ann.* 1, 11.

[5] W. Weber, *Princeps, Studien zur Geschicte des Augustus.* 1, Stuttgart 1934, pp. 9 *sqq.* nn. 62, 69.

colleague of himself in everything except *auctoritas*. The discovery of the wantonness of his daughter Julia brought him to disgrace her openly and to pursue the poet Ovid with unrelenting anger. The tremendous crisis of the Pannonian revolt roused him to vigorous action. Here was for a moment the need to defend the borders of Italy, and the need found the *princeps* at his post. The contrast with his reaction to the disaster of Varus is significant perhaps of the weakening of old age, but partly because it reveals the economical mind of the *imperator* who counted his legions so carefully—'Quintili Vare, legiones redde.'

It was in his very nature to reject the parade of power, for he was no mere 'hypocrite of genius' as he has been called. Resolved that the Roman world should be secure and be well-governed in the interests of Rome, he took for himself, as by instinct, the minimum of power necessary and assumed the minimum of pomp and ceremony. As evidence of this last may be adduced the reliefs of the Ara Pacis, where the *princeps* is not set apart from his family nor his family set apart from other citizens by any especial marks of distinction (pp. 546 *sqq.*). Caesar had endured, probably enjoyed, the splendid garb of a *triumphator*; Augustus preferred the plain toga which Livia had woven for him. One touch of vanity is recorded of him, that he was pleased when men dropped their eyes before his clear and steady gaze[1]. He avoided military display and did not pander unduly to the ambitions of generals. Himself no great commander, he was ready enough to risk his life in the high places of the field, but only when there was no other way to victory or to the mastery of his legionaries. Caesar had been a soldier among soldiers till the end; Augustus sedulously avoided the appeal that lay in the allocution 'commilitones.'

His countenance could abash the legionaries that had fought at Actium, but he was ready with tears and gestures to reveal his emotions and, if need be, to move the emotions of others. He studied elocution and cultivated a style of speech which set intelligibility before elegance. Sometimes a homely phrase, sometimes a touch of pedantry gave a personal note to his writing[2]. Yet he had not the foible of believing himself a man of letters, nor the foible of underrating the effectiveness of those who were[3]. For philosophers he had the respect which was dictated by good form. He may have had more: the possibility cannot be denied that

---

[1] Suetonius, *Aug.* 79; Julian, *Conv. Caes.* 309 B; Servius *ad Aen.* VIII, 689: see, however, Pliny, *N.H.* XI, 143, Aur. Vict. *epit.* I.

[2] Suetonius, *Aug.* 84 *sqq.*

[3] Suetonius, *Aug.* 85, 2; 89; *Horatii vita*, p. 45 R.; Macrobius, *Sat.* II, 4, 2.

the ideas of Plato or Panaetius, reflected in the writings of Cicero, had an influence over him[1]. But no such assumption is necessary; and the *auctoritas* of Augustus was rooted in Roman ideas conceived before Greek speculation affected the political thought of the Republic[2]. Nor need he have thought that either Greek philosophers or Cicero must teach him statecraft or the duty of a ruler, and abstract speculation can have had little attraction for his matter-of-fact mind. There was in him a trace of superstition in small matters[3], so that he may have been a valetudinarian in religion, but within strict limits. He loved comfort of body and mind, but held it lightly when there was work to be done. Once power was in his hand, he hated to tempt fortune. Daring as he had been when he could not afford to be anything else, he was not the man to risk hard-won gains, but to wait and wait until he could move cautiously and securely to his purpose. For those who ventured all to win something he had the sardonic reproof that they were like men who fished with a hook of gold, the loss of which would leave them poor, whatever they caught by its use[4]. The assemblage of qualities and capacities that made up his personality are not such as to strike the imagination of the world. In the sense that Alexander, Caesar or Napoleon surpassed other men in intellectual equipment, Augustus cannot be counted a man of genius. That he was not: he was the man that the world needed, and may claim to have been one of the greatest servants of the human race. The highest praise that he coveted was justly given by the sailors of a ship off Puteoli as the Princeps passed them on his way to die—*per illum se vivere, per illum navigare, libertate atque fortunis per illum frui*[5].

III. FOREIGN AND MILITARY POLICY

The foreign and military policy of Augustus, as has been seen, fell short of complete success. In the West and North there can be detected a far-sighted and strong advance of Roman security during the first two decades of his principate. In the East, apart from the abortive expedition to Arabia which may indirectly have had useful economic results, Roman policy in the same period discloses the realization that the Euphrates was a natural limit of the empire[6]. With a comparatively small expense of military effort reinforced by the use of diplomacy and of client-

---

[1] W. Kolbe, *Aus Roms Zeitwende*, pp. 65 *sqq.*
[2] See F. Schulz, *Prinzipien des römischen Rechts*, pp. 112 *sqq.*
[3] Suetonius, *Aug.* 90 *sqq.*   [4] Suetonius, *Aug.* 25.
[5] Suetonius, *Aug.* 98.   [6] See above, pp. 256 *sqq.*

kingdoms, that part of the Mediterranean world was made sufficiently secure. The defeat of Antony followed by a prudent settlement and the playing upon the dynastic cares of the King of Parthia produced a situation suited to the traditional methods of the older Roman statecraft. Twice only was there an important show of force, to support Tiberius and Gaius Caesar in the settlement of Armenia. Thus the main strength of the legions was available in the West: in Spain, on the Rhine or on the Danube, in Illyricum and round the northern borders of Italy itself. The conquest of Spain was completed, the Alps were made peaceful; most important of all, in the North-East the land-routes with Macedonia were secured by the occupation of Illyricum and the expansion of the empire to the Danube[1]. But in these military movements the part played by Augustus himself was small and his campaigns in Spain left work for Agrippa to finish. It may be suspected that the strategy of his early principate sprang from the brain of Agrippa, and it is possible that in Tiberius Agrippa found a worthy inheritor of his plans.

The earlier operations in Germany entrusted to Drusus were, as has been shown, of less vital consequence than the firm hold of the Danube and the communications behind it. But the death of Drusus removed Tiberius from Illyricum, and the failure to pierce that country with roads in the Roman fashion avenged itself later at the time of the great Pannonian Revolt. Yet there are good grounds to suppose that even during the voluntary exile of Tiberius the preparations for the overthrow of Maroboduus were advanced[2]. On the return of Tiberius to the Rhine this plan was brought to the very verge of accomplishment. It was a moment in the history of the Empire which was not to recur until the reign of Marcus Aurelius. But success was snatched away by a revolt which betrays at least one miscalculation by the Princeps or his advisers. Pannonia and Dalmatia had not been made secure by roads and by good or firm government. It is possible that there had been one other mistake in raising too many auxiliary regiments in this region without removing them from the influence of local patriotism. Indeed, the Romans had raised and trained against themselves a national army[3]. Granted that the Emperor roused himself to face the emergency and that the Roman generals and legions mastered the revolt and suffered no major disaster, it cannot be denied that the military power of Rome had been roughly shaken.

[1] See pp. 351 *sqq.*   [2] See pp. 365 *sqq.*   [3] See p. 230.

More striking, although less dangerous, was the achievement of Arminius in destroying the army of Varus. As has been pointed out[1], it was not necessary for Rome to occupy Germany and the enterprise did not offer positive gains worth the cost. Diplomacy playing on the rivalries of tribes and chiefs was enough for security, once it had been made plain that only the highest leadership could counter the skill and force of the Romans in war. But the disaster and the campaigns that followed it had effects more lasting than the temporary loss of the legend of invincibility. The concentration of eight legions on the Rhine meant that military policy was largely immobilized, and might mean a temptation to emperor-making[2]. Furthermore, the events that attended these successive crises showed that by the last decade of Augustus' principate there were no natural reserves of men in Italy who could be recruited for the legions on a large scale[3]. This fact attests, no doubt, the prosperity of Italy—for men did not need to become soldiers—but it betrays also a slackening of military spirit and some divorce of sympathy between the armies and the class from which the legions were mainly drawn. The armies were stationed far from Italy and the denial of family life to the legionaries weakened their ties with their own folk. The peasant who farmed in Italy can have had little sense of solidarity with his soldier brother who disappeared from sight for the best part of his life and, if he returned to Italy at all, returned to live as a petty *rentier* or, if he became a centurion, as a member of a local upper middle class[4]. The wars of the early Empire had little effect on economic or family life, the Roman People had been spared any great effort, and foreign policy was left without public criticism or public support. During the first decade of the Principate poets had echoed the highest hopes of a martial people, but with the development of the shrewd and wise, but unshowy, policy of Augustus, these voices lost their appeal to a people that sought peace and security.

Granted that the standing army was not capable of quick expansion, it is easy to point to the absence of a central strategic reserve[5], and to see in it a defect of policy. As years went by, the legions in Spain became more available to reinforce the other armies, and much could be done by the dexterous transference of troops from one frontier to another. But, apart from the nine

---

[1] See above, p. 380.   [2] See below, p. 787 *sq.*
[3] As the system developed and families with military traditions sprang up over a wider field, recruiting became easier. See p. 222.
[4] See p. 226.   [5] See p 224.

cohorts of the Praetorian guards and the marines of the fleets, the early Empire was short of troops at a central point. This weakness was endured by Augustus partly, we may conjecture, from economy, partly from a political instinct which forbade a concentration of force in Italy which might give to the new system the air of a military monarchy. The world had suffered so much from too many legions that it might well be content to take what risks were involved in having too few. The one great power outside and yet within reach of the Empire was Parthia, and Parthia was ill-equipped to force upon Rome a military emergency[1]. For a decade Maroboduus had been strong, but unwilling to match himself against the Empire even when the Pannonians and Arminius tempted him. Only twice in the reign of Augustus was Roman military action dictated by the will of Rome's enemies, and so long as the initiative lay with her, the existing military strength might just, though only just, meet all her needs.

It is to be remembered that in Syria and Egypt and for part of this period in Spain the legions were mainly engaged in police-duty and in public works, military or civil, rather than in guarding the frontiers[2]. This had an effect on their efficiency for serious wars, and in the two Eastern provinces these became almost local armies largely recruited from stocks of less military quality[3]. The more active legions in the main avoided the danger of seeing their men grow old together by the steady accession of recruits to replace the casualties of war. But the danger was there, and the military value of the Western armies no doubt varied from time to time, and where there was such variation it may have affected the *tempo* of military effort. Granted that the Roman government could, in general, choose its time for great enterprises, it was naturally economical to embark upon them when the legions concerned were at the height of their efficiency, because fewer troops needed to be used, and because, when legions were more veteran in character than at other times, each casualty might remove a claimant on the State who had more nearly served it to the end. Such moments were naturally followed by periods of comparative weakness, which could only be rapidly made good by drafts on the good-will of time-expired soldiers. Further, the policy of balancing the legions against the *auxilia* denied to Augustus the natural counterpart in arms of what had been the ancient Republican

[1] See above, p. 257 *sq.*
[2] See pp. 247, 281.
[3] Though Dessau 2483 attests the presence of the sturdy Galatians in the Egyptian garrison.

policy in citizenship. Had the legions been in part recruited from picked auxiliaries, the military problem would have been less difficult. But Rome and Augustus were not ready for that.

Such are the deductions that may fairly be made from the credit side of Roman military policy as it developed during the reign of Augustus. The loyalty of the army to the home government was secured by the provision, not by their generals but effectively by the *princeps*, of the grants of money and land that stood for pensions. Promotion, in most, if not all the armies, was ultimately derived from the *princeps*, and the constant transfer of picked centurions from one legion to another held the armies together by a kind of network of devotion to the *imperator*[1]. On the other hand, the almost permanent division of the army into frontier-groups was a new application of the maxim *divide ut imperes*. As there was little solidarity between the legions and the Italian lower middle class so there was little solidarity between the army groups. As the armies became conscious of their power, they became conscious of their local *esprit de corps*. Cadets of the imperial family served an apprenticeship in arms, and the elder and younger Drusus, Tiberius, and Germanicus held high commands in the field, but the place of the *princeps* was in Rome, even if his image stood between the standards of every legion or cohort. When Augustus died, no serving legionary had seen him in the camp, still less in the field, and the same is true of Tiberius. The early Principate was not, as has been seen, a military monarchy beyond all else, nor the creation or creature of the army. There is a great difference between the position of Augustus or of his successors and that of the First or Third Napoleon. If the legions were indifferent, the praetorians might at moments affect the policy of the State, but between the present, though slight, power of the guards and the distant and great, though divided, power of the frontier armies there was no consciousness of a common interest. From emperor to emperor due care was taken to ensure that if the *princeps* was not above all a soldier on the throne, no general should combine the power and the will to be one, until at last, half a century after Augustus' death, the 'secret of empire' was revealed. The armies and their generals for long remained the servants of the State, and saw in the *princeps* the head of the State and, as that, the head of the army.

There is one other topic that needs to be considered before a conclusion is reached. It is natural to think of the Empire as an aggregation of provinces, but it must not be forgotten that Roman

---

[1] See p. 226.

policy had for two centuries leaned on client-states, so that her power had had what have been well called 'invisible frontiers[1].' This policy Augustus inherited, and he was slow to change it. The armies of client-kingdoms were not to be despised and they played a part in the wars of his principate, though they slowly declined as the new system of the *auxilia* was developed. On the east and south from the Black Sea to the Pillars of Hercules there ran a chain of states, broken only here and there, which helped to bear the brunt of movements from without the Empire. No one of these was of great importance, but their affairs gave opportunities for state-craft and provided in part a sphere of policy in which the Senate might enjoy a consoling sense of influence. But most of these kingdoms bordered on Imperial provinces, and, besides, their rulers were very aware that at Rome it was the will of the *princeps* that prevailed. The trend of events, and perhaps the trend of policy, was towards their gradual extinction as opportunity offered, with the absorption of their military strength into the *auxilia* and the application of their financial resources to the budget of the Empire. In some regions, as in the Alpine districts, local chiefs were recognized so as to relieve the tasks of administration and to facilitate the pacification of the unruly and the employment of the soldierly elements in their population. It was but rarely that Rome had to put forth her power to protect these client-states or to support their rulers, and it cannot be doubted that on the balance the policy of Augustus justified itself.

To sum up the military achievement of Augustus, it may be argued that in the West and North the policy of the *princeps* met the needs of the Empire, and that, indeed, apart from the failure to secure the country between the Rhine and the Danube, the defence had been made good in the soundest and most economical ways. There is no essential contradiction between Augustus' claim to have extended the borders of every frontier province, and his final advice to maintain rather than advance the bounds of the empire. In the East, it cannot be denied that his policy for Armenia proved in the end a failure, though the failure was of compara-tively slight importance and could be retrieved when necessary as Tiberius quickly showed. It must also be admitted that the last decade of Augustus' reign witnessed a decline in Roman strength and prestige. There were elements of weakness in the military system on the side of recruiting and power to face a great emerg-ency. The professional character of the army made it a potential

---

[1] Kornemann, 'Die unsichtbaren Grenzen d. röm. Reiches,' *op. cit.* pp. 96 *sqq.*

menace to the State but the menace was for long kept far from actuality. The seas were kept safe, and the frontiers were held. The Empire became a kernel of peace within a husk of war, and few who have studied with care the history of the last century of the Republic will fail to acknowledge the greatness of what Augustus achieved.

IV. THE PRESENT AND THE FUTURE

In the previous section it has been suggested that one effect of the Empire was to make the citizen of the more civilized parts tend to cease to be *homo militaris*. In another chapter it is also suggested that the *homo politicus* tended to become the *homo oeconomicus*. It may fairly be assumed that the vast majority of the inhabitants of the Empire were more conscious of a steady rise in commercial enterprise and industrial and agrarian prosperity than of the political and military events that fill the pages of the historians. It is not without reason that the most brilliant account of the Empire that has been written in recent times should describe itself as social and economic. Whatever the future might have in store, the principate of Augustus was marked by an increase of happiness so far as that is secured by an increase of material goods and the certainty of their enjoyment. Nor was this enjoyment passive: it was accompanied by a sense of successful endeavour which filled the breast of a Trimalchio, as of his betters, with conscious pride. That with this there went suffering is true: many slaves and free men were driven hard with little or no share in the prosperity which they helped to produce. But in general the material benefits of the new order were widely spread.

The Augustan Empire was not consciously the Empire of a class. Those who live in an age in which class antagonism is promoted by social stresses and fostered by mass suggestion in speech and writing, may not readily realize how the differentiation of classes, which the Augustan régime undoubtedly tended to fix, fell short of producing a divided people. In economic matters the policy of Augustus was to remove hindrances, assist contacts and then leave trade and commerce to their own devices. Industrial advance, within the limits within which it moved[1], was not linked with a development of machinery which might produce unemployment, or rob skilled craftsmanship of its due reward. In the pursuit of luxuries the Empire might be living beyond its means, but the day when that fact was plain enough to arouse misgivings was yet to come.

[1] See p. 422 *sq.*

To turn first of all to Italy and Rome, the Principate, it is true, brought greater opportunities to classes of the population which had hitherto come short of their share in the advantages of Rome's progress. This is especially true of the middle class, who profited more than others from the Augustan peace and the economic unification of the Mediterranean world[1]. Yet the aristocracy, the middle class, the poorer citizens and the freedmen were not rivals for power who found the *princeps* active to assist them to the exclusion of others. Among the nobles pride or unsatisfied ambition or the temptations of leisure might produce sporadic discontent and even, though rarely and weakly, conspiracy. But of any true senatorial opposition there was hardly any sign. Between the apparent and the real position of the Senate there was an inconsistency which in later times was to have serious consequences[2]. But it must not be forgotten that the *princeps* was also *princeps senatus*, that he shared in the deliberations of the *Curia* and lent a part of his own personal prestige to that of the *patres*. The fact that the Senate was involved in a losing battle against the growth of the Imperial administration was probably obscure to most of Augustus' contemporaries, even if the *princeps* himself detected the inevitable result of what he was doing, slowly, unobtrusively but surely enough. The events which attended the accession of Tiberius show how little it was realized that the Senate, so far as it was not the recruiting ground for the Imperial administration, was destined to become either the shadow of a name—'magni nominis umbra'—or an aristocratic *fronde*. To most of the senators the *princeps* must have seemed most obviously the protector of the Senate against its old opponents, tribunes, generals, popular leaders; and ancient corporations are not quick to observe a slow ebbing of their power. The *equites* lost some sources of profit unhealthy to the State and the provinces, but the benefits of the extension and quickening of commerce and industry, together with the opportunities for careers of responsibility and power, attached them to the new order. The freedmen were given the one thing they needed most, a new self-respect and loyalty to the *princeps*. The poorer citizens at Rome gained what they prized, a city which received more than only *panem et circenses*, and lost what they no longer prized, the reality of power. In Italy there was the consciousness of being Romans in being Italians. The general attitude was that the more they had from

---

[1] See p. 387 *sq.*

[2] A. Momigliano, *L'opera dell' imperatore Claudio*, p. 50 (English edit. p. 25).

and through the *princeps* the better, except perhaps more of the reform of manners. The phrase in which Tacitus understates the motives for accepting the Principate—'militem donis, populum annona, cunctos dulcedine otii pellexit'—becomes less and less an adequate explanation of the continuance of the Imperial system. Had the rule of Augustus been either what it seemed to the age of Tacitus or what it has seemed to some historians, the Principate would hardly have survived his successors.

Throughout the provinces, despite the advantages they derived from economic activity and the spread of commerce[1], there was certainly not the sense of full active partnership in the benefits of the new order which might have been evoked by a policy less Italian and Roman than was the policy of Augustus. It was plain that many Romans believed that they were born booted and spurred where other men were born saddled and bridled. But so far as we can judge, there was little gross misgovernment or oppression. There is evidence for a *malaise* that afflicted mankind, and made it seek for means of quieting its perturbed spirit, but the *malaise* was not associated with the political or economic effects of the Principate.

The long life of Augustus extinguished the desire for any other form of government. What the Roman world wanted was a Principate; thus it was prepared to be ruled by a dynasty rather than have the danger of not being ruled by a *princeps* or the danger of a conflict for that position. The efforts made by Augustus to secure the succession in the direct line of the Julian house and their frustration have already been described. The final solution, in which the passing of the Principate to Tiberius was secured by the conferment on him of powers comparable with those of Augustus himself, provided for the desired continuity of rule. By the time that Augustus' will adopted Tiberius' mother Livia into the Julian house all had been done that could be done to give him the prestige that clung to the name of Divius Julius[2].

The abilities of Tiberius fully matched the task, but it may well be thought that it was unfortunate that Augustus did not die and make way for him ten years earlier, just as the last decade of Tiberius' reign might have been a better period for the Empire had he died *felix opportunitate mortis* and had the government passed to some other *princeps*, making a break with the strictly dynastic principle. The last decade of Augustus' principate, so far as can be deduced from the scanty evidence, produced valuable administrative reforms, including the establishment of the *aerarium*

[1] See p. 384 *sq.*   [2] See E. Ciaceri, *Tiberio*, p. 10.

militare, and revealed the progressive trend of government away from the Senate and towards the *princeps*. It is possible that the changes were made the more easily because of the great prestige of the aged Emperor. But Tiberius gained power at a time when he had lost initiative, and the Empire rested upon its oars. In the sphere of social life the tide of regeneration, never very high, had ebbed. In literature the pulse that had beat in the *Georgics* and *Aeneid* of Virgil and the Roman Odes of Horace was flagging. In the writings of Livy the sense of Roman greatness seems to have become dulled after his account of the Hannibalic war, and this may not be due alone to the disappearance from the scene of Rome's most formidable antagonist.

Further, there was in the Rome of the ageing Augustus no high or widespread intellectual or moral idealism. Philosophy was tending to become in part history teaching by examples, in part a conciliation of the mind, in part a guide for life. The day of the philosophic missionary or martyr had not yet come. Stoicism was moving towards Seneca, Epicureanism had won no inspiration from the *furor arduus* of Lucretius, Neopythagoreanism was a semi-mystical doctrine of release. The lesson of the Principate in all things was 'ducunt volentem fata, nolentem trahunt.' There was intellectualism, but not high intellectual adventure: there was scholarship, antiquarianism, criticism, but not the triumphs of science, mathematics or speculation. The burden of real government which the new Italians shouldered was stoutly borne, and the bearing of it was a great achievement. It was a 'glorious servitude,' not for the *princeps* alone, and the rewards that went with the great administrative careers were fully earned. The Italian people in the legions and in countless posts of service took on itself the duties to the world which the Populus Romanus had only half fulfilled. As has been shown above[1], the social policy of Augustus had a deeper purpose than the regimen of a sterile moralist—no less a purpose than the creation of a new Populus Romanus, co-extensive with the Italian people, with an aristocracy fit to lead, trained to lead from youth up, with a civilization strong enough not to lose itself in becoming the Latin civilization of Western Europe which abides to this day. In the provinces there was active local life and some degree of influence exerted on the central power through the activity of *concilia*. But, in general, outside Italy the sense of membership in the Empire was a sense of receiving direction from an earthly Providence, which gave justice, security and peace and the means of prosperity without

[1] Chap. XIV.

demanding too high a price for it. When all is said, it is a fair criticism of the new order, that its temptation was to be static in high matters, that political thought withered, so that the Empire lost the spirit of a common adventure, the welcome for what was new, without which the strongest and shrewdest political system is doomed in the end to become mechanical and sterile. '*Le tact des choses possibles*,' which nature had given to Augustus, was a great gift, and within the compass of his reign his practical achievement was of a kind that was unmatched in the history of antiquity. As will be seen, he left behind him problems which his successors failed to solve by his methods, and the next half-century saw the draining away of the capital of good-will with which he endowed the Principate. But in the creation of the new Roman People Augustus had given to the Empire a solid core, and in the system which he had built up, he had given to the Roman State a framework which stood firm.

CHAPTER XIX

TIBERIUS

I. THE SUCCESSION

THE death of Augustus left two questions of paramount importance to be decided; should the system of a Principate continue, and if so who should be *princeps* and fill Augustus' place. If the Principate was to continue, then the adopted son of Augustus, Tiberius Julius Caesar (to call him by the name that he had borne since his adoption on 26 June A.D. 4), by age, experience and by possession of power was the obvious candidate; indeed by virtue of his proconsular power he had already with perfect propriety sent despatches to the armies to announce Augustus' death. But he was a man of fifty-five, the best years of his life behind him, his character and judgment formed and hardened. Some retrospect is therefore essential if we are to appreciate the views he held and the principles upon which he would rule.

The details of his early career have already been seen (p. 151); few men were so hard worked and so little rewarded, and his marriage to Julia in order to act as guardian to the two grandsons of Augustus ended his patience. At the age of thirty-six, in disgust, he suddenly relinquished the path of duty, and turned to

Note. By far the fullest and most trustworthy ancient authority for the principate of Tiberius is Tacitus, *Ann.* I–VI, even though book V (detailing events between A.D. 29 and 32) is almost wholly lost. Tacitus could draw on a large number of original documents and on sources favourable and unfavourable; despite his obvious bias against the Julio-Claudian emperors he usually retains his critical sense, is honest, and rarely exaggerates. Suetonius' *Life of Tiberius* contains information of importance, but suffers from its inconvenient division into rubrics, from its lack of chronological narrative, and from over-facile generalizations. The account in Dio LVII and LVIII (and in his epitomators) provides a useful chronological framework, but is full of rhetoric and motivation of his own, and must be treated with great caution. Velleius Paterculus can see nothing but good in Tiberius and his minister Sejanus: from Strabo, Valerius Maximus, Seneca, Pliny the Elder, Josephus and Plutarch occasional items of interest can be gathered. For lost authors upon whom our surviving sources probably drew see the Appendix on Sources, pp. 866 *sqq.* The more important inscriptions and coins are noted in the text as they become relevant.

scholarly retirement at Rhodes, where he was to remain for eight years. He had learnt to love it when he had stayed there on his way back from Armenia, and here he could pursue undisturbed those studies which attracted him. He was abreast of the best Greek and Roman culture of the day, was fond of painting and sculpture, and had studied rhetoric under Theodorus of Gadara; poets and mathematicians were his friends, and to him scholars such as Apollonides dedicated their editions of authors or addressed their poems. Yet there was little geniality about his scholarship: it took the form rather of a fondness for curious questions and a Varronian love of out-of-the-way knowledge, coupled with a meticulous correctness and exactitude in all matters of ceremonial, form and etiquette (especially as regards things divine)[1] that made him a dragon to the young or inexperienced. At its best this bent of the man is seen in his hatred of superficiality or flattery and his contempt for shams (such as Apion of Alexandria), at its silliest in a pedantry that could apologize for the introduction of Greek words into an official edict. But in Rhodes he came under the influence of a remarkable man, Thrasyllus, astrologer and philosopher. Thrasyllus was no charlatan; he was renowned for his studies in Plato and music, but it was his mastery of astrology that attracted Tiberius and the attraction is intelligible. Tiberius was over thirty-six, by birth, endowments and upbringing he should have been destined for success, yet everything had gone awry: he had had to renounce his wife, he had lost his brother and had seen his own years of faithful service cast aside for younger men. Unable to appreciate Augustus' longing for direct heirs, unable to discern that it was his own austere personality that had docked him of favour, his proud and sensitive spirit found consolation in the thought that all was ruled by a destiny inexorable and impersonal, of which he, like others, was the victim. 'Fata regunt orbem: certa stant omnia lege': the words represent his own view as well as that of the poet who penned them in the years when Tiberius' influence was in the ascendant.

Indeed he had need of all the consolations of philosophy: he had to bear the disgrace and banishment of Julia, in 1 b.c. his tenure of tribunician power was not renewed, for he was still under the displeasure of those at Rome, and he tasted all the bitterness of a fall from greatness. Gaius Caesar scorned him and his courtiers referred to him as 'the exile'[2]; he experienced—and

[1] For instances see Seneca, *ad Marciam*, 15, 3 and Tacitus, *Ann.* III, 24, IV, 16, IV, 36, and VI, 12.
[2] The town of Nemausus overthrew his statues; Suetonius, *Tib.* 13.

long remembered—the enmity or coldness of such men as M. Lollius or Archelaus of Cappadocia (whom he had once helped), and the true friendship of Sulpicius Quirinius or Lucilius Longus. In the end Livia's entreaties wrung from Augustus permission for him to return to Rome in A.D. 2, but only with Gaius Caesar's approval and on the understanding that he should take no part in public affairs.

Then came the sudden amazing turn, Gaius and Lucius Caesar dead and himself adopted by Augustus, yet even so not left a free hand but forced to adopt Augustus' favourite grandson, Germanicus, the son of his brother Drusus, into his family as senior to his own son. But he was to work all the same, for there followed eight years fighting in Germany and Pannonia (pp. 368 *sqq.*), until on 23 October A.D. 12, he was allowed to celebrate a triumph for his victories[1]. The death of Augustus found him a disappointed and tired man, capable and experienced and with a wide knowledge of the needs of the Empire, but with the virtues of a subordinate rather than of a leader. Though he was a cautious and skilful general, in civil life and in dealing with the Senate he was not at ease. Long years under another's authority had made him diffident and self-critical and when called upon to face a sudden situation or a case without precedent he would waver and hesitate. He made a few friends whom he trusted devotedly—Longus, Thrasyllus, Sejanus: in other company he was reserved and awkward, unable to preside graciously at the pleasures and shows of the populace, unwilling to join in the extravagances and luxury of the nobles, and with a capacity for self-control that seemed inhuman. Such was the man on whose weary shoulders the burden of rule was to fall.

Apart from his weariness there were disquieting factors; the succession was by no means certain, there might be rivals ready to make a bid for power. Augustus himself had not been free from anxiety that disturbances might follow his death, and Tiberius was naturally aware of the possibility. Though Agrippa Postumus was put out of the way as soon as Augustus was dead[2], there had been friends prepared to rescue and rush him to the northern armies; there were, too, various nobles whose eminence, merits and wealth gave them a possible claim should candidature for a principate be discussed, men such as L. Arruntius, Asinius

---

[1] For the date see D. M. Pippidi in *Rev. des ét. lat.* XI, 1933, p. 435. For what may be a representation of the scene see Volume of Plates iv, 156, *a*.

[2] Possibly on Augustus' own order, though Tacitus puts the blame on Tiberius; see the present writer in *A.J.Ph.* XLIV, 1923, p. 145.

Gallus, or M'. Lepidus[1], and above all there was his nephew and adopted son Germanicus, a figure far more to the popular taste. Young, handsome and courageous, he was reputed to possess his father's Republican and democratic sentiments, and since A.D. 13 he had been in command of the armies of the Rhine. It may be suspected that tradition, so uniformly favourable to him and kindly to his memory[2], rests on writers who were glad to find in his gracious figure a foil to the dourness of Tiberius, but it is obvious that he had much to attract. Affable in manner, he was popular with the troops to whom he made concessions[3] and applied a gentler discipline than Tiberius had done. He was a poet, who had on his staff men of some literary eminence (such as Albinovanus Pedo or Suillius Rufus or P. Vitellius), and his poems (such as the *Aratea* tactfully dedicated to Tiberius) and some epigrams show skill and taste, though little more. He longed to equal and complete the exploits of his father Drusus in Germany, but had not the necessary gifts of leadership or insight; in war as in poetry he was perhaps too much the enthusiastic amateur. But his ambitions were fed and fostered by his wife Agrippina, proud of her descent from the divine Augustus, and he could be sure of support not only from those nobles who regarded war and conquest as the chief business of a Roman, but also from the newer nobility who might hope for fame and advancement from it[4]. All these considerations might well make Tiberius pause.

The first business was to arrange for the State funeral of Augustus and get the machinery of government working again. The bringing of the body to Rome must have taken some fifteen days and the first meeting of the Senate, which Tiberius had summoned by virtue of his tribunician power, cannot have taken place till early September. Some attempt was possibly made to induce Tiberius to accept the principate then and there, but he would not allow any business save that connected with the funeral of Augustus. The will of the dead ruler, bequeathing two-thirds of his estate to Tiberius and one-third to Livia, was read, and

---

[1] Tacitus, *Ann.* 1, 13. The insinuation that Tiberius soon got rid of all these possible claimants is unjustified.

[2] The portrait in Tacitus should be compared with the shorter eulogies that are to be found in Suetonius, *Calig.* 3 and Josephus, *Ant.* XVIII, [6], 207 *sqq.*

[3] He appears to have lightened the penalties for over-staying leave: *Dig.* XLIX, 16, 4, 13.

[4] This was first suggested by F. B. Marsh, *The Reign of Tiberius*, p. 67 *sq.*, but it should not be overstressed.

Tiberius heard the opening sentence, 'since cruel fate has robbed me of my sons Gaius and Lucius let Tiberius Caesar be my heir.' A public funeral was decreed, and a few days later amid all the pomp and ostentation that Roman ceremonial could provide, the pyre bearing the body was fired, while an eagle was let loose to fly heavenwards, symbolizing the assumption of Augustus among the immortals.

Some five or six days after the funeral the Senate again met, on 17 September. Godhead was decreed to the dead emperor under the style of Divus Augustus[1]; he was voted a temple and a body of priests. For Livia, who under the will was adopted into the gens Julia and became Julia Augusta, exceptional honours were at first proposed, but limited by Tiberius, whose sense of tradition and propriety rebelled: yet although in Italy such flattering titles as *mater patriae* or *mater Augusti* were never officially conferred or recognized, in Spain she appears as *Genetrix Orbis*, at Smyrna as *Iulia Augusta Augusti mater*[2], and in the East she was often worshipped under the name of the local goddess[3]. But by now four weeks had elapsed since the death of Augustus and the question of the future form of government was urgent. If the Principate, as planned and put into execution by its founder, was to continue, there was one obvious candidate, and it is reasonable to believe that Augustus, in his last days, had made careful arrangements with his friends and confidants, and with Tiberius himself in that last long interview on the day before his death. Upon Tiberius the year before he had had conferred by law a proconsular imperium equal to his own and a renewal of his tribunician power; in his will he had bequeathed to him two-thirds of his estate and the name Augustus. After Augustus' death a notable step had been taken when the consuls swore an oath of loyalty to Tiberius and administered the oath to Senate, Knights and People, for though the action had no constitutional significance its moral effect was strong. The one thing now needful was to make Tiberius' supremacy definite and acknowledged, but his election must above all appear as the free unanimous choice of Senate and People forced upon a reluctant but dutiful man.

This is undoubtedly what was secured, but Tacitus' account leaves the procedure uncertain. It may be conjectured that the consuls proposed a motion that Tiberius should become Princeps

---

[1] *C.I.L.* I², p. 244 (Fasti Amiternini): 'feriae ex s.c. q.e.d. divo Augusto honores caelestes a senatu decreti.'

[2] See Volume of Plates iv, 202,*f*: Smyrna, *I.G.R.R.* iv, 1392.

[3] As, *e.g.* in Egypt, *I.G.R.R.* i, 1150.

Senatus in place of the deified Augustus[1], should retain his proconsular imperium and his tribunician power not for a period but
for life[2], and should have all such powers necessary for the protection of the State as Augustus had possessed. Against this
proposal of the consuls—for whatever its form, in substance it
offered him the government of the State—Tiberius, though
aware he must give way in the end, for long held out. His reluctance was natural enough: he knew well what a 'burdensome
slavery' rule could be, he realized the dangers and possible
rivalries, to his friends he likened himself to a man holding a wolf
by the ears, but he also knew that there must be a ruler beside
and above the Senate. So at last he pronounced the words of
acceptance, but even in doing so he intimated that he hoped the
day might yet come when the Senate would grant his old age
relief and rest. Such reluctance, natural enough in a man of the
experience and diffidence of Tiberius, made a great impression:
while admirers lauded his modesty, detractors saw in it merely
a shameless farce and an example of hypocrisy. Both views were
reasonable: while Tiberius' unwillingness was genuine enough,
the result of the session of the Senate was a foregone conclusion;
though he was dead, Augustus imposed his will on Tiberius as
effectively as in life. From 17 September the new Principate had
officially begun[3].

II. ITALY AND THE SENATE

There was only one standard which the new *princeps* could
follow, that of his predecessor, and his reign demonstrated a rigid
respect for the Augustan tradition and observed carefully all his

[1] The position of Princeps Senatus was vacant by the death of Augustus.
By offering it to Tiberius, while confirming his existing proconsular imperium and his tribunician power, the consuls would bring him a step nearer
the Principate. The title of *Princeps Senatus* is not to be confused with the
unofficial name of Princeps, used often by Augustus of himself and by the
Augustan poets of Augustus; see Mommsen, *Staatsrecht*, II[3], p. 894 and
III, p. 971.

[2] Although no renewal was necessary the customary *Ludi decennales*
were celebrated in 24 and 34: Dio LVII, 24, LVIII, 24.

[3] The texts are Vell. Pat. II, 123–124; Tacitus, *Ann.* I, 7–13; Suetonius,
Tib. 22–24, and Dio LVII, 2–3. For the date here accepted see E. Hohl
in *Hermes*, LVIII, 1933, p. 106, though it must be admitted that there is no
absolutely clinching piece of evidence; for another view see A. Lang,
Beiträge zur Geschichte des Kaisers Tiberius, p. 5. The position of Tiberius
could be truly, though unofficially, described as *imperator perpetuus*, as in the
Gozo inscription, Dessau 121.

instructions[1]. For some years Tiberius achieved a fair measure of success in ruling. All authorities agree in recognizing a good early period (the *mitia* or *prima tempora* of his Principate), but not on the point at which it ended. A convenient line of demarcation can be found in the year 26 when Tiberius withdrew from Rome, for this withdrawal had grave consequences. The domestic policy of the first twelve years shows well the strength and weakness of his methods.

Adherence to the Augustan canon meant first and foremost gracious co-operation with the Senate, for the Senate was to be a partner in government. Its members were men of experience and training, it had provinces of its own to govern, and it now possessed jurisdiction over Italy in matters social and religious; in addition it could serve the Princeps as a legislative organ, and it was already in process of becoming a court for criminal jurisdiction, where serious cases or influential culprits could be tried (pp. 169 *sqq.*). At the very beginning of the reign its importance was enhanced by a momentous change that Tiberius carried out, nothing less than the complete transference of the elections from People to Senate. Not that Tiberius was the author of this change; he simply brought into operation a scheme that Augustus had devised and left in writing. But from this time onward the Senate became the sole electoral body, while the People apparently raised no voice in protest.

Thus co-operation between the Senate and Princeps was of the first importance, and Tiberius was assiduous in attendance. During the early years of his Principate a large number of *senatus consulta* were passed: while some were of a routine nature, adding to or interpreting already existing laws[2], others such as that against prostitution by women of rank or that which allowed a condemned criminal ten days grace (p. 631), either accorded with his known views or were even promoted by him[3]. Throughout Tiberius showed the Senate great deference and an almost too anxious respect, consulting it often even on minor matters and occasionally on some, such as the enlistment or discharge of soldiers, which were not its concern at all[4]. He was scrupulously careful to avoid

[1] Strabo v, 288; Tacitus, *Agric.* 13; *Ann.* 1, 72, 77; 11, 87; 1v, 37.

[2] As for instance measures passed in 20 and 29 supplementing the provisions of the *Lex Cornelia de Falsis*: *Dig.* xlvii, 13, 2 and xlviii, 10, 1, 2: Mommsen, *Strafrecht*, p. 671.

[3] Tacitus, *Ann.* 11, 85 and 111, 51; Suetonius, *Tib.* 35, 2 and 75, 2; *Dig.* xlviii, 5, (11) 10, 2.

[4] Suetonius, *Tib.* 30.

influencing opinion by proclaiming his own view too quickly, and tolerated considerable freedom of speech and expression. He entered the Senate-house unescorted, and would rise to greet the consuls or yield place to them. Any important commission or body of inquiry would always contain a majority of senators and was often composed entirely of them. Instances are easily found: the continued floods on the Tiber and the resulting damage were met by the appointment of a Board of Curators of the banks and bed of the river. Tiberius himself apparently nominated the first five members, all senators, but subsequent Curators appear to have been chosen *ex senatus consulto*: about the same time there was also established a Board for Public Sites, its duty being to investigate what was and what was not public property and to adjudicate in disputed cases; to this Board, too, senators were appointed, as also to a commission whose business it was to copy out and reinscribe public records that had become illegible and also to find the text of those which had been lost or destroyed. A senatorial commission was appointed to relieve the damage inflicted by an earthquake on some great cities in Asia Minor (p. 650 *sq.*), though in order to avoid possible conflict with the consular governor of the province, the chief commissioner was only of praetorian rank. When in A.D. 22 Tiberius wished for the conferment of *tribunicia potestas* upon his son Drusus he approached the Senate, as Augustus had done. It still dealt with boundary questions in its own provinces (as for instance with the *Dentheliates ager*)[1], and it alone could give exemption from the operation of the laws and allow towns such as Massilia or Trebia to benefit from legacies left to them[2]. And Tiberius' deference to the order was paralleled by his readiness to help senatorial families who had fallen undeservingly on evil days: to such he made large grants of assistance, to enable them to preserve their position and to live in a manner befitting their rank, but they had to prove their case before their peers, and to wastrels he would give no heed[3].

In the sphere of religion and morals, which the Senate had always regarded as peculiarly its own, Tiberius consulted it frequently: not that he was himself a believer in the State religion, as a religion, but he knew the value of traditional observances and set his face resolutely against foreign practices or cults. In the

[1] Tacitus, *Ann.* IV, 13. The dispute between Sidon and Damascus (Josephus, *Ant.* XVIII [VI, 3], 153) was in an imperial province and would have come before the imperial *legatus*.

[2] Tacitus, *Ann.* IV, 43; Suetonius, *Tib.* 31.

[3] Tacitus, *Ann.* I, 75; II, 38 (misrepresented by Suetonius, *Tib.* 47).

first days of his rule he felt bound, as an augur, to ask the Senate
to grant him dispensation for having touched the dead body of
Augustus, and on several occasions he displayed his knowledge of
Roman religious lore and ceremony, as in 23 over the rights and
privileges of the various priesthoods, or in 32 when he rebuked
two men for ignorance of procedure with regard to the Sibylline
books. In the year 19 a scandal connected with the worship of
Isis led to a searching investigation (p. 495); the convicted priests
were crucified, the image of Isis flung into the Tiber and the
temple was destroyed, while her followers and worshippers were
compelled to burn their robes and gear. Similarly, when some
Jews were found to have obtained money under false pretences
from a Roman lady, Tiberius persuaded the Senate to expel the
Jews and their rites from Italy, while four thousand of the strongest
were sent to Sardinia to act as a police force there. And, as before,
the Senate dealt with all such matters as rights of asylum in temples
and the reception or rejection of the cults.

Still more clearly was the bias of Tiberius visible over the great
shows and games. He did not approve of them: he disliked both
the waste of money and the popular licence and rioting. Several
times complaints about the conduct of actors were brought before
the Senate, and in 23 they were finally expelled from Italy: in
addition he placed restrictions upon the number of pairs of gladiators
to be exhibited and manifested so general a disapprobation of the
building of theatres or giving of games (as for instance at Trebia or
Pollentia)[1], that the very gladiators complained of the lack of
opportunity for showing their prowess[2]. This parsimony over
games and spectacles and this cheerless austerity were some of the
most unpopular things in his Principate.

More pressing were the problems to be faced from the social
legislation of Augustus. Anxiety to ensure a large free population
for Italy, to preserve due grades and distinctions in that population,
and to prevent indiscriminate manumission and the flooding of
Italy with foreign blood had led Augustus to pass or encourage
various laws such as the Lex Aelia Sentia of A.D. 4 and the Lex
Papia Poppaea of A.D. 9 (chap. XIV). The aims and effectiveness of
the Lex Papia Poppaea have been discussed elsewhere, but one
of the great evils of this formidable statute (as of the Lex Julia de
Maiestate) was that it encouraged a class of informers and offered

---

[1] Suetonius, *Tib.* 31 and 37.
[2] Seneca, *dial.* I, 4, 4. After the disaster at Fidenae in 27 a *senatus
consultum* forbade the giving of games by men whose income fell below
400,000 sesterces: Tacitus, *Ann.* IV, 62, 63.

high rewards to them: such encouragement had its natural result; much of the law still needed interpretation, everywhere vexatious trials were set on foot, and no one felt safe. There began 'a mania for accusations'[1], and hundreds were like to be involved, but Tiberius saw the extent of the danger and instituted a special commission of fifteen senators to moderate the working of the law by equitable interpretation of knotty points or of undue harshness[2]. So too with the problems presented by the freedman class, where new legislation appears to have been necessary. The details are controversial and only an outline can be given here. In the ordinary way a *libertinus*, not being of free birth, could not hope for municipal magistracies or other offices; but often these *libertini* were the most vigorous and enterprising section of a community and worth encouraging, and the *princeps* could apparently confer free birth (*ingenuitas*) by giving such the right to wear a gold ring (p. 188 *sq.*). So great, however, were the privileges conferred by this right that many claimed it fraudulently, and in 23 a *senatus consultum* was passed strictly limiting the right of wearing the ring to those who could show free descent for two generations and had equestrian census. But such an enactment, ambiguous in its terms and reactionary in its sentiment, could only cause further trouble, and in the very next year one of the consuls introduced a Lex Visellia to deal with the question. It must have been comprehensive, but we know of only two clauses: the first, granting full citizenship to all Junian Latins (p. 431) who served for only six years in the corps of Vigiles, reveals how easy it was for such men to rise to full citizenship; the second debarred those who were not *ingenui* from gaining magistracies or dignities in a municipality, 'unless they are upheld by the grant of the gold ring from the *princeps*.' Even so, ambition and office-seeking were stronger than the fear of the law, and in the reign of Claudius we hear of over four hundred prosecutions for unlawful claims[3].

In all such matters Tiberius worked through and with the Senate, and his moderation and prudence often saved it from mistakes. When the Senate could only propose consultation of the Sibylline books to cope with the Tiber floods it was Tiberius who suggested a commission of Curators, and when in 16 an attempt was made to introduce some foolish sumptuary legislation he joined with Asinius Gallus in deprecating it as futile and likely

[1] Seneca, *de benef.* III, 26.
[2] Tacitus, *Ann.* III, 25–28. Actually the one alteration of which we hear was in the direction of greater strictness: Suetonius, *Claud.* 23.
[3] Pliny, *N.H.* XXXIII, 29–34.

to lead to petty litigation. He showed like commonsense in face
of a demand for a special court for lampoons and libel, and a
downright phrase of his speech on this has been preserved[1]: 'we
really have not so much spare time as to warrant involving ourselves in still more business; if you once open this window, you
will prevent any other business being transacted, for everyone's
private quarrels will be brought before you on this excuse.' To
Tacitus his presence in the Senate and participation in the debates
(as in the law-courts) seems a mockery; in reality, Tiberius often
prevented the senators from throwing all burdens and decisions
on the *princeps* and reminded them of their dignity and duties.

Throughout he was morbidly careful to avoid unusual powers
or titles or anything which might hinder the smooth working of
the Augustan scheme. He refused to allow the oath of allegiance
to him to be renewed yearly. After his accession he only held the
consulship three times, never for more than half a year, and always
to do honour to a possible heir or partner, to Germanicus in 18,
to his son Drusus in 21, and to Sejanus in 31. When acting as
judge himself he retained the traditional custom of calling in a
select number of his friends as advisers, the *consilium Caesaris*. He
did not use the title *Imperator* as a *praenomen*[2], he refused the title
pater patriae both in 15 and 19; he would not allow any to address
him as 'lord' or 'master' save his own slaves, but laid down the
rule that 'I am *dominus* to my slaves, and *imperator* to my soldiers,
but to all the rest I am *princeps*'[3]. But the very fact that he had
to refuse or deprecate such forms of address shows the tendency
of the times, and in addition he could not disguise or soften a
certain bluntness or harshness which must have made even his
kindnesses appear ironical and caused a natural fear in approaching
him. 'You're rather late in waking up' was the greeting he gave
to a request for help from Acilius Buta, a notorious spendthrift,
and a proposal that November should be called *Tiberius* was met
by the query 'and what will you do if you have thirteen Caesars?'
Some time after the death of Drusus in 23 the people of Ilium,
suddenly aware that they had sent no embassy to offer sympathy,
hastily dispatched one; Tiberius listened, and then in his turn
begged to offer them his condolences upon the death of a dis-

---

[1] Suetonius, *Tib.* 28.

[2] The inscriptions in which he is given this title (or its Greek equivalent
αὐτοκράτωρ) are unofficial: see C. A. Holtzhausser, *An epigraphic Commentary on Suetonius's Life of Tiberius*, p. 26 sq., and J. R. Rietra, *C. Suetoni
Tranquilli Vita Tiberi*, c. 24–c. 40, p. 16.

[3] Dio LVII, 8, 2.

tinguished fellow-citizen—Hector[1]. The words are the echo of
a hard clear mind, but neither Caesar nor Augustus would have
answered thus, and his replies raised one more barrier between
himself and his people.

III. GERMANICUS AND DRUSUS

With the gloominess of Tiberius the popularity and charm of
Germanicus stood in strong contrast. But he did little to warrant
the favour shown him: the frontier-problems of the Rhine and his undistinguished campaigns have been related elsewhere (pp. 376 *sqq.*),
and Tiberius can scarcely have approved of what went on during
the three years 14–16. On hearing of the death of Augustus the
Rhine armies mutinied, demanding shorter service and higher
pay: Germanicus could not cope with them firmly; a first emotional
appeal missed fire, he met their demands by a forged letter from
Tiberius, and instead of restoring discipline by his own presence
he encouraged the more loyal legionaries to use mob-law and then
arrived to shed tears over the result. Obsessed with the idea of
emulating his father's exploits and conquering all Germany he had
carried out a census in Gaul and requisitioned supplies for a
grandiose effort. But nothing came of it, even Tacitus has to
admit that Germanicus blundered, though Tiberius (in an effort
to please) offered him a triumph in 15, and bestowed triumphal
insignia on three of his *legati*, Caecina, Silius and Apronius. And
Germanicus' theatrical instinct led him now to visit the rotting
remains of the Varian legions amid the gloom and loneliness of the
Teutoburger Wald[2], now to disguise himself and penetrate the
tents of his troops to test their feeling; when a serious disaster
overwhelmed his returning transports he could scarcely be refrained from committing suicide. Tiberius must have despised the
amateurish efforts of his adopted son, while the popularity both
of him and of his wife Agrippina, who on one occasion had
appeared in public and allayed a panic, left him uneasy. Recall
was the only way out, but it must be honourable. Still reasons
could easily be found: the many victories of Germanicus had re-
established Roman prestige, his task on the Rhine was accomplished and could be crowned by a triumph; affairs in the East

[1] Dio LVII, 18, 2: the name Tiberius was given to the October–November
month in Asia; *C.I.L.* I, i, p. 335. Suetonius, *Tib.* 52, 2: and cf. the
story of the officious servant in Phaedrus, II, 5.

[2] Tacitus, *Ann.* I, 61 and 62; the second chapter shows that Tiberius'
disapproval, which was quite justifiable, was directed against any disharten-
ment of the troops and against Germanicus' neglect of augural propriety.

too needed the presence of a member of the imperial house, who could win experience of a second frontier. So Germanicus reluctantly returned; with his five children in the chariot he celebrated an imposing triumph on 26 May, 17; the Greek laureate poet Crinagoras hymned it, and the exiled Ovid spurred his tired Muse once more; a triumphal arch was erected, and a largesse was distributed in Germanicus' name to the citizens.

Yet subsequent events proved the correctness of Tiberius' decision, though some imputed it to jealousy. Only a few years later the chief opponents of Rome, Arminius and Maroboduus, both fell victims to treachery (p. 783); Arminius was assassinated, Maroboduus was given a retreat in Italy, and Tiberius hailed this as the successful culmination of his patient diplomacy. And he was right; another fifty years were to pass before Rome experienced any serious trouble from German tribes. The Hermunduri remained friendly and Tiberius initiated an interesting experiment in frontier-guarding: numbers of Suebi and Marcomanni, who had accompanied king Maroboduus or the successful usurper Catualda (who was later driven out in his turn), were settled on the far bank of the Danube between the rivers Marus and Cusus (the March and the Eipel in Czecho-Slovakia), under a native chieftain called Vannius, and so became a client-state and an outpost to break the shock of possible invasions. Here, as elsewhere (p. 649), the far-seeing Tiberius began processes, some of which were not taken up or did not come to fruition till the second century, but it is a tribute to his judgment that they were all adopted in the end.

The need of a special commissioner in the East had been one reason for Germanicus' recall. The new Parthian king Artabanus had planned to set his brother Orodes upon the vacant throne of Armenia, king Vonones whom he had expelled had taken refuge at Antioch in Syria and was rumoured to have brought a vast treasure with him, the aged Archelaus of Cappadocia was suspected of treason and had been summoned to Rome, and the kings of the smaller states of Commagene and Cilicia had recently died; Judaea and Syria were begging for a diminution of tribute. Such a state of affairs could only be settled satisfactorily by one man with supreme control over all the Eastern provinces, who could view all these different problems as parts of one connected whole, and with such an exalted command only a member of the imperial house could be entrusted. The Senate granted to Germanicus a *maius imperium* over all governors in the Eastern provinces, and to mark the impressiveness of the occasion Tiberius himself assumed the consulship for A.D. 18 together with Germanicus. All the same he was in a dilemma: he must send Germanicus, he must give him power and position, yet inwardly he was uneasy; he distrusted the weakness and amiability of the young man, dominated by the strong ambition of Agrippina, left uncontrolled in the East, where the *legatus* of Syria, Creticus Silanus, had betrothed his daughter to Germanicus' second son, Nero. Some counterpoise was needed and here Tiberius' choice was unfortunate; in place of Silanus he sent to Syria Cn. Piso, a typical noble of the old Republican type, arrogant, harsh, unyielding. Tacitus mentions a rumour that Tiberius gave Piso 'secret instructions,' but Tiberius was neither fool nor knave and Piso's own temperament would be effective enough without instructions.

Germanicus did not hurry; he had with him a distinguished circle of *comites*, eminent both in war and in letters, and he travelled leisurely, visiting places of historic interest. In Dalmatia he met his cousin Drusus, and then passed by Actium, Athens, and Lesbos into Asia; at Ilium, the associations of the spot inspired him to an address to Hector:

'Myrmidonas periisse omnes dic, Hector, Achilli
Thessaliam et magnis esse sub Aeneadis.'

Everywhere he and his family were greeted with processions and honours: Chios instituted a holiday on his birthday, Clazomenae, Eumeneia, and Pergamum have left inscriptions, Patara celebrated him and Drusus as *Theoi epiphaneis*, to Andriaca he was 'Saviour and Benefactor,' Synnada struck coins in his honour, and two towns in Asia Minor, Caesarea-Germanica in Bithynia and Germanicopolis in West Cilicia, took a new name to celebrate his visit. Coins and inscriptions testify triumphantly to his extraordinary popularity and bear out Tacitus' sober judgment that 'it would not be easy to reckon up the number of statues or places where he was worshipped.'

While he departed for his main task in Armenia (p. 746) his *legati* were busy. Q. Veranius organized Cappadocia as a province to be under an equestrian procurator, retaining apparently most of the old divisions (p. 745), transferring the king's estates to the imperial *patrimonium*, and lightening the royal taxes to make Roman rule more acceptable; even so the new revenue accruing from Cappadocia was a very important addition (p. 746). To the south and east lay the wealthy and fertile kingdom of Commagene: Q. Servaeus arranged for its transformation into a province under a pro-praetorian legate in charge perhaps of a legion[1]; Cilicia, which was smaller, was simply incorporated in the province of Syria. In Armenia all went well, and the new king whom Germanicus installed was to rule for something over fifteen years, a surprising duration for an Armenian monarch (p. 746)[2].

Returning to Syria Germanicus opened up negotiations with Artabanus, who was willing to renew the treaty of friendship, but requested that Vonones should be removed farther west; this was done, and the unfortunate exile was killed shortly afterwards while attempting escape[3]. Other countries and states, too, opened negotiations with the Roman prince or came into closer connection; the good will of the desert caravan-city of Palmyra was important, and she now received apparently a resident representative of Rome and allowed one of her citizens, Alexandros, to undertake a mission on behalf of Germanicus to Sampsiceramus of Emesa and to Mesene. Perhaps Germanicus actually visited the city, for in the great court of the temple of Baal there has been found a dedication to Tiberius, Germanicus and Drusus by the commander of the Tenth Legion[4].

Winter was now approaching and Germanicus decided to take the rest, of which he felt in need, in Egypt. His choice could not have been more unfortunate, for it ignored the restrictions placed on visits to that jealously-guarded land. Perhaps Germanicus argued that, on the precedent of Gaius Caesar, his *maius imperium* made a request for leave to visit Egypt unnecessary; probably he never thought at all; Tiberius, naturally irritated, complained roundly in the Senate. The rest of his trip was marked by similar thoughtlessness, his curious passion for oracles drove him to visit the sanctuary of Apis (which Augustus had refused to do), he wore Greek dress in Alexandria (like Antony), to relieve a local famine he supplied cheap corn to the people of Alexandria from

---

[1] Tacitus, *Ann.* II, 56.

[2] For a coin commemorating the installation of Artaxias see Volume of Plates iv, 208, *c*. It is by no means certain, though it is commonly stated, that Germanicus issued this. Such an action would have been so treasonable that it is easier to suppose that it belongs to the series issued by Gaius in memory of his father. See *Rom. Imp. Coin.* I, p. 104, nos. 8, 9, and 10, with the footnote by H. M(attingly).

[3] Suetonius, *Tib.* 49, reports this, unjustly, as an instance of avarice.

[4] In *O.G.I.S.* 629 [=*I.G.R.R.* III, 1056] is mentioned ὁ ἐν Παλμύροις τεταγμένος: for Alexandros' mission see J. Cantineau in *Syria*, XII, 1931, pp. 116 *sqq.* (No. 18), and for the dedication H. Seyrig, *ib.* XIII, 1932, pp. 255 *sqq.*

the reserve granaries[1], and the early months of A.D. 19 were spent in a pleasure trip up the Nile[2]. Two edicts of his reflect his own benevolence and the enthusiastic welcome he received: such popularity did nothing to weaken Tiberius' mistrust, and the whole visit was disastrous in its effects. On his return fresh trouble broke out: in the previous year Piso had refused to detail troops for Armenia, though Germanicus had turned a blind eye on this and other pieces of contumacy: now he found that Plancina, Piso's wife, had been currying favour with the troops and that Piso himself had done all he could to upset his authority and arrangements. This could not be borne: Tacitus records laconically 'Piso determined to leave Syria,' but for an imperial legate to leave his province of his own accord would be inexcusable, and it is more reasonable to assume that Germanicus, using his higher power, bade him leave[3]; such a command, though its legality might be disputed or its intention misinterpreted, even Piso would not dare disobey. Shortly after, however, Germanicus fell ill at Antioch; the meagre information available suggests some kind of fever, but he was convinced that Piso had poisoned him, and in this belief, with a last prayer to Agrippina to avenge his murder, he died on 10 October. The body was hastily cremated at Antioch, and despite the wintry season Agrippina, bearing the ashes, at once took ship for Rome.

The death of Germanicus can scarcely be regarded as a loss to the Empire. His friends might fondly compare the circumstances of his death with those of Alexander the Great, and Tacitus reserves for him the most glowing colours on his palette, but dispassionate examination can find little more in him than a versatile and amiable mediocrity. The grief that the provinces and Rome felt for him was genuine enough, but there is nothing to show that Germanicus would have made a worthy *princeps*[4]. But his death opened a rift between Agrippina and Tiberius which had far-reaching consequences; nothing could persuade the widow that the emperor had not somehow engineered the

[1] These were not the granaries that supplied Rome: U. Wilcken in *Hermes*, LXIII, 1928, p. 48.
[2] Wilcken, *Chrestomathie der Papyruskunde*, no. 413.
[3] Tacitus, *Ann.* II, 70: 'addunt plerique iussum provincia decedere,' and cf. 76 and 78.
[4] The popularity of the house of Germanicus in Gaul, especially in Aquitania, is remarkable; *C.I.L.* XIII, 1036—40 are all to Germanicus or to his brother Claudius and to their house: cf. the town of Germanicomagus also in Aquitania.

death of her husband, and from that day there were two parties in the State. Unfortunately Tiberius did little to avert such ill-feeling; although he sent Drusus with two praetorian cohorts to escort the ashes to Rome, neither he nor Livia appeared at the exequies, and in an edict he rebuked the people for undue indulgence in mourning. The effect upon Agrippina and her adherents can be imagined. Vengeance was her only thought, and the task was made lighter by the folly of Piso, who after unseemly rejoicings over Germanicus' death determined to win back by force from Cn. Sentius Saturninus (who had been chosen to act as *legatus* for the time) the province from which he had been excluded. Repulsed, he prepared to stand his trial at Rome, and after appealing vainly to some influential senators, found an advocate in the moderate M'. Lepidus.

The usual procedure would have been to bring him before the *quaestio de veneficis*, but, however democratic in theory the Principate might be, the alleged murder of the son of the Princeps could not be treated as an ordinary crime; though Tiberius refused to have the case tried before his own tribunal—which would have been intolerably embarrassing—he referred the case to the Senate, thereby making it out as a matter of State importance. In the court of the Senate the consuls normally presided, but on this occasion Tiberius opened proceedings in a speech of studied moderation.

The charges against Piso were apparently threefold, poisoning Germanicus, contumacy towards his superior, and attempted invasion of a province by force. Piso's defenders could and did demonstrate the absurdity of the accusation of poisoning[1], and Piso himself put in a counter-charge that Germanicus had expelled him from Syria in order to further treasonable designs, but acquittal was impossible; the senators were sure there had been foul play somewhere, the mob outside was riotous and ready to lynch the accused, and Tiberius would never overlook insubordination and violence in one of his own *legati*. Seeing his case hopeless Piso, to save his name and estate, committed suicide. So ended a sensational trial, but an air of mystery remained about it which Tacitus' narrative does nothing to dispel, and there were many left willing to believe that Tiberius had brought about the death of his heir.

The obvious successor was now Drusus, Tiberius' only son by Vipsania, and therefore doubly dear to him. He was about

---

[1] Tacitus, *Ann.* III, 14.

the same age as Germanicus but had been kept more in the background; he was not quaestor till 11 and apparently never held the praetorship, though he was given the consulship by his father in 15. Tradition may be right in calling him cruel, but generally he appears as an ordinary young man of good breeding but no great talent, fond of his wife Livilla (the daughter of the elder Drusus), and so greatly attached to his cousin Germanicus that courtiers could compare the two to the Dioscuri[1]. Simultaneously with the mutiny in Germany mutiny broke out in the Pannonian legions, and Tiberius dispatched his son with a strong body of *comites* to deal with it: granted that an opportune eclipse (27 Sept. A.D. 14) came to his aid, he displayed a firmness in marked antithesis to the emotionalism of Germanicus, and later seems to have carried out the negotiations with Maroboduus and the settlement of the *regnum Vannianum* (p. 783) competently[2]. Tiberius' joy is intelligible when in 19 Livilla gave birth to twin sons, who were named Tiberius (Gemellus) and Germanicus, for now the line was secure, and the provinces were quick to recognize this; at Ephesus and in Cyprus we find priests of the young twins[3]. It was natural enough that Tiberius should bestow on him a second consulship, for 21 (during which he himself retired into Campania to give the young man experience of responsibility)[4], and, well-satisfied, should in the next year ask the Senate for a grant of *tribunicia potestas* for him. The young man was popular, he treated the children of Germanicus kindly, he was gaining experience. One figure alone he could not tolerate, the man on whom his father was coming to depend more and more, the Prefect of the Praetorian Guards, Sejanus: with him and with his ambitions he came into collision.

The name is one of the most famous and sinister in Roman history. L. Aelius Sejanus was of Etruscan descent, his father L. Seius Strabo a distinguished knight, and he himself, as his name indicates, had at some period been adopted by a member of the gens Aelia. From the start his qualities found favour, for Augustus chose him as one of the *comites* for C. Caesar, when he went Eastward in 1 B.C., and possibly on this journey he first met Tiberius. In 14 he was raised by Tiberius to share with his father

---

[1] Volume of Plates iv, 200, *j*.

[2] For this he was allowed to celebrate a triumph on 28 May A.D. 20 'ex Illyrico.' *C.I.L.* xiv, 244.

[3] *S.E.G.* iv, 515; *I.G.R.R.* iii, 997. Volume of Plates iv, 202, *g*.

[4] That he was not very successful is suggested by R. S. Rogers in *Class. Phil.* xxvii, 1932, p. 75.

the Prefecture of the Praetorians; shortly after, on the appointment of his father as Prefect of Egypt, he was left in sole command, and his position and his own talents enabled him to strengthen the hold he had already won upon Tiberius.

The reasons for his rise are not far to seek, though Tacitus can find no explanation beyond the 'anger of the gods with Rome.' By birth he belonged to a class to which the Principate was opening a new and dazzling future, the competent Equites. Possessed of great physical strength and of a soldierly bearing, discreet, trustworthy and efficient, he was the very man to appeal to the practical Tiberius. His office was a responsible one, responsible not only for the safety of the *princeps* but also for law and order throughout the peninsula; 'nihil aeque Tiberium anxium habebat quam ne composita turbarentur,' and though Sejanus did not often have to employ the praetorians their use was prompt and effective[1].

Sometime between A.D. 21 and 23 the Prefect succeeded in persuading Tiberius that discipline and efficiency would be better served by concentrating the nine praetorian cohorts at Rome, and new barracks covering over forty acres were built on high ground near the Porta Viminalis. In other ways, too, the favour of the Princeps was manifest; he proposed to marry Sejanus' daughter to a son of his nephew Claudius[2], and he referred in the most complimentary terms to his lieutenant, calling him 'partner of my labours' and 'my helper in government.' The hot-tempered Drusus found this hard to bear, and on one occasion actually struck the favourite[3], but his opposition did not accomplish much; the very year after he had been granted tribunician power he died[4].

Again fate had dealt Tiberius a cruel blow. He found himself, at the age of sixty-four, bereft of son and successor and forced to fall back on the children of Germanicus, for the twin-sons of Drusus were far too young, and indeed one of them (Germanicus) died the same year. Yet another helper was taken from him, Lucilius Longus, one of his most intimate friends, who had shared his withdrawal to Rhodes. Tiberius had little left him apart from a few scholars and the faithful prefect who stood by his side

---

[1] As against Pollentia (Suetonius, *Tib.* 37), or in the threatened slave war in South Italy (Tacitus, *Ann.* IV, 27).

[2] Tacitus, *Ann.* III, 29; Suetonius, *Claud.* 27.

[3] Tacitus, *Ann.* IV, 3: see K. Scott in *Class. Phil.* XXV, 1930, p. 7.

[4] The date, September 14, 23, is now known from the Verulae calendar. Fever was said to be the cause of death; see p. 638.

to support him during the funeral ceremony of his son[1]. And his grief, though deep-hidden by his habitual reserve and by a feverish devotion to his duties, could not but be exasperated by the confident joy of Agrippina, who could now count on the succession of one of her numerous sons. As in duty bound, Tiberius commended Nero and Drusus, the two eldest, to the Senate, but he was unwilling to see the young men's heads turned by premature honours, and when in the year 24 priests included the names of Nero and Drusus in the New Year vows for the safety of the *princeps* they received a rebuke. Slowly Sejanus began to see a fine avenue for his ambition: were Agrippina's children once out of the way, who but the faithful Sejanus was fit to be guardian for Tiberius' surviving grandson? Given time and care it should not be difficult to prejudice Tiberius against Agrippina or her sons or to lead them on to their own destruction. His position as Chief of the Police gave him advantages, and he found to his hand a weapon of formidable possibilities, the law of *maiestas*. The greater use of this law and the growing ascendancy of the favourite mark a second stage in the Principate of Tiberius.

IV. *MAIESTAS* AND THE POWER OF SEJANUS

Every State, however small, has sooner or later to protect itself not only against enemies without but also against malevolent citizens; as its constitution develops and changes, so do the sanctions safeguarding it and the conception of what constitutes treason. The progress of this conception at Rome has been seen elsewhere[2]: with the Principate a new law of treason, the Lex Iulia de maiestate, became necessary. In his own person the *princeps*, as the holder of *imperium*, the possessor of tribunician sacrosanctity, and head of the State religion, was a visible symbol of the might and majesty of Rome, and conspiracy against his life would be treason; in 23 B.C. the young Tiberius had secured the condemnation of Fannius Caepio for conspiring to kill Augustus[3]. But much in this law, as in the Lex Papia Poppaea, required interpretation; conspiracy was punishable, but what of insults by word or deed, or against statues or representations? And what was the position of members of the emperor's family? Augustus was thought to have gone too far when he treated adultery with

---

[1] Seneca, *ad Marciam*, 15, 3.
[2] See vol. IX, p. 86 *sq.*, 160 *sq.*, and pp. 169 *sqq.* in this volume.
[3] Suetonius, *Tib.* 8; see above, p. 136.

Julia as treason, but relationship to the *princeps* and protection by a bodyguard suggested a privileged position.

However necessary the new law, there were dangers in its scope and application which were only slowly realized. It encouraged the rise of a class of professional informers, *delatores*,—for there was no public prosecutor in Rome,—and the informer was rewarded, if successful, with one-quarter of the goods of the accused. The vagueness too of the conception of *maiestas* meant that it was liable to be tacked on to any and every charge, in the hope of securing prejudice against the accused. So long as the *princeps* could exercise a sane and moderating influence, so long as he felt secure, all would be well; let him once feel insecure or allow his fears or personal feelings to be worked upon and the law would become an instrument of terror.

It was unfortunate that Augustus should have left to his successor two laws, the Lex Iulia de maiestate and the Lex Papia Poppaea, of uncertain application and of wide scope, depending upon the odious assistance of common informers; the early years of Tiberius witnessed a number of accusations for treason, brought by some doubtless in good faith, but by others as a speculation. In this period of transition it will be seen that Tiberius showed both moderation and ironical good-sense, and that when consulted he refused resolutely to admit trivial charges or interpret libels or malicious utterances against himself as treasonable, but this is not immediately discernible from the pages of the *Annals*. For Tacitus both by reason of his own life and prejudices could not give a fair account (p. 871 *sq.*); knowing how formidable an engine the Law of Treason had become in his days, he saw in Tiberius, whose *Memoirs* Domitian had studied so carefully, the author of its abuse and in his moderation merely hypocrisy, and his pulse beats quicker as he approaches the hated topic. He relates the earliest cases that men may know 'from what beginnings and with what subtlety on the part of Tiberius this horrid form of destruction crept into the State'; the earliest informers, poor abjects, set the example of a life which, rendering them rich and formidable, brought ruin first on others and finally on themselves; he describes the affair of Libo Drusus in greater detail because it was the 'first appearance of an evil that cankered the State'; he introduces the case of Appuleia Varilla (p. 630 *sq.*) with the grim words, 'meanwhile the Law of Treason was attaining its full stature,' even though he reveals a few lines afterwards that Tiberius expressly refused to admit a charge of *maiestas* against her[1].

---

[1] *Ann.* i, 73, 74; ii, 27, 50.

It would thus be unreasonable to expect from Tacitus an unbiassed view, and the only way to win this is by careful examination. Space does not admit of a full analysis, which has already been exactly and triumphantly carried out by scholars[1], and in any account of the Empire it would be an error in proportion to assume that the law of *maiestas* is the most significant feature of Tiberius' rule. What it is important to remember is that the interpretation and application of the statute was still in a fluid state: although cases would normally be tried in a praetorian *quaestio*, in so delicate a matter a praetor could hardly be blamed for consulting the consuls or the *princeps*. But the steady development of the Senatorial court as a regular tribunal for cases of extortion (p. 171), and the growing tendency for it to take cognisance of such ordinary criminal charges as that of murder, when committed by persons of rank, led to the displacement of the *quaestiones* in such cases and to the growth of a feeling that senators should be tried by their peers. A charge of treason, in the sense of revolutionary designs, would usually affect men of outstanding power and influence; that is why little is said of praetorian courts and so much of hearings before the Senate. It would be the duty of the consuls, as presidents of the courts, to consider the applicability of all such charges, and to decide whether a case should be proceeded with or not, though here their decision might be overridden by the *princeps*' tribunician veto. The first accusations, as might be expected, were brought in the hope of getting a widened definition and establishing precedents: one man was accused of allowing an actor (a person technically *infamis*) to be a member of a guild of worshippers of *Divus Augustus*; another of perjury by the deity of Augustus; Granius Marcellus, an ex-governor of Bithynia (who was also accused of extortion), of slanders on Tiberius and of substituting the head of Tiberius on a statue of Augustus[2]. Such futilities were at once dismissed by Tiberius with the scorn and anger they deserved and the men set free, save that Marcellus was very properly sent before the court for extortion; but while Tiberius' good sense is praiseworthy, justice must not be withheld from Tacitus, who on this topic is often treated as though he were a rhetorical charlatan, and accused of introducing these cases with unnecessary solemnity of indig-

---

[1] Notably by E. Ciaceri in *Processi Politici e Relazioni Internazionali*, pp. 249–308, and by Marsh, *op. cit.* pp. 289–295.

[2] The removal of a statue inscribed with the *princeps*' name is matter for an accusation in the second of the Augustan edicts from Cyrene. See Malcovati, *op. cit.* p. 42 and J. G. C. Anderson in *J.R.S.* XVII, 1927, p. 39.

nation, seeing that nothing came of them. But Tacitus is perfectly right: the very triviality of the charges exhibits only too clearly the mean mentality and petty cupidity of the informers whom such legislation had created[1]. If suspicion were once aroused, the issue might be very different, as the affair of Libo Drusus in 16 showed.

The evidence in this case is by no means clear. The sources imply that Libo was accused of revolutionary designs, that is, of plots against the Emperor and his two sons (all of whom were in Rome in the autumn of 16) and of magical practices, and he was naturally tried by the Senate. Tacitus suggests that he was merely an empty-headed fool in the hands of unscrupulous black-guards and that the charges were interpreted too severely; the most serious piece of evidence appears to have been a notebook of his, in which mysterious marks were attached to the names of Tiberius, Germanicus and Drusus, and various senators. Belief in magical arts was strong, Tiberius himself was a victim of the grossest superstitions[2], and Libo, convinced there was no escape, returned home to commit suicide. Tiberius declared on oath that he would have pardoned him, had he lived, in spite of his guilt. For that his guilt was regarded as proven is shown not only by Velleius[3], but also by an entry in the *Fasti Amiternini* mentioning the holiday decreed for 13 September, the day when Libo's 'murderous designs' were detected in the Senate, and it is signifi-cant that his trial was followed by a general decree banishing astrologers and professors of magic from Italy[4]. Henceforward magic or the use of magical arts might be charged as treasonable, and terrible new possibilities were opened up.

Better founded were accusations akin to the old *perduellio*, where men were punished for conspiring against the peace and welfare of the State; such cases were those of Antistius Vetus, accused of helping King Rhescuporis to disturb the general peace (p. 645), Vibius Serenus, accused of stirring up revolt in Gaul (p. 644 *sq.*), and M. Caecilius Cornutus, charged with complicity. Even here it should be noted that Vetus was punished with the normal penalty of *aquae et ignis interdictio*, and that when a severer penalty was proposed for Serenus, Tiberius interposed in the interests of clemency. Sometimes a charge of treason was tacked on to others,

---

[1] With such petty charges compare the incident related by Seneca, *de benef.* III, 26.

[2] Pliny, *N.H.* XV, 135; XVI, 190, 194; XXVIII, 23: Suetonius, *Tib.* 19, 69.

[3] II, 130.

[4] *C.I.L.* I[2], i, p. 244; Tacitus, *Ann.* II, 32; R. S. Rogers in *Class. Phil.* XXVI, 1931, p. 203 *sq.* They soon returned: see p. 694.

as can be seen in the trials of Aemilia Lepida and of M. Silanus[1]:
Lepida was accused of an embarrassing variety of crimes, and
finally convicted, though not of *maiestas*, for Tiberius refused to
admit the charge; Silanus was guilty of extortion and cruelty, and
though punished by exile, it remains doubtful whether it was for
maiestas, since bad government was a sufficiently heinous offence
in Tiberius' eyes.

Two other cases, where the written or spoken word was
concerned, offer greater uncertainties. In the first a poet, Clutorius
Priscus, who had earned a handsome reward for an elegy on the
death of Germanicus, was vain enough to compose and recite,
when Drusus fell ill in 21, a poem to show how he could celebrate
Drusus' death. He was brought before the Senate, perhaps on a
charge of magical arts (where Libo's case would be a precedent),
and condemned: although the moderate M'. Lepidus pleaded for
the *aquae et ignis interdictio* 'exactly as though he were guilty
under the law of treason,' the mass of senators voted for instant
execution. (It should be noted that Tiberius was absent from
Rome at the time.) In the second Cremutius Cordus, a historian
of repute, was accused by agents of Sejanus in 25. But though
Tacitus puts into his mouth a spirited defence, the exact charge is
doubtful; if he was really accused of praising Brutus and Cassius
as 'the last of the Romans,' a phrase which Brutus himself had
used over Cassius, it must have been interpreted as treasonable
praise of men condemned by the Lex Pedia as traitors and outlaws,
and therefore no fit subject for eulogy[2]. Dio's statement that
Cordus had recited his *Histories* before Augustus can only be true
of parts of it, for one surviving fragment shows a definitely anti-
Augustan tone[3]. In the end Cordus committed suicide and his
books were publicly burnt by the aediles, though copies survived
among friends.

But while we may discern in these trials too much zeal on the
part of Sejanus and too little independence of judgment on the
part of the senators, and while Tacitus paints the growth of the
evil in dark colours, there is much to show that Tiberius tried to
exercise a moderating influence. He would not at first recognize
slanderous utterances against himself as falling under *maiestas*: he
refused to proceed against Appuleia Varilla in 17, and though

---

[1] Tacitus, *Ann.* III, 22, 23 and 66.

[2] Ciaceri, *op. cit.*, p. 296. The phrase used of Cassius by Valerius Maximus,
'numquam sine praefatione publici parricidii nominandus' (I, viii, 8), shows
what orthodoxy was at the time.

[3] Dio LVII, 24. See fragment 4 in Peter, *Hist. Rom. Fragmenta*, p. 287.

Cominius was convicted in 24 of libel against him he pardoned him; punishment for this offence was apparently not inflicted till 25, when Votienus Montanus was banished[1]. He interceded in favour of a knight, Ennius, who was accused of melting down a statue of him; he would not regard adultery with a member of the imperial house as *maiestas*; he caused the punishment in 21 of two Roman knights and in 25 of a senator, Firmius Catus, for bringing malicious accusations, and he could warn a delator not to mar his speeches by over-vehemence[2]. More still, after the execution of Clutorius Priscus he persuaded the Senate to pass a decree that no decisions should be entered on the records in the *aerarium* before the lapse of ten days; this meant that in future a condemned man had ten days of grace, in which much might happen. There is irony in the reflection that the ruler who, according to Tacitus, was responsible for 'reintroducing' the law of treason, actually made for a condemned man an innovation of clemency. 'But the Senate,' comments Tacitus, 'was not left free to repent, and Tiberius was not softened by the interval[3].'

This then was the instrument that Sejanus found ready for him, a law of treason of widening scope and a body of professional informers who could be disciplined by him. His first task was to rouse the fears of Tiberius against Agrippina and her sons. It is often assumed that they were innocent victims of Sejanus' cunning; but it must be remembered that Agrippina had never forgiven Tiberius, that descent from the divine Augustus might give her sons a strong claim to the succession[4], and that she had a considerable body of support. There was possible danger here, and Sejanus slowly struck down her chief adherents by *maiestas* trials, and fomented the jealousy of Drusus against his elder brother Nero by suggesting that he would be the obvious successor once Nero were out of the way[5]. C. Silius, a former governor of Germany, and his wife Sosia Galla, two friends of Agrippina, were condemned for extortion and removed, and a cousin Claudia Pulchra was found guilty of adultery and banished. Agrippina regarded these as attacks upon herself and loaded Tiberius with reproaches; she fell ill and when Tiberius visited her besought him with tears to let her

---

[1] Tacitus, *Ann.* II, 50, IV, 31, and IV, 42 (this last combined with Euseb.-Hieronymus, p. 149, ed. Schöne). Cf. these cases with the execution, in 35, of Sextus Paconianus in prison, 'ob carmina illic in principem factitata' (*Ann.* VI, 39).

[2] Tacitus, *Ann.* III, 70; III, 37; IV, 31; III, 19.   [3] Tacitus, *Ann.* III, 51.

[4] Tacitus, *Ann.* IV, 52 and cf. *Rev. Arch.* XXXIV, 1931, pp. 17–19.

[5] Tacitus, *Ann.* IV, 60, and cf. VI, 24.

take another husband; such a step would merely mean more complications and Tiberius left her abruptly. Now at last Sejanus could play the two off against each other: so-called friends warned her that Tiberius intended to poison her, and when at table she would scarcely touch food; to Tiberius Sejanus pointed this out as suspicious and contumacious conduct; Nero was provoked to incautious utterances, all of which were faithfully reported.

Unpleasantnesses such as these seem finally to have decided Tiberius to carry out a long-cherished plan and withdraw from Rome. He was sixty-seven and wearied with the cares of rule; the death of Drusus had been a crushing blow (he could not bear to see about the court people who reminded him of his son)[1], and in his agony then he had spoken of resignation. It was whispered too that he found the temper of his august mother hard to bear, and was sensitive about some facial disfigurement from which he was suffering[2]. If to all these we add disgust with the intrigues at court, and the fear of danger (sedulously fostered by Sejanus), there was reason enough for withdrawal. For his retreat he had chosen the island of Capreae, which Augustus had purchased from Naples some fifty years ago and on which he had built a large number of villas. On this four-mile island, with its heavenly climate, difficult of access and remote on some hill he might hope for solitude and peace. The friends he took with him, apart from Sejanus, evince a genuine love of scholarship and science as practised in those days; Thrasyllus with his philosophy and star-lore, Cocceius Nerva, a distinguished jurist and man of culture, Curtius Atticus, renowned for eloquence, and grammarians and men of letters[3].

Yet the withdrawal was a fatal mistake and had the most serious consequences. Though Tiberius worked on steadily and remitted none of his care for the Empire, it looked like despair and desertion of duty, and while it lost him prestige with the people, its effect on the Senate was to emphasize glaringly its inferiority and dependence on the *princeps*. There was no longer a first citizen attending its sessions, allowing freedom of speech and calling the senators 'my good masters': henceforward the Senate received letters and despatches, requesting, suggesting,

[1] Hence his dismissal of M. Julius Agrippa from Rome; Josephus, *Ant.* XVIII [6, 1], 146.

[2] Tacitus, *Ann.* IV, 57. Galen XIII, p. 836 (Kühn) mentions a prescription 'πρὸς ἕρπητας ὁ Τιβερίου Καίσαρος.'

[3] Plutarch, *de defect. oraculorum*, 419 E, mentions the συχνοὶ φιλόλογοι Tiberius used to have about him in Rome.

ordering, and felt itself helpless before the will of an inaccessible despot. More ominous, the position of Sejanus was materially strengthened; Tiberius' trust in him was unbounded; though he did not grant his request to marry Livilla, he could assure him that there was no eminence too lofty for his virtues and loyalty; the very journey to Capreae gave renewed proofs of Sejanus' unselfish devotion, for when the roof of a grotto in which they were dining collapsed he saved the life of Tiberius at the peril of his own. Whatever Sejanus said was likely to be credited, and the way was now clear against Agrippina. Another prominent adherent of hers was removed, Titius Sabinus; information against him was obtained by secreting witnesses between ceiling and roof, and on New Year's Day 28 a despatch from Tiberius accused Sabinus of conspiring against him and of corrupting his freedmen; the death penalty was passed and (contrary to law) carried out immediately, and a letter of thanks arrived from Tiberius declaring he was afraid of plots. It was the first occasion that death had been decreed for *maiestas*[1], and it was decreed because of Tiberius' expressed fears. The narrative in Tacitus is designed to imply that these fears were mainly the invention of Sejanus, but a passage in Pliny the Elder who speaks of an incident which happened 'when Titius Sabinus and his slaves were being punished in connection with the case of Nero, son of Germanicus,' suggests a different view; it is not impossible that Agrippina and her son, if not themselves guilty of plotting, were the focus of a conspiracy, and that there was some danger[2]. However that may be, when in the year 29 the empress mother died, Tiberius finally took action against his daughter and grandson.

The death of Augustus' widow demands more than a passing mention. She died at the advanced age of eighty-six[3]: for sixty years she had been a prominent figure at Rome, famous for her beauty, dignity and discretion; she had undoubtedly exercised a great influence upon her husband, and always for mildness and clemency, yet in the *Annals* she hardly ever appears save in a bad light and trailing a catalogue of crimes that would do credit to a Borgia: it is hinted that she caused the deaths of Marcellus, then

---

[1] Dio LVII, 22, 5 reports under A.D. 23 the execution of an Aelius Saturninus for ἔπη οὐκ ἐπιτήδεια against Tiberius: the present writer regards this as an error of Dio's. Cf. Marsh, *op. cit.* p. 281.

[2] Pliny, *N.H.* VIII, 145. In A.D. 31 a false Drusus gained some support from imperial freedmen and from the populace in the Greek East: Tacitus, *Ann.* v, 10; Dio LVIII, 25, 1 (under the year 34).

[3] Dio LVIII, 2: Pliny *N.H.* XIV, 60 is not an error.

of Gaius and Lucius Caesar, overthrew the two Julias, perhaps
poisoned Augustus, and hastened the death of Agrippa Postumus
'novercalibus odiis'; the final verdict is—'a complaisant wife well
matched with the cunning of her husband and the hypocrisy of
her son[1].' This farrago of nonsense is only comprehensible if it is
noted that accusations fall against her mainly on the question of
succession, that they are simply the result of the jealousy and
hatred of the Julias and Agrippinas and their party, and that
Tacitus reflects their propaganda. They drew the portrait of the
scheming stepmother and found a malicious delight in supposing
that afterwards the son, who (according to them) owed her so much,
could not bear her masterful temper and neglected her in her last
illness. It is likely enough that Tiberius found her difficult: Rome
was unaccustomed to queens or queen-mothers, and the question
of her rank or precedence was not easy. His sense of decorum
was shocked by undue prominence given to a woman (be it
Livia or Agrippina), and so he moderated the honours proposed
for her in 14 and limited the right of coinage she possessed in
Alexandria: but the tendency of the age was against him and it is
noticeable that on the Paris cameo, depicting the departure of
Germanicus for the Orient, Julia Augusta is represented as sitting
beside, though on a lower throne than the *princeps*[2]. At first he
appears to have treated her with great consideration; he consulted
with her and took her opinion, and he even allowed her to inscribe
her name before his on at least one monument. News of an illness
in 22 brought him back hastily from the retreat he had sought in
Campania, and he permitted the Senate to vow special games and
an altar to Pietas Augusta for her recovery[3]. On Capreae, however, he became more negligent: the altar was not dedicated until
twenty years had passed, he did not attend her funeral, and did
not hasten to carry out the provisions of her will[4]. The laudation
was pronounced by Gaius Caesar, the youngest son of Germanicus, who was then in his seventeenth year. In spite of malignant
tradition we may believe that she well deserved the honorific titles
that many provincial cities gratefully gave her and that she was
fully worthy of the great age in which she lived.

[1] Tacitus, *Ann.* v, 1.

[2] J. Vogt, *Alexandr. Münzen*, 1, p. 6 and p. 20 *sq.* For the Paris cameo
('Grand Camée de France') see p. 568 and Volume of Plates iv, 156, *b*.

[3] Tacitus, *Ann.* ii, 50; cf. Tiberius' reference to Livia in the Gytheum
letter, lines 9 and 10: Tacitus, *Ann.* iii, 64 and Dessau 8744a (wrongly
numbered as 8844a) and 202.

[4] Tacitus, *Ann.* v, 1 and 2: Suetonius, *Tib.* 51, 2: Dessau 202.

V. THE FALL OF SEJANUS AND THE LAST YEARS

The death of Julia Augusta marked the beginning of two years momentous for Tiberius and his line, for Sejanus could at last bend all his energies against the house of Germanicus. Unfortunately it is just here that Tacitus suddenly fails us, practically all of Book V of the *Annals* being lost, and for the ensuing period of excitement and terror there remain a few sections of Suetonius, some pieces of information in Josephus, and some nineteen chapters of Dio Cassius, the first seven of which are not Dio at all but later compilation. Dio and Suetonius are so frequently detected in error, where they can be checked by Tacitus or others, that it would be uncritically optimistic to hope that their information is any better just at this point, and the fall of Sejanus offers Dio not only some welcome omens but also full field for the display of his moralizing and dramatic tendencies. Still some outline can be reconstructed.

Shortly after Livia's death despatches arrived from Tiberius containing bitter complaints against the character and morals of Nero and the 'contumacy' of Agrippina. The majority of the senators hesitated; outside a mob was clamouring that the despatches were a forgery, and though shouting loyally for Tiberius it bore aloft the images of Agrippina and her sons. An angry letter from Tiberius followed, the Senate was submissive,— and all that can safely be said is that Agrippina and Nero were both sentenced to banishment; both were removed in chains, in closed litters, with strict orders to the soldiers on no account to stop or talk with anyone; the mother, after being kept in custody for a while near Herculaneum, was sent to Pandateria, Nero, after being adjudged *hostis*, to Pontia. Such punishment and such precautions would scarcely have been taken unless conspiracy had been alleged; we may assume that Agrippina and her son were charged with treasonable designs to flee to the German armies and overthrow Tiberius, and (though certainty is impossible) it looks as though Cotta Messallinus, Avillius Flaccus and possibly Domitius Afer were prominent in accusation[1]. That the two were guilty of imprudent speech and rash hopes is likely enough, that there was serious danger is most improbable[2], and the fact that so many former friends and lieutenants of Germanicus were

[1] Documents of the trial certainly existed; Suetonius, *Claud.* 15 and 30. For flight to the northern armies see Tacitus, *Ann.* IV, 67.
[2] For a different view see R. S. Rogers in *Trans. Amer. Phil. Soc.* LXII, 1931, pp. 141 *sqq.* So long as Sejanus was loyal, there was no danger.

afterwards implicated in the fall of Sejanus suggests that a number had deserted Agrippina for the winning side.

The way was now growing clearer: some time in 30 Nero was terrorized into committing suicide[1]; could Sejanus but sweep aside Drusus and Gaius the only possible successor would be the emperor's sole surviving grandson, Tiberius Gemellus, and the only possible guardian for so young a boy the incorruptible Sejanus. During the year 30 all went smoothly and his position grew stronger each day; he had many supporters, he had influential connections with most of the northern armies, though in Syria the legions never placed his image with that of the Princeps[2], and at last Tiberius promised him marriage with a member of the imperial family[3], and nominated him as consul for the year 31 with himself as colleague. Such treatment could mean only one thing, that Sejanus was destined for succession. He had induced Tiberius to send Drusus to Rome, where he was accused by Cassius Longinus and kept a prisoner in the palace. Only Gaius remained, and against him Sejanus had his agent ready[4].

And then something happened or rather two things; the suspicions of Tiberius were aroused and in the end Sejanus lost patience. Men might support Sejanus against Agrippina or Nero but not against the whole family of the popular Germanicus; somehow a hint reached Antonia, the mother of Germanicus and sister-in-law of Tiberius, and she sent a confidential messenger to warn Tiberius. The first sign was the sudden summons of Gaius, hitherto neglected in Rome, to Capreae, where he was given the *toga virilis*; he would be far safer on the island than in Rome whither Sejanus had departed to hold the consulship for 31. But for some months Tiberius took no overt action, not so much through fear, as through agonizing doubt. How could he be sure? If the news were true, once Sejanus got wind that he were suspected, then he had no other way of escape than removing the man who suspected him, and Tiberius' life was no longer safe. The Emperor must proceed cautiously: he praised Gaius and bestowed on him a priesthood; he found his action was popular, but at the same time he gave priesthoods to Sejanus and his son.

Sejanus had entered on his consulship full of confidence: a

---

[1] Marsh, *op. cit.* p. 194.

[2] Marsh, *op. cit.* pp. 190 *sqq.*; Suetonius, *Tib.* 48, 2.

[3] Suetonius, *Tib.* 65; 'spe adfinitatis et tribuniciae potestatis deceptum.' This must mean that the marriage did not take place, in spite of Dio LVIII, 7, 5: the bride would have been Livilla.

[4] Sextus Paconianus was to be his accuser: Tacitus, *Ann.* VI, 3.

fragmentary[1] inscription suggests that he made an inflammatory speech to the people; he got one of his creatures to overthrow Curtius Atticus (thus removing an honest man from Capreae), and it is said that he was granted the *imperium proconsulare* by the Senate. But Tiberius' attitude began to give him anxiety, for the princeps was slowly making it plain to the Senate that the favourite was not all-powerful. He sometimes addressed him by all his titles, but at others showed him scant respect or vetoed excessive adulation, and as he himself resigned the consulship in May Sejanus had to follow suit. Worse was to come: Sejanus had promoted an attack on the influential L. Arruntius, who was governing Nearer Spain from Rome as imperial *legatus*; Tiberius intervened to quash the proceedings, had the accusers punished, and caused the Senate to pass a decree forbidding attacks upon imperial *legati* during their term of office.

This decision, which can be dated between 1 July and 1 October of 31[2] (and more probably in the earlier months), was a definite setback for Sejanus, and taken with the ambiguous attitude of Tiberius apparently threw him completely off his balance. By now he had expected to receive all the necessary titles and powers, yet Tiberius was still hesitating. Did he suspect? Amid fear and exasperation Sejanus lost patience; he wrote to his friends in the provinces, tested the loyalty of the urban cohorts and was promised money from the military chest by P. Vitellius. But whatever his intentions they were betrayed by one Satrius Secundus, and Tiberius took the necessary counter-measures, though he must have doubted whether any remained loyal to him. He determined to appoint Sertorius Macro as Prefect of the Guards, and early in October sent him with a despatch to the Senate and secret instructions to P. Memmius Regulus, the consul-suffect on 1 October, whom he could trust; if necessary Drusus was to be released from custody and shown to the people; but for days the old man watched from one of the heights of Capreae for the signal that was either to reassure him or hurry his flight in the ships that waited beneath him.

On the night of 17 October Macro arrived in Rome and made all ready: meeting Sejanus early on the 18th he assured him that the despatch he brought was a request from Tiberius to the *patres*

[1] *C.I.L.* VI, 10213 (= Dessau 6044). It may be that Sejanus promised the restoration of elections to the people.

[2] For this see Dio LVIII, 8, 3; Suetonius, *Tib.* 41 and 63; and Tacitus, *Ann.* VI, 7 and 27, as combined and interpreted by R. S. Rogers in *Class. Phil.* XXVI, 1931, p. 31.

to grant tribunician power to the favourite; it would have been the
final touch, making him definitely *consors imperii*, and Sejanus
walked joyfully into the trap. Macro now showed the praetorians
his appointment and took them back to the camp, after placing
the despatch in the consul's hands and leaving Graecinus Laco with
his Vigiles to guard the meeting. The famous letter then read was
planned by its length and ambiguity to lull the suspicions of
Sejanus and prevent any sudden act; at the beginning Tiberius
wrote of perils that threatened him and asked for one of the
consuls to be sent with a military escort; the letter wound on its
long course and suddenly at the end came denunciation. Sejanus
was seized and removed in custody; then when the senators saw
that the praetorians were quiet and the mob gave no sign he was
strangled that very evening. Six days later his eldest son was
executed, and on the 26th Apicata, his divorced wife, committed
suicide[1], but not before she had composed and sent to Tiberius a
document that added the final shock to his agony of mind. He
had already had to bear the horror of betrayal by the one man he
had trusted and now he learnt that his son, Drusus, had not died
a natural death; Livilla had committed adultery with Sejanus and
the pair had poisoned him. And meanwhile the senators were
passing decrees—for 18 October to be a public holiday, for a statue
of Liberty to be set up, begging Tiberius to accept the title of
pater patriae—while provinces and cities hailed the overthrow
of a pernicious enemy and worshipped the 'foresight' of
Tiberius[2]. But for nine months Tiberius did not move from his
villa: even Regulus was repulsed[3]; he could face no one.

The few remaining years of Tiberius' life were spent away
from Rome, mostly at Capreae, though towards the end a restless-
ness beset him and he moved from place to place. Not content,
however, with leaving him to old age and misery, tradition has
branded him so that the name of Tiberius has come to stand for
unnatural vice and sensuality. Yet it is significant that such
stories occur in no first-century writer; the testimony of Philo,
who extols Tiberius in order to blacken Gaius the deeper, may be

[1] The exact dates are given by the *Fasti Ostienses*, and serve to correct the
sensational story in Dio LVIII, 11.
[2] For examples see Dessau 157 and 158. The inscription in A. B. West,
Corinth, VIII, no. 110 (a priest of *Providentia Augusta et Salus publica*),
pp. 90 *sqq.* probably belongs to this date. For *Providentia* as an attribute of
Tiberius see Val. Max. *Praef.* and cf. coins of Tiberius in *B.M. Coins Rom.
Emp.* I, CXXXIX *sq.*
[3] Suetonius, *Tib.* 65; cf. Dio LVIII, 13, 3.

exaggerated but it remains impressive in its favourable tone. And though Seneca and Pliny admit Tiberius' gloomy nature, and have silly stories to illustrate his love for drink, they never even hint at such vices: there is the same silence in Plutarch, though he actually speaks of the long sojourn of Tiberius on Capreae, and in Josephus too; even Juvenal has only a scornful fling at the aged emperor surrounded by a herd of astrologers on his rock at Capreae[1]. But in Tacitus and Suetonius, and to a lesser degree in Dio Cassius, the accusation is definite and detailed, and we can only conjecture that the first two were able to draw upon some *chronique scandaleuse* accessible and eagerly read in Stoic-aristocratic circles. Apart from the intrinsic untrustworthiness of such scandals, which are a commonplace of ancient polemic, the general good health of Tiberius (he lived to be seventy-seven), the company which he took with him to Capreae, which showed his interest in scholarship and learning, and the fact that scandal tends to gather round a solitary and retired life inexplicable to the mob, must all weigh against them. In the end they are all part of the hostile portrait of Tiberius as really vicious from birth, though repressed and hypocritical at first, and only breaking out when all control was removed at the end of his life[2].

At the worst, the verdict, to those who are accustomed to appreciate ancient historical evidence, must be *non liquet*. But those defenders of Tiberius who obstinately maintain that even after the disasters of 31 he remained unaltered have a difficult thesis. Seriously to suggest that Tiberius' mind was unaffected by the shocks that suddenly cumulated on it, argues strange ignorance. His reason must nearly have given way under the assaults of fear, self-pity, and craving for revenge. Even on his stronghold at Capreae he scarcely felt secure and ordered careful watch against unauthorized landings; if he were ever to come to Rome he begged the Senate to give adequate protection to one who was 'an old man and alone[3].' As for the followers of Sejanus, punishment must be ruthless. And this brooding over revenge was accompanied by periods of despair and frenzy so intense that his very despatches to the Senate bore evidence of a soul tortured and distracted; when Agrippina died in October 33 he boasted that he

---

[1] Philo, *Legatio*, 142 *sqq.* and 167 *sqq.*; Seneca, *Epist. Mor.* 83, 14–5; Pliny, *N.H.* xiv, 144–5; Plutarch, *de exilio, Mor.* 602 E; Juvenal, x, 93–5.

[2] Compare the insinuations of Tacitus about the retirement on Rhodes (*Ann.* 1, 4) with the detailed and favourable account in Suetonius, *Tib.* 11–13.

[3] Suetonius, *Tib.* 60 and 65, 1; cf. Tacitus, *Ann.* vi, 2 and 15.

had not had her strangled or her body thrown down the *Scalae
Gemoniae*[1]; the opening of another despatch is preserved by
Tacitus and Suetonius: 'what to write to you, Conscript Fathers,
or how to write or what not to write at this time, may heaven bring
me to a worse death than I feel myself dying daily if I know[2].' To
Tacitus this sentence is merely a proof that vice is its own punishment.

The interrogation of the guilty and suspect (and all friends of
Sejanus were suspect) was carried out with savage rigour, and
Tiberius was pitiless, for who could suffer as much as he had
suffered? Something of a reign of terror prevailed. Some of the
accused, such as Junius Blaesus or P. Vitellius, committed suicide,
some were kept in custody for Tiberius to question, as Junius
Gallio or Mamercus Scaurus, others (like Q. Servaeus or Sextus
Paconianus) turned informer and were presumably acquitted; the
end of some, such as Julius Africanus or Seius Quadratus, is
completely unknown. But many less notable had been involved;
it is said that the prisons were crowded with *Seianiani*[3]; the suspense and dread of those months must have been shattering.
The account given by Tiberius in his own *Memoirs* was that he
punished Sejanus for his mad designs against the children of
Germanicus: very few helpers of Sejanus escaped; Drusus, who
had aided him against Nero, was allowed to starve to death in the
palace; Livilla was driven to kill herself.

The last four years of Tiberius are pictured by Tacitus as of
unrelieved gloom, during which *maiestas* pursued its devastations.
It is indeed likely enough that in these last years few people in
eminent positions could feel secure, and the shadow of accusation
fell very near; this explains the reluctance of many to accept
provincial governorships against which Tacitus declares that
Tiberius publicly complained[4]. Yet Tacitus himself records instances where the *delatores* were punished, every accusation was
not successful, and it is not easy to find a case of a clearly
innocent person being victimized. Indeed Tacitus has to
mingle, with the execution of the condemned, deliberate
suicides, such as those of Cocceius Nerva or Arruntius, and
natural deaths, such as those of Aelius Lamia or M.' Lepidus,

---

[1] Suetonius, *Tib.* 53.
[2] Tacitus, *Ann.* VI, 6: Suetonius, *Tib.* 67. Marsh, *op. cit.* p. 202, and
Rogers, *Hermes*, LXVIII, 1933, p. 121 show that the letter was occasioned by
a charge against Cotta Messallinus.
[3] Cf. the story about Sabinus in Seneca, *Controv.* IX, iv, 17 *sqq.*
[4] Tacitus, *Ann.* VI, 27: cf. Dio LVIII, 23, 5.

as though to place the blame for all these on Tiberius. But though the picture is rhetorically coloured, it is noteworthy that some cases were cruelly or unduly delayed, because Tiberius could not make up his mind[1]. The hesitation and indecision, so characteristic of Tiberius, grew worse still in these latter years, and he cannot be exempted from blame over the trials for *maiestas*. An elaborate analysis of these has been carried out by Ciaceri[2]: after making all possible deductions, he concludes that some sixty-three persons had to face trial for treason during the reign of Tiberius, and he regards this figure as not large. Against this two points must be urged: the first, that nearly all of Book Five of the *Annals* is missing and that Tacitus only mentions the more notable and noble victims and disregards slaves or lowborn. The second objection is more general: Tiberius' reign lasted a little over twenty-two years; all cannot be well within a State when in so short a period sixty-three persons can be accused and tried for treason; granted that some of these cases were due to the zeal or plotting of Sejanus, yet a ruler is ultimately responsible for his ministers, and we cannot acquit Tiberius. His diffidence and hesitation, coupled later with fear and suspicion, allowed the growth of a grave evil.

A certain hardening too in his attitude towards the trials must be admitted. In the year 23 he aggravated the penalty for *maiestas*, interdiction from fire and water, by depriving those convicted of the power to make a will, one of the most definite marks of citizenship, and in the same year Vibius Serenus, after condemnation, instead of being allowed to choose his place of exile, was deported to Amorgos[3]. Here we have the beginnings of a penalty that soon developed fully, *deportatio*, involving loss of citizenship, confiscation of all goods save a competence, and deportation to an island. And when in A.D. 24 the Senate were discussing a proposal to abolish the customary rewards to the informers if the party accused of *maiestas* committed suicide before the end of the trial, Tiberius resisted vehemently, declaring that informers were the guardians of the Law[4].

[1] Some cases unnoticed by Tacitus need mention: Eutychus, kept in prison for several months, Josephus, *Ant.* XVIII, [6, 6], 179; Lampon of Alexandria had to wait two years for trial, but was then set free, Philo, *in Flaccum*, 128; P. Pomponius Secundus, kept in custody for seven years, Dio LIX, 6, 2.

[2] See *Processi Politici*, pp. 298 *sqq.* Cf. Josephus' general verdict in *Ant.* XVIII, [6, 5], 170.

[3] Dio LVII, 22; Tacitus, *Ann.* IV, 13; Mommsen, *Strafrecht*, p. 957 *sq.*

[4] Tacitus, *Ann.* IV, 30.

Yet even in old age and solitude Tiberius found time to supervise carefully as ever both Italy and the Empire; in foreign
affairs (see p. 649) there was no slackening of power or interest,
and it was the same at home. When a land and financial crisis
suddenly occurred in Italy in A.D. 33 Tiberius was able to set money
in circulation again by a princely loan of one hundred million
sesterces, to be managed by a board of Senators, from which
debtors could borrow over a period of three years free of interest.
To complaints of the people about the high price of corn he
replied by publishing the amount and sources of the corn he was
bringing to Rome and showing it was more than Augustus had
brought. When a fire damaged the Aventine and surrounding
regions in 36, Tiberius succoured the homeless by another great
gift of one hundred million sesterces. Donations such as these
show how securely based were the imperial finances, and his
thrifty policy enabled him to leave a sum of two thousand seven
hundred million sesterces in the treasury for his successor.

In the autumn of 36 Tiberius began to show signs of failing.
He was troubled over the question of an heir, for Gemellus was
too young and the claims of Germanicus' son, Gaius, could not
be passed over; he had been made a priest in 31, and given the
quaestorship in 33 with the right to hold office five years before the
legal age; his favour was courted both by the Praetorian Prefect,
Macro, and by the Jewish prince, Julius Agrippa, who had
returned to Italy in the spring of 36 leaving a train of unpaid
debts in the East. Tiberius bade him attend upon Gemellus, but
Herod preferred the society of Gaius, into whose ears he instilled
tales of what an absolute monarch might do, were Tiberius but
out of the way. An imprudent conversation, overheard by the
charioteer Eutychus, led to his denunciation and eventual imprisonment in the autumn of 36. But Gaius could not be set aside
and in 35 Tiberius had made a will in which he and Gemellus were
nominated as joint-heirs. On March 16, 37, the end came in
the villa of Lucullus at Misenum: feeling his strength failing
Tiberius took off his ring to hand it over, then gripped it again,
called for his attendants, staggered a few paces and fell, solitary
and hesitant in death as in life.

But so quiet a death little suited the imagination of those who
wished to contemplate the 'tyrant' Tiberius ending unhappily and
the 'madman' Gaius beginning badly. They persuaded themselves
that Tiberius' skill in astrology brought him sorrow; he foresaw
that Gaius would kill Gemellus and rule evilly, and he wept over it.
And Gaius must have poisoned or suffocated him, perhaps through

Macro or—better still—with his own hands. The crowd in Rome received the news of his death with fierce joy, crying 'Tiberius to the Tiber.' Something of the tragic destiny of the man has been seen in preceding pages, but no final verdict can be passed until his government of the provinces has been considered: here we can view him removed from the background of court life, which he loathed, and from association with a Senate, which he was apt to despise, employing his talents and experience for the service of the empire.

VI. THE GOVERNMENT OF THE EMPIRE

The first duty of a *princeps* was to safeguard the empire and assure tranquillity: Tiberius' own experience and his obedience to Augustus' advice combined to make him avoid wars or expeditions, with their consequent expense, and trust more in diplomacy: 'consiliis et astu res externas moliri, arma procul habere.' The measures that he took along the frontiers call for separate treatment (chaps. XXII, XXIII): inside the empire he effected such changes in the administration or government of regions as seemed necessary for safety. Client-kings or rulers who proved unsatisfactory were removed: soon after his accession he sent for King Archelaus of Cappadocia and brought him to trial before the Senate, possibly on the charge of treasonable designs, and he deprived C. Julius Laco of the tyranny that he held in Sparta. The aged Archelaus died in Rome, Laco was destined to return to power[1]. Tiberius' knowledge of Illyricum taught him that it was more economical for the whole Balkan peninsula to be under one control, and he arranged for the Senatorial provinces of Achaea and Macedonia to be combined with the imperial province of Moesia, placing the whole under the supervision of Poppaeus Sabinus. Where it seemed advantageous to incorporate client-kingdoms, as Cappadocia and Commagene, they were taken over, while friendly relations were maintained with regions beyond the frontiers, such as the new realm of Vannius or the older Bosporan kingdom.

While Germany and Parthia were left to internal dissension, occasionally fostered from Rome, and the frontiers secured against attack, three minor wars within its borders troubled the general tranquillity of the empire. The province of Africa suffered during the first ten years from a revolt of the Musulamii, under a leader who had learnt Roman discipline and methods of

---

[1] On Archelaus see below, p. 744; on Laco, Strabo VIII, 366, Ditt.³ 789, Tacitus, *Ann.* VI, 18 and West, *op. cit.* VIII, pp. 47 *sqq.*

warfare, Tacfarinas, and aided by the bordering Mauri[1]. The
nomad tribes found their freedom of movement hampered by the
slow advance of a settled urban civilization, and the clash soon came.
At first Roman generalship could not cope with the mobile
squadrons of a guerilla enemy and little was done, though Tiberius
was eager and ready to reward a senatorial commander, such as
Furius Camillus, with triumphal insignia. But Africa was too large
a province, its contribution to the corn-supply too important for
prolonged dislocation to be tolerable; in A.D. 20 Tiberius dispatched the Ninth legion from Pannonia to reinforce the army
and gently reminded the Senate that it was their duty to choose
a capable commander. An uncle of Sejanus, Junius Blaesus, won
some successes, for which he was greeted as *imperator* in A.D. 22,
—the last time a private citizen secured that honour,—but it was
left for P. Dolabella, who split his forces into four flying columns,
finally to rout and kill Tacfarinas. For assistance given in this
campaign Ptolemy of Mauretania (who had succeeded his father
Juba in the winter of 23/24) received formal recognition as
socius et amicus and gifts suitable to that distinction; on his coins he
displays these gifts and the temple of the god Tiberius[2]. Even this
petty war demonstrated the Senate's weakness: it is significant
that when Tiberius asked it to choose a good commander it
shirked responsibility by placing the decision on him[3]. Pacification could now begin: the Ninth legion had returned to Pannonia
in A.D. 23; the troops of the Third were put to useful work,
laying roads, constructing bridges and improving communications[4]. The tranquillity and growing prosperity of the province is
reflected in public works and buildings that sprang up during the
reign, notably at Bulla Regia and Thugga[5].

While Spain appears to have been undisturbed, Gaul suffered
from one movement of revolt, though not of any seriousness. Its
leaders were the Romanized Gauls, Julius Florus and Julius
Sacrovir, working among the Aedui and Treveri. The campaigns
of Germanicus had drained the resources of the country, and once
Germanicus was withdrawn a personal element for loyalty was
lacking; Roman governors and *negotiatores* had not learnt moderation all in a day, there were many debt-ridden men who would

---

[1] The main source is Tacitus, *Ann.* II, 52; III, 20–1; 32; 35; 73–4;
IV, 23–4. Cf. Dessau 939 and 2637.
[2] Tacitus, *Ann.* IV, 25, 26: coins, Müller, *Numismatique*, III, nos. 184–5.
[3] Tacitus, *Ann.* III, 32 and 35.
[4] *C.I.L.* VIII, 10018: 10023 (= Dessau 151): 10568.
[5] See *e.g. Journ. des Savants*, 1914, pp. 215 *sqq.*, 473 *sqq.*: Dessau 162.

flock to the standard of revolt, and possibly feeling had been exasperated by the suppression of the Druids and the disarmament of the natives[1]. Whatever its causes, it was not a widespread movement, and was easily crushed once the governors of Upper and Lower Germany, C. Silius and Visellius Varro, had settled their jealousies, though Silius spoilt the effect of his victory over Sacrovir by extortion and avarice, for which he was to pay later in Rome. But the lesson of the revolt was the usefulness of the Rhine legions as a police force rather than any real disaffection among Gauls, and the emperor Claudius was not merely tactful when he praised the century-long loyalty of that nation. For the rest peace prevailed and was gratefully acknowledged, as inscriptions from bodies of *negotiatores* or from guilds testify[2].

The only serious trouble arose in Thrace, where the Odrysian kingdom had been divided by Augustus between two members of the royal house; Rhescuporis, a brother of the late king Rhoemetalces, was given the mountainous and wilder parts in the west, while his nephew Cotys ruled the eastern half with its cultivable land and Greek cities on the coast. He had himself some reputation as a writer as well as a warrior, so that Ovid could appeal to him as a brother poet[3]. But Rhescuporis, anxious to extend his domains, and foolishly encouraged by the wealthy Antistius Vetus, first entrapped and then killed his nephew; this could not be tolerated, and Tiberius entrusted L. Pomponius Flaccus, who had experience of the country, with the task of bringing him to Rome to stand his trial before the Senate. There he was accused by Cotys' wife, Antonia Tryphaena, a remarkable woman, in whose veins flowed the blood of Antony (p. 112 *sq.*); he was sentenced to exile in Alexandria where he was later killed. His son Rhoemetalces II, since he was acquitted of complicity with his father, was allowed to inherit his kingdom, but the children of Cotys and Antonia were too young to succeed; their mother apparently retired to Cyzicus, but they were brought up at Rome in the house of the widowed Antonia, where afterwards they met the young Gaius. For the time being the kingdom was placed under the guardianship of a Roman resident officer, Trebellenus

---

[1] Pliny, *N.H.* xxx, 13. The date of this *senatus consultum* is unknown, but would accord well with A.D. 16, when *mathematici* and *magi* were expelled from Italy; Tacitus, *Ann.* II, 32. For a possible disarmament see Strabo IV, 178 and S. Reinach, *Cultes, Mythes, et Religions*, III, p. 184.

[2] *C.I.L.* XIII, 3026, 941, and 4481.

[3] *ex Ponto*, II, 9, 65. But his flattery was outdone by Antipater, *Anth. Pal.* XVI, 75.

Rufus; though he was subsequently recalled, Tiberius did not restore the kingdom to the family; perhaps he intended to annex it. But Thracians were not easily kept in order; a rising of the Odrysae and Coelaletae, who besieged Rhoemetalces in Philippopolis in 21, was dispersed; four years later they were in arms again, since levies and tribute pressed them hard, and the movement was serious enough to call for the intervention of the able Poppaeus Sabinus and earned him triumphal insignia. But the whole region must have been unsettled, and piracy broke out again: Cyzicus blocked up the channels that cut through the isthmus connecting her with the mainland, and Ilium recorded its thanks to a procurator of Drusus for putting down pirates in the Hellespont[1]. In Thrace itself we hear that Tiberius planted a city called Tiberia (possibly a re-foundation of Philippopolis), and gave a new city-wall to Apollonia[2]: if there is a kernel of truth in Malalas' statement, it must be that Rhoemetalces gave this name to his capital in gratitude and loyalty, just as Herod Antipas founded the city of Tiberias on the Sea of Galilee.

Apart from actual wars Tiberius took prompt action to put down disorders and guard against outbreaks. In his reign, if not shortly before, the City Prefecture, controlling the city cohorts, and responsible for order in the city, became a permanent office; brigandage in Sardinia was checked, a riot at Pollentia was punished by putting the leading citizens in chains, a threatened slave war in south Italy was stifled, and a daring attempt by a slave of Agrippa Postumus to impersonate his master, which might have assumed dangerous proportions, was checked by prompt action. The rights of asylum which many famous temples in the East possessed threatened to become an abuse, and Tiberius asked the Senate, as the proper authority, to deal with the whole question; while tradition was respected, some check appears to have been imposed, though details are not given[3]. Cyzicus, for an outbreak in which Roman citizens were roughly handled, lost the freedom it had possessed for a century[4], and to guard against brigands in Asia Minor and keep the hilly districts under control two cities were founded, one Tiberiopolis in the mountains between Mysia and Western Phrygia, the other Tiberia (or

---

[1] *I.G.R.R.* iv, 146 (Cyzicus); 219 (Ilium).
[2] Malalas, x, 236 and *I.G.R.R.* i, 659: see W. Weber in *Festgabe für A. Deissmann*, p. 20.   [3] Tacitus, *Ann.* iii, 60–63; iv, 14.
[4] Except for five years, 20–15 B.C., during which Augustus had deprived it of freedom for a similar offence (Dio LIV, 7, 6; 23, 7). Their punishment by Tiberius was in A.D. 25 (Tacitus, *Ann.* iv, 36).

Tiberiopolis) on the site of Pappa, not far from Antioch by Pisidia, which itself saw renewed building activity during the reign[1].

The finances of the empire were in a sound condition at his accession but Tiberius kept a keen watch for possible wastage or extravagance. All *beneficia* which Augustus had granted lapsed automatically at his death: his successor did not confirm them without question, but investigated each claim carefully[2]. Although at the time he was forced to recognize the privilege of discharge after sixteen years' service which Germanicus had granted to the mutineers on the Rhine, and even to extend it to the Pannonian legions, he knew that the military chest (p. 195) was unequal to the strain and, once the mutinous spirit had subsided, in A.D. 15 he arranged that normally discharge would not take place until after twenty years' service[3]. During his reign the imperial estates must have been steadily growing: to take but a few instances, the estates of King Archelaus of Cappadocia became imperial property, we hear of copper-mines in Gaul owned by Julia Augusta, of a silver-mine in Rutene territory worked by slaves of Tiberius, of the gold and copper-mines of Sextus Marius in Spain which were confiscated in A.D. 33, and of the estate at Jamnia which Salome bequeathed to Julia Augusta[4]; the management of these numerous concerns meant an increasing army of slaves and freedmen, such as those who controlled the *arca Liviana* at Thyatira, or Herennius Capito at Jamnia. But the central executive in Rome, though growing, was still relatively small: though we hear of one freedman *a rationibus* (a clerk for accounts), of another *acceptor a subscriptionibus* (secretary for petitions), and of a third *supra hereditates* (presumably controlling the accounts of the *vicesima hereditatum*) during this reign[5], they were not yet the all-powerful and arrogant ministers of a generation later. Tacitus notes with approval the small number of freedmen in the palace, and when in 23 the procurator of Asia, Lucilius Capito, was alleged to have used soldiers to enforce his demands, Tiberius,

---

[1] Sir W. M. Ramsay, *Hist. Geog. Asia Minor*, pp. 147, 398 *sqq.* and cf. *J.H.S.* xxii, 1906, p. 100 *sq.*; Head, *H.N.*[2], p. 687 and p. 709; D. M. Robinson in *A.J.A.* xxviii, 1924, p. 435 *sq.*

[2] Suetonius, *Titus* 8.

[3] Tacitus, *Ann.* i, 36, 52, and 78.

[4] A *servus Archelaianus* among the imperial slaves, *C.I.L.* vi, 4776. Pliny, *N.H.* xxxiv, 3; *C.I.L.* xiii, 1550: Tacitus, *Ann.* vi, 19; Josephus, *Ant.* xviii [2, 2], 31.

[5] See *C.I.L.* vi, 8409c and 5181, and Scribonius Largus, 162.

expressly declaring that he had only given him power over the imperial slaves and revenues, disowned him and his actions[1].

There was nothing of the exactions or of the scandalous riches of imperial freedmen that marred later reigns. Tacitus comments favourably on the indifference that Tiberius at first displayed towards others' money: he refused to accept legacies or claim *bona caduca* if any heirs could establish a reasonable claim. Careful conservation of all resources enabled him, while he would not waste a penny on unnecessary shows or donatives or *congiaria*, to give spectacular grants when need was pressing—a hundred million sesterces after a fire on the Aventine in 36, the same sum during the financial difficulties of 33, and in 19 he spent what must have amounted to much the same in lowering the price of corn to the populace when rates were high[2]. And though he refused a demand for reduction of taxation he bore it in mind: in A.D. 15 the people had murmured against the burden of the one per cent. tax on public sales, but Tiberius pointed out that it was the main prop of the military chest and could not be reduced; nevertheless, in 17 when the incorporation of Cappadocia as a province brought fresh revenues to the Empire, he remembered the complaint and reduced the tax to one-half per cent., at which figure it remained until the generosity of Gaius cancelled it altogether[3].

Such a proceeding, however, might mean that Tiberius was benefiting Italy from the spoils of the provinces, and leads us to consider his treatment of the provincials. Fortunately, on this point one of his own utterances is preserved; when a governor sent him more than the stipulated amount in taxes, his reply was sardonic but typical, 'you should shear my sheep, not flay them'; and if it was the governor of Egypt, Aemilius Rectus, as Dio relates, he was relieved next year of his governorship[4]. Both Tacitus and Philo concur in praising Tiberius' government of the provinces; his choice of governors seems to have been good, and if a man proved unsatisfactory he was soon removed. Competent governors were retained long—too long, it was complained —in their posts, and here Tiberius had his own ironical explanation; man was by nature greedy but the longer he stayed in a province, once he had satisfied himself, his appetite would diminish

---

[1] Tacitus, *Ann.* IV, 6, 7; 15, 3.
[2] Tacitus, *Ann.* IV, 64; VI, 45 (cf. *C.I.L.* XIV, Suppl. 4535): VI, 17; II, 87.
[3] Tacitus, *Ann.* I, 78; II, 42. The statement in Dio (LVIII, 16, 2; cf. LIX, 9, 6) that Tiberius later raised it to one per cent. is a blunder.
[4] Dio LVII, 10, 2; Suetonius, *Tib.* 32, 2 generalizes here as often; J. Lesquier, *L'armée romaine d'Égypte,* p. 510.

and the provincials would suffer less. But he was a shrewd judge of ability, and men like Poppaeus Sabinus (who was practically in charge of the Balkans) or L. Apronius or C. Galerius, the prefect of Egypt, were kept in their positions for a long term of years and knew their provinces well. One phenomenon, however, seems difficult to explain, the absentee governorships of L. Arruntius and Aelius Lamia[1], who, although nominated to Spain and Syria, were detained in Rome. Both Suetonius and Tacitus ascribe it to fear of leaving a prominent noble a free hand in a province, but in that case why award the honour at all? There were precedents for such governorships certainly, Pompey from 53 B.C. onwards and Lepidus in 42, and the experiment, which might have resulted in a sort of Secretariat for a Province, was worth trying; but the reign of Claudius produced something different.

A notable example of a good choice was the governorship of L. Vitellius in Syria; his dealings with Parthia are discussed elsewhere (p. 748 *sq.*), but in other quarters he displayed equal efficiency. He crushed with promptitude a rising of a mountain tribe, the Cietae in Western Cilicia[2], and when Philip the tetrarch died in A.D. 34 he was probably entrusted with the incorporation of his tetrarchy (comprising Gaulanitis, Trachonitis, and Batanea) into the province of Syria: it should be noted, however, that the revenues accruing from it were not paid into the common chest but kept in a separate fund[3], for possibly the same arrangement was made over other principalities held in abeyance, such as Eastern Thrace. Had Tiberius lived it looks as though the kingdom of Aretas of Nabataea would also have been absorbed, for Aretas had gone to war with Herod Antipas, and Vitellius received orders to march south against him; but before the orders could be carried out Tiberius was dead. But it is Vitellius' actions in Judaea that earn him a title among good governors, and here he came into conflict with the procurator, Pontius Pilate, whose tenure of office, from A.D. 26 to 36, revealed him as a man whose character and capacity fell below those of the ordinary provincial official. But it has been made famous by the trial and crucifixion of Jesus Christ, which took place probably in 33[4]. What is relevant for the purpose of this chapter is the fact of Pilate's obvious

---

[1] Possibly the Pacuvius mentioned in Seneca, *Epist. Mor.* 12, 8–9, and Tacitus, *Ann.* II, 79 acted as deputy for Lamia in Syria.

[2] Tacitus, *Ann.* VI, 41; Head, *H.N.*[2], p. 719 and 717.

[3] Josephus, *Ant. Jud.* XVIII, [4, 6], 108.

[4] So J. K. Fotheringham in *Journ. Theol. Stud.* XXXV, 1934, p. 146. For the origins and rise of Christianity see below, Vol. XI.

anxiety to avoid disturbance or riot. For the Jews had been exasperated by his procuratorship; in ten years he had piled blunder on blunder in his scorn for and misunderstanding of the people he was sent to rule; the final blunder was a needless massacre of some Samaritans, who had gathered on Mt Gerizim. The Council of Samaria naturally protested; Vitellius at once deprived Pilate of his office and packed him off to Rome to await trial. But he did more and by so doing showed a nice understanding of Jewish feeling: he gained permission from Tiberius to restore the High Priest's vestments, which were in Roman hands, to the custody of the Jews themselves, he remitted an unpopular market tax, and next year, when the priests begged him not to desecrate Jewish soil by bringing his men and their standards through it, he sent his troops round by another way, while he himself entered Jerusalem to offer sacrifice[1].

Such could be a good governor: against the bad Tiberius was implacable. There is evidence to suggest that he encouraged the provincial assemblies to act as organs for public opinion and forward complaints or instigate prosecutions. An ex-governor and a procurator of Asia were put on trial for extortion, one was condemned, the other escaped by suicide, and similar cases from other provinces are recorded[2]. Indeed Tiberius' severity was notorious: a procurator, Mela, recalled from his province, killed himself sooner than face trial, and C. Galba was forbidden to draw lots for a province because he had frittered away his fortune. In the imperial provinces Tiberius apparently completed the abolition of the farming of the tax-collecting to companies and used his own officials[3]. This was some safeguard against extortion, as was a resolution proposed by Cotta Messallinus in A.D. 24, which made governors responsible for their wives' delicts in a province.

Apart from these safeguards there were more positive benefits to record: in A.D. 17 a great earthquake, followed by fire, devastated Asia Minor and shook some of her finest cities, such as Sardes, Magnesia, Philadelphia, and Cyme, and this shock was the forerunner of others which later damaged Cibyra and Ephesus[4]. Prompt relief followed, for Tiberius persuaded the Senate to

---

[1] Vitellius' governorship, Josephus, *Ant.* xviii [4], 85–95 (cf. xv [11], 403–406), and 106–125.

[2] C. Silanus and Lucilius Capito from Asia, Tacitus, *Ann.* iii, 66–69 and iv, 15; Caesius Cordus from Cyrene, iii, 70; Vibius Serenus from Spain, iv, 13; Pomponius Labeo from Moesia, vi, 29.

[3] Hirschfeld, *Die kais. Verwaltungsbeamten*[2], 68 *sqq.*

[4] Strabo, xii, 579; Pliny, *N.H.* ii, 200; Tacitus, *Ann.* ii, 47; iv, 13.

concede a five-year remission of tribute to Sardes and himself made a grant of ten million sesterces to the city, and similar help was given to the others. Five years later the restored cities erected a colossal statue of Tiberius by the temple of Venus Genetrix, surrounded by symbolical representations of themselves[1], while Sardes instituted a city-cult of Tiberius as a god and henceforward styled itself 'Caesarian Sardes'; Asian cities commemorated the Emperor as founder at one stroke of twelve cities and coins celebrated the restoration. A few years later the gratitude of Asia, on hearing of the condemnation of Capito and Silanus, overflowed into a request to be allowed to dedicate a temple to himself, Livia, and the Senate; after much wrangling as to the site Smyrna enjoyed the honour of housing this curious triad[2]. This could be allowed, for it had a precedent in Augustus' times, but when Further Spain, grateful for the condemnation of Vibius Serenus, begged leave to erect a temple to Tiberius alone, permission was refused. The city of Olba in Western Cilicia celebrated Tiberius as founder and saviour, and Antioch in Syria, if we can believe Malalas, owed a whole series of buildings—city-wall, colonnades, theatre and temples—to his munificence[3].

One other activity remains to be mentioned,—that is road-making. In Africa, in Spain (especially in the north-west and the Montes Mariani) and in Narbonese Gaul repairs were carried out and new roads driven: an ambitious programme of construction was initiated in Dalmatia by the legate P. Cornelius Dolabella in 16, when the legionaries were employed on making at least four roads, some of which penetrated right into the interior, into the territory of the Ditiones and Daesitiatae, and so helped to quicken the pacification of these restless regions, and link up communication with Moesia (p. 803); in Moesia itself the men of the Fourth and Fifth legions cut a road along the cliff-face of the right bank of the Danube not far from the Iron Gates[4]. This constructional activity continued unabated not only in Tiberius' early years but during those when he was supposed to be sunk in sloth on Capreae; it is a minor proof, but corroborative of other proofs, that there was a directing head still in the Empire.

[1] Phlegon (*Frag. Gr. Hist.*, no. 257), xiii; a replica of this monument erected at Puteoli in A.D. 30 (Dessau 156) bears the additional names of Ephesus and Cibyra.

[2] Sardes, *I.G.R.R.* iv, 1523, 1502. Other cities, *ib.* 900, 911, 1351, 1514. A coin of 22/3, *Civitatibus Asiae Restitutis*; Volume of Plates iv, 202, *h, i*.

[3] Olba, *I.G.R.R.* iii, 845. Antioch; Malalas, x, 232–236. An aqueduct at Nicopolis *ad sinum Issicum*, *C.I.L.* iii, 6703 and *Eph. Ep.* v, 1336.

[4] *C.I.L.* iii, 1698 (= Dessau 2281) and 13813[b].

The interest of the Principate of Tiberius lies not only in the tragic history of the Princeps, but in the fact that it was the testing of the Augustan system, whether it could endure, not only on its administrative but also on its personal side. Tiberius did what he could, but he had been too long in subordination to another; his adherence to the policy of Augustus was sound, it was the best he could do, but it was a second-best; self-criticism and diffidence made it difficult for him to take an independent line, he possessed none of that constructive leadership which the Claudius he despised so thoroughly was to show. Abroad and in the provinces he kept the Augustan system going, his rule was firm and just and met with due recognition from the grateful provincials, his choice of governors was good. But at home the story was different: he lacked the graciousness in dealing with men and the tact that Augustus had possessed in so supreme a degree; slowly there came a growing irritation at the incompetence and hesitancy of a Senate, which dared not decide for itself and was apt to fling back all important questions to the *princeps*. When he retired, in weariness and sorrow, to Capreae the situation was not a whit improved; to us it is clear that he worked on and remitted none of his labours, but to contemporaries it was a cowardly desertion of his post. A stream of despatches reached the Senate, but they seemed like the orders of a despot to his subjects, no longer the recommendations of one who pretended to be an equal. And in the last years, though he could still take vigorous action where necessary, as against Artabanus or Aretas, a definite slackening is perceptible; he completed but would not dedicate the temple of Augustus (for it meant coming to a Rome that he loathed), he no longer published the State accounts, he gave up the *consilium principis* in judicial cases. Most serious of all was the neglect of Gaius, to whom he gave no responsible office and no opportunity of gaining experience in administration or government. Presumably he dared not let him out of his sight or trust him in Rome, but his neglect was to bear terrible consequences. Good general and administrator though he was, worthy descendant of the Neros to whom Rome owed so much, he worked on lines already laid down for him and broke no new ground. Later tradition, often too personal in its verdicts, forgot the patient years of labour and recorded only the malignity of his enemies who made him a monster of vice and hypocrisy. Such accusations modern scholarship can refute and point the way to a truer judgment, but from the consequences of his own personality it cannot save him.

CHAPTER XX

GAIUS AND CLAUDIUS

I. GAIUS[1]

SCARCELY was Tiberius dead before Macro was on his way to Rome to make the path smooth for Gaius' accession, for Gaius was as yet only *privatus* and in Tiberius' will he and his cousin Gemellus had been nominated as co-heirs; but there was no one to uphold the rights of the eighteen-year-old boy against a son of the popular Germanicus. The Senate readily agreed to set aside the will of Tiberius, on the ground that he was insane, and on 18 March 37, Gaius became *princeps*, with the usual titles, and began his first day of tribunician power. Ten days later he entered Rome and on the 29th soldiers bore the body of Tiberius into the city: Gaius asked for divine honours for Tiberius, but the Senate could not bring itself to grant this, and the matter was simply allowed to drop; a public funeral was, however, given to the body on the 3rd of April, and with that all traces of the old reign of gloom and anxiety were swept away. Everywhere relief and joy were expressed in almost delirious terms. As Gaius passed on his way to Rome the populace flocked out to bless him and call him its

---

Note. The *Annals* of Tacitus are missing for the period between 37 and 47, after which books XI and XII provide first-rate material for the second half of Claudius' reign. For any account of Gaius we have to fall back upon Suetonius' *Caligula* and Dio, book LIX, neither of which is satisfactory, being based mostly upon bitterly hostile and sensational material, and uncertain in chronology; yet their portrait, though overdrawn, contains much of truth. Philo and Josephus represent naturally a pro-Jewish point of view against a persecutor; Seneca and Pliny contain references of value. For the reign of Claudius, Suetonius and Dio are better and provide useful information. Inscriptions and papyri now become of great importance and have helped to correct and ameliorate the traditional literary portrait of Claudius; the principal ones are cited in the text. For the lost sources see the Appendix on Sources, pp. 866 *sqq.*

[1] Caligula was the affectionate nickname given by the Rhine legionaries to Gaius, who as a baby was dressed as a soldier, boots and all; he naturally rejected the nickname when a man (cf. Tacitus, *Ann.* 1, 41 with Seneca, *de const. sap.* 18, 4).

darling, but the provinces were not a whit behind: 'on all sides', says Philo, 'you could see nothing but altars and sacrifices, men and women decked in their holiday best and smiling,' while Eastern cities greeted the long-hoped-for accession of the new sun-god, Gaius Caesar Augustus Germanicus[1].

Yet a moment's reflection upon the young man's descent and upbringing might have given them pause. Through his mother Agrippina he traced back descent to Julia, on his father's side to Antony, and in his descendants Antony took revenge for Actium. He had been born on the 31st of August A.D. 12, brought up in the Rhine camps, and after his father's triumph in A.D. 17 accompanied him to the East: then came the death of Germanicus at Antioch and nearly ten years of living with his widowed mother, who instilled suspicion of Tiberius as murderer of his father, suspicion which must have seemed confirmed when he saw her and his brother Nero sent into exile and Drusus removed to custody. In 29 he moved to the house of his grandmother Antonia, where he would meet the three young Thracian princes Polemo, Rhoemetalces and Cotys (p. 645); unexpectedly the neglected boy was summoned to Capreae to receive the *toga virilis*, an augurate, a priesthood and praise from his great-uncle, with whom he was now to live. In 33 he became quaestor and was granted the right of holding office five years before the usual age; this marked him out, towns in Italy and the provinces selected him for honours[2], and shrewd men such as Macro or Julius Agrippa saw that he must be heir and was worth cultivating. Now after six years of repression and caution, of fear and suspicion, of living in an atmosphere of intrigue, the young man, with his excitable and perverse ancestry, and for years severely kept in order, suddenly found himself in possession of almost unimaginable powers and everyone's adoration.

It would have taken a far stronger and more disciplined mind to withstand so violent a change; although Gaius was not lacking in sharpness and wit, as displayed in his oratory or sayings, he was fatally inexperienced; he had held no magisterial office of importance and commanded no army, and had had nothing even of the

[1] Philo, *Legatio*, 12:Ditt.[3] 797 (Assos) and Dessau 190 (Aritium) show the kind of oath of allegiance taken by cities and peoples. Eastern cities such as Assos and Cyzicus (*I.G.R.R.* IV, 145) hail him as νέος Ἥλιος, perhaps on the initiative of Alexandria, where coins figure Gaius with radiate crown and on the reverse a half-moon; J. Vogt, *Die alexandrinischen Münzen*, p. 22 *sq.* and cf. Dio LIX, 26, 5.

[2] A duumvirate at Pompeii in 34, *C.I.L.* x, 901 and 902.

training which sons of noble houses might expect[1]. It is not surprising that, after a few months inspired by the vague universal benevolence that sudden prosperity often produces, he should have realized (helped by advisers such as Agrippa) the sweets and possibilities of autocracy and finally been ruined by its overpowering influence. Herein Josephus is correct in contrasting the earlier and the later Gaius, his mind overbalanced by power[2]. Most of our sources, however, content in the thought that Gaius was 'mad,' present a nightmarish disorder of events and actions, in which the character of Gaius has been so distorted by hatred and sensationalism that we cannot hope to see clear, and can only deplore the loss of the more sober Tacitus[3].

But at first the young man was a paragon: family affection had always been strong in the house of Germanicus, and Gaius demonstrated this when in stormy weather he brought back the ashes of his mother and brother from their islands[4]; to his grandmother Antonia he granted the title of *Augusta* and the honours Livia had enjoyed, he adopted Tiberius Gemellus and by nominating him *princeps iuventutis* marked him out as heir, chose his uncle, the despised Claudius, as colleague for his first consulship, 1 July 37, and gave to his sisters the privileges of Vestal Virgins; he gained for Tiberius a public funeral and paid punctually not only the legacies due from his estate but also those from Livia's, which Tiberius had simply neglected. In his first days he announced his programme, a return to Augustan ideas and to co-operation with the Senate, to whom he exhibited the greatest deference and respect. For example, he asked its permission to exceed the legal number of gladiators.

In fact there was to be a complete and decisive reversal of the policy of Tiberius: he denounced his rule to the Senators and showed himself the exact opposite; political exiles were brought home, informers and sycophants punished, elections were to be

---

[1] Tac. *Ann.* vi, 48 and cf. A. Momigliano in *La Personalità di Caligola*, Annali d. Reg. Scuola Normale Sup. di Pisa, S. ii, Vol. i, 1932, p. 1.

[2] Josephus, *Ant.* xviii [7, 2], 256. προϊὼν δὲ ἐξίστατο τοῦ ἀνθρωπίνως φρονεῖν ὑπὸ μεγέθους τῆς ἀρχῆς ἐκθειάζων ἑαυτόν.

[3] Tacitus, however, had no doubts of the disordered mind of Gaius: *Hist.* iv, 48, *Ann.* xiii, 3.

[4] This claim of *pietas* appears in his coinage both in West and East, Germanicus and the Elder Agrippina being frequently figured: *B.M. Coins Rom. Emp.* i, pp. 147, 153; W. Wruck, *Die syrische Provinzialprägung*, p. 52 *sq.* Cf. the Egyptian month-names in *Pap. Ryl.* ii, 149, such as Σωτήρ, Γερμανικεῖος, Δρουσιεύς, and Νερωνεῖος.

given back to the People, there were to be no unpopular taxes, histories and writings that had been banned and burnt could circulate again, and actors were allowed to return, for the people was to have its shows and games once more, in which the *princeps* took as much pleasure as they. To make the work of the jurymen less onerous a fifth *decuria* was added to the existing four. No longer would arrogant despatches from a distant ruler reach the Senate, for in their midst was now a prince young, humane and sympathetic, who could refuse to accept more than a small part of statues and gifts offered by a Greek *koinon*, 'so that you shall burden yourselves less with expenses[1].' The age of gold might have returned, and the solemn dedication on 30th of August of the templum Divi Augusti, which Tiberius had not yet done, was carried through with impressive ceremonial[2].

But some six months after his accession, in mid-October, Gaius fell dangerously ill; the empire was in agony, for should he die the danger of civil war could not be far distant; sacrifices and anxious vows were everywhere offered. Gaius recovered, but henceforward we observe a change: intoxicated by a sense of power he was determined that no one should share it with him, no one dictate to him; Agrippa was at hand to whisper how a monarch should behave, and now he got rid of his adopted son Tiberius Gemellus, and drove his prosy father-in-law M. Junius Silanus to suicide; Macro (whose patronage he could not tolerate and whose merits he had not been allowed to forget) and his wife Ennia were ordered to kill themselves and it may be that the Alexandrian Isidorus had a hand in their overthrow. And unfortunately on the 10th of June 38 there died the one person to whom he was devoted, whom he had named as his heir, and who might have exercised a restraining influence upon him, his sister Drusilla; in his first grief he thought of suicide but consoled himself finally by commanding a long period of mourning, and by ordaining her deification; as *Diva Drusilla* or *Panthea* or *Thea Nea Aphrodite Drusilla* she was to be worshipped by Italy and provinces alike[3].

Soon an awkward need made itself felt, money. For the newly restored games and largesses Gaius needed cash, and he had

---

[1] Dessau 8792.

[2] The temple is possibly represented on a coin of 37–8: *B.M. Coins Rom. Emp.* I, p. 153, no. 41 (Volume of Plates iv, 204, *d*), but cf. O. L. Richmond in *Essays and Studies presented to William Ridgeway*, pp. 198–211.

[3] *I.G.R.R.* iv, 145 (Cyzicus), 78 (Miletus), 1098 (Halasarna in Cos), 1721 (Samos): for the West see Dessau 196 and 197. Coins of Miletus are found with the legend θεὰ Δρουσίλλα.

dug deeply already into the ample reserves (said to have been 2,700,000,000 sesterces) bequeathed to him by the thrift of his predecessor; on a favourite charioteer he bestowed two million sesterces, to Livius Geminius (who swore he had seen Drusilla soaring heavenward) he gave a million, to Antiochus whom he installed as king of Commagene (p. 750) a hundred million, while bequests totalling forty-five millions were paid out of Tiberius' will, not to mention the cost of the rejoicings which accompanied the dedication of the temple of Augustus or Gaius' birthday or the restored games.

If the need for money thus became acute Gaius found ways of meeting it. The chemists of the time suggested he might win gold from orpiment, but he soon discovered surer methods. There is a possibility that the death of Macro put him in possession of information about the trials of his mother and brother, and that he realized what an instrument for extortion lay to his hand in *delatio*; for now he openly praised the policy of Tiberius, abused the senators as 'satellites of Sejanus' and became accessible to informers; trials, confiscations and executions began again. But he manifested a more dangerous trend still: the blood of Augustus, as he declared, flowing pure and untainted in his veins[1], gave him a divine title to rule, and henceforward he began to equate himself with divinity, though at first only with demigods such as Castor and Pollux. Finding his every act applauded and meeting with no opposition he became more and more conscious of his own pre-eminence and the more eager to make his supremacy in every sphere patent.

For when Nero boasted that none of his predecessors had understood what was permitted to a *princeps* he was wrong; Gaius had understood, and in that comprehension he was a logical man among fools. If Drusilla was divine how much more so he who had ordained her deification; and if divine he could brook no limitations, as his speech often showed; when writing to his procurators in 40 he could remind them that they need not spare money for, through him, they possessed a right over every man's property. And yet with the curious contrariety of megalomania, while at one moment delighted by the reception of honours and titles from the Senate at another he would be furious, for his

---

[1] For the divine right to rule see Philo, *Legatio*, 52 *sqq.*; and S. Eitrem, in *Symbolae Osloenses*, XI, 1932, p. 22. Hence Gaius' claim to have been born of incest between Augustus and Julia, Suetonius, *Calig.* 23; hence, too, his forbidding Lollia Paulina, whom he divorced, to wed any other man, Suetonius, *Calig.* 25.

acceptance of them suggested that there was some body which stood high enough to favour him. He would have no rival or equal: he began to hear cases on appeal even from the Senate, and the great senatorial nobles or commanders of armies were especial objects of suspicion; on them his attack first fell especially as he was preparing a great expedition to the North and wished to be secure from revolutionary movements. In the summer of 39 Calvisius Sabinus was recalled from his governorship of Pannonia and put on trial; his wife Cornelia was accused not only of adultery but of currying favour with the troops, like an Agrippina or Plancina. In Africa Gaius took away the control of the legion from the senatorial governor and entrusted it to an imperial officer. Senators such as Titius Rufus or Junius Priscus were compelled to commit suicide[1]. Eminence in any walk of life excited his envy: from young Cn. Pompeius Magnus, the holder of a once mighty name, he cut off the title *Magnus*[2], he belittled the genius of Virgil, and visited orators with his special jealousy; Domitius Afer, whose brilliance might over-shadow his own, saved himself only by tactful admiration, and the younger Seneca escaped because he was rumoured to be dying of consumption. Jurisconsults must not oppose him or venture to offer their opinions, for he was Law incarnate and the sole source of decisions[3]. The praetorians he could trust, and he apparently increased their numbers[4], but mindful of the dangerous powers of Sejanus or Macro he divided the prefecture among two. With this bent of mind he was turning definitely towards the institution of monarchy, and for this two things were necessary, the open public recognition of his manifest divinity and the military glory of a conqueror. His deification is noticed elsewhere (p. 496 *sq.*), but one of his most sensational acts is placed by Dio in the summer of 39, when he is said to have made a bridge of boats across the Bay of Baiae and ridden upon the sea in triumph, wearing the breastplate of Alexander the Great. The new Alexander, longing for a world to conquer, would naturally look for glory in Germany and the North, where his ancestors had won their laurels.

[1] Dio LIX, 18; Tacitus, *Hist.* I, 48 and IV, 48.
[2] Dio LX, 5, 8–9. But Dessau 9339 suggests that this did not happen till sometime in 40.
[3] Philo, *Legatio*, 119; Suetonius, *Calig.* 34.
[4] The number of cohorts was raised from 9 to 12 either by Gaius or by Claudius; see Daremberg-Saglio IV, i, p. 632 and literature there cited.

II. GERMANY AND JUDAEA

In the North there was, in fact, much that needed the attention of an *imperator*. There was trouble in Germany itself, there had been raids in which the Canninefates, for example, had taken part[1], there was opportunity for effective intervention in Britain with its reputed wealth, whence a chieftain Amminius had fled to Gaius' protection (p. 796). Such were his pretexts; more sinister was the suspicion that his two sisters Agrippina and Julia were intriguing with M. Aemilius Lepidus (whose marriage to Drusilla might be thought to give him some claim to the throne) and were relying on support from Cn. Lentulus Gaetulicus, the too popular legate of Germany. It is certainly possible that dissatisfaction was finding vent in plots, and a suspected conspiracy would explain the extraordinary haste of Gaius' departure for the North in September 39, would explain also the facts that Lepidus and Gaetulicus were both executed by mid-October[2], that Gaius wrote to the Senate informing them that he had escaped from a vast conspiracy, and drove Julia and Agrippina into exile, while the latter, in hideous burlesque of her mother's journey twenty years before, was forced to bear the ashes of her lover Lepidus back to Rome[3]. This may have been followed by some triumphant raids upon the German tribes, after which Gaius spent the winter in Gaul, entering upon his third consulship alone at the beginning of 40 at Lugdunum, receiving the congratulations of the Senate, auctioning imperial property at fancy prices and confiscating the estates of the richer Gauls; among his victims was Agricola's father. Possibly in the spring of 40 he contemplated an invasion of Britain, but nothing came of it, and possibly fear of what might happen in Rome if he delayed his return too long brought him back: preparations for a triumph of unprecedented splendour were begun, client-kings were summoned to take their part[4], and Gaius declared that he was no longer going to work with the

---

[1] Tacitus, *Hist.* IV, 15; Suetonius, *Galba*, 6, 3. It is probable that Gaius created two new legions for Germany, see below, p. 788 *sq.*.

[2] On 27 October the *fratres Arvales* sacrificed 'ob detecta nefaria consilia Cn. Lentuli Gaetulici.' *C.I.L.* VI, 32346.

[3] Gaius consecrated three daggers, said to belong to Lepidus, Agrippina, and Julia, in the temple of Mars Ultor at Rome: Suetonius, *Calig.* 24, 3 and Dio LIX, 22, 7.

[4] These were the 'reges, qui officii causa in urbem advenerant,' Suetonius, *Calig.* 22; Agrippa and Antiochus accompanied him on his return from Gaul, Dio LIX, 24.

Senate but to overthrow it; on 31 August he entered Rome again[1].

So much may be tentatively put forward as a sketch of Gaius' Northern journey, the rest is hidden under such a smoke-screen of ridicule, hatred and misrepresentation that it cannot be discerned. We are asked to believe that his campaigns were a farce, with provincials dressed up in red wigs to look like Germans (it is worth noting that the same kind of caricature was later made of Domitian's German campaigns); he flies panic-stricken at the first sound of alarm, he has his uncle Claudius, at the head of a congratulatory embassy from the Senate, ducked in the Rhone, on the shores of the Channel he bids his legionaries collect sea-shells as spoils of victory—and so on *ad nauseam*. On all this one need merely remark that the soldiers would have certainly revolted against such a mountebank, and they did not.

Arrived back in Rome he soon made his object clear; whereas he had started on the model of Augustus he would now no longer be a *princeps* ruling in conjunction with the Senate; rather he would be monarch and master, worshipped as a god (it mattered not which, for he could manifest his deity under any form)[2], and ruling his empire as a sort of Great King over a series of vassals. On his return from Gaul he had with him Agrippa and Antiochus of Commagene, who were viewed with deep disfavour in Rome as 'tyranny-teachers'; other client-kings (including Ptolemy of Mauretania) had been summoned to attend, and he himself very nearly assumed the diadem of autocracy. In this, as in much else, his reign shows a complete reversal of Tiberian tendencies; Tiberius, in care for the frontiers, had disestablished client-kingdoms bordering upon the Euphrates; Gaius distributed kingdoms in the East lavishly, and perversely enough struck down two clients whom Tiberius had left unmolested; Mithridates of Armenia had offended in some manner, he was put in custody and then dismissed to exile[3], while Ptolemy by drawing upon himself the attention of the populace in the theatre aroused his jealousy and was bidden kill himself. Mauretania was to be annexed, but the people, under a loyal freedman, Aedemon, flew to arms, and a war in that difficult country was a legacy that Gaius left to his successor (p. 674).

But for all his other princely friends he found situations in the

---

[1] 'Ovans urbem natali suo ingressus est,' Suetonius, *Calig.* 49. But *C.I.L.* VI (iv, 2) 32347 suggests that he was in the vicinity of Rome by June 1.

[2] Cf. the title of Drusilla, Πανθέα.

[3] Seneca, *de tranquill. animi*, 11, 12 and cf. Tacitus, *Ann.* XI, 8.

first year of his reign; to the sons of king Cotys, his boyhood's companions, he granted three kingdoms, Lesser Armenia to Cotys, Pontus-with-Bosporus to Polemo, and the old half-kingdom of Thrace, which had been the father's (p. 645), to Rhoemetalces, so that the Thracians had now two Rhoemetalces ruling over them simultaneously. Perhaps he regarded these donations as a demonstration of *pietas*, for the three young princes could claim a common descent through their mother Antonia Tryphaena from Mark Antony. But these did not exhaust his generosity; Laco, dynast of Sparta, who had incurred the disfavour of Tiberius, was restored to his post, an obscure Sohaemus was raised to be king of the Ituraean Arabians[1], and prince Antiochus, son of the former king of Commagene (p. 620), received back his father's possessions with part of the coast of Cilicia added, while in reparation for the loss of revenue during that period he was given one hundred million sesterces[2]. (Possibly the city of Caesarea Germaniceia in Commagene was founded by him, for its Era may have begun in 38.) Chief in his favour was the astute and ambitious Agrippa, who had supported his cause in early days and could claim to have suffered imprisonment for his zeal, and for several years his restless nature played a large part in Roman politics. Gaius released him from prison and kept him by his side; only after the death of Drusilla did he allow him to return (? late July 38) to the kingdom of Trachonitis and Ituraea that he had granted him. But Agrippa was fated to stir up trouble wherever he went, and when he put in at Alexandria on his voyage a seemingly slight incident led to incalculable results.

The Alexandrians had no love for Jewish princes and had possibly not forgotten that the new king had only a few years back stolen away to Italy owing a huge debt. The mocking welcome that they gave him swelled into an anti-Jewish riot, actually aided and abetted by the governor of Egypt, Avillius Flaccus (p. 309), and though Gaius recalled him to stand his trial, the mischief was done. The enmity between Jew and Greek in Alexandria now spread to Syria, ready to blaze up at a moment's notice, and it is likely enough that the warfare between the two nations at Antioch, which Malalas[3] chronicles in 39–40, has a foundation in fact. But in the year 40 an unlucky incident led to an explosion in the very home of Judaism.

[1] Ditt.³ 789; A. B. West, *Corinth*, VIII, ii, pp. 47 *sqq*. Dio LIX, 12, 2.
[2] Suetonius, *Calig.* 16, 4; Dio LIX, 8, 2; *I.G.R.R.* IV, 940. Later (? winter of 40), Gaius apparently took back his gift (Dio LX, 8).
[3] X, 244, 18 *sqq*.

This time the disorder was not due to Agrippa, though he had already succeeded in improving his position against his uncle Antipas. Antipas, who thought that a personal journey to Rome would give him the advantage, found to his surprise that his nephew had anticipated him by a letter accusing him of intrigues with Sejanus and general disloyalty; he was banished to Gaul and Agrippa was rewarded with his uncle's realm of Galilee and Peraea. The trouble in Judaea was due to Jewish and not Greek intolerance and arose from a riot in Jamnia. This sea-coast town was the centre of an imperial estate (it had been bequeathed by Salome to Livia) with a mixed population of Jews and Greeks, managed by a procurator Herennius Capito, who had been cheated some years before by Agrippa and cherished no goodwill towards his nation. Some Greeks and others erected an altar to Gaius, probably in the spring of A.D. 40 and to celebrate his German victories[1]: the Jews tore it down, and Capito wrote angrily to his master. Gaius had returned to Italy some two months before August, more convinced of his godhead than before; he had already given a cool reception to a Jewish embassy from Alexandria (headed by Philo), and now, determined to end this stubborn disloyalty, he sent orders to Petronius (who replaced Vitellius as *legatus* of Syria) to set up a colossal statue of himself in Jerusalem, using two legions if necessary to overawe resistance[2]. Petronius advanced as far as Ptolemaïs; in frenzied fear for their Temple the Jewish population deserted their farms and fields,

[1] Philo, *Legatio*, 197 *sqq.* The dedication to Gaius at Kula, in Lydia (*I.G.R.R.* IV, 1379), presumably belongs to this date. So too perhaps the dedication by A. Minicius Rufus at Cyrene and datable to 40, though the emperor's name is lost (*ib.* I, 1036); if so, Rufus would probably be the *legatus* of the Legio X Fretensis mentioned on the dedication discovered at Palmyra in 1931 (*Syria*, XIII, 1932, p. 255).

[2] The main texts for events in Judaea are Philo, *Legatio*, 188–338, Josephus, *Bell. Jud.* II [10, 1], 185–[10, 5], 203 and *Ant.* XVIII [8, 1], 257–[8, 9], 309. It is possible to place the winter voyage of Philo to Rome (*Legatio*, 190) in the winter months of either 38–39 or 39–40. Though no decisive evidence is to hand, the latter date seems preferable, because if Gaius received Philo in the summer of 39 the incident at Jamnia must be put in the spring of 39 (for Philo heard of it after he landed in Italy, *Legatio*, 184 *sqq.*); but it seems entirely out of keeping with Gaius' character that, having given an order for the erection of his statue in Jerusalem in the summer of 39, he should wait at least a year before taking further action. The present writer believes that the altar at Jamnia was erected in the spring of 40 to commemorate Gaius' German victories, and that all the correspondence between Petronius and Gaius can be fitted into the period between summer of 40 and February or March 41, when Petronius got news of Gaius' murder.

neglecting the autumn sowing, and gathered to protest; Petronius realized the gravity of the situation and advised the workers of Sidon, where the statue was to be made, to take their time. King Agrippa did his best to intercede with Gaius: whatever happened, whether we believe with Philo that he moved Gaius' mind by a long and philosophical letter, or follow Josephus who declares that he gave him a lavish banquet, somehow he succeeded in getting the order rescinded. But in a few months Gaius veered again: he was projecting a visit to Alexandria and Egypt, where he would manifest his divinity, and he now gave orders for a statue for Jerusalem to be made in Rome and wrote a cold letter to Petronius containing a command for suicide. Revolt must have followed, but on the 24th January 41 Gaius was killed and Jewry released from fear; the news travelled fast and reached Petronius soon enough to enable him to peruse with calm the death-warrant, now invalid, which he received a few days later.

III. TYRANNY

While revolt had broken out in Mauretania and was near breaking out in Judaea matters were not mending in Rome. Gaius had returned as the sworn enemy of the Senate, and though his future plans are uncertain, it looks as though he intended to embark upon a long coasting voyage to Alexandria, perhaps following in the tracks of his father Germanicus; finally in Egypt would be celebrated that triumph which he had refused to hold in Rome (where he had contented himself with an *ovatio*), and surrounded by his client-kings the Great King would appear in all his divine glory to his worshippers. The provincials had already recognized the divinity of Gaius: on coins of Amphipolis and Ilium he is entitled *theos*[1], and in Miletus a temple was erected to him[2], but in the autumn of A.D. 40 (if we can believe Dio) two temples were erected to him actually in Rome, one by the Senate, the other by himself: the temple of Castor and Pollux was a mere vestibule to his palace. And this deification was profitable too: his uncle Claudius and his own wife Caesonia, whom he had married in the winter of 39/40, had to pay down two million sesterces for the privilege of priesthood. For Gaius' need for money had not diminished; on his return to Rome he clapped new taxes on every

[1] R. Münsterberg in *Numism. Zeitsch.* XIX, 1926, p. 1.
[2] Berl. Abh. 1911, *Siebenter vorläufiger Bericht über Ausgrabungen in Milet und Didyma*, p. 65, which controls the statement of Dio LIX, 28, 1; the temple is possibly that shown on coins, *B.M. Cat., Ionia*, p. 198, no. 143.

available source of income, on the sale of eatables, on litigation, on
prostitutes, on the daily earnings of porters and carriers, and when
the populace in the theatre shouted against these new burdens he
sent soldiers to cut them down. In three and a half years he had
alienated all classes, but deliverance appeared doubtful, for a conspiracy that was formed against him was betrayed from within by
Anicius Cerealis, and the members of it executed with a savagery
that appalled. Some names we know, but doubtless more perished
nameless, and it was not only the cruelty of Gaius that made men
shiver but the hard joy he took in it. Extremely sensitive himself
to personal insult or physical pain, he took pleasure in inflicting
them on others; rumour declared that his favourite order to his
executioners was 'kill him so that he can *feel* he is dying.' Though
something must be allowed for exaggeration and for the sensationalism of the political pamphlet[1],—and we know that as late
as the autumn of 40 he could pity and reward an actress, Quintilia,
for the tortures she endured for her lover's sake[2],—yet it must be
admitted that in the main these stories ring true, and that in the
year 40 a tyrant was ruling in Rome.

For though Gaius, after the suppression of this conspiracy
and a servile display of the Senate, professed himself reconciled,
yet no one could feel his life secure. A governor with a record as
good as Vitellius, recalled from Syria, only saved himself by abasement and gross flattery to the new deity, and others were ready
enough to introduce *proskynesis* and Eastern customs; indeed to
one man whom he had pardoned Gaius graciously extended his
foot to kiss[3]. Memmius Regulus in Greece nearly lost his life for
delay in dispatching the statue of Olympian Zeus to his master,
Petronius of Syria was in equal danger, Cassius Longinus was
summoned from Asia on suspicion, and we can discern too the
beginnings of the long quarrel between philosophy and the
Principate. In 39 a rhetorician, Carrinas Secundus, had been
driven into exile for reciting a conventional exercise against
tyranny, and (probably in 40) Gaius attacked a little band of
Stoics and philosophers, including Julius Kanus and his friends,
Antiochus of Seleuceia and Rectus. What was the ground of

---

[1] On this sensational pamphlet literature see T. S. Jerome, *Aspects of the
Study of Roman History*, pp. 380–421, and M. P. Charlesworth in *Camb.
Hist. Journal*, vol. IV, 1933, p. 105.

[2] Josephus, *Ant.* XIX [1, 5], 36; her lover, Pomponius or Pompedius (the
name is doubtful, see Boissevain, on Dio LIX, 26, 4), had been accused of
conspiracy.

[3] Philo, *Legatio*, 116; Seneca, *de benef.* II, xii, 1, 2; Dio LIX, 27.

accusation is unknown, but Kanus was sentenced to death, and
Rectus followed him three days after. Henceforward philosophy
could be suspect, and though Seneca, some twenty years later,
deplored the notion that the devotees of philosophy were stubborn
opponents of government and officials, the suspicion remained
and more victims were to fall under Claudius and Nero[1].

With Senate and nobles outraged and fearful, and with the
mob hostile, the final touch of folly would be to offend the officers
of the army. Yet Gaius did so: he insulted beyond endurance a
tribune of the Praetorian Guards, Cassius Chaerea by name, and
now at last a plot was made which had some hope of success, for
not only were some of the nobles involved, but also the influential
palace freedman Callistus, Chaerea himself and the two prefects of
the praetorians. It was essential to act soon for Gaius was planning
his trip to Alexandria, and once in the East he would be safer. On
24 January 41 the first blow was dealt by Chaerea, and the hated
body was struck and pierced again and again by the conspirators,
who then rushed to summon the Senate and announce the return
of 'Liberty.' Caesonia was stabbed by a centurion, and her
daughter was dashed against a wall. Such was the end of Gaius
and his family; his corpse was hastily burned and buried in the
Lamian gardens, but restless as he had been in life so he was
rumoured to be in death; men said his uneasy spirit haunted the
gardens until he was properly buried.

But though Gaius had been removed the evil that he had done
remained and that was grave. Four years' extravagance and folly
had emptied the Treasury and brought the city near famine, yet
men could not look back on one useful piece of legislation or one
notable work. His grandiose schemes to cut through the Isthmus
of Corinth or build harbours of refuge for the corn-ships near the
Straits of Messana came to nothing; he pulled down the Aqua
Virgo and forgot to rebuild it[2]. On a young man without experience or training, and so without any sense of responsibility,
his position as the ruler of the Empire had a shattering effect:
he merely viewed it as so many opportunities for gratifying
his pleasures or exhibiting his power[3]. The precise nature of the
malady from which he suffered may never be determined; all our
sources agree in recording the frenzied energy that hurried him

---

[1] Dio LIX, 20, 6; Seneca, *de tranquill. animi*, 14, 4–10; Plutarch, Frag.
140, *Mor.* VII, p. 167 *sq.* (Bern.); Seneca, *Epist. Mor.* 73.

[2] Pliny, *N.H.* IV, 10; Josephus, *Ant.* XIX [2, 5], 205–6; Dessau 205.

[3] Josephus' verdict, *Ant.* XIX, [2] 201 *sqq.*

on, and Suetonius has a pitiful picture of sleepless nights, when he
would wander restlessly through the Palace crying for the dawn;
in any case it is matter more for the psychiatrist than the historian.
Far worse than the effects upon Gaius were the results of his
rule on Senate and people. His autocracy was unconcealed: when
two consuls offended him he deprived them of their office and
smashed their fasces, he ordered the Arval Brethren to co-opt as
he wished, he apparently began the minting of imperial money in
Rome[1]. Such an exercise of power drove home on the Senate the
lesson that the absence of Tiberius had begun, that Senate and
nobles were helpless before a *princeps* backed by military power and
guarded by praetorians; we read that when Gaius appeared in the
Senate-house to praise the policy of Tiberius and to reintroduce
delation the Senators listened and voted honours to him for his
clemency, that when an imperial freedman Protogenes attacked
one of their number as being Caesar's enemy the rest fell on him
and dispatched him with their knives, and we ask 'Could self-
abasement and servility farther go?' The fury with which his
name and memory were attacked, as witnessed by the tradition
about him, is a measure of the hatred and shame of the senatorial
order, impotent save against the dead. In the provinces and on
the frontiers Gaius left no great military success, no considerable
undertaking; on the contrary he had weakened the defensive
efficiency of the Empire by his restitution of the system of client-
kings, driven the people of Mauretania to rebellion, and in Judaea
ruined the effect of Vitellius' conciliation (p. 649 *sq.*); the Jews
looked on Gaius as a second Antiochus Epiphanes, bent on destroying their race and religion[2]; from that time onwards they could never
trust a Roman ruler again, and to that extent Gaius precipitated
the tragedy of the Jewish revolt and the fall of Jerusalem. Such
were the results to which the Principate of Augustus, based on a
scheme of family succession, had apparently led, and naturally
enough the Senate was ready to debate whether a principate should
continue at all; but the Senate was no longer master of the situation.

[1] Dio LIX, 20, 1, 2; *co-optatio ex tabella imperatoris,* Wissowa in P.W. II,
p. 1469; Mattingly in *J.R.S.* VII, 1917, p. 59.
[2] See vol. VIII, pp. 510 *sqq.* Josephus treats Gaius' murder as God's
punishment on a persecutor of the Jews, *Ant.* XIX [1, 2], 15–6, and in later
Jewish tradition, *e.g.* Yosiphon, this comes out strongly; see I. Lévi in *Rev.
Ét. Juives,* XCI, 1931, p. 134. The exact opposite occurs in Greek Eastern
tradition, for which (*e.g.* Malalas) Gaius is μεγαλόψυχος.

IV. CLAUDIUS. CAPITAL AND COURT

The Senate met; the session lasted until a late hour of the night, for though the consuls Cn. Sentius Saturninus and Q. Pomponius Secundus were fervent for liberty and a restoration of the Republic, more thought of release from the Julian house than of abolishing the Principate; if the system were to continue there was no lack of candidates, wealthy men such as Annius Vinicianus or Valerius Asiaticus in Rome, or governors of provinces like Servius Sulpicius Galba or Furius Camillus Scribonianus, both of whom were urged on by their friends. But the Senate was not the final arbiter. Amid the confusion and licence that followed the murder of Gaius some Praetorians found his uncle Claudius in hiding, recognized him as a Germanicus and hurried him to the camp to greet him as Imperator. The Senate thought to bully him out of it, and sent an embassy headed by two tribunes, Veranius and Brocchus, bidding him return. But the conclusion was foregone: Claudius had as his intermediary King Agrippa, who saw a chance of reaping an even richer harvest than he had from Gaius' accession, the Senate was not at one, the mob shouted for a *princeps*, and the urban cohorts who had at first protected the Senate soon joined with the Praetorians. On 25 January, escorted by the Praetorians to whom he gave a handsome donative (the first given by a *princeps* for his accession, and an evil precedent)[1], he was duly recognized by the Senate, received the titles of Imperator, Augustus, and Pontifex Maximus, and the tribunician power, and henceforward as Tiberius Claudius Caesar Augustus Germanicus ruled the empire for nearly fourteen years[2].

The new *princeps* was in his fiftieth year when Fortune brought him to power by a turn of her wheel so strange that Tacitus sees in it convincing proof of the chance that mocks human affairs. He had been despised by his mother and his family as an invalid and an imbecile: infantile paralysis in some form left its mark upon his frame: in a civilization that admired bodily grace and fitness Claudius had an ungainly gait, weak knees, a shaking head, a slobbering mouth and a thick uncouth utterance. Yet though neglected and allowed no part in public affairs, though on the Arch

---

[1] Coins, with legend IMPER. RECEPT. and PRAETOR. RECEPT. recall the part played by the Praetorians in Claudius' accession. Volume of Plates, iv, 204, *a*, *c*.

[2] The praenomen of Imperator he did not use; the title of Pater Patriae he accepted in 42; the name Germanicus was his by birth-right, and he himself, though a Claudian, of set policy took the cognomen Caesar.

at Pavia he is named last of all the imperial house[1], Augustus had discerned his latent ability. People and soldiers felt a sympathetic respect for a son of Drusus and brother of Germanicus, and the Equites chose him on occasion as their representative. Disappointed in his hopes of a career, he flung himself on scholarly studies, with Livy as a guide and friend; he read deeply and wrote voluminously—we hear of histories of Carthage and of Etruria, of a defence of Cicero (answering Asinius Gallus' attacks), of treatises on Dice and the Alphabet[2]. He ranked among the most erudite men of his time; Pliny the Elder cites him four times as an authority; to him scientists and savants could write or might dedicate their treatises[3]; before the Senate he could unfold his learning in early Roman history or his knowledge of the antiquities of Cos, on other occasions instruct his subjects on cures for snake-bite or calm their superstitious fears with the explanation of the causes of an eclipse.

Yet though when he was called upon to rule, apart from an augurate and a two-months' consulship in 37 and occasional presiding at the Games, he lacked (in this resembling Gaius) all administrative experience, he was after all a Claudius, with generations of political capacity behind him, and his historical studies had taught him something of the meaning and mission of Rome denied to those contemporaries who jeered at him. At the best they could glimpse in him merely an unpractical amiability; they could not see beyond the uncouth figure and ludicrous mishaps of their ruler, and so we hear *ad nauseam* of the Claudius who wished to see all men wearing the toga, whose first recitation was a fiasco, who was ducked in the Rhone or drenched by the outburst of the Fucine tunnel, the butt of Gaius' parties, the timid slave of his wives or freedmen who played skilfully on his fears and his affections. The discovery of inscriptions and papyri and closer study of his acts and utterances enable us to pass a very different verdict. But it will be well first briefly to review the events of his life and reign at Rome as represented by the tradition and after that consider the other evidence.

---

[1] Dessau 107.

[2] Inscriptions belonging to his principate often contain the reformed letters which he advocated; AI for AE, the sign Ⅎ for consonantal *v*, the Ↄ for *bs* or *ps*, and the for the Greek *upsilon*. Suetonius, *Claud.* 41, cf. F. Bücheler, *Kleine Schriften*, pp. 1, 106.

[3] For example the Latin doctor Scribonius Largus, or Thessalus of Tralles, or an Arabian sheikh Aretas, for whom see F. Cumont in *Rev. Phil.* L, 1926, pp. 13 *sqq.* (and cf. *ib.* XLII, 1918, p. 85).

Claudius' first task was to secure his position by appeasing all parties and by effacing, as far as possible, the unfortunate memory of the reigns of his two predecessors. Chaerea and the chief conspirators had to be removed or remove themselves: that was unavoidable, for the murder of a Caesar could not be condoned, but to all others, even to possible rivals, he showed a forgiving spirit. Asiaticus and Saturninus he counted among his friends, Galba took part in the expedition to Britain, and Veranius was promoted later to be imperial governor of Lycia. The Senate he treated with the utmost deference and he evinced his readiness to return to the normal constitutional principate: it is probable that he restored to the Senate the right of elections which Gaius had in 37 returned to the People (p. 655 *sq.*); he only held four consulships in all, the second in 42, the third in 43, the fourth in 47 and the fifth in 51. For eighteen months in 47 and 48 he held the censorship with his trusted friend L. Vitellius, during which he carried out a *lectio Senatus*, numbered the people and celebrated Secular Games[1]. A year after came the solemn taking of the *Augurium Salutis* and a performance of the Lusus Troiae. All this was on the Augustan model; he was not going to be as either of his predecessors; coins proclaimed the return of Augustan peace and Augustan liberty and his strongest oath was by the divine Augustus[2]. Much of Gaius' ill-doing was reversed: his papers were burnt, his exiles recalled, the new taxes he had imposed were gradually abolished, his thefts from Athens and other towns restored, the temple of Castor and Pollux was returned to the twin brethren, and Protogenes and another favourite freedman Helicon were put to death. Although Gaius' memory was never officially condemned, Claudius removed many statues and reminders of him unobtrusively, and referred openly to his folly and madness[3].

But reaction against Gaius was not to imply the gloom and inactivity of Tiberius: throughout his reign Claudius gratified the people with gladiatorial shows, games and imposing spectacles

[1] These games celebrated the 800th anniversary of the founding of Rome, according to Varronian chronology. See M. P. Nilsson in *P.W. s.v. Saeculares Ludi* etc., cols. 1717 *sqq.*

[2] Mattingly-Sydenham, *Rom. Imp. Coin.* i, pp. 126, 130; Suetonius, *Claud.* 11, 2. Volume of Plates, iv, 204, *b.*

[3] In many inscriptions Gaius' name is erased: Dessau 194, 5984; *I.G.R.R.* i, 1057, iv, 146; *C.I.L.* xi, 720. The scornful references (*e.g.* in Josephus, *Ant.* xix [5, 2], 280–5 and [5, 3], 287–91) were deliberate and not (as some suppose) lack of tact; it was essential to assure the world that such things would not happen again.

such as his triumph for Britain, his display of the British chieftain Caratacus, the Secular Games, the reception of an embassy from Ceylon (p. 307), or the opening of the Fucine tunnel (p. 695 *sq.*). The army-commanders were placated by ready grants of titles and distinctions[1], and the troops rejoiced in a son of Drusus and brother of Germanicus under whom there was plenty of campaigning and who for various successes gained took the title of *Imperator* no less than twenty-seven times[2]. Upon the Seventh and Eleventh Legions, which refused to support a disloyal governor in 42 (p. 671), he bestowed the titles of *Claudia, Pia, Fidelis,* and in 46 he granted to all legionaries (who were not allowed to marry during their term of service) the *privilegia maritorum.* Names such as Corbulo, Galba, Vespasian, Hosidius Geta and Suetonius Paulinus, who were all to become famous later, reveal how capably generals were chosen and explain the good discipline and contentment of the army. Although he put a stop to the colossal building-schemes of Gaius, a great deal of useful and necessary work was carried out on roads and aqueducts (p. 582), and the corn-supply was safeguarded by the construction of a new harbour and moles near Ostia and by the grant of special privileges to corn-shippers.

Admirable though much of this was, yet among the nobles in Rome itself Claudius' rule failed to find favour, and that for two reasons due to the gradual development of the Principate. The property of the princeps had within three generations swollen far beyond the limits of the richest private household; this, coupled with the vast amount of business that normally fell to his lot, meant that his secretaries and stewards were becoming, in effect, State officials whose influence was great and permanent, and this influence was exercised by freedmen, mostly of Greek or Asiatic origin, whose antecedents, arrogance, and power were alike displeasing to the Roman aristocracy. The other factor was the tendency, which had been promoted by Gaius, to invest not only the princeps, but also members of his family, especially his wife, with a privileged position (p. 699). Herein lay new and dangerous possibilities, for these freedmen possessed power without office or responsibility and would not be shocked by breaches in a tradition of which they were ignorant or disdainful, while the wife of the

[1] Thus P. Gabinius Secundus received the cognomen of Chaucius for his defeat of the Chauci, and *ornamenta triumphalia* were granted to various generals: Suetonius, *Claud.* 24.

[2] As Claudius had wisely refused the praenomen of *Imperator*, this repeated assumption of the title was a compliment to generals and troops.

Princeps held a position for which there was no precedent or parallel. To the freedmen, Callistus, Narcissus, Pallas and others, their posts meant riches beyond their dreams, to Messallina, who was Claudius' wife at his accession[1], it meant pleasure without restraint; she had borne two children, the elder a girl Octavia, the younger a son and heir whom Claudius had proudly shown to the people, usually called (after his father's British triumph) Britannicus, and she was sure of her hold on her husband. Claudius relied—naturally enough considering his scholarly bent—upon his wife and freedmen in all matters that did not interest him, and between them they gratified their utmost desires, putting out of the way all whom they feared or whose possessions they coveted.

For although Claudius is said to have sworn that he would not regard insults by speech or action against himself as treasonable[2], other ways lay open; before the court of the *princeps* himself (p. 169) men and women could be accused, Messallina or the freedmen could employ the services of L. Vitellius or Suillius Rufus, who played on the superstition or timidity of their master and could be sure of a conviction. Tradition records a large number of victims during the thirteen years, 35 senators and 300 knights, but the sources at our disposal do not render a proper check possible. Some of these undoubtedly perished as adherents of conspiracies. Thus in 42 Furius Camillus Scribonianus in Dalmatia was induced to revolt; but his two legions soon deserted him, he himself committed suicide, and accomplices such as Annius Vinicianus, Pomponius Secundus or Caecina Paetus followed his example; others implicated must have been executed[3]. A few years later a plot by Statilius Corvinus and Gallus Asinius was discovered, resulting in the death of Statilius and the banishment of Gallus, and in 47 we hear of an attempted assassination by a knight, Cn. Nonius[4]. Many, however, fell victims to the jealousy or anger or cupidity of Messallina; Julia daughter of Drusus, Julia daughter of Germanicus (accused of adultery with the young savant Seneca, who was exiled to Corsica), Catonius Justus the Praetorian Prefect, Cn. Pompeius Magnus and his mother Scribonia, Crassus Frugi and the wealthy Valerius Asiaticus were the most notable names, but we should probably place in these early years and ascribe to the avarice of Messallina the trials of

[1] She was his third wife. His first was Plautia Urgulanilla, the second Aelia Paetina; see the Genealogical Table at the end of the volume.
[2] Dio LX, 3, 6.   [3] Dio LX, 15; Suetonius, *Claud.* 13; 35.
[4] Dio LX, 27, 5; Suetonius, *Claud.* 13.

many of those 'herds of knights' whom Suillius was later charged with sending to execution, and which helped to swell the total[1]. But in the end Messallina over-reached herself: her amours with an actor such as Mnester or with unimportant knights might be overlooked and could be hidden from Claudius, but in her final infatuation for C. Silius, handsome, wealthy and noble, there lay the peril of a revolution. Against all warnings she persisted and Narcissus destroyed her: he took charge of the bewildered Claudius and ordered her execution, while Silius with numerous friends and associates was hurried to death[2].

A new wife had now to be found for Claudius. While Narcissus recommended a return to Aelia Paetina, Pallas supported the claims of Agrippina the younger, Claudius' niece, twice a widow, with a son born of her first marriage to Cn. Domitius Ahenobarbus. She had somehow managed to escape the attentions of Messallina; as one of the few surviving children of Germanicus and as a descendant of Divus Augustus she might be a danger if married to a citizen, and union with Claudius would solve many difficulties. But marriage with an uncle seemed incestuous and it needed all the persuasions of Vitellius—in a speech which must have sounded like a burlesque of the Claudian manner[3]—to rouse the Senate to demand it. The marriage was solemnized early in 48 and life in the palace took on a very different aspect; whereas Messallina had cared for nothing but pleasure Agrippina was a woman of high ambition and indomitable will, who loved power and wealth and the open display of both. Formality and decorum prevailed: she herself, greeted as Augusta and allowed unprecedented privileges[4], used to appear by the side of her husband at great public functions, splendidly dressed and usurping the place of a consort. At the same time she began to intrigue for the setting-aside of Britannicus in favour of her own son, L. Domitius Ahenobarbus, to whom she was devoted; Seneca was recalled from Corsica in 49, given a praetorship and appointed as his tutor (p. 700), and the two Praetorian Prefects, Rufrius Crispinus and

---

[1] Dio LX, 8, 5; 18, 3, 4; 27, 4; 29–31; Seneca, *Apocol.* 11, 2; Tacitus, *Ann.* XI, 1–3; 4–5; XIII, 43.

[2] The story is narrated at length in Tacitus, *Ann.* XI, 26–38. It is only fair to record on Messallina's behalf that she was but fifteen when she married Claudius, probably in A.D. 39; the disparity in age between the two and the easy standards prevalent then in Rome explain much.

[3] If the speech in Tacitus, *Ann.* XII, 5–6 is anything like reality.

[4] For the title Augusta, her privileges and high place see Tacitus, *Ann.* XII, 26, 37, 42, 56, and Pliny, *N.H.* XXXIII, 63. Cf. Vogt, *op. cit.* p. 6, and F. Sandels, *Die Stellung der kaiserlichen Frauen...*, pp. 23, 77.

Lusius Geta[1], were replaced in A.D. 51 by Afranius Burrus, on whom she could rely.

But though greater strictness prevailed at court the new marriage brought no change in judicial terrorism. Agrippina was completely unscrupulous: she had not hesitated to poison her second husband Crispus Passienus for the estates that she knew he would leave her, and now, in her determination to secure herself and her son, she struck down all those whose rivalry she feared or whose riches she coveted, and the pretext used was mostly the dreaded one of magic; on this charge or the like she got rid of the younger Scribonianus and of Statilius Taurus, of Lollia Paulina or Domitia Lepida[2]. In 52, following the condemnation of Taurus, the Senate passed a decree, similar to the one that had followed the condemnation of Libo Drusus, against all *mathematici* and such-like practitioners, in whose power Agrippina and Claudius believed as credulously as the meanest of their subjects. Thus treason-trials and delation began to be employed again, and though it was no part of Claudius' policy to frighten or uproot the old aristocracy, his wives and freedmen between them practically brought about such a state of things; these judicial murders were the worst aspect of his Principate and cannot be extenuated.

The last few years of Claudius witnessed a struggle for power among those behind the throne. Narcissus, who had been all-influential and who was possessed by a not ignoble devotion to his master, found that Pallas was against him and had the formidable gratitude and support of Agrippina herself; while he worked for Britannicus the other two made every effort to advance Nero and push Britannicus into the background. At last in the year 50 Agrippina prevailed upon her husband formally to adopt Nero as a guardian for the younger Britannicus—there was really only five years difference between them—and after that the rest was easy. In 51, at the age of thirteen, he assumed the *toga virilis*, and was designated to hold the consulship in his twentieth year; in the meantime he was to hold a proconsular imperium outside the city and to have the title of Princeps Iuventutis. In 53 he made his first public appearance, speaking before the Senate on behalf of various communities such as Bononia and Ilium, and in this year he was also married to Octavia the daughter of Claudius. Every-

[1] *I.G.R.R.* I, 1118 (= *O.G.I.S.* 666) shows that Geta (like Macro before him) was solaced by promotion to the governorship of Egypt.

[2] Tacitus, *Ann.* XII, 52 (Scribonianus), 59 (Taurus), 22 (Lollia Paulina), and 64–5 (Domitia). For the possible connection of the underground basilica of the Porta Maggiore with the Taurus of this trial see above, p. 500.

thing had gone according to plan, and nothing could have been more 'Augustan'; just as Tiberius had been given the hand of Augustus' daughter Julia in order to act as guardian to the young Caesares, so now Nero. Agrippina could look forward with complete confidence to seeing Nero emperor when Claudius should die, and even to playing a large part in the ruling of the Empire thanks to the influence she would exert over her young and devoted son. But before narrating the way in which she achieved her ends it is necessary to consider Claudius' work in the provinces and in the administration of the Empire, for only here can his true importance be appreciated.

V. THE PROVINCES AND CLIENT-KINGS

In his provincial and foreign policy Claudius was remarkably energetic: new territories were added to the Empire, many of the older client-kingdoms were incorporated and others were brought into closer contact with the imperial administration. More stress was laid on the military functions of the *princeps* as protector and enlarger of the realm: the defensive caution of Tiberius was abandoned—save along the line of the Rhine and Danube—and the pretences of Gaius were transformed into real soldiering. In this as in the succeeding section any connected account can be no more than a reconstruction, based partly upon such information as the literary sources can spare from the more absorbing topic of home affairs, and partly upon epigraphic material which, valuable as it is, often raises as many questions as it solves. But in spite of these limitations some attempt at a general account must be made, for Claudius' Principate marks a great advance in several directions.

In reviewing his administration it is convenient to move from south-west to south-east and to begin with Africa. Although at first no change was made here and the division between the senatorial governor and the imperial commander of the legion initiated by Gaius was retained, Claudius was ready to alter it if necessary, and when a revolt of the Musulamii troubled the province[1] he appointed one of his most trusted generals, Galba, as governor (p. 690)—presumably of the whole area and with control over the legion—and Galba held office for two years with credit. Farther west Mauretania was the scene of more serious fighting: Gaius had obviously intended annexation in the autumn of 40— indeed the provincial Era of Mauretania begins from that year[2]—

[1] Aurelius Victor, *de Caesaribus*, IV, 2.
[2] *C.I.L.* VIII, 8630, and cf. S. Gsell, *Hist. anc. de l'Afrique du Nord*, VIII, p. 284 *sq.*

but a freedman of the murdered king, Aedemon by name, kindled
a successful revolt against the annexers and summoned help from
various desert tribes; it needed some three or four years campaigning under distinguished commanders, such as Suetonius
Paulinus and Hosidius Geta, with the help of native levies, before
the country was properly pacified[1]. Mauretania was divided into
two provinces, Caesariensis and Tingitana (with capitals at Iol-
Caesarea and Tingi), each under an imperial equestrian procurator.
It would be a mistake to picture the new territory as wild and
uncivilized, for King Juba had done the work allotted to him well
and the old Punic tradition still survived in several towns, as their
coinage testifies; in fact these towns, or rather some of them, were
now used for new settlements or received privileges which would
enable them to become nuclei of Romanization round which less
advanced communities could cluster. Thus colonies of veterans were
sent to Iol and Tipasa, to Lixus and Tingi, and inscriptions have
recently revealed an act of political liberality which can scarcely
have been isolated. A native of Western Mauretania, who had
held high office in his community of Volubilis, during the revolt
of Aedemon raised levies among his townsmen and fought for the
Romans. To him and to his followers Claudius, when the request
was made to him, granted Roman citizenship and the right of legal
marriage *cum peregrinis mulieribus,* and to their town the status of
a municipality. Furthermore, not only did he attach to the new
municipality certain of the surrounding tribes as 'incolae,' but
also granted it the right of disposing of the goods of its citizens
who had died intestate during the war—goods which would have
normally accrued to the Aerarium—and exemption from imperial
taxation for ten years[2]. These latter grants were certainly exceptional, for only in exceptional circumstances will a government
surrender its claim upon monies due to it, but the gift of citizenship
and municipal rights was in the truest Roman tradition of granting

---

[1] Fighting can scarcely have begun till the spring of 41: Pliny, *N.H.* v,
11 corrects Dio LX, 8, 6. For the native levies see *C. R. Ac. Inscr.* 1915,
p. 396 (= *C.I.L.* VIII, 21823). In connection with this war Umbonius Silo
(governor of Baetica) was expelled from the Senate for not supplying enough
grain to the armies, Dio LX, 24, 5.

[2] The inscriptions about Volubilis in *C. R. Ac. Inscr.* 1915, p. 396 and
1924, p. 77. The account here given follows G. De Sanctis in *Atti Acc.
Torino,* LIII, p. 453; for other views see L. Constans in *Mus. B.* XXVIII, 1924,
p. 103; Wuilleumier in *Rev. E. A.* XXVIII, 1926, p. 323 and for the rest
of the literature see the Bibliography, section II, c, 2. On the legal aspect of
Claudius' interfering with the *bona vacantia* see E. Cuq in *C. R. Ac. Inscr.*
1916, p. 262.

privileges where the beneficiaries had earned them by service and merit, and throughout Claudius remained true to this policy.

A smaller accession of territory, though a more sensational one and more satisfying to Claudius' pride, was made in Britain. Quite apart from the political and military reasons for the expedition (p. 797) one most important consideration was that Claudius could thus prove himself a true son of the conqueror Drusus and keep the regard of the legionaries and generals; in fact he journeyed specially to Britain in the autumn of 43 in order to be present at the final victory. A colony of veterans was planted at Camulodunum (Colchester), the fringes of the new province were guarded by client-kingdoms, and in this reign or the next a new squadron, the *classis Britannica*, was formed to protect the coasts and shipping of the Channel. It was the achievement of which Claudius was most proud and to which his mind often returned: in 44 he celebrated a triumph, invitations for which he issued all over the Empire; provinces, cities, communities and associations innumerable sent him golden crowns and congratulatory embassies, and minor poets seized their opportunity[1]. Aulus Plautius, the victorious general, was granted the honour of an *ovatio* on returning from his term of office in 47, and Claudius formally advanced the *pomoerium* as a symbol that he had enlarged the territory of the Roman people[2].

In Spain the foundation of a new town, Claudionerium, and steady road-making in the north-west bears witness to the increasing importance of that mineral region, but apart from that and possibly the unification of Nearer Spain after its division by Augustus (p. 345) Claudius left little impression. Far different was his treatment of Gaul, the land of his birth: the conquest of Britain opened up fresh opportunities for trade and business activity; new roads were constructed in the regions of Normandy and Brittany, and new market-towns, Forum Claudii Vallensium (the former Octodurus) in the Valais, Forum Claudii Ceutronum in the Tarentaise—both upon important Alpine routes—and Claudiomagus (in Touraine) came into existence. Colonies were sent to Lugdunum Convenarum in Aquitania and to the town of the Ubii on the Rhine, which was now linked by a new road with the camp at Moguntiacum. Even more important was the willingness that Claudius betrayed in bestowing privileges on inhabitants of Gaul; it is not

---

[1] Pliny, *N.H.* XXXIII, 54; *P. Lond.* 1178 records the answer of Claudius to an embassy from the Sacred Association of Athletes at Sardes; for the poems see *Anth. Lat.* (ed. Riese), nos. 419–26.

[2] Tacitus, *Ann.* XII, 23, and *Not. degli Scavi*, x, 1913, p. 68.

unlikely that whole communities, such as the tribe of the Ceu-
trones, received the *ius Latii*, but in addition some individuals
gained the full Roman citizenship if their merits seemed to warrant
the grant. To many this citizenship was enough and their ambition was satisfied; the richer and more influential, chiefs and sons
of nobles, wanted more still—the public recognition of their right
to hold office in Rome and so win entry to the Senate. Men from
other provinces had already held magistracies, as had Valerius
Asiaticus and other senators from Narbonese Gaul, but so far
no one from the more recently conquered provinces of Gallia
Comata had been allowed the privilege, not on account (as it
would seem) of any legal hindrance or because their citizenship
was of any minor status, but because of a deep-rooted prejudice
against them. During his exercise of censorial power in 47/48
Claudius was approached by some of the Gallic notables, and he
seized the occasion to outline his policy to the Senate; Tacitus
preserves a pithy and coherent summary, and the famous bronze
at Lyon a considerable fragment, of the rambling oration that he
pronounced[1]. His theme was simple—that the State must not be
afraid of new measures and that Rome had grown great by freely
admitting precedents and by drawing the conquered to herself in
generous union. It is easy to point out that the thought was not
original, that Philip V of Macedon had long ago discerned the
reason for Rome's success[2] and that it was by now a commonplace
among historians and writers. But for a hundred who will pay
lip-service to political generosity there may rarely be found one
with courage and insight enough to carry it into practice. Such a
one was Claudius, and whatever the Senate might say he clung to
his resolution; it is very probable that he straightway brought into
the Senate by the use of the power of *adlectio* some of the greater
Gallic nobles, who might have scorned to go through the round of
petty offices required to qualify them for normal entry to the
Senate; but his speech was probably followed by a *senatus consultum*
affirming the full right of all Roman citizens in Gaul to stand for
office in Rome itself, and henceforward no presiding officer would
dare refuse their names: the first to attain the coveted honour were
the oldest Gallic allies of Rome, the Aedui.

Such liberality could scarcely have been shown to the Gauls

[1] The two texts, Dessau 212 and Tacitus, *Ann.* XI, 23–5, 1 are unfortunately least explicit where explicitness would be most valuable; hence
a vast body of literature on the subject, conveniently summed up by Ph. Fabia
in *La Table claudienne de Lyon.* See the bibliography to this chapter,
section II, B, 4.   [2] Ditt.[3] 543.

had they not been at once protected and watched over by the
legions upon the Rhine: the safeguarding of the long line stretching
from the Atlantic to the Black Sea is described elsewhere, but it
should be noted that though at either end of the line—in Britain
and in the Bosporus—Claudius made advances, along the Rhine
and Danube he pursued steadily the diplomatic policy that he had
inherited (pp. 785 and 804). The Cherusci consented to accept a
king from Rome, and though Vannius was expelled from the land
in which Tiberius had placed him (p. 619), he and his followers
were settled in Pannonia, while his two successors Vangio and
Sido were recognized as joint rulers; two fleets patrolled the whole
length of the Danube. Raetia and Noricum were two important
connecting links between north Italy and the upper Danube
frontier, and Claudius displayed activity here. One of the greatest
works of his censorship was the re-organization of communications
throughout this region. A road 350 miles long, the Via Claudia
Augusta, ran from Altinum over the Reschen-Scheideck Pass to
the Danube at Druisheim near Donauwörth, through the scene of
his father Drusus' earliest independent campaign, and a subsidiary
road connected this with towns in the valley of the Drave such as
Aguntum and Teurnia[1]. Noricum itself, which Augustus had
at first governed through a *praefectus*, now became an imperial
province under an equestrian procurator; its peaceful and advanced state may be gathered from the facts that no troops
garrisoned it and that Claudius gave municipal rights to various
important centres, Aguntum, Teurnia, Virunum and Celeia.

Towards the East Pannonia, which received a colony at
Savaria, and Moesia were more backward regions where less
could be done for Romanization and where governors had to be
constantly on the watch, even prepared to lead legions as far to the
north-east as the Bosporan kingdom (p. 806). In addition the
Greek cities of the Dobrudja and near the mouth of the Danube
looked to Rome for protection and jurisdiction and we find
governors of Moesia settling boundaries and confirming rights[2].
One change of considerable importance was made: the client-
kingdom of Thrace had always been a source of anxiety, owing to
the turbulent nature of its subjects and no less to the intermittent
feuds in the royal family itself, and, when in or before 46 King
Rhoemetalces III was murdered by his own wife, Claudius decided
to end the Thracian question once and for all by annexation. The

[1] W. Cartellieri, *Die römische Alpenstrassen...*, pp. 7, 45.
[2] Inscription from Istros first published by V. Pârvan in *An. Ac. Rom.*
XXXVIII, 1916, p. 556, and reprinted in *S.E.G.* I, 329.

process cost some fighting, but the kingdom was finally transformed into a province under an equestrian procurator; a colony was settled at Apri and a *koinon* of Thracian cities for the worship of the Caesars appears as from this date[1]. The work of pacification was thorough and we hear of no more uprisings.

For the eastern half of the empire the evidence is more fragmentary, but enough remains (when combined from coins and inscriptions) to indicate that Claudius was as active here as in the West. In Syria he planted a colony at Ptolemaïs Ace composed of veterans from the four legions (III Gallica, VI Ferrata, X Fretensis, and XII Fulminata) that made up the Syrian army, and apparently bestowed some privileges on Tyre, which from now on took the title Claudiopolis[2]. Beyond the frontier the existence of a Claudian tribe in Palmyra[3] suggests the spread of Roman influence and a desire to honour the emperor. But it was in the peninsula of Asia Minor that he left the greatest impression; we have evidence for road-making along the coast in Bithynia (near Amastris) and in Pamphylia (near Adalia)[4], and many cities, presumably for benefits received, adopted the name of the Emperor. Such were Bithynium, lying on the road between Nicomedeia and Amisus, which styled itself Claudiopolis, while in Paphlagonia there was a Neoclaudiopolis and in northern Pisidia Seleuceia Sidera became Claudio-Seleuceia and worshipped its benefactor as god manifest[5]; in Lycaonia the towns of Iconium, Derbe and Laodicea Catacecaumene similarly added the name of the Emperor to their titles, while in the territory of the Galatian Trocmi there appeared yet another Claudiopolis[6]. To the east the province of Cappadocia received a colony at Archelaïs (the older Garsaura), and the fortress-town of Claudiopolis (? Claudias) guarded one of the bends of the Euphrates. It would be unjust to assume that this was no more than the ostentation of a *princeps* or the adulation of provincials. These foundations or newly privileged cities served either to promote trade and intercourse, lying as many of them did upon important routes, or else to protect or hold in check

---

[1] *I.G.R.R.* I, 707 (Philippopolis), mentioning Rufus υἱὸς Ῥούφου τοῦ Θρακάρχου.

[2] Head[2], p. 793 (Volume of Plates iv, 202, *j*); *I.G.R.R.* I, 132.

[3] de Vogüé, *Inscr. palmyr.* no. 35.

[4] *C.I.L.* III, 6983; Dessau 215.

[5] Head[2], pp. 511, 507, 710, and *I.G.R.R.* III, 328.

[6] Head[2], pp. 714–15; Ptolemy v, 4, 9. For the problems presented by Ninica-Claudiopolis in Cilicia and Claudiopolis in the Calycadnus valley see Sir W. M. Ramsay in *Jahreshefte*, VII, 1904, Beiblatt, col. 76; the foundation was probably Domitian's.

mountainous or frontier districts, so that here again Claudius was completing the work initiated by Augustus when he planted his five colonies in Pisidia and Lycaonia (p. 272). This care for pacification and order explains a change in status which was carried through in 43: the communities of Lycia had been allowed to remain free but used this freedom merely to quarrel among themselves; Claudius decided that they were unfit for freedom and accordingly transformed them into an imperial province under a praetorian *legatus Augusti pro praetore*, the first of whom was Q. Veranius.

In the client-kingdoms Claudius mostly left undisturbed the arrangements of his predecessor, which it would have been unfriendly as well as unjust to upset, but as he gave the kingdom of Bosporus to Mithridates, he was bound to compensate Polemo for the loss, and so presented him with part of Cilicia (p. 752); for the rest, Cotys retained Armenia Minor, Antiochus IV was restored to Commagene and a strip of coast-land in Cilicia, and Sohaemus kept Ituraea, while a brother of King Agrippa was granted the principality of Chalcis. In this region, however, one kingdom and one king demand longer notice because of the light thrown upon Roman policy.

King Agrippa had calculated well in supporting Claudius; his reward was not only the confirmation of the privileges of the Alexandrian Jews in particular and of Jews throughout the empire in general but the enlargement of his own kingdom, which now comprised Judaea proper, Samaria, Trachonitis, Auranitis, Abilene and districts round Lebanon. It amounted to a reconstitution of the realm of Herod the Great, and was at once a generous present to a friend and a skilful move for reducing and soothing the anger and indignation Gaius had stirred up among the Jews. For the time being it was highly successful, for Agrippa used his opportunities with his customary ability. By October 41 he was back in Jerusalem. While he never concealed his friendship to Rome and her ruler, calling himself *Philokaisar* and *Philoromaios* on his coins and inscriptions, and while he made magnificent presents to a Gentile city like Berytus, he yet managed to keep on good terms with the Jewish population and priesthood, by whom his memory was treasured after death[1]. But his restless intriguing spirit created uneasiness; in 42 he began the refortification of Jerusalem, and the governor of Syria, Vibius Marsus, promptly intervened. The next year came a meeting with various other kings at Tiberias, Herod of Chalcis (who had married Agrippa's

[1] H. L. Strack-P. Billerbeck, *Kommentar zum Neuen Testament aus Talmud und Midrasch*, pp. 34, 124, 709 *sq.*

daughter Berenice), Antiochus IV of Commagene (whose son was to marry his daughter Drusilla), Polemo of Pontus, Cotys of Armenia Minor and Sampsiceramus of Emesa. It looked suspiciously like the formation of some common policy among the frontier-kingdoms, and Vibius abruptly broke up the conference[1]. Agrippa had to swallow his annoyance and his death in 44 relieved Rome of any more anxiety, but it is significant that Claudius allowed himself to be advised that the young son, Agrippa, then at Rome, had better not succeed to the large kingdom of his father; it was turned into a province and placed apparently under two procurators[2]. The decision was unfortunate; even so direct Roman rule over a sensitive race might have been mitigated by good rulers, but the procurators sent out were little credit to the imperial administration, and their choice reveals the influence that his freedmen could exert over Claudius.

Yet the reason for the decision is not far to seek: it was certainly not hostility to the young Agrippa, for in A.D. 50 Claudius sent him out to rule Chalcis after his uncle's death and three years later added to it Philip's tetrarchy together with Batanaea, Trachonitis and Abilene. It should be remembered that the marriage-alliances offered by King Agrippa often carried with them a request to embrace the Jewish religion in its strictest form including circumcision, and however friendly Claudius might be personally to Agrippa or however ready to see injustices to the Jews righted, he could not view with favour the formation of a block of frontier-kingdoms united both by marriage-ties and religion. He had no wish to see Judaism spreading any farther, just as he had no wish to see Druidism among Roman citizens; his putting-down of Druidism and his expulsion of the Jews from Rome in 49 (p. 500) are all pieces of the same policy.

It should be noted that though some five or six provinces were thus added to the empire equilibrium was not maintained between senatorial and imperial; true, Claudius restored Achaea and Macedonia to the Senate[3], but the new territories of Mauretania and Britain (to say nothing of Thrace and Judaea) made a vast accession to the area ruled directly by the *princeps*. Some of the kingdoms remaining were brought into a closer relationship to the

---

[1] Josephus, *Ant.* XIX [8, 1], 338–41.

[2] Josephus, *Ant.* XIX [8, 2], 351 places Agrippa's death definitely in A.D. 44; Tacitus, *Ann.* XII, 23 may be a confusion with Herod of Chalcis who died in 48. On the chronological question see K. Lake, *Beginnings of Christianity*, v, pp. 450 *sqq.*

[3] Dio LX, 24.

princeps by a device which seems to have been an invention of
Claudius himself; inscriptions reveal that Cogidubnus in Britain
(p. 800), Cottius in the Alps (who now regained the royal title
which had been borne by his father), and Laco dynast of Sparta,
were ready to call themselves *legatus* or *procurator Augusti* and
so were in effect imperial officials rather than bound by treaty to
the Roman People[1]. And though Britain and Lycia were reserved
for senators, the two Mauretanias and Judaea and Thrace were to
be governed by Equites.

Within the enlarged empire Claudius carried on zealously the
improvement of communications, the suppression of brigandage
or rioting, and all those duties which fell to the *princeps* as protector of the State; what those entailed has already been seen under
the reigns of Augustus and Tiberius and there is no need to enter
into complete detail. Few provinces but bear traces of his road-
making, while disorders were punished and put down speedily. A
German chief, Gannascus, who was indulging in piratical raids
upon the north Gallic coast, was hunted down and killed. In
Cilicia the mountain Cietae, after twenty years quiet, revolted
again and laid siege to Anemurium, but Antiochus IV, aided by
some cavalry sent from Syria, had little difficulty in suppressing
them. Some differences among the citizens of Delphi, upon which
the pro-consul of Achaea, L. Junius Gallio, duly reported were
serious enough to need a despatch from Claudius, in which he
protests his veneration for Apollo, but the main text is unfortunately missing[2]. The punishment of the Lycians has already been
seen; a riot in A.D. 44 at Rhodes, in which some Roman citizens
were crucified, was answered by deprivation of liberty, but the city
was too eminent to be degraded for long and when in 53 Nero
pleaded its cause before the Senate it regained its freedom.

One city alone presented a lasting problem, Alexandria, with
its bi-racial population; embassies from Greeks and Jews were
heard by Claudius in his first year, and a late tradition records that
Philo was bidden declaim his writings in the Senate-house and
that members were amazed—a statement that will surprise no
one who has endured to read much of him. Although Claudius

---

[1] *C.I.L.* VII, 11; Dio LX, 24, 4, and Dessau 94; West, *op. cit.* VIII, p. 68.
[2] This is the Gallio of Acts xviii, 12–17: the text of the letter in Ditt.[3]
801 D is datable to the first seven months A.D. 52. Assuming that Gallio's
malaria (Seneca, *Epist. Mor.* 104) made it inadvisable for him to stay more than
a year, his proconsulship could be dated from July 51 to July 52, and this
date is important for the chronology of St Paul's travels see Lake, *op. cit.*
pp. 462 *sqq.* But the assumption, though likely, cannot be proved.

confirmed the privileges of the Alexandrian Jews, nine months later came a statesmanlike letter in which he counselled both parties to keep the peace and live at unity within their city; otherwise he would have to show them 'what the wrath of an aggrieved *princeps* can be'—no idle threat as the Lycians were to find (see above, p. 680). For the moment things quietened down so that by April of 42 a dedicator could celebrate the Peace and Concord of Claudius[1], but hostility still smouldered below the surface. And the evil was not confined to Alexandria but spread up into Palestine and Syria: Malalas[2] retains a confused tradition of trouble between Greeks and Jews in Antioch at the end of Gaius' reign (p. 661), and when in 44 the Jews had to mourn the death of their protector Agrippa the Greeks of Caesarea gleefully poured libations to Charon. The pages of Philo's invective against Flaccus, Josephus' controversies with Apion, or the fragments of that strange literature christened by modern scholars 'Pagan Acts of the Martyrs' (wherein the champions of Alexandrian Hellenism, an Isidorus or Hermaiscus, rebuke the 'brutality' of Roman emperors and complain against the domination of the emperor's councils by 'godless Jews') can still give some pale idea of the vehement hatreds these racial enmities inspired, and which caused Rome a natural anxiety[3].

Government seems to have been equitable save where a freedman's avarice or ambition interfered, as in Judaea where the atrocious conduct of Felix was shielded by his brother Pallas (p. 854). We hear of a governor exiled for taking bribes, of charges of extortion preferred against Statilius Taurus after his tenure of Africa and against C. Cadius Rufus the pro-consul of Bithynia[4]. Indeed, Claudius took special care that the guilty should not escape justice, by refusing to give a post to a retiring official until an interval had elapsed in which he could be brought to trial[5]. Disaster or hardship were substantially relieved: Apamea, badly damaged by an earthquake, had its tribute remitted over five years, and like help was given to the cities of Crete and to Ephesus and Smyrna when they too were shaken[6]; Byzantium, exhausted

---

[1] *I.G.R.R.* I, 1165 (= *O.G.I.S.* 663).   [2] x, 244, 18 *sqq.*

[3] For the literature on the Isidorus *Acta*, etc., see the bibliography to Chapter x, section B, 8, Jews.

[4] Dio LX, 25, 4; Tacitus, *Ann.* XII, 59 and 22. Xiphilinus, p. 145, records an anecdote that Narcissus cheated Claudius to save Junius Cilo (whom he wrongly terms governor of Bithynia) from trial for extortion.

[5] Dio LX, 25, 4

[6] Perhaps the Κλαυδία βουλή at Tralles represents gratitude for a grant of help after the earthquake; Head[2], p. 660.

by recent wars in Bosporus and Thrace, received a remission
for five years; the court physician Xenophon was able to gain
immunity for his native island of Cos, and Ilium was granted
complete exemption from all burdens in the year 53 when Nero
pleaded its cause[1]. The list could be extended, but there is no need
to do so, or gather more proofs that Claudius possessed a deep
and genuine sense of the responsibility of the position to which
he had been called; it was customary for the newly chosen imperial
legates to thank the emperor for the favour vouchsafed them, but
Claudius would not have it and took a different view: 'it is I who
should thank them,' he declared, 'because they willingly help me
in bearing the burden of rule[2].' For rule was a burden, and justice
difficult because of the wickedness or the lack of interest of mankind, against which he inveighed more than once[3]. But to everything, whether it was a large and comprehensive scheme for
lightening both Italy and the provinces of the heavy cost of the
imperial postal service, or regulations for the precise date by
which senatorial governors—who were sometimes reluctant to
leave the capital—should depart for their provinces, he gave the
same minute and conscientious attention.

Few of his contemporaries could appreciate this sense of
responsibility any more than they could understand his attitude
towards citizenship or municipal rights. Yet Claudius was wiser
than they. His historical studies had convinced him that Rome
owed much to her readiness in former times to incorporate in the
citizen body men of merit; and on one of the few occasions when
she had obstinately refused she had nearly succumbed to civil war;
he realized that Gallic or Spanish or African notables, Greek and
Asiatic doctors, scientists and men of letters could all play a useful
part in the State. He was sometimes prepared to stretch a point
even, as is shown by the famous case of the Anauni, Tulliasses and
Sinduni, tribes attributed to the municipality of Tridentum. These
tribes, thanks to their bond with Tridentum, had in the course of
years usurped the rights of full citizens, and an informer had
questioned their status. Claudius, in an edict[4], while he recognized
the weakness of their claim, nevertheless graciously confirmed to
the tribesmen *de iure* all the rights they had held *de facto*, and the
reasons he gives are interesting: many of the men were serving

---

[1] Tacitus, *Ann.* XII, 63; 61; 58.   [2] Dio LX, 11, 7.
[3] As in the Tegea edict, Dessau 217, or the letter to Ephesus, *S.E.G.* IV,
516 B. With this may be compared his remark about the lack of interest
in *bonae artes*, Tacitus, *Ann.* XI, 15.
[4] Dessau 206.

already in his Praetorian Guard, or were holding a centurion's post in the legions, or were on the roll of jurors at Rome, and any cancellation would also involve grave injury to the flourishing town of Tridentum itself. It was a wise decision, but one need only compare it with the treatment he meted out to freedmen who had usurped equestrian rank—reducing them to slavery[1]—to discern that what weighed with him on this occasion were considerations of equity and past service, and no mere vague unregulated enthusiasm. Citizenship was a pearl of price, and a Roman citizen must speak the Roman language; he did not hesitate to take it away from a distinguished Greek who had shown that he did not know Latin[2].

Yet if contemporaries in Rome could not appreciate, the provincials whether in East or West could and did, and numerous inscriptions, as in the time of Tiberius, testify to the regard in which he was held, more especially in the Greek East, where the number of Tiberii Claudii (many of whom owed their citizenship to him)[3] is large and important. In Rome and Italy Claudius would not accept the title Imperator and refused worship as a god; to the Greek East he was *Autokrator* and *Theos* naturally and by no constraint. Though at Amastris an imperial official might show an elegant respect for Claudius' scruples by a dedication 'pro Pace Augusta et in honorem Tib. Claudii Germanici Augusti,' in Pisidia, Caria or Lydia he was a god and worshipped as such, and Ephesus celebrated as 'the marriage of gods' the union of Claudius and Agrippina[4]. It was their mode of showing gratitude, as they had done to other rulers before, but to few could it have been shown more justly than Claudius.

VI. CLAUDIUS AS RE-ORGANIZER AND LEGISLATOR

While Tiberius had followed rigidly the instructions of Augustus Claudius was not afraid of innovation. The progressiveness that has been seen in his treatment of the provinces is no less visible at home and in Italy. The Senate slowly begins to lose something of its status as a partner and the *princeps* gains by the

---

[1] Suetonius, *Claud.* 25.
[2] Dio lx, 17, 4; Suetonius, *Claud.* 25.
[3] But see C. S. Walton in *J.R.S.* xix, 1929, p. 42 *sq.*
[4] Amastris, Dessau 5883; Caria, *I.G.R.R.* iii, 83, and Pisidia, *ib.* 328: dedication to Claudius and Apollo at Nymphaeum, J. Keil in *Anatolian Studies presented to Sir W. M. Ramsay*, p. 247; Ephesus and the *theogamia*, Head, *H.N.*[2], p. 577.

gradual centralization of power into his hands, and by possessing a large and properly organized body of officials through which to administer this power. This re-organization is usually associated with the names of the influential freedmen of Claudius—Narcissus, Pallas, Callistus, Polybius and others—and it is therefore possible to assume that it was due to clever and unscrupulous servants who imposed a scheme of things at once profitable to themselves and gratifying to their vanity upon a weak master, an assumption which can find some support from the literary tradition, which loved to depict the Emperor as the credulous slave of his wives and freedmen, a picture true only of his latest years[1]. Yet apart from the presumption that a ruler is entitled to credit for what his subordinates do well—for the choice of ministers is his—another consideration makes the view less likely. Thanks to the discoveries of inscriptions and papyri the world of to-day possesses a considerable number of documents issued under Claudius' seal during the years of his Principate, all bearing the stamp of a distinctive style and mode of thought[2] that agrees well with what we know of Claudius and not at all with what we hear of Narcissus or of other freedmen. It is reasonable to infer that the attitude towards imperial problems and the political conceptions revealed in these documents are those of Claudius, and we can feel sure that the will that directed these various measures—here removing burdens, there cancelling inequities, taking a paternal interest in the affairs of his subjects and counselling them to live in concord—was the will of Claudius himself, not that of his freedmen.

The first signs were a re-ordering of the personal staff of the *princeps*, for which the time was overdue. The deaths of Livia or Antonia or Germanicus had added vastly to the imperial private estate, while the confiscated property of such men as Silius or Sejanus (which had been claimed, fairly enough, for the fiscus) and the wholesale robberies of Gaius meant an enormous increase in what may be called the Crown lands; when to all this is added the creation of new provinces, the burden of responsibilities and of routine business devolving on the *princeps* must have been formidable in its extent. Claudius could not possibly oversee all himself and he took the decisive step of creating special departments of what may be termed a Civil Service, each department

---

[1] Hirschfeld, *op. cit.* pp. 471 *sqq.*, but cf. Rostovtzeff, *op. cit.* p. 89 (citing J. G. C. Anderson).

[2] On the style of Claudius see esp. J. Cameron in *C.Q.* xx, 1926, p. 45 and J. Stroux in *Sitz. der Bay. Akad.* VIII, 1929, no. 8.

being controlled by a freedman—with a staff of other freedmen or slave assistants at his disposal—to deal with the various branches of his duties.

The most influential, though perhaps not the most noticeable, of these new posts was the office of Secretary-General, *ab epistulis*, held by Narcissus. All correspondence, whether in Greek or Latin, must have been opened, scanned and sorted in his bureau, before being forwarded to the proper department, reports from governors, letters and dispatches from accredited officials, addresses from cities or communities[1]; his knowledge alone made him indispensable and gave him a decisive voice in the deliberations of the *princeps*. Second only to him stood the Financial Secretary, *a rationibus*, Pallas. A notable development in Claudius' reign is the centralization of financial power in the hands of the emperor: inscriptions reveal an imperial procurator controlling the collection of the *vicesima hereditatum* even in a Senatorial province, and new imperial officials diverted the tax on manumission (*vicesima libertatis*) from the Aerarium to the emperor's[2] chest. And the evidence, sparse though it is, suggests that out of the various accounting departments one central Treasury-chest was now established, and called the Fiscus[3]. Over this complicated and vast machine the 'custos principalium opum,' as Pallas is termed in a magniloquent decree passed in his favour by the Senate, must have presided, and it may be assumed that he also exercised supervision over the procurator of the *patrimonium*, which now became a separate post. Opportunities for money-making in this sphere must have been extensive, and Pallas acquired an evil renown for wealth and arrogance; but tradition represents Narcissus as the real power behind the throne until the last years when the combination of Agrippina and Pallas proved too strong for him. These two offices were the most important, but there were others: there were the secretary *a libellis*, whose task it was to deal with all petitions and requests that were offered in person to the *princeps*, and to which a reply would be given by *subscriptio*; also the secretary *a cognitionibus*, whose business it would be to set in order and prepare all correspondence, papers and *dossiers* relating to the judicial cases brought before the *princeps*, and his influence must

---

[1] On the distinction between *epistula* and *libellus* see U. Wilcken in *Hermes*, LV, 1920, pp. 1 *sqq.*

[2] Dessau 1546; *C.I.L.* VI, 8450*a* and 8451; Hirschfeld, *op. cit.* pp. 96, 106.

[3] Ditt.[3] 800 (Lycosura) recalls how Nicasippos ἀπέδωκεν ἐκ τοῦ ἰδίου βίου τῷ φίσκῳ; cf. Seneca, *de clementia*, VII, 6, 3.

have been all the greater for the lively interest that Claudius displayed in jurisdiction[1]. The exact functions of the secretary *a studiis* are more doubtful, but it is not improbable that he was responsible for looking after the private library of the *princeps*, and helped him with references and material for his speeches and edicts. Others too there may have been, but the five here mentioned were outstanding, and their institution can confidently be dated to Claudius' reign and initiative.

At first glance this may not appear so much. No one would deny that secretaries similar to these had existed before, that we know of secretaries among the slaves and freedmen of Tiberius (p. 647) and that Philo mentions a freedman of Gaius, Homilus by name, whose duty it apparently was to receive letters and petitions[2]. Nevertheless Claudius' action marks a great advance: separate departments were now first constituted, each with a specialized personnel and definite sphere of activity, which gave the princeps an organization and efficiency superior to anything previously known in Rome, and more significant still, the heads of these departments not only had the power but were slowly in appearance given the status and dignity of public officials. Narcissus was allowed to wear the dagger of military office (*pugio*) and to address the soldiers; he was given the *ornamenta quaestoria* and Pallas the *ornamenta praetoria*; another freedman, Antonius Felix, commanded Roman troops in Judaea, and on another, Harpocras, was conferred the magisterial privilege of giving civic games.

A further step was taken in 53, when Claudius persuaded the Senate to grant to the imperial procurators in the provinces the right of jurisdiction: hitherto any contested claim of the fiscus would naturally have come before the senatorial or imperial governor for his decision; henceforward the procurators were competent in this sphere. The measure was presumably designed to increase efficiency by expediting the collection of monies due, but even though the competence of the procurators was limited to financial cases, it established an independent authority in the province, who was not prepared to truckle to the governor, and might easily overstep the not very clearly defined limits of his power. In the reign of Nero the imperial governor of Galatia and the procurator of an imperial domain at Tymbrianassus are found acting as equals in deciding a boundary question between Saga-

[1] In the *Apocolocyntosis* (15) it is therefore a fitting punishment that Claudius is finally handed over to act as a clerk to Menander, who is the *a cognitionibus* for Aeacus, the judge of the underworld.

[2] Homilus 'ἐπὶ τῶν πρεσβειῶν,' Philo, *Legatio*, 181.

lassus and the domain[1]. Slowly there was beginning to grow up a new nobility beside the senatorial aristocracy. Though there existed senators who would accept office under the *princeps* or co-operate with him others were too proud or too timid, and in addition Claudius had not, during his early years, moved sufficiently in senatorial society to have a large number of friends there upon whom he could rely. Naturally enough he fell back on knights or freedmen and those who had been his associates during the days of his obscurity; they were not too proud to hold unimportant offices at first and could be advanced by their own competency. He re-organized the *cursus honorum* of the equestrian order (though his re-organization was not lasting), and was prepared to promote to its ranks men even of Greek or Asiatic birth; thus Xenophon, the court physician and his brother Tiberius Claudius Cleonymus were military tribunes in Roman legions[2]. As the monarchies of sixteenth-century France or England in breaking loose from the feudal nobility and moving towards centralized power found their best instruments in a class distinct from the old nobility, so did the Principate.

Still all this was a development within the *princeps'* own province: far more momentous therefore was the gradual appropriation by Claudius of powers which till now had fallen within the sphere of the Senate. The old *quaestores classici* had outlived their usefulness; the two surviving ones were now abolished, for the Prefects of the fleets at Misenum and Ravenna could attend to their duties[3], and the Ostian quaestor was replaced by an imperial procurator of the new harbour (*procurator portus Ostiensis*). For Claudius, warned by the threat of a shortage of corn which occurred just after Gaius' death, determined to safeguard the supply and storage, and, more significant still, to make the cost a charge on the fiscus. Compensation for damage from storm was offered to transporters, bounties and privileges to ship-builders, and some three miles north of Ostia extensive harbour-works were begun, to protect shipping, and new granaries were built. In the capital, the imperial *praefectus annonae*, with a staff of freedman procurators, presided over the supply and accounting, though the distribution was apparently still managed by the senatorial *praefectus*

---

[1] *I.G.R.R.* III, 335 (Sagalassus). In Tacitus, *Agric.* 9, Agricola is praised for being 'procul a contentione adversus procuratores.'

[2] Suetonius, *Claud.* 25; Ditt.[3] 804 and 805.

[3] A. Momigliano, *L'opera dell' imperatore Claudio*, pp. 99 *sqq.* The reference in the English edition (which appeared too late to be used for this chapter) is pp. 51 *sqq.*

frumenti dandi[1]. Other departments, too, the Princeps took into his charge. The care of the roads and streets in Rome was transferred from the quaestors to imperial officials and the cost placed on the fiscus. Aqueducts had been so far controlled by a consular *curator aquarum* with senatorial assistants; when Claudius constructed his new aqueducts—the Anio Novus and Aqua Claudia, works of his censorship—he also added a freedman procurator with a staff of slaves to look after them, and this item too was presumably charged to the fiscus. To connect the imperial harbour near Ostia with the Tiber a new channel was dug, which helped also to lessen the risks of flooding, and henceforward the five members of the Board of Curators of the Tiber held office 'ex auctoritate principis[2].' The Senate was losing its power even over those departments which had been left to it by Augustus in Italy and which had so far been regarded as peculiarly its own.

In yet other ways Claudius encroached on the authority of the Senate. Since 23 B.C. the management of the Aerarium Saturni had lain with two praetors selected by lot (p. 195); its accounts were apparently in some disorder, and so in 42 Claudius had three ex-praetors appointed, with *imperium*, to collect all debts owing to it[3]; two years later, when order had presumably been re-established, he made an apparent return to older tradition by restoring the supervision to two quaestors. It may have looked like compensation for the abolition of the quaestorial provinces, but these quaestors were not chosen by lot, as of old, but were nominated by the *princeps* to hold office for three years, and in effect the old Republican treasury was now controlled by imperial officials[4]. If Dio's statement could be trusted, on some occasions Claudius actually nominated governors for the senatorial provinces, but the only attested instance is that of Galba in Africa from 44 to 46 (p. 674), and this was presumably an appointment for a special purpose, like the recommendation of M'. Lepidus and Junius Blaesus by Tiberius in A.D. 20, and it may be equally inferred that Claudius presented the name of Galba to the Senate[5].

[1] Suetonius, *Claud.* 18–20; Seneca, *de brev. vit.* 18 *sq.*; Hirschfeld, *op. cit.* p. 236, no. 3; Momigliano, *op. cit.* p. 97 (Eng. edit. p. 50).

[2] Mommsen, *Staatsrecht*, II³, p. 1050.

[3] Dio LX, 10, 4. Similarly an ex-praetor, Acilius Strabo, was sent to investigate the illegal occupation of domanial land in Cyrene; Tacitus, *Ann.* XIV, 18.

[4] Tacitus, *Ann.* XIII, 29; Suetonius, *Claud.* 24; Dio LX, 24; cf. Mommsen, *op. cit.* II³, p. 559, and Momigliano, *op. cit.* p. 93 (Eng. edit. p. 46).

[5] Dio LX, 25, 6; Suetonius, *Galba* 7. Dio is not always impeccable on such matters, and it looks here as though he is generalizing from the particular case of Galba.

This being so, it is not surprising that the *princeps* began to take control to some extent of the Senate. Attendance at meetings was strictly enforced and absenteeism punished; the debates ought to be serious and real, not merely a matter of formal assent. Claudius therefore took over the right to grant leave of absence to senators, by a decree of the Senate itself, though members were free to visit their estates in Sicily, and in Narbonese Gaul after 49, without such permission [1]. His tenure of the censorship in 47/48 gave him an opportunity to revise the list thoroughly, to cast out unsuitable members and bring in men of standing even from the provinces, for he meant the Senate to be worthy of its high position and to include in it the best brains of the empire. Men might be helped in their official career by the grant of honorary rank, and by this fictitious service (*militia imaginaria*) could advance more rapidly. But he had no intention of superseding the Senate or of making himself absolute master of it; he only held the censorship once and for the traditional eighteen months, not continuously as Domitian was to do, and he did not unduly influence the Senate's composition. Indeed he preferred to use its prestige for many of his enactments, and the number of *senatus consulta* passed during his reign is considerable. Since the majority of them were inspired by Claudius it is fitting to review his legislative activity here.

Many elements can be noted that seem at first curiously juxtaposed—an interest in law and the courts, an eagerness to put down abuses, a paternalist spirit and common-sense practicality. But they are all component parts in a character that had a natural bent for tidiness and good order and was not afraid of reform. It is typical of his strong practicality that he abolished the custom that had grown up in the Senate of reciting at the start of each year certain speeches of Augustus and Tiberius, and suppressed many holidays and festivals in order to save time and expedite business, especially in the courts [2]. For jurisdiction was a passion with him: he was accused of spending too much time in the courts and supervising everything, but it may be conjectured that after four years of Gaius the administration of law had not improved. Men could not tell what the new emperor would be like; it had become terribly easy for informers to bring malicious or trivial charges, which no praetor would dare dismiss for fear of wrath from above; a man accused might easily find himself in a prejudiced position, and Claudius announced publicly his determina-

---

[1] Dio LX, 11, 8; 25, 6, 7; Tacitus, *Ann.* XII, 23.
[2] Dio LX, 10, 2; 17, 1.

tion to break 'the tyranny of the accusers[1].' There can be no doubt that many abuses in the judicial system were put straight. Time-wasting tactics got short shrift: as defendants, fearing an adverse verdict, were apt either not to appear or else to send excuses, he gave warning that he would decide against all absentees after a stated interval; if the jurors could not come to a decision in the proper time, he suggested roundly that they would have to sit during the vacation; while if a prosecutor put in a charge and then left it pending, the praetor was now empowered to cite him—after the expiry of the period allowed for collecting evidence—and (if he did not then appear or offer reasonable excuse) to pronounce him guilty of *calumnia*, which would involve the deprivation of civil rights.

Certain minor reforms attest his care: in order to fill up the roll of the five decuries (p. 656), Claudius lowered the age limit to 24 years, though he retained the former limit of 25 for the court of the *recuperatores* and for more serious cases. The huge fees paid to advocates had become a scandal; he realized that to re-enact the hoary Lex Cincia (invoked by traditionalists) would be absurd and impracticable, but he persuaded the Senate to set some legal bounds to the amount payable. But while he speeded up procedure and cleared away much lumber by this work he had no wish to abolish good old customs: he praised and recommended to defendants the traditional practice of wearing mourning to excite sympathy, which appears to have been dying out. Though the sources are apt to dwell on the ludicrous side of Claudius' jurisdiction, he certainly used his influence—even sometimes beyond the law—in favour of equity; punishments were altered in accordance with the merits of the case, and those who had been non-suited through some technicality, as, for example, by demanding more than the precise sum allowed, had their actions restored[2].

In estimating the achievement of Claudius in law-giving it is convenient to consider it as a whole without distinguishing the means employed, whether through the mouthpiece of the Senate or by edict or even by an occasional *lex lata*. Some of the measures passed belong more perhaps to the history of Roman law[3] and need but brief mention here: such are the transference from praetors

---

[1] *Berl. Griech. Urkunden*, 611, upon which and upon Dio LX, 28, 6 the following sentences are based. The writer accepts J. Stroux' contention (*Bay. S.B.* VIII, 1929, no. 8) that the two parts of the papyri belong to one speech. For literature see the Bibliography, section B, II, 5.

[2] Suetonius, *Claud.* 14.

[3] For the history of Roman law under the Empire see Vol. XI.

to consuls of the nomination of guardians for those not *in sua potestate*, and the extension to governors in the provinces of the power to adjudicate on *fideicommissa*; while in Rome itself the consuls, whose duty it had been, were relieved of an unnecessarily heavy burden by shifting the minor cases to two praetors appointed by the *princeps*[1]. Other laws were designed to buttress the structure of society and to preserve the distinctions between grades; Claudius made clear his own attitude by the punishment meted out to freedmen who had usurped equestrian census—and there were many such—whom he ordered to be sold into slavery, as he also did to those who failed to show the proper *obsequium* to their former masters[2]; two *senatus consulta* passed before 47 emphasized the close dependence of a freed slave upon his patron. One, the *S.C.* Largianum of 42, assigned the property of a dead Junian Latin in the first place to the manumitter, and in the second to such of his children as had not been individually disinherited, and finally to his external heirs; the other, the *S.C.* Ostorianum, declared that if a patron specifically assigned a freedman to one of his sons, that son must count as his patron, but that in the event of his death the freedman would then come under the patronage of the remaining children of the manumitter. Later, towards the end of his reign and on the prompting of Pallas, Claudius strove to combat the contamination of free by slave blood through a *senatus consultum* which laid down that a free woman who deliberately entered into concubinage with a slave belonging to another owner, if against the owner's express will, should herself become his slave, while if he consented, though she retained her free status any child of hers would be a slave[3].

Herein Claudius was the upholder of the Augustan hierarchical system of society and of its rigorous enforcement; in other enactments we can trace a spirit, at its worst paternalist, at its best humane and liberal. He himself always refused to accept legacies to the injury or exclusion of natural heirs, and where a man had been condemned and confiscation of goods followed he insisted that the son's *peculium* should be respected. An early edict of his forbade wives to become surety for their husbands and this principle was extended generally (in the *S.C.* Vellaeanum of A.D. 46) so as to prevent a woman becoming surety for any man; such a law might be justified on various grounds, but it is noteworthy that

---

[1] Suetonius, *Claud.* 23; *Dig.* I, 2, 2, 32.
[2] Pliny, *N.H.* xxxiii, 33; Suetonius, *Claud.* 23; *Dig.* xxxvii, 14, 5.
[3] Tacitus, *Ann.* xii, 53, as corrected on some points by Gaius I, 84 and 160.

Ulpian regards it as intended to protect women from victimization, 'since owing to the weakness of their sex they are exposed to many such perils[1],' and its protection was not afforded to those women who meant to act fraudulently; a like intention may perhaps be seen too in the law which freed women from the restriction of agnate guardianship. Some relief was given to the operations of the Lex Papia Poppaea by modifying a clause that had been added under Tiberius (p. 616); henceforward if a man over sixty married, provided that his wife was under fifty, both would escape penalties[2]. Ironical critics have amused themselves by suggesting that the occasion for the modification may have been Claudius' own marriage to Agrippina, but as Claudius was not sixty at the time and as the hardships of the law had already caused trouble (p. 616) this clause may well have been mitigated earlier in the reign[3]. A like humanity may be seen in a law passed in 47 which forbade money-lenders to make advances of money to a young man against his father's death, and still more in an edict issued by Claudius as censor: masters had been accustomed to expose sick slaves in a temple of Aesculapius on an island in the Tiber and so leave them till recovery or death; Claudius decreed that if a slave, thus exposed, recovered he should be a free man, and that if a master, wishing to evade this ruling, killed him to save further expense, he should be put on trial as a murderer[4]. In this care for slaves and weaklings, as in many other of his views, he was in advance of his time and looks forward to the days of Hadrian or the Antonines, who re-enacted or carried further principles that he had laid down. No better compliment could be paid.

Other measures still attest his care for antiquity or for tradition or for the old Roman religion. The art of *haruspicina* which had played so great a part in Roman history was in danger of dying out; Claudius bewailed the lack of interest in such good institutions, and the Senate ordered the college of *pontifices* to take such steps as they deemed needful for its preservation. On the other hand astrologers and soothsayers, who had crowded back again to the capital (p. 629), were once more banished, following the trial of Furius Scribonianus in 52. But the religious policy of the

[1] *Dig.* XVI, 1, 2.   [2] Suetonius, *Claud.* 23, 1.
[3] One law does however reflect the conditions of the marriage, the *senatus consultum* passed in 47 sanctioning marriages between a man and his brother's daughter, though not his sister's: Tacitus, *Ann.* XII, 5–7; Gaius I, 62. For an interesting treatment of the questions, though not convincing to the present writer, see A. Piganiol in *Mélanges Cagnat*, pp. 153 *sqq.*
[4] Tacitus, *Ann.* XI, 13; Suetonius, *Claud.* 25, 2; *Dig.* XL, 8, 2.

Emperor is described elsewhere (p. 498 *sq.*); it will be enough to remark that for all his scholarly conservatism, as in other matters, so here he was no foe to innovations that could plead merit.

One other piece of legislation remains to be discussed, for its full purpose is not usually understood. A *senatus consultum* was passed in the early years of the reign (the *S.C.* Hosidianum) imposing a heavy penalty on those who should buy houses or buildings for the purpose of making a profit by their demolition, and declaring all such sales to be invalid[1]. In the preamble, which refers plainly to the oncoming Ludi Saeculares, is contained a tirade against those who indulge in so destructive a form of money-making and spread ravages as of war in a peaceful country. It is not unusual to find in municipal charters clauses forbidding an owner (without the previous consent of the decurions) to pull down property unless he gives a pledge to rebuild or restore: what excites curiosity here is the size of the fine to be paid by delinquents—double the purchase price—and the fierceness of the denunciation of the practice, and the natural question also arises how a man could hope (save in an exceptional case) to make much profit by demolition and sale of materials. The answer is to be sought in the history of Italian agriculture during the two past generations. Tiberius had pointed out to an audience in the Senate how little Italy produced of its own food-supply, and though he had done much to alleviate the financial and agrarian crisis of 33 (p. 642), the inevitable result of that crisis had been to bring still more land into the hands of wealthy creditors, who had no desire to live on their new estates or indeed to live as farmers at all but preferred to dismantle and pull down existing buildings and turn farms to grazing-land. It is against this class of speculator and absentee landlord that the severity of the law is directed, for it will be observed that it exempts specifically from penalty all who are prepared to settle on their estates (*rerum suarum possessores futuri*) and work for their improvement[2].

The evil was old indeed, but Claudius was doing what he could. Another example of his anxiety about agriculture may be seen in what is commonly regarded merely as a spectacular feat of engineering, the draining of the Fucine Lake in the Marsian Hills. The fluctuations in its level and the unhealthiness of its marshes

---

[1] Bruns, *Fontes*[7], 54; Dessau 6043.
[2] For the view here adopted see F.-G. de Pachtère in *Mélanges Cagnat*, pp. 169 *sqq.*, and for the growth of large estates during the first century see Rostovtzeff, *op. cit.* p. 115 (German edition, p. 84 *sq.*). See, however, W. E. Heitland, *Agricola*, p. 290 *sq.*

endangered the safety of the dwellers around and any land reclaimed could be put to profitable use, for private companies had offered to attempt the work provided they were allowed the land in freehold. During eleven years some 30,000 men were employed in tunnelling for over three miles through the limestone of Monte Salviano, and the opening was celebrated by an elaborate spectacle to which people flocked from miles around[1]. More important, however, was the fact that some hundreds of acres of land were reclaimed for cultivation, upon which *possessores* could and did settle. In this care for agriculture Claudius was at one with the opinion of his day; the philosopher Musonius Rufus preached a return to the land, declaring that the working of a farm was no hindrance to a philosopher, and might even be an incentive and example to his pupils of the life of strenuous endeavour[2]. That the draining of the lake was not more effective and beneficial was imputed to the avarice of Narcissus; the tunnel was apt to get blocked and need clearing, and Italian farming did not benefit to the extent it might have[3].

But the comparative failure of the enterprise had another and an unexpected result. Agrippina seized the opportunity to accuse Narcissus to her husband, and Narcissus hit back; the latent antagonism between the two broke out openly and Agrippina saw with dismay that Nero might yet be disappointed of the succession by a repentant Claudius. The time had come to act. Once Agrippina's mind was made up the rest was easy. To secure her own safety and the succession of Nero she decided to murder Claudius. Against her she had Narcissus, but Pallas was on her side; Seneca and Burrus would support her from gratitude if nothing else, and though they were of provincial birth they commanded respect in Roman circles. Narcissus left Rome in the autumn of 54 to take a cure at Sinuessa and Agrippina had her chance. She poisoned her husband with a dish of mushrooms[4], and to make assurance doubly sure called in the physician Xenophon to administer the *coup de grâce*. She could not at once pro-

---

[1] Tacitus, *Ann.* XII, 56–7; Suetonius, *Claud.* 20, 21, 6; Dio LX, 11, 5 and 33, 6.

[2] Musonius (Hense), XI, pp. 57–63. Cf. Heitland, *op. cit.* pp. 276–80.

[3] Dessau 302 records a cleaning of the tunnel and a reinstitution of the *possessores*.

[4] The fact is certain though details naturally vary, but Nero's later jest about mushrooms being 'the food of the gods' has no point unless it refers to the last meal of Claudius. See Pliny, *N.H.* XXII, 92; Tacitus, *Ann.* XII, 66, 67; Suetonius, *Claud.* 44, and Dio LX, 34, 35.

ceed with the proclamation of her son, for her astrologers warned
her the hour was not yet propitious, so the news of Claudius'
death was kept back: but Burrus was given his instructions and
Seneca busied himself with Nero's inaugural speeches.

VII. THE GOOD AND EVIL OF THE REIGN

Thus after a reign of a little less than fourteen years Claudius
vanished from the scene. The preceding sections have described his
various activities, and now some final estimate must be attempted.
In the provinces there were many to remember him gratefully, in
Rome fewer, yet in spite of the executions that stained his Principate he was not the victim of any revulsion of feeling such as
followed Tiberius or Gaius, his memory was not condemned, and
he was the first of the successors of Augustus to be given the
honour of deification. The really unpopular parts of his rule are
easily discerned from Nero's opening programme to the Senate:
what men had objected to was Claudius' absorption in the courts,
the abuse of trials *intra cubiculum principis*, the power of the freedmen, and the gradual encroachment upon the rights of the Senate;
all this the young ruler promised he would renounce[1].

It was the Senate in fact which most had felt itself in danger
from Claudius, but what that meant must be carefully defined.
Claudius had no idea of dispossessing the Senate[2] or of antiquating
it, like Gaius; his historical sense was too keen. But he did intend
the Senate to take its duties seriously and to share his views as
to the responsibilities of a ruling class. Some were prepared to
co-operate with him—there was no lack of willing governors for
the provinces—but if they were not they must make room for those
whom the Princeps knew to be more able or more conscientious or
better fitted. On some of the Senate's functions in Italy he undoubtedly did encroach, but the great bulk of its duties was left
unharmed, and he did all he could to safeguard its prestige and
high position[3] and to recall the more inert to a realization of these.
'If these proposals,' he said, in recommending some judicial
reforms, 'are approved by you, show your assent at once plainly
and sincerely. If, however, you do not approve them then find

[1] Tacitus, *Ann.* XIII, 4; Suetonius, *Nero*, 10. The *Apocolocyntosis* after
ridiculing Claudius' passion for hearing trials declares that the new ruler
'legum silentia rumpet.'

[2] The automatic recognition of treaties made by Claudius or his generals
was apparently temporary, for Britain only; Dio LX, 23, 6.

[3] Special seats in the theatre were assigned by Claudius to senators;
Dio LX, 7, 4.

some other remedies, but here in this temple now, or if you wish to take a longer time for consideration, take it, so long as you recollect that wherever you meet you should produce an opinion of your own. For it is extremely unfitting, Conscript Fathers, to the high dignity of this order that at this meeting one man only, the consul designate, should make a speech (and that copied exactly from the proposal of the consuls), while the rest utter one word only, "Agreed," and then after leaving the House remark "There, we've given our opinion"[1].' This was the lesson that Claudius would have the Senate learn, but earnest though he was he could impart it with a touch of humour that lightened it, and these are not the words of a master who holds the whip-hand, but of one reasoning with equals.

Indeed, as senators these nobles had nothing to fear from Claudius; what was dangerous was to be rich or popular with the army or a descendant of the divine Augustus. Riches attracted the greed and envy of the freedmen or wives of Claudius; and if in addition the victim possessed a famous name, or the loyalty of the legions, or claimed descent from Augustus, then the simplest way to incriminate him was to suggest that he was a conspirator or possible rebel and have the case heard in secrecy. There was little likelihood of pardon from an emperor whose timidity or superstition was only too easily excited, who was well aware of his own bodily infirmities and remembered that his predecessor had been assassinated. But this does not prove that the Senate was useless or abject: there were no heroics from a Thrasea Paetus (p. 730), because there was no call for them; there was plenty of honest discussion. Nor was it as servile as is sometimes supposed. Even in the days when Agrippina's power was high she could not save one of her agents (Tarquitius Priscus, who had successfully attacked Statilius Taurus for her) from ignominious expulsion. The Senate could still be a partner as Augustus had wished.

But though Claudius could look to the Senate to supply him with governors and generals—an Aulus Plautius or a Didius Gallus—and confidential advisers such as L. Vitellius (in whose charge he left the empire during his journey to and from Britain), for his personal assistants he turned mostly to the equites. Though there were incompetents, a man such as L. Julius Vestinus, who carried out important duties with skill and tact, could win his praise as an 'ornament of the equestrian order,' and into this order he was ready to promote freedmen of tried merit or centurions of good service, such as the Baebius Atticus who governed

1 *B.G.U.* 611.

Noricum as procurator at the crown of his career[1]. On this order a *princeps* was bound to rely ultimately for the bulk of his higher civil servants, and a generation later we find Vitellius choosing his chief secretaries from it rather than from the unpopular freedmen. And there is evidence that Claudius was prepared to bestow knighthood and important office upon Greeks or Jews or men of non-Roman extraction from the Eastern provinces; the instances of Xenophon and his brother Cleonymus have already been noticed, Tiberius Julius Alexander was chosen to govern Judaea and under Nero gave honourable service in Egypt, and these were not the only able non-Romans to win honour and a career from the emperor. For the equestrian order therefore privileges were carefully guarded, and in his censorship, on the accusation of Flavius Proculus, Claudius punished with enslavement some four hundred men who had usurped these privileges[2].

Such was his attitude to the two great orders of Roman society; what he did for the more efficient government of the Empire and towards the gradual equalization of the provincials with Romans has already been discussed. His treatment of the provinces arose out of no mere amiability but from a very real sense of the continuity of the Roman historical process, a process that owed its impulse to the wise admission of precedent: 'illa potius cogitetis,' was his reply to possible objectors, 'quam multa in hac civitate *novata* sint.' He used the past not as so many do as a contrast or as an objection to the future but as a justification and encouragement for still bolder measures.

Were this the whole story Claudius would unhesitatingly be entitled to a place among the greater rulers of Rome, but it is not. Inevitably, with the new efficient secretariate and with increased centralization, the Principate began to draw near to the outward form of a monarchy; the *princeps* and his family were becoming a royal family, raised above the citizens and protected by body-guards, his house a palace with courtiers, ceremonial and intrigues. The wife of the *princeps* begins to assume an importance that would have scandalized Augustus or Tiberius: magistrates celebrated the birthday of Messallina and offered vows for her, and at the British triumph she was allowed to follow her husband's chariot in a *carpentum*, a carriage reserved for Vestal Virgins and priests on solemn occasions. Agrippina was still more exalted; men had spoken jeeringly of Messallina as a queen[3], but she

---

[1] *C.I.L.* v, 1838 (= Dessau 1349).
[2] Pliny, *N.H.* xxxiii, 33; Suetonius, *Claud.* 25.
[3] Pliny, *N.H.* xxix, 20.

nearly turned the gibe into earnest; at public spectacles, even at military parades, she would appear gorgeously robed by the side of Claudius, the privilege of using the *carpentum* and the title *Augusta* were conferred upon her in 50, and Colonia Agrippinensis (Cologne) was named in her honour. The Princeps Iuventutis, Nero, like some young Hellenistic prince, was given the head of the Alexandrian Museum, Chaeremon the Stoic, for his tutor in Greek[1], and the most famous literary man of his day, Seneca, for his instructor in things Roman.

Nor was this all. While this development was contrary to Roman tradition and sentiment and to Augustus' intentions, there were men happy enough to forward a process which proved profitable to themselves. While smaller fry like Suillius Rufus or Tarquitius Priscus grew rich on accusations, greater men such as Seneca or Vitellius adapted themselves to furthering their rulers' purposes. When Messallina coveted the gardens of Valerius Asiaticus it was on Vitellius' eloquence that she relied to secure condemnation, and when Agrippina wished to break the betrothal between Junius Silanus and Octavia—so that she could be married to Nero—who but the faithful Vitellius could be found to inform Claudius of the distressing rumour that Silanus had committed incest with his sister, Junia Calvina[2]? Thanks to such courtiers and their fellows the language of a divine monarchy was beginning to make headway and phrases Tiberius had deprecated were now freely applied. Men could speak of the majesty of the ruler (*tanta maiestas ducis*), of Claudius' sacred hands or sacred duties, Scribonius Largus writes openly of 'our god Caesar.' The fulsome tone of the *senatus consultum* passed in honour of Pallas, which the younger Pliny reproduces with a commentary of indignant interjections[3], reveals to what a depth flattery of the freedmen could sink. For these court officials, despised and hated, were also to be feared and propitiated and liked to abase the pride of a Roman: 'I have seen,' writes Seneca, 'the former master of Callistus stand before his door and be refused admittance while others passed in[4],' and Seneca himself from his exile in Corsica courted the goodwill of Polybius in language that pains his admirers.

---

[1] H. R. Schwyzer, *Chairemon*, pp. 8–12.

[2] Tacitus, *Ann.* XII, 3, 4, 8. Silanus was a great-great-grandson of Augustus, in fact as closely connected as Nero, and it needed an extremely grave charge to move Claudius to break the betrothal.

[3] Pliny, *Epist.* VI, 6; Tacitus, *Ann.* XII, 53. The proposer was the Stoic hero Barea Soranus; cf. *Ann.* XIV, 21.   [4] Seneca, *Epist. Mor.* 47, 9.

But the most serious evil of Claudius' Principate was the power that he unwittingly surrendered to his wives and freedmen of enriching themselves by the sale of offices, immunities or grants of citizenship[1], or by the more brutal methods of confiscation and murder; the number of the victims, senators and knights, dwelt long in the memory of the Roman nobility. Our sources depict, therefore, an emperor weak, absent-minded, and deaf, prematurely aged through a long series of illnesses and by bouts of self-indulgence and gluttony, falling more and more under the domination of wills stronger than his own—a picture which the history of his last three or four years at home and abroad tends to confirm. It is true, but it is not the whole truth. Here as always the difference between Rome and the provinces must be borne in mind. In the edicts and letters that have survived we can judge for ourselves another aspect of Claudius, and the judgment must be favourable. Apart altogether from their content, the importance of which has been discussed above, in every one of them—whether he is counselling the Jews to show for others' religion something of the respect he does for theirs, or reminding senators what is due from their position, or confirming the disputed rights of the Anauni, even if it is merely a plain letter of acknowledgment to the guild of Dionysiac artists in Miletus—there is always present something strongly individual, revealing a nature sometimes pedantic or digressive, but kindly and understanding, not lacking in sense of humour, eager to promote order and justice, and genuinely anxious for the well-being of the ruled. His readiness to grant citizenship, to bring provincials into the Senate, and to found colonies, smacks of Caesar rather than of Augustus, but two generations had passed since the battle of Actium and he could attempt things that Augustus dared not. The good that he did endured and developed into the heritage of the empire, the evil was soon forgotten with Nero and civil wars following, the grotesque figure no longer seen. This was the ruler whom Agrippina killed to set her son upon the throne, herself to fall among his early victims.

[1] Dio LX, 17, 8 may be exaggerated but certainly contains a kernel of truth.

CHAPTER XXI

NERO

I. NERO'S ACCESSION. THE FIRST PHASE

CLAUDIUS once dead, the accession of Nero, expected by all—senators as well as soldiers—was carried through without a hitch. On 13 October 54[1] the Praetorians, who had been promised a donative of 15,000 sesterces—the same amount as that which Claudius had paid—hailed him as Imperator, and his recognition by the Senate followed immediately, no opposition being offered by any of the provincial armies. This unanimity arose, somewhat paradoxically, from two quite different motives. The legionaries and the provincials, whom Claudius had so

Note. Our literary tradition about Nero is derived, as a whole, in all probability from the *Histories* of Pliny the Elder: the present writer also holds that the two authors cited by Tacitus by the side of Pliny (Fabius Rusticus and Cluvius Rufus) had already been used by Pliny, so that Tacitus ordinarily only knows of them what Pliny passes on. (See p. 867.) Our information is consequently one-sided; we do not know the name of even one of those favourable historians whose existence Josephus attests (*Antiquitates*, xx [8, 3], 154). Hence the capital difficulty of estimating the Principate of Nero fairly. Whenever the check afforded by contemporary documents (especially coins and inscriptions) is lacking, the historian runs the risk of trusting his sources either too much or too little. Besides, since the drama of Nero's court is above all one of character, we must admit our inability to penetrate the innermost workings of the heart of the chief actors: no one can pretend to understand Nero, Agrippina, or even Seneca fully. The *Octavia*, a tragedy wrongly attributed to Seneca (cf. vv. 629 *sqq.* which may allude to the death of Nero), cannot be used for any historical reconstruction. If the base of its story is to be referred to the same source as Tacitus and Dio (*i.e.* probably Pliny), the details either are obviously the fruit of poetical imagination or else possess extremely questionable value, although the author probably wrote as early as the reign of Vespasian or (at the latest) of Titus.

[1] In reckoning the years of tribunician power the present writer accepts the thesis of H. F. Stobbe, *Philologus*, xxvii, 1872, p. 23, who regards the notice TRIB. POT. VII in the *Acta Arvalium* for A.D. 60 as mistaken (*C.I.L.* VI, 2042 b) and the diploma in Dessau 1987 as not belonging to the year 60: both are contradicted by coins and by Dessau 8902. All irregularities are thus removed from the reckoning beginning 4 Dec. 54. Cf. H. Dessau, *Gesch. d. Kaiserzeit*, II, p. 196 *n.*, and H. Mattingly, *J.R.S.* xx, 1930, pp. 79 *sqq.*

favoured, hoped naturally enough for a continuance of his policy: Nero was not yet seventeen, and it was obvious that the direction of affairs would lie in the hands of Agrippina and the two men she trusted, Seneca and Burrus; from a daughter of Germanicus and from two men of provincial birth army and provinces might look for much. On the other hand, the Roman aristocracy might with equal reason expect that Agrippina, her ambitions now presumably satisfied, would return to the liberal traditions of her house and would forgo suspicion and accusation, and that there would be an end to the all-pervading legal activity of Claudius' principate.

Thus the new government, anxious both to preserve the good-will of the provinces and to abolish the unpopular parts of Claudius' rule in Rome, stamped its early proceedings with a somewhat contradictory character. On the one hand, Claudius was deified, like Augustus, and coins commemorated *Divus Claudius*: on the Caelian hill the construction of a temple in his honour was at once begun (though the structure was a few years later transformed into a distributing-station for the Aqua Claudia): at the funeral Nero read a formal *laudatio* of the dead ruler, certainly composed for him by Seneca; one of the tribes of Alexandria—which were now re-organized, though the details escape us—received the name of *Philo-klaudios*, symbolizing Nero's love for his step-father[1]. And this was not the only formal manifestation, for when the Senate rescinded certain measures of Claudius—among them the duty imposed upon quaestors-designate of arranging for the gladiatorial games —Agrippina intervened with a protest, and the Senate had some difficulty in gaining its way. On the other hand, Nero intimated to the Senate his desire to put an end to the merging together of the private administration of the imperial house and the govern-ment of the State that had characterized the reign of Claudius, and above all to restore to the Senate its judicial powers. He claimed Augustus as his model: so had Claudius before him, but Augustus now became in official thought the term of reference that marked the difference between the new rule and that of Claudius. 'The new Augustus,' is the title given Nero by con-temporary Alexandrian coins, and the name of one of the re-organized tribes at Alexandria expresses in another form this special reverence for his great-great-grandfather[2]. This contrast

---

[1] Cf. E. Breccia, *Bull. Soc. Arch. Alex.* x, 1908, pp. 180 *sqq.*; U. Wilcken, *Arch. Pap.* v, 1913, pp. 182–4; G. Schumann, *Hellenistische und griechische Elemente in der Regierung Neros*, p. 12. (Note 22 gives a list of the papyri containing the new tribe names.)

[2] προπαπποσεβάστειος. Cf. also Ditt.³ 808, 810, Dessau 228.

finds its most forcible expression in the *Apocolocyntosis* of Seneca, where the divine Augustus is one of the most formidable accusers of Claudius, and where Apollo, the Augustan deity, predicts a return to justice and liberality.

Indeed this opposition to the policy of Claudius rapidly gained the upper hand. Mildness and clemency were the tendencies most strongly stressed by the new government in contrast to the judicial murders and cruelty of the past years. *Clementia* was the watchword that Seneca suggested to Nero for his public speeches and which he himself used as a title for the work that he dedicated towards the end of A.D. 55 to his imperial pupil: by '*clemency*' he meant a synthesis of all the virtues of a government, justice, goodwill (*concordia*), and love of peace—to employ the phrases that recur constantly on coins and in the names of the Alexandrian tribes. Poets too shared in propaganda for the programme, lulling themselves with the fancy of a new age of gold and helping to spread the fancy: such were Calpurnius Siculus in his *Bucolics*, the anonymous author of the *Carmina Einsidlensia*[1], and Lucan in the first book of the *Pharsalia*. All of them depicted the reign of Nero as initiating a new era of happiness.

All the same, the favours fell solely on the aristocracy, which was well pleased with the respect that Nero and his advisers showed for it. Every day he gave fresh proof of mildness or of modesty: he refused the title of *pater patriae*, recognizing that he was too young for it[2]; he would not allow the erection of statues in his own honour or consent that the beginning of the year should be moved to December, in which his own birthday fell; he stopped the prosecution of two charges of *maiestas*, against a senator and against a knight; he restored Plautius Lateranus, who had been degraded on the ground of adultery with Messallina, to his rank as senator; he cut down the rewards of informers under the Lex Papia Poppaea (p. 455)[3]; finally, he won the enthusiasm of all by exempting L. Antistius Vetus, who was his colleague in the consulship to which he had been nominated for 1 January 55, from taking the customary oath *in acta principis*, thus removing all distinction between himself and his colleague. He relieved the Praetorians of the surveillance of the games (although he was forced to restore it next year, possibly from fears for his personal

[1] *Anth. Lat.* (ed. Riese) no. 726. The present writer regards the efforts so far made to identify the author as lacking a satisfactory basis.

[2] Suetonius, *Nero* 8. Coins however prove that he allowed himself to be persuaded soon enough (about the end of 55) to take the title. Cf. O. T. Schulz, *Die Rechtstitel und Regierungsprogramme auf römischen Kaisermünzen*, p. 20, n. 55.　　　[3] The date of this is not attested. Suetonius, *Nero*, 10.

safety). There was no lack of assistance for the impoverished nobles, for whom a series of subsidies was expressly instituted in 58. It could even be said that the new *princeps* favoured certain conservative, or even reactionary, tendencies of the aristocracy, which emerged again, as in questions concerning the control of freedmen and slaves, where Nero, in contrast to his predecessor, posed as a protector of the interests of masters. Though he would not approve off-hand the Senate's proposal in 56 to cancel the manumission of freedmen who showed 'ingratitude' to their *patroni*, he recognized how reasonable was their anxiety to preserve the subordination of freedmen to their patrons and so granted them the right to deal with individual cases. And in 57 he allowed them to carry still further the resolutions of the *senatus consultum Silanianum* of A.D. 10 (p. 166) by decreeing that when a master had been killed by his slaves, even those who had been manumitted by his will (and so were still slaves at the time of the murder) must share the torture and punishments of the other slaves. Nor was this harshness merely permissive: in 61, when a slave murdered his master, L. Pedanius Secundus the prefect of the city, all his fellow-slaves, some 400, were condemned to death as accomplices, although the populace cried out against such archaic severity. One suggestion, however, that the freedmen who were in the same house should be deported from Italy, he did oppose, and that on the ground that this would mean a violation of older laws. Before that, in 57, there had occurred another sensational instance of a return to old-fashioned judicial practices, when the Senate handed a noble lady, Pomponia Graecina, *superstitionis externae rea*[1], over to her husband to try before a domestic court, and the significance of this was in no way lessened by the fact that he acquitted her.

This deference towards the Senate was seen in the delegation to it of many cases, especially accusations of extortion against governors, and a further proof was given in 61 when it was decided that in all civil cases on appeal to the Senate a deposit must first be made, as was customary in cases that went on appeal to the emperor. In coinage, too, the authority of the Senate was recognized and restored. Hitherto the right of coining gold and silver had been reserved exclusively to the emperor; now on the Neronian coins of these two metals there appears the legend 'EX s(enatus) c(onsulto).' Two points on these coins call for particular comment: first, the avoidance of the title *Imperator* as a praenomen, so that the usual formula is NERO CAES. AUG. IMP., and second, the adoption of the civic crown of oak as a type; for from the days

---

[1] Probably she was not, as tradition held, a convert to Christian but rather to Jewish practices (see below, p. 715).

of Brutus this had been a symbol for liberty and for the restoration
of senatorial authority[1]. The higher magistracies such as the consulship and praetorship also experienced the effects of Nero's
favour in an enhancement of their privileges and prestige in contrast with their old rivals, the tribunate and aedileship; these latter
found their rights of fining and powers of coercion curtailed and
restricted[2]. Artificial though much of this might be, the general
effect of this deference and respect for things Republican must
have been heightened by Nero's readiness to hold the office of
consul: in fact when he had been three times *consul ordinarius*, in
55, 57, and 58, the Senate on the last occasion decided to offer
him a perpetual consulship, presumably in the hope that with the
continued exercise of this magistracy he would be led more and
more into the straight path of Republican tradition.

But he refused it, and his refusal is significant. Whoever looks
below these particular measures to the real trend of affairs during
the first five years of Nero will observe no restitution of Republican liberties but a stronger current of absolutist tendencies.
No emperor before had ever in his lifetime been placed on such a
pinnacle by perpetual harping on the sovereign benefits that he
was bestowing on humanity. Everything was made to depend
upon him or derive from him alone; the very liberty which he apparently granted to his subjects lost its meaning when it was
recognized not as a right but as the gracious concession of a
sovereign being. Indeed it was, as his responsible advisers understood it, a form of clemency, and clemency has always been a
virtue of sovereigns and not of Republics. From the very beginning a tendency is visible, more marked perhaps in the East, to
exalt the person of the emperor, which finds expression in what
may be called the phrases of an imperial mystical creed. The
events of those years in which all recognize absolutism merely
continued a process that had begun and been developed in this
much praised *quinquennium*[3]. In the East the emperor is hailed

---

[1] See Volume of Plates iv, 204, *e*, *f*. The oak-crown, with the significant
words, *o(b) c(ives) s(ervatos)*, appears also on an altar dedicated to Nero by the
cives Remi, Dessau 235.

[2] The account of these reforms in Tacitus, *Ann.* XIII, 28, is obscure.
The present writer adopts the explanation given by B. Kübler in *Festschrift
Hirschfeld*, pp. 56–8.

[3] The famous verdict, however, of Trajan (Aurelius Victor, *Caes.* V, 2)
'procul differre cunctos principes Neronis quinquennio' probably refers, as
J. G. C. Anderson has shown in *J.R.S.* I, 1911, pp. 173 *sqq.*, to the later
building activity of Nero.

as restorer and saviour of the world and as the bringer of good things[1]: so too the collective cult of the imperial house, that is of the deified dead emperors and of the living emperor, spreads throughout the Eastern provinces and gains in strength and organization[2]. But in the West the same sentiments are discernible: in 55, to celebrate some initial successes in the Parthian War (p. 759), the statue of Nero was carried into the temple of Mars Ultor[3], and the exaltation of Nero in the *Apocolocyntosis* or in the proem to Lucan's *Pharsalia*, written about A.D. 60, together with the hints at the divinity of the Emperor, are sufficient to indicate the gulf between the dominant sentiment at court and the feeling that might have been expected from one who put on his coins the civic crown of oak. In practice, though there were many small measures in favour of the senatorial aristocracy, the direction of the government rested firmly in the hands of the Emperor and of his advisers, and the Emperor, as we have seen, carefully avoided compromising his position so far as to accept a perpetual consulship.

In reality, quite apart from the need for taking account of the favour which Claudius' policy had won in the provinces, the reaction of the new government was less marked than it imagined. It abolished the abuses that had disgraced the reign of Claudius such as the secret trials *intra cubiculum principis*, but its aim differed little. That aim was to win over members of the upper classes to help readily and efficiently as advisers or executive officers in the Augustan scheme by encouraging them and allaying their fears: trials, confiscations, and hasty condemnations were to be stopped; some harmless manifestations of Republican tradition were tolerated and even fostered, but these were only means to the end, and even in these means the government never overstepped the limits of its own convenience and so did not hesitate, from the beginning, to entrust some of the most important State offices to men who by their birth and education could not have the sympathies of the old traditional aristocracy. Thus the governorship

---

[1] Thus on coins of Alexandria Nero is equated with the city's protecting deity, appearing as Νέος Ἀγαθὸς Δαίμων, or in papyri as Ἀγαθὸς Δαίμων τῆς οἰκουμένης: Pap. Oxy. VII, 1021 = Wilcken, *Chrest.* 113; *O.G.I.S.* 666. Cf. the names of the new Alexandrian tribes, Ἀγαθοδότειος, Νεοκόσμιος, Σωσικόσμιος and the like; Schumann, *op. cit.* p. 12, n. 22.

[2] For the earliest documentation see Ditt.[3] 790, 808.

[3] Tacitus, *Ann.* XIII, 8. He thus became σύνναος with Mars, a form of association with deity which had been granted to no living person since Caesar. See vol. IX, p. 720.

of Egypt was in 55 actually entrusted to an Alexandrian who was also an astrologer, Ti. Claudius Balbillus[1].

One effective check there was upon the power of Nero, that is upon his advisers for the time being, and that was the power of his mother, but obviously such a check not only did not favour the aspirations of the aristocracy but was even in sharp antithesis to them. There is no doubt that Agrippina at first enjoyed a kind of co-regency with her son, although naturally this co-regency had not the definite status and the clear legal form which the co-regency of Tiberius with Augustus had possessed, with its share in the pro-consular and tribunician power. The power of Agrippina rested merely on the prestige of a daughter of Germanicus and on the gratitude of her son and his immediate helpers for the share that she had taken in securing for Nero the succession to the throne. On the coins of the early years she appears facing her son on the obverse in perfect equality[2]; and an inscription recently discovered speaks of an imperial procurator in the province of Achaea as *procurator Caesaris et Augustae Agrippinae*[3] while the inscriptions and coins that give Agrippina the title of *Augusta Mater Augusti* are numerous. The first to feel her power was the Senate, who, if we are to believe Tacitus, was compelled to gather on the Palatine so that the Empress, if she could not be personally present at their deliberations, could at any rate hear them from a convenient place.

Even so, the authority of Agrippina could not last long, for it was incompatible with that sovereign height on which her son had been placed. While on the one hand we may blame Seneca and Burrus for instigating and favouring this unbounded exaltation of Nero, in order to hinder the authority of the mother from equalling that of the son and to limit her influence upon him, on the other it is obvious that the very logic of his sovereignty must urge Nero to put bounds to the prestige of his mother and to drive her back into the shade; the saviour of the world could have no one as an equal. In fact neither Nero, with his ambitious character, nor Seneca and Burrus, jealous of their influence over the Emperor, were disposed to approve of the co-regency with Agrippina. Reasons for a difference soon arose. While Agrippina was in agreement with Seneca and Burrus in getting rid of some of the more influential

[1] The identification of the astrologer with the prefect of Egypt was made by Fr. Cumont, *Mél. d'arch. et d'hist.* XXXVII, 1918–19, p. 33 and independently by C. Cichorius, *Röm. Studien*, pp. 393 *sqq*.

[2] See Volume of Plates iv, 204, *e*.

[3] See A. B. West, *Corinth*, vol. VIII, ii, p. 50, no. 68.

freedmen who had surrounded Claudius—such as Narcissus, or Callistus, of whom we know nothing after the death of Claudius and who was almost certainly relieved of his office, she did not mean that the freedmen who were faithful to her and had secured her power in the time of Claudius should be dismissed. Pallas, in particular, the financial secretary, had been supported by her, but so long as he remained in office it could not be claimed that the rule of the freedmen had been eliminated, quite apart from the fact that Seneca was to show he had ideas of his own upon financial policy and that these ideas were likely to be very different from those favoured by Pallas during the reign of Claudius. Not that Seneca and Burrus meant to break up the organization created by Claudius, which suited well enough their own resolve not to yield all the most important posts to members of the aristocracy, but they aimed at subordinating it to the proper political authority and so were eager to get rid of those old officials who knew no intermediary between them and their sovereign. This was the more necessary for Seneca because he held no precise legal office and so had not an established position over the freedmen who were at the head of different branches of the administration; unable to exercise the control that comes from presiding regularly over a body of officials he felt it the more necessary to have in these posts men whom he could trust. Pallas was therefore at the beginning of 55 removed from his office, and in his place was put probably a freedman of the name of Phaon[1]; and all the threats of Agrippina, who foresaw in the ruin of her favourite the beginning of her own, could not succeed in saving him.

In fact her threats merely endangered her own position the more and perhaps helped definitely to bring ruin on Britannicus, if it is true that Agrippina in her rage foolishly hinted at the possibility of setting up the true son of Claudius against the adoptive son. But even without her threats his fate was sealed. Suspicion against all possible rivals to the throne and the use of any means to be rid of them were becoming as much a tradition of the Julio-Claudian family as of any ancient monarchy. Hardly was Claudius dead before the proconsul of Asia, M. Junius Silanus (brother of the L. Silanus who had been betrothed to Octavia) was murdered because he was a distant descendant of Augustus and so, had he availed himself of the popularity which he enjoyed, might have been able to raise a claim to the Principate. Once Britannicus was marked down for destruction the only difficulty

---

[1] The arguments of Schumann, *op. cit.* p. 57 *sq.*, are here accepted.

was to make his death appear natural; if we are to follow the account of our sources, shortly after the dismissal of Pallas in 55, he was at last removed by the use of poison, the effects of which resembled at first an attack of epilepsy. But no one was deceived by this; nor is the pitiful death of a youth whose spirit and character more than matched his birth condoned by the Tacitean reflection *antiquas fratrum discordias et insociabile regnum*.

Seneca and Burrus cannot well have been unaware of the plot against Britannicus; in any event here as on other occasions they showed themselves prepared to accept a *fait accompli* complacently. Though Nero's character showed a precocious development in cruelty, sensuality and artistic enthusiasm, his advisers, especially Seneca, actually encouraged these tendencies in the hope of keeping him bound to them by detaching him from his mother, and possibly too of drawing his attention away from political problems so that they could rule without a rival. For the time, if such was their design, it succeeded admirably. Nero, who from his young days had flitted with the ease of a dilettante from one art to another, painting, sculpturing, composing verses, singing and dancing, went on with these activities, trying to perfect himself under the greatest masters of each art, such as the harpist Terpnus who was reckoned as the most skilful of his time: artists sought him out and flattered him as their natural friend and protector[1]. At the same time he fell in love with a freedwoman called Acte and began to gather round him a company of young men of society and fashion, such as M. Salvius Otho, the future emperor, Claudius Senecio, or the friend of Seneca, Annaeus Serenus, commander of the night watch, who affected to be the chief lover of Acte in order to avert the suspicion of Agrippina; with these and other companions Nero went out on nocturnal adventures that soon began to swell the list of disorders in the city. In return Agrippina, who saw her son led astray and separated from her by these love affairs and these friendships, evinced an increasing scorn and began to pose as protectress of her unfortunate daughter-in-law, Octavia, and in this way fatally widened the gulf. Nero began to see in his mother more and more an obstacle. Nor did her own character, headstrong, suspicious, proud, and if not ignorant of affection certainly prone to forget it, serve as a check. After a series of clashes and attempts at reconciliation, Agrippina was deprived of her guard of honour and removed from the palace. Her new residence was to be in the house

---

[1] The dedication of the epigrams of Lucilius to Nero falls in the early years of the reign. Cf. Cichorius, *op. cit.* p. 372.

that had once belonged to Antonia, the mother of Germanicus. Coins mirror faithfully the decline of her power, for after the series already mentioned in which Agrippina is on an equality with Nero, there follow others in which at first her portrait appears only on the reverse and then vanishes altogether.

Naturally there were those who, seeing the once powerful Empress in distress, were only too pleased to try to aggravate it. That same year a matron, Junia Silana, who had her own reasons for hatred of Agrippina, procured the dancer Paris to accuse her to Nero of meaning to marry as her fourth husband a grandson of Tiberius, Rubellius Plautus, and put him up as a claimant to the Empire against her son. But the falsity of the accusation was soon detected, as was a second one, which only concerned Agrippina indirectly, in which Pallas and Burrus were charged with plotting to place Faustus Cornelius Sulla, the husband of Claudius' daughter, Antonia, on the throne. Suspicion rested only upon Cornelius Sulla, and this owing to the tendency mentioned above to suspect all connections of the imperial house; three years later, in 58, he was exiled to Massilia on the charge of having plotted to ambush the Emperor as he was returning from his usual nightly amusements.

II. THE POLICY OF SENECA AND BURRUS

The enforced withdrawal of Agrippina left Seneca and Burrus in complete control of policy. Nero took little part in the government, and even on the rare occasions when he did come forward, we cannot be sure how much is due to him and how much to his mentors. For example, his sympathy for Rhodes, to which he sent a reassuring letter in 55[1], and whose autonomy he had defended earlier before Claudius, was probably inspired by Seneca, and the interest he evinced in Egypt—as attested by an enactment that evoked the gratitude of Ptolemaïs in Upper Egypt in the year 60[2] —may have been equally inspired by his tutor, who wrote a work (now lost) upon that country; and if Nero approved the monarchical sentiment that showed signs of spreading slowly over the Empire from that centre, his tutor, too, was not averse from such speculations.

In the meantime Seneca and Burrus guided imperial policy

---

[1] Ditt.[3] 810, and notes. Cf. the praises of Nero in *Anth. Pal.* IX, 178.

[2] *O.G.I.S.* 668. The details are uncertain; cf. G. Glotz in *Rev. Arch.* XVIII, 1911, pp. 256 *sqq.*, and G. Plaumann in *Arch. Pap.* VI, 1913, pp. 178 *sqq.*

with a firm hand. They aimed steadily at enhancing the prestige
of imperial authority but they wished this prestige to be based
upon the securing of justice and economic prosperity for the
Empire. Their anxiety to bring about a change in economic
policy is especially notable, for it had no connection with the
government of former emperors and to a great extent determines
the policy of this period.

Claudius' policy, which aimed at bringing under the direct
control of the emperor all the finances of the State, even those that
came within the competence of the Senate, was maintained unaltered. By substituting in 56 two *praefecti aerarii Saturni* (chosen
from ex-praetors) for the quaestors who up to then had managed
the treasury, control was placed more firmly in the hands of the
emperor, and was also entrusted to men of greater seniority and
so of more experience than the quaestors. A proof of the effective
unity of the two treasuries was given a year later when 40 million
sesterces were transferred from the fiscus to the aerarium in order
to maintain its credit, since its revenues were steadily diminishing
owing to the increasing centralization of returns in the fiscus. By
making prosecution for extortion against ex-governors easier, as
is seen in the long series of such trials in the first years of the
reign, a check was put on ill-treatment of the provincials. In
addition, governors of provinces were forbidden to win the good
will of their subjects as a means of avoiding accusations by giving
theatrical spectacles. So, too, the agrarian prosperity of the provinces was safeguarded. For that reason in 59 the government
determined that the old royal estates of the kings of Cyrene which
had passed to Rome should remain in the possession of those who
had illegally occupied them, in order to avoid upsetting the
economic life of that region, notwithstanding the fact that an
imperial commissioner with praetorian power, Acilius Strabo,
who had been sent by Claudius to settle the dispute between
the fiscus and the occupiers (p. 690 n. 3) had declared that their
occupation was legally invalid.

Above all there were visions of a radical reform of the economic
life of the Empire, either by an alteration in the tributary system
or by an increase in commerce. The age of gold was not to be
simply a dream of contemporary poets; it was an aspiration of the
statesmen as well. This is shown by the famous project for reform
of the tribute which was brought before the Senate for discussion
in 58, for, despite the words of Tacitus (*Ann.* XIII, 50), it seems
improbable that this project originated with Nero rather than with
his advisers, Seneca and Burrus. The proposal was to abolish all

indirect taxes, that is the *portoria* and *vicesimae* that tended to hamper the economic life of the Empire, in the hope obviously that the greater yield from the direct taxes, that would have been made possible by the increase in commerce due to this freedom of trade, would compensate for the abolition. Anyone who remembers the complaints and the scandals which the Roman system of farming out indirect taxes had always aroused can understand that such a project must have been considered with great care, although it is not surprising that the numerous practical difficulties to which the abolition would have given rise prevented its being put into practice. After the discussion in the Senate, Seneca and Burrus had to content themselves for the time being with less far-reaching measures which merely diminished the evil. Thus, certain special customs rights were abolished and in order to safeguard the food of the city populace corn-ships were not to be reckoned as part of the taxable property of their owners, and measures were taken to facilitate the shipment of corn. The food-supply of Rome was a particular care of the administration, and in order to guarantee it the work undertaken by Claudius on the harbour of Ostia was completed[1]. The people of Rome received, apart from the usual distribution of corn, extraordinary largesses, such as the two *congiaria* of 400 sesterces per head which were distributed, one in 57, the other at a date unknown, and were celebrated by the issue of appropriate coins.

The foreign policy of the new government, so far as the frontiers are concerned, is described elsewhere (see below, chaps. XXII, XXIII). From the very beginning of the reign the task of dealing with Armenia and with Parthia was resolutely taken in hand. A rebellion in Britain was decisively crushed and in A.D. 64–5 the vassal kingdom of Pontus governed by Polemo II was incorporated in the empire[2]. The Black Sea was protected from pirates by a fleet, while the assumption of this responsibility for its safety led to a curtailment of the nominal independence of the Bosporan kingdom. The Danube frontier was made good against the barbarians by arms and diplomacy. Finally, in the closing years of his

---

[1] It is probable that, besides the issue of the well-known commemorative coins (Volume of Plates iv, 204, *g*), we should connect the raising of Puteoli to the rank of a colony in the year 60 with the conclusion of this task, since that could well be interpreted as compensation offered for the loss Puteoli suffered from the competition of the new port.

[2] The transformation of the vassal kingdom of the *Alpes Cottiae* into a small province administered by a procurator, and the grant of Latin citizenship to the peoples of the *Alpes Maritimae* belong to this year too.

principate, Nero appears to have planned an offensive against the
Sarmatians, which might have resulted in a marked extension of
the bounds of the empire. This later policy may be attributed to
the grandiose ambitions which visited the mind of the Princeps,
but it may fairly be supposed that the initial impulse towards a
vigorous frontier activity proceeded from the statecraft of Seneca and
Burrus. It may, indeed, have been due not only to the traditional
care of Romans for security and prestige. The increasing expenses
that fell upon the private treasury of the Emperor, his unbounded
extravagance, the need to safeguard Roman commerce and possibly
the hope of extending it supplied temptations which may have
appealed to the men who were at the head of the government.
Addicted themselves to luxury, they were not content only to
exploit the vast estates they had received from the generosity of
the Emperor, but took part also in commercial and banking enterprises which were closely connected with the course of politics.
The most notorious instance is Seneca, who not only had large
estates, especially in Egypt, but lent out money to provincials, so
that one of the reasons alleged for the rebellion in Britain was
inability to stand the burdensome rate of interest that he exacted.
But many other officers of State must have imitated him, and their
vast riches were long remembered[1].

The widening range of Roman policy meant that special care
must be paid to the morale of the army, which had already experienced severe reverses in Armenia, and so new military colonies,
or new settlements in older colonies, were devised to meet this need;
practically all were in Italy, either because the greater part of the
legionaries came from Italy or as a help in combating the increasing depopulation of the peninsula. The honour of settlement
in Nero's birthplace, Antium, was reserved for the praetorians;
other veterans were placed in a new colony at Nuceria and in the
older colonies of Capua and Tarentum. Probably veterans were also
settled at Tegeanum in Campania[2], and at Pompeii, for we know
that Nero raised both these to the status of colonies, though
possibly the grant to Pompeii may have been meant as a recompense for loss it had suffered in an earthquake in 63[3]. It is likely

[1] For the farms and estates of the freedman *a libellis* Ti. Claudius Dory-
phorus see the texts in Schumann, *op. cit.* p. 50.
[2] For the site of Tegeanum see A. Sogliano in *Rend. Lincei*, VI, 1897,
p. 393; cf. Dessau 6444.
[3] The *Liber Coloniarum* gives Aesernia, Atina, Beneventum, Castri-
monium and Saepinum as colonies of Nero, but inscriptions do not confirm
this statement; possibly some veteran settlements were made in these towns

too that there was a settlement at Luceria[1], while the Augustan colony of Aroë Patrensis in Greece became Colonia Neronia Patrensis and welcomed some veterans.

But the continuation of this vast scheme must have meant that the Emperor could not remain always indifferent to politics or consider himself under permanent guardianship; in fact Nero as he grew older longed more and more for liberty of action so as to be able to gratify his dominant passion for greatness and popularity. In spite of the differences between Agrippina and Seneca and Burrus they were agreed in upholding at least an outward tone of traditionalism in all their actions. Nero on the contrary wanted to express his admiration for Greek art and life in definite enterprises; he wanted to alter Roman fashions. And in his private life he wished for no more hindrance and for that reason he probably felt himself oppressed by the presence of his mother and of his ministers. We may imagine that Agrippina above all, whose influence did not disappear with her banishment from the court, must have become for a time to Nero's excited imagination the very embodiment of the whole order of things from which he wanted to break loose. And it is not too bold to suppose that he saw in his mother the greatest obstacle to his freeing himself from Octavia, who was merely a dead weight on his life, and so involved both in one common hatred.

His love for Poppaea was only the most important episode of this revulsion which induced Nero in the five years between 58 and 62 to free himself from all those who fettered his freedom. Poppaea Sabina, daughter of a Roman matron, who owing to her beauty had fallen a victim to Messallina, had inherited all the sensual charm of her mother and was also credited with a quick and versatile mind; unscrupulous in satisfying her own ambition, she was anxious to rise out of the circle of ordinary life and for that reason she was drawn towards eastern cults and perhaps towards Judaism, although Josephus, who knew her, does not venture to call her a proselyte but simply a believer in the supreme god ($\theta\epsilon o\sigma\epsilon\beta\eta\varsigma$)[2]. She had been the wife of Rufrius Crispinus, the

at Nero's wish. For the texts see B. W. Henderson, *The Life and Principate of the Emperor Nero*, p. 465. Pais' belief, that the references to Claudius Nero in the *Liber* refer usually to Tiberius seems improbable; *Mem. Linc.* xvi, 1920, pp. 80, 84, etc.

[1] Ritterling in *P.W. s.v. Legio*, col. 1264.

[2] $\theta\epsilon o\sigma\epsilon\beta\eta\varsigma$ is used to describe those who leaned to Judaism but were not officially proselytes (Juster, *op. cit.* i, p. 275). Besides his initiation into the cult of Mithras (p. 502), Nero had also a transient phase of devotion to the Dea Syria (Suetonius, *Nero*, 56).

Prefect of the Praetorians before Burrus, and had borne him a son; she then married M. Salvius Otho, the favourite companion of Nero, so that Nero had leisure to make her acquaintance and to feel the attraction of her personality, which in its mixture of sensuality, love of luxury and vague spiritual aspirations was extremely akin to his own. Common sympathy soon changed into passionate love and in order to satisfy it Nero removed his friend by giving him the governorship of Lusitania[1].

But Poppaea could not be content with being merely the mistress of the Emperor; she wished to become Empress and to achieve this she helped in her way to sharpen the discord between Nero and his mother and wife. It reached a point at which Nero, utterly unbalanced, plotted with Anicetus, a freedman who had been his tutor and was now in charge of the fleet at Misenum, to murder his mother. One evening in March 59 (during the festival of the Quinquatrus), Agrippina was invited by her son to a banquet at Baiae and afterwards at midnight was placed on a ship, so constructed as to founder, for the return voyage to Antium. The 'accident' duly happened, but Agrippina succeeded in saving herself by swimming to one of her villas on the Lucrine lake: well aware of the plot against her, she preferred to feign ignorance and to send a faithful freedman to tell her son she had been saved from a catastrophe. But in the excitement of the moment the court was ready for anything and apparently even Seneca and Burrus felt it was now impossible to turn back. On the pretext that Agrippina's messenger was really an assassin sent to kill the Emperor, Anicetus, with his sailors, was bidden to invade the villa to which Agrippina had withdrawn, and kill her.

When the matricide was over, although popular account declared that Nero was terrified and for long haunted by the ghost of his mother, he did all he could, in co-operation with his ministers, to spread the story that Agrippina had tried to murder her son and on hearing of the failure of her plan had killed herself. Such was the tenour of the despatch he sent to the Senate from Naples, whither he had retired. Naturally all hastened anxiously to join in paeans of thanksgiving for the 'deliverance' of their Emperor; the festival of the Quinquatrus had games added in celebration of the event, while the birthday of Agrippina was declared *dies nefastus*. Re-assured by such enthusiasm, Nero, who at first had not dared to return to Rome, hastened there and

---

[1] This is the substance of the account in Tacitus, *Ann.* XIII, 45–6, which is certainly deliberately altered from the absurd tradition that he followed in *Hist.* I, 13.

received triumphal homage. But everyone was aware of the reality and the popular conscience reacted against this flattery by circulating lampoons against the emperor. However insensitive absolutism may render men to crimes, it is certain that nothing was to contribute so much to destroy the prestige of Nero and to prepare his fall as the impression created by this act; the Sibylline Oracles written shortly after his death mention him above all as 'murderer of his mother[1].'

III. THE PRINCEPS AND ROMAN SOCIETY

But for Nero the murder meant freedom and he could now devote fresh zest to the task that for some years he had promised himself of reforming the education of the young Roman nobles. It was the first time that he had taken a step in public life which was entirely his own and certainly not in agreement with the aims of his ministers. As early as 57 he had tried to alter the character of the Roman games to bring them as near as possible to the Greek. After building a new amphitheatre in the Campus Martius, he had introduced the rule that no combat should be carried on to the death, for such brutality was repellent not only to his own sensibilities but also to the whole character of the Greek games. And since the competitors in the Greek games had been no slaves, or criminals, or professionals, but the flower of free men, he made senators and knights of old family descend into the arena to the great scandal of Rome. But in 59 he went further still; he succeeded in introducing Greek games into Rome and in organizing the young men for their practice. Whether he knew it or not, the Greek civilization that he was imitating in this way had nothing to do with that of the classical period, founded upon freedom, but was simply Hellenistic and based upon monarchy. This is clearly shown by his establishment of a corps of *Augustiani* in this year, with the object of gathering in the young men of the upper classes and making them join with him in gymnastic and artistic exhibitions[2]: he aimed at eradicating their Republican traditions and turning them into a bodyguard of nobles for the emperor's person. Although perhaps Nero was unaware of it, these innovations too played their part in the trans-

---

[1] See *Orac. Sibyll.* v, 145, 363 *sqq.* (Geffcken).

[2] It was an imitation of such bodies as those of the βασιλικοὶ παῖδες in Hellenistic capitals. This fact was partially seen by H. Schiller, *Röm. Kaiserreich unter...Nero,* and fully demonstrated by M. Rostovtseff in *Klio, Beiheft* III, 1905, pp. 74 *sqq.*

formation of principate into monarchy which was steadily going on, with this difference only that there was none of the prudence and respect for tradition which had marked the handling of Burrus and Seneca. The fact that this establishment played so little part, save in the games, and later vanished altogether, was due partly to lack of conviction in its members, but still more to a complete lack of any serious intention in Nero.

The *Augustiani* made their first appearance in 59. After many exhibitions of himself as charioteer in the circus which he had constructed for his private use in the Vatican valley, Nero celebrated the first shaving of his beard by the institution of Ludi Iuvenales, which he organized informally in his own gardens across the Tiber; in the singing contests he competed himself. A year later, giving up all pretence of informality, he established five-yearly games, called certamen quinquennale or Neronia, in imitation of the Olympic games, to include athletic contests, chariot-driving, and competitions in music, poetry and oratory[1]. The games were repeated in 65, but lapsed after the death of Nero, and were not re-introduced until the reign of Gordian the Third in 240. Nero competed as harper in the poetical contests, but also won the prize for oratory. Although he had already succeeded in obtaining the participation of his *Augustiani* in the literary events and in chariot-driving, for the athletic events at both these festivals he must almost certainly have fallen back upon professionals, since otherwise our sources could not have failed to notice the scandal. His propaganda for athleticism, however, continued unabated; he built a gymnasium in Rome in 61, and, though it was burned down a year later, he had reconstructed it by 66. At its inauguration he distributed oil to the senators and knights who took part in the exercises, exactly like a Hellenistic king. In order to make the idea of life in the gymnasium more pleasing to the Romans he built the famous baths (Thermae Neronianae) close to his gymnasium, the luxury of which made Martial ask

'Quid Nerone peius?
Quid thermis melius Neronianis?[2]'

Indeed by this time luxury had reached a height of which vivid descriptions are given by Petronius, one of the most re-

---

[1] The imitation was carried so far as to allow the Vestal Virgins to view the games, since the priestesses of Demeter had this right at Olympia.

[2] Martial, VII, 34. On the antipathy of the Romans towards the athletic sports introduced by Nero see Juvenal VII, especially lines 221–30.

fined associates of Nero, in his *Satyricon*, and by Seneca in the
mordant criticisms of his various ethical treatises. And in this
life the most incompatible elements, from art to the pleasures of
the kitchen (in which Apicius won himself a name), from sport to
a passion for collecting, from the most refined connoisseurship to
the grossest sensuality, were strangely blended; the fact that they
could all exist together shows that even the highest things, such
as Art, had become merely the object for dilettantism. Lucan was
the poet of the court, and his skill in mingling flattery for his
sovereign with a certain austere strain of good-old-times Republicanism perhaps helped to increase his attractiveness. Nero himself composed poetry, not so badly, if we can judge from the
meagre fragments that remain[1]. A poem on 'The Sack of Troy'
was perhaps his most important work[2]; others were a composition
called *Luscius* and an ode dedicated to the blonde tresses of Poppaea.
Since exhibition at the games was not enough for him, in 64 he
determined to display his skill as poet and harper to the Greek or
Graecized public at Naples, because it was more worthy of hearing
him; but owing apparently to some accident he was unable to
carry his programme through. It looks as though he had thoughts
of making an artistic tour in Greece even then, but after reaching
Beneventum, for unknown reasons, turned back.

Naturally enough there was no lack of those who felt the
emptiness and immorality of such a type of life: the most implacable dissector of this society, Seneca, did not withdraw from
it until driven by outward circumstances, but other men lived
aloof, pouring into a satire or an epigram their sufferings and their
impotent scorn. These were the men who had been brought up on
Stoicism, whom we shall find in later years forming the stricken
political opposition of the intellectuals; here we need only mention
two of them, in whom the literary opposition achieved its clearest
expression. Aulus Persius Flaccus, the poet who died in 62 at the
age of twenty-eight, wrote satires which, even though they do not
contain direct allusions to the art of Nero and much less quotations
from his verses[3], show throughout from the first word to the last
a reaction against the Neronian world: the other is Annaeus
Cornutus, the Stoic philosopher and tutor of Lucan, who brought

[1] Morel, *Fragm. poet. Lat.* pp. 131–2.

[2] The lines of Petronius, *Satyricon*, 89 and 90, are probably a good-
humoured skit on the Emperor's poem.

[3] According to the scholiast on *Satire* 1, verses 93–4 and 99–102, p. 269
and 271 Jahn (ed. 1843) should be reckoned as Nero's. But see E. Haguenin
in *Rev. Phil.* N.S. XXIII, 1899, p. 301.

exile upon himself by telling Nero bluntly that a poem upon Roman history, which he had in mind, would be useless.

These incursions of the Emperor into the daily life of the capital were only one aspect, merely the beginning, of his greater influence in the whole of politics. We can mark the change by the increasingly suspicious temper of the government. In 60 the apparition of a comet, the fall of a thunderbolt on an imperial villa at Subiaco, and some trifling indisposition of Nero gave rise to rumours of a change on the throne. That was enough for a possible claimant, Rubellius Plautus, to be given the order to withdraw to his estates in the province of Asia. And now in 62 trials for treason began again, and for some lampoons upon the Emperor the praetor Antistius Sosianius and a certain Fabricius Veiento were condemned, the one being sent to an island, the other banished. With the Emperor in that state of mind, we can understand how a chance such as the death of Burrus became the occasion for the greatest political change in the whole reign. All our sources declare that Burrus was poisoned, and Tacitus alone raises any doubt. But the ancients had nothing to confirm this rumour and we must incline to disbelieve it; in any case it is historically unimportant. What is important is the fact that Nero did not select, as he would have done some years before, a successor whom Seneca would approve, but returned to old practice and filled the prefectship of the praetorians with two men, upon whom Seneca knew he could not rely, Faenius Rufus, already prefect of the corn-supply, and Ofonius[1] Tigellinus, a Sicilian of low birth, who, after a vicious past for which he had been banished from Italy, had succeeded in obtaining the prefecture of the vigiles and soon showed himself the more influential of the two. To Seneca, whose work could only go on thanks to the unconditional support of Burrus, that is of the praetorians, such a choice meant that he no longer enjoyed the confidence of the Emperor and was indeed an implicit invitation to retire. An ideal which he had always preached in his books though he had never put it into practice, that of a simple life in retirement, devoted to the improvement of the mind in philosophic meditation, now gained a stronger hold on him. Down to this time the conflict between his ethical ideals and his ambitions had been to a large extent minimized or concealed by the knowledge that he was working usefully for the benefit of mankind; we need not doubt that it was this knowledge, and not mere ambition, that made

[1] For this *praenomen*, not Sofonius, see Ph. Fabia in *Rev. Phil.* N.S. xxi, 1897, p. 160.

Seneca ready to tolerate the crimes of Nero. Now, the time for retirement come, his resignation took the form of a conciliation with himself. His withdrawal, in spite of long and fine speeches to the contrary, was naturally acceptable to the Emperor.

No longer restrained by his former advisers, but urged on by the zealous Tigellinus, Nero allowed himself to be drawn deeper into suspicion. Sulla was murdered at Massilia, Rubellius Plautus in Asia, without, as far as we know, any exact charge being made against them. In 64 Decimus Junius Silanus Torquatus, upon whom, as upon all the Silani, fell the suspicion of claiming the throne through their descent from Augustus, had to commit suicide in order to escape the imperial police. It was now easy for Poppaea, who had found a support in Tigellinus, to persuade Nero in 62 to free himself from Octavia and raise her to the throne. After attempts to fasten on Octavia charges of adultery, attempts which failed owing to the persistent denials of her slaves, she was formally divorced on the ground of barrenness, and twelve days later Nero married Poppaea. Octavia was exiled to Campania, but she was followed by the sympathy of the people who, when the ungrounded rumour spread abroad that Nero had called her back to his side, burst into demonstrations of joy. Terrified, Nero now let himself be drawn into a fresh scheme designed to remove the burden for ever. He began a new trial for adultery against his ex-wife, and in this trial the prefect of the fleet at Misenum, Anicetus, who had been his agent in the murder of Agrippina, figured as the accomplice of Octavia; he admitted to being her lover, and depicted this adulterous relation as an attempt of Octavia to gain the fleet at Misenum and incite it to rebellion. Our sources in this mysterious story represent Anicetus as willingly helping to ruin Octavia; but the reality appears more complex. It looks as though Nero profited by the occasion to remove from one of the most important offices an inconvenient witness of his worst crime; nor must we exclude the possibility that Tigellinus co-operated on his own behalf in a desire to withdraw the Emperor from the influence of the freedman. In any case, Anicetus must have been placed in the dilemma either of confessing his guilt in adultery and receiving a light sentence for it or else of being accused and facing the whole consequences. He preferred the first alternative and ended his life in comfortable exile in Sardinia, while Octavia was banished to the island of Pandateria, which had a sinister renown in the Julian family, and shortly afterwards was brutally put to death.

IV. THE FIRE IN ROME

This series of crimes enraged the aristocracy and alienated the affection of the Roman people from the Emperor. And now in 64, one of the most famous events of his reign, the fire of Rome, increased his unpopularity. On the night of 18 July, while Nero was taking a country holiday at Antium, there broke out in the Circus Maximus a fire which spread and raged furiously over practically all Rome for nine days, and gave rise to those scenes of panic, crime and robbery that in older days usually accompanied such calamities. Of the fourteen Augustan regions, only I (Porta Capena), V (Esquiliae), perhaps VI (Alta Semita), and certainly XIV (Trans Tiberim) were spared; III (Isis et Serapis), X (Palatium), and XI (Circus Maximus) were almost completely destroyed; while VII (Via Lata) and IX (Circus Flaminius), unharmed at first, suffered greatly from a fresh outbreak of the fire after the sixth day. All the other regions suffered in greater or less degree although tradition exaggerated the extent of the damage. The Forum, part of the Palatine, above all the Capitol escaped, but apart from an incalculable number of works of art which had been collected in the Republican period and in the early Empire, some of the most venerable monuments attributed to the regal period or to an even earlier age, such as the great altar attributed to Evander, the temple of Juppiter Stator ascribed to Romulus, the *regia* and the temple of Vesta ascribed to Numa, and the temple of Diana ascribed to Servius Tullius, were completely destroyed.

As soon as he heard news of the fire Nero sped back to Rome since a new building, perhaps not yet completed, the *Domus Transitoria*, that connected the palace of the Caesars on the Palatine with the gardens of Maecenas on the Esquiline, had been attacked by the flames. He energetically directed the work of putting out and isolating the fire and arranged relief organizations. On his initiative all public buildings and the imperial gardens were thrown open to those who were rendered homeless, and a city of huts and tents raised in the Campus Martius; furthermore, he provided for the proper feeding of this crowd of people by artificially lowering the price of corn and by requisitioning it from the country round. In spite of that, public opinion accused Nero of being the author of the fire and of having watched it from the lofty Tower of Maecenas while singing his own Sack of Troy. Naturally there are no reasons for believing in the main charge of arson, although only one of our sources speaks of it as uncertain[1]; the more so that, as has been observed, a deliberate attempt to set fire to Rome could scarcely have gone undetected on a night of full moon as was that of 18 July 64, and under the clear sky of a Roman summer[2]. Nor does the accusation become more credible if the story of Nero's singing from the Tower of Maecenas is taken as authentic, which it is not. On the other hand, it is easy to find reasons for such a charge: in disasters the populace always looks for a scapegoat, and in this particular one the name of Nero was ready to hand not only because of the previous crimes that had stained it but still more on account of the grandiose works which were undertaken by him in order to rebuild Rome after the fire; thus it could appear quite likely that he had deliberately fired Rome in order to rebuild it according to his own taste.

Indeed the rebuilding of Rome proceeded rapidly under the direction of the architects Severus and Celer, who were commissioned to clean and embellish the city, to lay it out upon more modern lines[3] and to guard against further fires. Nero himself paid towards the rebuilding of houses and this meant additions to his already heavy budget. His expenses were still more increased by the building of the new imperial palace, the so-called *Domus Aurea* (in substitution for the *Domus Transitoria*), which would, when built, have spread over a large extent of ground between the Caelian and the Esquiline. The work was unfinished when Vespasian pulled it down and placed the Coliseum upon a portion of it; but all the same the ancients could tell of the marvels of its parks, its lakes and its woods, of its waters which flowed from the sea or from the sulphur springs of Tivoli, of its three colonnades, one of which stretched for a mile, of its dining-rooms, the roof of which could be opened for showers of flowers to be thrown upon the guests, and of the colossal statue of Nero, 120 feet high, the work of Zenodorus, which stood in the vestibule. Of all this magnificence we have still a small but vivid witness in the lovely '*Volta Dorata*[4],' which has been known since the Renaissance thanks to the investigations of the artists at the court of Leo X. In order to decorate the city in general and his palace in particular, Nero used the art treasures that his freedman Acratus had been collecting for some years in Greece and in Asia; Secundus Carrinas had been

[1] Tacitus, *Ann.* xv, 38.
[2] C. Hülsen, *A.J.A.* XIII, 1909, p. 45.
[3] A. Boethius, *The Neronian* 'nova urbs,' in *Corolla Archaeologica*, p. 84.
[4] Platner-Ashby, *A Topographical Dictionary of Rome*, p. 170, Pl. 22.

given him as a partner, probably after the fire, in order to hasten
the work. We have no exact figures for the extent of these de-
portations since our sources either confuse them with those that
were carried out by Nero during his tour in Greece or else as usual
exaggerate them. The evidence of the panic that these requisitions
produced, so that Rhodes used the favour of the Emperor to gain
exemption from it, shows even more plainly than notices, such as
that of Pausanias that five hundred statues were removed from
Delphi, how hateful this order was.

Lavish expenditure reached its height in this same year 64
with the project of linking Ostia by a canal to Lake Avernus, near
Cumae (which was in its turn already linked with Puteoli), in
order to facilitate the sea connections of Rome, and perhaps also
to put an end to the antagonism between the harbour of Ostia and
that of Puteoli. But the work had to be given up for lack of
money which, from 64 onwards, in consequence of all this extravagance, became embarrassing. All the forced contributions that
were imposed upon Italians and provincials for the rebuilding of
Rome did not suffice to make up for it. Nero went on his
way ruthlessly in the following years with partial or total confiscations of private estates, whether he profited by political condemnations, or simply put wealthy people out of the way, as
happened probably about this time in a celebrated case in Africa
where six landowners, who possessed half of all the estates there,
were put to death in order that he could claim their estates[1]. This
lack of money explains the curious story of a Roman knight,
Caesellius Bassus, who succeeded, in all good faith, in arousing
great hopes by his boast that he had had revealed to him in a dream
the secret hiding place of the buried treasure of Dido; he actually
persuaded the Emperor to order search to be made for it. And
it is to economic difficulties that we owe, probably in the first
instance, the deterioration of the coinage; the weight of the *aureus*
was reduced, about 64, from 1/40th to 1/45th of a pound and that
of the *denarius* from 1/84th to 1/96th. But doubtless other and
more technical reasons contributed to the change as is shown by
the fact that it was accompanied by an improvement in the
monetary system, since besides sesterce and dupondius, the As,
semis, and quadrans were minted in orichalcum and a semis in
copper was added to the As and quadrans. Possibly, too, a desire
to stabilize the value of the copper and orichalcum coins in relation to silver and gold, and by so doing to give Roman coins

---

[1] Cf. J. Carcopino, *L'inscription d'Aïn-El-Djemala* in *Mél. d'arch. et
d'hist.* XXVI, 1906, pp. 435 *sqq.*

values which could be brought into easy relations with those of the Greek coins, so that the equivalence of the one to the other was made more easy, also had some influence. Even so the date of the reform, at the very beginning of the financial crisis, suggests that diminution in weight was looked upon as an expedient, perhaps purely temporary, to lessen the amount paid out by the Treasury. The reform lasted in its essentials (that is in the lowering of the weight of the gold and silver coins) down to Caracalla, while for the type of coins in orichalcum or copper, Galba, or perhaps Nero himself, finally returned to the simpler Augustan system.

But these financial measures merely intensified the hostility of the Romans towards their emperor, and the conviction that Nero had been the incendiary deepened. Extremely sensitive, as his whole life shows, to popular opinion, he must have thought it would be useful to distract notice from himself by persecuting the Christians, who were by now distinct from the Jews. The testimony of sources[1] generally leaves no doubt that persecution was directed against the Christians as Christians, and we must suppose that Nero, in unloosing the attack, aimed rather at directing the fury of the people upon a section that was notoriously hated, and so winning back the favour of the mob, than at attributing the charge of firing Rome specifically to the Christians. It is true that the Jews too were hated; but their manner of life was less secret than that of the Christians and they were certainly protected by Poppaea. It is obvious that among the charges on which we may imagine the Christians were brought to trial, one that occurred most easily would be the accusation of being incendiaries. Naturally, too, in the excitement of the moment this charge was bound to prevail over all the others and must have determined in some part the penalties which the Christians had to undergo; if they were not thrown to beasts in the amphitheatre, they were, by a sort of retaliatory justice, used as living torches to light nocturnal games in the imperial gardens and in the Vatican circus. But it would be wrong to deduce from this that a definite charge of incendiarism was preferred against the Christians; such a charge can only have been an item in the complex of guilt which was attributed to the *nomen Christianum*.

It has been objected that if the persecution was directed against the Christians as such, it should have extended over all the empire, since the empire was dependent throughout upon its

----

[1] See Note 8, p. 887 *sq.*

emperor. Full and convincing evidence alone could prove either hypothesis, that the persecution was limited to Rome or extended over all the empire; but our evidence is meagre and doubtful. Apart from a forged inscription from Spain[1], and one from Pompeii, which can scarcely bear the weight that some have put upon it[2], there remain only the notices of the *Apocalypse* among the texts which can be held as trustworthy[3]; these notices allude however to isolated incidents and are merely valuable in so far as they tend to show that the *Apocalypse* was written about the year 68 and had reference to the Neronian persecution. The most probable hypothesis is that the persecution soon lost its force, whether owing to the Emperor's wearying of it or to greater discretion on the part of the Christians, and so was limited to Rome, though isolated echoes occurred in the provinces.

The late texts that accuse the Jews of having denounced the Christians have no value although, once granted the existing lack of sympathy, the Jews could scarcely have regarded a persecution of the Christians with disfavour. But once admitted that the Jews were exempted from the persecution because of their protection by Poppaea, their exemption is extremely important, for it shows that Nero had no intention of checking the proselytism of Oriental cults, especially Judaism, which was then active, but merely exploited a widespread public sentiment in order to distract attention from himself. The persecution had a political rather than a religious import, but the deep echo that it awoke in the consciousness of the Christians (who were now for the first time definitely recognized as such by the government), and the ascription of the deaths of St Peter and St Paul to it (whether rightly or wrongly does not matter), have helped to give it a significance for history and for the reputation of Nero in after times that by itself it could not have.

V. THE PISONIAN CONSPIRACY

The persecution of the Christians did not succeed in restoring the credit of Nero; rather, if we can believe Tacitus, it roused pity for the victims even among those who hated them, since the aim of the persecution was too open. Discontent reigned among the populace, but still more among the aristocracy, which now recognized more and more that it was being played with by the Emperor, its members persecuted, and the Senate deprived of all importance; besides, Nero's crimes and his artistic displays, which

---

[1] *C.I.L.* II, *231.   [2] *C.I.L.* IV, 679.   [3] Especially chapter II, 13.

were so contrary to Roman custom, could not but revolt them. One thing which must, most of all, have shocked the aristocracy, even though of recent date, was the large number of Orientals, especially freedmen, who had been given some of the highest posts in the empire; the more so because the monarchical character of Nero's rule was thus stressed and his Oriental subjects were the more ready to accept it. Balbillus held the prefecture of Egypt from 55 to 59 and was succeeded by the son of a Graeco-Oriental nurse of Nero, C. Caecina Tuscus, who held it until 65; on his fall another Oriental freedman Ponticus[1] ruled during the interim in 66 and was succeeded by a renegade Alexandrian Jew, Tiberius Julius Alexander, who some years before had given valuable help to Corbulo in the war in Armenia. The son of a Greek courtesan, C. Nymphidius Sabinus, held the prefecture of the praetorians in partnership with Tigellinus from 65 to 68, and Tigellinus himself was scorned for his low birth and for his ante-cedents. Claudius Athenodorus, the prefect of the corn supply in 67, was a freedman who had been raised to the rank of knight; freedmen also the two prefects who were successively in command of the fleet at Misenum, Anicetus and Moschus. The procurator of Judaea, Antonius Felix, was a freedman and, among his succes-sors, Gessius Florus was a Greek. Other freedmen were Patroclus, who was in charge of the public games, Polyclitus, who was sent to Britain in 61 to mend a quarrel between Suetonius Paulinus and the procurator Julius Classicianus, Acratus, who was sent over to Greece and Asia on an infamous mission to plunder works of art, and finally Helius, who during the tour of Nero in Greece re-mained as his representative in Italy.

All then—whether those who cherished a hope of complete restitution of Republican forms or those (henceforward the more numerous) who simply desired to replace Nero by an emperor who was more worthy and more respectful of tradition and privilege, whether soldiers who scorned the low-born men, such as Tigellinus, whom they saw placed in command of them, or finally the intel-lectual class who had been brought up on Stoic thought and taught to regard hatred of tyranny and the cult of freedom as ends in themselves—all were now agreed in being unable to endure the government of Nero any longer. A group of these banded them-selves together in 65 (after long preparations extending back perhaps to 62), in the so-called Pisonian conspiracy, the aim of which was to murder Nero. The majority of the conspirators

[1] Schumann, *op. cit.* p. 58. Cf. C. S. Walton, *Oriental Senators in the Service of Rome*, in *J.R.S.* XIX, 1929, pp. 44 *sqq.*

apparently wished to put in his place C. Calpurnius Piso, who belonged to the old Roman nobility, had won fame as a speaker, was
a generous protector of artists and was celebrated by an anonymous
poet in a poem which has come down to us[1]. Others perhaps
thought of Seneca, principally as a possible restorer of Republican
liberty, and so must have found themselves near to the smaller group
of real Republicans in the conspiracy. To apportion the names that
have come down to us between these sections is extremely difficult,
the more so as although they were for the moment united, we
cannot exclude the possibility of a compromise once the blow had
succeeded. We may be certain that among the republicans were
the *consul designatus*, Plautus Lateranus and the poet Lucan, who
had been disgusted by Nero's artistic jealousies; he could no
longer love the Emperor while hating the Empire, as he had done
at first, and this change inspired the greater seriousness and depth
of Republican sentiment which is visible in the last books of the
Pharsalia.

A military group, headed by the prefect of the praetorians
Faenius Rufus, who was jealous of his colleague Tigellinus, and
some tribunes and centurions, were apparently supporters of
Seneca. But the majority of the senators and knights were naturally enthusiastic for Piso. The knights numbered five, among
whom was Claudius Senecio who had been one of the intimate
friends of Nero. The number of senators is uncertain; beyond
Piso, Plautius Lateranus and Lucan, there were certainly two
others implicated, Afranius Quintianus and Flavius Scaevinus;
but the complicity of seven others is dubious and of five others,
apart from their complicity, we cannot even be sure that they were
of senatorial rank[2]. There can be no doubt that Seneca shared in
the conspiracy; his friendship with Piso, of which indeed he had
been accused in 62, was common knowledge and in 65 he could
not deny it; besides he was the uncle of one conspirator, and other
conspirators favoured his claims. It appears therefore unlikely that
he could have been kept in the dark, nor can we lightly accuse Nero
of having condemned him to death without just cause of suspicion.

The conspirators, after some hesitation as to the best method
of attacking Nero, decided to make the attempt during the games
held for the feast of Ceres in the Circus Maximus at the end of
April. But some news had already slipped out, when a freedwoman called Epicharis, who was in the secret, tried to draw into
the conspiracy an officer of the fleet at Misenum. This officer,

---

[1] *Incerti laus Pisonis*. Poet. Lat. min. 1, p. 225.
[2] See the table in Henderson, *op. cit.* p. 486.

Volusius Proculus, brought the matter to the notice of Nero but was not able to give further details since Epicharis had not mentioned any names, and for that reason the inquiry could not proceed further. But on the very night before the day fixed for the deed, a freedman called Milichus denounced his patron, the senator Scaevinus, and also a knight Antonius Natalis to the Emperor as conspirators. How he came to be aware of the plot was not certainly known even to the ancients. After first denying it, Natalis, when placed under torture and also urged on by promises of pardon, revealed the plot, together with the names of Seneca and Piso; Scaevinus followed him and added fresh names. After that the inquiry pursued the course usual in all detected conspiracies. Some persisted uselessly in denial, like the heroic Epicharis, who died under torture; Lucan sank, it is said, so low as to accuse his mother. The prefect Faenius Rufus for a time sat among the judges until he was unmasked by Scaevinus. Some, such as Piso and Lateranus, were killed, others had time to commit suicide and faced death as Stoicism had taught them; such was Lucan, who died reciting his own verses. Seneca received the order for death tranquilly and had his veins opened, but only after long agony found rest at last. His wife Paulina was saved by order of Nero, although she had already tried to take her life. Others who had been charged, since they were held harmless or less culpable, were sent into exile. Among those who were driven to suicide was the consul Atticus Vestinus, apparently innocent, but suspect for his Republican sentiments and perhaps still more for having married Statilia Messallina, a favourite of the Emperor. If we also include the daughter of Claudius, Antonia (who was killed a few months afterwards on the charge of having shared in the conspiracy), nineteen persons were executed, thirteen exiled and four tribunes cashiered, without counting some victims who were involved later and indirectly. Antonius Natalis was pardoned and Milichus received, amid lavish gifts, the title of saviour.

The conspiracy must have made a deep impression upon Nero owing to the men who were implicated in it. His suspicious nature was exacerbated and he enlarged that body of secret service agents, which was so hated and feared in Rome and was one of the first things abolished by Vespasian; it is enough to record two notorious members, Aquilius Regulus and Eprius Marcellus. In fact the Pisonian conspiracy marked the definite breach between Nero and the aristocracy.

Henceforward Tigellinus had a free hand in the task of purging the State of the suspected. L. Junius Silanus, the last of that unfortunate family, was killed; the relatives of Rubellius Plautus, his wife Pollitta, his father-in-law L. Antistius Vetus, and his wife's aunt Sextia, were driven to suicide. The aged jurist C. Cassius Longinus was banished to Sardinia, Musonius Rufus, notable as a philosopher, was relegated to Gyaros. In the following year, 66, commands to commit suicide grew more numerous: two brothers of Seneca, Gallio and Annaeus Mela, the father of Lucan, had to kill themselves[1] on suspicion of belonging to Piso's group, and the suicide of Mela carried with it that of Anicius Cerealis, who was accused, it is hard to see why, in a document attached to the will of Mela, of having taken part in the Pisonian conspiracy. So, too, Rufrius Crispinus, already exiled to Sardinia for the same conspiracy, was killed on information laid by Antistius Sosianus who hoped in this way to return from the banishment to which he had been sentenced in 62. Two nobles, P. Anteius and Ostorius Scapula, were condemned to death. Tacitus gives as a reason for their condemnation a horoscope that they had had drawn up by a companion of Antistius's exile, which would have served to show their longing to see a change in the future; but we are not bound to believe that the foundation of their accusation was so unsubstantial. Among particular victims of the hatred of Tigellinus there fell an ex-praetor Minucius Thermus, and the refined C. Petronius, the arbiter of elegance, who represented, though with a half-amused detachment, the luxurious life of the court. At Cumae he received the order to kill himself; he went to his death with the same lofty *insouciance* with which he had lived, and, with a last smile, smashed with his own hand his precious vases which he knew Nero coveted.

The persecution at last reached that small group of Stoics which had not so far been mixed up in any conspiracy but throughout had shown its proud scorn of tyranny. Thrasea Paetus, the senator who used to celebrate with garlands and libations the birthdays of Brutus and Cassius, who never sacrificed for the emperor, and kept away from the Senate whenever honours were decreed to the imperial family, was now condemned to death by the Senate for treason. He would not allow the young tribune Rusticus Arulenus, who was to be his panegyrist (and probably a distant source of Tacitus) and afterwards his imitator under Domitian, to postpone his fate by intercession; he refused to appear in his own defence in the Senate and awaited the announcement of his condemnation

[1] The account given here follows Dio LXII, 25, which is not in disagreement with Tacitus, *Ann.* XVI, 17, if we suppose that Tacitus mentioned the death of Gallio in the lost part of the *Annals*.

discussing in a Socratic manner with his friends the immortality of the soul. His son-in-law, Helvidius Priscus, and Paconius Agrippinus were condemned to exile, and a famous passage of Epictetus records the serenity with which Paconius greeted his punishment[1]. Finally, a former proconsul of Asia, Barea Soranus and his daughter Servilia were condemned to death; and the fact of their having consulted astrologers about the fate of the Emperor was, if not the chief accusation, as tradition records, at any rate severe testimony against them.

Even so, opposition was not broken. In 66 a new conspiracy, called the Vinician, from the name of its leader Annius Vinicianus, who had married the daughter of Corbulo, was discovered at Beneventum. We have no details about it; it seems probable that its aim was to substitute Corbulo for Nero and that it implicated more than one of the great commanders. In fact we cannot separate this conspiracy from what happened a few months later during the tour of Nero in Greece: the two governors of Upper and Lower Germany, Scribonius Rufus and Scribonius Proculus, were bidden to join Nero in Greece and hardly had they arrived before they received the order for death. So, too, Corbulo, while he disembarked at Cenchreae on the Saronic Gulf to rejoin his emperor, received the fatal order, and he too obeyed. The only possible explanation of this occurrence is that Nero had waited for a chance to lure these generals away, all unsuspecting, from their armies so as to punish them for attempted treachery without their being able to bring their troops behind them in resistance.

Although we can be sure that the account of all these victims of Nero[2], given us by hostile writers, has partially distorted the truth, concealing the real culpability of many of the condemned, it is none the less clear that the Emperor by this time had roused against him all thoughtful and conscientious men in Rome. The justification for their hostility lies in the very lightness with which Nero freed himself of them; for such lightness was a sign that he no longer valued those who preserved any sense of personal dignity and so were not ready to submit to him. For the principate in its transformation into a monarchy demanded the submission of all and the repression of all activity that was not at its service; and owing to the lack of all moral sense in Nero submission to the Empire too soon became submission to the personal caprices of the Emperor. And while the propaganda for this monarchical idea had aroused the hostility of the Roman aristocracy, this hostility in its turn drove Nero more and more to stress it and oppose the

[1] I, 2, 12 *sqq.*   [2] See Pliny, *Epp.* v, 5, 3.

divine being of the emperor, all-seeing and all-provident, to the ideals of Republican freedom. The figure of the emperor towered ever higher, and his character as Saviour of the World, already expressed in the name of an Alexandrian tribe, received still greater emphasis in the East[1]. And though after the Pisonian conspiracy he had refused the offer of a temple at Rome to himself as Divus Nero[2], perhaps because he realized that an anticipation of his apotheosis might be described by his enemies as of ill omen, the tendency to deification was becoming more openly expressed. Little emphasis can be placed on the vague exaltation in the proem of the *Pharsalia* or on the fact that he is called god (*theos*) on some coins of Asia Minor[3], for that compliment was also paid to emperors like Tiberius and Claudius, whose attitude towards deification was conservatively reluctant. But it is significant that he is identified with different deities, with Zeus explicitly at Acraephiae and on coins of Sicyon, and implicitly on Roman coins where the aegis is figured[4]. More frequent are identifications with Hercules or Apollo, that is with gods who represented those activities that he loved above all; in Rome, on his return from Greece, he was greeted as Hercules, and coins of Patrae bear the legend *Herculi Augusto*[5]. It is said by Dio that the senators acclaimed him as Nero-Apollo on the occasion of his triumphal return, and not only is he given the attributes of Apollo on coins and statues, but a recently-discovered inscription (from Athens) actually equates him with Apollo[6]. Closely connected with this is his identification with the sun-god Helios, a title which is applied to him in the Acraephiae inscription and also in one from Sagalassus in Pisidia[7] and is echoed in literature in the *Apocolocyntosis* and in an epigram from the Palatine anthology[8].

[1] Thus he is ὁ σωτὴρ τῆς οἰκουμένης in the Ptolemaïs inscription (A.D. 60–2), O.G.I.S. 668 *sq.*, and ὁ τοῦ παντὸς κοσμοῦ κύριος at Acraephiae, Ditt.[3] 814. Probably his identification on an inscription from Cos with Asclepius (*I.G.R.R.* IV, 1053) is to be connected with this title, just as ἀγαθὸς θεός is to be linked with the identification mentioned earlier, p. 707 n. 1, with ἀγαθὸς δαίμων.   [2] Tacitus, *Ann.* xv, 74.

[3] *E.g.* on coins of Cyme and Synaüs, which bear the legend θεὸς Νέρων, E. A. Sydenham, *The Coinage of Nero*, 1920, p. 48.

[4] Sydenham, *op. cit.* p. 23 and Volume of Plates iv, 204, *h*, *g*: Riewald, *de imp. Rom. cum certis dis et comparatione et aequatione*, p. 290.

[5] Sydenham, *op. cit.* p. 138.

[6] Dio LXIII, 20; on a new inscription from Athens see P. Graindor, *B.C.H.* LI, 1927, p. 260, αὐτοκράτορι [Νέρω]νι Καίσαρι Σεβαστῷ νέῳ Ἀπόλλωνι.   [7] Νέος Ἥλιος, *I.G.R.R.* III, 345.

[8] *Anth. Pal.* IX, 178. See above, p. 704.

Finally, the radiate crown which he wears on coins of this period is an attribute originally reserved for deified emperors (see also above, p. 501).

This religious elevation of the Emperor was naturally reflected in the whole imperial family. When the baby daughter of Poppaea, Claudia, died after a few months in 63, she was deified as *Diva Claudia*. So too Poppaea, who died in 65, apparently from a kick dealt her by Nero in a moment of anger, was deified and her body embalmed like that of oriental monarchs. His third wife, Statilia Messallina, whom he married in 66, shared the deification of her husband in the decree of Acraephiae, which ordains also the erection of a statue to her in the local temple of Apollo Ptoios[1].

Yet another aspect of the elevation of the Emperor is the changing of names of months and even of places in his honour. After the Pisonian conspiracy, the month of April became *Neroneus*, and the months of May and June were changed respectively to *Claudius* and *Germanicus*, perhaps rather in celebration of the other names of the Emperor than in memory of his adoptive father and of his grandfather. In Egypt the month of Pharmuthi received the name of *Neroneios Sebastos*. Among cities Caesarea Philippi, the capital of the kingdom of Agrippa II, became *Neronias*, and Artaxata in vassal Armenia emerged as *Neroneia*. Greater importance would have attached to two other changes, which may have been projected: the Acraephiae inscription leaves little doubt that Nero meant to rechristen the Peloponnese as the island of Nero[2], and this helps to explain (though not necessarily to confirm) Suetonius' assertion that Rome was to become *Neropolis*[3].

Coins above all afford us some conception of the way in which every occasion was exploited to heighten the glory of the Emperor. The rebuilding of Rome is commemorated by a series of coins that bear the name of the city, and by another series that picture different buildings that were reconstructed, such as the temple of Vesta, while another issue, after the Pisonian conspiracy, refers thankfully to the *Securitas Augusti*, the *Genius Augusti* and *Juppiter Custos*[4]. The culminating point in the glori-

[1] The name of Messallina has been erased but the restoration is certain.
[2] The present writer accepts the interpretation of the phrase in l. 13, τὴν ἕως νῦν Πελοπόννησον, first proposed by M. Holleaux in *B.C.H.* XII, 1888, pp. 510 *sqq.*   [3] Suetonius, *Nero*, 55.
[4] See Sydenham, *op. cit.* pp. 117, 76, 119 and cf. the coins which figure the eagle of Capitoline Juppiter, Volume of Plates iv, 204, *i, j*; 206, *a, b, c*. For a possible reference to Ζεὺς Καπετώλιος on Alexandrian coins see Vogt, *op. cit.* p. 32.

fication of the Emperor was reached in 66, when Tiridates came
to receive from Nero the crown of Armenia. After festivities at
Naples, the coronation took place in the Forum at Rome: Dio
declares that the prince abased himself before Nero as his god
(LXIII, 5), and worshipped him as Mithras (see also p. 773). The
temple of Janus was closed and coins proclaimed the peace which had
been earned so laboriously for the Roman People by sea and land;
pace p. R. terra marique parta Janum clusit is the legend upon one,
while others celebrate the *Victoria Augusti* and bear the inscription
Ara Pacis. We may find it hard to understand so great an uproar
over a solution that was merely a compromise and that in substance
unravelled none of the eastern frontier problems, but though we
may discount the exaggerations of officialdom, the spectacle, after
so many years of grievous warfare, of the Parthians recognizing
the superiority of Rome and of a Parthian prince coming to Rome
to make his submission[1] must have produced the liveliest emotion
and the highest hopes; and all this could not fail to work on so
excitable an imagination as Nero's and confirm his own conception
of his greatness. The great 'Column of Nero' at Mainz, dedicated
to *Juppiter Optimus Maximus*, 'pro salute Neronis Claudi Augusti,'
should almost certainly be assigned to this year, and is probably
connected with these very ceremonies in Rome[2]. At the top of the
column stood Juppiter, below in bas-reliefs there file before us
Apollo, Hercules, Juppiter again, Vulcan (perhaps signifying the
conquest of the fire at Rome), Mars and Neptune (symbols of
victory by land and sea), Minerva and Mercury (symbolizing the
encouragement given by Nero to learning and commerce), Fortuna, Felicitas, Salus, and other abstract deities[3]. It has justly been
called 'an imperial hymn in stone'; all the identifications with
gods and goddesses that the emperor most revered and all the
most widespread symbols are here united to show how Nero holds
in his hands the destinies of the world.

[1] The supposed connection between the journey of Tiridates and the
story of the Magi may be abandoned; see Fr. Cumont in *Mem. Pont. Accad.
Arch.* S. III, vol. III, 1932, p. 81.

[2] See Volume of Plates, iv, 194. The text here follows H. Drexel,
Röm.-Germ. Korr.-Blatt, VIII, 1915, p. 65: cf. F. Koepp, in *Germania
Romana*, IV, pp. 8–10. The establishment of the community of the *canabarii*
as a municipium was merely the occasion for its erection.

[3] For the vexed question of the interpretation of the various symbols see
F. Quilling, *Die Juppitersäule des Samus und Severus* and 'Nachtrag.'

VI. THE JOURNEY TO GREECE

The lord of the world now made ready, after these ceremonies at Rome, to give definite convincing proof of his majesty, for after such a prelude he must astonish men by his acts, and he was now in a state of mind to do so. The liberation of Greece, the piercing of the Isthmus of Corinth, not to mention artistic and athletic exhibitions at the most important centres—for this third item was as important to Nero's mind as the other two—were only to be the first acts of his enterprise. Afterwards he had in mind to journey to Alexandria and embark upon a grandiose policy of expansion towards the East and possibly towards the South (see below, pp. 776 *sqq.*). A concentration of legions was ordered in Egypt, but the outbreak of the Jewish revolt and the political events in the West combined to thwart his purposes, and for this reason, too, his schemes did not get beyond the tour in Greece.

The Emperor set out from Rome at the end of September in 66[1], accompanied by several thousand *Augustiani* and praetorians under the command of Tigellinus, leaving the capital in charge of his freedmen, among whom was Helius. Some weeks afterwards, he staged his first artistic appearance in Greece as a singer at Corcyra, and a few days after that at Actium took part in the games founded by Augustus. Thence he reached Corinth[2]; and, on 28 November, at the Isthmian games, specially celebrated on the spot where the proclamation of Flamininus had been made, he announced the gift of freedom to the Greeks in a speech which is still preserved in the Acraephiae inscription, and in which genuine love of Hellas is mingled with the most naïve self-praise ending in the complacent final exclamation, 'Other men have given freedom to individual cities, Nero alone has freed a whole province.' Naturally this gift did not mean that Greece was to be detached from the empire: free federate cities were bound to follow the external policy of Rome, and quite apart from the arbitrary intervention of provincial governors, any territory that had been proclaimed free

---

[1] The prayer of the Arval Brothers on 25 September, 'pro salute et reditu impera[toris Neronis Claudi Caesaris Augusti et Messallinae coniugis eius]' (*C.I.L.* vi, 2044), can only refer to the journey to Greece, in the opinion of the present writer, even though Messallina apparently did not accompany Nero.

[2] The year 66, and not 67, has been shown to be the right one by J. Vogt, *Alex. Münzen*, pp. 34–5. Objections based on Suetonius, *Nero*, 24 (see most recently Schumann, *op. cit.* p. 75) leave untouched the decisive fact that, by 1 July 67, Sardinia was a senatorial province: the liberation of Greece must therefore fall before this date.

by a mere unilateral gesture, ran the risk of seeing its freedom revoked by the same will that had granted it; freedom meant merely a limited autonomy, but it did carry exemption from the payment of tribute, which was a very great advantage for a region so impoverished as Greece. And if we add that the Greeks, immersed as ever in past glories, ascribed to the act a value far above its real, we can understand the enthusiasm that Nero's gesture evoked in them: a more emotional memory was preserved by the very fact that this dream of liberty was so soon dissolved by Vespasian's revocation of the grant. The enthusiasm of the miracle-worker, Apollonius of Tyana, who saw clearly enough the incompetence of Nero, is only one voice amid many.

The Senate received Sardinia as a recompense for the province that had been taken from them. After this proclamation, Nero passed the whole of the winter in Greece without, as far as we know, accomplishing anything noteworthy. In the spring he took part in the national games, which at his express wish were all summoned to meet in the same year, so that he could have the honours of a victor in all four; for this reason the Isthmian games, which had already been celebrated in the preceding autumn, were now repeated. In addition Nero appeared at the games at Argos. He had already in 65 at the Quinquennial games shown himself frequently in public and had performed men's and women's parts in tragedy. Now, besides acting as driver in the chariot races, he competed as harper and as tragedian, and had the programme of the games altered so that he could appear at Olympia as harper and at the Isthmus as tragic actor. It goes without saying that he won first prize at all competitions in which he took part, and even in those in which he did not, although he was anxious to compete seriously and bestowed Roman citizenship upon his competitors as a reward for their loyalty and skill.

Towards September, at Corinth, he began work on another great enterprise, which had previously attracted Gaius, that of uniting the Saronic Gulf with the Gulf of Corinth. True, this project was not of great importance for the trade of the empire; its advantages would have been limited to Greece, and so no great effort was made in antiquity either before or after Nero to put it into execution; in spite of Nero's solemn inauguration, after a few months' work it was allowed to lapse in the turmoil of the year 68. But the cutting of the isthmus appealed to Nero, not because of any economic advantages, but because of the unprecedented boldness of the scheme. There is, indeed, ample evidence of the great impression that the attempt made upon the ancients, an impression so profound that it was considered as an offence against heaven[1]. This explains the solemnity with which the work was begun; hymns were sung to Amphitrite, to Poseidon, to Melikertes and to Leukothea, and Nero himself cut the first sod; praetorians and prisoners, especially prisoners of war, were employed on the labour.

In the intervals between these enterprises, towards the end of 67, Nero toured all Greece, visiting famous places, collecting works of art, taking an interest in local life and imposing taxation on the rich to maintain himself and his suite. We need not linger over the tales of abnormal cruelty and lust that our sources attribute to Nero at this time, for such stories represent simply the rumours that were circulating in Italy against the absent emperor, and indicate his growing unpopularity. But even the most sceptical historian must admit that Nero's tour in Greece presents psychological problems which are hard to solve; apart from the fundamental fact that he took his rôle of competitor with such intense seriousness (for he must have known victory was secure), it is enough to mention that he would not visit either Sparta or Athens—a whim for which we can find no reason save the rather improbable one that these cities, being already free, could not have had any gratitude to show to the Emperor.

VII. THE DECLINE OF NERO'S POWER

But in any event the journey, though it may have excited Greece and made a deep impression on the East, had been most damaging for the prestige of Nero in the West. There was no lack, of course, of the usual official propaganda, and Roman coins afford a pale reflection of the ceremonies that must have accompanied every event in Greece, such as the arrival, Nero's victories, and the liberation of Greece. An echo of this is found in the Alexandrian coins which not only figure a series of protectors of the games (Zeus of Olympia and of Nemea, Apollo Pythius, Poseidon Isthmius, and Hera of Argos[2]), but at this time associate Nero with Augustus and Tiberius, thus making his philhellene policy appear a continuation of that of the founders of the dynasty. But all this propaganda could not lull the unrest that began to master

---

[1] Cf., for example, the notices in the Sibylline Oracles, viii, 155 *sqq.* (Geffcken), Philostratus, *Apollonius,* iv, 24 and pseudo-Lucian, *Nero sive de fossione Isthmi.*

[2] See Volume of Plates iv, 206, *d–h.*

the empire; the loathing of the aristocracy, cut off from the Emperor by a sea of blood[1], began to have an effect on the loyalty of the troops. The fate of Corbulo, the greatest soldier of the time, and of the two commanders of Upper and Lower Germany, was at once a symptom of the distrust of the generals and a reason for further distrust and anger (see above, p. 731). Nor had the inferior officers or troops any feeling of devotion to the Emperor that might have put a check on the intentions of the higher commands. Nero had kept far away from battles or from the great permanent camps of the armies, and he had taken no share in the campaigns against Parthia and the putting down of the rebellion in Britain. Now a dangerous revolt in Judaea was keeping some sixty thousand men, under the command of Vespasian, fully occupied while the Emperor was amusing himself in Greece (p. 859). Naturally the soldiers must have been more devoted to their generals than to their emperor and were easily persuaded to embark on adventures that promised them booty, promotion, relaxation of discipline and a privileged position. With this lowering of the prestige of the central power, the nationalist and separatist feelings of different regions sprang into life again, roused by envy of the privileges bestowed on Greece. In consequence those provincials who were in command of an army combined a Roman soldier's hatred of Nero with a provincial's ambitions for greater liberty, if not autonomy, in his own country, and in the same ambiguous manner as Vindex and Civilis ended as rebels.

Towards the end of 67, though as yet there were no open outbreaks, affairs began to look so dark that Helius, the freedman governor of Rome, asked Nero to return and, seeing that he could not make up his mind, went in person to Corinth to implore him. It is unnecessary to imagine that Helius had an inkling of any particular conspiracy; we may assume that he had insight enough to read the signs of the coming storm. In Rome irritation had been increased by a famine, due to the irregular arrival of corn from Egypt, possibly because both corn and corn-ships had been impounded for the supply of the army in Palestine and also, though in a less degree, of the imperial suite. About January 68 Nero returned to Italy and for a moment succeeded in reviving the emotions of the mob by his presence. At Naples he appeared

[1] For the hard facts of the imperial persecutions, so far as the Senate alone is concerned, see the statistics given by J. Willems, *Le Sénat romain en l'an 65 après Jésus Christ* in *Le Musée belge*, IV, 1900, pp. 236 *sqq.*; V, 1901, pp. 82 *sqq.*; VI, 1902, pp. 100 *sqq.*

as victor in the sacred games of Greece and, according to custom, entered the city through a breach made in the walls on a chariot drawn by white horses. Passing by Antium and Albanum, he reached Rome, where the same ceremony had been prepared for him, and through an arch in the Circus Maximus, past the Velabrum and the Forum, he climbed to the temple of Apollo on the Palatine, to whom he dedicated 1808 crowns that he had won in Greece. But apparently, lost in memories of the past year, he found it difficult to live save in a city of Greek customs, for by March he was back in Naples, where news reached him that the governor of Gallia Lugdunensis, the romanized Gaul, C. Julius Vindex, was in open revolt (p. 810).

This revolt, with its anti-Neronian cry of 'freedom from the tyrant,' aimed at getting a pledge from any successor which would recognize more or less complete autonomy for Gaul, but it was scarcely a real threat to the empire, since a few months were enough for the general of the legions in Upper Germany, Verginius Rufus, to put it down. Nor is it likely that, with the collapse of this movement, any greater success would have attended the revolt begun by the governor of Hispania Tarraconensis, Sulpicius Galba, who on 2 April 68 made common cause with Vindex, refused obedience to Nero, and by declaring himself the legate of the Senate and Roman People put forward, doubtless in agreement with Vindex, a claim to the throne. With Gaul once pacified, this outbreak would have been isolated in the Spanish peninsula, where Galba after eight years residence enjoyed great popularity. Even so, he only won two supporters, Otho, the governor of Lusitania, and Caecina, the quaestor of Baetica, while the forces of men and money at his disposal, even after enrolling a legion of provincials (which afterwards became the VII Galbiana) and of other light-armed troops drawn from marines and non-romanized Iberians, were quite inadequate for a march upon Italy. But in Rome all were only waiting for the chance to betray Nero, and though the Senate on the first news of the revolt declared Galba a public enemy and confiscated his estates in Italy, it did so with an ill grace and soon was ready to treat with his emissaries. Orthodox Republicanism, as we have seen, lived on now only in a few, but even these few must have recognized that without support from an army they could not get rid of Nero; hence they could do nothing short of recognizing Galba. On the other hand, Tigellinus, who disappears at this moment from the scene, did not help Nero by his advice. The fact is certain, though his reasons are difficult to define. Nero by himself was quite incapable of organizing seriously any resistance. He levied a new legion from marines (the Legio I Adiutrix), but mobilization was so slow that it could take no part in ensuing events. He sent his mistress, Calvia Crispinilla, to urge the legatus in Africa, Clodius Macer, to intervene in his favour, but Crispinilla did not work seriously for him, while Clodius revolted and struck money on his own account. Instead of taking command personally against the rebels, Nero entrusted the troops that he had intended for his expeditions to the East to Petronius Turpilianus, commanding in Britain, and to Rubrius Gallus[1]; they were recalled in time (among them the Legio I Italica), but though sent into Gaul they achieved nothing, whilst the conduct of Verginius Rufus who, though he would not accept the crown, put himself at the disposition of the Senate, was equivalent to an act of rebellion.

Nero's own feelings varied rapidly between extremes of despair and excessive confidence and though the extravagances attributed to him—such as his intention to poison the Senate, burn Rome and slip away to Egypt—must have been legendary, such well-attested actions as his defiant assumption of a sole consulship towards the end of April in the hope of making a demonstration of force, betray his bewilderment. In Rome the populace, who were waiting for bread and saw ships arrive loaded with sand for the stage on which the emperor was performing, grew more and more riotous. In such a situation all that was needed, now that Tigellinus had fled, was for the prefect Nymphidius Sabinus to suborn the praetorian guard to make common cause with the Senate, for Nero to find himself without helpers and lost. He now tried (the evening of 8 June) to escape, perhaps towards Egypt, which he rightly believed loyal, and whilst waiting for his freedman to get the fleet ready passed a night in the Servilian gardens on the road to Ostia. But by now the rebellion of the praetorians was in being; the officers refused to follow him and shortly after, at midnight, the company on guard deserted. Meanwhile, Nymphidius, accompanied by the senators, went down to the barracks of the praetorians and, by telling them Nero had fled and promising a donative of 30,000 sesterces for each man, persuaded them to proclaim Galba emperor. Nero by now had found refuge in the villa of his freedman Phaon, lying some four miles from the city between the Via Salaria and the Via Nomentana,

---

[1] The account of Schiller, *op. cit.* p. 281, n. 4, is here followed. The behaviour of Petronius Turpilianus is extremely mysterious, but Boissevain, *Cassius Dio*, III, p. 91, shows that he remained faithful to Nero.

Perhaps he still hoped to escape if he could elude the first search-parties. But when he learnt that he had been declared a public enemy by the Senate, who had at once recognized Galba, with the pursuing horsemen almost upon him, he plunged a sword into his throat, helped by one of the few who had followed him, his freedman, Epaphroditus. A centurion who burst in hoping to capture him found him dying and, while he strove to staunch the wound, heard him groan 'Too late, this is loyalty indeed.' It is said that before this, in the agony of his contemplated suicide, he walked about whimpering 'What an artist dies in me' (*qualis artifex pereo*)[1]. His two nurses, Ecloge and Alexandra, and the ever-faithful Acte saw him buried in the tomb of the Domitii in the Campus Martius. It was 9 June 68.

Nero was just thirty years and six months old. The mysterious circumstances of his death favoured, as it happened, the spread of a belief, especially in the East, that he was not dead but had got away safely. Hence impostors could arise, giving themselves his name and trying to raise the mob; one such appeared immediately in 69 and, after arousing great expectations in Greece and Asia, which found an echo even in Parthia, ended by killing himself in the island of Cythnus, where he had been driven by a storm. Another in 79, Terentius Maximus, like his predecessor profited from the prestige of Nero's name with the Parthians to turn for help to them, but he, too, after being exposed, ended badly, it is not known how.

But obviously this posthumous fame of Nero is not due merely to the mysterious circumstances of his death; it is rooted in the very character of his government, which was the first to give to his subjects the feeling of imperial authority as something super-eminent and above the law, sometimes terrible but sometimes beneficent; in comparison Gaius' experiment had passed unnoticed. In the West the phenomenon had a limited importance. Naturally there were those who regretted him, especially since in him the Julio-Claudian line perished, and for that reason his tomb was for long covered with flowers and Otho, exploiting this dynastic loyalty, represented himself as the legitimate successor of Nero. But this good-will, like the hostility which was far more widespread and became official with the advent of the Flavians, remained always political and moral and never religious. In the East, on the other hand, the liberation of Greece, the journey of the Parthian prince to do homage, and the cutting of the Isthmus of Corinth appeared as

[1] In the interpretation given to *artifex* (τεχνίτης) the present writer follows R. Cantarella, *Il Mondo Classico*, 1, 1931, fasc. 2, pp. 53 *sqq.*

so many proofs of the supernatural being of Nero and obliterated
the memory of his crimes. Hence the conviction that he was
destined to return and reign—a conviction that, as Dio Chrysostom shows, was still widespread in the time of Trajan and from
which those impostors who took his name profited greatly. On
the other hand, among Jews and Christians, who had in their
different ways suffered severely during his reign, and whose
higher moral sense revolted more deeply against crimes such as
the matricide, the figure of Nero assumed diabolic proportions.
His expected return to the throne from somewhere beyond the
Euphrates (where he was imagined to be lurking) is regarded by
the Jewish Sibylline Oracles as the momentary triumph of Satan,
which precedes the final victory of Justice. Christian tradition
was to identify him more definitely either with Antichrist or with
the messenger who precedes Antichrist and prepares the way for
his advent before the end of the world. This implied antithesis
between the Church of Christ and the Empire of Antichrist
suggests that a strange truth underlay the tradition that chose, as
the personification of the Empire opposed to the Church, the
emperor who first put into practice his conception of unlimited
power, offset—even though in ignorance—the salvation of Christ
by a salvation of his own, and like Christ wished to be called the
saviour of the world.

CHAPTER XXII

THE EASTERN FRONTIER FROM TIBERIUS TO NERO[1]

I. EGYPT. THE MISSION OF GERMANICUS TO THE EAST AND THE RESTORATION OF ROMAN PRESTIGE

BETWEEN the death of Augustus and that of Nero one or two changes of some importance took place in Egypt. It has been mentioned that the legionary establishment was reduced to two legions some time before A.D. 23, but that the reduction was in all probability made in the later years of Augustus. The position which the third legion had held at the southern apex of the Delta was still guarded by an auxiliary regiment[2]. Another change was the concentration of the two remaining legions at Alexandria, evidently with the object of overawing the turbulent Alexandrians: the capital of Egypt thus came to share the lot of Rome, which had the praetorian cohorts barracked outside its gates. The legion now brought to Nicopolis, to be quartered with that already there, was III Cyrenaica, which had probably been stationed either at Coptos or at Thebes. Both these towns continued to have garrisons, composed of legionary detachments and some auxiliary troops, from which soldiers were doubtless drawn to man the military posts in the Arabian Desert. The exact date of the transference of the legion is not certain, but probability points to the reign of Gaius or the early years of Claudius, when the disturbed situation resulting from the anti-Semitic outbreak of A.D. 38 would naturally suggest the strengthening of the garrison as a measure of precaution[3]. The barracking of two legions together in one fortress led to the appointment of a single

---

[1] See Map 3, facing p. 31, Map 4, facing p. 47, and Map 9, facing p. 255.

[2] P. Hamb. 2 attests the presence of an *ala Vocontiorum* in A.D. 59.

[3] Mommsen (*C.I.L.* III, 6809) dated the transference to A.D. 38, because Philo, *In Flaccum*, 111, narrating the events following the riot of that year, speaks of the στρατάρχης at Alexandria, a term which Mommsen equated with the title quoted in the next note. But the word may mean *praef. legionis*, as Mommsen himself had formerly interpreted it (*Gesamm. Schriften*, VI, p. 178, n. 2).

praefectus castrorum, who is described in an epitaph set up outside Egypt as 'prefect of the Egyptian army[1].'

In the East the reign of Tiberius opened with confusion. Armenia had no recognized ruler. On his expulsion from Parthia Vonones, as has been seen, fled thither in the hope of securing the crown, and having been accepted as king by a section of the nobility, sent envoys to ask the consent of the Roman government[2]. Naturally, however, his presence in Armenia could not be tolerated by his victorious rival Artabanus, who threatened war, and Tiberius, who had the meanest opinion of his spirit, refused to recognize him and about A.D. 16 ordered the governor of Syria, Creticus Silanus, to intern him in Antioch, where he was allowed to retain his royal title and enjoy the wealth he had brought with him from Parthia[3].

Cappadocia also was without a ruler. Soon after his accession Tiberius summoned to Rome the aged king Archelaus and brought him to trial before the Senate on a charge of revolutionary activities, the precise nature of which is not recorded[4]. In 20 B.C. Archelaus had had his dominions enlarged by the addition of Lesser Armenia, left vacant by the death of Artavasdes, and of eastern Lycaonia with the adjacent mountainous region of Cilicia Tracheia[5]. About A.D. 10 he became temporarily insane, and Augustus appointed a procurator to take charge of his kingdom and withdrew from him part of his Cilician territory, the districts of Cennatis and Lalassis in the valley of the Calycadnus, which he gave to Ajax, high-priest of Olba (Oura), a member of an old priestly family[6]. Tiberius bore the king no goodwill. Although in his early manhood he had secured his acquittal when brought to trial before Augustus by his subjects, Archelaus had paid him no attention during his stay in Rhodes (on the advice, says Tacitus, of the intimate friends of Augustus), but had courted the young Gaius during his mission to the East. The result of the trial is not recorded, but the king died shortly afterwards in A.D. 17.

[1] *Praefectus exercitu qui est in Aegypto*, Dessau 2696. His rank (he had held the first centurionate only once) shows that he was not commander of the legions (see above, p. 286).

[2] Josephus, *Ant.* XVIII [2, 4], 50.   [3] Tacitus, *Ann.* II, 4.

[4] Tacitus, *Ann.* II, 42; Dio LVII, 17. W. E. Gwatkin (*Cappadocia as a Roman procuratorial province*) makes the plausible conjecture that the charge was concerned with attempts on his part to help his relative Tigranes IV to recover the Armenian throne.   [5] Strabo XII, 535, 537; XIV, 671; Dio LIV, 9.

[6] His coinage begins in A.D. 10–11 (*B. M. Cat. Lycaonia*, etc. pp. lii, 119). Volume of Plates IV, 208, *e*.

About the same time two other client-kings died, Antiochus III of Commagene, and Philopator, king of a Cilician vassal state bordering on north Syria, a descendant of Tarcondimotus, whom Pompey in 63 B.C. had recognized as ruler of a district round Hieropolis-Castabala (Budrûm). Confirmed in his principality by Caesar, Tarcondimotus received from Antony the title of king, and fell fighting for him in the campaign of Actium (p. 102). His son Philopator transferred his allegiance to Augustus, but he was nevertheless deposed[1], and it was not until 20 B.C. that his brother Tarcondimotus II received back the greater part of his father's dominion. He was succeeded by Philopator, probably his son, who died in A.D. 17. 'The deaths of Antiochus and Philopator,' says Tacitus[2], 'unsettled their people, the majority of whom desired a Roman governor and the minority a king. The provinces, too, of Syria and Judaea, exhausted by their burdens, were asking for a reduction of their tribute.'

Such was the position of affairs. The task of settling them was entrusted by Tiberius to Germanicus[3], who was invested by decree of the Senate with proconsular authority superior to that of the governors of imperial and senatorial provinces beyond the sea. He arrived in the East in A.D. 18. Tiberius had decided to annex Cappadocia and Commagene. This was a step in the right direction, which extended Roman territory to the Euphrates along its middle course. The change to Roman administration was carried out by two members of Germanicus' suite. Commagene was organized by Q. Servaeus and added to the province of Syria, to which it naturally belonged both geographically and strategically; its incorporation was essential for the defence of the frontier. Cappadocia was organized by Q. Veranius. Its treatment hardly justified its annexation. Instead of being utilized for the establishment of a military frontier along the upper Euphrates, which would have exerted a decisive influence on the maintenance of Roman authority in Armenia, it was constituted a third-class province governed by a procurator of equestrian rank, who merely took the place of the king and had no regular troops under his command[4]. This personal form of government was, no doubt, naturally suggested by the backward state of the country's development. A land which had a political and social system of a feudal character did not lend itself to the type of provincial organization which was based on city communities. But it is clear that what made Cappadocia an attractive acquisition was its

---

[1] Dio LI, 2.

[2] *Ann.* II, 42.

[3] Tacitus, *Ann.* II, 43, 56 *sqq.*

[4] Cf. Tacitus, *Ann.* XII, 49.

financial rather than its military value. Although some of the
royal taxes were reduced in amount—a measure calculated to win
the goodwill of the feudal aristocracy—the revenues received by
the imperial exchequer were such as to permit Tiberius to reduce
by half the unpopular tax of one per cent. on public sales (*centesima
rerum venalium*), which was one of the mainstays of the military
treasury. Besides the tribute, a considerable revenue was derived
from the extensive royal domains, which passed to the emperor,
and from the numerous mines[1] (some of them at least royal properties), which yielded crystal, onyx, mica (*lapis specularis*) for
glazing, rock salt, the famous 'Sinopic' *miltos* (probably cinnabar)[2]
and argentiferous ore, which supplied the mint at Caesarea
Mazaca with metal for the silver coinage issued by the kings and
by the Roman emperors from the time of Tiberius[3]. The new
province probably included all the territory held by the late king
except eastern Lycaonia and Cilicia Tracheia, which were left in
the possession of his son Archelaus, who was still king of that
region in A.D. 36, when he caused a revolt by ordering a census on
the Roman model to be taken for taxation purposes[4].

The fate of the Cilician principality is not recorded, but an
inscription erected at Hieropolis in honour of Styrax, 'father of
the kings,' probably implies that it continued to exist under the
rule of a collateral branch of the old royal family[5].

The most urgent matter, however, with which Germanicus had
to deal was the succession to the Armenian throne. He had
ordered Piso, the recently appointed governor of Syria, to bring
or send under his son's command a legionary force to Armenia,
but the order was insolently ignored, and he proceeded without it
to Artaxata, where he crowned as king a member of the Pontic
royal family, Zeno, son of Polemo I by his second wife Pythodoris,
who had lost her husband in 8 B.C. but continued to rule the
greater part of his kingdom with distinguished success. Zeno was
the choice of the Armenians themselves. The young man had been
brought up by his sagacious mother in the Armenian fashion and
had endeared himself to the aristocracy by his love of hunting and
feasting and the other recreations of that class. Before a great

---

[1] Strabo XII, 540; Pliny, *N.H.* XXXI, 73 *sqq.*, 84; XXXVI, 160.

[2] *J.H.S.* XXXVI, 1916, pp. 10 *sqq.*

[3] *B. M. Cat. Rom. Emp.* I, p. cxl *sq.*; Head, *H.N.*[2] p. 752 *sq.* For the
political organization and sources of wealth of Cappadocia, cf. Gwatkin,
op. cit. chap. II, with *C.R.* XLV, 1931, p. 189.   [4] Tacitus, *Ann.* VI, 41.

[5] Heberdey-Wilhelm, *Reisen in Kilikien* (Denkschr. Akad. Wien), p. 28,
no. 64.

concourse of nobles and people Germanicus placed the tiara on his head and the crowd acclaimed him as King Artaxias, the name borne by the founder of Armenian independence[1]. The Parthian king Artabanus acquiesced, and sent envoys to express his desire for a renewal of pledges of friendship with Rome and to suggest a personal meeting on the bank of the Euphrates, at the same time requesting that Vonones should not be kept in Syria to carry on intrigues with Parthian nobles. Germanicus sent a courteous reply and removed Vonones to Pompeiopolis in Cilicia. The interview was apparently not declined, but it did not take place[2]. In the following year Vonones bribed his guards and attempted to escape, but he was captured and killed, without authority, by the officer who had been responsible for his safe custody.

II. THE RENEWAL OF PARTHIAN INTERFERENCE IN ARMENIA AND THE REPRISALS OF TIBERIUS

The choice of Zeno proved a happy one, and peace reigned in the East until his death about A.D. 34. Then trouble arose again[3]. A long and prosperous reign and successful wars against bordering peoples had made Artabanus arrogant, and he determined to challenge Roman authority in Armenia, convinced that no vigorous opposition would be offered by the aged Tiberius from his secluded retreat in Capreae. Placing his eldest son Arsaces on the Armenian throne, he sent an insulting message to the Emperor, demanding the restoration of the treasure left by Vonones in Syria and Cilicia and claiming, under threat of invasion, all the old territories of the Persian and Seleucid empires[4]. But he

---

[1] The ceremony of investiture was commemorated by an issue of silver coins from the mint of Caesarea, showing on the obverse the head and name of Germanicus and on the reverse the coronation of the king, with the legend 'Artaxias/Germanicus' vertically inscribed on left and right. But these coins were perhaps struck by the emperor Gaius (H. Mattingly, *Coins of the Rom. Emp.* i, p. cxlviii). Volume of Plates iv, 208, *c*.

[2] The interesting fact that Germanicus had entered into diplomatic relations with Parthian vassal States is revealed by an Aramaic inscription of Palmyra, which records that he sent a Palmyrene citizen on a mission to Mesene and to Orabzes, doubtless the ruler of an adjoining State (*Syria*, XII, 1931, p. 139; XIII, 1932, p. 266; cf. above, p. 621). Speculation about his purpose is unprofitable.

[3] The sources are Tacitus, *Ann.* VI, 31 *sqq.*; Josephus, *Ant.* XVIII [4, 4], 96–105; Dio LVIII, 26; LIX, 27.

[4] His alleged letter to Tiberius, reproaching him with the murder of his kindred and his subjects and with his dissolute life, and counselling him to

reckoned without his host. He had already alienated his grandees. In 35 a deputation of Parthian nobles went secretly to Rome and begged Tiberius to send them as a candidate for the throne Phraates, the youngest of the four sons of the former king of that name, who had resided in Rome for nearly half a century. This suited the plans of Tiberius, who resolved to teach Artabanus a lesson without undertaking a war against Parthia. He furnished Phraates with everything necessary for his enterprise and sent him off to Syria. The old man, on arriving there, made a brave attempt to throw off his Roman habits and adapt himself to those of Parthia, but the change was too much for him, and he fell ill and died. Tiberius replaced him by a younger Arsacid, also resident in Rome, Tiridates by name, a grandson of the old king Phraates; and he appointed as governor of Syria a capable administrator, L. Vitellius, who had been consul in 34, with authority to take charge of the situation. Meanwhile he had taken steps to set up a counter king of Armenia in the person of Mithridates, brother of the Iberian king Pharasmanes; the two had been at strife, but Pharasmanes was reconciled by the prospect of the honourable removal of his brother and was induced[1] to aid him in seizing the throne. Mithridates began his enterprise by bribing the attendants of Arsaces to poison him. Then an Iberian host burst into Armenia and seized Artaxata. To retrieve the situation, Artabanus sent another son Orodes with a Parthian force, which was to be supplemented by hired auxiliaries; and when he was routed by the Iberians, aided by the Albanians and by Sarmatians called in from beyond the Caucasus, he marched himself in full strength against the allies. But he fared little better, and he was forced to retire by the news that Vitellius was about to invade Mesopotamia.

His failure proved disastrous to him. Vitellius used the arts of diplomacy to foment the disaffection of leading Parthian magnates, and Artabanus was obliged to flee to Hyrcania, with which he was connected by family ties; there he wandered in destitution, supporting life by his bow. Tiridates now had his chance, and Vitellius escorted him with an imposing force of legionaries and auxiliaries across the Euphrates, where he was joined by

gratify the just hatred of the Romans by a voluntary death (Suetonius, *Tib.* 66), was no doubt a Roman *canard*. Such a letter could hardly have been written by a king who, after the Parthian fashion, had killed every potential rival of Arsacid stock who had reached adult years.

[1] By heavy bribes from Tiberius, alleges Josephus, with no support from Tacitus. He makes the same allegation against Vitellius in the case of the Parthian nobles, where again Tacitus is silent.

Ornospades, the governor of Mesopotamia, who had won Roman citizenship as a reward for his services in the great Pannonian-Dalmatian revolt, and by other Parthian notables. Here the Roman legate left him to make or mar his fortune, and returned with his troops to Syria. Tiridates enjoyed a triumphal progress to Ctesiphon, where he was crowned by the competent authority, Surenas. But Parthian disunion once more turned the tables. Two governors of very important provinces[1] who had asked for a short postponement of the coronation and then failed to attend it, returned to their allegiance to Artabanus, who, thus encouraged, rapidly collected a 'Scythian' force of Dahae and Sacae, and pushed southward towards Seleuceia. Tiridates, himself a coward in the face of danger, listened to the advice of his chief supporter to retreat to Mesopotamia, where reinforcements could be collected and the arrival of Roman troops awaited; but his forces melted away, and Tiridates made his way back to Syria with a few followers. He had humiliated the King of Kings, and presumably no more was expected of him.

Tiberius judged that Artabanus would now be ready to make his peace, and on his instructions Vitellius marched again to the Euphrates, where the pageantry of A.D. 1 was repeated. At an interview on the middle of a bridge thrown across the river—a symbol of the equal status of the contracting parties—the king, in return for the recognition of his independent sovereignty, accepted the Roman settlement in Armenia; and not long afterwards he appears to have sent to Rome as a hostage his son Darius[2], whose name recalled his father's arrogant claim to all Roman territory which had once been Persian. It was a signal triumph of astute diplomacy, as effective as any that could have been won by the expenditure of blood and money. Tiberius did not long survive his victory; and hatred of his memory and flattery of his successor distorted the facts about the conference[3] by representing that it was

---

[1] One of them, whose name was Phraates (Tacitus, *Ann.* VI, 42), may have been satrap of Susiana, if he is identical with the Phraates named in the letter of Artabanus, dated Dec. A.D. 21, recently discovered at Susa. The letter is addressed to Antiochus and Phraates, of whom the former was probably *epistates* of Susa and the latter satrap of Susiana (Fr. Cumont, *C.R. Acad. Inscr.* 1932, p. 249). [2] Cf. Suetonius, *Cal.* 19, 2.

[3] Suetonius, *Cal.* 14, 3; *Vit.* 2, 4; Dio LIX, 27, 3. As Tacitus ends his account in VI, 44 with the flight of Tiridates, he too evidently assigned the conference to the reign of Gaius. See E. Täubler, *Parthernachrichten*, pp. 38 *sqq.* The responsibility for the Roman version probably lay with Vitellius himself, who was driven to adulation of Gaius (p. 664); Dessau, *Gesch. d. röm. Kaiserzeit*, II, p. 87.

due to the desire of Artabanus to win the friendship of Gaius (or, inconsistently, to the consummate diplomacy of Vitellius), and that the king crossed the river to do obeisance to the Roman standards and the images of the emperors (Augustus and Gaius), an admission of vassalage which no Parthian king would have made save with the sword at his throat. The truth has been preserved by Josephus.

III. THE EAST UNDER GAIUS AND CLAUDIUS. THE BOSPORAN KINGDOM

The brief reign of Gaius had a disturbing effect on Eastern affairs. The equilibrium secured by the successful policy of Tiberius he destroyed by summoning the Armenian king Mithridates to Rome for some unrecorded reason and setting up no one in his place. After keeping him in custody for a time, he allowed him to go into voluntary exile[1]. Armenia remained without a king for the rest of Gaius' reign, and was thus abandoned to the Parthians, who appear to have taken possession of it[2]. The able L. Vitellius was recalled from Syria and forced to descend to the most abject servility to save his head.

Gaius also set back the development of frontier defence, slow enough as it was, by his policy of restoring to the status of dependencies territories which had been incorporated in the empire by his predecessor, in order to provide kingdoms for the Oriental princes who had been the playmates and companions of his youth in Rome. In 37 Commagene, now for twenty years part of the province of Syria, was re-established as a client-kingdom for Antiochus, son of the former king, who shared with Herod Agrippa the reputation of being the Emperor's instructor in tyranny; and, in accordance with Gaius' practice when he restored client-states, the new king was refunded the revenue, amounting to 100 million sesterces, which the exchequer had received in the interval[3]. There were also added to his dominions two regions in southern Asia Minor, which till then had been under the rule of Archelaus, son of the last Cappadocian king, the greater part of Cilicia Tracheia and eastern Lycaonia[4]. But hardly had he been installed when he was deposed (A.D. 40), to be reinstated by Claudius[5].

[1] Tacitus, *Ann.* XI, 8; Dio LX, 8, 1; Seneca, *de tranquill. animi*, 11, 12.
[2] Tacitus, *Ann.* XI, 9.   [3] Dio LIX, 8, 2; 24, 1; Suetonius, *Cal.* 16.
[4] Dio LIX, 8, 2; he struck coins at Laranda with the legend ΛΥΚΑΟΝΩΝ (*B. M. Cat. Lycaonia*, etc. p. xxi). Volume of Plates IV, 208, *d*.
[5] Dio LX, 8, 1; Josephus, *Ant.* XIX [5, 1], 276.

On the north of Cappadocia Gaius re-created client-kingdoms for other two of his youthful friends, Polemo and Cotys, sons of Antonia Tryphaena, daughter of Polemo I of Pontus, who had married the Thracian king Cotys[1]. The former was granted the Pontic kingdom which had been ruled by his grandmother, queen Pythodoris, till about A.D. 23. After her death her kingdom, if not actually annexed, was placed under wardship in default of male heirs of an age to succeed. It was now restored in A.D. 38 to Polemo II despite his youth, and he was also given the kingdom of Bosporus, once part of his grandfather's dominions, but it is doubtful whether he ever set foot in the country, since its coinage shows that sovereign rights were exercised by queen Gepaepyris, widow of the late king Aspurgus, till A.D. 39 and thereafter, at least for a time, conjointly by her and her stepson Mithridates[2]. At the same time Polemo's younger brother Cotys was made king of Armenia Minor, once ruled by Polemo I and subsequently included in the kingdom of Cappadocia, with which it had probably been annexed.

In Syria a fragment of the old Ituraean principality, a so-called tetrarchy centring round Arca in the northern Lebanon, was granted in 38 to a native prince Sohaemus, who held it till his death in 49, when it was incorporated in the province[3]. This was probably no more than a change of *personnel*, but farther south territory was withdrawn in 37 from Roman administration to provide a kingdom for another of Gaius' friends, Herod Agrippa (M. Julius Agrippa), grandson of Herod the Great. Released from custody shortly after the death of Tiberius, he was made king of the Haurân and the adjacent regions east of the Jordan, which had formed the north-eastern portion of Herod's kingdom and had then passed to his son, the tetrarch Philip, on whose death in 34 it had been incorporated in the province of Syria, although the incorporation was probably intended to be temporary, since the tribute accruing from the tetrarchy was kept in it. To Agrippa's dominion was added at the same time another portion of the old Ituraean principality, the 'tetrarchy' of Abilene in the Anti-Lebanon, north-west of Damascus; and three years later (40) his kingdom was further enlarged by the addition of Galilee and Peraea, the tetrarchy of his brother-in-law Herod

---

[1] Dio LIX, 12, 2 (who wrongly calls Polemo son of Polemo I).

[2] Coins of Gepaepyris as sole ruler, Volume of Plates iv, 208, *h*; in association with Mithridates, *ib.* iv, 208, *i*. Two aurei, dated 39/40 and 41/2, bear the name of Mithridates on the reverse and the emperor's head on the obverse (Volume of Plates iv, 208, *l*). Cf. U. Kahrstedt in *Klio*, x, 1910, p. 303.

[3] Tacitus, *Ann.* XII, 23; Dio LIX, 12, 2.

Antipas, who was deposed through his influence and exiled to Lugdunum in Aquitania[1].

The policy of establishing protectorates on the fringe of the empire, even at the expense of incorporated territory, was maintained by Claudius[2]. On his accession he reinstated Antiochus in Commagene and left the other vassal princes in possession of their dominions, making only some territorial rearrangements. In 41 he revoked the grant of the Bosporan kingdom to Polemo and recognized the sovereignty of its *de facto* ruler Mithridates, bestowing on Polemo by way of compensation the Cilician principality of Olba, Cennatis and Lalassis in the valley of the Calycadnus. In the same year he rewarded Herod Agrippa for the help he had given him in securing the throne by adding to his realm Judaea and Samaria, which had been governed by a Roman procurator since A.D. 6, thereby making his kingdom co-extensive with that of Herod the Great. Simultaneously he bestowed on Agrippa's brother Herod the kingdom of Chalcis, the central portion of the old Ituraean principality. In reconstituting Herod's kingdom, Claudius was actuated not merely by personal motives but by the desire to remove the danger of direct contact between Romans and Jews; but he did not adhere to this wise policy. When Agrippa died three years later (44) and his son was too young to succeed, his kingdom was re-converted into the procuratorial province of Judaea[3]; but in 50 the young Agrippa was appointed to succeed his uncle Herod of Chalcis, who had died two years before, and ruled the kingdom till 53, when Claudius created a new realm for him by separating most of the Transjordan region from the province of Judaea and adding to it the two Syrian fiefs of Abilene and Arca. This kingdom, which Nero seems to have enlarged in 61 by the inclusion of Peraea and a strip of Galilee, he held till nearly the end of the first century.

Mithridates, king of the Bosporus, did not long retain his crown[4]. Dreaming of the glory of his ancestor the great Mithri-

---

[1] Josephus, *Ant.* XVIII [4, 6], 106 *sqq.*; [6, 10], 236 *sq.*; [7, 2], 252; XIX [8, 2], 351; *Bell. Jud.* II [9, 6], 183.

[2] The authorities are Dio LX, 8; Josephus, *Ant.* XIX [5, 1], 276; [8, 2], 351; [9, 2], 362; XX [5, 2], 104; [7, 1], 138; *Bell. Jud.* II [11, 5], 215 *sqq.*; [12, 1], 223; [12, 8], 247; VII [5, 1], 97. For the Cilician principality, G. F. Hill, *B. M. Cat. Lycaonia*, etc. p. liv. Volume of Plates iv, 208, *f.*

[3] Cf. Tacitus, *Ann.* XII, 23 (under the year 49).

[4] For this paragraph the sources are an excerpt from Dio preserved in a fragment of the *Historiae* of Petrus Patricius, a sixth-century writer, who confuses the Bosporan with the Iberian Mithridates (Dio LX, 28, 7, ed. Boissevain), and Tacitus, *Ann.* XII, 15–21.

dates, he made preparations to free himself from dependence on Rome, disregarding the protests of his stepmother, queen Gepae-pyris. His rebellious attitude is reflected by his gold coins, on which he boldly placed his full name and title, in defiance of established practice. When Gepaepyris threatened flight, he sought to conceal his purpose by sending his half-brother Cotys with a friendly message to Claudius; but Cotys betrayed his whole ambitious scheme and was rewarded with the kingdom, to which he was conducted, in A.D. 44 or 45[1], by a Roman force under Didius Gallus, governor of Moesia, who was decorated with the triumphal insignia for his service[2]. After installing the youthful king, Didius withdrew the bulk of his army, leaving only a few auxiliary cohorts under a Roman knight, Julius Aquila, to support him. Scorning both of them, Mithridates attempted to recover his throne. With the aid of Maeotian and Sarmatian tribes[3], particularly the Siraci who occupied the valley of the Achardeus (probably the Jegorlyk, a tributary of the Manytch), he drove out the king of the Dan-daridae, who inhabited the delta of the Hypanis (Kuban) and bordered on the Siraci, and prepared to invade the Bosporan kingdom. On learning this, Aquila and Cotys secured the alliance of Eunones, king of the Sarmatian Aorsi, who adjoined the Siraci in the region between the lower Tanais (Don) and the north-west coast of the Caspian. With the assistance of his cavalry, the Roman troops defeated the enemy, overran Dandarica and stormed Uspe, a stronghold of the Siraci, slaughtering the inhabi-tants; whereupon Zorsines, king of the Siraci, made peace, gave hostages, and prostrated himself before the image of Claudius, while Mithridates threw himself on the mercy of Eunones, who sent envoys to the Emperor asking that he should not be led in triumph nor suffer the death penalty. Claudius consented, and Mithridates was taken as a prisoner to Rome, where he displayed a defiant attitude on being exhibited to the people; but he was set free and lived in the capital till the reign of Galba, who put him to death as an accomplice of Nymphidius Sabinus (p. 813).

[1] The earliest coin of Cotys is dated 45–6.
[2] Dessau 970, an inscription set up at Olympia, probably before Greece and Macedonia were detached from the province of Moesia in A.D. 44.
[3] Cf. Pliny, *N.H.* VI, 17.

IV. THE RECOVERY AND LOSS OF ARMENIA[1]

The Armenian question was tackled by Claudius as soon as political conditions in Parthia offered an opportunity of recovering control without a serious military effort. At the opening of his reign there were dynastic troubles in the Arsacid kingdom. In or just before A.D. 40 Artabanus died, and was succeeded by Vardanes, probably the eldest of his numerous sons. Within a few months he was deposed by his brother Gotarzes[2], but the cruelties of the new king soon alienated his subjects and led to the restoration of Vardanes in June, A.D. 42, at the latest. Gotarzes retired to his father's old home in the far north, where he collected reinforcements from the Dahae and Hyrcanians and renewed the contest in the following year[3], causing Vardanes to withdraw to 'the plains of Bactria' (the land of Margiana on the Bactrian border). News of this state of anarchy was sent by the Iberian king Pharasmanes, brother of the exiled Mithridates, with a promise of help in regaining Armenia, and Claudius encouraged the ex-king to seize the opportunity, sending a Roman force with him. With the aid of the Iberians, who broke Armenian resistance by a single battle, Mithridates secured the throne, and the Roman troops remained in Armenia to support him, being placed in garrison at Gorneae within a short distance of Artaxata.

Meanwhile the two Parthian princes were preparing for a decisive battle when they suddenly became reconciled on discovering that a plot was being hatched against them by their own countrymen, and they came to an agreement whereby Vardanes retained the throne, while Gotarzes accepted the position of a vassal king and retired to Hyrcania[4]. Vardanes now aspired to the recovery of Armenia, but he desisted when C. Vibius Marsus, governor of Syria from A.D. 42 to 45, threatened an invasion of

---

[1] For this section the important source is Tacitus, whose account is divided into two parts (*Ann.* XI, 8–10; XII, 10–14), the first of which narrates the events of several years up to A.D. 47, and the second those of 48 and 49. The chronology depends on the dated coins of the Parthian kings. Dio LX, 8, 1 places the departure of Mithridates for Armenia in A.D. 41. Josephus, *Ant.* XX [3, 4], 69–74, is very brief and not accurate.

[2] There is a coin of Vardanes dated Aug. 40, while the first coin of Gotarzes is dated 40–1. The reading of the former has been wrongly doubted (see Täubler, *op. cit.* p. 18).

[3] In 43–4 Gotarzes again issued money.

[4] He is probably the Γωτάρζης Γεόποθρος (Gevputhran) of the Bisitûn inscription, *O.G.I.S.* 431. If Herzfeld be right in holding that he was nephew and adoptive son of Artabanus (p. 278, above), Hyrcania was his ancestral fief.

Mesopotamia. Gotarzes did not long remain quiescent. At the solicitation of discontented Parthian nobles he attemped to win back the throne, but he was defeated on the banks of the Erindes[1] and took refuge, no doubt, among the Dahae. Elated by success, Vardanes became overbearing and fell by the hand of assassins in 45. Gotarzes was then called again to the throne, but his cruelty made him intolerable to nobles and people, and in 47 a secret embassy arrived in Rome to request Claudius to send out as king Meherdates, son of Vonones and grandson of Phraates, who lived as a hostage in the capital. Claudius consented and instructed the governor of Syria, C. Cassius Longinus, to escort him to the Euphrates.

At Zeugma he was received by his Parthian supporters, but once more the Parthians 'were readier to ask a king from Rome than to keep him.' Meherdates allowed himself to be lured by his false friend Abgar, king of Osroëne, to waste time in Edessa, and then to make a long detour across the snow-clad mountains of southern Armenia towards the Tigris, despite the earnest entreaties of the governor of Mesopotamia, a member of the great Parthian family of the Karēn, to make haste and take the direct route. When he reached Adiabene, he found another false friend in its king Izates, who declared in his favour but was secretly a supporter of Gotarzes. Continuing his march towards Ctesiphon, he captured Nineveh and Gaugamela and came up against Gotarzes in a defensive position behind the river Corma (perhaps the el-Adhem), which covered the approach to the capital. Gotarzes played for time to increase his forces and to tempt the fidelity of his opponent's allies. Izates and Abgar deserted with their troops, and Meherdates, fearing further desertions, resolved to stake his fortunes on a decisive battle, which was hotly contested until his most capable supporter, the Karēn, pushing his advantage too far, was intercepted by the enemy. In despair Meherdates trusted the promises of a client of his father, to find himself treacherously handed over to the victor, who contented himself with cutting off his ears, a mutilation which disqualified him for the Parthian throne. Not long afterwards Gotarzes died, in or soon after May 51. Following a regular custom of the Arsacids, he had put to death all the members of that family on whom he could lay his hands, and the throne passed to Vonones, king of Media (Atropatene), who after a reign of two or three months was succeeded in August 51 by his son Vologases, the offspring of a

[1] Probably identical with the Charindas, which was perhaps the river that flows by Barferush into the Caspian (Kiessling, *Hyrkania*, in *P.W.* cols. 468, 506).

Greek concubine[1]. The new monarch was to prove an able, vigorous, and sagacious ruler.

The civil war in Parthia and the adventure of Meherdates assured Armenia some eight years of immunity from Arsacid interference. Then the land became once more a scene of turmoil, which continued till the death of Claudius and ended in the annihilation of Roman influence. The history of these years casts a lurid light on the character of the central government during the later years of Claudius' reign, and affords a striking illustration of the disastrous effect produced by laxity of control on the behaviour of Roman officials on the outskirts of the empire[2].

It opens with a gruesome story of heartless treachery and cold-blooded family murder. The Iberian king Pharasmanes, who had taken the main part in establishing and restoring his brother Mithridates as king of Armenia, had a son Radamistus, a tall, handsome and popular prince, whose impatience to succeed to the throne drove his old father to suggest to him the seizure of Armenia, which was easily to be won by craft. The son swallowed the bait and, under pretext of a quarrel with his father, paid a visit to his uncle—who was also his father-in-law and brother-in-law—and being received with every mark of kindness used his opportunity to tempt the Armenian notables from their allegiance to the king, whose severe régime had earned him the dislike of all classes of the people. He then feigned reconciliation with his father, and returned home to demand and receive a military force for a *coup d'État*. Mithridates, caught unawares, was driven to take refuge in the fort of Gorneae, held by the Roman garrison under the command of an auxiliary prefect, Caelius Pollio, a man with a reputation for shameless venality, who had as his second in command a centurion named Casperius. Unable to storm the fort, Radamistus laid siege to it, and offered a bribe to Pollio, who was ready to accept it. The honest centurion protested against the betrayal of a client-king set up by Rome and, stipulating for a truce, departed for Iberia with the resolve to deter Pharasmanes from prosecuting the war, if he could, and in case of failure to report the state of affairs to the governor of Syria, Ummidius Quadratus. Freed from the centurion's restraint, Pollio urged Mithridates to come to terms, but the king hesitated, guessing his intentions. Meanwhile the centurion failed to extract anything but vague promises from Pharasmanes, who sent a secret message

---

[1] The king's name, Volgasi in Pahlavi, is variously spelled by ancient authors and by the coins of succeeding kings of the same name.

[2] For this period the authority is Tacitus, *Ann.* XII, 44–51.

to his son to press the attack by every possible means. Radamistus raised his price, and Pollio bribed his soldiers to threaten to abandon the defence of the fort. The unfortunate king was obliged to agree to a conference and left the fort, only to be murdered together with his wife—the sister of the murderer—and his sons. When the news reached Syria, the aged governor summoned his council. Most of his advisers, careless of the honour of Rome, advocated leaving things alone, and this view was adopted; but to avoid the appearance of condoning the crime and to save their faces, if Claudius should send other orders, they sent a message to Pharasmanes requiring him to withdraw from Armenian territory and remove his son.

Then the procurator of Cappadocia, Julius Paelignus, a favourite of Claudius, whose idle hours in earlier life he used to amuse, took it upon himself to intervene, without the knowledge of the responsible authority, the governor of Syria. He collected a force of provincial militia, as though to recover Armenia (in the ironical phrase of Tacitus), but he soon found himself left defenceless by the desertion of his men, and made his way to Radamistus, who bribed him to authorize his assumption of the royal insignia and to attend his coronation. On hearing of these disgraceful proceedings, Quadratus dispatched Helvidius Priscus with a legion to deal discreetly with the situation[1]. Meantime Vologases, convinced no doubt that Radamistus could not count on Roman support, prepared to seize the opportunity of securing the throne for his brother Tiridates, who might prove a menace to him, unless he were provided with a kingdom; whereupon Quadratus hastily recalled the legion, lest its continued presence in Armenia should provoke a war with Parthia. In the year 52[2], in all probability, Vologases advanced into Armenia, which submitted without resistance, both capitals, Artaxata and Tigranocerta, falling into his hands. Radamistus fled and Tiridates was installed in his place, but the severity of the following winter and a deficiency of supplies led to an outbreak of pestilence, which forced Vologases to withdraw. Tiridates also retired, and the following year saw

[1] About the Roman force at Gorneae nothing further is recorded. An excerpt from Dio (Exc. Vales. 237 = Dio LXI, 6, 6), referring to A.D. 54, speaks of a certain Laelianus, who had been *praef. vigilum*, being sent as successor to Pollio in Armenia and proving even more avaricious than he; whatever the explanation of this statement may be, it cannot be believed that the garrison remained in Armenia during the Parthian occupation.

[2] On the chronology of these events, which Tacitus groups together under A.D. 51, cf. B. W. Henderson in *C.R.* xv, 1901, pp. 159 *sqq.*

Radamistus back again in his kingdom, ruling with an increased harshness which was intended to cow the people but goaded them into insurrection. He found safety in headlong flight to his Iberian home. The Parthians then re-occupied Armenia and Tiridates recovered the throne. All this time the somnolent imperial government remained wholly passive and only awoke from its torpor when Claudius quitted the scene (Oct. 13, A.D. 54).

V. THE ARMENIAN WAR OF NERO'S REIGN: THE FIRST PHASE

The news of the final expulsion of Radamistus and of the re-occupation of Armenia by the Parthians reached Rome soon after the accession of Nero. An Armenian embassy arrived in the capital; it was evidently sent by the Romanizing party, and its mission can only have been to solicit the intervention of the government[1]. The youthful emperor's advisers, Seneca and Burrus, handled the situation with a vigour characteristic of the accession of new men to power. Preparations for war were immediately set on foot[2]. Orders were sent to Syria to bring up the legions to their proper strength by the enrolment of recruits from the adjoining provinces. The two neighbouring client-kings, Antiochus IV of Commagene and Herod Agrippa II, were instructed to get forces ready for the invasion of Parthia, while two districts adjoining Armenia on either side of the northern Euphrates, Armenia Minor on the west and Sophene on the east, were placed under client-kings, the former being given to Aristobulus, son of Herod of Chalcis and cousin of Herod Agrippa, and the latter to Sohaemus, a prince of the royal house of Emesa in Syria[3]. While Quadratus was allowed to retain his post as governor of Syria, the conduct of the war was entrusted to a capable soldier, Cn. Domitius Corbulo, who had won a reputation under Claudius as a vigorous officer and a strict disciplinarian, and whose appointment was welcomed by the Roman public as a token of serious determination to restore the influence and prestige of Rome in the East. For a war against Armenia the natural base of operations was Cappadocia, and this province was placed under Corbulo's

[1] Tacitus, *Ann.* XIII, 5.

[2] The history of the Armenian-Parthian war falls into three periods, for all of which the main source is Tacitus. The events of the first period down to A.D. 60 are narrated in *Ann.* XIII, 6–9; 34–41; XIV, 23–6. Dio LXII, 19–20 adds nothing.

[3] Hardly identical with the king of Emesa, C. Julius Sohaemus, who succeeded in A.D. 54 (Josephus, *Ant.* xx [8, 4], 158; Dessau 8958).

control together with the adjacent province of Galatia, which contained the best fighting material in the East[1]. For the administration of Galatia C. Rutilius Gallicus was appointed a subordinate *legatus*[2]. The war was to be carried on with an army consisting of half the legionary and auxiliary troops in Syria, with the addition of some auxiliary regiments of foot and horse which were then wintering in Cappadocia.

Early in A.D. 55 Corbulo hastened to take up his command. At Aegeae on the Cilician coast he found Quadratus awaiting his arrival with half the Syrian army; the old man was jealous of the new commander and feared a loss of prestige if the transfer of the troops were made in Syria itself. The legions handed over were III Gallica and VI Ferrata. Both legates then proceeded to dispatch messages to the Parthian king offering peace on condition that he was prepared to show the same respect to Rome as his predecessors had done by giving hostages. Vologases was not in a position to fight. The threat of war, conveyed by the military preparations of Rome, had awakened once more the spirit of discord in the Parthian empire, and the king was faced by a rival who is usually thought to have been his own son Vardanes, and who appears to have been already in open revolt, for the Parthian troops had been withdrawn from Armenia[3]. Vologases accordingly yielded to the demand, which enabled him to get rid of a number of suspected nobles of Arsacid stock, without tying his hands. The delivery of the hostages led to an unedifying exhibition of the jealousy between Quadratus and Corbulo. The former sent a centurion to receive them, and they were handed over to him, whereupon Corbulo dispatched a higher officer to take them over, and an altercation ensued which ended in leaving the decision to the hostages themselves and the envoys who had brought them; and they gave the preference to Corbulo. The quarrel between the two legates was diplomatically composed by Nero, who assigned equal credit to each by a proclamation that for the successes won by Quadratus and Corbulo the imperial *fasces* should be wreathed with laurel.

The struggle against the pretender to the throne, about whose fortunes Tacitus is strangely silent, and the revolt of Hyrcania, which broke out at the latest in 58 and may have started in support

[1] Mommsen, *Hermes*, xv, 1880, p. 295; with *C.R.* xlv, 1931, p. 190. His title was *legatus Augusti pro praetore* (Dessau 232).

[2] Dessau 9499, *legatus* (not *pro praetore*) *provinciae Galaticae*; cf. Groag in *P.W.* s.v. Rutilius (19), col. 1257.

[3] See Note 3, p. 879.

of the pretender, kept Vologases fully occupied[1]. Fortune could have offered no more favourable opportunity for the reconquest of Armenia. Yet Tiridates remained in undisturbed possession of his kingdom for more than two years after Corbulo's arrival in the East. The cause of Corbulo's inaction was that his troops were in a state of utter demoralization; they contained veterans who had no proper equipment and knew nothing of the practice of arms, but had devoted themselves to carrying on a petty traffic in the towns where their time had been spent (see above, p. 228). Corbulo's first task was to discharge the old and infirm and to fill up the units with recruits levied in Galatia and Cappadocia; his next was to drill, discipline, and harden his troops. An additional legion, X Fretensis, was brought up from Syria[2], where it was replaced by IV Scythica from Moesia, which was accompanied by its auxiliary complement of horse and foot[3].

Late in A.D. 57 this reorganized and partially disciplined force was led across the frontier into Armenia[4], where it was to complete its training under canvas amid the snow and frost and piercing cold of that Alpine land. It was a trying ordeal for the soldiers, most of them softened by the Syrian climate; the winter was more than usually severe: sentries died at their posts, men lost limbs by frost-bite, but iron discipline was maintained and desertions were relentlessly punished by death.

The site selected by Corbulo for his winter camp is not recorded, but it may well have been the lofty plateau of Erzerûm, over 6000 feet above the sea, the watershed between the northern Euphrates and the Araxes, which was within easy reach of his base in Cappadocia and well on the way towards Artaxata, which was to be his first objective when active operations began. In any case this was the route he followed when in 58[5] he struck his camp as soon as spring was well advanced (not earlier than the end of May) and marched against Tiridates, who was already in the field, supported by a force sent by Vologases, and was engaged in plundering districts which he suspected of Roman sympathies.

[1] See Note 3, p. 879.
[2] Though only part of it is mentioned in the campaign of 58 (Tacitus, *Ann.* XIII, 40, 3).
[3] Tacitus' statement that it came *ex Germania* (*Ann.* XIII, 35, 4) is a mistake: B. Filow, *Klio*, Beiheft VI, pp. 8 *sqq.*; Ritterling in *P.W.* s.v. *Legio*, col. 1558 *sq.*   [4] Tacitus, *Ann.* XIII, 36.
[5] Active operations began in 58, *eius anni principio* (Tacitus, *Ann.* XIII, 34, 4), and therefore the preceding winter was that of 57–8.

Corbulo hoped to bring him to an engagement, but he was too wise to risk a pitched battle and with his mobile horsemen kept up a guerilla warfare, eluding every force sent against him, until he forced the Roman commander to change his tactics. Dividing his army into separate columns, which were sent to attack several points at the same time, he arranged with various allies to make simultaneous raids into Armenia from the south-west and north-east. Antiochus of Commagene was instructed to invade the districts nearest to his kingdom; Pharasmanes of Iberia, who was anxious to reinstate himself in the good graces of Rome and with that object had disavowed and put to death his son Radamistus, did not wait for an invitation to fall upon his hated neighbours; while the adjoining tribe of the Moschi (or perhaps rather the Heniochi[1]) were won over to the Roman side and raided Armenia from the north.

Thus harried on nearly every side, Tiridates opened communications with Corbulo. But his tone was not that of a suppliant: his message was a remonstrance against the invasion as a breach of the friendship which had been renewed between Rome and Parthia by the delivery of hostages, and a threat that, if Rome persisted in seeking to drive him from the kingdom that had long been in his possession, she would have cause to regret once more her challenge of Arsacid valour and good fortune. If Vologases had not yet moved, it was because he, like Tiridates himself, preferred to rely on the justice of their cause. Corbulo knew that Vologases was occupied by the Hyrcanian revolt, and he advised Tiridates to address a petition to Nero, to whom he should look for recognition and security of tenure.

Corbulo's reply discloses the policy of the Neronian government, for it can hardly be doubted that he was acting on instructions[2]. Tiridates was to be permitted to retain the kingship, provided that he was prepared to accept it as a gift from Rome and thereby to acknowledge her overlordship. This was a departure from the policy laid down by Augustus: for effective suzerainty was now to be substituted a nominal suzerainty, whereby the country was to become an appanage for a Parthian prince of the ruling house on condition that all concerned accepted investiture by the Roman emperor. Of the wisdom of this compromise there can be no doubt: it was recommended by past experience, it sacrificed no

[1] See Note 5, p. 880.

[2] While it is hardly open to doubt that this policy (adopted in the end) was that which Corbulo favoured throughout the war, there is nothing to suggest that it was not also the policy of the government at the start.

vital Roman interest, and it saved the time-honoured Roman claim to overlordship, while suiting the conditions of the problem.

Neither Tiridates, however, nor Vologases[1] was yet prepared to accept this solution. As the parleys led to no result, Tiridates proposed an interview with Corbulo under conditions which betrayed a treacherous purpose, and when the Roman general required that it should take place in the presence of both armies, Tiridates failed to attend. On the renewal of hostilities he attempted to intercept the Roman supply trains as they wended their way from Trapezus (Trebizond) over the mountains to Erzerûm, but the attempt was foiled by the chain of military posts established to guard the line of communications. Corbulo now determined to force the elusive king to stand on the defensive by marching against Artaxata. Several forts which no doubt defended the approaches to the capital were first stormed; the strongest of all, Volandum[2], was taken under the direction of the commander-in-chief, and it was treated with great severity, the non-combatants being sold by auction and the place given over to plunder. Moving then against the capital, Corbulo avoided the direct road which crossed the Araxes by a bridge under the walls of the city, and was therefore within range of the defenders' missiles, and forded the river higher up. As he approached the city, Tiridates appeared and sought by the usual Parthian tactics to lure the Roman troops to break formation and isolate themselves by rash pursuit, but he failed in his efforts and vanished at nightfall. Corbulo, supposing he had retired to the capital, ordered a camp to be entrenched, intending to invest the city under cover of darkness; but when his scouts discovered that the king had fled to Media or Albania, he deferred his advance till the morning. Then the city, warned by the fate of Volandum, opened its gates; its surrender saved the lives of its inhabitants, but as the Roman army was too small both to hold the city and to carry on the war, and as its capture would have been valueless if it were left ungarrisoned, Corbulo set fire to it and levelled it with the ground.

The news of the capture of Artaxata reached Rome in 58, doubtless towards the end of the year, and was received with great rejoicing. Nero was saluted *Imperator* for the fifth, or more probably the sixth time[3], and the Senate surpassed itself in the

---

[1] Tacitus, *Ann.* XIII, 34, 4.

[2] Perhaps identical with Olane, a stronghold and royal treasury near the city, Strabo XI, 529; it may have stood on the site of Igdir.

[3] Nero was *Imp. VI* on Jan. 3, 59 (Dessau 229, l. 41): cf. H. Stuart Jones, *Rev. Arch.* III, 1904, p. 263.

extravagance of its decrees in celebration of the victory. Besides a vote of statues and triumphal arches and consulships for a series of years to Nero, it was resolved that the day of the victory, the day of its announcement, and that on which it had been brought before the Senate should all be added to the number of festival days; and other resolutions of like tenor were adopted, till C. Cassius Longinus, the famous jurist, was moved to the observation (which was not taken amiss) that, as the whole year would not suffice for the rendering of due thanks to the gods, it was advisable to keep some days free for business.

With the fall of Artaxata the campaign of 58 appears to have ended. Where the Roman army passed the winter is not stated; but the locality is indicated by Corbulo's next movement, which started from the region of Artaxata. As the city would have furnished welcome winter-quarters in a most inclement climate, it is difficult to believe that Tacitus' narrative is exact in recording its destruction immediately after its surrender; it is probable that, in order to complete the story of its fate, he has anticipated an event which took place in the following spring[1].

Next year Corbulo determined to march against the second Armenian capital, Tigranocerta, in the basin of the upper Tigris[2]. This involved cutting himself adrift from his lines of communication and supply, and traversing some 300 miles of difficult country, where his troops would have to depend on what provisions they could find. The route he chose may be guessed from two geographical data given by Tacitus, that he passed along the borders of the Mardi and traversed the *regio Tauraunitium*, the district of Mûsh[3]. He probably crossed the Egri-Masis range on the west of Mt Ararat, which forms its eastern limit, to the upper waters of the southern arm of the Euphrates, the Arsanias (Murad Su), and followed the course of that river to the vale of Mûsh, whence the pass of Bitlis, the gate of the Armenian highlands, offered easy access through the Taurus range to the lowlands of Mesopotamia.

On the march the army encountered no serious resistance; flank attacks by the Mardi, a robber tribe which dwelt in the mountain region north-east and east of the Lake of Van, were met by launching the Iberian horsemen against them; but the troops suffered severely from the fierce summer heat, the lack of any but

---

[1] See Note 4, p. 880.

[2] Its exact site is still uncertain (see vol. IX, p. 366).

[3] The Taronitis of Strabo XI, 528, the Tarûn of Arab geographers: H. Hübschmann in *Indo-germ. Forschungen*, XVI, 1904, pp. 325 *sqq.*

animal food, and scarcity of water (a surprising and perhaps a rhetorical touch) until they reached the rich grain-growing districts on the north of lake Van, where the corn stood ripe in the fields. After reducing two forts in this region, Corbulo advanced into the fertile plain of Mûsh, which fringes the northern slopes of Taurus. On the southern side of the mountain Tigranocerta was reported to be waiting to open its gates, and the inhabitants sent the Roman general a propitiatory gift of a golden crown; but before he arrived, the Armenian notables changed their minds and were contemplating resistance, until the head of a captured grandee, hurled from a *ballista*, chanced to fall in the midst of their council of war and terrified them into surrender[1]. The conqueror prudently abstained from penal measures, but resistance was still offered by the outlying fort of Legerda, which has been identified with Lidja, a town on the higher slopes of Taurus, to the south of the easy pass which is traversed by the southward road from Erzerûm.

With its reduction the season's campaign probably closed[2]. Its success had been facilitated by the revolt of the Hyrcanians, who had sent an embassy to Rome to ask for alliance in recognition of their service in detaining Vologases. The envoys were now on their way home, and to prevent their capture by the Parthians when they crossed the Euphrates, Corbulo gave them an escort to the Persian Gulf, whence they reached Hyrcania by a route which avoided territory under effective Parthian rule, probably by way of the kingdom of Persis and its dependency Carmania[3]. About the result of the embassy nothing is recorded.

The Roman army doubtless passed the winter in Tigranocerta. In the spring of 60[4] Tiridates made a final attempt to invade Armenia from Media Atropatene, but he was repulsed without serious difficulty and forced to abandon the struggle. Corbulo then proceeded to complete the subjugation of the country by a series of punitive expeditions against disaffected districts. Meantime the home government had been considering the situation created by Corbulo's successes and the disappearance of Tiridates from the scene, and it decided to revert to the old policy of setting

[1] Frontinus, *Strat.* II, 9, 5.

[2] The fall of Tigranocerta was the occasion of Nero's seventh imperatorial acclamation (*Act. Frat. Arv.* of Jan. 1, 60: *C.I.L.* VI, 2042 *d*, 17).

[3] Cf. W. Schur, *Orientpolitik*, p. 75, n. 2; J. Markwart, *Iberer*, p. 89.

[4] As may be inferred from the facts that Tigranocerta was occupied late in the autumn and that the campaigning season in Armenia ended about October.

a Romanized prince on the Armenian throne. Its choice fell on an Oriental long resident in Rome, Tigranes, a nephew of Tigranes IV (p. 277) and a great-grandson of both Herod the Great and Archelaus, the last king of Cappadocia[1]. This return to a policy which past experience had discredited was foredoomed to failure[2]. The new king was naturally welcomed only by the minority which leaned to Rome. A Roman force of a thousand legionaries, three auxiliary regiments of infantry and two of cavalry was left in Armenia to support him, while the neighbouring client-kings who had co-operated in the war—Antiochus, Aristobulus, Polemo and Pharasmanes—were rewarded by the grant of portions of Armenia adjoining their territories, a measure which may have interested them in the maintenance of the new régime but which could not fail to increase the ill-will of many of the Armenian nobles towards Tigranes. These arrangements made, Corbulo withdrew to the province of Syria, which had been assigned to him on the death of Quadratus.

VI. THE PARTHIAN INTERVENTION AND ITS RESULTS

Vologases had remained a passive spectator of the expulsion of Tiridates and the installation of a Roman nominee in his stead[3]. His hands were still tied by the Hyrcanian revolt and by many wars arising out of it; but at the outset he had renewed the treaty of friendship with Rome by the delivery of hostages[4], and when his hands were freed, he studied to avoid a direct conflict with Roman troops; indeed, both powers affected to treat the Armenian question as a side-issue between Tiridates and Rome. Now, however, he was goaded into action by the unprovoked aggression of Tigranes, who proceeded in 61[5] to violate Parthian sovereignty by invading and systematically plundering the feudatory kingdom of Adiabene, apparently with the intention of occupying it

[1] Josephus, *Ant.* xviii [5, 4], 140.

[2] The contention of Schur, that this and the next change of policy were merely feints to force the acceptance of what was the government's consistent policy from start to finish, may be mentioned.

[3] For the remaining period of the war we have some excerpts from Dio (LXII, 20–26), who seems to have drawn on Pliny's *History* (cf. above, p. 702): but the main source is Tacitus, *Ann.* xv, 1–17; 24–31. For the visit of Tiridates to Rome, Dio LXIII, 1–7; Suetonius, *Nero*, 13.

[4] Tacitus, *Ann.* xiii, 37, 4, *redintegrata amicitia*; xv, 1, 1, *continui foederis reverentia*.

[5] Tacitus groups together the events of 61 and 62, but the dividing line is marked by the allusion to winter-quarters in *Ann.* xv, 6.

permanently. The narrative of Tacitus conveys the impression that Tigranes acted on his own initiative, hoping (we may suppose) to raise himself in the esteem of his subjects and to mitigate the effect produced by the curtailment of Armenian territory. But the presence of a Roman force in Armenia suggests a doubt whether he could have ventured on such an enterprise without the approval of the Roman commandant and of Corbulo and without the sanction of the Roman government, and has led to the conjecture that the invasion was designed to relieve Parthian pressure on Hyrcania. However that may have been—and it is to be noted that the Roman troops appear to have taken no part in the invasion —the resentment of the injured king Monobazus, the successor of Izates, and of the Parthian nobility, reinforced by the plaints of the exiled Tiridates, forced Vologases to intervene. In the presence of his council he bound the diadem round his brother's head and sent a Parthian magnate Monaeses, with a body of horse which formed the king's customary escort, and Monobazus with his Adiabenian levies to drive Tigranes out of Armenia, while he himself settled his differences with the Hyrcanians, apparently by conceding them independence[1], and mobilized his forces to threaten Syria.

On receipt of this intelligence, Corbulo took such measures as were possible to assist Tigranes. He could not defend his province and at the same time be responsible for the conduct of military operations in Armenia. He, therefore, promptly wrote to Nero to say that Armenia needed a separate general for her defence in view of the Parthian threat to Syria; and he then dispatched to the aid of Tigranes the two legions he could best spare, IV Scythica and XII Fulminata[2], under the command of two experienced officers, Verulanus Severus and Vettius Bolanus. These legions had taken no part in the war, and the twelfth, which had long been in Syria, was presumably in no better condition for active service than the other Syrian legions had been six years before; but, as the real danger point was Syria, the seasoned legions were quite properly retained for its defence. As it was plainly advisable not to engage in serious fighting in Armenia pending the arrival of a new commander, Corbulo gave the two legates

[1] That the independence of Hyrcania was maintained for a century at least is inferred from the fact that in the reign of Antoninus Pius *Indi Bactri Hyrcani legatos misere iustitia tanti imperatoris comperta* (Aur. Victor, *Epit.* xv, 4). Cf. A. von Gutschmid, *Gesch. Irans*, p. 130; Kiessling in *P.W.* s.v *Hyrkania*, col. 508; Markwart, *op. cit.* p. 89.

[2] As is clear from Tacitus, *Ann.* xv, 6, 5.

secret instructions to act with deliberation and not to hurry matters: they were to do no more than might be necessary to ensure the king's safety[1]. He then hastened to put Syria in a state of defence, moving his legions forward to the Euphrates, mobilizing the provincial militia, fortifying the river crossings and guarding the wells.

Meanwhile Monaeses had shut up Tigranes in Tigranocerta, which he vainly attempted to take; while Vologases fixed his headquarters at Nisibis, whence he could menace Syria or assist Monaeses. Here he received a message from Corbulo remonstrating against the siege of a Roman protégé and Roman soldiers and requiring him to raise it, otherwise he would himself invade Mesopotamia. Vologases was not in a happy position. He was anxious, then as always, to avoid war with Rome. The Parthians were making no progress at Tigranocerta, which was well provisioned; his own horsemen could find no fodder for their mounts, a swarm of locusts having devoured every green thing; and he was threatened with attack from two sides. So he sent a conciliatory reply: he would send envoys to Rome to ask for Armenia and conclude a lasting peace—thereby expressing his willingness to accept the conditions originally offered; and he called off Monaeses and retired himself. An armistice was arranged[2], but not without concessions on the Roman side, which were not publicly announced at the time. When it became known that Tigranes had quitted Armenia and that the Roman legions had been withdrawn and sent to winter in hurriedly constructed huts in Cappadocia, a section of the Roman public inferred (rightly enough) that these concessions were part of the armistice terms, and surmised that they had been made by Corbulo on his own responsibility to allow time for the arrival of another general, who should relieve him of the risk of losing the glory he had already won. The motive suggested was wholly unjust to Corbulo, who, though as jealous of his reputation as other worthy Romans, was not the man to flinch from risks. If Corbulo really acted on his own responsibility in withdrawing the Roman troops and letting Tigranes fall, his action was at any rate endorsed by the imperial government, which realized the blunder

---

[1] The ambiguous phrase of Tacitus, *quippe bellum habere quam gerere malebat* (*Ann.* XV, 3, 1), has usually been interpreted as a censure of Corbulo, but it need not be so taken. Corbulo desired to let the war drag for the time rather than to prosecute it vigorously.

[2] An excerpt from Dio (LXII, 20, 4) represents Vologases as taking the initiative in arranging the truce, but the motive attributed to him is inadequate, and this version cannot stand against the circumstantial account of Tacitus.

it had made—and was preparing to plunge into another. The Parthian embassy received an evasive answer[1], and Nero embarked on a new policy, the implications of which can hardly have been understood either by him or his advisers, Seneca and Burrus. Armenia was to be annexed, and L. Caesennius Paetus, who had just held the consulship, was appointed to annex it. A worse choice could not have been made: Paetus was an incompetent soldier, an insufferable braggart, and an absolute poltroon. Reaching Cappadocia in 62[2], he signalized his arrival by pouring contempt on the achievements of Corbulo and proclaiming that the rule of a phantom king in Armenia would soon be replaced by Roman administration. After that, it was natural that there should be no love lost between the two legates.

The legions at Paetus' disposal were the Fourth and Twelfth, which had wintered in Cappadocia, and a new legion, V Macedonica, which had been ordered to the East from Moesia and had reached Pontus, together with auxiliaries from Galatia, Cappadocia and Pontus. Without awaiting the arrival of the new legion, Paetus determined to begin his offensive. His plan was to strike at Tigranocerta, which had been evacuated by the Roman troops and was not held by the Parthians; and he took the direct route which crossed the Euphrates at Îsoghli, opposite Tomisa, and ran to the fertile plain of Kharput, the *Kalon Pedion* of antiquity[3], whence it ascended the ridge of Taurus by the easy pass that skirts Lake Geuljik and debouches on the Mesopotamian side at Arghana. In the plain of Kharput lay the fortified city of Arsamosata (Tacitus calls it *castellum* merely) on the southern bank of the Arsanias, at some distance to the east of its junction with the tributary now called Peri Su[4]. On reaching the plain, Paetus proceeded to construct a base camp, choosing for its site Rhandeia[5], a place near Arsamosata but on the north bank of the river, which was not connected with Cappadocia by any good route and left unsecured his line of communications along the south bank. Nor could he wait to complete the camp: it was only half finished when he led his troops across Taurus to ravage districts which Corbulo had left untouched. After long marches, which resulted in nothing beyond the capture of some strongholds and the collection of considerable plunder, he retired on the near approach of winter to Rhandeia and sent a pompous despatch to Nero to

[1] Dio LXII, 20, 4.
[2] The date is fixed by reckoning back from Tacitus, *Ann.* xv, 24, *veris principio* (A.D. 63).
[3] Polybius VIII, 25, 1.
[4] See Note 5, p. 880.
[5] Dio LXII, 21, 1.

announce the practical completion of the war, with the result that the emperor assumed his ninth imperatorial acclamation[1]. Then he granted indiscriminate furloughs to his soldiers.

But the campaigning season was not yet over. Vologases had been making demonstrations against the Syrian frontier, but when Corbulo strengthened his defence of the river by constructing a pontoon bridge, doubtless at Zeugma, in face of the Parthian horsemen, and occupying the hills on the opposite side[2] with auxiliary and legionary troops, the king abandoned all hope of forcing the passage of the river, and turned northwards to launch his army against Paetus. On the news of his approach, Paetus concentrated his two weakened legions in the unfinished camp; then, changing his mind and scorning the advice of his officers, he marched out to meet the Parthians, but when a small reconnoitring party was cut off, he returned in dismay. Recovering confidence when he found the Parthian advance slower than he expected, he thought to stop it by dispersing his forces. On the crest of the pass, north of Lake Geuljik, he posted 3000 picked infantry (nearly half his legionary force[3]), and in the plain of Kharput he placed his best cavalry, while he detached a cohort to protect his wife and son and other non-combatants in Arsamosata. The rest of his troops he kept in camp at Rhandeia. Then he was prevailed upon to let Corbulo know that he was pressed. Corbulo got ready a force of some 8000 men, but made no haste to dispatch it: the message was not urgent, and it would not occur to him that an army of two legions with auxiliaries could not defend a fortified camp against Parthians, who were notoriously incapable of pressing a siege and would be unable, from lack of supplies and forage, to maintain a blockade in winter[4].

Vologases was not deterred by the attempt to block the road by isolated detachments. He crushed the legionaries, swept the cavalry aside, and appeared before the camp, which was a scene of utter demoralization. The men were panic-stricken; their general lost his head, and sent a piteous appeal to Corbulo, who now hurried to the rescue, marching by day and night through Commagene and Cappadocia, to find on his arrival at the Euphrates that Rhandeia had capitulated by agreement when he was only three days' march distant. Vologases, hearing of his approach, had

---

[1] C.I.L. ii, 4888.

[2] Near the village of Tell Musa opposite Balkis (described by E. Sachau, *Reise in Syrien u. Mesopotamien*, p. 178). [3] Cf. Tacitus, *Ann.* xv, 12, 5.

[4] Dio lxii, 21, 2. Tacitus' motive, 'the greater the peril, the greater the glory of the rescue,' is doubtless a rhetorical commonplace.

pressed the siege, and although he made no attempt to storm the camp, he succeeded in driving Paetus to surrender on terms. The legions were allowed to depart on condition that all Roman troops should quit Armenia and that all forts and supplies should be handed over; when these conditions were carried out, Vologases was to be free to send an embassy to Nero. To complete his humiliation, the king ordered Paetus to build a bridge over the river as a monument of his victory; which done, the Roman soldiers fled pell-mell to safety, keeping to the northern bank until they were out of sight of the enemy, with their general at their head covering 40 miles in a day and abandoning his wounded as he fled. Yet this prince of cowards was lightly dismissed by his emperor with an ironical jest. The man was not unworthy of his master.

Such was the issue of the only direct collision between Roman and Parthian troops during the whole course of the war. In a brief interview with Paetus on the bank of the Euphrates Corbulo behaved with moderation, but rejected his suggestion of a joint invasion of Armenia, as being outside his instructions: it was his duty to return to his province, which might be attacked by the Parthians. Paetus then retired to pass the winter in Cappadocia, and to send to Rome a false report, which implied that all was well on the Eastern front. In his memoirs Corbulo did not spare his disgraced rival. Among other statements, one of them perhaps exaggerated[1], he said that Paetus had sworn before the standards and in presence of the king's witnesses that no Roman should set foot in Armenia until it was known whether Nero assented to the peace. Tacitus doubts this statement—which shows that he did not regard the memoirs as wholly trustworthy—but it corresponded to what actually happened, and he admits that there was no uncertainty about the shameful details of the flight. Arrived in Syria, Corbulo received a message from Vologases requesting him to destroy his fortifications on the east bank of the Euphrates and treat the river as the boundary as hitherto, and to this he agreed on the king's yielding to his counter-demand for the withdrawal of Parthian garrisons from Armenia. Once more the Armenians were left without a ruler.

VII. THE CONCLUSION OF PEACE

At the beginning of the following spring (A.D. 63) Parthian envoys appeared in Rome with a letter from Vologases, which revealed the true state of affairs and made a moderate proposal

[1] Tacitus, *Ann.* xv, 16, 1, compared with xv, 8, 1.

which amounted to an acceptance of the terms offered by Rome in 55. His claim, he said, to Armenia had been decided by the fortune of war, but Tiridates was ready to do homage for it before the Roman standards and the effigies of the Emperor, and, but for the obligation of his priestly office, he would even have been willing to go to Rome to receive the diadem. It was not, however, the Roman way to treat with a triumphant foe, even though he offered the terms which had originally been offered to him, and Nero's advisers counselled the resumption of hostilities, but the presentation of gifts to the envoys conveyed a plain hint that the issue was narrowed down to a point of ceremony: if Tiridates presented his petition in person, he would not ask in vain. To extort compliance with this condition, an imposing display of force was arranged. Paetus was recalled, and Corbulo was appointed commander-in-chief of all the forces in the East, which were reinforced by the addition of a third Danubian legion, XV Apollinaris from Pannonia, and by detachments of picked troops from Illyricum and Egypt. While his official title was the normal one of *legatus Augusti pro praetore*, he was granted an authority overriding that of all governors of neighbouring provinces (*maius imperium*) and placing client-kings and princes under his orders[1]. In Syria he was succeeded by C. Cestius Gallus, who took over the administration of the province but had no independent military authority, although the troops left in Syria remained under his charge; these consisted of the Tenth legion and the two demoralized legions, IV and XII, sent back from Cappadocia. The other two Syrian units, the seasoned Third and Sixth, were dispatched to Melitene, where they were joined by V Macedonica from Pontus and the recently transferred XV Apollinaris. These four, with the auxiliary horse and foot and the contingents furnished by client-princes, made up a force of some 50,000 men, the most powerful yet assembled on the eastern front.

With this army Corbulo crossed the Euphrates, but he had not advanced far along the route once followed by Lucullus and recently by Paetus, when envoys of Tiridates and Vologases met him with overtures of peace. He received them in a friendly manner and sent them back with a message of advice: it was for the advantage of Tiridates to accept Armenia undevastated as a gift, and Vologases would best consult Parthian interests by an alliance with Rome. This counsel he drove home by an immediate attack on the Armenians who had been the first to turn against Rome, which had the desired effect. Vologases asked for a truce

[1] Dessau 232; *C.R.* xlv, 1931, p. 190.

for the provinces attacked, and Tiridates requested an interview, suggesting Rhandeia as the meeting-place, to which Corbulo did not object, as the contrast between the present and the past would enhance his glory and, it may be added, the prestige of Rome. Tiridates declared himself willing to go to Rome and 'bring the Emperor a novel glory, an Arsacid as a suppliant while Parthia flourished'; and it was agreed that he should lay his diadem before Nero's effigy and only resume it from his hand. The ceremony took place amid a brilliant military display, and Tiridates left to visit his brothers, Vologases and Pacorus, and his mother before undertaking the long journey to Rome, handing over his daughter as a hostage. The only stipulation made by the Parthian king, who had already gone to Ecbatana, was that Tiridates should not be subjected to any indignity on his way to Rome or in the capital itself.

The preparations for the journey of an eastern potentate were naturally not made in a day, and during the interval Corbulo kept at least part of his army together and continued to occupy some of the frontier districts: in 64–5 the presence of the Third legion at Kharput (Ziata) is attested by three inscriptions, which record in the same formula the completion of what was no doubt a fort[1]. It was not till 66 that Tiridates arrived in Italy after a nine months' journey, escorted by bodies of Parthian and Roman cavalry and accompanied by his wife and sons, the sons of Vologases and Pacorus and Monobazus, and a great retinue. The journey was made overland by way of the Hellespont, because a long voyage would have entailed defilement of the divine waters of the sea, which was forbidden by the Mazdean religion[2]; and it cost the huge sum of 800,000 sesterces a day, which was charged (very improperly) to the public treasury[3]. From North Italy Tiridates was conveyed in an imperial chariot to Naples, where Nero entertained him, afterwards accompanying him to Rome for the coronation ceremony. The capital was gaily decorated with festoons and lights, and crowded with people who filled the streets and the forum and climbed to the housetops to get a view, while the route

[1] One of these inscriptions is Dessau 232, dated 13 Oct. 64–5.
[2] Pliny, *N.H.* xxx, 16. The crossing from Brundisium to Dyrrhachium, which he made on his return journey, would take only about 24 hours. The same scruple was expressed by Vologases when, in declining Nero's invitations to Rome, he said: 'It is far easier for you than for me to cross such a wide expanse of sea' (Dio LXIII, 7, 2). Similar prohibitions of the pollution of water are found in the Avesta (Cumont, *Mystères de Mithra*, I, p. 104 *sq.*).
[3] According to Dio LXIII, 2, 2.

was lined by soldiers with gleaming arms and standards. Next morning Nero in triumphal garb, accompanied by the Senate and the Praetorian guard, entered the forum and seated himself on the rostra, to which Tiridates and his suite advanced through lines of troops, and did obeisance to the Emperor, hailing him as his master and adoring him as an emanation of Mithras. Then Nero proclaimed him king of Armenia and placed the diadem on his head as he sat at his feet; he was saluted *imperator* and in celebration of the triumph of the Roman arms he deposited a laurel wreath in the Capitol. From this time, as his coins attest, he assumed the *praenomen* of *Imperator*. The ceremony of investiture was followed by a special performance in Pompey's theatre, the whole interior having been gilded for the occasion and the properties adorned with gold—a display which led the people to apply the adjective 'golden' to the day itself. A costly banquet and public exhibitions by Nero of his favourite arts completed the entertainment of the guest, whose parting was sped by a princely gift from the Emperor (estimated variously at one or two hundred million sesterces) and a number of skilled workmen to rebuild Artaxata, which arose from its ruins under the short-lived name of Neroneia.

VIII. THE SEQUEL OF THE WAR AND THE MILITARY PROJECTS OF NERO

So ended ten years of marches and talk, punctuated by a disgraceful episode, which went by the name of war. The public homage done in Rome by an Arsacid prince was certainly a triumph such as no emperor had hitherto enjoyed, and it duly impressed the public, which hardly realized that the price paid for it was the virtual abandonment of Armenia to Parthia. The Arsacids were now recognized as the legitimate rulers of that harassed land, which really became—what Armenian historical tradition wrongly supposed it had been since the third century B.C.—an appanage of the Parthian crown; and Rome's right of enfeoffment left her only the shadow of the authority she had claimed for a century. It is not surprising that Nero's concession, crowned by the splendour of the reception accorded to Tiridates, won him popularity in Parthia, which lasted for many years after his death. Yet the compromise, reached after several oscillations of policy which showed that the Roman statesmen of the day had no clear grasp of the conditions of the problem, was a reasonable settlement: it saved Roman prestige, satisfied the well-founded claim of the Parthian empire, and led to a stable peace on the eastern frontier, which lasted for half a century, disturbed only by an occasional passing cloud. This result showed that the settlement suited the conditions imposed by the geographical situation of Armenia and by its social and cultural ties with Parthia.

The removal of the one real obstacle to friendly relations between the two empires did not, however, remove the need of a proper system of frontier defence. The establishment of such a system was left to Vespasian, but the way was prepared by Nero when he annexed in 64–5[1] the vassal kingdom of Pontus, ruled since 38 by Polemo II. Polemo retired to the Cilician kingdom (Olba, Cennatis and Lalassis) which had been given him in 41 in lieu of Bosporus[2], and his Pontic realm was added to the province of Galatia, which was the important frontier province of Asia Minor in the Julio-Claudian period and grew to a vast size by the attachment to it of each fresh annexation (except Cappadocia). The incorporation of Polemo's Pontus advanced Roman territory to the frontier of Lesser Armenia and placed under direct imperial rule the whole of the Black Sea coast from Amisus (Samsûn) to the slopes of the Caucasus, with the ports of Side (Polemonium), Cerasus and Trapezus[3].

The annexation was hardly prompted by a realization of the need of organizing the frontier towards Armenia; otherwise Armenia Minor, which was of paramount importance from that point of view, would not have been left, as it was, under the rule of a client-prince. It seems to have been rather part of a policy, initiated in the previous year, which aimed at securing direct control of the coast lands of the Black Sea. The Euxine was to become a Roman lake, which would be made safe for navigation and from whose shores watch could be kept on the Sarmatian tribes that occupied the whole *hinterland* from the region of the Danube delta to the Caucasus and the Caspian. Commerce apart, the sea routes from Moesia and Thrace and from the Bosporan kingdom to Trapezus were of great military importance.

[1] The exact date is furnished by the Era of the Pontic cities Neocaesarea, Zela, Cerasus and Trapezus, which is proved by their coins to have begun in Oct. 64 (Kubitschek in *P.W.* s.v. *Aera*, xxxv; Babelon-Reinach, *Recueil général des monnnaies grecques d'Asie Mineure*, I, 1).

[2] He was still ruling there in the reign of Galba (*B. M. Cat. Lycaonia*, etc. pp. xxx, liv). See Volume of Plates iv, 208, *g*.

[3] The Pontic kingdom no doubt included Colchis, as it had done under Polemo's predecessors (Strabo XI, 499).

For Roman troops operating in Armenia or stationed near its borders the Euxine provided the chief line of communication with their centres of supply and reinforcement; the land route from the Thracian Bosporus through Bithynia-Pontus to the Euphrates was still undeveloped, at least in its eastern section, and transport over it was at best slow and laborious. But the Euxine needed vigilant policing; piracy had always been rife on its waters, and its prevalence in the Augustan age has already been noted. Till A.D. 64 the task of keeping it in check had been left to the kings of Pontus and the Bosporus; with the annexation of Polemo's realm the responsibility was taken over by Rome, the royal squadron being utilized to form the nucleus of a Pontic fleet, which some years later numbered forty ships and had its head-quarters at Trapezus[1].

More formidable, however, was the Sarmatian menace, which had been brought home to the Roman government by the events of the last few years. The various Sarmatian tribes in the steppes of South Russia had been steadily moving westwards towards the Danube, driven forward by the advance of fresh swarms from central Asia. Before A.D. 50 the Iazyges had established themselves at the expense of the Dacians in the great plain between Theiss and Danube, and by A.D. 62 the Roxolani (the Blond Alans) are found not far from the region of the lower Danube in contact and in friendly relations with the Germanic Bastarnae and the Thracian Dacians. The increasing pressure of these tribes on the Danube frontier is attested by the epitaph of Plautius Silvanus Aelianus, governor of Moesia in the years following A.D. 60[2]. About 62 Plautius had to suppress a threatening movement of the Sarmatians, in which the adjoining tribes were involved, and after restoring order in what is now Rumanian territory, he had to intervene in the Crimea, where the Scythians who held the interior of the peninsula were besieging the Greek city of Cher-sonesus, close to Sebastopol. By dispatching a force, which could easily be transported by sea, or possibly by the mere threat of war, he compelled the Scythian king to raise the siege. His interven-tion appears to have been followed by a drastic curtailment of the nominal independence of the Bosporan kingdom, which had been ruled since 45/6 by Cotys I. This is an inference which may reasonably be drawn[3] from a solitary gold coin of A.D. 62/3

[1] Josephus, *Bell. Jud.* II [16, 4], 367.
[2] See p. 806; Dessau 986; Dessau in *Jahreshefte*, XXIII, 1926, pp. 346 *sqq.*
[3] Despite Dessau's doubts (*Gesch. d. röm. Kaiserzeit*, II, p. 205, n. 1). For the coin see Volume of Plates IV, 208, *m.*

(Bosporan Era 359) which is devoid of any reference to the king—his royal monogram being replaced by an imperial one, Nέρ(ων) K(αîσαρ)—and from a copper coin bearing Nero's head and name without any allusion to the king. Whether Cotys had died or whether, if still alive, he was deposed or more probably reduced to the position of a Roman functionary, cannot be determined; his last coin belongs to A.D. 62, and he is heard of no more[1]. The next extant coin, an *aureus* of his son Rhescuporis, bearing the date 68–9 and the heads of Vespasian and Titus, shows that the monarchy was re-established with its old rights after Nero's death.

A natural sequel to the virtual incorporation of the Bosporan kingdom would be a Roman military occupation, and such an occupation not only of Bosporan territory but of the whole Caucasian coast has been inferred from the speech which Josephus puts into the mouth of the Jewish king Agrippa in A.D. 66[2]. In the course of a survey of the legionary forces at the disposal of the Roman emperor, designed to impress on the Jews the folly of rebellion, Agrippa is made to say that the Heniochi, Colchi and Tauri, the Bosporani and the tribes that dwell round the Euxine and the Sea of Azov are kept in subjection by 3000 legionary troops, and that 40 ships of war 'now maintain peace on that hitherto savage and unnavigable sea.' Josephus' information was plainly drawn from an official source, but as there are reasons for believing that the document in question really belonged to the reign of Vespasian[3], it can hardly be regarded as good evidence for military measures taken by Nero.

Nevertheless the territories brought under direct control in 63 and 64 were to be used by Nero as a base of operations for an offensive against the Sarmatians, which was said to be part of an

---

[1] A gold coin dated 365 (= A.D. 68–9), alleged to bear Cotys' monogram and the heads of Vitellius and his father, the censor, has been cited as evidence for the restoration of Cotys by that date, but the description is undoubtedly incorrect. All the descriptions and reproductions of the coin, beginning with Köhne (*Musée Kotschoubey*, p. 227) and ending with Burachkov (*Gen. Catal.* p. 252, no. 115), go back to Sestini's *Lettere*, 11, p. 170, no. 23. Berthier-de-La-Garde in his *Corrections* to Burachkov pointed out that the heads are those of Vespasian and Titus. The coin is an example of the first *aureus* of Rhescuporis, the monogram of which could obviously be misread as that of Cotys. Volume of Plates iv, 208, *n*.

[2] *Bell. Jud.* 11 [16, 4], 345 *sqq.* A. von Domaszewski, *Rh. Mus.* XLVII, 1892, pp. 208 *sqq.*; M. Rostovtzeff, *Klio*, 11, 1902, pp. 80 *sqq.*; Schur, *op. cit.* p. 89.

[3] Ritterling, in *P.W.* s.v. *Legio*, cols. 1261 *sqq.*

ambitious scheme of conquest in the East. In 66 (or perhaps 67) military preparations began with the creation of a new legion, composed of Italians six feet tall, which was given the title of *Legio I Italica*; Nero dubbed it the 'Phalanx of Alexander the Great,' a description which reveals the grandiose ideas that were fermenting in his brain[1]. Other legions could be drawn from the Eastern army, now that peace was established on the Parthian frontier. The objective of the campaign was the Caspian Gates, and Tacitus specifies the Albani as the foe who was to be attacked[2]. By the 'Caspian Gates' was obviously not meant the famous pass south of the Caspian Sea, on the road which led from Media to Parthyene and central Asia. The name was also commonly given to the pass of Darial, the 'Gate of the Alans'—properly, says Pliny, called the 'Caucasian Gates'—through which ran the main route over the central Caucasus from Harmozica (or Harmastus), near Tiflis, in Iberia to the valley of the river Terek[3]. This was the 'Caspian route' (*Caspia via*) by which in A.D. 35 the Iberians had brought a horde of Sarmatians over the Caucasus to attack the Parthians[4]. These Sarmatians were, as Josephus states, the Alani, whose name was not known to the Romans till A.D. 64–5 and was easily confused with Albani, as it evidently was by Tacitus' authority[5]. The Alans were the latest wave of the barbarian flood which had been moving westwards from central Asia, and at this time they were settled in the steppes between

---

[1] Suetonius, *Nero*, 19.

[2] Tacitus, *Hist.* I, 6; Suetonius, *loc. cit.*; Dio LXIII, 8, 1.

[3] Ptolemy calls it the Sarmatian Gates (v, 8, 5; 9; pp. 911, 914, ed. Müller). Pliny (*N.H.* VI, 30; 40) says that the pass was wrongly labelled the 'Caspian Gates' on the map sent to Rome by members of Corbulo's army, who explored the country by Nero's order (cf. Dio, *loc. cit.*), and that Nero's threat 'was said to be directed against the Caspian Gates instead of the Gates which led through Iberia into the country of the Sarmatians,' the true Caspian Gates being the defile traversed by Alexander the Great (further defined in 43–4).

[4] Tacitus, *Ann.* VI, 33; Josephus, *Ant.* XVIII [4, 4], 97, who likewise calls the pass the Caspian Gates. It is to be noted that the Caucasus was formerly called Caspius after the tribe of the Caspii (Strabo XI, 497).

[5] This suggestion is due to Mommsen; the confusion of the two names is frequent in later MSS. The first mention of Alani is in Lucan, *De bello civ.* VIII, 223; X, 454 (written in 64–5). It is true that a campaign against the Alans would have involved complete control over Albania, which was not one of Corbulo's allies in the Armenian war and shortly before had been at enmity with Iberia, but the scale of Nero's preparations (see below) does not commend the statement that this small state was to be the primary object of attack.

the Caucasus and the Caspian. When the migratory movement was stemmed on the west by Plautius Silvanus, it threatened to seek an outlet towards the south, and an overflow in this direction took place within a few years, when the floodgates on the Danube, temporarily opened by the denudation of the frontier during the civil war, were closed again by a strengthened defence[1].

These conditions are sufficient to account for Nero's projected campaign; but what precisely his purpose was, cannot be said. Certain it is that an offensive, even had it been successful, would have had no permanent effect in removing the Sarmatian pressure on the Roman provinces and vassal kingdoms; while the maintenance of a military frontier in the steppes of South Russia, added to all its other commitments, would have been wholly beyond the power of the Roman Empire[2].

Besides the Caucasian expedition Nero is said to have contemplated a campaign against the kingdom of Ethiopia. As early as the autumn of 61 he sent a party of praetorian soldiers with a tribune and two centurions (the latter perhaps belonging to the Egyptian army) to explore the country[3]; and about a year after their return, in 64, he meditated a visit to the provinces of the East, especially Egypt, but was deterred by a bad omen[4]. The exploratory mission was, ostensibly at any rate, a friendly one, and it met with a friendly reception. With the help of the 'king' of Ethiopia (evidently a sub-king, since the ruler of Meroë at this time was, as Pliny states, a queen-regent Candace[5]) and the letters of recommendation which he gave them to neighbouring 'kings,' the explorers accomplished a long journey up the Nile beyond Meroë to the marshes of the White Nile, and brought back geographical and zoological information, together with a map and a report to the effect that the Ethiopian kingdom was in a state of utter decay: Meroë itself was sparsely inhabited. Plainly this poverty-stricken country was not a desirable acquisition; it was friendly towards Rome; and Seneca, who was still at the helm when the expedition was sent out, says nothing of any

---

[1] Josephus, *Bell. Jud.* VII [4, 3], 94.

[2] For a different view of Nero's purpose, see Note 6, pp. 880 *sqq.*

[3] Seneca, *Nat. Quaest.* VI, 8, 3–4; Pliny, *N.H.* VI, 181 *sqq.*; XII, 19; Dio LXIII, 8, 1. The date has been made very probable by Schur, *op. cit.* p. 41 *sq.*: Seneca's sixth book was written in 63, and such a long and difficult journey would require about a year and a half.

[4] Tacitus, *Ann.* XV, 36, 1; Suetonius, *Nero*, 19, 35.

[5] See above, p. 242 n. 1.

military policy, but states that its purpose was to discover the source of the Nile[1].

These facts cast suspicion on the truth of the report that the object of the expedition was to collect information for an Ethiopian campaign[2]. In all probability Pliny is the only ultimate authority for it, and it is notorious that he was animated by a fierce hatred of Nero and lost no opportunity of placing him in the most unfavourable light[3]. Pliny's statement may indeed derive support from the dispatch of certain bodies of troops to Alexandria: in the summer of 66 there were in the Egyptian capital 2000 men of the African army, including the *ala Siliana*, which was to play a part in the war between Otho and Vitellius; later in the same year arrived one of Corbulo's legions, XV Apollinaris, and in the following year came legionary detachments from Germany[4]. The African troops had been sent on to await the Emperor's arrival, but the presence of the rest may be otherwise explained. If Tacitus is to be trusted, the legionary detachments were destined for the Caucasus campaign, and they may have been sent by way of Egypt to avoid the slow and laborious march by land, while the legion may (as in 71) have been on its way back to Pannonia[5]. On these points certainty is not attainable; but if Nero's programme really included an Ethiopian war, it is difficult to divine the motives that prompted him. It may be that he was allured by the prospect of a cheap triumph[6]. The view that his object was to safeguard the commercial interests of the empire by securing the decaying Meroïtic kingdom against the encroachment of the expanding Axumite kingdom of Abyssinia, which threatened to monopolize the African ivory trade, will hardly bear close scrutiny[7].

Whatever Nero's intentions may have been, his plans were disturbed by the outbreak of the serious rebellion in Judaea, for

[1] *Ad investigandum caput Nili.* It was a scientific expedition sent by Nero, *ut aliarum virtutum ita veritatis in primis amantissimus.* It may well be that its dispatch was suggested by Seneca himself, who was keenly interested in matters of geography and ethnography.

[2] Pliny, *N.H.* VI, 181: *renuntiavere...Neroni...missi ab eo... ad explorandum, inter reliqua bella et Aethiopicum cogitanti.* Cf. Leuze in *Or. Lit. Zeit.* XXVII, 1924, p. 346.   [3] See Appendix on Sources, p. 867.

[4] Josephus, *Bell. Jud.* II [18, 8], 494; III [1, 3], 8; Tacitus, *Hist.* I, 31, 70.

[5] Tacitus, *Hist.* I, 6; Josephus, *op. cit.* VII [5, 3], 117. Cf. Ritterling, *op. cit.* col. 1260 *sq.*

[6] Cf. H. Kortenbeutel, *Ägypt. Handel,* p. 61.

[7] See Note 6, pp. 880 *sqq.*

the suppression of which three legions had to be detailed. But they were not abandoned. Steps were taken to restore the military balance by ordering reinforcements from the West. From Britain was summoned the Fourteenth legion, which had distinguished itself in crushing the revolt of Boudicca, and was selected as a 'crack' regiment, while detachments were drawn from the other three British legions and from the legions of Germany and Illyricum[1]. But the storm-clouds gathering in the West forced the emperor to return to Italy at the beginning of 68 and to recall the troops for the protection of his throne. Fortunately for Rome the founder of the next dynasty was a man of robust practical sense who realized that what the empire needed was, not enlargement, but consolidation and defence, and who immediately set about the establishment of a scientific frontier in the East and sought to meet the Sarmatian peril by assisting the king of Iberia to hold the gate of the Caucasus and by strengthening the kingdom of Bosporus.

[1] Tacitus, *Hist.* 1, 6; 11, 11.

CHAPTER XXIII

THE NORTHERN FRONTIERS FROM TIBERIUS TO NERO

I. ROMAN FRONTIER POLICY

SUB Tiberio quies: here as elsewhere the Principate of Tiberius was a period of peace and retrenchment. An ambitious plan of conquest in the north had ended in disaster, unsuspected dangers had been revealed, even victory was costly or barren. Had the destinies of the Empire been guided by a ruler lacking the caution and the experience of Tiberius, he could have followed no other policy.

In A.D. 6 fifteen legions were stationed in the lands bounded by Rhine and Danube. The same garrison was maintained after A.D. 9, but with a changed distribution and a changed purpose. There were now five armies, each under a consular legate, those of Upper and Lower Germany, of Pannonia and Dalmatia (Illyricum had been divided in or shortly after A.D. 9), and of Moesia. It was not intended that the legions should be employed to make fresh conquests; and frontier defence was not their main function—it was the control of the interior that more urgently demanded their attention. The loyalty and tranquillity of the Gallic provinces under Augustus did not conceal from the Romans the presence of danger. Their apprehensions, which were confirmed by the revolt of Florus and Sacrovir in A.D. 21 (p. 644), were strengthened still further by the formidable rising of Vindex—whatever may have been his aims, thousands flocked to the standard of a descendant of an Aquitanian royal house. Raetia and Noricum appeared to be safe; but the Pannonians and Dalmatians, a recent conquest, had risen

Note. The *Annals* of Tacitus, in their surviving parts, supply some valuable details about the Rhine frontier, but the *Histories* and the *Germania* together are more important. There is very little to be gleaned from other literary sources—and for this reason it is all the more regrettable that Tacitus should have so little to say about the Danube. Inscriptions are now indispensable—with their help the movements of the legions can often be traced with remarkable accuracy; moreover, the purely archaeological evidence contributes some valuable results. But here too the Danubian lands are poorly represented. See Map 13, facing p. 347.

at the first opportunity. They were crushed, but only with difficulty, and though this was the last of their revolts, the character of the land and of its inhabitants forbade the Romans to assume that it would be so. That after A.D. 9 law and order should have endured unbroken in Bosnia is a remarkable testimony to the thoroughness of the final subjugation, if not to the influences of civilization. Farther to the south-east were other warlike peoples that needed watching. Their resistance had been broken by Piso in his great Thracian War which lasted for three years, and the Balkans had thus been pacified; but here too trouble might again be expected sooner or later. This view of the function of the legions is confirmed by the fact that in Spain after A.D. 9 a large garrison remained, of three legions[1].

Hampered by these grave responsibilities, the legions would perhaps not have been able to guard the frontiers as well. They did not need to. Care had been taken that the enemies of Rome beyond the great rivers should be kept weak, disunited and harmless. This had been one of the objects of three great expeditions beyond the Danube in the decade before the attack on Maroboduus; they had not been all in vain and no further intervention on a comparable scale was needed. A similar aim, it might be argued, was the only real justification for the campaigns of Germanicus; whether it was attained might, however, be doubted, for the power of Arminius emerged strengthened rather than weakened. However that may be, when the Roman pressure relaxed, the feuds of tribe against tribe, of faction against faction, could pursue their unimpeded course. Roman encouragement was seldom required. In the year following the recall of Germanicus, Arminius turned his arms against Maroboduus. The Semnones and the Langobardi deserted the king, a loss which can hardly have been compensated by the accession to his cause of Inguiomerus, the uncle of Arminius. A battle ensued which illustrated how much the Germans had already learnt from their warfare against disciplined armies. Although the issue was indecisive, Maroboduus was seriously weakened and his empire began to crumble. In vain that he appealed for Roman aid: Roman diplomacy turned the scales against him. Before long an exile, Catualda, appeared on the scene and expelled him from his capital and his kingdom. The fallen monarch sought refuge on Roman territory. He was interned at Ravenna where he lingered

---

[1] IV Macedonica, VI Victrix and X Gemina. An inscription, Dessau 2648, records an otherwise unattested Asturian rising in Nero's reign.

on for eighteen years. Such was the melancholy fate of the first statesman in the history of the German peoples. The career of Arminius the liberator had been more dramatic, his end was sudden and violent. In emulation of Maroboduus he aspired to kingly power among the Cherusci, and was treacherously slain by his own kinsmen (A.D. 19).

The triumph of Roman policy had been rapid and complete, and its fruits were not lost. In order to illustrate the economy with which the frontier could often be held it will be convenient to pursue further the story of Roman relations with the Germans of Bohemia and Moravia, the Marcomanni and the Quadi. Catualda succumbed almost at once to an attack of the Hermunduri; his followers and those of Maroboduus were established north of the Danube, with Vannius of the nation of the Quadi as their king. Vannius enjoyed a long and prosperous reign until at last, in A.D. 50, he was assailed by the Hermunduri, the Lugii and other tribes which were supporting his nephews Vangio and Sido against him. Vannius fell, for the governor of Pannonia had been instructed not to intervene, and Vangio and Sido divided the kingdom between them. Like their neighbours to the east, the princes of the Sarmatae Iazyges, they maintained a steady loyalty to Rome. But in A.D. 89, during Domitian's war against the Dacians, these friendly relations were disturbed. The situation was critical—Roman policy had been based upon the risky but by no means irrational calculation that there would not be serious trouble on different parts of the frontier at the same time. To check the Sarmatians Domitian therefore made peace with Dacia, and against the Marcomanni and Quadi he negotiated with the tribes in their rear, the Semnones and the Lugii[1]. But this was not enough. The most vulnerable section of the whole northern frontier of the empire, the Middle Danube eastwards from Vienna, had been laid bare; it now required the protection of several more legions.

The emperors of the Julio-Claudian house were not confronted by any problem of this gravity, a bitter disappointment to their historian who complained that his task was dull and tedious. The frontiers were secure and satisfactory, and there was another reason for not going beyond them—the responsibility and the glory of war could not be resigned to a subject, conquest must be achieved, if at all, by or at least in the presence of the emperor himself. After a generation of peace, however, the accession of a youthful prince might promise a change; but the designs of

---

[1] Dio LXVII, 5, 2–3.

Gaius were never clearly revealed, and it was Claudius who disregarded the testament of Augustus and added Britain to the empire. The remarkable tranquillity of the European frontiers appeared to justify this step. The Rhine was still thought to require eight legions, it is true; but over a vast extent of territory between the camps of Vindonissa near Bâle and Carnuntum a little to the east of Vienna, there was no legion at all—military protection was almost absent because superfluous. In Raetia the auxiliary troops were at first scattered over the country, and were not posted along the line of the Danube until the time of Claudius. Noricum too has no history: and although the area under Roman control on the Lower Danube was extended, such was the peace on and within the frontiers that legions could be withdrawn to the East. For a time (A.D. 63–8) during Nero's reign only five were left instead of seven. But danger was soon to threaten from beyond the river, and by the end of the century the centre of interest shifts to the Danube. During this period, however, the Rhine is still the more important military frontier.

II. THE RHINE

When a political boundary corresponds to a geographical limit such as the sea or the mountains, virgin forest or barren desert, it may be called a natural frontier. Though a river is not a limit of this kind, it may form a convenient line of demarcation and lend itself to military defence, especially if its valley is such as to offer good lateral communications. For various reasons the whole length of the Rhine was not equally well suited for these purposes; above Mainz its passage across the plain was capricious and unregulated, below Mainz it plunged into winding gorges, near Nymwegen the stream divided. Indeed, after the annexations made by the Flavians, it was to form the frontier of the Empire only for a comparatively short stretch, below Coblence; and in this period it is not always easy to discern exactly where the frontier was conceived to run, for beyond the river were Roman outposts and native tribes in varying degrees of dependence.

The Island of the Batavians and Canninefates was always regarded as within the empire. These tribes paid no tribute but supplied soldiers. To the north-east dwelt the Frisii; beyond them were the Chauci, who had probably, like the Frisii, remained loyal after the disaster of Varus. The Chauci appear to have been neglected after A.D. 16, but the Frisii were governed by a Roman military officer. In A.D. 28 the Frisians revolted, inflicting a

defeat on the Romans, and enjoyed impunity and independence
until in A.D. 47 Corbulo reasserted Roman authority over them.
This did not content his ambition. The Chauci had already been
defeated by Gabinius Secundus in A.D. 41[1], but before the arrival
of Corbulo they had made piratical raids on the Gallic coast.
He resolved to chastise, if not to subjugate them, but was arrested
in his enterprises by the jealousy or the prudence of the Emperor.
He obeyed the summons, but with reluctance, and his posts were
withdrawn across the Rhine. Whether this meant the total
abandonment of Roman control over the Frisians is uncertain.
They are hostile in A.D. 69–70, but later contribute auxiliary
regiments to the army. Along the Rhine north-east of Vetera was a
strip of territory which the Romans kept empty of inhabitants and
preserved for the requirements of their own garrisons. In Nero's
reign first the Frisii and then the Angrivarii sought to occupy
these lands, but were repulsed by force or threats. Beyond this
zone lived the Bructeri, against whom there were hostilities in the
Flavian period, to the south along the Rhine were the Tencteri
and next to them the Usipi, neither of which tribes appeared to be
formidable, while the Mattiaci, dwelling between the Lahn and
the Main, were friendly if not already dependent. It was in their
territory that Curtius Rufus employed his troops in silver mining,
and Pliny the Elder inspected the hot springs of Aquae Mattiacae
(Wiesbaden)[2], where Roman occupation had probably been
permanent and unbroken since the days of Drusus. There was
probably an earth-fort at Wiesbaden itself; another was constructed at Hofheim, a few miles to the east, in A.D. 40–2, but
appears to have been destroyed by the Chatti in A.D. 50[3]. There
was as yet, however, no permanent bridge across the river at
Mainz. Above Mainz the protection of the frontier, if such it can
be called, presented no difficulty. Southern Germany had a thin
and mixed population with no large tribes. The Suebi Nicretes in
the neighbourhood of Heidelberg were a small and innocuous
people, and it was not likely that an enemy would emerge from the
Black Forest. As yet this region has no history; Baden-Baden
may, however, have attracted visitors, and beyond the Upper
Rhine northwards from Vindonissa an earth-fort of Claudian date
has been discovered at Hüfingen.

The presence of this line of weak or dependent tribes made the
task of frontier defence easy and economical. But there was one

---

[1] Dio LX, 8, 7, cf. Suetonius, *Claudius*, 24.　　　[2] *N.H.* XXXI, 20.
[3] E. Ritterling, 'Das frührömische Lager bei Hofheim' (= *Nassauische
Annalen* XL, 1912).

large and formidable nation of Germans in dangerous proximity, the Chatti. They were not only a hardy and warlike stock—they preserved an iron discipline when they marched forth to war; and, if this were not remarkable enough, they carried with them rations of food and tools for entrenching[1]. In A.D. 50 the legate of Upper Germany, Pomponius Secundus, had to check one of their incursions, and they were to be heard of again. The Chatti had neighbours and enemies who could be employed against them, to the north the Cherusci and on the east the Hermunduri. The Cherusci, it is true, were but a shadow of their former greatness; and their internal discords were intensified rather than assuaged when in A.D. 47 Italicus, the son of Arminius' renegade brother Flavus, was sent from Rome to be their king. None the less, they might be a cause of anxiety to the Chatti, and later Domitian is found supporting their king Chariomerus[2]. The Hermunduri needed no encouragement to serve the interests of Rome. Like the Alemanni and the Burgundians in a later age the Hermunduri and the Chatti disputed the possession of certain salt-springs. In A.D. 58 a great battle was fought with results disastrous to the Chatti.

A frontier is no less a frontier when it does not happen to be bristling with camps and forts. There had been no legions on the Rhine in the generation between Caesar and Drusus, and there were hardly any on the Danube in the Julio-Claudian period. Drusus, however, had brought up the legions from the interior of Gaul and established them on the Rhine in positions from which they were to invade and conquer Germany. Here they remained. Before the Varian disaster there had been five legions on the Rhine and two in Raetia: there were now, and there continued to be for the greater part of the century, eight legions along the Rhine, from Vetera to Vindonissa. After A.D. 9, or perhaps rather after A.D. 17, their arrangement was as follows. At Vetera (Xanten) were the legions V Alaudae and XXI Rapax, at Oppidum Ubiorum (Cologne) I and XX (Valeria Victrix). In A.D. 50 a colony of veterans was established at the town of the Ubii, which thereafter became known as Colonia Claudia Ara Agrippinensium; but the legions had departed long before, during the reign of Tiberius, I to Bonna (Bonn), XX to Novaesium (Neuss). In Upper Germany legions XIV Gemina and XVI were stationed at Moguntiacum (Mainz), II Augusta at Argentorate (Strasbourg), XIII Gemina at Vindonissa (Windisch). Argentorate and Vindonissa had not been legionary camps before A.D. 9, for they could

---

[1] Tacitus, *Germ.* 30.   [2] Dio LXVII, 5, 1.

not have served as bases for invading Germany; nor did this part of the frontier require any protection. But it was the duty of this great army of eight legions to intervene, if necessary, in Gaul. The colony of Lugdunum had an urban cohort; but, except perhaps for a few auxiliary regiments and detachments of legionary troops, the Gallic provinces were without garrisons.

While the army was still regarded as a field-army, the camps of the legions were not fortresses, but merely bases for mobile troops. In Augustan days the winter-camp of a legion is still rudimentary, often abandoned at the opening of the campaigning season and rebuilt at its close, as the excavations at Vetera have clearly shown. In the course of the next fifty years or so, as the legion gradually loses mobility, its camp begins to acquire permanence and stability: the ramparts of earth, reinforced with timber, become more massive, the inner appointments more comfortable. Indeed some camps were constructed in stone during this period (Argentorate and Vindonissa), but this practice does not become general on the Rhine before the time of the Flavians.

Like the camps of the legions, the earth-forts occupied by the auxiliary regiments gradually assume strength and permanence. The defence of the Rhine had formerly been entrusted to the tribes dwelling along its bank. This system was not completely superseded—at least it is sometimes difficult to draw a distinction between the militia of a tribe and a regular regiment, for in this period most of the regiments serving on the Rhine are themselves Gallic or Rhenish in origin. The regiments of Vangiones and Nemetes which helped Pomponius Secundus in repelling a raid of the Chatti were stationed in their own territory; and the Helvetii garrisoned a fort with their own troops and at their own cost[1].

It was therefore a simple task to preserve inviolate the western bank of the Rhine. The garrisons were more than adequate to repel an invasion, even if Roman policy had not rendered that danger remote and improbable. A fleet patrolled the river, raiders were deterred, even harmless natives were not suffered to cross the stream how and where they pleased[2]. But on that frontier was a menace to the security of the empire far more formidable than the Germans—eight legions conscious of their power[3]. And so the

---

[1] Tacitus, *Hist.* 1, 67.
[2] Tacitus, *Hist.* iv, 64. On the frontier of Raetia, however, an exception was made in favour of the Hermunduri, who were allowed to cross the Danube freely (*Germ.* 41).
[3] Cf. Tacitus, *Ann.* 1, 31.

history of the Rhine armies is a large part of the history of the first
century. Two of their commanders were elevated to the purple,
Vitellius by force of arms, Trajan by adoption; three others,
Lentulus Gaetulicus, Verginius Rufus and Antonius Saturninus,
were suspected or unsuccessful. Six of the legions lay in contagious
proximity on a short stretch of the Rhine from Moguntiacum to
Vetera. The armies of the Danube, scattered over a wide area,
were better behaved; continuous warfare occupied and diverted
the British legions. But expeditions beyond the Rhine were unnecessary and inexpedient. Baffled of conquest, Corbulo set his
troops to dig a canal; other generals followed his example, but
public works or mining were a sorry substitute for the discipline of
war. The choice of the commanders of the armies was a delicate
question—birth, ambition or even ability were qualities suspect to
the emperor and often fatal to themselves. Competent men of no
family like Verginius Rufus were favoured, and aged mediocrity
became a qualification for military command. But an elderly
martyr to gout like Hordeonius Flaccus was unable to control the
troops, and even a Vitellius was acceptable when once they had
tasted blood and were eager to elevate any candidate providing he
were their own. To secure the loyalty of his armies and the peace
of the world it was advisable for an emperor to visit them; a
neglect of this elementary precaution was perhaps the ultimate
cause of the fall of Nero. The Emperor Gaius, however, showed
some discernment—two years after his accession he appeared
upon the Rhine (A.D. 39).

In the ten years of his governorship of Upper Germany
Lentulus Gaetulicus had won the affection of his troops and built
up for himself an almost impregnable position. Not long after the
arrival of Gaius he was put to death on a charge of conspiracy
against the Emperor; it might therefore appear that what brought
Gaius to the Rhine was the danger from Gaetulicus, that his
gigantic military preparations were undertaken to deceive a
domestic rather than to intimidate a foreign enemy. None the less,
even if this be admitted, Gaius may also have contemplated new
conquests in Britain or in Germany. In the absence of direct
evidence, a solution of the problem whether it was Gaius or
Claudius who raised the two new legions XV Primigenia and
XXII Primigenia would be of paramount importance[1]. For Gaius
as against Claudius there are no conclusive arguments, and almost

---

[1] E. Ritterling, *P.-W. s.v. Legio*, cols. 1244–9, has argued in favour of the
attribution to Gaius, H. M. D. Parker in *The Roman Legions*, pp. 93–8, for
Claudius.

the only argument of any value is an inference from the numbers which were given to the legions. XV was surely chosen in order that that legion should garrison Upper Germany along with XIII, XIV and XVI: XXII to fit in with XX and XXI in Lower Germany (while the legions with the low numbers I, II and V were perhaps to be withdrawn from the Rhine). Yet when the legions are rearranged after the Claudian invasion of Britain it is found on the contrary that XV has been placed in Lower Germany, XXII in Upper Germany. It might therefore be argued that the emperor who distributed the legions in A.D. 43 to the neglect of this numerical sequence was not the same as he who had raised them with such a nice regard for it. But this is not all—it appears that XV Primigenia had indeed been stationed for a time in Upper Germany, as the theory of the numbers demands, for there have been discovered at Weisenau near Mainz four gravestones of its soldiers, all of whom died in their first year of service[1]. Gaius, therefore, is the probable creator of the two legions. It follows that he meditated, sooner or later, a war of conquest; it does not follow, however, that the expedition which he made across the Rhine from Mainz was of any great importance. The four soldiers of the legion XV Primigenia, if they fell in battle, may have fallen in the campaign against the Chatti conducted by Galba, the successor of Gaetulicus[2]. Similarly the building of an earth-fort at Hofheim in A.D. 40–2 is in itself of no great significance, whether it occurred during the presence of Gaius on the Rhine or after his departure.

Whatever may have been the designs of Gaius, they were postponed or abandoned. If it was he who created the two new legions, there was an added reason to incite Claudius to his conquest of Britain—eight legions on the Rhine were a danger, ten were a catastrophe. Claudius took to Britain three of the Rhine legions (II, XIV and XX); this did not mean, however, that the permanent establishment on the Rhine was thereby weakened, salutary though that would have been, for there were three legions to take their place, the two which had been recently enrolled and IV Macedonica, withdrawn from Spain. The legions were now rearranged. At Vetera were V Alaudae and XV Primigenia; XVI was at Novaesium; I at Bonna. In Upper Germany IV Macedonica and XXII Primigenia shared the double camp of Moguntiacum. XXI Rapax seems to have spent several years at Argentorate before going to Vindonissa where it was required to take the place of XIII Gemina which was dispatched to Pannonia in A.D. 45–6

---

[1] *C.I.L.* XIII, 11853–6.   [2] Dio LX, 8, 7; cf. Suetonius, *Galba*, 6.

(see below, p. 804). This reduced the garrison to seven legions, which still occupied the same positions when, in the year of the Four Emperors, they felt themselves called upon to play a part worthy of their power and their prestige.

In the meantime the other three legions and the Ninth from Pannonia had conquered and held Britain for the Roman Empire.

III. THE ROMANS AND BRITAIN

Julius Caesar's invasion proved that Britain was within reach of Rome; not that it was within her grasp. A Roman army under vigorous leadership could land in Britain and carry out a campaign there. It could break up the most powerful confederacy in the island and impose its own terms on the tribes. But, on the other side of the account, Caesar had demonstrated that this could only be done by overcoming great difficulties and by running grave risks. The Channel was a dangerous sea; expeditions to its further shore could never be lightly undertaken; and therefore invasions like that of Caesar could never permanently impose the will of Rome on a recalcitrant British prince. Unless the Britons were ready to be subservient, it was idle to hope for the development of a client-kingdom across the Channel, and no less idle to expect that a governor of Gaul would be able to govern Britain as well. These were the lessons that Caesar's invasion taught him and his successors.

It also taught the Britons something. They found that, north of the Channel, Rome could neither protect her friends nor exact more than a momentary obedience from her enemies. Hence, if there was any disposition on their part to truckle to Rome before that event, the event must sensibly have diminished it. Caesar failed to increase Rome's prestige in Britain; and in such circumstances a failure to gain prestige amounts to a loss of it.

We do not know whether the Britons ever paid the tribute Caesar made them promise, or, if they paid it at first, how soon they stopped; but we do know that within a generation or less their other and more important promise had been broken. The enemy against whom Caesar had been operating in Britain had been the Belgic confederacy under Cassivellaunus; he had found allies in the Trinovantes, a non-Belgic tribe which had good reason to fear Belgic encroachments; and at his departure he had (in his own words) given Cassivellaunus orders to leave the Trino-

Note. For the ancient sources for this and the following section (mainly Tacitus and Suetonius) see the Bibliography.

vantes alone. But there is no reason to think that Rome even protested when the Catuvellauni conquered the Trinovantes and planted among them a new Belgic town at Lexden, by Colchester, soon to become the virtual capital of Britain under Cunobelinus. The date of this decisive step is not known, but it was most probably taken not by Cassivellaunus himself but by Tasciovanus, perhaps his son or grandson, who came to the throne about 20–15 B.C.

This was not the only way in which the Belgic element gained in power and territory soon after Caesar's invasion. Commius broke with Caesar in the crisis of Vercingetorix' revolt, and after its failure despaired of pardon; he fled to Britain, and soon afterwards we find him reigning as king of the British Atrebates at Silchester. There were no Atrebates in Britain, so far as we can tell, at the time of Caesar's campaigns there; it seems that they and other new Belgic immigrants came over afterwards and settled down in Hampshire and Berkshire, gradually extending westward into Wiltshire and Somerset[1].

By the time of Claudius, the Belgic area thus includes not only Kent and Hertfordshire, the two original centres, but Essex and a part of East Anglia, marching with the non-Belgic Iceni somewhere near Newmarket, and with the non-Belgic Dobuni in the Cherwell valley. It includes all Berkshire except its northern fringe, and all Hampshire. Its influence is felt in west Sussex, in Dorset and in Wiltshire; and as far west as Glastonbury scattered bands of the same race are, if not settling, at least raiding and destroying.

This region was the heritage of two royal houses, that of Cassivellaunus and that of Commius. Cunobelinus, son of Tasciovanus, reigned at Colchester from about A.D. 5 to between A.D. 40 and 43; coins struck by his brother Epaticcus are found in Surrey and Wiltshire, and it has been fancied that he inherited

---

[1] The distinction between two Belgic areas in Britain is now generally recognized. One, in Kent and Hertfordshire, spreading into Essex but stopping short of the Iceni and Dobuni, is the so-called Aylesford-Swarling area; the other, including the Atrebates and the 'Belgae' of Ptolemy (which must have been an artificial canton formed by the Romans for purposes of local government out of scattered Belgic settlements; C. F. C. Hawkes and G. C. Dunning, *Belgae*, pp. 294–5) had a different culture characterized by 'bead-rim' pottery resembling that of Normandy instead of 'pedestal-urns' like those of the Marne valley. The Belgae of this second area are thought (by J. P. Bushe-Fox, *Swarling*, p. 33; Hawkes and Dunning, *op. cit.* pp. 280 *sqq.*) to have reached Britain after Caesar's invasion. Doubt is thrown on the Cambridgeshire extension of the first area by R. E. M. Wheeler, *Belgic Cities of Britain*, p. 35.

the former district and then, with the westward movement of
Belgic power, conquered the latter. Commius, as we saw, created
a new kingdom at Silchester; his sons Tincommius, Verica, and
Eppillus, are thought to have had kingdoms in Sussex, Hampshire and Kent. But Tincommius was expelled from Britain, and
took refuge with Augustus, together with another British king,
Dubnovellaunus, who seems to have been driven from Essex into
Kent by the house of Cassivellaunus and, later, driven from Kent
also; and these incidents seem parts, or effects, of a process by
which the older dynasty at last acquired the ascendency over all
its rivals, so that, during the reign of Augustus, Cunobelinus
came to be called king of Britain. How far his power extended
we cannot precisely tell; but we may suppose him to have been
immediate sovereign of all south-eastern England, except for a
few regions—that of the Iceni in East Anglia and that of the Regni
in west Sussex are the only examples to which we can point—
where independent kings must have recognized him, not without
jealousy, as overlord. Whether in any effective sense he controlled
the Dobuni of the Cotswolds, the Dumnonii of the west, the
Welsh tribes, or the northern midlands and the great Brigantian
confederacy, we do not know; certainly the Brigantes had a dynasty
of their own, which may well have been completely independent.

With this political consolidation went an advance in wealth and
a progressive adoption of Roman ways. The Belgic settlement had
already improved British agriculture and increased the density of
the population; and with these changes the trade between Britain
and Gaul, already appreciable in Caesar's time, expanded also.
We begin to find in Britain not only objects evidently imported
from northern Gaul, but bronze and silver goods from Italy, in
growing bulk. The most remarkable among many instances comes
from a burial-mound at Lexden, containing large quantities of
Roman and Celtic metal goods, among them a head of Augustus
cut from a Roman silver coin and mounted in a medallion as if for
use as a brooch; it is just conceivable that the tomb was that of
Cunobelinus himself. Writing about the same time, Strabo tells
us that there was a large export of corn, cattle, gold, silver, iron,
hides, slaves, and hunting-dogs, and a corresponding import of
jewellery, glassware and other manufactured goods[1].

The same romanizing tendency appears in the British coinage.
Coins minted in Gaul reached Britain about the beginning of the
first century before Christ; but it was not until the Belgic invasion

[1] iv, 199. P. G. Laver in *Archaeologia*, LXXVI, 1927, p. 241; cf. Hawkes
and Dunning, *op. cit.* p. 259. See also above, p. 406 *sq.*

that any were struck in Britain itself, and the earliest British inscribed coins are those of Commius. These earlier examples are decorated with barbaric types derived, through a long chain of copies and modifications, from the gold staters of Philip II of Macedon, which were introduced to the central Gaulish tribes by their intercourse with Rome late in the second century. But in the next generation after Commius a new set of types came into use. Cunobelinus, Verica, Eppillus, and their contemporaries introduced such motives as a vine-leaf, an eagle, a gorgon head, and other types directly copied from the coinage of Rome and Magna Graecia[1]. At the same time, the iron currency-bars which Caesar had found still used in Britain were being superseded by minted coins, until, by the time of the Claudian invasion, they had altogether disappeared.

These changes in Britain could not be a matter of indifference to Rome. Even if Gaul were tranquil, the growth of a rich and powerful monarchy across the Channel would keep alive the unsolved problem bequeathed to posterity by Caesar. And for some time Gaul was not tranquil. The Bellovaci revolted in 46 B.C., the Aquitani in 39, the Morini and Treveri in 30 and 29, the Aquitani again shortly afterwards. The leading Britons, who had learnt to recognize in Rome an enemy, but one whose power was too remote to be formidable, must have looked upon these rebellions with favour, or even lent them aid; and Augustus repeatedly showed how far he was from being satisfied with the position of affairs. In 34, according to Dio, he actually set out on a British campaign, but was recalled by news of a revolt in Dalmatia. He returned to the same project, we are told, in 27, but the affairs of Gaul proved more pressing; he tried to deal with Britain by diplomatic means, but these broke down, and in the next year he is again said to have resolved on invasion, but was once more turned from the plan by urgent matters nearer home, in Spain and the Alps[2]. If Dio's stories are true, we must credit Augustus with the design of conquering and permanently occupying a part, at any rate, of Britain; Dio hints that he wished to outdo Caesar, and he must have learnt from Caesar's example that no permanent results could come from a mere raid. It is probable that the stories, as an account of his actions, are not true. Britain was dangerous, but so was Parthia; and Augustus, who always had plenty to do nearer home, was inclined to shirk remote frontier problems. It

[1] Volume of Plates iv, 206, *i, j*.
[2] Dio XLIX, 38, 2; LIII, 22, 5, 25, 2. Horace, *Odes*, I, 35, 29; III, 5, 2–4.

was more characteristic of him to advertise an intention which he did not really entertain, than to abandon an enterprise he had once undertaken. For our present purpose it is not important to decide between these alternatives. The decision affects our view of Augustus' character, but not our view of the British question as it existed in his time. Whether he actually planned the conquest of Britain, only to be diverted from it by other tasks, or whether, recognizing from the first that these other tasks had a prior claim, he only allowed others to think he was planning it, in either case he was bearing witness to an unsolved problem on the north-western frontier, and the necessity of solving it, sooner or later, by conquest.

After the Gaulish settlement of 27 B.C. the project of conquering Britain dropped into the background. Gaul tranquillized, Britain was less dangerous. Augustus could afford to change, if not his real policy, at least his ostensible policy, and make public what may very well have been his private opinion from the first, that for the present Britain had best be left alone.

The change of policy is reflected in two passages of Strabo which, with their curiously argumentative and apologetic tone, must embody an 'inspired' answer to the question 'why is the conquest of Britain not being pushed forward?' In the first place, Strabo tells us, some of the British kings are good friends of Augustus, and a great part of the island is now in close relations with Rome, so that there is no need for a military occupation; secondly, the tribute resulting from annexation would have to be set off against the cost of maintaining a garrison *plus* the loss of *portoria* on trade between Britain and Gaul, so that it would not pay. The financial argument is probably, within limits, genuine, though it must not be taken too seriously; it reads more like a plausible excuse for disappointing popular hopes, than a candid statement of the grounds of Augustus' policy. The political argument is plainly sophistical, as Augustus himself implicitly confessed in his *Res Gestae*, where Britain is conspicuously absent from his list of countries whose rulers 'sought my friendship,' and the most he could claim was that he had been visited by two exiled kings, whose names are identifiable as the Dubnovellaunus and Tincommius of British coins. Strabo's passage in fact contains some *suggestio falsi* as well as much *suppressio veri*; Augustus, like Caesar, shelved the British question without solving it[1].

---

[1] Strabo II, 115–16; IV, 200. *Res Gestae* 32, where the British *reges* are Dumnobellaunus and Tim.... Their visit reappears in Strabo IV, 200. For the coins see Volume of Plates iv, 206, *k* to *m*.

During the reign of Augustus Britain was undergoing a certain degree of romanization in manners; and, if the above reading of Strabo's words is correct, Augustus wished his contemporaries to think that with this Romanization in manners went a friendly or submissive attitude towards Rome in politics. But the two things do not necessarily go together; and the tacit admissions of the *Res Gestae* point to a very different reality. When that document was written, Cunobelinus had been reigning for nearly ten years, and during the whole of that time it is plain that he had never once attempted to make his peace with Augustus. Such neglect, amounting to defiance, was natural enough. Caesar's expedition had come to nothing; and Rome's prestige in British eyes, shaken by that failure, had not been restored by the empty rumours of invasion that had been heard in the earlier part of Augustus' reign. The Britons felt themselves safe, and believed that the Channel would be the permanent frontier of the Roman Empire. We cannot suppose that Augustus shared that belief. He knew from the experience of Caesar how close were the connections between Britain and Gaul; he knew that a powerful and not un-civilized monarchy was growing up across the Channel; he knew that the spirit of this monarchy was unfriendly to Rome; and, since Julius had proved that there was no third alternative except to conquer Britain or to leave it alone, he must still have intended that, some day, it should be conquered. In the meantime, like the subtle politician he was, he kept his intention to himself.

Tiberius also knew how to play a waiting game. During his reign the situation changed little. The power of Cunobelinus was increasing, and his policy remained unaltered; there is no evidence that the overtures to Rome which he never made in Augustus' lifetime were forthcoming after his death. But towards the end of Tiberius' reign new factors began to appear, both in Britain and at Rome.

In Britain, so long as Cunobelinus held the reins of power, affairs were directed by a ruler too strong to be easily assailable—Britain was now far more able to defend itself than it had been in the days of Julius—and too wise to provoke a war, whether by needlessly annoying Rome or by creating an opposition likely to turn traitor and invite Roman help; and the British *reguli* who sent home certain castaway soldiers of Germanicus evidently meant to maintain a correct attitude. But Cunobelinus was growing old, and the anti-Roman policy which he had pursued in a cautious and moderate manner was taken up by his sons Togodumnus and Caratacus in a spirit of something like fanaticism. It was natural that a pro-Roman party also should appear at the court of the aged king, and the leader of this seems to have been another son, Amminius. Matters were moving towards a crisis in which Roman intervention would be natural, if not inevitable.

On the side of Rome, it can hardly be doubted that Augustus shelved the British question because he could not afford the troops to deal with it in the one effective way. But in the later years of Tiberius the military problems which blocked the road to Britain began to disappear. The East was quiet at last, and it was becoming evident that Spain no longer needed the large garrison Augustus had left there. The time was approaching when the whole problem of the north-western frontier would have to be reconsidered; and when that was done, the conquest of Britain was a necessary part of any permanent settlement.

The abortive invasion of Gaius, in A.D. 40, may have been ill-judged in its hasty inception and hasty abandonment; but in the light of these new factors it is clear that Gaius had good reasons for his project. It was part of a sweeping scheme for the reorganization of the north-western frontier, of which the other chief element was an invasion of Germany. What seems to have happened is that Gaius, correctly judging that the conquest of Britain could not be much longer deferred, assembled an expeditionary force on the Channel, and was visited by Amminius, an exiled son of Cunobelinus, promising submission. Gaius publicly interpreted this act as equivalent to the annexation of Britain; perhaps deceived by the claims of Amminius, who may have represented himself as certain to be occupying the throne before long, perhaps merely seizing the excuse to defer an enterprise whose dangers were notorious. In either case, the story implies that Cunobelinus had never done anything which could be twisted into an act of submission to Rome. To his own people Gaius could now announce that the threat of invasion had at last brought Britain to her senses; but to the Britons he had merely given fresh reason to believe that Rome was afraid of attacking them[1].

[1] Suetonius, *Calig.* 44, 2; Tacitus, *Agric.* 13, 4. The British prince called Adminius by Suetonius appears on coins as Amminius. His visit cannot have been the reason for Gaius' projected invasion, for Gaius appears to have received him when he was already in the field, perhaps even on the shore of the Channel.

IV. THE CONQUEST OF BRITAIN

The conquest of Britain, which had been the distant goal of Roman policy ever since Augustus, became with Gaius a project ripe for immediate execution, and in that state he bequeathed it to Claudius. Between A.D. 40 and 43 no decisive event happened; but various considerations helped to precipitate the invasion.

The exile of Amminius was a triumph for the more violently anti-Roman party at Colchester. It showed that when Cunobelinus died, as he did soon afterwards, that party would dictate the official policy of Britain. Togodumnus and Caratacus were ready to defy Rome openly; at the same time they saw their discontented kinsmen and vassals—first Amminius, then Bericus—slipping away to Rome and, no doubt, promising to find support in Britain for an invading army. In their false sense of security, not realizing that Rome's hands were now free to deal with them, they allowed themselves to threaten reprisals upon the Empire that harboured these exiles. They went so far as to take hostile action, perhaps in the shape of a raid on the Gallic coast.

It was a sufficient *casus belli*; but Claudius would not have used it unless the conquest of Britain had been a project necessary on other grounds and feasible for military reasons. The true motives for the conquest of Britain were those which had been permanent factors in the British question ever since Julius had first raised it. Of these permanent factors the need to attack Druidism in its home was one temporary aspect. The increasing wealth of Britain may have modified the financial arguments of Augustus; and the expediency of employing the army on a glorious enterprise may have appealed to the successor of Gaius; but it is doubtful if Britain ever really paid for its occupation, and the expeditionary force was so backward in its pursuit of glory that it mutinied to escape the dangers of the Channel. Whatever part was played by economic causes or personal motives, the determining element was reasons of State; and the right way of putting the question why Claudius invaded Britain is to ask, not why it was done, but why it was done then and not earlier. The conquest was merely the execution, at the right moment, of a policy long accepted.

The primary objective, as in Caesar's time, was the conquest of the Belgic tribes[1]. Their capital was now not Verulam[2] but

---

[1] Hawkes and Dunning, *op. cit.* pp. 313–16.

[2] Wheeler, in his forthcoming report on excavations at Verulam, shows that the Belgic city there had superseded Cassivellaunus' *oppidum* at Wheathampstead.

Colchester; but otherwise the strategic situation was unaltered, and Caesar's plan of campaign was still the best. The main seat of the Belgic monarchy was north of the Thames; Kent was an outlying province of the same people, and Kent was the natural gate to Britain. In Sussex and East Anglia there were tribes hostile to the Belgae and ready to welcome the Romans as friends and deliverers; but strategy and policy alike forbade the Roman force to land in their territory. Not only was it a longer and more dangerous sea voyage to their shores, but they do not seem to have shown their hand until after the expedition had reached Britain.

Aulus Plautius' army of four legions and auxiliaries was not much superior in strength to that of Caesar in 54 B.C. He sailed, Dio tells us, in three divisions, and it has been conjectured that these landed at the three ports of Richborough, Dover and Lympne. Excavation has brought to light traces of a very large encampment, dating from the earliest days of the Roman occupation, at Richborough, and this was always the official seaport of Roman Britain; but there is no evidence of early camps at Dover or Lympne, and even if detachments were landed at these other places it is clear that Richborough became the naval base of the expeditionary force. The army can only have been divided in one way: a main body of two legions with auxiliaries under Plautius himself, and two units of half this size. Plautius, whose staff-work throughout the campaign was excellent, cannot be credited with the elementary blunder of dividing his forces in the face of the enemy and risking the total loss of 10,000 men in the event of the British main body encountering one of his detachments; Dio's story can only mean that the smaller units were ordered to make feints, perhaps at Dover and Lympne, while the main body sailed round to Richborough, there to be joined by the rest. A study of Caesar's narrative might easily have suggested such a plan. It was, however, unnecessary. The Britons had learnt of the mutiny, and thought that Gaius' fiasco of three years before was to be repeated. Accordingly they took no measures of defence—an extraordinary proof of the contempt into which Roman prestige had fallen—and Plautius landed at Richborough unopposed.

Togodumnus and Caratacus had begun the war with a grave mistake; but they now did their best to retrieve it. Hurrying into Kent with what troops they could instantly muster, they instructed their main forces, as soon as they could be mobilized, to hold the line of the Medway. They themselves, though too weak to fight a general action, could perhaps delay the Romans' advance until the Medway position could be occupied in force. They found their

Kentish subjects already engaged in guerilla warfare against Plautius, and put themselves at their head; but Plautius was equal to the occasion and succeeded in defeating first Caratacus and then Togodumnus, who fell in the engagement. The defence of the Medway proved formidable and was obstinately maintained; but after a two days' battle the Britons were driven back on their next position, the line of the Thames.

A small trading settlement had lately begun to grow up on the site of London, and the Thames had been bridged[1]; just below this were the fords for which the retreating Britons made. Pursued by the Roman vanguard they crossed the river, and inflicted a check on their pursuers in the marshes of the Lea valley. The Romans fell back, and the Britons were able to organize a defensive position on the left bank of the Thames.

It had always been part of the plan of campaign that Claudius should show himself to the army. The official version of the plan was that if Plautius found himself in difficulties he was to send for the Emperor; but in point of fact the difficulties of the Thames crossing were exaggerated in order to give an excuse for the Emperor's appearance, and it had probably been settled in advance that there should be a check at the Thames for this purpose. The long halt while the expeditionary force awaited Claudius' arrival served also a further end: Caratacus, like Cassivellaunus, found his army melting away as the weeks went by and his unwilling vassals, emboldened by his initial failures, went over to the winning side. When Claudius came up with fresh troops and elephants, all effective resistance was over: the Thames was crossed without delay and the emperor rode into Camulodunum among the cheers of his troops.

The Belgic kingdom founded by Cassivellaunus, and extended over a great part of Britain by Cunobelinus, had fallen. Its immediate territories became a Roman province, with its capital at Camulodunum and Aulus Plautius as its first governor. But outside these territories lay the land of various non-Belgic tribes which had unwillingly recognized the house of Cassivellaunus as overlords, but were now glad enough to see its fall and pay their respects to its conqueror.

Two of these can be identified with certainty. North-east of the Belgic area lay the kingdom of the Iceni. Archaeology shows

[1] The whole of the Thames estuary has subsided relatively to the sea about 15 feet since Roman times; *Roman London*, pp. 13–14. For the supposed pre-Claudian trading-settlement, cf. T. D. Pryce and F. Oswald in *Archaeologia*, LXXVIII, 1928, pp. 100–1.

that they were untouched by the peculiar civilization of the Belgae; the narrative of the conquest shows that they were left alone in the first years of the Roman invasion; and as late as Nero's time they still had a king, Prasutagus, of their own. Plainly their part in the Claudian invasion was parallel to that of the Trinovantes in the Julian: fearing and hating the Belgic power which was Rome's chief enemy, they submitted to Rome as soon as they could do so with safety, and thus bought a temporary and nominal freedom.

The same action was taken by the Regni, whose capital was Chichester. Their territory was cut off from the chief Belgic area by the dense and hardly penetrable forest of the Weald; archaeologically we know it as a backwater untouched by the movements of peoples and cultures that impinged upon Britain in Kent on the one side and in Dorset on the other. Here too we find, side by side with a non-Belgic type of civilization, a native king, Cogidubnus, kept on his throne by Claudius with the title *rex (et) legatus Augusti in Britannia*. His status—the invention, it would seem, of Claudius—was somehow intermediate between that of a client-king and that of the governor of an imperial province; and we can hardly doubt that the same title was conferred on Prasutagus.

It is possible that a similar attitude was taken up by the Dobuni, whose hill-forts still crown the heights and spurs of the Cotswolds: but of that we have no direct evidence, for the Dobuni must not be confused with the Boduni, an East Kentish tribe whose submission was received by Aulus Plautius in the early days of the invasion.

With the occupation of the Belgic capital and the voluntary submission of Cogidubnus and Prasutagus, the primary objective of the invasion was attained. But the Roman plan of campaign envisaged the complete conquest of Britain; and for that purpose the army was once more divided into three columns. Plautius himself, with the Fourteenth and Twentieth legions, operated north-westward along the line of Watling Street; Vespasian, with the Second (Augusta), moved west and south-west into what had been the realm of Commius; and the Ninth, on the right wing, advanced northward. The midlands, heavily timbered but sparsely inhabited, cannot have given much trouble either to the centre or to the right: but Vespasian on the left had to deal with the Atrebates, who inherited a Belgic military tradition and hostility to Rome, the various other Belgic clans that had settled in what was to be Wessex, and the Durotriges, a partially Belgicized tribe whose capital, Maiden Castle, is the most stupendous fortification of any age in England.

By A.D. 47, when Aulus Plautius was succeeded by Ostorius Scapula, the whole Belgic area was permanently pacified, and the conquerors' main task seemed at an end. Scapula drew a frontier, the Fosse Way, from Lincoln to South Devon, so as to include all the Belgic tribes together with the client-kingdoms of Cogidubnus and Prasutagus; the Dobuni and Coritani were partly included, the frontier-road passing through the centre of their territories —evidently they were not hostile—and the tribes outside this frontier might be expected to yield before a judicious mixture of conciliation and force.

This expectation was very nearly fulfilled. There were three tribes or groups of tribes immediately in question: the Dumnonii in Devon and Cornwall, the Silures, Ordovices and Degeangli in Wales, and the Brigantes north of the Humber. The Dumnonii submitted without striking a blow. The Brigantes were divided in counsel, but their queen Cartimandua was on the whole ready to become a client of Rome. Only in Wales trouble arose, and that was brewed by Caratacus. Heir to the empire of Cunobelinus, he had failed alike in policy and in war, and had alienated his subjects and lost his crown; now, a defeated and discredited exile, he accomplished the extraordinary feat of rousing first the Silures, and then the whole of Wales, to resistance. Even his defeat in 51, though it ended his career—he fled to the Brigantes, and Cartimandua gave him up to Ostorius—did not destroy his work; he had lit a fire in Wales which it cost Rome thirty years to extinguish.

Behind the Ostorian frontier the work of romanization went rapidly forward. London, under the new impulse to trade which followed the conquest, leapt into prominence as a commercial town thronged with native and foreign merchants. At Camulodunum, the capital of the province, a colony was planted, whose members settled down to a peaceful life on the lands of the dispossessed Belgic nobles, and the temple of the deified Claudius, where Colchester Castle now stands, seemed to symbolize the ascendency which the idea of Rome had established for ever in the minds of Britons. At Verulamium the old earthworks in Prae Wood were deserted, and a new city by the river, with the rank of a *municipium*, grew quickly in size and wealth[1]. The Belgic area, which had now become Roman Britain, had reconciled itself

---

[1] London: *Royal Comm. on Anc. Monuments: Roman London*; R. E. M. Wheeler, *London in Roman Times*; Pryce and Oswald, *loc. cit.* pp. 73–110. Colchester: Wheeler and Laver, 'Roman Colchester' in *J.R.S.* ix, 1919, pp. 139 *sqq.*; excavations in progress. Verulamium: excavations in progress. Brief reports annually in *J.R.S.*

to its new political status and was continuing, with accelerated pace, its old process of Romanization in manners. The event had amply justified both articles in the Roman policy: deferring the decisive step until the death of Cunobelinus, and taking it then.

One element in the Roman policy was less successful. Owing to the tradition of the Belgic dynasty, Claudius was obliged to bring its own dominions directly under an imperial governor; but there remained native Britain, the dominions of kings friendly to Rome. Of these, Cogidubnus proved loyal; but Prasutagus or his people found the rule of Rome less easy to accept, and as early as 47 they resented the action of Ostorius when, drawing the Fosse frontier, he placed them in the conquered half of the country. They broke out in revolt, which Ostorius was obliged to suppress; but they still fancied that their monarchy, the symbol of their independence, was secure. It was probably Rome's intention from the first to treat these kingdoms as transitional; to absorb them, on the death of their present holders, into the imperial province. When therefore Prasutagus died in 61, his widow Boudicca was informed that she was not to succeed him. The Iceni were made aware, with every circumstance of indignity, that they had misunderstood their position. Instead of introducing the new régime with tact and moderation, the Roman officials left nothing undone to outrage the feelings of their new victims. The Iceni rose, Boudicca at their head; the Trinovantes were swept into the revolt; the centres of Romanization went up in flame; and the rebellion was only put down, at terrible cost to both sides, after a crisis in which it seemed that the Roman armies might easily be annihilated and Roman rule brought to an end.

The Icenian revolt, complete though its failure was, shows that the conquest of Britain had been no mere military parade. The comparative ease with which the first stage had been achieved was not due to lack of spirit or fighting power in the Britons; it was due to political events and conditions which were acutely watched and justly weighed at Rome. The only serious trouble which the Romans encountered in the conquest of Britain arose when they failed to control political factors in the situation: when Caratacus, against all reasonable expectation, made the Silures instruments of his hatred for Rome, or when subordinate officials, in the governor's absence, alienated the good will of the Iceni.

V. THE DANUBE

The lessons of the great revolt of the Pannonians and Dalmatians (A.D. 6–9) were not lost upon the Romans. War and famine had thinned the rebel tribes; they were further weakened by the sending of their levies to serve in other lands. The auxiliary regiments stationed at various points in Pannonia and Dalmatia were at first almost all of foreign origin, but gradually lost their foreign character with the spread of local recruiting. After their rapid and easy conquest of Illyricum in 13–9 B.C. the Romans had neglected to make its subjugation permanent by driving roads through the interior. This oversight was now repaired—early in the reign of Tiberius the legions of Dalmatia were employed in the construction of a series of roads which penetrated the rough and mountainous interior of Bosnia[1]. A similar, even if less intense, activity must have been displayed elsewhere—in the north and north-west of Spain it is attested by adequate evidence[2]; but for the provinces bounded by the Danube there is hardly any evidence at all. In A.D. 14 soldiers of the Pannonian legions were improving the road across the Julian Alps between Aquileia and Emona; and Claudius was to build a road where the armies of his father Drusus had passed, across the Alps to Augusta Vindelicorum in Raetia and then as far as the bank of the Danube[3]; and an inscription of the year A.D. 33–4 shows that in Moesia a road was being hewn in the rock along the gorge of the Danube above the Iron Gates[4].

Two consular governors and the *legati* of five legions had charge of all Illyricum from the Adriatic to the Danube. Their duties were considerably lightened by a delegation of authority which was a characteristic of Roman administration, and one of the secrets of its success. Roman prefects controlled the Bosnian tribes of the Maezaei and Daesitiates[5], and among the Iapudes a native chieftain was tolerated[6]. As the inhabitants gradually accustomed themselves to the peace which had been imposed upon them, some of the garrisons could be removed.

After the division of Illyricum in A.D. 9 the new province of

---

[1] Dessau 2478, 5829, 5829 a. Cf. M. Abramić, *Vjesnik za arh. i hist. Dalmatinsku* XLIX, 1926–7, pp. 139–55.

[2] For example *C.I.L.* II, 4868 (*c.* A.D. 11–12); 4773; 4905 (= Dessau 152); 4883.   [3] *C.I.L.* V, 8002 (= Dessau 208) and 8003.

[4] Dessau 2281. For road-building in Thrace in the time of Nero, cf. Dessau 231.

[5] *C.I.L.* IX, 2574.   [6] Dessau 4878 b.

Dalmatia (which embraced most of Bosnia and extended north-wards almost to the Save) was garrisoned by two legions placed at important strategic points commanding routes into the interior. Legion XI was at Burnum (near Kistanje, a little to the south-west of Knin), legion VII at Gardun, about eight miles south-east of Sinj[1]. The camps of the three legions of Pannonia cannot be accurately determined. The legion VIII Augusta appears to have been at Poetovio, where the great highway to the North crossed the Drave. Claudius was to plant a colony at Savaria on the same road, and veterans may have been established at Scarbantia even earlier[2]. But the terminus of the road, Carnuntum on the Danube (Petronel, some twenty miles east of Vienna) is the position of cardinal importance. Tiberius had intended it for winter-quarters at the end of the campaign of A.D. 6; and it has been conjectured that the legion XV Apollinaris came to Carnuntum not long after the beginning of the reign of Tiberius if not earlier[3]. The strategic importance of Sirmium is clearly revealed in the wars of Augustus, but it is not known whether Sirmium was a legionary camp in the time of his successors. In the absence of evidence Siscia has been claimed as the station of the third legion, IX Hispana. This legion was absent in Africa for a few years (A.D. 20–4) and in A.D. 43 was permanently withdrawn to Britain; but when VIII Augusta departed to Moesia, c. A.D. 45–6, its place was taken at Poetovio by a legion from Germany, XIII Gemina. The two Dalmatian legions received the title of 'Claudia pia fidelis' as a reward for their rapid desertion of a rebellious governor in A.D. 42. In A.D. 57, if not earlier, one of them, VII, was sent to Moesia.

The Pannonian section of the Danube frontier neither received nor required much protection. The setting up of the client-kingdom of Vannius in A.D. 19 (p. 783) relieved Rome from anxiety about the most critical portion of it. A single legion at Carnuntum, though at some distance from its two fellows, would not be in any danger and might be of use. The Dacians had once been the eastern neighbours of the Germans, in dangerous proximity to Pannonia. But at some time between A.D. 20 and 50 the Sarmatae Iazyges poured over the Carpathians, swept them out of the

[1] The ancient name is not known; it has sometimes been supposed, without any direct evidence, that it was Delminium.

[2] Scarbantia bears the name Julia in Pliny (*N.H.* III, 146) and so may have been a foundation of Tiberius (cf. Ritterling, *P.-W. s.v. Legio*, col. 1243).

[3] Cf. Ritterling, *op. cit.* cols. 1748–9. A passage in Tacitus (*Ann.* XII, 29) cannot be taken as evidence that there was no legion stationed on the Danube before A.D. 50.

Hungarian plain and confined them to Transylvania[1]. They were a welcome ally against a common enemy, and they repaid toleration with loyalty—at least until the time of Domitian. An officer in charge of the Boii and Azalii eastwards of Carnuntum bore the title of *praefectus ripae Danuvii*[2]. There was a fleet to patrol the river, and there were probably a few regiments stationed here and there along its bank.

The lower reaches of the Danube did not share this tranquillity. The Dacians made light of the submission to which Augustus claimed he had reduced them, the Sarmatians were always ready to participate in a raid. In A.D. 6 Caecina Severus the legate of Moesia had been called back to deal with these enemies, and there was again trouble in the closing years of the reign of Augustus. Troesmis and Aegissus, situated not far from the mouth of the Danube, were assailed and sacked[3]. Though Roman aid was forthcoming it was tardy, for the legions were far away. No permanent protection could yet be given to the Greek cities of the Dobrudja, which were left to their own devices or to such assistance as the kingdom of Thrace might provide. The extent and the status of Moesia are alike obscure. Probably a few years before A.D. 6 the legions hitherto under the proconsul of Macedonia were transferred to an imperial legate of Moesia (p. 367 *sq.*); but Moesia was perhaps not a province in the strict sense of the term, but a military zone, like the two Germanies[4]. A not inconsiderable part was administered by an equestrian officer, 'the prefect of the tribes of Moesia and Treballia[5].' Somewhere along the Moesian stretch of the Danube, as on the Pannonian, a *praefectus ripae* appears to have been stationed[6]; and there may even have been another official of this type farther down the river on the Dobrudja, a *praefectus ripae Thraciae* or a *praefectus orae maritimae*[7]. In A.D. 15 Achaia and Macedonia were transferred from the Senate to the *princeps* and attached to Moesia, an arrangement which lasted until A.D. 44. The consular governor in charge of this large province, the administration of which presents analogies to Tarraconensis, seems to have delegated the governorship of Moesia to one of his legates. Which were the camps of the two legions in the time of Tiberius, IV Scythica and V Macedonica, is not known. One or both of them may still have been in the

---

[1] Pliny, *N.H.* IV, 80–1. [2] Dessau 2737.

[3] Ovid, *Ex Ponto*, I, 8 and IV, 7. [4] Cf. Appian, *Ill.* 30.

[5] Dessau 1349. [6] *Ann. épig.* 1926, no. 80.

[7] The existence of some such officer is attested by *S.E.G.* I, no. 329 in the time of Claudius.

interior. Naissus (Nish), a very important strategic position
where five roads met, had perhaps been the site of a legionary
camp in the days of Augustus; the function of the legions of
Moesia was still, almost of necessity, the control of the interior
rather than the protection of the frontier, and Thrace, as in the
days of Augustus, called for their intervention more than once.

The kingdom of Thrace was an institution of value as long as it
could impose order upon its turbulent subjects. But Rome could
not look on with equanimity when its princes emulated in discord
and crime the notoriety of the house of Herod. After the death of
the able Rhoemetalces Augustus divided the kingdom between
his brother Rhescuporis and his son Cotys. They quarrelled; the
perfidious uncle entrapped and slew the nephew. In A.D. 19 he was
deposed, and a Roman resident guided the affairs of eastern Thrace
in the name of the children of Cotys (p. 645 *sq.*). Rhoemetalces,
son of Rhescuporis, was allowed to hold his father's kingdom of
western Thrace, but soon he and the Roman resident earned the
ill-will of the Thracians, who, in A.D. 21, rose and besieged
Philippopolis, but were easily dispersed: five years later a serious
insurrection was quelled by Poppaeus Sabinus, the consular
governor of Moesia. At length, in A.D. 45–6, after disturbances
provoked by the assassination of Rhoemetalces (the last king, one
of the sons of Cotys) at the hand of his wife, the kingdom was
abolished and Thrace became a procuratorial province.

Macedonia and Achaia had been restored to proconsuls two
years before, and the legate of Moesia could now give to the
Lower Danube and the Pontic Shore the attention it had so long
lacked[1]. The accession of a third legion to the garrison of
Moesia, VIII Augusta from Pannonia, is evidence of added
responsibilities; and if a legionary camp had not already existed at
Oescus on the Danube, facing the valley of the Aluta, one was now
established there, and perhaps another at Novae some forty miles
to the east[2]. The camp of the other legion was probably Vimi-
nacium. The direct control of Rome extended to the Lower Danube,
her influence was dominant far beyond it (see above, p. 380). The
historians are silent; but a lengthy inscription records and perhaps
exaggerates the exploits of a legate of Moesia in Nero's reign,
Plautius Silvanus Aelianus[3]. He brought more than a hundred

---

[1] *S.E.G.* 1, 329 (letters of several Roman governors to the city of Istros).
[2] There is not enough evidence to confirm definite statements about the
camps of the Moesian legions in this period.
[3] Dessau 986 (see above, p. 775). Similar activity on the part of a governor
of Pannonia late in Nero's reign seems to be indicated by Dessau 985.

thousand natives across the river to pay homage and tribute to the majesty of Rome, quelled an incipient disturbance among the Sarmatians and successfully negotiated with the chieftains of many peoples, Dacians, Bastarnae, and Roxolani. In this way, no doubt more by diplomacy than by force of arms, he secured the peace of the frontier. It was perhaps very much like a repetition of the campaigns of Lentulus in the days of Augustus (p. 367 *sq.*). And so the suzerainty of Rome was acknowledged far beyond the frontier, but it does not appear that the bounds of the province of Moesia were thereby extended[1]. Indeed, it may be doubted whether the governor commanded strong enough forces for extensive conquests, since during Nero's reign the Danube armies had been called upon to supply three legions for the East. IV Scythica was withdrawn in A.D. 57–8, but its place was no doubt taken by VII Claudia pia fidelis from Dalmatia. The departure of V Macedonica, however, in A.D. 61–2 reduced the garrison of Moesia to two legions (VII and VIII), and it is probably this weakening of the army which is referred to on the inscription of Silvanus[2]. As for Pannonia, in 63 XV Apollinaris departed from Carnuntum, but X Gemina came from Spain (which was now left with a single legion, VI Victrix) to fill the gap and maintain the total of two legions. In the last year of Nero the arrival of a Syrian legion, III Gallica, brought the army of Moesia again to a strength of three legions. When the time came they refused to be outdone by the German armies in the game of emperor-making.

[1] Neither the words of the inscription, *per quem* (*sc. quae* = 'by which acts') *pacem provinciae et confirmavit et protulit*, nor the events to which they refer, justify that assumption.

[2] *quamvis parte(m) magna(m) exercitus ad expeditionem in Armeniam misisset.*

CHAPTER XXIV

THE YEAR OF THE FOUR EMPERORS

I. GALBA

WHEN Nero died in A.D. 68 nearly a hundred years had passed since the battle of Actium. During this period, though many wars had been waged on the frontiers, the Empire was saved from the civil strife which had darkened the last days of the Republic. The names of Pharsalus, Philippi, Perusia, and Mutina recalled such painful memories[1] that many critics of the Principate were reconciled to its existence by the thought that, whatever its defects, it had secured for the Roman world the blessing of internal peace. The task of Augustus had certainly been rendered easier by the fact that the world was, in the words of Tacitus[2], 'wearied of civil discord,' and was therefore prepared to welcome a strong government at almost any cost. It was this feeling which secured the continuance of the system which he had founded even under less able successors. Men were so well aware that a disputed succession would almost inevitably lead to civil war that they were prepared to accept as their ruler any candidate who could trace descent by birth or adoption from the deified Augustus. Although in theory the Principate ended on the death of each *princeps*, the hereditary principle had been recognized in practice, and the imperial family had come to occupy a position of unrivalled prominence in the State.

Note. Tacitus (*Histories*) is very much the most important source for the history of the years A.D. 69–70, but his references to the events A.D. 68 are only incidental. For the latter Plutarch's and Suetonius' Lives of Galba are valuable, but these writers are of quite secondary importance for the period covered by Tacitus. The resemblances between Tacitus and Plutarch (*Galba* and *Otho*) are so marked that the use of a common source, possibly Pliny the Elder, has generally been assumed. The value of Fabia's careful discussion of this problem in his book *Les Sources de Tacite* is diminished by his assumption that Tacitus almost slavishly followed one main source. This assumption has been challenged by Groag, Schanz and others (cf. the present writer in *Journal of Philology*, xxxv, 1920, p. 204 *sq.*). Suetonius (*Galba, Otho, Vitellius, Vespasian*) adds little to Tacitus except personal details, and the fragments of Dio are of little value.

---

[1] Tacitus, *Hist.* I, 50. [2] *Ann.* I, I.

While it is a mistake to describe the early Principate as a military monarchy, there can be no doubt that the loyal support of the army was essential to the emperor. Tiberius came to the throne with an established reputation as a general, and even the unwarlike Claudius took a personal part in the invasion of Britain. As the *princeps* received the salutation of *imperator* when a victory had been gained by one of his generals it was only reasonable to demand that he should not be absolutely devoid of military capacity and experience. The reign of Nero had seen some remarkable military achievements in Britain and the East, but these achievements had been gained by Suetonius Paulinus and Corbulo, and the Emperor had never even visited in person the scene of operations. His musical performances and artistic ambitions put such a severe strain on the loyalty of the armies that the idea began to be entertained that more was required from an emperor than descent from Augustus, and that a more worthy holder of the office could be found outside the imperial family. If, when the situation became critical in the spring of A.D. 68, Nero had shown some personal energy and put himself at the head of an army, his authority might have been restored, for the forces arrayed against him were not very powerful, and he was not without friends and admirers. But his nerve collapsed and he found in suicide the only escape from his difficulties.

What had finally driven Nero to despair was the action of the Senate in declaring him a public enemy, but at such a crisis this body was not in a position to play a really decisive part. Though the higher officers of the army were to be found among its members, it had since the time of Augustus exercised no military authority, and had been compelled when the throne was vacant simply to ratify the choice of the soldiers. As has been shown above (p. 740), the support given to Galba by Nymphidius Sabinus and the praetorians determined the action of the Senate in outlawing Nero. The troubled period which followed made clear the essential weakness of the Senate's position: it could do nothing to influence events, and was compelled to confer the imperial titles on a succession of men who owed their success to the sword.

Discontent with the rule of Nero had been growing since the death of Burrus and the fall of Seneca had removed from his side the two men who had guided the policy of the Empire during the earlier part of his reign. The feeling which prevailed in senatorial circles had been shown in the Pisonian conspiracy, and soon the commanders of armies began to be alarmed for their own safety and to fear that they might share the fate of Corbulo and the

Scribonii. But the first move came not from one of the great armies but from C. Julius Vindex, a romanized Gaul, who was at the time governor of one of the three 'unarmed' Gallic provinces, probably Lugdunensis. He got into communication with various army-commanders in the west, and sounded their feelings, and finally in the spring of 68 rose openly against the tyrant, whom in a manifesto he was bold enough to describe as among other things a bad lyre-player[1]. In his place he suggested the name of Servius Sulpicius Galba, governor of Nearer Spain, one of the very few members of an ancient family who at that time occupied an important command. To him Vindex wrote offering to support him in a bid for the principate with an army of 100,000 Gauls and received a not discouraging reply. What were the ultimate objects of Vindex has been the subject of much controversy[2]. It is possible that the idea of an Imperium Galliarum, independent of Rome, originated with him, but definite proof is to seek. In any case his influence in Gaul was limited. While some important tribes— notably the Aedui, Arverni, and Sequani—answered his appeal, an equally important group—the Treveri and Lingones—was prepared to take up arms against him. It seems probable that though the primary aim of Vindex was not the independence of Gaul or (as has been suggested) the restoration of the Republic, but rather the substitution for Nero of a more worthy successor, the legions on the Rhine regarded him as the leader of a nationalist movement whom it was their duty to crush. The rising of Florus and Sacrovir under Tiberius had shown that no Gallic revolt could succeed so long as it was opposed by the Rhine armies, whose twofold duty it was to protect the frontier against invasion and to keep an eye on the provinces of Gaul.

While Vindex was besieging the colony of Lugdunum, which remained faithful to Nero in contrast to the neighbouring city of Vienna, which gave active support to the rebel, he learned that Verginius Rufus, commander of the army of Upper Germany, was advancing against him with at least three legions and strong *auxilia*, and with his raw levies drew out to meet him. Near Vesontio (Besançon) the two armies met. What followed is not quite clear, though afterwards Rufus claimed credit for the defeat of Vindex. It was said that the two leaders parleyed and actually came to an agreement, but that the legions insisted on fighting against the wish of their commander, who expressed sorrow when,

---

[1] Suetonius, *Nero*, 41.
[2] See B. W. Henderson, *The Life and Principate of the Emperor Nero*, pp. 395 *sq.*, 496 *sq.*

after the loss of 20,000 of his troops, Vindex committed suicide[1]. Probably this story was put into circulation after the accession of Galba, whose relations with Vindex were close, in order to protect Verginius. Tacitus always connects him with the defeat of Vindex, and it is probable that, as has been said, he thought it his duty to suppress what he took to be a movement against the integrity of the empire. Elated by their victory the troops immediately offered the principate to Rufus. Though now and subsequently he refused the honour, there is no reason to suppose that he was inspired by any devotion to Nero personally. He probably considered that he was disqualified by being the son of an *eques*. It is legitimate to regret his decision, for there can be little doubt that he would have been successful against Galba, whose military strength was so much weaker, and that his accession would have spared the Roman world the misery from which it was at last saved by Vespasian, a man who on grounds of birth had no greater claim to the throne.

Though the rising of Vindex ended in disaster to himself it was successful in bringing Nero's rule to an end, for it is doubtful whether Galba would have thrown off his allegiance if the suggestion had not come from Gaul that he should come forward as a 'champion of the human race[2].' He had indeed been warned that Nero was compassing his death, but the elderly governor of a province in which only one legion was stationed would scarcely have acted as he did unless he had hoped for armed support elsewhere. On April 2 he allowed himself to be hailed at New Carthage as *Legatus senatus populique Romani*, and prepared to make his action effective by raising in the province a new legion and auxiliary troops. In this he was supported by T. Vinius, the *legatus* of the Spanish legion, whom Galba dispatched to Rome to look after his interests, by M. Salvius Otho, governor of the neighbouring province of Lusitania, and by A. Caecina, quaestor of Baetica, who was appointed a legionary legate. When the news of the defeat of Vindex reached Spain, things looked black for Galba, and he retired to the remote city of Clunia, where he is said to have contemplated suicide. But about the middle of June his freedman Icelus arrived with the news that Nero was dead and that Galba had been accepted as emperor by the Senate and the praetorians.

It is not surprising that the candidature of Galba was welcome to the senators, for, unlike his possible rival Verginius, he was a man of ancient lineage who traced his descent from several leading

---

[1] Dio LXIII, 24.
[2] Suetonius, *Galba*, 9. This claim is reflected by the legend SALVS GENERIS HVMANI on Galba's coins. Volume of Plates iv, 206, *n*.

nobles of the Republic. He had reached the consulship as far back as the reign of Tiberius, and at the time of his accession was 73 years of age. Under Gaius he had governed Upper Germany with vigour, and on the death of the Emperor in 41 had been considered as a possible successor. Since 60 he had been in Spain, where his administration had towards the close of his eight years of office shown a decline in energy. He was undoubtedly too old a man to perform adequately the difficult task to which he was called. Probably most of his supporters regarded him as a stop-gap, and it is in this sense that we should interpret the well-known epigram of Tacitus, 'omnium consensu capax imperii nisi imperasset[1].' For there was nothing in his previous career to show that he possessed outstanding qualities of intellect or character, still less that elasticity of mind which would have alone enabled him to deal with so difficult a situation.

Though Galba had been recognized by the Senate his success was not everywhere greeted with enthusiasm. On the death of Nero the German legions had made a second unsuccessful attempt to persuade Verginius to aim at the throne, and delayed some time before taking the oath of allegiance to the new emperor, who shortly afterwards recalled Verginius, treating him with cold respect. His successor was not likely to increase the popularity of Galba on the Rhine: Hordeonius Flaccus was a lame man of advanced years whose period of rule in Germany was destined to end in disaster. The governor of Lower Germany, Fonteius Capito, was suspected, perhaps unjustly, of designs against Galba, and was summarily murdered by two of his officers, one of whom, Fabius Valens, who was to play an important part in the events of the following year, expected more gratitude from Galba than he actually received. Trouble also arose in Africa, where L. Clodius Macer, *legatus* of Numidia, refused to recognize the new régime, raised a second legion, and threatened the corn-supply of Rome. His coins show that he posed as a champion of the Republic[2]. Galba sent orders for his murder, which were promptly carried out.

In Rome itself the accession of Galba was marked by bloodshed. The prefect of the praetorians, Nymphidius Sabinus, who had persuaded his soldiers to renounce their allegiance to Nero, had evidently hoped to become the right-hand man and possibly the successor of the aged emperor. Accordingly when Cornelius Laco was appointed in his place he lost his head and actually

---

[1] *Hist.* I, 49.
[2] H. Mattingly and E. A. Sydenham, *Roman Imperial Coinage*, vol. I, p. 193 *sq.*; see Volume of Plates iv, 208, *a*, *b*.

attempted to seize the empire for himself. This was too much for
the troops, who were not prepared to support the son of a freedwoman, even if he claimed to be an illegitimate son of Gaius, and
he was cut down by them. Galba would have been well advised to
show some appreciation of this proof of loyalty by paying the
donative which Nymphidius had promised to the praetorians on
his behalf, and which was commonly granted on the accession of
a new emperor. His soldierly remark that he 'chose his men and
did not buy them[1]' was in the circumstances a tactless one. A bad
impression was also made by the execution without trial of the
consul-designate Cingonius Varro, who had stood in close relations
to Nymphidius, and of Petronius Turpilianus, an ex-consul, whose
only fault was that he had been chosen by Nero to command an
army against the rebels.

Galba showed a similar want of sense in his policy in Gaul,
where the situation called for tactful handling. The tribes which
had joined Vindex were rewarded by gifts of citizenship and by
reduction of taxes, while the Treveri and Lingones were deprived
of territory, and Lugdunum was punished by confiscation of its
revenues. The conduct of Verginius Rufus in refusing the throne
met with no appreciation, and he was deprived of his command.
Thus although the legions on the Rhine took the oath of allegiance,
their support was half-hearted, and Galba's behaviour produced
discontent which was soon to burst out into open rebellion.

The unpopularity of the new emperor was increased by his
choice of advisers. He was supposed to be entirely in the hands of
three men, to all of whom Tacitus gives a very bad character,
Titus Vinius, his legionary legate in Spain, who was chosen to be
the colleague of the Emperor in the consulship, Cornelius Laco,
the new prefect of the praetorians, and the freedman Icelus, who
was given equestrian rank. Vinius was friendly with Otho, who
accompanied Galba from Spain, and who was believed to be a
suitor for the hand of his daughter. It must have been a disappointment to the Senate who had welcomed Galba's accession that
he chose his associates from men who were regarded with little
respect.

It was not till the autumn of 68 that the Emperor, who had been
met at Narbo by a deputation of the Senate and perhaps of the
praetorians, entered the city of Rome. Outside the walls an unfortunate incident occurred. Galba was met by the former soldiers
of the fleet whom Nero in his last days had trained for legionary
service and who now appealed for recognition as a regular legion.

---

[1] Tacitus, *Hist.* I, 5.

Some dispute arose which led to bloodshed, and this was afterwards magnified into the statement that thousands of innocent men had been massacred[1].

The behaviour of Galba in Rome did nothing to remove the bad impression created by the events which have been described. With the laudable desire of restoring the finances of the State which had suffered from Nero's extravagance, he took steps which caused offence without producing much revenue. A commission of thirty *equites* was appointed to recover from the recipients nine-tenths of the sums which Nero had lavished on his favourites, but the money had been spent and the efforts of the commission were futile. The Emperor's meanness alienated both the population of Rome which had been kept in a good temper by Nero's festivals, and the soldiers who failed to receive the promised donative. Though some of the less prominent members of Nero's entourage were put to death, the notorious Tigellinus, who was held responsible for the worst actions of his master, was saved through the influence of Vinius and retired to a life of luxury at Sinuessa, until on the accession of Otho he was driven to commit suicide.

News of the unpopularity of Galba in Rome had reached the legions on the Rhine. Accordingly when on the first of January 69 they were called upon to renew the oath of allegiance the two legions stationed at Mainz overthrew the statues of the Emperor, imprisoned the centurions who opposed them, and called upon the Senate and People of Rome to choose a successor. When this news arrived in Rome a few days later Galba felt that he must take the step which was long overdue of adopting as his son a man who might support and eventually succeed him. In this matter he showed the want of tact which had characterized him throughout. On January 10 he announced that his choice had fallen on a certain Piso Licinianus, who was descended from Crassus on his father's and from Pompey on his mother's side, but who had no qualifications other than noble birth and a blameless and austere character. His family had been persecuted by Claudius and Nero, and he himself had just returned from exile. The praetorians received the news of the adoption of Piso without enthusiasm, though their prefect Laco had been his principal supporter, but from the Senate he had naturally a more cordial reception.

Piso was destined to occupy the position of heir-apparent for not more than five days. His selection by Galba had been a great blow to Otho, who had hoped to succeed him, and whose prospects of doing so had seemed up to the present distinctly good. Not

[1] Tacitus, *Hist.* I, 37.

only had he the support of Vinius, but he was on cordial terms with Galba himself, who often dined at his house: on these occasions Otho had taken the opportunity of acquiring popularity with the soldiers by making gifts of money to the troops who accompanied the Emperor. Among the praetorians he had two agents who by gifts and promises had prepared the way for the step which he had no doubt for some time considered that it might be necessary to take. When the adoption was announced Otho felt that the time had come for immediate action and that otherwise he would be in imminent danger of bankruptcy if not of death or exile.

The fifteenth of January 69 was fixed for the attempt. On the morning of that day Otho was called away while attending on Galba, who was sacrificing before the temple of Apollo. At the 'golden milestone' in the forum he was met by 23 praetorians, who placed him in a litter and hurriedly conveyed him to the camp, where he was hailed emperor by the soldiers with such enthusiasm that the officers did not dare to resist. In a speech he inveighed against the cruelty and avarice of Galba and his subordinates and called for their death.

The position of the Emperor was now quite hopeless. There were indeed in the city a few troops other than the praetorians, the remnants of a force raised by Nero for the wars in the East which he had been planning at the end of his reign, drawn from the legions of Germany and the Danube. Of these the German troops were not ill-disposed to Galba, who had treated them well, but when it came to the point they did not fight for him, and the Danubian soldiers were actively hostile. The legion which he had raised in Spain he had rather rashly sent off to Pannonia[1], and the soldiers of the fleet (now Legio I Adiutrix) had not forgotten their reception on his arrival. Literally the only troops at the emperor's disposal were a single cohort which was on duty at the palace. It was difficult for him to know what had actually happened. A rumour reached him that Otho had been killed, and a soldier arrived waving a bloodstained sword and claiming to have done the deed. These reports encouraged Galba, contrary to the advice of Vinius, to descend into the forum and see what he could do by his personal influence. The buildings which surrounded the forum were thronged with people who looked on with horror at the last scene in the life of the Emperor. When Otho heard that he had left the palace he ordered his troops to act. 'And so Roman soldiers, as though they were seeking to expel Vologeses or Pacorus from

---

[1] The Spanish legion (VI Victrix) had been left in the province, the garrison of which had been increased by X Gemina from Pannonia.

the ancestral throne of the Arsacids and not to massacre their aged and unarmed emperor, scattered the plebs before them and trampled on senators, as with threatening arms they galloped into the forum[1].' The few soldiers who accompanied Galba deserted him. He fell from his litter near the Lacus Curtius, and was killed as he lay on the ground. His death was followed by the murder of Vinius in spite of his protests that he was Otho's friend. The unfortunate Piso was struck down in the temple of Vesta, where he had taken refuge, and Laco and Icelus soon shared his fate. The heads of the murdered men were fixed on poles and carried among the military standards but were afterwards secured by the relations of the dead and given burial. The body of Galba was buried by one of his slaves in his private gardens.

Such was the tragic end of Galba. During the seven months of his reign he had committed a succession of blunders, and can fairly be considered responsible for his failure. But the task which he had too lightly undertaken was one of incredible difficulty, which could only have been successfully performed by a man of outstanding brilliance. Galba was, in the words of Tacitus, 'of mediocre ability, rather lacking in bad than endowed with good qualities[2].' It is true that Vespasian succeeded in establishing a stable government though his birth was low and his character prosaic. But in the months which had elapsed since the death of Galba Italy had twice experienced the horrors of civil war, and was prepared to accept almost any ruler who could give it peace.

II. OTHO

The new emperor received a cordial welcome from those elements in the population of the city which had resented the austerity and meanness of Galba's rule, for he had at one time been a close intimate of Nero, and had not yet attained the age of thirty-seven. Otho was a man of good though not of ancient family. His grandfather had entered the Senate under Augustus, and his father had been given patrician rank by Claudius. His friendship with Nero had come to an end in 58 when a quarrel arose between them over his beautiful wife Poppaea, as a result of which the young husband, though only of quaestorian rank, was appointed governor of the province of Lusitania in order that the Emperor might monopolize the lady, who afterwards became his wife[3]. It is not surprising that after this treatment Otho, who had governed his province in

---

[1] Tacitus, *Hist.* I, 40.   [2] Tacitus, *Hist.* I, 49.
[3] *Ann.* XIII, 45–6; *Hist.* I, 13. See above, p. 716.

quite a creditable fashion during ten long years, gave his support to Galba when he rose against the tyrant. There is some evidence that his character had matured, and that in happier circumstances he might have proved not unworthy of the high position to which he attained. But his reign, which had begun amid scenes of brutal assassination, was destined to last only three months, and he was to fall a victim to the hostility of the German armies, for which not he but Galba was responsible.

After the horrible scenes of January 15 Otho showed considerable moderation in the exercise of his power. He rescued from the praetorians the eminent soldier Marius Celsus, who had remained faithful to Galba to the last, and treated him with great respect. He realized that tact was required in his dealings with the Senate, which had obediently conferred on him the *tribunicia potestas* and the other customary powers, for he knew that this official recognition would increase his prestige in the provinces[1]. With his brother he held the consulship till March 31, when he was succeeded by Verginius Rufus. He allowed the praetorians to choose two prefects to succeed Laco, and settled some long-standing grievances about the conditions of service. When a body of soldiers, who had heard a rumour of a plot against his life, burst into the palace demanding a massacre of senators, he dealt with the matter firmly but without undue severity.

Otho must have been well aware that he could not retain his power without fighting for it. It is true that the legions of the Danube and the Euphrates at once took the oath of allegiance to him and that he hoped to secure the loyalty of Spain, where he was known and on some communities of which he bestowed favours. But on the Rhine the situation had developed so rapidly that a conflict with the German armies was inevitable, and Otho would have been well advised to make preparations for the defence of Italy sooner than he did.

As has been said, the news of the refusal of the legions of Upper Germany to swear allegiance had reached Galba about a week before his death, though it is uncertain whether he ever knew of the extent of the disaffection. Immediately after his accession Otho must have been informed that another claimant to the throne had been proclaimed on the Rhine. The news of what had happened at Mainz had reached the army of Lower Germany on January 2 and called for immediate action. About a month earlier the command had been taken over by Aulus Vitellius in succession to the murdered Fonteius Capito. Vitellius was the son

[1] Tacitus, *Hist.* I, 76, 84; II, 32.

of a distinguished senator who had held the consulship three times, had rendered valuable military services to Tiberius, and had been the colleague of Claudius in the censorship[1]. Though, as events were to show, no more unsuitable candidate for the principate could have been found, he had made himself popular with the soldiers since his arrival by removing some of their grievances. Accordingly he was hailed as emperor by his own troops and immediately afterwards by those of Upper Germany also.

The principal agents in this movement were not Vitellius himself but two *legati legionum*, Alienus Caecina and Fabius Valens. Caecina was one of the numerous people whom Galba had alienated. As quaestor of Baetica he had supported him and been given command of Legion IV in Upper Germany, but more recently the Emperor had earned his hostility by accusing him of embezzling public money. Valens, *legatus* of Legion I at Bonn, was an older man, who had been responsible for the death of Fonteius Capito and had kept Galba informed about the doings of Verginius, services which he thought had not been adequately appreciated. The neighbouring tribes, the Treveri and Lingones, who deeply resented their treatment by Galba after the defeat of Vindex, welcomed with enthusiasm the action of the armies, and it was not long before the governors of the adjacent provinces, Belgica, Lugdunensis, and Raetia, signified their adherence. Aquitania, the Spanish provinces and Gallia Narbonensis hesitated for a little, but eventually decided for Vitellius, and Britain was nominally on his side, so that he had the support of all the western part of the Roman Empire. On the other hand, the legions of the Danube and Euphrates and the provinces of Egypt and Africa declared at once for Otho, not, says Tacitus, from any party feeling but because he held the city and had been recognized by the Senate. The stage seemed to be set for a great struggle between East and West.

The advance of the German armies to Italy had begun before the news arrived of the death of Galba and the accession of Otho. The new emperor was personally unknown in Germany, but it cannot have been forgotten that he had supported Galba at the time of the rising of Vindex. The fact that he owed his success to the praetorians would not endear him to the legionaries, who felt towards the garrison of Rome a mixture of dislike and envy. In any case things had gone too far to stop. Otho made advances to Vitellius, offering him a peaceful place of retreat, but the energetic supporters of the latter took good care that they were refused.

[1] Coins of Vitellius often show the image of his father; Volume of Plates iv, 206, *o*.

The forces which were to invade Italy were divided into two armies under the command of Caecina and Valens, while Vitellius himself was to follow with a third army. Caecina, who had at his disposal some 30,000 soldiers of the army of Upper Germany, was to advance through Switzerland over the so-called Pennine Alps by the Great St Bernard Pass. A somewhat larger body of troops under Valens took the much longer route through Gaul to Lyons and thence down the Rhone and over the western Alps to the Plain of Lombardy. This army consisted of large detachments from the legions of Lower Germany, and another legion (I Italica) which happened to be at Lyons joined it when that city was reached. Eight Batavian cohorts, which normally were attached to Legion XIV, and were at the time quartered in the territory of the Lingones, were put under Valens' command, and proved a somewhat troublesome element in his forces. The army with which the Vitellian leaders invaded Italy must have numbered about 100,000 men, to whom Otho without the assistance of the Danubian legions could oppose merely the city troops and one legion (I Adiutrix) which had been raised quite recently and was without experience of active service. Great as was the prestige of the praetorians, they had seldom seen service in the field.

The advance of Valens through Gaul was a terrifying experience for the tribes which had joined Vindex, for they could only escape from plunder and massacre by giving active assistance to the Vitellians. Even as it was, a panic broke out in Metz which caused the death of 4000 men. The colony of Vienna, which had been the headquarters of the rebellion, barely avoided destruction. Cities and individuals paid large sums to Valens in order to avoid giving house-room to his troops. Even more unpleasant incidents marked the progress of the army of Caecina. On its way to the Alps it had to pass through the territory of the Helvetii, where it came into conflict with the local militia, which was on bad terms with Legion XXI at Vindonissa and was not inclined to support Vitellius. Fury was not unnaturally roused by the conduct of the Helvetii in arresting a party of soldiers under a centurion which had been sent to invite the legions of Pannonia to throw off their allegiance to Otho. The result was that the territory of the tribe was laid waste, many thousands killed, and the capital Aventicum with difficulty saved from destruction by an appeal to Vitellius himself.

While Caecina was still north of the Alps he received good news from Italy. The *ala Siliana*, which had served under Vitellius in Africa, and was glad to do him a service, declared for him and secured the adherence of the principal cities north of the Po.

Though Caecina was tempted to cross the Arlberg Pass and gain the support of Noricum before crossing the Alps he decided that delay would be dangerous and that his first duty was to occupy North Italy before Otho was able to do so. Accordingly he led his whole army through the snow of the St Bernard Pass and by the beginning of March had reached Cremona, which was inadequately defended by a single cohort of Pannonians. The city of Placentia on the south bank of the river Po had already been occupied by the Othonians.

Otho was now in a difficult but not entirely hopeless situation. The provinces which had sworn allegiance to him contained seventeen legions, but most of these were far away and time was on the side of his opponents. In the East the Jewish war was only in suspense, and in Moesia the situation was such that it would probably have been dangerous to reduce the garrison. At this very time the province was invaded by 9000 cavalry of the Roxolani, and though they were annihilated by M. Aponius the governor, the presence of a strong body of Roman troops on the lower Danube was obviously desirable. On the other hand the four legions of Pannonia and Dalmatia were not far from Italy, and there was every reason to hope for their support if the communications with the north-east were kept open and the Vitellians prevented from closing the roads which ran south-west from Aquileia. Several experienced generals were at Otho's disposal, Suetonius Paulinus, who had crushed the rebellion of Boudicca, Marius Celsus, who had served under Corbulo, and Annius Gallus. But the troops actually in Rome were unlikely without reinforcement to prove a match for the German legions. Their number cannot have exceeded 25,000 and they were lacking in military experience. Otho was actually reduced to arming a body of 2000 gladiators.

Though much precious time was wasted by Otho during the first weeks of his short principate, when he decided on action he showed a true appreciation of the military situation. It was indeed too late to close the Alpine passes or to recover the western part of the plain of Lombardy, but he saw that the line of the Po must be held at all costs. Accordingly the army which was dispatched (probably early in March) under Annius Gallus and Vestricius Spurinna was instructed to occupy the important city of Placentia, where the Via Aemilia crossed the river, and to keep open the lines of communication with Aquileia. Spurinna established himself in Placentia, and Gallus probably crossed the Po at Hostilia and occupied Mantua or Verona. Soon after Otho himself left Rome with the rest of his army accompanied by Paulinus and Celsus. The large number of senators who followed him did not go farther than Mutina, a considerable distance south of the river.

A part of Otho's inadequate forces was employed on an enterprise which, if it had been better timed, more efficiently led, and organized on a larger scale might have proved very embarrassing to the invading army. A body of troops was dispatched by sea to Narbonese Gaul with the object of hampering the advance of Valens. It is possible that Otho supposed that the Vitellians would approach Italy along the Ligurian coast, but in any case if a large army had been landed at Fréjus and had marched rapidly up-country it might have delayed Valens long enough to enable Otho to defeat Caecina before the arrival of his colleague. But the campaign was hopelessly bungled. The force employed was far too small and was under the command of officers of low rank for whom the troops had no respect. The expedition was dispatched too late to hinder the advance of Valens. As the fleet sailed up the coast it burned villages and plundered the inhabitants. The town of Albintimilium, the capital of the Maritime Alps, was sacked. When the news of these doings reached Valens, who may already have crossed the Alps, he felt that some action was necessary, and detached certain auxiliary troops including a squadron of Treveri under Julius Classicus, who was soon to be well known as a leader of the revolt against Rome in Gaul. Some of these troops occupied Fréjus, while the remainder moved east against the Othonians. In the battle which followed the Vitellians were defeated, but instead of advancing inland Otho's soldiers retired to Albingaunum in Liguria, while the Vitellians occupied Antipolis. The army of Valens had not been seriously weakened nor delayed: on the other hand the Othonian army on the Po had been deprived of some troops which could ill be spared.

The operations in the north of Italy began in a way which was not discouraging for Otho. The small force—three praetorian cohorts, 1000 legionaries, and some cavalry—which had occupied Placentia showed an aggressive spirit that Spurinna found quite embarrassing. But the arrival of Caecina at the head of his army convinced the soldiers that they could not expect to do more than hold the city for Otho. This they did successfully, so that Caecina was compelled to abandon all hope of securing the crossing and to content himself with the occupation of Cremona. The reinforcements which Gallus was bringing to Placentia were able to return as their services were not required. The body of gladiators under Martius Macer took up a position opposite Cremona and made raids across the river which did great execution among Caecina's troops. Here also the officers incurred unpopularity by restraining the eagerness of their men. Rightly or wrongly their loyalty to Otho was distrusted, and this suspicion affected the Emperor himself with unfortunate results.

The greater part of the Othonian army took up its position at Bedriacum, a village on the Via Postumia about twenty-two miles east of Cremona, at a point where it was joined by the road from Verona, along which reinforcements from the Danube were expected to arrive. Some troops, both legionaries and auxiliaries, had already reached Bedriacum from Pannonia and Dalmatia, so that Otho's forces were probably not greatly inferior in numbers to the army which Caecina had brought from Germany. Caecina was annoyed by his failure to capture Placentia and was eager to gain some success before the arrival of Valens. But the plan which he adopted nearly involved him in disaster. He hoped by a feint attack to entice the Othonian army into an ambush which he had placed in the woods which lined the Via Postumia at a point about twelve miles from Cremona. Unfortunately for him, this rather simple plan was betrayed to the enemy, who turned it to their own ends. When Caecina's cavalry retired the army of Paulinus and Celsus followed, but halted before reaching the point where the Vitellian ambush was stationed. The soldiers emerged prematurely from their hiding place and poured out on to the road. By a skilful series of movements the Othonian generals drew them into a position where they were completely surrounded. If Paulinus had at once given the order to attack a very serious blow would have been inflicted on Caecina's army, but he delayed and thus enabled the Vitellians to escape, though considerable execution was done on them as they retired. The battle of Locus Castorum, as it was called, discredited Caecina and did not increase the popularity of Paulinus with his men. Skilful as his dispositions had been during the battle, his failure to make full use of his success encouraged his enemies to suggest disloyalty. But he was probably wise not to lead his wearied army to Cremona, where he would certainly have encountered fresh troops.

Soon after this the situation was altered to Otho's disadvantage by the arrival at Cremona of the army of Valens. His advance had been delayed by a serious mutiny which nearly cost the commander his life: his proposal to detach the Batavian cohorts for the defence of Narbonese Gaul had aroused the fury of the soldiers. Another mutiny was nearly caused by the news of Caecina's misadventure at Locus Castorum which reached the army at Ticinum. The combined Vitellian forces at Cremona must have numbered nearly 100,000 men. Both sections were eager for battle, the army of Caecina in order to wipe out the memory of its reverses, the army of Valens in order to silence the complaints about its late arrival. The generals decided however that a frontal attack along the Via Postumia was undesirable. They hoped that the enemy would take the offensive, and in the meantime started work on a bridge over the Po close to Cremona, which when completed would enable them to turn the position of the Othonians.

A council of war was now held at Bedriacum at which Otho himself was present. Strong arguments in favour of delay were put forward by Suetonius Paulinus, who pointed out that the enemy's forces had reached their maximum strength, while they themselves had everything to gain by waiting for reinforcements. Their communications, he said, both with the capital and with the East were secure, and their emperor enjoyed the advantage of having been recognized by the Senate and People of Rome. On the other hand, the enemy would soon find it difficult to obtain supplies, and if the war lasted till the summer the German troops would suffer from the heat. Though similar views were expressed by Celsus and Gallus, Otho pressed for an immediate attack, and was supported by his brother Titianus and by Proculus, the prefect of the praetorians, who considered that use should be made of the undoubted enthusiasm of the soldiery before it had time to grow cold. The Emperor had his way and it was decided to attack at once. The army was put under the command of Titianus, and the more experienced generals were subordinated to him. Otho withdrew across the Po to Brixellum, taking with him a considerable body of troops. There seems to be no good reason against accepting the opinion of Tacitus[1] that the absence of the Emperor from the battle weakened the morale of the soldiers, who were devoted to him and distrusted their other commanders.

The so-called first battle of Bedriacum has been the subject of much controversy[2]. There is some reason to think that the original intention of the Othonians was not to march direct to Cremona but to reach a point where they might threaten the communications of the enemy. However this may be, the intention was not carried out and the conflict took place not far from the walls of the city. When the army halted for the night some six miles from Bedriacum

---

[1] *Hist.* II, 33, 39.
[2] B. W. Henderson, *Civil War and Rebellion in the Roman Empire*, p. 100 *sq.*; E. G. Hardy, *Studies in Roman History*, II, p. 197 *sq.*; Mommsen, *Ges. Schriften*, IV, p. 354 *sq.*

Paulinus and Celsus strongly opposed a farther advance but were not listened to by Titianus and Proculus, who received urgent messages from Otho ordering an immediate attack. The result was that when Otho's troops came into touch with the enemy they were weary after a long march over difficult country, distrustful of their leaders, and demoralized by rumours that the Vitellians were prepared to make peace. Their opponents on the other hand were warned of their approach and had plenty of time to make preparations. The battle consisted of a number of separate encounters, in one of which Otho's new legion (I Adiutrix) distinguished itself by capturing the eagle of the veteran XXI Rapax. But elsewhere things went badly for the Emperor. Legion XIII from Pannonia proved no match for V Alaudae, and the praetorians failed to justify their reputation. The arrival of the Batavian cohorts, fresh from a defeat of the Othonian gladiators, finally decided the result of the battle. The whole of Otho's army took to flight along the Via Postumia, and was cut down as it fled by the pursuing Vitellians. Paulinus and Proculus slipped away, but the other generals tried to rally the troops, though they recognized that the situation was hopeless. The praetorians murmured that they had been betrayed, that much of the army was still at Bedriacum or with Otho and that the legions of Moesia had not yet arrived. When the Vitellian army reached a point five miles from Bedriacum it halted, hoping, as proved to be the fact, that it would be spared the necessity of assaulting the camp. The next day surrender was offered and before long the soldiers of the two armies were fraternizing with each other.

When the news of the defeat reached Otho at Brixellum he abandoned all hope, and although the praetorians who were with him and envoys of the Moesian legions tried to persuade him that success was yet possible he decided to put an end to the bloodshed by taking his own life. After destroying all papers which might compromise his adherents he retired to his room and the next morning was found dead. Otho seems to have had the power of inspiring personal devotion, for some of the praetorians committed suicide at his tomb, but, on the whole, it is difficult to pass a favourable judgment on him or to agree with the view that Tacitus has done him less than justice. There are indeed a few obscurities in the narrative of the historian, but he seems to have been well informed about the details of the campaign, for which good sources of information were available. Otho can hardly be excused for lingering two months in Rome before setting out to face the Vitellians and for taking no effective steps to secure that the Danubian legions should reach Italy in time to be of use. The dispatch of an adequate force to North Italy in January might have stopped the advance of Caecina before it reached the Po. Even Placentia does not seem to have been occupied until the very last minute. The expedition to Narbonese Gaul, which shows some trace of military imagination, was badly mismanaged and did little to hamper the movements of Valens. Finally at Bedriacum he distrusted the able generals, whose services he was fortunate to command, and by removing himself to a distance from the battle failed to gain the full advantage from the personal attachment of the troops which was his chief asset.

III. VITELLIUS

When the news reached Vitellius of the success of his generals before Cremona and of the death of Otho he was still in Gaul preparing to advance into Italy. He had held a levy for the purpose of reinforcing the depleted legions on the Rhine and had summoned from Britain a detachment of 8000 men. At Lyons he was met not only by Caecina and Valens but by Suetonius Paulinus and other generals of Otho, who disgraced themselves by pleading that the battle had been lost through their treachery. All were pardoned by Vitellius and Marius Celsus was even allowed to hold the consulship to which he had been nominated by Galba. It would have been wise to show the same clemency to certain centurions who were put to death in cold blood, an act which infuriated the Danubian legions, whose support it might at this stage have been possible to secure.

The first problem to be settled was how to treat the defeated troops. Vitellius decided to send Legion I Adiutrix to Spain and Legion XIV, which had arrived in Italy soon after the battle, back to its old quarters in Britain. The Batavian cohorts, who had quarrelled violently with their former associates when both were stationed at Turin, were dispatched to Germany, where they were soon to give further trouble (see below, p. 843). Of the Danubian legions VI and XI were sent back to their provinces, while XIII, all of which had been engaged at Bedriacum, was given the humiliating task of building amphitheatres at Cremona and Bononia. The detachments of the Moesian legions which had reached Aquileia returned to their province in a very bad temper. Vitellius was probably unwise in disarming and discharging the praetorians who had fought for Otho, and in creating sixteen new cohorts drawn entirely from the soldiers of the German army. This humiliation of what had regarded itself as a *corps d'élite* was deeply resented, and Vespasian was to find enthusiastic supporters among the ex-praetorians. In dealing with his own army Vitellius showed an unjustifiable confidence in the strength of his position. Many Gallic auxiliaries were sent back to their own country, and from motives of economy recruiting for the army was stopped and soldiers were invited to ask for discharge.

It was, however, a large army, amounting to 60,000 men, which accompanied Vitellius to Rome. About the end of May he reached Cremona in order to visit the scene of the battle, where bodies were still lying unburied, and after attending gladiatorial shows in the new amphitheatres at Cremona and Bononia he proceeded south. During his advance the troops were given the same license to plunder as they would have enjoyed had they been marching through hostile territory. Not only did they often use their weapons against the peaceful inhabitants but they quarrelled among themselves, legionaries taking up arms against auxiliaries. Seven miles from Rome some citizens who out of curiosity had come to meet the advancing army were nearly massacred because they had treated the soldiers with what was considered undue familiarity. Vitellius entered Rome like a conqueror, escorted by four legions with their eagles and by detachments of four others, as well as by twelve *alae* of cavalry and thirty-four cohorts of auxiliary infantry. The conditions under which the troops lived in the city completed the process of demoralization which had begun during the advance. They were quartered all over Rome in temples and porticoes, subject to no kind of discipline. Many Germans and Gauls died of disease contracted in the low-lying region of the Vatican during the hot Italian summer.

Vitellius had been unduly elated when the news arrived that the Eastern legions had sworn allegiance to him, and did not realize that his army would soon be required to fight again. In Rome he showed a certain geniality in his behaviour, supporting in person his candidates for the consulship and attending regularly the meetings of the Senate, where he allowed views opposed to his own to be expressed. He refused at first the title of Augustus, and his power was crumbling before he allowed himself to be called Caesar. Caecina and Valens were appointed consuls for September and October, but the Emperor did not hold the consulship himself, though at the very end of his life he adopted the style of *consul perpetuus*. He posed as the successor of Nero, to whose shades he made offerings. But his personal character earned for him nothing but contempt, and his gluttony was such that it cost the State 900 million sesterces during his short reign, though he declared himself unable to find the money necessary for important purposes. His freedman Asiaticus was as prominent as Icelus had been under Galba. Caecina and Valens did nothing to enhance the prestige of the new régime, and vied with each other in ostentation, seizing property which rightly belonged to the exiles who had returned under Galba and Otho.

While Vitellius was feasting in Rome, attending games and gladiatorial shows, and allowing his army to lose its efficiency, events were occurring which were soon to bring his reign to a dis-honourable close. The legions of the Danubian provinces were restless and discontented[1]. They would probably have supported Verginius Rufus if he had been willing to aim at the throne on the death of Nero, and might even have joined the Rhine armies in fighting for Vitellius if the invitation to do so had reached them in time. As it was they had taken the oath of allegiance to Otho, and were indignant that the battle of Bedriacum had been fought before they arrived in full strength. The treatment by Vitellius of Legion XIII, which had taken part in the battle, was regarded as an insult: the people of Cremona were soon to pay a heavy price for the amphitheatre built for them by the soldiers. The detachments of the Moesian legions which had reached Aquileia when the news of Otho's death arrived had behaved with such violence that they feared the vengeance of Vitellius.

If any of the governors of the three Danubian provinces—Pannonia, Moesia, Dalmatia—had been a man of high birth or personal distinction it is almost certain that the army would have set him up as a rival to Vitellius. But, as it happened, all three were complete nonentities, and one of them, Tampius Flavianus, governor of Pannonia, was related to the Emperor. The most vigorous personality among the legionary officers, Antonius Primus, *legatus* of Legion VII, was only of praetorian standing. It was accordingly necessary to look elsewhere for a leader, and he was found in T. Flavius Vespasianus, governor of Judaea. The armies of the Danube and the Euphrates were united by fairly close ties. One of the Moesian legions—III Gallica—had come quite recently from the East, and three of the eastern legions[2] had been transferred by Nero from the Danube to the Euphrates.

The prestige of the army of the East had been considerably increased by its achievements under Corbulo, and its reputation now ranked high. Normally the supreme command had been in

---

[1] The legends FIDES and CONSENSVS EXERCITVVM on his coins express what Vitellius wished to be believed. Volume of Plates iv, 206, *p, q*.

[2] IV Scythica, V Macedonica, XV Apollinaris.

the hands of the *legatus* of Syria, but on the outbreak of the Jewish revolt Nero had appointed as governor of Judaea Vespasian, a man of consular standing, giving him command of three legions, while the remaining three were under C. Licinius Mucianus, governor of Syria. Except in Judaea the eastern frontier was now peaceful, for Nero's settlement of the Armenian question had established good relations between Rome and Parthia. It is therefore a little surprising that the oath of allegiance had been taken by the eastern legions to Galba, Otho, and Vitellius. Vespasian had even sent his son Titus to Rome to salute Galba on his accession.

But by the summer of 69 a strong feeling had arisen in the East that the rule of Vitellius could not be tolerated. Rumours had arrived about the situation in Italy, and the representatives sent by the Emperor made a bad impression. It was well known that the discontented legions on the Danube would gladly support a new claimant to the throne. The governor of Egypt, Ti. Julius Alexander, was eager for a change. Thus it seemed probable that not less than fourteen legions, half of the whole Roman army, together with auxiliary troops and the forces of client-kings, would be at the disposal of a new candidate. The only question was who this candidate was to be. Mucianus had not at first been on cordial terms with Vespasian, but the attractive Titus had won the heart of the childless governor of Syria, and the two were now good friends. If Mucianus had been willing he could probably have become emperor, but he preferred to be Vespasian's right-hand man. He had literary and scientific interests and was lacking in ambition. Accordingly he used his influence with the troops in favour of Vespasian, who was at first very unwilling to accept the honour which was being thrust upon him, realizing as he did the difficulty of concentrating on Italy his large but scattered forces.

Vespasian is a good example of the type of man to whom the Principate provided a career in public life which would certainly have been closed to them under the Republic. His father was an undistinguished member of the equestrian order, who ended his days as a moneylender among the Helvetii, but this did not prevent his two sons from entering the Senate and rising to eminent positions. The career of Vespasian had been creditable but not specially distinguished. He had done well in Britain as *legatus* of a legion during the Claudian invasion and been awarded the insignia of a triumph. In 51 he had held the consulship, and since then had governed Africa, where he acquired much less popularity than Vitellius. Since 67 he had been dealing successfully with the troublesome Jewish revolt and had earned the admiration of his soldiers by his interest in them and his willingness to expose himself to danger.

The scruples of Vespasian were overcome by Mucianus, who pointed out that if he did not act he would be treated by Vitellius as Corbulo had been treated by Nero. Vitellius, he said, owed his success mainly to the bad generalship of Otho. The victorious army was rapidly crumbling, while he would have a large and enthusiastic force behind him. Egypt was the first province openly to declare for Vespasian. On July 1 the legions at Alexandria took the oath of allegiance to him, and their example was followed two days later by the army of Judaea. Before the middle of the month he was recognized in Syria, where Mucianus had cleverly spread the report that Vitellius intended to transfer the eastern legions to the Rhine, a suggestion which infuriated the troops, whose ties with the province in which they were stationed were very close. Vespasian was soon assured of the support of all the eastern provinces and of the client-kings of Sophene and Commagene, who commanded considerable forces. A conference was held at Berytus at which it was decided to send embassies to Parthia and Armenia to secure that no hostile action should be taken while the civil war was in progress. The command against the Jews was entrusted to Titus. Vespasian resolved to proceed to Egypt, the chief granary of Rome, hoping by control of that province and of Africa to starve the city into submission, while Mucianus set off for the West with Legion VI and 13,000 soldiers of other units. In the meantime money was raised by confiscating the property of the wealthier provincials, but Vespasian was careful not to show undue generosity in promising donatives to his men. A message was sent to the praetorians disbanded by Vitellius offering reinstatement if they joined Vespasian.

When Mucianus started on his march through Asia Minor to Byzantium his plan of campaign was still uncertain. Much would depend on the attitude of the Danubian armies which was not yet known. As the Pontic fleet was ordered to sail to Byzantium the possibility of an invasion of Italy by sea was evidently contemplated. The shortest route to Italy was by the Via Egnatia to Dyrrhachium and thence across the Adriatic to Brundisium, but this line of advance would only be possible if the Flavians controlled the sea. As it turned out, the defection of the Ravenna fleet from Vitellius would have enabled Mucianus to reach Brundisium safely, but when he left Syria there was no reason to anticipate this favourable turn of events.

The news of Vespasian's bid for power was received with

enthusiasm on the Danube. In Moesia Legion III, which considered that it belonged to the army of Syria, declared for him at once, and won the support of the other two legions (VII and VIII). The governor of the province, Aponius Saturninus, followed suit in a half-hearted fashion. The two legions of Pannonia (VII Galbiana and XIII) took his side with alacrity. Their leader was the restless and energetic Antonius Primus, who was to be the most important agent in securing the success of Vespasian. He was a protégé of Galba, who restored him to the Senate from which he had been expelled for forgery under Nero, and gave him command of the new legion which he had raised in Spain. In spite of this he offered his services to Otho, who rather unwisely failed to make use of him. Antonius found a keen supporter in Cornelius Fuscus, procurator of Pannonia, a man of senatorial birth who had voluntarily entered the equestrian order, and had been appointed to his present post by Galba. The governor of Pannonia took fright and slipped away to Italy, leaving the management of affairs in the hands of Antonius. In Dalmatia the single legion (XI) showed less eagerness to support Vespasian, and the decisive victory had been gained before it decided to do so.

A conference was held at the headquarters of Legion XIII at Poetovio to discuss the plan of campaign. The question to be decided was whether the army of the Danube should take the offensive at once against the Vitellians or wait for Mucianus to arrive. It was pointed out that Vitellius still possessed a large army, which had received reinforcements from Britain, and that their own troops were less numerous than those which had been defeated at Bedriacum, and it was urged that it would be wise to occupy the passes over the Julian Alps and wait for the Syrian army. On the other hand Antonius emphasized the fact that the Vitellian legions had been demoralized by their residence in Italy, and suggested that delay would give Vitellius time to bring reinforcements from the provinces which still supported him and to use his fleets against them. If, he said, the legions feared to advance, he was prepared to attack at the head of the auxiliaries alone. The enthusiasm of Antonius, who was supported by Fuscus, so inspired the soldiers that it was decided to do as he wished. Messages were sent to the governor of Moesia to bring up his legions with all speed. A detachment was sent to the valley of the Inn to prevent the procurator of Raetia, who was faithful to Vitellius, from advancing over the Brenner. In order to secure the safety of the frontier it was decided to attach to the army of invasion the chiefs of the Sarmatae Iazyges, and also Sido and Italicus the joint kings of the Marcomanni, who occupied the territory just north of Pannonia. Accompanied by Arrius Varus, a veteran officer of Corbulo, Antonius advanced to Aquileia with a force of auxiliaries, and then occupied without opposition Opitergium, Altinum, Patavium, and Ateste. Not far from the latter town he was successful in a skirmish with a Vitellian detachment which had thrown a bridge across the Adige.

Vitellius had concealed as long as possible the bad news which reached him from the east and north, but at last even he had to realize that something must be done. Reinforcements were summoned from Germany, Britain and Spain, but without result. The only province which showed any enthusiasm for him was Africa, where his successful proconsulship was not forgotten. It soon became clear that he would have to trust to the troops which had invaded Italy earlier in the year, and to the generals Caecina and Valens who had led them to victory. Unfortunately for him Valens, the more trustworthy of the two, was ill when the army was dispatched from Rome, so that it had to be put under the command of Caecina, who was meditating treachery.

It was essential for Vitellius, as it had been for Otho, that the line of the Po should be strongly held. Now, however, the point of greatest strategical importance was Hostilia rather than Placentia, for the enemy was advancing from the north-east, and would attempt to cross the river at that city. It was accordingly to Hostilia that the greater part of Caecina's army proceeded, while some auxiliaries, followed by Legions I Italica and XXI Rapax, were sent to occupy Cremona. Caecina had under his command four legions with their eagles and large detachments of four German and three British legions together with auxiliaries. All the sixteen cohorts of praetorians were left behind in Rome. This force was impressive in numbers, but its quality had greatly deteriorated during the last five months. It was, however, devoted to Vitellius, and under competent and honest leadership might have proved a match for the brilliant but headstrong Antonius.

On his way north Caecina visited Ravenna in order to confer with Lucilius Bassus, prefect of the fleet, who had a grievance against Vitellius because he had not been appointed prefect of the praetorians, and it was arranged that both should throw off their allegiance. In the meantime, however, they concealed their intentions and Caecina followed his army to Hostilia, where he took up a strong position north of the town, between the Po and the Tartarus. Tacitus is probably right in thinking that if he had attacked at once before the Flavian army had reached its full

strength he would have had every prospect of success[1]. Instead
of doing so he remained inactive waiting for the news of the
defection of the fleet. This was secured without difficulty by
Bassus, as most of the sailors were natives of the provinces of
Pannonia and Dalmatia, which sympathized with Vespasian.
Though Bassus made no secret of his own sympathies he was put
under formal arrest and sent to Atria, where he was presently set
at liberty. The command of the fleet was taken over by Cornelius
Fuscus.

Caecina was less successful with his troops than Bassus had
been. At a secret meeting he persuaded some of the officers to do
as he wished, but when the common soldiers heard of this there
was an outburst of indignation: they threw Caecina into chains
and declared that they were confident of their ability to defeat the
Danubian legions a second time. They chose as their leaders,
instead of Caecina, Fabius Fabullus, *legatus* of Legion V and Cassius Longus, prefect of the camp. But the treachery of its commander had a demoralizing effect on the army, which decided to
abandon its position before Hostilia and join its comrades before
Cremona. Accordingly it threw open to the Flavian army the
direct road to Rome by Hostilia and Bononia, and set out on the
long march to Cremona by Mutina, Parma and Placentia[2].

The delay and treachery of Caecina had been a godsend to the
Flavians, and had given Antonius time to collect an imposing
army. After the two Pannonian legions had joined him at Patavium
he advanced to Verona, which was made the base of operations,
as the surrounding country was suitable for cavalry and the town
commanded the road from the north over the Brenner. Here the
army was increased by the arrival of the three legions from Moesia
accompanied by the governor of the province, Aponius Saturninus.
His presence in the city as well as that of the governor of Pannonia, who had rejoined his legions, was distinctly embarrassing
for the *de facto* commander Antonius, who was no doubt considerably relieved when an outburst of indignation among the soldiers
against the two consulars enabled him to secure their escape.

Antonius was now in command of an army which resented the
duty of fortifying Verona and clamoured to be led against the
enemy. In advancing beyond Aquileia he had acted in direct disobedience to the orders of Vespasian and Mucianus, who wished
to postpone the offensive till the army of the East had arrived.
Up till now fortune had been favourable to him, but he could

[1] *Hist.* III, 9.
[2] See Mommsen, *Ges. Schriften*, IV, p. 363 *sq.*

only justify his disobedience by gaining a decisive victory. He therefore decided to attack the Vitellian army at Cremona before it could be placed under the command of Valens, for whose military capacity he had some respect. Valens had left Rome on the arrival of the news of Caecina's treachery, accompanied, we are told, by a train of courtesans and eunuchs, and on hearing of the defection of the fleet had merely sent to Rome for reinforcements and awaited events. If he had hurried on to Hostilia his arrival might have restored the morale of Caecina's army and proved fatal to the plans of Antonius. When three cohorts and a squadron of cavalry arrived from the city he was content to send them to garrison Ariminum, while he disappeared over the Apennines with the wild idea of making his way to Gaul and raising a new army against Vespasian. The unfortunate troops at Cremona were left without a leader.

When Antonius learned that Hostilia had been evacuated and that Caecina's legions were on their way to Cremona he felt that energetic action was more than ever necessary, if the attack were to be delivered before the two armies had united. Accordingly there followed what has been described as a race to Cremona[1]. In two days the Flavian army reached Bedriacum, where the legions were left to fortify the camp, while Antonius with 4000 cavalry advanced four miles along the Via Postumia. Arrius, who pressed on still farther, came into contact with the enemy, who drove him back in such confusion that a disaster was only prevented by the personal efforts of Antonius. By this time the Vitellian cavalry were exhausted, while the better led Flavians reformed their ranks and advanced a second time in the direction of Cremona, driving the enemy before them. Four miles from the town Legions I and XXI were drawn up in line, but they failed to shelter the retreating cavalry and merely held their ground till a fiery charge of the Moesian cohorts forced them to retire under the walls of Cremona. In spite of the setback earlier in the day the operations had begun well for the Flavians.

By this time the legions had arrived from Bedriacum and clamoured for an immediate attack although it was late in the afternoon and Antonius vigorously opposed the proposal, pointing out that all the advantages were on the side of the enemy. When it became known that the Vitellian legions had arrived after marching thirty miles in one day and in spite of their exhaustion were preparing to attack it was clear that the struggle would not be long delayed. The Flavian army was drawn up in battle order on both

[1] Henderson, *op. cit.* p. 189.

sides of the Via Postumia, the Thirteenth Legion being in the centre. If Valens or some other competent general had been in Cremona he would undoubtedly have urged his soldiers to postpone the attack till the next day. The wearied troops would have passed the night in comfortable quarters, while their opponents would have had to bivouac in the open far from their base. But the Vitellians were even more eager than the Flavians to fight at once. The result was a confused battle which lasted the whole night. At times the Vitellians did well. Galba's Legion VII was hard pressed, losing six of its leading centurions, and was only saved from destruction by the arrival of a body of ex-praetorians whom their treatment by Vitellius had rendered strong supporters of Vespasian. When the moon rose the Flavians had the advantage, for it shone full on the faces of their opponents. At dawn Legion III, as the Eastern custom was, saluted the rising sun. This action, which was misinterpreted by the Vitellians to mean that Mucianus and his army had arrived, led them to abandon their resistance and flee in confusion to their camp outside Cremona.

The next task of the victorious army was to attack this strongly fortified camp, for Bedriacum was too far away and there was no time to construct a camp of their own. The defenders put up a stout resistance and caused heavy casualties among the assailants, who only rallied when the rumour spread that the reward of success would be the sack of Cremona. At length part of the rampart collapsed and the soldiers of Legions III and VII forced their way through the gate which faced towards Bedriacum. The defenders flung themselves from the ramparts and the Flavian army occupied the camp.

The troops of Antonius were now prepared to assault Cremona itself, which was at the time crowded with civilians attracted by the annual fair, but the siege had scarcely begun when the Vitellian officers decided that nothing was to be gained by further resistance. They even released Caecina in the hope that he would secure for them better terms, and he issued from the gate wearing his official robes as consul and preceded by lictors. The traitor was protected from the fury of the soldiers by Antonius and sent to Vespasian, who spared his life and even took him into favour. He could do nothing to save Cremona from its fate. The defeated soldiers withdrew from the town, in which the victors were allowed to work their will. It had been twice in one year the headquarters of a Vitellian army and had been the scene of a gladiatorial show given by Caecina in honour of the first battle of Bedriacum. The soldiers of Legion XIII had not forgotten that they had been mocked by the inhabitants while building the amphitheatre. For four days the city was given over to murder, rapine, and lust, and at the end was burned to the ground. It was soon afterwards rebuilt, but its sufferings during these days were never forgotten.

As the result of the bold strategy of Antonius the ultimate victory of Vespasian was now assured. Vitellius could not hope to receive any reinforcements from the Rhine, where the rising of Civilis, for which Antonius was in part responsible, had already broken out, and in any case the Flavians controlled the Alpine passes. The attempt of Valens to cause trouble in the south of Gaul had proved fruitless, and he himself was taken prisoner near Massilia. The Spanish legions, led by I Adiutrix which had fought for Otho, took the oath of allegiance to the new emperor, and their example was followed by the troops in Britain, where Vespasian's achievements were not forgotten. Much misery would have been avoided if Vitellius had followed the example of Otho, and, recognizing that his cause was hopeless, committed suicide. If he had possessed any courage or military ability he might with the considerable army which he still retained have at any rate delayed the Flavian advance, for the army of Antonius was demoralized and Mucianus was far from Italy. But, deprived of the two generals who had gained him the throne, he revealed his hopeless incapacity and his unworthiness of the devotion of the soldiers who were still prepared to die for him.

The news of the battle of Cremona was received by Vespasian and Mucianus with somewhat mixed feelings. They must have been relieved that the rashness of Antonius had not led to disaster, but Mucianus was not too anxious that the Flavian army should enter Rome before his arrival. His own advance had been delayed by the need of dealing with a serious attack on Moesia by the Dacians, who crossed the Danube at a time when they believed the province to be almost denuded of troops. It was fortunate for Rome that the army of Mucianus was at hand, for the situation on the Rhine was critical and a simultaneous rising on the Danube would have imposed a terrible strain on the resources of the empire. But Mucianus repelled the invasion successfully, a new governor was appointed, and the army of the province was reinforced from the defeated legions of Vitellius, which were thus usefully employed at a safe distance from Italy.

It was not thought desirable explicitly to forbid Antonius to advance towards Rome. The battle of Cremona had been fought at the end of October, and the weather was beginning to make

campaigning difficult. There were floods in the valley of the Po
and enough snow lay on the Apennines to hamper an invading
army. There was therefore no time to be lost if the Flavian army
were to cross the mountains before the road was blocked. The
force which Valens had left in Ariminum was blockaded by the
fleet, so that the whole of Italy north of the Apennines was now in
Flavian hands. Antonius advanced with a picked force to Fanum
Fortunae, where the Via Flaminia leaves the coast, sending back
word to Verona for the remainder of his troops to follow at once.
The condition of his army was none too good; like the Vitellians
earlier in the year his soldiers were demoralized by the advance
through Italy, and showed little respect for their officers. But, as
Tacitus remarks[1], the Flavian leaders were helped now as on other
occasions not less by luck than by their own skill.

While his soldiers had been fighting for him in North Italy
Vitellius had shown a terrible lack of energy. 'Hidden in the shade
of his gardens like a lazy animal which lies torpid if you give it
food, he paid no regard to the past present or future[2].' The news
of the treachery of Caecina brought him to Rome, but the reinforcements which he sent to Valens were quite inadequate. It was
long before he admitted the truth about the disaster at Cremona,
the details of which were reported to him by a centurion, who
committed suicide in order to prove that he was telling the truth.
Even now if he had acted with energy something might have been
done. He had at his disposal sixteen praetorian cohorts, composed
of his old German legionaries, four urban cohorts, and a legion
(afterwards II Adiutrix) raised from the marines as well as a considerable body of cavalry. If this force, which was about as large
as that which Otho had commanded, had advanced rapidly along
the Via Flaminia and across the Apennines, it might well have
given trouble to Antonius. As it was the greater part of it was sent
to Mevania, about 80 miles north of Rome, where the road
entered the mountains, and was followed by Vitellius himself,
whose gross incompetence in military matters was here ludicrously
displayed. When he heard that the fleet at Misenum had abandoned
him he was stricken with panic and insisted on returning to Rome,
taking with him seven of the praetorian cohorts. The remainder of
the army was withdrawn from its advanced position and retired
to Narnia, thirty miles nearer the city. This pusillanimous behaviour merely encouraged the rebels in the south, who were
assisted by a rising in Samnium and elsewhere. L. Vitellius, the
Emperor's brother, who had been left in Rome, could probably have

[1] *Hist.* III, 59.   [2] *Hist.* III, 36.

dealt with the rebellion with the troops at his disposal, and the six cohorts and 500 cavalry who were sent under him to Campania could have been more profitably employed in the north.

When the Flavian army had forced its way through the snow of the Apennines and descended into the plains it was astonished to find that it could proceed without opposition as far as Carsulae, ten miles from the diminished forces of Vitellius. There it halted for some time hoping for a proposal which would make fighting unnecessary. Petilius Cerialis, a distinguished officer who had escaped from the city, brought the news that Vespasian's brother, Flavius Sabinus, prefect of the city, was negotiating with the Emperor. When the officers of the small Vitellian force at Narnia learned that the Flavian legions had joined the advance guard at Carsulae they considered that further resistance was hopeless and began to desert to the enemy. The flight to Rome of the two praetorian prefects convinced even the common soldiers, who had been prepared to fight, that there was no disgrace in surrender. Their last hope vanished when they were shown the head of Valens, who had been executed at Urbinum. The surrendering troops were received with honour and left at Narnia and Interamna in charge of a small detachment. After this success Antonius ought to have marched straight to Rome. Unfortunately he halted at Ocriculum in the hope that Sabinus would persuade Vitellius to resign and the troops in the city to surrender voluntarily. Cerialis was indeed sent on with a body of cavalry, but was instructed not to hurry. The Flavian leaders failed to realize that, however willing Vitellius might be to accept a peaceful settlement and to retire to a life of luxury in Campania, his soldiers would not tolerate such conduct and were prepared to fight to the end.

In the city Flavius Sabinus had rejected the advice that he should declare openly for his brother trusting to the urban cohorts whom he as prefect of the city commanded, and in the hope of avoiding bloodshed had preferred to negotiate with Vitellius. A conference was held in the temple of Apollo at which the Emperor agreed to abdicate. On December 18 when the news arrived that the army at Narnia had surrendered he descended from the palace in mourning attire accompanied by his family with the intention of laying down the insignia of office in the temple of Concord and of retiring to his brother's house. But the crowd barred the way and forced him to return to the palace. Feeling was now so high that Sabinus was in great danger and thought it best to take refuge in the Capitol with a little band of adherents. During the night he brought there his own family and Vespasian's

son Domitian, and sent an urgent message to Antonius, but took
no steps to summon the urban cohorts and arrange for an adequate
defence. Probably he did not yet realize to what lengths the
Vitellian soldiers were prepared to go. It was useless to protest to
Vitellius that the compact had been broken, for he was 'no longer
Emperor but only a cause of war.'

Next day the Vitellians tried to force their way into the citadel.
The defenders blocked the gate with statues and threw down
stones and tiles upon the assailants, who swarmed over the roofs
of adjoining houses. As both sides lacked artillery, firebrands were
used freely, with the result that the famous temple caught fire and
was burned to the ground. Domitian escaped, disguised as a
temple-servant, but the unhappy Sabinus was captured and in spite
of the protests of Vitellius murdered and thrown into the Tiber.

On receiving the message of Sabinus Antonius left Ocriculum,
where his troops had been celebrating the Saturnalia, and on the
evening of the day on which the Capitol had fallen reached Saxa
Rubra, across the Mulvian Bridge, where he learned that Sabinus
was dead. Vitellius was arming the mob to defend the city and
simultaneously sending envoys to the Flavians asking for a settlement. Antonius would have been glad to postpone till the next
day his entry into Rome, but his soldiers would not listen. The
army advanced in three columns and was desperately opposed at
every point, while the populace looked on, as at a gladiatorial
show, cheering the victors and robbing the defeated. The baths
and eating-houses were crowded with spectators. The Vitellians
fought with a bravery worthy of a better cause till the survivors
were driven back to the praetorian camp, where a last stand was
made. Even now there was no talk of surrender and the defenders
were cut down with wounds in front. Vitellius himself had tried to
escape to his brother, who was at the head of an army at Tarracina,
but fearing to expose himself he returned to the palace, where he
attempted to lie in hiding. He was dragged from his hiding-
place and, his hands tied behind his back, led through the forum
past the place where Galba had fallen, to the Gemonian stairs where
he was cut down among the jeers of the mob (Dec. 20, A.D. 69).

Vitellius had even fewer personal qualifications than Otho for
the high position which he had for a few months occupied. He
was simply an amiable and self-indulgent man who was unfortunate
enough to be the instrument of other people's ambitions. The
devotion shown to him by his soldiers cannot be attributed to any
respect felt for his personal, still less for his military qualities, but
rather to the fact that he was the chosen nominee of the German

armies. Rivalry between army-groups was, as has been pointed out elsewhere (p. 224 *sq.*), one of the weakest features of the Augustan system. It was latent in ordinary times, but the victory of the Vitellians over Otho's troops at Bedriacum had aroused in the Danubian legions a desire for revenge of which Vitellius was the unfortunate victim.

On the death of Vitellius all resistance collapsed. When he heard of his brother's death L. Vitellius, who was in Campania with six praetorian cohorts dealing with the rebels, realized that it was useless to continue the struggle. He surrendered with his cohorts to a force which had been sent to Bovillae, and on his arrival in Rome was put to death, a martyr to a cause unworthy of his merits. His troops were put under arrest, but later on some at least were permitted to remain members of the praetorian guard of the new emperor.

The behaviour of the Flavian army in Rome recalled its doings in Cremona, and Antonius was unable to prevent it from committing murder and robbery. Domitian devoted himself to pleasure and exercised no authority. It must have been a great relief to the population of the city when Mucianus, who before his arrival had been awarded the insignia of a triumph for his defeat of the Dacians, reached Rome in January 70. Vespasian and Titus were elected consuls for the early months of the year. Antonius had to be contented with the insignia of the consulship and Fuscus and Arrius with those of the praetorship, while Arrius was appointed prefect of the praetorians. The services of these men could not be overlooked, but Vespasian and Mucianus were determined to keep them in their place. For six months Mucianus was practically ruler of Rome, and it was not till the summer that the Emperor arrived in the city. By that time the Capitol had been rebuilt and dedicated, and a beginning had been made with the reconstitution of the praetorian cohorts.

The steps taken by Vespasian to re-establish the *pax Romana* will be described elsewhere. By the end of the year 70 the rising on the Rhine had been crushed and Jerusalem captured. His reign of ten years was one of comparative peace, and he was able to devote himself almost entirely to the work of re-organization. The 'year of the four emperors' left such a horrible memory that when Domitian met his end in 96 without an heir the armies were prepared to let the Senate choose a successor. It was not till 193 that the accession of an emperor was again the cause of civil war.

CHAPTER XXV

REBELLION WITHIN THE EMPIRE

I. ROMAN POLICY IN GAUL

IN order that the significance of the events now to be described
may be grasped it is necessary to state in outline the policy which
had been pursued by the Roman government in Gaul and on the
Rhine since Tiberius had decided that an extension of the frontier
to the Elbe was undesirable. In the first century A.D., as at the
present time, the Rhine did not form a boundary between two
races. Many tribes included in the Roman Empire were akin to
the 'free' Germans on the right bank of the river[1]. No attempt
had been made to impose Roman ways on these tribes, which had
been allowed to retain their native institutions, but it was hoped
that they would with time come to realize the advantages of membership in the Empire, would identify their interests with those
of their Gallic neighbours, and would learn to think of Italy rather
than of free Germany as their 'spiritual home.' They had been
freely drawn upon for military service in the *auxilia*, and their
contingents were frequently under the command of their own chiefs,
who had received Roman citizenship and bore Roman names.
Most of these units were in the Julio-Claudian period employed
in the neighbourhood of their homes, a fact which shows an almost excessive confidence on the part of the government in the
power of military discipline. But before the year A.D. 69 there
had been no reason to think that this confidence had been misplaced, and German soldiers had rendered valuable service not
only on the Rhine but in Britain.

A similar policy had been pursued in Gaul proper. No interference had been made with native institutions. The tribal system

Note. For the history of the risings on the Rhine and in Gaul we are
entirely dependent on the narrative of Tacitus in the *Histories* (IV–V),
which is commonly supposed to be based on the writings of Pliny the
Elder (see Ph. Fabia, *Sources de Tacite*, p. 199 f. and F. Münzer, *Bonn.
Jahrb.* CIV, p. 98). As military history this is one of the most satisfactory
parts of Tacitus' work. He was possibly governor of Belgica under
Domitian, and probably derived much of his information from personal
enquiries. See Map 13, facing p. 347.

[1] Tacitus, *Germ.* 28.

had been left intact, and the main object of Roman rule had been
to maintain peace among communities which had been at an
earlier date constantly at war. 'Before you came under our rule,'
says a speaker in Tacitus[1], 'Gaul saw nothing but wars and attempts at domination. The only use which we have made of our
victory is to keep the peace.' The survival of traditional rivalries
among Gallic tribes was not altogether unwelcome to Rome, so
long as it did not lead to actual hostilities, for she was not anxious
to create a sense of national unity, which under able leaders might
have been a source of danger to herself. Individual Gauls were
given opportunities of rising to high positions under the government. As early as the reign of Claudius some were admitted to
the Senate; many were given the citizenship and commanded
auxiliary units; a few, like Vindex, had even governed provinces.
The annual assembly of the *concilium Galliarum* at Lyons brought
together friends of Rome from all three provinces, on one of
whom was conferred the distinguished title of 'priest of Roma
and Augustus.' The speaker quoted above scarcely exaggerates
when he says that the advantages of membership of the Empire
were open to Gauls as freely as to Italians: 'nihil separatum
clausumve.'

The policy of Rome was thus to attach leading Gauls to herself,
and to trust to tribal rivalries to prevent discontented elements
from fomenting a rising of the whole country against her rule.
This policy had been successful against Florus and Sacrovir under
Tiberius, and as recently as 68 had led to the defeat of Vindex,
whose conqueror Verginius had been actively assisted by the
Treveri and Lingones. At the time of Nero's death few would
have prophesied that it would soon again be put to the test.

A word must be added on the relations which existed at this
period between Gauls and Germans. Rome justified her presence
in Gaul by claiming to confer on the country security against the
German peril. She hoped that the inhabitants of her Gallic provinces in spite of any ties of blood would come to regard the
Germans as barbarians and would co-operate with her in holding
the line of the Rhine. That this policy had met with some success
is clear from Tacitus' account of the rising of Civilis. The assistance rendered by the Gauls to the German rebels was belated,
half-hearted, and confined to a few tribes. On the other hand
Civilis and his Germans were unwilling to identify their interests
with those of their Gallic allies, and refused to swear allegiance to
the 'Imperium Galliarum[2].' Many Gauls must have feared that

---

[1] Tacitus, *Hist.* IV, 74.   [2] Tacitus, *Hist.* IV, 61.

Civilis would prove a second Ariovistus. That the Rhine was coming to be regarded as the frontier between civilization and barbarism is shown by the unwillingness of the inhabitants of Cologne to remove the barriers set by the Romans to free inter- course between them and their kinsfolk on the opposite bank[1].

The temporary success of the rising against Rome in A.D. 69–70 does not justify a condemnation of the policy which had hitherto been pursued, though it taught some important lessons. German 'nationalism' was not yet extinct on Gallic soil, and it was made clear that the loyalty of German chieftains who had received Roman military training could not yet be fully trusted and that it was dangerous to employ them in the neighbourhood of their homes. But Gaul as a whole was not dissatisfied with Roman rule, and Gallic national feeling was too weak to cause alarm. Finally, the military situation at the time of the rising was unique, and very unlikely to recur. At no time was the army on the Rhine so small and so incompetently led as when it had been depleted by Vitellius for his campaigns against Otho and Vespasian.

II. THE FIRST SUCCESSES OF THE REBELS

When the Flavian army was advancing into Italy in the summer of 69 Antonius Primus, fearing that Vitellius might receive rein- forcements from the Rhine, communicated to the Batavian chief Julius Civilis a request to take such action as would detain on the river the Roman forces which had been left in the north, and a similar appeal, we are told, reached him from Hordeonius Flaccus, the governor of Upper Germany, whose sympathies were with Vespasian. These invitations were welcome to Civilis, who, in spite of his Roman citizenship and his twenty-five years of service in the army, had no love of Rome and had already in recent years been twice suspected of disloyalty. Though it was a matter of indifference to him whether Vitellius or Vespasian was emperor, he was prepared in the first instance to pose as a supporter of the latter, hoping that in the event of success he would be able to throw off the pretence and come forward as a champion of German and perhaps of Gallic independence.

The Batavians, who occupied the so-called Island between the Waal and the Lek on the Lower Rhine, had long been allies of Rome, and had taken part in the campaigns of Germanicus against the Germans east of the river. Though they paid no tribute they were expected to provide soldiers for the *auxilia*, in which Civilis

[1] Tacitus, *Hist.* IV, 65.

had commanded a cohort. At the time when the revolt broke out recruiting officers of Vitellius were at work among the tribe, discrediting the cause of their emperor by their violence and corruption. Thus Civilis had no difficulty in collecting a force strong enough to overcome the resistance of the small Roman garrison in the Island. He secured the adhesion of his neighbours the Canninefates and the Frisii; in the first engagement with the enemy he was joined by a cohort of Tungri, a tribe of German stock who lived well inside the province of Belgica, and by his fellow-tribesmen who served in the Rhine fleet. More valuable reinforcements soon arrived in the form of eight veteran cohorts of Batavians which normally were attached to the army of Britain, and had formed part of the force with which Valens had invaded Italy. When the invitation of Civilis was received by these cohorts at Mainz, which they had reached on their way back to Britain, they decided to disobey the order of Vitellius to recross the Alps, and to join their fellow-countrymen. The rather half-hearted opposition of the legion stationed at Bonn was overcome without difficulty, and they met with no further resistance in their march to the north.

The very considerable force now commanded by Civilis was definitely of German stock. His early successes gained for him the support of the Bructeri and Tencteri on the right bank of the Rhine. But the envoys which he sent to the tribes of Gaul found little response, and it was not till a later stage in the revolt that certain of them were willing to co-operate; indeed at the outset very considerable reinforcements were sent from Gaul to the Roman generals.

Civilis was now strong enough to attack the nearest legionary headquarters, Castra Vetera at the mouth of the Lippe, where were stationed those soldiers of the Fifth and Fifteenth Legions who had not been taken to Italy. Though the garrison numbered barely five thousand men, about half of its normal strength, and the camp was in no way prepared for a siege, an indignant answer was given to the envoys of Civilis who urged the legionaries to swear allegiance to Vespasian. After a vain attempt to storm the camp it was invested by Civilis, who knew that it was badly supplied with provisions and that many civilians had taken refuge within the fortifications.

Hordeonius Flaccus, who must now have regretted his previous relations with Civilis, could not allow him to capture Vetera. Accordingly a relieving force was collected at Mainz consisting of soldiers of the Fourth and Twenty-Second legions under the command of Dillius Vocula, legate of the Twenty-Second. On its march down the river the army received reinforcements at Bonn from the First and at Neuss (Novaesium) from the Sixteenth Legions. Flaccus accompanied the expedition as far as Neuss, but handed over the supreme command to the younger and more vigorous Vocula. The advance of the relieving army was hampered by difficulties of supply and by the unruly conduct of the troops, who professed to distrust their leaders. A long halt was made at Gelduba, only twenty-five miles from Vetera, where the timely arrival of some Spanish cohorts enabled Vocula to repel an attack of Civilis. Even after this victory there was some delay, but at last Vetera was reached, and the wearied garrison sallied out to join the relieving force in repelling the Germans.

By this time the news of the defeat of the Vitellians at Cremona had arrived and been communicated to Civilis, who was thus forced to abandon the pretence that he was fighting for Vespasian. The Roman troops took the oath to the new emperor without enthusiasm, for they had suspected their leaders of disloyalty to Vitellius and had perhaps heard that Civilis had been instigated to rebellion by Flaccus. The situation was, however, now clear. The task of the Roman forces was to defend the integrity of the Empire against open rebellion.

The relief of Vetera was not followed, as might have been expected, by the reinforcement of the garrison or the total evacuation of the position. The fortifications of the camp were strengthened, a thousand soldiers withdrawn and incorporated in the army of Vocula, and non-combatants removed to Neuss. The rest of the garrison (some four thousand men) were provided with food and left where they were to face a second siege. It cannot be doubted that Vocula hoped to return before long and relieve the place, which in the meantime would have occupied the attention of part of the enemy's forces. But his intentions are certainly obscure[1], and it is not surprising that the army was discontented and suspected its general of treachery. The relief of Vetera had done little to weaken the enemy, who controlled the river and hampered communications along the road which followed the bank.

Hordeonius Flaccus was quite incapable of controlling the troops who were now concentrated at Neuss. In vain he distributed in the name of Vespasian a sum of money which had been sent by Vitellius. The soldiers dragged the old man from his bed and put him to death; Vocula would have shared his fate if he had

---

[1] See B. W. Henderson, *Civil War and Rebellion*, pp. 276–84.

not disguised himself as a slave. When, however, the news arrived
that the trouble had spread to Upper Germany, and that Mainz
itself was besieged, discipline was to some extent restored, and
Vocula was able to collect an army from soldiers of the First,
Fourth, and Twenty-Second Legions and march south to its relief.
He was successful in defeating the assailants, who expected no
opposition, and Mainz was for the time saved for Rome. But the
situation was very critical. The garrison of Vetera could not be
expected to hold out for long, and the recent events at Neuss had
shown how untrustworthy were the troops on which Vocula was
forced to depend.

As has been said, the appeals of Civilis for assistance had at the
earlier stages of the revolt been rather coldly received by the Gauls.
The Treveri had actually run a palisade round the whole of their
territory, and vigorously repelled a German attack. But after the
murder of Flaccus the discontented elements in the Gallic tribes
considered that the time for action had arrived. The leaders of the
movement were, like Civilis himself, men of high birth, who had
obtained citizenship and had served as officers in the Roman army.
Julius Classicus of the Treveri had commanded a squadron
of his fellow-tribesmen in the advance of Valens on Italy, and
Julius Tutor of the same tribe had been appointed by Vitellius
'prefect of the banks of the Rhine.' The third leader, Julius
Sabinus of the Lingones, claimed descent from Julius Caesar. Encouraged by the news from Italy, and especially by the burning
of the Capitol, which they interpreted as an omen of the downfall
of Roman power, these men did not realize that the success of
Vespasian would be lasting and that he would soon be strong
enough to crush a rebellion. At a secret meeting in Cologne, at
which representatives of the Ubii and the Tungri were present,
they decided to raise their tribes against the Romans. It was
suggested that the troops on the Rhine should be immediately
massacred, but it was ultimately decided to aim at securing their
adhesion and to keep silence until Vocula and the few other
officers of high rank had been disposed of. The conspirators were
evidently sanguine enough to believe that initial success would
bring the whole of Gaul over to their side, and that an 'Imperium
Galliarum' could be created, independent of Rome and ruled presumably by one of themselves. But their plans were not worked
out in detail and were doomed to failure. The rebellion made
little headway outside the tribes to which the leaders belonged.
Sabinus was vigorously opposed by the neighbouring tribe of the
Sequani, and the Treveri were unable to secure the support even

of the Mediomatrici whose territory adjoined their own on the Moselle.

The position of Vocula was now a very terrible one. Though he was aware of what was going on, he felt it his duty to lead his untrustworthy troops to the relief of the garrison of Vetera. At Cologne he dispatched Claudius Labeo, a Batavian rival of Civilis, to stir up trouble among the German tribes, and then advanced north. When he was approaching Vetera Classicus and Tutor thought that the moment had come to show their true colours and deserted to the enemy. Vocula fell back on Neuss with such troops as were prepared to follow him. There after making a fruitless appeal for loyalty to Rome he was murdered by a deserter from the legions sent by Classicus. The two remaining legionary legates were put in chains, and the troops actually swore allegiance to the Gallic Empire. As Mommsen truly says, 'in Roman military history Cannae and Carrhae and the Teutoburg Forest are glorious pages compared with the double disgrace of Novaesium.'

The fate of the wretched garrison of Vetera was soon decided. As all hope of relief had vanished and all food was exhausted the survivors surrendered under promise of their lives. But five miles from the camp they were treacherously attacked, and perished either on the spot or in the flames of the burning fortress. The legionary legate Lupercus was assassinated on his way as an offering to the prophetess Veleda. The soldiers of the First and Sixteenth Legions were sent to Trèves. All the legionary headquarters north of Mainz were set on fire and nowhere on the Rhine was Roman authority recognized. The leaders of the revolt had some difficulty in saving the city of Cologne, which had the status of *colonia*, and where many non-German veterans had been settled, so that it was naturally regarded by the tribes of the right bank as the centre of Roman influence. Accordingly they clamoured for its destruction, but were forced to be content with permission to cross the river under certain conditions and with the abolition of the dues which had been charged on goods entering Roman territory. That the adhesion of Cologne to the rebels was due simply to compulsion is shown by its subsequent behaviour. As soon as the collapse of the revolt seemed to be impending all Germans stationed in the city were murdered and a cohort of Chauci and Frisii left by Civilis in the neighbourhood was rendered intoxicated and burnt to death.

III. THE TURN OF THE TIDE

It was soon clear that the leaders of the Gallic revolt had greatly overestimated the amount of support that they were likely to obtain. When it was known that an army was approaching from across the Alps a conference of representatives of the tribes of Gaul was held in the territory of Rome's old allies the Remi, at which opinion was very definitely hostile to the rebellion. The other Gauls did not forget that the Treveri and Lingones had taken the lead in opposing Vindex, and apart from this the rivalry which existed between the tribes rendered common action impossible. In spite of the opposition of Valentinus, the representative of the Treveri, a letter was sent to that tribe urging the cessation of hostilities. Though no notice was taken of this communication little was done by the rebels to prepare for the impending attack. Civilis wasted time in trying to capture his fellow-countryman Claudius Labeo. Classicus was entirely inactive, and Tutor took no steps to close the Alpine passes.

No want of vigour was shown by Mucianus, the representative of Vespasian in Rome, in dealing with the situation. Two experienced generals, Petilius Cerialis and Annius Gallus, were put at the head of an army which eventually consisted of as many as nine legions, five of which came from Italy, three from Spain, and one from Britain. Gallus was probably instructed to deal with the Lingones and secure Upper Germany, while Cerialis was given the more difficult task of defeating the Treveri and then of advancing north against Civilis and his German allies. An attempt made by Tutor to stop the advance of the Twenty-First Legion and some auxiliary troops from Raetia came to nothing. In spite of a preliminary success he was deserted by the ex-legionaries in his army and by most of the recruits whom he had raised on the Rhine, and was forced to retreat with what remained of his force to a point near Bingen, north of Mainz, where he suffered a second defeat. At this point the Treveri would probably have submitted if they had not been more deeply committed by the action of Tutor and Valentinus in murdering the two surviving legionary legates of the old Rhine army.

Cerialis, who had now reached Mainz, made a good impression by dismissing the recruits who had been raised in Gaul, asserting that Rome could deal with the revolt without Gallic assistance. Deciding that his first duty was to reduce the Treveri, he advanced rapidly to the valley of the Moselle, where at Rigodulum, six miles below Trèves, he easily disposed of the resistance put up by

Valentinus against the advice of Civilis and Classicus. Valentinus himself was captured and sent to Italy for execution. The Roman army occupied Trèves, where it was met by the wretched remains of the First and Sixteenth Legions, whom Cerialis treated with surprising indulgence. He forbade his soldiers to taunt them with their perfidy and included them in his army.

The surviving leaders of the revolt were not prepared to allow the Treveri to submit without making a further effort. The advice of Tutor to attack at once was accepted, though Civilis was in favour of delaying till a large army could be collected from across the Rhine. A surprise attack was made on the Roman camp which had been constructed opposite the town, and only the personal efforts of Cerialis prevented a disaster. His appeal to the repentant legionaries to show their sincerity by fighting bravely was responded to, and when the veteran Twenty-First Legion had a chance of showing its quality the badly disciplined barbarians suffered a severe defeat. The three leaders disappeared to the north, where the arrival of the Fourteenth Legion from Britain rendered their presence necessary; on its approach the Nervii and Tungri had returned to their allegiance and a body of the former tribe had even been armed against the rebels.

The 'Imperium Galliarum' had now completely collapsed, and the only tribes which supported Civilis were those which had begun the revolt. The city of Cologne, as was noted above, abandoned him at once. The wife and sister of Civilis and the daughter of Classicus were seized and held as prisoners. As the presence of Cerialis in the town was urgently required, he proceeded there without delay in order to protect the inhabitants and to avenge certain minor successes gained by the rebels.

The vigour and ability of Civilis were abundantly displayed in the last stage of the rebellion, during which he made a very gallant stand against the army of Cerialis, now reinforced by four legions. A bitter fight took place on the site of Vetera, where the ground had been skilfully flooded so as to hamper the movements of the Romans. Things looked very bad for them till a deserter enabled Cerialis to send round cavalry to take the enemy in the rear. Even when Civilis and his allies retired to the Island the war was far from over. The armies were separated by the river Waal, which had been deepened by the destruction of a mole built by Drusus in 9 B.C. to divert the water of the Rhine from the Waal to the Lek. Across this raids could more easily be made by the Batavians than by the Romans. They captured the fleet which Cerialis brought down the river and for some time completely controlled the stream. When at last Civilis withdrew still farther to the north and the Romans crossed into the Island without opposition the war was over. Both sides were probably anxious to make peace before winter, and so Civilis agreed to a conference with Cerialis on a bridge which spanned one of the numerous rivers of the district. At this point the narrative of Tacitus ends and we do not know what settlement was reached. The fate of Civilis and the other leaders is uncertain. The Batavians were treated with leniency and seem to have been allowed to retain the privileged position which they had occupied before they had been so misguided as to challenge the power of Rome.

The reorganization of the Rhine army which followed the suppression of the revolt shows that Vespasian profited by the lessons which it had taught. The defence of the frontier was entrusted to an almost completely new set of legions, drawn from other parts of the empire, and unlikely to sympathize with any Gallic or German national movement. Of the legions which had been affected by the revolt four were disbanded and one (V Alaudae) was transferred to Moesia. The Twenty-Second was allowed to survive and is found in Lower Germany, possibly as a tribute to the memory of its *legatus* Dillius Vocula. A new legionary camp, garrisoned by the Tenth Legion, was established at Nymwegen in close proximity to the territory of the Batavians. Further, although recruits for the *auxilia* continued to be drawn from Gallic and German tribes, it was no longer considered wise to employ them near their own homes under leaders of their own stock. In the subsequent period units bearing Gallic or German titles are to a much greater extent than before found in other provinces, where as a result of the development of local recruiting they tended to lose their national character (see above, p. 229 *sq*.). The commanders of such troops were normally men who had no ties of blood with the districts with which the units were associated.

No radical change however was made in the policy sketched at the beginning of this chapter. By its means the regions west of the Rhine were gradually linked closer and closer to Rome, and no attempt was made to establish Gallic independence until in the third century the Empire as a whole seemed to be in danger of collapse.

IV. THE ROMAN GOVERNMENT OF PALESTINE[1]

Far different from the issue of the rebellion in the West was to be that of the revolt of the Jews which ran its course about the same time. Palestine continued to be a distracted country. The hatred of the conquered for their conquerors was complicated by the ill-feeling between the upper and lower classes; to the one class, which was more or less resolutely Sadducee, belonged a few priestly families who monopolized the higher offices, especially that of the High Priest, the other was strongly Pharisee in sentiment and supported by most of the lesser priests and the Levites. And since this division involved social questions too, and the lower classes clamoured for some such redistribution of land as the Mosaic law ordered, or dreamed of a communism like that of the Essenes (vol. ix, p. 424 *sq.*), and were already rising to action, the upper classes found their natural protectors in the Romans. In Palestine, as in Greece, Rome protected the great landowners, and for such obvious advantages these were prepared to abate their national pride and to live on terms with the Romans. Not so the populace: their hatred and scorn for their rulers—Gentile, unclean and idolatrous—was only increased by recognition of the fact that Rome was the champion of the rich, a class to whom the Jewish Law in its entirety, whether written or oral, was not a vital matter, and who showed signs of adopting Roman customs, just as in the days of the Seleucid conquest they had adopted Greek. To the ordinary Jew the duty of paying tribute to the Romans, the sight of the Temple commanded by the Roman garrison in the neighbouring Tower of Antonia, the thought that the vestments of the High Priest were in Roman hands (p. 324) and the knowledge that the traditional administration of justice was limited by the intervention of the Roman governor, which was inevitable in spite of the large share left to Jewish courts—all these things were a continual offence.

The complete lack of understanding and consequently of tolerance that most of the Jews evinced for the Romans was matched on the Roman side: indeed the Roman lack of sympathy was so great as to overpower their natural administrative sagacity, which bade them respect the religious traditions of Judaism. If the procurators could not hide their antipathy in their daily con-

[1] The main source for the narrative of this and the following sections is Josephus, *Bell. Jud.*; *Ant.* xx; *Vita.* But the accounts in the *Bell. Jud.* and the *Vita* are often divergent, because Josephus' intention is different in each. Evidence for the reconstruction followed here will be found in the present writer's *Ricerche sull' organizzazione della Giudea sotto il dominio romano.* For the subsidiary sources see the Bibliography. See Map 10, facing p. 317.

tacts with their subjects, far less could their underlings and the soldiers, drawn from the non-Jewish population of Palestine: hence arose numberless small *fracas*, rendered serious simply because the Romans, in conflicts between Jews and non-Jews, usually took (whether rightly or wrongly) the side of the latter. But occasionally the provocation came direct from Rome, and produced not isolated outbreaks but an almost general uprising; such, for example, was the attempt of Gaius to impose the imperial cult on the Jews, and this attempt marked the beginning of a series of disorders that was to culminate in the rebellion of 66. In 36 L. Vitellius had apparently begun a more conciliatory policy (p. 650) but it was rudely interrupted when Gaius determined to set up his own image in the Temple itself (see above, p. 662). So formidable was the feeling aroused that the legate of Syria, P. Petronius, who had been ordered to carry through the erection of the statue, dared not risk it and persuaded Gaius to give up the idea, but this disturbance, reinforced by the news of similar disturbances in other parts of the empire, especially at Alexandria, greatly widened the gulf between Jews and Romans.

The one way of restoring some calm to Judaea was to hand it back to a vassal king of the Jewish faith, for this would give the Jews a feeling of greater autonomy and put an end to the constant friction between governors and governed. This was the solution that Claudius favoured: shortly after his accession he practically reconstituted for his friend Agrippa the old kingdom of Herod the Great (p. 680). Although Agrippa was probably at heart indifferent to Pharisaism, he showed himself able to work in concert with the more orthodox Jews and so has left a good memory of himself in many traditions of the Talmud. The few years of his reign, A.D. 41–4, might really have begun the task of pacification had he not aroused the suspicion of the Romans by a policy of co-operation and agreement with other vassal kings that culminated in the Congress of Tiberias, which was dissolved by the governor of Syria (p. 680 *sq.*). The precise aims of Agrippa must remain doubtful, but the mere hint of a possible coalition between vassal states was enough for Rome to place Judaea again under a procurator when Agrippa died, although his son Agrippa II enjoyed the personal favour of the Emperor and, like his father, was always treated as a sort of representative at court of the interests of the Jews[1].

[1] It is also possible that the bad financial administration of Agrippa I (cf. Josephus, *Ant.* xix [8, 2], 352) helped to bring about the re-absorption of Judaea into the empire.

With the reappearance of the procurators the enmity of the Jews towards Rome flared up again, all the more because the government of Agrippa had been popular whereas the return to Rome looked like a return to slavery; by this sudden attack of prudence Roman statecraft had missed a unique opportunity of securing the tranquillity of Judaea. Doubtless the position was made worse by the incompetence of the several governors, an incompetence which is magisterially rebuked in a solemn and famous sentence of Tacitus[1]; but it is perfectly clear that if their conduct had been contrary to the aims of the government in Rome they could not long have continued in the system. On the other hand, it is equally clear that the fundamental thesis advanced in the *Jewish War* of Josephus—that a minority of extremists overcame the moderate party in Judaea and carried it to rebellion—is only true in the restricted sense that in this, as in all other rebellions, an extremist minority (the so-called Zealots) succeeded in dragging the majority, who thought as they did though with less intensity, in their train. But it is useless to try to allot responsibility between individuals, when the real conflict was between minds incapable of any mutual sympathy, for it was a conflict between the Jewish ideal of a State subordinated to the national religion, and the cosmopolitanism of Imperial Rome in which religion itself was subordinated to the State.

Cuspius Fadus, the procurator in 44, showed at once the line of policy he favoured by demanding the return of the High-Priestly garments whose keeping Vitellius had allowed to the Jews. A long agitation followed until Claudius, on the advice of Agrippa II, definitely recognized the right of the Jews. But the ferment did not cease: the anti-Roman agitations gathered strength and took that Messianic colouring that was peculiar to them; a prophet, Theudas, gathered around him bands of disciples by promising wonders and ended by urging them to rise against Rome. With the speculative uneasiness that beset men of his time Fadus may have feared that Theudas really could work miracles; he had the prophet killed and his head sent to Jerusalem. Owing to the meagreness of our sources we do not know exactly what followed, but obviously discontent increased. However, Rome recognized that Fadus could no longer remain at his post, for he was soon succeeded (the exact date is unknown) by the apostate Jew, Tiberius Alexander, who remained in office until 48: the choice was unfortunate, in view of the

---

[1] *Hist.* v, 10, 'Duravit tamen patientia Iudaeis usque ad Gessium Florum procuratorem: sub eo bellum ortum.'

hatred that Jews felt for apostates. And though we know nothing of his government it is likely that it marked a definite step forward in the discontent of the people, which was aggravated by the famine that began to torment Palestine after the death of Agrippa I.

Under his successor, Ventidius Cumanus (48–52), a soldier who was on guard at the Temple committed an offence during Passover which provoked the gravest riots in Jerusalem. The subsequent murder of an imperial slave brought on reprisals by the Romans, who sacked some villages not far from Jerusalem near which the murder had taken place, and since in the plundering a roll of the Law was profaned, fresh disturbances arose, quieted only by the execution of the offender. Soon after came a second incident: Galilean Jews, on pilgrimage to Jerusalem, were killed by Samaritans; this provoked a mass movement of Jews against Samaria; the procurator failed to arrest its progress and only put it down with bloodshed. The question of culpability for these affairs came before the *legatus* of Syria who could, however, reach no decision, since judgment for Samaritans would have implied censure upon the procurator of Judaea, and so referred the case to Claudius. Claudius decided that Ventidius must be put on his trial and entrusted the inquiry to the governor of Syria and to a brother of the freedman Pallas, Antonius Felix, who had been sent out to Samaria with the rank of procurator. The inquiry led to the execution of the Samaritan leaders and the exile of Ventidius, and Felix was now placed in charge of all Palestine. But even these acts of tardy justice meant a loss of prestige for Rome, which had thus to disown its own official, and the gangs of those extremist Pharisees who had already taken a great part in the attack on the Samaritans emerged from the conflict bolder than before. In these bands the economic agitation, already associated for some time with the political unrest, found its most vigorous expression[1]; they systematically robbed large estate-owners, hence the name of 'brigands' which Josephus gives them.

The new procurator proceeded against these bands at once, but he could not avoid acts which made him personally hated; for example, he took a Jewish princess, Drusilla, sister of Agrippa II, from her lawful husband, Azizus, the judaizing King of Emesa, in order to marry her himself; and even from the Roman side

[1] On the economic situation the statement of Josephus, *Ant.* xx [9,7], 219, that after the completion of the Temple, *c.* A.D. 64, the authorities had to relay the streets of Jerusalem, in order to provide fresh employment for the workmen, is very significant.

severe judgments were passed upon him. Though the 'brigands' were dispersed, they arose again in another form as 'Men of the Knife,' fanatics armed with daggers who gave up attacks on landed estates and took to ambushing and murdering the friends of Rome. The refusal to pay tribute became more general and Messianic hopes spread more widely than ever; while they helped to feed Christianity, they also filled up the ranks of the rebels. An Egyptian Jew succeeded in gathering several thousands around him on the Mount of Olives by promising to cause the fall of the walls of Jerusalem: during the governorship of Porcius Festus, who succeeded Felix about 60, another visionary promised freedom from all evils to all who would follow him to the desert. Both these bands could only be dispersed by the aid of Roman soldiers. And now there began outbreaks between the Jews and the Gentile inhabitants of Palestine. Long quarrels accompanied the Jewish claim to rights of equal citizenship (*isopoliteia*) at Caesarea, and Nero's decision against them served only to increase their hatred. Internal conflicts between the priestly classes to secure the rights of tithe also grew more bitter. In the days of Felix the High Priest Jonathan was killed by the 'Men of the Knife.' Josephus asserts that the assassins acted on the instructions of the procurator Felix, who for the moment was in agreement with them, an assertion which is naturally difficult to control and not made by Josephus in his preceding work[1]; but whether this is true or not, it is beyond doubt that the High Priesthood, though philo-Roman, was never really in complete understanding with the procurators, possibly owing to personal antipathies, but above all because the violent partisan quarrels in the High Priesthood could not be favoured by Rome since they only aggravated the situation. An example of this turbulence was the action of the High Priest Ananus in the period that intervened between the death of Festus and the arrival of the new procurator, Albinus (? 62–4). He summarily condemned his opponents, among whom apparently was James, the brother of Jesus, and had to be deposed scarcely three months after he had taken office.

The situation was further complicated because, perhaps in 61, Rome had added a part of Galilee and of Peraea to the realms of Agrippa II (p. 338), and had moreover granted him the power to appoint or dismiss the High Priest that Herod of Chalcis had enjoyed after the death of Agrippa I. Although he was in agreement with the Priesthood in its general aims, his

[1] Josephus, *Ant.* xx [2, 1], 62 compared with *Bell. Jud.* ii [13, 3], 256.

control provoked ill-will such as is revealed in an absurd episode which, however, gave rise to a diplomatic incident of some importance in the time of Festus. In order to prevent Agrippa from watching from his palace all that was happening in the precincts of the Temple, the priests built a high wall. Agrippa, supported by Festus, protested. The decision was left to Nero, who solved the matter by a compromise, allowing the wall to remain but detaining the High Priest Ishmael, who had gone to Rome personally to plead his cause, and so giving Agrippa the chance of making another appointment. If we add that Agrippa, like his father, could never remain in lasting agreement with the Romans, because as a Jew and representative of Jewish interests he was influenced by the nationalism of his co-religionists, we shall realize how many contradictory elements there were to weaken the forces in favour of Rome, which were already in a minority. The continual changes in the High Priesthood show clearly the weakness of the philo-Roman party, and were in turn a cause of the final weakness of the Priesthood itself.

V. THE JEWISH REBELLION

Albinus, who succeeded the unimportant governor Festus, initiated in his brief term a policy of mildness which caused him to be accused of corruption[1]. But the next procurator, Gessius Florus (64–6), returned to the policy of a strong hand, and so gave the final impulse to the rebellion. In 66 he confiscated seventeen talents from the Temple treasury, possibly as a partial set-off for alleged arrears of tribute; but this pretext, apart from having no legal basis, so shocked the religious sentiment of the people that they broke into riot. Gessius replied by allowing a cohort to plunder some quarters of Jerusalem, and this is the moment (16th Artemision, about May) from which Josephus makes the Jewish war against Rome begin. In reality the inhabitants of Jerusalem were prepared to make the submission which Gessius demanded, and to welcome honourably two cohorts which came up from Caesarea. But apparently these cohorts were not responsive and behaved arrogantly, and this provoked a new outburst, during which the people succeeded in cutting the communications between the Tower of Antonia and the Temple where fortifications were being run up. Gessius had to withdraw from Jerusalem leaving there one of the cohorts as reinforcement for the garrison.

---

[1] The estimates Josephus gives of Albinus' work in *Bell. Jud.* II [14, 1], 272 *sqq.* and in *Ant.* xx [9, 2], 204 *sqq.* are at variance. But the facts seem to justify the interpretation given in the text.

Agrippa II hastened back from Alexandria, hoping to move the people from their attitude, but all in vain: the crowd demanded the suspension of the daily sacrifice for the Emperor, and succeeded in storming the fortress of Masada, on the western bank of the Dead Sea (the modern Sebbeh), and did not even give way when 3000 of Agrippa's cavalry, who were stationed in the upper city where Herod's palace lay, arrived to reinforce the peace party. The mob now captured the Tower of Antonia and drove from it the garrison, which took refuge in some towers of the palace of Herod, and even this was besieged. Agrippa's little force soon surrendered, glad to withdraw with the honours of war; shortly after the Roman garrison followed, and at this same time (about September 66) the High Priest Ananias also fell a victim.

The rebellion spread over all Palestine; Jews and non-Jews set about killing each other; the effects were even felt in Alexandria where Tiberius Alexander had great difficulty in repressing a revolt of the Jews. In Caesarea, in Scythopolis, and finally in Tyre, the Jews were massacred until the troops that the governor of Syria, Cestius Gallus, sent into Palestine to restore calm had to turn and safeguard Jews and non-Jews alike. But the Jews greeted them as enemies, and began fortifying Jerusalem; though Cestius had with him the whole of the Twelfth Legion (Fulminata), numerous detachments from other legions and a large body of auxiliaries, and although he reached the gates of Jerusalem, he did not dare assault it for he feared an attack on his flanks. He finally decided to withdraw, but well-timed sallies of the Jews converted his withdrawal into a rout, and at Beth-horon he had to leave in their hands his baggage train and his artillery (November 66), a prize which was to prove of great value during the actual siege.

So unexpected and so sensational a success naturally strengthened the hands of the war-party; their opponents dared not proclaim themselves openly and even thought it advisable to express approval for fear of losing control over the country. So the High Priest's party, although it had been notoriously on the side of peace, decided to assume the direction of the war which it now considered inevitable. Palestine was divided into various military zones, each under a commander, and the defence of Jerusalem was entrusted to Ananus, the ex-High Priest, who had his own reasons for enmity to the Romans[1], and to Joseph the son of

---

[1] See p. 854. For the importance of the ex-High Priest at this time cf. J. Jeremias, *Jerusalem zur Zeit Jesu*, p. 14 sq.

Gorion. But the lukewarm spirit in which they undertook the war can be gauged by their choice of a general, or of one of the generals[1], for the important district of Galilee, which was likely to bear the brunt of the Roman offensive: they sent there a young priest, barely thirty years old, Joseph son of Matthias, the future historian Flavius Josephus. Born about A.D. 37 he had passed through the schools of the Pharisees, Sadducees and Essenes, and had then spent three years in the desert under an ascetic called Banus, but after that had returned to civil life and gained some reputation as a Pharisee of moderate and philo-Roman views. He had therefore been sent to Rome to win pardon for some priests imprisoned there, had won the favour of Poppaea through a Jewish mime at the court, and finally succeeded in his mission. The dispatch of a philo-Roman general to Galilee showed that the government had no desire for war to the bitter end with Rome, and was merely manœuvring to find the best mode of concluding an honourable peace. But in the agitated state of the country such a policy of compromise could never succeed, and this is clearly shown by what happened in Galilee, the only district upon which Josephus gives us information. Confused and contradictory though this information is it probably represents well enough the complications of the situation, which must have been matched in the rest of Palestine. The rivalries of the different cities, of different classes, and of individuals, and their attitude, alternately favourable and unfavourable, towards Agrippa II (to whom a part of Galilee belonged), meant that neither anti-Romans nor philo-Romans could agree among themselves.

On his arrival in Galilee Josephus was soon drawn into the maelstrom. His chief support he found in the moderate elements which were scattered about the country and were specially strong in Taricheia, a city that had revolted from Agrippa II. But he had difficulties with all his supporters, even in Taricheia; for instance, on one occasion, Josephus, who had no wish to antagonize Agrippa, appropriated some plunder that had been taken from one of the king's officials, with the intention of returning it; but his action provoked riots in Taricheia which he could only appease by making the populace believe that he was going to use the money on building new walls for the city. Naturally the more fervent zealots were against Josephus; from their centre at Gischala, where their leader, John, son of Levi, was tyrant, they aimed at bringing Galilee under their sway. To defend

---

[1] Josephus, in *Bell. Jud.* II [20, 4], 568, asserts he was the only general, while in *Vita* [7], 29 he mentions two colleagues.

himself against these Josephus had to stoop to an alliance with gangs of 'bandits' whom he took into his pay, but upon whose loyalty he could not absolutely rely; these bandits were probably zealots who had found that John, rich merchant as he was, could not at that time accept their whole programme[1]. Among the cities in which John had the largest following was Tiberias, which had also broken away from Agrippa II; here his influence was only limited by a strong philo-Roman minority. True there was yet another party in the city, a more moderate one, headed by Justus, son of Pistus, but Josephus could not avail himself of it owing to his personal enmity with its head, an enmity that was to develop into a literary rivalry too, for afterwards Justus published his own account of the war.

This rivalry also paralyzed the party of Justus, and owing to his awkward situation he swayed now towards John of Gischala, now towards Agrippa; thus Josephus found himself, in Tiberias at any rate, obliged to put down extremist movements whether anti-Roman or philo-Roman. In addition one city, Sepphoris, remained loyal to Rome and though once occupied by Josephus freed itself and admitted a garrison sent there by Cestius; another city, Gamala in Gaulanitis, which had also revolted from Agrippa, was besieged by his troops without success for seven months and could not be used effectively by Josephus as a unit in his defensive scheme; and finally disturbances arose in every place almost as soon as the Roman troops of Cestius drew near in their raids.

The central government at Jerusalem meanwhile was doing nothing to help; instead, whether from dissatisfaction at his work or because it was gradually coming under extremist influences, it decided to send four commanders into Galilee to replace Josephus. Josephus was fully equal to maintaining his own position by a dexterous use of his friends against the newcomers, but this episode too only helped to increase the general confusion. Naturally enough he was unable not only to offer any systematic opposition to the Romans, but to give any aid to his government apart from defending his own position. Such was the situation when Nero, in February 67, appointed Titus Flavius Vespasianus with the rank of *legatus* to carry on the war.

---

[1] For a commercial speculation of his see Josephus, *Vita* [13], 74–76: he may possibly, at first, have been pro-Roman, as Josephus says *Vita* [10], 43; but cf. the observations of A. Baerwald, *Flavius Josephus in Galiläa*, p. 44.

VI. THE CAMPAIGNS OF VESPASIAN

Vespasian started off at once and picked up two legions at Antioch, the Vth (Macedonica) and the Xth (Fretensis). Then at Ptolemaïs he met his son Titus, who was bringing with him the XVth (Apollinaris) from Egypt. With the auxiliary cohorts, the cavalry squadrons and the militia of the client-kings (among whom naturally was Agrippa) his army must have amounted to some 50,000 or 60,000 men. By the beginning of June he was already on the frontier of Galilee and began a series of campaigns characterized by extreme prudence and great care in keeping his army united as far as possible. Such tactics, though they prolonged the war, were justified by the extreme pugnacity which the Jews, in spite of their internal dissensions, displayed, preferring a species of guerilla warfare, especially in each city, to open fighting, where the Roman superiority was indisputable. Open fighting scarcely occurred at all; Josephus tried to concentrate his army near the village of Garis, two and a half miles from Sepphoris, where Vespasian had placed a garrison of 6000 men; but it melted away before coming to blows, and with the remainder he had to take refuge in the hill-fortress of Jotapata, north of Sepphoris, where for forty-seven days in June and July he was besieged by Vespasian. When it was captured, he and forty companions took refuge in an underground reservoir, and decided to kill each other, in accordance with the established custom not to fall into the hands of the enemy. But Josephus, probably by a trick, succeeded in being one of the last two left and persuaded his companion to surrender with him to the Romans. Brought before Vespasian he attracted his attention by prophesying his elevation to the throne, and for this he obtained a pardon that, when the prophecy came true, was changed into open good-will and the gift of his freedom[1].

Meanwhile the Romans, after a brief rest at Caesarea, resumed the struggle in Galilee, where the opposition was now broken up into various local units; while Tiberias immediately opened its gates, Taricheia, Gischala, and, above all, Gamala made a fierce resistance which protracted matters until late autumn. After wintering at Caesarea, in the spring of 68 Vespasian began the encirclement of Jerusalem, occupying with

---

[1] The fact that Talmudic tradition credits Johanan ben Zakkai with the same prophecy does not lessen the trustworthiness of Josephus' statement, backed as it is by Suetonius, *Vesp.* 5 and Dio LXVI, 1, 4, and so probably contained in the Memoirs of Vespasian.

ease Samaria, Peraea, Idumaea, and the coast region of Judaea, properly so called. By June a few isolated hill-fortresses such as Herodium, Masada and Machaerus (in Peraea) alone remained in the hands of the Jews, but as Vespasian was preparing for the final attack upon Jerusalem the news of Nero's suicide (June 68) determined him to suspend operations until his command was confirmed by Nero's successor. The succeeding complications resulted in his remaining inactive for a whole year, until June 69.

The Jews used this interval not only to strengthen the defences of Jerusalem but also to begin the struggle again in the rest of Judaea. But this bold effort was practically useless because they were incapable of organizing an army that could oppose the Romans. In fact, the struggle became mere brigandage upon the Romans in which Simon bar Giora ('son of the proselyte') won great fame; his most successful *coup* was the occupation of Hebron, from which he gained much booty. Even more damaging to the Jews than their military incompetence were their internal dissensions. By the end of 67 the concentration in Jerusalem of gangs of zealots who had been hunted out of the rest of Palestine gave the upper hand to the extremists who were still dominated by John of Gischala with his band. All whom he suspected of philo-Roman tendencies he imprisoned or killed; for a high priest nominated from one of the aristocratic priestly families he substituted one drawn by lot. The moderate elements, headed by some of these dispossessed priestly families and helped by the population, which naturally had suffered much from the lawless bands that were camping in the city, attempted counter-measures, but though the zealots were at first driven back into the inner court of the Temple they succeeded in admitting secretly into the city bands of Idumaeans who were certainly inspired not so much by hatred of Rome as by loathing for the Jewish upper classes, whom they thought responsible for their oppression. With their aid John of Gischala made himself master of the whole city and drove out his opponents[1].

There was no change in the situation till the spring of 69 when the band of Simon bar Giora, who found his raids in the country severely hampered, entered the city. The inhabitants at first gave him a warm welcome, but soon realized from the quarrels that immediately followed between the rival captains that they had

---

[1] The Christian community took no part in these struggles. It must have left early, and have withdrawn to the Greek city of Pella in Peraea, where it remained undisturbed during the whole war.

gained nothing by opposing Simon to John. In the reaction a third party of local zealots, headed by Eleazar, son of Simon, was formed and barricaded itself in the Temple; the rest of the hill to the east, upon which the Temple stood (the lower city), with the Tower of Antonia, was in the hands of John, and Simon occupied the western hill (the upper city). Partisan fury rose to such a height that the reserves of corn in the city were destroyed.

VII. THE SIEGE AND FALL OF JERUSALEM

Meanwhile, in June 69, after the victory of Vitellius, Vespasian decided to take the field again, reoccupied Hebron, and restored order throughout all the territory around Jerusalem; but once more the war was interrupted owing to the proclamation of Vespasian as *princeps* which occurred shortly after (p. 829). The command was transferred to Titus, but after long delays in Alexandria and Caesarea he only really began operations in the spring of 70. His three legions, whose effective strength had been lowered by the dispatch of detachments to the West with Mucianus, were reinforced by the Twelfth Legion which was recalled to share in the campaign, and Tiberius Alexander, with his valuable experience of Jewish circles, was appointed chief of staff[1]. The siege of Jerusalem was now begun without delay. Upon the approach of the enemy internal quarrels broke out for a moment with even greater violence, possibly because the various leaders realized that they must eliminate their rivals in order to gain the necessary unity in defence. At the Passover John of Gischala succeeded in penetrating into the Temple and removing Eleazar. Even now, in spite of the decimation of the peace party, a few dared advise peace, but naturally they were forced to keep silence; it was probably at this moment that the most notable of them, the famous teacher and Pharisee, John, the son of Zakkai (Johanan ben Zakkai), succeeded in escaping in a coffin, according to tradition, to the Roman camp. The danger that had now become pressing owing to the Roman attack upon the so-called third encircling wall, that surrounded both the city and also the suburb of Bezetha, warned John and Simon that they must come to an agreement; the first continued to maintain the defence of the Tower of Antonia and of the Temple, the second that of the upper city.

[1] An inscription from Aradus, *O.G.I.S.* 586, calls him ἐπ]άρχου τοῦ Ἰουδαι[κοῦ στρατοῦ].

Thus the defence was reinforced, but none the less it did not prove possible to prevent the third wall from falling into the hands of the Romans by May. Five days later the second wall fell and the Romans began their attack on the more elaborate system of fortifications that made up the first wall. Two legions were launched against the upper city and two against the Tower of Antonia, while Josephus, who was now on the staff of Titus, vainly advised the besieged to surrender. The Jews succeeded at first in destroying the platforms raised by the besiegers, but they could not prevent their reconstruction or the building of a wall of circumvallation which was designed to cut off all provisions. In spite of heroic attempts to destroy these works, in June the Tower of Antonia fell and siege was laid to the Temple, which was defended by its own system of fortifications. The daily sacrifices in the Temple had at last to be suspended and the agony of famine began. In August, on the day that corresponds to the 9th Ab in the Jewish calendar, the Roman troops succeeded in firing the gate of the Temple and broke into it. Jewish tradition treats this day as that of the destruction of the Temple; in reality it was not until the next day, apparently on the order of Titus himself[1], that the Temple was burnt by the soldiers and a terrible massacre began. The head of the resistance, John of Gischala, with a band of his soldiers succeeded in retreating safely into the upper city, which continued to be defended, since it was separated from the lower city by a wall.

Upon this all the efforts of the Roman soldiery were now turned, once Titus refused to grant the right of free departure which the besieged claimed as a condition of surrender. The struggle ended in September amid scenes of renewed slaughter and with the almost complete destruction of the city. Simon bar Giora was taken to Rome to be killed at the foot of the Capitol in the victors' triumph; John of Gischala was spared, but spared for imprisonment for life. Titus returned to Italy with his booty, among which was the table of the Shewbread and the seven-branched candlestick which had been saved from the burning Temple; afterwards, apparently, these were carried by Genseric's Vandals to Africa, where they were recaptured by Belisarius and

---

[1] Sulpicius Severus, *Chron.* II, 30, in a passage deriving from Tacitus, asserts that Titus gave a deliberate order for the destruction of the Temple. This passage has undergone Christian modification, but this modification affects only the reasons for Titus' decision and not the decision itself. Josephus' denial, *Bell. Jud.* VI [4, 3], 241, is clearly tendencious.

taken to Constantinople. Titus celebrated his triumph, together
with his father and his brother Domitian, in 71[1]. But the struggle
in Palestine was not yet finished, for the three fortresses of Herodium, Machaerus and Masada continued to hold out. The new
governor, Lucilius Bassus, who, like Vespasian, was of senatorial
rank, received the task of reducing them, which passed to his
successor, Flavius Silva. Herodium was easily captured; not so
Machaerus, whose defenders in the end were allowed to leave
with the honours of war. The resistance of Masada, in which a
group of Sicarii under the command of Eleazar, son of Jairus, had
taken refuge, was prolonged until April 73, and when further
resistance appeared impossible its defenders killed themselves.

Outside Palestine the destruction of Jerusalem had not the
immediate echoes that might be expected. The Roman government had to put down outbursts of anti-Semitic feeling here and
there, as at Antioch, and rapidly put an end to Jewish disorders
in Cyrene and in Egypt. But it created a complicated and deplorable state of feeling that was to find an outlet fifty years later
in the time of Trajan and Hadrian.

From the purely juridical point of view the status of Judaea was
little altered. It remained, as before, a separate province, though
its equestrian procurator was now made subordinate to a *legatus*,
of senatorial rank, who commanded the Tenth Legion (Fretensis), which was left there as a garrison. Caesarea continued to
be the seat of the governor, though now raised to the rank of a
colony with the title of Colonia Prima Flavia Augusta Caesarensis.
The Jews outside Palestine and those in Palestine who had
supported Rome naturally retained their status as ordinary provincials. Those who had fought but escaped death or enslavement, and so were regarded as *dediticii*, must soon have been
merged in the remainder of the Jewish people, so that, generally
speaking, apart from the multitude of slaves, the *status civitatis* of
the Jews was not permanently altered[2]. But within this framework
their lot was radically changed. Landed property in Palestine
underwent a profound transformation, though much of the truth

---

[1] The present Arch of Titus was only erected after his death: the inscription on another arch, now non-existent, erected in his lifetime has been
preserved; see Dessau 264.

[2] For example, the 40,000 of *Bell. Jud.* vi [8, 2], 386 were certainly
dediticii. See J. Juster, *Les Juifs dans l'empire romain*, ii, p. 19 and
A. Büchler, *The economic condition of Judaea after the destruction of the
second Temple*, p. 3.

about it remains obscure. Apparently the whole territory, apart from some portions of Galilee and Peraea, which had belonged to Agrippa II and were now restored to him with some undefined extension[1], became imperial domain. Most of this land was farmed out, some districts near Jerusalem served for the army of occupation, 800 veterans were assigned lots at Emmaus, about three miles from Jerusalem (not to be confused with Emmaus Nicopolis), and there were the usual grants to those whom the Emperor favoured; here Josephus profited, since he was able to withdraw to Rome and enjoy there the pension and the rights of Roman citizenship that Vespasian bestowed on him. All the cities that had resisted the Romans were sacked and partially destroyed, while those of their citizens who had been captured were sold into slavery: still there were many fugitives to spread abroad the seeds of future revolts.

The most serious measure of all remains to be mentioned: by abolishing the Sanhedrin and the High Priesthood and by forbidding the resumption of the worship of the Temple at Jerusalem the Romans destroyed the political and religious centre of Judaism. Even the schismatic temple at Leontopolis in Egypt (vol. VIII, p. 517) was closed in 73, although it was in decay, in order to prevent its becoming a centre of attraction after the closing of the Jerusalem Temple. A seal was set on this severance of the ties that bound Jews to their centre by an order diverting the poll-tax of two drachmae, that they had been accustomed to pay to the Temple of Jerusalem, to the temple of Capitoline Juppiter instead: from this arose the *fiscus Judaicus*. But this does not mean that the existence of the Jewish nation was no longer recognized: the religious privileges that the Jews originally enjoyed were maintained, and since they passed on to successive generations they presuppose the recognition of the national unity of the Jews. Further, the creation of the *fiscus Judaicus*, clearly on the same lines as the *fiscus Asiaticus* and the *fiscus Alexandrinus*, implies the recognition of the Jews as a separate entity. There is no proof that the Jews of the Diaspora lost particular rights in any place where, as for example at Alexandria, they already possessed them. Far more serious was the fact that even those who had taken no part in the war were subjected to the humiliation of a payment to Capitoline Juppiter[2].

---

[1] Photius, *Bibl.* 33.

[2] The inscription from Smyrna, of Hadrianic date (*I.G.R.R.* IV, 1431), in which are mentioned οἱ ποτὲ Ἰουδαῖοι, reflects a purely local state of affairs, and no generalizations can be drawn from it. They may possibly be converted Jews.

From the point of view simply of the religious development of Judaism the destruction of the Temple marked the end of a process that had been in operation from at least the days of the Maccabees. With the abolition of the High Priesthood and of the Sanhedrin Sadduceeism vanished, and Pharisaism—with its characteristic institution of the Rabbi—was left triumphant. A few saw this clearly and believed that a fresh field for development lay open to Judaism: the representative of this school of thought was Johanan ben Zakkai who during the siege of Jerusalem persuaded Vespasian to grant him leave to open a school at Jamnia, which became a new centre for Judaism; so much so that later Jews were to look on it as a new Sanhedrin. But the great majority of the people, although they might find satisfaction for their religious needs in the Synagogue which henceforth took the place of the Temple, could not easily accept the humiliation of defeat, the most galling mark of which was the ruin of the Temple. The Temple that they no longer needed for their religion lived on as a symbol of their nation and the memory of the Temple was to inspire all the struggles and all the Messianic hopes of the succeeding centuries.

APPENDIX

THE LITERARY AUTHORITIES FOR ROMAN HISTORY
44 B.C.–A.D. 70.

The purpose of this Appendix is to give a short valuation of the ancient literary authorities whose works have been used in writing the history of the period covered by this volume, 44 B.C.–A.D. 70, and also to give some indication of the material that was available to them, though it is now lost to us. It would, however, be impossible, save at great space, to enumerate all the writers, and here will be found only the more important; for lesser names, and for more elaborate treatment of Source-Criticism, the reader is referred to the standard histories of Greek and Roman Literature and to the articles mentioned in the bibliographies to the various chapters. No treatment of epigraphic or numismatic material is attempted, though Augustus' *Res Gestae* is regarded as a 'literary' document: similarly the chronographic writers, Jerome, Eusebius, Syncellus, and the like, will not be found here. The evidence afforded by the jurists (whose writings will be treated of in Volume XI) is also not discussed. It should be noted, too, that as the value and trustworthiness of an author may vary according to the period he is describing, the verdicts here passed hold simply for the period of the present volume. Sources that have not survived are discussed before those that are still existent, and Latin authors before those who wrote in Greek.

Non-existent Sources

(a) Latin

For the early period one of the most important names is that of ASINIUS POLLIO (75 B.C.–A.D. 4), statesman, general, and patron of artists and men of letters. He was no respecter of persons or reputations and no detractor of his own performance. His *History*, which began with 60 B.C., certainly included events down to the Battle of Philippi, and may have extended as far as the defeat and death of Sextus Pompeius, which Octavian proclaimed as the end of Civil War. Some of his prejudices and hatreds can still be discerned in the pages of Appian, who draws largely from him.

LIVY is also completely lacking, and the meagre *Epitome* helps little save to show (when compared with the *Res Gestae* of Augustus) that, though he could treat Pompey with respect, he was wise enough to be orthodox in his sympathies towards the parties that fought at Actium. It could hardly be otherwise, yet the loss of Books CXVI–CXLII in which he narrated fully the events between 44 and 9 B.C. is indeed grievous, and can scarcely be compensated by the shorter account of Dio Cassius, who draws largely upon him. Both from Pollio and from Livy we should have had a fullness of treatment and a moderation in tone which are not to be found in their lesser brethren.

AUFIDIUS BASSUS lived into the reign of Nero, and apparently wrote two works, a history of the Roman wars against the Germans, and an annalistic history; of the first work nothing is known, the second certainly included the death of Cicero, and went down at least as far as the consulship of Tiberius and Sejanus, A.D. 31. It may have gone farther, possibly to A.D. 47, for from the title that the younger Pliny gives to his uncle's *History—a fine Aufidii Bassi*—it has been conjectured that Aufidius stopped at some point in the course of a reign and not at the death of a *princeps*. Of his political views we know nothing, though various conjectures have been made. A contemporary of his, M. SERVILIUS NONIANUS, who made a name for himself as an orator, also wrote a history, but no fragments have survived unless Suetonius, *Tib.* 61, can be ascribed to him. Both men probably published their works in the last years of Claudius or early years of Nero, and both had considerable repute, but they can be little more than names to us.

A. CREMUTIUS CORDUS, a Senator who lived through the reign of Augustus, later apparently offended Sejanus by his outspokenness and wit, and in his old age was put on trial by two of the Prefect's creatures (A.D. 25). He was accused of praising Brutus and of calling Cassius 'the last of the Romans' (p. 630): he defended the independent attitude he had adopted, but preferred to commit suicide rather than await the issue of the trial. His *Annales* seem to have embraced the period of the Civil Wars and of Augustus, and to have been moderately Republican in tone, but if he really 'proscribentis in aeternum proscripsit' (Seneca, *ad Marciam*, 26, 1), he cannot have been quite as inoffensive as our sources suggest. Greater interest attaches to CLUVIUS RUFUS. Born about the beginning of the Christian era, an orator of distinction, favoured by Nero but not abusing his influence, he took part in the Civil Wars of 68–70, and probably wrote his History after Vespasian's accession. If we accept Mommsen's hypothesis that Josephus, *Ant. Jud.* XIX, 1–270, is based upon him, we possess something whereby to judge his attitude and manner: combining this with other fragments we may conjecture that his history, like his life, showed a prudent moderation towards the Principate, and that he would not repeat the worst even about Gaius or Nero; its limits are unknown but may plausibly be reckoned from the death of Augustus to the accession of Vespasian. His work was certainly used later by Tacitus, Suetonius, and Dio Cassius, and was probably of major importance. Less known is an elder contemporary of Tacitus and the younger Pliny, FABIUS RUSTICUS, a distinguished orator and a protégé of Seneca. The surviving fragments suggest that he consistently upheld Seneca's character and blackened Nero's. His work was probably published some time between 74 and 83 —he seems unaware that Britain is an island—and it has been conjectured that it comprised events between the battle of Actium and the death of Nero.

Among these shadowy personalities C. PLINIUS SECUNDUS (the Elder Pliny) stands out in strong contrast, a useful public servant and an indefatigable worker and writer, whose life extended from A.D. 23–4 to 79. In history his two important works were *Bellorum Germaniae libri XX* and *a fine Aufidii Bassi XXXI*. From the surviving fragments of them and from the historical allusions in his encyclopaedic *Historia Naturalis* it is not difficult to guess his outlook: moderate and practical, he approved the rule of Augustus, Claudius and Vespasian, regarded Tiberius as 'the gloomiest of mortals,' and reserved his severer judgments for the extravagance of Gaius, and especially of Nero, 'faex generis humani et hostis.' It is possible that his thirty-one books *a fine Aufidii Bassi* began *c.* A.D. 47, and went down to 70 or 71. There can be no doubt that he was one of the main sources for Tacitus in the later books of the *Annals* (see *Ann.* XIII, 20, where Cluvius Rufus and Fabius Rusticus are also mentioned), even though Tacitus apparently sneers at his passion for trivial detail or improbable rumours (*Ann.* XIII, 31; XV, 53), and it is extremely likely that he is the authority who underlies the remarkable agreement observable between Plutarch, Tacitus and Suetonius, in narrating the events of 69 and 70. The fullness of his work and the fact that he was contemporary with the happenings that he described, the good geographical information contained in the *Historia Naturalis* and the tantalizing occasional references there, make the total loss of this work grievous indeed.

A few other writers are mentioned in our surviving sources: Bruttedius Niger, Cn. Cornelius Lentulus Gaetulicus, the Elder Seneca, Julius Secundus (to whom Plutarch owes some details about Otho), Pompeius Planta (who wrote of the Civil War of A.D. 69–70), and Tib. Claudius Balbillus, a prefect of Egypt. Yet though the Elder Seneca wrote Histories, it remains extremely doubtful if they were ever published, and the fragments usually ascribed to him may really be his son's. And whether the others were writing history or occasional pieces is difficult to ascertain, and cannot be decided unless fresh evidence is discovered.

So much for historians proper. There remains a long list of others who, while they did not write professed history, yet provided materials for historians by composing *Commentarii*, memoirs or 'experiences,' as they might now be called. Chief among them is the Emperor AUGUSTUS who wrote an account of his own life and deeds in thirteen books down to the Cantabrian War (probably to the end of 25 B.C.). The few surviving fragments suggest that the work was intended (naturally enough) to promote his fame and good name, but it is rash to infer (as some critics do) that therefore Augustus' account must invariably be wrong and that of his enemies right. Its influence must have been immense on Augustan writers, such as Nicolaus of Damascus, Livy and Velleius; later, Plutarch, Pliny, Suetonius, Appian and Dio Cassius all use it as a storehouse for quotation with varying comments. The Emperor TIBERIUS also composed a Memoir 'summatim breviterque' in his old age, again justificatory, though Suetonius (*Tib.* 61) rejects the one statement he specifically quotes from it. More important were those of the Emperor CLAUDIUS, who described his own early days, and probably the first years of his reign: it is perhaps to these that Suetonius owes the detailed knowledge he displays of his legislation and measures. His other numerous learned works, though used by the elder Pliny and Tacitus, were not concerned with the history of the period. The Emperor VESPASIAN, too, wrote an account of his life and exploits, including possibly those in Britain, and certainly those in Judaea. Another of the imperial writers was Agrippina the Younger, 'quae Neronis principis mater vitam suam et casus suorum posteris memoravit' (Tacitus, *Ann.* IV, 53). It is reasonable to suppose that a writer who is cited by Tacitus for Tiberius' rudeness to the elder Agrippina, and by Pliny for an incident of the birth of Nero, is largely responsible for the favourable picture of Germanicus and the darker one of Tiberius that have survived in later writers, and that as she glorified her father, so she did what she could to augment the fame of her son Nero, by stories about his sun-blest birth and miraculous escapes from dangers (Suetonius, *Nero*, 6 and Tacitus, *Ann.* XI, 11).

There must now be noticed a number of men who served with distinction in war and were prepared to record it. Q. DELLIUS, an officer who knew when to desert a losing cause, was an eye-witness of Antony's campaigns against Parthia, for which he was drawn upon by Plutarch, and helped to swell the chorus of hate and detraction against Cleopatra. C. SUETONIUS PAULINUS is cited for details of his Mauretanian campaigns (though not of his British) by Pliny, as is CN. DOMITIUS CORBULO, one of Nero's most distinguished victims, for details of his campaigns in Armenia, both by Pliny and Tacitus. It is possible that C. LICINIUS MUCIANUS contributed information about the campaigns of A.D. 68–70, in which he was the champion of the Flavian cause, but Pliny only cites him for marvels and wonders. Finally, M. VIPSTANUS MESSALLA, who also took the Flavian side in the Civil War, is quoted once by Tacitus, and ANTONIUS JULIANUS, who was a commander in the Jewish War under Titus, apparently commemorated his experiences in a book *de Iudaeis*. Tenuous though much of the evidence is, it yet possesses importance as helping to show how vast a mass of literature there must have been to read through, consult and criticize, before Tacitus could begin writing his *Histories* or his *Annals*, or Suetonius his *Lives*.

A class of its own is formed by pamphlets or broadsheets in praise of or attacking some prominent figure, or written for a party purpose. The *Philippics* of Cicero are an outstanding example of this class, but there were many more, now fortunately unknown: Antony in his *de ebrietate sua* and Augustus in his *de vita sua* did not hesitate, while defending their own conduct, to throw the vilest charges at one another. They were naturally backed up, and often outdone, by their supporters. Antony had Cassius of Parma, and possibly such men as Aquilius Niger and Julius Saturninus, whom Suetonius quotes for charges against Augustus (*Aug.* 11 and 27). Augustus had the support of the constant Caesarian C. Oppius, and of those who deserted to him, Q. Dellius, Sextus Titius and Munatius Plancus, while Cornelius Nepos (? in his *Exempla*) praised his temperance, Julius Marathus and C. Drusus recounted the wonders that had accompanied his birth and childhood, and Baebius Macer told of the *sidus Iulium* that was thought to have appeared for his glory. But there were not wanting men to glorify the lost cause of the aristocratic Republic and its last champions: L. Calpurnius Bibulus, P. Volumnius, and a Greek rhetorician, Empylus, all wrote praises of Brutus, and in the reign of Tiberius praise of Brutus and Cassius proved fatal to Cremutius Cordus, as did a *Life of Cato* to P. Clodius Thrasea Paetus in Nero's reign. Indeed, Thrasea Paetus and others of Nero's victims in their turn found biographers and admirers, for L. Junius Arulenus Rusticus wrote a life of Thrasea which roused the anger of Domitian, and Pliny the Younger laments the untimely death of C. Fannius, who was composing a monograph on the fate of those 'occisorum aut relegatorum a Nerone.' How much of this pamphleteering underlies Tacitus' *Annals* we can only guess, but it certainly has a share.

(b) Greek

In the Eastern half of the Empire there must have been many—local historians, city-chroniclers, collectors of the marvellous—who served as sources for existent writers. Here it is only necessary to mention three of the chief, Nicolaus, Timagenes, and Phlegon.

NICOLAUS was a learned Greek from Damascus, who wrote on a variety of topics, including an *Universal History* in 144 books, and received the compliment of being chosen by Herod the Great to be his secretary, spokesman, and chronicler. The post must have called for talents and dexterity of no common order, but Nicolaus was successful. Josephus plainly relies on him largely for Books XIV–XVII of his *Jewish Antiquities* and much of his style here probably reproduces that of Nicolaus. Fragments of another work of his on the youth and training of Augustus are extant; they are good journalism but not necessarily untrue. TIMAGENES of Alexandria was less fortunate: he lived at Rome from about 50 B.C., but his scurrility and attacks upon Augustus and Livia finally lost him the imperial favour and he took refuge with Asinius Pollio. There, in revenge, he burnt the account he had written of Augustus' deeds. Little is known about his other *Histories*, but there can be small doubt that they provided much of the scandalous and sensational gossip that crops up in Suetonius and others about Augustus and his private life. Lastly, PHLEGON of Tralles, a freedman of the Emperor Hadrian, compiled various erudite treatises, including some on history (the *Olympiads*) and on *Marvels and Wonders*; from surviving fragments of this last work we learn of the statue dedicated to Tiberius by the cities of Asia after A.D. 17 (p. 650), and an eclipse which he mentioned in the thirteenth Book of his *Olympiads* is thought to be identifiable with the 'great darkness' recorded as following the Crucifixion.

EXISTING SOURCES

(a) Latin

Among surviving writers the earliest is CICERO. His own letters give a full and vivid picture of what was happening in the Roman world between March 44 and June 43 B.C., then they fail. His *Philippics*, too, are contemporary documents of importance: much of the abuse of Antony and praise of Octavian contained in them came in very opportunely for Augustus later, in much the same way as Cicero's *de Republica* and *de legibus* gave material and precedent to Augustus for his legislation and acts. The collected correspondence of Cicero also preserves (in the *ad familiares*) some highly characteristic letters from Lepidus, Asinius Pollio, Munatius Plancus and others. The two books of letters between Cicero and M. Brutus (the genuineness of which seems now agreed) are important not only for the historical details they contain but also for the light they throw on Brutus' character. The same cannot be said of the Greek letters of Brutus; though most scholars now accept the authenticity of those going under his name they add little to our knowledge, and the answers appear to be simply a literary exercise of first-century date.

Of the compositions of AUGUSTUS the only one that has survived in almost complete form is his own account of his achievements, the *Res Gestae*. A copy in Greek and Latin known as the *Monumentum Ancyranum* still stands on the walls of what was the Augusteum at Ancyra in Galatia: four fragments of the Greek version were found at Apollonia in Galatia, and considerable and important fragments of the Latin at Antioch-by-Pisidia. It gives a list of the various honours conferred upon Augustus, of the sums of money he spent upon the State, and lastly of his achievements in war and peace, and the original was set up outside the Mausoleum that Augustus built for his family. Though he gave some final touches to the document as late as A.D. 12–13 there can be little doubt that in substance it was complete by A.D. 6, and that the greater part even of this had received its first form by 8 B.C. If there were earlier draftings than this it is impossible to fix them with any certainty. Moreover, though Augustus from time to time made additions, alterations, and corrections to his first draft of 8 B.C. he revised and worked over the whole with care, so that slight discrepancies of style and order alone indicate different stages in its composition. In its proud consciousness of achievement and in its severe reserve it is no unworthy monument of the Emperor, and its plain and lucid style illustrates well his aim 'sensum animi quam apertissime exprimere' (Suetonius, *Aug.* 86).

VELLEIUS PATERCULUS, in his short history composed to celebrate the consulship of his patron M. Vinicius in A.D. 30, devotes some seventy chapters of Book II (58–131) to events following 44 B.C., based largely on the official Augustan account, as a comparison with the *Epitome* of Livy and with the *Res Gestae* shows. He had served as an officer under Tiberius and becomes panegyrical when he contemplates the campaigns of his general and his achievements as *princeps*; he is equally full of praise for his minister Sejanus. Apart from his account of the later German and Pannonian campaigns (A.D. 4–12) Velleius' work is important in two ways: it gives a favourable picture of Tiberius as a soldier and general, and it reveals how even an honest man, as Velleius was, could hardly escape the growing tendency of the times to flatter the *princeps* and his helpers. This tendency is plainer still in VALERIUS MAXIMUS, who dedicated his nine-volume collection of *Exempla* of virtues and vices to the heavenly providence of Tiberius, and who retails some scraps of information about victims of the Proscription of 43–42, and about famous men of the Augustan principate. The younger SENECA lived through the reigns of Tiberius, Gaius and Claudius, and most of Nero's, and though he wrote no professed historical work, his numerous moralizing treatises contain first-hand contemporary information, often of real value. But his feelings change with the times, and his early flattery of Claudius, or of his freedmen, turns into bitter mockery of the Emperor when dead. Few things could exceed the savagery of the *Apocolocyntosis divi Claudii* (which is almost universally acknowledged to be Seneca's), where every feature of Claudius' person is ridiculed, and he himself damned by the verdict of the very Emperor, Augustus, whom he professed to hold as his model. Such are treatises written 'recentibus odiis.'

Very different is the work of our most important surviving authority, CORNELIUS TACITUS—the *praenomen* is still uncertain—though here only essentials can be mentioned. He was born probably early in the reign of Nero (*c.* A.D. 55), married the daughter of Agricola in 77, and passed through most of the stages in the official career under the Flavian emperors. Praetor in 88, he was then away from Rome for four years in some provincial post; he returned to find his father-in-law dead—it was rumoured that Domitian had poisoned him—and to witness the tyranny of the last years of Domitian's reign; on his death he attained the consulship in 97, with the Emperor Nerva as his colleague. He was proconsul of Asia about 112, and died probably early in Hadrian's reign. Thus he had an advantage denied to many of the historians mentioned here, of knowing the workings of the system he was to describe. He had received the thorough training in rhetoric common to the time, he was an impressive orator, and he had already completed three studies in different *genres* before he undertook the writing of his two great historical works: these were the *Histories*, covering the years from 69 to 96, probably in twelve books, of which only the first four and a few chapters of the fifth survive, and the *Annals*, from 14 to 68, probably in eighteen books, of which we now possess Books I–IV, a fragment of V, VI, about half of Book XI, the whole of XII–XV, and a few chapters of Book XVI. Of the three preliminary studies the *Dialogus de oratoribus* (now generally agreed to be his and possibly published as early as A.D. 81), discusses the reasons for the admitted decline of oratory under the Principate, and finds them in the lack of party strife and politics and in the all-pervading influence of the *princeps*; the *de vita Julii Agricolae* is a biography of his father-in-law, published in 98, when his hatred of Domitian could find free vent; and the *de origine et situ Germanorum*, published in the same year as his *Agricola* but later, is a study of the land and climate of Germany and of the history and social and religious structure of the German tribes. The value of these last two works for the early history of Roman Britain and of the Germans needs no underlining.

It is clear therefore that Tacitus had an experienced pen, practical knowledge, and personal experience; to this he added a grasp of the literature and a thoroughness in investigating sources which his friend the younger Pliny unreservedly admired. But he approached his task with certain inevitable preconceptions; his reading of history combined with his own experience showed him that since the Republic had been superseded by the Principate, two men, emerging victorious from bloody Civil Wars, had founded dynasties that began with a programme of peace, reconciliation, and restoration of security, and yet went down in cruelty and bloodshed. One emperor alone had changed for the better, Vespasian (*Hist.* I, 50): on all the others, power had exercised a demoralizing effect (cf. *Ann.* VI, 48 and XV, 53). This feeling, coupled with the strong impress left by the Stoic circles among which he moved, makes him take a moral view of the function of history—'praecipuum munus annalium reor ne virtutes sileantur utque pravis dictis factisque ex posteritate et infamia metus sit' (*Ann.* III, 65). But though this view naturally affects his presentation of events and colours his painting of the emperors, he never forgoes the first duty of a historian, laborious and critical investigation of evidence in order to reach a true and impartial account. Though occasionally he appears to group events more with a view to literary effect than to their strict sequence in time, it would be difficult to produce an instance where he has deliberately mis-stated or falsified facts, and easy to cite passages where he carefully rejects and passes over versions and rumours which might suit his book better, but which he eschews. His portrait of the slow degeneration of Tiberius or Claudius is severe, but with his preconceptions, and on the evidence before him, he could not write otherwise: he depicted Tiberius as he does because the evidence before him all pointed that way. Modern research tends ultimately not so much to prove Tacitus false or malignant, but rather to illustrate and stress aspects of the history of the Empire in which Tacitus was not interested.

Thus it comes about that the facts he reports are usually accurate enough and rarely refuted by modern discoveries, but his interpretation must often be challenged. For some three generations Tacitus has been subjected to the most merciless and often unfair analytical scrutiny, even accused of '*l'hystérie du mensonge*,' but the trend of present-day scholarship is towards the recognition of his integrity and essential greatness. He is by far the most complete and the most trustworthy author that we possess for the early Principate.

From Tacitus it is a long descent to C. SUETONIUS TRANQUILLUS, yet his writings contain much that is useful and illuminating. A humbler friend in the younger Pliny's circle, a born researcher and antiquarian, for a short time he was secretary to Hadrian; but the rest of his life was uneventful, devoted to learning and to writing. Save for a few literary biographies, *The Lives of the Twelve Caesars* alone survives from his voluminous output. It is obvious that he read widely and gathered information everywhere: he often quotes from or bases his view upon official or semi-official documents, *e.g.*, the *Res Gestae*, speeches and letters of various emperors, yet he often reproduces the merest gossip, or popular songs, or rumours perpetuated in hostile anti-Caesarian literature. In consequence *The Lives* is a curious patchwork, for Suetonius makes no organic whole of them, but arranges each under a series of Rubrics or Headings (*e.g.* Public Life and Offices, Campaigns, Treatment of Friends, Virtues, Vices, *etc.*), in which good and worthless elements may be juxtaposed. So the value of a life varies greatly according to the material available: he is excellent on Augustus and good on Claudius (where it has been conjectured that he used Claudius' own account of his life), fairly balanced upon Tiberius, though with a good deal of sensational detail, and definitely hostile to Gaius and Nero, against whom obviously an evil tradition existed. It is likely enough that for the Year of the Four Emperors (A.D. 69) he used the same basic source (perhaps Pliny) as Tacitus and Plutarch, and a comparison of what Tacitus omits and what Suetonius retains is instructive. One great merit he has, that he often preserves speeches and utterances unaltered and material uncontaminated, whereas more consciously literary authors, such as Tacitus and Dio, are too apt for reasons of style or regard for 'the dignity of history' to avoid direct quotation, and work the substance into their narrative. Occasionally he takes trouble over a disputed question, such as the birthplace of Gaius, at another time he can complacently exclaim, 'at quod discrepat in medio sit.' Yet within his limits he preserves material of great value.

There remain for final mention some late epitomators, Florus, Eutropius, Aurelius Victor, and Orosius. Under the name of JULIUS FLORUS we possess four (perhaps originally two) books on the *Wars of the Romans*, rhetorical and inaccurate, probably composed during the reign of Hadrian. To the fourth century belongs the *Breviarium* of Eutropius, an epitome of Roman History from Romulus down to the emperor Valens, to whom the work was dedicated: so too a couple of biographical works, *de viris illustribus* and *Caesares*, usually ascribed to a certain SEXTUS AURELIUS VICTOR. PAULUS OROSIUS, a Spaniard and pupil of St Augustine, published in 417 the seven books of his *Historiae adversus Paganos*, compiled with the genial aim of proving that the miseries of his Christian times were no more than those of the Pagan centuries. All these epitomes derive whatever value they possess for the early period of this volume from the fact that they all used an abridged version of the lost books of Livy; occasionally, but only occasionally, they preserve figures or facts of some worth. For the period after Augustus they merely repeat monotonously the tradition that was finally fixed after the time of Tacitus and Suetonius.

A brief account only need be given here of some technical or semi-technical works. VITRUVIUS POLLIO published, probably about 14 B.C., the ten books of his *de Architectura*, which contain some valuable information about the period when Rome was being transformed and beautified by the building works of Augustus and of his friends. SEXTUS JULIUS FRONTINUS, who was *praetor urbanus* in 70, governor of Britain between 74 and 77, and finally *curator aquarum* under Nerva in 97, was the author of several treatises: of these the four books of *Strategemata* (published in the late years of Domitian) afford some items of interest for our period, and a monograph, possibly originally entitled *Commentarius de aquis* and published about A.D. 100, gives important information about the water-supply of Rome and its organization under the early Empire. Some three hundred years later FLAVIUS VEGETIUS RENATUS compiled from various sources, including the Elder Cato and Frontinus, an *Epitoma rei militaris* which, in spite of inaccuracies and uncertain chronology, provides material of some value for the history of the imperial armies.

(b) Greek

STRABO, of Amasia (c. 40 B.C.–A.D. 25), a Greek who spent much of his time in Rome, and had realized that henceforth Greek and Roman were one culture, wrote, in addition to the seventeen books of his *Geography*, a history of which unfortunately only fragments remain. But his geographical books, which were completed in first draft by about 6 B.C., and then later apparently roughly revised so as to include some of the events of the first ten years of Tiberius, are a mine of information for the whole of the Empire, based on excellent sources. On the Northern frontier wars, on relations with Parthia, on the Arabian expedition of Aelius Gallus, on the internal conditions of Italy and the provinces, and on the Principate as it looked to the world of his day, he gives the most valuable evidence, disinterested and (for the time) accurate.

PHILO, of Alexandria (c. 30 B.C.–A.D. 45), uncle of Tiberius Alexander (pp. 852, 861) was a wealthy Jew, steeped in Greek, and especially Platonic, philosophy, who devoted most of his large output to explaining and allegorizing the books of the Bible, but two nearly complete parts remain from a treatise on 'The Wonderful Works of God' (περὶ Ἀρετῶν), usually called the *in Flaccum* and the *Legatio ad Gaium*. These, despite an overload of declamation, contain an extremely graphic picture of the famous 'Jew-hunt of Alexandria' in A.D. 38 (p. 310) and of an embassy of Alexandrian Jews, of which Philo himself was a member, to the Emperor Gaius. But the rhetoric is strong: Tiberius is praised with enthusiasm to make Gaius' wickedness appear the blacker, and the figure of King Agrippa I, though possibly more moral, is less natural than in the pages of Josephus. But when the necessary deductions have been made, his evidence is not unimportant.

The Jewish general and Roman citizen, FLAVIUS JOSEPHUS (A.D. 37–

? 100), provides material of great interest in this period, not only for affairs in Judaea and Syria—he is practically the sole source for the reign of Herod the Great and for the history of his descendants—but also for affairs in Rome. Not only does he preserve, usually in an abbreviated form, edicts and rescripts of various emperors concerning the Jews, but he also gives an interesting account of the last days of Tiberius and of the assassination of Gaius, that clearly derives from a good Roman original (possibly Cluvius Rufus); in the earlier part his view of Cleopatra derives from Herod's defender, Nicolaus. More important still is his narrative of the events that led up to the Jewish revolt, and of the actual course of the revolt itself, in much of which he played a leading part; but in his writings he has the difficult task of portraying himself satisfactorily as at once a pious Jew and patriot, and yet a friend and supporter of the Romans (see p. 884). Whatever the exact purpose of his *Jewish Antiquities*, in twenty books, from Creation to A.D. 66, published in 94, his *Vita* published later is frankly apologetic against the attacks of his enemies, and his *Jewish War*, in seven books, which was published earlier, and apparently first written in Aramaic, is a pro-Roman document, and issued, as he declares, under official approval. But where his own personal attitude or behaviour is not in question, he is a source of undeniable merit.

PLUTARCH, of Chaeronea in Boeotia (*c.* A.D. 50–120), the writer of the famous *Parallel Lives*, in his *Cicero* and *Brutus* offers admirable material, based on first-hand evidence, such as that of Cicero's confidential secretary Tiro and of Brutus' companions and friends. In his *Antony*, however, he is obviously out of sympathy with the protagonist, though he draws on Dellius, and towards the end on the memoirs of Cleopatra's physician, Olympus; even so it is one of the finest of his *Lives*. Of his biographies of the emperors, apart from those of *Galba* and *Otho* (where the elder Pliny appears to have been his principal source), nothing remains, though some scraps in the *Moralia* suggest that they contained plenty of those anecdotes and personal touches 'reflecting character,' that Plutarch sought out.

A writer of considerable value for the early period is APPIAN, a Greek from Alexandria, who rose to hold a minor official position under the Antonines. In Books XV–XVII of his *Roman Histories* (usually numbered as Books III–V of the Civil Wars), he covers the period from 44 to 35 B.C. with some fullness, and in Book XXIII (the *Illyrica*) he recounts Octavian's campaigns of 35 and 34 in Dalmatia, using Octavian's autobiography. Much of these books, being mainly military, is admirable in facts and figures, whereas he is uneasy and incorrect upon constitutional matters, as the end of the Second Triumvirate. Down to the battle of Philippi he draws largely upon Asinius Pollio, which accounts for his bias against Cicero and Munatius Plancus; after 42 B.C., it looks as though he used Messalla Corvinus and Augustus' autobiography as well. Naturally he finds much to say in favour of Octavian, though it is noticeable that he looks on Mark Antony and his brother L. Antonius with sympathy. In these books Appian gives us some of his best.

DIO CASSIUS COCCEIANUS, whose *floruit* falls about A.D. 200, and who wrote a history of Rome, in eighty books, from the foundation of the city to A.D. 229, is a writer of curious contradictions. Of Greek descent, but a Roman citizen and with a distinguished career (including the consulship) in the service of the Empire, a would-be Thucydides, an admirer of Severan autocracy, deeply conscious of the high office of the historian, yet often descending to puerile anecdotes and to catalogues of omens, he is almost an epitome of the strong and weak points of the later Graeco-Roman civilization. Books XLIV–LXV, retailing the history of the period covered by this volume, are fairly complete, save for the reign of Nero and years of the Civil War, where we have to depend upon epitomators. From Books XLIV–LIV Livy was probably his main source, which means that he is apt to be pro-Augustan and anti-Antonian, though a strong secondary source, anti-Augustan (perhaps Timagenes), crops up from time to time: for the reigns of the Julio-Claudians no certainty can be established, but it may be noted that he follows a tradition extremely hostile to Seneca. The lengthy speeches he inserts in the body of his narrative are unhistorical—as, *e.g.*, the alleged conversation between Octavian and his advisers in Book LII, which reflects Dio's own age and views and not those of Octavian (p. 127)—and their style curiously streaked with reminiscences of Greek drama or of Thucydides. His statements on matters of constitutional importance in the development of the Principate are often refuted by better evidence, and where it is not possible to check what he says on these matters he is not to be readily credited with precision, the more so that he is by no means consistent in his translation of Roman terms into Greek. Yet in spite of obvious faults, we owe him gratitude on many counts: he preserves an indispensable chronological framework, he appears—as he claims himself—to have worked carefully at his sources and to have formed a view of his own, and without his aid we should be badly adrift for long sections of Roman history.

Some writers of considerably later date round off the list. JOHN MALALAS of Antioch in Syria compiled in the sixth century an universal history in twelve books, and much of Book X refers to the period comprised in this volume. Malalas' main interest naturally lies in Eastern affairs, especially in those of his native Antioch; indeed he shows a fine disregard for Western geography and chronology. But amid a mass of rather trivial anecdotes he does occasionally preserve items—*e.g.*, about building-benefactions, or about riots between Jews and Christians—that appear to be founded on genuine city-tradition. Among works of Byzantine scholars we possess excerpts from the great *Encyclopaedia* of historical extracts which the Emperor Constantine Porphyrogenitus had drawn up in the tenth century, and to the same century probably belongs the *Lexicon* of SUIDAS, which includes articles on the emperors. Later still, JOHN XIPHILINUS, in the eleventh century, and JOHN ZONARAS, in the twelfth, made epitomes of Dio Cassius, which thus preserve the Dionic tradition where Dio himself is lacking. But all these late works must be used with considerable caution.

NOTES

1. OPPIDUM MARIBA IN FINIBUS SABAEORUM

It is argued in the text (p. 251) that Mariba or Marsyaba, the farthest point reached by Aelius Gallus, is not to be identified with the Sabaean capital Mariaba. Pliny's account shows that in this part of Arabia there were several places bearing similar names, and it is an attractive suggestion that the town in question was Maryama, an ancient site with considerable remains on the left bank of the Wadi Baihan in the district of El-Kasab, south-east of Marib. Strabo probably wrote 'Maryaba': permutation of the labials *m* and *b* is not infrequent in the transcription of Arabic names, and it was rare for foreign names to be accurately reproduced by Greek and Latin writers or their informants. Maryama is the Maryamat of a South Arabian inscription and the Μαριάμα of Ptolemy VI, 7, 37 (see C. Landberg, *Arabica*, V, pp. 21, 82; Tkač in *P.W.* s.v. *Saba*, col. 1356 *sqq.*; Grohmann, *ib.* s.v. *Marsyaba*). This identification accords with Pliny's statement that the limit of Gallus' advance was Caripeta, corresponding to Harib, no great distance away; and Strabo's Rhammanitae were probably Pliny's Rhadamaei and the Radmān of Arabian geographers and inscriptions, whose name still remains attached to the region of Maryama and Harib. They may well have been part of the Calingi, to whom Pliny assigns the town of Mariba and whose name perhaps reappears in the great group of tribes called by Arabic writers Kahlan (A. Sprenger, *Alte Geographie Arabiens*, p. 178; Tkač, *loc. cit.* col. 1367).

J. G. C. A.

2. THE POSITION HELD BY QUIRINIUS FOR THE HOMANADENSIAN WAR

The view adopted in the text (p. 271 *sq.*), that Quirinius conducted the campaign as governor of Galatia and Pamphylia, has been put forward by R. Syme[1], who is probably right in believing that the same province was held by Piso at the time when he was summoned to Thrace (in 13 or 12 B.C.), and by Plautius Silvanus in A.D. 6[2]. The union of Pamphylia with Galatia, which is probably recorded under Nero[3] and is definitely attested under Galba[4], was in itself natural, and it was necessary at a time when the Taurus tribes had to be coerced. The fact that in later time Galatia was governed by a senator of praetorian rank, whereas Quirinius was a consular, presents no real difficulty; in the reign of Augustus, when conditions were still unsettled, administrative practice was not yet governed by hard and fast rules, and some provinces were placed at one time under ex-praetors and at another under ex-

---

[1] *J.R.S.* XXIII, 1933, XXVII, 24, and more fully in *Klio*, XXXVII, 1934, pp. 1 *sqq.*, 131 *sqq.*

[2] Dio LIV, 34, 6, and the Pamphylian inscription cited below.

[3] Statius, *Silv.* I, 4, 77; Groag in *P.W.* s.v. *Rutilius Gallicus*, col. 1258.

[4] Tacitus, *Hist.* II, 9.

consuls, as circumstances dictated[1]. The suggestion of E. Groag that Quirinius conducted the war as proconsul of Asia is not probable: his campaign against the Marmaridae (p. 347), which is cited as a parallel, would be analogous only in so far as concerns the placing of legionary troops under a proconsul, for the province of Asia did not extend to the Homanadensian country[2]. The view almost universally accepted has been that Quirinius conducted the war as governor of Syria, for Syria was the only consular province in the East with an army and it was from Syria that troops were normally drawn for service in Asia Minor[3]. Now Quirinius was governor of Syria in A.D. 6[4], whereas the Homanadensian campaign preceded his appointment as adviser to Gaius Caesar in A.D. 2; but there was believed to be evidence that he had already governed the province at an earlier date, and it was concluded that the war took place under his first administration. According to the much discussed passage of St Luke (ii, 1–2), Quirinius was governor of Syria just before the birth of Christ; and a fragmentary inscription found in the territory of Tibur (Dessau 918), which mentions a *rex* and was interpreted as recording a second tenure of the province of Syria in the time of Augustus, was restored by Mommsen as the sepulchral *elogium* of Quirinius, the *rex* being identified as Amyntas. In the list of the known governors of Syria there is a gap after 4 B.C., and Mommsen fixed 3–2 B.C. as the date of the war.

This view is beset with grave difficulties. (1) A second tenure of Syria or indeed any other consular province under one and the same emperor by a senator who was not a member of the imperial house is unparalleled, and the Tiburtine inscription speaks, not of a second tenure, but of a second legateship with Syria as the province assigned: the words are [*legatus pr. pr.*] *divi Augusti* [*i*]*terum Syriam et Ph*[*oenicen optinuit*...]. (2) The statement of St Luke is in conflict with several undoubted facts and disaccords with his reference in Acts v, 37 to 'the census,' which, when compared with the evidence of Josephus[5], is seen to imply the census of A.D. 6/7, taken when Judaea became a Roman province. (3) The attribution of the Tiburtine fragment to Quirinius involves several difficulties, which are set forth by Groag[6]. He claims the inscription for M. Plautius Silvanus, consul in 2 B.C., but this attribution is also unacceptable. The clause above quoted can only mean that the man commemorated was legate of Augustus for a second time with Syria as his province; but the Syrian command (if held at all by Silvanus) was not—on Groag's own showing—his second legateship, and a dedication to him recently discovered in Pamphylia[7] shows that he was *legatus pro praetore* there, in all probability as a consular just before his command in Pannonia and Illyricum, A.D. 7–9.　　　　　　　　　　　　J. G. C. A.

---

[1] Gallia Comata (Dio LIII, 26, 4; LIV, 20, 5; Vell. Pat. II, 97), Nearer Spain (usually consular but praetorian in 22, Dio LIV, 5, 1) and Macedonia (usually praetorian but consular *c.* 19–18, Dio LIV, 20, 3) are quoted by Syme.
[2] Groag in *Jahreshefte*, XXI–XXII, 1924, Beiblatt, p. 460 and in *P.W.* s.v. *Sulpicius Quirinius*, col. 831. 　　[3] Tacitus, *Ann.* VI, 41; XII, 55.
[4] Josephus, *Ant.* XVIII [1, 1], 1; [2, 1], 26; Dio LV, 27, 6.
[5] *Ant.* XX [5, 2], 102; *Bell. Jud.* II [8, 1], 118; [17, 8], 433.
[6] *Jahreshefte*, pp. 448 *sqq.*
[7] *Annuario della Scuola Arch. di Atene*, VIII–IX, 1925–6, p. 363.

3. THE PARTHIAN PRETENDER OF A.D. 55

It is not certain that the pretender was Vardanes, son of Vologases. The MS. text of Tacitus, *Ann.* XIII, 7, 2 is *exortusque in tempore aemulus Vologaeso filius Vardanis*, where the last word is usually emended to *Vardanes*. An objection to the MS. text is that we should have expected Tacitus to give his name, which was not likely to have been unknown. Von Gutschmid retained the MS. reading (*Gesch. Irans*, p. 130), and he is followed by W. Schur, *Orientpolitik*, p. 72 *sq.*, who conjectures that the pretender (probably, he thinks, an illegitimate scion of the Hyrcanian branch of the royal house, see above, p. 278) was king of Hyrcania, and that consequently his rebellion and the Hyrcanian revolt, which had broken out before 58, were one and the same thing. The identity of the two movements is certainly an attractive hypothesis, but Tacitus does not connect them, and his failure to do so is hardly to be explained away by his 'use of two different sources for Eastern events.' It is, however, possible that the Hyrcanians rose in support of the pretender; the intervention of the northerners in dynastic affairs was frequent.

The MS. text of Tacitus is also retained by E. Herzfeld, who rejects the theory of the Hyrcanian origin of the house of Artabanus and thinks it more than probable that the *filius Vardanis* was Orthagnes, whose name appears, with the title of βασιλεὺς βασιλέων μέγας, on coins of Gundofarr (Gondophares, Hyndopherres) and who was thus proclaimed as Gundofarr's candidate for the Parthian throne against his uncle Vologases. Gundofarr, he argues, belonged to the family of the Surēn, whose hereditary domain was Drangiane-Sacastane (Seïstan) and Arachosia; he was a determined foe of Artabanus and his successors of the Arsacid female line, broke away from Parthia, and in A.D. 19–20 became ruler of Indian Sakastan with the title 'great king of kings' (*Sakastan*, pp. 91 *sqq.*). On this view it may be remarked that Gundofarr's support of a grandson of Artabanus in A.D. 55 would have been a political *volte face*.

Several numismatists have assigned to the pretender a series of tetradrachms issued between A.D. 54–5 and Panemos (June) 58, which bear a different portrait from that on the early coinage of Vologases (A.D. 50–1 to 53–4), showing a more youthful face with round beard (instead of a somewhat pointed one) and a wart on the temple. This series is succeeded by a third (A.D. 60–1 to 67–8), on which the portrait is sufficiently unlike that of the early coins to have led some numismatists to assign the group to a different king, who is supposed—with no support from historical evidence—to have succeeded Vologases about 60. If the attribution of the intermediate group be correct, it would indicate the duration of the struggle for the throne. Wroth, however, held that the differences in the portraiture are not sufficient to compel their assignation to different rulers and considered them to be successive issues of Vologases (*B.M. Cat. Parthia*, pp. L *sq.*, 178 *sqq.*); and this view is supported by the occurrence of wide variations in portraiture on Parthian coins and by the facts that the bust on the middle group does not look like that of a man 20 years or so younger than the king of the first group, and that the two portraits do not overlap. See Volume of Plates iv, 210, *k* for a coin assigned by some to the pretender.

J. G. C. A.

4. THE DATE OF THE DESTRUCTION OF ARTAXATA

It is pointed out in the text (p. 763) that a difficulty is created by the impression which the narrative of Tacitus conveys that the destruction of Artaxata by Corbulo followed immediately on its surrender. On account of this fact and because of the words *utendum recenti terrore* in *Ann.* XIV, 23, it has been held that in the portion of his narrative of the war which he gives under the year 58 Tacitus has anticipated some of the events of 59. E. Egli, *Feldzüge in Armenien*, pp. 283 *sqq.*, and B. W. Henderson, *C.R.* XV, 1901, p. 211, have maintained that the fall of Artaxata belongs to 59 and that the campaign of that year begins at XIII, 39 (after the failure of the negotiations, which are supposed to have taken place during the winter); but this view is open to the objections that there is no hint of a new year beginning at that point, that it makes Tacitus break off his narrative in the middle of 59, and that it makes him antedate by a year the Senate's decrees, although he expressly assigns them to 58 by passing on with *deinde* (c. 42, 1) to other events of that year.

J. G. C. A.

5. TWO POINTS OF ARMENIAN TOPOGRAPHY

Among Corbulo's allies in 58 the text of Tacitus names the Insochi, *gens ante alias socia Romanis* (*Ann.* XIII, 37). Ritter's emendation *Moschi* has been generally accepted, but *Heniochi* is suggested by M. Cary (*C.R.* XXV, 1911, p. 107). The latter seems preferable, although the name is correctly given in *Ann.* II, 68. The Moschi had moved, or had been moved by Mithridates Eupator, from their old abode between the river Acampsis (mod. Chorok) and the head waters of the Cyrus (mod. Kûr) to the watershed between the Phasis and the Cyrus, which still bears the name of the Meschic Mountains (cf. Pliny, *N.H.* VI, 13, *Phasis oritur in Moschis*). The Heniochi had moved from the slopes of the Caucasus to the mountain country on both sides of the Acampsis, extending inland as far as the upper Cyrus, where they bordered on the Iberians (Pliny, *N.H.* VI, 26). Cf. Kiessling in *P.W.* s.v. *Heniochoi*, cols. 265, 272 *sq.*

Arsamosata is the Armenian Ašmušat, the Shamshat or Shimshat of Arab geographers, one of whom locates it a mile above the junction of Nahr Salkit (probably the Peri Su) with the Arsanias (*J.H.S.* XVII, 1897, p. 25), while another describes it as fully two days' march east of Kharput. It may be identical with the extensive ruins at Naǧaran, E.S.E. of Kharāba (E. Huntington quoted in *Verh. Berlin. Ges. f. Anthropol.* 1900, p. 149; W. Tomaschek, *Kiepert-Festschrift*, p. 138; J. Markwart, *Südarmenien*, p. 240).

J. G. C. A.

6. THE POLICY OF NERO IN THE SOUTH-EAST
AND THE NORTH-EAST

The views expressed in the text (pp. 778 *sqq.*) differ radically from those advanced by W. Schur in his *Orientpolitik des Kaisers Nero*, which develops ideas put forward by E. Kornemann[1]. He holds that, in planning both the Caucasian and the Ethiopian expeditions, Nero was resuming a commercial

---

[1] *Janus*, I, 1921, pp. 55 *sqq.*

policy conceived by Seneca and Burrus and partially carried out by them. Its aim was to secure control of two trade-routes which brought to the Roman market the products of India and China and were both in the hands of middlemen—the south-eastern sea route, which was exploited by the southern Arabs, and the north-eastern land route, which ran from Bactria by way of the Caspian Sea and Albania to the Euxine[1]. After Nero's accession political crises interfered with the traffic over both routes; the northern must have been practically closed by the revolt of Hyrcania, while in the south the expanding kingdom of Axum threatened to capture the Arabian-Indian trade and endanger the supply of oriental goods, for which there was a steadily increasing demand. Dependence on middlemen who had become, or might become, foes began to make itself unpleasantly felt.

I. The South-Eastern policy. The theory is briefly as follows. The ambitions of the Axumite kingdom, which is first mentioned in the *Periplus of the Erythraean Sea* (written, it is held, about A.D. 90), began to exercise the minds of Seneca and Burrus at the time of the pause in the Armenian war, a year before the dispatch of the exploratory expedition to Ethiopia in the autumn of 61. The kingdom, it is argued, was founded not by the king mentioned in the *Periplus* (Zoscales) but by the nameless king of at least a generation earlier who commemorated his conquests in the inscription of Adulis (*O.G.I.S.* 199), relating how he had extended his dominion northwards from Abyssinia to the borderlands of Egypt and southwards along the Somali coast, and then, crossing the sea, had occupied the Arabian coast from the Sabaean frontier to Leuke Kome. His encroachment on Arabia was bound to cause anxiety at Rome, for his ultimate object was to conquer Yemen and seize its trade. To secure the weak and amenable Sabaean-Himyarite State against his attack, Rome concluded a treaty of friendship and alliance with it (*Per.* 23) and on the basis of this treaty occupied Aden (*ib.* 26). She also secured indirect control of the island of Socotra, which was leased by the king of Hadramût (*ib.* 31) and was doubtless leased to a syndicate of Roman traders from Egypt. Since the security of the Arabian kingdom was the most urgent matter, the treaty was no doubt made before the mission was sent to Ethiopia, and it may therefore be dated to the summer of 60. The occupation of Aden and the control of Socotra led naturally to the opening of direct intercourse by sea between Egypt and India. The Ethiopian expedition was to be the complement of this South Arabian policy. Its object was to check the further expansion of Axum, and to prevent it from securing a monopoly of the African ivory trade, by establishing a protectorate over the decaying kingdom of Meroë and reviving the old trade-route down the Nile, which its decline had allowed to fall into disuse. The purpose of the military preparations was to nip in the bud any attempt by the kingdom to resist attachment, however loose, to the Roman empire.

This alluring theory requires critical examination.

(1) The *Periplus*, a sailor's guide written by an experienced Egyptian merchant, was composed some time in the course of the first century A.D., but not in the nineties of Domitian's reign. This date is based on the belief that it was later than the *Natural History* of Pliny, since it is not used as a source in VI, 96–106, and later than 87, because it speaks of trade between

---

[1] Strabo XI, 498, 509; Pliny, *N.H.* VI, 52.

India and China by way of Bactria (ch. 64), whereas Chinese sources indicate a complete suspension of this trade from A.D. 23 to 87[1]. The first argument is manifestly invalid, and the second will not stand. What the Chinese evidence proves is the severance of the old political connection between China and the states through which passed the routes to Bactria, but this fact is not incompatible with the continuance of trade, particularly the intermittent sort of trade of which the *Periplus* speaks; during the interval, too, these states resumed friendly relations with China and sought the restoration of their old political connection[2]. Moreover, Domitian's reign is ruled out by the fact that the author mentions Malichus as the contemporary king of the Nabataeans[3] (ch. 19). The only king of that name who comes into question is Malichus II, who reigned from about A.D. 40 to 71 (or 75). His successor was Rabel II, who ruled certainly till 96 (or 101) and probably till 106. The existence of a Malichus III, who is supposed to have succeeded Rabel in 101, has been inferred from two inscriptions by Dussaud and Macler[4], but is problematical. Schürer has shown that the inference is uncertain[5], and the Nabataean coinage ends with Rabel. There can therefore be small doubt that the *Periplus* was written during the reign of Malichus II, and an earlier rather than a later date in his reign is indicated by the probable identification of another ruler mentioned in ch. 27, Eleazos, king of Hadramût, whom Arabic scholars have equated with Ilī'azzu Ialīt, named in an inscription of A.D. 26[6].

(2) The author of the *Periplus* limits the territory of the Axumite kingdom to the region lying (approximately) between Suakin and the straits of Bâb el-Mandeb, and he knows nothing of any territory possessed by the king in Arabia nor of any political authority or influence exerted by him there, as Mommsen pointed out long ago (*Prov. of the Rom. Empire*, II, p. 281). The expansion of the kingdom across the Red Sea had plainly not yet taken place, and consequently the urgent cause assigned for Roman intervention in South Arabia is not a *vera causa*.

(3) It is widely believed, on the strength of *Per.* 26, νῦν δὲ οὐ πρὸ πολλοῦ τῶν ἡμετέρων χρόνων Καῖσαρ αὐτὴν κατεστρέψατο, that at some time during the Julio-Claudian period the Roman government subjugated the port of Aden, then called Eudaemon Arabia, in order to secure

[1] Kornemann, *loc. cit.* These arguments are repeated and accepted by E. Herzfeld (*Sakastan*, pp. 89 *sqq.*). The second argument is derived from A. Herrmann, *Ztschr. d. Ges. f. Erdk. zu Berlin*, 1913, p. 553, n. 3. The historical evidence furnished by the Chinese Annals is summarized in the latter's *Alte Seidenstrassen* (Sieglin's *Quellen u. Forsch.* XXI), 1910, p. 7 *sq.*

[2] See the translation of the relative portion of the Chinese Annals of the Han Dynasty in *Journ. Anthrop. Inst.* 1882, p. 114 *sq.* Dr Herrmann informs the present writer that he has long since ceased to adhere to the inference drawn in 1913.

[3] A date 'nearer the beginning than the end' of the reign which Schur substitutes in *Klio*, XX, 1926, p. 222, is therefore equally unacceptable.

[4] *Voyage archéol. au Safâ*, 1901, pp. 169 *sqq.*

[5] *Gesch. d. jüdischen Volkes*, I⁴, p. 741 *sq.*

[6] Cf. Tkač in *P.W.* s.v. *Saba*, col. 1464.

for Egyptian traders a monopoly in Arabian and Indian waters. But the statement of the *Periplus* involves serious difficulties. There is no trace of a permanent occupation of the port, without which no lasting injury would have been inflicted on Arabian trade; and it is incredible to the present writer that Roman literature would have been wholly silent about an important Roman success in Arabia Felix, fraught with the consequences ascribed to it, when the adventure of Aelius Gallus obtained so much notice; above all, the silence of Pliny, who could not have failed to know the fact, and his emphatic declaration that Gallus was the only person up to his own time who had carried the Roman arms into South Arabia (*N.H.* VI, 160) appear to be irreconcilable with the assertion of the *Periplus*. These considerations lend support to the suggestion of J. H. Mordtmann, based on the use of the word Καῖσαρ, that the author of the *Periplus* blundered[1]: he had heard tell of Gallus' expedition to Eudaemon Arabia (as the country was called by Augustus) and he thought that its objective was the port of that name with which he was familiar. It is hardly open to question that Καῖσαρ, applied by an ordinary Egyptian Greek to an emperor no longer alive, should mean Augustus. But whether Mordtmann has hit the mark or not, a Roman occupation of Aden, for which the sole evidence is the statement of an Egyptian merchant who was not a highly educated man, can hardly rank as an undoubted historical fact.

(4) That the Roman government secured indirect control of Socotra is a pure hypothesis, which is not warranted by the statement of the *Periplus*.

(5) It is not obvious how Roman commercial interests would be seriously prejudiced if the African ivory reached Egypt by way of the Axumite kingdom and the Red Sea—as it did at the time when the *Periplus* was written (ch. 4)—instead of passing through the Meroïtic kingdom, a route which, moreover, is supposed to have already fallen into disuse.

(6) The contention that direct intercourse by sea between Egypt and India was not opened till Nero's reign is disproved by the evidence of Strabo, which shows that even in the time of Augustus the maritime trade was far from being wholly in the hands of the southern Arabs (see above, p. 252 *sq.*), and by the numerous gold and silver coins of the Julio-Claudian emperors found in India, of which a very large proportion are issues of Augustus and Tiberius. The view, advanced by Kornemann and adopted by Schur, that by ἡ Ἰνδική Strabo means, not India, but the Indian Sea, i.e. the sea that washes the south coast of Arabia, has been refuted by Leuze (*O.L.Z.* XXVII, 1924, p. 346), and has been abandoned by Schur, but without any substantial modification of his conclusions (*Klio, loc. cit.* p. 221).

II. The Caucasian expedition. The Caucasian campaign is also believed to have been a resumption of the commercial policy of Seneca and Burrus. Schur supports the statement of Tacitus that it was directed against the Albani, and he holds that the 'Caspian Gates' meant the narrow pass of Derbend between the Caucasus and the Caspian; this was the pass to which Corbulo's explorers really gave the name of the 'Caspian Gates,' and Pliny 'must himself have been the victim of the error which he combats so vigorously' (p. 68).

[1] *Anzeige von Glasers Skizze I* in *Ztschr. d. deutsch. morgenl. Gesellschaft,* XLIV, 1890, p. 180

The Albani, he points out, had thrown off their allegiance to Rome at the end of Claudius' reign, and they were not on the Roman side during the Armenian war. Roman prestige demanded a punitive expedition against them, all the more because the cession of Armenia necessitated its 'military encirclement' by a ring of client states. But there was also an important economic motive. In 58 Rome had made an alliance with Hyrcania, and this alliance was now to be exploited in order to gain control of the Caspian-Euxine trade-route. The first step was to secure a base of operations on the Euxine, and this was done by incorporating the kingdoms of Pontus and Bosporus. The next was to occupy the land-bridge between the Euxine and the Caspian: Iberia had already been won back, and only Albania barred the way to Hyrcania and Bactria.

In this view there are two cardinal points. The first is the accuracy of Tacitus which is supported by an effort to discredit the trustworthiness of Pliny. But it is plainly impossible to get away from Pliny's detailed and precise testimony. If the 'Caspian Gates' really meant the pass of Derbend, the question may be asked why the objective of a campaign against Albania was described, with uniform consistency, as a pass lying at the extreme northern point of its territory towards Sarmatia; *ex hypothesi* what mattered to Rome was the possession of the Albanian plain south of the Caucasus. The other crucial point is the alleged alliance with Hyrcania. There is admittedly no evidence for it, however great may have been the advantages—military, political and commercial—which it is supposed to have offered to Rome.

Moreover, it is improbable that the Caspian-Euxine route carried any considerable volume of traffic. Its importance is likewise exaggerated by Prof. D. Magie, who argues that the object of Rome's policy of maintaining supremacy in Armenia and in the Iberian-Albanian isthmus was to retain control of the western section of the trade-route, which Pompey had brought into her hands (*Report of the Amer. Hist. Assoc. for* 1919, p. 302).   J. G. C. A.

7. JOSEPHUS AS A SOURCE FOR THE HISTORY OF JUDAEA

The purpose of this note is simply to discuss the value of the evidence for events in Judaea falling within the period of this volume which is offered by Josephus in his four works, the *Bellum Judaicum, Antiquitates Judaicae, contra Apionem,* and the autobiography (*Vita*). His career is dealt with in chap. XXV; on his value as an authority for Roman history see the Appendix upon Sources, p. 874 *sq.*

The *Bellum* was first composed in Aramaic for circulation among the Jews of the East (*Bell.* I, *proem.* 6). We may fairly suppose that it was written at the wish of Vespasian to persuade the Jewish groups in the Parthian kingdom, in Adiabene and elsewhere, to accept the *fait accompli* of the destruction of the Temple and not to foment discontents among their fellows in the Empire. The translation, or rather revision, in Greek was made with the help of assistants (*c. Apion.* 1 [9], 50) between A.D. 75 (cf. *Bell.* VII [5, 7], 158) and 79, when Vespasian, to whom Josephus dedicated the work, died. *Ant.* XX [12, 1], 259, 267 and other passages show that Josephus meant, after finishing the *Antiquities*, to revise once again his history of the war; but he did not do so. R. Eisler (*The Messiah Jesus*, etc. 1931) has claimed that the Slavonic text of the *Bellum* represents in substance the translation of a Greek text intermediate between the Aramaic and our present Greek text, which would have borne the title *About the Capture* [*of Jerusalem*], a title given to the existing text of the majority of the MSS., whereas Josephus plainly called it *About the Jewish War* or something similar (*e.g. Ant.* xx [11, 1], 258). In general Eisler's theory has little to support it (cf. A. Goethals, *Anti-Eisler; un peu de polémique*, Paris, 1932 and J. M. Creed, *The Slavonic Version of Josephus' History of the Jewish War*, Harv. Theol. Rev. xxv, 1932, p. 277); but some details of the Slavonic text are still unexplained, especially those raised by S. Reinach in *Rev. Arch.* 5th Ser. xxx, 1929, p. 18 = *Amalthée* II, p. 336 (which V. Ussani's reply, *Rend. Acc. Pont. Archeol.* N.S. VIII, 1932, p. 227 falls short of solving), and by R. Laqueur, *H.Z.* CXLVIII, 1933, p. 326. In the *Bellum* the history proper of the rebellion, A.D. 66–70, is preceded by a long introduction, which gives a fairly detailed account from the revolt of the Maccabees down to the struggles following the death of Herod and then various episodes of the period between 4 B.C. and A.D. 66. The source for this first section is certainly Nicolaus of Damascus, whose *Universal History* in 144 books, finished after the death of Herod, gave full space to events in Judaea. On some points, however, Josephus parts company with him: thus he regards Herod as an Idumaean, while Nicolaus called him Jew (as we know from *Ant.* XIV [1, 3], 9). Even so he avoids all polemic, mainly so as not to injure the feelings of Agrippa II, who was a descendant of Herod and his patron at that time (*Vita* [65], 359 *sqq.*). We need not therefore assume an anonymous writer between Nicolaus and Josephus. For the history of the succeeding period Josephus uses, besides his own personal memories, written sources which cannot be identified, except the *commentarii* of Vespasian and of Titus (mentioned in *Vita* [65], 342 and 358 and in *c. Apion.* 1 [10], 56), upon which he certainly drew for the movements of the Roman troops and for other details. The aim of the whole work is to show how the Jews were misled by an extremist minority, and at the same time to exalt the bravery of the Jews and thereby magnify the importance of the achievements of Vespasian and Titus. Noteworthy are the way in which Josephus exonerates Titus from all responsibility for the firing of the Temple, and the small part he gives to the Messianic movements that accompanied the political upheaval.

Of the *Jewish Antiquities* we need only speak as far as concerns the age of Herod and the events that preluded the Great Rebellion (Books XIV onward). The work was completed in A.D. 93–94 (xx [12, 1], 267) and dedicated to an Epaphroditus, not the freedman of Nero but the scholar and patron mentioned by Suidas; among other points that distinguish it from the *Bellum* we may note its greater detachment from the circle of the Herodians. Thus Josephus declares that his account roused the anger of the descendants of Herod, and stresses the fact that he belongs to a priestly family connected with the Hasmonaeans (the right interpretation in R. Laqueur, *Der jüdische Historiker Flavius Josephus*, pp. 130 *sqq.*). Consequently the history of Herod appears in less favourable light and Josephus deplores the overthrow of the rule of the Hasmonaeans (XIV [16, 4], 490–1). For most of Book XIV and for large parts of Books XV–XVII he follows Nicolaus, but he sometimes attacks him (xiv [1, 5], 9; xvi [7, 1], 183) and then corrects and completes him from other sources; these new sources show most clearly in contradictions of the previous account in *Wars*. Thus in *Bell. Jud.* 1 [18, 2], 351 the siege of Jerusalem in 37 B.C. is made to last five months, that is—since it began at the end of winter (cf. *Ant.* xiv [15, 14], 465)—until about July; but in the source of *Ant.* xiv [16, 4], 487 it is extended to the Fast of Kippur (about October), obviously to make a parallel with the end of the siege by Pompey, which is placed on this day—rightly or wrongly—by *Ant.* xiv [4, 3], 66 and Strabo xvi, 763. So too in *Bell.* 1 [22, 2], 437 the brother of Mariamme who was made High Priest is given his Jewish name Ionathes, while in *Ant.* xv [3, 3], 51 he has the Greek name Aristobulus.

In general, the chief corrections in Book xiv come from the *Historical Commentaries* of Strabo, in forty-three books, and those in Books xv–xvii are due to the use of a biography of Herod, which was not concerned to defend his memory. Possibly it was by Ptolemy (? of Ascalon), in so far as the only surviving fragment (cf. Ammonius, *de adfinium vocabulorum differentia*, ed. Kulenkamp, 1822, *s.v.* Ἰδουμαῖοι) suggests that it did not regard Herod as a Jew, but as an Idumaean, and so had no court flavour. The *Memoirs* of Herod, which Josephus cites once (xiv [6, 3], 174), must have been already used and cited by this biography. Most of the parts that go back to Nicolaus are in reality a superficial working-over of the corresponding parts of the *Wars*, but there is definite proof that on some points the source was re-read: for example, a comparison of xiv [5, 3], 88 with *Wars* 1 [8, 4], 166. In Books xviii–xx, as far as Jewish history is concerned, the narrative of *Wars* has been expanded with much new material of uncertain origin; some of it (*e.g.* the List of High Priests in xx [10, 1], 224 *sqq.*) is doubtless due to a written source, but most of it can be readily explained by the personal recollections and religious upbringing of the writer. There is thus no reason to believe that in the *Antiquities* either there was an anonymous intermediary between Josephus and his sources. We must admit that in the *Antiquities* Josephus again used helpers with varying stylistic mannerisms; for instance, his assistant for Books xvii–xix was a marked imitator of Thucydides (H. St John Thackeray, *Josephus, the Man and the Historian*, pp. 109 *sqq.*).

The *Life*, in its existing form, was certainly composed after A.D. 100—the year in which Agrippa II died (Photius, *Cod.* 33)—for his death is presupposed (*Vita*, [65], 359). But in reality it was first written as an Appendix to the *Antiquities*, as the last sentence conclusively shows. It seems clear then (as was first observed by G. Hölscher in *P.W.* ix, cols. 1941–2, and more fully demonstrated by B. Motzo, *Saggi di storia e letteratura giudeo-ellenistica*, p. 241) that the *Life* was originally published in A.D. 93–94 as an Appendix to the *Antiquities* and in a second edition after A.D. 100. The reason for this second edition must have been the publication, shortly after Agrippa's death, of a history of the Jewish War by Justus of Tiberias (cf. p. 858): indeed much of the present *Life* is polemic against him. Of the character of Justus' work we know nothing: F. Jacoby's rather hesitant hypothesis (in *P.W. s.v.* cols. 1344 *sq.*), that it is one with a chronicle by the same author (possibly called *Stemmata*) and of uncertain limits, does not seem justified. Yet the trustworthiness of Justus' information, at least as regards events in Judaea, is confirmed by Josephus himself; in attacking Justus he has to drop the pose of a great general, which he had assumed in the *Bellum* when describing affairs in Galilee, and so to give an account of them which agrees far more with the situation in which he actually found himself.

A. M.

8. THE PERSECUTION OF THE CHRISTIANS

The solution of this difficult problem given in the text (p. 725) is based upon the following considerations:

1. None of our sources, with the exception of Tacitus, knows of any connection between the persecution and the fire. Obviously, in the opinion of these sources the Christians were persecuted as being Christians. The evidence of Suetonius, *Nero* 16, is of fundamental importance, since it is not Christian.

2. Tacitus wavers between two explanations: that is, between the persecution of the Christians as Christians and the persecution of the Christians as incendiaries. In *Ann.* xv, 44 the sentence *ergo abolendo rumori Nero reos subdidit et quaesitissimis poenis adfecit quos per flagitia invisos vulgus Christianos appellabat* implies that the Christians were accused as incendiaries. But to the present writer it appears indubitable that a subsequent sentence presupposes a charge of being Christians: *igitur primum correpti qui fatebantur, deinde indicio eorum multitudo ingens haud proinde in crimine incendii quam odio humani generis convicti* (vel *coniuncti*) *sunt.* Granted that Tacitus does not believe that the Christians were guilty of incendiarism he cannot possibly have meant us to understand anything after *qui fatebantur* but *se Christianos esse*; for had he wished to say that they confessed to having fired Rome he must, in some way, have made it clear that the confession was extorted by force and was therefore without foundation. The proof that *qui fatebantur* presupposes a confession of being Christians is given in another sentence; *unde quamquam adversus sontes et novissima exempla meritos miseratio oriebatur.* Tacitus did not hold the Christians *sontes* as regards the crime of incendiarism; he did believe them guilty of the crime of being Christians. The interpretation which regards the word *sontes* as representing not the thought of Tacitus but the thought of those who believed them guilty of incendiarism is improbable in itself, and besides is contradicted by the phrase *novissima exempla meritos*, which undoubtedly reproduces the thought of Tacitus about the *exitiabilis superstitio.*

3. The wavering of Tacitus between the two explanations—which is the reason for the obscurity of the passage—cannot in its turn be explained except on the supposition that he combined two versions, one of which was common to him and Suetonius. Instead of trying to find an agreement between the two versions, Tacitus, as often elsewhere, has simply left them side by side.

4. Of the two versions, if we start without preconceived ideas, far the better documented appears to be that which is common to both Tacitus and Suetonius, which must go back to a contemporary of Nero (such as Pliny) and is confirmed by all Christian tradition. The other version must be regarded as an over-simplified interpretation of the persecution, made with the intention of putting Nero in an unfavourable light and suggested above all, as is shown below, by one of the things that the Christians may have been charged with during their trial.

5. It will be understood that the assertion that in the time of Nero the Christians were accused as Christians means merely that the Christians were regarded as constituting an illegal association guilty of crime, and not that their religious conceptions were attacked as such. We are not informed under what precise category the crimes attributed to them fell, since *odium humani generis* can scarcely be regarded as a specific accusation in law. But we may conjecture that every Christian, in so far as being such, could be regarded as guilty of *maiestas* (as stirring up civil strife), or more simply as guilty of *vis* (public violence), and it is likely that among the charges that were levelled at them was that of having set fire to Rome.   A. M.

9. THE DATE OF THE LEX JUNIA

This note makes no attempt to survey the literature which has grown up round the dispute about the date of the Lex Junia: its purpose is rather to provide a brief statement of the more important evidence, and to indicate the reasons which lead the writer to regard one interpretation as, on the whole, more plausible than its rival. From the name generally given to the measure itself (Lex Junia), as from the phrases used to designate the status which it created (Latinitas Juniana) and those to whom the status belonged (Latini Juniani), no clue about the date of the law is to be got for any conclusion more precise than that it was probably passed at a time when some Junius was consul. There is, however, one passage which might seem to offer a more accurate indication: the author of the first book of the *Institutes* appears to have described the law in question as a 'Lex Junia Norbana[1]' (though it may be noticed that both in the Latin tradition and in the corresponding sentence of the Greek paraphrase the manuscripts show several variants of the second name)[2]. If this could be accepted as proof that a Junius and a Norbanus had combined to give the law its title, there would be little doubt that it should be assigned to A.D. 19, when M. Junius M. f. Silanus and L. Norbanus [Balbus] were *consules ordinarii*[3]. Unfortunately, however, there are considerations which point to a different conclusion, and against them it is an open question whether a single text from the sixth century—even with such support as can be invoked to confirm it—may legitimately be allowed to prevail.

The exact year in which the Lex Junia was passed is a matter of less interest than its relation in time to the Lex Aelia Sentia of A.D. 4. Since there can be no question that it was the Lex Junia which created the form of Latinitas enjoyed by slaves informally manumitted[4], it follows that, if this kind of Latinitas was mentioned or assumed in A.D. 4 by the authors of the Lex Aelia Sentia, the Lex Junia itself must have been enacted at some earlier date. On this issue the evidence of Gaius may be taken first. In three places[5] he writes in a way which, if other testimony were lacking, would almost

---

[1] *Inst.* 1, 5, 3.
[2] For the Greek see *Institutionum Graeca Paraphrasis Theophilo antecessori vulgo tributa*...Rec....E. C. Ferrini. Pars prior (Berlin, 1883), p. 23.
[3] Tacitus, *Ann.* II, 59, 1; Dessau 5982, l. 12 *sq.*
[4] Gaius III, 56; *Frag. Dos.* 12.
[5] 1, 29, 31 and 66 (of which the last is imperfectly preserved): *cf.* 1, 80.

certainly be taken as proof that Junian Latinity was already a recognized
status when the Lex Aelia Sentia was drafted. He is dealing with the rights
which the Lex Aelia Sentia conferred on certain freedmen who, having
married either a Roman citizen or a Latin colonist or one of their own position, could satisfy an appropriate magistrate that a child born of the union
had reached the first anniversary of its birth. The freedmen concerned are
clearly those freed by informal manumission, whom any statute, so far as we
can say, must have treated as slaves at all times until the Lex Junia came to
give them Junian Latinity. In these passages, however, by contemplating
something which could be described as marriage between them and women of
Roman or colonial Latin status, Gaius clearly assumes that they were not
slaves, and this assumption implies that by the time of the Lex Aelia Sentia
they had already acquired Latinitas Juniana. Thus the doctrine of these
texts confirms Gaius in his explicit description of the freedmen in question
as Latins at the date when the Lex Aelia Sentia was passed, and the sense of
his argument makes it difficult to accept the suggestion that, in calling them
so, he is using by anticipation a name which in fact did not become appropriate until some later period.

So far the testimony of Gaius indicates that the Lex Junia was earlier
that the Lex Aelia Sentia, and this indication may be supported by two passages derived from Ulpian[1]. In the former of these the words 'quoquo modo
manumissi sunt' are hard to understand unless they include informal manumission; and, if that be so, the regulation here ascribed to the Lex Aelia
Sentia—that slaves of bad character, 'quoquo modo manumissi sunt,' became
dediticii—almost necessarily implies that the Lex Junia was the earlier law.
For, if the Lex Junia had not yet been passed, the Lex Aelia Sentia would
have had the absurd effect of giving freedom—as *dediticii*—to such informally
manumitted slaves as were rogues while leaving those of good character in
what legally was slavery.

On the other hand, there is one place[2] in which Gaius mentions the Lex
Aelia Sentia and the Lex Junia in that order, which might be taken as an
indication of their chronological sequence, and there are two passages in the
Epitome of Ulpian pointing to the same conclusion. One of them[3], if the
last three words be ignored, is phrased in a way which cannot be regarded as
accurate if the Lex Junia had been passed before the Lex Aelia Sentia. The
other[4] is in direct conflict with Gaius and, if it were right, would destroy the
argument for the priority of the Lex Junia based on Gaius I, 29, 31 and 66
(see above); for the arrangements contemplating marriage of freedmen
informally manumitted, which Gaius ascribes to the Lex Aelia Sentia,
thereby implying that the Lex Junia had already been passed, are here assigned to the Lex Junia itself.

In attempting to decide between Gaius and Ulpian it is first of all to be
recalled that not only was the doctrine of Gaius set down earlier than that of
Ulpian, but it is preserved in a manuscript which, so far as it is legible, gives
an unabbreviated text of his *Institutes*, whereas the relevant teaching of
Ulpian is only accessible in the version, more or less incomplete and more or
less garbled, produced by an epitomator. This consideration may be thought
to commend the authority of Gaius, and to it a second can be added. The

---

[1] *Ulpiani Epit.* I, 11; VII, 4.

[2] I, 80.   [3] I, 12.   [4] III, 3.

passage of the Ulpianic *Epitome* (III, 3) which is in open disagreement with Gaius comes near to being contradicted by another in the same work[1]. For these reasons it appears to the present writer that, on the issue which divides these authorities most sharply, the evidence of Gaius should probably be accepted. In that case the awkwardness of the language in 1, 12 would have to be ascribed to Ulpian's epitomator, and the peculiar order in which the Lex Aelia Sentia and the Lex Junia are mentioned by Gaius[2] might be explained by the fact that the Lex Aelia Sentia is undoubtedly the more germane to his argument at this point. Thus it seems possible to hold that the conclusion to be drawn, if not without hesitation, from the evidence of our legal sources is that the Lex Junia was passed before the Lex Aelia Sentia. Nevertheless, it must be plainly stated that the meaning of these texts is not beyond dispute. Even though such an interpretation is not perhaps the most natural, if demonstrative proof were forthcoming from some other quarter that the Lex Junia was a later measure than the Lex Aelia Sentia, they could be interpreted without great difficulty to accord with the version of the social legislation which would then be imperative. A recent treatment of the legal evidence so as to bring it into agreement with the theory which would put the Lex Junia in A.D. 19 is given by A. Steinwenter in his article 'Latini Iuniani' in Pauly-Wissowa-Kroll, *Real-Encyclopädie* (XII, cols. 910 *sqq.*).

Two historical considerations may be mentioned next. First, unless the account given in Chapter XIV is altogether misconceived, the task of social re-organization undertaken by Augustus was one which would make it surprising if he left his successor to solve the great problem set by slaves informally manumitted. And, secondly, though the Lex Junia was by no means an encouragement to the enfranchisement of slaves (see above, p. 432), its spirit is closer to that of the Augustan legislation as revealed in the Lex Aelia Sentia than to that of the principate of Tiberius as seen in the *senatus consultum* of A.D. 23[3] and the Lex Visellia of A.D. 24 (see above, p. 616).

Such in brief are the reasons which lead the present writer to the conclusion that the Lex Junia is probably to be placed in some year during the rule of Augustus earlier than the passing of the Lex Aelia Sentia in A.D. 4. The question of its precise date is less important. Cicero[4], writing in 44 B.C., gives a *terminus post quem* for its enactment, and thereafter the first plausible occasion is to be found in 25 B.C. when M. Junius M. f. Silanus was consul with Augustus. Nevertheless, though Agrippa was at Rome, Augustus himself spent this year in Spain, and for that reason the time was not one at which a major measure in the legislative programme is naturally to be expected. It is possible, indeed, that, if the description of the Lex Junia as a Lex Junia Norbana is a mere mistake, the error arose from a mis-reading of records which showed M. Junius M. f. Silanus and C. Norbanus C. f. Flaccus as successive colleagues of Augustus in the consulships of 25 and 24 B.C. respectively; but this consideration does little to commend 25 B.C. as the date of the law. The alternative is 17 B.C., when C. Junius C. f. Silanus was consul with C. Furnius C. f. and when Augustus himself was in Rome, actively engaged with the social reforms. For these reasons, if it is right to hold that the Lex Junia was earlier than the Lex Aelia Sentia, 17 B.C. would appear to the present writer to be the most probable year for its enactment.

H. M. L.

---

[1] VII, 4.   [2] 1, 80.   [3] Pliny, *N.H.* XXXIII, 32.   [4] *Topica*, 2, 10.

LIST OF ABBREVIATIONS

[See also General Bibliography, Parts II, IV, and for papyri the
bibliography to chapter x]

Abh. Arch.-epig.	Abhandlungen d. archäol.-epigraph. Seminars d. Univ. Wien.
Aeg.	Aegyptus. Rivista italiana di egittologia e di papirologia.
A.J.A.	American Journal of Archaeology.
A.J. Num.	American Journal of Numismatics.
A.J. Ph.	American Journal of Philology.
Ann. épig.	L'Année épigraphique.
Ann. Serv.	Annales du Service des Antiquités de l'Égypte.
Arch. Anz.	Archäologischer Anzeiger (in J.D.A.I.).
Arch. Pap.	Archiv für Papyrusforschung.
Arch. Relig.	Archiv für Religionswissenschaft.
Ath. Mitt.	Mitteilungen des deutschen arch. Inst. (Athenische Abteilung).
Atti Acc. Torino	Atti della r. Accademia di scienze di Torino.
Bay. Abh.	Abhandlungen d. bayerischen Akad. d. Wissenschaften.
Bay. S.B.	Sitzungsberichte d. bayerischen Akad. d. Wissenschaften.
B.C.H.	Bulletin de Correspondance hellénique.
Berl. Abh.	Abhandlungen d. preuss. Akad. d. Wissenschaften zu Berlin.
Berl. S.B.	Sitzungsberichte d. preuss. Akad. d. Wissenschaften zu Berlin.
B.J.	Bonner Jahrbücher.
B.M. Cat.	British Museum Catalogue.
B.P.W.	Berliner Philologische Wochenschrift.
B.S.A.	Annual of the British School at Athens.
B.S.R.	Papers of the British School at Rome.
Bursian	Bursian's Jahresbericht.
C.I.G.	Corpus Inscriptionum Graecarum.
C.I.L.	Corpus Inscriptionum Latinarum.
C.J.	Classical Journal.
C.P.	Classical Philology.
C.Q.	Classical Quarterly.
C.R.	Classical Review.
C.R. Ac. Inscr.	Comptes rendus de l'Académie des Inscriptions et Belles-Lettres.
Dessau	Dessau, Inscriptiones Latinae Selectae.
Ditt.³	Dittenberger, Sylloge Inscriptionum Graecarum. Ed. 3.
D.S.	Daremberg et Saglio, Dictionnaire des antiquités grecques et romaines.
Eph. Ep.	Ephemeris Epigraphica.
F.Gr. Hist.	F. Jacoby's Fragmente der griechischen Historiker.
F.H.G.	C. Müller's Fragmenta Historicorum Graecorum.
Germ.	Germania.
G.G.A.	Göttingische Gelehrte Anzeigen.
Gött. Abh.	Abhandlungen d. Gesellschaft d. Wissenschaften zu Göttingen.
Gött. Nach.	Nachrichten von der königlichen Gesellschaft der Wissenschaften zu Göttingen. Phil.-hist. Klasse.
Harv. St.	Harvard Studies in Classical Philology.
H.Z.	Historische Zeitschrift.
I.G.	Inscriptiones Graecae.
I.G.R.R.	Inscriptiones Graecae ad res Romanas pertinentes.
Jahreshefte	Jahreshefte d. österr. archäol. Instituts in Wien.

J.D.A.I.	Jahrbuch des deutschen archäologischen Instituts.
J. d. Sav.	Journal des Savants.
J.E.A.	Journal of Egyptian Archaeology.
J.H.S.	Journal of Hellenic Studies.
J.I. d'A.N.	Journal International d'Archéologie Numismatique.
J.P.	Journal of Philology.
J.R.S.	Journal of Roman Studies.
Mém. Ac. Inscr.	Mémoires de l'Académie des Inscriptions et Belles-Lettres.
Mem. Acc. Lincei	Memorie della r. Accademia nazionale dei Lincei.
Mem. Acc. Torino	Memorie della r. Accademia di scienze di Torino.
Mnem.	Mnemosyne.
Mus. B.	Musée belge.
N. J. f. Wiss.	Neue Jahrbücher für Wissenschaft und Jugendbildung.
N. J. Kl. Alt.	Neue Jahrbücher für das klassische Altertum.
N.J.P.	Neue Jahrbücher für Philologie.
N.S.A.	Notizie degli Scavi di Antichità.
Num. Chr.	Numismatic Chronicle.
Num. Z.	Numismatische Zeitschrift.
O.G.I.S.	Orientis Graeci Inscriptiones Selectae.
O.L.Z.	Orientalistische Literaturzeitung.
Phil.	Philologus.
Phil. Woch.	Philologische Wochenschrift.
P.W.	Pauly-Wissowa-Kroll's Real-Encyclopädie der classischen Altertumswissenschaft.
Rend. Linc.	Rendiconti della r. Accademia dei Lincei.
Rev. Arch.	Revue archéologique.
Rev. Belge	Revue Belge de philosophie et d'histoire.
Rev. Bib.	Revue biblique internationale.
Rev. E. A.	Revue des études anciennes.
Rev. E. G.	Revue des études grecques.
Rev. E. J.	Revue des études juives.
Rev. E. L.	Revue des études latines.
Rev. H.	Revue historique.
Rev. Hist. Rel.	Revue de l'histoire des religions.
Rev. N.	Revue numismatique.
Rev. Phil.	Revue de philologie, de littérature et d'histoire anciennes.
R.-G. K. Ber.	Berichte der Römisch-Germanischen Kommission.
Rh. Mus.	Rheinisches Museum für Philologie.
Riv. Fil.	Rivista di filologia.
Riv. stor. ant.	Rivista di storia antica.
Röm. Mitt.	Mitteilungen des deutschen arch. Inst. Römische Abteilung.
Sächs. Abh.	Abhandlungen d. sächs. Akad. d. Wissenschaften zu Leipzig.
S.B.	Sitzungsberichte.
S.E.G.	Supplementum epigraphicum Graecum.
St. Fil.	Studi italiani di filologia classica.
Symb. Osl.	Symbolae Osloenses.
Wien Anz.	Anzeiger d. Akad. d. Wissenschaften in Wien.
Wien S.B.	Sitzungsberichte d. Akad. d. Wissenschaften in Wien.
Wien. St.	Wiener Studien.
Z. d. Sav.-Stift.	Zeitschrift d. Savigny-Stiftung f. Rechtsgeschichte, Romanistische Abteilung.
Z.N.	Zeitschrift für Numismatik.

BIBLIOGRAPHIES

These bibliographies do not aim at completeness. They include modern and standard works and, in particular, books utilized in the writings of the chapters. Some technical monographs, especially in journals, are omitted, but the works that are registered below will put the reader on their track.

The works given in the General Bibliography for Greek and Roman History are, as a rule, not repeated in the bibliographies to the separate chapters.

The first page only of articles in journals is given.

GENERAL BIBLIOGRAPHY

I (a). GENERAL HISTORIES

Albertini, E. *L'Empire romain*. (Vol. iv in the *Peuples et Civilisations* Series directed by L. Halphen and P. Sagnac.) Paris, 1929.

Barbagallo, C. *Roma Antica*, ii. *L'Impero romano*. (Vol. ii of *Storia universale*.) Turin, 1932.

Bloch, G. *L'Empire romain. Évolution et décadence*. Paris, 1922.

Boak, A. E. R. *A History of Rome to* A.D. 565. Ed. 2. New York, 1929.

Bury, J. B. *A History of the Roman Empire from its Foundation to the death of Marcus Aurelius* (27 B.C.–A.D. 180). 6th Impression. London, 1913.

Chapot, V. *Le monde romain*. Paris, 1927.

Dessau, H. *Geschichte der römischen Kaiserzeit*. Berlin. Vol. i, 1924; vol. ii, i, 1926; vol. ii, ii, 1930.

von Domaszewski, A. *Geschichte der römischen Kaiser*. 2 vols. Ed. 3. Leipzig, 1922.

Drumann, W. *Geschichte Roms in seinem Übergange von der republikanischen zur monarchischen Verfassung*. Ed. 2, edited by P. Groebe. Vol. i, 1899, Berlin. Vol. ii, 1902; vol. iii, 1906; vol. iv, 1908; vol. v, 1919; vol. vi, 1929, Leipzig.

Duruy, V. *Histoire des Romains depuis les temps les plus reculés jusqu'à l'invasion des Barbares*. Paris, 1882–85. Vols. iv–vii.

Ferrero, G. *The Greatness and Decline of Rome*. Vols. iii–v, translated by H. J. Chaytor. London, vol. iii, 1907; vol. iv, 1908; vol. v, 1909.

Frank, T. *A History of Rome*. London, n.d. [1923].

—— *An Economic History of Rome*. Ed. 2. Baltimore, 1927.

Homo, L. *Le haut-empire*. (Vol. iii of *Histoire romaine* in the *Histoire générale* directed by G. Glotz.) Paris, 1933.

Jullian, C. *Histoire de la Gaule*. Vol. iv, Le Gouvernement de Rome. Ed. 4. Paris, 1929.

Kornemann, E. and J. Vogt. *Römische Geschichte* in Gercke-Norden, *Einleitung in die Altertumswissenschaft*. Ed. 3, iii, 2. Leipzig-Berlin, 1933.

Marsh, F. B. *The Founding of the Roman Empire*. Ed. 2. Oxford, 1927.

Mommsen, Th. *The Provinces of the Roman Empire from Caesar to Diocletian*. (English Translation by W. P. Dickson in 1886, reprinted with corrections in 1909.) London, 1909.

Niese, B. *Grundriss der römischen Geschichte nebst Quellenkunde.* 5te Auflage neubearbeitet von E. Hohl. (Müller's *Handbuch der klassischen Altertumswissenschaft,* Band III, Abt. 5.) Munich, 1923.

Nilsson, M. P. *Imperial Rome,* translated by G. C. Richards. London, 1926.

Pais, E. *Dalle guerre puniche a Cesare Augusto.* 2 vols. Rome, 1918.

Rostovtzeff, M. *The Social and Economic History of the Roman Empire.* 1926. Ed. 2 (in German), *Gesellschaft und Wirtschaft im römischen Kaiserreich.* Leipzig, n.d. [1930]: ed. 3 (in Italian), *Storia economica e sociale dell' impero Romano.* Florence, 1933.

—— *A History of the Ancient World.* Vol. II, Rome. Oxford, 1927.

Schiller, H. *Geschichte der römischen Kaiserzeit.* Gotha. Vol. I, i & ii, 1883; vol. II, 1887.

Stevenson, G. H. *The Roman Empire.* London, 1930.

Stuart Jones, H. *The Roman Empire,* B.C. 29–A.D. 476. 3rd Impression, London, 1916.

Toutain, J. *L'économie antique.* Paris, 1927.

Wells, J. and R. H. Barrow. *A Short History of the Roman Empire to the death of Marcus Aurelius.* London, 1931.

I (b). MONOGRAPHS ON AUGUSTUS

Gardthausen, V. *Augustus und seine Zeit.* Leipzig. Erster Teil: erster Band, 1891; zweiter Band, 1896; dritter Band, 1904. Zweiter Teil: erster Halbband, 1891; zweiter Halbband, 1896; dritter Band, 1904. Bibliographische Nachträge zu Teil II, n.d.

Holmes, T. Rice. *The Architect of the Roman Empire.* Oxford. Vol. I, 1928; vol. II (27 B.C.–A.D. 14), 1931.

Seeck, O. *Kaiser Augustus.* Bielefeld-Leipzig, 1902.

Shuckburgh, E. S. *Augustus: The Life and Times of the Founder of the Roman Empire* (B.C. 63–A.D. 14). London, 1903.

II. WORKS OF REFERENCE, DICTIONARIES, ETC.

Abbott, F. F. and A. C. Johnson. *Municipal Administration in the Roman Empire.* Princeton, N.J., 1926.

Daremberg, Ch. and E. Saglio. *Dictionnaire des antiquités grecques et romaines d'après les textes et les monuments.* Paris, 1877–1919. (D.S.)

De Ruggiero, G. *Dizionario Epigrafico di Antichità romane.* Rome. 1895– . (Diz. Epig.)

Friedländer, L. and G. Wissowa. *Darstellungen aus der Sittengeschichte Roms.* Ed. 10. Leipzig, 1919–21.

Gercke, A. and E. Norden. *Einleitung in die Altertumswissenschaft.* Ed. 2, Leipzig-Berlin, 1914. Ed. 3 in course of publication. (Gercke-Norden.)

Hirschfeld, O. *Die kaiserlichen Verwaltungsbeamten bis auf Diocletian.* Ed. 2. Berlin, 1905.

Lübker, Friedrich. *Reallexikon des klassischen Altertums für Gymnasien.* Ed. 8 (by J. Geffcken and E. Ziebarth). Leipzig, 1914. (Lübker.)

Marquardt, J. *Römische Staatsverwaltung.* Leipzig. Ed. 2. Vol. I, 1881; vol. II, 1884; vol. III, 1885.

Mommsen, Th. *Abriss des römischen Staatsrecht.* Ed. 2. Leipzig, 1907.

—— *Römisches Staatsrecht.* Leipzig. Vol. I (ed. 3), 1887; vol. II, I (ed. 3), 1887; vol. II, 2 (ed. 3), 1887; vol. III, I, 1887; vol. III, 2, 1888.

—— *Römisches Strafrecht.* Leipzig, 1899.

von Müller, Iwan. *Handbuch der Altertumswissenschaft.* (In course of revision under editorship of W. Otto.) Munich, 1886–   . (Müllers Handbuch.)

Platner, S. B. *A Topographical Dictionary of Ancient Rome.* (Completed and revised by T. Ashby.) Oxford, 1929.

Roscher, W. H. *Ausführliches Lexikon der griechischen und römischen Mythologie.* (Under editorship of K. Ziegler.) Leipzig, 1884–   . (Roscher.)

Sandys, Sir J. E. *A Companion to Latin Studies.* Ed. 3. Cambridge, 1929.

Stuart Jones, H. *A Companion to Roman History.* Oxford, 1912.

Wissowa, G. *Pauly's Real-Encyclopädie der classischen Altertumswissenschaft.* Neue Bearbeitung. (Under editorship of W. Kroll.) Stuttgart, 1894–   . (P.W.)

III. CHRONOLOGY

Bickermann, E. *Chronologie,* in Gercke-Norden, Band III, Heft 5. Leipzig-Berlin, 1933.

Goyau, G. *Chronologie de l'empire romain.* Paris, 1891.

Griffin, M. H. and G. A. Harrer. *Fasti Consulares.* A.J.A. XXXIV, 1930, pp. 360 *sqq.*

Kubitschek, W. *Grundriss der antiken Zeitrechnung,* in Müllers Handbuch, I, 7. Munich, 1928.

Leuze, O. *Bericht über die Literatur zur Chronologie (Kalendar und Jahrzählung) in die Jahren* 1921–1928. Bursian, CCXXVII, 1930, pp. 97–139.

Liebenam, W. *Fasti Consulares imperii Romani von 30 v. Chr. bis 565 n. Chr.* Bonn, 1909.

IV. NUMISMATICS

Bernhart, M. *Handbuch zur Münzkunde der römischen Kaiserzeit.* Halle a.S., 1926.

Cohen, H. *Description historique des monnaies frappées sous l'empire romain.* Ed. 2. Paris, 1880–92.

Head, B. V. *Historia Numorum.* Ed. 2 (assisted by G. F. Hill, George Macdonald, and W. Wroth). Oxford, 1911. (H.N.²)

Mattingly, H. *British Museum Catalogue of Coins of the Roman Empire.* Vol. I (Augustus to Vitellius). London, 1923. (Mattingly.)

Mattingly, H. and E. A. Sydenham. *The Roman Imperial Coinage.* Vol. I (Augustus to Vitellius). London, 1923. (Mattingly-Sydenham.)

Milne, J. G. *Catalogue of Alexandrian Coins in the Ashmolean Museum.* Oxford, 1932.

Münsterberg, R. *Die römische Kaisernamen der griechischen Münzen.* Num. Z. LIX, 1926, p. 1.

—— *Die Kaisernamen der römischen Kolonialmünzen. Ib.* p. 51.

Schulz, O. Th. *Die Rechtstitel und Regierungsprogramme auf römischen Kaisermünzen, von Caesar bis Severus.* (Studien zur Geschichte und Kultur des Altertums, XIII, 4.) Paderborn, 1925.

Vogt, J. *Die alexandrinischen Münzen.* Stuttgart, 1924.

Wruck, W. *Die syrische Provinzialprägung von Augustus bis Trajan.* Stuttgart, 1931.

CHAPTERS I—IV

THE AVENGING OF CAESAR: THE TRIUMVIRS: THE WAR OF THE EAST AGAINST THE WEST: THE TRIUMPH OF OCTAVIAN

PART I. AFFAIRS IN ITALY, SICILY, AND THE WESTERN PROVINCES

I. SOURCES

A. *Primary*

(a) Contemporary Documents.

1. Lex tabulae Heracleensis, dicta Iulia municipalis. Dessau 6085; Bruns, *Fontes*[7],18; Abbott and Johnson, 24. See A. von Premerstein, *Die Tafel von Heraclea und die Acta Caesaris*, Z. d. Sav.-Stift. XLIII, 1922, p. 45, and for previous treatments of the topic see Bibliography to Vol. IX, Chapters XV–XVII, p. 956.
2. Lex Coloniae Genetivae Iuliae seu Ursonensis. Dessau 6087; Bruns, *Fontes*[7], 28; Abbott and Johnson, 26. See A. von Premerstein's article cited above.
3. Lex Falcidia. Bruns, *Fontes*[7], 19; *Dig.* XXXV, 2, 1.
4. Laudatio ?Turiae. Dessau 8393; Bruns, *Fontes*[7], 126: *C.I.L.* VI, 37053.
5. Edictum de privilegiis veteranorum. Bruns, *Fontes*[7], 69; H. Malcovati, *Caesaris Augusti Imperatoris operum fragmenta*[2], XCVI, p. 36; U. Wilcken, *Grundzüge und Chrestomathie der Papyruskunde*, 462.
6. An edict of Octavian and letters to the town of Rhosos, first published by P. Roussel, in *Syria*, XV, 1934, p. 33.
7. *C.I.L.* I[2], pars i, *Fasti Consulares*, pp. 158–161; *Acta Triumphorum*, pp. 179–180; *Feriale Cumanum*, p. 229.

See also the following inscriptions in Dessau, 41, 42, 76–81, 108, 885, 886, 889, 893 and 893[A], 895, 896, 1945, 2672, 6085, 6087, 6317, 8393, 8891, 8893. See also *C.I.L.* V, 2603 as completed by *N.S.A.* 1915, p. 139 (= *Ann. épig.* 1916, 60); *Ann. épig.* 1922, 96 (date of second battle of Philippi).

(b) Contemporary Speeches and Writings.

Caesaris Augusti Imperatoris operum fragmenta iteratis curis collegit, recensuit, praefata est, appendicem criticam addidit Henrica Malcovati. Turin, 1928, pp. 2; 15; 36–37; 60–71.

Res Gestae divi Augusti iterum ed. Th. Mommsen, Berlin, 1883. For the Antiochene version see (Sir) W. M. Ramsay and A. von Premerstein, *Monumentum Antiochenum: die neugefundene Aufzeichnung der Res Gestae divi Augusti im Pisidischen Antiochia* (Klio, Beiheft XIX), Leipzig, 1927, which contains a convenient summary of previous important literature; the newest text conveniently in Malcovati, *op. cit.* pp. 78–105, and in C. Barini, *Res Gestae Divi Augusti*, Milan, 1930. See further below, C. 5.

Cicero, *Epistulae ad Atticum* (ed. L. C. Purser), XIV–XVI. *Epistulae ad M. Brutum* (ed. L. C. Purser), I–II. *Epistulae ad Familiares* (ed. L. C. Purser), IX, 14; X; XI; XII, 1–16; 20–30; XV, 20; XVI, 23, 24.

The Correspondence of M. Tullius Cicero, arranged...by R. Y. Tyrrell and L. C. Purser. Dublin. Vol. V (ed. 2), 1915; Vol. VI (ed. 2), 1933.

Cicero, *Philippicae* (ed. A. C. Clark), I–XIV. *M. Tulli Ciceronis in M. Antonium Orationes Philippicae prima et secunda.* Ed. J. D. Denniston, Oxford, 1926.

(c) Coins.

Babelon, E. *Description historique et chronologique des monnaies de la République romaine*. Paris, 1885–86. Vol. I, pp. 129–134; 158–206; 433–435; 465–467. Vol. II, pp. 32–67; 240–245.

Cohen, H. *Description historique des Monnaies frappées sous l'Empire romain*. Paris. Ed. 2. Vol. I, 1880, pp. 21–62; 72–74.

Grueber, H. A. *Coins of the Roman Republic in the British Museum*. London, 1910. Vol. I, pp. 554–594. Vol. II, pp. 1–17; p. 373; pp. 392–417; pp. 510–514; pp. 560–565; pp. 577–581.

Hill, G. F. *Historical Roman Coins*. London, 1909. pp. 112–136.

Mattingly, H. *Roman Coins*. London, 1928. pp. 83–85.

Mattingly, H. and Sydenham, E. A. *The Roman Imperial Coinage*. Vol. I, London, 1923. pp. 41–44.

For a unique copper coin of M. Agrippa see H. Mattingly, in *Num. Chr.* (Ser. 5) XIV, 1934, p. 2.

B. *Secondary*

Appian, *Hannib.* (ed. L. Mendelssohn), 13; *Libyca*, 136; *Ill.* 12–29. *Bella Civilia* (ed. P. Viereck), II, 118 (494)–V, 145 (602).

Dio Cassius (ed. U. P. Boissevain), XLIV, 20–LIII, 2, 7.

Josephus, *Antiquitates Judaicae* (ed. S. A. Naber), XIV [12, 2], 301; [14, 4], 381–[14, 5], 389. *Bellum Judaicum* (ed. S. A. Naber), I [12. 4], 242; [14. 4], 282–5.

Epitomizers of Livy: *Periochae*, 116–134; Orosius VI, 18–20; VII, 6, 5; Florus II, xiv–xxi; xxvi [IV, 3–12]; Eutropius VII, 1–8; Incerti, *de viris illustribus*, 79–85.

Nicolaus of Damascus, περὶ τοῦ Βίου Καίσαρος καὶ τῆς αὐτοῦ ἀγωγῆς (?), in Jacoby, *F. Gr. Hist.* II A, pp. 391–420.

Pliny, *N.H.* (ed. C. Mayhoff). *Praef.* 31; II, 93, 98; III, 36; IV, 42, 47; VII, 57, 147–149; IX, 55, 85; X, 110; XII, 13; XV, 136; XVI, 7; XXVI, 125; XXXI, 41; XXXIII, 39; XXXIV, 58; XXXV, 200; XXXVI, 104, 121; XXXVII, 9–10.

Plutarch, *Moralia* (ed. G. Bernardakis). Vol. II, p. 96 (*Apophthegmata*, 206 F); p. 390 (*de fortuna Rom.* 319 B); V, p. 25 (*an seni gerenda*, 784 D).

Plutarch, *Vitae* (edd. Cl. Lindskog and K. Ziegler); *Antony*, 14–87; *Brutus*, 17–53 (*Comp. Bruti cum Dione*, 2, 4, 5); *Cato Minor*, 73. (Ed. C. Sintenis); *C. Caesar*, 67–69; *Cicero*, 42–49 (*Comp. Dem. cum Cicerone*, 3, 4).

Polyaenus (ed. J. Melber). VIII, 24, 7.

Pseudo-Ciceronis, *Epistula ad Octavianum* (ed. L. C. Purser).

Scriptores Historiae Augustae (ed. E. Hohl). I, x, 7, 6.

Seneca, *Epistulae Morales* (ed. O. Hense). 82, 12; 83, 25; 91, 14.

Seneca, *Quaestiones naturales* (ed. A. Gercke), I, 2, 1; IV, *praef.* 21, 22: *de beneficiis* (ed. C. Hosius), III, 32, 5; *de clementia* (ed. C. Hosius), I, 9, 1; 10, 1, 4; II, 1.

Strabo (ed. A. Meineke). IV, 194, 205, 207, 208; V, 244–45, 258–59, 268, 270, 272; VI, 296, 305, 313–15.

Strabonis ἱστορικῶν ὑπομνημάτων Fragmenta collegit et enarravit adjectis quaestionibus Strabonianis P. Otto. (Leipziger Studien zur Klassischen Philologie, Supplementheft XI.) Leipzig, 1889.

Suetonius, *de vita Caesarum libri viii* (rec. M. Ihm). *Divus Iulius*, 82, 3–85; 88, 89. *Divus Augustus*, passim. *Tiberius*, 4, 2–7, 1. *Claudius*, I, 1. *Nero*, 3. *Galba*, 3, 2.

C. Suetoni Tranquilli Divus Augustus, edited with historical introduction, commentary, appendices and indices by E. S. Shuckburgh. Cambridge, 1896.

Tacitus, *Annals* (ed. C. Halm; ed. S. G. Andresen). I, 1; 2; 9, 4, 5; 10, 1, 2; II, 27, 2; 53, 2; III, 18, 1; 28, 3; 72, 2; IV, 5, 1; 34, 8; 43, 1; 44, 2; V, 1, 2, 3; VI, 11, 3; 51, 1, 2; XI, 7, 4; 25, 3; XIII, 6, 4.
—— *dialogus de oratoribus* (ed. H. Furneaux), 17, 2; 28, 6.
Valerius Maximus (ed. C. Kempf), VI, 4, 5; 7, 2, 3; 8, 4–7; VIII, 3, 3; IX, 5, 4; 11, 5–7; 13, 3.
Velleius Paterculus (ed. A. Bolaffi), II, 56–89.

C. *Source-criticism*

The items are given in chronological order.

1. *General.*

Wachsmuth, C. *Einleitung in das Studium der alten Geschichte.* Leipzig, 1895.
Peter, H. *Die geschichtliche Literatur über die römische Kaiserzeit bis Theodosius I und ihre Quellen.* Leipzig, 1897, 2 vols.
Leo, F. *Die griechisch-römisch Biographie nach ihrer literarischen Form.* Leipzig, 1901.
Rosenberg, A. *Einleitung und Quellenkunde zur römischen Geschichte.* Berlin, 1921.
Levi, M. A. *Appendice sulle Fonti.* In *Ottaviano capoparte*, vol. II, Florence, 1933, pp. 189–260.

2. *Appian.*

Bailleu, P. *Quomodo Appianus in bellorum civilium libris II–V usus sit Asinii Pollionis historiis.* Diss. Göttingen, 1874.
Soltau, W. *Appians Bürgerkriege.* Phil. Suppl. bd. VII, 1899, p. 597.
Schwartz, Ed. Art. in P.W. *s.v.* Appianus, col. 216.
Kornemann, E. *Die unmittelbare Vorlage von Appians Emphylia.* Klio, XVII, 1920, p. 33.

3. *Dio.*

Grasshof, M. *De fontibus et auctoritate Dionis Cassii.* Bonn, 1867.
Fischer, J. Gu. *De fontibus et auctoritate Cassii Dionis in enarrandis a Cicerone post Caesaris mortem a.d. xvi K. Apr. de pace et Kal. Ian. anni a Chr. n. 43 habitis orationibus.* Diss. Leipzig, 1870.
Beckurts, F. *Zur Quellenkritik des Tacitus, Sueton und Cassius Dio.* Diss. Braunschweig, 1880.
Schwartz, Ed. Art. in P.W. *s.v.* Cassius Dio (40).
Vrind, G. *De Cassii Dionis Historiis.* Mnem. LIV, 1926, p. 321.

4. *Josephus* (see also below, p. 992).

Destinon, J. v. *Die Quellen des Flavius Josephus in der jüdischen Archaeologie B. XII–XVII.* Kiel, 1882.
Korach, L. *Über den Wert des Josephus als Quelle für die römische Geschichte.* (Teil 1. Bis zum Tode des Augustus.) Leipzig Diss. Breslau, 1895.
Albert, K. *Strabo als Quelle des Flavius Josephus.* Würzburg Diss. Aschaffenburg, 1902.
Hölscher, G. *Die Quellen des Josephus für die Zeit vom Exil bis zum jüdischen Kriege.* Marburg Diss. Leipzig, 1904.
Hölscher, G. Art. in P.W. *s.v.* Josephus.
Laqueur, R. *Der jüdische Historiker Flavius Josephus.* Giessen, 1920.
Thackeray, H. St J. *Josephus the Man and Historian.* New York, 1929.

5. *Res Gestae Divi Augusti.*

A full bibliography is provided in H. Malcovati, *op. cit.* pp. lvii–lxii, down to the year 1927. Attention is called to the following studies:

Wilcken, U. *Zur Entstehung des Monumentum Ancyranum.* Hermes, XXXVIII, 1903, p. 618.

Vulić, N. *Quando fu scritto il Monumentum Ancyranum?* Riv. stor. ant. XIII, 1909, p. 41.

Besnier, M. *Récents Travaux sur les Res gestae divi Augusti.* Mélanges Cagnat, Paris, 1912, pp. 119–151.

Kornemann, E. *Mausoleum und Tatenbericht des Augustus.* Leipzig-Berlin, 1921. (This sums up many previous contributions to *Klio.*)

—— Art. in P.W. *s.v.* Monumentum Ancyranum.

Harrer, G. A. *Res gestae Divi Augusti.* Studies in Philology, XXIII, 1926, p. 387.

Dessau, H. *Mommsen und das Monumentum Ancyranum,* Klio, XXII, 1928, p. 261.

Wilcken, U. *Zu den Impensae der Res Gestae divi Augusti.* Berl. S.B. 1931, p. 772.

Rudberg, G. *Zu Monumentum Ancyranum.* Symb. Osl. X, 1932, p. 148.

Wilcken, U. *Zur Genesis der Res Gestae divi Augusti.* Berl. S.B. 1932, p. 225.

Ensslin, W. *Zu den* Res gestae Divi Augusti. Rh. Mus. LXXXI, 1932, p. 335.

6. *Strabo.*

Pais, E. *Straboniana.* Riv. Fil. XV, 1886/7, p. 97.

Otto, P. *De Strabone Appiani et Plutarchi fonte* in *Strabonis...Fragmenta.* Leipzig, 1889, pp. 245 *sqq.*

Pais, E. *The time and place in which Strabo composed his Historical Geography* in *Ancient Italy.* Chicago, 1908, pp. 379–428.

—— in *Italia Antica,* vol. I, 1922, pp. 269–316.

Anderson, J. G. C. *Some questions bearing on the date and place of composition of Strabo's Geography,* in *Anatolian Studies presented to Sir William Mitchell Ramsay,* Manchester, 1923, pp. 1–13.

Sihler, E. G. *Strabo of Amaseia: His Personality and His Works.* A.J. Ph. XLIV, 1923, p. 134.

Honigmann, E. Art. in P.W. *s.v.* Strabon.

7. *Suetonius.*

Macé, A. *Essai sur Suétone.* Paris, 1900.

Ciaceri, E. *Alcune osservazioni sulle fonti di C. Suetonio Tranquillo nella Vita di Augusto.* Catania, 1901.

Fürst, W. *Suetons Verhältnis zu der Denkschrift des Augustus.* Diss. Erlangen, 1904.

Gottanka, F. *Suetons Verhältnis zu der Denkschrift des Augustus.* Programm des K. Luitpold-Gymnasiums in München. Munich, 1904.

von Wölfflin, E. *Sueton und das Monumentum Ancyranum.* Arch. f. Lat. Lexik. und Grammatik, XIII, 1904, p. 193.

Mueller, H. *Suetons Verhältniss zum M.A.* Würzburg Progr. 1914.

Hache, F. in Bursian, CCXXVI, 1930, pp. 207–232. (Report on Literature on Suetonius between 1918 and 1928.)

Funaioli, G. Art. in P.W. *s.v.* Suetonius (4).

8. *Tacitus.*

See Bibliography to Chapter XIX, *Tiberius,* section I. A. 5*d,* Sources and Source-criticism (p. 963 *sq.*).

9. *Velleius Paterculus.*

Faust, F. *De Vellei Paterculi rerum Scriptoris fide.* Diss. Giessen, 1891.

Burmeister, F. *De fontibus Vellei Paterculi.* Diss. Halle, 1893.

Münzer, F. *Zur Komposition des Velleius* (aus der Festschrift zur 49ten Versammlung Deutscher Philologen und Schulmänner). Basel, 1907, pp. 247–278.

Raff, P. *Le fonti storiche di Velleio Paterculo.* Lucera, 1925.

10. *Miscellaneous* (grouped under authors).

Blumenthal, F. *Die Autobiographie des Augustus.* Wien. St. xxxv, 1913, pp. 113 *sqq.* and 267 *sqq.*; xxxvi, 1914, pp. 84 *sqq.*

Bosch, C. *Die Quellen des Valerius Maximus.* Stuttgart, 1929.

Patsch, C. *Zu Nicolaus von Damascus.* Wien. St. xii, 1890, p. 231.

Witte, K. *De Nicolai Damasceni fragmentorum Romanorum fontibus.* Berlin, 1900.

Duttlinger, R. *Untersuchungen über den historischen Wert des* Βίος Καίσαρος *des Nicolaus Damascenus.* Heidelberg Diss. Zürich, 1911.

Hall, C. M. *Nicolaus of Damascus' Life of Augustus.* (Smith College Classical Studies.) Northampton (Mass.), 1923.

Rühl, F. *Die griechischen Briefe des Brutus.* Rh. Mus. lxx, 1915, p. 315.

Cichorius, C. *Die griechischen Brutusbriefe und ihre Verfasser* in *Römische Studien,* Berlin-Leipzig, 1922, pp. 434–438.

Kornemann, E. *Der historische Schriftstellerei des C. Asinius Pollio.* Jahrb. f. class. Phil. Suppl. xxii, 1896, p. 555.

Groebe, P. Art. *s.v.* Asinius (25) Pollio in P.W.

Daebritz, R. *Zu Asinius Pollio.* Phil. lxx, 1911, p. 267.

Hammer, J. *Prolegomena to an Edition of the Panegyricus Messallae.* New York, 1925.

Gudeman, A. *The Sources of Plutarch's Life of Cicero.* Philadelphia, 1902.

Wachsmuth, C. *Timagenes und Trogus.* Rh. Mus. xlvi, 1891, p. 478.

II. Modern Literature

A. *General Works*

Besides the relevant parts of the general histories of the Empire and monographs on Augustus cited in Section I of the General Bibliography, the following should be noted as relevant to the period:

Becht, E. *Regeste über die Zeit von Caesars Ermordung bis zum Umschwung der Politik des Antonius.* Freiburg i.B. 1911.

Ciaceri, E. *Cicerone e i suoi tempi.* Milan. Vol. ii, 1930, pp. 333–399.

Daniel, R. *M. Vipsanius Agrippa. Eine Monographie.* Diss. Breslau, 1933.

von Domaszewski, A. *Die Heere der Bürgerkriege in den Jahren 49 bis 42 vor Christus.* Neue Heid. Jahrb. iv, 1894, p. 157 (esp. pp. 175–188).

Fitzler, K. and O. Seeck. Art. in P.W. *s.v.* Julius (132) (Augustus), cols. 275–342.

Groebe, P. Art. in P.W. *s.v.* Antonius (30), cols. 2595–2614.

Holmes, T. Rice. *The Architect of the Roman Empire.* Oxford, 1928.

Kappelmacher, A. Art. in P.W. *s.v.* Maecenas (6).

Levi, M. A. *Ottaviano capoparte.* 2 vols. Florence, 1933.

Miltner, F. Art. in P.W. *s.v.* Seekrieg (Römer), cols. 896–898.

Reinhold, M. *Marcus Agrippa. A biography.* Geneva–New York, 1933.

von Rohden, P. Art. in P.W. *s.v.* Aemilius (73), cols. 556–561.

B. *Antony in Power*

Bondurant, B. C. *Decimus Junius Brutus Albinus.* Chicago, 1907.

Deutsch, M. E. *Caesar's Son and Heir.* Univ. Calif. Public. in Class. Arch. ix, 1928, no. 6, p. 149.

Deutsch, M. E. *Antony's Funeral Speech.* Univ. Calif. Public. in Class. Arch. ix, 1928, no. 5, p. 127.

Liegle, J. *Pietas.* Z.N. xlii, 1932, p. 59.

Münzer, F. *D. Junius Brutus Albinus* (55a) in P.W. Supplementband V.

von Premerstein, A. *Die Tafel von Heraclea und die Acta Caesaris.* Z. d. Sav.-Stift. xliii, 1922, p. 45.

Schelle, E. *Beiträge zur Geschichte des Todeskampfes der römischen Republik.* Dresden, 1891.

Schmidt, O. E. *Die letzten Kämpfe der römischen Republik.* Jahrb. f. class. Phil. Suppl. xiii, 1884, p. 663.

Schwartz, Ed. *Die Vertheilung der römischen Provinzen nach Caesars Tod.* Hermes, xxxiii, 1898, p. 185.

C. *The young Octavius*

Anton, [n. i.] *De sideribus Augusti nataliciis quae coniicienda videantur.* Halle, 1861.

Blumenthal, F. *Die Autobiographie des Augustus.* Wien. St. xxxv, 1913, p. 113; p. 267; xxxvi, 1914, p. 84.

Deonna, W. *La légende d'Octave Auguste Dieu Sauveur et maître du monde.* Rev. Hist. Rel. lxxxiii, 1921, pp. 32 *sqq.*, pp. 163 *sqq.*; lxxxiv, 1921, pp. 77 *sqq.*

Ensslin, W. *Zu den Res Gestae divi Augusti.* iii. *Zu c.* 13, ii 44. Rh. Mus. lxxxi, 1932, p. 362.

von Frauenholtz, E. *Imperator Octavianus Augustus in der Geschichte und Sage des Mittelalters.* Historisches Jahrbuch xlvi, 1926, p. 86.

Gundel, W. *Textkritische und exegetische Bemerkungen zu Manilius.* Phil. xxxv, 1926, pp. 331 *sqq.* (on ii, 507 and the *thema* of Augustus).

Housman, A. E. *Manilius, Augustus, Tiberius Capricornus and Libra.* C.Q. vii, 1913, p. 109.

Kleinstück, H. *Antike Beobachtungen zur meteorologischen Optik.* In *Festschrift zu Franz Polands fünfundsiebzigstem Geburtstag.* Leipzig, 1932, cols. 237 *sqq.*

McCarthy, J. H. *Octavianus puer.* C.P. xxvi, 1931, p. 362.

Mommsen, Th. *Das Datum der Erscheinung des Kometen nach Caesars Tod.* Ges. Schriften, iv, pp. 180–182.

—— *Das Augustische Festverzeichniss von Cumae.* Ges. Schriften, iv, pp. 259–270.

von Voigt, W. *Unter welchen Gestirnen wurde Cäsar, Agrippa und Tiberius geboren?* Phil. lviii, 1899, p. 170.

D. *Mutina*

Bardt, C. *Plancus und Lepidus im Mutinensischen Kriege.* Hermes, xliv, 1909, p. 574.

Frank, T. *Tulliana.* 1. *triumviris, Ad Att.* xvi, 11. 1. A.J. Ph. xli, 1920, p. 275.

Groebe, P. *De legibus et senatus consultis anni* 710. Berlin, 1893.

von Hagen, A. *De bello Mutinensi quaestiones criticae.* Marburg, 1886.

Simon, L. *Die Spuren einer unbekannten Philippika Ciceros.* N.J. Kl. Alt. xiv, 1911, p. 412.

Solari, A. *Claterna.* Riv. Fil. (N.S.) vii, 1929, p. 97.

Sternkopf, W. *Plancus, Lepidus und Laterensis im Mai* 43. Hermes, xlv, 1910, p. 250.

—— *Die Verteilung der römischen Provinzen vor dem Mutinensischen Kriege.* Hermes, xlvii, 1912, p. 321.

van Wageningen, J. *De C. Asinii Pollionis ad Antonium transitione.* Mnem. xlvii, 1919, p. 77.

E. *The Triumvirate and the Proscription. Philippi*

Collart, P. *Note sur les mouvements de troupes qui ont précédé la bataille de Philippes.* B.C.H. LIII, 1929, p. 351.
—— *Brutus et Cassius en Thrace.* B.C.H. LV, 1931, p. 423.
Conway, R. S. *The Proscription of 43 B.C.* Harvard Lectures on the Vergilian Age. Cambridge, Mass. 1928, pp. 3–13.
Hirschfeld, O. *Die sogenannte Laudatio Turiae.* Kleine Schriften, Berlin, 1913, p. 824.
Hülsen, Chr. *Zum Kalendar der Arvalbrüder: Das Datum der Schlacht bei Philippi.* In *Strena Buliciana.* Zagreb, 1924, pp. 193 *sqq.*
Kloevekorn, H. *De Proscriptionibus a. a. Chr. 43 a M. Antonio, M. Aemilio Lepido, C. Iulio Octaviano triumviris factis.* Diss. Regiomontani, 1891.
Kromayer, J. and G. Veith. *Antike Schlachtfelder,* IV, Berlin, 1924–31, pp. 654–661.
—— *Schlachtenatlas zur antiken Kriegsgeschichte.* Röm. Abt. IV. Leipzig, 1924, Blatt 23.
Rothstein, M. *Caesar über Brutus.* Rh. Mus. LXXXI, 1932, p. 324.
Warde Fowler, W. *On the Laudatio Turiae and its Additional Fragments.* Roman Essays and Interpretations. Oxford, 1920, p. 126.

F. *Perusia and After*

Bayet, J. *Virgile et les triumvirs "agris diuidundis,"* Rev. E.L. VI, 1928, p. 270.
Cantarelli, L. *Origine e governo delle provincie africane sotto l'impero.* Riv. stor. ant. V, 1900, p. 91.
Frothingham, A. L. *Propertius and the arae Perusinae.* C.P. IV, 1909, p. 345.
Ganter, F. L. *Die Provinzialverwaltung der Triumvirn.* Diss. Strassburg, 1892.
—— *Q. Cornuficius.* Phil. LIII, 1894, p. 132.
Gsell, S. *Histoire ancienne de l'Afrique du Nord.* Vol. VIII. (Jules César et l'Afrique. Fin des royaumes indigènes.) Pp. 182–199. Paris, 1928.
Heitland, W. E. *A great agricultural emigration from Italy?* J.R.S. VIII, 1918, p. 34.
Klingner, F. *Virgil's Erste Ekloge.* Hermes, LXII, 1927, p. 129.
Levi, M. A. *La guerra perugina. Contrasti di idee e di masse in Roma e in Italia negli ultimi anni della Repubblica Romana.* In *Résumés des communications présentées au septième congrès international des sciences historiques.* Warsaw, 1933, pp. 60–62.
Pais, E. *I nummi di L. Mussidius Longus ed il loro significato per la storia del triumvirato romano.* Rend. Linc. (Ser. V) XXXIII, 1924, p. 15.
Reid, J. S. *Human Sacrifice at Rome and other notes on Roman religion.* J.R.S. II, 1912, pp. 41–44.
Reitzenstein, R. *Ein litterarischer Angriff auf Octavian.* (No. II of "Drei Vermutungen zur Geschichte der römischen Litteratur" in Festschrift Theodor Mommsen.) Marburg, 1893.
Schwenn, Fr. *Die Menschenopfer bei den Griechen und Römern.* Giessen, 1915.

G. *Brundisium and Misenum*

Carcopino, J. *La paix de Misène et la peinture de Bellori.* Rev. Arch. XXII, 1913, p. 253.
Conway, R. S. *The Youth of Vergil.* Bulletin of the John Rylands Library, July, 1915.
Frank, T. *Vergil. A biography.* New York, 1922, p. 30.
Kromayer, J. *Die Zeit des Brundusinisches Friedens und Antonius' Abreise nach Syrien i. J.* 39. Hermes, XXXIX, 1904, p. 556.

Oppermann, H. *Vergil und Oktavian.* Hermes, LXVII, 1932, p. 196.

Pais, E. *Un epigrafe di Casinum e la data del trattato di Brindisi.* In *Dalle guerre puniche a Cesare Augusto,* I, pp. 369 *sqq.* Rome, 1918.

Sciama, R. *A propos de la paix de Pouzzoles.* Rev. Arch. XXIII, 1914, p. 340.

Rostagni, A. *Virgilio Minore. Saggio sullo svolgimento della poesia virgiliana.* Turin, 1933.

Warde Fowler, W. *Note on* Culex—*Lines* 24–41. C.R. XXVIII, 1914, p. 119.

For literature upon the Fourth Eclogue of Virgil and its interpretation see further, p. 911.

H. *Sicily. The End of the Civil Wars*

Aiello, A. *La Spedizione di Ottaviano a Tauromenium e la Via di Ritirata di L. Cornificio* A.U.C. 718–36 A.C. in *Raccolta di Studi di Storia antica.* Catania, 1893–6. Vol. II, p. 181.

Burck, E. *Die Komposition von Vergil's Georgika.* Hermes, LXIV, 1929, p. 279.

Carcopino, J. *Le Mariage d'Octave et de Livie et la naissance de Drusus.* Rev. Hist. CLXI, 1929, p. 225. (Cf. Bull. Soc. nat. Antiq. de France, 1929, p. 147.)

Casagrandi, V. *Raccolta di Studi di Storia Antica.* 2 vols. Catania, 1893–6. (Contains numerous studies on the history of this period.)

—— *Il promontorio "Taurianum."* Riv. stor. ant. II, 1896, fasc. i, p. 66.

Cichorius, C. *Marineoffiziere Octavians* in *Römische Studien,* Leipzig-Berlin, 1922, pp. 257–261.

Cuntz, O. *Zur Geschichte Siziliens in der Cäsar.-augusteisch. Epoche.* Klio, VII, 1907, p. 460.

Gow, J. *The Frog of Horace,* Satires, *I.* 5. C.R. XV, 1901, p. 117. (And cf. E. S. Shuckburgh, *ib.* p. 166.)

Grasso, G. *Lo* ΣΚΥΛΑΚΙΟΝ ΟΡΟΣ *di Appiano e l'itinerario di Ottaviano da Vibona a Tauromenio nel* 718/36. Riv. stor. ant. XII, 1908, p. 19.

Hadas, M. *Sextus Pompey.* New York, 1930.

Holm, A. *Geschichte Siciliens im Alterthum.* Vol. III, Leipzig, 1898, pp. 196–214 and 452–464.

Janssen, J. *De die quo Nero Claudius Drusus natus est.* Mnem. XLVIII, 1920, p. 94.

Klein, J. *Die Verwaltungsbeamte von Sicilien und Sardinien.* Bonn, 1878, pp. 64–66 and 136–7.

Kromayer, J. *Chronologische Bestimmung des Vertrages von Tarent.* In *Die rechtliche Begründung des Principats* (Marburg Diss. 1888), pp. 51–57.

I. *Octavian's Illyrian Campaigns*

Casson, S. *Macedonia, Thrace and Illyria.* Oxford, 1926, pp. 287–327 (Illyria).

Cons, H. *La province romaine de Dalmatie.* Paris, 1881, pp. 136 *sqq.*

Degrassi, A. *Ricerche sui limiti della Giapidia.* (Estratto dall' "Archeografo Triestino" volume del centenario, 1929/30.) Trieste, 1930, pp. 263 *sqq.*

Dobiáš, J. *K Octavianovým výpravám illyrským v letech* 35–33 *př. Kr.* Listy filologické, XLVIII, 1921, pp. 65–75; 213–223.

—— *A propos des expéditions illyriennes d'Octavianus en* 35–33 *av. J.-C.* Summary in "Czecho-Slovak Research Work, III, 1921" of the above article.

—— *Studie k Appianově knize Illyrské.* (Études sur le livre illyrien d'Appien.) In Czech, with French résumé. Prague, 1930.

Fluss, M. Arts. in P.W. *s.vv.* Illyrier and Liburni.

Gribaudi, D. *Synodium.* Riv. Fil. (N.S.) III, 1925, p. 413.

Kahrstedt, U. *Studien zur politischen und Wirtschafts-Geschichte der Ost- und Zentralalpen vor Augustus.* Gött. Nach. 1927, p. 1.

Kromayer, J. *Kleine Forschungen zur Geschichte des zweiten Triumvirats. V. Die illyrischen Feldzüge Octavians.* Hermes, xxxiii, 1898, p. 1.

Patsch, C. *Die Lika in römischer Zeit.* (Schriften der Balkankommission. Ant. Abt. i.) Vienna, 1900.

—— *Zur Geschichte und Topographie von Narona.* (Schrift. d. Balkankomm. Ant. Abt. v.) Vienna, 1907.

—— *Wissenschaftliche Mitteilungen aus Bosnien und der Herzegowina.* xii, 1912, p. 92.

Schmid, W. *Metulum und Fluvius Frigidus. Eine Erwiderung.* Jahreshefte, xxi–xxii, 1922–24. (Beiblatt.) col. 495.

—— *Der Feldzug Oktavians gegen die Japoden und die Einnahme Metulums.* R.-G. K. Ber. xv, 1923–24, 1926, p. 178.

Swoboda, E. *Octavian und Illyricum.* Vienna, 1932; and see *L'Acropole*, viii, 1933, p. 104.

Syme, R. Review of Swoboda in *J.R.S.* xxiii, 1933, p. 66.

Veith, G. *Die Feldzüge des C. Julius Caesar Octavianus in Illyrien in den Jahren 35–33 v. Chr.* (Schriften der Balkankommission, Ant. Abt. vii.) Vienna, 1914.

—— *Metulum und Fluvius Frigidus,* and *Nachtrag zu Metulum und Fluvius Frigidus.* Jahreshefte, xxi–xxii, 1922–24. (Beiblatt.) cols. 479 and 507.

Vulić, N. *Contributi alla storia della guerra di Ottavio in Illiria nel* 35–33 *e della campagna di Tiberio nel* 15 A.C. Riv. stor. ant. vii, 1903, p. 489.

—— *La guerre d'Octave en Illyrie.* L'Acropole, vii, 1932 (July–Dec.), p. 1; and see *ib.* viii, 1933, p. 108.

Vulpe, R. *Gli Illiri dell' Italia imperiale romana.* Ephemeris Dacoromana, iii, 1925, p. 137.

Zippel, G. *Die römische Herrschaft in Illyrien bis auf Augustus.* Leipzig, 1877, pp. 225 *sqq.*

J. *The Duration of the 'Second Triumvirate'*

(The items are arranged in chronological order to show the development of the discussion.)

Mommsen, Th. *Römisches Staatsrecht,* vol. ii³, pp. 707 *sq.* and 718 *sq.*

Kromayer, J. *Die rechtliche Begründung des Principats.* Diss. Marburg, 1888.

Gardthausen, V. *Augustus und seine Zeit.* i, ii, Leipzig, 1896, pp. 175 *sqq.*

Cicotti, E. *La fine del II triumvirato.* Riv. Fil. xxiv, 1896, (N.S.) 2, p. 80.

Caspari, M. O. B. *On the* Iuratio Italiae *of* 32 B.C. C.Q. v, 1911, p. 230.

Kolbe, W. *Der zweite Triumvirat.* Hermes, xlix, 1914, p. 273.

Schultz, O. Th. *Das Wesen des römischen Kaisertums der ersten zwei Jahrhunderte.* Paderborn, 1916, pp. 2–8.

Bauer, A. *Das Staatsstreich des Octavianus im Jahre* 32 *v. Chr.* H.Z. cxvii, 1917, p. 11.

Kornemann, E. *Mausoleum und Tatenbericht des Augustus.* Leipzig-Berlin, 1921, pp. 96–101.

Wilcken, U. *Der angebliche Staatsstreich Octavians im Jahre* 32 *v. Chr.* Berl. S.B. 1925, p. 69.

Dessau, H. *Der Staatsstreich des Jahres* 32 *v. Chr.* Phil. Woch. xlv, 1925, p. 1017.

van Groningen, B. A. *De Octaviani Caesaris ante principatum conditum imperio.* Mnem. liv, 1926, p. 1.

Holmes, T. Rice. *The duration of the Triumvirate and the alleged* coup d'état *of* 32 B.C. (In *The Architect of the Roman Empire,* vol. i, pp. 231 *sqq.*)

Schulz, O. Th. In review of Kornemann's *Doppelprinzipat* in Z. d. Sav.-Stift. li, 1931, p. 496, especially p. 498 *sq.*

Schulz, O. Th. *Das dritte Triumvirat Oktavians.* Z.N. XLII, 1932, p. 101.

On the edict of Octavian *de privilegiis veteranorum*, B.G.U. II, 628, see U. Wilcken, *Grundzüge und Chrestomathie der Papyruskunde*, p. 545 *sq.*; P. F. Girard, *Textes de droit romain*[5], p. 172 *sq.*; O. Th. Schultz, *Der dritte Triumvirat Oktavians*, p. 107 *sq.*

K. *The Winning of Italy and the Break between Octavian and Antony*

Bormann, E. *Cn. Domitius Calvinus* in *Festschrift für O. Benndorf.* Vienna, 1898, pp. 283 *sqq.*

Carcopino, J. *Le calendrier de Veroli.* C.R. Ac. Inscr. 1923, p. 64.

Charlesworth, M. P. *Some Fragments of the Propaganda of Mark Antony.* C.Q. XXVII, 1933, p. 172.

Gagé, J. *Les sacerdoces d'Auguste et ses réformes religieuses.* Mél. d'arch. et d'hist. XLVIII, 1931, p. 75.

Kalinka, E. *Die von Sueton berichteten Schmähungen auf Oktavian.* Wien S.B. CXCVII, 1922, Abh. 6, vi, pp. 39–48.

Kromayer, J. *Die Militärcolonien Octavians und Caesars in Gallia Narbonensis.* Hermes, XXXI, 1896, p. 1.

Rasch, F. *De Ludo Troiae.* Progr. Jena, 1882.

Richmond, O. L. *The Augustan Palatium.* J.R.S. IV, 1914, p. 193.

Scott, K. *Octavian's Propaganda and Antony's* de sua ebrietate. C.P. XXIV, 1929, p. 133.

—— *The Political Propaganda of 44–30 B.C.* Mem. Amer. Acad. Rome, vol. XI, 1933, p. 1.

Shipley, F. W. *C. Sosius: his coins, his triumph and his temple of Apollo.* In *Papers in memory of J. M. Wulfing.* St Louis, 1930, pp. 73–87.

—— *Chronology of the building operations in Rome from the death of Caesar to the death of Augustus.* Mem. Amer. Acad. Rome, IX, 1931, p. 7.

(Some of these items also refer to the topics of Part II of the Bibliography.)

L. *The West after Actium*

(a) *Messalla in Aquitania.*

Hammer, J. *Prolegomena to an edition of the* Panegyricus Messallae. New York, 1925.

Hirschfeld, O. *Aquitanien in der Römerzeit.* Kleine Schriften, Berlin, 1913, pp. 209–238, esp. p. 214 *sq.*

Kuthan, R. *De duabus Messalae Expeditionibus.* In *Festsschrift für Grohovi.* Prague, 1923, pp. 35–41.

McCracken, G. *Tibullus, Messalla and the Via Latina.* C.P. LIII, 1932, p. 344.

Postgate, J. P. *Messalla in Aquitania.* C.R. XVII, 1903, p. 112.

(b) *The Balkans and the Campaigns of Crassus.*

Bauer, A. *Die Herkunft der Bastarnen.* Wien S.B. CLXXXV, Abh. 2, 1918.

Columba, G. M. *Le sedi dei Triballi.* Stud. stor. ant. class. III, 1910, p. 203.

Filow, B. *Die Legionen der Provinz Moesia von Augustus bis auf Diokletian.* Klio, Ergänzungsband I, Leipzig, 1906.

Groag, E. Art. in P.W. *s.v.* Licinius (58) (Crassus).

Kazarow, G. *Die ethnographischen Stellung der Päonen.* Klio, XVIII, 1923, p. 20.

Pârvan, V. *Getica: o protoistorie a Daciei.* Bucharest, 1926, pp. 82–91.

von Premerstein, A. *Die Anfänge der Provinz Moesiens.* Jahreshefte, I, 1898, Beiblatt, col. 158.

Stout, S. E. *The governors of Moesia*. Diss. Princeton, 1911.
Vulić, N. *La nationalité des Péoniens*. Mus. B. xxx, 1926, p. 107.
—— *Die Sitze der Triballer zur Römerzeit*. Wien. St. xxiv, 1902, p. 336.

(c) *Octavian in Italy*. (The works marked * are relevant also to the following two chapters.)

*Abele, T. A. *Der Senat unter Augustus*. (Studien zur Geschichte und Kultur des Altertums.) Paderborn, 1907.
Blumenthal, F. *Auguria salutis*. Hermes, xlix, 1914, p. 246.
Costa, G. *L' 'augurium salutis' e l' 'auguraculum' capitolino*. Bull. Com. Arch. Rom. xxxviii, 1910, p. 118.
Dessau, H. *Livius und Augustus*. Hermes, xli, 1906, p. 142.
*Ferrabino, A. *La rinunzia di Augusto*. Nuova Antologia, 1931, July 1, p. 66.
Gagé, J. *Romulus-Augustus*. Mél. d'arch. et d'hist. xlvii, 1930, p. 138.
—— *Les sacerdoces d'Auguste et ses réformes religieuses*. *Ib*. xlviii, 1931, p. 75.
*Hardy, E. G. Lectio Senatus *and* Census *under Augustus*. C.Q. xiii, 1919, p. 43.
*Heinze, R. *Auctoritas*. Hermes, lx, 1925, p. 348.
Hirschfeld, O. *Augustus ein Inschriftenfälscher?* Kleine Schriften, 1913, p. 398.
Jörs, P. *Die Ehegesetze des Augustus*, in *Festschrift Theodor Mommsen*... Marburg, 1893, pp. 3–28.
*McFayden, D. *The History of the Title 'Imperator' under the Roman Empire*. Diss. Chicago, 1920.
*Muller, F. (Jzn). "*Augustus*." Med. d. kon. Akad. van Wetenschappen te Amsterdam, 63, A, 1927, no. 11.
*Oltramare, A. *La réaction cicéronienne et les débuts du Principat*. Rev. E.L. x, 1932, p. 58.
*Rosenberg, A. Art. in P.W. s.v. *Imperator*, col. 1145.
Scott, K. *The identification of Augustus with Romulus-Quirinus*. Trans. Amer. Phil. Assoc. 1925, p. 82.
*Stobart, J. C. *The Senate under Augustus*. C.Q. iii, 1909, p. 296.

PART II. AFFAIRS IN THE EAST AND THE CAMPAIGN OF ACTIUM

I. Sources

A. *Primary* (*for Coins see* I, D, *below*)

Letters and rescripts of Antony: *O.G.I.S.* 453–5; F. Preisigke, *Sammelbuch*, 4224 (see II, B, *s.v.* Brandis); J. Keil, *Jahreshefte*, xiv, 1911, Beiblatt, cols. 124–5; Suetonius, *Augustus*, 69; Josephus, *Antiquitates*, xiv [2, 3], 306; [4], 314 and [5], 319; cf. Dio L, 1, 3 = Plutarch, *Ant.* 55.
—— —— of Cleopatra: G. Lefebvre, *Mélanges Holleaux*, 1913, p. 103. [?*B.G.U.* viii, no. 1730. See above, p. 37, n. 6.]
—— —— of Octavian: Ditt.[3] 768 (= fr. 74 Malcovati): cf. Dio L, 1, 4 = Plutarch, *Ant.* 55.
Inscriptions, Greek. *O.G.I.S.* 194–6, 357–61; 654 (= *C.I.L.* iii, Supp. 2, 14147[5]); 752. *C.I.G.* 2715, 2717[b], 2282–3, 4523 (2282 = F. Durrbach, *Choix des inscriptions de Délos*, no. 171). Ditt.[3] 769, 786–7. *I.G.* ii[2], 1043; v, 1, 970. *S.E.G.* iv, 246. *Monumenta Asiae Minoris antiqua*, iii, nos. 63–7. *B.C.H.* xi, 1887, pp. 151, no. 56; 225; lv, 1931, facing p. 85.
Lefebvre, G. *Ann. Serv.* 1908, p. 241 no. 4 = Preisigke, *Sammelbuch*, 1570.
Ramsay, Sir W. M. *J.H.S.* 1918, p. 140, cf. p. 143.
Kougéas, S. B. Ἑλληνικά, 1, 1928, p. 8 no. 1.

Inscriptions, Latin. Fasti and Acta Triumphorum. *C.I.L.* I, 2nd ed. 1893, pp. 50, 61–2, 76–7, 214, 244, 248, see pp. 54, 160–1, 180, 323, and add Dessau II, 2, p. 993.

Monumentum Ancyranum, cc. 3, 24–5, 27, 29, 32.

C.I.L. VI, 701–2, 1798; XII, p. 382.

—— Egyptian. Stele from the Bucheum at Armant of year 1 of Augustus, no. 13 in Sir R. Mond and O. H. Myers, *The Bucheum* (Hieroglyphic inscriptions, ed. H. W. Fairman). Vol. II. London, 1934.

Literary. Malcovati, H. *Caesaris Augusti Imperatoris operum fragmenta*, 2nd ed. Turin, 1898, frs. 136–7, 177–8 (177–8 = Peter, *Hist. rom. rel.* II, p. 62, frs. 15, 14).

M. Valerius Messalla Corvinus, in Peter, II, p. 67, frs. 6–8, 10.

Isidore of Charax, *Parthian Stations*, § 1.

Pliny, *N.H.* XXXII, 3.

Nicolaus of Damascus, *F. Gr. Hist.* II A, p. 324 *sq.* frs. 1, 2 (see II C, p. 229); Socrates of Rhodes, *ib.* II B, p. 927; Q. Dellius, *ib.* II B, p. 929, and Olympus, *ib.* pp. 929–30 (see *F.H.G.* III, pp. 926–7); Athenodorus, *F.H.G.* III, p. 485 (title and note).

Horace, *Epode* IX; *Odes* I, 37; III, 6.

Virgil, *Eclogue* IV; *Aeneid*, VIII, 678–714.

Propertius II, 1, 30 *sqq.*; III, 11; IV, 6.

Oracula Sibyllina, III, 46–54; 75–92; 350–61, 367–80.

Anth. Graec. VI, 236; VII, 645; IX, 235, 553, 752.

The Zamaspes poems from Susa: Fr. Cumont, *C.R. Ac. Inscr.* 1930, p. 212; 1931, p. 241.

B. Secondary

Inscriptions: *O.G.I.S.* 377 (with the notes), 753; *I.G.R.R.* IV, 1375; E. Breccia, *Iscriz. greche e latine*, p. 32 no. 48ª; G. Perrot and E. Guillaume, *Exploration archéologique de la Galatie et de la Bithynie*, pp. 29 no. 20, 32 no. 22; perhaps *S.E.G.* IV, 535.

Papyri. *B.G.U.* IV, nos. 1182, 1198; U. Wilcken, *Chrestomathie*, no. 115; F. G. Kenyon, *Rev. Phil.* XIX, 1895, p. 177.

Parchment from Doura, see II, E, under Rostovtzeff and Welles.

Literary (the most important sources are placed first).

Appian, *Bella Civilia*, V.

Plutarch, *Antony*; *Mor.* 61 A, 207A, 319 E–320 A, 814 D; *Publicola*, 17.

Dio XLVIII, 1–LI, 19.

Epitomizers of Livy: *Periochae*, 125, 127–8, 130–3; Orosius VI, 18–19; Florus II, xix–xxi (II, 4, 9–11); Eutropius VII, 5–7; Incerti, *de viris illustribus*, 79, 85–6.

Josephus, *Antiquitates*, XIV [12, 1], 297–end; XV [1–7, 3], 1–217, [10, 1], 344–349. *Bellum Judaicum*, I, 12, 4–20, 4 (242–397). *C. Apionem*, II, 56–60.

Strabo VII, 325; XI, 523, 530, 532; XII, 543, 547, 558–60, 562, 567–9, 571, 574–5, 578; XIII, 595; XIV, 637, 649, 669, 671–2, 674–6, 685; XV, 697; XVI, 748, 751, 756, 765; XVII, 794–7.

Suetonius, *Augustus*, 10, 13, 16–18, 31, 63, 69–70, 86.

Velleius Paterculus II, 78–9, 82–7.

Justin XLII, 4, 7–5, 8, with Trogus, *Prol.* XLII.

Tacitus, *Annals*, I, 2, 10; II, 3, 53; III, 62; IV, 34, 43. *Hist.* V, 9.

Frontinus I, 1, 6; II, 2, 5; 3, 15; 5, 36–7; IV, 1, 37.

Pliny, *N.H.* VII, 135; IX, 119; XIV, 148; XVIII, 22; XXI, 12; XXXIII, 82, 132.

Valerius Maximus I, 1, 19; 7, 7; III, 8, 8; IX, 15, ext. 2.

Zonaras X, 22 (511)–36 (531).

Galen, Θηριακὴ πρὸς Πίσωνα, in Kühn, *Medicorum graec. opera*, XIV, pp. 236–7.

Porphyry, *F.H.G.* III, pp. 724–5, *F. Gr. Hist.* (= Eusebius Armen. tr. Kaerst), II B, pp. 1202–3.

Eusebius, ed. Schoene, I, pp. 167–70, 212 (= *Excerpta Latina Barbari* 36ᵇ); II, pp. 140–1.

Servius on Virgil, *Aeneid*, VIII, 678–714.

Pseudo-Acro (ed. Keller 1902), Scholia on Horace, *Odes* I, 37.

Porphyrion (ed. Meyer 1874), Commentaries on Horace, *Epode* IX and *Odes* I, 37.

Seneca Rhetor, *Suasoriae*, I, 7; Seneca, *Quaest. Nat.* IV, 2; Aelian, *de nat. animal.* IX, 61; Gellius, *N.A.* XV, 4; Malalas IX, 218–220; Ammianus XXII, 16, 9; Macrobius, *Saturnalia*, II, 13; Philostratus, *Vit. Soph.* I, 5; Zenobius V, 24; Sophronius, *F.H.G.* IV, p. iii; Suidas, διεφθαρμένος, ἡμίεργον, Θεόδωρος ποιητής.

Charles, R. H. *The Chronicle of John, Bishop of Nikiu*, ch. 67. London-Oxford, 1916.

Incerti, *de Augusti bello Aegyptiaco carmen* (Baehrens, *Poet. Lat. Min.* I, 214), ed. J. Ferrara, Pavia, 1908, *sub tit. Poematis latini reliquiae ex vol. Herculanensi evulgatae.*

Oracula Sibyllina, XI, 245–260, 272–314.

C. *Cleopatra's chronology*

1. Documents of Cleopatra and Ptolemy Caesar with a single date.
   O.G.I.S. 194, 742; *P. Oxy.* XIV, 635; *P.S.I.* V, 549; F. Preisigke, *Sammelbuch,* 1570; G. Lefebvre, *Mélanges Holleaux*, p. 103; W. Spiegelberg, *P. Cairo Dem.* no. 31232; *id.*, *Die demotischen papyri Loeb*, no. 63 with W. Otto's *Zusatz.*
2. Documents with a double date.
   18 = 3. *P. Ryl.* II, no. 69.
   19 = 4. *O.G.I.S.* 195.
   20 = 5. *O.G.I.S.* 196; J. G. Tait, *Greek Ostraca in the Bodleian Library*, 1930, p. 38, no. 222.
   21 = 6. Coins of Berytus: J. N. Svoronos, Tὰ νομίσματα τοῦ Κράτους τῶν Πτολεμαίων, II, p. 314 nos. 1886–9; G. F. Hill, *Phoenicia*, British Museum Catalogue, pp. 53 no. 14, 54 no. 15, and Plate XL, 2.
   22 = 7. *P. Oxy.* XII, 1453.

D. *Coins (see generally Head, H.N.²)*

(1) *Antony and other Romans and client-states*

Bahrfeldt, M. *Ueber die Chronologie der Münzen des Marcus Antonius.* Atti del congresso internaz. di scienze storiche, VI, p. 187. Rome, 1904.

—— *Die Münzen der Flottenpräfekten des Marcus Antonius.* Num. Zeits. (Wien), XXXVII, 1905, p. 9.

—— *Provinziale Kupferprägung aus dem Ende der römischen Republik: Sosius, Proculeius, Crassus.* J.I. d'A.N. XI, 1908, p. 215.

—— *M. Antonius, Octavia und Antyllus.* J.I. d'A.N. XII, 1910, p. 89.

—— *Die römische Goldmünzenprägung während der Republik und unter Augustus.* Halle, 1923.

Cohen, H. *Médailles Impériales*, 2nd ed., Leipzig, 1930 (reprint from 2nd edit. Paris, 1880–92), vol. I, pp. 35–58 (Antony).

Gardner, P. *Thessaly to Aetolia*, B.M. Cat. 1883, pp. 102–3 (Nicopolis).

—— *Peloponnese*, B.M. Cat. 1887, pp. 23, 83, 102, 127–8.

Grueber, H. A. *Roman bronze coinage from* B.C. 45–3. Num. Chr. 1904, p. 185.

—— *Coins of the Roman Republic in the British Museum*, 1910; I, pp. 566–end, II, pp. 8–12, 486–534 (Antony and others).

Grueber, H. A. *Coinage of the triumvirs, Antony, Lepidus, and Octavian.* Num. Chr. IV, 1911, p. 109.

Hill, G. F. *Historical Roman coins,* 1909, nos. 81–84.

—— *Phoenicia,* B.M. Cat. 1910, pp. 44, 53, 54, 130, 204, and Pl. XL, 2 (Antony and Cleopatra).

—— *Lycaonia, Isauria, and Cilicia,* B.M. Cat. 1910, pp. xxix, cxxx, 237.

—— *Palestine,* B.M. Cat. 1914, pp. 108, 212, 220.

Mattingly, H. *Coins of the Roman Empire in the British Museum,* I, 1923, p. 18, no. 95, and pp. 99–106, nos. 602–4, 615, 622, 625, 631, 633, 647–54 (Augustus).

—— *Roman Coins.* London, 1928.

Robinson, E. S. G. *Cyrenaica,* B.M. Cat. 1927, pp. ccxxi, 117, 127.

Willers, H. *Geschichte der römischen Kupferprägung.* Leipzig-Berlin, 1909, pp. 111–125.

Wroth, W. *Galatia, Cappadocia, and Syria,* B.M. Cat. 1899, pp. 2–4, 43–4, 157–8, 280–1.

(2) *Cleopatra*

Forrer, L. *Les monnaies de Cléopatre VII Philopator, reine d'Égypte.* Rev. Belge de Numismatique, LVI, 1900, pp. 5, 149, 277.

Kahrstedt, U. *Frauen auf antiken Münzen.* Klio, X, 1910, pp. 261, 276.

Macdonald, Sir G. *Catalogue of the Greek coins in the Hunterian collection,* vol. III, Glasgow, 1905, pp. 218, 398–400; Pls. LXXV, 1, LXXXIV, 19–21.

Poole, R. S. *The Ptolemies, Kings of Egypt,* B.M. Cat. 1883, pp. 122 *sqq.*

Regling, K. reviewing Svoronos, Z.N. XXV, 1906, pp. 393–8.

—— *Die tetradrachmen der Kleopatra VII.* J.I. d'A.N. XI, 1908, p. 244.

Svoronos, J. N. Τὰ νομίσματα τοῦ Κράτους τῶν Πτολεμαίων, Athens, 1904– ; I, pp. υμη´–υπθ´ (= IV, pp. 358–396, German trans.), II, pp. 305–18; III, Pls. LXII, LXIII.

(3) *Parthia*

Allotte de la Fuye. *Monnaies Arsacides surfrappées.* Rev. N. VIII, 1904, p. 174.

De Morgan, J. *Numismatique de la Perse antique;* Fasc. I, Introduction–Arsacides. Paris, 1927. (Vol. III, 1 of E. Babelon, *Traité des monnaies grecques et romaines.*)

Wroth, W. *Parthia,* B.M. Cat. 1903.

II. Modern Literature

A. *On the sources*

See the works on Appian and Asinius Pollio cited above, pp. 898, 900, and add

Bürcklein, A. *Quellen und Chronologie der römisch-parthischen Feldzüge in den Jahren 713–18.* Berlin, 1879.

Hartmann, K. *Ueber das Verhältniss des Cassius Dio zur Parthergeschichte des Flavius Arrianus.* Phil. LXXIV, 1917, p. 73.

Hirschfeld, O. *Dellius ou Sallustius.* Mélanges Boissier, Paris, 1903, p. 293.

B. *Antony and Cleopatra. History (special studies)*

See also the Histories of Ptolemaic Egypt by E. R. Bevan (London, 1927) and A. Bouché-Leclercq (Paris, 1903). For histories of Rome see the General Bibliography.

Brandis, C. G. *Ein Schreiben des Triumvirs Marcus Antonius an den Landtag Asiens.* Hermes, xxxii, 1897, p. 509.

Charlesworth, M. P. *The fear of the Orient in the Roman Empire.* Cambridge Hist. Journ. ii, 1926, p. 9.

Craven, L. *Antony's Oriental Policy until the defeat of the Parthian expedition.* Univ. of Missouri Studies, iii, 1920, no. 2.

Cuntz, O. *Legionäre des Antonius und Augustus aus dem Orient.* Jahreshefte xxv, 1930, p. 70.

Dessau, H. *De regina Pythodoride.* Eph. Ep. ix, 1913, p. 691.

Dobiáš, J. *La deuxième donation faite par Antoine à Cléopâtre, en 34.* Listy filologické, xlix, 1922, pp. 183, 257. (Summary in French in *Rev. d. travaux scientifiques tchéco-slovaques,* iv–vi, 1922–4, p. 262.)

—— *La donation a' Antoine à Cléopâtre en l'an 34 av. J.-C.* Mélanges Bidez (Annuaire de l'Institut de philologie et d'histoire, ii, Brussels, 1934), p. 287.

Finch, S. L. *The name Marcus Antonius in C.I.L. vol.* vi. C.P. xxiv, 1929, p. 402.

Gardthausen, V. *Die Scheidung der Octavia und die Hochzeit der Kleopatra.* N.J. Kl. Alt. xxxix, 1917, p. 158.

Hill, G. F. *Olba, Cennatis, Lalassis.* Num. Chr. 1899, p. 181.

Kahrstedt, U. *Syrische Territorien in Hellenistischer Zeit,* pp. 88 *sq.,* 97 *sqq.* Berlin, 1926.

Keil, J. *Die Synodos der ökumenischen Hieroniken und Stephaniten.* Jahreshefte xiv, 1911, Beiblatt, col. 123.

Kjellberg, E. *C. Julius Eurykles.* Klio, xvii, 1921, p. 44.

Kortenbeutel, H. *Eingabe an den Statthalter G. Turranius.* Aeg. xiii, 1933, p. 247.

Kromayer, J. *Kleine Forschungen zur Geschichte des zweiten Triumvirats.* Hermes, xxix, 1894, p. 556; xxxi, 1896, p. 70; xxxiii, 1898, p. 1; xxxiv, 1899, p. 1.

Lumbroso, G. *Lettere al Prof. Calderini* xi, xii. Aeg. iii, 1922, pp. 46–8.

Macurdy, G. H. *Hellenistic Queens.* Baltimore–London, 1932.

Mahaffy, J. P. *Cleopatra VI.* J.E.A. ii, 1915, p. 1.

Nöldeke, Th. *Über Mommsens Darstellung der römischen Herrschaft und römischen Politik im Orient.* Zeits. d. deutsch. morg. Gesell. xxxix, 1885, p. 349.

Otto, W. *Herodes.* Stuttgart, 1913 (in P.W. Suppl. Bd. ii).

Ramsay, Sir W. M. *Studies in the Roman Province Galatia,* iii. J.R.S. xii, 1922, p. 147.

Roussel, P. *Le miracle de Zeus Panamaros.* B.C.H. lv, 1931, p. 70.

Sands, P. C. *The Client princes of the Roman Empire under the Republic.* Cambridge, 1908. (See review by J. G. C. Anderson in *J.H.S.* xxx, 1910, p. 181.)

Sbordone, Fr. *La morte di Cleopatra nei medici greci.* Riv. Indo-greco-italica, xiv, 1930, fasc. i–ii, p. 1.

Seeck, O. *Die Zusammensetzung der Kaiserlegionen.* Rh. Mus. xlviii, 1893, p. 602.

Stähelin, F. Art. *s.v.* Kleopatra (20) in P.W.

Stein, A. *Untersuchungen zur Geschichte und Verwaltung Aegyptens unter römischer Herrschaft.* Stuttgart, 1915.

Strack, M. L. *Kleopatra.* H.Z. xix, 1916, p. 473.

Tarn, W. W. *Antony's Legions.* C.Q. xxvi, 1932, p. 75.

Thiersch, H. *Die Alexandrinische Königsnekropole.* J.D.A.I. xxv, 1910, pp. 57–9, 66 *sqq.*

Wilcken, U. *Zum Germanicus-papyrus.* Hermes, lxiii, 1928, p. 48.

Wilhelm, A. *Ein Grabgedicht aus Athen.* Mélanges Bidez, p. 1007.
Articles in P.W.: Antigonos, 9 (Wilcken); Antiochos, 37, 38 (Wilcken); Antonius, 30 (Groebe); Archelaos, 15 (Wilcken); Ariarathes, 10 (Niese); Artavasdes, 1 (Baumgartner), 2 (Wilcken); Artaxias, 2 (Baumgartner); Asandros, 4 (Wilcken); Athenodoros, 19 (v. Arnim) and in Supp. Bd. v (Philippson); Bogudes, 2 (Klebs); Canidius, 2 (Münzer); Deiotarus, 2, 4 (Niese); Dellius (Wissowa); Domitius, 23 (Groag); Fulvia, 113 (Münzer); Hybreas, 1 (Radermacher); Iamblichos, 1 (Stein); Ituraea (Beer); Kleon, 6 (Stein); Labienus, 5 (Münzer); Lykomedes, 9, 10 (Obst); Lysanias, 6 (Stein); Maecenas, 6 (A. Kappelmacher); Malchos, 3 (Fluss); Mardoi (Weissbach); Sosius, 2 (Fluss).

There are various popular *Lives* of Cleopatra, which do not call for mention.

C. *The religious aspects and Virgil*

Alföldi, A. *Der neue Weltherrscher der vierten Ekloge Vergils.* Hermes, LXV, 1930, p. 369.
Bennett, H. *Vergil and Pollio.* A.J.Ph. LI, 1930, p. 324.
Blumenthal, Fr. *Der ägyptische Kaiserkult.* Arch. Pap. v, 1913, p. 317.
Boll, Fr. *Sulla quarta Ecloga di Virgilio.* Memorie delle R. Accad. d. Scienze dell' Instituto di Bologna, v–VII, 1920–3, p. 3.
Carcopino, J. *Virgile et le mystère de la IVᵉ Églogue.* Ed. 3. Paris, 1930.
Corssen, P. *Die vierte Ecloge Virgils.* Phil. LXXXI, 1926, p. 26.
Funaioli, G. *Ancora la IV ecloga di Virgilio e il XVI epodo di Orazio.* Mus. B. 1930, p. 55.
Heinen, H. *Zur Begründung des römischen Kaiserkultes.* Klio, XI, 1911, pp. 137–143.
Herrmann, Erwin. *Kleopatra's angeblicher Schlangentod.* Phil. Woch. 1931, col. 1100.
Herrmann, L. *Les Masques et les Visages dans les Bucoliques de Virgile.* Brussels, 1930. Ch. v.
Jeanmaire, H. *La politique religieuse d'Antoine et de Cléopâtre.* Rev. Arch. XIX, 1924, p. 241.
—— *Le Messianisme de Virgile.* Paris, 1930.
Mayor, J. B., W. Warde Fowler and R. S. Conway. *Virgil's Messianic Eclogue.* London, 1907.
Nock, A. D. *Notes on Ruler-cult,* I–IV. J.H.S. XLVIII, 1928, pp. 33–6.
—— Σύνναος Θεός. Harvard St. XLI, 1930, pp. 4, 21, 55.
Norden, E. *Die Geburt des Kindes.* Leipzig, 1924.
Ribezzo, Fr. *Millenario cumano e messianismo cesareo nella IV Ecloga di Virgilio.* Riv. Indo-greco-italica, XIV, 1930, fasc. III–IV, p. 1.
Rose, H. J. *The departure of Dionysos.* Annals of Arch. and Anthr. XI, 1924, p. 25.
—— *Some neglected points in the Fourth Eclogue.* C.Q. XVIII, 1924, p. 113.
Slater, D. A. *Was the Fourth Eclogue written to celebrate the marriage of Octavia to Mark Antony?* C.R. XXVI, 1912, p. 114.
Spiegelberg, W. *Weshalb wählte Kleopatra den Tod durch Schlangenbiss?* Ägyptologische Mitteilungen, Bay. Abh. 1925, Abh. 2 no. 1.
Tarn, W. W. *Alexander Helios and the Golden Age.* J.R.S. XXII, 1932, p. 135.
Taylor, L. R. *The Divinity of the Roman Emperor.* Middletown, Conn. 1931, chap. v.
Wagenvoort, H. *Vergils Vierte Ekloge und das Sidus Julium.* Med. d. Kon. Akad. van Wetenschappen te Amsterdam, 67, A, 1929, no 1.
Weber, W. *Der Prophet und sein Gott.* Leipzig, 1925.
Weinreich, O. Reviewing Boll and Norden in *Phil. Woch.* 1924, col. 890.

D. *The Actium Campaign*

Bentley, R. Notes to Horace, Epode ix, in his *Horace*. Ed. 3. Amsterdam, 1738.
Eichler, Fr. and E. Kris. *Die Kameen im Kunsthistorischen Museum*. Vienna, 1927, p. 50 (list of cameos and gems relating to Actium).
Ferrabino, A. *La battaglia d' Azio*. Riv. Fil. lii, 1924, p. 433.
Jurien de la Gravière, J.-P.-E. *La marine des Ptolemées*, i. Paris, 1885.
Kromayer, J. *Die Entwickelung der römischen Flotte von Seeraüberkriege des Pompeius bis zur Schlacht von Actium*. Phil. lvi, 1897, p. 426.
—— *Die Vorgeschichte des Krieges von Actium* (Kleine Forschungen, vi). Hermes, xxxiii, 1898, p. 13.
—— *Der Feldzug von Actium und der sogenannte Verrath der Kleopatra* (Kleine Forschungen, vii). Hermes, xxxiv, 1899, p. 1.
—— *Antike Schlachtfelder*, iv, p. 662: *Nachtrag zur Schlacht von Actium 31 v. Chr.* Berlin, 1931.
—— *Actium. Ein Epilog*. Hermes, lxviii, 1933, p. 361.
Levi, M. A. *La battaglia d' Azio*. Athenaeum, x, 1932, p. 1. (See Appendix iv in the writer's *Ottaviano capoparte*.)
Maximowa, M. *Un camée commémoratif de la bataille d'Actium*. Rev. Arch. xxx, 1929, p. 64.
Pichon, R. *La bataille d'Actium et les témoignages contemporains*. Mélanges Boissier, p. 397. Paris, 1903.
Tarn, W. W. *The battle of Actium*. J.R.S. xxi, 1931, p. 173.
Wagenvoort, H. *De Horatii epodo nono*. Mnem. lix, 1932, p. 403.
Wilkinson, L. P. *Horace, Epode* ix. C.R. xlvii, 1933, p. 2.

E. *Parthia*

[See further the bibliography to vol. ix, ch. xiv.]

Cumont, Fr. *Nouvelles Inscriptions grecques de Suse*. C.R. Ac. Inscr. 1930, p. 212.
—— *Inscriptions grecques de Suse. Ib.* 1931, p. 233.
Darmesteter, J. *Les Parthes à Jérusalem*. Journ. Asiat. (N.S.) iv, 1894, p. 43.
Günther, A. *Beiträge zur Geschichte der Kriege zwischen Römer und Parthern*. Berlin, 1922.
Gutschmid, A. von. *Geschichte Irans*. Tübingen, 1888.
Kromayer, J. *Der Partherzug des Antonius* (Kleine Forschungen, iv). Hermes, xxxi, 1896, p. 70.
Mommsen, Th. *The Provinces of the Roman Empire*, ii, ch. ix. (Eng. trans. 1886.)
Rawlinson, G. *The sixth great oriental monarchy*. London, 1873.
Rostovtzeff, M. I. and C. B. Welles. *A parchment contract of loan from Dura-Europus on the Euphrates*. Yale Classical Studies, ii, 1930, p. 1.
Tarn, W. W. *Tiridates II and the young Phraates*. Mélanges Glotz. Paris, 1932, p. 831.

CHAPTERS V–VIII, XVIII

THE PRINCEPS: *SENATUS POPULUSQUE ROMANUS*: THE IMPERIAL ADMINISTRATION: THE ARMY AND NAVY: THE ACHIEVEMENT OF AUGUSTUS

I. ANCIENT SOURCES

A. CONTEMPORARY DOCUMENTS

(*a*) *Inscriptions*

1. *Res gestae divi Augusti*. See Bibliography to chaps I–IV, Part I, I A (*b*), p. 896, and for modern literature, p. 899.
2. *Lex Quinctia de aquaeductibus*. (Bruns, *Fontes*[7], 22.)
3. *Edictum Augusti de aquaeductu Venafrano*. (Bruns, *Fontes*[7], 77.)
4. Edicts of Cyrene and *S. C. Calvisianum de repetundis*.
   Oliverio, G., *La stele di Augusto rinvenuto nell' agora di Cirene*, Notiziario Arch. del ministero delle Colonie, IV, Milan-Rome, 1927; cf. Anderson, J. G. C., in *J.R.S.* XVII, 1927, pp. 33 ff.; Stroux, J. and L. Wenger, in *Bay. Abh.* XXXIV, 2, Munich, 1928 (reviewed by Anderson in *J.R.S.* XIX, 1929, p. 229, and V. Arangio-Ruiz in *Riv. Fil.* LVIII, 1930, p. 220); von Premerstein, A., *Die fünf neugefundenen Edikte des Augustus aus Kyrene*, Z. d. Sav.-Stift. XLVIII, 1928, p. 419, and *Zu den kyren-äischen Edikten des Augustus*, *ib.* XLIX, 1931, p. 431 (with full bibliography).

See also the documents named in the Bibliography cited above, I A (*a*), Nos. 4, 7; the following inscriptions (those of importance for the Constitution are cited in the text)—Dessau, 70–143, 241, 244 (Lex de imperio Vespasiani); 862; 889; 906; 908; 911–30; 944; 973; 1335; 5050 (Ludi saeculares); 5922–5; 5935–41; 6043; 6123; 8894–8; 8995; Ann. épig. 1927, No. 88; C.I.G. I, 309; Ditt.[3] 780; 785 *ad fin.*; 799; I.G. III, 575, VII, 349; I.G.R.R. I, 1055–6; 1294; 1295; 1322. III, 312; 720; 940. IV, 7; 9; 33, col. b, ll. 13–43, col. c; 64; 65, *a*, *b*; 68, *a*, *b*; 200; 204; 682; 1693; 1717; 1718; 1756; O.G.I.S. 459; 460–9; 532; see Rushforth, G. M°N., *Latin Inscriptions illustrating the history of the Early Roman Empire*. Ed. 2. Oxford, 1930, nos. 1–6, 24–32, 34–47, 70.

(*b*) *Papyri*

B.G.U. 611 (see J. Stroux, Bay. S.B. 1928).
B.G.U. 628 (see Bibliography cited above, I A (*a*), No. 5).

(*c*) *Coins*

See General Bibliography IV and Bibliography to Chaps. I–IV, Part I, I A (*c*).

B. LITERARY SOURCES

Dio LII–LVI.
Frontinus, *de aquaeductibus*, 99–130.
Josephus, *Ant.* XV [10, 2], 250; XVI [3, 3], 86, [6, 4], 167; XVII [9, 5], 225. *Bell. Jud.* II [2, 4], 25.
Livy, *Epit.* 134–42.
Strabo VI, 288; XVII, 840.
Suetonius, *Augustus, passim*; also *Div. Iul.* 41, 2; *Tib.* 8, 10, 31; *Nero* 10.

Tacitus, *Ann.* I, 2–10, 15, 72, 77, 81; II, 28, 79; III, 4, 10, 12, 17, 24, 28–30;
    IV, 21, 26, 37; VI, 11; XII, 26; XIII, 4.
Velleius Paterculus, II, 89–128.

References are given to the important passages from the above in the relevant
sections of the text: occasional references to the topics of the above chapters are found
in the Augustan poets, especially Horace, *Odes* and *Carmen Saeculare*, Ovid, *Fasti*
and *Tristia*, and other authors. Cf. e.g. Philo, *Legatio*, 143; Seneca, *de Clem.* I, 10, 1;
Pliny, *N.H.* VII, 147; Plutarch, *Antonius*, 87, etc.

For the criticism of the literary sources see the Bibliography to chaps I–IV, Part I,
I, C (for Tacitus the Bibliography to Chap. XIX, I A (v) (*d*)).

The works of the classical lawyers are important for the Constitution. See especially
Gaius IV, 30; Paulus, *Sent.* XXVI, 1, and the following passages in the Digest: I, 2, 2,
32 and 47 (Pomponius); I, 4, 1 (Ulpian); I, 12, 1; I, 17; V, 13 (rubric); XVI, 1, 2, 1
(S. C. Vellaeanum); XXIX, 5, 1 (Ulpian) and 14 (Paulus); XLVIII, 2, 3 Pr. (Paulus);
XLVIII, 19, 32 (Ulpian); XLIX, 2, 1 (Ulpian).

On the Imperial Constitutions cf. Gaius I, 5, Dig. I, 2, 2, 12 (Pomponius), I, 4 pr.
1 (Ulpian), and on the validity of *senatus consulta* cf. Gaius III, 32, Dig. I, 1, 7 pr.
(Papinian).

For the history of the Army and Navy the most important evidence for organization
is to be found in inscriptions:

Res Gestae, esp. 3, 16, 17.
Dessau, esp. cap. IX (Tituli Militares).
    Literary works of value are:
Velleius Paterculus II, 88–95.
Tacitus, *Hist.*, *Agricola*, and some passages in *Ann.* (*e.g.* 1, 16 *sqq.*, IV, 4–5, XIII, 35,
    XIV, 27, XVI, 13).

Isolated statements of importance are to be found in Josephus, Suetonius and Dio.

For the personality of Augustus the main source is Suetonius, *Augustus*. Collections
of sayings are preserved in Macrobius, *Sat.* II, 4, and in Plutarch's *Moralia* (*Apophth.
imper. et regum*). The letters and other writings of Augustus are collected in H. Malcovati, *Caesaris Augusti Imperatoris operum fragmenta*. Ed. 2. Turin, 1928.

II. MODERN LITERATURE

For general histories and monographs on Augustus see the General Bibliography;
see also the works marked with an asterisk in the Bibliography to Chaps. I–IV,
Part I, II, L (*c*).

A. The Constitution and Character of the Principate

Mommsen, Th. *Römisches Staatsrecht*, II, 2. Ed. 3, Leipzig, 1887, is fundamental.

For a recent treatment of the subject see

Hammond, M. *The Augustan Principate*. Harvard University Press, 1933 (with
    bibliography).

The following is a selection of the most important works giving representative
views on the establishment and underlying ideas of the Principate and personality
and aims of Augustus (reference is made in the text to the views of other scholars,
e.g. L. Mitteis, *Römisches Privatrecht*, p. 352, and O. Hirschfeld, *Die kaiserlichen
Verwaltungsbeamten*, p. 470).

von Beseler, G. *Vom Wesen des römischen Prinzipates* in *Jüristische Miniaturen.* Leipzig, 1929, pp. 151 *sqq.*

Betti, E. *Sulla fondazione del principato in Roma.* Rendiconti del r. Istituto Lombardo di scienze e lettere, XLVIII, 1915, p. 464 (with full bibliography).

—— *Il Carattere giuridico del principato di Augusto.* Città di Castello, 1915.

Brassloff, S. *Staat und Gesellschaft in der römischen Kaiserzeit.* Vienna-Leipzig, 1933.

Ciccotti, E. Art. Augustus in Diz. epig.

Cuq, E. *Le Conseil des empereurs d'Auguste à Dioclétien.* Mém. Ac. Inscr. IX, 1884, pp. 311 *sqq.*

von Domaszewski, A. *Die philosophischen Grundlagen des augusteischen Prinzipats* in *Festgabe für E. Gothein.* Munich-Leipzig, 1923, pp. 63–71.

Ferrabino, A. *La rinunzia di Augusto.* Nuova Antologia, LXVI, 1931, p. 66.

de Francisci, P. *La costituzione augustea,* in *Studi in onore di Pietro Bonfante nel XL anno d' insegnamento.* Milan, 1930, I, pp. 11 *sqq.*

—— *Storia del diritto romano,* vol. II. Rome, 1929. I, Tit. II, cap. I, II.

Gelzer, M. *Caesar und Augustus* in *Meister der Politik* I, Ed. 2. Stuttgart, 1923.

Greenidge, A. H. J. *Roman Public Life.* London, 1901.

Hammond, M. *The significance of the speech of Maecenas in Dio, Book LII.* Trans. Amer. Phil. Assoc. LXIII, 1932, p. 88.

Hardy, E. G. *Imperium Consulare or Proconsulare* in *Studies in Roman History.* First series, Ed. 2, London, 1910, pp. 283 *sqq.*

Heinze, R. *Kaiser Augustus.* Hermes, LXV, 1930, p. 385.

—— *Auctoritas.* Hermes, LX, 1925, p. 348.

—— *Die Augusteische Kultur.* Ed. 2. Leipzig-Berlin, 1933.

Herzog, E. *Geschichte und System der römischen Staatsverfassung,* vol. II, 1. Kaiser-zeit. Leipzig, 1891.

Homo, L. *Les institutions politiques romaines.* Paris, 1927, pp. 243–87.

Jolowicz, H. F. *Historical Introduction to the Study of Roman Law.* Cambridge, 1932, chap. XIX.

Kaerst, J. *Scipio Aemilianus, die Stoa und der Prinzipat.* N. J. f. Wiss. V, 1929, p. 653.

Köstermann, E. 'Statio Principis.' Phil. LXXXVII, 1932, pp. 358, 430.

Kolbe, W. *Von der Republik zur Monarchie,* in *Aus Roms Zeitwende.* Leipzig-Berlin, 1931, pp. 39–65.

Kornemann, E. *Doppelprinzipat und Reichsteilung im Imperium Romanum.* Leipzig-Berlin, 1930.

Kromayer, J. *Die rechtliche Begründung des Principats.* Marburg, 1888.

Levi, M. A. *Kaiser Augusto.* Rome, 1929.

Marsh, F. B. *The Founding of the Roman Empire.* Ed. 2, Oxford, 1927.

McFayden, D. *The history of the title Imperator under the Roman Empire.* Diss. Chicago, 1920.

—— *The Princeps and the senatorial provinces.* C.P. XVI, 1921, p. 34.

—— *The newly discovered Cyrenean Inscriptions and the alleged imperium maius proconsulare of Augustus.* C. P. XXIII, 1928, p. 388.

Meyer, E. *Kaiser Augustus,* in *Kleine Schriften,* I. Halle, 1924, pp. 441 *sqq.*

—— *Caesars Monarchie und das Principat des Pompejus.* Ed. 2, Stuttgart-Berlin, 1919.

Meyer, P. *De Maecenatis Oratione a Dione ficta.* Berlin, 1891.

Münzer, D. *Die Entstehung des römischen Prinzipats. Ein Beispiel des Wandels von Staatsformen.* Münster, 1927.

Pelham, H. F. *The 'imperium' of Augustus and his successors,* in *Essays.* Oxford, 1911, pp. 60–86.

—— *The domestic policy of Augustus. Ib.* pp. 89–151.

Reitzenstein, R. *Die Idee des Prinzipats bei Cicero und Augustus.* Gött. Nach. 1917, pp. 399 *sqq.*, 481 *sqq.*

Rosenberg, A. Art. *s.v. Imperator* in P.W.

Rostovtzeff, M. *Augustus.* University of Wisconsin Studies in Language and Literature. No. 15, 1922, p. 134.

Schönbauer, E. *Untersuchungen zum römischen Staats- und Wirtschaftsrecht,* I. *Wesen und Ursprung des römischen Prinzipats.* Z. d. Sav.-Stift. XLVII, 1927, p. 264.

Schulz, F. *Prinzipien des römischen Rechts.* Munich-Leipzig, 1934, p. 112 *sqq.*

Schulz, O. T. *Das Wesen des römischen Kaisertums der ersten zwei Jahrhunderte.* Studien zur Geschichte und Kultur, VIII, 2. Paderborn, 1916.

Seeck, O. Art. *s.v. Consistorium* in P.W. cols. 926–7.

Siber, H. *Zur Entwicklung der römischen Prinzipatsverfassung.* Sächs. Abh. XLII, 3. Leipzig, 1933.

Weber, W. *Der Prophet und sein Gott.* Leipzig, 1925, pp. 28 *sqq.*

Willrich, H. *Augustus bei Tacitus.* Hermes, LXII, 1927, p. 54.

B. SPECIAL TOPICS

(a) The significance of the name Augustus

Hirst, G. *The Significance of 'Augustior' as applied to Hercules and Romulus: a note on Livy* I, 7, 9. A. J. Ph. XLVII, 1926, p. 347.

Muller, F. Jzn. *'Augustus.'* Med. d. Kon. Ak. van Wetenschappen te Amsterdam, 63, A, 1927, no. 11.

See review by A. von Premerstein in *Phil. Woch.* 1929, cols. 845–851.

Reiter, S. *Augustus:* Σεβαστός (id.). Phil. Woch. 1930, col. 1199.

Taylor, L. R. *Livy and the name Augustus.* C.R. XXXII, 1918, p. 158.

(b) The helpers of the Princeps

Ciaceri, E. *Tiberio successore di Augusto.* Milan, 1934, ch. II.

Daniel, R. *M. Vipsanius Agrippa; eine Monographie.* Breslau, 1933.

Marsh, F. B. *The Reign of Tiberius.* Oxford, 1931, pp. 34–44.

Reinhold, M. *Marcus Agrippa; a biography.* Geneva and New York, 1933.

Rogers, R. S. *L. Arruntius.* C.P. XXVI, 1931, p. 172.

Willrich, H. *Livia.* Leipzig-Berlin, 1911.

Arts. in P.W. *s.vv.* Calpurnius (99) Piso (Groag), Claudius (139 = Drusus) (Stein), Iulius (154 = Tiberius) (Gelzer), Livius (Livia 37) (Ollendorff), Maecenas (6) (A. Kappelmacher), Munatius Plancus (30) (Hanslik), Statilius Taurus (34) (Nagl), and Sulpicius (90) Quirinius (Groag).

(c) The senatorial and equestrian orders

Abele, T. A. *Der Senat unter Augustus.* Studien zur Geschichte und Kultur des Altertums. Paderborn, 1907.

Cichorius, C. *Die Neuordnung der Staatsämten durch Augustus* in *Römische Studien,* Leipzig, 1922, pp. 285–291.

Fischer, F. *Senatus Romanus qui fuerit Augusti temporibus.* Göttingen-Berlin, 1908.

Gelzer, M. *Die Nobilität der Kaiserzeit.* Hermes, L, 1915, p. 395.

Hardy, E. G. *Lectio Senatus and Census under Augustus.* C.Q. XIII, 1919, p. 43.

Jerome, T. S. *Aspects of the Study of Roman History.* New York, 1923, pp. 286–318.

Kübler, F. Art. *s.v. Equites Romani* in P.W.
Marsh, F. B. *Op. cit.* chap. VIII.
Mommsen, Th. *Römisches Staatsrecht*, III. Leipzig, 1887, pp. 12 *sqq.* (Der souveräne Senat des Prinzipats.)
Stein, A. *Der römische Ritterstand*, in Münchener Beitrage zur Papyrusforschung und antiker Rechtsgeschichte. Munich, 1927.
Stobart, J. C. *The Senate under Augustus.* C.Q. III, 1909, p. 296.

(d) Legislation

de Francisci, P. *Storia del diritto romano*, II (1). Rome, 1929, Tit. II, Chap. IV, §§ 1–5, pp. 318–74.
—— *Intorno alla massima 'princeps legibus solutus est.'* Bull. dell' Istituto di diritto romano, XXXIV, 1925, p. 321.
Jolowicz, H. F. *Op. cit.* chap. XXI.
Jörs, P. Art. *s.v. Constitutio principum* in P.W.
McFayden, D. *The lex data of the Roman Republic as a precedent for the legislation of the Princeps.* Papers in memory of J. M. Wulfing, pp. 64–72, St Louis, Washington University, 1930, pp. 64–72.
Rotondi, G. *Leges publicae populi Romani.* Milan, 1912. (Leges Juliae, pp. 442–54.)
Weiss, E. Art. *s.v. Leges Iuliae* (2) in P.W.

(e) The administration of justice.

In addition to the relevant chapters in the general histories of Roman law (see vol. IX, p. 967 *sq.*) the following may be consulted:

de Francisci, P. *Le fonti del diritto privato e il processo della loro unificazione in Roma*, in *Nuovi studi di diritto, economia e politica.* Rome, 1928.
Jolowicz, H. F. *Op. cit.* chap. XXIII.
McFayden, D. *The rise of the Princeps' jurisdiction within the city of Rome.* Washington University Studies, Humanistic Series, X, 2, 1923.
Mitteis, L. *Römisches Privatrecht bis auf die Zeit Diokletians*, vol. I. Leipzig, 1908.
Mommsen, Th. *Römisches Strafrecht.* Leipzig, 1899.
Strachan-Davidson, J. L. *Problems of the Roman Criminal Law.* Oxford, 1912.
Wenger, L. *Institutionen des römischen Zivilprozessrechts.* Munich, 1925.
Wlassak, F. *Römische Prozessgesetze.* Leipzig, vol. I, 1882, vol. II, 1891.

(f) Foreign Policy

See the Bibliographies to Chaps. IX and XII.

(g) Client-kingdoms.

Kornemann, E. *'Die unsichtbaren Grenzen des römischen Reichs*,' in *Staaten-Männer-Völker.* Berlin-Leipzig, 1934.
Sands, P. C. *The Client Princes of the Roman Empire under the Republic.* Cambridge, 1906, pp. 127 *sqq.*

C. Finance

Dessau, H. *Geschichte der römischen Kaiserzeit.* I, Berlin, 1924, chap. 4. Das Finanzwesen (important).
Ensslin, W. *Zu den* Res Gestae divi Augusti. Rh. Mus. LXXXI, 1932, p. 335.
Frank, T. *'Dominium in Solo Provinciali' and 'Ager Publicus.'* J.R.S. XVII, 1927, p. 141.

Frank, 'T. *On Augustus and the Aerarium.* J.R.S. XXIII, 1933, p. 143.

Kubitschek, W. Art. *s.v. Census* in P.W.

Marquardt, J. *Römische Staatsverwaltung.* Vol. II, Ed. 2. Leipzig, 1884, pp. 182 *sqq.*

Rostowzew, M. I. *Studien zur Geschichte des römischen Kolonates.* (Beiheft zum Arch. Pap. I.) Leipzig, 1910.

—— Art. *Fiscus* in Diz. Epig.

—— *Geschichte der Staatspacht in der römischen Kaiserzeit bis Diocletian.* Phil. Suppl. IX, 1901–4, No. 3.

Stuart Jones, H. *Administration* in *The Legacy of Rome.* Oxford, 1923, pp. 91–139 (relevant also to sections D and E).

Wilcken, U. *Zu den impensae des Res Gestae Divi Augusti.* Berl. S.B. 1932, XXVII, p. 772.

D. Administration in Rome

Baillie Reynolds, P. K. *The Vigiles of Imperial Rome.* Oxford, 1926.

Cardinali, G. Art. *Frumentatio* in Diz. Epig.

Dessau, H. *Geschichte der römischen Kaiserzeit,* I. Berlin, 1924, chap. 6. Die Hauptstadt.

Mancini, G. Art. *Cura, Curator,* in Diz. Epig.

Rostowzew, M. Art. *s.v. Frumentum* in P.W.

De Ruggiero, E. Art. *Aqua* in Diz. Epig.

Thédenat, H. Art. *cura aquarum* in D.S.

E. Provinces

(a) Policy and imperial administration

Arnold, W. T. *Studies in Roman Imperialism.* Manchester, 1906.

—— *The Roman System of Provincial Government to the Accession of Constantine the Great.* New ed. Oxford, 1906.

Hirschfeld, O. *Die kaiserlichen Verwaltungsbeamten bis auf Diocletian.* Ed. 2. Berlin, 1905.

Marquardt, J. *Römische Staatsverwaltung.* Ed. 2. Leipzig, 1881, I, pp. 497 *sqq.*

Mattingly, H. *The Imperial Civil Service of Rome.* Cambridge, 1910.

(b) Provinces

1. General.

Chapot, V. *Le Monde romain.* Paris, 1927.

Dessau, H. *Geschichte der römischen Kaiserzeit.* II, 2. *Die Länder und Völker des Reichs im ersten Jahrhundert der Kaiserzeit.* Berlin, 1930.

Marquardt, J. *Römische Staatsverwaltung.* Ed. 2. Leipzig, 1881. Vol. I, pp. 242 *sqq.*

Mommsen, Th. *The Provinces of the Roman Empire from Caesar to Diocletian.* London, 1909.

2. Separate provinces.

(On Egypt see the Bibliography to Chap. x, on Judaea that to Chap. xi and Chap. xxv, on Roman Germany and the Danube region that to Chap. xii.)

Albertini, E. *Les Divisions administratives de l'Espagne romaine.* Paris, 1923.

Bouchier, E. S. *Spain under the Roman Empire.* Oxford, 1914.

—— *Syria as a Roman Province.* Oxford, 1916.

Broughton, T. R. S. *The Romanization of Africa Proconsularis.* Baltimore, 1929.

Chapot, V. *La province romaine proconsulaire d'Asie depuis ses origines jusqu'à la fin du Haut-Empire.* Paris, 1904.

Fluss, M. Art. *s.v.* Moesia in P.W.
Gsell, S. *Histoire ancienne de l'Afrique du Nord*, VIII. Paris, 1928, pp. 183 *sqq.*
Jullian, C. *Histoire de la Gaule.* Vol. IV, *Le Gouvernement de Rome.* Ed. 4. Paris, 1929.
Marchetti, C. Art. Hispania in Diz. Epig.
Schulten, A. Art. *s.v.* Hispania in P.W.
Stähelin, F. *Die Schweiz in römischer Zeit.* Ed. 2. Basel, 1931.
Sutherland, C. H. V. *Aspects of Imperialism in Roman Spain.* J.R.S. XXIV, 1934,
    p. 31.
Syme, R. *Galatia and Pamphylia under Augustus.* Klio, XXVII, 1934, p. 122.
Toutain, F. Art. Gallia, Galliae, in Diz. Epig.

(c) Provincial organization and local government

Abbott, F. F. and A. C. Johnson. *Municipal Administration in the Roman Empire.*
    Princeton; Oxford, London, 1926.
Guiraud, P. *Les Assemblées provinciales.* Paris, 1887.
Hardy, E. G. *The provincial Concilia from Augustus to Diocletian* in *Studies in*
    Roman History, First Series. Ed. 2. London, 1910, pp. 235 *sqq.*
Kornemann, E. Art. *s.v. Concilium* in P.W. cols. 803–820.
Liebenam, W. *Städteverwaltung im römischen Kaiserreiche.* Leipzig, 1900.
Reid, J. S. *The Municipalities of the Roman Empire.* Cambridge, 1913.
Vaglieri, D. Art. *Concilium* in Diz. Epig.

F. The Army and Navy

Chapot, V. *La flotte de Misène.* Paris, 1896.
Cheesman, G. L. *The Auxilia of the Roman Imperial Army.* Oxford, 1914.
Cichorius, C. Arts. *s.vv. Ala* and *Cohors* in P.W.
Dessau, H. *Geschichte der römischen Kaiserzeit*, I. Berlin, 1924, pp. 211–316.
    (A masterly survey of the whole question.)
von Domaszewski, A. *Die Rangordnung des römischen Heeres.* B.J. 117, 1908.
Fiebiger, L. Art. *s.v. Classis* in P.W.
Kromayer, J. and Veith, G. *Heerwesen und Kriegführung der Griechen und Römer.*
    Munich, 1928, pp. 470–626.
Lammert, F. *Die römische Taktik zu Beginn der Kaiserzeit und die Geschichtschrei-*
    bung. Leipzig, 1931.
Lesquier, J. *L'armée romaine d'Égypte d'Auguste à Dioclétien.* Cairo, 1918.
Liebenam, W. Art. *s.v. Exercitus* in P.W.
Marquardt, J. *Römische Staatsverwaltung*, II². Leipzig, 1884, pp. 443 *sqq.* (Still
    useful.)
Mommsen, Th. *Die Conscriptionsordnung der römischen Kaiserzeit.* Ges. Schriften,
    VI, pp. 20–117.
—— *Die Gardetruppen der römischen Republik und der Kaiserzeit.* Ges. Schriften,
    VI, pp. 1–16.
Parker, H. M. D. *The Roman Legions.* Oxford, 1928.
Ritterling, H. Art. *s.v. Legio* in P.W. (This elaborate and invaluable study (1924)
    supersedes all earlier discussions of the subject.)
Stein, E. *Die kaiserlichen Beamten und Truppenkörper im römischen Deutschland*
    unter dem Prinzipat. Vienna, 1932.
Stevenson, G. H. *The Roman Empire.* London, 1930, pp. 170–89.
Syme, R. *Some notes on the legions under Augustus.* J.R.S. XXIII, 1933, p. 14.

CHAPTER IX

THE EASTERN FRONTIER UNDER AUGUSTUS

The ancient sources are cited at the relevant places in the text of the chapter.

Besides the relevant portions of the histories of Schiller, Mommsen, Gardthausen and Dessau, cited in the General Bibliography I, and the Parthian histories of Rawlinson (*The sixth great oriental monarchy*. London, 1873) and von Gutschmid (*Geschichte Irans*. Tübingen, 1888), see the following:

1. *The Defence of Egypt*

von Domaszewski, A. *Die Rangordnung des römischen Heeres.* B. J. 117, 1908, p. 120 *sq.*

Griffith, F. Ll. *Meroitic Studies*, iv. J.E.A. iv, 1917, p. 159.

Lesquier, J. *L'armée romaine d'Égypte d'Auguste à Dioclétien.* Cairo, 1918.

Mommsen, Th. *Res Gestae divi Augusti.* Ed. 2. Berlin, 1883, p. 108.

Parker, H. M. D. *The Roman Legions.* Oxford, 1928, p. 193.

Reisner, G. A. *The Pyramids of Meroë and the Candaces of Ethiopia.* Sudan Notes and Records, v, 1922, p. 173.

—— *The Meroïtic Kingdom of Ethiopia.* J.E.A. ix, 1923, p. 63.

Ritterling, E. Art. *s.v.* Legio in P.W. (cols. 1220, 1223, 1235, 1506, 1706, 1791).

Rostovtzeff, M. *Storia Economica e Sociale dell' Impero Romano.* Florence, 1933. pp. 351 *sqq.*

Syme, R. *Some Notes on the Legions under Augustus.* J.R.S. xxiii, 1933, p. 14.

Wilcken, U. *Grundzüge und Chrestomathie der Papyruskunde.* Berlin, 1912, pp. 381 *sqq.*

2. *The Romans and Arabia*

Glaser, E. *Skizze der Geschichte und Geographie Arabiens*, Bd. ii. Berlin, 1890, p. 43.

—— *Die Abessinier in Arabien und Afrika.* Munich, 1895.

Hardy, E. G. *The Monumentum Ancyranum.* Oxford, 1923, p. 121.

Hartmann, M. *Die arabische Frage mit einem Versuche der Archäologie Jemens.* Der islamische Orient, Bd. ii. Leipzig, 1909, pp. 38, 470.

Kammerer, A. *Essai sur l'histoire antique d'Abyssinie.* Paris, 1926, ch. vii.

—— *Pétra et la Nabatène.* Paris, 1929–30, ch. xi, 4.

Maiuri, A. *La Successione 'Elio Gallo—C. Petronio' nella lista dei prefetti dell' Egitto.* Saggi di Storia Antica e di Archeologia (presented to Beloch). Rome, 1910, p. 321.

Milne, J. G. *A history of Egypt under Roman rule*, ed. 3. London, 1924, p. 277.

Mommsen, Th. *Res Gestae*, p. 106.

Nielsen, D. *Handbuch der altarabischen Altertumskunde*, i. Copenhagen, 1927. (Kap. ii by F. Hommel, Kap. iii by N. Rhodokanakis.)

Rostovtzeff, M. *Caravan Cities.* Oxford, 1932. (For the caravan trade and Petra.)

Sprenger, A. *The Campaign of Aelius Gallus in Arabia.* Journ. Roy. Asiatic Soc. 1873, p. 121.

—— *Die alte Geographie Arabiens.* Bern, 1875.

Tkač, J. Art. *s.v.* Saba in P.W.

Art. in P.W. *s.vv.*: Egra (Tkač), Leuke Kome (Moritz), Mariaba (Grohmann), Marsyaba (Grohmann), Syllaios (Stein).

3. *The Parthian and Armenian problem*

Chapot, V. *La Frontière de l'Euphrate*. Paris, 1907. (Pp. 3, 72, 76, 84, 375.)

Cumont, F. *Études Syriennes*. Paris, 1917, pp. 119, 221.

Dobiáš, J. *Séleucie sur l'Euphrate*. Syria, VI, 1925, p. 253.

—— *Histoire de la province romaine de Syrie* (translation from Czecho-Slovakian in preparation). [Original inaccessible to the present writer.]

Furneaux, H. *The Annals of Tacitus*, II. Ed. 2. Oxford, 1907. Introd. ch. IV.

Holmes, T. Rice. *The Architect of the Roman Empire*, II. Oxford, 1931.

Jones, A. H. M. *The Urbanization of the Ituraean Principality*. J.R.S. XXI, 1931, p. 265.

Parker, H. M. D. *The Roman Legions*. Oxford, 1928, p. 126.

Ritterling, E. Art. *s.v. Legio* in P.W. (cols. 1220, 1224, 1231, 1235 and under the individual legions).

Syme, R. *Some Notes on the Legions under Augustus* (see above), pp. 24 *sqq.*

Art. in P.W. *s.vv.*: Artabanos, 7 (Cauer), Artavasdes, 2 (Wilcken), Artaxias (Baumgartner), Erato (Stein), Ituraea (Beer), Iulius-Augustus (Fitzler-Seeck), Iulius-Gaius (Gardthausen), Iulius-Tiberius (Gelzer), M. Lollius, 11 (Groag).

4. *The Bosporan Kingdom*

Brandis, C. G. Art. *s.v.* Bosporos in P.W.

Latyshev, V. V. Introduction to *Ios. P.E.* II, 1890, pp. XXXVI *sqq.* (in Latin).

Minns, E. H. *Scythians and Greeks*. Cambridge, 1913, pp. 591, 600.

Rostovtzeff, M. *Queen Dynamis of Bosporus*. J.H.S. XXXIX, 1919, p. 88.

—— *Iranians and Greeks in South Russia*. Oxford, 1922, ch. VII.

Art. in P.W. *s.vv.*: Asandros, 4 (Wilcken), Aspurgos (von Rohden), Dynamis (Stein), Scribonius, 3 (Stein).

5. *The Homanadensian War*

(Arranged in chronological order in order to show the progress of the discussion.)

Mommsen, Th. *Res Gestae*, ed. 2, p. 160.

Cheesman, G. L. *The Family of the Caristanii at Antioch in Pisidia*. J.R.S. III, 1913, p. 253.

Ramsay, Sir W. M. *Colonia Caesarea (Pisidian Antioch) in the Augustan age*. J.R.S. VI, 1916, p. 83.

—— *The Homanadeis and the Homanadensian War*. J.R.S. VII, 1917, p. 228. [Review by C. Torr, *Rev. Arch.* V[e] sér. XII, 1920, p. 154.]

Bleckmann, F. *Die erste syrische Statthalterschaft des P. Sulpicius Quirinius*. Klio, XVII, 1921, p. 104.

Dessau, H. *Zu den neuen Inschriften des Sulpicius Quirinius*. Klio, XVII, 1921, p. 252.

Groag, E. *Prosopographische Beiträge*, VII. Jahreshefte, XXI–XXII, 1924, Beiblatt, col. 445.

—— Art. *s.v.* Sulpicius (90) Quirinius in P.W.

Taylor, L. R. *Quirinius and the Census of Judaea*. A.J.Ph. LIV, 1933, p. 120.

Broughton, T. R. S. *Some Notes on the War with the Homonadeis*. *Ib.* p. 134.

Syme, R. *Galatia and Pamphylia under Augustus*. Klio, XXVII, 1934, p. 122.

CHAPTER X

EGYPT UNDER THE EARLY PRINCIPATE

A. Ancient Sources.

1. *Literary Texts*

For the literary sources for the political history of Egypt in this period see the Bibliographies to chapters IX and XXII.

For Egypt and its connections see particularly Strabo XVI and XVII; Philo, *In Flaccum* and *Legatio ad Gaium*, and Josephus, *Contra Apionem*.

2. *Documents*

A. *General*

Preisendanz, K. *Papyrusfunde und Papyrusforschung.* Leipzig, 1933.
Preisigke, F. und F. Bilabel. *Sammelbuch griechischer Urkunden aus Aegypten*, Berlin, 1915– (S.B.). This includes both papyri and inscriptions.

B. *Inscriptions*

Reports on new inscriptions and the literature relating to them may be found in the bibliography of inscriptions which M. N. Tod periodically contributes to the *J.E.A.* Many new inscriptions are published in the *Ann. Serv.* and the *Bull. de la Soc. Roy. d'Arch. d'Alexandrie.*

Breccia, E. *Iscrizioni greche e latine.* Catal. gén. des ant. ég. du Musée d'Alexandrie. Cairo, 1911.
Milne, J. G. *Greek Inscriptions.* Catal. gén. des ant. ég. du Musée du Caire. Oxford, 1905.

C. *Papyri*

(All collections of any importance which contain non-literary papyri from any part of the Roman period are here included.)

B.G.U. = *Aegyptische Urkunden aus den Museen zu Berlin.* Griechische Urkunden, I–V, 1895–1919; VII, 1926.
P. Achmîm = P. Collart, *Les papyrus grecs d'Achmîm à la Bibliothèque Nationale de Paris*, in *Bull. de l'Inst. français d'arch. orientale*, Cairo, XXXI, 1930, p. 35.
P. Amh. = B. P. Grenfell and A. S. Hunt, *The Amherst Papyri.* II. London, 1901.
P. Bad. = Fr. Bilabel, *Veröffentlichungen aus den badischen Papyrus-Sammlungen. Griechische Papyri*, II, IV. Heidelberg, 1923–4.
P. Bankakten = H. Frisk, *Bankakten aus dem Faijûm.* Göteborg, 1931.
P. Basel = E. Rabel, *Papyrusurkunden der Öffentlichen Bibliothek der Universität zu Basel.* Berlin, 1917.
P Berl. Frisk = H. Frisk, *Vier Papyri aus der Berliner-Sammlung.* Aeg. IX, 1928, p. 281.
P. Berl. Leihgabe = T. Kalén and others, *Berliner Leihgabe griechischer Papyri.* Uppsala, 1932.
P. Berl. Möller = S. Möller, *Griechische Papyri aus dem Berliner Museum.* Göteborg, 1929.
P. Bour. = P. Collart, *Les papyrus Bouriant.* Paris, 1926.
P. Cairo Preis. = Fr. Preisigke, *Griechische Urkunden des Ägyptischen Museums zu Kairo.* Strassburg, 1911.

P. Col. = *Columbia Papyri*. Greek Series. II. W. L. Westermann and C. W. Keyes, *Tax Lists and Transportation Receipts from Theadelphia*. New York, 1932.

P. Corn. = W. L. Westermann and C. J. Kraemer, *Greek Papyri in the Library of Cornell University*. New York, 1926.

P. Fay. = B. P. Grenfell, A. S. Hunt and D. G. Hogarth, *Fayûm Towns and their Papyri*. London, 1900.

P. Flor. = G. Vitelli and D. Comparetti, *Papiri Fiorentini*, vols. I–III. Milan, 1906–15.

P. Freib. = *Mitteilungen aus der Freiburger Papyrussammlung*. 2. J. Partsch, *Juristische Texte der römischen Zeit*. Heidelberg, 1916.

P. Gen. = J. Nicole, *Les Papyrus de Genève*. 1. Geneva, 1896–1906.

P. Giss. = O. Eger, E. Kornemann, P. M. Meyer, *Griechische Papyri im Museum des oberhessischen Geschichtsvereins zu Giessen*. 1. Leipzig, 1910–12.

P. bibl. univ. Giss. = H. Kling and H. Büttner, *Mitteilungen aus der Papyrussammlung der Giessener Universitätsbibliothek*. I, III. Giessen, 1924, 1931.

P. Goodsp. = E. J. Goodspeed, *Greek Papyri from the Cairo Museum*, etc. University of Chicago Decennial Publications, 1st Series, vol. v, 1904.

P. Göt. = H. Frisk, *Papyrus grecs de la Bibliothèque Municipale de Gothembourg*. Göteborg, 1929.

P. Graux = H. Henne, *Papyrus Graux*, in *Bull. de l' Inst. français d'Arch. Orientale*, Cairo, XXI, 1923, p. 189, XXVII, 1927, p. 1.

P. Grenf. I = B. P. Grenfell, *An Alexandrian Erotic Fragment and other Greek Papyri chiefly Ptolemaic*. Oxford, 1896.

P. Grenf. II. = B. P. Grenfell and A. S. Hunt, *New Classical Fragments and other Greek and Latin Papyri*. Oxford, 1897.

P. Gron. = A. G. Roos, *Papyri Groninganae*. (Verh. d. Kon. Ak. v. Wetensch. te Amsterdam.) Amsterdam, 1933.

P. Hamb. = P. M. Meyer, *Griechische Papyrusurkunden der Hamburger Stadtbibliothek*. 1. Leipzig, 1911–24.

P. Iand. = *Papyri Iandanae*. Cum discipulis edidit Carolus Kalbfleisch. Nonliterary texts in parts 2 (L. Eisner), 3 (L. Spohr), 4 (G. Spiess), 6 (G. Rosenberger). Leipzig, 1913–34.

P. Lond. = *Greek Papyri in the British Museum*. I, 1893, and II, 1898, ed. by F. G. Kenyon; III, 1907, ed. by F. G. Kenyon and H. I. Bell; *Jews and Christians in Egypt*, 1924, ed. by H. I. Bell (P. Lond. 1912, letter of Claudius).

P. Louvre = Brunet de Presle, *Notices et Extraits des Manuscrits de la Bibliothèque impériale*, XVIII. *Notices et textes des papyrus grecs*.

P. Marmarica = M. Norsa and G. Vitelli, *Il papiro Vaticano greco II*. Città del Vaticano, 1931.

P. Meyer = P. M. Meyer, *Juristische Papyri: Erklärung von Urkunden zur Einführung in die juristische Papyruskunde*. Berlin, 1920.

P. Mich. Tebt. = A. E. R. Boak, *Michigan Papyri*, vol. II. *Papyri from Tebtunis*, Part 1. Ann Arbor, 1933.

P. Milan. = *Papiri Milanesi*. Per cura della scuola di papirologia dell' Università Cattolica del S. Cuore. Parte 1. Milano, 1928.

P. Neutest. = P. M. Meyer, *Griechische Texte aus Ägypten*. Berlin, 1916. (Papyri, pp. 3–103.)

P. Oslo. = S. Eitrem and L. Amundsen, *Papyri Osloenses*. II. Oslo, 1931.

P. Oxy. = B. P. Grenfell and A. S. Hunt, *The Oxyrhynchus Papyri*, Parts I–XVII. London, 1898–1927.

P. Princ. Kase = E. H. Kase, Jr., *A Papyrus Roll in the Princeton Collection*. Baltimore, 1933.

P. Rain. Führer = *Papyrus Erzherzog Rainer: Führer durch die Ausstellung.* Vienna, 1894.

P. Rein. = Th. Reinach, *Papyrus grecs et démotiques.* Paris, 1905.

P. Rev. Belge de phil. et hist. IV = M. Hombert, *Quelques papyrus des Collections de Gand et de Paris,* in *Rev. Belge,* IV, 1925, pp. 633–76.

P. Ross.-Georg. = *Papyri russischer und georgischer Sammlungen.* II, 1929. *Ptolemäische und frührömische Texte,* ed. by O. Krüger; III, 1930, *Spätrömische und byzantinische Texte,* ed. by G. Zereteli and P. Jernstedt.

P. Ryl. = J. de M. Johnson, V. Martin and A. S. Hunt, *Catalogue of the Greek Papyri in the John Rylands Library, Manchester.* II. Manchester, 1915.

P.S.I. = *Pubbl. della Soc. It. per la ricerca dei Pap. greci e latini in Egitto. Pap. greci e latini.* I–X. Florence, 1912–1932.

P. Strassb. = F. Preisigke, *Griechische Papyrus der Kaiserlichen Universitäts- und Landesbibliothek zu Strassburg.* I. Leipzig, 1912.

P. Tebt. = B. P. Grenfell, A. S. Hunt and E. J. Goodspeed, *The Tebtunis Papyri.* Part II. London, 1907.

P. Würzb. = U. Wilcken, *Mitteilungen aus der Würzburger Papyrussammlung.* (Abh. Pr. Ak. d. Wiss. 1933, No. 6.) Berlin, 1934.

Princ. Univ. = A. C. Johnson and H. B. Van Hoesen, *Papyri in the Princeton University Collections.* Baltimore, 1931.

Sitol. Pap. = K. Thunell, *Sitologen-Papyri aus dem Berliner Museum.* Uppsala, 1924. (Republished with a new commentary in P. Berl. Leihgabe.)

Stud. Pal. = C. Wessely, *Studien zur Palaeographie und Papyruskunde.* Nonliterary texts of the Roman period are to be found in Parts 2, 4, 5, 7, 14, 17, 20, 22.

D. *Ostraca*

Amundsen, L. *Ostraca Osloensia.* Oslo, 1933.

Gardiner, A. H., H. Thompson, and J. G. Milne. *Theban Ostraca.* Oxford, 1913.

Meyer, P. M. *Griechische Texte aus Ägypten.* II. Ostraka der Sammlung Deissmann (pp. 107–205). Berlin, 1916.

Preisigke, F. *Die Prinz Joachim Ostraka.* Strassburg, 1914.

Tait, J. G. *Greek Ostraca in the Bodleian Library at Oxford and various other Collections.* I. London, 1930.

Viereck, P. *Ostraka aus Brüssel und Berlin.* Berlin, 1922.

—— *Griechische und Griechisch-Demotische Ostraka der Universitäts- und Landesbibliothek zu Strassburg im Elsass.* I. Berlin, 1923.

Wilcken, U. *Griechische Ostraka aus Aegypten und Nubien.* 2 vols. Berlin, 1899.

B. Modern Literature

(The literature relating to papyri is now so extensive that only a selection can here be referred to. Several of the works cited contain bibliographies. A general reference may be given to the periodicals which give special attention to Graeco-Roman Egypt, viz. *Aeg., Ann. Serv., Arch. Pap., Bull. de l'Inst. franç. d'archéologie orientale, Bull. de la Soc. Roy. d'Archéologie d'Alexandrie, Chronique d'Égypte, Études de Papyrologie, J.E.A., Revue égyptologique, Studien zur Palaeographie und Papyruskunde,* and to the articles dealing with Egyptian institutions in P.W.

1. *General Works*

Deissmann, A. *Licht vom Osten.* Ed. 4. Tübingen, 1923. (English edition: *Light from the Ancient East.* London, 1927.)

Martin, V. *La Fiscalité romaine en Égypte aux trois premiers siècles de l'Empire.* Geneva, 1926.

Milne, J. G. *A History of Egypt under Roman Rule.* Ed 3. London, 1924.
—— *The Ruin of Egypt by Roman Mismanagement.* J.R.S. XVII, 1927, p. 1.
Modica, M. *Contributi papirologici alla ricostruzione dell' ordinamento dell' Egitto sotto il dominio greco-romano.* Rome, 1916.
Rostovtzeff, M. *Roman Exploitation of Egypt in the First Century A.D.* Journ. of Econ. and Business Hist. I, 1929, p. 337.
—— *The Problem of the Origin of Serfdom in the Roman Empire.* Journ. of Land and Public Utility Economics, 1926, p. 198.
Schubart, W. *Ägypten von Alexander dem Grossen bis auf Mohammed.* Berlin, 1922.
—— *Einführung in die Papyruskunde.* Berlin, 1918.
Stein, A. *Untersuchungen zur Geschichte und Verwaltung Aegyptens unter römischer Herrschaft.* Stuttgart, 1915.
Van Hoesen, H. B. *Roman Cursive Writing.* Princeton, 1915.
Wilcken, U. und L. Mitteis. *Grundzüge und Chrestomathie der Papyruskunde.* I–II. Leipzig-Berlin, 1912.
—— *Griechische Ostraka aus Aegypten und Nubien.* I. Leipzig-Berlin, 1899.

2. *The Status of Egypt*

Blumenthal, Fr. *Der ägyptische Kaiserkult.* Arch. Pap. V, 1913, p. 317.
Gardthausen, V. *Kratesisjahre des Augustus.* B.P.W. XL, 1920, p. 619.
Groningen, B. A. van. *L'Égypte et l'Empire.* Aeg. VII, 1926, p. 189.
Levi, M. A. *L'esclusione dei senatori romani dall' Egitto Augusteo.* Aeg. V, 1924, p. 231.
Solazzi, S. *Di una pretesa legge di Augusto relativa all' Egitto* Aeg. IX, 1928, p. 296.

3. *Religion, Priests and Temples*

(Some useful works of a more general character, omitted here for reasons of space, will be found in the bibliography to Chapter IV of vol. VII.)

Otto, W. *Priester und Tempel im hellenistischen Ägypten.* Leipzig-Berlin, 1905–8.
Reinach, Th. *De quelques articles du 'Gnomon de l'Idiologue' relatifs au culte égyptien.* Rev. Hist. Rel. LXXXV, 1922, p. 16.
Hopfner, Th. *Fontes Historiae Religionis Aegyptiacae.* Bonn, 1922–1925.
Bilabel, Fr. *Die gräko-ägyptischen Feste.* Neue Heid. Jahrb. 1929, p. 1.
Nock, A. D. ΣΥΝΝΑΟΣ ΘΕΟΣ. Harv. St. XLI, 1930, p. 1.
Schubart, W. *Orakelfragen.* Zeitschr. f. ägypt. Spr. u. Altertumsk. LXVII, 1931, p. 110.
Woess, Fr. von. *Das Asylwesen Ägyptens in der Ptolemäerzeit und die spätere Entwicklung.* Munich, 1923.
For religion as exemplified in art see:
Kaufmann, C. M. *Ägyptische Terrakotten.* Cairo, 1913.
Perdrizet, P. *Bronzes grecs d'Égypte de la collection Fouquet.* Paris, 1911.
—— *Les terres cuites grecques d'Égypte de la collection Fouquet.* Nancy-Paris, 1921.
Vogt, J. *Die griechisch-ägyptische Sammlung E. von Sieglin.* II. *Terrakotten.* Leipzig, 1924.
Weber, W. *Die ägyptisch-griechischen Terrakotten.* Berlin, 1914.

4. *Army and Navy.*

Lesquier, J. *L'armée romaine d'Égypte d'Auguste à Dioclétien.* Cairo, 1918. With bibliography.
In addition references may be given to:
Degrassi, A. *Il papiro 1026 della Società italiana e i diplomi militari romani.* Aeg. X, 1929, p. 242.

Winter, J. G. *In the Service of Rome* in *C.P.* xxii, 1927, p. 237.

Zingerle, J. *Römisch-Militärisches aus Ägypten*. Arch. Pap. ix, 1928, p. 5.

5. *Administration and Taxation.*

General: Oertel, Fr. *Die Liturgie.* Leipzig, 1917.

—— Hirschfeld, O. *Die kaiserlichen Verwaltungsbeamten bis auf Diocletian.* Ed. 2. Berlin, 1905. (Egypt, pp. 343–409.)

Prefect: Cantarelli, L. *La serie dei prefetti di Egitto:* i, *da Ottaviano Augusto a Diocleziano.* Rome, 1906. A later list is that in Lesquier's *L'armée romaine d'Égypte*, pp. 509–18.

Epistrategus: Martin, V. *Les épistratèges.* Geneva, 1911.

Archidicastes: Jörs, P. *Erzrichter und Chrematisten.* Z. d. Sav.-Stift. xxxvi, 1915, p. 230; xxxix, 1918, p. 52; xl, 1919, p. 1.

—— Koschaker, P. *Der Archidikastes.* Z. d. Sav.-Stift. xxviii, 1907, p. 254; xxix, 1908, p. 1.

Idios Logos: Plaumann, G. *Der Idioslogos.* Berl. Abh. 1918, no. 17; commentary by W. Graf Uxkull-Gyllenband, 1934.

—— Schubart, W. *Der Gnomon des Idios Logos.* Berlin, 1919 [= B.G.U. v] Text republished with commentary by P. M. Meyer, *Jur. Pap.* no. 93.

—— Carcopino, J. *Le gnomon de l'idiologue et son importance historique.* Rev. E.A. xxiv, 1922, pp. 101, 211.

—— Jones, H. Stuart. *Fresh Light on Roman Bureaucracy.* Oxford, 1920.

—— Reinach, Th. *Un code fiscal de l'Égypte romaine. Le Gnomon de l'Idiologue.* Nouv. Rev. Hist. de Droit fr. et étr. xliii, 1919, p. 583, xliv, 1920, p. 5.

—— Roberts, C. H. and T. C. Skeat, *A Sale of ὑπόλογος at Tebtunis.* Aeg. xiii, 1933, p. 455.

—— Seckel, E. and Paul M. Meyer. *Zum sogenannten Gnomon des Idioslogos.* Berl. S.B. 1928, xxvi.

—— Wilhelmson, K. *Zum römischen Fiskalkauf in Ägypten* in *Acta et Comm. Univ. Tartuensis*, B, xviii. 5.

Strategos: Hohlwein, N. *Le stratège du nome.* Mus. B. xxviii, 1924, pp. 125; 193; xxix, 1925, pp. 5; 85; 257.

—— Martin, V. *Stratèges et basilicogrammates du nome Arsinoïte à l'époque romaine.* Arch. Pap. vi, 1913, p. 137.

Basilicogrammateus: Biedermann, E. *Studien zur ägyptischen Verwaltungsgeschichte in ptolemäisch-römischer Zeit: Der* Βασιλικὸς Γραμματεύς. Berlin, 1913.

—— See also under Strategos.

Taxation: See especially vol. i of Wilcken's *Griechische Ostraka*; vol. ii of P. Rylands, which contains much valuable material with admirable commentaries; and V. Martin, *Un document administratif du nome de Mendès*, in Wessely's *Studien zur Palaeographie und Papyruskunde*, xvii, 1917, p. 9.

—— Corn tax: Calderini, A. ΘΗΣΑΥΡΟΙ. Milan, 1924.

—— Customs: Clauson, N.Y. *A Customs House Registry from Roman Egypt.* Aeg. ix, 1928, p. 240.

—— —— Fiesel, L. *Geleitszölle im griechisch-römischen Ägypten und im germanisch-romanischen Abendland.* Gött. Nach. 1925, p. 57.

Census: Calderini, A. *Di due specie di schede del censimento individuale romano d'Egitto*, in Rend. R. Ist. Lombardo, lv, 1922; *La composizione della famiglia secondo le schede di censimento dell'Egitto romano.* Milan, [1923]; *Le schede di censimento dell'Egitto romano secondo le scoperte più recenti.* Rome, 1932; *La più antica scheda di censimento romano proveniente dall'Arsinoïte*, in Rend. R. Ist. Lombardo, lxiv, 1931.

6. *Law and the Administration of Justice*

(A selection only.)

General: Meyer, P. M. *Juristische Papyri*. Berlin, 1920.
—— Mitteis, L. *Grundzüge und Chrestomathie der Papyruskunde*. 2 Band: *Juristischer Teil*. Leipzig-Berlin, 1912.
———— *Reichsrecht und Volksrecht in den östlichen Provinzen des römischen Kaiserreichs*. Leipzig, 1891.
———— *Römisches Privatrecht bis auf die Zeit Diokletians*. 1. Leipzig, 1908.
—— Naber, J. C. *Observatiunculae de Iure Romano*, in *Mnem.* XVII, 1889 and following volumes. (Papyri are often treated in these notes.)
—— Taubenschlag, R. *Geschichte der Rezeption des römischen Privatrechts in Ägypten*, in *Studi in onore di P. Bonfante*, 1, p. 369.
—— Weiss, E. *Griechisches Privatrecht auf rechtsvergleichender Grundlage*. Leipzig, 1923.
—— Wenger, L. *Rechtshistorische Papyrusstudien*. Graz, 1902.
Criminal: Taubenschlag, R. *Das Strafrecht im Rechte der Papyri*. Leipzig-Berlin, 1916.
Hypothecation: Schwarz, A. B. *Hypothek und Hypallagma*. Leipzig-Berlin, 1911.
—— Weiss, E. *Pfandrechtliche Untersuchungen*. 1 Abteilung. Weimar, 1909.
Inheritance: Arangio-Ruiz, V. *La successione testamentaria secondo i papiri greco-egizii*. Naples, 1906.
—— Kreller, H. *Erbrechtliche Untersuchungen auf Grund der graeco-aegyptischen Papyrusurkunden*. Leipzig-Berlin, 1919.
—— Segrè, A. *Ricerche di diritto ereditario romano*. Rome, 1930.
Oaths: Seidl, E. *Der Eid im römisch-ägyptischen Provinzialrecht*. Munich, 1933.
Obligations: Weber, Fr. *Untersuchungen zum gräko-ägyptischen Obligationenrecht*. Munich, 1932.
Personal: Arangio-Ruiz, V. *Persone e famiglia nel diritto dei papiri*. Milan, 1930.
—— Sethe, K. und J. Partsch. *Demotische Urkunden zum ägyptischen Bürgschaftsrechte vorzüglich der Ptolemäerzeit*. Leipzig, 1920.
—— Taubenschlag, R. *Die materna potestas im gräko-ägyptischen Recht*. Z. d. Sav.-Stift. XLIX, 1929, p. 115.
———— *Vormundschaftsrechtliche Studien*. Leipzig-Berlin, 1913.
———— *Das Sklavenrecht im Rechte der Papyri*. Z. d. Sav.-Stift. L, 1930, p. 140.
—— Wenger, L. *Die Stellvertretung im Rechte der Papyri*. Leipzig, 1906.
Procedure: Wilcken, U. *Der ägyptische Konvent*. Arch. Pap. IV, 1908, p. 366.
—— Zucker, Fr. *Beiträge zur Kenntnis der Gerichtsorganisation im ptolemäischen und römischen Ägypten*. Phil. Supplementband XII.

7. *The Document*

Arangio-Ruiz, V. *Lineamenti del sistema contrattuale nel diritto dei papiri*. Milan, n.d.
Berger, A. *Die Strafklauseln in dem Papyrusurkunden*. Leipzig-Berlin, 1911.
Bickermann, E. *Beiträge zur antiken Urkundengeschichte*, in *Arch. Pap.* VIII, 1927, and following volumes.
Boak, A. E. R. *The Anagraphai of the Grapheion of Tebtunis and Kerkesouchon Oros*. J.E.A. IX, 1923, p. 164.
Caldara, A. *I connotati Personali nei documenti d' Egitto dell' età greca e romana*. Milan, 1924.
Eger, O. *Zum ägyptischen Grundbuchwesen in römischer Zeit*. Leipzig-Berlin, 1909.
Hasebroek, J. *Das Signalement in den Papyrusurkunden*. Berlin-Leipzig, 1921.

Jörs, P. Δημοσίωσις und ἐκμαρτύρησις. Z. d. Sav.-Stift. XXXIV, 1913, p. 107.

Lewald, H. *Beiträge zur Kenntnis des römisch-ägyptischen Grundbuchrechts*. Leipzig, 1909.

Preisigke, Fr. *Das Wesen der βιβλιοθήκη ἐγκτήσεων*. Klio, XII, 1912, p. 402.

Schwarz, A. B. *Die öffentliche und private Urkunde im römischen Ägypten*. Leipzig, 1920.

Segrè, A. *I documenti agoranomici in Egitto nell' età imperiale*. Bull. dell' Ist. di Diritto Romano, XXXV, 1927, p. 61.

—— *Note sul documento greco-egizio del grapheion*. Aeg. VII, 1926, p. 97.

—— *Note sul documento nel diritto greco-egizio*. Bull. dell' Ist. di Dir. Rom. XXXIV, 1925, p. 67.

—— *Note sulla forma del documento greco-romano*. Bull. dell' Ist. di Dir. Rom. XXXV, 1927, p. 69.

Steinacker, H. *Die antiken Grundlagen der frühmittelalterlichen Privaturkunde*. Berlin, 1927.

Steinwenter, A. *Beiträge zum öffentlichen Urkundenwesen der Römer*. Graz, 1915.

Wilcken, U. *Zu den Edikten*. Z. d. Sav.-Stift. XLII, 1921, p. 124.

—— *Zu den Kaiserreskripten*. Hermes, LV, 1920, p. 1.

von Woess, Fr. *Untersuchungen über das Urkundenwesen und den Publizitätsschutz im römischen Ägypten*. Munich, 1924.

8. *Cities, Nomes, and Nationalities*

Municipalities: Jouguet, P. *La vie municipale dans l'Égypte romaine*. Paris, 1911.

—— Preisigke, Fr. *Städtisches Beamtenwesen im römischen Ägypten*. Halle, 1903.

—— van Groningen, B. A. *Le gymnasiarque des métropoles de l'Égypte romaine*. Groningen, 1924.

—— Schmitz, H. *Die hellenistisch-römischen Stadtanlagen in Aegypten*. Diss. Freiburg, 1921.

Alexandria: Breccia, E. *Alexandrea ad Aegyptum*. Bergamo, 1922. (With bibliography.)

—— Bell, H. I. *Alexandria*. J.E.A. XIII, 1927, p. 171.

—— —— *Jews and Christians in Egypt*. London, 1924.

—— Gardthausen, V. *Die alexandrinische Bibliothek*. Zeitschr. d. Deutschen Vereins f. Buchw. u. Schrifttum, V, 1922, p. 73.

—— Lösch, S. *Epistula Claudiana*. Rottenburg a. N., 1930.

—— Schubart, W. *Alexandrinische Urkunden aus der Zeit des Augustus*. Arch. Pap. V, 1909, p. 35.

—— Seston, W. *L'empereur Claude et les Chrétiens*. Rev. d' hist. et de phil. relig. XI, 1931, p. 275.

—— See also below, Jews.

Canopus: Breccia, E. *Monuments de l'Égypte gréco-romaine*. Tome I, 1926. *Le rovine e i monumenti di Canopo* (pp. 9–84).

Ptolemaïs: Plaumann, G. *Ptolemais in Oberägypten*. Leipzig, 1910.

Antinoopolis: Kühn, E. *Antinoopolis*. Diss. Göttingen, 1913.

Arsinoite nome: Grenfell, B. P., A. S. Hunt and D. G. Hogarth. *Fayûm Towns and their Papyri*, pp. 1–74.

—— —— *The Tebtunis Papyri*. Part II, pp. 343–424.

—— Paulus, Fr. *Prosopographie der Beamten des* ΑΡΣΙΝΟΙΤΗΣ ΝΟΜΟΣ *in der Zeit von Augustus bis auf Diokletian*. Diss. Greifswald, 1914.

—— Wessely, C. *Topographie des Faijûm (Arsinoites Nomus) in griechischer Zeit*. Denkschr. der K. Akad. d. Wiss. 50, no. 1. Vienna, 1904.

—— Single localities: Arsinoe. Wessely, C. *Die Stadt Arsinoe (Krokodilopolis) in griechischer Zeit*. (Sitzungsber. K. Akad. d. Wiss. 145.) Vienna, 1903.

· —— —— Karanis: Boak, A. E. R., and E. E. Peterson. *Karanis*. Ann Arbor, 1931, 1933.

—— —— —— Wessely, C. *Karanis und Soknopaiu Nesos*. (Denkschr. der K. Akad. d. Wiss. 47, no. 4.) Vienna, 1902.

—— —— Philadelphia: *B.G.U.* VII, pp. 1–13.

—— —— —— Viereck, P. *Philadelpheia*. Leipzig, 1928.

—— —— Theadelphia: Breccia, E. *Monuments de l'Égypte gréco-romaine*. Bergamo, Tome I, 1926. *Teadelfia e il tempio di Pneferôs* (pp. 87–131).

Hermopolis: Méautis, G. *Hermoupolis-la-Grande*. Lausanne, 1918.

Oxyrhynchus: Rink, H. *Strassen- und Viertelnamen von Oxyrhynchus*. Diss. Giessen, 1924.

—— Breccia, E. *Le Musée Gréco-Romain*, 1931–1932. Bergamo, 1933. *Fouilles d' Oxyrhynchos*, pp. 36–47.

Nationalities: Heichelheim, F. *Die auswärtige Bevölkerung im Ptolemäerreich*. Klio, Beiheft 18, 1925. (Supplement in *Arch. Pap.* IX, 1928, p. 47.)

—— Milan. *Studî della Scuola Papirologica*, III. *Ricerche etnografiche sui papiri greco-egizî*, pp. 3–85.

—— Schönbauer, E. *Studien zur Personalitätsprinzip im antiken Recht*. Z. d. Sav.-Stift. XLIX, 1929, p. 345.

—— Greeks and Egyptians: Bickermann, E. *Beiträge zur antiken Urkundengeschichte*. I. *Der Heimatsvermerk und die staatsrechtliche Stellung der Hellenen im ptolemäischen Ägypten*. Arch. Pap. VIII, 1927, p. 216; II. Ἀπογραφή, Οἰκογένεια, Ἐπίκρισις, Αἰγύπτιοι, *ib*. IX, 1928, p. 24.

—— Schubart, W. *Die Griechen in Ägypten*. Leipzig, 1927. (Beihefte zum 'Alten Orient,' 10); *Rom und die Ägypter nach dem Gnomon des Idios Logos*, in *Zeitschr. f. äg. Spr. u. Altertumskunde*, LVI, 1920, p. 80.

—— Jews: A select bibliography of the extensive literature in Bell, H. I. *Juden und Griechen im römischen Alexandreia* (Beihefte zum 'Alten Orient,' 9, Leipzig, 1926), pp. 49–50. Of the works there cited the most important are, on the Jews in general: Schürer, E. *Geschichte des jüdischen Volkes im Zeitalter Jesu Christi*, Ed. 4, 1901, 1909; Juster, J. *Les Juifs dans l'Empire Romain* (1914); Fuchs, L. *Die Juden Ägyptens* (1924); on Alexandrian anti-Semitism, Wilcken, U. *Zum alexandrinischen Antisemitismus*, Abh. Kön. sächs. Ges. d. Wiss. XXVII, 1909, pp. 783–839; Weber, W. *Eine Gerichtsverhandlung vor Kaiser Traian*, Hermes, L, 1915, p. 47; von Premerstein, A. *Zu den sogenannten alexandrinischen Märtyrerakten*, Phil. Supplementband XVI, Heft II. Add now: Hopkins, C. *The Date of the Trial of Isidorus and Lampo before Claudius*. Yale Class. Stud. I, 1928, pp. 171–7; Uxkull-Gyllenband, W. Graf. *Ein neues Bruchstück aus den sogenannten heidnischen Märtyrerakten*, Berl. S.B. 1930, p. 664; Bell, H. I. *A New Fragment of the Acta Isidori*. Arch. Pap. X, 1931, p. 5; von Premerstein, A. *Das Datum des Prozesses des Isidoros in den sogennanten heidnischen Märtyrerakten*, Hermes, LXVII, 1932, p. 174; Goodenough, E. R. *The Jurisprudence of the Jewish Courts in Egypt*. New Haven, 1920.

—— Persians of the Epigone: the literature is again extensive. See especially Pringsheim, F. *Die Rechtsstellung der* Πέρσαι τῆς ἐπιγονῆς, Z. d. Sav.-Stift. XLIV, 1924, p. 396; Tait, J. G. ΠΕΡΣΑΙ ΤΗΣ ΕΡΙΓΟΝΗΣ, Arch. Pap. VII, 1924, p. 175.

9. *Agriculture*

Boak, A. E. R. *Irrigation and Population in the Faijûm.* Geogr. Rev. XVI, 1926, p. 353; and *Notes on Canal and Dike Work in Roman Egypt.* Aeg. VII, 1926, p. 215.

Bry, M. J. *Essai sur la vente dans les papyrus gréco-égyptiens.* Paris, 1909.

Calderini, A. *Ricerche sul regime delle acque nell' Egitto greco-romano.* Aeg. I, 1920, pp. 37; 189.

Dubois, Ch. *L'olivier et l'huile d'olive dans l'ancienne Égypte.* Rev. Phil. XLIX, 1925, p. 60; LIII, 1927, p. 7.

Ricci, C. *La Coltura della Vite e la fabbricazione del vino nell' Egitto greco-romano.* Milan, 1924.

Rostowzew, M. *Studien zur Geschichte des römischen Kolonates.* Leipzig, 1910.

Schnebel, M. *Die Landwirtschaft im hellenistischen Ägypten.* I. Munich, 1925.

Waszyński, S. *Die Bodenpacht.* Leipzig-Berlin, 1905.

Westermann, W. L. *Aelius Gallus and the Reorganization of the Irrigation System of Egypt under Augustus.* C.P. XII, 1919, p. 237; and *The 'Uninundated Lands' in Ptolemaic and Roman Egypt.* C.P. XV, 1920, p. 120.

10. *Trade, Industry, Finance, Currency, Metrology.*

General: Rostovtzeff, M. I. *The Social and Economic History of the Roman Empire.* Oxford, 1926. (The German and Italian editions (see Gen. Bibl.) are more up-to-date.)

Trade: Charlesworth, M. P. *Trade Routes and Commerce of the Roman Empire.* Cambridge, Ed. 2, 1926, pp. 16–34.

—— Chwostow, M. *History of the Oriental Commerce of Roman Egypt.* (In Russian.) Kazan, 1907.

—— Kortenbeutel, H. *Der ägyptische Süd- und Osthandel in der Politik der Ptolemäer und römischen Kaiser.* Inaug.-Diss. Berlin-Charlottenburg, 1931.

—— Warmington, E. H. *The Commerce between the Roman Empire and India.* Cambridge, 1928.

Industry: Chwostow, M. *The Textile Industry in Graeco-Roman Egypt.* (In Russian.) Kazan, 1907.

—— Fitzler, K. *Steinbrüche und Bergwerke im ptolemäischen und römischen Ägypten.* Leipzig, 1910.

—— Lewis, N. *L'industrie du Papyrus dans l' Égypte Gréco-Romaine.* Paris, 1934.

—— Reil, Th. *Beiträge zur Kenntnis des Gewerbes im hellenistischen Ägypten.* Leipzig, 1913.

Banking: Desvernos, J. *Banques et Banquiers dans l'Égypte Ancienne,* in *Bull. Soc. Roy. d'Arch. d'Alex.* No. 23, 1928, p. 303.

—— Preisigke, F. *Girowesen im griechischen Ägypten.* Strassburg, 1910.

—— Westermann, W. L. *Warehousing and Trapezite Banking in Antiquity.* Journ. of Econ. and Business Hist. III, 1930, p. 30.

Economics: Heichelheim, F. *Wirtschaftliche Schwankungen der Zeit von Alexander bis Augustus.* Jena, 1930.

—— Segrè, A. *Circolazione monetaria e prezzi nel mondo antico ed in particolare in Egitto.* Rome, 1922.

—— —— *Il mutuo e il tasso d' interesse nell' Egitto greco-romano.* Atene e Roma (N.S.), V, 1924, p. 119.

Currency: Milne, J. G. *The Alexandrian Coinage of Augustus.* J.E.A. XIII, 1927, p. 135.

—— Vogt, J. *Die Alexandrinischen Münzen.* Stuttgart, 1924.

Metrology: Segrè, A. *Metrologia e circolazione monetaria degli antichi.* Bologna, 1928. See too the earlier works there cited.

11. *Chronology*

Hohmann, F. *Zur Chronologie der Papyrusurkunden*. Berlin, 1911.

Scott, K. *Greek and Roman Honorific Months*. Yale Class. Stud. II, 1931, p. 201.

12. *Art and Social Conditions*

Bell, H. I. *Hellenic Culture in Egypt*. J.E.A. VIII, 1922, p. 139.

Bendel, P. *Qua ratione Graeci liberos docuerint, papyris, ostracis, tabulis in Aegypto inventis illustratur*. Münster, 1911.

Calderini, A. *La composizione della famiglia secondo le schede di censimento dell' Egitto romano*. Milan, [1923].

—— *Piccola letteratura di provincia nei papiri*. Aeg. II, 1921, p. 137.

—— *Pensiero e sentimento nelle epistole private greche dei papiri*. Studî della Scuola Papirologica (Milan), II, 1917, p. 9.

—— and M. Mondini. *Repertorio per lo studio delle lettere private dell' Egitto greco-romano*. Ib. p. 109.

Ghedini, G. *Di alcuni elementi religiosi pagani nell' epistole private greche dei papiri*. Studî della Scuola Papirologica (Milan), II, 1917, p. 51.

Grassi, T. *Musica, mimica e danza secondo i documenti papiracei greco-egizî*. Ib. III, 1920, p. 117.

Hornickel, O. *Ehren- und Rangprädikate in den Papyrusurkunden*. Diss. Giessen, 1930.

Kenyon, F. G. *The Library of a Greek of Oxyrhynchus*. J.E.A. VIII, 1922, p. 129.

Luckhard, F. *Das Privathaus im ptolemäischen und römischen Ägypten*. Diss. Bonn, 1914.

Majer-Leonhard, E. Ἀγράμματοι *in Aegypto qui litteras sciverint qui nesciverint ex papyris Graecis quantum fieri potest exploratur*. Frankfurt a.M. 1913.

Manteuffel, G. *De opusculis Graecis Aegypti e papyris, ostracis lapidibusque collectis*. Warsaw, 1930.

—— *Die Papyri als Zeugen griechischer Kleinliteratur*, in *Chron. d'Égypte*, 1932, p. 243.

Martin, V. *Les manuscrits antiques des classiques grecs*. Geneva, 1919.

Mondini, M. *Lettere femminili nei papiri greco-egizî*. Studî della Scuola Papirologica (Milan), II, 1917, p. 29.

Oldfather, C. H. *The Greek Literary Texts from Greco-Roman Egypt*. Madison, 1923.

Olsson, B. *Papyrusbriefe aus der frühesten Römerzeit*. Diss. Uppsala, 1925.

Preisigke, F. *Antikes Leben nach den ägyptischen Papyri*. Leipzig-Berlin, 1916.

San Nicolò, M. *Ägyptisches Vereinswesen zur Zeit der Ptolemäer und Römer*. Munich, 1913, 1915.

Schubart, W. *Die Frau im griechisch-römischen Ägypten*. Internationale Monatsschrift f. Wiss. Kunst u. Technik, 1916, cols. 1503–38.

—— *Ein Jahrtausend am Nil*. Ed. 2, Berlin, 1923.

—— Οἰκογένεια. Raccolta Lumbroso, 1925, pp. 49–67.

Winter, J. G. *Life and Letters in the Papyri*. Ann Arbor, 1933.

Zehetmair, A. *De appellationibus honorificis in papyris Graecis obviis*. Diss. Marburg, 1912.

Ziebarth, E. *Aus der antiken Schule*. Ed. 2, Bonn, 1913.

CHAPTER XI

HEROD OF JUDAEA

A. ANCIENT SOURCES

I. *Inscriptions*

I.G. III, 551; *O.G.I.S.* 414–7; *C.R. Ac. Inscr.* 1927, p. 243; Vogelstein-Rieger, *Geschichte der Jüden in Rom*, Berlin, 1896, no. 124.

II. *Coins*

F. W. Madden, *Coins of the Jews*, London, 1881, p. 99 (Antigonus); 105 (Herod); 114 (Archelaus). See also Th. Reinach, *Les monnaies juives*, Paris, 1887 (English trans. by G. F. Hill, London, 1903).

III. *Literary Sources*

(*a*) *Principal*

Josephus, *Bell. Iud.* I [10, 10], 216–II [8, 14], 166; *Ant.* XIV [11, 2], 271–XVII. (Zonaras, V, 10–26 is excerpted from Josephus.)

(*b*) *Secondary*

Appian, *Bell. Civ.* V, 74, 319.
Assumptio Mosis (in E. Kautzsch, *Apokryphen und Pseudepigraphen des Alten Testaments*, Tübingen, 1900, or in R. H. Charles, *The Apocrypha and Pseudepigrapha of the Old Testament in English*, Oxford, 1913).
Chronicon Paschale (ed. Dindorf), I, p. 367.
Dio XLIX, 22, 32; LI, 7; LIV, 9; LV, 27.
The Ethiopic 'Book of Enoch,' chapters 92 *sqq.* (in Kautzsch, *op. cit.* and Charles, *op. cit.* See also R. H. Charles, *The Ethiopic version of the Book of Enoch with the fragmentary Greek and Latin versions*, Oxford, 1906; *The Book of Enoch or I Enoch*. Ed. 2. Oxford, 1919).
Eusebius, *Hist. eccles.* I, 6–8.
Julius Africanus, *apud* Georg. Syncell. (ed. Dindorf), I, 561, 581.
St Justin, *Dialogus contra Tryphonem*, 52, 3.
Macrobius, *Sat.* II, 4, 11.
Mark, iii, 6; xii, 13.
Matthew, ii; xxii, 16.
Nicolaus of Damascus, frags. 131–36 (Jacoby, *F. Gr. Hist.* IIA, pp. 420–5).
Persius, *Sat.* V, 179 *sqq.*
Philo, *Legatio ad Gaium*, 23 (152 *sqq.*); 37–38 (294 *sqq.*); 40 (311 *sqq.*).
Plutarch, *Ant.* 36.
Strabo, XVI, 765.
The Talmudic and Rabbinical tradition in J. Dérenbourg, *Essai sur l'histoire et la géographie de la Palestine*, I, Paris, 1867, p. 145; or in H. L. Strack and P. B. Billerbeck, *Kommentar zum Neuen Testament aus Talmud und Midrasch* I, Munich, 1922, pp. 88–89; 944; II, p. 411. For the description of the Temple of Herod Mishna, tractate *Middoth*, should be consulted, though with caution (cf. *Middot*, Text, Übersetzung und Erklärung von O. Holtzmann, Giessen, 1913). See also Th. Reinach, *Textes d'auteurs grecs et romains relatifs au Judaïsme*, Paris, 1895.

IV. *Modern Works upon the Sources*

Generally, and for fuller bibliographical notices, consult E. Schürer, *Geschichte des jüdischen Volkes im Zeitalter Jesu Christi*, 1, 3. Ed. 4, Leipzig, 1901, pp. 46–8 (Strabo); 48 (Herod's *Memoirs*); 48–50 (Ptolemy, the biographer of Herod); 50–57 (Nicolaus of Damascus); 58–63 (Justus of Tiberias); 74–106 (Josephus). On Josephus see also Note 7, p. 884. The following notices concern only the period of Herod.

Besides the works of Albert, Destinon, Hölscher, and Korach, cited in the Bibliography to Chaps. I–IV, Part I, sect. I, C, 4 (p. 898), the following should be noted:

Asbach, J. *Zu Nikolaos von Damaskos*. Rh. Mus. XXXVII, 1882, p. 295.

Büchler, A. *The sources of Josephus for the history of Syria in Antiquities*, XII, 3–XIII, 14. Jew. Quart. Rev. IX, 1897, p. 311 (pp. 325–39, Nicolaus as source).

Laqueur, R. *Ephoros. I. Die Proömien*. Hermes, XLVI, 1911, pp. 167–76 (the proems of Josephus as an indication of the sources).

Luther, H. *Josephus und Justus von Tiberias*. Diss. Halle, 1910 (pp. 49–54; Writings of Justus).

Motzo, B. *Ircano II nella tradizione storica*. Studi Cagliaritani di storia e filologia. Vol. I, 1927, p. 1.

Nestle, E. *Judaea bei Josephus*. Zeits. deutsch. Pal. Ver. XXXIV, 1911, p. 65.

Niese, B. *Bemerkungen über die Urkunden bei Josephus Archaeol. B.* XIII–XIV–XVI, Hermes, XI, 1876, p. 466.

—— *Der jüdische Historiker Josephus*. H.Z. LXXVI, 1896, p. 193.

Otto, P. *Strabonis Ἱστορικῶν Ὑπομνημάτων fragmenta*. Leipz. Stud. XI, Suppl. 1889, p. 225.

Schemann, F. A. C. *Die Quellen des Flavius Josephus in der Jüd. Archäologie, B.* XVIII–XX = Polemos II, cc. viii–xiv, 3. Diss. Marburg, 1887.

Täubler, E. *Die nicht bestimmbaren Hinweise bei Josephus und die Anonymus-hypothese*. Hermes, LI, 1916, p. 211.

Unger, G. F. *Zu Josephus. v. Das verlorene Geschichtswerk*. Bay. S.B. 1897, p. 223.

Articles in P.W. *s.vv.* Herodes (W. Otto), Suppl. bd. II, cols .1–15; Josephus (G. Hölscher); Justus v. Tiberias (F. Jacoby).

B. MODERN WORKS

Works and articles earlier than 1900 are not cited, since for these reference may be made to the bibliography in Schürer, *op. cit.* 1[4], pp. 4–31.

I. *General*

The fundamental work on the reign of Herod is the article *s.v.* Herodes by W. Otto in P.W. Suppl. bd. II, cols. 1–158, completed by the articles *s.vv.* Herodes Antipas (*ib.* cols. 168–91); Herodes Archelaos (cols. 190–200); and Herodianoi (cols. 200–2).

Klausner, J. *The History of Israel.* III (*The Herodian Age*). Jerusalem, 1924 (in Hebrew).

Lagrange, M.-J. *Le Judaïsme avant Jésus-Christ*. Paris, 1931, p. 164.

Meyer, E. *Ursprung und Anfänge des Christentums*. Vol. II, Stuttgart-Berlin, 1921, p. 319.

Oesterley, W. O. E. *A History of Israel*. Vol. II, Oxford, 1932, pp. 350–78.

Renan, E. *Histoire du peuple d'Israël*. Vol. V, Paris, 1893, p. 205.

Schlatter, A. *Geschichte Israels von Alexander dem Grossen bis Hadrian*. Ed. 3. Stuttgart, 1925, p. 231.

Schürer, E. *Geschichte des jüdischen Volkes im Zeitalter Jesu Christi.* 1, 3–4 ed., Leipzig, 1901, p. 354.

Täubler, E. *Staat und Umwelt: Palästina in der hellenistisch-römischen Zeit*, in *Tyche*, Leipzig, 1926, p. 116.

Vickers, J. *The History of Herod.* Ed. 2. London, 1901.

Wellhausen, J. *Israelitische und jüdische Geschichte.* Ed. 4, Berlin, 1901, pp. 323 *sqq.*

Willrich, H. *Das Haus des Herodes zwischen Jerusalem und Rom.* Heidelberg, 1929.

II. *Works of Detail*

(a) *Economic and Social Conditions*

There is at present no special monograph on the subject, but many indications can be found, especially in the following works:

Bertholet, A. *Die Stellung der Israeliten und der Juden zu den Fremden.* Freiburg-Leipzig, 1896, p. 243.

Büchler, A. *Das Synedrion in Jerusalem.* Vienna, 1902.

—— *Der galiläische 'Am ha-'Areṣ.* Vienna, 1906.

Felten, J. *Neutestamentliche Zeitgeschichte oder Judentum und Heidentum zur Zeit Christi und der Apostel.* 2 vols. Regensburg, 1910.

Grant, F. C. *The economic background of the Gospels.* Oxford, 1926.

Herz, J. *Grossgrundbesitz in Palästina im Zeitalter Jesu.* Paläst. Jahrb. xxiv, 1926, p. 98.

Jeremias, J. *Jerusalem zur Zeit Jesu: Kulturgeschichtliche Untersuchung zur neutestamentlichen Zeitgeschichte.* 1, iiA, B, Leipzig, 1923– .

Jones, A. H. M. *The Urbanization of Palestine.* J.R.S. xxi, 1931, p. 78.

Juster, J. *Les Juifs dans l'empire romain.* 2 vols. Paris, 1914.

Kittel, G. *Die Probleme des palästinischen Spätjudentums und des Urchristentums.* Stuttgart, 1926.

Klausner, J. *Jesus of Nazareth, his life, times, and teaching.* (Engl. trans. from the Hebrew.) London, 1929, p. 175.

Schwalm, M. B. *La vie privée du peuple juif à l'époque de Jésus Christus.* Paris, 1910.

Works on Pharisaism and Sadduceeism should also be consulted; see vol. ix, pp. 933–4.

(b) *Herod's Public Works*

For general works on the topography of Jerusalem and of Palestine see vol. iii, p. 728; vol. ix, p. 931.

Dalman, G. *Der zweite Tempel zu Jerusalem.* Paläst. Jahrb. v, 1909, p. 29.

Eckardt, R. *Das Praetorium des Pilatus.* Zeits. deutsch. Pal. Ver. xxxiv, 1911, p. 39.

Haefeli, L. *Cäsarea am Meer. Topographie und Geschichte der Stadt nach Josephus und Apostelgeschichte.* Münster, 1923, p. 9 (Neutestamentliche Abhandlungen x, 5).

Harvard Excavations at Samaria (by G. A. Reisner, C. S. Fischer, D. G. Lyon). Vol. 1, Cambridge, Mass. 1924, p. 166.

Hasak, M. *Die königliche Halle des Herodes, die Marienkirche Justinians und die Moschee al-Akṣa auf dem Tempelplatz in Jerusalem.* Zeits. deutsch. Pal. Ver. xxxvi, 1913, p. 300.

Hollis, F. J. *The archaeology of Herod's Temple, with a commentary on the tractate Middoth.* London, 1934.

Schulten, A. *Masada, die Burg des Herodes und die römischen Lager.* Zeits. deutsch. Pal. Ver. lvi, 1933, p. 1.

Smith, G. A. *Jerusalem. The topography, economics and history from the earliest times to* A.D. 70. Vol. II, London, 1908, p. 469.

Thomsen, P. *Denkmäler Palästinas aus der Zeit Jesu.* Leipzig, 1916 (II, 1, *Das Land der Bibel*).

Vincent, H. *L'Antonia et le Prétoire.* Rev. Bib. XLII, 1933, p. 83.

(c) Miscellaneous

Brann, M. *De Herodis, qui dicitur magni, filiis patrem in imperio secutis.* I. Breslau Diss. 1873.

—— *Die Söhne des Herodes.* Monatsschrift f. Gesch. u. Wiss. d. Judentums (M.G.W.J.), XXII, 1873, pp. 241, 305.

Darmesteter, J. *Les Parthes à Jérusalem.* Journ. Asiat. (Sér. IX) VIII, 1894, p. 43.

Dobiáš, J. *La donation d'Antoine à Cléopâtre en l'an 34 av. J.-C.* Mélanges Bidez, Brussels, 1934, p. 287.

Gardthausen, V. *Die Eroberung Jerusalems durch Herodes.* Rh. Mus. L, 1895, p. 311.

Herzfeld, L. *Wann war die Eroberung Jerusalems durch Pompeius und wann die durch Herodes?* M.G.W.J. IV, 1885, p. 11.

Kahrstedt, U. *Syrische Territorien in hellenistischer Zeit.* Gött. Abh. XIX (2), 1926, pp. 108–10.

Korach, L. *Die Reisen des Herodes nach Rom.* M.G.W.J. XXXVIII, 1894, p. 529.

Kromayer, J. *Die Eroberung Jerusalems durch Herodes.* Hermes, XXIX, 1894, p. 556.

—— *Zeit und Bedeutung der ersten Schenkung Marc Antons an Cleopatra.* Ib. XXIX, 1894, p. 571.

Momigliano, A. *Ricerche sull' organizzazione della Giudea sotto il dominio romano* (63 a.C.–70 d.C.), Annali Scuola Normale Superiore di Pisa, N.S. III, 1934, p. 183.

CHAPTER XII

THE NORTHERN FRONTIERS UNDER AUGUSTUS

I. GENERAL

A. ANCIENT SOURCES

See above, p. 341, *note*. The more important references will be mentioned under the separate sections below. The military inscriptions will be found in Ritterling's article *s.v. Legio* in P.W. Only a brief selection can be given below.

B. MODERN WORKS

Besides general histories of the period the following works may be consulted:

von Domaszewski, A. *Die Beneficiarierposten und die römischen Strassennetze.* Westdeutsche Zeitschr. XXI, 1902, p. 158.

Kiepert, H. *Formae Orbis Antiqui.*

Mommsen, Th. *Res Gestae Divi Augusti.* Ed. 2. Berlin, 1883.

—— *The Provinces of the Roman Empire.* Ed. 2. London, 1909.

Ritterling, E. Art. *s.v. Legio* in P.W.

Syme, R. *Some Notes on the Legions under Augustus.* J.R.S. XXIII, 1933, p. 14.

II. THE SPANISH WARS

A. ANCIENT SOURCES

1. *Inscriptions*

C.I.L. I², pp. 50, 77, 181. Dessau 103, 8895. *C.I.L.* II, 2703. *Ann. épig.* 1921, n. 6. For the roads in the North-west, cf. *Viae Tarraconensis* in *C.I.L.* II and *Eph. Ep.* VIII.

2. *Coins*

Mattingly, H. and E. Sydenham. *The Roman Imperial Coinage,* I. London, 1923, p. 82, nn. 221 *sqq.* (coins of P. Carisius).

Cohen, H. *Description historique des monnaies frappées sous l'empire romain.* Ed. 2. Paris, 1880–92. Vol. I.

3. *Literary evidence*

Horace, *Ep.* I, 12, 26. Livy XXVIII, 12; *Epit.* 135. Strabo III, esp. 164–6. Vell. Pat. II, 90, 4. Suetonius, *Aug.* 81, 85. Dio LIII–LVI *passim.* Florus II, 33 [IV, 12]. Orosius VI, 21, 1–11. Cassiodorus, *Chron.,* ann. 730. Isidorus, *Orig.* 15, 1, 69.

B. MODERN WORKS

Albertini, E. *Les divisions administratives de l'Espagne romaine.* Paris, 1923.

Arnold, W. T. *Studies of Roman Imperialism.* Manchester, 1906, pp. 123–157.

Besnier, M. *Itinéraires épigraphiques d'Espagne.* Bull. Hispan. XXVI, 1924, p. 1.

Blázquez, A. *Cuatro téseras miliares.* Boletin de la Real Academia de la Historia, LXXVII, 1920, pp. 99–107.

Haebler, A. *Die Nord- und Westküste Hispaniens.* Leipzig, 1886.

Kornemann, E. *Die Entstehung der Provinz Lusitanien.* Festschrift für O. Hirschfeld. Berlin, 1903, p. 221.

Magie, D. *Augustus' War in Spain* (26–25 B.C.). C.P. XV, 1920, p. 323.
Marchetti, M. Art. Hispania in Diz. Epig.
Oman, (Sir) C. *A History of the Peninsular War*, I. Oxford, 1902. Sect. II, I, *Military geography of the Peninsula*, pp. 72–88.
Richmond, I. A. *The first years of Emerita Augusta.* Arch. Journ. 89, 1930, p. 98.
Ritterling, E. *De legione Romanorum x̄ Gemina.* Leipzig, 1885, pp. 19–36.
Schulten, A. Art. *s.v.* Hispania in P.W.
Syme, R. *The Spanish War of Augustus* (26–25 B.C.). A.J. Ph. LV, 1934, p. 293.

III. NORTHERN AFRICA

A. ANCIENT SOURCES

1. *Inscriptions*

C.I.L. I², p. 50. Dessau 120, 8966.

2. *Literary evidence*

Strabo XVII, 828. Vell. Pat. II, 116, 2. Pliny, *N.H.* V, 36–7. Dio LV, 28, 3–4. Florus II, 31 [IV, 12]. Orosius VI, 21, 18.

B. MODERN WORKS

Broughton, T. R. S. *The Romanization of Africa Proconsularis.* Baltimore, 1929.
Cagnat, R. *L'Armée romaine d'Afrique.* Ed. 2. Paris, 1913, pp. 1–9.
von Domaszewski, A. *Kleine Beiträge zur Kaisergeschichte*, 3. *Der Marmariden-Krieg unter Augustus.* Phil. LXVII, 1908, p. 4.
Groag, E. Art. *s.v.* P. Sulpicius (90) Quirinius in P.W.
Gsell, S. *Inscriptions latines de l'Algérie*, I. Paris, 1922, p. 286.
—— *Histoire ancienne de l'Afrique du Nord*, VIII. Paris, 1928, pp. 201–250.
de Pachtère, F. *Les camps de la troisième légion en Afrique au premier siècle de l'empire.* C.R. Ac. Inscr. 1916, p. 273.
Pallu de Lessert, A. C. *Fastes des provinces africaines*, I. Paris, 1896.
Tissot, C. *Géographie comparée de la province romaine d'Afrique*, I–II. Paris, 1884–8.

IV. NORTH ITALY AND THE ALPINE LANDS

A. ANCIENT SOURCES

To the references in the footnotes may be added the following:

1. *Inscriptions*

Dessau 86, 1348, 2689.

2. *Literary evidence*

Horace, *Odes*, IV, 4 and 14. *Consolatio ad Liviam*, 383 *sqq.* Livy, *Epit.* 135 and 138. Strabo IV and V, *passim.* Vell. Pat. II, 98. Florus II, 22 [IV, 12]. Appian, *Ill.* 15 and 29. Dio LIII, 25, 3–4; LIV, 22, 1–5; 24, 3. Ammianus XV, 10, 7. Eusebius, ed. Schoene, p. 142 *sq.* Orosius VI, 21, 22–3.

B. MODERN WORKS

Calderini, A. *Aquileia Romana.* Milan, 1930, pp. 31–37 and 191–234.
Cartellieri, W. *Die römischen Alpenstrassen über den Brenner, Reschen-Scheideck und Plöckenpass.* Phil. Suppl. bd. XVIII, 1. Leipzig, 1926.

Detlefsen, D. *Das Pomerium Roms und die Grenzen Italiens.* Hermes xxi, 1886, p. 522.

von Duhn, F. *Die Benutzung der Alpenpässe im Altertum.* Neue Heidelberger Jahrbücher, ii, 1892, p. 55.

Egger, R. *Führer durch die Antikensammlung des Landesmuseums in Klagenfurt.* Vienna, 1921, pp. 1–4.

—— *Teurnia.* Ed. 2. Vienna-Leipzig, 1926, pp. 1–4.

Ferrero, E. *L'Arc d'Auguste à Suse.* Turin, 1901.

Haug, F. Art. *s.v.* Raetia in P.W.

Heuberger, R. *Raetien,* vol. i. Innsbruck, 1932.

Kahrstedt, U. *Studien zur politischen und Wirtschaftsgeschichte der Ost- und Zentralalpen vor Augustus.* Gött. Nach. 1927, i, p. i.

Nissen, H. *Italische Landeskunde,* i. Berlin, 1883, pp. 136–173; ii, 1902, pp. 1–111.

Oberziner, G. *Le Guerre di Augusto contro i popoli Alpini.* Rome, 1900.

Patsch, C. *Alte und neue Prätorianerinschriften aus Aquileia.* Arch.-ep. Mitt. aus Österreich-Ungarn, xiv, 1891, p. 100.

Ritterling, E. *Die römischen Münzen aus Oberhausen bei Augsburg.* Zeitschr. des hist. Vereins für Schwaben u. Neuburg, 40, 1914, p. 162.

Scheffel, P. H. *Verkehrsgeschichte der Alpen,* i. Berlin, 1908.

Schmid, W. *Römische Forschung in Österreich* 1912–1924. C. *Die Noriker.* R.-G. K. Ber. xv, 1923/4, p. 189.

Stähelin, F. *Die Schweiz in römischer Zeit.* Ed. 2. Basel, 1931.

Vollmer, F. *Inscriptiones Baivariae Romanae.* Munich, 1915.

Wagner, F. *Die Römer in Bayern.* Ed. 4. Munich, 1928.

Zippel, G. *Die römische Herrschaft in Illyrien bis auf Augustus.* Leipzig, 1877, pp. 247–297.

V. ILLYRICUM AND THE BALKANS

A. ANCIENT SOURCES

1. *Inscriptions*

Res Gestae 30, 31. Dessau 918 (?), 921, 2270, 2532, 2673, 8965. *Fasti Praenestini* (*C.I.L.* i², p. 231; *Ann. épig.* 1922, n. 96). *C.I.L.* iii, 7386. *I.G.R.R.* i, 654. *Ann. épig.* 1933, n. 85.

2. *Literary evidence*

Ovid, *Ex Ponto,* ii, 1, 45–6; *Tristia,* ii, 197–200. *Consolatio ad Liviam,* 387–8. Strabo vii, *passim.* Vell. Pat. ii, 39, 96, 98, 101, 108–116. Seneca, *Epp.* 83, 14. Pliny, *N.H.* iii, 139–150; vii, 45. Frontinus, *Strat.* ii, 1, 15. Suetonius, *Aug.* 21; *Tib.* 9, 16, 21. Appian, *Ill.* 29–30. Dio xlix, 37, 3; liv–lvi. *passim.* Livy, *Epit.* 139–142. Florus ii, 24, 25, 27, 28, 29 [iv, 12]. Orosius vi, 22, 2. Cassiodorus, *Chron., ann.* 746.

B. MODERN WORKS

Most of the works mentioned in the bibliography to chapters I–IV for the campaigns of Octavian and of M. Licinius Crassus (pp. 903 *sq.*, p. 905) will here be required. In addition the following:

1. *General*

Evans, (Sir) A. *Antiquarian researches in Illyricum*, i–iv. Reprinted from *Archaeologia*, xlviii, 1883; xlix, 1885.

—— *The Adriatic Slavs and the Overland Route to Constantinople*. Geog. Journ. 1916, p. 241.

Jireček, C. *Die Heerstrasse von Belgrad nach Constantinopel und die Balkenpässe*. Prague, 1877.

Jung, J. *Römer und Romanen in den Donauländern*. Ed. 2. Innsbruck, 1887.

Nischer, E. *Die Römer im Gebiete des ehemaligen Österreich-Ungarn*. Vienna, 1923.

Patsch, C. *Beiträge zur Völkerkunde von Südosteuropa*, v. *Aus 500 Jahren vorrömischer und römischer Geschichte Südosteuropas*, 1: *Bis zur Festsetzung der Römer in Transdanuvien*. Wien S.B. 1932.

2. *Dalmatia and Pannonia*

Abramić, M. *Führer durch Poetovio*. Vienna, 1925.

—— *O novim miljokazima i rimskim cestama Dalmacije*. Vjesnik za arh. i hist. Dalmatinsku, xlix, 1926–7, p. 139.

Balliff, P. *Römische Strassen in Bosnien und der Hercegowina*. Vienna, 1893.

Čremošnik, G. and D. Sergejevski. *Novitates Musei Sarajevoensis*, 9. Sarajevo, 1930, pp. 8–9 (inscription of a *princeps Daesitiatium*).

Cuntz, O. *Legionäre des Antonius und Augustus aus dem Orient*. Jahreshefte xxv, 1929, p. 70.

Hoernes, M. *Altertümer der Hercegowina*, ii. Wien S.B. 1882. Section iv, *Römische Strassen und Orte im heutigen Bosnien*, pp. 926–946.

Patsch, C. *Arch.-ep. Untersuchungen zur Gesch. der r. Provinz Dalmatien*, iv, pp. 54–62 (Die Marzeii). Wissenschaftliche Mitt. aus Bosnien u. der Herzegowina, vii, 1900.

—— *Historische Wanderungen im Karst und an der Adria*, i. *Die Herzegowina einst und jetzt*. Vienna, 1922.

Richter, E. *Beiträge zur Landeskunde Bosniens und der Herzegowina*. Wissenschaftliche Mitt. aus Bosnien u. der Herzegowina, x, 1907.

Ritterling, E. *Die Statthalter der Pannonischen Provinzen*. Arch.-ep. Mitt. aus Österreich-Ungarn, xx, 1897, p. 1.

Tomaschek, W. *Die vorslawische Topographie der Bosna, Herzegowina, Crnagora, etc.* Mitt. der k.-k. geogr. Gesellschaft in Wien, xxiii, 1880, pp. 497–528, 545–567.

Die Occupation Bosniens u. der Hercegowina durch k.-k. Truppen im Jahre 1878. Verlag des k.-k. Generalstabes. Vienna, 1879 (esp. pp. 41–59).

3. *Moesia and Thrace* (for the Black Sea, see p. 921)

Collart, P. *Inscriptions de Philippes*. B.C.H. lvi, 1932, pp. 207 *sqq.*

von Domaszewski, A. *Die Entwicklung der Provinz Moesia*. Neue Heid. Jahrb. i, 1891, p. 190.

Fluss, M. Art. *s.v.* Moesia in P.W.

Kazarow, G. *Beiträge zur Kulturgeschichte der Thraker*. Sarajevo, 1916.

Pârvan, V. *I primordi della civiltà Romana alle foci del Danubio*. Ausonia, x, 1921, p. 192.

von Premerstein, A. *Die Anfänge der Provinz Moesien*. Jahreshefte i, 1898, Beiblatt col. 145.

Stout, S. E. *The Governors of Moesia*. Diss. Princeton, 1911.

Syme, R. *Lentulus and the Origin of Moesia*. J.R.S. xxiv, 1934 (part 2).

Tomaschek, W. *Die alten Thraker*, 1. Wien S.B. 128, 1893, p. 1.

Weiss, J. *Die Dobrudscha im Altertum.* Sarajevo, 1911.

4. *Rome and the Transdanuvian Peoples*

Devrient, E. *Hermunduren und Marcomannen.* N.J. Kl. Alt. iv, 1901, p. 51.

Dobiáš, J. *Zadunajská výprava M. Vinicia.* Časopis Musea královstí českého, xcvi, 1922, pp. 81 *sqq.*, 213 *sqq.*

Gnirs, A. *Zur Topographie des Markomannenlandes.* Charisteria A. Rzach. Reichenberg, 1930, p. 41.

—— *Die römischen Schutzbezirke an der oberen Donau.* Augsburg-Vienna, 1929.

Groag, E. Art. *s.v.* P. Sulpicius (90) Quirinius in P.W., cols. 822 *sqq.*

Kirchoff, A. *Thüringen doch Hermundurenland.* Leipzig, 1882.

Nischer-Falkenhof, E. *Das römische Reich und die Sudetenländer.* Sudeta, iv, 1928, p. 40.

Pič, J. L. *Le Hradischt de Stradonitz en Bohême.* Leipzig, 1906, pp. 104–136.

von Premerstein, A. *Ein Elogium des M. Vinicius Cos. 19 vor Chr.* Jahreshefte vii, 1904, p. 215.

—— *Der Daker- und Germanensieger M. Vinicius (Cos. 19 v. Chr.) und sein Enkel (Cos. 30 und 45 n. Chr.)*, 1. Jahreshefte xxviii, 1933, p. 140.

Syme, R. *Lentulus and the Origin of Moesia.* J.R.S. xxiv, 1934 (part 2).

Winkelsesser, C. *De rebus divi Augusti auspiciis in Germania gestis quaestiones selectae.* Diss. Detmold, 1901, pp. 23–37.

5. *The Pannonian Revolt*

Abraham, A. F. *Zur Gesch. der germanischen und pannonischen Kriege unter Augustus* Progr. Berlin, 1875.

Bauer, A. *Zum Dalmatisch-pannonischen Krieg 6–9 n. Chr.* Arch.-ep. Mitt. aus Österreich-Ungarn, xvii, 1894, p. 135.

Groag, E. *M. Plautius Silvanus (Prosopographische Beiträge*, vii). Jahreshefte xxi–xxii, 1924, Beiblatt col. 445.

Hirschfeld, O. *Zur Gesch. des pannonisch-dalmatischen Krieges.* Kleine Schriften, p. 387.

Kaer, P. *Sull' ubicazione di Andetrium.* Zara, 1895.

Rau, R. *Zur Gesch. des pannonisch-dalmatischen Krieges der Jahre 6–9 n. Chr.* Klio, xix, 1924, p. 313.

Saria, B. *Bathinus Flumen.* Klio, xxiii, 1929, p. 92.

—— *Bathinus—Bosna.* Klio, xxvi, 1933, p. 279.

Syme, R. *Galatia and Pamphylia under Augustus: the Governorships of Piso, Quirinius and Silvanus.* Klio, xxvii, 1934, p. 139.

Vulić, N. *Dalmatsko-panonski ustanak 6–9 g. po Hr.* Glas srpske kraljevske akademije, cxxi, 1926, p. 55.

—— *Reka Bathinus.* Glas srpske kraljevske akademije, clv, 1933, p. 3.

Wissowa, G. *Neue Bruchstücke des römischen Festkalenders.* Hermes, lviii, 1923, pp. 373–7 (on the date of Tiberius' triumph). See D. M. Pippidi in *Rev. E.L.* xi, 1933, p. 435.

VI. GERMANY

A. Ancient Sources

The ancient evidence for this section and for the subsequent history of the Rhine frontier (chap. xxiii) will be found collected in the following works:

Byvanck, A. W. *Excerpta Romana. De Bronnen der Romeinische Geschiedenis van Nederland.* Gravenhage, 1931.

Riese, A. *Das rheinische Germanien in der antiken Litteratur.* Leipzig, 1892.
—— *Das rheinische Germanien in den antiken Inschriften.* Leipzig and Berlin, 1914.
Ritterling, E. *Fasti des römischen Deutschland unter dem Prinzipat.* (Beiträge zur Verwaltungs- und Heeresgeschichte von Gallien und Germanien, II.) Vienna, 1932.
Stein, E. *Die kaiserlichen Beamten und Truppenkörper im römischen Deutschland unter dem Prinzipat.* (Beiträge etc., I.) Vienna, 1932.

The most important evidence is the following:

1. *Inscriptions*

Res Gestae 26. Dessau 2244, 2263, 8898, 9463.

2. *Literary evidence*

Horace, *Odes*, IV, 9 (M. Lollius); 14, 51–2. *Anth. Pal.* VII, 741. Strabo IV and VII, *passim.* Vell. Pat. II, 97, 104–9, 117–121. Valerius Maximus V, 5, 3. Frontinus, *Strat.* II, 9, 4; III, 15, 4; IV, 7, 8. Pliny, *N.H.* II, 167; VII, 84; XI, 55. Tacitus, *Germ.* 28–9; *Ann.* I, 31–51, 55–71; II, 5–26, 45–7, 62–3; XII, 39. Suetonius, *Aug.* 21, 23; *Tib.* 9, 16–20, 25, 52; *Calig.* I; *Claud.* I; *Nero*, 4. Dio LIV–LVI, *passim.* Livy, *Epit.* 138–142. Julius Obsequens 71–2. Florus II, 30 [IV, 12]. Orosius VI, 21, 24–7.

B. MODERN WORKS

1. *General*

Delbrück, H. *Geschichte der Kriegskunst*, II. Ed. 2. Berlin, 1921.
Fabricius, E. *Die Besitznahme Badens durch die Römer.* Heidelberg, 1905, pp. 22–31.
Hertlein, F. *Die Geschichte der Besetzung des römischen Württemberg.* (Die Römer in Württemberg, I.) Stuttgart, 1928.
Jullian, C. *Histoire de la Gaule*, IV. Paris [1913].
Koepp, F. *Die Römer in Deutschland.* Ed. 3. Bielefeld and Leipzig, 1926.
Mommsen, Th. *Die germanische Politik des Augustus.* Reden und Aufsätze. Berlin, 1905, pp. 316–343.
Norden, E. *Die germanische Urgeschichte und Tacitus Germania.* Ed. 3. Leipzig and Berlin, 1923.
Riese, A. *Forschungen zur Geschichte der Rheinlande in der Römerzeit.* Programme. Frankfort, 1889.
Sadée, E. *Rom und Deutschland vor Neunzehnhundert Jahren.* B.J. 124, 1917, p. 1.
Schmidt, L. *Geschichte der deutschen Stämme bis zum Ausgang der Völkerwanderung*, I–II. Berlin, 1910–1918.
Stähelin, F. *Die Schweiz in römischer Zeit.* Ed. 2. Basel, 1931.
Wilcken, U. *Zur Genesis der Res Gestae Divi Augusti.* Berl. S.B. 1932, p. 232.

2. *Archaeological evidence for Roman military sites and campaigns*

Bohn, O. *Arretina aus Vindonissa.* Germ. XI, 1928, p. 2.
Bolin, S. *Die Funde römischer und byzantinischer Münzen im freien Germanien.* R.-G. K. Ber. XIX, 1929, p. 86.

Fabricius, E., F. Hettnert and O. von Sarwey. *Der Obergermanisch-raetische Limes des Römerreiches.* Heidelberg. Abt. B: Vol. ii, Nr. 26, Friedberg (Lief. 39, 1913); nr. 28, Höchst am Main (Lief. 27, 1912); nr. 29, Hofheim (Lief. 7, 1897); nr. 31, Wiesbaden (Lief. 31, 1909).

Grenier, A. *Manuel d'archéologie gallo-romaine*, i. Paris, 1931.

Kahrstedt, U. *Lager mit Claviculae.* B.J. 138, 1933, p. 144 (on Kneblinghausen).

Koepp, F. *Die Bauten des römischen Heeres.* Germania Romana, Ein Bilder-Atlas. Ed. 2, i, Bamberg, 1924.

Krüger, H. *Die Vorgeschichtlichen Strassen in den Sachsenkriegen Karls des Grossen.* Korrespondenzblatt des Gesamtvereins, 80, 1932, p. 223.

Laur-Belart, R. *Grabungen der Gesellschaft Pro Vindonissa im Jahre 1931.* Anz. für schweiz. Altertumskunde, xxxiv, 1932, pp. 102–104.

Lehner, H. *Drususkastelle und Tiberiuskastelle.* B.J. 114/5, 1906, p. 206.

—— *Vetera. Die Ergebnisse der Ausgrabungen bis 1929.* Römisch-germanische Forschungen, iv. Berlin, 1930.

—— *Das Römerlager Vetera bei Xanten.* Bonn, 1926.

Nissen, H. *Geschichte von Novaesium.* B.J. 111/2, 1904, p. 1.

Oelmann, F. *Das Standlager der Ala Vocontiorum bei Soissons.* Germ. iv, 1920, p. 7.

Oxé, A. *Wann wurde das Legionslager Vindonissa angelegt?* Germ. xi, 1928, p. 127.

—— *Das römische Bonn.* Bonn, 1925.

Schuchhardt, K. *Vorgeschichte von Deutschland.* Ed. 2. Munich and Berlin, 1934, pp. 230–251.

Schumacher, K. *Siedelungs- und Kulturgeschichte der Rheinlande von der Urzeit bis in das Mittelalter.* i. *Die vorrömische Zeit.* Mainz, 1922, c. 7, pp. 210–218. ii. *Die römische Periode.* Mainz, 1923.

Sprater, F. *Die Pflalz unter den Römern*, i. Speier, 1929.

In addition numerous articles in the *Berichte* of the Römisch-germanische Kommission (1903–   ), the *R.-G. Korrespondenzblatt* (1908–1916) and its successor, *Germania* (1917–   ). The excavations at Haltern and Oberaden are recorded in the *Mitt. aus Westfalen* (i–vii, Münster, 1899–1922).

3. *The German Wars*

(a) *General and miscellaneous.*

Asbach, J. *Die Überlieferung der germanischen Kriege des Augustus.* B.J. 85, 1888, p. 14.

—— *Nochmals das bellum Germanicum des Florus.* B.J. 114/5, 1906, p. 442.

Dragendorff, H. *Neues zur Geschichte der römischen Occupation Germaniens.* i, *Die Frühzeit.* R.-G. K. Ber. iii, 1906/7, p. 151.

—— *Zur Geschichte der frührömischen Okkupation Germaniens.* R.-G. K. Ber. v, 1909, p. 73.

Gebert, W. *Limes.* B.J. 119, 1910, p. 158.

Groag, E. Art. *s.v.* M. Lollius (11) in P.W.

Kornemann, E. *Zur den Germanenkriegen unter Augustus.* Klio, ix, 1909, p. 422.

Kropatschek, G. *Der Drususfeldzug 11 v. Chr.* B.J. 120, 1911, p. 19.

Oxé, A. *Der Limes des Tiberius.* B.J. 114/5, 1906, p. 99.

Ritterling, E. *Zur Geschichte des römischen Heeres in Gallien unter Augustus.* B.J. 114/5, 1906, p. 159.

Seyffert, P. *Quaestiones ad Augusti bella Germanorum Critica*, i. Diss. Erlangen, 1887.

Winkelsesser, C. *De rebus divi Augusti auspiciis in Germania gestis quaestiones selectae.* Diss. Detmold, 1901.

(*b*) *The Problems of Haltern, Oberaden and Aliso.*

Kolbe, W. *Review of Prein.* Gnomon VIII, 1932, pp. 96–101.

Kropatschek, G. *Das Alisoproblem.* Deutsche Geschichtsblätter, XII, 1, 1910, p. L

Prein, O. *Aliso bei Oberaden und die Varusschlacht.* Münster, 1930.

Sadée, E. *Über den Stand der Alisofrage.* B.J. 130, 1925, p. 302.

Schulten, A. *Eine neue Römerspur in Westfalen.* B.J. 124, 1917, p. 88.

(*c*) *Varus.*

Franke, A. Art. *s.v. Teutoburgiensis saltus* in P.W., with 'Korrekturzusatz' in col.
1171, mentioning eleven papers that appeared between 1931 and 1933.

Henke, O. and B. Lehmann. *Die neueren Forschungen über die Varusschlacht.*
Gymnasial-Bibliothek, Heft 52. Gütersloh, 1910.

Kolbe, W. *Forschungen uber die Varusschlacht.* Klio, XXV, 1932, p. 141.

Koepp, F. *Lichter und Irrlichter auf dem Wege zum Schlachtfeld des Varus.* Westfalen, XIII, 1927, pp. 49 *sqq.* and 97 *sqq.*

Klotz, A. *Der Untergang des Varus.* B.P.W. 1932, col. 199.

Kornemann, E. *P. Quinctilius Varus.* N.J. Kl. Alt. XXV, 1922, p. 42.

Meyer, Edm. *Untersuchungen über die Schlacht im Teutoburger Walde.* Berlin,
1893.

Mommsen, Th. *Die Örtlichkeit der Varusschlacht.* Ges. Schriften, IV, p. 200.

Oldfather, W. A. and H. V. Canter. *The defeat of Varus and the German frontier
policy of Augustus.* Univ. of Illinois Studies in Social Science, 4, 1915.

Sadée, E. *Review of Oldfather and Canter.* B.P.W. 1916, cols. 459–473.

Wilisch, E. *Der Kampf um das Schlachtfeld im Teutoburger Wald.* N.J. Kl. Alt.
XII, 1909, p. 322.

(*d*) *Germanicus.*

Bersu, G. (along with Heimbs, Lange and Schuchhardt). *Der Angrivarisch-
Cheruskische Grenzwall und die beiden Schlachten des Jahres 16 n. Chr.
zwischen Arminius und Germanicus.* Präh. Zeitschr. XVII, 1926, p. 100.

Dahm, O. *Die Feldzüge des Germanicus.* Trier, 1902. (Westdeutsche Zeitschr.,
Ergänzungsheft XI.)

Hofmeister, H. *Die Chatten,* I. *Mattium: Die Altenburg bei Niedenstein.* Frankfurt, 1930.

Kessler, G. *Die Tradition über Germanicus.* Leipzig Diss. Berlin, 1905.

Knoke, F. *Die Kriegszüge des Germanicus in Deutschland.* Ed. 2. Berlin, 1922.

Schumacher, K. *Beiträge zur Topographie und Geschichte der Rheinlande,* III, 10.
Der Feldzug des Germanicus gegen die Chatten im Jahre 15 n. Chr. Mainzer
Zeitschr. VII, 1912, p. 71.

Wolff, G. *Die geographischen Voraussetzungen der Chattenfeldzüge des Germanicus.*
Hess. Zeitschr. 50, 1917 (Kassel), p. 53.

CHAPTER XIII

THE ECONOMIC UNIFICATION OF THE MEDITERRANEAN REGION. INDUSTRY, TRADE, AND COMMERCE

I. Ancient Sources

The main literary sources are Strabo, Petronius' *Cena Trimalchionis*, Pliny's *Natural History* and the *Periplus maris Erythraei*.

In the view of the present writer, the *Periplus* does not presuppose the effects of Neronian policy, nor is there any compelling reason to date it as late as the time of Domitian. (Cf. also Note 6 [p. 881 *sq.*] which places it about A.D. 50.) The literary sources are reinforced by the abundant epigraphic, archaeological and papyrus material.

II. Modern Works

A. *General*

Besides the works of Chapot, Friedländer-Wissowa, Homo and, above all, Rostovtzeff (*Social and Economic History*) cited in the General Bibliography, see also:

1. *On Political and Social Conditions.*

Barrow, R. H. *Slavery in the Roman Empire.* London, 1928.
Cavaignac, E. *La paix romaine.* Paris, 1928.
Duff, A. M. *Freedmen in the early Roman empire.* Oxford, 1928.
Frank, T. *Race mixture in the Roman empire.* Amer. Hist. Rev. xxi, 1915–16, p. 689.
Kornemann, E. *Die historischen Nachrichten des* Periplus Maris Erythraei *über Arabien.* Janus, i, 1921, p. 55.
Reid, J. S. *The Municipalities of the Roman empire.* Cambridge, 1913.
Schur, W. *Die Orientpolitik des Kaisers Nero.* Klio, Beiheft xv, 1923. Cf. Klio xx, 1925–26, pp. 215 *sqq.*
Wilcken, U. *Zu den* Impensae *der* Res Gestae divi Augusti. Berl. S.B. 1931, p. 772.

2. *On Industry, Trade and Commerce.*

Brewster, E. H. *Roman Craftsmen and Tradesmen of the early Roman empire.* University of Pennsylvania Press, 1917.
Charlesworth, M. P. *Trade Routes and Commerce of the Roman empire.* Ed. 2. Cambridge, 1926.
Frank, T. *An economic history of Rome.* Ed. 2. Baltimore, 1927.
Hatzfeld, J. *Les trafiquants italiens dans l'Orient hellénique.* Bibl. des écoles franç. 115. Paris, 1919.
Oertel, F. Anhang zu R. Pöhlmann's *Geschichte der sozialen Frage und des Sozialismus in der antiken Welt.* Ed. 3. Munich, 1925. Vol. ii, pp. 514 *sqq.*
Pârvan, V. *Die Nationalität der Kaufleute im römischen Kaiserreiche.* Diss. Breslau, 1909.
Schaal, H. *Vom Tauschhandel zum Welthandel.* Leipzig, 1931.
Toutain, J. *L'économie antique.* Paris, 1927.
Wilcken, U. *Alexander der Grosse und die hellenistische Wirtschaft.* Schmollers Jahrbuch, xlv (2), 1921, p. 45.
Articles in D.S.: *mercatura* (Cagnat-Besnier), *negotiator* (Cagnat); in P.W.: *Industrie und Handel* (Gummerus), *Monopole* (Heichelheim).

B. *Special Topics*

1. *Ramifications of Industry, Trade and Commerce.*

Cartellieri, W. *Die römischen Alpenstrassen über den Brenner, Reschen-Scheideck und Plöckenpass mit ihren Nebenlinien.* Leipzig, 1926.

Chwostow, M. *Geschichte des Orienthandels des griechisch-römischen Ägyptens* (332 v. Chr.–284 n. Chr.). Kazan, 1907. (In Russian.) Cf. M. Rostovtzeff, Arch. Pap. IV, 1907, p. 298.

Gummerus, H. *Die südgallische Terrasigillata Industrie nach den Graffiti aus La Graufesenque.* Soc. Scient. Fennica, Comm. Hum. Lit. III, 1932, p. 39.

Hagen, J. *Römerstrassen der Rheinprovinz.* Ed. 2. Bonn, 1931.

Herrmann, A. *Die Verkehrswege zwischen China, Indien und Rom um* 100 *n. Chr.* Leipzig, 1922.

—— *Lou-lan, China, Indien und Rom im Lichte der Ausgrabungen am Lobnor.* Leipzig, 1931.

Kisa, A. *Das Glas im Altertum.* Leipzig, 1908.

Lehmann-Hartleben, K. *Die antiken Hafenanlagen des Mittelmeeres.* Klio, Beiheft. XIV, 1923.

Oswald, F. and T. D. Pryce. *Terra Sigillata.* London, 1922.

Oxé, A. *Arretinische Reliefgefässe vom Rhein, Frühgallische Reliefgefässe vom Rhein* (Materialien für röm.-german. Keramik, Hefte 5, 6), 1933, 1934.

Schmidt, A. *Drogen und Drogenhandel im Altertum.* Leipzig, 1924.

Warmington, E. H. *The Commerce between the Roman Empire and India.* Cambridge, 1928.

Willers, H. *Neue Untersuchungen über die römische Bronzeindustrie von Capua und von Niedergermanien.* Hanover-Leipzig, 1907.

Numerous articles in P.W. *e.g. s.vv. Banken* in Suppl. IV, cols. 71 *sqq.* (Laum), *Eisen* (Blümner), *Gold* (Blümner), *Kupfer* (Blümner), *Lana* (Orth), *Silber* (Blümner).

2. *Particular Areas.* (Only a brief selection of works is here possible.)

Brusin, G. *Aquileia. Guida storico e artistico.* Udine, 1929.

Calderini, A. *Aquileia Romana.* Milan, 1930.

Carcopino, J. *Ostie.* Paris, 1929.

Chwostow, M. *Études sur l'organisation de l'industrie et du commerce dans l'Égypte gréco-romaine.* (In Russian.) Vol. I, L'industrie textile. Kazan, 1914.

Dragendorff, H. *Westdeutschland zur Römerzeit.* Ed. 2. Leipzig, 1919.

Ebert, M. *Südrussland im Altertum.* Bonn and Leipzig, 1921. esp. Chap. VII *ad fin.*

Fiesel, L. *Geleitszölle im griechisch-römischen Ägypten und im germanisch-romanischen Abendland.* Gött. Nach. 1925, p. 57.

Gsell, S. *Histoire ancienne de l'Afrique du Nord.* Vols. VII, VIII. Paris, 1928.

Haverfield, F. and G. Macdonald. *The romanization of Roman Britain.* Ed. 4. Oxford, 1923.

Jouguet, P. and M. Rostovtzeff. *Dédicace Grecque de Médamoud.* Bull. de l'Inst. Franç. d'Arch. Or. XXXI, 1930.

Jullian, C. *Histoire de la Gaule.* Vols. IV, V. Ed. 2. Paris, 1921, 1926.

Koepp, F. *Die Römer in Deutschland.* Ed. 3. Bielefeld and Leipzig, 1926.

Kunkel, O. *Pommersche Urgeschichte in Bildern, Text und Tafel.* Stettin, 1931.

Mau, A. *Führer durch Pompeji.* Ed. 6. Leipzig, 1928.

Reil, Th. *Beiträge zur Kenntnis des Gewerbes im hellenistischen Ägypten.* Borna-Leipzig, 1913.

West, L. C. *Commercial Syria under the Roman Empire.* Trans. Amer. Phil. Ass. Vol. LV. 1924, p. 159.

Wilcken, U. in Mitteis–Wilcken, *Grundzüge und Chrestomathie der Papyruskunde.* Leipzig, 1912.

Numerous articles in P.W. *e.g. s.vv.* Hispania (Schulten), Syria (Honigmann).

CHAPTER XIV

THE SOCIAL POLICY OF AUGUSTUS

I. ANCIENT AUTHORITIES

(The references given in the chapter are to the following collections and editions.)

1. *Inscriptions*

Corpus Inscriptionum Latinarum. Berlin. Vol. I. Inscriptiones Latinae antiquissimae ad C. Caesaris mortem. Editio altera. 1893–1918. Vol. VI. Inscriptiones urbis Romae Latinae. Pars prima, 1876; partis quartae fasciculus posterior, 1902.

Dessau, H. *Inscriptiones Latinae Selectae*. Berlin. Vol. I, 1892; vol. II, 1, 1902; vol. II, 2, 1906; vol. III, 1, 1914; vol. III, 2, 1916.

The Monumentum Ancyranum, edited by E. G. Hardy. Oxford, 1923.

Res gestae divi Augusti. Ex monumentis Ancyrano et Apolloniensi iterum edidit Th. Mommsen. Berlin, 1883.

Conway, R. S. *The Italic Dialects edited with a grammar and glossary*. 2 vols. Cambridge, 1897.

2. *Legal Documents*

Der Gnomon des Idios Logos, bearbeitet von E. Seckel und W. Schubart. Erster Teil: der Text, von W. Schubart. Ägyptische Urkunden aus den staatlichen Museen zu Berlin. Griechische Urkunden, v. Band, 1. Heft. Berlin, 1919.

Plaumann, G. *Der Idioslogos. Untersuchungen zur Finanzverwaltung Ägyptens in hellenistischer und römischer Zeit*. Berl. Abh. Jahrgang 1918. Phil.-hist. Klasse, Nr. 17. Berlin, 1919.

Seckel, E. (and P. M. Meyer). *Zum sogenannten Gnomon des Idioslogos*. Berl. Sitz. Phil.-hist. Klasse, 1928, p. 424.

Reinach, Th. *Un code fiscal de l'Égypte romaine*. Nouvelle revue historique de droit français et étranger, XLIII, 1919, 583; XLIV, 1920, 5.

Iurisprudentiae anteiustinianae reliquias...editione sexta...ediderunt E. Seckel et B. Kuebler. Leipzig. Volumen prius, 1908; voluminis alterius fasciculus prior, 1911; voluminis alterius fasciculus secundus, 1927. The Fragmentum quod dicitur Dositheanum (*Frag. Dos.*) will be found in Vol. I of this collection, pp. 419 *sqq.*; the Fragmenta iuris Romani Vaticana (*Frag. Vat.*) in Vol. II, 2, pp. 191 *sqq.*; and the work commonly known as 'Mosaicarum et Romanarum legum Collatio' (*Collatio*), *ib.* pp. 324 *sqq.* The treatise printed in Vol. I, pp. 436 *sqq.*, under the title 'Ulpiani liber singularis Regularum,' is cited in Chapter XIV as *Ulpiani Epit.* See

Die Epitome Ulpiani des Codex Vaticanus Reginae 1128, herausgegeben von F. Schulz. Bonn, 1926.

Gai Institutiones, with a translation and commentary by the late E. Poste. Fourth edition, revised and enlarged by E. A. Whittuck, with an historical introduction by A. H. J. Greenidge. Oxford, 1904.

Codex Theodosianus. Rec. P. Krueger. Berlin. Fasc. I (libri I–VI); 1923 Fasc. II (libri VII–VIII); 1926.

Corpus Iuris Civilis. Berlin. Volumen primum: *Institutiones* rec. P. Krueger; *Digesta* rec. Th. Mommsen, retractavit P. Krueger. Editio stereotypa quarta decima. 1922. Volumen secundum: *Codex Iustinianus.* Rec. et retractavit P. Krueger. Editio stereotypa nona. 1915.

Institutionum Graeca Paraphrasis Theophilo antecessori vulgo tributa...Rec.... E. C. Ferrini. Pars prior. Berlin, 1883.

Rotondi, G. *Leges publicae populi Romani.* (Estratto dalla *Enciclopedia giuridica Italiana.*) Milan, 1912.

3. *Literary Sources*

Appiani Historia Romana. Lipsiae. Vol. II. Ed. L. Mendelssohn: editio altera correctior curante P. Viereck, 1905.

M. Tulli Ciceronis scripta quae manserunt omnia. Lipsiae. De Officiis. Rec. C. Atzert. De virtutibus. Rec. O. Plasberg. 1923.

Cassii Dionis Cocceiani Historiarum Romanarum quae supersunt. Ed. U. P. Boissevain. Volumen II. Berolini, 1898.

C. Iuli Caesaris Commentarii. Recensuit R. Du Pontet. 2 vols. Oxonii, 1900.

Catulli Carmina rec....R. Ellis. Oxonii. n.d.

M. Tulli Ciceronis Orationes. Oxonii. Cum Senatui gratias egit. Cum populo gratias egit. De domo sua. De haruspicum responso. Pro Sestio. In Vatinium. De provinciis consularibus. Pro Balbo. Rec. G. Peterson. 1911.

Dionysi Halicarnasensis Antiquitatum Romanarum quae supersunt, ed. C. Jacoby. Lipsiae. Vol. I, 1885; vol. II, 1888; vol. III, 1891; vol. IV, 1905. Supplementum indices continens, 1925.

Sexti Pompeii Festi De Verborum Significatu quae supersunt cum Pauli epitome. Ed. W. M. Lindsay. Lipsiae, 1913.

A. Gellii Noctium Atticarum libri xx. Ed. C. Hosius. 2 vols. Lipsiae, 1903.

Q. Horati Flacci opera rec....E. C. Wickham. Editio altera, curante H. W. Garrod. Oxonii, 1912.

Titi Livi ab urbe condita. Recc. R. S. Conway et C. F. Walters. Oxonii. Tom. II: libri VI–X, 1919.

Titi Livi ab urbe condita libri. Editionem primam curavit G. Weissenborn: editio altera, quam curavit M. Müller. Lipsiae. Pars III, fasc. II, 1909; pars IV, fasc. I, 1912.

T. Livi periochae omnium librorum, fragmenta Oxyrhynchi reperta, Iulii Obsequentis prodigiorum liber. Ed. O. Rossbach. Lipsiae, 1910.

M. Val. Martialis Epigrammata rec....W. M. Lindsay. Oxonii, 1902.

T. Macci Plauti Comoediae. Rec....W. M. Lindsay. Oxonii. 2 vols. 1903.

C. Plini Secundi Naturalis Historiae libri xxxvii. Ed. C. Mayhoff. Lipsiae. Vol. I, 1906; vol. II, ed. 2, 1909; vol. III, 1892; vol. IV, 1897; vol. V, 1897.

Plutarchi Vitae Parallelae. Recc. Cl. Lindskog et K. Ziegler. Lipsiae. Vol. II, fasc. I, 1932. Vol. III, fasc. 2, 1926.

The Elegies of Propertius, edited...by H. E. Butler and E. A. Barber. Oxford, 1933.

M. Fabii Quintiliani Institutionis Oratoriae libri duodecim. Rec. E. Bonnell. Lipsiae. Vol. I, 1884; vol. II, 1889.

M. Fabii Quintiliani Institutionis Oratoriae libri XII. Ed. L. Radermacher. Pars prior. Lipsiae, 1907.

L. Annaei Senecae De Beneficiis libri VII, De Clementia libri II. Iterum ed. C. Hosius. Lipsiae, 1914.

C. Suetoni Tranquilli De Vita Caesarum libri VIII. Rec. M. Ihm. Lipsiae, 1907.

C. Suetoni Tranquilli Divus Augustus, edited by E. S. Shuckburgh. Cambridge, 1896.

Cornelii Taciti Annalium ab excessu divi Augusti libri. Rec. C. D. Fisher. Oxonii, 1906.

Valerii Maximi Factorum et Dictorum Memorabilium libri novem. Iterum rec. C. Kempf. Lipsiae, 1888.

P. Vergili Maronis opera rec. F. A. Hirtzel. Oxonii, 1900.

II. MODERN WORKS

The lists which follow are not intended to set out the whole literature of the subject. Their purpose is to indicate works to which the writer desires to acknowledge his indebtedness and those wherein references to other publications may easily be found.

1. *General*

See the works of Dessau, Gardthausen, Holmes, Homo, Kornemann, Rostovtzeff, Seeck and Shuckburgh cited in General Bibliography I, and those of Marquardt and Mommsen cited in General Bibliography II.

Ciccotti, E. Art. *Augustus* (*Imp. Caesar Divi f.*) in Diz. Epig. vol. I, p. 879.

Duméril, A. *Auguste et la fondation de l'empire romain.* Annales de la Faculté des Lettres de Bordeaux: Année 1890, p. 1.

Ferrero, G. *The Greatness and Decline of Rome.* London. Vol. IV, *Rome and Egypt*, translated by H. J. Chaytor, 1908. Vol. V, *The Republic of Augustus*, translated by H. J. Chaytor, 1909.

Fitzler, K. and O. Seeck. Art. *C. Iulius C. f. Caesar, später Imp. Caesar Divi f. Augustus.* P.W. X, col. 275.

Hammond, M. *The Augustan Principate.* Cambridge, Mass. 1933.

Heinze, R. *Die Augusteische Kultur.* Ed. 2. Leipzig-Berlin, 1933.

Meyer, Ed. *Kaiser Augustus.* In *Kleine Schriften*, vol. I (ed. 2—Berlin, 1924), p. 423.

Rostovtzeff, M. *Augustus.* University of Wisconsin Studies in Language and Literature, Number 15, p. 134.

In the following sections of this bibliography works are grouped so far as possible in the order in which they become relevant to the text of the chapter.

2. *The Social Problem and the Policy of Augustus*

Arnold, W. T. *The Domestic Policy of Augustus* in *Studies of Roman Imperialism* (Manchester, 1906), p. 161.

Bouché-Leclercq, A. *Les lois démographiques d'Auguste.* Rev. Hist. LVII, Janvier–Avril 1895, p. 241.

Frank, T. *Aspects of Social Behavior in Ancient Rome.* Cambridge, Mass. 1932.

Gouraud, Général, *Ce que nous apprennent les commentaires de César.* Pro Alesia, Nouvelle Série, 12e–14e Année, 1927, nos. 47–48, p. 99.

Homo, L. *Problèmes sociaux de jadis et d'à présent.* Paris, 1922.

Pelham, H. F. *The Domestic Policy of Augustus* in *Essays by Henry Francis Pelham*, collected and edited by F. Haverfield (Oxford, 1911), p. 89.

Petri, F. *Die Wohlfahrtspflege des Augustus.* N.J. f. Wiss. III, 1927, p. 268.

Beloch, (K.) J. *Die Bevölkerung der griechisch-römischen Welt.* Leipzig, 1886.

Ciccotti, E. *Il problema demografico nel mondo antico.* Metron IX, no. 2, 1931.

Zumpt, C. G. *Über den Stand der Bevölkerung und die Volksvermehrung im Alterthum.* Abh. der Akad. der Wiss. zu Berlin, 1840, phil.-hist. Kl., p. 1.

Dessau, H. *Die Vorrede des Livius*, in *Festschrift zu Otto Hirschfelds sechzigstem Geburtstage* (Berlin, 1903), p. 461.

Leaf, W. *Horace* Carm. 1. 14. J.P. xxxiv, 1918, p. 283.

Mommsen, Th. *Rede zur Feier der Geburtstage König Friedrichs II und Kaiser Wilhelms II* in *Reden und Aufsätze* (Berlin, 1912—dritter Abdruck), p. 168.

von Domaszewski, A. *Der Festgesang des Horaz auf die Begründung des Principates.* Rhein. Mus. lix, 1904, p. 302 (reprinted in *Abhandlungen zur römischen Religion* [Leipzig, 1909], p. 111).

Fowler, W. Warde, *Notes on Horace, Odes,* iii. 1–6, in *Roman Essays and Interpretations* (Oxford, 1920), p. 210.

Mommsen, Th. *Die Akten zu dem Säkulargedicht des Horaz* in *Reden und Aufsätze* (Berlin, 1912—dritter Abdruck), p. 351.

Fowler, W. Warde, *The* Carmen Saeculare *of Horace and its Performance, June 3rd, 17 B.C.* in *Roman Essays and Interpretations* (Oxford, 1920), p. 111.

Carter, J. B. *The Religion of Numa and Other Essays on the Religion of Ancient Rome.* London, 1906.

Fowler, W. Warde, *Roman Ideas of Deity in the Last Century before the Christian Era.* London, 1914.

3. *Slaves and Freedmen*

The date of the Lex Junia will be found discussed in the works marked †.

Barrow, R. H. *Slavery in the Roman Empire.* London, 1928.

†Buckland, W. W. *The Roman Law of Slavery.* Cambridge, 1908.

Frank, T. *The Sacred Treasure and the Rate of Manumission.* A.J. Ph. liii, 1932, p. 360.

†Duff, A. M. *Freedmen in the Early Roman Empire.* Oxford, 1928.

Weiss, E. Art. *s.v. Manumissio* in P.W.

Wlassak, M. *Die prätorischen Freilassungen.* Z. d. Sav.-Stift. xxvi, 1905, p. 367.

†Schneider, A. *Die lex Iunia Norbana.* Z. d. Sav.-Stift. v, 1884, p. 225.

†—— *Die Latini Iuniani und das Berliner Fragment de dediticiis.* Z. d. Sav.-Stift. vi, 1885, p. 186.

†—— *Noch einmal die 'Latini Iuniani' und Ulp.* i. 12. Z. d. Sav.-Stift. vii, 1886, 1. Heft, p. 31.

†Holder, E. *Zur Frage vom gegenseitigen Verhältnisse der Lex Aelia Sentia und Iunia Norbana.* Z. d. Sav.-Stift. vi, 1885, p. 205.

†—— *Erwiderung.* Z. d. Sav.-Stift. vii, 1886, 1. Heft, p. 44.

†Romanet Du Caillaud, *De la date de la loi* Junia Norbana. C. R. Ac. Inscr. Quatrième série: tome x, séances de l'année 1882, p. 198; tome xi, séances de l'année 1883, p. 431.

†Steinwenter, A. Art. *s.v. Latini Iuniani* in P.W.

4. *Marriage, Divorce and Concubinage*

Manigk, A. Art. *s.v. Manus* in P.W.

Kunkel, W. Art. *s.v. Matrimonium* in P.W.

Corbett, P. E. *The Roman Law of Marriage.* Oxford, 1930.

Heineccius, I. G. *Ad legem Iuliam et Papiam Poppaeam commentarius,* in *Io. Gottlieb Heineccii...operum tomus tertius* (Geneva, 1767).

Jörs, P. *Ueber das Verhältnis der Lex Iulia de maritandis ordinibus zur Lex Papia Poppaea.* Diss. Bonn, 1882.

—— *Die Ehegesetze des Augustus.* Marburg, 1894. First published in *Festschrift Theodor Mommsen zum fünfzigjährigen Doctorjubiläum überreicht von P. Jörs, E. Schwartz, R. Reitzenstein* (Marburg, 1893).

Kübler, B. *Über das Ius liberorum der Frauen und die Vormundschaft der Mutter.* Z. d. Sav.-Stift. xxx, 1909, p. 154 and xxxi, 1910, p. 176.

Cuq, E. *Les lois d'Auguste sur les déclarations de naissance,* in *Mélanges Paul Fournier* (Paris, 1929), p. 119.

Weiss, E. *Zur Rechtsstellung der unehelichen Kinder in der Kaiserzeit.* Z. d. Sav.-Stift. xlix, 1929, p. 260.

Leonhard, R. Art. *s.v. Divortium* in P.W.

Levy, E. *Der Hergang der römischen Ehescheidung.* Weimar, 1925.

Solazzi, S. *Studi sul divorzio.* Bull. dell' Istituto di diritto romano, xxxiv, 1925, p. 295.

Meyer, P. *Der römische Konkubinat nach den Rechtsquellen und den Inschriften.* Leipzig, 1895.

Plassard, J. *Le concubinat romain sous le Haut Empire.* Toulouse-Paris, 1921.

5. *The* Regiones *and* Vici *of Rome*

Gatti, G. *Ara marmorea del 'Vicus Statae Matris.'* Bullettino della Commissione archeologica comunale di Roma, xxxiv, 1906, p. 186.

6. *Juventus*

Rostowzew, M. *Römische Bleitessarae.* Leipzig, 1905. (Beiträge zur alten Geschichte, Beiheft iii.)

Della Corte, M. *Iuventus.* Arpino, 1924.

Taylor, L. R. Seviri equitum Romanorum *and Municipal* Seviri: *a study in pre-military training among the Romans.* J.R.S. xiv, 1924, p. 158.

Nock, A. D. *Seviri and Augustales,* in *Mélanges Bidez* (Annuaire de l'Institut de philologie et d'histoire orientales, ii, Brussels, 1934), pp. 627 *sqq.*

Forbes, C. A. *NEOI. A Contribution to the Study of Greek Associations.* Philological Monographs published by the American Philological Association, Number ii. Middletown, Connecticut, 1933.

Van Buren, A. W. *The Ara Pacis Augustae.* J.R.S. iii, 1913, p. 134.

CHAPTER XV

RELIGIOUS DEVELOPMENTS FROM THE CLOSE OF THE REPUBLIC TO THE REIGN OF NERO

The ancient sources are listed in the bibliographies to the earlier chapters.

For detailed surveys of the modern literature, see reports in Bursian (last by Fr. Pfister, *Supp.* ccxxix, 1930: published separately as *Die Religion der Griechen und Römer*. Leipzig, 1930), Arch. Relig. (last by O. Weinreich and L. Deubner, xxiii, 1925); Year's Work in Classical Studies (by H. J. Rose); J.E.A. (by A. D. Nock, in bibliography of Graeco-Roman Egypt, written in collaboration with H. I. Bell and others).

I. GENERAL WORKS

(A list supplementary to that in the bibliography to Vol. viii, chap. xiv.)

Altheim, Fr. *Römische Religionsgeschichte*, iii. Die Kaiserzeit. Berlin-Leipzig, 1933. (Appeared too late to be used for this chapter).

Cumont, F. *Les religions orientales dans le paganisme romain*. Ed. 4. Paris, 1929.

—— *After Life in Roman Paganism*. New Haven, 1922.

Halliday, W. R. *The Pagan Background of early Christianity*. Liverpool, 1925.

Heinze, R. *Die Augusteische Kultur*. Ed. 2. Leipzig-Berlin, 1933.

Leipoldt, G. *Die Religionen in der Umwelt des Urchristentums* (H. Haas, *Bilderatlas zur Religionsgeschichte*, Lieferung 9/11). Leipzig, 1926.

Nock, A. D. *Conversion*. Oxford, 1933.

—— *Early Gentile Christianity and its Hellenistic Background* (in *Essays on the Trinity and the Incarnation*, ed. A. E. J. Rawlinson). London, 1928.

Peterson, R. M. *The Cults of Campania*. Rome, 1919 (appeared 1923).

Reitzenstein, R. *Die hellenistischen Mysterienreligionen*. Ed. 3. Leipzig, 1927.

Rostovtzeff, M. *Mystic Italy*. New York, 1927.

Toutain, J. *Les cultes païens dans l'empire romain*, i. Paris, 1907– .

Wendland, P. *Die hellenistisch-römische Kultur in ihren Beziehungen zu Judentum und Christentum*. Eds 2 and 3. Tübingen, 1912.

von Wilamowitz-Moellendorff, U. *Der Glaube der Hellenen*, ii. Berlin, 1932.

Wilhelm, Fr. *Das römische Sakralwesen unter Augustus als Pontifex Maximus*. Diss. Strassburg, 1915.

II. RULER-WORSHIP

Bickermann, E. *Die römische Kaiserapotheose*. Arch. Relig. xxvii, 1929, p. 1.

Blumenthal, F. *Der ägyptische Kaiserkult*. Arch. Pap. v, 1913, p. 317.

Deonna, W. *La légende d'Octave Auguste Dieu Sauveur et maître du monde*. Rev. Hist. Rel. lxxxiii, 1921, p. 32, 163; lxxxiv, 1921, p. 77.

Eitrem, S. *Zur Apotheose*. Symb. Osl. x, 1932, p. 31; xi, 1932, p. 11 (to be continued).

Gagé, J. *Romulus-Augustus*. Mél. d'arch. et d'hist. xlvii, 1930, p. 138.

—— *La Victoria Augusti et les auspices de Tibère*. Rev. Arch. (5 Sér.) xxxii, 1930, p. 1.

—— *Les sacerdoces d'Auguste et ses reformes religieuses*. Mél. d'arch. et d'hist. xlviii, 1931, p. 75.

—— *Divus Augustus*. Rev. Arch. (5 Sér.) xxxiv, 1931, p. 11.

—— *Un thème de l'art impérial romain. La Victoire d'Auguste*. Mél. d'arch. et d'hist. xlix, 1932, p. 61.

Geiger, Fr. *De sacerdotibus Augustorum municipalibus*. Diss. Phil. Hal. 1913.

Heinen, H. *Zur Begründung des römischen Kaiserkultes, Chronologische Uebersicht von 48 v. bis 14 n. Chr.* Klio, XI, 1911, p. 129.

Immisch, O. *Zum antiken Herrscherkult* (in *Aus Roms Zeitwende. Das Erbe der Alten*, Zweite Reihe, 20. Leipzig, 1931).

Kornemann, E. *Zur Geschichte der antiken Herrscherkulte*. Klio, I, 1901, p. 51.

Mommsen, Th. *Das Augustische Festverzeichniss von Cumae*. Ges. Schriften, IV, p. 259.

Muller, F. (Jzn.). "*Augustus.*" Med. d. kon. Akad. van Wetenschappen te Amsterdam, 63, A, 1927, no. 11.

Nock, A. D. ΣΥΝΝΑΟΣ ΘΕΟΣ. Harv. St. XLI, 1930, p. 1.

—— *Seviri and Augustales*. Mélanges Bidez. Brussels, 1934, pp. 627 *sqq*.

Pippidi, D. M. *Le "Numen Augusti."* Rev. E.L. IX, 1931, p. 83.

Riewald, P. *De imperatorum Romanorum cum certis dis et comparatione et aequatione*. Diss. Phil. Hal. 1912.

Scott, K. *Mercur-Augustus und Horaz C.* I. 2. Hermes, LXIII, 1928, p. 15.

—— *The Dioscuri and Imperial Cult*. C.P. XXV, 1930, p. 379.

—— *Drusus nicknamed Castor*. C.P. XXV, 1930, p. 155.

—— *Greek and Roman honorific months*. Yale Class. Stud. II, 1931, p. 199.

—— *The significance of statues in precious metals in Emperor worship*. Trans. Amer. Phil. Ass. LXII, 1931, p. 101.

Stein, A. *Untersuchungen zur Geschichte und Verwaltung Ägyptens unter römischen Herrschaft*, ch. I. Stuttgart, 1915.

—— *Zur sozialen Stellung der provinzialen Oberpriester*. ΕΠΙΤΥΜΒΙΟΝ Heinrich Swoboda dargebracht. Prague, 1927, p. 300.

Taylor, L. R. *The Worship of Augustus in Italy during his lifetime*. Trans. Am. Phil. Ass. LI, 1920, p. 116.

—— *The Divinity of the Roman Emperor*. (Philological Monographs published by the American Philological Association, I.) Middletown, Conn. 1931. (See reviews by M. P. Charlesworth, C.R. XLVI, 1932, p. 225, A. D. Nock, Gnomon, VIII, 1932, p. 513, U. Kahrstedt, G.G.A. 1933, p. 200, A. von Premerstein, Phil. Woch. LIII, 1933, col. 1114).

Toutain, J. *Observations sur quelques formes de loyalisme particulières à la Gaule et à la Germanie romaine*. Klio, II, 1902, p. 194.

III. OTHER SPECIAL TOPICS

Altheim, Fr. *Almus Sol*. N. J. f. Wiss. VIII, 1932, p. 141.

Blumenthal, F. *Ludi saeculares*. Klio, XV, 1918, p. 217.

Carcopino, J. *Attideia*. Mél. d'arch. et d'hist. XL, 1923, pp. 135, 237.

Drexel, Fr. *Die Götterverehrung in römischen Germanien*. R.-G.K. Ber. XIV, 1922.

Gagé, J. *Observations sur le Carmen saeculare d'Horace*. Rev. E.L. IX, 1931, p. 290.

Giannelli, G. *I Romani ad Eleusi*. Atti Acc. Torino, L, 1914–15, p. 319.

Hardy, E. G. *Studies in Roman History*. London, 1906.

Henzen, W. *Acta fratrum Arvalium*. Berlin, 1870.

Juster, J. *Les juifs dans l'empire romain*. Paris, 1914.

Kroll, W. *Die Religiosität in der Zeit Ciceros*. N. J. f. Wiss. IV, 1928, p. 519.

—— *Die Kultur der Ciceronischen Zeit*. (Das Erbe der Alten, Zweite Reihe, 22. Leipzig, 1933.)

Lortz, J. *Tertullian als Apologet*. II (Münsterische Beiträge zur Theologie herausgegeben von F. Diekamp und R. Stapper), pp. 203–21. Münster, 1928.

Merrill, E. T. *Early Christian History Essays*. London, 1924.

Metzmacher, G. *De sacris fratrum Arvalium*. Jahrb. für Liturgiewissenschaft, IV, 1924, p. 1.

Mommsen, Th. *Der Religionsfrevel nach römischen Recht*. Ges. Schriften, III, p. 389.

Nock, A. D. *The Augustan Restoration*. C.R. XXXIX, 1925, p. 60.

—— Art. *s.v. Kornutos* in P.W. Supp. bd. v, col. 995.

—— *Cremation and Burial in the Roman Empire*. Harv. Theol. Rev. XXV, 1932, p. 321.

Rostovtzeff, M. *Augustus*. University of Wisconsin Studies in Language and Literature, No. 15, 1922, p. 134 (and Röm. Mitt. XXXVIII/XXXIX, 1923/4, p. 281).

Snijder, G. A. S. *Ein Priester der Magna Mater aus Smyrna*. Oudheidkundige Mededeelingen uit's Rijksmuseum van Oudheden te Leiden (Nuntii ex Museo antiquario Leidensi), Nieuwe Reeks, XIII, i, 1932.

Strong, A. *Apotheosis and After Life*. London, 1915.

Taylor, L. R. *The History of the Secular Games*. A.J.Ph. LV, 1934, p. 101.

Wissowa, G. *Interpretatio romana. Römische Götter im Barbarenlande*. Arch. Relig. XIX, 1916, p. 1.

Wuilleumier, P. *Tarente et le Tarentum*. Rev. E.L. X, 1932, p. 127.

CHAPTER XVI

THE LITERATURE OF THE AUGUSTAN AGE

It is impossible here to give more than a selection from the vast literature upon the Augustan Age writers. What follows is a list of books which may be found helpful. Texts of most of the authors will be found in the Teubner Library or the Oxford Classical Texts. The Loeb Library contains completed translations into English of many of the writers of the period, and others are in process of appearing.

Modern Works

1. *General*

Dimsdale, M. S. *History of Latin Literature*. London, 1915.
Duff, J. Wight, *A Literary History of Rome*. (Contains bibliographies of the various writers.) Ed. 7, London, 1927.
Mackail, J. W. *Latin Literature*. London, 1895.
Nettleship, H. *Lectures and Essays on Subjects connected with Latin Literature and Scholarship*. Oxford, 1st series, 1885, 2nd series, 1895.
Patin, H. J. G. *Études sur la Poésie latine*. Ed. 4. Paris, 1900.
Pichon, R. *Histoire de la littérature latine*. Ed. 5. Paris, 1912.
Sikes, E. E. *Roman Poetry*. London, 1923.
Teuffel's *History of Roman Literature* (enlarged and revised by L. Schwabe), English translation by G. C. W. Warr. London, 1900.
Tyrrell, R. Y. *Latin Poetry*. London and New York, 1895.
Ussani, V. *Storia della Letteratura Latina*. Milan, 1929.

2. *The Elegiac Poets and Ovid*

(*a*) Propertius. Texts: C. Hosius, Leipzig, 1932; J. S. Phillimore, Oxford, 1907; O. L. Richmond, Cambridge, 1928.
    Text and Commentary: H. E. Butler and E. A. Barber, Oxford, 1933.
    Index Verborum Propertianus, by J. S. Phillimore, Oxford, 1906.
(*b*) Tibullus. Texts: F. W. Levy, Leipzig, 1927; J. P. Postgate, Oxford, 1914.
(*c*) Ovid. Texts:
    (1) *Complete:* R. Merkel, R. Ehwald, F. Levy and F. W. Lenz, 1880–1932, Leipzig, 3 vols. in 4. A complete text, by various editors, will be found in Postgate's Corpus Poetarum Latinorum, vol. 1, part 2. In the Oxford Classical Texts only vol. 1 (*Tristia, Ex Ponto*, etc.) edited by S. G. Owen, 1915, has so far appeared. In the Paravia series there are *Ars Amatoria* (C. Marchesi), *Fasti* (C. Landi), *Metamorphoses* (P. Fabbri), and *Tristia* (C. Landi).
    (2) *Separate works:*
Epistulae ex Ponto. O. Korn. Leipzig, 1868.
Fasti. Introduction, Translation, and Commentary by Sir J. G. Frazer, in 5 vols. London, 1929.
Heroides. A. Palmer. Dublin, 1898.
Ibis. Text and Commentary by R. Ellis. Oxford, 1881.
Metamorphoses. Text by H. Magnus. Berlin, 1914.

Metamorphoses. Text and German Commentary by M. Haupt and O. Korn, revised by R. Ehwald. Leipzig, 1915–16.

Tristia. Book II. Text, Translation and Commentary by S. G. Owen. Oxford, 1924.

3. *Horace*

(*a*) Texts and editions:

Complete Works. J. G. Orelli and J. G. Baiter (Ed. 4, revised by W. Hirschfelder and W. Mewes), 2 vols., Zürich, 1886–92; O. Keller and A. Holder (with Index Verborum), Ed. 2, 2 vols., Leipzig, 1899–1925; E. C. Wickham, vol. I (Odes and Epodes), Ed. 3, Oxford, 1896, vol. II (Satires and Epistles), Oxford, 1891.

Satires. A. Palmer. Ed. 4. London, 1891. P. Lejay, Paris, 1911.

Epistles. A. S. Wilkins, London, 1885. (Reprinted with Appendix of additional notes, 1892.)

Odes and Epodes. T. E. Page, London, 1895.

Ars Poetica. A. Rostagni, Turin, 1930.

(*b*) English translations:

Complete Works, by E. C. Wickham, *Horace for English Readers*, Oxford, 1903. Odes, by W. E. Gladstone, London, 1894; by H. Macnaghten, Cambridge, 1926. Satires and Epistles, by F. Howes, London, 1845; by J. Conington, London, 1892.

(*c*) Works on Horace:

Boissier, G. *Nouvelles Promenades Archéologiques, Horace et Virgile.* Ed. 2. Paris, 1890.

Campbell, A. Y. *Horace. A new interpretation.* London, 1924.

Frank, T. *Catullus and Horace.* New York, 1928.

Glover, T. R. *Horace. A Return to Allegiance.* Cambridge, 1932.

Goad, C. *Horace in the English Literature of the Eighteenth Century.* New Haven, Conn., 1918.

Hauthal, F. *Acronis et Porphyrionis Commentarii in Q. Horatium Flaccum.* Berlin, 1864.

Sellar, W. Y. *Horace and the Elegiac Poets.* Ed. 2. Oxford, 1899.

Verrall, A. W. *Studies Literary and Historical in the Odes of Horace.* London, 1884.

4. *Virgil*

(*a*) Text:

J. Conington, 1858, London. (*Bucolics* and *Georgics*, 5th ed. revised by H. Nettleship and F. Haverfield, 1898. *Aeneid*, I–VI, 4th ed. by H. Nettleship, 1884; VII–XII, 3rd ed., 1883.) T. L. Papillon and A. E. Haigh, Oxford, 1892. O. Ribbeck, 2nd ed., Leipzig, 1894–5. H. Nettleship, revised by J. P. Postgate, London, 1912 (Medici Society). J. W. Mackail, *The Aeneid*, Oxford, 1930.

Servius, *Commentarii*, edited by G. Thilo and H. Hagen, Leipzig, 1881–7.

(*b*) English translations:

Aeneid: J. Conington (Verse), ed. 3, 1870; (Prose), 1884. J. W. Mackail (Prose), 1908. C. J. Billson (Verse), Oxford, 1923. F. Richards (Verse), 1931. *Eclogues:* Lord Burghclere, 1904.

(*c*) Works on Virgil:

Butler, H. E. *The Sixth Book of the Aeneid.* Oxford, 1920.

Comparetti, D. *Vergil in the Middle Ages.* Eng. trans. by E. F. M. Benecke, London, 1895.

Crump, M. M. *The Growth of the Aeneid.* Oxford, 1920.

De Witt, N. W. *Virgil's Biographia Litteraria.* Toronto, 1923.

Frank, T. *Vergil: a Biography.* New York, 1922.

Fowler, W. Warde, *Virgil's Gathering of the Clans.* Ed. 2, Oxford, 1918.

—— *Aeneas at the Site of Rome.* Ed. 2, Oxford, 1918.

—— *The Death of Turnus.* Oxford, 1919.

Glover, T. R. *Virgil.* Ed. 6. London, 1930.

Haarhoff, T. J. *Vergil in the Experience of South Africa.* Oxford, 1931.

Heinze, R. *Virgils Epische Technik.* Ed. 3. Leipzig, 1915.

Henry, J. *Aeneidea.* Dublin, 1873–89.

Knight, W. F. J. *Vergil's Troy.* Oxford, 1932.

Leland, C. G. *The unpublished legends of Virgil.* London, 1899.

Mayor, J. B., W. Warde Fowler and R. S. Conway. *Virgil's Messianic Eclogue.* London, 1907.

Norden, E. *Aeneis.* Buch VI. Ed. 3, Berlin, 1926.

Rand, E. K. *In Quest of Virgil's Birthplace.* Cambridge, Mass., 1930.

—— *The Magical Art of Virgil.* Cambridge, Mass., 1931.

Royds, T. F. *The Beasts, Birds, and Bees of Virgil.* Ed. 2. Oxford, 1922.

—— *The Eclogues, Bucolics, and Pastorals of Virgil.* Oxford, 1914.

Sainte-Beuve, C. A. *Étude sur Virgile.* Paris, 1891.

Sellar, W. J. *The Roman Poets of the Augustan Age: Vergil.* Ed. 3. Oxford, 1897.

Skutsch, F. *Aus Vergils Frühzeit,* I and II. Leipzig, 1901, 1906.

Spargo, F. W. *Virgil the Necromancer.* Cambridge, Mass., 1934.

5. *Manilius: the* Aetna

Manilius. Texts: A. E. Housman. Editio maior, London, vol. I, 1903; II, 1912; III, 1916; IV, 1920; V, 1930. Editio minor, Cambridge, 1932.

Text, Commentary and Translation: Book II, by H. W. Garrod, Oxford, 1911.

Aetna. Text, by E. Schwartz, Bonn, 1933 (Lietzmann's *Kleine Texte,* no. 166).

Text, Commentary, and Translation, by R. Ellis, Oxford, 1901.

6. *Minor Prose-Writers*

For works upon Asinius Pollio, the *Res Gestae* of Augustus, and Strabo, see the Bibliography to Chapters I–IV, Part I, C, 5, 6, and 10 (pp. 898–90).

(*a*) Diodorus Siculus. *Bibliotheca Historica.* Ed. F. Vogel, Leipzig. Vol. I, 1888; II, 1890; III, 1893; ed. C. T. Fischer, IV, 1906; V, 1906.

(*b*) Dionysius of Halicarnassus. *Antiquitatum Romanarum quae supersunt.* Ed. C. Jacoby, Leipzig. Vol. I, 1885; II, 1888; III, 1891; IV, 1905.

(*c*) Vitruvius. Text: F. Krohn. Leipzig, 1912.

Translation: M. H. Morgan. Cambridge, Mass., 1914.

(See also bibliography to chap. XVII).

7. *Livy*

Text: R. S. Conway and C. F. Walters. Oxford, 1914–. (Books I–XXV so far issued.)

Works on Livy:

Bornecque, H. *Tite-Live.* Paris, 1933.

Modica, M. *Tito Livio.* Catania, 1928.

Riemann, O. *Etudes sur la langue et la grammaire de Tite-Live.* Ed. 2. Paris, 1885.

Soltau, W. *Livius' Geschichtswerk, seine Komposition und seine Quellen.* Leipzig, 1897.

Taine, H. *Essai sur Tite-Live.* Ed. 7. Paris, 1904.

CHAPTER XVII

THE ART OF THE AUGUSTAN AGE

I. General

These items are supplementary to those cited in the Bibliography to Chap. xx of Vol. IX, p. 965 *sq.* As a rule only recent works are cited.

Grenier, A. *Le Génie Romain.* Paris, 1926.

Lawrence, A. W. *Classical Sculpture.* London, 1929, Chap. xv.

Picard, C. H. *Chronique de la Sculpture Étrusco-Latine*, i–vi, 1928–1934 (Rev.E.L.) (contains admirable summaries).

Pijoan, J. *El Arte Romano hasta la muerte di Diocleziano*, vol. v of Historia General del Arte. Madrid, 1934. (Valuable for its many illustrations of little known and unpublished works.)

Rodenwaldt, G. *Die Kunst der Antike.* (*Hellas und Rom.*) Propyläen-Kunstgeschichte, III, Berlin, 1927, pp. 501 *sqq.*

—— *Ara pacis und S. Vitale.* B.J. 133, 1929, p. 228.

Rumpf, A. *Griechische und römische Kunst*, in Gercke and Norden's *Einleitung.* Ed. 4. II, 3. Leipzig-Berlin, 1931.

Snijder, G. A. S. *Het Probleem der Romeinsche Kunst.* Tijdschrift voor Geschiedenis 1934. (See also for earlier contributions above, vol. IX, p. 305, n. 2.)

Strong, E. *Roman Sculpture from Augustus to Constantine.* London, 1907, largely superseded by *La Scultura Romana.* Florence, 1923.

—— *Art in Ancient Rome.* 2 vols. London, 1929.

Wickhoff, F. *Roman Art* (transl. by E. Strong). London, 1900.

Walters, H. B. *The Art of the Romans.* London, 1911.

II. Special Works

Altheim, F. *Römische Religionsgeschichte*, vol. III, Berlin–Leipzig, 1934, pp. 53 *sqq.*

Bieber, M. *Die Venus Genetrix des Arkesilaos.* Röm. Mitt. XLVIII, 1933, p. 261.

Brendel, O. *Immolatio Boum.* Röm. Mitt. XLV, 1930, p. 204 *sq.* (Boscoreale cups.)

Deubner, M. L. *Eine unbekannte Ara Pacis.* Röm. Mitt. XLV, 1930, p. 37.

Gagé, J. *La Théologie de la victoire impériale.* Rev. H. 171, 1933, p. 1.

—— *Recherches sur les Jeux séculaires.* Paris, 1934.

—— *La victoire impériale dans l'empire chrétien.* Rev. d'hist. et de phil. relig. XIII, 1933, p. 370. (See also works of Gagé cited above, p. 951.)

Gsell, S. *Statues du Temple de Mars Ultor à Rome.* Rev. Arch. XXXIV, 1899, p. 37.

Loewy, E. *Orazio ed Ara Pacis.* Atti 1° Congresso naz. di Studi Romani, 1928, p. 104.

Poinssot, L. *L'autel de la gens Augusta à Carthage.* Tunis-Paris, 1929.

Rizzo, G. E. *La Base di Augusto.* Rome, 1933.

—— *L'Eneide e l'Arte Antica.* Boll.... Studi Mediterranei, 1930, no. 5.

Rostovtzeff, M. *Augustus.* Univ. of Wisconsin Studies in Language and Literature, Number 15, 1922 (and *Röm. Mitt.* XXXVIII–XXXIX, 1923–4, pp. 281 *sqq.*)

Strong, E. *Apotheosis and After Life.* London, 1915.

Taylor, L. R. *The Divinity of the Roman Emperor.* Middletown, Conn., 1931.

Weickert, C. *Rodenwaldt's Sarkophag Caffarelli and Snijder's Romeinsche Kunstgeschiedenis.* Gnomon, III, 1927, p. 215. (Critical survey of recent studies in Roman art.)

III. PORTRAITURE

Of the very large recent literature on Augustan and Julio-Claudian portraiture, only general works and a few monographs of outstanding importance are here cited. For special articles see the bibliographical material in the Volume of Plates.

Blümel, C. *Römische Bildnisse.* (Cat. of Roman portraits in the Berlin Museum.) Berlin, 1933.

Brendel, O. *Ikonographie des Kaisers Augustus.* Heidelberg Diss. Nürnberg, 1931.

Curtius, L. *Ikonographische Beiträge zum Porträt der römischen Republik und der julisch-claudischen Familie.* Röm. Mitt. XLVII, 1932, p. 202; *ib.* XLVIII, 1933, p. 182.

—— *Neue Erklärung des grossen Pariser Kameo mit der Familie des Tiberius.* Röm. Mitt. XLIX, 1934, p. 119.

de Grüneisen, W. *Le Portrait.* Paris, 1911.

Ippel, A. *Römische Porträts* (in H. Schaal's *Bilderhefte zu Kunst und Kunstgeschichte des Altertums*). Bielefeld-Leipzig, 1927.

Johnson, F. E. *Corinth.* IX. *Sculpture.* Cambridge, Mass., 1931, pp. 70 *sqq.*

Maiuri, A. *La Villa dei Misteri.* Rome, 1931. pp. 223 *sqq.* (For portrait of Livia.)

Michalowski, C. *Les portraits hellénistiques et romains* (*Délos* 13). École Française d'Athènes. Paris, 1932.

Paribeni, R. *Il Ritratto nell' arte Antica.* Milan, 1934.

Poulsen, Fr. *Porträtstatuen in norditalienischen Provinzmuseen.* Copenhagen, 1928.

—— *Sculptures Antiques de Musées de Provinces Espagnols.* Copenhagen, 1933. (Many examples of Republican and Julio-Claudian portraiture.)

—— *Iconographie Romaine.* Rev. E.A. XXXV, 1933, p. 333.

Waldhauer, O. *Roman Portraits in the Hermitage.* Petrograd, 1923. (In Russian.)

West, R. *Römische Porträt-Plastik.* Vol. 1. Munich, 1933.

IV. PAINTING, MOSAIC, STUCCO AND SILVER WORK: THE MINOR ARTS

Blake, M. E. *The Pavements of the Roman Buildings of the Republic and Early Empire.* Mem. Amer. Acad. Rome, VIII, 1930, p. 9.

Eichler, F. and E. Kris. *Die Kameen im Kunsthistorischen Museum.* Vienna, 1927.

Herrmann, P. *Denkmäler der Malerei des Altertums.* Munich, 1906 (in cont.).

Hinks, R. P. *Catalogue of the Greek, Etruscan and Roman paintings and mosaics in the British Museum.* London, 1933. (With good bibliography.)

Ippel, A. *Mosaikstudien.* Röm. Mitt. XLV, 1930, p. 80.

Lippold, G. *Gemmen und Kameen des Altertums und der Neuzeit.* Stuttgart, 1922.

von Lorentz, F. Art. *s.v. Mosaik* in P.W.

Maiuri, A. *La Casa del Menandro e il suo tesoro di argenteria.* 2 vols. Rome, 1933

Nogara, B. *Le Nozze Aldobrandine.* Rome, 1907.

—— *I mosaici antichi conservati nei palazzi pontifici del Vaticano e del Laterano.* Milan, 1910.

Pernice, E. *Gefässe und Geräthe aus Bronze,* and *Hellenistische Tische, Zisternenmündungen, Beckenuntersätze, Altäre und Truhen.* = Parts IV and V of Winter and Pernice, *Die Hellenistische Kunst in Pompeji.* Berlin, 1925 and 1932.

Pernice, E. and Fr. Winter. *Der Hildesheimer Silberfund.* Berlin, 1901.

Pfuhl, E. *Malerei und Zeichnung der Griechen.* Munich, 1923.

—— *Meisterwerke griechischer Zeichnung und Malerei.* Munich, 1924. English translation by J. D. Beazley, London, 1926.

Reinach, A. *Textes grecs et latins relatifs à l'histoire de la peinture ancienne.* Recueil Milliet, Paris, 1921.

Reinach, S. *Répertoire des Peintures grecques et romaines*. Ed. 2. Paris, 1929.

Ronczewski, K. *Gewölbeschmuck im römischen Altertum*. Berlin, 1903.

Rostowzew, M. *Die hellenistisch-römische Architekturlandschaft*. Röm. Mitt. XXVI, 1911, p. 1.

Villefosse, H. de. *Le Trésor de Boscoreale*. Mon. Piot, 1899.

Wadsworth, L. *Stucco reliefs of the first and second centuries still extant in Rome*. Mem. Amer. Acad. Rome, IV, 1925, p. 9.

Walters, H. B. *Catalogue of the engraved gems and cameos (Greek, Etruscan and Roman) in the British Museum*. Rev. Ed. London, 1926.

V. ARCHITECTURE, TOWN PLANNING

The official publication *Capitolium*, 1926–, gives short articles, well illustrated though often only preliminary, of new excavations and discoveries in Rome.

Bartoli, A. *Il Valore Storico delle recenti Scoperte al Palatino e al Foro*. Pavia, 1932.

Bendinelli, G. *Arco Imperiale eretto in 'Augusta Torinorum' nel 1° Sec. D.C.* Rassegna mensile 'Torino.' Nov. 1933.

Boethius, A. *Remarks on the development of domestic architecture in Rome*. A.J.A. XXXVIII, 1934, p. 158.

—— *The Neronian 'Nova Urbs.'* Corolla Archeologica, Lund, 1932, p. 84.

Brendel, O. *Archäologische Funde aus Italien, etc. von Okt. 1932 bis Okt. 1933*. J.D.A.I. XLVIII, 1933, Arch. Anz., cols. 600 *sqq.* (Important for Fora of Caesar and of Augustus, Curia, etc.)

Calza, G. *Un nuovo frammento di fasti-annali (anni 108–113)*. N.S.A. 1932, p. 188.

Giglioli, G. Q. *Il sepolcreto Imperiale* (Mausoleum of Augustus). Capitolium, VI, 1930, p. 532.

Lugli, G. *I Monumenti Antichi di Roma e Suburbio*. Ed. 2. Rome, 1931.

Maiuri, A. *Il Palazzo di Tiberio ('Villa Jovis') a Capri*. Atti 3° Congresso Nazionale di Studi Romani, 1934.

—— *Brevi Note sulla Vita di Augusto a Capri*. Atti r. Accad. di Archeologia... di Napoli, N.S. XIII, 1933–4, p. 211.

Muller, F. (Jzn.). *"Augustus."* Med. d. kon. Akad. van Wetenschappen te Amsterdam, 63, A, 1927, no. 11, pp. 275–345. (With new plan of Palatine, not known in time for use in writing the chapter.)

Paribeni, R. *Iscrizioni dei Fori Imperiali*. N.S.A. 1933, p. 431.

Reinhold, M. *Marcus Agrippa, a biography*. Geneva-New York, 1933. (Important for buildings of Agrippa.)

Ricci, C. *La Via dell' Impero*. Rome, 1932.

—— *Il Foro di Cesare* (new excavations). Illustrazione Italiana, 26 Nov. 1933.

Richmond, I. A. *Commemorative Arches and City Gates in the Augustan age*. J.R.S. XXIII, 1933, p. 149.

Shipley, F. W. *Chronology of the Building Operations in Rome from the death of Caesar to the death of Augustus*. Mem. Amer. Acad. Rome, IX, 1931, p. 7.

—— *Agrippa's Building Activities in Rome*. Washington Univ. Studies, 1933.

Vitruve. Ed. A. Choisy. 4 vols. Paris, 1909.

Vitruvius. Trans. M. H. Morgan. Cambridge, Mass., 1914.

—— Text and translation by F. Granger, Loeb Library, London-New York. Vol I, 1931, vol. II, 1934.

CHAPTER XVIII

THE ACHIEVEMENT OF AUGUSTUS

(See above, pp. 913 *sqq.*)

CHAPTER XIX

THE PRINCIPATE OF TIBERIUS

I. Ancient Sources

A. *Contemporary Documents*

(i) *Inscriptions*

1. Tiberius and Gythium. S. B. Kougéas, Ἐπιγραφικαὶ ἐκ Γυθείου Συμβολαί in Ἑλληνικά, I, 1928, pp. 7 *sqq.*, pp. 152 *sqq.* See G. De Sanctis in *Riv. Fil.* VI, 1928, p. 586; H. Seyrig in *Rev. Arch.* XXIX, 1929, p. 84; E. Kornemann, *Neue Dokumente zum lakonischen Kaiserkult*, Breslau, 1929; L. Wenger in *Z. d. Sav.-Stift.* Rom. Abt. XLIX, 1929, p. 308; M. Rostovtseff in *Rev. Hist.* CLXIII, 1930, p. 1; S. Eitrem in *Symb. Osl.* X, 1932, p. 43.

2. Lex Narbonensis. Dessau 6964. See Krascheninnikov in *Phil.* LIII, 1894, p. 161; L. R. Taylor in *The Divinity of the Roman Emperor*, 1931, pp. 280–82; A. B. Abaecherli, *The Dating of the Lex Narbonensis*, in *Trans. Amer. Phil. Ass.* LXIII, 1932, p. 256.

3. Senatusconsulta in A.D. 20 (*Dig.* I, 16, 4, 2 and XLVIII, 2, 12, 3), A.D. 29 (*ib.* XLVIII, 10, 1, 2) and A.D. 31 (*ib.* XLVIII, 2. 12, 1).

4. *C.I.L.* I², pars i. Various *Fasti*, including *Praenestini* (pp. 230–39), *Vallenses* (240–41), *Amiternini* (243–45), and *Antiates* (247–49); and p. 335 (*mensis* Τιβέριος in Asia).

5. Acta Fratrum Arvalium, in *C.I.L.* VI, pars iv (fasc. ii), 1902, pp. 3261–3275. (Additamenta in *pars* vi, fasc. i, 1933).

6. *C.I.L.* II, 49, 1516, 2038; III, 6703 (see Eph. Ep. v, 1336, and L. Jalabert & R. Mouterde, *Inscr. grec. et lat. de la Syrie*, I, 164), 13813ᵇ; VI, 1235 & 1237, 4776, 8409ᶜ, 32340; VIII, 10568; X, 7527; XIII, 941, 1036–40, 1550, 4481, 4635; XIV, 244, 3472, and *Suppl. Ostiense*, 1930, pp. 655–657.

7. Ann. épig. 1906, 144; 1907, 30; 1910, 176; 1912, 11; 1914, 172; 1917/18, 122 (*Fasti Ostienses*); 1920, 1; 1921, 3; 1927, 158, 162; 1929, 99 & 100 (Gythium); 1933, 204 (Palmyra).

8. Dessau 107, 108, 113–189, 939, 1514, 2281, 2637, 3335, 4613ᵈ, 5829 & 5829ᵃ, 6044, 6124, 8744ᵃ (wrongly numbered as 8844ᵃ), 8898, 8967, 9643.

9. Ditt.³ 782, 791 A, B.

10. *I.G.R.R.* I, 119, 429, 659, 777, 853, 864, 880, 906, 1150. III, 721, 845, 895, 997, 1056, 1086, 1344. IV, 144–47, 180, 207, 219, 257, 900, 911, 1042, 1213, 1351, 1392, 1407, 1502, 1514, 1523.

11. *S.E.G.* I, 286, 387, 390. IV, 515, 707.

12. For some inscriptions concerning Germanicus in the East see *I.G.* III, i, 448, 452, 453; Ditt.³ 792; *I.G.R.R.* IV, 206; 326, 327, 328, 330, 464; 723; 948; 979, 980; 1549; III, 680; 715, 716; Ditt.³ 797. Cf. H. Seyrig in *Syria*, XIII, 1932, pp. 255 *sqq.*

Collart, P. *Inscriptions de Philippes*, B.C.H. LVI, 1932, p. 192, no. 4. *Corinth.* (Results of Excavations conducted by the American School of Classical Studies at Athens.) Volume VIII, Part II (Latin Inscriptions, 1896–1926 edited by A. B. West). Cambridge, Mass., 1931, Nos. 15, 17, 67 and 68 (C. Julius Laco), and 110. Graindor, P. *Inscriptions attiques d'époque romaine.* B.C.H. LI, 1927, p. 254, no. 18.

(ii) *Papyri*

1. Edicts of Germanicus in Egypt. U. von Wilamowitz-Moellendorff and F. Zucker, *Zwei Edikte des Germanicus auf einem Papyrus des Berliner Museums*, Berl. S.B. 1911, pp. 794–821. Cf. the articles by Cichorius and Wilcken cited below, section II, D.
2. B.G.U. 636, 3: P. Oxy. II, 240, 259: P. Ryl. II, 133. Mitteis-Wilcken, *Grundzüge und Chrestomathie...*, I, ii, 13; 413; 414.

(iii) *Coins*

In addition to the relevant pages in the numismatic works by Cohen, Mattingly, Mattingly and Sydenham, Milne, Münsterberg, Vogt, and Wruck, cited in the General Bibliography, see also:

Dieudonné, A. *Les monnaies grecques de Syrie*, in Rev. N. xxx, 1927, p. 35 and p. 37. H. Mattingly, *Some historical Coins of the First Century* A.D. A. "*Divus Tiberius*," J.R.S. x, 1920, p. 36. L. Müller, *Numismatique de l'ancienne Afrique*. Vol. III, Copenhagen, 1863, pp. 103–125 (Juba II, esp. nos. 55–57 and 71); pp. 125–137 (Ptolemy II, esp. nos. 184–85). For coins struck in honour or commemoration of Germanicus and Drusus see *B.M.Cat. Lydia*, p. 251 (Sardes), *B.M.Cat. Caria*, p. 167 (Tabae), *B.M.Cat. Phrygia*, p. 246 (Hierapolis); Germanicus alone, Imhoof-Blumer, *Kleinasiatische Münzen*, I, Vienna, 1901, p. 293. For a coin, possibly of King Vannius, see *Wien. Num. Zeits.* XII, 1880, p. 114.

(iv) *Literary Sources*

Anthologia Palatina. VII, 391; IX, 219; 283; 287; XVI, 61; 75. (IX, 17, 18 and 387 are ascribed to Germanicus.)

Aulus Gellius (ed. C. Hosius), *Noct. Att.* V, 6, 14.

Digesta, I, 16, 4, 2; XLVII, 13, 2; XLVIII, 2, 12, 1 and 3; 5, 11 (10), 2; 10, 1, 2; XLIX, 16, 4, 13.

Dio, LVI, 30–47; LVII; LVIII; LIX, 6, 2, 3.

Diogenes Laertius (ed. G. Cobet). IX, 12, 109.

Galen, in C. G. Kühn, *Medic. Graec. opera*, XIII, p. 836.

Germanici Caesaris Aratea. (Ed. 2. A. Breysig, 1899.)

Josephus, *Antiquitates*, XVIII [2, 2], 33–[5, 3], 129; [6, 1], 143–[6, 10], 236; *Bellum Judaicum*, II [9, 1], 168–[9, 5], 180.

Julian, *Convivium (Caesares)*, 309 C–310 A. *Epist. ad Themistium*, 265 C, D.

John Malalas (ed. A. Schenk, *Die römische Kaisergeschichte bei Malalas*, Stuttgart, 1931), pp. 232, 10–243, 3.

Marcus Aurelius, XII, 27.

Ovid, *ex Ponto*, III, iv, 87–114; IV, xiii, 23–32.

Phaedrus (ed. J. P. Postgate). II, v, 7–25; III, *prol.* 33–44.

Phlegon of Tralles, in *F. Gr. Hist.* II B, no. 257, frag. 36, pp. 1182/3.

Pliny, *N.H.* III, 82: VII, 149: VIII, 145; 185; 197: XI, 187: XIV, 60: XV, 135: XVI, 190; 194: XIX, 110: XXVI, 9: XXVIII, 23: XXX, 13: XXXIII, 32: XXXIV, 62: XXXV, 70.

Pliny Minor, *Epist.* V, 3.

Plutarch, *Moralia, Quomodo adulator...*, 60 C, D (I, p. 145): *de amicorum multitudine*, 96 C (I, p. 233): *de tuenda sanitate...*, 136 E (I, p. 333): *de defectu oraculorum*, 419 D, E (III, p. 93): *de garrulitate*, 508 A–C (III, p. 316): *de invidia et odio*, 537 B (III, p. 389): *de exilio*, 602 E, F (III, p. 559): *Quaest. conviv....*, 62 A–C (IV, p. 34): *an seni r.p. gerenda?*, 794 B (V, p. 50): *de anima*, 10 (VII, p. 30): one fragment of the Τιβερίου Βίος (VII, p. 148).

Scribonius Largus (ed. G. Helmreich), 97; 120; 162.

Seneca, *de providentia*, 4, 4; *de ira*, I, 18, 3–6; III, 21, 5; *ad Marciam*, 1; 15, 3; 22, 4–8; *ad Polybium*, 15, 5; *de tranquillitate*, 11, 11; *de beneficiis*, II, 7–8; III, 26; *de clementia*, I, 1, 6.

—— *Epistulae Morales*. 12, 8; 55, 3; 70, 10; 83, 14, 15; 95, 42; 108, 22; 122, 10, 11.

Seneca Rhetor (ed. A. Kiessling, 1872), *Suas*. II, 12; *Controv*. IX, 4, 17 *sqq*.

Strabo (ed. A. Meineke), III, 156; IV, 178; V, 288; XII, 534, 579; XIII, 618, 627; XVII, 828, 831, 840.

Suetonius, *Augustus*, 86, 2; 97–101; *Tiberius*, passim; *Calig*. 1–16; 19, 3; 21; 30, 2; 31; 37, 2; 38, 3; *Claud*. 5–6; 23; 25, 3; *Nero*, 5, 2; *Galba*, 5, 2; *Vitell*. 2; *Titus*, 8, 1; *Domit*. 20.

Holtzhausser, C. A. *An Epigraphic Commentary on Suetonius's Life of Tiberius*. Philadelphia Thesis, 1918. *C. Suetoni Tranquilli vita Tiberii*—c. 24–c. 40 neu kommentiert von Dr. J. R. Rietra. Amsterdam, 1928.

Suidas, *Lexikon* (ed. Gaisford), *s.v.* Τιβέριος.

Tacitus, *Agricola*, 13, 3; *Historiae*, II, 65, 95; *Annales*, I–VI *passim*; XI, 21; XIII, 3, 45; XV, 44; XVI, 29.

—— *Annals*, I–VI (H. Furneaux: ed. 2, Oxford, 1896). XI–XVI (H. Furneaux, revised edition by H. F. Pelham and C. D. Fisher, 1907).

Velleius Paterculus II, 123–131 (see K. Scott in *C.P.* XXVI, 1931, p. 205 on an emendation for c. 126, 2).

(v) *Criticism of the Sources*

Besides the works by Leo, Peter, Rosenberg, and Wachsmuth cited on p. 898 the following works are generally applicable to the Julio-Claudians after Augustus:

Appelquist, H. S. *De praecipuis rerum Gai, Claudii, Neronis scriptoribus*. Diss. Helsingfors, 1889.

Gercke, A. *Seneca-Studien*. Jahrb. f. class. Phil. Supplbd. XXI, 1896. II. *Historisch-biographische Untersuchungen über Seneca und seine Zeit*. Pp. 159–328.

Knabe, C. A. *De fontibus historiae imperatorum Julianorum*. Diss. Halle, 1864.

Momigliano, A. *Osservazioni sulle Fonti per la storia di Caligola, Claudio, Nerone*. Rend. Linc. VIII, 1932, p. 293.

Stevenson, G. H. *Ancient Historians and their Sources*. J.P. XXXV, 1920, p. 205.

(a) *Dio*.

Besides the general works cited on p. 898 the following should be noted:

Bergmans, J. *Die Quellen der vita Tiberii (Buch 57 der Historia Romana) des Cassius Dio*. Heidelberg Diss. Amsterdam, 1903.

Sickel, G. *De fontibus a Cassio Dione in conscribendis rebus inde a Tiberio usque ad mortem Vitelli gestis adhibitis*. Diss. Göttingen, 1876.

(b) *Josephus*.

Besides works cited on p. 898 see also:

Bloch, H. *Die Quellen des* Flavius Josephus *in seiner Archaeologie*. Leipzig, 1879.

von Destinon, J. *Die Chronologie des Josephus*. Kiel, 1880.

—— *Untersuchungen zu Flavius Josephus*. Kiel, 1904.

Drüner, H. *Untersuchungen über Josephus*. Diss. Marburg, 1896.

Liempt, L. van. *De testimonio Flaviano*. Mnem. LV, 1927, p. 109.

Niese, B. *Zur Chronologie des Josephus*. II. Die römischen Kaiserjahre. Hermes, XXVIII, 1893, pp. 208–216.

Norden, E. *Josephus und Tacitus über Jesus Christus und eine messianische Prophetie*. N.J. Klass. Alt. XXXI, 1913, p. 637.

Pharr, C. *The Testimony of Josephus to Christianity.* A.J.Ph. XLVIII, 1927, p. 137.

Schemann, F. A. C. *Die Quellen des Flavius Josephus in der jüdischen Archaeologie.* (Buch XVIII–XX = Polemos, II, cap. VII–XIV, 3.) Hagen, 1887.

Stein, E. *De Flavii Josephi arte narrandi.* Eos, XXXIII, 1930/31, p. 641.

Täubler, E. *Die Parthernachrichten bei Josephus.* Berlin, 1904.

—— *Die nicht bestimmbaren Hinweise bei Josephus und die Anonymushypothese.* Hermes, LI, 1916, p. 211.

(*c*) *Suetonius.*

See works cited on p. 899.

(*d*) *Tacitus.*

The following works will be found useful:

1. *General.*

Boissier, G. *Tacite.* Ed. 4, Paris, 1923.

Drexler, H. *Bericht über Tacitus für die Jahre* 1913–1927. Bursian, CCXXIV, Suppl. bd. 1929, p. 257.

Fraenkel, Ed. *Tacitus.* Neue Jahrb. f. Wiss. und Jugendbildung, VIII, 1932, pp. 218–233.

Klingner, F. *Tacitus.* Die Antike, VIII, 1932, p. 151.

Marchesi, C. *Tacito.* Messina-Roma, 1924.

Reitzenstein, R. *Tacitus und sein Werk.* (Neue Wege zur Antike, IV.) Leipzig-Berlin, 1926.

Art. *s.v.* P. Cornelius Tacitus in P.W. (Schwabe.)

2. *Life and Views.*

Brakman, C. *Tacitus quae de Astrologia iudicaverit.* Mnem. LVI, 1928, p. 70.

Fabia, Ph. *La carrière sénatoriale de Tacite.* J. d. Sav. 1926, p. 193.

—— *L'Irréligion de Tacite.* J. d. Sav. 1914, p. 250.

Halliday, W. R. *A Sidelight upon Tacitus.* Liverpool Ann. Arch. IX, 1922, p. 27.

Hammer, S. *Ramenta Tacitina.* Eos, XXV, 1921/2, p. 10.

Lord, L. E. *Note on Tacitus' Summary of the Reign of Augustus.* C.R. XLI, 1927, p. 41.

Meister, R. *Die Tacitusinschrift von Mylasa.* Jahreshefte, XXVII, 1932, Beiblatt, pp. 233–244.

von Pöhlmann, R. *Die Weltanschauung des Tacitus.* Ed. 2, Munich, 1913.

Reid, J. S. *Tacitus as a Historian.* J.R.S. XI, 1921, p. 191.

Vogt, J. *Tacitus als Politiker.* Stuttgart, 1924.

Willrich, H. *Augustus bei Tacitus.* Hermes, LXII, 1927, p. 54.

3. *Sources, Composition, and Art.*

Bretschneider, K. *Quo ordine ediderit Tacitus singulas Annalium partes.* Diss. Strassburg, 1905.

Courbaud, E. *Les procédés d'art de Tacite dans les "Histoires."* Paris, 1918.

Everts, P. S. *De Tacitea historiae conscribendae ratione.* Diss. Kerkrade, 1926.

Fabia, Ph. *Les sources de Tacite dans les Histoires et les Annales.* Paris, 1893.

Glaser, K. *Bemerkungen zu den Annalen des Tacitus.* Mitt. d. Ver. Klass. Phil. in Wien, VI, 1929, p. 34.

Graf, W. *Untersuchungen über die Komposition der Annalen des Tacitus.* Bern Diss. Thun, 1931.

Hanssen, R. *Die Quellenanführungen in Tacitus' Historiae und Annales.* Symb. Osl. XII, 1933, p. 81.

Hirschfeld, O. *Die Bücherzahl der Annalen und Historien des Tacitus.* Kleine Schriften, Berlin, 1913, p. 842.

—— *Zur annalistischen Anlagen des Taciteischen Geschichtwerkes.* Kleine Schriften, p. 855.

Leo, F. *Die staatsrechtlichen Exkurse in Tacitus' Annalen.* Gött. Nach. 1896, p. 191.

Marsh, F. B. *Tacitus and Aristocratic Tradition.* C.P. xxi, 1926, p. 289.

Marx, F. A. *Untersuchungen zur Komposition und zu den Quellen von Tacitus' Annalen.* Hermes, lx, 1925, p. 74.

—— *Die Quellen der Germanenkriege bei Tacitus und Dio.* Klio, xxvi (N.F. viii), 1933, p. 323.

Mommsen, Th. *Das Verhältniss des Tacitus zu den Acten des Senats.* Ges. Schriften, vii, p. 252.

Münzer, F. *Die Quellen des Tacitus für die Germanenkriege.* B. J. 104, 1899, p. 66.

Slijper, E. *De Tacito, graecos auctores, Herodotum in primis, imitante.* Mnem. lvii, 1929, p. 106.

Stein, A. *Die Protokolle des römischen Senats und ihre Bedeutung als Geschichtsquelle für Tacitus.* Progr. Prague, 1903. (And cf. B.P.W. 1916, 1038–40.)

—— *Tacitus als Geschichtsquelle.* N.J. Kl. Alt. xviii, 1915, p. 361.

4. *The Tacitean Portrait of Tiberius.*

Besides the general works in section 1 the following should be consulted

Freytag, L. *Tiberius und Tacitus.* Berlin, 1870.

Gentile, I. *L'imperatore Tiberio e la moderna critica storica.* Milan, 1887.

Harrer, G. A. *Tacitus and Tiberius.* A.J.Ph. xli, 1920, p. 57.

Jerome, T. S. *The Tacitean Tiberius.* C.P. vii, 1912, p. 265.

—— *Aspects of the Study of Roman History.* New York, 1923, pp. 319–380.

Ritter, J. *Die taciteische Charakterzeichnung des Tiberius.* Gymnasial-Programm, Rudolstadt, 1895.

Wiesner, E. *Tiberius und Tacitus.* (Kritische Beleuchtung des taciteischen Berichtes über die Regierung Tibers bis zum Tode des Drusus.) Krotoschin-Ostrowo, 1877.

(*e*) *Velleius Paterculus.*

See works cited on p. 899 *sq.* and also:

Goeke, W. *De Velleiana Tiberii imagine iudicium.* Diss. Jena, 1876.

Raff, P. *Le fonti storiche di Velleio Paterculo.* Lucera, 1925.

Schaefer, W. *Tiberius und seine Zeit im Lichte der Tradition des Velleius Paterculus.* Leipzig Diss. Halle, 1912.

(*f*) *Miscellaneous. Lost and late writers.*

Carcopino, J. *Un inscription de M. Servilius Nonianus.* Bull. de la Soc. nat. des Antiq. de France, 1931, pp. 108–115.

Castiglioni, L. *Lattanzio e le Storie di Seneca padre.* Riv. Fil. (N.S.) vi, 1928, p. 454.

Detlefsen, D. *Ueber des älteren Plinius Geschichte seiner Zeit und ihr Verhältniss zum Tacitus.* Phil. xxxiv, 1876, p. 40.

Klotz, A. *Das Geschichtswerk des älteren Seneca.* Rh. Mus. lvi, 1901, p. 429.

Mommsen, Th. *Cornelius Tacitus und Cluvius Rufus.* Originally published 1870: in *Ges. Schriften*, vii, p. 224.

Motzo, R. B. *I Commentari di Agrippina madre di Nerone.* Studi Cagliaritani di Storia e Filologia. Vol. i, Cagliari, 1927, p. 19.

—— *Gli Annali di Servilio Noniano.* Studi Cagliaritani.... p. 62.

—— *I libri della guerra di Germania di Aufidio Basso.* Studi Cagliaritani... p. 58.

Münzer, F. *Aufidius und Plinius*. Rh. Mus. LXII, 1907, p. 161.
—— *Beiträge zur Quellenkritik der Naturgeschichte des Plinius*. Berlin, 1897.
Nissen, A. *Die Historien des Plinius*. Rh. Mus. XXVI, 1871, p. 497.
Patzig, E. *Johannes Antiochenus und Johannes Malalas*. Leipzig, 1892.
Pelka, W. *Zu Aufidius Bassus*. Rh. Mus. LXI, 1906, p. 620.
Schenk, A. (Graf von Stauffenberg). *Die römische Kaisergeschichte bei Malalas*. Stuttgart, 1931.
Weber, W. *Studien zur Chronik des Malalas* in *Festgabe für A. Deissmann*. Tübingen, 1927, p. 20.
von Wölfflin, E. *Plinius und Cluvius Rufus*. Archiv f. Lat. Lexik. und Grammatik, XII, 1902, p. 345.

II. MODERN WORKS

A. *General*

(Works marked † in this and the following bibliography
were not accessible to the writer)

Besides the relevant pages in the works cited in the General Bibliography, many of the following are generally relevant for the whole reign:

Baker, G. P. *Tiberius Caesar*. London, 1929.
Beesly, E. S. *Catiline, Clodius, and Tiberius*. London, 1878.
Dieckmann, H. *Die effektive Mitregentschaft des Tiberius*. Klio, XV, 1918, p. 339.
Fluss, M. *Bericht über die Literatur zur Geschichte der römischen Kaiserzeit bis auf Diocletian (14–284 n. Chr.) aus dem Jahren* 1894–1913. Bursian, CLXXXIX, 1921, p. 53.
Gagé, J. *Divus Augustus. L'idée dynastique chez les empereurs julio-claudiens*. Rev. Arch. XXXIV, 1931, p. 11.
—— *La Victoria Augusti et les auspices de Tibère*. Rev. Arch. XXXII, 1930, p. 1.
Gelzer, M. *Die Nobilität der Kaiserzeit*. Hermes, L, 1915, p. 395. Cf. W. Otto, *ib.* LI, 1916, p. 73.
Groag, E. *Zur Ämterlaufbahn der Nobiles in der Kaiserzeit*. Strena Buliciana. Zagreb, 1924, p. 253.
Hentig, H. von. *Über den Cäsarenwahnsinn, die Krankheit des Kaisers Tiberius*. Munich, 1924. [But cf. E. Hohl in *Deut. Lit. Zeitung*, 1925, p. 269.]
Ihne, W. *Zur Ehrenrettung des Kaisers Tiberius*. Strassburg, 1892.
Kahrstedt, U. *Frauen auf antiken Münzen*. Klio, X, 1910, p. 261 (esp. p. 293).
Kornemann, E. *Doppelprinzipat und Reichsteilung im Imperium Romanum*. Leipzig-Berlin, 1930, pp. 26–60.
Lang, A. *Beiträge zur Geschichte des Kaisers Tiberius*. Jena, 1911.
Marsh, F. B. *The Reign of Tiberius*. London, 1931.
Pelham, H. F. *The early Roman emperors*. In *Essays*, 1911, pp. 21–48 (esp. pp. 33–37).
Sandels, F. *Die Stellung der kaiserlichen Frauen aus der iulisch-claudischen Hause*. Giessen Diss. Darmstadt, 1912.
Schott, W. *Studien zur Geschichte des Kaisers Tiberius*. Bamberg, I, 1904, II, 1905.
Schwab, J. *Leben und Charakter des Tiberius Claudius Nero nach Velleius und Tacitus bis zum Jahre 29 n. Chr.* Progr. Tetschen a. E. 1912.
Spengel, A. *Zur Geschichte des Kaisers Tiberius*. Bay. S.B. 1903. Heft I, pp. 3–63.
Tarver, J. C. *Tiberius the Tyrant*. London, 1902.
†Tuxen, S. L. *Kejser Tiberius*. Copenhagen, 1896.
von Voigt, W. *Unter welchem Gestirnen wurde Cäsar, Agrippa und Tiberius geboren?* Phil. LVIII, 1899, p. 170.

B. *The Accession*

Bickermann, E. *Die römische Kaiserapotheose.* Arch. Relig. XXVII, 1929, p. 1.

Charlesworth, M. P. *Livia and Tanaquil.* C.R. XLI, 1927, p. 55.

—— *Tiberius and the death of Augustus.* A.J.Ph. XLIV, 1923, p. 145.

Fabia, Ph. *L'avènement officiel de Tibère.* Rev. Phil. XXXIII, 1909, p. 28.

Haverfield, F. *Four notes on Tacitus.* J.R.S. II, 1912, p. 199 (Note on *Ann.* I, 14).

Hohl, E. *Wann hat Tiberius das Prinzipat übernommen?* Hermes, LXVIII, 1933, p. 106.

Poplawski, M. St. *L'Apothéose de Sylla et d'Auguste.* Eos, XXX, 1927, p. 273.

Scott, K. *Tiberius' Refusal of the Title of Augustus.* C.P. XXVII, 1932, p. 43.

C. *Italy and the Senate*

Groag, E. *Zum Konsulat in der Kaiserzeit.* Wien. St. XLVII, 1929, p. 143.

Heidel, W. A. *Why were the Jews banished from Italy in* 19 A.D.? A.J.Ph. XLI, 1920, p. 38.

Jörs, P. *Die Ehegesetze des Augustus.* (Die Lex Papia Poppaea, p. 49 *sq.*) In *Festschrift Theodor Mommsen...*, Marburg, 1893.

Kornemann, E. *Neues vom Kaiser Tiberius.* Forschungen und Fortschritte, V, 1929, p. 342.

Kuntz, O. *Tiberius Caesar and the Roman Constitution.* Univ. Washington Publ. in soc. sciences. II, 1924.

La Piana, G. *Foreign Groups in Rome during the first century of the Empire.* Harv. Theol. Rev. XX, 1927, p. 183.

Marsh, F. B. *Tiberius and the Development of the Early Empire.* C.J. XXIV, 1928/29, p. 14.

Merrill, E. T. *The Expulsion of the Jews from Rome under Tiberius.* C.P. XIV, 1919, p. 365.

Neumann, K. J. Art. *s.v.* dominus in P.W., col. 1306 *sq.*

Rogers, R. S. *The Date of the Banishment of the Astrologers.* C.P. XXVI, 1931, p. 203.

Scott, K. *The* Diritas *of Tiberius.* A.J.Ph. LIII, 1932, p. 139.

Stella Maranca, F. da. *Di alcuni Senatusconsulti nelle iscrizioni latine.* Rend. Linc. Ser. VI, Vol. I, 1925, p. 504.

Taylor, L. R. *Tiberius' Refusals of Divine Honours.* Trans. Am. Phil. Assoc. LX, 1929, p. 87.

Zmigryder-Konopka, Zdz. *Les Romains et la circoncision des Juifs.* Eos, XXXIII, 1930/31, p. 334.

D. *Germanicus and the East*

Cantineau, J. *Textes palmyréniens du temple de Bêl.* Syria, XII, 1931, pp. 116 *sqq.*, no. 18.

Casagrandi, V. *Germanico Cesare secondo la mente di Tacito.* In *Storia e archeologia Romana*, Genova, 1886, pp. 163–177.

—— *Il Partito dell' opposizione repubblicana sotto Tiberio e la morte di Germanico Cesare. ib.* pp. 181–212.

Cichorius, C. *Die ägyptischen Erlasse des Germanicus*, in *Römische Studien*, pp. 375–388.

von Domaszewski, A. *Eine Inschrift des P. Suillius Rufus.* Rh. Mus. LXVII, 1912, p. 151.

Ferber, C. *Utrum metuerit Tiberius Germanicum necne quaeritur.* Kiel Diss. Hamburg, 1890.

Hohl, E. *Ein römischer Prinz in Aegypten.* Preuss. Jahrb. CLXXXII, 1920, p. 344.

Kessler, G. *Die Tradition über Germanicus.* Berlin, 1905.

Kroll, W. *Kleinigkeiten.* [Includes *Zu den Fragmenten des Germanicus.*] Wochens. f. klass. Phil. xxxv, 1918, col. 304.

Mommsen, Th. *Die Familie des Germanicus.* Ges. Schriften iv, pp. 271–290.

Müller, A. *Strafjustiz in römischen Heere.* N.J. Kl. Alt. xvii, 1906, p. 550 (esp. p. 565).

Pascal, C. *Un epigramma di Germanico.* Athenaeum, N.S. iii, 1925, p. 33.

Rogers, R. S. *Quinti Veranii, Pater et Filius.* C.P. xxvi, 1931, p. 172.

Seyrig, H. *Antiquités syriennes.* (I. *L'incorporation de Palmyre à l'empire romain.*) Syria, xiii, 1932, pp. 255 *sqq.*

Steup, J. *Eine Umstellung im zweiten Buche der Annalen des Tacitus.* Rh. Mus. xxiv, 1869, p. 72.

Viertel, A. *Tiberius und Germanicus.* Göttingen Gymn. Prog. 1901.

Wilcken, U. *Zum Germanicus Papyrus.* Hermes, lxiii, 1928, p. 48.

E. *Drusus and the Succession*

Abraham, F. *Tiberius und Sejan.* Berlin, 1888.

Cichorius, C. *Zur Familiengeschichte Seians.* Hermes, xxxix, 1904, p. 461.

Richmond, I. A. *The Relation of the Praetorian Camp to Aurelian's Wall of Rome.* B.S.R. x, 1927, p. 12.

Scott, K. *Drusus, nicknamed "Castor."* C.P. xxv, 1930, p. 155.

—— *The Dioscuri and the Imperial Cult.* C.P. xxv, 1930, p. 379.

F. Maiestas *and the Rise of Sejanus*

(*a*) *General treatment of* maiestas.

Ciaceri, E. *L'imperatore Tiberio e i processi di lesa majestà.* Processi politici e Relazioni internazionali. Rome, 1918, pp. 249–308.

Dürr, F. *Die Majestätsprocesse unter dem Kaiser Tiberius.* Progr. Heilbronn, 1880.

Marsh, F. B. *Tacitus and the Tiberian Terror* and *The Law of Treason under Tiberius* in *The Reign of Tiberius.* Oxford, 1931, pp. 284–288; 289–295.

Mommsen, Th. *Römisches Strafrecht.* Leipzig, 1899. (Esp. pp. 537–94, *Das Staatsverbrechen.*)

Schott, W. *Die Kriminaljustiz unter dem Kaiser Tiberius.* Erlangen, 1893.

(*b*) *Particular Topics.*

Columba, M. *Il Processo di Cremuzio Cordo.* Atene e Roma, iv, 1901, p. 361.

Maroni, C. *Uno sguardo ai fasti dei prefetti al pretorio.* Riv. stor. ant. iv, 1899, Fasc. iv, p. 338.

Rogers, R. S. *Lucius Arruntius.* C.P. xxvi, 1931, p. 31.

—— *The career of Aemilia Lepida and the Roman criminal law.* Trans. Amer. Phil. Ass. 1930, p. xlv.

—— *Two Criminal Cases tried before Drusus Caesar.* C.P. xxvii, 1932, p. 75.

Strazzulla, V. *Il processo di Libone Druso.* Riv. stor. ant. xii, 1908, p. 62; p. 243.

(*c*) *Livia.*

Barini, C. C. *La tradizione superstite ed alcuni giudizi dei moderni su Livia.* Rend. Linc. Ser. v, Volume xxxi, 1922, p. 25.

Degrassi, A. *Iscrizione municipale di Cuma.* Riv. Fil. (N.S.) iv, 1926, pp. 371 *sqq.*

Willrich, H. *Livia.* Leipzig-Berlin, 1911, pp. 32–44; 55–70.

G. *The Fall of Sejanus*

Calza, G. *Scoperta di un frammento di Fasti.* N.S.A. XIV, 1917, p. 180.
Charlesworth, M. P. *The banishment of the elder Agrippina.* C.P. XVII, 1922, p. 260.
Cichorius, C. *Der Astrologe Ti. Claudius Balbillus.* Rh. Mus. LXXVI, 1927, p. 102.
Lugand, R. *Le viol rituel chez les Romains.* Rev. Arch. XXXII, 1930, p. 36.
Rogers, R. S. *The Conspiracy of Agrippina.* Trans. Amer. Phil. Ass. LXII, 1931, p. 141.
Willenbücher, H. *Tiberius und die Verschwörung des Sejan.* Gutersloh, 1896.

H. *The Last Years*

Boutterin, M. *La Villa de Tibère à Capri.* Mon. Ant. Suppl. VI, 1914.
Carcopino, J. *Attideia.* Mél. d'Arch. et d'Hist. XL, 1923. II. ii. *L'archigalle de Parrhasios*, pp. 267–299. iii. *Les conséquences d'une correction*, pp. 299–307.
Cichorius, C. *Tiberius als Schriftsteller* in *Römische Studien*, pp. 388–390.
—— *Der Astrologe Thrasyllos und sein Haus. Ib.* pp. 390–398.
Cortellini, N. *A proposito di alcune date incerte dell' ultimo decennio del regno di Tiberio.* Riv. stor. ant. III, 1898, Fasc. i, p. 15.
Rogers, R. S. *Der Prozess des Cotta Messalinus.* Hermes, LXVIII, 1933, p. 121.

I. *The Government of the Empire*

Besnier, M. *Fouilles et découvertes récentes en Tunisie.* J. d. Sav. 1914, p. 211 (p. 217 *sq.* Bulla Regia).
Bickel, E. *Die politische und religiöse Bedeutung des Provinzialoberpriesters im römischen Westen.* B. J. 133, 1928, p. 1.
Cagnat, R. *La ville romaine de Thugga.* J. d. Sav. 1914, p. 473.
—— *L'armée romaine d'Afrique.* Ed. 2. Paris, 1908, pp. 9–24.
Calder, W. M. *The Tarcondimoti of Cilicia.* J.R.S. VI, 1916, p. 105.
Cantarelli, L. *Tacfarinata.* Studi Romani e Bizantini, Rome, 1915, pp. 199–208.
—— *La serie dei Prefetti di Egitto.* Mem. Acc. Lincei, XII, 1906, p. 47.
Griffin, M. H. and G. A. Harrer. *Fasti Consulares.* A.J.A. XXXIV, 1930, p. 360.
Gwatkin, W. E. *Cappadocia as a Roman procuratorial province.* University of Missouri Studies. Vol. V, No. 4, Oct. 1930.
Hirschfeld, O. *Über ein Senatusconsultum vom Jahre 20 nach Chr.* Kleine Schriften, Berlin, 1913, p. 404.
Honigmann, E. Art. *s.v.* Kommagene in P.W.
Keil, J. *Die Kulte Lydiens* in *Anatolian Studies presented to Sir William Mitchell Ramsay*, Manchester, 1923, p. 239.
Lambrino, S. *Histria romaine à la lumière des fouilles.* Rev. E.L. IX, 1931, p. 77.
Lange, H. *Die Wörter* AEQUITAS *und* JUSTITIA *auf römischen Münzen.* Z. d. Sav.-Stift. LII, 1932, p. 296.
Lesquier, J. *L'armée romaine d'Égypte d'Auguste à Dioclétien.* Mémoires...de l'Institut français d'archéologie orientale du Caire. Cairo, LI, 1918.
—— *Les Préfets d'Égypte d'Auguste à Dioclétien* in *L'armée romaine d'Égypte...*, pp. 509 *sqq.*
Mehlis, C. *Die πόλεις Helvetiens.* Phil. Woch. 1924, col. 183.
Mommsen, Th. *Observationes Epigraphicae; XVIII. Dedicatio facta ob victoriam de Tacfarinate.* Eph. Ep. II, 1875, pp. 264–270.
Pansa, G. *L'Epoca del proconsolato in Asia di C. Asinio Pollione.* Riv. Ital. Num. XXII, 1909, p. 365.
Pârvan, V. *A propos du "basileus" Cotys de Callatis.* Dacia, I, 1924, p. 363.
—— *I primordi della civiltà Romana alle foci del Danubio.* Ausonia, X, 1921, p. 192.

von Premerstein, A. *Die Anfänge der Provinz Moesiens.* Jahreshefte, 1, 1898, Beiblatt, col. 194.

Ramsay, (Sir) W. M. *Historical Geography of Asia Minor.* London, 1890, pp. 398 *sqq.*

Reinach, S. *Cultes, Mythes et Religions.* Paris, 1905, Vol. III, pp. 182–185.

Robinson, D. M. *A Preliminary Report on the Excavations at Pisidian Antioch and at Sizma.* A.J.A. XXVIII, 1924, p. 435.

Schmidt, L. *Das regnum Vannianum.* Hermes, XLVIII, 1913, p. 292.

Schwarz, E. *Ueber das Reich des Vannius.* Sudeta, VII, 1931, p. 145.

—— *Wo lag das Swebenreich des Vannius?* Forschungen und Fortschritte, IX, 1933, p. 35.

van Sickle, C. E. *The Repair of Roads in Spain.* C.P. XXIV, 1929, p. 77.

Stout, S. E. *The Governors of Moesia.* Diss. Princeton, 1911.

Weber, W. *Studien zur Chronik des Malalas.* In *Festgabe für A. Deissmann,* Tübingen, 1927, pp. 20 *sqq.*

Wilhelm, A. *Zu Inschriften aus Kleinasien* in *Anatolian Studies presented to Sir William Mitchell Ramsay,* Manchester, 1923, pp. 418–431.

Ziegler, I. *Die Königsgleichnisse der Midrasch beleuchtet durch die römische Kaiser zeit.* Breslau, 1903, chap. 3.

CHAPTER XX

GAIUS AND CLAUDIUS

A. Gaius

I. Ancient Sources

A. *Contemporary Documents*

(i) *Inscriptions*

Acta Fratrum Arvalium, *C.I.L.* vi, pars iv, fasc. 2 (1902), 32344, 32345, 32346, 32347–47 *a*.

Dessau, 171–199, 205, 206, 5948–50, 6396, 6397, 8791, 8792 (= part of *I.G.* vii, 2711), 8899, 9339.

Ditt.³ 789, 797, 798, 799 (= *I.G.R.R.* 251, 145, 146).

I.G. vii, 2711 *sqq.*

I.G.R.R. i, ?1036, 1057, 1086, 1248; iii, 612, 703; iv, 76, 78, 145, 146, 251, 981, 1001, 1022, 1098, 1102, 1379, 1615, 1657.

O.G.I.S. 472 and 473.

(ii) *Coins*

In addition to the relevant pages in works cited in the General Bibliography, see:

Cortellini, N. *Le Monete di Caligola in Cohen.* Riv. Ital. Num. xi, 1908, p. 239.

Dattari, G. *Regno di Caligola.* Riv. Ital. Num. xiii, 1900, p. 378.

B. *Literary Authorities*

Athenaeus, iv, 148 c, d.

Dio, lvii, 5, 6, 7; lvii, 8, 1, 2; 23, 1–4; 25, 2; 28; lix, *passim*; lx, 5, 8, 9; 6, 6, 8; 8, 1.

Frontinus, *de aquaeductibus* (ed. F. Bücheler), 13.

Josephus, *Ant.* xviii [6, 8], 205–[7, 9], 309; xix [1], 1–[2, 5], 211; *Bell. Jud.* ii [9, 5], 178–[10, 5], 203.

Julian, *Convivium (Caesares)*, 310 a, b.

Philo, *In Flaccum: Legatio ad Gaium* (edd. L. Cohn and S. Reiter in vol. vi of the Cohn-Wendland Edition of Philo).

Pliny, *N.H.* iv, 10; v, 2; v, 11; vii, 45; xiv, 56; xxxii, 4; xxxiii, 33; 79; xxxv, 18; xxxvi, 111; 122; xxxvii, 17.

Plutarch, *Moralia, de superstitione*, 170 f, Frag. 140; *Vitae, Romul.* 20; *Ant.* 87, 8; *Galb.* 9.

Seneca, *de constantia sapientis*, 18; *de ira*, ii, 33; iii, 18; *de tranquillitate animi*, ii, 10; 14, 4–10; *ad Polybium*, 13, 4; *ad Helviam*, 10, 4; *de beneficiis*, ii, 12; iv, 31, 2; *nat. quaest.* iv, praef. 17: *Apocolocyntosis*, 11, 2; *Epist.* 4, 7; 77, 18.

Suetonius, *Tib.* 54, 1; 62, 3; 73, 2; 75, 2; 76; *Calig. passim*; *Claud.* 7; 9, 1; 10, 1; 11, 1; 11, 3; 20, 1; 26, 3; 38, 3; *Nero*, 6, 3; 30, 1; *Galba* 6, 2, 3; 7, 1; *Otho*, 6, 1; *Vitell.* 2, 5; 4; 17, 2; *Vesp.* 2, 3; 5, 3.

　R. R. Rosborough, *An Epigraphic Commentary on Suetonius's Life of Gaius Caligula.* Pennsylvania Diss. Philadelphia, 1920.

Suidas (ed. Adler), *s.v.* Γάϊος, i, p. 503 *sq.*

Tacitus, *Agric.* 4, 13; *Germ.* 37; *Hist.* iv, 48; v, 9; *Ann.* i, 32, 41, 69; v, 1; vi, 3, 5, 9, 20, 45, 46, 48, 50; xi, 3; xiii, 3; xv, 72; xvi, 17.

C. *Works on the Sources and Source-Criticism*

In addition to the works cited in the Bibliography to Chapter XIX, I A (v), the following should be consulted:

Balsdon, J. P. V. D. *Notes concerning the Principate of Gaius.* J.R.S. XXIV, 1934, p. 13.

Charlesworth, M. P. *The Tradition about Caligula.* Camb. Hist. Journal, IV, no. 2, 1933, p. 105.

Jerome, T. S. *The Historical Tradition about Gaius*, 37–41 A.D. (Ch. XVIII in *Aspects of the Study of Roman History.*) New York and London, 1923.

Krüger, P. *Philo und Josephus als Apologeten des Judentums.* Diss. Leipzig, 1906.

Lugand, R. *Suétone et Caligula.* Rev. E.A. XXXII, 1930, p. 9.

Momigliano, A. *Osservazioni sulle Fonte per la Storia di Caligula, Claudio, Nerone.* Rend. Linc. VIII, 1932, p. 293.

Mommsen, Th. *Bruchstücke der Saliarischen Priesterliste.* Hermes, XXXVIII, 1903, p. 125.

—— *Cornelius Tacitus und Cluvius Rufus.* Gesammelte Schriften, VII, pp. 224–252.

Willrich, H. *Judaica.* Göttingen, 1900, pp. 40–51.

II. MODERN WORKS

(a) General

Besides the relevant pages in the general histories mentioned in the General Bibliography the following should be consulted:

Gelzer, M. *s.v.* Iulius (133) (Caligula) in P.W., cols. 381 *sqq.*

Holleaux, M. *Inscription d'Acraephiae.* B.C.H. XII, 1888, p. 305.

Ireland, W. W. *The Blot upon the Brain.* Ed. 2, 1893, Edinburgh. Paper IV, 'The Insanity of Power,' pp. 88–150.

Kahrstedt, U. *Frauen auf antiken Münzen.* Klio, X, 1910, pp. 295 *sqq.*

†Linnert, U. *Beiträge zur Geschichte Caligulas.* Jena Diss. Nürnberg, 1909.

Momigliano, A. *La Personalità di Caligola.* Annali d. R. Scuola Normale Superiore di Pisa, Serie II. 1, 1932, p. 1.

Mommsen, Th. *Die Familie des Germanicus.* Ges. Schriften, IV, p. 271.

—— *Iusiurandum in C. Caesarem Augustum.* Ges. Schriften, VIII, p. 461.

Quidde, L. *Caligula.* (*Eine Studie über römische Cäsarenwahnsinn.*) Ed. 3. Leipzig, 1894.

Sachs, H. *Bubi Caligula.* Ed. 2, Vienna, 1932. (Ed. 1 translated by H. Singer, *Caligula*, London, 1931.)

Vaglieri, D. Art. Caligula in Diz. Epig.

Venturini, L. *Vita di Caligola.* Various articles in *Riv. stor. ant.* III, 1898, and IV, 1899.

†—— *Caligola.* Milan, 1906.

Wiedemeister [n.i.]. *Der Cäsarenwahnsinn der Julisch-Claudischen Imperatoren-familie geschildert an den Kaisern Tiberius, Caligula, Claudius, Nero.* Ed. 2. Leipzig, 1886.

Willrich, H. *Caligula.* Klio, III, 1903, pp. 85, 288, 397.

(*b*) *The Northern Campaigns and Affairs in the East*

(i) *Gaul, the Rhine, and Britain*

Balsdon, J. P. V. D. *op. cit.* J.R.S. xxiv, 1934, pp. 16–18.

Dalmasso, L. *Caligola al Reno.* Riv. stor. ant. xi, 1907, p. 470.

Janssen, J. *Ad expeditionem Gai principis in Germaniam.* Mnem. xlviii, 1920, p. 205.

Jullian, C. *Histoire de la Gaule,* iv², pp. 161–4.

Mommsen, Th. *Relief aus Kula.* Ath. Mitt. xiii, 1888, p. 18.

Lizop, R. *Les Convenae et les Consoranni.* Toulouse-Paris, 1931, pp. 32 *sqq.*

Riese, A. *Der Feldzug des Caligula an den Rhein.* Neue Heidelberger Jahrb. vi, 1896, p. 152.

Ritterling, E. *Zum Germanenkrieg d. J. 39–41 n. Chr.* Röm.-Germ. Korrespondenzblatt, vi, 1913, p. 1.

Teuber, G. *Beiträge zur Geschichte der Eroberung Britanniens durch die Römer.* Breslau, 1909, pp. 1 *sqq.,* 82 *sqq.*

(ii) *Egypt, the Jews, and the East*
(See also the Bibliography to Chapter x, B, 8.)

Balsdon, J. P. V. D. *ib.* pp. 19–24.

Bell, H. I. *Juden und Griechen im römischen Alexandreia.* Leipzig, 1926, pp. 16–24.

D[e] S[anctis], G. *Miscellanea.* II. I Giudei e le fazioni dei ludi (incorporating a letter from Prof. J. Dobiaš). Riv. Fil. liii, 1925, p. 245.

Goodenough, E. R. *Philo and Public Life.* J.E.A. xii, 1926, p. 77.

Groag, E. *Prosopographische Bemerkungen* (III. Lurius Varius). Wien. St. l, 1932 (publ. 1933), p. 202.

Heinemann, J. Art *s.v. Antisemitismus* in P.W. Supplementband v.

†Luria, S. (Anti-Semitism in the ancient world.) In Russian. Leningrad, 1922.

von Premerstein, A. *Zu den sogenannten alexandrinischen Märtyrakten.* Phil. Supplementband xvi, ii, 1923, esp. pp. 4–14.

Radermacher, L. *Zur Charakteristik neutestamentlicher Erzählungen.* Arch. Relig. xxviii, 1930, p. 31.

Reiter, S. Ἀρετή *und der Titel von Philo's 'Legatio.'* In ΕΠΙΤΥΜΒΙΟΝ *Heinrich Swoboda dargebracht,* Reichenberg, 1927, pp. 228–237.

Schürer, E. *Geschichte des jüdischen Volkes im Zeitalter Jesu Christi.* Leipzig, 1901, i⁴, pp. 495–506.

Scott, K. *Greek and Roman honorific months.* Yale Classical Studies, ii, 1931, esp. pp. 245 *sqq.*

Seston, W. *L'empereur Claude et les Chrétiens.* Rev. d'hist. et de philos. relig. xi, 1931, p. 275.

(*c*) *Tyranny*

Eitrem, S. *Zur Apotheose.* Symb. Osl. x, 1932, p. 49 (*Caligula*); *ib.* xi, 1932 p. 11 (*Die heilige Ehe*); p. 22 (*Das Herrscherblut und die Domus Augusta*).

Haussoullier, B. *Caligula et le temple d'Apollon Didyméen.* Rev. Phil. xxii, 1899, p. 147.

Lévi, I. *Jésus, Caligula et Claude dans une interpolation de Yosiphon.* Rev. E. J. xci, 1931, p. 134.

Mattingly, H. *The Mints of the Early Empire.* J.R.S. vii, 1917, p. 59.

Riewald, P. *De imperatorum Romanorum cum certis dis et comparatione et aequatione.* Diss. Phil. Hal. xx, 3, 1912.

Van Deman, E. B. *The House of Caligula.* A.J.A. xxviii, 1924, p. 368.

Wiegand, Th. *Siebenter vorläufiger Bericht über Ausgrabungen in Milet und Didyma.* Berl. Abh. 1911, p. 65. (Cf. *Rev. Arch.* xx, 1912, p. 440.)

B. Claudius

I. Ancient Sources

1. *Contemporary Documents*

Only the most important documents and those used in writing the sections on Claudius can be included here, together with a reference to the publications where they are most conveniently accessible.

(a) *Inscriptions*

1. Ann. épig. 1914, 173; 1915, 105; 1916, 42 and 1924, 66 (the Volubilis inscriptions); 1919, 10; 1923, 13; 1928, 63, 150; 1929, 74; 1930, 72.
2. Dessau 107, 198–224, 964, 966, 967, 968, 969, 970, 972, 975, 986, 1349, 1546, 1978, 1986, 4375, 5004, 5639, 5747^b, 5830, 5883, 5889, 5926, 5952, 5971, 6043 (= Bruns, *Fontes*[7], 54), 6797, 7061, 7076, 8848 (= I.G.R.R. III, 263), 8900.
3. Ditt.[3] 800, 801, 804, 805, 806.
4. I.G.R.R. I, 434, 707, 980, 1013, 1014, 1118 (= O.G.I.S. 664), 1155, 1161, 1165 (= O.G.I.S. 663), 1262; III, 83, 263, 328, 344, 577, 692, 717, 768, 788, 971, 1209, 1540; IV, 12, 43, 81, 208, 209, 463, 558, 559, 584, 899, 902, 914, 1023, 1026 (= Ditt.[3] 806), 1099, 1103, 1123, 1145, 1146, 1179, 1331, 1332, 1491, 1505 (better in *Sardis*, vol. VII, i, no. 10), 1608 (cf. S.E.G. IV, 641), 1711, 1733.
5. O.G.I.S. 418, 663, 664, 665.
6. S.E.G. I, 329; II, 453; IV, 516, 641; VI, 647, 834.

See also: *Ath. Mitt.* XXXVII, 1912, pp. 217 *sq.* (Samos); Corinth, vol. VIII, part II (Latin Inscriptions, 1896–1926), edited by A. B. West, Cambridge, Mass., 1931, Nos. 11, 67, and 86; Sardis, vol. VII (Greek and Latin Inscriptions), Part I by W. H. Buckler and David M. Robinson, Leyden, 1932, Nos. 10, 11, 39.

For Legislation and Edicts see also: Bruns, *Fontes*[7], 50–54, 79. *Digest*, I, 2, 2, 32; XVI, 1, 2 (= Bruns, *Fontes*[7], 50); XXXVII, 14, 5; XXXVIII, 4, 1 (= Bruns, *Fontes*[7], 51); XL, 8, 2. Gaius, *Institutiones*, I, 62, 84, 160; III, 63. Josephus, *Antiq. Jud.* XIX [5, 2], 280–285; XIX [5, 3], 287–291; XX [1, 2], 11–14.

(b) *Papyri*

Bell, H. I. *Jews and Christians in Egypt*. London, 1924, pp. 23–37. (For subsequent literature upon this letter of Claudius see the Bibliography to Chapter X, B, 8.)

Kenyon, F. G. and H. I. Bell. *Greek Papyri in the British Museum*, vol. III, no. 1178.

Stroux, J. *Eine Gerichtsreform des Kaisers Claudius*. Bay. S.B. VIII, 1929, no. 8. (This gives an improved text of B.G.U. 611 together with a commentary.)

(c) *Coins*

In addition to the relevant pages in works cited in the General Bibliography, the following should be consulted:

B.M. Cat. Palestine, pp. xcvii and 236–238 (alliance-coin of King Agrippa I).

Imhoof-Blumer. F. *Britannicus auf Münzen*. Num. Z. VIII, 1915, p. 85.

Imhoof-Blumer, F. *Kleinasiatische Münzen.* Vienna, 1901, pp. 416 *sq.* (Claudiconium; and cf. *I.G.R.R.* III, 1474).
Madden, F. W. *Coins of the Jews.* [London], 1881, p. 137.

For changes in the style of cities, due to action by Claudius, as shown on coinage see Head, *H.N.²*: pp. 507 (Neoclaudiopolis), 511 (Claudiopolis), 660 (Tralles), 710 (Claudio-Seleuceia), 713–714 (Claudiconium), 786 (Gaba), 793 (Ptolemaïs-Ace), 802 (Tiberias).

2. *Literary Sources*

Aulus Gellius, *Noct. Att.* XIII, 14, 7.
Dio, LV, 27, 33; LVIII, 11; LIX, 6, 23, 28; LX, *passim*; LXII, 2.
Frontinus, *de aquaeductibus*, 13–15, 105.
Josephus, *Ant. Jud.* XIX [3, 1], 212–[9, 2], 366; XX [1, 1], 1–[1, 3], 16; [2, 4], 37; [5, 1], 99–[8, 2], 152; *Bell. Jud.* II [11, 1], 204–[12, 8], 249.
Pliny, *N.H.* III, 119, 141, 146; V, 2, 20; VI, 8; VII, 159; XVI, 202; XXII, 92; XXIX, 8, 20, 22, 54; XXXIII, 63, 134; XXXV, 93, 94, 201; XXXVI, 57, 60, 70, 122–25.
Pliny Minor, *Epistulae*, I, 13, 3; III, 16, 7–9; VII, 29; VIII, 6.
Scribonius Largus, *Epist. ad Callistum*, p. 5; c. 60; c. 163.
Seneca, *Apocolocyntosis* [Ludus de morte Claudii]; *ad Polybium*; *de beneficiis*, I, 15, 5; VI, 19, 2–4; *de clementia*, I, 23, 1; *nat. quaest.* VII, 17, 2; VII, 21, 3; *Epist.* 47, 9.
Suetonius, *Calig.* 15, 2; 21; 23, 3; *Claud.*; *Nero*, 6, 2–4; 7, 1, 2; *Galba*, 7, 1; 14, 3; *Otho*, 1, 2, 3; *Vitell.* 2, 4, 5; 4; *Vesp.* 4, 1; *Domit.* 4, 3.
    Smilda, H. *C. Suetonii Tranquilli vita Divi Claudii.* Diss. Groningen, 1896.
Suidas, *Lexikon* (ed. Gaisford), *s.v.* Κλαύδιος.
Tacitus, *Agricola*, 13, 5; *Annals*, I, 54; III, 2, 3, 18, 29; IV, 31; VI, 32, 46; XI and XII, *passim*; XIII, 2, 3, 6, 14, 29, 32, 42, 43; XIV, 18, 63.

For the new letters introduced by Claudius see Quintilian, *Inst. Orat.* I, 7, 26; Martianus Capella (ed. A. Dick), III, 245; and Priscian, *Inst. Gramm.* (ed. A. Keil), I, 42.

3. *Modern Works on the Sources and Source-Criticism*

In addition to the works cited in the Bibliography to Chapter XIX, 1, A (v) see the following:

Albertini, E. *La Composition dans les Ouvrages philosophiques de Sénèque.* Paris Thesis, 1923.
Bickel, E. *Die Datierung der Apocolocyntosis.* Phil. Woch. XLI, 1924, p. 845.
Bücheler, F. *Divi Claudii* Ἀποκολοκύντωσις. Kleine Schriften, I, 1915, p. 439.
Ciaceri, E. *Claudio e Nerone nelle storie di Plinio.* Processi Politici e Relazioni Internazionali. Rome, 1918, p. 387.
Grigull, Th. *De auctoribus a Tacito in enarranda Divi Claudii vita adhibitis.* Diss. Münster, 1907.
Momigliano, A. *Osservazioni sulle Fonti per la storia di Caligola, Claudio, Nerone.* Rend. Linc. (Ser. VI), VIII, 1932, pp. 293, 336.
Smilda, H. *C. Suetonii Tranquilli vita Divi Claudii.* Diss. Groningen, 1896.
Viedebannt, O. *Warum hat Seneca die Apokolokyntosis geschrieben?* Rh. Mus. LXXV, 1926, p. 142.
Wagenvoort, H. Ἀποκολοκύντωσις. Mnem. (III S.) I, 1933/4, p. 4.
Weinreich, O. *Senecas Apocolocyntosis.* Berlin, 1923.

II. Modern Works

(a) General: the life and reign of Claudius

Albertini, E. *La clientèle des Claudii*. Mél. d'arch. et d'hist. xxiv, 1904, p. 247 (esp. pp. 270 *sqq.*).

Bickel, E. *Der Schluss der Apokolokyntosis*. Phil. xxxi, 1921, pp. 219 *sqq.*

Bücheler, F. *De Tiberio Claudio Caesare grammatico*. Kleine Schriften, 1915, p. 1 (and also *Claudianum*, p. 106).

Cumont, Fr. *Astrologues romains et byzantins*. I. *Balbillus*. Mél. d'arch. et d'hist. xxxvii, 1918–1919, pp. 33 *sqq.*

—— Écrits Hermétiques. (II. *Le médecin Thessalus et les plantes astrales d'Hermès Trismégiste*.) Rev. Phil. xlii, 1918, p. 8.

—— *Le sage Bothros ou le phylarque Arétas*. Rev. Phil. l, 1926, p. 13.

Double, L. *L'empereur Claude*. Paris, 1876.

Fabia, Ph. *La Mère de Néron*. Rev. Phil. xxxv, 1911, p. 144.

Faider, P. *Sénèque et Britannicus*. Mus. B. xxxiii, 1929, p. 171.

Ferrero, E. Art. Claudius in Diz. Epig.

Frank, T. *Claudius and the Pavian Inscription*. C.Q. ii, 1908, p. 89.

Green, W. M. *Appropriations for the Games at Rome in* 51 a.d. A.J.Ph. li, 1930, p. 249.

Josserand, Ch. *Le testament de Claude*. Mus. B. xxxiv, 1930–1932, p. 285.

Kroll, W. *De Claudii morte*. Raccolta Ramorino, Milan, 1925, p. 197.

Marchesi, M. *Seneca*. Messina, 1920.

Momigliano, A. *L' Opera dell' Imperatore Claudio*. Florence, 1932. (The English translation, published in May 1934, could not be used in the writing of this chapter.)

Mommsen, Th. *Inschrift des Bogens von Pavia*. Ges. Schrift. viii, p. 93.

Neppi Modona, Aldo. *La personalità dell' imperatore Claudio*. Il Mondo Classico, ii, 1932, p. 321.

Rogers, R. S. *Quinti Veranii, Pater et Filius*. C.P. xxvi, 1931, p. 175.

Ruth, T. De C. *The Problem of Claudius*. Johns Hopkins Diss. 1916. Baltimore, 1924.

Stähelin, Felix. *Kaiser Claudius*. (Basler Aulavortrag.) Basel, 1933.

Stella Maranca, F. da, *L. Anneo Seneca nel* "Consilium Principis." Rend. Linc. xxxii, 1923, p. 282.

Vivell, K. *Chronologisch-kritische Untersuchungen zur Geschichte des Kaisers Claudius*. Diss. Heidelberg, 1911.

(b) Administration and Public Works in Italy and the Provinces

Albertini, E. *L'inscription de Claude sur la Porte Majeure et deux passages de Frontin*. Mél. d'arch. et d'hist. xxvi, 1906, p. 305.

Cantarelli, L. *Gallione proconsole di Acaia e San Paolo*. Rend. Linc. xxxii, 1923, p. 157.

Carcopino, J. *Ostie*. Paris, 1929.

Dessau, H. *Zur Reihenfolge der Statthalter Moesiens*. Jahreshefte, xxiii, 1926 Beiblatt, col. 345.

von Domaszewski, A. *Kleine Beiträge zur Kaisergeschichte: 6. Die Verwaltung Judäas unter Claudius und Nero*. Phil. lxviii, 1908, p. 9.

Herzog, R. *Nikias und Xenophon von Kos*. H.Z. cxxv, 1922, p. 189.

Lambrino, S. *Observations sur un nouveau diplôme militaire de l'empereur Claude*. Rev. Phil. v, 1931, p. 250.

Lehmann-Hartleben, K. *Die antiken Hafenanlagen des Mittelmeeres*. Leipzig, 1923, pp. 182–191 (Ostia).

Lesquier, J. *L'armée romaine d'Égypte d'Auguste à Dioclétien.* Cairo, 1918, p. 510.
Rostovtseff, M. *Pontus, Bithynia and the Bosporus.* B.S.A. XXII, 1916–1918, p. 1 (esp. pp. 15–22).
Seltman, C. T. *The Administration of Bithynia under Claudius and Nero.* Num. Chr. VIII, 1928, p. 100.
Wall, B. *Porticus Minucia.* Corolla Archaeologica. Lund, 1932, p. 31.
West, A. B. and L. R. Taylor. *The Euryclids in Latin Inscriptions from Corinth.* A.J.A. 1926, XXX, pp. 389 *sqq.*

On the drainage of the Fucine Lake see Article *s.v. Emissarium* in D.S., and the books there cited.

(c) The re-organization of the empire: legislation and edicts, etc.

1. General

Cardinali, G. Art. *Frumentatio* in Diz. Epig.
Hirschfeld, O. *Die kaiserlichen Verwaltungsbeamte....* Ed. 2, 1905, pp. 1–39, 471–475.
Momigliano, A. *Op. cit.* pp. 79–134.
Rostovtseff, M. Arts. *s.vv. ab epistulis* and *fiscus* in P.W.
—— Arts. *fiscus* and *hereditates* in Diz. Epig.
Wilcken, U. *Zu den Kaiserreskripten.* Hermes, LV, 1920, p. 1.

2. The Volubilis Inscriptions

Chatelain, L. (on the first inscription). In *C.R. Ac. Inscr.* 1915, p. 396.
Constans, L. *Notes sur deux inscriptions de Volubilis.* Mus. B. XXVIII, 1924, p. 103.
Cuq, E. (on the first inscription). In *C.R. Ac. Inscr.* 1916, p. 262; 1918, p. 227; 1920, p. 343; and in *J.d. Sav.* 1917, p. 481.
De Sanctis, G. In *Atti di reale Acc. di Torino*, LIII, p. 453; and in *Riv. Fil.* LIII, 1925, p. 372.
Wuilleumier, P. *Le Municipe de Volubilis.* Rev. E.A. XXVIII, 1926, p. 323.

3. The Anauni Edict

Mommsen, Th. *Edict des Kaisers Claudius über das römische Bürgerrecht der Anauner vom J. 46 n. Chr.* Ges. Schriften, IV, pp. 291–322.
Jung, J. *Über Rechtsstellung und Organisation der alpinen civitates in der römischen Kaiserzeit.* Wien. St. XII, 1890, pp. 98–120.
Pais, E. In *Dalle guerre puniche a Cesare Augusto*, II, Rome, 1918, pp. 375 *sqq.*

4. On the ius honorum of the Gauls

(The items are arranged in chronological order to show the progress of the discussion.)

Münzer, F. *Die Verhandlung über das* Ius honorum *der Gallier im Jahre* 48. Festschrift für O. Hirschfeld, Berlin, 1903, p. 34.
Cunningham, H. J. *Claudius and the* Primores Galliae. C.Q. VIII, 1914, p. 132. (Same title in C.Q. IX, 1915, p. 57.)
Hardy, E. G. *Claudius and the* Primores Galliae: *a Reply and a Restatement.* C.Q. VIII, 1914, p. 282.
Pelham, H. F. [*Two*] *Notes on the Reign of Claudius.* (1) Claudius and the Chiefs of the Aedui. (2) Claudius and the Quaestura Gallica. In *Essays*, Oxford, 1911, pp. 152–158.

Grupe, G. *Über die oratio Claudii de iure honorum Gallis dando und Verwandtes.*
 Z. d. Sav.-Stift. XLII, 1921, p. 31.
Fabia, Ph. *La Table Claudienne de Lyon.* Lyon, 1929.
De Sanctis, G., in Riv. Fil. (N.S.) VII, 1929, p. 575.
Carcopino, J. *Sur la date du discours de Claude.* C.R. Ac. Inscr. 1930, p. 58.
—— *La Table Claudienne de Lyon* (reviewing Fabia). J. d. Sav. 1930, pp. 69, 116.
Fabia, Ph. *À propos de la table Claudienne.* Rev. E.A. XXXIII, 1931, pp. 117 *sqq.*

5. *On B.G.U. 611*

Fliniaux, A. *Une réforme judiciaire de l'empereur Claude (B.G.U. 611), à propos de
 travaux récents.* Rev. Hist. Droit Franç. 4e Série, X, 1931, p. 509.
Stroux, J. *Eine Gerichtsreform des Kaisers Claudius* (B.G.U. 611). Bay. S.B.
 VIII, 1929.
von Woess, F. *Die oratio des Claudius über Richteralter, Prozessverschleppung und
 Anklägertyrannei.* B.G.U. 611. Z. d. Sav.-Stift. LI, 1931, pp. 336 *sqq.*

6. *Miscellaneous*

Bachofen, J. J. *Das vellejanische Senatusconsult, seine ursprüngliche Fassung und
 spätere Erweiterung.* In *Ausgewahlte Lehren des römischen Civilrechts*, Bonn,
 1848, p. 1.
—— *Die Bestimmungen der römischen Kaiser über Erhaltung und Wiederherstellung
 der Privatgebaüde in Rom und Italien. ib.* p. 185.
de Pachtère, F. G. *Les* campi Macri *et le sénatus-consulte Hosidien.* Mél. Cagnat,
 Paris, 1912, p. 169.
Piganiol, A. *Observations sur une loi de l'empereur Claude.* Mél. Cagnat, Paris,
 1912, p. 153.

BIBLIOGRAPHY

CHAPTER XXI

NERO

A. ANCIENT SOURCES

1. *Inscriptions*

The chief Latin inscriptions will be found in Dessau, 225–36; 1742; 1987; 2595; 4914; 5622; 5640; 7386; 7396; 8901–2. (To these should be added the inscriptions already cited in the text.)

The chief Greek inscriptions will be found in Ditt.³ 807–14; I.G.R.R. I, 1034–5; III, 15, 335, 986; IV, 209, 560, 1125, 1053, 1061; O.G.I.S. 55, 475, 538, 666–8; S.E.G. IV, 530, 563. See also those already cited in the text and in J.R.S. XX, 1930, p. 43; Jahreshefte, XXVI, 1930, Beiblatt, col. 51.

2. *Papyri*

References to the principal papyri are given in the text. See also U. Wilcken, *Griechische Ostraka*, Leipzig, 1899 and P. M. Meyer, *Griechische Texte aus Aegypten*, Berlin, 1916, index *s.v.* Nero.

3. *Coins*

In addition to the works cited in the General Bibliography see also:

Gabrici, E. *La cronologia delle monete di Nerone stabilita sopra nuove ricerche icono-grafiche*. Riv. Ital. Numism. X, 1897, p. 275.
Kenner, F. *Die Scheidemünze des Kaisers Nero*. Num. Z. X, 1878, p. 230.
Pick, B. *Ueber einige Münzen der römischen Kaiserzeit*. Z.N. XVII, 1890, p. 180.
Soutzo, M. C. *Étude sur les monnaies impériales romaines*. Rev. N. 4 S. II, 1898, p. 659; III, 1899, p. 9.
Sydenham, E. A. *The Coinage of Nero*. London, 1920.

4. *Iconography*

Bernoulli, J. *Römische Ikonographie*. II, 1, Berlin-Stuttgart, 1886, p. 385.

5. *Literary*

(a) Main Sources

Dio Cassius, LXI–LXIII (cf. LXIV, 9; LXVI, 19).
Suetonius, *Nero*.
Tacitus, *Annals*, XIII–XVI.

(b) Secondary Sources

This list does not claim to be exhaustive. Sources for the 'legend' of Nero will be found in the studies cited in Section B, 2 (g), and especially in C. Pascal, *Nerone nella storia aneddotica e nella leggenda*. Only passages of special significance are cited here.

Anth. Lat. (ed. Riese), 725; 726 (= Baehrens, *Poet. lat. minores*, III, p. 61).
Anth. Pal. IX, 178.
Aurelius Victor, *De Caesar.* 5.
Calpurnius, *Eclogae* (= Baehrens, *Poet. lat. minores*, III, p. 69).

Digesta, XXXVI, 1, 1.

Dio Chrysostom, *Orat.* XXI, XXXI, XXXII.

Epictetus I, 1, 26–31; I, 2, 12–18; IV, 5, 17.

Eusebius, *Hist. Eccles.* II, 25; IV, 26.

Eutropius, *Breviarium*, 14.

Gaius, *Instit.* II, 197; II, 253.

[St John], *The Apocalypse.*

Josephus, *Ant.* XX [8], 148 *sqq.*

Lactantius, *De mortibus persecutorum*, 2.

Laus Pisonis (= Baehrens, *Poet. lat. minores*, I, p. 225).

Liber Coloniarum, p. 230 Lachmann (p. 50 Pais); p. 231 L. (p. 52 P.); p. 233 L.
    (p. 56 P.); p. 237 L. (p. 68 P.)

[Lucian.] *Nero, sive de fossione Isthmi.*[1]

Martial, VII, 21; 34; VIII, 70; X, 48; XI, 33; *Spect.* 2; 28 (besides numberless minor
    allusions).

Nero, *Fragmenta* (Morel, *Fragm. poet. lat.* pp. 131–2).

Octavia praetexta.

Oracula Sibyllina, IV, 119 *sqq.*; V, 28–34, 137 *sqq.*, 363 *sqq.*; VIII, 88–90, 140 *sqq.*;
    XII, 78 *sqq.* (ed. Geffcken).

Orosius, VII, 7.

Pausanias, II, 17, 6; 37, 5; V, 12, 8; 25, 8; 26, 3; VII, 17, 3–4; IX, 27, 3–4; X, 7,
    1; X, 19, 2.

St Peter, *Epistula*, I.

Philostratus, *De Tyanensi Apollonio libri* (ed. Conybeare), *passim.*

Pliny, *N.H.* IV, 10; VII, 45–6; XXII, 92; XXIII, 154; XXXIV, 45–7; 84; XXXVI, 111–13.

Pliny Minor, *Epist.* V, 5.

Plutarch, *Galba*; *Otho*; *Quomodo adulator*, 60 D (I, p. 146 Bernardakis); *De cohibenda
    ira*, 462 (III, p. 201); *De garrulitate*, 505 (III, p. 310); *De sera num. vind.* 567
    (III, p. 465); *Praecepta gerend. reipubl.* 810 (V, p. 90); 815 D (V, p. 103). His
    Life of Nero is lost.

Polyaenus, *Strateg.* VIII, 62.

Quintilian, *Inst. Orat.* VIII, 5, 18.

Statius, *Silvae*, II, 7 (Genethliacon Lucani ad Pollam).

Suetonius, *Vita Lucani.*

Sulpicius Severus, *Chronic.* II, 28–9, ed. Lavertujon.

Tertullian, *Apolog.* 5.

The works of Lucan, Persius, Petronius, and above all the younger Seneca are
important: all Seneca's writings, especially the *Apocolocyntosis* and the *de Clementia*,
contain valuable material for the general life of the period.

6. *Modern Works on the Sources*

(a) *Dio, Suetonius and Tacitus*

Besides the general studies on these authors (see pp. 898 *sq.*, 962, 963 *sq.*) the
following should be consulted:

Appelquist, H. S. *De praecipuis rerum Gai Claudii Neronis scriptoribus.* Helsing-
    forsiae, 1889.

Callegari, E. *Dei fonti per la storia di Nerone.* Atti Ist. Veneto, Ser. 6, VI, 1887,
    pp. 1099, 1397; VII, 1888, pp. 153, 219.

---

[1] But see the notice in P.W. XIII, 1752, where grounds are given for attributing this
dialogue to one of the two Philostrati.

Christensen, H. *De fontibus a Cassio Dione in vita Neronis enarranda adhibitis.* Berlin, 1871.

Ciaceri, E. *Claudio e Nerone nelle storie di Plinio.* (Processi Politici e Relazioni internazionali.) Rome, 1918, p. 387.

Momigliano, A. *Osservazioni sulle fonti per la storia di Caligola, Claudio, Nerone.* Rend. Linc., Ser. 6, VIII, 1932, p. 293.

Motzo, B. *I commentarii di Agrippina madre di Nerone.* Studi di Storia e Filologia, Cagliari, 1927. (Studi Cagliaritani di Storia e Filologia, I.) p. 19.

Reitzenstein, R. *Ein Stück hellenistischer Kleinliteratur.* Gött. Nach. 1904, p. 327.

(b) The Octavia *as a source*

Fuller information will be found in Herrmann, cited below.

Baehrens, W. *Die Octavia praetexta und Seneca.* Phil. Woch. 1923, col. 668.

Birt, Th. *Nochmals zur Octavia des sog. Seneca.* Phil. Woch. 1923, col. 740.

Cima, A. *La tragedia romana Octavia e gli annali di Tacito.* Pisa, 1904. (Cf. Riv. Fil. XXXIV, 1906, p. 529.)

Flinck, E. *De Octaviae praetextae auctore.* Helsingfors, 1919.

Herrmann, L. *Octavie, tragédie prétexte.* Paris, 1924.

Ladek, F. *De Octavia praetexta.* Diss. Phil. Vindobon. III, 1, 1891.

—— *Zur Frage über die histor. Quellen der Octavia.* Zeitschr. f. oesterr. Gymn. 1905, pp. 673, 865, 961.

Nordmeyer, G. *De Octavia fabula.* Leipzig, 1892. (Cf. Jahrb. f. class. Phil. XIX, Suppl. 1893, p. 257.)

Pease, A. St. *Is the Octavia a play of Seneca?* C.J. XV, 1920, p. 388.

Santoro, A. *Appunti sull' Ottavia.* Classici e Neolatini, VIII, 1912, p. 182.

Ussani, V. *Su l' Octavia.* Riv. Fil. XXIII, 1905, p. 449.

B. Modern Works

1. *General*

Besides the general histories cited in the General Bibliography, especially Dessau, von Domaszewski, and Schiller, the following should be noted:

Baring-Gould, G. *The tragedy of the Caesars.* London, 1892, II, p. 54.

Ferrero, G. *Néron.* Revue de Paris, 1906, p. 449.

Henderson, B. *The life and principate of the emperor Nero.* London, 1903.

Pelham, H. F. *Essays on Roman History.* Oxford, 1911, p. 43.

Raabe, A. H. *Geschichte und Bild von Nero nach den Quellen bearbeitet.* Utrecht, 1872.

Ranke, L. von. *Weltgeschichte.* III, 1, Leipzig, 1883, p. 109.

Schiller, H. *Geschichte des römischen Kaiserreichs unter Nero.* Berlin, 1872. (And see O. Hirschfeld's review in *G.G.A.* 1873, p. 74.)

Art. in P.W. Suppl. bd. III, *s.v.* Domitius Nero, cols. 349 *sqq.* (E. Hohl).

2. *Special Topics*

(a) *The Court. Literature and Art*

Bloch, G. *Remarques à propos de la carrière d'Afranius Burrus...d'après une inscription récemment découverte.* Annuaire de la Faculté des Lettres de Lyon, III, Paris, 1885, p. 1.

Boethius, A. *The Neronian "nova urbs."* Corolla Archeologica, Lund, 1932, p. 84.

Bücheler, F. *Zur höfischen Poesie unter Nero.* Rh. Mus. XXVI, 1871, p. 235 (= Kleine Schriften, II, p. 1).

Cichorius, C. *Chronologisches zu den Gedichten des Lucilius.* Römische Studien, Leipzig-Berlin, 1922, p. 372.

Dirichlet, G. *Der Philosoph Seneca als Quelle für die Beurteilung der ersten römischen Kaiser.* Königsberg, 1890.

Fabia, Ph. *Le troisième mariage de Néron.* Rev. Phil. N.S. xix, 1895, p. 218.

—— *L'adultère de Néron et de Poppée.* Rev. Phil. N.S. xx, 1896, p. 12.

—— *Comment Poppée devint impératrice.* Rev. Phil. N.S. xxi, 1897, p. 221.

—— *Le gentilice de Tigelin.* Rev. Phil. N.S. xxi, 1897, p. 160.

—— *Le règne et la morte de Poppée.* Rev. Phil. N.S. xxii, 1898, p. 333.

—— *Néron acteur.* Lyons, 1906.

—— *Sénèque et Néron.* J. d. Sav. 1910, p. 260.

—— *La mère de Néron. À propos d'un plaidoyer pour Agrippina.* Rev. Phil. N.S. xxxv, 1911, p. 144.

Faider, P. *Études sur Sénèque.* Ghent, 1921, p. 209.

Ferrero, G. *Le donne dei Cesari.* Milan, 1925, p. 119.

Friedländer, L. *Der Philosoph Seneca.* H.Z. (N.F.) li, 1900, p. 193.

Friedrich, W. L. *Burrus und Seneca Reichsverweser unter Nero.* B.P.W. 1914, col. 1342.

Haguenin, E. *Perse a-t-il attaqué Néron?* Rev. Phil. N.S. xxiii, 1899, p. 301.

Hartman, J. J. *De Nerone, Poppaea, Othone.* Mnem. N.S. xxvi, 1898, p. 314.

Heikel, J. A. *Senecas Charakter und politische Thätigkeit aus seinen Schriften beleuchtet.* Acta Soc. Scient. Fennicae, xvi, 1888, p. 1.

Hochart, P. *Études sur la vie de Sénèque.* Paris, 1885.

Kornemann, E. *Doppelprinzipat und Reichsteilung im imperium romanum.* Leipzig-Berlin, 1930, p. 57.

Loth, A. *Acte, sa conversion au christianisme.* Rev. Quest. hist. xviii, 1875, p. 58.

Marchesi, C. *Seneca.* Messina, 1920, Parte i, La Vita.

Parmeggiani, L. *Claudia Atte liberta di Nerone.* Riv. stor. ant. viii, 1904, p. 455.

Pascal, C. *Seneca.* Catania, 1906.

Paul, L. *Die Vergottung Neros durch Lucanus.* Jahrb. class. Phil. cxlix, 1894, p. 409.

Sandels, Fr. *Die Stellung der Kaiserlichen Frauen aus dem jülischen-claudischen Hause.* Giessen Diss. Darmstadt, 1912.

Silvagni, U. *Le donne dei Cesari.* Ed. 3, Turin, 1927, p. 290.

Stahr, A. *Agrippina die Mutter Neros.* Ed. 2, Berlin, 1880.

Stella Maranca, F. da, *L. Anneo Seneca nel Consilium Principis.* Rend. Linc., Ser. v, xxxii, 1923, p. 282.

Van Deman, E. B. *The sacra via of Nero.* Mem. Amer. Acad. in Rome, v, 1925, p. 115.

de la Ville de Mirmont, H. *Afranius Burrhus, la légende traditionnelle, les documents épigraphiques et historiques.* Rev. Phil. N.S. xxxiv, 1910, p. 23.

Walz, R. *La vie politique de Sénèque.* Paris, 1909.

—— *A propos d'Afranius Burrus.* Rev. Phil. N.S. xxxiv, 1910, p. 244.

Weege, F. *Das Goldene Haus des Nero.* J.D.A.I. xxviii, 1913, p. 127.

(b) Nero, Greece and the Hellenistic East

Birt, Th. *Zur Phylenordnung Alexandrias.* Rh. Mus. lxv, 1910, p. 317.

Blumenthal, F. *Der ägyptische Kaiserkult.* Arch. Pap. v, 1913, p. 316.

Deissmann, A. *Licht vom Osten.* Ed. 4. Tübingen, 1923, pp. 301–2.

Fabia, Ph. *Néron et les Rhodiens.* Rev. Phil. N.S. xx, 1896, p. 188.

Gatti, G. *Nerone e la libertà ellenica.* Bull. Ist. Diritto Romano, ii, 1889, p. 136.

Gerster, M. B. *L'Isthme de Corinthe, tentatives de percement dans l'antiquité.* B.C.H. viii, 1884, p. 225.

Glotz, G. *Les 6475 dans les cités grecques d'Egypte*. Rev. Arch. 4 Sér. XVIII, 1911, p. 256.

Holleaux, M. *Discours de Néron prononcé à Corinthe pour rendre aux Grecs la liberté*. B.C.H. XII, 1888, p. 510.

—— *Discours prononcé par Néron à Corinthe en rendant aux Grecs la liberté*. Lyons, 1889.

Plaumann, G. *Die ἐν 'Αρσινοίτῃ ἄνδρες Ἕλληνες 6475*. Arch. Pap. VI, 1920, p. 178.

Schumann, G. *Hellenistische und griechische Elemente in der Regierung Neros*. Leipzig, 1930.

Schur, W. *Die Orientpolitik des Kaisers Nero*. Klio, Beiheft XV, Leipzig, 1923.

—— *Zur Neronischen Orientalpolitik*. Klio, XX, 1925, p. 215.

Vogt, J. *Die alexandrinische Münzen*. Stuttgart, 1924, p. 26.

Wilcken, U. *Kaiser Nero und die Alexandrinischen Phylen*. Arch. Pap. V, 1913, p. 182.

(c) The Opposition

See also the general works, especially Henderson, and the bibliography to Chapter XXV.

Barbagallo, C. *La catastrofe di Nerone*. Catania, 1915.

Boissier, G. *L'opposition sous les Césars*. Ed. 1, Paris, 1875.

Ciaceri, E. *La congiura pisoniana contro Nerone*. Processi Politici e Relazioni internazionali. Rome, 1918, p. 363.

Giri, G. *Della credibilità del delitto di Lucano contro la madre*. Classici e Neolatini, VIII, 1912, p. 47.

Mancini, C. *Storia di P. Helvidio Prisco*. Atti Real. Acc. Arch. Napoli, 1883, p. 59.

Sievers, G. R. *Nero und Galba*. *Studien zur Geschichte der römischen Kaiser*, Berlin, 1870, p. 107.

de la Ville de Mirmont, H. *C. Calpurnius Piso et la conspiration de l'an* 818/65. Rev. E. A. XV, 1913, p. 405; XVI, 1914, pp. 45, 197, 295.

Willems, J. *Le sénat romain en l'an 65 après Jésus-Christ*. Mus. B. IV, 1900, p. 236; V, 1901, p. 89; VI, 1902, p. 100.

(d) The Great Fire at Rome and the Persecution of the Christians

This is selective and comprises those works which the author has found most useful in writing the chapter: only Henderson's *Nero* is important among general works.

Allard, B. *Les Chrétiens ont-ils incendié Rome sous Néron?* Paris, 1904.

Arnold, C. F. *Die Neronische Christenverfolgung*. Leipzig, 1888.

Batiffol, P. *L'église naissante*. Rev. Bib. III, 1894, p. 503.

Caiati, G. *Una nuova ipotesi sulle origini dell' incendio neroniano*. Rivista d' Italia, 1916, p. 705.

Callewaert, C. *Le délit de Christianisme dans les deux premiers siècles*. Rev. Quest. hist. LXXIV, 1903, p. 28.

Cézard, L. *Histoire juridique des persécutions contre les Chrétiens de Néron à Septime Sévère*. Paris, 1911, p. 3.

Coen, A. *La persecuzione neroniana dei Cristiani*. Atene e Roma, III, 1900, cols. 249; 297; 329.

Conrat, M. *Die Christenverfolgungen im Römischen Reiche vom Standpunkte der Juristen*. Leipzig, 1897.

Corssen, P. *Die Zeugnisse des Tacitus und Pseudo-Josephus über Christus.* Zeits. f. neutest. Wissensch. XIV, 1913, p. 114.

Cuq, E. *De la nature des crimes imputés aux Chrétiens d'après Tacite.* Mél. d'arch. et d'hist. VI, 1886, p. 115.

Guérin, L. *Étude sur le fondement juridique des persécutions dirigées contre les Chrétiens.* Nouvelle Revue Historique, XIX, 1895, pp. 601, 714.

Hardy, E. G. *Christianity and the Roman Government.* London, 1894, p. 54.

Hirschfeld, O. *Die neronische Christenverfolgung.* Kleine Schriften, p. 407.

Hochart, P. *Études au sujet de la persécution des Chrétiens sous Néron.* Paris, 1885.

Hülsen, C. *The burning of Rome under Nero.* A.J.A. XIII, 1909, p. 45.

Klette, E. Th. *Die Christenkatastrophe unter Nero nach ihren Quellen, insbesondere nach Tac. ann.* XV, 44 *von neuem untersucht.* Tübingen, 1907 (and cf. the review by G. Andresen, in *Jahresberichte d. philol. Vereins zu Berlin,* XXXIV, 1908, p. 362).

Linck, K. *De antiquissimis veterum quae ad Jesum Nazarenum spectant testimoniis.* Religionsg. Versuche und Vorarbeiten, XIV, 1913, pp. 88–9.

Meyer, E. *Ursprung und Anfänge des Christentums.* Stuttgart-Berlin, III, 1923, p. 500.

Mommsen, Th. *Der Religionsfrevel nach römischem Recht.* Ges. Schriften, III, p. 389.

Nestle, W. "*Odium generis humani*" (*zu Tac. ann.* XV, 44). Klio, XXI, 1926, p. 91.

Pascal, C. *L' incendio di Roma e i primi Cristiani.* Ed. 2, Turin, 1900 (= *Fatti e Leggende di Roma antica,* Catania, 1903, p. 117).

—— *Di una nuova fonte per l' incendio neroniano.* Atene e Roma, IV, 1901, col. 137.

Pirro, A. *Tacito e la persecuzione neroniana dei Cristiani.* Studi Storici Ant. Class. IV, 1911, p. 152.

Profumo, A. *Le fonti e i tempi dell' incendio neroniano.* Roma, 1905.

Renan, E. *L'antéchrist.* Paris, 1873.

Schiller, H. *Ein Problem der Tacituserklärung.* Comment. Phil. in honorem Th. Mommsenii, Berlin, 1877, p. 41.

Schoenaich, G. *Die neronische Christenverfolgung.* Breslau, 1911.

Weiss, J. E. *Christenverfolgungen, Geschichte ihrer Ursachen im Römerreiche.* Munich, 1899, p. 30.

Werner, P. *De incendiis urbis Romae aetate imperatorum.* Leipzig, 1906.

Zeller, E. *Das odium generis humani der Christen.* Zeitschr. wiss. Theol. XXXIV, 1891, p. 359.

(e) Chronology

Constans, M. L. *Les puissances tribuniciennes de Néron.* C.R.Ac. Inscr. 1912, p. 385.

Holzapfel, L. *Römische Kaiserdaten.* Klio, XII, 1912, p. 483 (the date of Nero's death).

Mattingly, H. *The date of the tribunicia potestas of Nero and the coins.* Num. Chr. Ser. IV, XIX, 1919, p. 199.

—— '*Tribunicia potestate.*' J.R.S. XX, 1930, pp. 79–80.

Stobbe, H. F. *Die Tribunenjahre der Römischen Kaiser.* Phil. XXXII, 1872, p. 23.

On the chronology of the imperatorial salutations see E. Maynial in Rev. Arch. XXXIX, 1901, p. 167, and *ib.* N.S. IV, 1904, p. 172, and H. Stuart Jones, *ib.* N.S. III, 1904, p. 263.

(*f*) *Miscellaneous*

Anderson, J. G. C. *Trajan on the Quinquennium Neronis.* J.R.S. I, 1911, p. 173.

Cantarella, R. *Le ultime parole di Nerone morente.* Il Mondo Classico, I, 1931, fasc. 2, p. 53.

Cumont, F. *L'iniziazione di Nerone da parte di Tiridate d' Armenia.* Riv. Fil. N.S. XI, 1933, p. 145.

Haverfield, F. *A note on the Quinquennium Neronis.* J.R.S. I, 1911, p. 178.

Hirschfeld, O. *Der Brand von Lugdunum.* Rh. Mus. LII, 1897, p. 294.

Janne, H. *Une affaire de Christianisme sous Néron* (65 apr. J.-C.). L'Antiquité Classique, II, 1933, p. 331.

Pais, E. *Il liber coloniarum.* Mem. Acc. Lincei, Ser. V, Vol. XVI, 1920, pp. 55–94; 377–411.

Quilling, F. *Die Juppitersäule des Samus und Severus.* Leipzig, 1918.

Sogliano, A. *Colonie Neroniane.* Rend. Linc. Ser. V Vol. VI, 1897, p. 389.

(*g*) *Nero in Art and Legend*

Callegari, E. *Nerone nell' arte figurativa contemporanea.* Venice, 1891.

—— *Nerone e la sua corte nella storia e nell' arte.* I, L' arte antica e mediana. Venice, 1892.

Geffcken, J. *Studien zur älteren Nerossage.* Gött. Nach. 1899, p. 441.

Gnoli, D. *Nerone nell' arte contemporanea.* Studi Letterari, Bologna, 1883, p. 241.

Graf, A. *Roma nella memoria e nelle immaginazioni del medio evo.* Turin, 1882, I, p. 332.

Kampers, F. *Die deutsche Kaiseridee in Prophetie und Sage.* Munich, 1896, pp. 5–15 (Ed. 2 of *Kaiserprophetieen und Kaisersagen im Mittelalter,* 1895).

Nordmeyer, G. *Der Tod Neros in der Legende.* Festschrift des Gymnasiums Adolfinum zu Mörs, 1896, p. 27.

Pascal, C. *Nerone nella storia aneddotica e nella leggenda.* Milan, 1923.

Pincherle, A. *Gli oracoli sibillini giudaici.* Rome, 1922, pp. 113–19.

Reville, A. *Néron l'Antichrist, Essais de Critique Religieuse.* Ed. 2, Paris, 1869, p. 79.

CHAPTER XXII

THE EASTERN FRONTIER FROM TIBERIUS TO NERO

The ancient sources are cited at the relevant places in the text of the chapter.
Besides the relevant portions of the histories of Schiller, Mommsen, Dessau, Rawlinson, and von Gutschmid cited in the General Bibliography and Bibliography to chapter IX, see:

1. *Egypt and Arabia*

von Domaszewski, A. *Die Rangordnung d. röm. Heeres* (see above, p. 920), pp. 119 *sqq.*
Lesquier, J. *L'armée romaine d'Égypte* (see above, p. 920), pp. 119–132.
Rostovtzeff, M. *Zur Geschichte der Ost- und Südhandels in ptolemäisch-römischen Ägypten.* Arch. Pap. IV, 1908, p. 306.
Tkač, J. Art. *s.v.* Saba in P.W. cols. 1461 *sqq.*
Kornemann, E. *Die historischen Nachrichten des Periplus Maris Erythraei über Arabien.* Janus, I, 1921, p. 55.
Schur, W. *Die Orientpolitik des Kaisers Nero.* Klio, Beiheft XV, 1923, pp. 45 *sqq.*
Charlesworth, M. P. *Some Notes on the Periplus Maris Erythraei.* C.Q. XXII, 1928, p. 92.
Kortenbeutel, H. *Der ägyptische Süd- und Osthandel in der Politik der Ptolemäer und römischen Kaiser.* Diss. Berlin, 1932, pp. 58–63.

2. *Armenia and Parthia: the Eastern Frontiers*

Egli, E. *Feldzüge in Armenien vom 41–63 n. Chr.* Untersuchungen zur röm. Kaisergeschichte, herausg. von Max Büdinger, I. Leipzig, 1868, pp. 265 *sqq.*
Furneaux, H. *The Annals of Tacitus*, II (see above, p. 921), pp. 103 *sqq.*
Günther, A. *Beiträge zur Geschichte der Kriege zwischen Römern und Parthern.* Berlin, 1922, p. 75.
von Gutschmid, A. *Gotarzes.* Kleine Schriften, III. Leipzig, 1892, pp. 43 *sqq.*
Gwatkin, W. E. *Cappadocia as a Roman procuratorial province.* Univ. of Missouri Studies, V. Columbia, Miss. 1930.
Henderson, B. W. *The Chronology of the wars in Armenia* A.D. 51–63. C.R. XV, 1901, pp. 159, 204, 266.
—— *The Life and Principate of the emperor Nero.* London, 1903, chs. V–VI.
Herzfeld, E. *Sakastan: geschichtliche Untersuchungen zu den Ausgrabungen am Kūh i Khwādja.* Archaeol. Mitteilungen aus Iran, IV, 1932, pp. 1 *sqq.*
Latyshev, V. V. *Ios. P.E.* II, St. Petersburg, 1890, pp. xlii–xlv.
Magie, D. *Roman Policy in Armenia and Transcaucasia.* Ann. Report of Amer. Hist. Assoc. for 1919, I, 1923, p. 297.
Markwart, J. *Iberer und Hyrkanier.* Caucasia, fasc. 8, 1931, p. 78.
Marsh, F. B. *The Reign of Tiberius.* Oxford, 1931, pp. 78, 211.
Minns, E. H. *Scythians and Greeks.* Cambridge, 1913, pp. 597 *sqq.*
Momigliano, A. *Corbulone e la politica Romana verso i Parti.* Atti del II° Congresso Nazionale di Studi Romani. Rome, 1931, p. 368.
Parker, H. M. D. *The Roman Legions.* Oxford, 1928, pp. 132, 181.
Ritterling, E. Art. *s.v.* Legio in P.W. (cols. 1242, 1254 *sqq.* and under the individual legions).
Rostovtzeff, M. *Iranians and Greeks in South Russia.* Oxford, 1922, pp. 117, 153.
Schiller, H. *Geschichte des römischen Kaiserreichs unter der Regierung des Nero.* Berlin, 1872, p. 91.

Schoonover, D. T. *A Study of Cn. Domitius Corbulo as found in the "Annals" of Tacitus.* Diss. Chicago, 1909.

Schur, W. *Die Orientpolitik d. Kaisers Nero* (see Section 1).

—— *Untersuchungen zur Geschichte der Kriege Corbulos.* Klio, xix, 1925, p. 75.

—— *Zur Neronischen Orientpolitik.* Klio, xx, 1925, p. 215.

—— *Die orientalische Frage im römischen Reiche.* N.J. f. Wiss. 11, 1926, p. 270.

Täubler, E. *Die Parthernachrichten bei Josephus.* Diss. Berlin, 1904.

—— *Zur Geschichte der Alanen.* Klio, ix, 1909, p. 14.

Willrich, H. *Caligula.* v. *Der Orient unter Gaius.* Klio, iii, 1903, p. 297.

See also:

Andresen, G. Review of Henderson's *Chronology* in *Jahresber. d. philol. Vereins zu Berlin*, xxvii, 1901, p. 318.

—— Review of Schur's *Untersuchungen, ib.* xlix, 1924, p. 145.

and the following critiques of Schur's *Orientpolitik*: G. De Sanctis, *Riv. stor. ital.* N.S. iii, 1925, p. 199. W. Ensslin, *B.P.W.* 1924, p. 579. E. Hohl, *Deutsche Literaturzeitung*, xlv, 1924, p. 915. O. Leuze, *O.L.Z.* xxvii, 1924, p. 343.

On Armenian topography besides the works cited in Vol. ix, p. 928, see:

Hübschmann, H. *Die altarmenischen Ortsnamen.* Indo-germ. Forschungen, xvi, 1904, pp. 177 *sqq.*

Markwart, J. *Südarmenien und die Tigrisquellen.* Studien zur armenischen Geschichte, iv. Vienna, 1930.

Articles in P.W. *s.vv.*: Antiochos IV (Wilcken), Archelaos, 15 (Wilcken), Artaxias, 3 (Wilcken), Domitius Corbulo (Stein, Suppl. bd. iii), Domitius-Nero (Hohl), Gotarzes (Stein), Hyrkania (Kiessling), M. Iulius Agrippa, I and II (Rosenberg), Iulius-Germanicus (Gelzer), Izates (Weissbach), Kotys (2), 9, 10 (Kahrstedt), Mithridates, 16, 33 (Geyer), Radamistus (Stein), Sohaemus, 3 (Stein).

CHAPTER XXIII

THE NORTHERN FRONTIERS FROM TIBERIUS TO NERO

PART I. THE RHINE AND THE DANUBE (Sections I, II and V)

I. THE RHINE

A. ANCIENT SOURCES

1. *Inscriptions*

Cf. above, p. 941 (Bibliography to c. XII, Section VI). The following inscriptions may here be mentioned:

Dessau 950. Acta Fratrum Arvalium, *C.I.L.* VI, 32346. *C.I.L.* XIII, 11513–4, 11853–6.

2. *Literary evidence*

Cf. above, p. 941 (Bibliography to c. XII, Section VI). The following are the most important passages:

Pliny, *N.H.* XXXI, 20. Tacitus, *Ann.* II, 45–6, 88; III, 40–7; IV, 72–4; VI, 30; XI, 16–20; XII, 27–8; XIII, 53–7. Suetonius, *Tib.* 41; *Calig.* 43–51; *Claud.* 24; *Galba*, 6, 8. Dio LIX, 21–2; LX, 8, 7; 30, 4–6. Eutropius VII, 12, 2.

B. MODERN WORKS

Almost all the items referred to above in the bibliography to c. XII, section VI, 1 and 2, will here be required. For Gaius on the Rhine, see the bibliography to Ch. XX, A, 2, (*b*) i. In addition, the following:

Barthel, W. R.-G. K. Ber. VI, 1910–11, pp. 123–5 (criticism of Hofmann's views).

Bohn, O. *Rheinische 'Lagerstädte.'* Germ. X, 1926, p. 25.

Dahm, O. *Der römische Bergbau an der unteren Lahn.* B.J. 101, 1897, p. 117.

—— *Der Raubzug der Chatten nach Obergermanien im Jahre 50 n. Chr. Ib.* p. 128.

Forrer, R. *Strasbourg-Argentorate*, I. Strasbourg, 1927.

Hofmann, H. *Zur Frage der vorflavischen Okkupation des rechten Rheinufers.* Mainzer Zeitschr. VI, 1911, p. 31.

Klinkenberg, J. *Die ältesten bekannten Bürger Kölns.* (Reprinted from Jahrbuch des Kölnischen Geschichtsvereins, XII, 1930.)

Münzer, F. *Die Quellen des Tacitus für die Germanenkriege.* B.J. 104, 1899, p. 66 (the elder Pliny on the Rhine).

Revellio, P. *Kastell Hüfingen.* Germ. X, 1926, p. 16; XI, 1927, p. 98.

Ritterling, E. *Ein Offizier des Rheinheeres aus der Zeit des Caligula.* Germ. I, 1917, p. 170.

—— *Das frührömische Lager bei Hofheim i. T.* (=Nassauische Annalen, 40). Wiesbaden, 1913.

Sadée, E. *Über den Stand der Alisofrage.* IV. *Einiges zur Gesch. des rechtsrheinischen Vorgeländes von Vetera in der Kaiserzeit seit 16 n. Chr.* B.J. 130, 1925, pp. 306–309.

II. THE DANUBE

A. ANCIENT SOURCES

1. *Inscriptions*

Dessau 231, 938, 962, 969, 970, 971, 985, 986, 1349, 1987, 2281, 2478, 2737, 5829, 5829*a*, 9197. *C.I.L.* II, 3272; V, 8002 (= Dessau 208); 8003. *S.E.G.* I, 329. *Ann. épig.* 1926, n. 8, 19.

2. *Literary evidence.*

Ovid, *Ex Ponto*, I, 8, 11–20; IV, 7, 9, 75–80, 119–120; *Tristia*, II, 197–200. Josephus, *Bell. Jud.* II, 16, 4. Tacitus, *Germ.* 41–2; *Hist.* III, 5; *Ann.* I, 76, 80; II, 44, 62–7; III, 38–9; IV, 46–51; VI, 39; XII, 29–30. Pliny, *N.H.* IV, 80–1. Suetonius, *Tib.* 41; *Claud.* 25. Appian, *Ill.* 30. Dio LVIII, 25, 4.

B. MODERN WORKS

Many of the items quoted above in section V of the bibliography of c. XII above are relevant, especially the exhaustive study of C. Patsch, Wien S.B., 1932. In addition:

Abramić, M. *Novi natpisi iz Poetovija*. Časopis za Zgodovino in Narodopisje. Maribor, 1931, p. 177.

Cuntz, O. *Römische Inschriften aus Emona*. Jahrbuch für Altertumskunde, VII, 1913, pp. 195–200.

Dessau, H. *Zur Reihenfolge der Statthalter Moesiens*. Jahreshefte XXIII, 1926, Beiblatt, col. 345.

von Domaszewski, A. *Zur Geschichte der römischen Provinzialverwaltung*, I. *Moesia und Hispania Citerior*. Rh. Mus. 45, 1890, p. 1.

Fabia, P. *Sur une page perdue et sur les livres* XVI, XVII, XVIII *des Annales de Tacite*. Rev. E.A. XXXIV, 1932, p. 139.

Groag, E. Art. *s.v.* P. Memmius (29) Regulus in P.W.

Lambrino, S. *Observations sur un nouveau diplôme de l'empereur Claude*. Rev. Phil. (IIIe Série), V, 1931, p. 251.

Pârvan, B. *Histria*, IV. Analale Academiei Române. Mem. Sect. Ist. XXXVIII, 1915/6. Bucarest, 1916.

Schmidt, L. *Das Regnum Vannianum*. Hermes, XLVIII, 1913, p. 292.

Schwarz, E. *Über das Reich des Vannius*. Sudeta, VII, 1931, p. 145.

Stein, A. *Römische Reichsbeamte der Provinz Thracia*. Sarajevo, 1921.

Der römische Limes in Oesterreich, XII, 1914, pp. 166 *sqq.*; XVI, 1926, pp. 8 *sqq.*; XVII, 1933, pp. 76 *sqq.*

PART II. BRITAIN (Sections III–IV)

A. ANCIENT SOURCES

1. *Literary*

Frontinus, *Strat.* II, 13, 11.

Horace, *Odes*, I, 35, 39; III, 5, 2–4.

Strabo, II, 115–116; IV, 200–201.

Suetonius, *Calig.* 19; 44; 46; *Claud.* 17; *Nero*, 18; *Vesp.* 4.

Tacitus, *Ann.* XII, 31–40; XIV, 29–39; *Agric.* 5; 10–16.

On Tacitus, *Agricola*, see H. Furneaux and J. G. C. Anderson, Tacitus, *de vita Agricolae*, Oxford, 1922; on Tacitus, *Annals*, see H. Furneaux, H. F. Pelham and C. D. Fisher, *Annals* XI–XVI, Oxford, 1907.

2. *Epigraphic*

The British material is (*a*) C.I.L. VII; (*b*) supplements in Eph. Epigr. III, IV, VII, IX; (*c*) Haverfield, F., *Roman Britain in* 1913 and *Roman Britain in* 1914; (*d*) annually in J.R.S. from vol. XI.

Very few inscriptions refer to this period. The chief are: Res Gestae 32; C.I.L. VI, 920 = Dessau 216 (Claudius); C.I.L. VII, 11 (Cogidubnus), 12 (Nero), 1201 (pig of Mendip lead, A.D. 49), and some tombstones, *e.g.* C.I.L. VII, 155, Eph. Epigr. VII, 903, J.R.S. XVIII, no. 5.

B. MODERN WORKS

Atkinson, D. *The Governors of Britain from Claudius to Diocletian.* J.R.S. XII, 1922, p. 60.

British Museum Guide to Early Iron Age Antiquities. London, 1925.

British Museum Guide to Antiquities of Roman Britain. London, 1922.

Brooke, G. C. *The Distribution of Gaulish and British Coins in Britain.* Antiquity, VII, 1933, p. 268.

Bulleid, A. and H. St G. Gray. *The Glastonbury Lake Village.* Glastonbury, 1911.

Bushe-Fox, J. P. *Excavations at Hengistbury Head, Hants.* London, 1915.

—— *Excavation of the Late Celtic Urnfield at Swarling, Kent.* London, 1925.

—— *First (second) Report on the excavation of the Roman Fort at Richborough, Kent.* London, 1926, 1928.

Collingwood, R. G. *The Fosse.* J.R.S. XIV, 1924, p. 252.

Curwen, E. C. *Excavations in the Trundle, Goodwood,* 1928. Sussex Arch. Collections.

Evans, A. J. *On a Late Celtic Urnfield at Aylesford.* Archaeologia, LII, 1891, p. 315.

Evans, J. *The Coins of the Ancient Britons.* London, 1864.

Haverfield, F. and G. Macdonald. *Roman Occupation of Britain.* Oxford, 1924.

Hawkes, C. F. C. *Hill-forts.* Antiquity, V, 1931, p. 60.

Hawkes, C. F. C. and G. C. Dunning. *The Belgae of Gaul and Britain.* Archaeol. Journ. LXXXVII, 1930, p. 150.

Hawkes, C. F. C., J. N. L. Myres and C. G. Stevens. *St Catherine's Hill.* Proc. Hants. Field Club, XI, 1930.

Holmes, T. Rice. *Ancient Britain and the Invasions of Julius Caesar.* Oxford, 1907.

Laver, P. G. *The Excavation of a Tumulus at Lexden, Colchester.* Archaeologia, LXXVI, 1927, p. 241.

Leeds, E. T. *Celtic Ornament in the British Isles down to* A.D. 700. Oxford, 1933.

Oman, C. W. C. *England before the Norman Conquest.* London, 1910.

Pryce, T. D. and F. Oswald. *Roman London: its initial occupation as evidenced by early types of Terra Sigillata.* Archaeologia, LXXVIII, 1928, p. 73.

Royal Commission on Historical Monuments. *Roman London.* London, 1928.

Wheeler, R. E. M. *London in Roman Times.* London, 1930.

—— *A Prehistoric Metropolis: the first Verulamium.* Antiquity, VI, 1932, p. 133.

—— *Belgic Cities of Britain.* Antiquity, VII, 1933, p. 21.

Wheeler, R. E. M. and P. G. Laver. *Roman Colchester.* J.R.S. IX, 1919, p. 139.

CHAPTER XXIV

THE YEAR OF THE FOUR EMPERORS

A. Ancient Sources

Dio, fragments of Books LXIII–LXIV (Boissevain's edition, vol. III, pp. 84–134).
Josephus, *Bell. Jud.* IV [9, 2], 491–502; [9, 9], 545–549; [10, 1], 585–[11, 5], 663.
Plutarch, *Galba; Otho.* See E. G. Hardy, *Plutarch's Lives of Galba and Otho*, with Introduction and explanatory notes. London, 1890.
Suetonius, *Galba; Otho; Vitellius; Vesp.* 5–7; *Domit.* 1. See G. W. Mooney, *C. Suetoni Tranquilli de vita Caesarum libri* VII–VIII, with introduction, translation, and commentary. Dublin, 1930.
Tacitus, *Hist.* I–V. See W. A. Spooner, *The Histories of Tacitus*, with introduction, notes, and an index. London, 1891. (Besides the Oxford and Teubner texts of the *Histories* that by J. van der Vliet, Groningen, 1910, should be mentioned).

B. Modern Works

In addition to the relevant pages in the general histories of the Empire cited in the General Bibliography, the following publications should be noted:

Fabia, Ph. *L'ambassade d'Othon aux Vitelliens.* Rev. Phil. XXXVII, 1913, p. 53.
—— *La journée du 15 Janvier 69 à Rome.* Ib. XXXVI, 1912, p. 78.
—— *La lettre de Pompeius Propinquus à Galba.* Klio, IV, 1904, p. 42.
—— *Les prétoriens de Vitellius.* Rev. d'hist. de Lyon, III, 1903, p. 89.
—— *Vitellius à Lyon.* Rev. Phil. XXXVIII, 1914, p. 33.
Feliciani, N. *L'anno dei quattro imperatori.* Riv. stor. ant. XI, 1907, p. 3; p. 378.
Groag, E. *Zur Kritik von Tacitus' Quellen in die Historien.* Jahrb. f. class. Phil. Suppl. bd. XXIII, 1897, p. 709.
Hardy, E. G. *Studies in Roman History.* (Second Series.) London, 1909, pp. 130–268.
—— *Tacitus as a military historian in the Historie .* J.P. XXXI, 1910, p. 123.
Henderson, B. W. *Civil War and Rebellion in the Roman Empire.* London, 1908.
—— *Life and Principate of the Emperor Nero.* London, 1903.
Holzapfel, L. *Römische Kaiserdaten.* Klio, XII, 1912, p. 483; XIII, 1913, p. 289; XV, 1917, p. 99.
Köster, F. *Der Marsch der Invasionsarmee des Fabius Valens von Niederrhein nach Italien.* Münster, 1927.
Momigliano, A. *Vitellio.* St. Fil. IX, 1931, p. 117.
Mommsen, Th. *Der letzte Kampf der römischen Republik.* Ges. Schriften, IV, p. 333.
—— *Die Zwei Schlachten von Bedriacum in Jahre 69 n. Chr.* Ib. p. 354.
Nischer, E. *Die Schlacht bei Cremona.* Klio, XX, 1927, p. 187.
Paul, L. *Kaiser Marcus Salvius Otho.* Rh. Mus. LVII, 1902, p. 76.
Valmaggi, L. *Sulla campagna flavio-vitelliana del* 69. Klio, IX, 1909, p. 252.

The following articles in P.W. *s.vv.* Antonius (89) Primus (Rohden), Caecina Alienus (Groag), Fabius (151) Valens (Goldfinger), Flavius (206) Vespasianus (Weynand), Julius (534) Vindex (Fluss), Licinius (116 a) Mucianus (Kappelmacher), Salvius (21) Otho (Nagl), and Sulpicius (63) Galba (Fluss).

CHAPTER XXV

REBELLION WITHIN THE EMPIRE

PART I. THE RHINE (Sections I–III)

A. ANCIENT SOURCES

Tacitus, *Hist.* IV, 12–37, 54–79, 85, 86; V, 14–26. (For texts and editions see Bibliography to Chapter XXIV, section A.)

Tacitus provides the only continuous narrative of any value. Scattered references to events of the rebellion will be found in Dio, LXVI, 3, 3; Frontinus, *Strat.* IV, 3, 14; Josephus, *Bell. Jud.* VII [4, 2], 75–88; Martial, II, 2; Plutarch, *Amatorius*, 25, p. 700; Silius Italicus, III, 607–8; and Suetonius, *Domit.* 2, 1.

B. MODERN WORKS

Bang, M. *Die Germanen im römischen Dienst bis zum Regierungsantritt Constantins I.* Berlin, 1906.
Fabia, Ph. *Le premier consulat de Petilius Cerialis.* Rev. Phil. XXXIV, 1910, p. 5.
Henderson, B. W. *Civil War and Rebellion in the Roman Empire.* London, 1908.
Jullian, C. *Histoire de la Gaule.* Vol. IV, pp. 183–223.
Mommsen, Th. *The Provinces of the Roman Empire.* London, 1909, vol. I, pp. 127–145.
Münzer, F. *Die Quelle des Tacitus für die Germanenkriege.* B.J. 104, 1899, p. 85.
Nissen, T. *Der batavische Krieg.* B.J. 111–112, 1904, p. 82.
Vulič, N. *Petilius Cerialis.* Klio, VII, 1907, p. 457.

See also the article in P.W. *s.v.* Julius (186) Civilis (E. Stein).

PART II. JUDAEA (Sections IV–VII)

I. ANCIENT SOURCES

Acts of the Apostles, V, 36 *sq.*; XI, 28; XXI, 38.
Dio, LXVI, 1; 4–8.
Eusebius, *Hist. eccl.* III, 5, 2–3.
Josephus, *Bell. Jud.*; *Ant.* XX; *Vita.*
Orosius, VII, 9.
Procopius, *de bello gothico*, I, 12; *de bello vandalico*, II, 9 (Dindorf).
Suetonius, *Vesp.* 5; *Tit.* 4–5.
Sulpicius Severus, *Chron.* II, 30.
Tacitus, *Ann.* XII, 54; *Hist.* V, 9–13.
Theophanes, *Chronographia*, I, pp. 109, 199 (De Boor).
Zonaras, VI, 12–29 (derived from Josephus).

On passages from the Talmud (though of small importance for the reconstruction of events) see J. Dérenbourg, *Essai sur l'histoire et la géographie de la Palestine*, I, Paris 1867, p. 247.

On coins see E. Schürer, *Geschichte des jüdischen Volkes im Zeitalter Jesu Christi*, I, 3–4 ed., Leipzig, 1901, p. 765 (with Bibliography).

See also the useful collection edited by Th. Reinach, *Textes d'auteurs grecs et romains relatifs au Judaïsme*, Paris, 1895.

The latinized version of the *Bellum Judaicum*, the so-called Hegesippus or Josippus, edited by Weber-Caesar, Marburg 1864, has been republished by V. Ussani in the *Corpus Script. Eccl. Lat.* vol. LXVI, 1932. Of the Slavonic version only the first four books in a German translation are so far available: *Flavius Josephus vom Jüdischen Kriege, Buch I–IV, nach der slavischen Uebersetzung deutsch herausgegeben...von* A. Berendts u. K. Grass, Dorpat, 1924–27. It is impossible to take up any definite stand about the problems raised by this version (especially after the appearance of R. Eisler's Ἰησοῦς βασιλεὺς οὐ βασιλεύσας, Heidelberg, 1928–30) until the whole text has been published. See above, p. 885.

II. Modern Works on the Sources

The notices about Josephus are concerned only with the *Bellum Judaicum* and the *Vita*. Fuller details in Schürer, *op. cit.* I, 1901, p. 57 (The memoirs of Vespasian); p. 58 (Antonius Julianus); pp. 58–63 (Justus of Tiberias); pp. 78–106 (Flavius Josephus).

Baerwald, A. *Josephus in Galiläa, sein Verhältniss zu den Parteien, insbesondere zu Justus von Tiberias und Agrippa II.* Breslau, 1877.

Bernays, J. *Ueber die Chronik des Sulpicius Severus.* Gesamm. Abhandl. II, 1885, p. 159.

Drexler, H. *Untersuchungen zu Josephus und zur Geschichte des Jüdischen Aufstandes* 66–70. Klio, XIX, 1924, p. 277.

Laqueur, R. *Der jüdische Historiker Flavius Josephus.* Giessen, 1920.

Luther, H. *Josephus und Justus von Tiberias.* Halle, 1910.

Motzo, B. *Due edizioni della "vita" di Giuseppe.* Saggi di Storia e Letteratura Giudeo-ellenistica. Florence, 1925, p. 214.

—— *Gli avvenimenti di Galilea in 'Bell.' e in 'Vita.'* Ib. p. 226.

Niese, B. *Der jüdische Historiker Josephus.* H.Z. LXXVI, 1896, p. 193.

Schalit, A. *Josephus und Justus.* Klio, XXVII, 1932, p. 67.

Thackeray, H. St J. *Josephus, the Man and the Historian.* New York, 1929.

Weber, W. *Josephus und Vespasian.* Stuttgart, 1921.

Zeitlin, S. *Megillat Taanit as a Source for Jewish Chronology and History in the Hellenistic and Roman Periods.* Jew. Quart. Review, X, 1919–20, pp. 74, 263.

The articles in P.W. *s.v.* Josephus (Hölscher); Justus v. Tiberias (F. Jacoby).

III. Works on the War

A. On the military operations

Of the general histories apart from those cited in the General Bibliography see especially:

Graetz, H. *Geschichte der Juden.* Ed. 4, vol. III, Leipzig, 1888, p. 448.

Schürer, E. *Op. cit.* I, p. 564 (for fuller bibliographical detail).

See also, for the antecedents of the rebellion, E. Meyer, *Ursprung und Anfänge des Christentums*, III, Stuttgart-Berlin, 1923, p. 42 and A. Momigliano, *Ricerche sull' organizzazione della Giudea sotto il dominio romano* (63 a.C.–70 d.C.), Annali Scuola Normale Superiore di Pisa, N.S. III, 1934, p. 183.

Among more detailed works (besides the works on Sources, cited above, practically all of which contain a reconstruction of the events, especially of those in Galilee), see:

Büchler, A. *Zur Verproviantirung Jerusalems im Jahre 69/70 n. Chr.* Breslau, 1900 (in *Gedenkbuch zur Erinnerung an David Kaufmann*).

Cagnat, R. *L'armée romaine au siège de Jérusalem.* Rev. E.J. XXII, 1891, p. xxviii.

Fabia, Ph. *Pline l'ancien a-t-il assisté au siège de Jérusalem par Titus?* Rev. Phil. N.S. xvi, 1892, p. 149.

Reinach, S. *L'arc de Titus.* Rev. E.J. xx, 1890, p. lxv.

de Saulcy, F. *Les derniers jours de Jérusalem.* Paris, 1866.

Valeton, I. M. J. *Hierosolyma capta.* Mnem. xxvii, 1899, p. 78.

Zeitlin, S. *La Révolution Juive de 65–70, La Révolution Française et La Révolution Russe.* Paris, 1930. (Cf. the same author's *The Am Haarez*, Jew. Quart. Review, N.S. xxiii, 1932, p. 45.)

B. The juridical status of the Jews after A.D. 70

Büchler, A. *The Economic Conditions of Judaea after the Destruction of the Second Temple.* London, 1912, *passim.*

Ginsberg, M. S. *Fiscus Judaicus.* Jew. Quart. Review, N.S. xxi, 1930, p. 281.

Juster, J. *Les Juifs dans l'empire romain.* ii, Paris, 1914, p. 282.

Momigliano, A. *Ricerche sull' organizzazione della Giudea sotto il dominio romano* (63 a.C.–70 d.C.). Annali Scuola Normale Superiore di Pisa, N.S. iii, 1934, p. 183.

Mommsen, Th. *Der Religionsfrevel nach römischem Recht.* Ges. Schriften, iii, p. 416.

Article in P.W. *s.v.* fiscus (Rostovtzeff), cols. 2403–5.

GENERAL INDEX

Where the only mention of a name does not record a fact of historical importance about it, the name is usually omitted. Romans are indexed under the most familiar part of their name, whether praenomen, nomen or cognomen. In case of doubt, a cross-reference is given. For identification, dates of consulship (cos., or cos. suff.) are given.

Cleopatra VII, queen of Egypt, character and aims of, 35 *sqq.*; mystical daughter of Re, 36, 38; her reign, 36 *sqq.*; her popularity in Egypt, 35 *sqq.*; attitude towards native religion, 36; care for agriculture, 37; later tradition about, 38; ring of, 38 *sq.*; initiate of Dionysus, 39; flight from Rome after murder of Caesar, 4; summoned to Tarsus by Antony to meet charge of aiding Cassius, 35, 39 *sq.*; Antony accompanies her to Alexandria, 40 *sq.*; gives birth to twins, 41; marries Antony, 55, 66, 76; receives gifts of territory from Antony, 67; as Aphrodite-Isis, 67 *sq.*; re-names twins, 68, significance of names, 68; visits Herod, and leases balsam gardens to him, and bitumen monopoly to Malchus, 70; meets Antony at Leuke Kome, 75; dream of world rule, 76; winters at Ephesus, 95; mobilizes fleet, 95; at Samos, 96; honoured by Athens, 96; outburst against in Rome, 98; Octavian declares war on her alone, 98 *sq.*; flight from Actium to Alexandria, 105; alleged treachery to Antony, 107; captured by Proculeius, 108; interview with Octavian, 109 *sq.*; suicide of, 110; reason for using an asp, 110 *sq.*; Roman hatred and fear of, 111; coinage, 37, 67, 81 *n.*, 101
— Jewess, wife of Herod, 333
— Selene, daughter of Antony and Cleopatra, 68, 174 *n.*, 215; gifts of territory to from Antony, 80; cared for by Octavia, 112; married to Juba II, 112
Cleopatris (Arsinoe), 250
Client-kings, 600 *sq.*; their importance to Rome, 34, 258; Antony's policy towards, 34; change in method of choosing, 48, 51 *sq.*; called up by Antony, 95; Augustus' settlement of, 113 *sqq.*, 174 *sq.*, 215 *sq.*; military service demanded of, 232; policy of Tiberius, 643, of Gaius, 660 *sq.*, of Claudius, 680; and ruler-worship, 488
Clodius Macer, proconsul of Africa, 227 *n.*; revolts against Nero, 740; refuses to recognize Galba, 812; coinage, 740, 812
Cocceius, L., Nerva (cos. 36 B.C.), 46 *n.*; mediates between Octavian and Antony, 43
Coelaletae, rising of, 646
Cogidubnus of Britain, 682, 800 *sq.*
cognitio, 168, 170, 172, 173 and *n.*
cohors, see under *auxilia*
Coinage, of Africanus Fabius Maximus, 178; of Agrippa, 122 *n.*; of Alexandria, 308, 654 *n.*, 703, 707 *n.*, 737; of Antigonus, 48; of Antioch, 271 *n.*; of Antiochus IV, 750 *n.*; of L. Antonius,

28 *n.*; of M. Antonius, 31 *n.*, 50 *n.*, 56 *n.*, 59 *n.*, 68, 69 and *n.*, 72, 78, 80 *sqq.*, 94 *n.*, 100 *n.*; of Antony and Cleopatra, 67; of Antony's fleet prefects, 52; of Archelaus, 744 *n.*; of Artabanus III, 278 *n.*; of Artaxias, 621 *n.*, 747; of Asander, 267; of cities of Asia Minor, 732; of Attambelos I, 79 *n.*; of Augustus, 17 *n.*, 31 *n.*, 113, 123, 127, 130, 197 *sq.*, 208, 263 *sqq.*, 285 *n.*, 478, 577; of Berytus, 100 *n.*, 281 *n.*; of Bosporan kings, 269 and *nn.*, 751 and *n.*, 775 *sq.*; British, 792 *sq.*; of M. Brutus, 19; of Claudius, 161 *n.*, 667 *n.*, 669 *n.*; of Cleopatra, 37, 81 *n.*, 101; of Clodius Macer, 740, 812; of P. Clodius, 473; of Commune Asiae, 198; of Cotys I, 753 *n.*, 776 *n.*; of Cyme, 732 *n.*; of Dynamis, 267, 269; of Eastern cities, 620; of Epaticcus, 791; of Gaius, 621 *n.*, 655 *n.*, 656 *n.*; of Galba, 725; of Gepaepyris, 751; of Germanicus, 621 *n.*, 747 *n.*; of Gondofarr, 879; of Gotarzes, 754 *n.*; of Herod, 326, 336 *n.*; of Agrippa I, 680; of Ilium, 663; India, Julio-Claudian coins found in, 418, 883 *n.*; of Labienus, 47; of Livia, 634; of Mauretanian towns, 675; of Miletus, 656 *n.*; of Mithridates of Bosporus, 753; of Nero, 702 *n.*, 703 *sqq.*, 708, 713 *n.*, 733 *sqq.*, 737; of Pacorus, 48 and *n.*; of Parthian kings, 754 *n.*, 756 *n.*; of Patrae, 732; of Paullus Fabius Maximus, 178; of Phraates IV, 79 *n.*; of Sextus Pompeius, 4 *n.*, 15 *n.*, 57 *n.*; of Pontic cities, 774 *n.*; of Proculeius, 52; of Ptolemy of Mauretania, 644; of Rhescuporis, 776 *n.*; of Sabaean and Sabaean-Himyarite kings, 249; of Scarpus, 101 *n.*; of Sicyon, 732; of Sosius, 52, 54; of Synaüs, 732 *n.*; of Synnada, 620; of Tarcondimotus, 52; of Tiberius, 308, 638 *n.*; of Turullius, 101; of Vardanes, 754 *n.*; of Vitellius, 818 *n.*; of Vologases, 756 *n.*; of Vonones, 278 *n.*
Colchester, *see under* Camulodunum
Colchi, Colchis, 776; export from, 402
collegia, abolished by Augustus, 459
Cologne, 848; a military colony, 227; murder of Batavian rebels at, 846; glass-blowing at, 406
Colonia Caesarea, garrison colony at Corinth, 270
Colonies for veterans, 120 and *n.*; military, planted by Augustus, 206 *sq.*; of Caesar for time-expired soldiers, 221; C. Gracchus and transmarine colonies, 221
Comama, in Pisidia, colony at, 272
Comana in Cappadocia, priest-kings of, pretenders to throne, 34

726 *sqq.*; victims of, 729 *sq.*; persecution of Stoics, 730 *sq.*; Vinician conspiracy, 731; divine honours paid to, 732 *sq.*; journey to Greece, 735 *sqq.*; gives freedom to Greece, 735; attempts to cut Isthmus of Corinth, 736 *sq.*; policy in East, 758 *sqq.*, 881 *sqq.*; Armenia, 764, 773; annexes Pontus, 774; alleged intention to invade Caucasus, 735, 777 *sq.*, 880 *sqq.*, and Ethiopia, 778 *sq.*, 880 *sqq.*; decline of power, 737 *sqq.*; revolts in Judaea and Gaul, 738 *sqq.*; return to Rome, 739; attempts to escape, 740 *sq.*; death, 741; causes of unpopularity, 809 *sq.*; false Neros, 741; Jewish and Christian views of, 742; coinage, 702 *n.*, 703 *sqq.*, 707 *sq.*, 713 *n.*, 732 *sqq.*, 737
— son of Germanicus, 162 *n.*, 620; presented to Senate by Tiberius, 626; banishment of, 635; suicide of, 636
— Tib. Claudius (praet. 42 B.C.), proposes rewards for Caesar's murderers, 2; attempts to lead slave revolt in Campania, 29; flight from Italy, 29; restored from exile, 46; divorces Livia, who marries Octavian, 56 *sqq.*
Neroneia, *see under* Artaxata
Neronia, certamen quinquenniale, established by Nero, 718
— Patrensis (Aroë), 715
Neronias (Caesarea Philippi), 733
Nerva, M. Cocceius, 177 *n.*
— — — with Tiberius at Capreae, 632; suicide of, 640
— P. Silius (cos. 20 B.C.), subdues Venostes, 348
Nervii, and Civilis, 843, 845, 848
Nestor, philosopher, 51
New Carthage, 811; silver mines of, 408
Nicaea, temple to Roma at, 485
Nicander of Colophon, *Theriaca* of, 521
Nicolaus of Damascus, 36, 39 *n.*; at Herod's court, 115, 327; pleads with Agrippa for rights of Jews in Asia Minor, 331; source of Josephus, 870, 885
Nicomedia, temple to Roma and Augustus at, 485
Nicopolis, in Epirus, founded by Octavian, 113; synoecized with cities of Acarnania and Epirus, 113; Herod contributes to, 329
— in Egypt, 743
Nigidius Figulus, Neopythagorean, 471, 508
Nile river, valley of, 240; river patrol of, 243; and famines in Egypt, 37; Roman exploration of sources of, 312, 778
Ninica-Claudiopolis, 679 *n.*
Nola, relief from, 553

Nonius, Cn., attempts to assassinate Claudius, 671
Norbanus Flaccus (cos. 33 B.C.), in Civil War, 22 *sqq.*
— Sorex, actor, portrait of, 562
Noreia, iron and gold from, 411
Noricum, 211, 232; under equestrian procurator, 215; annexation of, 348, 360 *sq.*; an imperial province, 678; iron and gold fields of, 395, 411
Novae, legionary camp at, 806
Novaesium (Neuss), 786, 844, 846
novi homines in Senate and in office, 177 *sq.*, 184 *sq.*
Nuceria, veteran colony at, 714
Numerius Atticus and deification of Augustus, 488
Numidia (Africa Nova), 346; exports from, 410
Ny Carlsberg, portrait of Livia at, 564
Nymphaeum, dedication to Claudius and Apollo at, 685 *n.*
Nymwegen, legionary camp at, 849

Oberhausen, archaeological remains at, 350 *n.*
Obodas, Nabataean king, 250, 254, 331 *n.*
Octavia, sister of Octavian, 5, 51; marries Antony, 44, 51; winters with Antony at Athens, 52 *sqq.*; mediates between Octavian and Antony at Tarentum, 54, 58 *sq.*; sent home by Antony, 55; tribunician sacrosanctity conferred on, 64, 121; brings men and stores to Antony, 77, 92; tends Cleopatra's children, 114; beauty of her character, 51, 77; head of on Antony's Dionysus coinage, 69
— daughter of Claudius and Messallina, 671; betrothed to Silanus, 700, 715; married to Nero, 673; divorced and murdered, 721
Octavius, Octavian, *see under* Augustus
— C., father of Augustus, 5
Odrysae, 174, 215, 356; given charge of holy place of Dionysus, 118; rising of, 646
Oescus, legionary camp at, 806
Olba, in Cilicia, 70; honours Tiberius, 651 and *n.*
— Cennatis, Lalassis, Cilician principality, 752
Olbasa, colony at, 272
Olympus, physician to Cleopatra, 31
Oppius, C., 869
— Statianus, 93 *n.*, 94; *legatus* of Antony in Armenia, 73
Ops, temple of, treasures of embezzled by Antony, 4
oratio principis, 168 and *n.*
Ordovices, British tribe, 801

Piso, Cn. Calpurnius, Frugi (cos. 23 B.C.), 46, 136, 193
—— —— (cos. 7 B.C.), 169 sq.; governor of Syria, quarrel with Germanicus, 622; ordered to leave Syria, 622; suspected of poisoning Germanicus, 622; charges against, 623; suicide of, 623
— L. Calpurnius, Caesoninus (cos. 58 B.C.), attacks Antony in Senate, 10
—— —— Licinianus adopted by Galba, 814
—— —— (cos. 15 B.C.), *praefectus urbi*, 201; governor of Galatia, 214; rising in Thrace quelled by, 357
Plancina, wife of Cn. Piso, 622
Plancus, L. Munatius (cos. 42 B.C.), 12 sq., 27, 29, 869; supports amnesty for Caesar's murderers, 2; correspondence with Cicero, 13; protests loyalty to Senate, 14, but joins Antony, 17; colonies founded by, 18; in Perusine War, 29; meets Antony at Athens, 42; governor of Asia, 49; deserts to Octavian and divulges Antony's will to, 97; proposes conferring name of Augustus on Octavian, 130; censor, 143 sq.; tomb of, 572
Plautia Urgulanilla, wife of Claudius, 671 n.
Plautius, Aulus, granted *ovatio* for operations in Britain, 676, 798 sqq.
— Lateranus, 704; in Pisonian conspiracy, 728 sq.
— M., Silvanus (cos. 2 B.C.), in Pannonian rebellion, 372 sq.
— Silvanus Aelianus, and Sarmatians and Scythians, 775, 778; relieves Chersonesus, 775; inscription to, 806
Plautus, Rubellius, suspected by Nero, 720
Pliny, the Elder, 867; naval commander at Misenum, 237
— the Younger, correspondence with Trajan, 165 n.
Plotius Firmus, Praetorian Prefect, 233
Plutarch, on Antony and Cleopatra, 31 n.; works of, 875
Poenina Vallis (Valais), tribes of, 348, 350
Poetovio, 353, 804; conference of Vespasian's supporters at, 830
Pola, destroyed, 84; restored as Colonia Pietas Julia, 88
Polemo I, king of Pontus and Bosporus, holds Laodicea-on-the-Lycus against Parthians, 47; grant of kingdom to by Antony, 52; Cilicia Tracheia given to Cleopatra, 67; Cleopatra receives Pontus and Armenia Minor from Antony, 69, 70 and n.; captured by Medes, 74; guards Armenian frontier for Antony, 95; makes peace with Octavian, 114; deprived of Armenia Minor by, 114; 'friend of the Roman people,' 175;

intervenes in Bosporus, 267 sqq.; king of Bosporus, 268; marries Dynamis, 268, and Pythodoris, 268; captured by 'Aspurgians' and executed, 269
— II, king of Pontus and Bosporus, 661, 751, 765; grant of Bosporus revoked by Claudius, 680, 752; retires from Pontus to Cilicia, 774
— M. Antonius, *see under* Antonius
politeumata, non-Egyptian racial unions in Egypt, 297 sq.
Polla, sister of Agrippa, portico of, 572
Pollentia, 615; riot at, 646
Pollio, C. Asinius (cos. 40 B.C.), 13, 27 sq., 42, 327; joins Antony with two legions, 17 sq.; assigns allotments to veterans in Cisalpine Gaul, 20; Antony's envoy at Misenum, 43 sqq.; subdues Parthini, 46, 49, 84; breaks with Antony, but remains neutral, 94 n., 102; historian, 1 n., 30 n., 530, 866
— Caelius, commander in Armenia, 756 sq.
— P. Vedius, freedman, equestrian rank conferred on by Augustus, 189
Pollitta, wife of Rubellius Plautus, 730
Polybius, freedman of Claudius, 686, 700
Polyclitus, freedman of Nero in Britain, 727
Pompeii, 392 sq., 714; Cloth Hall at, 394; manufactures of, 396 sq.; Gaius duumvir of, 654 n.
Pompeius, Cn. (the Great), theatre of restored by Octavius, 88, 573
— Magnus, deprived of title 'Magnus' by Gaius, 658; victim of Messallina, 671
— Planta, historian, 868
— Sextus, 5 n.; won over to Senate by Lepidus, 12; in charge of fleet and coast of Italy, 15; proscribed, 21; seizes towns in Sicily, and aids fugitive proscribed, 21, 23; settlement with Octavian, 30; offers services to Antony, 30; seeks alliance with Antony, 42; operations with Antony, 43; raids Etruria and threatens corn-supply, 45; gains from treaty of Misenum, 45 sq.; discontent at non-transference of Achaea, 56 sq.; war with Octavian in Sicily, 55 sqq.; deserted by Menas, 56, 59 sq.; naval successes, 57; defeated at Naulochus, 61 sq.; plunders temple of Hera at Lacinium, 62; death, 62, 77; character of, 55 sq.; coinage, 4 n., 15 n., 57 n.
Pomponia Graecina, *superstitionis externae rea*, 503, 705
Pomponius Hylas, Columbarium of, 567
— P., Secundus, 641 n., 671
— Q., Secundus (cos. A.D. 41), 667; subdues Chatti, 786 sq.
Pont du Gard, 579

INDEX TO MAPS

Maps have each their own index, and reference is made here only to the number of the map. The alphabetical arrangement ignores the usual prefixes (lake, etc.).

INDEX OF PASSAGES REFERRED TO

(Classical authors p. 1043; biblical texts p. 1055; inscriptions p. 1055; ostraca and papyri p. 1057. Reference to pages includes the notes at the foot of the page)

ps.-Acro
on Hor. *Od.* I, 37, 23   36

Aetna
32	522
92	522
617–19	522
633	522

Ammianus Marcellinus
XIV, 2	273
XVI, 10, 2	350
XXII, 16, 9	38

Anon.
Bell. Alex. 68, 2	244
de vir. ill. 86	110
Incerti Laus Pisonis	728
(*Poet. Lat. Min.* I, p. 225)	
Laudatio Turiae	129
Periplus maris Erythr.	
4	883
6	393, 399, 418
7	409
8	418
10	413
19	389, 882
23	252, 881
26	881 *sq.*
27	882
31	881
49	393, 418
56	413
64	882

Anth. Lat. (ed. Riese) nos
419–26	676
no. 726	704

Anth. Pal. IX, 178	711, 732
IX, 752	38
XVI, 75	645

Appian
Bell. Civ. I, 104, 489	435
II, 10, 35	384
II, 102, 424	577
III, 13, 46–7	7
III, 31, 120 *sqq.*	11
III, 39, 157 *sqq.*	11
III, 82, 337 *sqq.*	16
III, 85, 351	27
III, 92, 381	17
III, 97, 402	19
IV, 38, 162	116

Appian
Bell. Civ. IV, 53, 226–56	27
IV, 74, 315	23
IV, 86, 367	23
IV, 89, 374	17
IV, 99, 415	23
IV, 107, 447	23
IV, 108, 454	23
IV, 115, 479	22
IV, 115, 480	61
IV, 117, 494	61
V, 3, 12	26
V, 4, 19	191
V, 8, 33	3
V, 12, 45	6
V, 12, 46	27
V, 12, 47	26
V, 17, 68–71	105
V, 20, 79–80	28
V, 26, 102–3	28
V, 26, 104	43
V, 51, 216	39, 41
V, 66, 278–9	44
V, 67, 282	45
V, 73, 313	46
V, 75, 318	51
V, 75, 319	52, 321
V, 75, 321	
	27, 30, 49
V, 80, 339	57
V, 85	91
V, 93, 387	54
V, 95, 396	59
V, 95, 398	59
V, 98, 406	30
V, 103, 428	60
V, 104, 430	30
V, 104, 430–2	60
V, 108, 447	61
V, 117, 494	61
V, 121, 503	62
V, 131, 543	152
V, 132, 546	473
Ill. 13	83
15–28	83
16	87 *sq.*
17	87
22	85
27	6
28	59, 88
30	805
Mithr. 120	266

Apuleius
Met. II, 18	565

Arrian
VII, 11, 9	83

Athenaeus
XI, 497B	37

Augustine
Conf. I, 13, 21	539
de Civ. Dei, V, 2	521

Augustus
(see also under *Res Gestae Divi Augusti* (p. 1057))

Caes. Aug. Imp. operum fragmenta (Malcovati²)
XCVI, p. 36	63
CLXVIII, p. 63	150
pp. 5–22	591
pp. 8–12	592
p. 42	402

Aulus Gellius
N.A. I, 10, 4	524
II, 15, 4	452
II, 24, 14–15	456
X, 23, 4	444
X, 23, 5	440
XIII, 12, 2	450
XIV, 7	138
XV, 7	276

Aurelius Victor
Caes. IV, 2	674
V, 2	706
Epit. I	398, 595
XV, 4	766

Caesar
Bell. Civ. III, 3	191
III, 31	191
III, 103	191
Bell. Gall. I, 39	186
III, 21, 3	405
VI, 1, 3	426
VII, 22, 2	405

Cassius Dio, *see* Dio Cassius

Catullus
LXIV	467
LXVIII, 124 (LXVIIIA, 84)	438

CLIENT DYNASTIES

KINGS OF ARMENIA

Artavasdes I (captured by Antony and taken to Alexandria)	56–34 B.C.
Artaxes	33–20 B.C.
Tigranes II	20–c. 8 B.C.
Tigranes III	c. 8 B.C.–A.D. 1
Short reign of a pretender Artavasdes II sent out by Rome	
Ariobarzanes	c. A.D. 2–4
Artavasdes III	c. 4–c. 6

Short reigns of Tigranes IV and Erato (widow of Tigranes III); then an interregnum. Between A.D. 11 and 16 the Armenian throne is occupied by Vonones, unrecognized by either Rome or Parthia

Artaxias	18–c. 34
Arsaces	c. 34–36
Mithridates (exiled by Gaius, but restored by Claudius)	36–51
Short usurpation of Radamistus	51
Tiridates	51–60
Tigranes V	60–62

From 63 onwards Tiridates is restored, and recognized as a client-king by Rome; he receives the diadem from Nero's hands in Rome in 66

KINGS OF THE BOSPORUS

Asander (his wife, Dynamis, strikes her own coins in 17/16 B.C.)	c. 44–17 B.C.
Scribonius (marries Dynamis)	17–16
Polemo (marries Dynamis)	14–8
Dynamis (marries Aspurgus)	8 B.C.–A.D. 7/8

Unknown ruler for two years (p. 269)

Aspurgus (becomes *amicus Caesaris populique Romani* and receives Roman citizenship in 14/15)	A.D. 10/11–37/8
Gepaepyris (widow of Aspurgus)	37/8–39
Mithridates (for a time jointly with Gepaepyris)	39–44/5
Cotys (perhaps degraded in 62)	44/5–62

Interregnum

Rhescuporis	68/9–c. 90

KINGS OF THRACE

A list of these can only claim approximate certainty. After Sadales of Thrace died childless, c. 42 B.C., leaving his kingdom to Rome, we hear of various Thracian dynasts, Rhescuporis, Sitas, and the Rhoemetalces who deserted to Octavian at Actium, but of no one king. It appears possible, however, that a brother of Rhoemetalces, named Cotys, was king at the time of Actium, and that he died shortly after, leaving a son who was a minor under the guardianship of Rhoemetalces.

Cotys	died c. 25 B.C.
Rhescuporis I (under guardianship of Rhoemetalces)	c. 25–11 B.C.
Rhoemetalces I	c. 11 B.C.–A.D. 12

The kingdom was now divided, Augustus granting the Western portion to Rhescuporis II, a brother of Rhoemetalces I, and the Eastern to Cotys II, a son of Rhoemetalces I.

WESTERN THRACE

	A.D.
Rhescuporis II (exiled to Alexandria and later killed)	12–19
Rhoemetalces II (son of the above)	19–?40

EASTERN THRACE

	A.D.
Cotys II (murdered by Rhescuporis II)	12–19

During the minority of Cotys' three children the kingdom is administered by Trebellenus Rufus

Rhoemetalces III (νεώτερος) (murdered by his wife)	37/8–46

On the murder of Rhoemetalces III, the whole of Thrace is turned into a province by Claudius.

For further information consult Th. Mommsen in *Eph. Epig.* II, 1875, p. 252; J. W. Crowfoot in *J.H.S.* XVII, 1897, p. 321; R. M. Dawkins and F. W. Hasluck in *Ann. Brit. School at Athens*, XII, 1905/6, p. 175; and H. Dessau in *Eph. Epig.* IX, 1913, p. 696. Also articles by U. Kahrstedt in P. W. *s. vv.* Kotys (6–8), Ῥασκούπορις, Ῥοιμητάλκης.

For kings and tetrarchs of the House of Herod see Genealogical Table

MAP 14

ROMAN BRITAIN
IN THE
JULIO-CLAUDIAN PERIOD

Scales

0   10   20   30   40   50
English Miles

0 10 20 30 40 50 60
Kilometres

INDEX TO NAMES

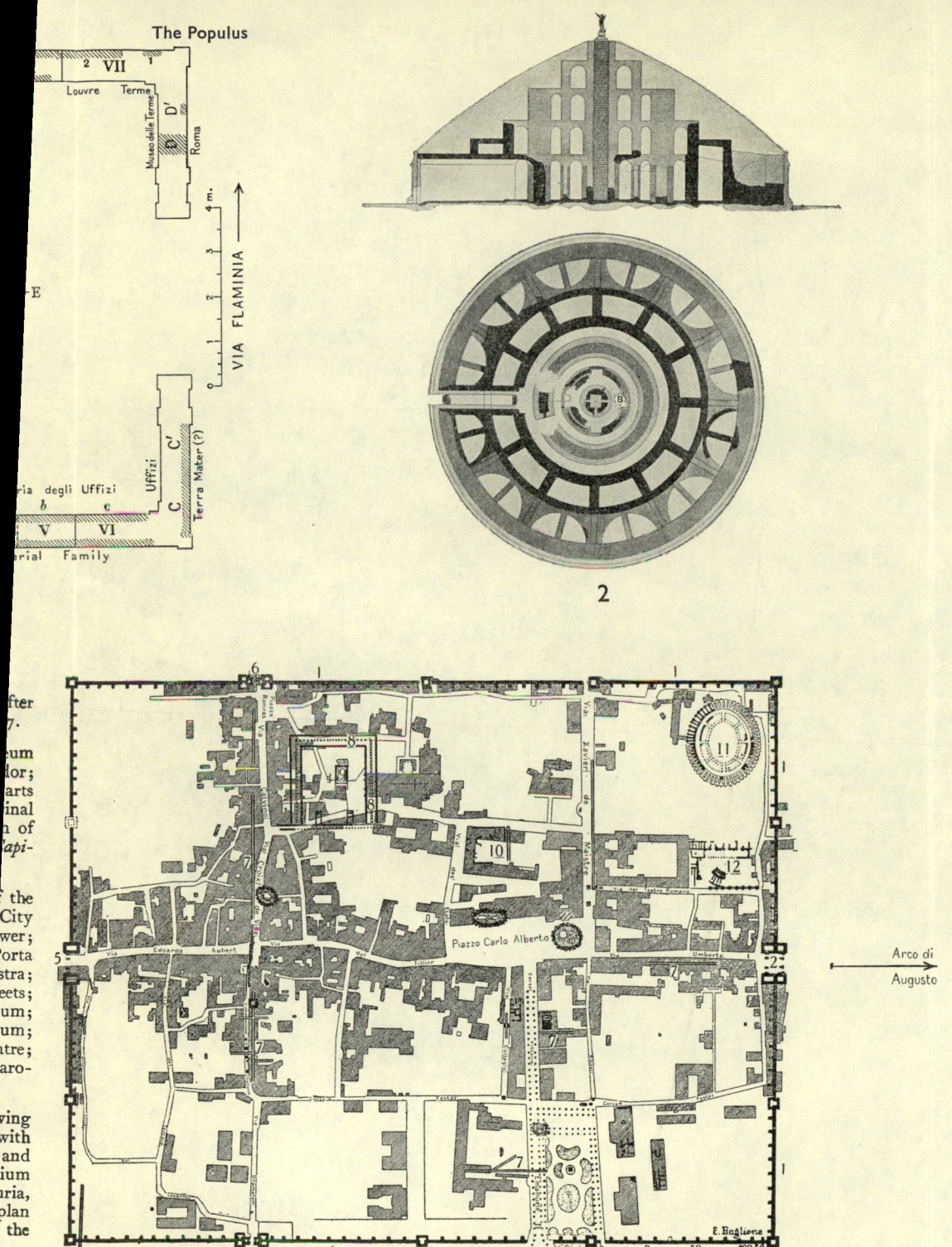

The Populus

VII
Louvre
Terme
D'
Museo delle Terme
Roma

VIA FLAMINIA

ria degli Uffizi
Uffizi
Terra Mater (?)
V
VI
rial Family

2

after
7.
um
or;
arts
inal
n of
api-

the
City
wer;
Porta
stra;
eets
um;
ium
atre
Baro-

wing
with
and
rium
Curia,
plan
the

6

11

10

12

Piazza Carlo Alberto

Arco di
Augusto

3

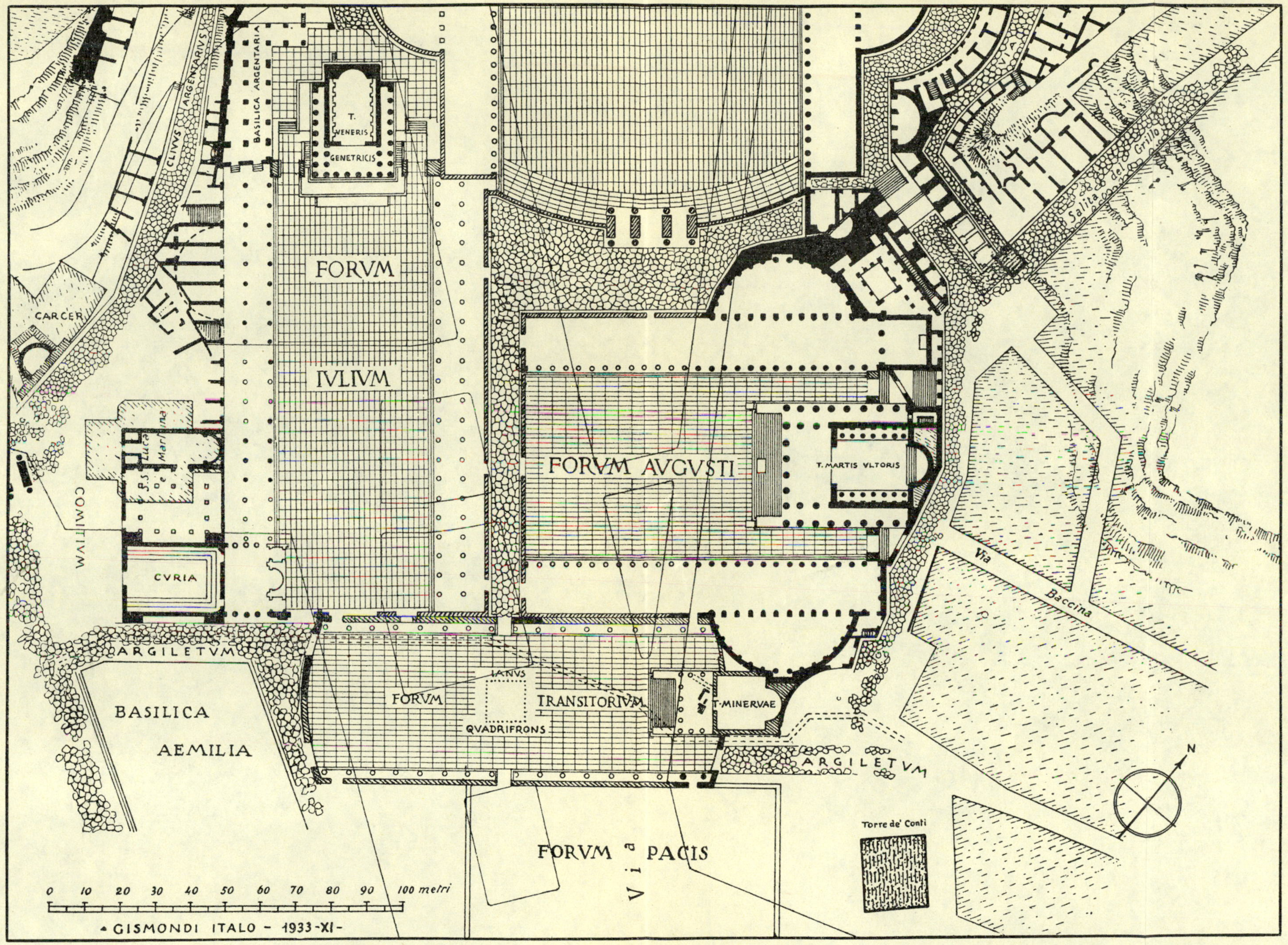

E. Bagliero
600 RA

CARCER

CLIVUS ARGENTARIVS

BASILICA ARGENTARIA

T. VENERIS GENETRICIS

FORVM

IVLIVM

FORVM AVGVSTI

T. MARTIS VLTORIS

COMITIVM

B. J.
Maribiana

Salita del Grillo

CVRIA

ARGILETVM

BASILICA
AEMILIA

FORVM TRANSITORIVM

IANVS
QVADRIFRONS

T. MINERVAE

ARGILETVM

Via Baccina

FORVM a PACIS

Via   Pacis

Torre de' Conti

N

0 10 20 30 40 50 60 70 80 90 100 metri

· GISMONDI ITALO · 1933 · XI ·

4

To face p. 582